A Concordance to the Poems of
THEODORE ROETHKE

edited by
GARY LANE

programmed by
ROLAND DEDEKIND

The Scarecrow Press, Inc.
Metuchen, N.J.   1972

From THE COLLECTED POEMS OF THEODORE ROETHKE

Many of the poems in the collection from which this concordance was made appeared originally in The New Yorker and Poetry. Others appeared in The New York Times, The Nation, Saturday Review, "Night Crow," Copyright 1944 by Saturday Review Association, Inc., The Atlantic Monthly, "The Dance," Copyright 1952 by the Atlantic Monthly Company, "The Exulting," "His Words," "Memory," "The Wall," "What Now?," Copyright 1956 by Atlantic Monthly Co., Yale Review, The American Scholar, "Big Wind," Copyright 1947 by The United Chapters of Phi Beta Kappa, The New Republic, "Carnations," "Child on Top of a Green House," "Flower-Dump," "Weed Puller," "Moss-Gathering," Copyright 1946 by Editorial Publications, Inc., "Elegy," "Love's Progress," "The Shimmer of Evil," "Slug," Copyright 1955 by New Republic, Inc., The Virginia Quarterly Review, The Commonweal, "Double Feature" as "Episode Seven," Copyright 1942 by Commonweal Publishing Co., Inc., The Tiger's Eye, "A Field of Light," Copyright 1948 by The Tiger's Eye, The Sewanee Review, "Judge Not," Copyright 1947 by The University of the South, Harper's Bazaar, "My Papa's Waltz," Copyright 1942 by Hearst Magazines, Inc., and "Last Words," Copyright 1946 by Hearst Magazines, Inc., Harper's, "Old Florist," Copyright 1946 by Harper & Brothers, American Mercury, "Pickle Belt," Copyright 1943 by The American Mercury, Inc., Partisan Review, Botteghe Oscure, "The Other," Copyright 1956 by Botteghe Oscure, "Her Becoming," Copyright 1958 by Botteghe Oscure, The Hudson Review, The Kenyon Review, "I Waited," Copyright 1956 by Kenyon College, Poems in Folio, Flair, Landmarks and Voyages. The Poetry Society Supplement for 1957, Poetry London-New York, Encounter, New World Writing, Ladies' Home Journal, Poetry Northwest, New Poems by American Poets, No. 2, The Pocket Book of Modern Verse, Folkways Album (No. FL 9736), and Critical Quarterly.

PREFACE

My experience with the symbolic and associative texture of Theodore Roethke's language urged this book. As both a lover and a teacher of Roethke's poems, I have come more and more to see his work as a tension-riddled but integral whole--his is perhaps the most unified body of poetry since Yeat's-- and come more and more to feel the need for tracing the sinews that tug at and bind it. This concordance should facilitate such investigation. With it, the reader wishing to assess, for example, the poet's relation to nature and her creatures can collect them--"staid aardvark" to "odious yak," a veritable zoo--quickly and efficiently. With it, the scholar can follow the development of symbols surely and thoroughly.

After nearly three months of part-time work on programming, card punching, and proofreading, the concordance was compiled in about 29 minutes on an IBM 360 computer. It includes, on pages 1- 436, each word and the lone number--10¢--in Roethke's poetry; in addition, because of the poet's fondness for hyphenated compounds, a separate listing of their components is provided on pages 437-458. The searcher will thus find in the first part of the con- cordance 33 occurrences of the word "shape"; if he turns to the second part, he will find as well, again under "shape," the compounds "sea-shape," "cloud- shape," and "meadow-shape." A word frequency table, on pages 459-484, concludes the book.

With the kind permission of Doubleday and Company and Faber and Faber, this concordance has been correlated to The Collected Poems of Theodore Roethke. Except as noted below, each line is printed exactly as it appears in the Collected Poems, and beside each is its CP page number, poem title or a shortened version of it, and line number. Where several poems have the same title --three are called "Song," for example, two "The Waking"--they are distinguished by parenthesized numbers following the titles. Line numbers of T and ST are given to titles and section titles, re- spectively, of the poems.

In order to save space, I have suppressed the listing of the words below, all of which, I think, are unlikely to interest. A suppressed word is fol- lowed, not by the lines that use it, but by a single, parenthesized number, its frequency of occurrence. My choices are of course somewhat arbitrary, but I hope and suspect that any quarrels will be with what I list fully rather than what I omit.

Suppressed Words

a	for	is	our	through
am	from	it	ours	to
an	had	its	she	us
and	has	me	that	was
are	have	my	the	we
at	he	neither	their	were
be	her	no	theirs	with
been	hers	nor	them	you
but	him	not	these	your
by	his	of	they	yours
can	I	on	this	
either	in	or	those	

I have made only one correction in Doubleday's text, replacing the semi-colon in line three of "For an Amorous Lady" with the comma that Roethke surely intended. Several changes, however, were necessitated by our program. First, because the computer could not conveniently distinguish the apostrophe from the single quotation mark, I have made all of Roethke's quotation marks double. Then, because the computer could not easily distinguish the period that marks a sentence's end from that which designates abbreviation, words like "Mrs." and "Mr."--though correctly printed within lines of poetry--are indexed as "Mrs" and "Mr". Finally, where a very occasional line ends in a broken or hyphenated word--this occurs some four or five times in all--the entire word appears on the line that begins it. Several inconsistencies are Roethke's own: "traveler" and "traveller" for instance, or "elm tree," "elm-tree," and "elmtrees."

Without the help of several people, this work could never have been completed. Roland Dedekind forsook three months of spare time to write, test, and revise the program, turning with wry tolerance back to the task each time a new idea of mine necessitated revision. Rogert Vogelsinger created several proofreading programs for us, and super- vised both tests and final run on Bethlehem Steel Corporation's IBM 360; his personal generosity and unfailing kindness cheered me through an arduous and exacting task. Finally, my wife Carmen, fel- low lover of Roethke's poems, took time out of her busy graduate student's career to read me aloud, slowly and with punctuation, the whole of the Col- lected Poems.

GARY LANE

NOTE: Most of Roethke's 209 poems have titles short enough to fit the 15 columns of space available in this book. For those that do not, the editor has devised shortened forms evocative of the original. The table that follows lists those poems whose titles in this Concordance are not identical to the titles in the Collected Poems.

Concordance Title	"Collected Poems" Title	CP Page
AGNST DISASTER	Against Disaster	19
ALL EARTH, AIR	All the Earth, All the Air	121
AMOROUS LADY	For an Amorous Lady	23
AT OYSTER RIVER	Meditation at Oyster River	190
BEFORE STUDY	Prayer before Study	24
BOY AND BUSH	The Boy and the Bush	182
CHILD ON GRNHSE	Child on Top of a Greenhouse	43
CLAIRVOY WIDOW	Ballad of the Clairvoyant Widow	27
COMING OF COLD	The Coming of the Cold	14
CUTTINGS (LATE)	Cuttings (later)	37
DIM-WIT COUSIN	My Dim-Wit Cousin	25
ELEGY (1)	Elegy	144
ELEGY (2)	Elegy	223
EPIDERM MACABRE	Epidermal Macabre	19
FIELD OF LIGHT	A Field of Light	62
FIRST MEDITATN	First Meditation	157
FOLLIES OF ADAM	The Follies of Adam	262
FOR STEVENS	A Rouse for Stevens	266
FOURTH MEDITATN	Fourth Meditation	168
FRAU BAUMAN	Frau Bauman, Frau Schmidt, and Frau Schwartze	44
GIVE WAY, GATES	Give Way, Ye Gates	79
HARSH COUNTRY	The Harsh Country	265
MIGHWAY: MICH	Highway: Michigan	33
I CRY, LOVE!	I Cry, Love! Love!	92
IN EVEING AIR	In Evening Air	240
IN HYDROTHERAPY	Meditation in Hydrotherapy	256
IN LATE SUMMER	A Walk in Late Summer	149
IN VIOLENT WARD	Heard in a Violent Ward	228
JOURNY INTERIOR	Journey to the Interior	193
KITTY-CAT BIRD	The Kitty-Cat Bird	177
LADY AND BEAR	The Lady and the Bear	117
LIGHT BREATHER	A Light Breather	101
LIGHT BRIGHTER	The Light Comes Brighter	11
LONG LIVE WEEDS	"Long Live the Weeds"	18
MANIFESTATION	The Manifestation	235
MEADOW MOUSE	The Meadow Mouse	227
MID-CNTRY BLOW	Mid-Country Blow	12
MONOTONY SONG	The Monotony Song	181
O, THOU OPENING	O, Thou Opening, O	97
O LULL ME, LULL	O Lull Me, Lull Me	83
OLD LADY'S WRDS	Old Lady's Winter Words	103
ONCE MORE, RND	Once More, the Round	251
ORDERS FOR DAY	Orders for the Day	7
PRAISE PRAIRIE	In Praise of Prairie	13
PRAISE TO END!	Praise to the End!	85
REPL TO CENSURE	Reply to Censure	20

ROAD TO WDLAWN	On the Road to Woodlawn	22
SAGINAW SONG	The Saginaw Song	267
SANITARIUM	Lines upon Leaving a Sanitarium	257
SENSIBILITY! LA	Sensibility! O La!	81
SENTENTIOUS MAN	The Sententious Man	131
SHAPE OF FIRE	The Shape of the Fire	64
SHIMMER OF EVIL	"The Shimmer of Evil"	143
SIR JOHN DAVIES	Four for Sir John Davies	105
SONG (1)	Song	211
SONG (2)	Song	236
SONG (3)	Song	258
SQUEEZE-BOX	Song for the Squeeze-Box	111
SUPPR W LINDSAY	Supper with Lindsay	273
THE TREE, BIRD	The Tree, the Bird	248
THE WAKING (1)	The Waking	51
THE WAKING (2)	The Waking	108
TO A LADY ED	Reply to a Lady Editor	113
UNEXTINGUISHED	The Unextinguished	17
VERNAL SENTIMNT	Vernal Sentiment	24
VERSE W ALLUSNS	Verse with Allusions	25
WHAT TELL BONES	What Can I Tell My Bones?	171
WHERE KNOCK IS	Where Knock Is Open Wide	71
WISH YOUNG WIFE	Wish for a Young Wife	217
WORDS FOR WIND	Words for the Wind	123

	PAGE	TITLE	LINE

A (1539)

AARDVARK
    THE PENSIVE GNU, THE STAID AARDVARK, ... 23   AMOROUS LADY   1

ABETTOR
    IN TRUTH, THE EYE'S THE ABETTOR OF 8   PRAYER   15

ABIDE
    SPEAK AND ABIDE. 62   FIELD OF LIGHT   21
    HOW SWEETLY I ABIDE. AM I A BIRD? 165   HER BECOMING   16
    I, LIVING, STILL ABIDE 215   HIS FOREBODING   2
    WHEN WE ABIDE YET GO 237   THE TRANCED   3

ABIDES
    THE MOON STILL ABIDES. 82   SENSIBILITY! LA   43
    WHAT SPEECH ABIDES? 220   THE ABYSS   25

ABIDING
    WITH THE BIRD, THE ABIDING LEAF, ... 251   ONCE MORE, RND   6

ABJURE
    A SCENE FOR THE SELF TO ABJURE!-- 233   THE PIKE   10

ABLE
    IT WAS STAND ON YOUR FEET AS LONG AS YOU'RE ABLE, ... 112   SQUEEZE-BOX   35

ABOMINABLE
    A FLASH INTO THE BURNING HEART OF THE ABOMINABLE; 221   THE ABYSS   56

ABOUT
    THE SEASON'S WRECKAGE LIES ABOUT, ... 14   COMING OF COLD   26
    HIS FINGERS MAKE A HAT ABOUT HIS HEAD. 16   THE BAT   3
    THEY THOUGHT ABOUT SATURDAY PAY, ... 46   PICKLE BELT   3
    MOVE ABOUT. 83   O LULL ME, LULL   7
    CARES ABOUT THE DANCE OF DEAD UNDERWEAR, OR THE SAD WALTZ
        OF PAPER 98   O, THOU OPENING   26
    IT IS HARD TO CARE ABOUT CORNERS, ... 104   OLD LADY'S WRDS   59
    --ABOUT GETTING RID OF OUR MONEY. 111   SQUEEZE-BOX   12
    "I'M SERIOUS ABOUT MY SINGING CAREER!" 115   THE SERPENT   24
    HE THINKS ABOUT IT FOR A YEAR; 116   THE SLOTH   3
    WHEN THE WORST IS ABOUT TO ARRIVE; 172   WHAT TELL BONES   35
    A FUNNY THING ABOUT A CHAIR: 178   THE CHAIR   1
    THERE'S THIS TO REMEMBER ABOUT THE GNU: 180   THE GNU   1
    TO MAKE REMARKS ABOUT MY--GRRR! 181   MONOTONY SONG   11
    WAS I TOO GLIB ABOUT ETERNAL THINGS, ... 241   THE SEQUEL   1

ABOVE
    OF MARSH GRASS HEAPED ABOVE A MUSK-RAT HOLE. 15   THE HERON   4
    THEN POINTS HIS HEAVY BILL ABOVE THE WOOD. 15   THE HERON   10
    SLOW SWINGS THE BREEZE ABOVE HER HEAD, ... 17   NO BIRD   5
    WANTS SINGLENESS OF SPIRIT ABOVE ALL ELSE: 24   POETASTER   2
    WITH EVERYTHING BLOOMING ABOVE ME, ... 39   WEED PULLER   11
    THE WINDLESS PERPETUAL MORNING ABOVE A SEPTEMBER CLOUD. 43   CARNATIONS   7
    ABOVE THE BLUE SNOW. 58   THE LOST SON   153
    I SIT ABOVE THE BACK WHEELS, WHERE THE JOLTS ARE HARDEST, ... 158   FIRST MEDITATN   22
    FOR A MOMENT THEY STAND ABOVE ME, ... 158   FIRST MEDITATN   56
    I SEE THE FLOWER OF ALL WATER, ABOVE AND BELOW ME, THE
        NEVER RECEDING, ... 194   JOURNY INTERIOR   52
    SILENCE OF WATER ABOVE A SUNKEN TREE: 201   THE FAR FIELD   100
    I RETURN TO THE TWITTERING OF SWALLOWS ABOVE WATER, ... 204   THE ROSE   73
    WHO LIVED ABOVE A POTTING SHED FOR YEARS. 224   OTTO   4
    ABOVE THE BLUE AIR, IN THE SLIGHT HAZE BEYOND, ... 232   THE THING   3
    THE MIST ABOVE ME SINGS WITH ITS SMALL FLIES. 246   THE MARROW   2
    GODHEAD ABOVE MY GOD, ARE YOU THERE STILL? 246   THE MARROW   13
    I ROSE, A HEAVY BULK, ABOVE THE FIELD. 247   I WAITED   5

ABSENT
    WITH THE SAME ABSENT GAZE: 130   THE OTHER   20

ABSOLUTE
    THE MURMUR OF THE ABSOLUTE, THE WHY 201   THE FAR FIELD   89
    THE NAKED ABSOLUTE. 238   THE MOMENT   8

ABSOLUTES
    LONGING FOR ABSOLUTES THAT NEVER COME. 171   WHAT TELL BONES   13

ABSORBED
    A DRUNK MAN STUMBLES BY, ABSORBED IN SELF-TALK. 33   IDYLL   2

ABSTRACT
    AND SCORN THE ABSTRACT ENTITIES. 25   VERSE W ALLUSNS   4

ABSURD
    HIS ABSURD WHISKERS STICKING OUT LIKE A CARTOON-MOUSE, ... 227   MEADOW MOUSE   7
    DIVINITY ITSELF MALIGN, ABSURD; 237   THE TRANCED   7
    I'LL FACE ALL THAT, AND THE DIVINE ABSURD: 272   DUET   5

ABYSS
    THE GROUND NEEDS THE ABYSS, ... 121   ALL EARTH, AIR   19

	PAGE	TITLE	LINE
ABYSS (CONTINUED)			
I LIVE NEAR THE ABYSS. I HOPE TO STAY	134	THE PURE FURY	26
THE ABYSS	219	THE ABYSS	T
AND THE ABYSS? THE ABYSS?	219	THE ABYSS	5
AND THE ABYSS? THE ABYSS?	219	THE ABYSS	5
"THE ABYSS YOU CAN'T MISS:	219	THE ABYSS	6
SO THE ABYSS--	221	THE ABYSS	50
THE WIDE, THE BLEAK ABYSS	238	THE MOMENT	4
ACADEMIC			
ACADEMIC	23	ACADEMIC	T
ACCELERATION			
ACCELERATION IS THEIR NEED:	33	HIGHWAY: MICH	11
ACCENTS			
IN ACCENTS MEASURED BY THE BLOOD.	22	SILENCE	3
ACCEPT			
ACCEPT CARESSES IN THE DARK;	23	AMOROUS LADY	2
ACCORDING			
FISH FEED ON FISH, ACCORDING TO THEIR NEED:	155	THE DYING MAN	66
ACCOUNTING			
DETERIORATION'S SCRUPULOUS ACCOUNTING	25	DIM-WIT COUSIN	7
ACCOUTERMENTS			
WITH FALSE ACCOUTERMENTS OF SENSE,	19	EPIDERM MACABRE	14
ACCUSERS			
THE HALF-GROWN CHRYSANTHEMUMS STARING UP LIKE ACCUSERS,	43	CHILD ON GRNHSE	3
ACHE			
I ACHE FOR ANOTHER CHOICE.	89	UNFOLD! UNFOLD!	4
ACHIN'			
BUT ALAS, ALACK, AND ME ACHIN' BACK,	268	SAGINAW SONG	45
ACKNOWLEDGE			
AND I ACKNOWLEDGE MY FOOLISHNESS WITH GOD,	196	THE LONG WATERS	8
ACQUIRES			
ACQUIRES, FOR A TIME, THE SANDPIPER'S INSOUCIANCE,	191	AT OYSTER RIVER	39
ACRES			
BEHIND THE EYE; THE LOST ACRES AT THE EDGE OF SMOKY CITIES.	159	FIRST MEDITATN	75
ACRID			
THE DILL BEARS UP ITS ACRID CROWN;	14	COMING OF COLD	14
ACROSS			
THEY DART ACROSS A CORNER OF THE EYE.	8	THE SIGNALS	4
HE JERKS A FROG ACROSS HIS BONY LIP,	15	THE HERON	9
BLEAK CLOUDS ACROSS THE HEAVY SKY,	15	COMING OF COLD	50
UNTIL THOUGHT CRACKLES WHITE ACROSS THE BRAIN.	17	UNEXTINGUISHED	12
CLIMBED TO HER ATTIC WINDOW AND GAZED ACROSS THE SILL.	27	CLAIRVOY WIDOW	2
AS YOU LOOK ACROSS MY CITY, IN GOD'S COUNTRY?"	27	CLAIRVOY WIDOW	4
COLD, COLD ACROSS THE FLESH	31	LULL	2
FLINGING LONG STRINGS OF WET ACROSS THE ROOF-TOP,	41	BIG WIND	29
I STROLLED ACROSS	51	THE WAKING (1)	1
I CAME ACROSS A TIME,	71	WHERE KNOCK IS	13
ACROSS HER PULSING THROAT;	123	WORDS FOR WIND	22
ACROSS MY LAWN THE SOFT-BACKED CREATURES COME;	149	IN LATE SUMMER	3
LEANING ACROSS A SILL TO GREET THE DAWN?	154	THE DYING MAN	44
A FUME REMINDS ME, DRIFTING ACROSS WET GRAVEL;	160	FIRST MEDITATN	91
COMING ACROSS SNOW IN EARLY EVENING?	161	I'M HERE	5
ACROSS A FIELD, INTO A LITTLE WOOD.	166	HER BECOMING	51
THE DOE WITH ITS SLOPED SHOULDERS LOPING ACROSS THE HIGHWAY,	190	AT OYSTER RIVER	27
ACT			
THE EYES REJOICE IN THE ACT OF SEEING AND THE FRESH AFTER-IMAGE;	163	I'M HERE	79
I WISH YOU WOULD ACT LIKE A BIRD REALLY SHOULD,	177	KITTY-CAT BIRD	6
HE WOULD ACT VERY SNIDE.	178	THE YAK	4
IT WAS NO RANDOM ACT, FOR THOSE TWO MEN	224	OTTO	20
THIS REACH BEYOND THIS DEATH, THIS ACT OF LOVE	243	THE MOTION	17
ACTING			
--OF ACTING MY POEM CALLED POEM.	113	TO A LADY ED	12
YOU ARE NOT ACTING WELL:	267	SAGINAW SONG	16
ACTIVE			
HANDS ACTIVE, EYES CHERISHED;	187	THE LONGING	8
A MIND TOO ACTIVE IS NO MIND AT ALL;	244	INFIRMITY	19
ACTIVITY			
ACTIVITY CENTRIPETAL.	24	BEFORE STUDY	10
ACTUAL			
IN A FIELD, IN THE ACTUAL AIR,	166	HER BECOMING	45
ADAM			
THE FOLLIES OF ADAM	262	FOLLIES OF ADAM	T

		PAGE	TITLE	LINE
ADAMANT				
	THE ADAMANT	9	THE ADAMANT	T
ADD				
	WE HUNT THE CAUSE OF RUIN, ADD,	30	THE RECKONING	5
	SAID, "I KNOW MY LEGS ADD UP TO TWO!	182	PHILANDER	2
ADDER-MOUTHED				
	ADDER-MOUTHED,	39	ORCHIDS	2
ADDLED				
	STOPPING TRAFFIC, INDIGNANT AS ADDLED OLD LADIES,	234	ALL MORNING	27
ADDS				
	ADDS UP A PAIR OF JIGGLING DOUBLE CHINS.	25	DIM-WIT COUSIN	8
ADIEU				
	IN ROBES OF GREEN, IN GARMENTS OF ADIEU.	201	THE FAR FIELD	86
ADMIRE				
	THE PURE ADMIRE THE PURE, AND LIVE ALONE;	133	THE PURE FURY	8
ADOLESCENCE				
	SO MUCH OF ADOLESCENCE IS AN ILL-DEFINED DYING,	162	I'M HERE	35
ADOLESCENT				
	WITHOUT STARING LIKE A LOUT, OR A MOPING ADOLESCENT;	163	I'M HERE	80
ADORE				
	SHE MOVES, AND I ADORE:	130	THE OTHER	17
	"ADORE AND DRAW NEAR.	222	THE ABYSS	86
	NOW I ADORE MY LIFE	251	ONCE MORE, RND	5
	THE MUSES, THEY MUST ALL ADORE HIM,	266	FOR STEVENS	18
ADORES				
	LOVE LIKES A GANDER, AND ADORES A GOOSE:	127	I KNEW A WOMAN	15
ADVANCE				
	AND THE IVY ADVANCE WITH ITS WHITE LIZARD FEET--	194	JOURNY INTERIOR	49
	FROM THE WORM'S ADVANCE AND RETREAT, FROM THE BUTTERFLY'S HAVOC,	196	THE LONG WATERS	21
ADVANCING				
	I SEE IN THE ADVANCING AND RETREATING WATERS	198	THE LONG WATERS	67
ADVANTAGE				
	HOLD TO ADVANTAGE DEARLY WON.	33	HIGHWAY: MICH	9
ADVERB				
	YOU BE AN ADVERB, I'LL BE A VERB,	272	DUET	6
ADVICE				
	NOW THAT'S A PIECE OF GOOD ADVICE	181	MONOTONY SONG	3
	AND HERE'S MORE ADVICE:	183	THE LIZARD	5
AFFIRMATIONS				
	SUCH AFFIRMATIONS ARE PERPETUAL.	135	THE RENEWAL	4
AFFRIGHTED				
	AFFRIGHTED FROM HER WITS,	136	THE SENSUALISTS	10
AFLAME				
	AND THERE I THRASHED, MY THIGHS AND FACE AFLAME.	132	SENTENTIOUS MAN	22
AFRAID				
	WE ARE AFRAID OF WHAT OUR EYES HAVE SEEN:	16	THE BAT	8
	IN THE SLOW RAIN, WHO'S AFRAID?	79	GIVE WAY, GATES	21
	WHO ISN'T UNWILLING, WHO ISN'T AFRAID	112	SQUEEZE-BOX	44
	BUT WHO'S AFRAID OF THAT?	138	THE SURLY ONE	6
	AND SHAPES MAKE ME AFRAID:	171	WHAT TELL BONES	14
	IN SLEEP, AFRAID. DEATH'S FACE RISES AFRESH,	190	AT OYSTER RIVER	25
	I WENT, NOT LOOKING BACK. I WAS AFRAID.	247	I WAITED	18
AFRESH				
	IN SLEEP, AFRAID. DEATH'S FACE RISES AFRESH,	190	AT OYSTER RIVER	25
AFTER				
	HIS IMAGE KEPT FOLLOWING AFTER,--	6	THE PREMONITION	10
	AND YOU, CAT AFTER GREAT MILK AND VASTY FISHES,	79	GIVE WAY, GATES	9
	AND AFTER EXCHANGING A PUNCH OR TWO,	111	SQUEEZE-BOX	5
	DAY AFTER SOMBER DAY,	139	PLAINT	1
	WHEN I FOLLOW AFTER THEM,	141	MEMORY	11
	AS MY EYES FOLLOW AFTER	152	THE SISKINS	23
	THE MOVEMENT IS FORWARD, AFTER A FEW WAVERS,	158	FIRST MEDITATN	27
	IS BEFORE, OR RIGHT AFTER, A BLIZZARD.	183	THE LIZARD	2
	AT EASE AFTER ROCKING THE FLESH TO SLEEP,	194	JOURNY INTERIOR	55
	AFTER THE MIDNIGHT CRIES.	194	JOURNY INTERIOR	64
	AFTER THE BLINDING MISERY,	221	THE ABYSS	52
	THE WEEK AFTER."	229	ON THE QUAY	6
	AND THE DUCKS NEAR LAKE WASHINGTON WADDLE DOWN THE HIGHWAY AFTER A RAIN,	234	ALL MORNING	26
	AFTER A WHILE THE LIGHT BEGAN TO WANE	274	SUPPR W LINDSAY	35
AFTER-IMAGE				
	THE AFTER-IMAGE NEVER STAYS THE SAME.	132	SENTENTIOUS MAN	20

	PAGE	TITLE	LINE

AFTER-IMAGE (CONTINUED)
| OR AFTER-IMAGE OF THE INNER EYE. | 155 | THE DYING MAN | 57 |
| THE EYES REJOICE IN THE ACT OF SEEING AND THE FRESH AFTER-IMAGE; | 163 | I'M HERE | 79 |

AFTERLIGHT
| THE LAST GEESE CROSSING AGAINST THE REFLECTED AFTERLIGHT, | 202 | THE ROSE | 17 |

AFTER-LIGHT
| TO STARE INTO THE AFTER-LIGHT, THE GLITTER LEFT ON THE LAKE'S SURFACE, | 67 | SHAPE OF FIRE | 88 |
| THE AFTER-LIGHT UPON ICE-BURDENED PINES; | 201 | THE FAR FIELD | 97 |

AFTERNOON
OR AFTERNOON OF LIGHT	139	PLAINT	10
IN A WORLD ALWAYS LATE AFTERNOON,	171	WHAT TELL BONES	10
SHE'D MUDDLE THE WHOLE AFTERNOON	179	MYRTLE'S COUSIN	9
WHEN THE ICE MELTS ALONG THE EDGES IN EARLY AFTERNOON.	191	AT OYSTER RIVER	48
AND THE BUNCHED LOGS PEEL IN THE AFTERNOON SUNLIGHT,	196	THE LONG WATERS	16

AFTERNOONS
| SIFT, ALMOST INVISIBLE, THROUGH LONG AFTERNOONS OF TEDIUM, | 46 | DOLOR | 11 |

AFTERWARDS
| AND AFTERWARDS I ALWAYS FELT MEAN, JOGGING BACK OVER THE LOGGING ROAD, | 40 | MOSS-GATHERING | 9 |

AGAIN
NIBBLE AGAIN, FISH NERVES.	55	THE LOST SON	70
IT WILL COME AGAIN.	58	THE LOST SON	171
I TAKE IT, AND I GIVE IT BACK AGAIN:	105	SIR JOHN DAVIES	20
I THOUGHT THAT ONCE, AND THOUGHT COMES ROUND AGAIN;	107	SIR JOHN DAVIES	87
YOU ASKED ME BEFORE, I'LL TELL YOU AGAIN:	114	DINKY	11
THEN OFF AGAIN TO SLEEP HE GOES,	116	THE SLOTH	10
A LIVELY THING CAN COME TO LIFE AGAIN.	129	SHE	12
AS IF ALL THINGS HAD DIED, AND ROSE AGAIN.	133	THE PURE FURY	6
SHE TRIES TO THINK, AND IT FLIES LOOSE AGAIN.	133	THE PURE FURY	11
WILL THE SELF, LOST, BE FOUND AGAIN? IN FORM?	135	THE RENEWAL	17
IF WE DO THIS AGAIN," --	136	THE SENSUALISTS	24
FALTERED; ROSE UP AGAIN;	145	THE BEAST	12
I TURNED AND TURNED AGAIN,	147	THE EXORCISM	20
I DOUBT I'LL USE IT AGAIN.	153	THE DYING MAN	5
AND WOULD THE SAME AGAIN.	154	THE DYING MAN	33
AND THEN I RAN AGAIN.	166	HER BECOMING	60
GLEAMING, FREEZING HARD AGAIN, CREAKING AT MIDNIGHT--	191	AT OYSTER RIVER	51
I'LL RETURN AGAIN,	200	THE FAR FIELD	47
WE MET TO LEAVE AGAIN	212	LIGHT LISTENED	19
THEN WE ROMPED OUT AGAIN,	214	THE HAPPY THREE	35
OUT AGAIN,	214	THE HAPPY THREE	36
OUT AGAIN,	214	THE HAPPY THREE	37
FOR THE WORLD INVADES ME AGAIN,	220	THE ABYSS	30
ENDING CURLED AROUND AND OVER AGAIN,	226	THE LIZARD	11
RISING AGAIN, SLOWLY,	226	THE LIZARD	25
I BROUGHT HER BACK IN AGAIN	228	THE GERANIUM	5
WHERE THEY DROPPED AGAIN	232	THE THING	11
AND IN BROAD DAY THE MIDNIGHT COME AGAIN!	239	IN A DARK TIME	15
AND WHEN I LOOK AGAIN,	240	IN EVEING AIR	16
WHAT WE PUT DOWN, MUST WE TAKE UP AGAIN?	243	THE MOTION	11
THE BIRD FLIES OUT, THE BIRD FLIES BACK AGAIN;	250	THE RIGHT THING	4
I SOON WILL BE MYSELF AGAIN.	256	IN HYDROTHERAPY	12

AGAINST
BUT WHEN HE BRUSHES UP AGAINST A SCREEN,	16	THE BAT	7
AGAINST DISASTER	19	AGNST DISASTER	T
AND PULLED THE GREEN SHADE AGAINST MORNING SUN.	29	THE REMINDER	8
LEAF-MOLD, MANURE, LIME, PILED AGAINST SLIPPERY PLANKS.	38	ROOT CELLAR	9
AS IF I HAD COMMITTED, AGAINST THE WHOLE SCHEME OF LIFE, A DESECRATION.	40	MOSS-GATHERING	13
THE SUN WAS AGAINST ME,	55	THE LOST SON	77
SCRAPING HER CHEEK AGAINST STRAW;	102	ELEGY FOR JANE	12
TOOK ARMS AGAINST OUR OWN OBSCURITY.	106	SIR JOHN DAVIES	54
OR THEY FLING THEMSELVES AGAINST TREE TRUNKS,	152	THE SISKINS	16
AGAINST THE IMMENSE IMMEASURABLE EMPTINESS OF THINGS.	156	THE DYING MAN	101
BUMPING AGAINST STICKS AND BOTTOM-STONES, THEN SWINGING	159	FIRST MEDITATN	70
MY THIGHS BRUSHING AGAINST FLOWER-CROWNS;	161	I'M HERE	22
BRACING MY BACK AGAINST A SAPLING,	161	I'M HERE	24
SLAPPING LIGHTLY AGAINST A SUNKEN LOG.	190	AT OYSTER RIVER	14
THE ICE PILING HIGH AGAINST THE IRON-BOUND SPILES,	191	AT OYSTER RIVER	50
OVER THE THIN, FEATHERY RIPPLES BREAKING LIGHTLY AGAINST THE IRREGULAR SHORELINE--	197	THE LONG WATERS	50

	PAGE	TITLE	LINE
AGAINST (CONTINUED)			
AND THE GULLS CRY AGAINST THE CROWS	202	THE ROSE	7
AND THE TIDE RISES UP AGAINST THE GRASS	202	THE ROSE	9
THE LAST GEESE CROSSING AGAINST THE REFLECTED AFTERLIGHT,	202	THE ROSE	17
PITTING MY BREAST AGAINST THE RUSHING AIR,	209	HER LONGING	18
OR BEATING AGAINST THE BLACK CLOUDS OF THE STORM,	209	HER LONGING	22
AGAINST THE STONE BREAKWATER,	230	THE STORM	1
AND THE SMALL STREET-LAMP SWINGING AND SLAMMING AGAINST THE LAMP POLE.	230	THE STORM	7
MY SHADOW PINNED AGAINST A SWEATING WALL.	239	IN A DARK TIME	10
AGED			
AGED THIRTEEN.	87	PRAISE TO END!	58
AGENCY			
OR AGENCY OUTSIDE ME.	173	WHAT TELL BONES	99
AGES			
BUT NOW THE INSTANT AGES,	80	GIVE WAY, GATES	43
THE INSTANT AGES ON.	154	THE DYING MAN	25
THE INSTANT AGES ON THE LIVING EYE;	244	INFIRMITY	13
AGING			
HE LIKES THE ATTIC OF AN AGING HOUSE.	16	THE BAT	2
AGING, I SOMETIMES WEEP,	130	THE OTHER	23
HERE IN OUR AGING DISTRICT THE WOOD PIGEON LIVES WITH US,	234	ALL MORNING	1
BY DYING INWARD, LIKE AN AGING TREE.	244	INFIRMITY	12
AGITATION			
I HAVE MARRIED MY HANDS TO PERPETUAL AGITATION,	56	THE LOST SON	109
AGO			
OH THAT WAS LONG AGO! I KEPT	6	THE PREMONITION	3
YOUR LITTLE MANHOOD LONG AGO WAS SMOTHERED.	25	DIM-WIT COUSIN	2
OR FRENCHMEN KILLED A HUNDRED YEARS AGO,	224	OTTO	26
AGONIES			
OUR SMALL SOULS HID FROM THEIR SMALL AGONIES,	238	THE TRANCED	21
AGONY			
TO WITLESS AGONY.	3	OPEN HOUSE	18
AGONY OF CRUCIFIXION ON BARSTOOLS.	187	THE LONGING	6
AND YET SHE DIED IN AGONY,	223	ELEGY (2)	16
AH			
AH, WHEN SHE MOVED, SHE MOVED MORE WAYS THAN ONE:	127	I KNEW A WOMAN	3
AH, HOW SHE LAUGHED TO SEE	262	FOLLIES OF ADAM	16
AHEAD			
I SMELL THE JUMPS AHEAD.	81	SENSIBILITY! LA	14
O SWEET FIELD FAR AHEAD, I HEAR YOUR BIRDS,	156	THE DYING MAN	88
RAN AHEAD OF MYSELF,	166	HER BECOMING	50
AIMING			
HE ALWAYS KNEW WHAT HE WAS AIMING AT.	224	OTTO	17
AIMLESS			
AND SMALL MOUTHS, STAY YOUR AIMLESS CHEEPING:	92	I CRY, LOVE!	23
A SPORTIVE, AIMLESS ONE,	145	THE BEAST	7
AIMLESSLY			
SO THEY CIRCLED AIMLESSLY FOR ALMOST A MINUTE,	232	THE THING	8
AIMLESSNESS			
PURE AIMLESSNESS PURSUED AND YET PURSUED	241	THE SEQUEL	3
AIR			
THE ELEMENT OF AIR WAS OUT OF HAND.	6	INTERLUDE	1
AT DUSK OUR SLOW BREATH THICKENS ON THE AIR.	12	SLOW SEASON	8
THE YIELD'S HALF DOWN AND HALF IN AIR,	14	COMING OF COLD	8
THE RICHES OF THE AIR BLOW THIN.	14	COMING OF COLD	21
TO CONFLAGRATION IN THE UPPER AIR.	17	UNEXTINGUISHED	3
DRAWING IN THE WARM AIR.	39	ORCHIDS	8
OUT INTO THE SWEET AIR,	42	TRANSPLANTING	20
AND THE AIR COOL, AS IF DRIFTING DOWN FROM WET HEMLOCKS,	43	CARNATIONS	3
THEY SEWED UP THE AIR WITH A STEM;	44	FRAU BAUMAN	22
OUT THROUGH THE VELVETY CHAINS TO THE COOL AIR OF NIGHT.	47	DOUBLE FEATURE	4
TURNED BY REVOLVING AIR	50	THE CYCLE	8
THE AIR GREW LOOSE AND LOUD.	50	THE CYCLE	12
AIR.	57	THE LOST SON	138
THROUGH THE CLEAR AIR, IN THE SILENCE.	58	THE LOST SON	163
THIS AIR COULD FLESH A DEAD STICK. SWEET JESUS, MAKE ME SWEAT.	61	THE LONG ALLEY	63
SWAYING OVER THE WALKS, IN THE WATERY AIR,	61	THE LONG ALLEY	75
SEND DOWN A RUSH OF AIR, O TORRENTIAL,	61	THE LONG ALLEY	83
AND I WALKED, I WALKED THROUGH THE LIGHT AIR;	63	FIELD OF LIGHT	51
THAT AIR AND SHINE: AND THE FLICKER'S LOUD SUMMER CALL:	66	SHAPE OF FIRE	70
TO HAVE THE WHOLE AIR!--	67	SHAPE OF FIRE	78

	PAGE	TITLE	LINE
AIR (CONTINUED)			
THE AIR, THE AIR PROVIDES.	83	O LULL ME, LULL	18
THE AIR, THE AIR PROVIDES.	83	O LULL ME, LULL	18
LACKING THE CANDOR OF DOGS, I KISS THE DEPARTING AIR;	86	PRAISE TO END!	26
YOUR FATHER TOSSED A CAT IN AIR,	86	PRAISE TO END!	36
ARCH OF AIR, MY HEART'S ORIGINAL KNOCK,	88	PRAISE TO END!	79
IN THE COLD AIR,	104	OLD LADY'S WRDS	63
TO YOU AND ME; SO TAKE THE LIVELY AIR,	108	THE WAKING (2)	14
SHE CAME TOWARD ME IN THE FLOWING AIR,	119	THE DREAM	9
ALL THE EARTH, ALL THE AIR	121	ALL EARTH, AIR	T
LOVING, I USE THE AIR	123	WORDS FOR WIND	3
IN RIVERY AIR, AT EASE,	125	WORDS FOR WIND	73
WHOSE THIN SONG HUNG IN AIR,	128	THE VOICE	9
THE EARTH, THE SOLID AIR--	128	THE VOICE	21
THE LIGHT AIR TAKES MY BEING'S BREATH AWAY;	134	THE PURE FURY	23
I PAW THE DARK, THE SHIFTING MIDNIGHT AIR.	135	THE RENEWAL	16
AND SHE IS WHAT I WOULD. IN THIS LIGHT AIR.	140	THE SWAN	17
ON THE LONG BANKS, IN THE SOFT SUMMER AIR.	149	IN LATE SUMMER	8
STAYED, IN THE STILL AIR.	150	SNAKE	5
AND THE FINCHES PITCH THROUGH THE AIR, TWITTERING;	152	THE SISKINS	7
THE LOOSE AIR SENT ME RUNNING LIKE A CHILD--	155	THE DYING MAN	55
HE QUIVERED LIKE A BIRD IN BIRDLESS AIR,	155	THE DYING MAN	64
AND THE AIR CLAPS BETWEEN US,	158	FIRST MEDITATN	35
THE AIR STILL, THE GROUND ALIVE,	165	HER BECOMING	14
IN A FIELD. IN THE ACTUAL AIR,	166	HER BECOMING	45
THE LIGHT AIR SLOWED: IT WAS NOT NIGHT OR DAY.	166	HER BECOMING	56
I LIVE IN AIR; THE LONG LIGHT IS MY HOME;	167	HER BECOMING	93
WHO TOOK THE DARKNESS FROM THE AIR?	173	WHAT TELL BONES	94
DOES HE POISE IN THE AIR,	183	THE WAGTAIL	4
IN A TOWER OF WIND, A TREE IDLING IN AIR,	195	JOURNY INTERIOR	70
AS A FIRE, SEEMINGLY LONG DEAD, FLARES UP FROM A DOWNDRAFT OF AIR IN A CHIMNEY,	198	THE LONG WATERS	63
ALWAYS, IN EARTH AND AIR.	201	THE FAR FIELD	81
WITH ALL THE AIR TO GREET HIM AS HE FLIES,	205	THE ROSE	109
PITTING MY BREAST AGAINST THE RUSHING AIR,	209	HER LONGING	18
THE CLOSE AIR FAINTLY STIRRED.	212	LIGHT LISTENED	7
A COLD AIR BROUGHT ITS RAIN,	212	LIGHT LISTENED	21
I SNIFF THE DARKENING AIR	215	HIS FOREBODING	17
I HAVE MERGED, LIKE THE BIRD, WITH THE BRIGHT AIR,	222	THE ABYSS	99
ABOVE THE BLUE AIR, IN THE SLIGHT HAZE BEYOND,	232	THE THING	3
AND THE BLUE AIR DARKENED.	232	THE THING	23
IN EVENING AIR	240	IN EVEING AIR	T
I SEE, IN EVENING AIR,	240	IN EVEING AIR	23
AN INTIMATE OF AIR AND ALL ITS SONGS?	241	THE SEQUEL	2
SWAYING IN AIR, LIKE SOME LONG WATER WEED.	241	THE SEQUEL	19
I SEEMED TO EAT THE AIR;	247	I WAITED	3
RIDING THE AIR, A WILLOW WITH ITS KIND,	248	THE TREE, BIRD	10
WITH EVERY SHIFT OF AIR, THOSE BEATING WINGS,	248	THE TREE, BIRD	15
THINK OF THE TASK OF AIR!--	260	THE CHANGELING	7
BIRDS TO THIS WATERY AIR?	261	THE CHANGELING	47
AIRS			
LIGHT AIRS! LIGHT AIRS! A PIERCE OF ANGELS!	61	THE LONG ALLEY	77
LIGHT AIRS! LIGHT AIRS! A PIERCE OF ANGELS!	61	THE LONG ALLEY	77
TO FOOLS AND FRAUDS: HE DOES NOT PUT ON AIRS	224	OTTO	3
AIR'S			
THE AIR'S QUIET UNDER THE SMALL LEAVES.	78	BRING THE DAY!	41
AIRY			
THIS FLESH HAS AIRY BONES.	99	O, THOU OPENING	82
THESE AIRY HIPPETY-HOP SKIPPERS,	152	THE SISKINS	20
AISLE			
LOVERS DISENGAGE, MOVE SHEEPISHLY TOWARD THE AISLE	47	DOUBLE FEATURE	2
ALACK			
--ALAS, ALACK FOR HARRY!	181	MONOTONY SONG	16
BUT ALAS, ALACK, AND ME ACHIN' BACK,	268	SAGINAW SONG	45
ALARM			
AND ROUT THE SPECTER OF ALARM.	19	AGNST DISASTER	12
ALAS			
THERE'S NO ALAS	74	I NEED, I NEED	14
--ALAS, ALACK FOR HARRY!	181	MONOTONY SONG	16
BUT ALAS, ALACK, AND ME ACHIN' BACK,	268	SAGINAW SONG	45
ALBINO			
THY SOFT ALBINO GAZE	81	SENSIBILITY! LA	10

	PAGE	TITLE	LINE
ALDER			
THE UPLAND OF ALDER AND BIRCHTREES,	193	JOURNY INTERIOR	13
PAST ALDER LANE, AND WE GABBED THERE A WHILE.	274	SUPPR W LINDSAY	47
ALDERMAN			
WITH THE DARK HEARSE, AND ENOUGH FLOWERS FOR AN ALDERMAN,--	223	ELEGY (2)	2
ALERT			
I'VE CRAWLED FROM THE MIRE, ALERT AS A SAINT OR A DOG;	88	PRAISE TO END!	81
I WAITED, ALERT AS A DOG.	100	THE VISITANT	7
ALGAE			
I WAS PRIVY TO OILY FUNGUS AND THE ALGAE OF STANDING WATER;	89	UNFOLD! UNFOLD!	25
ALGY'S			
AND OVER BY ALGY'S	77	BRING THE DAY!	13
ALICE			
SWEET ALICE S. MORRIS, I AM PLEASED, OF COURSE,	113	TO A LADY ED	1
ALIEN			
I HEAR YOU, ALIEN OF THE MOON.	82	SENSIBILITY! LA	44
ALIVE			
THE ARBOR IS ALIVE WITH FUME	14	COMING OF COLD	2
"I SEE THE RIVER HARBOR, ALIVE WITH MEN AND SHIPS,	28	CLAIRVOY WIDOW	19
LIPS NEITHER DEAD NOR ALIVE,	39	ORCHIDS	16
ALIVE, IN A SLIPPERY GRAVE.	39	WEED PULLER	16
FINER THAN FLOUR, ALIVE, MORE DANGEROUS THAN SILICA,	46	DOLOR	10
STILLNESS BECOMING ALIVE,	58	THE LOST SON	167
ONLY THE WOODS ARE ALIVE.	77	BRING THE DAY!	19
SO ALIVE I COULD DIE!	99	O, THOU OPENING	58
I'M REMINDED TO STAY ALIVE	104	OLD LADY'S WRDS	56
ALIVE AT NOON, I PERISHED IN HER FORM.	107	SIR JOHN DAVIES	94
I STAY ALIVE, BOTH IN AND OUT OF TIME,	131	SENTENTIOUS MAN	14
I LIVE, ALIVE AND CERTAIN AS A BULL;	140	THE SWAN	9
A MAN ALIVE, FROM ALL LIGHT I MUST FALL.	140	THE SWAN	12
REMIND ME TO STAY ALIVE.	154	THE DYING MAN	23
THE AIR STILL, THE GROUND ALIVE,	165	HER BECOMING	14
THE ONLY THING ALIVE IN HEAVEN'S EYE,	166	HER BECOMING	58
BY MIDNIGHT I LOVE EVERYTHING ALIVE.	173	WHAT TELL BONES	93
ALIVE WITH TINY STRIPED FISH, AND YOUNG CRABS CLIMBING IN AND OUT OF THE WATER.	190	AT OYSTER RIVER	5
THROUGH THE SWAMP ALIVE WITH QUICKSAND,	193	JOURNY INTERIOR	14
THE WEEDY EDGE, ALIVE WITH SMALL SNAKES AND BLOODSUCKERS,--	200	THE FAR FIELD	70
AS IF I SWAYED OUT ON THE WILDEST WAVE ALIVE,	205	THE ROSE	104
BY LUST ALONE WE KEEP THE MIND ALIVE,	243	THE MOTION	5
THE LIKELIEST GANDER ALIVE.	258	SONG (3)	18
A MAN, A MAN ALIVE.	271	THE REPLY	17
ALKALINE			
DOWN BY THE MUCK SHRINKING TO THE ALKALINE CENTER.	197	THE LONG WATERS	43
ALL			
MY TRUTHS ARE ALL FOREKNOWN,	3	OPEN HOUSE	7
HANDS, HARD AND VEINED ALL OVER,	7	ORDERS FOR DAY	1
TAKE TONGUE AND EAR--ALL ELSE I HAVE--	8	PRAYER	21
ALL NIGHT AND ALL DAY THE WIND ROARED IN THE TREES,	12	MID-CNTRY BLOW	1
ALL NIGHT AND ALL DAY THE WIND ROARED IN THE TREES,	12	MID-CNTRY BLOW	1
ALL SHADE IS LEAN, THE ANTIC BRANCH	14	COMING OF COLD	28
ALL THINGS ARE BROUGHT TO BARN AND FOLD.	15	COMING OF COLD	34
ALL SUMMER GREEN IS NOW UNDONE:	15	COMING OF COLD	42
ALL DISTANT SHAPES TURN BRIGHTER TO THE GAZE.	17	UNEXTINGUISHED	4
ALL THINGS UNHOLY, MARRED BY CURSE,	18	LONG LIVE WEEDS	5
MY SOURCES DRAINED OF ALL CONTENT,	19	AGNST DISASTER	3
ALL RANDOM, WASTED, AND DISPERSED,	19	AGNST DISASTER	5
AND ALL THE RUBBISH OF CONFUSION SOLD.	21	THE AUCTION	16
WANTS SINGLENESS OF SPIRIT ABOVE ALL ELSE:	24	POETASTER	2
THOUGH IT ALL HAPPENED BEFORE, I CANNOT GROW BITTER:	24	VERNAL SENTIMNT	7
DELIVER ME, O LORD, FROM ALL	24	BEFORE STUDY	9
THE LAWYERS ALL ARE CUNNING, THE BUSINESS MEN ARE FAT,	27	CLAIRVOY WIDOW	7
ALL PROFITS DISAPPEAR: THE GAIN	30	THE RECKONING	1
FOR ALL OUR SCRATCHING ON THE PAD,	30	THE RECKONING	7
ALL THE RINGS AND THE RELICS ENCRUSTED WITH SIN	32	SALE	19
ALL CROSS MY LINE OF SIGHT,	34	NIGHT JOURNEY	9
ALL PULSE WITH THE KNOCKING PIPES	38	FORCING HOUSE	5
TUGGING ALL DAY AT PERVERSE LIFE:	39	WEED PULLER	9
CRAWLING ON ALL FOURS,	39	WEED PULLER	15
TO LOOSEN WITH ALL TEN FINGERS HELD WIDE AND LIMBER	40	MOSS-GATHERING	1
ALL THE FAUCETS STOPPED?--	41	BIG WIND	5
WE STAYED ALL NIGHT,	41	BIG WIND	19
ALL IN ONE,	42	TRANSPLANTING	8

		PAGE	TITLE	LINE
ALL (CONTINUED)				
OR STAND ALL NIGHT WATERING ROSES, HIS FEET BLUE IN RUBBER BOOTS.		42	OLD FLORIST	10
A FEW WHITE CLOUDS ALL RUSHING EASTWARD,		43	CHILD ON GRNHSE	5
ALL THE COILS, LOOPS, AND WHORLS.		44	FRAU BAUMAN	24
THE FRUIT ROLLED BY ALL DAY.		46	PICKLE BELT	1
ALL THE MISERY OF MANILLA FOLDERS AND MUCILAGE,		46	DOLOR	3
PRICKLING WITH ALL THE ITCHES		46	PICKLE BELT	11
I SAID: ON ALL THESE, DEATH, WITH GENTLENESS, COME DOWN.		48	JUDGE NOT	10
AND ALL THE WATERS		51	THE WAKING (1)	25
OF ALL THE STREAMS		51	THE WAKING (1)	26
ALL THE LEAVES STUCK OUT THEIR TONGUES;		53	THE LOST SON	5
HATH THE RAIN A FATHER? ALL THE CAVES ARE ICE. ONLY THE SNOW'S HERE.		56	THE LOST SON	84
I'M COLD. I'M COLD ALL OVER. RUB ME IN FATHER AND MOTHER.		56	THE LOST SON	85
ALL THE WINDOWS ARE BURNING! WHAT'S LEFT OF MY LIFE?		56	THE LOST SON	106
DARK ALL THE WAY,		57	THE LOST SON	123
ONCE I STAYED ALL NIGHT.		57	THE LOST SON	134
MY GATES ARE ALL CAVES.		59	THE LONG ALLEY	20
I SAW THE SEPARATENESS OF ALL THINGS!		63	FIELD OF LIGHT	45
THESE FLOWERS ARE ALL FANGS. COMFORT ME, FURY.		64	SHAPE OF FIRE	9
THE BEARDED BOARDS IN THE STREAM AND THE ALL OF APPLES;		66	SHAPE OF FIRE	71
ALL HAVE PUPPIES.		71	WHERE KNOCK IS	8
I SANG I SANG ALL DAY.		72	WHERE KNOCK IS	38
HE WAS ALL WHITEY BONES		73	WHERE KNOCK IS	78
A DOVE SAID DOVE ALL DAY.		75	I NEED, I NEED	20
EVEN STEVEN ALL IS LESS:		75	I NEED, I NEED	23
THE OATS ARE ALL RIGHT.		76	I NEED, I NEED	56
IT WAS ALL HAY.		76	I NEED, I NEED	62
WHAT'S ALL THE SINGING BETWEEN?--		77	BRING THE DAY!	26
NOT ALL ANIMALS		83	O LULL ME, LULL	6
I'M ALL READY TO WHISTLE;		84	O LULL ME, LULL	36
ALL RISINGS		85	PRAISE TO END!	15
I DREAMT I WAS ALL BONES;		87	PRAISE TO END!	63
I'M AWAKE ALL OVER:		88	PRAISE TO END!	80
MY GHOSTS ARE ALL GAY.		88	PRAISE TO END!	100
YOU'RE BLISTERED ALL OVER		89	UNFOLD! UNFOLD!	14
ALL OPENINGS PRAISE US, EVEN OILY HOLES.		90	UNFOLD! UNFOLD!	40
SING, SING, YOU SYMBOLS! ALL SIMPLE CREATURES,		90	UNFOLD! UNFOLD!	45
ALL SMALL SHAPES, WILLOW-SHY,		90	UNFOLD! UNFOLD!	46
IN A SODDEN PLACE, ALL RAPS AND KNOCKS APPROVE.		93	I CRY, LOVE!	30
AND NOW ARE WE TO HAVE THAT PELLUDIOUS JESUS-SHIMMER OVER ALL THINGS,		98	O, THOU OPENING	21
I'M TIRED OF ALL THAT, BAG-FOOT. I CAN HEAR SMALL ANGELS ANYTIME. WHO		98	O, THOU OPENING	25
FOR THEY ARE ALL MY FRIENDS: I SAW ONE SLIDE		105	SIR JOHN DAVIES	7
BUT WHAT I LEARNED THERE, DANCING ALL ALONE,		105	SIR JOHN DAVIES	17
THE LIVING ALL ASSEMBLE! WHAT'S THE CUE?--		106	SIR JOHN DAVIES	41
LAY ALL THE LONELY PASTURES OF THE DEAD;		106	SIR JOHN DAVIES	51
ALL LOVERS LIVE BY LONGING, AND ENDURE:		107	SIR JOHN DAVIES	77
THE WORD OUTLEAPS THE WORLD, AND LIGHT IS ALL.		107	SIR JOHN DAVIES	96
THEY ALL SAT DOWN LIKE ME AND YOU		111	SQUEEZE-BOX	6
(IT TURNED OUT SHE HADN'T A FATHER AT ALL)		111	SQUEEZE-BOX	15
FOR WHENEVER I COULD, I DEALT THEM ALL IN		112	SQUEEZE-BOX	32
THE DOCTORS, THE LAWYERS, THE COPS ARE ALL PAID--		112	SQUEEZE-BOX	42
HE SAID, "LOOK, BIRDS, ALL THIS IS FUTILE:		115	THE SERPENT	19
ALL WHO REMEMBER, DOUBT. WHO CALLS THAT STRANGE?		120	THE DREAM	21
ALL THE EARTH, ALL THE AIR		121	ALL EARTH, AIR	T
ALL THE EARTH, ALL THE AIR		121	ALL EARTH, AIR	T
ALL INNOCENCE AND WIT,		121	ALL EARTH, AIR	11
ALL THINGS BRING ME TO LOVE.		125	WORDS FOR WIND	81
I LOLL, I LOLL, ALL TONGUE.		130	THE OTHER	16
TRUE LECHERS LOVE THE FLESH, AND THAT IS ALL.		131	SENTENTIOUS MAN	6
AND ALL DIMENSIONS QUIVERED TO ONE THING.		132	SENTENTIOUS MAN	24
AND FOUND OUT ALL I COULD OF ALL DESIRE;		132	SENTENTIOUS MAN	32
AND FOUND OUT ALL I COULD OF ALL DESIRE;		132	SENTENTIOUS MAN	32
AS IF ALL THINGS HAD DIED, AND ROSE AGAIN.		133	THE PURE FURY	6
GREAT BOEHME ROOTED ALL IN YES AND NO;		133	THE PURE FURY	13
LOVE ALTERS ALL. UNBLOOD MY INSTINCT, LOVE.		135	THE RENEWAL	10
MY HAIR'S ALL TANGLED ON YOUR HEAD,		136	THE SENSUALISTS	3
AND ALL THE BIRDS ARE STONE.		138	LOVE'S PROGRESS	22
A MAN ALIVE, FROM ALL LIGHT I MUST FALL.		140	THE SWAN	12
SING OF THAT NOTHING OF WHICH ALL IS MADE,		140	THE SWAN	19

	PAGE	TITLE	LINE
ALL (CONTINUED)			
AND SHE KNOWS ALL I AM.	141	MEMORY	4
LOVE'S ALL. LOVE'S ALL I KNOW.	141	MEMORY	8
LOVE'S ALL. LOVE'S ALL I KNOW.	141	MEMORY	8
THE WEATHER WEPT, AND ALL THE TREES BENT DOWN;	143	SHIMMER OF EVIL	1
--THERE WAS NO LIGHT; THERE WAS NO LIGHT AT ALL:	143	SHIMMER OF EVIL	5
FAR FROM THE MIRRORS ALL THE BUSHES RANG	143	SHIMMER OF EVIL	6
--THERE WAS NO LIGHT; THERE WAS NO LIGHT AT ALL:	143	SHIMMER OF EVIL	10
--THERE WAS NO LIGHT; THERE WAS NO LIGHT AT ALL.	143	SHIMMER OF EVIL	15
THEN ALL IS AS IT WAS.	148	THE SMALL	12
AND ALL THE STONES HAVE WINGS.	148	THE SMALL	24
BEFORE THE CAVING-IN OF ALL THAT IS;	149	IN LATE SUMMER	14
A THING ALL EARTHLY LOVERS UNDERSTAND.	149	IN LATE SUMMER	22
A TREE ALL OUT OF SHAPE FROM WIND AND RAIN,	150	IN LATE SUMMER	27
NOW THEY MOVE ALL TOGETHER!--	152	THE SISKINS	19
I DARED TO QUESTION ALL,	154	THE DYING MAN	32
ALL SENSUAL LOVE'S BUT DANCING ON A GRAVE.	154	THE DYING MAN	47
ALL EXULTATION IS A DANGEROUS THING.	155	THE DYING MAN	72
I SHALL UNDO ALL DYING BY MY DEATH.	155	THE DYING MAN	77
ALL WOMEN LOVED DANCE IN A DYING LIGHT--	156	THE DYING MAN	78
NOR CAN IMAGINATION DO IT ALL	156	THE DYING MAN	98
ALL JOURNEYS, I THINK, ARE THE SAME:	158	FIRST MEDITATN	26
AND FOR A WHILE WE ARE ALL ALONE,	158	FIRST MEDITATN	28
WITH A WIND FROM THE WEST AND THE TREES ALL IN MOTION.	158	FIRST MEDITATN	42
LIVING ALL MY HEART'S SUMMER ALONE,	161	I'M HERE	19
LEANING, OUT OF ALL BREATH,	161	I'M HERE	23
MY GERANIUM IS DYING, FOR ALL I CAN DO,	163	I'M HERE	75
BIRDS ARE AROUND. I'VE ALL THE SINGING I WOULD.	164	I'M HERE	93
ALL NATURAL SHAPES BECAME SYMBOLICAL.	166	HER BECOMING	57
A SMALL PLACE ALL IN FLAME.	167	HER BECOMING	77
ASK ALL THE MICE WHO CAPER IN THE STRAW--	167	HER BECOMING	86
I DRINK MY TEARS IN A PLACE WHERE ALL LIGHT COMES.	170	FOURTH MEDITATN	78
THE FIRST AND LAST OF ALL THINGS.	170	FOURTH MEDITATN	86
IT IS DIFFICULT TO SAY ALL THINGS ARE WELL,	172	WHAT TELL BONES	34
MOTHER, MOTHER OF US ALL, TELL ME WHERE I AM!	172	WHAT TELL BONES	53
HOW SLOWLY ALL THINGS ALTER.	173	WHAT TELL BONES	66
I LIVE IN LIGHT'S EXTREME; I STRETCH IN ALL DIRECTIONS;	173	WHAT TELL BONES	82
THE SUN! THE SUN! AND ALL WE CAN BECOME!	173	WHAT TELL BONES	84
I HAD A DONKEY, THAT WAS ALL RIGHT,	178	THE DONKEY	1
ALL OVER YOUR HAT,--	180	GOO-GIRL	8
BUT FOUND HE WASN'T THERE AT ALL,	181	MONOTONY SONG	14
AND YOU CAN SING IT ALL DAY LONG--	181	MONOTONY SONG	22
HE JUMPS ALL OVER. WHO	182	THE LAMB	3
HE STARTS TO YAWN--IT TAKES ALL DAY--	182	THE HIPPO	4
THE ROSE EXCEEDS, THE ROSE EXCEEDS US ALL.	188	THE LONGING	29
--HOW FREE; HOW ALL ALONE.	188	THE LONGING	36
--ALL BEGINNINGS COME.	188	THE LONGING	38
I WOULD UNLEARN THE LINGO OF EXASPERATION, ALL THE DISTORTIONS OF MALICE AND HATRED;	188	THE LONGING	42
IN THE CRADLE OF ALL THAT IS,	191	AT OYSTER RIVER	59
AND ALL FLOWS PAST--	194	JOURNY INTERIOR	34
I SEE THE FLOWER OF ALL WATER, ABOVE AND BELOW ME, THE NEVER RECEDING,	194	JOURNY INTERIOR	52
HOW THEY FILLED THE ORIOLE'S ELM, A TWITTERING RESTLESS CLOUD, ALL ONE MORNING,	199	THE FAR FIELD	28
WAKES ALL THE WAVES, ALL THEIR LOOSE WANDERING FIRE.	201	THE FAR FIELD	88
WAKES ALL THE WAVES, ALL THEIR LOOSE WANDERING FIRE.	201	THE FAR FIELD	88
ALL FINITE THINGS REVEAL INFINITUDE:	201	THE FAR FIELD	94
WHEN THE MIND REMEMBERS ALL,	204	THE ROSE	75
WITH ALL THE AIR TO GREET HIM AS HE FLIES,	205	THE ROSE	109
"WRITE ALL MY WHISPERS DOWN,"	208	HER WORDS	8
WHEN ALL	210	HER TIME	1
ALL'S KNOWN, ALL, ALL AROUND:	212	LIGHT LISTENED	13
ALL'S KNOWN, ALL, ALL AROUND:	212	LIGHT LISTENED	13
ALL RAGE WAS GONE.	213	THE HAPPY THREE	28
WHO KNOWS THE END OF IT ALL?	215	HIS FOREBODING	8
IS SHE THE ALL OF LIGHT?	215	HIS FOREBODING	16
THE EDGE OF ALL THE LAND, THE FINAL SEA?	221	THE ABYSS	63
KNOWS ALL."	222	THE ABYSS	88
I RECALL HOW SHE HARRIED THE CHILDREN AWAY ALL THE LATE SUMMER	223	ELEGY (2)	12
MAX LAURISCH HAD THE GREENEST THUMB OF ALL.	224	OTTO	7
ALL THINGS INNOCENT, HAPLESS, FORSAKEN.	227	MEADOW MOUSE	29

	PAGE	TITLE	LINE
ALL (CONTINUED)			
BUT THAT'S ALL RIGHT,--	228	IN VIOLENT WARD	3
THREW HER, POT AND ALL, INTO THE TRASH-CAN,	228	THE GERANIUM	23
ALL MORNING	234	ALL MORNING	T
ALL DURING MATING SEASON,	234	ALL MORNING	17
ALL BIRDS REMEMBERED, O NEVER FORGOTTEN!	235	ALL MORNING	45
ALL IN MY YARD, OF A PERPETUAL SUNDAY,	235	ALL MORNING	46
ALL MORNING! ALL MORNING!	235	ALL MORNING	47
ALL MORNING! ALL MORNING!	235	ALL MORNING	47
ALL FLOWED: WITHOUT, WITHIN;	238	THE MOMENT	10
YET IT'S THE NATURE OF ALL LOVE TO RISE:	238	THE TRANCED	22
ALL NATURAL SHAPES BLAZING UNNATURAL LIGHT.	239	IN A DARK TIME	18
AN INTIMATE OF AIR AND ALL ITS SONGS?	241	THE SEQUEL	2
AND ALL WILD LONGINGS OF THE INSATIATE BLOOD	241	THE SEQUEL	4
ALL WATERS WAVER, AND ALL FIRES FAIL.	242	THE SEQUEL	26
ALL WATERS WAVER, AND ALL FIRES FAIL.	242	THE SEQUEL	26
I FEEL THE AUTUMN FAIL--ALL THAT SLOW FIRE	242	THE SEQUEL	31
KNOWING HOW ALL THINGS ALTER IN THE SEED	243	THE MOTION	15
IN WHICH ALL CREATURES SHARE, AND THEREBY LIVE,	243	THE MOTION	18
A MIND TOO ACTIVE IS NO MIND AT ALL;	244	INFIRMITY	19
DEAD TO MYSELF, AND ALL I HOLD MOST DEAR,	244	INFIRMITY	23
MY EARS STILL HEAR THE BIRD WHEN ALL IS STILL;	244	INFIRMITY	28
RUNNING FROM GOD'S THE LONGEST RACE OF ALL.	245	THE DECISION	2
RISING OR FALLING'S ALL ONE DISCIPLINE!	245	THE DECISION	7
WHEN CONTEMPLATION DAZZLES ALL I SEE;	246	THE MARROW	8
TO SLEEP IS ALL MY LIFE. IN SLEEP'S HALF-DEATH,	246	THE MARROW	14
I SAW ALL THINGS THROUGH WATER, MAGNIFIED,	247	I WAITED	10
AND I BECAME ALL THAT I LOOKED UPON.	247	I WAITED	12
AND ALL THE WINDS CAME TOWARD ME. I WAS GLAD.	247	I WAITED	23
ALL BY ITSELF.	249	THE RESTORED	4
HIS BEING SINGLE, AND THAT BEING ALL:	250	THE RIGHT THING	11
AND THE EYE ALTERING ALL;	251	ONCE MORE, RND	8
ALL THAT DIVING AND PITCHING AND SWOOPING.	255	LIGHT POEM	5
LIGHT STAYED ALL NIGHT,	258	SONG (3)	14
ALL THINGS ARE VULNERABLE, STILL;	259	SONG (3)	47
YOU LARKS ALL DAY, YOU ROBINS RIGHT,	260	THE CHANGELING	22
HOW FREE! HOW ALL ALONE!	261	THE CHANGELING	39
BY ALL THE THINGS THAT ARE,	261	THE CHANGELING	41
AT EASE WITH ALL THAT FLOWS.	262	FOLLIES OF ADAM	14
ALL TRUE BONES SING ALONE.	263	FOLLIES OF ADAM	28
HE RODE ALL NIGHT, AND CAME	263	FOLLIES OF ADAM	32
THE MUSES, THEY MUST ALL ADORE HIM,	266	FOR STEVENS	18
ALL WOMEN, O, ARE BEAUTIFUL	268	SAGINAW SONG	60
BUT IT HAD A FLAVOR ALL ITS OWN,	270	GOB MUSIC	40
I'LL FACE ALL THAT, AND THE DIVINE ABSURD:	272	DUET	5
LET'S EAT BEFORE THE MOONLIGHT ALL RUNS OUT."	273	SUPPR W LINDSAY	29
WE'RE GETTING CLOSER TO IT ALL THE TIME."	274	SUPPR W LINDSAY	45
ALLEY			
THE LONG ALLEY	59	THE LONG ALLEY	T
AND A CHILD'S DIRTY SHIFT BILLOWS UPWARD OUT OF AN ALLEY,	230	THE STORM	18
DEAR SPARROWS OF THIS ALLEY,	261	THE CHANGELING	37
ALLEYS			
THE LONG ALLEYS OF STRING AND STEM;	61	THE LONG ALLEY	70
ALL-OF-A-SUDDEN			
YOU ALL-OF-A-SUDDEN GODS,	82	SENSIBILITY! LA	26
ALLOW			
MOTHER ME OUT OF HERE. WHAT MORE WILL THE BONES ALLOW?	64	SHAPE OF FIRE	7
ALL'S			
ALL'S EVEN WITH THE ODD,	123	WORDS FOR WIND	7
THOUGH ALL'S IN MOTION, WHO IS PASSING BY?	132	SENTENTIOUS MAN	19
ALL'S A SCATTERING,	192	AT OYSTER RIVER	69
ALL'S KNOWN, ALL, ALL AROUND:	212	LIGHT LISTENED	13
ALLUSIONS			
VERSE WITH ALLUSIONS	25	VERSE W ALLUSNS	T
ALLUVIAL			
BEFORE DESCENDING TO THE ALLUVIAL PLAIN,	200	THE FAR FIELD	65
ALMOST			
SIFT, ALMOST INVISIBLE, THROUGH LONG AFTERNOONS OF TEDIUM,	46	DOLOR	11
WHEN I STAND, I'M ALMOST A TREE.	78	BRING THE DAY!	32
I STRETCHED LIKE A BOARD, ALMOST A TREE.	90	UNFOLD! UNFOLD!	32
UNTIL HE FINDS THE THING HE ALMOST WAS	133	THE PURE FURY	19
THEN FLYING ALMOST STRAIGHT UPWARD,	152	THE SISKINS	3
A SHAPE WITHOUT A SHADE, OR ALMOST NONE,	167	HER BECOMING	88

	PAGE	TITLE	LINE
ALMOST (CONTINUED)			
COME THE FIRST TIDE-RIPPLES, MOVING, ALMOST WITHOUT SOUND, TOWARD ME,	190	AT OYSTER RIVER	2
MAKES ALMOST A WAVE OVER A BARRIER OF SMALL STONES,	190	AT OYSTER RIVER	13
AND THE BACK WHEELS HANG ALMOST OVER THE EDGE	193	JOURNY INTERIOR	4
FEATHERS OF THE LONG SWELL, BURNISHED, ALMOST OILY--	197	THE LONG WATERS	51
BEFORE THE ALMOST INVISIBLE	210	HER TIME	16
NEAR THE END, SHE SEEMED ALMOST TO HEAR ME--	228	THE GERANIUM	20
SO THEY CIRCLED AIMLESSLY FOR ALMOST A MINUTE,	232	THE THING	8
AND I LEAN, ALMOST INTO THE WATER,	233	THE PIKE	11
ALMOST-INVISIBLE			
ITS ALMOST-INVISIBLE WINGS, BUZZING, HITTING THE LOOSE LEAVES INTERMITTENTLY--	234	ALL MORNING	32
ALOFT			
ALOFT, AND ON THE GROUND.	128	THE VOICE	12
ALONE			
HAPPY ALONE IN HIS BEDROOM COUNTING HIS PULSE.	24	POETASTER	3
ALONE, HIS WIFE IS GRIEVING FOR WHAT HER HEART DESIRES.	27	CLAIRVOY WIDOW	14
NOW, WHEN I'M ALONE AND COLD IN MY BED,	44	FRAU BAUMAN	30
I WASN'T ALONE	51	THE WAKING (1)	15
THE MIND MOVED, NOT ALONE,	58	THE LOST SON	162
I WAS THERE ALONE	62	FIELD OF LIGHT	17
ALONE, I KISSED THE SKIN OF A STONE;	63	FIELD OF LIGHT	29
I'M ALONE WITH MY RIBS;	82	SENSIBILITY! LA	30
BUT I CAN'T GO LEAPING ALONE.	84	O LULL ME, LULL	32
BUMPKIN, HE CAN DANCE ALONE.	85	PRAISE TO END!	7
I'LL FEED THE GHOST ALONE.	85	PRAISE TO END!	11
THE RIVER'S ALONE WITH ITS WATER.	85	PRAISE TO END!	14
ALONE, IN A SLEEP-DAZE, I STARED AT BILLBOARDS;	89	UNFOLD! UNFOLD!	24
ALONE.	93	I CRY, LOVE!	58
POKING ALONE IN MY GARDEN.	103	OLD LADY'S WRDS	34
BUT WHAT I LEARNED THERE, DANCING ALL ALONE,	105	SIR JOHN DAVIES	17
IT WAS AND WAS NOT SHE, A SHAPE ALONE,	107	SIR JOHN DAVIES	71
KEEPS PACE WHEN I WALK ALONE.	123	WORDS FOR WIND	32
I BEAR, BUT NOT ALONE,	124	WORDS FOR WIND	59
OR COME TO LOVE ALONE?	130	THE OTHER	14
I WEEP FOR WHAT I'M LIKE WHEN I'M ALONE	132	SENTENTIOUS MAN	33
THE PURE ADMIRE THE PURE, AND LIVE ALONE;	133	THE PURE FURY	8
AND I WEPT THERE, ALONE.	145	THE BEAST	19
I WAS MYSELF, ALONE.	147	THE EXORCISM	25
IN THE WEAK LIGHT THEY WANDER, EACH ALONE.	149	IN LATE SUMMER	4
THE LONG DAY DIES; I WALKED THE WOODS ALONE;	150	IN LATE SUMMER	29
I BREATHE ALONE UNTIL MY DARK IS BRIGHT.	155	THE DYING MAN	51
I DIE INTO THIS LIFE, ALONE YET NOT ALONE.	155	THE DYING MAN	59
I DIE INTO THIS LIFE, ALONE YET NOT ALONE.	155	THE DYING MAN	59
I'VE THE LARK'S WORD FOR IT, WHO SINGS ALONE:	156	THE DYING MAN	90
ALONE, ON A BUS THROUGH WESTERN COUNTRY.	158	FIRST MEDITATN	21
AND FOR A WHILE WE ARE ALL ALONE,	158	FIRST MEDITATN	28
LIVING ALL MY HEART'S SUMMER ALONE,	161	I'M HERE	19
THE GRANDEUR OF A CRAZY ONE ALONE!--	167	HER BECOMING	90
I WAS ALWAYS ONE FOR BEING ALONE,	168	FOURTH MEDITATN	1
--HOW FREE; HOW ALL ALONE.	188	THE LONGING	36
OF DRIVING ALONE, WITHOUT LUGGAGE, OUT A LONG PENINSULA,	199	THE FAR FIELD	3
THE THRUSH SINGING ALONE, THAT EASY BIRD,	204	THE ROSE	61
WHO PASSED BY, ALONE.	208	THE APPARITION	4
ONCE WE WERE LEFT ALONE.	212	LIGHT LISTENED	4
TO NOTHINGNESS, ALONE.	215	HIS FOREBODING	13
I LIE HERE AND THINKING, "I AM NOT ALONE."	216	THE SHY MAN	19
OR THE TWO OF US, ALONE, BOTH SEEDY,	228	THE GERANIUM	17
BY LUST ALONE WE KEEP THE MIND ALIVE,	243	THE MOTION	5
HOW FREE! HOW ALL ALONE!	261	THE CHANGELING	39
ALL TRUE BONES SING ALONE.	263	FOLLIES OF ADAM	28
WITH HOPE, AND NOT ALONE,	265	HARSH COUNTRY	14
ALONG			
THE HAZE OF HARVEST DRIFTS ALONG THE FIELD	12	SLOW SEASON	3
SCUMS, MILDEWS, SMUTS ALONG STEMS,	38	FORCING HOUSE	3
LIKE WITCHES THEY FLEW ALONG ROWS	44	FRAU BAUMAN	19
HUNTING ALONG THE RIVER.	54	THE LOST SON	40
ALONG THE LOW GROUND DRY ONLY IN AUGUST,--	62	FIELD OF LIGHT	26
WALKED ALONG THE HIGHWAY,	87	PRAISE TO END!	53
LIGHT ALTERED LIGHT ALONG THE LIVING GROUND.	106	SIR JOHN DAVIES	34
JUST SEND ME ALONG THAT SWEET SEVENTY-FIVE;	113	TO A LADY ED	14
SHE STEPS ALONG THE STREET,	121	ALL EARTH, AIR	14

	PAGE	TITLE	LINE
ALONG (CONTINUED)			
AND WE BOUNCE AND SWAY ALONG TOWARD THE MIDNIGHT,	158	FIRST MEDITATN	23
AND ONE CRAB, TENTATIVE, HUNCHES HIMSELF BEFORE MOVING ALONG THE BOTTOM,	159	FIRST MEDITATN	62
OR THE WHIPPOORWILL, ALONG THE SMOKY RIDGES,	160	FIRST MEDITATN	89
RUNS FITFULLY ALONG THE STUBBLE,	160	FIRST MEDITATN	95
STANDING, SILENT, ON SANDY BEACHES OR WALKING ALONG GREEN EMBANKMENTS;	168	FOURTH MEDITATN	4
RUNNING ALONG THE NARROW FURROWS OF THE SHORE, THE ROWS OF DEAD CLAM SHELLS;	190	AT OYSTER RIVER	3
WHEN THE ICE MELTS ALONG THE EDGES IN EARLY AFTERNOON,	191	AT OYSTER RIVER	48
WHEN THE SLOW FREIGHT WINDS ALONG THE EDGE OF THE RAVAGED HILLSIDE,	204	THE ROSE	83
LIKE A LEECH, LOOPING MYSELF ALONG,	209	HER LONGING	7
ALONG THE SEA-WALL, A STEADY SLOSHING OF THE SWELL,	230	THE STORM	10
WHAT A SCUTTLING AND RAPPING ALONG THE DRAINPIPES,	234	ALL MORNING	21
ALOUD			
MY SECRETS CRY ALOUD.	3	OPEN HOUSE	1
ALREADY			
LET THE GESTURES FREEZE; OUR DOOM IS ALREADY DECIDED.	56	THE LOST SON	105
I'M A BISCUIT. I'M MELTED ALREADY.	77	BRING THE DAY!	21
ALSO			
IT WAS PLACE AND SHOW AND ALSO RAN	112	SQUEEZE-BOX	28
ALTER			
HOW SLOWLY ALL THINGS ALTER.	173	WHAT TELL BONES	66
KNOWING HOW ALL THINGS ALTER IN THE SEED	243	THE MOTION	15
ALTERED			
WHEN I LOOKED AT THE ALTERED SCENE, MY EYE WAS UNDECEIVED,	12	MID-CNTRY BLOW	7
THE BLOOD SLOWS TRANCE-LIKE IN THE ALTERED VEIN;	12	SLOW SEASON	15
LIGHT ALTERED LIGHT ALONG THE LIVING GROUND.	106	SIR JOHN DAVIES	34
THE GREEN, THE ALTERED LEAF,	125	WORDS FOR WIND	85
THE WAVES, ALTERED BY SAND-BARS, BEDS OF KELP, MISCELLANEOUS DRIFTWOOD,	191	AT OYSTER RIVER	32
ALTERING			
I WOULD DELIGHT IN MY HANDS, THE BRANCH SINGING, ALTERING THE EXCESSIVE BIRD;	188	THE LONGING	44
MY BODY ALTERS, ALTERING THE SOUL	246	THE MARROW	15
I COULD NOT BEAR ITS SONG, THAT ALTERING	248	THE TREE, BIRD	14
AND THE EYE ALTERING ALL;	251	ONCE MORE, RND	8
ALTERNATE			
ALTERNATE SNOW AND SLEET, NO ON-COMING TRAFFIC,	199	THE FAR FIELD	6
ALTERS			
LOVE ALTERS ALL. UNBLOOD MY INSTINCT, LOVE.	135	THE RENEWAL	10
MIST ALTERS THE ROCKS. WHAT CAN I TELL MY BONES?	172	WHAT TELL BONES	44
MY BODY ALTERS, ALTERING THE SOUL	246	THE MARROW	15
ALTES			
ALTES WUNDERKIND.	266	FOR STEVENS	16
ALWAYS			
BUT SOMETHING ALWAYS WENT OUT OF ME WHEN I DUG LOOSE THOSE CARPETS	40	MOSS-GATHERING	7
AND AFTERWARDS I ALWAYS FELT MEAN, JOGGING BACK OVER THE LOGGING ROAD,	40	MOSS-GATHERING	9
THERE WAS ALWAYS A SINGLE LIGHT	57	THE LOST SON	130
HE'S GONE FOR ALWAYS,	72	WHERE KNOCK IS	25
HAVE I COME TO ALWAYS? NOT YET.	74	WHERE KNOCK IS	86
WHAT FALLS AWAY IS ALWAYS. AND IS NEAR.	108	THE WAKING (2)	17
THEY SENT,--YOU ALWAYS SEND,--TO CUBA	115	THE SERPENT	15
THE LAST-ABANDONED STALK ALWAYS QUIVERING	152	THE SISKINS	14
THE SPIRIT MOVES, BUT NOT ALWAYS UPWARD,	157	FIRST MEDITATN	8
INACCESSIBLE, THE BOAT ALWAYS PULLING OUT	158	FIRST MEDITATN	50
A BIRD ALWAYS KEPT SINGING.	163	I'M HERE	73
I'M WHERE I ALWAYS WAS.	165	HER BECOMING	25
I WAS ALWAYS ONE FOR BEING ALONE,	168	FOURTH MEDITATN	1
IN A WORLD ALWAYS LATE AFTERNOON,	171	WHAT TELL BONES	10
BUT HE ALWAYS WANTED TO FLY MY KITE;	178	THE DONKEY	2
WHO ALWAYS DID THINGS BY THE DOZEN;	179	MYRTLE'S COUSIN	2
ALWAYS A SHARP TURN TO THE LEFT PAST A BARN CLOSE TO THE ROADSIDE,	193	JOURNY INTERIOR	25
ALWAYS, IN EARTH AND AIR.	201	THE FAR FIELD	81
THERE ALWAYS IS	219	THE ABYSS	10
HE ALWAYS KNEW WHAT HE WAS AIMING AT.	224	OTTO	17
MY EYE ALWAYS BEYOND THE SURFACE REFLECTION;	233	THE PIKE	12
IT IS NEITHER SPRING NOR SUMMER: IT IS ALWAYS,	235	ALL MORNING	39

	PAGE	TITLE	LINE
AM (57)			
AMBUSH			
THIS AMBUSH, THIS SILENCE,	188	THE LONGING	48
AMERICAN			
I THINK OF AMERICAN SOUNDS IN THIS SILENCE:	204	THE ROSE	59
AMISS			
FOR SOMETHING IS AMISS OR OUT OF PLACE	16	THE BAT	9
AMONG			
AMONG THE VIRULENT.	7	ORDERS FOR DAY	20
AMONG THE TREES THAT FACE THE CORNER LIGHT.	16	THE BAT	6
DOWN AMONG THE RUBBISH, THE BUG-RIDDLED FOLIAGE,	54	THE LOST SON	41
LIGHT AS A HAND AMONG BLOSSOMS,	78	BRING THE DAY!	39
AMONG THE UNWRINKLING FERNS	80	GIVE WAY, GATES	41
IT'S NECESSARY AMONG THE FLIES AND BANANAS, TO KEEP A CONSTANT VIGIL,	86	PRAISE TO END!	24
SOMEWHERE, AMONG THE FERNS AND BIRDS,	103	OLD LADY'S WRDS	12
MAY THEY SLEEP IN ROBES OF GREEN, AMONG THE ANCIENT FERNS;	169	FOURTH MEDITATN	58
YET MOVES GENTLY AMONG THE BIRDS.	170	FOURTH MEDITATN	74
THE BAREST SPEECH OF LIGHT AMONG THE STONES.	173	WHAT TELL BONES	71
AMONG THE SHY BEASTS, THE DEER AT THE SALT-LICK,	190	AT OYSTER RIVER	26
AMONG THE TIN CANS, TIRES, RUSTED PIPES, BROKEN MACHINERY,--	199	THE FAR FIELD	17
(I FOUND IT LYING AMONG THE RUBBLE OF AN OLD COAL BIN)	199	THE FAR FIELD	20
DOWN IN THE CORNER OF THE GARDEN, AMONG THE RAGGEDY LILACS,	204	THE ROSE	64
AND THE SEA REARRANGES ITSELF AMONG THE SMALL ISLANDS.	205	THE ROSE	97
AMONG THE HALF-DEAD TREES, I CAME UPON THE TRUE EASE OF MYSELF,	205	THE ROSE	99
AMONG MY EIGHT-LEGGED FRIENDS,	209	HER LONGING	5
AMONG US, WHO IS HOLY?	220	THE ABYSS	24
MOVING SERENELY AMONG THE LEEKS AND CABBAGES,	223	ELEGY (2)	20
THAT PLACE AMONG THE ROCKS--IS IT A CAVE,	239	IN A DARK TIME	11
AMOROUS			
FOR AN AMOROUS LADY	23	AMOROUS LADY	T
WHEN AMOROUS ARTS WE WOULD PURSUE,	23	AMOROUS LADY	11
AMORPHOUS			
OLD SECRETS TO AMORPHOUS SWARMS.	4	FEUD	16
AN (89)			
ANALOGIES			
DO THESE ANALOGIES PERPLEX? A SKY WITH CLOUDS,	235	MANIFESTATION	6
ANATOMY			
THE RAGS OF MY ANATOMY,	19	EPIDERM MACABRE	12
ANCESTORS			
FOR ANCESTORS WHO LOVED A WARLIKE SHOW,	224	OTTO	25
ANCESTRAL			
THE MENACE OF ANCESTRAL EYES;	4	FEUD	2
ANCIENT			
INFLAME WITH HATE. THIS ANCIENT FEUD	4	FEUD	18
GONE THE THREE ANCIENT LADIES	44	FRAU BAUMAN	1
THESE ANCIENT LEATHERY CRONES,	44	FRAU BAUMAN	32
HONORED, ON MY RETURN, BY THE ANCIENT FELLOWSHIP OF ROTTEN STEMS.	89	UNFOLD! UNFOLD!	26
MAY THEY SLEEP IN ROBES OF GREEN, AMONG THE ANCIENT FERNS;	169	FOURTH MEDITATN	58
THE DARK HEART OF SOME ANCIENT THING	260	THE CHANGELING	4
AND (1053)			
ANGEL			
COME OUT OF A CLOUD, ANGEL WITH SEVERAL FACES,	48	LAST WORDS	8
ANGEL WITHIN ME, I ASKED,	62	FIELD OF LIGHT	19
HE WON'T BE AN ANGEL,	72	WHERE KNOCK IS	29
DID SPACE SHAKE OFF AN ANGEL WITH A SIGH?	107	SIR JOHN DAVIES	69
O ANGEL, LET ME LOOSE!"	136	THE SENSUALISTS	6
ANGELS			
LIGHT AIRS! LIGHT AIRS! A PIERCE OF ANGELS!	61	THE LONG ALLEY	77
HOW MANY ANGELS DO YOU KNOW?--	77	BRING THE DAY!	12
HARDLY ANY OLD ANGELS ARE AROUND ANY MORE.	78	BRING THE DAY!	40
I'M TIRED OF ALL THAT, BAG-FOOT. I CAN HEAR SMALL ANGELS ANYTIME. WHO	98	O, THOU OPENING	25
THAT DAY WE TOOK FROM THE ANGELS:	258	SONG (3)	13
ANGER			
THE ANGER WILL ENDURE,	3	OPEN HOUSE	13
ANGORA			
WHEN HATTIE WRIGHT'S ANGORA DIED AS WELL,	224	OTTO	29
ANGUISH			
THIS ANGUISH SELF-REVEALED.	3	OPEN HOUSE	8
THAT ANGUISH OF CONCRETENESS!--	92	I CRY, LOVE!	25

	PAGE	TITLE	LINE
ANIMAL			
THIS ANIMAL REMEMBERING TO BE GAY.	105	SIR JOHN DAVIES	12
BETWEEN SUCH ANIMAL AND HUMAN HEAT	105	SIR JOHN DAVIES	25
EACH IS AN ANIMAL,"--	136	THE SENSUALISTS	16
LURKS THE BAD ANIMAL.	161	I'M HERE	11
A WIND CAME CLOSE, LIKE A SHY ANIMAL.	241	THE SEQUEL	22
I MOVED LIKE SOME HEAT-WEARY ANIMAL.	247	I WAITED	17
'TWIXT ANIMAL AND MAN DIVIDED,	264	THREE EPIGRAMS	13
ANIMALS			
NOT ALL ANIMALS	83	O LULL ME, LULL	6
WHILE ANIMALS EAT TO THE NORTH,	157	FIRST MEDITATN	9
HOW CLOSE WE ARE TO THE SAD ANIMALS!	171	WHAT TELL BONES	20
ANIMAL'S			
THE ANIMAL'S CANDID GAZE, A SHADE LESS THAN FEATHERS, LIGHT'S BROKEN	98	O, THOU OPENING	22
ANISETTE			
TO THEIR CARDS, THEIR ANISETTE.	230	THE STORM	27
ANKLE-DEEP			
THE WALKER TRUDGES ANKLE-DEEP IN LEAVES;	12	SLOW SEASON	11
ANKLES			
WITH ANKLES BRUISED FROM STUBBLE OF THE GRAIN.	13	PRAISE PRAIRIE	8
ANN			
WHERE'S ANN? WHERE'S LOU? WHERE'S JOCK-WITH-THE-WIND?	97	O, THOU OPENING	17
ANNOUNCE			
A CANNON CRACK ANNOUNCE AN EARLY THAW.	11	LIGHT BRIGHTER	4
ANNOUNCED			
THE SEA'S UNEQUAL LENGTHS ANNOUNCED THY BIRTH	81	SENSIBILITY! LA	8
ANONYMOUS			
THE CRANED NECKS, THE MOURNERS' ANONYMOUS FACES,	22	ROAD TO WDLAWN	7
ANOTHER			
DAYS OF ANOTHER SUMMER.	6	THE PREMONITION	2
EYES, STARING PAST ANOTHER	7	ORDERS FOR DAY	15
SHALL NEVER TOUCH ANOTHER EAR.	22	SILENCE	20
UP OVER A VIADUCT I CAME, TO THE SNAKES AND STICKS OF ANOTHER WINTER,	65	SHAPE OF FIRE	37
I KNOW ANOTHER FIRE.	76	I NEED, I NEED	67
AND MY THOUGHT HUNTS ANOTHER BODY.	80	GIVE WAY, GATES	44
WAY TO ANOTHER GRACE!--	83	O LULL ME, LULL	23
I HEAR, CLEARLY, THE HEART OF ANOTHER SINGING,	88	PRAISE TO END!	94
I ACHE FOR ANOTHER CHOICE.	89	UNFOLD! UNFOLD!	4
THIS FROG'S HAD ANOTHER FALL.	99	O, THOU OPENING	51
I'M KING OF ANOTHER CONDITION,	99	O, THOU OPENING	57
GREAT NATURE HAS ANOTHER THING TO DO	108	THE WAKING (2)	13
IT WAS FADE ME ANOTHER AND STICK OUT YOUR CAN;	112	SQUEEZE-BOX	27
IN ANOTHER BEING, AT LAST.	126	WORDS FOR WIND	105
YOU WERE TOO LONELY FOR ANOTHER FATE.	144	ELEGY (1)	6
ANOTHER JOIN MY SONG	146	THE SONG	25
I'M SURE I'VE BEEN A TOAD, ONE TIME OR ANOTHER.	151	SLUG	25
SPRINGING, ONE TO ANOTHER,	152	THE SISKINS	13
ANOTHER SHAPE THAN HERS	154	THE DYING MAN	29
HE TURNED HIS FACE: THERE WAS ANOTHER MAN,	155	THE DYING MAN	62
AND ANOTHER, OUTSIDE, IN THE BRIGHT DAY,	158	FIRST MEDITATN	41
SO THE SPIRIT TRIES FOR ANOTHER LIFE,	159	FIRST MEDITATN	66
ANOTHER WAY AND PLACE IN WHICH TO CONTINUE;	159	FIRST MEDITATN	67
A LONGING FOR ANOTHER PLACE AND TIME,	162	I'M HERE	37
ANOTHER CONDITION.	162	I'M HERE	38
NOR THE SOUND OF ANOTHER FOOTSTEP--	169	FOURTH MEDITATN	54
I'M WET WITH ANOTHER LIFE.	173	WHAT TELL BONES	95
BECOME ANOTHER THING;	198	THE LONG WATERS	74
OR PERHAPS WITH ANOTHER MIND, LESS PECULIAR;	200	THE FAR FIELD	43
AS IF ANOTHER MAN APPEARED OUT OF THE DEPTHS OF MY BEING,	205	THE ROSE	100
FROM ANOTHER BEATRICE.	216	HER WRATH	5
DO WE MOVE TOWARD GOD, OR MERELY ANOTHER CONDITION?	221	THE ABYSS	75
THEN ANOTHER, ANOTHER,	232	THE THING	15
THEN ANOTHER, ANOTHER,	232	THE THING	15
TO THE DARK BEGINNINGS OF ANOTHER DAY.	241	THE SEQUEL	24
ANSWER			
SPEAK TO THE STONES, AND THE STARS ANSWER.	90	UNFOLD! UNFOLD!	54
BUT THE BRIGHT DAY HAD NO ANSWER.	101	THE VISITANT	25
AND SHAPELESS NIGHT THAT MADE NO ANSWER BACK.	107	SIR JOHN DAVIES	90
I CANNOT ANSWER BACK;	123	WORDS FOR WIND	29
FROZEN BY A FATHER'S LIP, A MOTHER'S FAILURE TO ANSWER.	169	FOURTH MEDITATN	45

		PAGE	TITLE	LINE
ANTIC				
ALL SHADE IS LEAN, THE ANTIC BRANCH	....	14	COMING OF COLD	28
HE WALKS THE SHALLOW WITH AN ANTIC GRACE.	....	15	THE HERON	5
ANTIMACASSAR				
THE ANTIMACASSAR FOR THE SOFA IN RED,	....	32	SALE	9
ANTS				
NUDGING AND TICKLING OF ANTS AND SPIDERS,		255	LIGHT POEM	2
ANXIETY				
SHOULD DAME ANXIETY EVER COME NEAR	....	272	DUET	24
ANXIOUS				
AND CHILL THE ANXIOUS HEART;	....	31	LULL	3
ANY				
DO YOU SEE ANY SIGN OR SEMBLANCE OF THAT THING CALLED "HOPE"?"	....	27	CLAIRVOY WIDOW	18
LEAVES, DO YOU LIKE ME ANY?	....	78	BRING THE DAY!	33
HARDLY ANY OLD ANGELS ARE AROUND ANY MORE.		78	BRING THE DAY!	40
HARDLY ANY OLD ANGELS ARE AROUND ANY MORE.		78	BRING THE DAY!	40
LIKE ANY SUMMER DAY.	....	128	THE VOICE	24
READY FOR ANY CREVICE,		187	THE LONGING	22
AS CLOSE TO HIM AS ANY KITH OR KIN.	....	224	OTTO	6
BUT THAT'S ENOUGH FOR ANY MAN	....	267	SAGINAW SONG	29
ANYBODY				
I WAS FAR BACK, FARTHER THAN ANYBODY ELSE.	....	89	UNFOLD! UNFOLD!	21
ANYTHING				
AND FAR FROM ANYTHING MY OWN,	....	19	AGNST DISASTER	2
AND SING HE DID, LIKE ANYTHING!	....	115	THE SERPENT	10
ANYTIME				
I'M TIRED OF ALL THAT, BAG-FOOT. I CAN HEAR SMALL ANGELS ANYTIME. WHO	....	98	O, THOU OPENING	25
ANYWHERE				
YET DARED TO FIX HIS VISION ANYWHERE.	....	155	THE DYING MAN	65
APART				
NOW EACH MAN STANDS APART.	....	31	LULL	7
AND SO I STOOD APART,	....	128	THE VOICE	5
AS IF REALITY HAD SPLIT APART	....	135	THE RENEWAL	22
THUS I; AND SHOULD THESE REASONS FLY APART,		144	ELEGY (1)	9
WHIPPING THE LINE OF WHITE LAUNDRY, BENDING THE COTTONWOODS APART,	....	194	JOURNY INTERIOR	44
IT WOULD BLOW THE PLACE APART,--	....	268	SAGINAW SONG	40
APHORIST				
DAZZLE ME, DIZZY APHORIST.		97	O, THOU OPENING	5
APPALL				
THE EDGES OF THE SUMMIT STILL APPALL	....	156	THE DYING MAN	96
APPARENT				
FURY OF WIND, AND NO APPARENT WIND,	....	171	WHAT TELL BONES	28
APPARITION				
THE APPARITION	....	208	THE APPARITION	T
APPEAR				
THE FROG SCUM APPEAR ON THE POND WITH THE SAME FROTH OF GREEN,	....	24	VERNAL SENTIMNT	2
APPEAR IN THE FORM OF A SPIDER	....	54	THE LOST SON	22
APPEARANCES				
BODY AND SOUL TRANSCEND APPEARANCES	....	149	IN LATE SUMMER	13
APPEARED				
AS IF ANOTHER MAN APPEARED OUT OF THE DEPTHS OF MY BEING,		205	THE ROSE	100
APPENDAGE				
A FAT, FIVE-INCH APPENDAGE	....	151	SLUG	12
APPETITE				
THAT APPETITE FOR LIFE SO RAVENOUS	....	133	THE PURE FURY	16
APPLAUSE				
ONLY TO GAIN FRESH TRIUMPHS AND APPLAUSE.	....	28	THE FAVORITE	6
APPLES				
IN A GROVE OF APPLES.	....	51	THE WAKING (1)	16
THE BEARDED BOARDS IN THE STREAM AND THE ALL OF APPLES;		66	SHAPE OF FIRE	71
THE PLANTS WAVE ME IN, AND THE SUMMER APPLES;	....	88	PRAISE TO END!	86
A LAPFUL OF APPLES SLEEPS IN THIS GRASS.	....	92	I CRY, LOVE!	24
APPLES! HAVE A CARE!	....	261	THE CHANGELING	43
APPLEWORMS				
A WIND STIRRED IN A WEB OF APPLEWORMS;	....	101	THE VISITANT	26
APPREHENDED				
BUT HE WAS APPREHENDED, BARE,	....	264	THREE EPIGRAMS	9
APPROACHING				
IMPERIOUS YOUNGLING, THOUGH APPROACHING FORTY;	....	264	THREE EPIGRAMS	2

	PAGE	TITLE	LINE
APPROVE			
IN A SODDEN PLACE, ALL RAPS AND KNOCKS APPROVE.	93	I CRY, LOVE!	30
APRIL			
SOON FIELD AND WOOD WILL WEAR AN APRIL LOOK,	11	LIGHT BRIGHTER	13
THE APRIL CHEEPING, THE VIREO'S INSISTENCE,	161	I'M HERE	8
OF THE FIRST TREMBLING OF A MICHIGAN BROOK IN APRIL,	191	AT OYSTER RIVER	42
VANISHED LIKE APRIL SNOW;	213	THE HAPPY THREE	27
ARBITRATORS			
THE ARBITRATORS WAIT;	31	LULL	13
ARBOR			
THE ARBOR IS ALIVE WITH FUME	14	COMING OF COLD	2
THE ARBOR IS COOLER. FAREWELL, FAREWELL, FOND WORM.	64	SHAPE OF FIRE	18
ARBORS			
WHISTLING BETWEEN THE ARBORS, THE WINDING TERRACES;	230	THE STORM	5
ARBUTUS			
TO YOU ARBUTUS CALM, MYSTERIOUS AS A STONE?	261	THE CHANGELING	29
ARBUTUS-CALM			
SWAN-HEART, ARBUTUS-CALM,	124	WORDS FOR WIND	51
ARCH			
ARCH MY BACK, PRETTY-BONES, I'M DEAD AT BOTH ENDS.	85	PRAISE TO END!	9
ARCH OF AIR, MY HEART'S ORIGINAL KNOCK,	88	PRAISE TO END!	79
THE GREAT GODS ARCH MY BONES.	137	LOVE'S PROGRESS	5
ARCHAIC			
THE DESCENDANTS OF THE PLAYFUL TREE-SHREW THAT SURVIVED THE ARCHAIC KILLERS,	170	FOURTH MEDITATN	66
ARCHED			
A SHELL ARCHED UNDER MY TOES,	49	RIVER INCIDENT	1
ARCHNESS			
BEHIND THE CHILD'S ARCHNESS	161	I'M HERE	10
ARDENT			
THE HUSK LIVES ON, ARDENT AS A SEED;	170	FOURTH MEDITATN	83
ARDOR			
SUCH ARDOR TAMES ETERNITY, I THINK.	132	SENTENTIOUS MAN	30
ARDORS			
NOW MY ARDORS SLEEP IN A SLEEVE.	103	OLD LADY'S WRDS	3
ARE (115)			
ARID			
THE VAGUE, THE ARID,	220	THE ABYSS	22
ARISES			
A TREE ARISES ON A CENTRAL PLAIN--	150	IN LATE SUMMER	25
ARISTOCRACY			
THE ARISTOCRACY;	267	SAGINAW SONG	20
ARM			
IS THE SUN UNDER MY ARM?	82	SENSIBILITY! LA	45
AND IT STEPPED IN THE ROOM, UNDER HIS ARM,--	273	SUPPR W LINDSAY	6
ARMS			
HER WHITE ARMS REACHING TOWARDS ME.	100	THE VISITANT	14
TOOK ARMS AGAINST OUR OWN OBSCURITY.	106	SIR JOHN DAVIES	54
IN MY ARMS.	164	I'M HERE	98
MERCY HAS MANY ARMS.	173	WHAT TELL BONES	76
SMALL ENOUGH TO BE TAKEN IN, EMBRACED, BY TWO ARMS,--	191	AT OYSTER RIVER	46
MY THIN ARMS TO AND FRO,	207	THE YOUNG GIRL	10
HER ARMS MADE A SUMMER.	258	SONG (3)	23
AROUND			
AROUND A CENTRAL GRAIN	18	GENESIS	11
THAT RIFFLED AROUND MY KNEES.	49	RIVER INCIDENT	3
HARDLY ANY OLD ANGELS ARE AROUND ANY MORE.	78	BRING THE DAY!	40
TAIL AROUND, NOSING IN AND OUT OF THE CURRENT,	101	LIGHT BREATHER	9
ELM SWINGING AROUND	103	OLD LADY'S WRDS	27
THE WIND WANDERS AROUND THE HOUSE	104	OLD LADY'S WRDS	52
OUR SHADOWS MET, AND SLOWLY SWUNG AROUND;	120	THE DREAM	26
THE SHARP STARS SWING AROUND;	125	WORDS FOR WIND	64
JOURNEY AROUND A TREE;	137	LOVE'S PROGRESS	7
OF LICHEN AROUND STONES?	139	PLAINT	16
THE SMALL BIRDS SWIRL AROUND;	148	THE SMALL	1
MAKING A SLOW JOURNEY AROUND THE WELL-CURB.	151	SLUG	3
SCUTTLING DOWN AND AROUND LIKE YOUNG SQUIRRELS,	152	THE SISKINS	17
SETTLING IN SMALL BEADS AROUND WEEDS AND SUNKEN BRANCHES,	159	FIRST MEDITATN	61
AROUND, BACK INTO THE TINY MAINCURRENT, THE RUSH OF BROWNISH-WHITE WATER,	159	FIRST MEDITATN	71
ROMPING AROUND A FIRE,	163	I'M HERE	67
BIRDS ARE AROUND. I'VE ALL THE SINGING I WOULD.	164	I'M HERE	93
THE NUMINOUS RING AROUND THE OPENING FLOWER,	198	THE LONG WATERS	70

	PAGE	TITLE	LINE
AROUND (CONTINUED)			
A SEA-SHAPE TURNING AROUND,--	201	THE FAR FIELD	84
WINDING AROUND THE WATERS OF THE WORLD.	201	THE FAR FIELD	103
AND THE TICKING OF SNOW AROUND OIL DRUMS IN THE DAKOTAS,	204	THE ROSE	68
ALL'S KNOWN, ALL, ALL AROUND:	212	LIGHT LISTENED	13
I SING THE WIND AROUND	215	HIS FOREBODING	11
AROUND A CLOUD,	219	THE ABYSS	14
ENDING CURLED AROUND AND OVER AGAIN,	226	THE LIZARD	11
BUMBLING UP AND AROUND THE BAMBOO WINDBREAK;	226	THE LIZARD	21
AND THE HUMMINGBIRD DIPS IN AND AROUND THE QUINCE TREE,	234	ALL MORNING	29
THE LEAVES, THE TREES TURNED OUR TWO SHAPES AROUND.	237	THE TRANCED	15
FROM A KNOCKED OVER CHURN, AND FOAMED AROUND	273	SUPPR W LINDSAY	13
AROUSE			
TOUCH AND AROUSE. SUCK AND SOB. CURSE AND MOURN.	80	GIVE WAY, GATES	46
ARRANGED			
THE BRONZE WHEAT ARRANGED IN STRICT AND FORMAL ORDER;	29	THE REMINDER	3
OF VEAL SOAKED IN MARSALA AND LITTLE LARKS ARRANGED ON A			
LONG PLATTER,	232	THE THING	19
ARRANGERS			
MATCH-MAKERS, ARRANGERS OF PICNICS--	169	FOURTH MEDITATN	41
ARRIVALS			
MANY ARRIVALS MAKE US LIVE: THE TREE BECOMING	235	MANIFESTATION	1
ARRIVE			
AND SHOULD HE ARRIVE, WHY JUST LEAN YOURSELF BACK	113	TO A LADY ED	7
WHEN THE WORST IS ABOUT TO ARRIVE;	172	WHAT TELL BONES	35
ARROYO			
THE ARROYO CRACKING THE ROAD, THE WIND-BITTEN BUTTES, THE			
CANYONS,	193	JOURNY INTERIOR	7
ARSENICAL			
I NOTICE A TREE, ARSENICAL GREY IN THE LIGHT, OR THE SLOW	47	DOUBLE FEATURE	10
ART			
SOME LEARN THE ART OF THIEVING, AND SOME GROW UP TO BEG;	27	CLAIRVOY WIDOW	10
O PRIDE, THOU ART A PLUME UPON WHOSE HEAD?	188	THE LONGING	25
ARTS			
WHEN AMOROUS ARTS WE WOULD PURSUE,	23	AMOROUS LADY	11
AS			
THEMSELVES, THEIR PARLORS MUSTY AS A FUNERAL HOME.	5	PROGNOSIS	12
THE CHAOS GREW AS HOUR BY HOUR THE LIGHT	6	INTERLUDE	5
AS KNOWN PARTICULARS COME WHEELING BY,	8	THE SIGNALS	3
AS BRANCHES LOOSE LAST VESTIGES OF SNOW.	11	LIGHT BRIGHTER	10
UNTIL I COULD THINK THERE WERE WAVES ROLLING HIGH AS MY			
BEDROOM FLOOR;	12	MID-CNTRY BLOW	2
THE OAK STOOD WITH EACH LEAF STIFF AS A BELL.	12	MID-CNTRY BLOW	6
LOST HUES OF BIRDS THE TREES TAKE AS THEIR OWN.	12	SLOW SEASON	9
HERE DISTANCE IS FAMILIAR AS A FRIEND.	13	PRAISE PRAIRIE	11
AND NOSTRILS WIDEN AS THEY PASS	14	COMING OF COLD	10
THE HEART BEAT FASTER AS THE FAT WORDS ROLLED.	21	THE AUCTION	14
I REJOICE IN THE SPRING, AS THOUGH NO SPRING EVER HAD BEEN.	24	VERNAL SENTIMNT	8
AS YOU LOOK ACROSS MY CITY, IN GOD'S COUNTRY?"	27	CLAIRVOY WIDOW	4
THE LIBRARY USED AS A CARD ROOM INSTEAD	32	SALE	11
THE TABLE WHERE EVERYONE ATE AS HE SHOULD,	32	SALE	14
NOW AS FROM MAPLE TO ELM THE FLITTERMICE SKITTER AND TWIRL,	33	IDYLL	1
AS DARKNESS CREEPS UP ON THE WELL-GROOMED SUBURBAN TOWN,	33	IDYLL	5
NOW AS THE TRAIN BEARS WEST,	34	NIGHT JOURNEY	1
SLIPPERY AS FISH,	37	CUTTINGS (LATE)	10
NOTHING WOULD SLEEP IN THAT CELLAR, DANK AS A DITCH,	38	ROOT CELLAR	1
ROOTS RIPE AS OLD BAIT,	38	ROOT CELLAR	7
AS THE LIVE HEAT BILLOWS FROM PIPES AND POTS.	38	FORCING HOUSE	11
LIMP AND DAMP, DELICATE AS A YOUNG BIRD'S TONGUE;	39	ORCHIDS	5
AS IF I HAD BROKEN THE NATURAL ORDER OF THINGS IN THAT			
SWAMPLAND;	40	MOSS-GATHERING	10
AS IF I HAD COMMITTED, AGAINST THE WHOLE SCHEME OF LIFE, A			
DESECRATION.	40	MOSS-GATHERING	13
AS THE SEAMS HISSED	41	BIG WIND	12
CANNAS SHINY AS SLAG,	43	FLOWER DUMP	1
AND THE AIR COOL, AS IF DRIFTING DOWN FROM WET HEMLOCKS,	43	CARNATIONS	3
WEAK AS A WHIFFET;	44	FRAU BAUMAN	29
AS I TURNED FOR A BACKWARD LOOK,	47	THE RETURN	5
THEIR EYES, RICH AS PLUMS, STARING FROM NEWSPRINT,--	48	JUDGE NOT	3
IT'S SLEEK AS AN OTTER	55	THE LOST SON	58
AS MY OWN TONGUE KISSED	56	THE LOST SON	98
IS THE SEED LEAVING THE OLD BED? THESE BUDS ARE LIVE AS			
BIRDS.	56	THE LOST SON	102

		PAGE	TITLE	LINE
AS (CONTINUED)				
THE WORMS WERE DELIGHTED AS WRENS.		63	FIELD OF LIGHT	50
STILL AS A CHILD IN ITS FIRST LONELINESS;		67	SHAPE OF FIRE	85
AS AN OPAQUE VASE FILLS TO THE BRIM FROM A QUICK POURING,		67	SHAPE OF FIRE	93
IT WASN'T EVEN AS		71	WHERE KNOCK IS	14
AS YOU CAN SEE I GUESS I GUESS.		75	I NEED, I NEED	34
LIGHT AS A HAND AMONG BLOSSOMS,		78	BRING THE DAY!	39
PLEASED AS A KNIFE.		81	SENSIBILITY! LA	25
O MY LOVE'S LIGHT AS A DUCK		83	O LULL ME, LULL	12
I ROMPED, LITHE AS A CHILD, DOWN THE SUMMERY STREETS OF MY VEINS,		86	PRAISE TO END!	21
STRICT AS A SEED, NIPPY AND TWIGGY.		86	PRAISE TO END!	22
BE LARGE AS AN OWL, BE SLICK AS A FROG,		86	PRAISE TO END!	39
BE LARGE AS AN OWL, BE SLICK AS A FROG,		86	PRAISE TO END!	39
BE GOOD AS A GOOSE, BE BIG AS A DOG,		86	PRAISE TO END!	40
BE GOOD AS A GOOSE, BE BIG AS A DOG,		86	PRAISE TO END!	40
BE SLEEK AS A HEIFER, BE LONG AS A HOG,--		86	PRAISE TO END!	41
BE SLEEK AS A HEIFER, BE LONG AS A HOG,--		86	PRAISE TO END!	41
I'VE CRAWLED FROM THE MIRE, ALERT AS A SAINT OR A DOG;		88	PRAISE TO END!	81
I WAS PURE AS A WORM ON A LEAF; I CHERISHED THE MOLD'S CHILDREN.		89	UNFOLD! UNFOLD!	27
SOME ERRAND, OBSCURE AS THE WIND'S CIRCUIT,		92	I CRY, LOVE!	6
I CARE FOR A CAT'S CRY AND THE HUGS, LIVE AS WATER.		92	I CRY, LOVE!	16
OR HAPPY, CORRECT AS A HAT?		98	O, THOU OPENING	46
I WAITED, ALERT AS A DOG.		100	THE VISITANT	7
SLOW, SLOW AS A FISH SHE CAME,		100	THE VISITANT	10
SLOW AS A FISH COMING FORWARD,		100	THE VISITANT	11
STIRS AS A BLOSSOM STIRS,		101	LIGHT BREATHER	3
PLAYS AS A MINNOW PLAYS,		101	LIGHT BREATHER	7
I REMEMBER THE NECKCURLS, LIMP AND DAMP AS TENDRILS;		102	ELEGY FOR JANE	1
MY MARROW BEAT AS WILDLY AS MY PULSE.		106	SIR JOHN DAVIES	36
MY MARROW BEAT AS WILDLY AS MY PULSE.		106	SIR JOHN DAVIES	36
WE PLAYED WITH DARK AND LIGHT AS CHILDREN SHOULD.		107	SIR JOHN DAVIES	66
AS WE SAT THERE DRINKING THAT BATHTUB GIN		112	SQUEEZE-BOX	24
IT WAS STAND ON YOUR FEET AS LONG AS YOU'RE ABLE,		112	SQUEEZE-BOX	35
IT WAS STAND ON YOUR FEET AS LONG AS YOU'RE ABLE,		112	SQUEEZE-BOX	35
--AS I DANCE TO MY POEM CALLED POEM.		113	TO A LADY ED	16
AS I WAS CROSSING A HOT HOT PLAIN,		114	DINKY	9
AS THE BIRDS FLEW OFF TO THE END OF NEXT WEEK.		115	THE SERPENT	26
"I AM WHAT IS KNOWN AS A BIDDLY BEAR,--		117	LADY AND BEAR	5
AS HE WENT ON FISHING HIS WAY, HIS WAY,		117	LADY AND BEAR	29
AS HE WENT ON FISHING HIS WAY.		117	LADY AND BEAR	30
I MET HER AS A BLOSSOM ON A STEM		119	THE DREAM	1
A MAN RICH AS A CAT,		121	ALL EARTH, AIR	7
WHEN, EASY AS A BEAST,		121	ALL EARTH, AIR	13
MYSELF AS I SHOULD BE,		123	WORDS FOR WIND	6
AS A LOVELY SUBSTANCE WILL;		123	WORDS FOR WIND	19
I SWEAR SHE CAST A SHADOW WHITE AS STONE.		127	I KNEW A WOMAN	25
SHE MOVES AS WATER MOVES, AND COMES TO ME,		129	SHE	15
AS IF A LION KNELT TO KISS A ROSE,		131	SENTENTIOUS MAN	17
AS IF ALL THINGS HAD DIED, AND ROSE AGAIN.		133	THE PURE FURY	6
AS THE THICK SHADE OF THE LONG NIGHT COMES ON.		134	THE PURE FURY	28
I WALK AS IF MY FACE WOULD KISS THE WIND.		135	THE RENEWAL	12
AS IF REALITY HAD SPLIT APART		135	THE RENEWAL	22
A WOMAN STOOD, PURE AS A BRIDE,		136	THE SENSUALISTS	9
AND BREATHING HARD, AS THAT MAN RODE		136	THE SENSUALISTS	11
THEN EACH FELL BACK, LIMP AS A SACK,		136	THE SENSUALISTS	25
I LIVE, ALIVE AND CERTAIN AS A BULL;		140	THE SWAN	9
SHE TURNS, AS IF TO GO,		141	MEMORY	5
SHOULD EVERY CREATURE BE AS I HAVE BEEN,		144	ELEGY (1)	1
AS IF PURE BEING WOKE,		147	THE EXORCISM	5
THEN ALL IS AS IT WAS.		148	THE SMALL	12
AS IF OUT OF MY SIDE,		148	THE SMALL	16
BEYOND THE RIDGE TWO WOOD THRUSH SING AS ONE.		150	IN LATE SUMMER	30
THE EVENING WRAPS ME, STEADY AS A FLAME.		150	IN LATE SUMMER	32
BUT AS FOR YOU, MOST ODIOUS--		151	SLUG	28
BIRDS FURIOUS AS BEES.		152	THE SISKINS	18
LIGHT AS SEED BLOWING OFF THISTLES!		152	THE SISKINS	21
AS MY EYES FOLLOW AFTER		152	THE SISKINS	23
I KNOW, AS THE DYING KNOW,		153	THE DYING MAN	9
"A MAN SEES, AS HE DIES,		153	THE DYING MAN	11
NOW, AS THE CASEMENT BLURS.		154	THE DYING MAN	30
A BEAST CRIES OUT AS IF ITS FLESH WERE TORN,		156	THE DYING MAN	82

		PAGE	TITLE	LINE
AS	(CONTINUED)			
WITH A CHEEK SOFT AS A HOUND'S EAR.		157	FIRST MEDITATN	17
WHAT'S LEFT IS LIGHT AS A SEED;		157	FIRST MEDITATN	18
OFTEN I THINK OF MYSELF AS RIDING--		158	FIRST MEDITATN	20
THE LIGHTS TILTING UP, SKYWARD, AS WE COME OVER A LITTLE RISE,		158	FIRST MEDITATN	24
THEN DOWN, AS WE ROLL LIKE A BOAT FROM A WAVE-CREST.		158	FIRST MEDITATN	25
AS WHEN SILT DRIFTS AND SIFTS DOWN THROUGH MUDDY POND-WATER,		159	FIRST MEDITATN	60
THIN AND INSISTENT AS A CICADA,		159	FIRST MEDITATN	85
A BIRD, SMALL AS A LEAF,		163	I'M HERE	60
MY BREAST WILD AS THE WAVES.		165	HER BECOMING	10
LIGHT AS A PETAL FALLING UPON STONE.		165	HER BECOMING	12
AS A CHIP OR SHELL, FLOATING LAZILY WITH A SLOW CURRENT,		168	FOURTH MEDITATN	6
IN THE WHITE KINGDOMS, I WAS LIGHT AS A SEED,		168	FOURTH MEDITATN	15
I SEE THEM AS FIGURES WALKING IN A GREENY GARDEN,		170	FOURTH MEDITATN	63
THE HUSK LIVES ON, ARDENT AS A SEED;		170	FOURTH MEDITATN	83
I'M THICK WITH LEAVES AND TENDER AS A DOVE,		173	WHAT TELL BONES	89
AS IF RELEASED BY A SPIRIT,		173	WHAT TELL BONES	98
SHE WAS MAD AS A HARE,		179	MYRTLE	3
AS THOSE TWO QUIETLY TALKED,		182	BOY AND BUSH	7
BARE AS A BUD, AND NAKED AS A WORM.		188	THE LONGING	34
BARE AS A BUD, AND NAKED AS A WORM.		188	THE LONGING	34
THE WIND SLACKENS, LIGHT AS A MOTH FANNING A STONE:		190	AT OYSTER RIVER	17
A TWILIGHT WIND, LIGHT AS A CHILD'S BREATH		190	AT OYSTER RIVER	18
THE SUDDEN SUCKING ROAR AS THE CULVERT LOOSENS ITS DEBRIS OF BRANCHES AND STICKS,		191	AT OYSTER RIVER	53
AS THE PILED ICE BREAKS AWAY FROM THE BATTERED SPILES,		191	AT OYSTER RIVER	55
AS A BLIND MAN, LIFTING A CURTAIN, KNOWS IT IS MORNING,		195	JOURNY INTERIOR	74
AS LIGHT REFLECTS FROM A LAKE, IN LATE EVENING,		198	THE LONG WATERS	60
AS A FIRE, SEEMINGLY LONG DEAD, FLARES UP FROM A DOWNDRAFT OF AIR IN A CHIMNEY,		198	THE LONG WATERS	63
MOVING, ELUSIVE AS FISH, FEARLESS,		199	THE FAR FIELD	31
AS A SNAKE OR A RAUCOUS BIRD,		200	THE FAR FIELD	48
OR, WITH LUCK, AS A LION.		200	THE FAR FIELD	49
AS OF WATER QUICKENING BEFORE A NARROWING CHANNEL		200	THE FAR FIELD	59
AS WHEN A SHIP SAILS WITH A LIGHT WIND--		203	THE ROSE	31
THE SHRIEK OF NAILS AS OLD SHINGLES ARE RIPPED FROM THE TOP OF A ROOF,		204	THE ROSE	70
AS IF ANOTHER MAN APPEARED OUT OF THE DEPTHS OF MY BEING,		205	THE ROSE	100
AS IF I SWAYED OUT ON THE WILDEST WAVE ALIVE,		205	THE ROSE	104
WITH ALL THE AIR TO GREET HIM AS HE FLIES,		205	THE ROSE	109
I LIVED SERENE AS A FISH,		209	HER LONGING	2
AS HE WOULD OR WOULD NOT,--		209	HER RETICENCE	5
AS I WALKED BY THE HIGH SEA-WALL.		216	THE SHY MAN	4
AS I MOPED BY THE HIGH SEA-WALL.		216	THE SHY MAN	8
AS I WALKED BESIDE HER, THE O'CONNELL'S DAUGHTER,		216	THE SHY MAN	11
AS WE WALKED BY THE HIGH SEA-WALL.		216	THE SHY MAN	16
AS WE EMBRACE BY THE HIGH SEA-WALL.		216	THE SHY MAN	23
AS WE KISS BY THE HIGH SEA-WALL.		216	THE SHY MAN	26
AS WHEN THE DOOR SWINGS OPEN IN A FLORIST'S STOREROOM--		220	THE ABYSS	46
HER TONGUE, AT THE LAST, THICK, BLACK AS AN OX'S.		223	ELEGY (2)	17
AS CLOSE TO HIM AS ANY KITH OR KIN.		224	OTTO	6
AS CLOSE TO HIM AS ANY KITH OR KIN.		224	OTTO	6
HE POTTED PLANTS AS IF HE HATED THEM.		224	OTTO	9
WHEN HATTIE WRIGHT'S ANGORA DIED AS WELL,		224	OTTO	29
AS I LOOKED OUT AT THEM FROM THE HIGH HOUSE,		225	OTTO	35
HIS HEAD, STIFF AS A SCARAB, TURNED TO ONE SIDE,		226	THE LIZARD	5
THE TAIL STRAIGHT AS AN AWL,		226	THE LIZARD	9
AS HIS HEAD; HIS BAT-LIKE EARS		227	MEADOW MOUSE	15
A CAT RUNS FROM THE WIND AS WE DO,		230	THE STORM	19
THE SUDDEN SHUDDER AS THE JUTTING SEA-CLIFF COLLAPSES,		231	THE STORM	42
TRAILING A THING--WHAT WAS IT?--SMALL AS A LARK		232	THE THING	2
STOPPING TRAFFIC, INDIGNANT AS ADDLED OLD LADIES,		234	ALL MORNING	27
SUBJECT AND OBJECT SANG AND DANCED AS ONE;		237	THE TRANCED	17
SOUND, SILENCE SANG AS ONE.		238	THE MOMENT	9
SHE STAYED IN LIGHT, AS LEAVES LIVE IN THE WIND,		241	THE SEQUEL	18
AS CHANGES SHIMMER IN THE INNER EYE.		244	INFIRMITY	2
BREAKS ON ME AS MY MEAGER FLESH BREAKS DOWN--		244	INFIRMITY	15
AS A MAN TURNS TO FACE ON-COMING SNOW.		245	THE DECISION	12
IT WAS AS IF I TRIED TO WALK IN HAY,		247	I WAITED	6
THE SWEET LIGHT MET ME AS I WALKED TOWARD		248	THE TREE, BIRD	3
SMALL AS AN ELF,		249	THE RESTORED	3
SHE DROPPED AS IF SHOT.		249	THE RESTORED	6

	PAGE	TITLE	LINE
AS (CONTINUED)			
AND, PRAISING CHANGE AS THE SLOW NIGHT COMES ON,	250	THE RIGHT THING	16
AS WE DANCE ON, DANCE ON, DANCE ON.	251	ONCE MORE, RND	12
STILL AS THE WIND'S CENTER,	258	SONG (3)	29
STILL AS A CLAY SUNK	258	SONG (3)	30
AS SHE STEPS INTO SUMMER,	260	THE CHANGELING	8
HER HEAVEN-SENSE PURE AS A STONE.	260	THE CHANGELING	11
AS WATER TEACHES STONE. BELIEVE ME, EXTREMEST ORIOLE,	260	THE CHANGELING	19
TO YOU ARBUTUS CALM, MYSTERIOUS AS A STONE?	261	THE CHANGELING	29
HE'S PART OF ONE, AS A MATTER OF COURSE.	264	THREE EPIGRAMS	12
A COLOR PURE, O PURE AS GOLD,	269	GOB MUSIC	26
AS I GULPED IT DOWN, AS I GULPED IT DOWN.	270	GOB MUSIC	41
AS I GULPED IT DOWN, AS I GULPED IT DOWN.	270	GOB MUSIC	41
AS CRYPTIC AS A RUNE,	271	THE REPLY	7
AS CRYPTIC AS A RUNE,	271	THE REPLY	7
AS ROUND AND PURE AS THE MOON,	271	THE REPLY	8
AS ROUND AND PURE AS THE MOON,	271	THE REPLY	8
AND FRESH AS SALT-DRENCHED SKIN.	271	THE REPLY	9
YET FINE AS MAIDENHAIR,	271	THE REPLY	12
I'D SAY MY FACE IS JUST AS ROUND AS HIS,	273	SUPPR W LINDSAY	8
I'D SAY MY FACE IS JUST AS ROUND AS HIS,	273	SUPPR W LINDSAY	8
AND THAT MAKES THREE, COUNTING HIS FACE AS ONE.	273	SUPPR W LINDSAY	9
ASH			
THE FALL OF THE LAST ASH	103	OLD LADY'S WRDS	31
WHERE THE YELLOWISH PRONGS OF GRASS POKE THROUGH THE BLACKENED ASH,	196	THE LONG WATERS	15
THE WIND FANNING THE ASH OF A LOW FIRE.	201	THE FAR FIELD	79
ASHES			
AND POKES THE CRUMBLED COAL THE ASHES HID,	17	UNEXTINGUISHED	11
KISS ME, ASHES, I'M FALLING THROUGH A DARK SWIRL.	57	THE LOST SON	121
THESE LAZY ASHES.	86	PRAISE TO END!	50
ASK			
ASK THE MOLE, HE KNOWS.	55	THE LOST SON	67
THE STALKS ASK SOMETHING ELSE.	91	UNFOLD! UNFOLD!	62
WASPS COME WHEN I ASK FOR PIGEONS.	92	I CRY, LOVE!	2
I'M TRUE TO SOUP, AND HAPPY TO ASK:	99	O, THOU OPENING	55
YOU ASK HIM SOMETHING IN HIS EAR,	116	THE SLOTH	2
ASK ALL THE MICE WHO CAPER IN THE STRAW--	167	HER BECOMING	86
WHICH IS THE WAY? I ASK, AND TURN TO GO,	245	THE DECISION	11
ASKED			
I ASKED: MAY THE BLESSINGS OF LIFE, O LORD, DESCEND ON THE LIVING.	48	JUDGE NOT	6
ANGEL WITHIN ME, I ASKED,	62	FIELD OF LIGHT	19
SHE ASKED HER SKIN	77	BRING THE DAY!	8
IT'S TIME YOU STOOD UP AND ASKED	89	UNFOLD! UNFOLD!	10
YOU ASKED ME BEFORE, I'LL TELL YOU AGAIN:	114	DINKY	11
IF YOU ASKED FOR A RIDE,	178	THE YAK	3
SHE ASKED, WOMAN.	213	THE HAPPY THREE	12
FOR SHE ASKED NO QUARTER AND GAVE NONE,	223	ELEGY (2)	7
ASKER			
A MOUSE TAUGHT ME HOW, I WAS A HAPPY ASKER.	90	UNFOLD! UNFOLD!	35
ASKEW			
AND ONE EYE GAZED ASKEW. "WHY, BLAKE, HE'S DEAD,--	273	SUPPR W LINDSAY	22
ASKS			
THE MOUTH ASKS. THE HAND TAKES.	80	GIVE WAY, GATES	51
ASLEEP			
WE SIT IN THE PORCH SWING, CONTENT AND HALF ASLEEP.	33	IDYLL	8
THEY TEASED OUT THE SEED THAT THE COLD KEPT ASLEEP,--	44	FRAU BAUMAN	23
OR ASLEEP.	72	WHERE KNOCK IS	44
I'VE BEEN ASLEEP IN A BOWER OF DEAD SKIN.	86	PRAISE TO END!	47
ON THINGS ASLEEP, NO BALM;	187	THE LONGING	1
ASLEEP IN HER SKIN,	258	SONG (3)	2
A-SLEEPING			
LAST NIGHT YOU LAY A-SLEEPING? NO!	114	DINKY	13
ASPECT			
THE ASPECT OF HIS FLESHY CLOTHES,--	19	EPIDERM MACABRE	2
ASSEMBLE			
THE LIVING ALL ASSEMBLE! WHAT'S THE CUE?--	106	SIR JOHN DAVIES	41
ASSISTANT			
I GREW TIRED OF THE RITUAL OF NAMES AND THE ASSISTANT KEEPER OF THE MOLLUSKS:	65	SHAPE OF FIRE	36
ASSUME			
ONCE MORE THE TREES ASSUME FAMILIAR SHAPES,	11	LIGHT BRIGHTER	9

	PAGE	TITLE	LINE
ASSUME (CONTINUED)			
HE WILL ASSUME THAT YOU HAVE HEARD--	116	THE SLOTH	6
ASSYRIAN			
GRAVE, HIERATIC, A PIECE OF ASSYRIAN SCULPTURE,	234	ALL MORNING	10
ASTER			
OR A WIZENED ASTER IN LATE SEPTEMBER,	228	THE GERANIUM	4
ASTERS			
OR PINCHING-BACK ASTERS, OR PLANTING AZALEAS,	42	OLD FLORIST	2
ASTIR			
THAT TREMBLE OF SWEET NOTES SET MY HEART ASTIR,	216	THE SHY MAN	10
ASTONISHED			
ASTONISHED INTO PASSIONATE REPOSE.	131	SENTENTIOUS MAN	18
ASTONISHMENT			
THOUGH EVERYTHING'S ASTONISHMENT AT LAST,	107	SIR JOHN DAVIES	79
ASTOUNDED			
THE BIRDS, THEY WERE, THEY WERE ASTOUNDED;	115	THE SERPENT	11
ASTOUNDS			
MANY ASTOUNDS BEFORE, I LOST MY IDENTITY TO A PEBBLE;	88	PRAISE TO END!	88
ASTRIDE			
THEY STOOD ASTRIDE PIPES,	44	FRAU BAUMAN	16
OR, WITH SKINNY KNEES, TO SIT ASTRIDE A WET LOG,	200	THE FAR FIELD	45
AND MY FATHER STANDING ASTRIDE THE CEMENT BENCHES,	203	THE ROSE	53
AT (170)			
ATE			
THE TABLE WHERE EVERYONE ATE AS HE SHOULD,	32	SALE	14
DEW ATE THE FIRE.	76	I NEED, I NEED	66
IT'S A PIECE OF A PRINCE I ATE.	86	PRAISE TO END!	48
IF I ATE AND DRANK LIKE HIM,	266	FOR STEVENS	11
SO WE SAT DOWN AND ATE OURSELVES A MEAL,	274	SUPPR W LINDSAY	30
BUT WHAT WE ATE I CAN'T REMEMBER QUITE:	274	SUPPR W LINDSAY	31
ATTACKS			
FOR THE ATTACKS OF FALSE HUMILITY TAKE SUDDEN TURNS FOR THE WORSE.	86	PRAISE TO END!	25
ATTAINED			
DANTE ATTAINED THE PURGATORIAL HILL,	107	SIR JOHN DAVIES	73
ATTEND			
LET LIGHT ATTEND ME TO THE GRAVE!	8	PRAYER	22
ATTENDANT			
LIKE A NURSE HE SAT WITH ME FOR WEEKS, A SLY SURLY ATTENDANT,	220	THE ABYSS	38
ATTENDED			
ATTENDED WHAT WE DID. BEHIND, BEFORE,	106	SIR JOHN DAVIES	50
ATTENTION			
TO DISTRACT ATTENTION FROM THE SHORT-TAILED RIDICULOUS YOUNG ONES	234	ALL MORNING	19
ATTIC			
HE LIKES THE ATTIC OF AN AGING HOUSE.	16	THE BAT	2
CLIMBED TO HER ATTIC WINDOW AND GAZED ACROSS THE SILL.	27	CLAIRVOY WIDOW	2
--AND AN ATTIC OF HORRORS, A CLOSET OF FEARS.	32	SALE	4
AUCTION			
THE AUCTION	21	THE AUCTION	T
AUCTIONEER			
AN AUCTIONEER WAS WHIPPING UP A SALE.	21	THE AUCTION	3
AUDACIOUSLY			
SANG OUT AUDACIOUSLY	213	THE HAPPY THREE	31
AUGUST			
ALONG THE LOW GROUND DRY ONLY IN AUGUST,--	62	FIELD OF LIGHT	26
AND WE TURN BACK TO THE HEAT OF AUGUST,	220	THE ABYSS	48
AUK			
THE PASSENGER PIGEON, THE GREAT AUK, THE CAROLINA PARAQUET,	235	ALL MORNING	44
AUNT			
AND SO SHE WAS, IN HER WAY, AUNT TILLY.	223	ELEGY (2)	3
AUNTIES			
THOSE DOTING AUNTIES NEVER WOULD HAVE BOTHERED.	25	DIM-WIT COUSIN	4
AUSGEPOOPEN			
ER IST NIEMALS AUSGEPOOPEN,	266	FOR STEVENS	15
AUTHENTIC			
OR KNOWN, ONCE, THE SOUL'S AUTHENTIC HUNGER,	169	FOURTH MEDITATN	47
AUTUMN			
LATE AUTUMN FRUIT IS ROTTED NOW.	14	COMING OF COLD	27
I FEEL THE AUTUMN FAIL--ALL THAT SLOW FIRE	242	THE SEQUEL	31
AUTUMNAL			
THAT LATE AUTUMNAL BLOOM, IS DEAD.	15	COMING OF COLD	41

	PAGE	TITLE	LINE
AUTUMNAL (CONTINUED)			
LIKE THAT CLEAR AUTUMNAL WEATHER OF ETERNITY,	43	CARNATIONS	6
A WEDGE OF HEAVEN'S LIGHT, AUTUMNAL SONG.	173	WHAT TELL BONES	68
AWAKE			
MY LIPS AWAKE.	56	THE LOST SON	99
THE HERRINGS ARE AWAKE.	77	BRING THE DAY!	25
I'M AWAKE ALL OVER:	88	PRAISE TO END!	80
HOW I WISH THEM AWAKE!	169	FOURTH MEDITATN	55
YOURSELF AWAKE UNTIL YOU SLEEP,	181	MONOTONY SONG	26
SWAYS ME AWAKE. WHAT HO, AND THE FIELD'S MY FRIEND,	260	THE CHANGELING	14
AWAKENS			
NO BIRD AWAKENS HER.	17	NO BIRD	8
AWARE			
WE WALK AWARE OF WHAT IS FAR AND CLOSE.	13	PRAISE PRAIRIE	10
YET REMAIN ONLY HALF AWARE OF THE INTRANSIENT GLORY?	169	FOURTH MEDITATN	32
AWAY			
AWAY FROM SIMPLE FAITH	31	LULL	16
FURTHER AND FURTHER AWAY	49	NIGHT CROW	6
CRUMBLED AND FLOWED AWAY,	49	RIVER INCIDENT	8
THE FIEND'S FAR AWAY. LORD, WHAT DO YOU REQUIRE?	59	THE LONG ALLEY	21
SO UP AND AWAY AND WHAT DO WE DO	60	THE LONG ALLEY	37
BRICKS FLAKE BEFORE MY FACE. MASTER OF WATER, THAT'S TREES AWAY.	61	THE LONG ALLEY	80
MY UNCLE'S AWAY.	72	WHERE KNOCK IS	24
HER EYES WENT KISSING AWAY	72	WHERE KNOCK IS	36
THE WORM HAS MOVED AWAY.	73	WHERE KNOCK IS	69
WHAT SLIDES AWAY	80	GIVE WAY, GATES	61
A MOON AWAY.	87	PRAISE TO END!	70
THE LAST TIME I NEARLY WHISPERED MYSELF AWAY.	89	UNFOLD! UNFOLD!	20
THE SISTER SANDS, THEY SLIPPER SOFT AWAY.	92	I CRY, LOVE!	3
THE DEVIL ISN'T DEAD; HE'S JUST AWAY.	97	O, THOU OPENING	16
NEVER WISHING ITSELF AWAY,	101	LIGHT BREATHER	14
THE WHITE GRASS BENDING AWAY,	103	OLD LADY'S WRDS	20
HAS SCAMPERED AWAY IN A DRY WIND.	103	OLD LADY'S WRDS	38
WHAT FALLS AWAY IS ALWAYS. AND IS NEAR.	108	THE WAKING (2)	17
I TURNED MY FACE AWAY, AND YET SHE STAYED.	119	THE DREAM	14
WHAT FALLS AWAY WILL FALL;	125	WORDS FOR WIND	80
THE LONG NOON PULSED AWAY,	128	THE VOICE	23
SHE DANCES, AND THE GROUND BEARS HER AWAY.	129	SHE	10
THE LIGHT AIR TAKES MY BEING'S BREATH AWAY;	134	THE PURE FURY	23
I CRIED, AND BACKED AWAY.	146	THE SONG	5
CLOSE, AND YET FAR AWAY.	146	THE SONG	27
IT TURNED; IT DREW AWAY;	150	SNAKE	6
I BURNED THE FLESH AWAY,	154	THE DYING MAN	26
BUT THESE ROSES: I CAN WEAR THEM BY LOOKING AWAY.	163	I'M HERE	78
AND THEY'LL SOON STAY AWAY IN GREAT BUNCHES!"	180	GOO-GIRL	16
WHO SIGHS FROM FAR AWAY?	188	THE LONGING	41
AS THE PILED ICE BREAKS AWAY FROM THE BATTERED SPILES,	191	AT OYSTER RIVER	55
WHILE, FARTHER AWAY, THE HEAT-LIGHTNING FLASHES.	194	JOURNY INTERIOR	41
NOT TOO FAR AWAY FROM THE EVER-CHANGING FLOWER-DUMP,	199	THE FAR FIELD	16
THEN PITCHING AWAY IN HALF-FLIGHT,	200	THE FAR FIELD	34
THE WHEEL TURNING AWAY FROM ITSELF,	200	THE FAR FIELD	53
SLIDING AWAY FROM THE TRAVELER'S EYE,	203	THE ROSE	34
THE KILLDEER WHISTLING AWAY FROM ME,	204	THE ROSE	62
THE BULLDOZER BACKING AWAY, THE HISS OF THE SANDBLASTER,	204	THE ROSE	71
FANCIES SWAY AWAY	210	HER TIME	3
FLIES AWAY FROM MY FACE	210	HER TIME	15
PHOEBE NOT FAR AWAY	213	THE HAPPY THREE	30
OF BEING, BEING AWAY	215	HIS FOREBODING	4
WHO SENT HIM AWAY?	220	THE ABYSS	40
THE LORD GOD HAS TAKEN MY HEAVINESS AWAY;	222	THE ABYSS	98
I RECALL HOW SHE HARRIED THE CHILDREN AWAY ALL THE LATE SUMMER	223	ELEGY (2)	12
O WORLD SO FAR AWAY! O MY LOST WORLD!	225	OTTO	42
WHITISH AND SPREAD WIDE WHEN HE TRIED TO STRUGGLE AWAY,	227	MEADOW MOUSE	10
THEN THROWING ITSELF UP AND AWAY FROM THE IMPLACABLE SWIFT PURSUERS,	232	THE THING	6
NOT EVEN FEATHERS FROM SO FAR AWAY.	232	THE THING	17
AND THE HALF-SUNKEN BRANCH BENDS AWAY FROM THE GAZER'S EYE.	233	THE PIKE	9
FAR AWAY, CLOSE-AT-HAND, HIS CALL FLOATING OVER THE ON-COMING TRAFFIC,	234	ALL MORNING	3
FLAPPING AWAY HEAVILY WHEN A CAR BLASTS TOO CLOSE,	234	ALL MORNING	7
RISING, WHEELING AWAY WITH HARSH CRIES,	235	ALL MORNING	37

	PAGE	TITLE	LINE
AWAY (CONTINUED)			
FROM THE TEAR, FAR AWAY,	236	SONG (2)	2
A LIGHT LEAF ON A TREE, SHE SWAYED AWAY	241	THE SEQUEL	23
I WATCH A RIVER WIND ITSELF AWAY;	243	THE MOTION	8
ONE LOOK TOO CLOSE CAN TAKE MY SOUL AWAY.	246	THE MARROW	9
THE PRESENT FALLS, THE PRESENT FALLS AWAY;	248	THE TREE, BIRD	18
AND LOOKED AWAY.	262	FOLLIES OF ADAM	21
WE'LL SAIL AWAY FROM THE FRIGHTFUL SHORE	272	DUET	9
COME EASY TO THE SILL, THINGS LOST FROM FAR AWAY.	273	SUPPR W LINDSAY	4
WITH THAT HE HITCHED HIS PANTS AND HUMPED AWAY.	274	SUPPR W LINDSAY	50
AWFUL			
TO STOP THE SERPENT'S AWFUL RACKET:	115	THE SERPENT	13
AWKWARD			
AND THE NEW PLANTS, STILL AWKWARD IN THEIR SOIL	63	FIELD OF LIGHT	42
GROTESQUE, AWKWARD, HIS EXTENDED EYES LOOKING AT NOTHING IN PARTICULAR,	159	FIRST MEDITATN	63
AWL			
THE TAIL STRAIGHT AS AN AWL,	226	THE LIZARD	9
AXLE			
THE GREAT WHEEL TURNS ITS AXLE WHEN IT CAN;	105	SIR JOHN DAVIES	3
AZALEAS			
OR PINCHING-BACK ASTERS, OR PLANTING AZALEAS,	42	OLD FLORIST	2
AZURE			
RECOUNT EACH CHILDHOOD PLEASURE: THE SKIES OF AZURE	5	TO MY SISTER	5
BABBLE			
HEARING A CRASS BABBLE OF BIRDS.	258	SONG (3)	9
BABBLING			
BABBLING IN URINALS.)	147	THE EXORCISM	12
AND ONCE MORE THE TONGUES BEGIN BABBLING.	220	THE ABYSS	31
BABIES			
I AM UNDONE BY THE GURGLE OF BABIES AND PITCHERS,	255	LIGHT POEM	7
BABY			
SLEEPS THE BABY MOUSE I FOUND IN THE MEADOW,	227	MEADOW MOUSE	2
AND THE CYCLAMEN LEAVES GLISTEN LIKE THE BACKS OF BABY TURTLES.	260	THE CHANGELING	15
BACK			
MY SHAVING HAND JERKED BACK IN SUDDEN TERROR:	25	DIM-WIT COUSIN	11
AND AFTERWARDS I ALWAYS FELT MEAN, JOGGING BACK OVER THE LOGGING ROAD,	40	MOSS-GATHERING	9
THE LEAVES CURLED BACK IN ELABORATE CORINTHIAN SCROLLS;	43	CARNATIONS	2
DEEP IN THE BRAIN, FAR BACK.	49	NIGHT CROW	8
THE MOON SAID, BACK OF AN EEL,	54	THE LOST SON	29
AND THE BACK OF AN EEL,	55	THE LOST SON	55
MORNING-FAIR, FOLLOW ME FURTHER BACK	66	SHAPE OF FIRE	64
PAPA THREW HIM BACK.	73	WHERE KNOCK IS	61
KISSES COME BACK,	73	WHERE KNOCK IS	76
STOP THE LARKS. CAN I HAVE MY HEART BACK?	76	I NEED, I NEED	47
ARCH MY BACK, PRETTY-BONES, I'M DEAD AT BOTH ENDS.	85	PRAISE TO END!	9
THE WIND CAME AT MY BACK;	87	PRAISE TO END!	52
SWEET JESUS TOSSED ME BACK:	87	PRAISE TO END!	65
I CAN'T CRAWL BACK THROUGH THOSE VEINS,	89	UNFOLD! UNFOLD!	3
THE CLIFFS! THE CLIFFS! THEY FLING ME BACK.	89	UNFOLD! UNFOLD!	5
I WAS FAR BACK, FARTHER THAN ANYBODY ELSE.	89	UNFOLD! UNFOLD!	21
ON ITS WAY TO THE BACK PASTURE.	104	OLD LADY'S WRDS	53
I TAKE IT, AND I GIVE IT BACK AGAIN:	105	SIR JOHN DAVIES	20
I GAVE HER KISSES BACK, AND WOKE A GHOST.	106	SIR JOHN DAVIES	45
AND SHAPELESS NIGHT THAT MADE NO ANSWER BACK.	107	SIR JOHN DAVIES	90
AND SHOULD HE ARRIVE, WHY JUST LEAN YOURSELF BACK	113	TO A LADY ED	7
I CANNOT ANSWER BACK;	123	WORDS FOR WIND	29
WHEN SMALL BIRDS SIGHED, SHE WOULD SIGH BACK AT THEM;	127	I KNEW A WOMAN	2
WHEN WILL THAT CREATURE GIVE ME BACK MY BREATH?	134	THE PURE FURY	25
MY BACK IS JUST ONE BRUISE;	136	THE SENSUALISTS	4
THEN EACH FELL BACK, LIMP AS A SACK,	136	THE SENSUALISTS	25
YET WHISTLE BACK AT EVERY WHISTLING BIRD	140	THE SWAN	11
THE MOON DRAWS BACK ITS WATERS FROM THE SHORE.	140	THE SWAN	15
WITH HIS STRIPES OF SILVER AND HIS SMALL HOUSE ON HIS BACK,	151	SLUG	2
BACK INTO STRAIGHTNESS;	152	THE SISKINS	15
THE FIGURE AT MY BACK IS NOT MY FRIEND;	154	THE DYING MAN	38
THEN SETTLES BACK TO SHADE AND THE LONG NIGHT.	156	THE DYING MAN	81
AND THAT CRY TAKES ME BACK WHERE I WAS BORN.	156	THE DYING MAN	83
I SIT ABOVE THE BACK WHEELS, WHERE THE JOLTS ARE HARDEST,	158	FIRST MEDITATN	22
AROUND, BACK INTO THE TINY MAINCURRENT, THE RUSH OF BROWNISH-WHITE WATER,	159	FIRST MEDITATN	71

	PAGE	TITLE	LINE
BACK (CONTINUED)			
BRACING MY BACK AGAINST A SAPLING,	161	I'M HERE	24
IN THE BACK OF MY MIND, RUNNING WITH THE ROLLING WATER,	165	HER BECOMING	9
TILTING BACK THE SUNLIGHT.	168	FOURTH MEDITATN	11
MY BACK CREAKS WITH THE DAWN.	170	FOURTH MEDITATN	84
BEFORE THE MOON DRAWS BACK,	171	WHAT TELL BONES	8
THE POND LAPSES BACK INTO A GLASSY SILENCE.	172	WHAT TELL BONES	50
WHO TOOK ONLY TOADS ON HIS BACK:	178	THE YAK	2
I THINK HIS FORWARD'S COMING BACK!	182	THE HIPPO	2
I'D LIKE TO TALK BACK,	182	BOY AND BUSH	4
FALLS BACK, A SLUG, A LOOSE WORM	187	THE LONGING	21
AND THE BACK WHEELS HANG ALMOST OVER THE EDGE	193	JOURNY INTERIOR	4
SWIMMING SLOWLY, ITS BACK RUFFLED BY THE LIGHT CROSS-WINDS,	197	THE LONG WATERS	53
I, WHO CAME BACK FROM THE DEPTHS LAUGHING TOO LOUDLY,	198	THE LONG WATERS	73
WITH ITS THICK GRASSY SCUM AND CRABS SCUTTLING BACK INTO THEIR GLISTENING CRATERS.	203	THE ROSE	50
NEITHER FORWARD NOR BACK,	210	HER TIME	7
ON THE BACK LAWN.	213	THE HAPPY THREE	16
BACK TO THE HOUSE WE RAN,	214	THE HAPPY THREE	33
AND WE TURN BACK TO THE HEAT OF AUGUST,	220	THE ABYSS	48
AND I OBEY THE WIND AT MY BACK	221	THE ABYSS	66
AND YET MY THOUGHT TURNS BACK TO THEM,	225	THE CHUMS	3
BUT THIS MORNING THE SHOE-BOX HOUSE ON THE BACK PORCH IS EMPTY.	227	MEADOW MOUSE	20
I BROUGHT HER BACK IN AGAIN	228	THE GERANIUM	5
THE BOTTOM-STONES SHIMMER BACK THEIR IRREGULAR STRIATIONS,	233	THE PIKE	8
THEY SIT, THREE OR FOUR, HIGH IN THE FIR-TREES BACK OF THE HOUSE,	234	ALL MORNING	6
THE SHIFTING SHADE, THE CINDERS AT MY BACK.	245	THE DECISION	10
I WAS FLUNG BACK FROM SUFFERING AND LOVE	246	THE MARROW	19
SLOWLY I CAME BACK TO THE DUSTY ROAD;	247	I WAITED	15
I WENT, NOT LOOKING BACK. I WAS AFRAID.	247	I WAITED	18
GREW BACK A NEW WING,	249	THE RESTORED	16
THE BIRD FLIES OUT, THE BIRD FLIES BACK AGAIN;	250	THE RIGHT THING	4
BACK ON THE SEA-FOAM;	263	FOLLIES OF ADAM	33
BUT ALAS, ALACK, AND ME ACHIN' BACK,	268	SAGINAW SONG	45
A SWAYING LIGHT-CORD, THEN RAN HALF-WAY BACK.	273	SUPPR W LINDSAY	25
BACKED			
I CRIED, AND BACKED AWAY.	146	THE SONG	5
BACK-EDDY			
NUDGES INTO A BACK-EDDY, A SANDY INLET,	159	FIRST MEDITATN	69
BACKING			
THE BULLDOZER BACKING AWAY, THE HISS OF THE SANDBLASTER,	204	THE ROSE	71
BACKLOTS			
AND THE FIRST DUST OF SPRING LISTING OVER BACKLOTS,--	92	I CRY, LOVE!	27
BACKS			
WATCHING THE WIND RIFFLE THE BACKS OF SMALL BIRDS,	165	HER BECOMING	2
AND THE CYCLAMEN LEAVES GLISTEN LIKE THE BACKS OF BABY TURTLES.	260	THE CHANGELING	15
BACK-STREAM'S			
I KNOW THE BACK-STREAM'S JOY, AND THE STONE'S ETERNAL PULSELESS LONGING.	88	PRAISE TO END!	82
BACKWARD			
OF FLESH, BURN BACKWARD TO A BLACKENED HEAP.	17	UNEXTINGUISHED	8
AS I TURNED FOR A BACKWARD LOOK,	47	THE RETURN	5
TILTS, BACKWARD AND FORWARD.	93	I CRY, LOVE!	51
AND I SEEM TO GO BACKWARD,	158	FIRST MEDITATN	37
BACKWARD IN TIME:	158	FIRST MEDITATN	38
THE TAIL AND SMALLER LEGS SLIPPING AND SLIDING SLOWLY BACKWARD--	159	FIRST MEDITATN	65
NEITHER FORWARD NOR BACKWARD,	195	JOURNY INTERIOR	72
BACTERIAL			
AND BACTERIAL CREEPERS	50	THE MINIMAL	6
BAD			
LURKS THE BAD ANIMAL.	161	I'M HERE	11
BAG-FOOT			
I'M TIRED OF ALL THAT, BAG-FOOT. I CAN HEAR SMALL ANGELS ANYTIME. WHO	98	O, THOU OPENING	25
BAGS			
CHILDREN, THEIR BELLIES SWOLLEN LIKE BLOWN-UP PAPER BAGS,	48	JUDGE NOT	2
BAGS? WHO EVER SAID GOD SANG IN YOUR FAT SHAPE? YOU'RE NOT THE ONLY	98	O, THOU OPENING	27

		PAGE	TITLE	LINE
BAIT				
ROOTS RIPE AS OLD BAIT,	....	38	ROOT CELLAR	7
BALANCED				
PALE BLOSSOMS, EACH BALANCED ON A SINGLE JOINTED STEM,	...	43	CARNATIONS	1
AND SHE BALANCED IN THE DELIGHT OF HER THOUGHT,	....	102	ELEGY FOR JANE	4
BALANCES				
OR BALANCES WITH ONE LEG ON A HUMP	....	15	THE HERON	3
THE GREAT DAY BALANCES UPON THE LEAVES;	....	244	INFIRMITY	27
BALEFUL				
THE YOUNG, BROW-BEATEN EARLY INTO A BALEFUL SILENCE,	.....	169	FOURTH MEDITATN	44
BALL				
THE SUN A BALL OF FIRE COMING DOWN OVER THE WATER,	....	202	THE ROSE	16
BALLAD				
BALLAD OF THE CLAIRVOYANT WIDOW	....	27	CLAIRVOY WIDOW	T
BALM				
ON THINGS ASLEEP, NO BALM;	....	187	THE LONGING	1
BALTIMORE				
WITH BALTIMORE ORIOLES, MICHIGAN BOBOLINKS,		235	ALL MORNING	42
BAMBOO				
BUMBLING UP AND AROUND THE BAMBOO WINDBREAK;	....	226	THE LIZARD	21
BANANAS				
IT'S NECESSARY AMONG THE FLIES AND BANANAS, TO KEEP A				
CONSTANT VIGIL,	....	86	PRAISE TO END!	24
BAND				
THE SUMMER HOUSE SHAPED LIKE A VILLAGE BAND STAND	....	32	SALE	7
BANDANNAS				
WITH THEIR BANDANNAS STIFFENED WITH SWEAT,	....	44	FRAU BAUMAN	33
BANG				
IN THE KINGDOM OF BANG AND BLAB.	....	54	THE LOST SON	33
I DO NOT LIKE TO BANG OR TOOTLE."	....	115	THE SERPENT	20
BANK				
AND AT THAT THE LADY SLIPPED FROM THE BANK	....	117	LADY AND BEAR	26
THE BANK SWALLOWS VEER AND DIP,	....	152	THE SISKINS	1
BANKED-UP				
MY BANKED-UP VERTIGO	....	213	THE HAPPY THREE	26
BANKER'S				
I SEE A BANKER'S MANSION WITH TWENTY WOOD-GRATE FIRES,	...	27	CLAIRVOY WIDOW	13
BANKS				
ONCE I FISHED FROM THE BANKS, LEAF-LIGHT AND HAPPY:	......	86	PRAISE TO END!	19
ON THE LONG BANKS, IN THE SOFT SUMMER AIR.	....	149	IN LATE SUMMER	8
WHEN BANKS CONVERGE, AND THE WIDE RIVER WHITENS;	....	200	THE FAR FIELD	60
TO THE CLAY BANKS, AND THE WILD GRAPES HANGING FROM THE				
ELMTREES.	....	200	THE FAR FIELD	66
ON THE BANKS OF THE TOMBSTONE, THE WIND-HARPS HAVING THEIR				
SAY,	....	204	THE ROSE	60
BANTER				
OR THE SEA'S BANTER,--	....	229	ON THE QUAY	4
BARE				
THE HILLS ARE GREY, THE TREES ARE BARE,	....	15	COMING OF COLD	43
THE FIELDS ARE HARSH AND BARE, THE ROCKS		15	COMING OF COLD	45
AND THE WHOLE MOTION OF THE SOUL LAY BARE:	....	135	THE RENEWAL	23
I BARE A WOUND, AND DARE MYSELF TO BLEED.	....	155	THE DYING MAN	69
BARE AS A BUD, AND NAKED AS A WORM.	....	188	THE LONGING	34
BUT HE WAS APPREHENDED, BARE,	....	264	THREE EPIGRAMS	9
A TUNE SO BOLD AND BARE,	....	271	THE REPLY	11
BARED				
BARED FOR A HUNTER'S BOOT.	....	47	THE RETURN	13
BAREFOOT				
AND THEN STEP BAREFOOT ON A WORM	....	114	DINKY	7
BAREST				
THE BAREST SPEECH OF LIGHT AMONG THE STONES.	....	173	WHAT TELL BONES	71
BARGAINS				
THE BARGAINS FELL TO BIDDERS, ONE BY ONE.	....	21	THE AUCTION	10
BARK				
THE DANK BARK DRIES BENEATH THE SUN,	....	14	COMING OF COLD	32
I KEEP A DOG, AND BARK MYSELF.	....	138	THE SURLY ONE	4
DRY BARK FLEW IN THEIR FACES FROM HIS SHOT,--	....	224	OTTO	16
BARKED				
BARKED AND HOWLED,	....	55	THE LOST SON	76
THE SEA BARKED IN ITS CAVES.	....	258	SONG (3)	16
BARLEY				
A FIELD OF BARLEY SPREAD BENEATH THE SUN.	....	13	PRAISE PRAIRIE	4

	PAGE	TITLE	LINE
BARLEY-BREAK			
BUT BARLEY-BREAK AND SQUEEZE.	60	THE LONG ALLEY	38
BARN			
ALL THINGS ARE BROUGHT TO BARN AND FOLD.	15	COMING OF COLD	34
WHEN FROM UNDER THE BARN THE CAT BRINGS A SIMILAR LITTER,--	24	VERNAL SENTIMNT	5
THE SOUL RESIDES IN THE HORSE BARN.	59	THE LONG ALLEY	22
ALWAYS A SHARP TURN TO THE LEFT PAST A BARN CLOSE TO THE ROADSIDE,	193	JOURNY INTERIOR	25
BARNACLED			
OVER THE LOW, BARNACLED, ELEPHANT-COLORED ROCKS,	190	AT OYSTER RIVER	1
BAROQUE			
THE DRIVERS CREAKING THE SEATS OF THE BAROQUE HEARSES,	22	ROAD TO WDLAWN	2
BARREN			
THE BITTER ROCK, THE BARREN SOIL	18	LONG LIVE WEEDS	3
IN THE HOUR OF RIPENESS THE TREE IS BARREN.	64	SHAPE OF FIRE	14
BARRIER			
MAKES ALMOST A WAVE OVER A BARRIER OF SMALL STONES,	190	AT OYSTER RIVER	13
BARRIERS			
THOSE BARRIERS CIRCUMVENT	7	ORDERS FOR DAY	18
BARSTOOLS			
AGONY OF CRUCIFIXION ON BARSTOOLS.	187	THE LONGING	6
BARTENDERS			
BARTENDERS THINK NO ILL;	267	SAGINAW SONG	14
BARTER			
IN LOVE ARE NEVER KNOWN TO BARTER;	23	AMOROUS LADY	6
BASALT			
GLITTER OF BASALT AND MICA,	265	HARSH COUNTRY	3
BASE			
IN THE COUNTRY OF FEW LAKES, IN THE TALL BUFFALO GRASS AT THE BASE OF THE CLAY BUTTES,	189	THE LONGING	53
GREY FROM THE LONG WINTER, BURNT AT THE BASE IN LATE SUMMER.	193	JOURNY INTERIOR	10
BASIN			
THE UNALTERABLE PATHOS OF BASIN AND PITCHER,	46	DOLOR	6
BASK			
I BASK IN THE BOWER OF CHANGE;	88	PRAISE TO END!	85
AND THE CRABS BASK NEAR THE EDGE,	200	THE FAR FIELD	69
BASKETS			
AND LIFT UP A PATCH, DARK-GREEN, THE KIND FOR LINING CEMETERY BASKETS,	40	MOSS-GATHERING	2
BASSWOOD			
ODOR OF BASSWOOD ON A MOUNTAIN-SLOPE,	201	THE FAR FIELD	98
BAT			
THE BAT	16	THE BAT	T
BY DAY THE BAT IS COUSIN TO THE MOUSE.	16	THE BAT	1
OF FLYING LIKE A BAT DEEP INTO A NARROWING TUNNEL,	199	THE FAR FIELD	2
BATHTUB			
AS WE SAT THERE DRINKING THAT BATHTUB GIN	112	SQUEEZE-BOX	24
BAT-LIKE			
AS HIS HEAD; HIS BAT-LIKE EARS	227	MEADOW MOUSE	15
BATS			
THE BATS WEAVE IN AND OUT OF THE WILLOWS,	93	I CRY, LOVE!	41
WITH BATS, WEASELS, WORMS--I REJOICE IN THE KINSHIP.	151	SLUG	26
LIKE BATS IN DAYTIME,	152	THE SISKINS	4
THE BATS TWITTERED AT NOON.	162	I'M HERE	40
WHEN BATS FLY, CLOSE TO SLIGHTLY TILTING BROWNISH WATER,	198	THE LONG WATERS	61
BATTERED			
AND BATTERED FRUIT HAS CHOKED THE GRASS.	14	COMING OF COLD	7
WAS BATTERED ON ONE KNUCKLE;	45	MY PAPA'S WALTZ	10
AS THE PILED ICE BREAKS AWAY FROM THE BATTERED SPILES,	191	AT OYSTER RIVER	55
BAUMAN			
FRAU BAUMAN, FRAU SCHMIDT, AND FRAU SCHWARTZE	44	FRAU BAUMAN	T
BAY			
FOR SHE FINALLY LEFT TOWN ON THE BAY CITY FREIGHT	112	SQUEEZE-BOX	40
NO SOUND FROM THE BAY. NO VIOLENCE.	190	AT OYSTER RIVER	6
TO A LANDLOCKED BAY, WHERE THE SALT WATER IS FRESHENED	197	THE LONG WATERS	47
BAYS			
A COUNTRY OF BAYS AND INLETS, AND SMALL STREAMS FLOWING SEAWARD.	196	THE LONG WATERS	19
BE (106)			
BEACH			
THE BEACH RISES WITH THE WAVES.	83	O LULL ME, LULL	15
THE FLAT BOOM ON THE BEACH OF THE TOWERING SEA-SWELL,	231	THE STORM	41

	PAGE	TITLE	LINE
BEACHES			
STANDING, SILENT, ON SANDY BEACHES OR WALKING ALONG GREEN EMBANKMENTS;	168	FOURTH MEDITATN	4
BEACH-GRASS			
THE DEW REVIVES ON THE BEACH-GRASS;	190	AT OYSTER RIVER	20
BEACHY			
A BEACHY WETNESS.	162	I'M HERE	57
BEACON			
I WATCH A BEACON SWING	34	NIGHT JOURNEY	16
LIKE AN ENORMOUS BEACON,	265	HARSH COUNTRY	10
BEADS			
SETTLING IN SMALL BEADS AROUND WEEDS AND SUNKEN BRANCHES,	159	FIRST MEDITATN	61
BEAK			
THE BEAK OF FROST HAS PICKED THE BOUGH,	14	COMING OF COLD	23
HIS BEAK IS QUICKER THAN A HUMAN HAND.	15	THE HERON	8
OUT OF A NESTLING'S BEAK	123	WORDS FOR WIND	27
I'M NO LONGER A BIRD DIPPING A BEAK INTO RIPPLING WATER	220	THE ABYSS	41
BEANS			
THERE'S BEANS ON EVERY PLATE,	267	SAGINAW SONG	4
BEAR			
FEET, BEAR THE THIN BONES OVER	7	ORDERS FOR DAY	8
THE BEAR, EQUIPPED WITH PAW AND SNOUT,	23	AMOROUS LADY	3
WHEEL OF THE STARS, THE GREAT BEAR GLITTERING COLDER THAN SNOW,	47	DOUBLE FEATURE	11
MAKE ME A BIRD OR A BEAR!	80	GIVE WAY, GATES	39
I STILL BEAR.	80	GIVE WAY, GATES	58
A CAGED BEAR RARELY DOES THE SAME THING TWICE	105	SIR JOHN DAVIES	10
THE LADY AND THE BEAR	117	LADY AND BEAR	T
A LADY CAME TO A BEAR BY A STREAM.	117	LADY AND BEAR	1
TELL ME, DEAR BEAR THERE BY THE STREAM,	117	LADY AND BEAR	3
"I AM WHAT IS KNOWN AS A BIDDLY BEAR,--	117	LADY AND BEAR	5
SAYS A BEAR	117	LADY AND BEAR	11
YES, A BEAR HAS TO FISH WITH HIS PAW, PAW, PAW.	117	LADY AND BEAR	19
A BEAR HAS TO FISH WITH HIS PAW."	117	LADY AND BEAR	20
BUT THE BEAR JUST SAT THERE UNTIL SHE SANK;	117	LADY AND BEAR	28
I BEAR, BUT NOT ALONE,	124	WORDS FOR WIND	59
THAT GOD HIMSELF CAN SCARCELY BEAR.	144	ELEGY (1)	4
THAT CHRIST, SECURELY BOUND, COULD BEAR.	144	ELEGY (1)	8
I HAVE MYSELF, AND BEAR ITS WEIGHT OF WOE	144	ELEGY (1)	15
SHE COULD GROWL LIKE A BEAR,--	179	MYRTLE	4
ONE DAY HUGH WALKED UP TO A BEAR	181	MONOTONY SONG	5
THE BEAR SAID, SIR, YOU GO TOO FAR,	181	MONOTONY SONG	9
I COULD NOT BEAR ITS SONG, THAT ALTERING	248	THE TREE, BIRD	14
BEARD			
TODAY I SAW A BEARD IN A CLOUD.	76	I NEED, I NEED	48
SPEAK TO ME, FROSTY BEARD.	86	PRAISE TO END!	29
O WHAT'S THE WEATHER IN A BEARD?	114	DINKY	1
BEARDED			
THE BEARDED BOARDS IN THE STREAM AND THE ALL OF APPLES;	66	SHAPE OF FIRE	71
BEARING			
BEARING BEING ITSELF,	221	THE ABYSS	71
BEARING DOWN, WITH TWO STEADY EYES,	223	ELEGY (2)	22
BEARING ITS LIFE AND MORE, A DOUBLE SOUND,	248	THE TREE, BIRD	11
BEARS			
BUT THE TRUE SUBSTANCE BEARS	9	THE ADAMANT	7
THE DILL BEARS UP ITS ACRID CROWN;	14	COMING OF COLD	14
THE BRIAR BEARS ITS THORN, AND DROUGHT	14	COMING OF COLD	24
NOW AS THE TRAIN BEARS WEST,	34	NIGHT JOURNEY	1
SPEECH REVIVED, A GHOSTLY GOING OF TAME BEARS, A BRIGHT MOON ON GLEAMING	98	O, THOU OPENING	23
I'LL SING AND WHISTLE ROMPING WITH THE BEARS.	105	SIR JOHN DAVIES	6
THAT CAME TO BE THE BEARS AND YEATS WOULD KNOW.	105	SIR JOHN DAVIES	24
WE BIDDLY'S ARE PEE-CULIAR BEARS.	117	LADY AND BEAR	7
SHE DANCES, AND THE GROUND BEARS HER AWAY.	129	SHE	10
HEROES AND BEARS, AND OLD PHILOSOPHERS--	274	SUPPR W LINDSAY	42
BEAST			
WHEN, EASY AS A BEAST,	121	ALL EARTH, AIR	13
SHE FROLICKS LIKE A BEAST;	126	WORDS FOR WIND	101
A MAN'S A BEAST PROWLING IN HIS OWN HOUSE.	133	THE PURE FURY	17
A BEAST WITH FANGS, AND OUT FOR HIS OWN BLOOD	133	THE PURE FURY	18
THE BEAST	145	THE BEAST	T
AND THERE A GREAT BEAST PLAYED,	145	THE BEAST	6
A BEAST CRIES OUT AS IF ITS FLESH WERE TORN,	156	THE DYING MAN	82

	PAGE	TITLE	LINE
BEAST (CONTINUED)			
MY BREATH GREW LESS. I LISTENED LIKE A BEAST.	166	HER BECOMING	53
NOT A BEAST, NOT A BIRD,--	182	BOY AND BUSH	9
BEASTS			
OUT, OUT, YOU SECRET BEASTS,	167	HER BECOMING	78
AMONG THE SHY BEASTS, THE DEER AT THE SALT-LICK,	190	AT OYSTER RIVER	26
BEASTS OF THE HILL AND SERPENTS OF THE DEN.	239	IN A DARK TIME	6
BEAST'S			
YOU CHILD WITH A BEAST'S HEART,	80	GIVE WAY, GATES	38
BEAT			
HIS PULSE BEAT IS SO SLOW WE THINK HIM DEAD.	16	THE BAT	4
THE HEART BEAT FASTER AS THE FAT WORDS ROLLED.	21	THE AUCTION	14
YOU BEAT TIME ON MY HEAD	45	MY PAPA'S WALTZ	13
MY MARROW BEAT AS WILDLY AS MY PULSE.	106	SIR JOHN DAVIES	36
SPIRIT AND NATURE BEAT IN ONE BREAST-BONE--	131	SENTENTIOUS MAN	1
I HEAR A BEAT OF BIRDS, THE PLANGENT WINGS	173	WHAT TELL BONES	69
AND THEN I BEAT UPON A CAN,	269	GOB MUSIC	3
BEATEN			
REEDS BEATEN FLAT BY WIND AND RAIN,	193	JOURNY INTERIOR	9
BEATING			
OR A MOTH BEATING THE CURTAIN.	54	THE LOST SON	23
SOME MORNING THING CAME, BEATING ITS WINGS.	63	FIELD OF LIGHT	35
WHERE ARE YOU NOW, MY BONNY BEATING GRISTLE,	86	PRAISE TO END!	17
THE GROUND'S BEATING LIKE FLAME!	99	O, THOU OPENING	59
WHAT'S BEATING AT THE GATE?	154	THE DYING MAN	34
OR BEATING AGAINST THE BLACK CLOUDS OF THE STORM,	209	HER LONGING	22
THEIR FOUR WINGS BEATING TOGETHER,	210	HER TIME	13
THE FLAT-ROOFED HOUSES, COMING DOWN IN GUSTS, BEATING	230	THE STORM	24
WITH EVERY SHIFT OF AIR, THOSE BEATING WINGS,	248	THE TREE, BIRD	15
THE BIRD, THE BEATING BIRD, EXTENDING WINGS--.	248	THE TREE, BIRD	21
BEATRICE			
DID BEATRICE DENY WHAT DANTE SAW?	107	SIR JOHN DAVIES	76
FROM ANOTHER BEATRICE.	216	HER WRATH	5
BEATS			
WHAT BEATS IN ME	80	GIVE WAY, GATES	57
FOR OTHER TUNES AND OTHER WANTON BEATS	105	SIR JOHN DAVIES	21
BEATS SLOWER IN MY CARELESS SOLITUDE.	155	THE DYING MAN	68
WHO STOPS BEING A BIRD, YET BEATS HIS WINGS	156	THE DYING MAN	100
BEAUTIFUL			
THE BEAUTIFUL SURVIVING BONES	58	THE LOST SON	157
IN A BOAT OF BEAUTIFUL THINGS.	103	OLD LADY'S WRDS	24
THE TRULY BEAUTIFUL,	121	ALL EARTH, AIR	16
BEAUTIFUL, IN ITS WAY, LIKE QUICKSILVER--	151	SLUG	22
THE GENTLE AND BEAUTIFUL STILL-TO-BE-BORN;	170	FOURTH MEDITATN	65
BEAUTIFUL MY DESIRE, AND THE PLACE OF MY DESIRE.	204	THE ROSE	78
FROM THE ONE BEAUTIFUL THING IN HER YARD, THE PEACHTREE;	223	ELEGY (2)	13
A FLORIST DOES NOT WOO THE BEAUTIFUL:	224	OTTO	8
THE LUGUBRIOUSLY BEAUTIFUL PLAINT UTTERED AT REGULAR INTERVALS,	234	ALL MORNING	4
IN THE PLACE OF BEAUTIFUL STONES.	258	SONG (3)	7
ALL WOMEN, O, ARE BEAUTIFUL	268	SAGINAW SONG	60
BECAME			
BECAME A CLAM.	62	FIELD OF LIGHT	14
MY MISSION BECAME THE SALVATION OF MINNOWS.	90	UNFOLD! UNFOLD!	31
SLOWLY BECAME THE MOON.	123	WORDS FOR WIND	24
ALL NATURAL SHAPES BECAME SYMBOLICAL.	166	HER BECOMING	57
SILENCE BECAME A THING;	167	HER BECOMING	66
AND I BECAME ALL THAT I LOOKED UPON.	247	I WAITED	12
BECAUSE			
BECAUSE. BECAUSE.	115	THE SERPENT	4
BECAUSE. BECAUSE.	115	THE SERPENT	4
SHE LOVED THE WIND BECAUSE THE WIND LOVED ME.	119	THE DREAM	16
I LOVE BECAUSE I AM	167	HER BECOMING	84
BECAUSE NOBODY HEARD,	182	BOY AND BUSH	8
BECHSTEIN			
THE BECHSTEIN PIANO, THE FOUR-POSTER BED,	32	SALE	10
BECKON			
AND HOW THOSE FLOWERHEADS SEEMED TO FLOW TOWARD ME, TO BECKON ME, ONLY A CHILD, OUT OF MYSELF.	203	THE ROSE	55
BECKONED			
FOR A BLOND HILL BECKONED	265	HARSH COUNTRY	9
BECKONING			
BECKONING THROUGH HALLS,	56	THE LOST SON	89

	PAGE	TITLE	LINE
BECOME			
THIS FLAT LAND HAS BECOME A PIT	19	AGNST DISASTER	9
THE LEAVES, THE LEAVES BECOME ME!	61	THE LONG ALLEY	78
TO SEE CYCLAMEN VEINS BECOME CLEARER IN EARLY SUNLIGHT,	67	SHAPE OF FIRE	86
I'VE BECOME A SENTRY OF SMALL SEEDS,	103	OLD LADY'S WRDS	33
DID EACH BECOME THE OTHER IN THAT PLAY?	106	SIR JOHN DAVIES	55
IS SHE WHAT I BECOME?	130	THE OTHER	7
MY FRIENDS BECOME MORE CHRISTIAN, YEAR BY YEAR.	132	SENTENTIOUS MAN	38
I'VE BECOME A STRANGE PIECE OF FLESH,	157	FIRST MEDITATN	15
A LIGHT WIND RISES: I BECOME THE WIND.	167	HER BECOMING	95
TO BECOME LOST IN A LOVE,	169	FOURTH MEDITATN	31
WOMEN WHO BECOME THEIR POSSESSIONS,	169	FOURTH MEDITATN	39
WHAT'S BECOME OF CARE? THIS LAKE BREATHES LIKE A ROSE.	170	FOURTH MEDITATN	76
TO TRY TO BECOME LIKE GOD	172	WHAT TELL BONES	59
THE SUN! THE SUN! AND ALL WE CAN BECOME!	173	WHAT TELL BONES	84
BECOME ANOTHER THING;	198	THE LONG WATERS	74
BROODING ON GOD, I MAY BECOME A MAN.	246	THE MARROW	10
THE SMALL BECOME THE GREAT, THE GREAT THE SMALL;	250	THE RIGHT THING	8
BECOMES			
THE LIGHT BECOMES ME.	88	PRAISE TO END!	101
THE WOOD BECOMES A WALL.	148	THE SMALL	9
THE SPIRIT OF WRATH BECOMES THE SPIRIT OF BLESSING,	195	JOURNY INTERIOR	78
THE HILL BECOMES THE VALLEY, AND IS STILL;	250	THE RIGHT THING	5
BECOMING			
STILLNESS BECOMING ALIVE,	58	THE LOST SON	167
HER BECOMING	165	HER BECOMING	T
IS FAR FROM BECOMING GOD.	172	WHAT TELL BONES	60
BEYOND BECOMING AND PERISHING,	205	THE ROSE	102
MANY ARRIVALS MAKE US LIVE: THE TREE BECOMING	235	MANIFESTATION	1
YOU'RE BECOMING THAT HORROR, A TWO-LEGGED PIG	272	DUET	3
BED			
THE SMALL BROOK DIES WITHIN ITS BED;	15	COMING OF COLD	38
YOUR BED COLLAPSES FROM IMAGINED SINS.	25	DIM-WIT COUSIN	6
THE BECHSTEIN PIANO, THE FOUR-POSTER BED,	32	SALE	10
NOW, WHEN I'M ALONE AND COLD IN MY BED,	44	FRAU BAUMAN	30
THEN WALTZED ME OFF TO BED	45	MY PAPA'S WALTZ	15
IS THE SEED LEAVING THE OLD BED? THESE BUDS ARE LIVE AS BIRDS.	56	THE LOST SON	102
RISING SLOWLY OUT OF ITS BED,	67	SHAPE OF FIRE	84
WHO READS IN BED	99	O, THOU OPENING	69
"THE BED ITSELF BEGINS TO QUAKE,	136	THE SENSUALISTS	21
THE SPIKEY PURPLE BUSHES IN THE WINDING DRY CREEK BED--	194	JOURNY INTERIOR	37
I'D STAND UPON MY BED, A SLEEPLESS CHILD	225	OTTO	40
WE CREEP TO OUR BED, AND ITS STRAW MATTRESS.	231	THE STORM	28
BEDRAGGLED			
SHE LOOKED SO LIMP AND BEDRAGGLED,	228	THE GERANIUM	2
BEDROOM			
UNTIL I COULD THINK THERE WERE WAVES ROLLING HIGH AS MY BEDROOM FLOOR;	12	MID-CNTRY BLOW	2
HAPPY ALONE IN HIS BEDROOM COUNTING HIS PULSE.	24	POETASTER	3
BEDS			
WE GO TO OUR BEDS IN A HOUSE AT THE EDGE OF A MEADOW,	33	IDYLL	11
WHOLE BEDS OF BLOOM PITCHED ON A PILE,	43	FLOWER DUMP	3
THE WAVES, ALTERED BY SAND-BARS, BEDS OF KELP, MISCELLANEOUS DRIFTWOOD,	191	AT OYSTER RIVER	32
WHERE THE SALMON EASE THEIR WAY INTO THE KELP BEDS,	205	THE ROSE	96
BED-SITTING			
NOW IN THE MISERY OF BED-SITTING ROOM CONFUSION,	29	THE REMINDER	9
BEDSTEAD			
RUNNING OVER THE COVERLET, DOWN UNDER THE IRON BEDSTEAD.	231	THE STORM	35
BEE			
THE STEM THAT HOLDS THE BEE IS PRONE;	15	COMING OF COLD	39
AND A BEE SHAKING DROPS FROM A RAIN-SOAKED HONEYSUCKLE.	63	FIELD OF LIGHT	49
THE BLOSSOM STINGS THE BEE.	121	ALL EARTH, AIR	18
BEEF			
WITH COLD ROAST BEEF AND COFFEE FOR DESSERT--	274	SUPPR W LINDSAY	33
BEEN (17)			
BEER			
SO LONG ON GIN, BOBBIE PINS, HALF-SMOKED CIGARS, DEAD BEER,	228	THE GERANIUM	10
MY JUG, MY HONEY, MY CAN OF BEER,	272	DUET	22
BEES			
BEES AND LILIES THERE WERE,	77	BRING THE DAY!	1
BEES AND LILIES THERE WERE,	77	BRING THE DAY!	2

	PAGE	TITLE	LINE

BEES (CONTINUED)
BEES AND LILIES WERE THERE. .... 77 BRING THE DAY! 5
I KEEP DREAMING OF BEES. .... 99 O, THOU OPENING 81
BIRDS FURIOUS AS BEES. .... 152 THE SISKINS 18
I HEAR A NOISE OF BEES, A TRELLIS HUM, ... 155 THE DYING MAN 74
WHETHER THE BEES HAVE THOUGHTS, WE CANNOT SAY, ... 196 THE LONG WATERS 1
A SCENT BELOVED OF BEES; .... 201 THE FAR FIELD 99
ITS BEVY OF BEES, AND ITS WIND-BEATEN RICKETY SUN-CHAIRS. 226 THE LIZARD 29

BEETLES
BEETLES IN CAVES, NEWTS, STONE-DEAF FISHES, ... 50 THE MINIMAL 3
BEETLES SWEETENED MY BREATH. .... 89 UNFOLD! UNFOLD! 28

BEFALL
WHAT ELSE CAN BEFALL? .... 92 I CRY, LOVE! 4

BEFORE
A FLASH OF OBJECTS NEVER SEEN BEFORE. .... 8 THE SIGNALS 2
BEFORE OBLIVION CLOUDS THE BRAIN. .... 8 PRAYER 4
THE BUDS DRAW IN BEFORE THE COLD. .... 15 COMING OF COLD 37
BEFORE THE BREAKING OF A STRING, ... 22 SILENCE 8
PRAYER BEFORE STUDY .... 24 BEFORE STUDY T
THOUGH IT ALL HAPPENED BEFORE, I CANNOT GROW BITTER: ..... 24 VERNAL SENTIMNT 7
TODAY, WHILE SCRAPING HAIR BEFORE THE MIRROR, ... 25 DIM-WIT COUSIN 10
AND I KNEW I HAD BEEN THERE BEFORE, ... 49 RIVER INCIDENT 9
I HAD HEARD BEFORE. .... 55 THE LOST SON 74
BRICKS FLAKE BEFORE MY FACE. MASTER OF WATER, THAT'S TREES
    AWAY. .... 61 THE LONG ALLEY 80
THAT WAS BEFORE. I FELL! I FELL! .... 73 WHERE KNOCK IS 68
LET'S PLAY BEFORE WE FORGET! .... 83 O LULL ME, LULL 20
MANY ASTOUNDS BEFORE, I LOST MY IDENTITY TO A PEBBLE; .... 88 PRAISE TO END! 88
WE MET IN A NEST. BEFORE I LIVED. .... 93 I CRY, LOVE! 55
I'VE SEEN MY FATHER'S FACE BEFORE .... 97 O, THOU OPENING 14
ATTENDED WHAT WE DID. BEHIND, BEFORE, ... 106 SIR JOHN DAVIES 50
WE DANCED TO SHINING; MOCKED BEFORE THE BLACK .... 107 SIR JOHN DAVIES 89
YOU ASKED ME BEFORE, I'LL TELL YOU AGAIN: .... 114 DINKY 11
AND, THEN, BEFORE HE SAYS A WORD .... 116 THE SLOTH 4
BEFORE SHE EVER BREATHED, AND IN THAT DREAM .... 119 THE DREAM 2
WHERE ARE THE DEAD? BEFORE ME .... 122 ALL EARTH, AIR 22
BEFORE THE CAVING-IN OF ALL THAT IS; .... 149 IN LATE SUMMER 14
AND ONE CRAB, TENTATIVE, HUNCHES HIMSELF BEFORE MOVING
    ALONG THE BOTTOM, ... 159 FIRST MEDITATN 62
A SPIRIT PLAYS BEFORE ME LIKE A CHILD, ... 165 HER BECOMING 22
I SIGH BEFORE I SING. .... 167 HER BECOMING 83
BEFORE THE MOON DRAWS BACK, ... 171 WHAT TELL BONES 8
AND SOMETIMES LOOK BEFORE YOU LEAP .... 181 MONOTONY SONG 27
IS BEFORE, OR RIGHT AFTER, A BLIZZARD. .... 183 THE LIZARD 2
HOW GRACEFUL THE SMALL BEFORE DANGER! .... 192 AT OYSTER RIVER 67
THE FRIEND THAT RUNS BEFORE ME ON THE WINDY HEADLANDS, ... 198 THE LONG WATERS 71
AS OF WATER QUICKENING BEFORE A NARROWING CHANNEL ..... 200 THE FAR FIELD 59
BEFORE DESCENDING TO THE ALLUVIAL PLAIN, ... 200 THE FAR FIELD 65
AN OLD MAN WITH HIS FEET BEFORE THE FIRE, ... 201 THE FAR FIELD 85
OR THAT LONELY TIME BEFORE THE BREAKING OF MORNING .... 204 THE ROSE 82
BEFORE THIS LONGING, ... 209 HER LONGING 1
BEFORE THE ALMOST INVISIBLE .... 210 HER TIME 16
GLINT OF THE SUN, BEFORE .... 210 HER TIME 20
BEFORE THAT SIMPLE TUNE .... 271 THE REPLY 6
LET'S EAT BEFORE THE MOONLIGHT ALL RUNS OUT." .... 273 SUPPR W LINDSAY 29

BEG
SOME LEARN THE ART OF THIEVING, AND SOME GROW UP TO BEG; 27 CLAIRVOY WIDOW 10

BEGAN
--AND BEGAN TO DRINK UP THE MONEY. .... 111 SQUEEZE-BOX 7
STARED, AND BEGAN TO SING. .... 146 THE SONG 17
AFTER A WHILE THE LIGHT BEGAN TO WANE .... 274 SUPPR W LINDSAY 35

BEGETS
LOVE BEGETS LOVE. THIS TORMENT IS MY JOY. .... 243 THE MOTION 7

BEGIN
BEGIN WITH THE ROCK; .... 77 BRING THE DAY! 30
IT'S TIME TO BEGIN! .... 78 BRING THE DAY! 44
TO BEGIN! .... 78 BRING THE DAY! 45
I SEE THE RUBBLESTONES BEGIN TO STRETCH .... 135 THE RENEWAL 21
NOW THE PLACE TO BEGIN .... 183 THE LIZARD 3
AND THE DEAD BEGIN FROM THEIR DARK TO SING IN MY SLEEP. 195 JOURNY INTERIOR 79
BEGIN RISING WHITELY, ... 210 HER TIME 9
AND ONCE MORE THE TONGUES BEGIN BABBLING. .... 220 THE ABYSS 31

	PAGE	TITLE	LINE
BEGINNER			
BEGINNER,	171	WHAT TELL BONES	1
PERPETUAL BEGINNER,	171	WHAT TELL BONES	2
BEGINNING			
"IT WAS BEGINNING WINTER"	58	THE LOST SON	ST
IT WAS BEGINNING WINTER,	58	THE LOST SON	149
IT WAS BEGINNING WINTER,	58	THE LOST SON	154
YOU TREE BEGINNING TO KNOW,	79	GIVE WAY, GATES	24
NOW THE GILLS ARE BEGINNING TO CRY.	92	I CRY, LOVE!	18
THE MOON BEGINNING.	100	THE VISITANT	20
BEGINNINGS			
I QUAIL, LEAN TO BEGINNINGS, SHEATH-WET.	37	CUTTINGS (LATE)	11
BEGINNINGS START WITHOUT SHADE,	93	I CRY, LOVE!	33
A PRINCE OF SMALL BEGINNINGS, ENDURING THE SLOW STRETCHES OF CHANGE,	170	FOURTH MEDITATN	70
BEWARE THOSE PERPETUAL BEGINNINGS,	171	WHAT TELL BONES	23
--ALL BEGINNINGS COME.	188	THE LONGING	38
TO THE DARK BEGINNINGS OF ANOTHER DAY.	241	THE SEQUEL	24
BEGINS			
AT BRIDGEHEADS BUCKLED ICE BEGINS TO SHIFT,	11	LIGHT BRIGHTER	7
"THE BED ITSELF BEGINS TO QUAKE,	136	THE SENSUALISTS	21
I THINK A BIRD, AND IT BEGINS TO FLY.	155	THE DYING MAN	70
AND THE MIDCHANNEL BEGINS CRACKING AND HEAVING FROM THE PRESSURE BENEATH,	191	AT OYSTER RIVER	49
AND THE WHOLE RIVER BEGINS TO MOVE FORWARD, ITS BRIDGES SHAKING.	191	AT OYSTER RIVER	56
IN A DARK TIME, THE EYE BEGINS TO SEE,	239	IN A DARK TIME	1
HE WHO HIMSELF BEGINS TO LOATHE	257	SANITARIUM	9
BEGONIA			
WHY DON'T YOU, BEGONIA,	74	I NEED, I NEED	13
BEGUILE			
BEGUILE ME, CHANGE. WHAT HAVE I FALLEN FROM?	170	FOURTH MEDITATN	77
BEHAVED			
YOUR DONKEY IS BETTER BEHAVED, I TRUST.	178	THE DONKEY	4
BEHIND			
FLESH BEHIND STEEL AND GLASS IS UNPROTECTED	5	PROGNOSIS	5
BEHIND THE GREEN VISCID TRELLIS,	62	FIELD OF LIGHT	24
WHEN THE SUN HAS FALLEN BEHIND A WOODED ISLAND;	67	SHAPE OF FIRE	89
FISHING, I CAUGHT MYSELF BEHIND THE EARS.	89	UNFOLD! UNFOLD!	23
ATTENDED WHAT WE DID. BEHIND, BEFORE,	106	SIR JOHN DAVIES	50
COMING BEHIND HER FOR HER PRETTY SAKE	127	I KNEW A WOMAN	13
WHEN THERE'S A DAZZLING DARK BEHIND THE SUN?	155	THE DYING MAN	53
DOWN FROM BEHIND THE LAST RANGES,	158	FIRST MEDITATN	33
A GREAT WOODEN SLEIGH CAREENING BEHIND THEM,	158	FIRST MEDITATN	54
BEHIND THE EYE; THE LOST ACRES AT THE EDGE OF SMOKY CITIES.	159	FIRST MEDITATN	75
BEHIND THE CHILD'S ARCHNESS	161	I'M HERE	10
THEN A RUNNEL BEHIND ME, CREEPING CLOSER,	190	AT OYSTER RIVER	4
AND NO LIGHTS BEHIND, IN THE BLURRED SIDE-MIRROR,	199	THE FAR FIELD	7
THE LONELY BUZZ BEHIND MY MIDNIGHT EYES;--	248	THE TREE, BIRD	16
I RAN BEHIND HIM EVERY DAY	268	SAGINAW SONG	54
BEHOLD			
BEHOLD, IN THE LOUT'S EYE,	93	I CRY, LOVE!	38
AND I BEHOLD THE DARK SIDE OF A TREE	240	IN EVEING AIR	14
BEHOLD THE CRITIC, PITCHED LIKE THE CASTRATI,	264	THREE EPIGRAMS	1
BEHOLD, THE MOON!--	273	SUPPR W LINDSAY	5
BEING			
THE PARTICLES OF BEING LIE;	19	AGNST DISASTER	6
A FOOL CAN PLAY AT BEING SOLEMN	24	BEFORE STUDY	7
GOOD-BYE FOR BEING WRONG.	76	I NEED, I NEED	50
I HEAR MY BEING DANCE FROM EAR TO EAR.	108	THE WAKING (2)	5
BEING MYSELF, I SING	126	WORDS FOR WIND	90
IN ANOTHER BEING, AT LAST.	126	WORDS FOR WIND	105
AS IF PURE BEING WOKE,	147	THE EXORCISM	5
A BLAZE OF BEING ON A CENTRAL STEM.	149	IN LATE SUMMER	18
BEING DELIGHTS IN BEING, AND IN TIME.	150	IN LATE SUMMER	31
BEING DELIGHTS IN BEING, AND IN TIME.	150	IN LATE SUMMER	31
THE COLD SLIME COME INTO BEING,	151	SLUG	11
WHO STOPS BEING A BIRD, YET BEATS HIS WINGS	156	THE DYING MAN	100
I WAS ALWAYS ONE FOR BEING ALONE,	168	FOURTH MEDITATN	1
MAY THEY FLAME INTO BEING!--	169	FOURTH MEDITATN	62
OF BEING BORN FAILS ON HIS NAKED EARS.	201	THE FAR FIELD	90
AS IF ANOTHER MAN APPEARED OUT OF THE DEPTHS OF MY BEING,	205	THE ROSE	100
AND I REJOICED IN BEING WHAT I WAS:	205	THE ROSE	106

	PAGE	TITLE	LINE
BEING (CONTINUED)			
OF BEING, BEING AWAY	215	HIS FOREBODING	4
OF BEING, BEING AWAY	215	HIS FOREBODING	4
BEARING BEING ITSELF, ...	221	THE ABYSS	71
BEING, NOT DOING, IS MY FIRST JOY.	222	THE ABYSS	101
BEING, WE CAME TO BE	238	THE TRANCED	23
HIS BEING SINGLE, AND THAT BEING ALL:	250	THE RIGHT THING	11
HIS BEING SINGLE, AND THAT BEING ALL:	250	THE RIGHT THING	11
BEING'S			
THE LIGHT AIR TAKES MY BEING'S BREATH AWAY;	134	THE PURE FURY	23
BELCHES			
A DRUNKARD DRINKS, AND BELCHES IN HIS DRINK;	132	SENTENTIOUS MAN	29
BELIEVE			
BELIEVE ME, THERE'S NO ONE ELSE, KITTEN-LIMP SISTER.	59	THE LONG ALLEY	23
BELIEVE ME, KNOT OF GRISTLE, I BLEED LIKE A TREE;	79	GIVE WAY, GATES	1
I BELIEVE! I BELIEVE!--	88	PRAISE TO END!	90
I BELIEVE! I BELIEVE!--	88	PRAISE TO END!	90
SWAYING, WOULD YOU BELIEVE, ...	98	O, THOU OPENING	48
I KNOW A DANCE THE ELEPHANTS BELIEVE.	106	SIR JOHN DAVIES	40
IT WAS "WOULD YOU BELIEVE IT--FAWTHER'S TALL!"	111	SQUEEZE-BOX	14
THOSE WHO EMBRACE, BELIEVE.	125	WORDS FOR WIND	69
GOD COULD BELIEVE: I AM HERE TO FEAR.	144	ELEGY (1)	12
WHAT YOU SURVIVED I SHALL BELIEVE: THE HEAT, ...	144	ELEGY (1)	13
WHO CAN BELIEVE THE MOON?	167	HER BECOMING	74
THE SOUL KNOWS NOT WHAT TO BELIEVE, ...	171	WHAT TELL BONES	3
I WOULD BELIEVE MY PAIN: AND THE EYE QUIET ON THE GROWING			
ROSE;	188	THE LONGING	43
WHAT CAN THE SPIRIT BELIEVE?--	207	THE YOUNG GIRL	1
"I BELIEVE, I BELIEVE, IN THE MOON!--	208	HER WORDS	10
"I BELIEVE, I BELIEVE, IN THE MOON!--	208	HER WORDS	10
AS WATER TEACHES STONE. BELIEVE ME, EXTREMEST ORIOLE, ...	260	THE CHANGELING	19
BELIEVED			
THE SECOND DAWN I WOULD NOT HAVE BELIEVED:	12	MID-CNTRY BLOW	5
THE WEEDS BELIEVED ME, AND THE NESTING BIRDS.	63	FIELD OF LIGHT	47
BELIEVING			
BELIEVING:	200	THE FAR FIELD	46
BELL			
THE OAK STOOD WITH EACH LEAF STIFF AS A BELL.	12	MID-CNTRY BLOW	6
LIGHT DEEPENED TO A BELL, ...	212	LIGHT LISTENED	8
BELLIES			
CHILDREN, THEIR BELLIES SWOLLEN LIKE BLOWN-UP PAPER BAGS,	48	JUDGE NOT	2
BELLS			
LIGHTER THAN BELLS, ...	88	PRAISE TO END!	95
BELLY			
I HEARD YOUR LAUGHTER RUMBLE FROM MY BELLY.	25	DIM-WIT COUSIN	12
A FISH FLOATS BELLY UPWARD, ...	59	THE LONG ALLEY	2
ON BELLY AND NOSE	65	SHAPE OF FIRE	51
THEY'LL JUMP ON HIS BELLY, ...	72	WHERE KNOCK IS	28
DEEP IN THE BELLY OF A THING TO BE.	97	O, THOU OPENING	15
HIS TAIL CURLED UNDER HIM, HIS BELLY BIG	227	MEADOW MOUSE	14
I'LL JUMP ON YOUR BELLY, I'LL KICK YOUR BUM	272	DUET	19
BELONG			
TO WHOM DOES THIS TERRACE BELONG?--	226	THE LIZARD	27
BELOVED			
WHEN WE BROOD ON THE DEAD OR THE BELOVED;	156	THE DYING MAN	97
A SCENT BELOVED OF BEES;	201	THE FAR FIELD	99
BELOW			
IN RIVULETS; THE COLD ROOTS STIR BELOW.	11	LIGHT BRIGHTER	12
AND A LAKE BELOW MY KNEES.	34	NIGHT JOURNEY	11
THE ROOM WAS THIRTY-FIVE BELOW;	114	DINKY	14
BELOW, ON THE FERNY GROUND, ...	125	WORDS FOR WIND	72
AN OLD BRIDGE BELOW WITH A BUCKLED IRON RAILING, BROKEN BY			
SOME IDIOT PLUNGER;	194	JOURNY INTERIOR	32
I SEE THE FLOWER OF ALL WATER, ABOVE AND BELOW ME, THE			
NEVER RECEDING, ...	194	JOURNY INTERIOR	52
AND BELOW, IN A MIST OUT OF NOWHERE, ...	202	THE ROSE	29
AND A BLACK BULL NUDGED AT A WALL IN THE VALLEY BELOW, ...	232	THE THING	22
BELOW, THE BRIGHT SEA WAS, THE LEVEL WAVES, ...	247	I WAITED	22
BELT			
PICKLE BELT	46	PICKLE BELT	T
BEMUSED			
BEMUSED; PLEASED TO BE;	162	I'M HERE	31

	PAGE	TITLE	LINE

BEMUSEDLY
"THE SPIDER'S GONE," HE SAID BEMUSEDLY. .... 274 SUPPR W LINDSAY 39

BENCH
QUICK ON THE WOODEN BENCH, 42 TRANSPLANTING 9

BENCHES
UNDER THE CONCRETE BENCHES, ... 39 WEED PULLER 1
LEAN FROM THE TIERS AND BENCHES, ... 61 THE LONG ALLEY 72
AND THE MEN BENEATH THEM WHEELING IN DIRT TO THE CEMENT
   BENCHES, ... 158 FIRST MEDITATN 45
AND MY FATHER STANDING ASTRIDE THE CEMENT BENCHES, ... 203 THE ROSE 53

BEND
BEND DOWN, SMALL BREATHERS, CREEPERS AND WINDERS; .... 61 THE LONG ALLEY 71
LOST OPPOSITES BEND DOWN-- .... 140 THE SWAN 18

BENDING
THE WHITE GRASS BENDING AWAY, ... 103 OLD LADY'S WRDS 20
BENDING THEM DOWN TO THE GROUND; .... 152 THE SISKINS 11
WHIPPING THE LINE OF WHITE LAUNDRY, BENDING THE COTTONWOODS
   APART, ... 194 JOURNY INTERIOR 44
HANGING, BUNCHED LIKE YOUNG FRUIT, BENDING THE END BRANCHES, 199 THE FAR FIELD 32
BENDING THE TREES HALF-WAY DOWN TO THE GROUND, ... 231 THE STORM 31

BENDS
AND THE HALF-SUNKEN BRANCH BENDS AWAY FROM THE GAZER'S EYE. 233 THE PIKE 9
THE WAVE BENDS WITH THE FISH. I'M TAUGHT .... 260 THE CHANGELING 18

BENEATH
DECREASED BENEATH AN UNDIVIDED SKY. .... 6 INTERLUDE 6
A FIELD OF BARLEY SPREAD BENEATH THE SUN. 13 PRAISE PRAIRIE 4
THE DANK BARK DRIES BENEATH THE SUN, ... 14 COMING OF COLD 32
I MOVE BENEATH AN EVIL SKY. .... 19 AGNST DISASTER 8
THEIR WIVES GO OUT ON SUNDAY BENEATH THE LATEST HAT. 27 CLAIRVOY WIDOW 8
ONE DRIVER, PINNED BENEATH THE SEAT, 33 HIGHWAY: MICH 19
BENEATH THE ROCK AND CLAY, ... 50 THE CYCLE 2
BENEATH THE ROOTS OF TREES, 50 THE CYCLE 3
BENEATH THE HAIR. .... 64 SHAPE OF FIRE 23
THE VALLEY ROCKED BENEATH THE GRANITE HILL; 106 SIR JOHN DAVIES 59
NO MATTER WHICH ONE IS BENEATH. .... 136 THE SENSUALISTS 15
THE FURY OF THE SLUG BENEATH THE STONE. .... 156 THE DYING MAN 93
AND THE MEN BENEATH THEM WHEELING IN DIRT TO THE CEMENT
   BENCHES, ... 158 FIRST MEDITATN 45
AND THE MIDCHANNEL BEGINS CRACKING AND HEAVING FROM THE
   PRESSURE BENEATH, 191 AT OYSTER RIVER 49
THE STREAM SLIPPING BENEATH THE MOSSY LOGS, ... 222 THE ABYSS 94
RIDING BENEATH THE MOON, HID FROM THE MOON, ... 225 OTTO 36
WHERE HE TREMBLED AND SHOOK BENEATH A STICK .... 227 MEADOW MOUSE 3

BENIGN
I AM BENIGN IN MY OWN COMPANY. .... 167 HER BECOMING 87

BENT
EVEN THE HUSHED FORMS, THE BENT YELLOW WEEDS 57 THE LOST SON 147
THE WEATHER WEPT, AND ALL THE TREES BENT DOWN; .... 143 SHIMMER OF EVIL 1
BENT DOWN THEIR BIRDS: THE LIGHT WAVES TOOK THE WAVES; ... 143 SHIMMER OF EVIL 2
ITS SHADOW BENT IN HALF; .... 150 SNAKE 7
WHEN I BENT TO UNTANGLE MYSELF, ... 162 I'M HERE 48
WHEN LINDSAY BENT HIS HEAD .... 273 SUPPR W LINDSAY 19

BENZEDRINE
THE MINIONS OF BENZEDRINE AND PARALDEHYDE, ... 169 FOURTH MEDITATN 37

BERRIES
AND WINTERGREEN BERRIES AND LEAVES STILL STUCK TO THE TOP,-- 40 MOSS-GATHERING 5

BERTH
AND FROM MY PULLMAN BERTH .... 34 NIGHT JOURNEY 3

BESET
WHEREIN I AM BESET BY HARM, ... 19 AGNST DISASTER 10

BESIDE
THE SIDEBOARD BESIDE WHICH A TALL FOOTMAN STOOD .... 32 SALE 15
THERE BESIDE HIM SHE STOOD,-- .... 46 PICKLE BELT 7
OF THOSE SO CLOSE BESIDE ME, WHICH ARE YOU? .... 108 THE WAKING (2) 7
AND SHE WAS RIGHT, FOR THERE BESIDE .... 136 THE SENSUALISTS 7
AS I WALKED BESIDE HER, THE O'CONNELL'S DAUGHTER, ... 216 THE SHY MAN 11
FOR HERE CLOSE BESIDE ME IS O'CONNELL'S DAUGHTER, ... 216 THE SHY MAN 20

BESIDES
"AND BESIDES, IT SEEMS THERE'S A LAW: .... 117 LADY AND BEAR 9

BEST
THE BEST HE COULD DO WAS JIGGLE HIS BLUBBER. .... 178 THE WHALE 4
THE MOTTLED TIGER, BEST IN THE CORNER OF A DAMP PLACE, ... 197 THE LONG WATERS 40

	PAGE	TITLE	LINE

BEST (CONTINUED)
AND PICKED AND PICKLED THE BEST, TO BE LEFT ON RICKETY			
DOORSTEPS.	223	ELEGY (2)	15
TO THE BEST OF MYSELF I SING,	261	THE CHANGELING	32

BESTOW
| I BLEED MY BONES, THEIR MARROW TO BESTOW | 246 | THE MARROW | 23 |

BET
| SHE WAS TOO MUCH FOR ONE, YOU CAN BET YOUR LIFE: | 114 | THE COW | 3 |

BETOOK
| SO I BETOOK MYSELF | 213 | THE HAPPY THREE | 13 |

BETRAY
| HAVE SCALED YOUR WALLS, AND SPIES BETRAY | 4 | FEUD | 15 |

BETRAYED
| THE VEINS WITHIN OUR HANDS BETRAYED OUR FEAR. | 6 | INTERLUDE | 11 |

BETRAYERS
| TERROR OF COPS, BILL COLLECTORS, BETRAYERS OF THE POOR,-- | 223 | ELEGY (2) | 18 |

BETRAYING
| THE MEDIOCRE BUSY AT BETRAYING | 5 | PROGNOSIS | 11 |

BETTER
YOU'D BETTER WATCH THE THINGS YOU DO.	114	DINKY	17
YOU'D BETTER WATCH THE THINGS YOU DO.	114	DINKY	18
YOU'D BETTER NOT LAUGH; AND DON'T SAY, "POOH!"	177	KITTY-CAT BIRD	18
YOUR DONKEY IS BETTER BEHAVED, I TRUST.	178	THE DONKEY	4
WHY I COULD DO BETTER	179	MYRTLE	10
BETTER TO HUG CLOSE, WARY OF RUBBLE AND FALLING STONES.	193	JOURNY INTERIOR	6

BETWEEN
THEY SLIP BETWEEN THE FINGERS OF MY SIGHT.	8	THE SIGNALS	7
TWO YELLOW AND BLACK, AND ONE THAT LOOKS IN BETWEEN,--	24	VERNAL SENTIMNT	6
WHAT'S ALL THE SINGING BETWEEN?--	77	BRING THE DAY!	26
WRINKLING BETWEEN REEDS IN SHALLOWER WATER,	93	I CRY, LOVE!	47
MY HAIR BETWEEN ME AND THE SUN,	104	OLD LADY'S WRDS	42
BETWEEN SUCH ANIMAL AND HUMAN HEAT	105	SIR JOHN DAVIES	25
THE LINKS WERE SOFT BETWEEN US; STILL, WE KISSED;	107	SIR JOHN DAVIES	81
I WATCHED HER THERE, BETWEEN ME AND THE MOON;	119	THE DREAM	11
BETWEEN THOSE LOVELY TITS.	136	THE SENSUALISTS	12
AND THE AIR CLAPS BETWEEN US,	158	FIRST MEDITATN	35
SPEECH PASSED BETWEEN SMALL BIRDS;	167	HER BECOMING	65
I WOULD BE A STREAM, WINDING BETWEEN GREAT STRIATED ROCKS			
IN LATE SUMMER;	188	THE LONGING	46
THE TIDE RUSTLING IN, SLIDING BETWEEN THE RIDGES OF STONE,	191	AT OYSTER RIVER	34
OR THE TITTEBAWASEE, IN THE TIME BETWEEN WINTER AND SPRING,	191	AT OYSTER RIVER	47
UNDERNEATH, THE SLUGGISH WATER RUNNING BETWEEN WEEDS,			
BROKEN WHEELS, TIRES, STONES.	194	JOURNY INTERIOR	33
AT FIRST A SWIFT RIPPLING BETWEEN ROCKS,	200	THE FAR FIELD	63
MY PAPERS UP, BETWEEN	213	THE HAPPY THREE	6
I ROCK BETWEEN DARK AND DARK,	221	THE ABYSS	78
BETWEEN THE SPIRIT AND THE FLESH,--WHAT WAR?	223	ELEGY (2)	5
WHISTLING BETWEEN THE ARBORS, THE WINDING TERRACES;	230	THE STORM	5
BETWEEN THE WHITENING TREES, UP SANTA LUCIA,	230	THE STORM	20
FLASHING BETWEEN GOLD LEVELS OF THE LATE SUN,	232	THE THING	5
SLOWLY WE MOVED BETWEEN	237	THE TRANCED	18
I LIVE BETWEEN THE HERON AND THE WREN,	239	IN A DARK TIME	5
THE WAY GREW STEEPER BETWEEN STONY WALLS,	247	I WAITED	19
BETWEEN CLIFFS OF LIGHT	265	HARSH COUNTRY	5

BEVY
| ITS BEVY OF BEES, AND ITS WIND-BEATEN RICKETY SUN-CHAIRS. | 226 | THE LIZARD | 29 |

BEWARE
| BEWARE MOTHER MILDEW. | 55 | THE LOST SON | 69 |
| BEWARE THOSE PERPETUAL BEGINNINGS, | 171 | WHAT TELL BONES | 23 |

BEWILDERS
| BEWILDERS HIMSELF: | 259 | SONG (3) | 46 |

BEWITCHED
| NOT DREARILY BEWITCHED, | 172 | WHAT TELL BONES | 57 |

BEYOND
PLATITUDES GARNISHED BEYOND A FOOL'S GAINSAYING;	5	PROGNOSIS	9
HE LIVED BEYOND THE TOUCH OF MORTAL LAWS.	28	THE FAVORITE	8
BEYOND THE MOUNTAIN PASS	34	NIGHT JOURNEY	20
IT'S A WINK BEYOND THE WORLD.	79	GIVE WAY, GATES	20
A BIRD SINGING INTO THE BEYOND,	103	OLD LADY'S WRDS	7
I'D SAY IT TO MY HORSE: WE LIVE BEYOND	106	SIR JOHN DAVIES	37
SHOOK WITH A MIGHTY POWER BEYOND HIS WILL,--	107	SIR JOHN DAVIES	75
AND I SWAYED OUT BEYOND THE WHITE SEAFOAM;	120	THE DREAM	29
ON A WIDE PLAIN, BEYOND	124	WORDS FOR WIND	35

	PAGE	TITLE	LINE
BEYOND (CONTINUED)			
I GET A STEP BEYOND	125	WORDS FOR WIND	65
BEYOND THE LOOK OF LOVE.	137	LOVE'S PROGRESS	15
HE LOOKED BEYOND ME WHEN	146	THE SONG	2
BEYOND THE RIDGE TWO WOOD THRUSH SING AS ONE.	150	IN LATE SUMMER	30
WHAT'S BEYOND NEVER CRUMBLES LIKE AN EMBANKMENT,	159	FIRST MEDITATN	76
A PULSE BEYOND NOTHINGNESS,	171	WHAT TELL BONES	6
I'D BE BEYOND; I'D BE BEYOND THE MOON,	188	THE LONGING	33
I'D BE BEYOND; I'D BE BEYOND THE MOON,	188	THE LONGING	33
WATCHING FOR DANGEROUS DOWN-HILL PLACES, WHERE THE WHEELS WHINED BEYOND EIGHTY--	193	JOURNY INTERIOR	19
BEYOND MY OWN ECHO,	195	JOURNY INTERIOR	71
THE STAR WINKING BEYOND ITSELF,	196	THE LONG WATERS	26
MY EYES EXTEND BEYOND THE FARTHEST BLOOM OF THE WAVES;	198	THE LONG WATERS	75
BEYOND THE CLOVER, THE RAGGED HAY,	203	THE ROSE	46
BEYOND THE SEA PINE, THE OAK, THE WIND-TIPPED MADRONA,	203	THE ROSE	47
BEYOND BECOMING AND PERISHING,	205	THE ROSE	102
IN THE BIRD BEYOND THE BOUGH, THE SINGLE ONE	205	THE ROSE	108
YET IF WE WAIT, UNAFRAID, BEYOND THE FEARFUL INSTANT,	221	THE ABYSS	57
HOW CAN I DREAM EXCEPT BEYOND THIS LIFE?	221	THE ABYSS	61
ABOVE THE BLUE AIR, IN THE SLIGHT HAZE BEYOND,	232	THE THING	3
MY EYE ALWAYS BEYOND THE SURFACE REFLECTION;	233	THE PIKE	12
FROM BEYOND THE END OF A MOSSY LOG,	233	THE PIKE	15
A SEED PUSHING ITSELF BEYOND ITSELF,	235	MANIFESTATION	3
THIS REACH BEYOND THIS DEATH, THIS ACT OF LOVE	243	THE MOTION	17
I MOVE BEYOND THE REACH OF WIND AND FIRE.	244	INFIRMITY	24
I'LL SING BEYOND THE WIND	260	THE CHANGELING	26
I'LL SPIT OVER MY CHIN AND BEYOND THE CURB,	272	DUET	7
--FAR BEYOND, O BEYOND! DEAR KIERKEGAARD.	272	DUET	21
--FAR BEYOND, O BEYOND! DEAR KIERKEGAARD.	272	DUET	21
BIBBLE			
SO BIBBLE WHERE THE PEBBLE IS.	75	I NEED, I NEED	32
BICKER			
OUTSIDE, THE SAME SPARROWS BICKER IN THE EAVES.	161	I'M HERE	6
BICKERED			
WHILE THE WRENS BICKERED AND SANG IN THE HALF-GREEN HEDGEROWS,	200	THE FAR FIELD	36
BID			
I BID STILLNESS BE STILL.	240	IN EVEING AIR	22
BIDDERS			
THE BARGAINS FELL TO BIDDERS, ONE BY ONE.	21	THE AUCTION	10
BIDDLY			
"I AM WHAT IS KNOWN AS A BIDDLY BEAR,--	117	LADY AND BEAR	5
BIDDLY'S			
WE BIDDLY'S ARE PEE-CULIAR BEARS.	117	LADY AND BEAR	7
BIDS			
HIS NOBLE NATURE BIDS HIM GIVE.	23	AMOROUS LADY	8
BIG			
WHO RAN UP AND DOWN THE BIG CENTER STAIRS	32	SALE	2
BIG WIND	41	BIG WIND	T
THE BIG ROSES, THE BIG BLOODY CLINKERS.	57	THE LOST SON	133
THE BIG ROSES, THE BIG BLOODY CLINKERS.	57	THE LOST SON	133
BE GOOD AS A GOOSE, BE BIG AS A DOG,	86	PRAISE TO END!	40
WHEN HE TRIED TO SPOUT, THAT GREAT BIG LUBBER,	178	THE WHALE	3
HIS TAIL CURLED UNDER HIM, HIS BELLY BIG	227	MEADOW MOUSE	14
I'LL KEEP MY BIG MOUTH SHUT.	270	GOB MUSIC	37
O WHEN YOU WERE LITTLE, YOU WERE REALLY BIG:	272	DUET	1
BIGGER			
IT'S BIGGER THAN THAT.	54	THE LOST SON	45
AND THEIR SHADOWS, BIGGER,	152	THE SISKINS	5
HIS NOSE LOOKED EVEN BIGGER THAN IT WAS,	273	SUPPR W LINDSAY	21
BIGGEST			
FROM THE TOWN'S BIGGEST CROOKS.	267	SAGINAW SONG	36
BIKE			
I TOOK THE PLEDGE CARDS ON MY BIKE;	267	SAGINAW SONG	31
BILL			
THEN POINTS HIS HEAVY BILL ABOVE THE WOOD.	15	THE HERON	10
YOU CAN, WITH PLEASURE, BILL OR COO.	23	AMOROUS LADY	12
TERROR OF COPS, BILL COLLECTORS, BETRAYERS OF THE POOR,--	223	ELEGY (2)	18
I'VE COME TO LOVE. A VIREO WHETS ITS BILL.	244	INFIRMITY	26
AND THEN SEND YOU THE BILL.	267	SAGINAW SONG	18
BILLBOARDS			
ALONE, IN A SLEEP-DAZE, I STARED AT BILLBOARDS;	89	UNFOLD! UNFOLD!	24

	PAGE	TITLE	LINE
BILLOWING			
THE WIND BILLOWING OUT THE SEAT OF MY BRITCHES,	43	CHILD ON GRNHSE	1
THEIR SKIRTS BILLOWING OUT WIDE INTO TENTS,	44	FRAU BAUMAN	17
FAR DOWN A BILLOWING PLAIN,	240	IN EVEING AIR	15
BILLOWS			
AS THE LIVE HEAT BILLOWS FROM PIPES AND POTS.	38	FORCING HOUSE	11
AND A CHILD'S DIRTY SHIFT BILLOWS UPWARD OUT OF AN ALLEY,	230	THE STORM	18
BILLS			
O FORTUNATE HE WHOSE MAMMA PAYS THE BILLS!	24	POETASTER	4
BIN			
(I FOUND IT LYING AMONG THE RUBBLE OF AN OLD COAL BIN)	199	THE FAR FIELD	20
BINDINGS			
THE SILVER FISH RAN IN AND OUT OF MY SPECIAL BINDINGS;	65	SHAPE OF FIRE	35
BIRCHTREES			
THE UPLAND OF ALDER AND BIRCHTREES,	193	JOURNY INTERIOR	13
BIRD			
NO BIRD	17	NO BIRD	T
NO BIRD AWAKENS HER.	17	NO BIRD	8
FLEW A TREMENDOUS BIRD	49	NIGHT CROW	5
BIRD, SOFT-SIGH ME HOME,	53	THE LOST SON	9
HAS THE BIRD LEFT?	56	THE LOST SON	114
IS HE A BIRD OR A TREE? NOT EVERYONE CAN TELL.	64	SHAPE OF FIRE	3
O SMALL BIRD WAKENING,	78	BRING THE DAY!	38
A BIRD SINGS IN THE BUSH OF YOUR BONES.	79	GIVE WAY, GATES	5
MAKE ME A BIRD OR A BEAR!	80	GIVE WAY, GATES	39
SUCH OWLY PLEASURES! FISH COME FIRST, SWEET BIRD.	87	PRAISE TO END!	71
ON THE JACKPINE PLAINS I HUNTED THE BIRD NOBODY KNOWS;	89	UNFOLD! UNFOLD!	22
A BIRD SINGING INTO THE BEYOND,	103	OLD LADY'S WRDS	7
SEA-BEAST OR BIRD FLUNG TOWARD THE RAVAGED SHORE?	107	SIR JOHN DAVIES	68
THERE, UPSIDE DOWN (UNLIKE A BIRD),	116	THE SLOTH	5
A BIRD SANG LOW; THE MOONLIGHT SIFTED IN;	119	THE DREAM	7
A BIRD SANG FROM THE CENTER OF A TREE;	119	THE DREAM	15
A SMALL BIRD FLEW IN CIRCLES WHERE WE STOOD;	120	THE DREAM	19
ONE FEATHER IS A BIRD,	128	THE VOICE	1
THOSE NOTES WENT, LIKE THE BIRD,	128	THE VOICE	8
THE SHY CERULEAN BIRD;	128	THE VOICE	14
BIRD, GIRL, AND GHOSTLY TREE,	128	THE VOICE	20
IF SHE BUT SIGHS, A BIRD PUTS OUT ITS TONGUE.	129	SHE	3
TRUE, SHE CAN THINK A BIRD	137	LOVE'S PROGRESS	11
YET WHISTLE BACK AT EVERY WHISTLING BIRD.	140	THE SWAN	11
HE QUIVERED LIKE A BIRD IN BIRDLESS AIR,	155	THE DYING MAN	64
I THINK A BIRD, AND IT BEGINS TO FLY.	155	THE DYING MAN	70
WHO STOPS BEING A BIRD, YET BEATS HIS WINGS	156	THE DYING MAN	100
A SINGLE BIRD CALLING AND CALLING;	160	FIRST MEDITATN	90
A BIRD, SMALL AS A LEAF,	163	I'M HERE	60
A BIRD ALWAYS KEPT SINGING.	163	I'M HERE	73
HOW SWEETLY I ABIDE. AM I A BIRD?	165	HER BECOMING	16
A CHILD AT PLAY, A WIND-EXCITED BIRD,	165	HER BECOMING	23
BY SWOOPS OF BIRD, BY LEAPS OF FISH, I LIVE.	167	HER BECOMING	91
A BIRD SINGS OUT IN SOLITARINESS	171	WHAT TELL BONES	18
THE KITTY-CAT BIRD	177	KITTY-CAT BIRD	T
THE KITTY-CAT BIRD, HE SAT ON A FENCE.	177	KITTY-CAT BIRD	1
--SAID THE WREN TO THE KITTY-CAT BIRD.	177	KITTY-CAT BIRD	4
I WISH YOU WOULD ACT LIKE A BIRD, REALLY SHOULD,	177	KITTY-CAT BIRD	6
--SAID THE WREN TO THE KITTY-CAT BIRD.	177	KITTY-CAT BIRD	8
--SAID THE WREN TO THE KITTY-CAT BIRD.	177	KITTY-CAT BIRD	12
THE KITTY-CAT BIRD, HE MOPED AND HE CRIED.	177	KITTY-CAT BIRD	13
THAT THE KITTY-CAT BIRD JUST HOPPED INSIDE;	177	KITTY-CAT BIRD	15
--DID THE KITTY--THE KITTY-CAT BIRD.	177	KITTY-CAT BIRD	17
--OR YOU'LL END LIKE THE KITTY-CAT BIRD.	177	KITTY-CAT BIRD	21
NOT A BEAST, NOT A BIRD,--	182	BOY AND BUSH	9
FROM A CRAZY OLD JACK-DAW BIRD	183	THE WAGTAIL	7
I WOULD DELIGHT IN MY HANDS, THE BRANCH SINGING, ALTERING THE EXCESSIVE BIRD;	188	THE LONGING	44
WELTER OF TIN CANS, PAILS, OLD BIRD NESTS, A CHILD'S SHOE RIDING A LOG,	191	AT OYSTER RIVER	54
AND I WATCHED AND WATCHED TILL MY EYES BLURRED FROM THE BIRD SHAPES,--	199	THE FAR FIELD	29
AS A SNAKE OR A RAUCOUS BIRD,	200	THE FAR FIELD	48
THE THRUSH SINGING ALONE, THAT EASY BIRD,	204	THE ROSE	61
A SOUND SO THIN IT COULD NOT WOO A BIRD,	204	THE ROSE	77
IN THE BIRD BEYOND THE BOUGH, THE SINGLE ONE	205	THE ROSE	108
A BIRD MY BODY,	207	THE YOUNG GIRL	11

	PAGE	TITLE	LINE
BIRD (CONTINUED)			
THE LOVE-BEAT OF A BIRD.	212	LIGHT LISTENED	9
I'M NO LONGER A BIRD DIPPING A BEAK INTO RIPPLING WATER	220	THE ABYSS	41
I HAVE MERGED, LIKE THE BIRD, WITH THE BRIGHT AIR,	222	THE ABYSS	99
THEN THE FIRST BIRD	232	THE THING	13
GREEN, A BIRD TIPPING THE TOPMOST BOUGH,	235	MANIFESTATION	2
I HEARD A BIRD STIR IN ITS TRUE CONFINE;	241	THE SEQUEL	11
MY EARS STILL HEAR THE BIRD WHEN ALL IS STILL;	244	INFIRMITY	28
A BIRD KEPT HAUNTING ME WHEN I WAS YOUNG--	245	THE DECISION	3
THE TREE, THE BIRD	248	THE TREE, BIRD	T
THE WILLOW WITH ITS BIRD GREW LOUD, GREW LOUDER STILL.	248	THE TREE, BIRD	13
THE BIRD, THE BEATING BIRD, EXTENDING WINGS--	248	THE TREE, BIRD	21
THE BIRD, THE BEATING BIRD, EXTENDING WINGS--	248	THE TREE, BIRD	21
THE BIRD FLIES OUT, THE BIRD FLIES BACK AGAIN;	250	THE RIGHT THING	4
THE BIRD FLIES OUT, THE BIRD FLIES BACK AGAIN;	250	THE RIGHT THING	4
WITH THE BIRD, THE ABIDING LEAF,	251	ONCE MORE, RND	6
THE BIRD IN THE SMALL BUSH	259	SONG (3)	45
DIVERGENT BIRD,	261	THE CHANGELING	52
BIRD, BIRD DON'T EDGE ME IN;	271	THE REPLY	1
BIRD, BIRD DON'T EDGE ME IN;	271	THE REPLY	1
AND, LIKE YOU, BIRD, I SING,	271	THE REPLY	16
BIRD-BLOOD			
MY BIRD-BLOOD READY.	207	THE YOUNG GIRL	12
BIRD-FURTIVE			
NERVOUS AND COLD, BIRD-FURTIVE, WHISKERY,	157	FIRST MEDITATN	16
BIRDLESS			
HE QUIVERED LIKE A BIRD IN BIRDLESS AIR,	155	THE DYING MAN	64
BIRDS			
LOST HUES OF BIRDS THE TREES TAKE AS THEIR OWN.	12	SLOW SEASON	9
QUICKER THAN BIRDS, THEY DIPPED	44	FRAU BAUMAN	13
IS THE SEED LEAVING THE OLD BED? THESE BUDS ARE LIVE AS BIRDS.	56	THE LOST SON	102
ARE THE FLOWERS HERE? THE BIRDS ARE.	61	THE LONG ALLEY	64
THE GREAT ELM FILLED WITH BIRDS.	63	FIELD OF LIGHT	36
THE WEEDS BELIEVED ME, AND THE NESTING BIRDS.	63	FIELD OF LIGHT	47
SHALE LOOSENS. MARL REACHES INTO THE FIELD. SMALL BIRDS PASS OVER WATER.	64	SHAPE OF FIRE	11
WATER BIRDS WENT CHING. WENT CHING.	73	WHERE KNOCK IS	54
WENT TO VISIT THE WIND. WHERE THE BIRDS DIE.	73	WHERE KNOCK IS	72
HOW IS IT WITH THE LONG BIRDS?	79	GIVE WAY, GATES	18
WHEREFORE, O BIRDS AND SMALL FISH, SURROUND ME.	88	PRAISE TO END!	97
SOMEWHERE, AMONG THE FERNS AND BIRDS,	103	OLD LADY'S WRDS	12
WITH ITS DEEP SHADE, AND BIRDS.	103	OLD LADY'S WRDS	28
THE BIRDS, THEY WERE, THEY WERE ASTOUNDED;	115	THE SERPENT	11
HE SAID, "LOOK, BIRDS, ALL THIS IS FUTILE:	115	THE SERPENT	19
AS THE BIRDS FLEW OFF TO THE END OF NEXT WEEK.	115	THE SERPENT	26
I CRIED, AND THE BIRDS CAME DOWN	123	WORDS FOR WIND	15
THE BIRDS AND FISHES MOVE	125	WORDS FOR WIND	62
WHEN SMALL BIRDS SIGHED, SHE WOULD SIGH BACK AT THEM;	127	I KNEW A WOMAN	2
AND ALL THE BIRDS ARE STONE.	138	LOVE'S PROGRESS	22
BENT DOWN THEIR BIRDS: THE LIGHT WAVES TOOK THE WAVES;	143	SHIMMER OF EVIL	2
THE SMALL BIRDS SWIRL AROUND;	148	THE SMALL	1
BIRDS FURIOUS AS BEES.	152	THE SISKINS	18
O SWEET FIELD FAR AHEAD, I HEAR YOUR BIRDS,	156	THE DYING MAN	88
BIRDS ARE AROUND. I'VE ALL THE SINGING I WOULD.	164	I'M HERE	93
WATCHING THE WIND RIFFLE THE BACKS OF SMALL BIRDS,	165	HER BECOMING	2
SPEECH PASSED BETWEEN SMALL BIRDS;	167	HER BECOMING	65
YOU BIRDS, YOU WESTERN BIRDS.	167	HER BECOMING	79
YOU BIRDS, YOU WESTERN BIRDS.	167	HER BECOMING	79
YET MOVES GENTLY AMONG THE BIRDS.	170	FOURTH MEDITATN	74
I HEAR A BEAT OF BIRDS, THE PLANGENT WINGS	173	WHAT TELL BONES	69
BUT WHEN I BREATHE WITH THE BIRDS,	195	JOURNY INTERIOR	77
I SUFFERED FOR BIRDS, FOR YOUNG RABBITS CAUGHT IN THE MOWER,	199	THE FAR FIELD	24
THE MORNING BIRDS GONE, THE TWITTERING FINCHES,	202	THE ROSE	14
WAS IT HERE I WORE A CROWN OF BIRDS FOR A MOMENT	202	THE ROSE	26
WHEN EVERYTHING--BIRDS, MEN, DOGS--	210	HER TIME	23
A DELIRIUM OF BIRDS!	235	ALL MORNING	33
AND THOSE BIRDS FOREVER DEAD,	235	ALL MORNING	43
ALL BIRDS REMEMBERED, O NEVER FORGOTTEN!	235	ALL MORNING	45
A NIGHT FLOWING WITH BIRDS, A RAGGED MOON,	239	IN A DARK TIME	14
HEARING A CRASS BABBLE OF BIRDS.	258	SONG (3)	9
YOU BIRDS,	260	THE CHANGELING	23
BIRDS TO THIS WATERY AIR?	261	THE CHANGELING	47

	PAGE	TITLE	LINE
BIRD'S			
LIMP AND DAMP, DELICATE AS A YOUNG BIRD'S TONGUE;	39	ORCHIDS	5
BIRTH			
THE SEA'S UNEQUAL LENGTHS ANNOUNCED THY BIRTH	81	SENSIBILITY! LA	8
BISCUIT			
I'M A BISCUIT. I'M MELTED ALREADY.	77	BRING THE DAY!	21
BISHOP			
WHO'S BISHOP OF BREATHING?	83	O LULL ME, LULL	3
BIT			
"ONE COAT OF PRIDE, PERHAPS A BIT THREADBARE;	21	THE AUCTION	5
A BIT OF WATER CAUGHT IN A WRINKLED CREVICE, ...	168	FOURTH MEDITATN	8
ONE GREENISH LID LIFTS A BIT HIGHER, ...	226	THE LIZARD	23
A BIT OF THE LIKES OF IT.	270	GOB MUSIC	35
BITE			
BITE WITH HIS FEET;	71	WHERE KNOCK IS	2
AND THEY BITE.	73	WHERE KNOCK IS	63
I'LL BE A BITE. YOU BE A WINK.	73	WHERE KNOCK IS	74
DO THE DEAD BITE?	74	I NEED, I NEED	18
A MISTRESS OF ZEN, I'LL BITE YOUR THUMB, ...	272	DUET	18
BITING			
BITING THEMSELVES PERHAPS;	79	GIVE WAY, GATES	29
THE LIKES OF HIM IS BITING WHO, ...	86	PRAISE TO END!	32
BITTEN			
"MY SHOULDER'S BITTEN FROM YOUR TEETH;	136	THE SENSUALISTS	13
BITTER			
AND PUMPKINS SWEAT A BITTER OIL.	14	COMING OF COLD	17
WINDS BRING A FINE AND BITTER SNOW.	15	COMING OF COLD	52
THE BITTER ROCK, THE BARREN SOIL	18	LONG LIVE WEEDS	3
THOUGH IT ALL HAPPENED BEFORE, I CANNOT GROW BITTER:	24	VERNAL SENTIMNT	7
BLAB			
IN THE KINGDOM OF BANG AND BLAB.	54	THE LOST SON	33
BLACK			
I MISS THE POLISHED BRASS, THE POWERFUL BLACK HORSES, ...	22	ROAD TO WDLAWN	1
TWO YELLOW AND BLACK, AND ONE THAT LOOKS IN BETWEEN,-- ...	24	VERNAL SENTIMNT	6
THAT BLOSSOMED IN SOOT; A BLACK CAT LICKING ITS PAW;	29	THE REMINDER	2
THE WORLD RECEDES IN THE BLACK REVOLVING SHADOW;	33	IDYLL	9
HACKING AT BLACK HAIRY ROOTS,--	39	WEED PULLER	2
INTO A MOONLESS BLACK, ...	49	NIGHT CROW	7
AN OLD SCOW BUMPS OVER BLACK ROCKS.	64	SHAPE OF FIRE	5
WE DANCED TO SHINING; MOCKED BEFORE THE BLACK	107	SIR JOHN DAVIES	89
THEIR BLACK SHAPES BREAKING PAST;	158	FIRST MEDITATN	34
THEIR BLACK SKINS SHUDDERING:	159	FIRST MEDITATN	57
MY DESIRE FOR THE PEAKS, THE BLACK RAVINES, THE ROLLING MISTS	196	THE LONG WATERS	9
WHERE THE SLOW CREEK WINDS DOWN TO THE BLACK SAND OF THE SHORE	203	THE ROSE	49
I DIVE WITH THE BLACK HAG, THE CORMORANT, ...	209	HER LONGING	13
OR BEATING AGAINST THE BLACK CLOUDS OF THE STORM, ...	209	HER LONGING	22
HER TONGUE, AT THE LAST, THICK, BLACK AS AN OX'S.	223	ELEGY (2)	17
THEN A CRACK OF THUNDER, AND THE BLACK RAIN RUNS OVER US, OVER	230	THE STORM	23
AND A BLACK BULL NUDGED AT A WALL IN THE VALLEY BELOW, ...	232	THE THING	22
WHICH IS THE WAY? I CRY TO THE DREAD BLACK, ...	245	THE DECISION	9
BLACKBERRY			
HIDING DEEP IN THE BLACKBERRY BUSHES--	234	ALL MORNING	20
BLACKBURNIAN			
CAPE MAY, BLACKBURNIAN, CERULEAN,--	199	THE FAR FIELD	30
BLACKENED			
OF FLESH, BURN BACKWARD TO A BLACKENED HEAP.	17	UNEXTINGUISHED	8
UNDER THE BLACKENED LEAVES, ...	62	FIELD OF LIGHT	23
WHERE THE YELLOWISH PRONGS OF GRASS POKE THROUGH THE BLACKENED ASH, ...	196	THE LONG WATERS	15
BLACKENING			
I WOULD WITH THE FISH, THE BLACKENING SALMON, AND THE MAD LEMMINGS, ...	188	THE LONGING	39
BLACKNESS			
HAS DEEPENED TO THE BLACKNESS OF A POOL, ...	15	THE HERON	2
BLAKE			
WOULD BLAKE CALL YOU HOLY?	151	SLUG	29
WITH THE LIKES OF BLAKE, ...	228	IN VIOLENT WARD	5
AND I DANCE WITH WILLIAM BLAKE	251	ONCE MORE, RND	9
--"THAT MEANS BLAKE, TOO?"	273	SUPPR W LINDSAY	18
AND ONE EYE GAZED ASKEW. "WHY, BLAKE, HE'S DEAD,--	273	SUPPR W LINDSAY	22

	PAGE	TITLE	LINE
BLAKE (CONTINUED)			
"THAT'S NEVER BLAKE," SAID LINDSAY. "HE'D BE A WORM,	273	SUPPR W LINDSAY	26
WE NEED A BREED THAT MIXES BLAKE AND ME,	274	SUPPR W LINDSAY	41
BLAND			
GRACIOUS AND BLAND,	103	OLD LADY'S WRDS	10
BLANKETS			
THE SHEETS AND BLANKETS TURNED TO SNOW.	114	DINKY	15
RUBBING MY NOSE IN THE WOOL OF BLANKETS;	162	I'M HERE	30
BLAST			
WE SHIVER AT THE SIREN'S BLAST.	33	HIGHWAY: MICH	18
AND I LONG FOR THE BLAST OF DYNAMITE,	191	AT OYSTER RIVER	52
BLASTED			
BLASTED TO DEATH BY THE NIGHT WATCHMAN.	199	THE FAR FIELD	23
BLASTING			
BLASTING THE FROSTED WINDOWS,	158	FIRST MEDITATN	36
BLASTS			
FLAPPING AWAY HEAVILY WHEN A CAR BLASTS TOO CLOSE,	234	ALL MORNING	7
BLAZE			
OF WESTERN LIGHT LEAPS WITH INTENSER BLAZE	17	UNEXTINGUISHED	2
A BLAZE OF BEING ON A CENTRAL STEM.	149	IN LATE SUMMER	18
DARE I BLAZE LIKE A TREE?	171	WHAT TELL BONES	9
AND YOUR HAIR EVER BLAZE,	217	WISH YOUNG WIFE	8
BLAZES			
THOUGH SUMMER BLAZES IN THE VIREO'S EYE.	240	IN EVEING AIR	2
BLAZING			
FROM DARK TO BLAZING BRIGHT;	34	NIGHT JOURNEY	17
ALL NATURAL SHAPES BLAZING UNNATURAL LIGHT.	239	IN A DARK TIME	18
BLEACHED			
WITH BLEACHED VEINS	43	FLOWER DUMP	7
AND THE MOLD SANG IN THE BLEACHED VALLEYS UNDER THE ROSE.	102	ELEGY FOR JANE	9
BLEAK			
BLEAK CLOUDS ACROSS THE HEAVY SKY,	15	COMING OF COLD	50
THEN A BLEAK WASTED PLACE,	34	NIGHT JOURNEY	10
IN A COUNTRY OF BLEAK STONE,	146	THE SONG	9
THE BLEAK WIND EATS AT THE WEAK PLATEAU,	157	FIRST MEDITATN	11
THE BULKS CANNOT HIDE US, OR THE BLEAK SHEDS OF OUR DESOLATION,	166	HER BECOMING	39
IN A BLEAK TIME, WHEN A WEEK OF RAIN IS A YEAR,	187	THE LONGING	14
AND I LIE HERE THINKING IN BLEAK BOFIN TOWN	216	THE SHY MAN	18
THE WIDE, THE BLEAK ABYSS	238	THE MOMENT	4
KIN TO THE WIND, AND THE BLEAK WHISTLING RAIN.	248	THE TREE, BIRD	12
BLEED			
BELIEVE ME, KNOT OF GRISTLE, I BLEED LIKE A TREE;	79	GIVE WAY, GATES	1
I BARE A WOUND, AND DARE MYSELF TO BLEED.	155	THE DYING MAN	69
I BLEED MY BONES, THEIR MARROW TO BESTOW	246	THE MARROW	23
BLEEDS			
THIS SLAG RUNS SLOW. WHAT BLEEDS WHEN METAL BREAKS?	59	THE LONG ALLEY	11
BLENCH			
BUT AT LEAST WE KNOW ONE NEEDN'T BLENCH	272	DUET	16
BLESS			
BLESS ME AND THE MAZE I'M IN!	92	I CRY, LOVE!	20
GOD BLESS THE GROUND! I SHALL WALK SOFTLY THERE,	108	THE WAKING (2)	8
GOD BLESS THE ROOTS!--BODY AND SOUL ARE ONE!	250	THE RIGHT THING	7
BLESSED			
BLESSED BE TORPOR.	83	O LULL ME, LULL	5
BLESSED BY THE LIPS OF A LOW WIND,	197	THE LONG WATERS	45
BLESSED THE MEEK; THEY SHALL INHERIT WRATH;	244	INFIRMITY	17
BLESSEDNESS			
SO SINGULAR A BLESSEDNESS.	8	PRAYER	18
OF INWARD BLESSEDNESS?	139	PLAINT	5
BLESSING			
DENIES THE BLESSING OF THE SUN,	4	FEUD	10
THE SPIRIT OF WRATH BECOMES THE SPIRIT OF BLESSING,	195	JOURNY INTERIOR	78
BLESSINGS			
I ASKED: MAY THE BLESSINGS OF LIFE, O LORD, DESCEND ON THE LIVING.	48	JUDGE NOT	6
BLIND			
AS A BLIND MAN, LIFTING A CURTAIN, KNOWS IT IS MORNING,	195	JOURNY INTERIOR	74
AND THERE ON THE BLIND	220	THE ABYSS	34
BLINDING			
AFTER THE BLINDING MISERY,	221	THE ABYSS	52
BLISTERED			
YOU'RE BLISTERED ALL OVER	89	UNFOLD! UNFOLD!	14

	PAGE	TITLE	LINE
BLIZZARD			
IS BEFORE, OR RIGHT AFTER, A BLIZZARD.	183	THE LIZARD	2
BLOCKED			
THE WAY BLOCKED AT LAST BY A FALLEN FIR-TREE,	193	JOURNY INTERIOR	15
BLOND			
FOR A BLOND HILL BECKONED	265	HARSH COUNTRY	9
BLOOD			
EXHAUSTED FATHERS THINNED THE BLOOD,	4	FEUD	5
FROM ENEMIES THAT WHISPER TO THE BLOOD;	5	PROGNOSIS	6
BREATH, TURN THE OLD BLOOD OVER.	7	ORDERS FOR DAY	21
SOMETIMES THE BLOOD IS PRIVILEGED TO GUESS	8	THE SIGNALS	9
THE BLOOD SLOWS TRANCE-LIKE IN THE ALTERED VEIN;	12	SLOW SEASON	15
INVADES QUIESCENT BLOOD,	18	GENESIS	6
IN ACCENTS MEASURED BY THE BLOOD.	22	SILENCE	3
THE DINING ROOM CARPET DYED BRIGHTER THAN BLOOD,	32	SALE	13
--AND THE TAINT IN A BLOOD THAT WAS RUNNING TOO THIN.	32	SALE	20
THE WHILE MY BLOOD LEAPED WITH A WORDLESS SONG.	105	SIR JOHN DAVIES	14
A BEAST WITH FANGS, AND OUT FOR HIS OWN BLOOD	133	THE PURE FURY	18
IS THERE NO WAY OUT OF THAT COURSING BLOOD?	140	THE SWAN	4
I FELT MY SLOW BLOOD WARM.	150	SNAKE	9
MY ENEMIES RENEW ME, AND MY BLOOD	155	THE DYING MAN	67
AND ALL WILD LONGINGS OF THE INSATIATE BLOOD	241	THE SEQUEL	4
THIS WATER, HEATED LIKE MY BLOOD,	256	IN HYDROTHERAPY	5
BLOOD'S			
THE SAVAGE BLOOD'S OBSCENITY,	19	EPIDERM MACABRE	11
BLOODSUCKER			
THE TURTLES HAVE BLOODSUCKER SORES,	267	SAGINAW SONG	9
BLOODSUCKERS			
THE WEEDY EDGE, ALIVE WITH SMALL SNAKES AND BLOODSUCKERS,--	200	THE FAR FIELD	70
BLOODY			
THE BIG ROSES, THE BIG BLOODY CLINKERS.	57	THE LOST SON	133
BLOOM			
THAT LATE AUTUMNAL BLOOM, IS DEAD.	15	COMING OF COLD	41
WHOLE BEDS OF BLOOM PITCHED ON A PILE,	43	FLOWER DUMP	3
THE DRY BLOOM SPLITTING IN THE WRINKLED VALE,	197	THE LONG WATERS	30
MY EYES EXTEND BEYOND THE FARTHEST BLOOM OF THE WAVES;	198	THE LONG WATERS	75
WHEN FLOWERS GREW, THEIR BLOOM EXTENDED HIM.	224	OTTO	11
BLOOMING			
WITH EVERYTHING BLOOMING ABOVE ME,	39	WEED PULLER	11
BLOSSOM			
STIRS AS A BLOSSOM STIRS,	101	LIGHT BREATHER	3
I MET HER AS A BLOSSOM ON A STEM	119	THE DREAM	1
THE BLOSSOM STINGS THE BEE.	121	ALL EARTH, AIR	18
BLOSSOMED			
THAT BLOSSOMED IN SOOT; A BLACK CAT LICKING ITS PAW;	29	THE REMINDER	2
BLOSSOMS			
THE BLOSSOMS EXTENDING	42	TRANSPLANTING	19
PALE BLOSSOMS, EACH BALANCED ON A SINGLE JOINTED STEM,	43	CARNATIONS	1
THE BLOSSOMS SANG.	51	THE WAKING (1)	8
HANDS AND HAIR MOVED THROUGH A DREAM OF WAKENING BLOSSOMS.	66	SHAPE OF FIRE	74
LIGHT AS A HAND AMONG BLOSSOMS,	78	BRING THE DAY!	39
DRIFTING WITH THE BLOSSOMS,	168	FOURTH MEDITATN	16
ROCKING THE BLOSSOMS;	258	SONG (3)	15
BLOUSE			
OF A MAN-TAILORED BLOUSE; THE LIST OF SHOPPING DONE;	29	THE REMINDER	6
BLOW			
MID-COUNTRY BLOW	12	MID-CNTRY BLOW	T
THE RICHES OF THE AIR BLOW THIN.	14	COMING OF COLD	21
WINDS GATHER IN THE NORTH AND BLOW	15	COMING OF COLD	49
THE WINDS OF HATRED BLOW	31	LULL	1
FROM THE BLOW OF THE WIND,	229	ON THE QUAY	3
IT WOULD BLOW THE PLACE APART,--	268	SAGINAW SONG	40
BLOWING			
AND THEIR SNUFF-LADEN BREATH BLOWING LIGHTLY OVER ME IN MY FIRST SLEEP.	44	FRAU BAUMAN	35
LIGHT AS SEED BLOWING OFF THISTLES!	152	THE SISKINS	21
A GUST BLOWING THE LEAVES SUDDENLY UPWARD,	171	WHAT TELL BONES	29
BLOWN-UP			
CHILDREN, THEIR BELLIES SWOLLEN LIKE BLOWN-UP PAPER BAGS,	48	JUDGE NOT	2
BLOWS			
A FAR-OFF TRAIN BLOWS ITS ECHOING WHISTLE ONCE;	33	IDYLL	10
THE WIND BLOWS UP YOUR FEET,	267	SAGINAW SONG	2

	PAGE	TITLE	LINE
BLUBBER			
OF FATE, YOU BLUBBER IN SURPRISE.	4	FEUD	4
THE BEST HE COULD DO WAS JIGGLE HIS BLUBBER.	178	THE WHALE	4
BLUE			
THE BLUE SPRUCE LASHED LIKE A SURF AT THE DOOR.	12	MID-CNTRY BLOW	4
OR STAND ALL NIGHT WATERING ROSES, HIS FEET BLUE IN RUBBER BOOTS.	42	OLD FLORIST	10
ABOVE THE BLUE SNOW.	58	THE LOST SON	153
MOTHER OF BLUE AND THE MANY CHANGES OF HAY,	79	GIVE WAY, GATES	14
MY BLUE ORIGINAL DANDY, NUMB WITH SUGAR?	86	PRAISE TO END!	18
AND THE SUN COMES OUT OF A BLUE CLOUD OVER THE TETONS,	194	JOURNY INTERIOR	40
MINNOWS CAN HEAR, AND BUTTERFLIES, YELLOW AND BLUE,	196	THE LONG WATERS	3
THE BLUE JAY RASPING FROM THE STUNTED PINE.	196	THE LONG WATERS	28
OR WHEN TWO RIVERS COMBINE, THE BLUE GLACIAL TORRENT	200	THE FAR FIELD	61
THAT GENTLES ON A SUNNY BLUE PLATEAU.	201	THE FAR FIELD	92
LIKE THE BLUE SHINE ON FRESHLY FROZEN SNOW,	201	THE FAR FIELD	96
ABOVE THE BLUE AIR, IN THE SLIGHT HAZE BEYOND,	232	THE THING	3
AND THE BLUE AIR DARKENED.	232	THE THING	23
BLUEBIRD			
THE BLUEBIRD, LOVER OF HOLES IN OLD WOOD, LILTING ITS LIGHT SONG,	204	THE ROSE	66
BLUE-BLACK			
BLUE-BLACK FROM WHERE I AM SITTING,	190	AT OYSTER RIVER	12
BLUE-TAILED			
THEY FLICKER FASTER THAN A BLUE-TAILED SWIFT,	8	THE SIGNALS	5
BLUNDERING			
BOTH MOTH AND FLAME? THE WEAK MOTH BLUNDERING BY.	241	THE SEQUEL	6
BLURRED			
AND NO LIGHTS BEHIND, IN THE BLURRED SIDE-MIRROR,	199	THE FAR FIELD	7
AND I WATCHED AND WATCHED TILL MY EYES BLURRED FROM THE BIRD SHAPES,--	199	THE FAR FIELD	29
BLURS			
NOW, AS THE CASEMENT BLURS.	154	THE DYING MAN	30
BOARD			
NEXT DOOR THERE IS A LOVE-NEST OF PLASTER BOARD AND TIN,	27	CLAIRVOY WIDOW	15
I STRETCHED LIKE A BOARD, ALMOST A TREE.	90	UNFOLD! UNFOLD!	32
BOARDS			
THE BEARDED BOARDS IN THE STREAM AND THE ALL OF APPLES;	66	SHAPE OF FIRE	71
I DREAM OF NOTHING BUT BOARDS;	79	GIVE WAY, GATES	2
BOAST			
THEY DIDN'T BOAST; THEY DIDN'T SNIVEL,	111	SQUEEZE-BOX	3
BOAT			
HELD UP, WHILE THE ROWER BREATHES, AND THE SMALL BOAT DRIFTS QUIETLY SHOREWARD;	67	SHAPE OF FIRE	91
DON'T HIT HIM ON THE BOAT, I SAID.	73	WHERE KNOCK IS	59
IN A BOAT OF BEAUTIFUL THINGS.	103	OLD LADY'S WRDS	24
THEN DOWN, AS WE ROLL LIKE A BOAT FROM A WAVE-CREST.	158	FIRST MEDITATN	25
INACCESSIBLE, THE BOAT ALWAYS PULLING OUT	158	FIRST MEDITATN	50
THE STERN HIGH, DIPPING LIKE A CHILD'S BOAT IN A POND--	203	THE ROSE	37
BOBBIE			
SO LONG ON GIN, BOBBIE PINS, HALF-SMOKED CIGARS, DEAD BEER,	228	THE GERANIUM	10
BOBOLINK			
THE BOBOLINK SKIRRING FROM A BROKEN FENCEPOST,	204	THE ROSE	65
BOBOLINKS			
WITH BALTIMORE ORIOLES, MICHIGAN BOBOLINKS,	235	ALL MORNING	42
BODIES			
THEIR BODIES CANNOT LIE:	121	ALL EARTH, AIR	17
OUR BODIES LIGHT, AND LIGHTED BY THE MOON.	237	THE TRANCED	20
BODY			
AND MY THOUGHT HUNTS ANOTHER BODY.	80	GIVE WAY, GATES	44
TELL ME, BODY WITHOUT SKIN, DOES A FISH SWEAT?	89	UNFOLD! UNFOLD!	2
BE A BODY LIGHTED WITH LOVE,	98	O, THOU OPENING	44
IN THE SAME WAY: O WATCH HIS BODY SWAY!--	105	SIR JOHN DAVIES	11
WHO CAN EMBRACE THE BODY OF HIS FATE?	106	SIR JOHN DAVIES	33
THE BODY AND THE SOUL KNOW HOW TO PLAY	106	SIR JOHN DAVIES	47
THERE WAS A BODY, AND IT CAST A SPELL,--	106	SIR JOHN DAVIES	61
SHE HELD HER BODY STEADY IN THE WIND;	120	THE DREAM	25
BODY AND SPIRIT KNOW	126	WORDS FOR WIND	95
(I MEASURE TIME BY HOW A BODY SWAYS).	127	I KNEW A WOMAN	28
MY BODY HALF IN FLAME.	147	THE EXORCISM	2
BODY AND SOUL TRANSCEND APPEARANCES	149	IN LATE SUMMER	13
MAKING IT QUIVER WITH MY BODY;	161	I'M HERE	25
THE BODY, DELIGHTING IN THRESHOLDS,	163	I'M HERE	58

	PAGE	TITLE	LINE
BODY (CONTINUED)			
IN THE SUN, BUSY AT A YOUNG BODY,	165	HER BECOMING	7
IN THE CHANGING BODY.	168	FOURTH MEDITATN	22
IS MY BODY SPEAKING? I BREATHE WHAT I AM:	170	FOURTH MEDITATN	85
A BODY WITH THE MOTION OF A SOUL.	188	THE LONGING	27
I HAVE LEFT THE BODY OF THE WHALE, BUT THE MOUTH OF THE NIGHT IS STILL WIDE;	188	THE LONGING	51
AND I ROAM ELSEWHERE, MY BODY THINKING,	195	JOURNY INTERIOR	68
MY BODY SHIMMERS WITH A LIGHT FLAME.	198	THE LONG WATERS	66
IT TAKES IN THE WHOLE BODY;	207	THE YOUNG GIRL	2
A BIRD MY BODY,	207	THE YOUNG GIRL	11
NOR THE SOUL HAUNTING MY BODY,	209	HER RETICENCE	8
A PHOENIX, SURE OF MY BODY,	209	HER LONGING	19
SHE KEPT HER BODY STILL	212	LIGHT LISTENED	10
A LITTLE QUAKER, THE WHOLE BODY OF HIM TREMBLING,	227	MEADOW MOUSE	6
THE BODY MOVES, THOUGH SLOWLY, TOWARD DESIRE.	235	MANIFESTATION	10
OR IS THE BODY BUT A MOTION IN A SHOE?	237	THE TRANCED	5
BODY MET BODY, WE	238	THE MOMENT	11
BODY MET BODY, WE	238	THE MOMENT	11
I SAW A BODY DANCING IN THE WIND,	241	THE SEQUEL	9
SHE LEFT MY BODY, LIGHTER THAN A SEED;	241	THE SEQUEL	20
I GAVE HER BODY FULL AND GRAVE FAREWELL.	241	THE SEQUEL	21
THE SOUL HAS MANY MOTIONS, BODY ONE.	243	THE MOTION	1
HOW BODY FROM SPIRIT SLOWLY DOES UNWIND	244	INFIRMITY	35
MY BODY ALTERS, ALTERING THE SOUL	246	THE MARROW	15
GOD BLESS THE ROOTS!--BODY AND SOUL ARE ONE!	250	THE RIGHT THING	7
BOEHME			
GREAT BOEHME ROOTED ALL IN YES AND NO;	133	THE PURE FURY	13
BOFIN			
AND I LIE HERE THINKING IN BLEAK BOFIN TOWN	216	THE SHY MAN	18
IT HAPPENED O, IN BOFIN TOWN,	270	GOB MUSIC	38
BOG			
FROM THE SUCKING BOG.	65	SHAPE OF FIRE	52
BOGEY-HAUNTED			
WHOSE BOGEY-HAUNTED LOOK	7	ORDERS FOR DAY	16
BOG-HOLES			
BY THE MUDDY POND-EDGE, BY THE BOG-HOLES,	54	THE LOST SON	42
BOGS			
SQUIRMERS IN BOGS,	50	THE MINIMAL	5
BOILED			
BOILED EGGS FROM A CUP,--	179	MYRTLE'S COUSIN	4
BOILER			
THE WAY TO THE BOILER WAS DARK,	57	THE LOST SON	122
BOILERS			
INTO THE RUSTY BOILERS,	41	BIG WIND	9
BOLD			
THE BOLD WEAR TOUGHENED SKIN	20	REPL TO CENSURE	13
FEARLESS AND BOLD, HE DID HIS FELLOWS IN,	28	THE FAVORITE	5
BOLD IN FEAR THEREFORE;	60	THE LONG ALLEY	40
A TUNE SO BOLD AND BARE,	271	THE REPLY	11
BOLDLY			
WALK BOLDLY MY SISTER BUT DO NOT DEIGN TO GIVE	5	TO MY SISTER	10
BOLSTER			
GONE TO BOLSTER A ROAD.	103	OLD LADY'S WRDS	36
BOLT			
FROM THE BOLT, STUCK IN ITS GROOVE,	236	SONG (2)	7
BONE			
I'M NAKED TO THE BONE,	3	OPEN HOUSE	9
HAIR ON A NARROW WRIST BONE;	6	THE PREMONITION	9
IS LOCKED IN NARROW BONE.	18	GENESIS	4
THE FLYING FABRIC STITCHED ON BONE,	19	EPIDERM MACABRE	3
A SHRED OF BONE ITS HORN,	145	THE BEAST	8
THE FLESH DESERTS THE BONE.	153	THE DYING MAN	7
FLESH CRIES TO FLESH; AND BONE CRIES OUT TO BONE;	155	THE DYING MAN	58
FLESH CRIES TO FLESH; AND BONE CRIES OUT TO BONE;	155	THE DYING MAN	58
I CAN'T BURY THE BONE OF THIS MISERY LIKE A FASTIDIOUS DOG.	261	THE CHANGELING	31
BONE-ACHE			
WHAT A BONE-ACHE I HAVE.	85	PRAISE TO END!	3
BONES			
FEET, BEAR THE THIN BONES OVER	7	ORDERS FOR DAY	8
IN MY VEINS, IN MY BONES I FEEL IT,--	37	CUTTINGS (LATE)	6
SHOOTING UP LIME AND DUNG AND GROUND BONES,--	38	FORCING HOUSE	9
I SHOOK THE SOFTENING CHALK OF MY BONES,	53	THE LOST SON	6

	PAGE	TITLE	LINE
BONES (CONTINUED)			
MY VEINS ARE RUNNING NOWHERE. DO THE BONES CAST OUT THEIR FIRE?	56	THE LOST SON	101
THE BONES OF WEEDS KEPT SWINGING IN THE WIND,	58	THE LOST SON	152
THE BEAUTIFUL SURVIVING BONES	58	THE LOST SON	157
FLESH, YOU OFFEND THIS METAL. HOW LONG NEED THE BONES MOURN?	59	THE LONG ALLEY	12
THERE'S NO JOY IN SOFT BONES.	59	THE LONG ALLEY	26
MOTHER ME OUT OF HERE. WHAT MORE WILL THE BONES ALLOW?	64	SHAPE OF FIRE	7
HE WAS ALL WHITEY BONES	73	WHERE KNOCK IS	78
A BIRD SINGS IN THE BUSH OF YOUR BONES.	79	GIVE WAY, GATES	5
I KNOW MY OWN BONES:	83	O LULL ME, LULL	16
I DREAMT I WAS ALL BONES;	87	PRAISE TO END!	63
CAN THE BONES BREATHE? THIS GRAVE HAS AN EAR.	87	PRAISE TO END!	75
WENT WEEPING, LITTLE BONES. BUT WHERE?	92	I CRY, LOVE!	1
THE BONES ARE LONELY.	93	I CRY, LOVE!	32
THIS FLESH HAS AIRY BONES.	99	O, THOU OPENING	82
I KNEW A WOMAN, LOVELY IN HER BONES,	127	I KNEW A WOMAN	1
THESE OLD BONES LIVE TO LEARN HER WANTON WAYS:	127	I KNEW A WOMAN	27
DRY BONES! DRY BONES! I FIND MY LOVING HEART,	135	THE RENEWAL	19
DRY BONES! DRY BONES! I FIND MY LOVING HEART,	135	THE RENEWAL	19
THE GREAT GODS ARCH MY BONES.	137	LOVE'S PROGRESS	5
WAS IT YESTERDAY I STRETCHED OUT THE THIN BONES OF MY INNOCENCE?	168	FOURTH MEDITATN	12
HAVE THEY SEEN, EVER, THE SHARP BONES OF THE POOR?	169	FOURTH MEDITATN	46
WHAT CAN I TELL MY BONES?	171	WHAT TELL BONES	T
O MY BONES,	171	WHAT TELL BONES	22
MIST ALTERS THE ROCKS. WHAT CAN I TELL MY BONES?	172	WHAT TELL BONES	44
DO THESE BONES LIVE? CAN I LIVE WITH THESE BONES?	172	WHAT TELL BONES	52
DO THESE BONES LIVE? CAN I LIVE WITH THESE BONES?	172	WHAT TELL BONES	52
AND SHAKE THE SECRETS FROM MY DEEPEST BONES;	173	WHAT TELL BONES	87
PAIN WANDERS THROUGH MY BONES LIKE A LOST FIRE;	246	THE MARROW	11
I BLEED MY BONES, THEIR MARROW TO BESTOW	246	THE MARROW	23
LONG BONES ARE LOVELIEST: I LOVE LONG BONES.	260	THE CHANGELING	12
LONG BONES ARE LOVELIEST: I LOVE LONG BONES.	260	THE CHANGELING	12
ALL TRUE BONES SING ALONE.	263	FOLLIES OF ADAM	28
BONNY			
WHERE ARE YOU NOW, MY BONNY BEATING GRISTLE,	86	PRAISE TO END!	17
BONY			
HE JERKS A FROG ACROSS HIS BONY LIP,	15	THE HERON	9
BOOGER			
AND THERE WILL BE A BOOGER.	75	I NEED, I NEED	26
BOOK			
OR WAS THAT IN A BOOK? I THINK WITH PRIDE:	105	SIR JOHN DAVIES	9
WHAT BOOK, O LEARNED MAN, WILL SET ME RIGHT?	133	THE PURE FURY	2
SHE WOULD SIT WITH A BOOK ON HER KNEES,--	179	MYRTLE	6
BOOKS			
AND NONE HAS READ MY BOOKS,	225	THE CHUMS	2
I HELPED OUT WITH THE BOOKS;	267	SAGINAW SONG	32
BOOM			
THE FLAT BOOM ON THE BEACH OF THE TOWERING SEA-SWELL,	231	THE STORM	41
BOOMS			
THE LONG SURF OF THE STORM BOOMS	210	HER TIME	21
BOOPS			
I'M KING OF THE BOOPS!	92	I CRY, LOVE!	13
BOOR			
WHO LOVES THE SMALL CAN BE BOTH SAINT AND BOOR,	225	OTTO	31
I'M OFTEN A DRUNKEN BOOR;	268	SAGINAW SONG	46
BOOT			
BARED FOR A HUNTER'S BOOT.	47	THE RETURN	13
BOOTS			
OR STAND ALL NIGHT WATERING ROSES, HIS FEET BLUE IN RUBBER BOOTS.	42	OLD FLORIST	10
BOOZE			
ME BREATHING BOOZE AT HER,	228	THE GERANIUM	18
BORDER			
I REMEMBER THE CROSSING-TENDER'S GERANIUM BORDER	29	THE REMINDER	1
BORDERS			
THOUGH IT REJECT DRY BORDERS OF THE SEEN,	154	THE DYING MAN	42
BORE			
"THIS STUFF IS A BORE!	179	MYRTLE	9
BORED			
I NEVER AM BORED, HOWEVER FAMILIAR THE SCENE.	24	VERNAL SENTIMNT	4

	PAGE	TITLE	LINE
BORN			
I'M MORE THAN WHEN I WAS BORN;	84	O LULL ME, LULL	37
AND THAT CRY TAKES ME BACK WHERE I WAS BORN.	156	THE DYING MAN	83
OF BEING BORN FAILS ON HIS NAKED EARS.	201	THE FAR FIELD	90
BOSOM			
LUMINOUS ONE, SHALL WE MEET ON THE BOSOM OF GOD?	59	THE LONG ALLEY	29
BOTH			
BUT SNAKES, BOTH POISONOUS AND GARTER,	23	AMOROUS LADY	5
BOTH LOVE	78	BRING THE DAY!	36
ARCH MY BACK, PRETTY-BONES, I'M DEAD AT BOTH ENDS.	85	PRAISE TO END!	9
I STAY ALIVE, BOTH IN AND OUT OF TIME,	131	SENTENTIOUS MAN	14
WHO LOVES THE SMALL CAN BE BOTH SAINT AND BOOR,	225	OTTO	31
OR THE TWO OF US, ALONE, BOTH SEEDY,	228	THE GERANIUM	17
BOTH MOTH AND FLAME? THE WEAK MOTH BLUNDERING BY.	241	THE SEQUEL	6
GROWS SICK IN FLESH AND SPIRIT BOTH.	257	SANITARIUM	10
BOTHERED			
THOSE DOTING AUNTIES NEVER WOULD HAVE BOTHERED.	25	DIM-WIT COUSIN	4
BO-TREE			
AND MY THOUGHT FLIES TO THE PLACE BY THE BO-TREE.	222	THE ABYSS	100
BOTTLE-CAP			
NOW HE'S EATEN HIS THREE KINDS OF CHEESE AND DRUNK FROM HIS BOTTLE-CAP WATERING-TROUGH--	227	MEADOW MOUSE	12
BOTTOM			
AND ONE CRAB, TENTATIVE, HUNCHES HIMSELF BEFORE MOVING ALONG THE BOTTOM,	159	FIRST MEDITATN	62
WHEN YOU HIT THE DEEP PIT AT THE BOTTOM OF THE SWALE,	193	JOURNY INTERIOR	20
MY EYES STARE AT THE BOTTOM OF A RIVER,	201	THE FAR FIELD	73
A BOTTOM OF WATER.	233	THE PIKE	4
BOTTOMS			
THE BOTTOMS OF MIGRATING DUCKS	267	SAGINAW SONG	11
BOTTOM-STONES			
BUMPING AGAINST STICKS AND BOTTOM-STONES, THEN SWINGING	159	FIRST MEDITATN	70
THE BOTTOM-STONES SHIMMER BACK THEIR IRREGULAR STRIATIONS,	233	THE PIKE	8
BOUGH			
THE YOUNG FRUIT SWELL UPON THE PEAR-TREE BOUGH.	11	LIGHT BRIGHTER	16
WHEN I STOOD AT THE WINDOW, AN ELM BOUGH SWEPT TO MY KNEES;	12	MID-CNTRY BLOW	3
THE BEAK OF FROST HAS PICKED THE BOUGH,	14	COMING OF COLD	23
IN THE BIRD BEYOND THE BOUGH, THE SINGLE ONE	205	THE ROSE	108
GREEN, A BIRD TIPPING THE TOPMOST BOUGH,	235	MANIFESTATION	2
BOUGHT			
THEY BOUGHT A DRUM. HE WOULDN'T WHACK IT.	115	THE SERPENT	14
BOUNCE			
AND WE BOUNCE AND SWAY ALONG TOWARD THE MIDNIGHT,	158	FIRST MEDITATN	23
BOUND			
WHO LEAPS TO HEAVEN AT A SINGLE BOUND?	107	SIR JOHN DAVIES	80
THAT CHRIST, SECURELY BOUND, COULD BEAR.	144	ELEGY (1)	8
BOWER			
I'VE BEEN ASLEEP IN A BOWER OF DEAD SKIN.	86	PRAISE TO END!	47
I BASK IN THE BOWER OF CHANGE;	88	PRAISE TO END!	85
BOWL			
IN A HAND LIKE A BOWL	249	THE RESTORED	1
FROM MY HAND LIKE A BOWL.	249	THE RESTORED	12
BOX			
IN A SHOE BOX STUFFED IN AN OLD NYLON STOCKING	227	MEADOW MOUSE	1
WE'LL GIVE EACH OTHER A BOX ON THE EAR,	272	DUET	25
BOXES			
BULBS BROKE OUT OF BOXES HUNTING FOR CHINKS IN THE DARK,	38	ROOT CELLAR	2
NEAT IN THEIR BOXES, DOLOR OF PAD AND PAPER-WEIGHT,	46	DOLOR	2
BOY			
COULD MAKE A SMALL BOY DIZZY;	45	MY PAPA'S WALTZ	2
HELLO, HELLO. MY NERVES KNEW YOU, DEAR BOY.	65	SHAPE OF FIRE	32
I PLAYED IN FLAME AND WATER LIKE A BOY	120	THE DREAM	28
O MORE THAN A ROARING BOY,	169	FOURTH MEDITATN	51
AND SAID, OLD BOY, YOU'RE SHEDDING HAIR,	181	MONOTONY SONG	6
THE BOY AND THE BUSH	182	BOY AND BUSH	T
A BOY WHO HAD GUMPTION AND PUSH	182	BOY AND BUSH	1
BOYS			
AND BOYS MOON AT GIRLS WITH LAST YEAR'S FATUOUS FACES,	24	VERNAL SENTIMNT	3
THE BOYS I KNEW WHEN I WENT TO POT;	111	SQUEEZE-BOX	2
AND EVEN THE BOYS TURNED OUT TO BE MEN	112	SQUEEZE-BOX	23
HOPE'S HOLY WRISTS: THE LITTLE BURNING BOYS	143	SHIMMER OF EVIL	13
BRACING			
BRACING MY BACK AGAINST A SAPLING,	161	I'M HERE	24

	PAGE	TITLE	LINE
BRACKISH			
I DABBLE MY TOES IN THE BRACKISH FOAM SLIDING FORWARD, ...	190	AT OYSTER RIVER	15
BRAIN			
BEFORE OBLIVION CLOUDS THE BRAIN.	8	PRAYER	4
UNTIL THOUGHT CRACKLES WHITE ACROSS THE BRAIN.	17	UNEXTINGUISHED	12
A PEARL WITHIN THE BRAIN,	18	GENESIS	9
DEEP IN THE BRAIN, FAR BACK.	49	NIGHT CROW	8
IN THE FAIR NIGHT OF SOME DIM BRAIN,	81	SENSIBILITY! LA	4
HAVE TOSSED MY HEART AND FIDDLED THROUGH MY BRAIN.	105	SIR JOHN DAVIES	22
BRAMBLE			
WITH BURR, BRAMBLE, AND THORN;	145	THE BEAST	3
BRANCH			
AND SOON A BRANCH, PART OF A HIDDEN SCENE,	11	LIGHT BRIGHTER	17
ALL SHADE IS LEAN, THE ANTIC BRANCH	14	COMING OF COLD	28
THE MOULD UPON THE BRANCH IS DRY,	15	COMING OF COLD	44
HE'LL SIGH AND GIVE HIS BRANCH A HUG;	116	THE SLOTH	9
THE FLAT BRANCH OF THAT HEMLOCK HOLDS THE LAST OF THE SUN,	163	I'M HERE	83
I WOULD DELIGHT IN MY HANDS, THE BRANCH SINGING, ALTERING THE EXCESSIVE BIRD;	188	THE LONGING	44
THE ETERNAL ONE, THE CHILD, THE SWAYING VINE BRANCH,	198	THE LONG WATERS	69
AND THE HALF-SUNKEN BRANCH BENDS AWAY FROM THE GAZER'S EYE.	233	THE PIKE	9
BRANCHES			
AS BRANCHES LOOSE LAST VESTIGES OF SNOW.	11	LIGHT BRIGHTER	10
HER SONG TREMBLING THE TWIGS AND SMALL BRANCHES.	102	ELEGY FOR JANE	6
SETTLING IN SMALL BEADS AROUND WEEDS AND SUNKEN BRANCHES,	159	FIRST MEDITATN	61
THE SUDDEN SUCKING ROAR AS THE CULVERT LOOSENS ITS DEBRIS OF BRANCHES AND STICKS,	191	AT OYSTER RIVER	53
HANGING, BUNCHED LIKE YOUNG FRUIT, BENDING THE END BRANCHES,	199	THE FAR FIELD	32
BRASS			
I MISS THE POLISHED BRASS, THE POWERFUL BLACK HORSES,	22	ROAD TO WDLAWN	1
BRAVE			
THE BRAVE KEEP UNDEFILED	20	REPL TO CENSURE	11
BRAW			
DAN CUPID, I TELL YOU'S A BRAW LADDIE-BUCK;	113	TO A LADY ED	5
BRAYED			
AND THEN A JACKASS BRAYED. A LIZARD LEAPED MY FOOT.	247	I WAITED	14
BREAK			
COMPRESSION CANNOT BREAK	9	THE ADAMANT	9
THE GREAT FEET BREAK THE RIDGES OF THE SAND,	15	THE HERON	6
WHEN SPROUTS BREAK OUT.	37	CUTTINGS (LATE)	9
SHOULD A SONG BREAK A SLEEP?	99	O, THOU OPENING	74
MY NECK, IF NOT MY HEART, WILL BREAK	136	THE SENSUALISTS	23
I MET A WOMAN WHO COULD BREAK WIND	268	SAGINAW SONG	41
BREAKING			
THE FROST BE GONE, FOR GREEN IS BREAKING NOW;	11	LIGHT BRIGHTER	14
BEFORE THE BREAKING OF A STRING,	22	SILENCE	8
BREAKING INTO NAKEDNESS,	42	TRANSPLANTING	18
THEIR BLACK SHAPES BREAKING PAST;	158	FIRST MEDITATN	34
OVER THE THIN, FEATHERY RIPPLES BREAKING LIGHTLY AGAINST THE IRREGULAR SHORELINE--	197	THE LONG WATERS	50
I REMEMBER A STONE BREAKING THE EDDYING CURRENT,	197	THE LONG WATERS	55
OR THAT LONELY TIME BEFORE THE BREAKING OF MORNING	204	THE ROSE	82
THEN SLOWLY BREAKING WHITER IN THE DAWN;	225	OTTO	37
BREAKS			
BREAKS UP THE CRUST OF CINDERS THAT REMAIN,	17	UNEXTINGUISHED	10
IT BREAKS UPON MY SOLITUDE--	22	SILENCE	4
THIS SLAG RUNS SLOW. WHAT BLEEDS WHEN METAL BREAKS?	59	THE LONG ALLEY	11
A FIELD BREAKS LIKE THE SEA;	124	WORDS FOR WIND	37
SHE BREAKS MY BREATH IN HALF,	126	WORDS FOR WIND	100
AS THE PILED ICE BREAKS AWAY FROM THE BATTERED SPILES,	191	AT OYSTER RIVER	55
BREAKS ON ME AS MY MEAGER FLESH BREAKS DOWN--	244	INFIRMITY	15
BREAKS ON ME AS MY MEAGER FLESH BREAKS DOWN--	244	INFIRMITY	15
BREAKWATER			
AGAINST THE STONE BREAKWATER,	230	THE STORM	1
FOR THE GREAT LAST LEAP OF THE WAVE OVER THE BREAKWATER,	231	THE STORM	40
BREAST			
LIP, BREAST AND THIGH CANNOT POSSESS	8	PRAYER	17
MY BREAST WILD AS THE WAVES.	165	HER BECOMING	10
DARE I EMBRACE A GHOST FROM MY OWN BREAST?	165	HER BECOMING	21
PITTING MY BREAST AGAINST THE RUSHING AIR,	209	HER LONGING	18
A CHILD UPON HER BREAST,	268	SAGINAW SONG	57
BREAST-BONE			
SPIRIT AND NATURE BEAT IN ONE BREAST-BONE--	131	SENTENTIOUS MAN	1

	PAGE	TITLE	LINE
BREASTS			
NOR MY LIPS, MY BREASTS, MY THIGHS	209	HER RETICENCE	9
BREATH			
BREATH, TURN THE OLD BLOOD OVER.	7	ORDERS FOR DAY	21
AT DUSK OUR SLOW BREATH THICKENS ON THE AIR.	12	SLOW SEASON	8
EVEN THE DIRT KEPT BREATHING A SMALL BREATH.	38	ROOT CELLAR	11
AND THEIR SNUFF-LADEN BREATH BLOWING LIGHTLY OVER ME IN MY FIRST SLEEP.	44	FRAU BAUMAN	35
THE WHISKEY ON YOUR BREATH	45	MY PAPA'S WALTZ	1
BEETLES SWEETENED MY BREATH.	89	UNFOLD! UNFOLD!	28
THE BREATH OF A LONG ROOT,	125	WORDS FOR WIND	82
SHE BREAKS MY BREATH IN HALF;	126	WORDS FOR WIND	100
THE LIGHT AIR TAKES MY BEING'S BREATH AWAY;	134	THE PURE FURY	23
WHEN WILL THAT CREATURE GIVE ME BACK MY BREATH?	134	THE PURE FURY	25
THE GHOSTLY FIGURE SUCKED ITS BREATH,	136	THE SENSUALISTS	17
WHEN I STAYED FOR BREATH, I LAY	146	THE SONG	11
BREATHING A SLOWER BREATH,	147	THE EXORCISM	27
A BREATH IS BUT A BREATH: I HAVE THE EARTH;	155	THE DYING MAN	76
A BREATH IS BUT A BREATH: I HAVE THE EARTH;	155	THE DYING MAN	76
LEANING, OUT OF ALL BREATH,	161	I'M HERE	23
MY BREATH GREW LESS. I LISTENED LIKE A BEAST.	166	HER BECOMING	53
MY BREATH IS MORE THAN YOURS.	167	HER BECOMING	81
A TWILIGHT WIND, LIGHT AS A CHILD'S BREATH	190	AT OYSTER RIVER	18
MY BREATH BUT A SIGH.	208	THE APPARITION	10
AND OUR BREATH COMES MORE EASY,--	230	THE STORM	22
FROM THE GHOST WITHOUT BREATH,	236	SONG (2)	11
THAT ONCE COULD MELT THE DARK WITH ITS SMALL BREATH.	246	THE MARROW	16
NOT EVEN OUT OF BREATH?	262	FOLLIES OF ADAM	7
BREATHE			
THEY HAD MANY MOUTHS TO BREATHE WITH.	57	THE LOST SON	127
I BREATHE INTO A DREAM,	83	O LULL ME, LULL	25
CAN THE BONES BREATHE? THIS GRAVE HAS AN EAR.	87	PRAISE TO END!	75
MOST LOVINGLY: I BREATHE;	123	WORDS FOR WIND	4
WE BREATHE IN UNISON.	141	MEMORY	2
I BREATHE ALONE UNTIL MY DARK IS BRIGHT.	155	THE DYING MAN	51
IS MY BODY SPEAKING? I BREATHE WHAT I AM:	170	FOURTH MEDITATN	85
WHAT DREAM'S ENOUGH TO BREATHE IN? A DARK DREAM.	188	THE LONGING	28
BUT WHEN I BREATHE WITH THE BIRDS,	195	JOURNY INTERIOR	77
THE UNSINGING FIELDS WHERE NO LUNGS BREATHE,	196	THE LONG WATERS	11
TIMES FIVE A MAN; I BREATHE	271	THE REPLY	14
BREATHED			
BEFORE SHE EVER BREATHED, AND IN THAT DREAM	119	THE DREAM	2
BREATHER			
AND THE CRAB, THE QUIET BREATHER.	100	THE VISITANT	9
A LIGHT BREATHER	101	LIGHT BREATHER	T
BREATHERS			
BEND DOWN, SMALL BREATHERS, CREEPERS AND WINDERS;	61	THE LONG ALLEY	71
BREATHES			
WHO ELSE BREATHES HERE? WHAT DOES THE GRAVE SAY?	59	THE LONG ALLEY	19
HELD UP, WHILE THE ROWER BREATHES, AND THE SMALL BOAT DRIFTS QUIETLY SHOREWARD;	67	SHAPE OF FIRE	91
WHAT'S BECOME OF CARE? THIS LAKE BREATHES LIKE A ROSE.	170	FOURTH MEDITATN	76
BREATHING			
EVEN THE DIRT KEPT BREATHING A SMALL BREATH.	38	ROOT CELLAR	11
BREATHING.	39	ORCHIDS	18
THE ROSES KEPT BREATHING IN THE DARK.	57	THE LOST SON	126
WHO'S BISHOP OF BREATHING?	83	O LULL ME, LULL	3
MY FLESH IS BREATHING SLOWER THAN A WALL.	135	THE RENEWAL	9
I FEEL WE'RE BREATHING WITH THE DEAD;	136	THE SENSUALISTS	5
AND BREATHING HARD, AS THAT MAN RODE	136	THE SENSUALISTS	11
BREATHING A SLOWER BREATH,	147	THE EXORCISM	27
ME BREATHING BOOZE AT HER,	228	THE GERANIUM	18
BREATHING HEAVILY, HOPING--	231	THE STORM	39
BREED			
WE NEED A BREED THAT MIXES BLAKE AND ME,	274	SUPPR W LINDSAY	41
BREEDS			
TELLS ME MY DRINKING BREEDS A WILL TO DIE.	246	THE MARROW	4
BREEZE			
SLOW SWINGS THE BREEZE ABOVE HER HEAD,	17	NO BIRD	5
OR A BREEZE MOVES OVER THE KNEES FROM A LOW HILL,	198	THE LONG WATERS	64
BRIAR			
THE BRIAR BEARS ITS THORN, AND DROUGHT	14	COMING OF COLD	24

	PAGE	TITLE	LINE
BRIARS			
THE COWS AND BRIARS	55	THE LOST SON	81
BRIARY			
OUT OF THE BRIARY HEDGE, THE TANGLE OF MATTED UNDERBRUSH,	203	THE ROSE	45
BRICK			
OR POUND UPON A BRICK;	269	GOB MUSIC	4
BRICKS			
BRICKS FLAKE BEFORE MY FACE. MASTER OF WATER, THAT'S TREES AWAY.	61	THE LONG ALLEY	80
BRIDE			
AND THE WEAK BRIDEGROOM STRENGTHENS IN HIS BRIDE.	132	SENTENTIOUS MAN	42
A WOMAN STOOD, PURE AS A BRIDE,	136	THE SENSUALISTS	9
BRIDEGROOM			
AND THE WEAK BRIDEGROOM STRENGTHENS IN HIS BRIDE.	132	SENTENTIOUS MAN	42
BRIDGE			
OVER A RICKETY BRIDGE	54	THE LOST SON	38
AN OLD BRIDGE BELOW WITH A BUCKLED IRON RAILING, BROKEN BY SOME IDIOT PLUNGER;	194	JOURNY INTERIOR	32
AND A FISHERMAN DAWDLES OVER A WOODEN BRIDGE,	197	THE LONG WATERS	37
WHERE'S THE BRIDGE OF DANCING CHILDREN?	258	SONG (3)	24
BRIDGEHEADS			
AT BRIDGEHEADS BUCKLED ICE BEGINS TO SHIFT,	11	LIGHT BRIGHTER	7
BRIDGES			
BRIDGES OF IRON LACE,	34	NIGHT JOURNEY	6
AND THE WHOLE RIVER BEGINS TO MOVE FORWARD, ITS BRIDGES SHAKING.	191	AT OYSTER RIVER	56
BRIEF			
THE SPIEL RAN ON; THE SALE WAS BRIEF AND BRISK;	21	THE AUCTION	9
BRIGHT			
THE PAGEANTRY OF WINGS THE EYE'S BRIGHT TREASURE.	5	TO MY SISTER	6
FROM DARK TO BLAZING BRIGHT;	34	NIGHT JOURNEY	17
SPEECH REVIVED, A GHOSTLY GOING OF TAME BEARS, A BRIGHT MOON ON GLEAMING	98	O, THOU OPENING	23
BUT THE BRIGHT DAY HAD NO ANSWER.	101	THE VISITANT	25
ON A BRIGHT STONE.	103	OLD LADY'S WRDS	11
THE SHAPES A BRIGHT CONTAINER CAN CONTAIN!	127	I KNEW A WOMAN	4
I BREATHE ALONE UNTIL MY DARK IS BRIGHT.	155	THE DYING MAN	51
AND ANOTHER, OUTSIDE, IN THE BRIGHT DAY,	158	FIRST MEDITATN	41
THE MOUNTAIN WITH ITS SINGULAR BRIGHT SHADE	201	THE FAR FIELD	95
I HAVE MERGED, LIKE THE BIRD, WITH THE BRIGHT AIR,	222	THE ABYSS	99
BELOW, THE BRIGHT SEA WAS, THE LEVEL WAVES,	247	I WAITED	22
IN A COUNTRY OF BRIGHT STONE.	265	HARSH COUNTRY	16
BRIGHTER			
THE LIGHT COMES BRIGHTER	11	LIGHT BRIGHTER	T
THE LIGHT COMES BRIGHTER FROM THE EAST; THE CAW	11	LIGHT BRIGHTER	1
ALL DISTANT SHAPES TURN BRIGHTER TO THE GAZE.	17	UNEXTINGUISHED	4
THE DINING ROOM CARPET DYED BRIGHTER THAN BLOOD,	32	SALE	13
UNTIL MY EYES LOOK AT A BRIGHTER SUN	134	THE PURE FURY	27
ONE WHITE FACE SHIMMERS BRIGHTER THAN THE SUN	246	THE MARROW	7
HER NAILS BRIGHTER THAN SHELLS,	261	THE CHANGELING	55
BRIGHTLY			
DYING BRIGHTLY UNDER THE STREET LIGHTS SUNK IN COARSE CONCRETE,	193	JOURNY INTERIOR	29
BRIM			
AS AN OPAQUE VASE FILLS TO THE BRIM FROM A QUICK POURING,	67	SHAPE OF FIRE	93
BRIMMING			
I LEAN MY HEAD NEAR THE BRIMMING EDGE	269	GOB MUSIC	14
BRING			
WINDS BRING A FINE AND BITTER SNOW.	15	COMING OF COLD	52
BRING ME MY HAT, MY UMBRELLA AND RUBBERS,	48	LAST WORDS	9
BRING THE DAY!	77	BRING THE DAY!	T
BRING ME A FINGER. THIS DIRT'S LONESOME FOR GRASS.	79	GIVE WAY, GATES	7
ALL THINGS BRING ME TO LOVE.	125	WORDS FOR WIND	81
COULD BRING ME TO MY GOD?	139	PLAINT	8
BRING ME THE MEEK, FOR I WOULD KNOW THEIR WAYS;	149	IN LATE SUMMER	5
IS IT TO BRING THE LILY?	261	THE CHANGELING	45
IS IT TO BRING	261	THE CHANGELING	46
CAN BRING A GOOD MAN DOWN.	269	GOB MUSIC	19
WILL BRING A GOOD MAN DOWN.	270	GOB MUSIC	47
BRINGING			
BRINGING ME HOME FROM THE TWILIGHT FISHING.	221	THE ABYSS	67
BRINGS			
WHEN FROM UNDER THE BARN THE CAT BRINGS A SIMILAR LITTER,--	24	VERNAL SENTIMNT	5

	PAGE	TITLE	LINE
BRINGS (CONTINUED)			
THIS WIND BRINGS MANY FISH;	61	THE LONG ALLEY	86
MY FRIEND, THE RAT IN THE WALL, BRINGS ME THE CLEAREST MESSAGES;	88	PRAISE TO END!	84
AND THE SUN BRINGS JOY TO SOME.	157	FIRST MEDITATN	12
BRINGS THE SECRET--RIGHT IN HERE!	266	FOR STEVENS	8
BRISK			
THE SPIEL RAN ON; THE SALE WAS BRIEF AND BRISK;	21	THE AUCTION	9
BRISKED			
IN A FLICKER OF FIRE BRISKED BY A DUSTY WIND.	194	JOURNY INTERIOR	61
BRISTLED			
THEN BRISTLED LIKE A DOG.	47	THE RETURN	4
BRITCHES			
THE WIND BILLOWING OUT THE SEAT OF MY BRITCHES,	43	CHILD ON GRNHSE	1
HE, IN HIS SHRUNKEN BRITCHES,	46	PICKLE BELT	9
BROAD			
THE FULL MOON WAS SHINING UPON THE BROAD SEA;	216	THE SHY MAN	1
AND IN BROAD DAY THE MIDNIGHT COME AGAIN!	239	IN A DARK TIME	15
HOPE HAS ITS HUSH: WE MOVE THROUGH ITS BROAD DAY,--	243	THE MOTION	22
BROKE			
BULBS BROKE OUT OF BOXES HUNTING FOR CHINKS IN THE DARK,	38	ROOT CELLAR	2
THAT BROKE OVER THE WHOLE OF HER,	41	BIG WIND	27
THE WAVES BROKE EASY, CRIED TO ME IN WHITE;	107	SIR JOHN DAVIES	83
WHEN TRUE LOVE BROKE MY HEART IN HALF,	138	THE SURLY ONE	1
OR BROKE, BUT WOULD NOT GO.	147	THE EXORCISM	18
I BROKE FROM THAT LOW PLACE	147	THE EXORCISM	26
THE TIME WE BROKE FROM TIME;	212	LIGHT LISTENED	20
A BUD BROKE TO A ROSE,	240	IN EVEING AIR	11
BROKEN			
THE NIGHTMARE SILENCE IS BROKEN. WE ARE NOT LOST.	5	PROGNOSIS	16
AS IF I HAD BROKEN THE NATURAL ORDER OF THINGS IN THAT SWAMPLAND;	40	MOSS-GATHERING	10
THE ANIMAL'S CANDID GAZE, A SHADE LESS THAN FEATHERS, LIGHT'S BROKEN	98	O, THOU OPENING	22
WITH A BROKEN UMBRELLA,	171	WHAT TELL BONES	32
AN OLD BRIDGE BELOW WITH A BUCKLED IRON RAILING, BROKEN BY SOME IDIOT PLUNGER;	194	JOURNY INTERIOR	32
UNDERNEATH, THE SLUGGISH WATER RUNNING BETWEEN WEEDS, BROKEN WHEELS, TIRES, STONES.	194	JOURNY INTERIOR	33
TO A TREE LYING FLAT, ITS CROWN HALF BROKEN.	197	THE LONG WATERS	54
SURROUNDED BY SAND, BROKEN SHELLS, THE WRECKAGE OF WATER.	197	THE LONG WATERS	59
AMONG THE TIN CANS, TIRES, RUSTED PIPES, BROKEN MACHINERY,--	199	THE FAR FIELD	17
THE BOBOLINK SKIRRING FROM A BROKEN FENCEPOST,	204	THE ROSE	65
I'LL MAKE A BROKEN MUSIC, OR I'LL DIE.	240	IN EVEING AIR	6
BRONZE			
LONG SINCE, BRONZE WHEAT WAS GATHERED INTO SHEAVES.	12	SLOW SEASON	10
THE BRONZE WHEAT ARRANGED IN STRICT AND FORMAL ORDER;	29	THE REMINDER	3
AND THE BRONZE OF A DEAD BURDOCK AT THE EDGE OF A PRAIRIE LAKE,	197	THE LONG WATERS	42
BROOD			
DARLING OF AN INFECTED BROOD,	4	FEUD	7
WHEN WE BROOD ON THE DEAD OR THE BELOVED;	156	THE DYING MAN	97
HE WAS THE YOUNGEST SON OF A STRANGE BROOD,	224	OTTO	1
BROODING			
TOADS BROODING WELLS.	53	THE LOST SON	4
I'M TIRED OF BROODING ON MY NEIGHBOR'S SOUL;	132	SENTENTIOUS MAN	37
BROODING ON GOD, I MAY BECOME A MAN.	246	THE MARROW	10
BROODS			
UNTIL IT BROODS IN HER EYES.	137	LOVE'S PROGRESS	12
THE LILY BROODS. WHO KNOWS	165	HER BECOMING	26
BROOK			
THE OVENBIRD WILL MATCH THE VOCAL BROOK.	11	LIGHT BRIGHTER	15
THE SMALL BROOK DIES WITHIN ITS BED;	15	COMING OF COLD	38
OF THE FIRST TREMBLING OF A MICHIGAN BROOK IN APRIL,	191	AT OYSTER RIVER	42
BROTHER			
MY BROTHER THE VINE IS GLAD.	123	WORDS FOR WIND	8
BROTHER, HE'S OUR FATHER!	266	FOR STEVENS	20
BROUGHT			
ALL THINGS ARE BROUGHT TO BARN AND FOLD.	15	COMING OF COLD	34
QUITE-BY-CHANCE BROUGHT ME MANY COOKIES.	90	UNFOLD! UNFOLD!	36
ILLUMINATION BROUGHT TO SUCH A PITCH	135	THE RENEWAL	20
A COLD AIR BROUGHT ITS RAIN,	212	LIGHT LISTENED	21
TILL I CAUGHT HIM UP BY THE TAIL AND BROUGHT HIM IN,	227	MEADOW MOUSE	4

	PAGE	TITLE	LINE
BROUGHT (CONTINUED)			
I BROUGHT HER BACK IN AGAIN	228	THE GERANIUM	5
BROUGHT ME DOWN TO MY KNEES. O WHO CAN BE	241	THE SEQUEL	5
BROW			
AND MINUTES BURST UPON A BROW	4	DEATH PIECE	7
THERE IS A NOISE WITHIN THE BROW	22	SILENCE	1
BROW-BEATEN			
THE YOUNG, BROW-BEATEN EARLY INTO A BALEFUL SILENCE,	169	FOURTH MEDITATN	44
BROWN			
THE LANDSCAPE STILL PARTLY BROWN:	58	THE LOST SON	151
AND MIST LIFTING OUT OF THE BROWN CAT-TAILS;	67	SHAPE OF FIRE	87
THE COLOR, MY DEARS, WAS GUINNESS BROWN,	270	GOB MUSIC	39
BROWNISH			
WHEN BATS FLY, CLOSE TO SLIGHTLY TILTING BROWNISH WATER,	198	THE LONG WATERS	61
BROWNISH-WHITE			
AROUND, BACK INTO THE TINY MAINCURRENT, THE RUSH OF BROWNISH-WHITE WATER,	159	FIRST MEDITATN	71
BRUISE			
HIS CLUMSY FINGERS BRUISE	7	ORDERS FOR DAY	6
MY BACK IS JUST ONE BRUISE;	136	THE SENSUALISTS	4
BRUISED			
WITH ANKLES BRUISED FROM STUBBLE OF THE GRAIN.	13	PRAISE PRAIRIE	8
BRUSHES			
BUT WHEN HE BRUSHES UP AGAINST A SCREEN,	16	THE BAT	7
BRUSHING			
WITHOUT BRUSHING THE WET STONES,	100	THE VISITANT	16
MY THIGHS BRUSHING AGAINST FLOWER-CROWNS;	161	I'M HERE	22
BUBBLES			
ONLY A FEW BUBBLES LOOSENING FROM THE ILL-MATCHED TENTACLES,	159	FIRST MEDITATN	64
BUCK			
WITH BUCK STILL TIED TO THE LOG, ON COMES THE LIGHT.	47	DOUBLE FEATURE	1
BUCKING			
BUCKING INTO THE WIND-WAVES	41	BIG WIND	26
BUCKLE			
MY RIGHT EAR SCRAPED A BUCKLE.	45	MY PAPA'S WALTZ	12
BUCKLED			
AT BRIDGEHEADS BUCKLED ICE BEGINS TO SHIFT,	11	LIGHT BRIGHTER	7
AN OLD BRIDGE BELOW WITH A BUCKLED IRON RAILING, BROKEN BY SOME IDIOT PLUNGER;	194	JOURNY INTERIOR	32
BUCKSHOT			
RIDDLING THE SAND, LIKE A WIDE SPRAY OF BUCKSHOT,	230	THE STORM	14
BUD			
BARE AS A BUD, AND NAKED AS A WORM.	188	THE LONGING	34
A BUD BROKE TO A ROSE,	240	IN EVEING AIR	11
BUDS			
BUDS, LONG UNSEALED, OBSCURE THE NARROW LANE.	12	SLOW SEASON	14
THE BUDS DRAW IN BEFORE THE COLD.	15	COMING OF COLD	37
THE UNDERLEAVES, THE SMALLEST BUDS	42	TRANSPLANTING	17
IS THE SEED LEAVING THE OLD BED? THESE BUDS ARE LIVE AS BIRDS.	56	THE LOST SON	102
AND MY INTENT STRETCHED OVER THE BUDS AT THEIR FIRST TREMBLING.	66	SHAPE OF FIRE	69
LIGHTLY: SO BUDS UNLEAVE;	130	THE OTHER	4
THE SCENT OF THE HALF-OPENED BUDS CAME UP OVER ME.	162	I'M HERE	49
BUD-SHEATH			
STILL WET FROM ITS BUD-SHEATH,	101	LIGHT BREATHER	4
BUFFALO			
IN THE COUNTRY OF FEW LAKES, IN THE TALL BUFFALO GRASS AT THE BASE OF THE CLAY BUTTES,	189	THE LONGING	53
IN THE SUMMER HEAT, I CAN SMELL THE DEAD BUFFALO,	189	THE LONGING	54
THE BUFFALO CHIPS DRYING.	189	THE LONGING	56
BUG			
OR DROWN A BUG IN ONE SPIT OF TOBACCO JUICE,	42	OLD FLORIST	8
BUG-EYED			
A BUG-EYED EDIBLE ONE,	209	HER LONGING	8
BUG-RIDDLED			
DOWN AMONG THE RUBBISH, THE BUG-RIDDLED FOLIAGE,	54	THE LOST SON	41
BUGS			
IT WAS SAMOOTS MATUNA AND BUGS MORAN;	112	SQUEEZE-BOX	26
BUILD			
TO BUILD A COMPLEMENT TO RAGE,	22	SILENCE	12
BUILT			
A HOUSE FOR FLOWERS! HOUSE UPON HOUSE THEY BUILT,	224	OTTO	23

		PAGE	TITLE	LINE
BULB				
	THE BULB UNRAVELS. WHO'S FLOATING? NOT ME.	90	UNFOLD! UNFOLD!	41
	THE BULB GOES ON AND OFF, WEAKLY.	231	THE STORM	36
BULBS				
	BULBS BROKE OUT OF BOXES HUNTING FOR CHINKS IN THE DARK,	38	ROOT CELLAR	2
BULGE				
	THE SMALL CELLS BULGE;	37	CUTTINGS	4
BULK				
	A CLOUD MOVED CLOSE. THE BULK OF THE WIND SHIFTED.	100	THE VISITANT	1
	I ROSE, A HEAVY BULK, ABOVE THE FIELD.	247	I WAITED	5
BULKS				
	THE BULKS CANNOT HIDE US, OR THE BLEAK SHEDS OF OUR DESOLATION,	166	HER BECOMING	39
BULL				
	I LIVE, ALIVE AND CERTAIN AS A BULL;	140	THE SWAN	9
	AND A BLACK BULL NUDGED AT A WALL IN THE VALLEY BELOW,	232	THE THING	22
BULLDOZER				
	THE BULLDOZER BACKING AWAY, THE HISS OF THE SANDBLASTER,	204	THE ROSE	71
BULLHEAD				
	ON THE BULLHEAD, IN THE DAKOTAS, WHERE THE EAGLES EAT WELL,	188	THE LONGING	52
BULLHEADS				
	BULLHEADS HAVE WHISKERS.	73	WHERE KNOCK IS	62
BUM				
	I'LL JUMP ON YOUR BELLY, I'LL KICK YOUR BUM	272	DUET	19
BUMBLING				
	BUMBLING UP AND AROUND THE BAMBOO WINDBREAK;	226	THE LIZARD	21
BUMPING				
	BUMPING AGAINST STICKS AND BOTTOM-STONES, THEN SWINGING	159	FIRST MEDITATN	70
BUMPKIN				
	BUMPKIN, HE CAN DANCE ALONE.	85	PRAISE TO END!	7
BUMPS				
	THE SUMMER BUMPS OF HA:	60	THE LONG ALLEY	44
	AN OLD SCOW BUMPS OVER BLACK ROCKS.	64	SHAPE OF FIRE	5
BUMS				
	ON WELL-UPHOLSTERED BUMS	31	LULL	10
BUNCHED				
	THEN PLUMPING IN THE BUNCHED ROOTS,	42	TRANSPLANTING	6
	AND THE BUNCHED LOGS PEEL IN THE AFTERNOON SUNLIGHT,	196	THE LONG WATERS	16
	HANGING, BUNCHED LIKE YOUNG FRUIT, BENDING THE END BRANCHES,	199	THE FAR FIELD	32
BUNCHES				
	AND THEY'LL SOON STAY AWAY IN GREAT BUNCHES!"	180	GOO-GIRL	16
BUNCHING				
	THAT HUMP OF A MAN BUNCHING CHRYSANTHEMUMS	42	OLD FLORIST	1
BUNION				
	PRETENDS HIS DEAD BUNION GIVES EXQUISITE PAIN.	29	THE GENTLE	4
BUNYAN				
	PAUL BUNYAN IS PART RUSSIAN, DID YOU KNOW?--	274	SUPPR W LINDSAY	44
BURDEN				
	THE BURDEN OF THIS JOY.	124	WORDS FOR WIND	60
	A BURDEN TO THE SOUL.	215	HIS FOREBODING	7
BURDOCK				
	AND THE BRONZE OF A DEAD BURDOCK AT THE EDGE OF A PRAIRIE LAKE,	197	THE LONG WATERS	42
BURLAP				
	STUFFING THE HOLES WITH BURLAP;	41	BIG WIND	20
BURN				
	OF FLESH, BURN BACKWARD TO A BLACKENED HEAP.	17	UNEXTINGUISHED	8
	--BUT HOW SHE COULD BURN UP THE MONEY!	111	SQUEEZE-BOX	16
BURNED				
	I BURNED THE FLESH AWAY,	154	THE DYING MAN	26
	AND THERE I STAYED UNTIL THE DAY BURNED DOWN.	166	HER BECOMING	52
	AND SHIMMERING. THE SUN BURNED THROUGH A HAZE,	247	I WAITED	11
BURNING				
	ALL THE WINDOWS ARE BURNING! WHAT'S LEFT OF MY LIFE?	56	THE LOST SON	106
	HOPE'S HOLY WRISTS: THE LITTLE BURNING BOYS	143	SHIMMER OF EVIL	13
	WITHOUT BURNING.	160	FIRST MEDITATN	97
	I CAN'T LAUGH FROM A CRATER OF BURNING PITCH,	166	HER BECOMING	36
	MAY THEY BE TAKEN BY THE TRUE BURNING;	169	FOURTH MEDITATN	61
	A FLASH INTO THE BURNING HEART OF THE ABOMINABLE;	221	THE ABYSS	56
	THE BURNING LAKE TURNS INTO A FOREST POOL,	221	THE ABYSS	58
	BURNING IN SAND. "IT LOOKS LIKE I SHOULD GO,"--	274	SUPPR W LINDSAY	37
BURNISHED				
	FEATHERS OF THE LONG SWELL, BURNISHED, ALMOST OILY--	197	THE LONG WATERS	51

	PAGE	TITLE	LINE
BURNS			
WHAT BURNS ME NOW? DESIRE, DESIRE, DESIRE.	246	THE MARROW	12
BURNT			
GREY FROM THE LONG WINTER, BURNT AT THE BASE IN LATE SUMMER.	193	JOURNY INTERIOR	10
FROM A BURNT PINE THE SHARP SPEECH OF A CROW	246	THE MARROW	3
BURR			
WITH BURR, BRAMBLE, AND THORN;	145	THE BEAST	3
BURROWS			
THE MORLEYS AND THE BURROWS ARE	267	SAGINAW SONG	19
BURST			
AND MINUTES BURST UPON A BROW	4	DEATH PIECE	7
TO BURST THE FRUIT OF GOOD.	18	GENESIS	8
BURY			
I CAN'T BURY THE BONE OF THIS MISERY LIKE A FASTIDIOUS DOG.	261	THE CHANGELING	31
BUS			
ALONE, ON A BUS THROUGH WESTERN COUNTRY.	158	FIRST MEDITATN	21
BUSH			
I CAN'T CATCH A BUSH.	77	BRING THE DAY!	24
A BIRD SINGS IN THE BUSH OF YOUR BONES.	79	GIVE WAY, GATES	5
THE BOY AND THE BUSH	182	BOY AND BUSH	T
WOULD FREQUENTLY TALK TO A BUSH,	182	BOY AND BUSH	2
AND THE BUSH WOULD SAY, "MAC,	182	BOY AND BUSH	3
THE BIRD IN THE SMALL BUSH	259	SONG (3)	45
BUSHES			
THE BUSHES AND THE STONES DANCED ON AND ON;	119	THE DREAM	12
FAR FROM THE MIRRORS ALL THE BUSHES RANG	143	SHIMMER OF EVIL	6
THE SPIKEY PURPLE BUSHES IN THE WINDING DRY CREEK BED--	194	JOURNY INTERIOR	37
HIDING DEEP IN THE BLACKBERRY BUSHES--	234	ALL MORNING	20
BUSINESS			
THE LAWYERS ALL ARE CUNNING, THE BUSINESS MEN ARE FAT,	27	CLAIRVOY WIDOW	7
WE'LL BE AT THE BUSINESS OF WHAT MIGHT BE	80	GIVE WAY, GATES	36
BUSKS			
WHO BUSKS ME ON THE NOSE?	130	THE OTHER	6
BUST			
EVERY TIME I LET HIM, THE STRING WOULD BUST.	178	THE DONKEY	3
BUSY			
THE MEDIOCRE BUSY AT BETRAYING	5	PROGNOSIS	11
BUSY, OBVIOUS WITH OURSELVES,	158	FIRST MEDITATN	29
IN THE SUN, BUSY AT A YOUNG BODY,	165	HER BECOMING	7
THE WATER IS BUSY	258	SONG (3)	6
BUT (127)			
BUTCHER			
SHARPENED A BUTCHER KNIFE;	213	THE HAPPY THREE	2
ON THE QUAKING BUTCHER.	223	ELEGY (2)	23
BUTCHER'S			
LET THE KISSES RESOUND, FLAT LIKE A BUTCHER'S PALM;	56	THE LOST SON	104
BUTTER			
I JUMPED IN BUTTER.	90	UNFOLD! UNFOLD!	37
BUTTERFLIES			
MINNOWS CAN HEAR, AND BUTTERFLIES, YELLOW AND BLUE,	196	THE LONG WATERS	3
WREN-SONG IN TRELLIS: A LIGHT ECSTASY OF BUTTERFLIES COURTING,	255	LIGHT POEM	1
BUTTERFLY			
AN OLD WIND-TATTERED BUTTERFLY FLEW DOWN	243	THE MOTION	2
BUTTERFLY'S			
FROM THE WORM'S ADVANCE AND RETREAT, FROM THE BUTTERFLY'S HAVOC,	196	THE LONG WATERS	21
BUTTERNUTS			
THE PLACE WHERE BUTTERNUTS ARE FOUND.	14	COMING OF COLD	11
BUTTES			
IN THE COUNTRY OF FEW LAKES, IN THE TALL BUFFALO GRASS AT THE BASE OF THE CLAY BUTTES,	189	THE LONGING	53
THE ARROYO CRACKING THE ROAD, THE WIND-BITTEN BUTTES, THE CANYONS,	193	JOURNY INTERIOR	7
BUZZ			
OR MAKE THE DUST BUZZ WITH A LIGHT SPRAY,	42	OLD FLORIST	7
THE LONELY BUZZ BEHIND MY MIDNIGHT EYES;--	248	THE TREE, BIRD	16
BUZZING			
ITS ALMOST-INVISIBLE WINGS, BUZZING, HITTING THE LOOSE LEAVES INTERMITTENTLY--	234	ALL MORNING	32
KEEPS BUZZING AT THE SILL. WHICH I IS I?	239	IN A DARK TIME	21
BY (142)			

		PAGE	TITLE	LINE
C				
THOUGH HE HEAR A NOTE HIGHER THAN C	....	196	THE LONG WATERS	6
CABBAGE				
SOLACE OF KISSES AND COOKIES AND CABBAGE,	....	48	LAST WORDS	1
ARE THE ENTRAILS CLEAR, IMMACULATE CABBAGE?	....	89	UNFOLD! UNFOLD!	19
CABBAGE-BUTTERFLY				
A WHITE CABBAGE-BUTTERFLY DRIFTS IN,	....	226	THE LIZARD	20
CABBAGES				
MOVING SERENELY AMONG THE LEEKS AND CABBAGES,		223	ELEGY (2)	20
CADENCE				
I TAKE THIS CADENCE FROM A MAN NAMED YEATS;	....	105	SIR JOHN DAVIES	19
CADGED				
SO CAGED AND CADGED, SO CLOSE WITHIN	....	24	BEFORE STUDY	3
CAGE				
THE SPIRIT CRYING IN A CAGE	....	22	SILENCE	11
EVERYTHING'S CLOSER. IS THIS A CAGE?	....	77	BRING THE DAY!	17
LUCK! LUCK! THAT'S WHAT I CARE FOR IN A CAGE		273	SUPPR W LINDSAY	2
CAGED				
SO CAGED AND CADGED, SO CLOSE WITHIN		24	BEFORE STUDY	3
A CAGED BEAR RARELY DOES THE SAME THING TWICE	....	105	SIR JOHN DAVIES	10
CAKE				
DOWN A STEEP HILLSIDE ON A CAKE OF ICE,--	....	105	SIR JOHN DAVIES	8
CAKED				
WITH A PALM CAKED HARD BY DIRT,	....	45	MY PAPA'S WALTZ	14
CALIFORNIA				
WITH TOWHEES, FINCHES, CHICKADEES, CALIFORNIA QUAIL, WOOD DOVES,	....	235	ALL MORNING	40
CALL				
SHALL I CALL THE FLOWERS?	....	61	THE LONG ALLEY	65
CALL OFF THE DOGS, MY PAWS ARE GONE.	....	61	THE LONG ALLEY	85
THAT AIR AND SHINE: AND THE FLICKER'S LOUD SUMMER CALL:		66	SHAPE OF FIRE	70
BUT SHOULD YOU CALL HIS MANNER SMUG,	....	116	THE SLOTH	8
WOULD BLAKE CALL YOU HOLY?	....	151	SLUG	29
FAR AWAY, CLOSE-AT-HAND, HIS CALL FLOATING OVER THE ON-COMING TRAFFIC,	....	234	ALL MORNING	3
THERE'S LITTLE LEFT I CARE TO CALL MY OWN.	....	244	INFIRMITY	8
CALLED				
DO YOU SEE ANY SIGN OR SEMBLANCE OF THAT THING CALLED "HOPE"?"	....	27	CLAIRVOY WIDOW	18
RAIN SWEETENED THE CAVE AND THE DOVE STILL CALLED;		66	SHAPE OF FIRE	75
--AND SO LIKE MY POEM CALLED POEM.	....	113	TO A LADY ED	4
--AND RECITE HIM MY POEM CALLED POEM.		113	TO A LADY ED	8
--OF ACTING MY POEM CALLED POEM.	....	113	TO A LADY ED	12
--AS I DANCE TO MY POEM CALLED POEM.	....	113	TO A LADY ED	16
A SHAPE CALLED UP OUT OF MY NATURAL MIND;	....	241	THE SEQUEL	10
A NESTLING SIGHED--I CALLED THAT NESTLING MINE;		241	THE SEQUEL	12
THAT SOME HAVE CALLED SWAN CREEK;	....	267	SAGINAW SONG	8
WAS CALLED THE GOLDEN RHULE,--		267	SAGINAW SONG	28
"WHO CALLED ME POET OF THE COLLEGE YELL?	....	274	SUPPR W LINDSAY	40
CALLERS				
I HEAR THE OWLS, THE SOFT CALLERS, COMING DOWN FROM THE HEMLOCKS.	....	93	I CRY, LOVE!	40
CALLING				
A SINGLE BIRD CALLING AND CALLING;	....	160	FIRST MEDITATN	90
A SINGLE BIRD CALLING AND CALLING;	....	160	FIRST MEDITATN	90
HE COMES CALLING WITHOUT WIPING HIS SHOES!	....	183	THE WAGTAIL	8
A SMALL VOICE CALLING FROM A DRIFTING CLOUD.	....	248	THE TREE, BIRD	4
CALLS				
A CRACKED POD CALLS.	....	64	SHAPE OF FIRE	6
THE DEPTH CALLS TO THE HEIGHT	....	97	O, THOU OPENING	9
ALL WHO REMEMBER, DOUBT. WHO CALLS THAT STRANGE?	....	120	THE DREAM	21
THE DREAM'S AN INSTANT THAT CALLS UP HER FACE.	....	131	SENTENTIOUS MAN	11
CALM				
SHE SAILED UNTIL THE CALM MORNING,	....	41	BIG WIND	32
I NEED A POOL; I NEED A PUDDLE'S CALM.	....	171	WHAT TELL BONES	21
IN THE LILAC CHANGE, THE WHITE REPTILIAN CALM,		205	THE ROSE	107
AND I EMBRACE THIS CALM--	....	221	THE ABYSS	81
TO YOU ARBUTUS CALM, MYSTERIOUS AS A STONE?	....	261	THE CHANGELING	29
CAME				
UNTIL WE CAME TO A RIVER.	....	6	THE PREMONITION	6
THE RAIN STAYED IN ITS CLOUD; FULL DARK CAME NEAR;	....	6	INTERLUDE	9
I CAME WHERE THE RIVER	....	51	THE WAKING (1)	21
NOT EVEN THE MINNOWS CAME.	....	53	THE LOST SON	15

	PAGE	TITLE	LINE
CAME (CONTINUED)			
THE LIGHT IN THE MORNING CAME SLOWLY OVER THE WHITE	57	THE LOST SON	135
THEN CAME STEAM.	57	THE LOST SON	139
CAME TO LAKES; CAME TO DEAD WATER,	62	FIELD OF LIGHT	1
CAME TO LAKES; CAME TO DEAD WATER,	62	FIELD OF LIGHT	1
A SIGH CAME FAR.	63	FIELD OF LIGHT	28
SOME MORNING THING CAME, BEATING ITS WINGS.	63	FIELD OF LIGHT	35
UP OVER A VIADUCT I CAME, TO THE SNAKES AND STICKS OF ANOTHER WINTER,	65	SHAPE OF FIRE	37
I CAME ACROSS A TIME,	71	WHERE KNOCK IS	13
DARK CAME EARLY.	73	WHERE KNOCK IS	67
THE EVENING CAME	74	WHERE KNOCK IS	82
SOMETHING CAME BY ME,	77	BRING THE DAY!	14
THE WIND CAME AT MY BACK;	87	PRAISE TO END!	52
THE SUN CAME OUT;	87	PRAISE TO END!	55
BY SNAILS, BY LEAPS OF FROG, I CAME HERE, SPIRIT.	89	UNFOLD! UNFOLD!	1
SLOW, SLOW AS A FISH SHE CAME.	100	THE VISITANT	10
SHE CAME WITHOUT SOUND,	100	THE VISITANT	15
SHE CAME,	100	THE VISITANT	18
THAT CAME TO BE THE BEARS AND YEATS WOULD KNOW.	105	SIR JOHN DAVIES	24
A LADY CAME TO A BEAR BY A STREAM.	117	LADY AND BEAR	1
SHE CAME TOWARD ME IN THE FLOWING AIR,	119	THE DREAM	9
THE DEER CAME DOWN, OUT OF THE DAPPLED WOOD.	120	THE DREAM	20
I CAME TO LOVE, I CAME INTO MY OWN.	120	THE DREAM	32
I CAME TO LOVE, I CAME INTO MY OWN.	120	THE DREAM	32
I CRIED, AND THE BIRDS CAME DOWN	123	WORDS FOR WIND	15
AND TREES CAME CLOSER WITH A DENSER SHADE.	133	THE PURE FURY	21
I CAME TO A GREAT DOOR,	145	THE BEAST	1
THE GREY SHEEP CAME. I RAN,	147	THE EXORCISM	1
THE SCENT OF THE HALF-OPENED BUDS CAME UP OVER ME.	162	I'M HERE	49
WHAT CAME TO ME VAGUELY IS NOW CLEAR,	173	WHAT TELL BONES	97
THEN A REAL CAT CAME WITH A MOUTH SO WIDE,	177	KITTY-CAT BIRD	14
THE SHAPE THAT CAME FROM MY SLEEP, WEEPING:	198	THE LONG WATERS	68
I, WHO CAME BACK FROM THE DEPTHS LAUGHING TOO LOUDLY,	198	THE LONG WATERS	73
AMONG THE HALF-DEAD TREES, I CAME UPON THE TRUE EASE OF MYSELF,	205	THE ROSE	99
THE CURLEW'S SLOW NIGHT SONG CAME ON THE WATER.	216	THE SHY MAN	9
SUDDENLY THEY CAME FLYING, LIKE A LONG SCARF OF SMOKE,	232	THE THING	1
AND CAME TO A DARK RAVINE,	238	THE MOMENT	2
BEING, WE CAME TO BE	238	THE TRANCED	23
A WIND CAME CLOSE, LIKE A SHY ANIMAL.	241	THE SEQUEL	22
BUT NO WIND CAME.	247	I WAITED	2
SLOWLY I CAME BACK TO THE DUSTY ROAD;	247	I WAITED	15
AND ALL THE WINDS CAME TOWARD ME. I WAS GLAD.	247	I WAITED	23
HE RODE ALL NIGHT, AND CAME	263	FOLLIES OF ADAM	32
THE LARGEST CONTRIBUTIONS CAME	267	SAGINAW SONG	35
MY THIRST CAME ON, AND I HAD TO DRINK.	269	GOB MUSIC	31
CAN (89)			
CANCEL			
AND THE GREAT LEAVES CANCEL THEIR STEMS;	259	SONG (3)	50
CANDID			
THE ANIMAL'S CANDID GAZE, A SHADE LESS THAN FEATHERS, LIGHT'S BROKEN	98	O, THOU OPENING	22
CANDOR			
LACKING THE CANDOR OF DOGS, I KISS THE DEPARTING AIR;	86	PRAISE TO END!	26
CANKER			
THERE'S CANKER AT THE ROOT, YOUR SEED	4	FEUD	9
CANNAS			
GREAT CANNAS OR DELICATE CYCLAMEN TIPS,--	38	FORCING HOUSE	4
CANNAS SHINY AS SLAG,	43	FLOWER DUMP	1
CANNON			
A CANNON CRACK ANNOUNCE AN EARLY THAW.	11	LIGHT BRIGHTER	4
CANNOT			
I CANNOT PUT MY GLANCE UPON THEM TIGHT.	8	THE SIGNALS	8
THE THINGS THE EYE OR HAND CANNOT POSSESS.	8	THE SIGNALS	10
LIP, BREAST AND THIGH CANNOT POSSESS	8	PRAYER	17
COMPRESSION CANNOT BREAK	9	THE ADAMANT	9
THOUGH IT ALL HAPPENED BEFORE, I CANNOT GROW BITTER:	24	VERNAL SENTIMNT	7
WE CANNOT TRACE THE ERROR DOWN.	30	THE RECKONING	8
FOR WHOM WERE YOU MADE, SWEETNESS I CANNOT TOUCH?	59	THE LONG ALLEY	27
THE EDGE CANNOT EAT THE CENTER.	66	SHAPE OF FIRE	57
FELICITY I CANNOT HOARD.	88	PRAISE TO END!	83
SKIN, A THING YOU CANNOT SAY TO WHISPER AND EQUAL A WOUND?	98	O, THOU OPENING	24

	PAGE	TITLE	LINE
CANNOT (CONTINUED)			
THE SIDES OF WET STONES CANNOT CONSOLE ME,	102	ELEGY FOR JANE	16
I FEEL MY FATE IN WHAT I CANNOT FEAR.	108	THE WAKING (2)	2
THEIR BODIES CANNOT LIE:	121	ALL EARTH, AIR	17
I CANNOT ANSWER BACK;	123	WORDS FOR WIND	29
A MOUTH I CANNOT LEAVE.	137	LOVE'S PROGRESS	4
THE BULKS CANNOT HIDE US, OR THE BLEAK SHEDS OF OUR DESOLATION,	166	HER BECOMING	39
FOR THE SLEEK CAPTAINS OF INTUITION CANNOT REACH THEM;	169	FOURTH MEDITATN	52
WHETHER THE BEES HAVE THOUGHTS, WE CANNOT SAY,	196	THE LONG WATERS	1
THE WILD STREAM, THE SEA ITSELF CANNOT CONTAIN ME:	209	HER LONGING	12
TIME CANNOT OVERWHELM.	240	IN EVEING AIR	9
AND TELL MYSELF MY IMAGE CANNOT DIE.	244	INFIRMITY	4
WITHIN THIS TUB BUT CANNOT DROWN.	256	IN HYDROTHERAPY	2
SOME CANNOT PRAISE HIM: I AM ONE OF THOSE.	264	THREE EPIGRAMS	6
CANS			
WELTER OF TIN CANS, PAILS, OLD BIRD NESTS, A CHILD'S SHOE RIDING A LOG,	191	AT OYSTER RIVER	54
AMONG THE TIN CANS, TIRES, RUSTED PIPES, BROKEN MACHINERY,--	199	THE FAR FIELD	17
CANT			
TO THE CANT AND FURY OF	31	LULL	17
CAN'T			
CAN YOU NAME IT? I CAN'T NAME IT.	59	THE LONG ALLEY	17
I CAN'T LAUGH AT A PROCESSION OF DOGS.	64	SHAPE OF FIRE	13
A GHOST CAN'T WHISTLE.	73	WHERE KNOCK IS	50
I CAN'T TASTE MY MOTHER.	74	I NEED, I NEED	2
A SNEEZE CAN'T SLEEP.	74	I NEED, I NEED	5
I CAN'T MARRY THE DIRT.	77	BRING THE DAY!	20
I CAN'T CATCH A BUSH.	77	BRING THE DAY!	24
BUT I CAN'T GO LEAPING ALONE.	84	O LULL ME, LULL	32
MY DEAREST DUST, I CAN'T STAY HERE.	86	PRAISE TO END!	44
THIS SALT CAN'T WARM A STONE.	86	PRAISE TO END!	49
I CAN'T CRAWL BACK THROUGH THOSE VEINS,	89	UNFOLD! UNFOLD!	3
THIS FAT CAN'T LAUGH.	91	UNFOLD! UNFOLD!	57
SUCH A SWEET NOISE: I CAN'T SLEEP FOR IT.	92	I CRY, LOVE!	19
I CAN'T LAUGH FROM A CRATER OF BURNING PITCH,	166	HER BECOMING	36
HE CLOSELY RESEMBLES--BUT I CAN'T TELL YOU!	180	THE GNU	2
"THE ABYSS YOU CAN'T MISS:	219	THE ABYSS	6
"I'M MAIMED; I CAN'T FLY;	249	THE RESTORED	9
I CAN'T BURY THE BONE OF THIS MISERY LIKE A FASTIDIOUS DOG.	261	THE CHANGELING	31
A PICTURE WINDOW'S ONE YOU CAN'T	267	SAGINAW SONG	23
MAYBE IT'S WHITMAN'S SPIDER, I CAN'T TELL,	273	SUPPR W LINDSAY	28
BUT WHAT WE ATE I CAN'T REMEMBER QUITE:	274	SUPPR W LINDSAY	31
CANYONS			
THE ARROYO CRACKING THE ROAD, THE WIND-BITTEN BUTTES, THE CANYONS,	193	JOURNY INTERIOR	7
CAP			
THE ICE CAP AT MY RIGID NECK	256	IN HYDROTHERAPY	3
CAPE			
CAPE MAY, BLACKBURNIAN, CERULEAN,--	199	THE FAR FIELD	30
CAPER			
ASK ALL THE MICE WHO CAPER IN THE STRAW--	167	HER BECOMING	86
CAPTAINS			
FOR THE SLEEK CAPTAINS OF INTUITION CANNOT REACH THEM;	169	FOURTH MEDITATN	52
CAR			
OR SEND OFF A CAR WITH VAGUE LIFTS OF A HAND.	47	DOUBLE FEATURE	8
THE TRICK WAS TO THROW THE CAR SIDEWAYS AND CHARGE OVER THE HILL, FULL OF THE THROTTLE.	193	JOURNY INTERIOR	21
THE WIND VEERING THE CAR SLIGHTLY TO THE RIGHT,	194	JOURNY INTERIOR	43
WHERE THE CAR STALLS,	199	THE FAR FIELD	10
FLAPPING AWAY HEAVILY WHEN A CAR BLASTS TOO CLOSE,	234	ALL MORNING	7
CARD			
THE LIBRARY USED AS A CARD ROOM INSTEAD	32	SALE	11
CARDPLAYERS			
THE LAST WATCHER INDOORS, MOVING THE CARDPLAYERS CLOSER	230	THE STORM	26
CARDS			
TO THEIR CARDS, THEIR ANISETTE.	230	THE STORM	27
I TOOK THE PLEDGE CARDS ON MY BIKE;	267	SAGINAW SONG	31
CARE			
I DON'T CARE EITHER.	72	WHERE KNOCK IS	26
I DON'T CARE EITHER.	72	WHERE KNOCK IS	30
DIDDLE WE CARE	74	I NEED, I NEED	6
A COW'S A CARE AND WHO'S A COO?--	86	PRAISE TO END!	33

	PAGE	TITLE	LINE
CARE (CONTINUED)			
I CARE FOR A CAT'S CRY AND THE HUGS, LIVE AS WATER.	92	I CRY, LOVE!	16
IT IS HARD TO CARE ABOUT CORNERS,	104	OLD LADY'S WRDS	59
LOVE, LOVE, A LILY'S MY CARE,	123	WORDS FOR WIND	1
WHAT TIME'S MY HEART? I CARE.	125	WORDS FOR WIND	75
WHAT'S BECOME OF CARE? THIS LAKE BREATHES LIKE A ROSE.	170	FOURTH MEDITATN	76
O, BUT I SEEK AND CARE!	172	WHAT TELL BONES	61
WAKING'S MY CARE--	240	IN EVEING AIR	5
THERE'S LITTLE LEFT I CARE TO CALL MY OWN.	244	INFIRMITY	8
APPLES! HAVE A CARE!	261	THE CHANGELING	43
LUCK! LUCK! THAT'S WHAT I CARE FOR IN A CAGE	273	SUPPR W LINDSAY	2
CARED			
HE CARED SO MUCH FOR THE SPORT,	263	FOLLIES OF ADAM	31
CAREENING			
A GREAT WOODEN SLEIGH CAREENING BEHIND THEM,	158	FIRST MEDITATN	54
CAREER			
"I'M SERIOUS ABOUT MY SINGING CAREER!"	115	THE SERPENT	24
CAREFULLY			
I STEPPED CAREFULLY, LIKE A NEW-SHOD HORSE,	166	HER BECOMING	46
CARELESS			
WHO, CARELESS, SLIPS	65	SHAPE OF. FIRE	45
I WAS CARELESS IN GROWING.	104	OLD LADY'S WRDS	48
I KNOW HER CARELESS WAYS!--	130	THE OTHER	21
LEWD, TINY, CARELESS LIVES	147	THE EXORCISM	16
BEATS SLOWER IN MY CARELESS SOLITUDE.	155	THE DYING MAN	68
CARELESSNESS			
FOR CARELESSNESS CAN SMOTHER	7	ORDERS FOR DAY	3
CARES			
--WHO CARES? THE OLD OWL?	89	UNFOLD! UNFOLD!	15
CARES ABOUT THE DANCE OF DEAD UNDERWEAR, OR THE SAD WALTZ OF PAPER	98	O, THOU OPENING	26
THIS JOY OUTLEAPS THE DOG. WHO CARES? WHO CARES?	106	SIR JOHN DAVIES	44
THIS JOY OUTLEAPS THE DOG. WHO CARES? WHO CARES?	106	SIR JOHN DAVIES	44
CARESS			
I DARE CARESS THE STONES, THE FIELD MY FRIEND;	167	HER BECOMING	94
FOR HIM TO KISS OR CARESS	209	HER RETICENCE	4
CARESSES			
CARESSES OF THE HAND AND EYE.	19	EPIDERM MACABRE	8
ACCEPT CARESSES IN THE DARK;	23	AMOROUS LADY	2
CARESSING			
CLEANING AND CARESSING,	50	THE MINIMAL	10
CARGO			
CARRYING HER FULL CARGO OF ROSES.	41	BIG WIND	33
CARIBBEAN			
EXPLODES LIKE A ROSE, OR THRUSTS WINGS OVER THE CARIBBEAN.	159	FIRST MEDITATN	77
CARNAL			
FOR HEARKENING TO CARNAL EVILS	8	PRAYER	7
INCARNADINE AND CARNAL GHOST.	19	EPIDERM MACABRE	16
CARNATIONS			
CARNATIONS	43	CARNATIONS	T
CARNATIONS, VERBENAS, COSMOS,	43	FLOWER DUMP	4
CARNATIONS, RED	44	FRAU BAUMAN	8
FLATTENING THE LIMBER CARNATIONS.	231	THE STORM	33
CAROLINA			
THE PASSENGER PIGEON, THE GREAT AUK, THE CAROLINA PARAQUET,	235	ALL MORNING	44
CARP			
WHAT'S WEATHER TO ME? EVEN CARP DIE IN THIS RIVER.	164	I'M HERE	90
CARPET			
THE DINING ROOM CARPET DYED BRIGHTER THAN BLOOD,	32	SALE	13
ON THE FADED CARPET, THE STALE	228	THE GERANIUM	12
CARPETS			
BUT SOMETHING ALWAYS WENT OUT OF ME WHEN I DUG LOOSE THOSE CARPETS	40	MOSS-GATHERING	7
CARRIAGES			
THE CARRIAGES REEKING WITH VARNISH AND STALE PERFUME.	22	ROAD TO WDLAWN	4
CARRIED			
THAT I CARRIED SO LONG	211	SONG (1)	3
CARRION			
SMELLED THE CARRION AT ENTRANCES,	48	JUDGE NOT	8
CARROTS			
HE LIVES ON CARROTS, LEEKS AND HAY;	182	THE HIPPO	3
CARRYING			
CARRYING HER FULL CARGO OF ROSES.	41	BIG WIND	33

		PAGE	TITLE	LINE
CARS				
THE PAVEMENT SMOKES WHEN TWO CARS MEET	....	33	HIGHWAY: MICH	16
CARTOON-MOUSE				
HIS ABSURD WHISKERS STICKING OUT LIKE A CARTOON-MOUSE,	...	227	MEADOW MOUSE	7
CARVED				
A THING CARVED OF STONE OR WOOD, WITH THE DULL IRIDESCENCE				
OF LONG-POLISHED WOOD,	....	234	ALL MORNING	11
CASCADE				
AND THAT WRIST-THICK CASCADE TUMBLING FROM A CLEFT ROCK,		191	AT OYSTER RIVER	44
CASE				
IS IT A CASE OF JUST PICK AND CHOOSE?	....	183	THE WAGTAIL	2
CASEMENT				
NOW, AS THE CASEMENT BLURS..	....	154	THE DYING MAN	30
CAST				
MY VEINS ARE RUNNING NOWHERE. DO THE BONES CAST OUT THEIR				
FIRE?	....	56	THE LOST SON	101
OH, WHEN SHE WAS SAD, SHE CAST HERSELF DOWN INTO SUCH A				
PURE DEPTH,	....	102	ELEGY FOR JANE	10
THERE WAS A BODY, AND IT CAST A SPELL,--	....	106	SIR JOHN DAVIES	61
I SWEAR SHE CAST A SHADOW WHITE AS STONE.	....	127	I KNEW A WOMAN	25
AND THE IVY-BRANCH, CAST TO THE GROUND, PUTS DOWN ROOTS				
INTO THE SAWDUST,	....	197	THE LONG WATERS	34
CASTOREUM				
WORSE THAN CASTOREUM OF MINK OR WEASELS,	....	187	THE LONGING	4
CASTRATI				
BEHOLD THE CRITIC, PITCHED LIKE THE CASTRATI,	....	264	THREE EPIGRAMS	1
CASUAL				
A CASUAL MAN, I KEEP MY CASUAL WORD,	....	140	THE SWAN	10
A CASUAL MAN, I KEEP MY CASUAL WORD,	....	140	THE SWAN	10
A LATE ROSE RAVAGES THE CASUAL EYE,	....	149	IN LATE SUMMER	17
CAT				
WHEN FROM UNDER THE BARN THE CAT BRINGS A SIMILAR LITTER,--		24	VERNAL SENTIMNT	5
THAT BLOSSOMED IN SOOT; A BLACK CAT LICKING ITS PAW;	.....	29	THE REMINDER	2
TAKE THE SKIN OF A CAT	....	55	THE LOST SON	54
AND YOU, CAT AFTER GREAT MILK AND VASTY FISHES,	....	79	GIVE WAY, GATES	9
CAN A CAT MILK A HEN?	....	81	SENSIBILITY! LA	15
BY THE LIFTING OF THE TAIL OF A NEIGHBOR'S CAT,	....	82	SENSIBILITY! LA	35
YOUR FATHER TOSSED A CAT IN AIR,	....	86	PRAISE TO END!	36
MINCING LIKE A CAT.	....	87	PRAISE TO END!	54
A CAT GOES WIDER.	....	92	I CRY, LOVE!	9
A MAN RICH AS A CAT.	....	121	ALL EARTH, AIR	7
A CAT IN THE FORK OF A TREE,	....	121	ALL EARTH, AIR	8
A MAN CHASING A CAT,	....	171	WHAT TELL BONES	31
YOU MEW LIKE A CAT, YOU GRATE LIKE A JAY:	....	177	KITTY-CAT BIRD	9
THEN A REAL CAT CAME WITH A MOUTH SO WIDE,	....	177	KITTY-CAT BIRD	14
THE CAT RUNS FOR A ROOF	....	180	GOO-GIRL	11
SHE CROONS, LIKE A CAT TO ITS CLAWS;	....	208	HER WORDS	2
KILLED EVERY CAT THAT NEARED THEIR PHEASANT RUNS;	....	224	OTTO	28
A CAT RUNS FROM THE WIND AS WE DO,	....	230	THE STORM	19
WHEN OUR SPAYED FEMALE CAT YAWNS AND STRETCHES OUT IN THE				
SUNSHINE--	....	234	ALL MORNING	23
I GIVE THE CAT A KICK.	....	269	GOB MUSIC	6
CATALOGUES				
BE WITH ME, WHITMAN, MAKER OF CATALOGUES:	....	220	THE ABYSS	29
CATBIRD				
THE WREN, THE CATBIRD.	....	162	I'M HERE	34
THE MIMETIC CHORTLING OF THE CATBIRD	....	204	THE ROSE	63
CAT-BIRD				
HAUNT OF THE CAT-BIRD, NESTING-PLACE OF THE FIELD-MOUSE,		199	THE FAR FIELD	15
CATCH				
I CAN'T CATCH A BUSH.	....	77	BRING THE DAY!	24
SHAKING OUT MY CATCH IN THE MORNING SUNLIGHT,	....	209	HER LONGING	15
CATCHER				
HERO OF PHANTASIES AND CATCHER OF CHILLS,	....	24	POETASTER	1
CATCHING				
ITS WINGS CATCHING A LAST GLINT OF THE REFLECTED SUNLIGHT.		190	AT OYSTER RIVER	23
CATERPILLAR				
EVEN THE CATERPILLAR I CAN LOVE, AND THE VARIOUS VERMIN.		151	SLUG	27
A FURRED CATERPILLAR CRAWLS DOWN A STRING.	....	220	THE ABYSS	35
CAT-LIKE				
THOSE CAT-LIKE IMMACULATE CREATURES	....	169	FOURTH MEDITATN	48
CAT-MEWING				
THEIR CAT-MEWING OVER,	....	190	AT OYSTER RIVER	9

	PAGE	TITLE	LINE
CATS			
ARE THE RATS DANCING? THE CATS ARE.	79	GIVE WAY, GATES	8
LAY LIKE THE CATS DO	87	PRAISE TO END!	61
CONDUCTING HIS LONG WARS WITH THE NEIGHBORHOOD CATS,	234	ALL MORNING	16
IS THIS FARE FOR THE CATS AND DOGS?	261	THE CHANGELING	35
CAT'S			
TO THE CAT'S WISH?	60	THE LONG ALLEY	58
I CARE FOR A CAT'S CRY AND THE HUGS, LIVE AS WATER.	92	I CRY, LOVE!	16
CAT-TAILS			
AND MIST LIFTING OUT OF THE BROWN CAT-TAILS;	67	SHAPE OF FIRE	87
CATTLE			
THE FLOATING HAWKS, THE JACKRABBITS, THE GRAZING CATTLE--	194	JOURNY INTERIOR	38
CAUGHT			
FISHING, I CAUGHT MYSELF BEHIND THE EARS.	89	UNFOLD! UNFOLD!	23
CAUGHT IN THE DYING LIGHT,	154	THE DYING MAN	16
AND MY DRESS CAUGHT ON ROSE-BRIER.	162	I'M HERE	47
A BIT OF WATER CAUGHT IN A WRINKLED CREVICE,	168	FOURTH MEDITATN	8
AND THEN CAUGHT COLD AND UP AND DIED?	178	THE CEILING	2
AND THE TOM-CAT, CAUGHT NEAR THE PHEASANT-RUN,	199	THE FAR FIELD	21
I SUFFERED FOR BIRDS, FOR YOUNG RABBITS CAUGHT IN THE MOWER,	199	THE FAR FIELD	24
TILL I CAUGHT HIM UP BY THE TAIL AND BROUGHT HIM IN,	227	MEADOW MOUSE	4
CAUSE			
WE HUNT THE CAUSE OF RUIN, ADD,	30	THE RECKONING	5
THE CAUSE OF GOD IN ME--HAS IT GONE?	172	WHAT TELL BONES	51
CAUSED			
I SAW A SIGHT THAT CAUSED ME PAIN,	114	DINKY	10
CAVE			
MOTHER, MOTHER, STIR FROM YOUR CAVE OF SORROW.	64	SHAPE OF FIRE	16
RAIN SWEETENED THE CAVE AND THE DOVE STILL CALLED;	66	SHAPE OF FIRE	75
MY SWEETHEART'S STILL IN HER CAVE.	82	SENSIBILITY! LA	28
MY DESIRE'S A WIND TRAPPED IN A CAVE.	172	WHAT TELL BONES	45
THAT PLACE AMONG THE ROCKS--IS IT A CAVE,	239	IN A DARK TIME	11
CAVES			
BEETLES IN CAVES, NEWTS, STONE-DEAF FISHES,	50	THE MINIMAL	3
HATH THE RAIN A FATHER? ALL THE CAVES ARE ICE. ONLY THE SNOW'S HERE.	56	THE LOST SON	84
MY GATES ARE ALL CAVES.	59	THE LONG ALLEY	20
THE SEA BARKED IN ITS CAVES.	258	SONG (3)	16
CAVE'S			
BY THE CAVE'S DOOR,	55	THE LOST SON	72
CAVING-IN			
BEFORE THE CAVING-IN OF ALL THAT IS;	149	IN LATE SUMMER	14
CAW			
THE LIGHT COMES BRIGHTER FROM THE EAST; THE CAW	11	LIGHT BRIGHTER	1
CEDAR			
WITH WRENS, SPARROWS, JUNCOS, CEDAR WAXWINGS, FLICKERS,	235	ALL MORNING	41
CEDARS			
THERE WERE CLOUDS MAKING A ROUT OF SHAPES CROSSING A WINDBREAK OF CEDARS,	63	FIELD OF LIGHT	48
CEILING			
THE CEILING	178	THE CEILING	T
SUPPOSE THE CEILING WENT OUTSIDE	178	THE CEILING	1
LONG GAZING AT THE CEILING WILL	257	SANITARIUM	5
CEILING'S			
TO FIND OUT HOW THE CEILING'S FEELING.	178	THE CEILING	6
CELESTIAL			
I SEE YOU IN SOME CELESTIAL SUPERMARKET,	223	ELEGY (2)	19
CELL			
THE HIVE THAT HUMMED IN EVERY CELL	4	DEATH PIECE	3
CELLAR			
ROOT CELLAR	38	ROOT CELLAR	T
NOTHING WOULD SLEEP IN THAT CELLAR, DANK AS A DITCH,	38	ROOT CELLAR	1
WENT DOWN CELLAR,	74	I NEED, I NEED	8
US, UNDER THE CHAIR-RUNGS, TOWARD THE CELLAR DOOR.	273	SUPPR W LINDSAY	14
CELLS			
THE SMALL CELLS BULGE;	37	CUTTINGS	4
CEMENT			
AND THE MEN BENEATH THEM WHEELING IN DIRT TO THE CEMENT BENCHES,	158	FIRST MEDITATN	45
AND MY FATHER STANDING ASTRIDE THE CEMENT BENCHES,	203	THE ROSE	53
CEMETERY			
AND LIFT UP A PATCH, DARK-GREEN, THE KIND FOR LINING CEMETERY BASKETS,	40	MOSS-GATHERING	2

	PAGE	TITLE	LINE
CEMETERY (CONTINUED)			
THE CEMETERY WITH TWO SCRUBBY TREES IN THE MIDDLE OF THE PRAIRIE.	194	JOURNY INTERIOR	35
CENSURE			
REPLY TO CENSURE	20	REPL TO CENSURE	T
CENTAUR			
THE CENTAUR AND THE SIBYL ROMP AND SING	135	THE RENEWAL	2
THE CENTAUR	264	THREE EPIGRAMS	ST
THE CENTAUR DOES NOT NEED A HORSE;	264	THREE EPIGRAMS	11
CENTER			
A CENTER SO CONGEALED;	9	THE ADAMANT	10
WHO RAN UP AND DOWN THE BIG CENTER STAIRS	32	SALE	2
THE EDGE CANNOT EAT THE CENTER.	66	SHAPE OF FIRE	57
A BIRD SANG FROM THE CENTER OF A TREE;	119	THE DREAM	15
IN THE DEEP CENTER OF THE VOICE AND FIRE.	132	SENTENTIOUS MAN	34
DOWN BY THE MUCK SHRINKING TO THE ALKALINE CENTER.	197	THE LONG WATERS	43
I HAVE COME TO A STILL, BUT NOT A DEEP CENTER,	201	THE FAR FIELD	71
STILL AS THE WIND'S CENTER,	258	SONG (3)	29
CENTERED			
I AM TOO CENTERED ON THIS SPOT.	24	BEFORE STUDY	2
CENTRAL			
AROUND A CENTRAL GRAIN	18	GENESIS	11
DENSE IN THE CENTRAL STONE.	50	THE CYCLE	11
A BLAZE OF BEING ON A CENTRAL STEM.	149	IN LATE SUMMER	18
A TREE ARISES ON A CENTRAL PLAIN--	150	IN LATE SUMMER	25
CENTRIPETAL			
ACTIVITY CENTRIPETAL.	24	BEFORE STUDY	10
CERTAIN			
I LIVE, ALIVE AND CERTAIN AS A BULL;	140	THE SWAN	9
EXISTENCE MOVES TOWARD A CERTAIN END--	149	IN LATE SUMMER	21
CERTAINTY			
AND GRIEVE INTO THE CERTAINTY OF LOVE.	243	THE MOTION	6
CERTITUDE			
UNTIL THEY REACH THIS FINAL CERTITUDE,	243	THE MOTION	16
CERULEAN			
THE SHY CERULEAN BIRD;	128	THE VOICE	14
THE CERULEAN, HIGH IN THE ELM,	159	FIRST MEDITATN	84
CAPE MAY, BLACKBURNIAN, CERULEAN,--	199	THE FAR FIELD	30
CESSATION			
AND WITH WATER: THE WAVES COMING FORWARD, WITHOUT CESSATION,	191	AT OYSTER RIVER	31
CHAINS			
OUT THROUGH THE VELVETY CHAINS TO THE COOL AIR OF NIGHT.	47	DOUBLE FEATURE	4
CHAIR			
THE CHAIR OF HONOR, WITH A MISSING RUNG."	21	THE AUCTION	8
THE CHAIR	178	THE CHAIR	T
A FUNNY THING ABOUT A CHAIR:	178	THE CHAIR	1
TO KNOW A CHAIR IS REALLY IT,	178	THE CHAIR	3
CLEAR UNDER THE CHAIR;	180	GOO-GIRL	12
HE LEFT HIS PANTS UPON A CHAIR:	264	THREE EPIGRAMS	7
AND LINDSAY HEAVED HIMSELF FROM MY OLD CHAIR.	274	SUPPR W LINDSAY	38
CHAIR-RUNGS			
US, UNDER THE CHAIR-RUNGS, TOWARD THE CELLAR DOOR.	273	SUPPR W LINDSAY	14
CHAIRS			
THE WHAT-NOT, THE SETTEE, THE CHIPPENDALE CHAIRS	32	SALE	3
CHALK			
I SHOOK THE SOFTENING CHALK OF MY BONES,	53	THE LOST SON	6
CHANCE			
ONE WAY, A CHANCE TO BE SECURE:	30	THE RECKONING	10
ONLY MY SALT HAS A CHANCE.	91	UNFOLD! UNFOLD!	58
IT IS NO TRICK OF CHANGE OR CHANCE OF LIGHT.	150	IN LATE SUMMER	26
A CHANCE? PERHAPS. BUT THE ROAD WAS PART OF ME, AND ITS DITCHES,	193	JOURNY INTERIOR	23
O, MOTION O, OUR CHANCE IS STILL TO BE!	243	THE MOTION	24
CHANGE			
I BASK IN THE BOWER OF CHANGE;	88	PRAISE TO END!	85
I'LL CHANGE THE IMAGE, AND MY SHOES.	97	O, THOU OPENING	19
A SHAPE OF CHANGE, ENCIRCLED BY ITS FIRE.	119	THE DREAM	10
IN HELL THERE IS NO CHANGE.	139	PLAINT	3
IT IS NO TRICK OF CHANGE OR CHANCE OF LIGHT.	150	IN LATE SUMMER	26
A PRINCE OF SMALL BEGINNINGS, ENDURING THE SLOW STRETCHES OF CHANGE,	170	FOURTH MEDITATN	70
BEGUILE ME, CHANGE. WHAT HAVE I FALLEN FROM?	170	FOURTH MEDITATN	77
WHERE SHADOW CAN CHANGE INTO FLAME,	188	THE LONGING	49

		PAGE	TITLE	LINE
CHANGE (CONTINUED)				
DELIGHTING IN SURFACE CHANGE, THE GLITTER OF LIGHT ON WAVES,		195	JOURNY INTERIOR	67
I KNOW THIS CHANGE:		195	JOURNY INTERIOR	75
I FEEL A WEIGHTLESS CHANGE, A MOVING FORWARD		200	THE FAR FIELD	58
IN THE LILAC CHANGE, THE WHITE REPTILIAN CALM,		205	THE ROSE	107
THE CHANGE FROM DARK TO LIGHT OF THE SLOW MOON,		244	INFIRMITY	22
AND, PRAISING CHANGE AS THE SLOW NIGHT COMES ON,		250	THE RIGHT THING	16
SHIFTING IN SEA CHANGE,		265	HARSH COUNTRY	11
AND IF THE METER NEEDS A CHANGE		269	GOB MUSIC	5
CHANGED				
AND THE LEAVES CHANGED;		62	FIELD OF LIGHT	12
SHE CHANGED ME ICE TO FIRE, AND FIRE TO ICE.		131	SENTENTIOUS MAN	12
BUT MY LEAST MOTION CHANGED INTO A SONG,		132	SENTENTIOUS MAN	23
SHE CHANGED WITH CHANGING LIGHT.		212	LIGHT LISTENED	18
CHANGELESS				
IS IT THE SEA WE WISH? THE SLEEP OF THE CHANGELESS?		165	HER BECOMING	28
CHANGELING				
THE CHANGELING		260	THE CHANGELING	T
CHANGES				
MOTHER OF BLUE AND THE MANY CHANGES OF HAY,		79	GIVE WAY, GATES	14
HOW SLOW THE CHANGES OF A GOLDEN MEAN:		133	THE PURE FURY	12
THE GRASS CHANGES TO STONE.		141	MEMORY	12
THE LOST SELF CHANGES,		201	THE FAR FIELD	82
AS CHANGES SHIMMER IN THE INNER EYE.		244	INFIRMITY	2
THINGS OF HIGH WIT AND CHANGES OF THE MOON.		260	THE CHANGELING	27
CHANGING				
IN THE CHANGING BODY.		168	FOURTH MEDITATN	22
CHANGING WITH EVERY TWIST OF WIND,		196	THE LONG WATERS	10
THE ROAD CHANGING FROM GLAZED TARFACE TO A RUBBLE OF STONE,		199	THE FAR FIELD	8
SHE CHANGED WITH CHANGING LIGHT.		212	LIGHT LISTENED	18
CHANNEL				
AS OF WATER QUICKENING BEFORE A NARROWING CHANNEL		200	THE FAR FIELD	59
CHANTICLEER				
I WOULD BE A CHANTICLEER.		266	FOR STEVENS	12
CHAOS				
THE CHAOS GREW AS HOUR BY HOUR THE LIGHT		6	INTERLUDE	5
WE UNDID CHAOS TO A CURIOUS SOUND:		107	SIR JOHN DAVIES	82
CHAPTER				
--AND CLOSE UP THAT CHAPTER OF KIERKEGAARD.		272	DUET	8
CHAR				
JOHN RANSOM SHOULD BE HERE, AND RENE CHAR;		274	SUPPR W LINDSAY	43
CHARGE				
THE TRICK WAS TO THROW THE CAR SIDEWAYS AND CHARGE OVER THE HILL, FULL OF THE THROTTLE.		193	JOURNY INTERIOR	21
CHARITY				
AND CHARITY DISCOVER		7	ORDERS FOR DAY	19
CHARRED				
TO THE CHARRED EDGE OF THE SEA		196	THE LONG WATERS	14
CHASING				
A MAN CHASING A CAT,		171	WHAT TELL BONES	31
CHASTENED				
CHASTENED.		220	THE ABYSS	49
CHEAP				
A CHEAP CLOCK TICKING IN GHOSTLY CICADA VOICE.		29	THE REMINDER	12
CHECK				
AND CHECK THE PEDANTRY		20	REPL TO CENSURE	3
CHEEK				
THAT WATERY CHEEK		56	THE LOST SON	97
SCRAPING HER CHEEK AGAINST STRAW;		102	ELEGY FOR JANE	12
(I'D HAVE THEM SING IN CHORUS, CHEEK TO CHEEK).		127	I KNEW A WOMAN	7
(I'D HAVE THEM SING IN CHORUS, CHEEK TO CHEEK).		127	I KNEW A WOMAN	7
WITH A CHEEK SOFT AS A HOUND'S EAR.		157	FIRST MEDITATN	17
CHEEKBONES				
HOPE FLUSHED MY CHEEKBONES WITH A SCARLET DISK.		21	THE AUCTION	11
CHEEPING				
AND SMALL MOUTHS, STAY YOUR AIMLESS CHEEPING:		92	I CRY, LOVE!	23
THE APRIL CHEEPING, THE VIREO'S INSISTENCE,		161	I'M HERE	8
CHEESE				
NOW HE'S EATEN HIS THREE KINDS OF CHEESE AND DRUNK FROM HIS BOTTLE-CAP WATERING-TROUGH--		227	MEADOW MOUSE	12
CHERISH				
CHERISH THE EYES THE PROUD INCREDIBLE POISE		5	TO MY SISTER	9
IN THE DIRT AND DISORDER I CHERISH ONE SCRAP OF ILLUSION:		29	THE REMINDER	11

	PAGE	TITLE	LINE
CHERISH (CONTINUED)			
I CHERISH WHAT I HAVE	125	WORDS FOR WIND	76
CHERISHED			
I WAS PURE AS A WORM ON A LEAF; I CHERISHED THE MOLD'S CHILDREN.	89	UNFOLD! UNFOLD!	27
HANDS ACTIVE, EYES CHERISHED;	187	THE LONGING	8
CHERRIES			
RICH ME CHERRIES A FONDLING'S KISS, ...	60	THE LONG ALLEY	43
CHEWS			
THE RUMINANT, REASON, CHEWS A POISONED CUD.	5	PROGNOSIS	8
CHICKADEES			
AND THE WRENS SCOLD, AND THE CHICKADEES FRISK AND FROLIC,	234	ALL MORNING	24
WITH TOWHEES, FINCHES, CHICKADEES, CALIFORNIA QUAIL, WOOD DOVES, ...	235	ALL MORNING	40
CHICKEN-YARD			
AND THE FLICKER DRUMMED FROM HIS DEAD TREE IN THE CHICKEN-YARD.	200	THE FAR FIELD	37
CHILD			
O HE WAS FORTUNE'S CHILD, A FAVORITE SON	28	THE FAVORITE	9
CHILD ON TOP OF A GREENHOUSE	43	CHILD ON GRNHSE	T
STILL AS A CHILD IN ITS FIRST LONELINESS;	67	SHAPE OF FIRE	85
YOU CHILD WITH A BEAST'S HEART, ...	80	GIVE WAY, GATES	38
I ROMPED, LITHE AS A CHILD, DOWN THE SUMMERY STREETS OF MY VEINS, ...	86	PRAISE TO END!	21
A CHILD STARES PAST A FIRE	130	THE OTHER	19
WITH THE SMALL VOICE OF A CHILD, ...	146	THE SONG	26
THE LOOSE AIR SENT ME RUNNING LIKE A CHILD--	155	THE DYING MAN	55
A SPIRIT PLAYS BEFORE ME LIKE A CHILD, ...	165	HER BECOMING	22
A CHILD AT PLAY, A WIND-EXCITED BIRD.	165	HER BECOMING	23
A THIN HARSH SONG. THE DAY DIES IN A CHILD.	171	WHAT TELL BONES	19
THE ETERNAL ONE, THE CHILD, THE SWAYING VINE BRANCH, ...	198	THE LONG WATERS	69
AND HOW THOSE FLOWERHEADS SEEMED TO FLOW TOWARD ME, TO BECKON ME, ONLY A CHILD, OUT OF MYSELF.	203	THE ROSE	55
I'D STAND UPON MY BED, A SLEEPLESS CHILD	225	OTTO	40
MY THUMB OF A CHILD THAT NUZZLED IN MY PALM?--	227	MEADOW MOUSE	22
O WHO WOULD TAKE THE VISION FROM THE CHILD?--	243	THE MOTION	23
CHILD OF THE DARK, HE CAN OUT LEAP THE SUN, ...	250	THE RIGHT THING	10
A CHILD UPON HER BREAST, ...	268	SAGINAW SONG	57
CHILDHOOD			
RECOUNT EACH CHILDHOOD PLEASURE: THE SKIES OF AZURE	5	TO MY SISTER	5
CHILDREN			
THE ROOM THAT THE CHILDREN HAD NEVER BEEN IN, ...	32	SALE	18
WITH MOTHERS, SLEEP-HEAVY CHILDREN, STALE PERFUME, PAST THE MANAGER'S SMILE	47	DOUBLE FEATURE	3
CHILDREN, THEIR BELLIES SWOLLEN LIKE BLOWN-UP PAPER BAGS,	48	JUDGE NOT	2
I WAS PURE AS A WORM ON A LEAF; I CHERISHED THE MOLD'S CHILDREN.	89	UNFOLD! UNFOLD!	27
WE PLAYED WITH DARK AND LIGHT AS CHILDREN SHOULD.	107	SIR JOHN DAVIES	66
THE CHILDREN WAVING;	158	FIRST MEDITATN	52
AND THE LIVES OF THEIR CHILDREN?--	169	FOURTH MEDITATN	43
HAPPINESS LEFT TO DOGS AND CHILDREN--	187	THE LONGING	9
THE CHILDREN DANCING, THE FLOWERS WIDENING.	188	THE LONGING	40
TO A SCURRY OF SMALL DOGS AND A SHRIEK OF CHILDREN, ...	193	JOURNY INTERIOR	26
I RECALL HOW SHE HARRIED THE CHILDREN AWAY ALL THE LATE SUMMER	223	ELEGY (2)	12
WHERE'S THE BRIDGE OF DANCING CHILDREN?	258	SONG (3)	24
WE STRAYED LIKE CHILDREN, ...	265	HARSH COUNTRY	6
CHILD'S			
BEHIND THE CHILD'S ARCHNESS	161	I'M HERE	10
A TWILIGHT WIND, LIGHT AS A CHILD'S BREATH	190	AT OYSTER RIVER	18
WELTER OF TIN CANS, PAILS, OLD BIRD NESTS, A CHILD'S SHOE RIDING A LOG, ...	191	AT OYSTER RIVER	54
THE STERN HIGH, DIPPING LIKE A CHILD'S BOAT IN A POND--	203	THE ROSE	37
THE CHILD'S HAND REACHING INTO THE COILED SMILAX, ...	221	THE ABYSS	65
AND A CHILD'S DIRTY SHIFT BILLOWS UPWARD OUT OF AN ALLEY,	230	THE STORM	18
CHILD-WHIMPERING			
THEIR CHILD-WHIMPERING.	190	AT OYSTER RIVER	10
CHILL			
CHILL DEPTHS OF THE SPIRIT ARE FLUSHED TO A FEVER, ...	5	PROGNOSIS	15
AND CHILL THE ANXIOUS HEART;	31	LULL	3
THE WHOLE PLACE SHOOK WHENEVER I GOT A CHILL--	163	I'M HERE	64
CHILLS			
HERO OF PHANTASIES AND CATCHER OF CHILLS, ...	24	POETASTER	1

	PAGE	TITLE	LINE
CHILL'S			
THE CHILL'S GONE FROM THE MOON.	77	BRING THE DAY!	18
CHILLY			
A CHILLY NOISE;	62	FIELD OF LIGHT	8
THE SMALL WINDS MAKE THEIR CHILLY INDICTMENTS.	157	FIRST MEDITATN	3
CHIMNEY			
FOR THE THIN SOUND IN THE WINDY CHIMNEY,	103	OLD LADY'S WRDS	30
AS A FIRE, SEEMINGLY LONG DEAD, FLARES UP FROM A DOWNDRAFT OF AIR IN A CHIMNEY,	198	THE LONG WATERS	63
CHIMNEYS			
THE SWALLOWS FLEW IN AND OUT OF THE SMOKELESS CHIMNEYS.	162	I'M HERE	41
CHIN			
THE CHIN JUMPS TO THE NOSE.	60	THE LONG ALLEY	42
HOW WELL HER WISHES WENT! SHE STROKED MY CHIN,	127	I KNEW A WOMAN	8
IS JUST UNDER HIS CHIN,--	183	THE LIZARD	4
I'LL SPIT OVER MY CHIN AND BEYOND THE CURB,	272	DUET	7
CHING			
WATER BIRDS WENT CHING. WENT CHING.	73	WHERE KNOCK IS	54
WATER BIRDS WENT CHING. WENT CHING.	73	WHERE KNOCK IS	54
CHINK			
O LOVELY CHINK, O WHITE	83	O LULL ME, LULL	22
CHINKS			
BULBS BROKE OUT OF BOXES HUNTING FOR CHINKS IN THE DARK,	38	ROOT CELLAR	2
CHINS			
ADDS UP A PAIR OF JIGGLING DOUBLE CHINS.	25	DIM-WIT COUSIN	8
CHIP			
THE TOOL CAN CHIP NO FLAKE:	9	THE ADAMANT	11
AS A CHIP OR SHELL, FLOATING LAZILY WITH A SLOW CURRENT,	168	FOURTH MEDITATN	6
CHIPPENDALE			
THE WHAT-NOT, THE SETTEE, THE CHIPPENDALE CHAIRS	32	SALE	3
CHIPPEWA			
THE DOUGH I SPENT ON CHIPPEWA KATE,	112	SQUEEZE-BOX	39
CHIPS			
THE BUFFALO CHIPS DRYING.	189	THE LONGING	56
CHIRPING			
CHIRPING WITH FLEAS IN THE SAND,	165	HER BECOMING	3
CHIRR			
THE HIGH CICADAS CHIRR;	148	THE SMALL	2
CHOICE			
DEFER THE VICE OF FLESH THE IRREVOCABLE CHOICE	5	TO MY SISTER	8
I FOUND MY CHOICE POSSESSIONS ON THE LAWN.	21	THE AUCTION	2
I ACHE FOR ANOTHER CHOICE.	89	UNFOLD! UNFOLD!	4
OF HER CHOICE VIRTUES ONLY GODS SHOULD SPEAK,	127	I KNEW A WOMAN	5
THAT GHOST WAS MY OWN CHOICE,	128	THE VOICE	13
THE SOUL STANDS, LONELY IN ITS CHOICE,	168	FOURTH MEDITATN	20
THINGS WITHOUT HANDS TAKE HANDS: THERE IS NO CHOICE,--	244	INFIRMITY	31
OF MULTIPLE CHOICE AND EITHER/OR	272	DUET	10
CHOICES			
HER CHOICES WHISPER.	260	THE CHANGELING	6
CHOKED			
AND BATTERED FRUIT HAS CHOKED THE GRASS.	14	COMING OF COLD	7
CHOOSE			
KEEP FAITH WITH PRESENT JOYS REFUSE TO CHOOSE	5	TO MY SISTER	7
I PRAY THEE, LORD, THAT I MAY CHOOSE	8	PRAYER	2
IS IT A CASE OF JUST PICK AND CHOOSE?	183	THE WAGTAIL	2
CHORTLING			
THE MIMETIC CHORTLING OF THE CATBIRD	204	THE ROSE	63
CHORUS			
(I'D HAVE THEM SING IN CHORUS, CHEEK TO CHEEK).	127	I KNEW A WOMAN	7
AND THE DEEP CHORUS OF HORNS COMING UP FROM THE STREETS IN EARLY MORNING.	204	THE ROSE	72
CHRIST			
THAT CHRIST, SECURELY BOUND, COULD BEAR.	144	ELEGY (1)	8
SWEET CHRIST, REJOICE IN MY INFIRMITY;	244	INFIRMITY	7
CHRISTIAN			
MY FRIENDS BECOME MORE CHRISTIAN, YEAR BY YEAR.	132	SENTENTIOUS MAN	38
CHRISTOPHER			
AND CHRISTOPHER SMART,	228	IN VIOLENT WARD	6
CHRYSANTHEMUM			
THE ROSE, THE CHRYSANTHEMUM TURNED TOWARD THE LIGHT.	57	THE LOST SON	146
CHRYSANTHEMUMS			
THAT HUMP OF A MAN BUNCHING CHRYSANTHEMUMS	42	OLD FLORIST	1
THE HALF-GROWN CHRYSANTHEMUMS STARING UP LIKE ACCUSERS,	43	CHILD ON GRNHSE	3

		PAGE	TITLE	LINE
CHRYSANTHEMUMS (CONTINUED)				
CHRYSANTHEMUMS; THE STIFF		44	FRAU BAUMAN	9
CHUMS				
THE CHUMS		225	THE CHUMS	T
CHUNK				
--ON THAT CHUNK OF GRANDPA'S MONEY.		112	SQUEEZE-BOX	33
CHURN				
FROM A KNOCKED OVER CHURN, AND FOAMED AROUND		273	SUPPR W LINDSAY	13
CHURNING				
CHURNING IN A SNOWDRIFT		199	THE FAR FIELD	11
CICADA				
A CHEAP CLOCK TICKING IN GHOSTLY CICADA VOICE.		29	THE REMINDER	12
THIN AND INSISTENT AS A CICADA,		159	FIRST MEDITATN	85
AND THAT THIN CRY, LIKE A NEEDLE PIERCING THE EAR, THE INSISTENT CICADA,		204	THE ROSE	67
CICADAS				
THE HIGH CICADAS CHIRR;		148	THE SMALL	2
CICERO				
WAS THE UNDERBELLY OF CICERO;		111	SQUEEZE-BOX	18
CIGARETTE				
(WOULD A CIGARETTE DISTURB HIM?)		226	THE LIZARD	13
CIGARETTES				
THE GIN AND CIGARETTES,		136	THE SENSUALISTS	8
CIGARS				
SO LONG ON GIN, BOBBIE PINS, HALF-SMOKED CIGARS, DEAD BEER,		228	THE GERANIUM	10
CINDERS				
BREAKS UP THE CRUST OF CINDERS THAT REMAIN,		17	UNEXTINGUISHED	10
OVER SLIPPERY CINDERS		57	THE LOST SON	124
THERE'S NO FILTH ON A PLATEAU OF CINDERS.		59	THE LONG ALLEY	15
WITH JOTS AND JOGS AND CINDERS ON THE FLOOR:		79	GIVE WAY, GATES	27
I NO LONGER CRY FOR GREEN IN THE MIDST OF CINDERS,		173	WHAT TELL BONES	74
THE SHIFTING SHADE, THE CINDERS AT MY BACK.		245	THE DECISION	10
CINDERY				
THE CINDERY SNOW TICKS OVER STUBBLE.		104	OLD LADY'S WRDS	54
CIRCLED				
I CIRCLED ON LEATHER PAWS		47	THE RETURN	1
SO THEY CIRCLED AIMLESSLY FOR ALMOST A MINUTE,		232	THE THING	8
CIRCLES				
A SMALL BIRD FLEW IN CIRCLES WHERE WE STOOD;		120	THE DREAM	19
(SHE MOVED IN CIRCLES, AND THOSE CIRCLES MOVED).		127	I KNEW A WOMAN	21
(SHE MOVED IN CIRCLES, AND THOSE CIRCLES MOVED).		127	I KNEW A WOMAN	21
CIRCUIT				
SOME ERRAND, OBSCURE AS THE WIND'S CIRCUIT,		92	I CRY, LOVE!	6
CIRCULAR				
IN THE CIRCULAR SMELLS OF A SLOW WIND,		171	WHAT TELL BONES	11
CIRCULARITY				
IS CIRCULARITY SUCH A SHAME?		92	I CRY, LOVE!	8
CIRCUMFERENCE				
BY THE CIRCUMFERENCE OF HAND,		25	VERSE W ALLUSNS	2
CIRCUMSTANCE				
THE WHEELS OF CIRCUMSTANCE THAT GRIND		22	SILENCE	9
AT ODDS WITH CIRCUMSTANCE? THE DAY'S ON FIRE!		239	IN A DARK TIME	8
CIRCUMVENT				
THOSE BARRIERS CIRCUMVENT		7	ORDERS FOR DAY	18
CISTERN				
WATER ROARS INTO THE CISTERN.		231	THE STORM	37
CITIES				
BEHIND THE EYE; THE LOST ACRES AT THE EDGE OF SMOKY CITIES.		159	FIRST MEDITATN	75
THE SLAG-HEAPS FUME AT THE EDGE OF THE RAW CITIES:		187	THE LONGING	15
CITY				
AS YOU LOOK ACROSS MY CITY, IN GOD'S COUNTRY?"		27	CLAIRVOY WIDOW	4
FOR SHE FINALLY LEFT TOWN ON THE BAY CITY FREIGHT		112	SQUEEZE-BOX	40
CLAIM				
I DID NOT MOVE TO CLAIM WHAT WAS MY OWN.		21	THE AUCTION	4
I CLAIM; ONE TREE, A WOOD;		128	THE VOICE	2
CLAIRVOYANT				
BALLAD OF THE CLAIRVOYANT WIDOW		27	CLAIRVOY WIDOW	T
"CLAIRVOYANT WIDOW LADY, WITH AN EYE LIKE A TELESCOPE,		27	CLAIRVOY WIDOW	17
CLAM				
BECAME A CLAM.		62	FIELD OF LIGHT	14
RUNNING ALONG THE NARROW FURROWS OF THE SHORE, THE ROWS OF DEAD CLAM SHELLS;		190	AT OYSTER RIVER	3

		PAGE	TITLE	LINE
CLAMS				
SOFTLY SOFTLY, YOU'LL WAKE THE CLAMS.		85	PRAISE TO END!	10
CLAP				
I HEAR THE CLAP OF AN OLD WIND.		80	GIVE WAY, GATES	55
CLAPS				
AND THE AIR CLAPS BETWEEN US,		158	FIRST MEDITATN	35
CLARE				
AND THAT SWEET MAN, JOHN CLARE.		228	IN VIOLENT WARD	7
CLAW				
NOT EVEN THE END OF HIS CLAW, CLAW, CLAW,		117	LADY AND BEAR	17
NOT EVEN THE END OF HIS CLAW, CLAW, CLAW,		117	LADY AND BEAR	17
NOT EVEN THE END OF HIS CLAW, CLAW, CLAW,		117	LADY AND BEAR	17
NOT EVEN THE END OF HIS CLAW.		117	LADY AND BEAR	18
THE FANG AND THE CLAW, THE CLUB AND THE KNOUT, THE IRRATIONAL EDICT,		170	FOURTH MEDITATN	67
CLAWS				
SHE CROONS, LIKE A CAT TO ITS CLAWS;		208	HER WORDS	2
CLAY				
BENEATH THE ROCK AND CLAY,		50	THE CYCLE	2
RINGED ROUND WITH CRUMBLED CLAY:		146	THE SONG	15
IN THE COUNTRY OF FEW LAKES, IN THE TALL BUFFALO GRASS AT THE BASE OF THE CLAY BUTTES,		189	THE LONGING	53
TO THE CLAY BANKS, AND THE WILD GRAPES HANGING FROM THE ELMTREES.		200	THE FAR FIELD	66
STILL AS A CLAY SUNK		258	SONG (3)	30
CLEAN				
WHEN I HAD TRIED TO CLEAN		213	THE HAPPY THREE	5
CLEANING				
CLEANING AND CARESSING,		50	THE MINIMAL	10
CLEAR				
UNTIL CLEAR EYES PUT ON THE LOOK OF SLEEP.		12	SLOW SEASON	4
LIKE THAT CLEAR AUTUMNAL WEATHER OF ETERNITY,		43	CARNATIONS	6
THROUGH THE CLEAR AIR, IN THE SILENCE.		58	THE LOST SON	163
ARE THE ENTRAILS CLEAR, IMMACULATE CABBAGE?		89	UNFOLD! UNFOLD!	19
THE SMALL! THE SMALL! I HEAR THEM SINGING CLEAR		149	IN LATE SUMMER	7
WHAT CAME TO ME VAGUELY IS NOW CLEAR,		173	WHAT TELL BONES	97
CLEAR UNDER THE CHAIR;		180	GOO-GIRL	12
CLEARED				
AND WHEN YOU THINK THE SKY HAS CLEARED		114	DINKY	3
CLEARER				
TO SEE CYCLAMEN VEINS BECOME CLEARER IN EARLY SUNLIGHT,		67	SHAPE OF FIRE	86
CLEAREST				
RAGE WARPS MY CLEAREST CRY		3	OPEN HOUSE	17
MY FRIEND, THE RAT IN THE WALL, BRINGS ME THE CLEAREST MESSAGES;		88	PRAISE TO END!	84
STIRRING THE CLEAREST WATER.		102	ELEGY FOR JANE	13
CLEARLY				
I HEAR, CLEARLY, THE HEART OF ANOTHER SINGING,		88	PRAISE TO END!	94
SPEAK IT FROM THE FACE OUT CLEARLY:		266	FOR STEVENS	13
CLEFT				
AND THAT WRIST-THICK CASCADE TUMBLING FROM A CLEFT ROCK,		191	AT OYSTER RIVER	44
CLIFF				
CLIFF DISAPPEAR IN A LAST		210	HER TIME	19
CLIFFS				
THE CLIFFS! THE CLIFFS! THEY FLING ME BACK.		89	UNFOLD! UNFOLD!	5
THE CLIFFS! THE CLIFFS! THEY FLING ME BACK.		89	UNFOLD! UNFOLD!	5
THE FAR FIELD, THE WINDY CLIFFS OF FOREVER,		200	THE FAR FIELD	51
BETWEEN CLIFFS OF LIGHT		265	HARSH COUNTRY	5
CLIFF-SIDE				
THEN RETIRE TO A ROCK HIGHER UP ON THE CLIFF-SIDE.		190	AT OYSTER RIVER	16
CLIMB				
YOU FEEL DISASTER CLIMB THE VEIN.		4	FEUD	8
THE SALMON CLIMB THE RIVERS, THE RIVERS NUDGE THE SEA,		28	CLAIRVOY WIDOW	25
MAY THE HIGH FLOWER OF THE HAY CLIMB INTO THEIR HEARTS;		169	FOURTH MEDITATN	56
A FALLEN MAN, I CLIMB OUT OF MY FEAR.		239	IN A DARK TIME	22
CLIMBED				
CLIMBED TO HER ATTIC WINDOW AND GAZED ACROSS THE SILL.		27	CLAIRVOY WIDOW	2
CLIMBING				
NASTURTIUMS, THE CLIMBING		44	FRAU BAUMAN	6
ALIVE WITH TINY STRIPED FISH, AND YOUNG CRABS CLIMBING IN AND OUT OF THE WATER.		190	AT OYSTER RIVER	5
THE CLIMBING, THE ENDLESS TURNING,		221	THE ABYSS	53

	PAGE	TITLE	LINE
CLIMBS			
THE LOWLY WORM CLIMBS UP A WINDING STAIR;	108	THE WAKING (2)	11
AND THE VINE CLIMBS;	259	SONG (3)	49
CLINGING			
STILL CLINGING TO YOUR SHIRT.	45	MY PAPA'S WALTZ	16
THE LEECH CLINGING TO A STONE WAITED;	100	THE VISITANT	8
CLINGS			
--AND A FUME OF DECAY THAT CLINGS FAST TO THE WOOD.	32	SALE	16
CLINKERS			
THE BIG ROSES, THE BIG BLOODY CLINKERS.	57	THE LOST SON	133
CLOAK			
THE CLOAK OF EVIL AND DESPAIR,	19	EPIDERM MACABRE	6
CLOCK			
A CHEAP CLOCK TICKING IN GHOSTLY CICADA VOICE.	29	THE REMINDER	12
CLOSE			
CLOSE TO THE HEELS OF MY FATHER,	6	THE PREMONITION	4
WE WALK AWARE OF WHAT IS FAR AND CLOSE.	13	PRAISE PRAIRIE	10
SO CAGED AND CADGED, SO CLOSE WITHIN	24	BEFORE STUDY	3
SWAYING CLOSE TO THE FACE,	39	ORCHIDS	3
OR SCOOP OUT A WEED CLOSE TO FLOURISHING ROOTS,	42	OLD FLORIST	6
STAY CLOSE. MUST I KILL SOMETHING ELSE?	60	THE LONG ALLEY	31
THAT WAS A CLOSE KNOCK. SEE WHAT THE WILL WANTS.	61	THE LONG ALLEY	62
THE POKE OF THE WIND'S CLOSE,	84	O LULL ME, LULL	31
PRICKLE-ME, TICKLE-ME, CLOSE STEMS.	85	PRAISE TO END!	6
ON THE ROCKS SOUTH OF QUIET, IN THE CLOSE REGIONS OF KISSING,	86	PRAISE TO END!	20
DIPPING AND VEERING CLOSE TO THE MOTIONLESS WATER.	93	I CRY, LOVE!	44
THOSE CLOSE TO THE GROUND	97	O, THOU OPENING	11
A CLOUD MOVED CLOSE. THE BULK OF THE WIND SHIFTED.	100	THE VISITANT	1
THE TREE, THE CLOSE WILLOW, SWAYED.	101	THE VISITANT	27
I HAVE LISTENED CLOSE	103	OLD LADY'S WRDS	29
SHE KISSED ME CLOSE, AND THEN DID SOMETHING ELSE.	106	SIR JOHN DAVIES	35
OF THOSE SO CLOSE BESIDE ME, WHICH ARE YOU?	108	THE WAKING (2)	7
BUT IF I MOVE TOO CLOSE,	130	THE OTHER	5
"YOU HAVE ME PINNED SO CLOSE;	136	THE SENSUALISTS	2
THE CLOSE DARK HUGS ME HARD,	138	LOVE'S PROGRESS	21
CLOSE, AND YET FAR AWAY.	146	THE SONG	27
IN MY WAY, CLOSE COUSIN	151	SLUG	5
HOW CLOSE WE ARE TO THE SAD ANIMALS!	171	WHAT TELL BONES	20
MY FACE ON FIRE, CLOSE TO THE POINTS OF A STAR,	172	WHAT TELL BONES	55
BETTER TO HUG CLOSE, WARY OF RUBBLE AND FALLING STONES.	193	JOURNY INTERIOR	6
ALWAYS A SHARP TURN TO THE LEFT PAST A BARN CLOSE TO THE ROADSIDE,	193	JOURNY INTERIOR	25
WHEN BATS FLY, CLOSE TO SLIGHTLY TILTING BROWNISH WATER,	198	THE LONG WATERS	61
THE MOON LOLLING IN THE CLOSE ELM, A SHIMMER OF SILVER,	204	THE ROSE	81
FLICK OVER THE CLOSE WHITECAPS,	210	HER TIME	11
THE CLOSE AIR FAINTLY STIRRED.	212	LIGHT LISTENED	7
THEN A CLOSE TOWHEE, A	213	THE HAPPY THREE	29
FOR HERE CLOSE BESIDE ME IS O'CONNELL'S DAUGHTER,	216	THE SHY MAN	20
TOO CLOSE IMMEDIACY AN EXHAUSTION:	220	THE ABYSS	45
AS CLOSE TO HIM AS ANY KITH OR KIN.	224	OTTO	6
WHEN I COME CLOSE TO HIM?	227	MEADOW MOUSE	18
FLAPPING AWAY HEAVILY WHEN A CAR BLASTS TOO CLOSE,	234	ALL MORNING	7
VEERING CLOSE TO MY HEAD,	234	ALL MORNING	30
YE LITTLES, LIE MORE CLOSE!	240	IN EVEING AIR	7
A WIND CAME CLOSE, LIKE A SHY ANIMAL.	241	THE SEQUEL	22
THE CLOSE DIRT DANCING ON A SUNLESS STONE	243	THE MOTION	20
ONE LOOK TOO CLOSE CAN TAKE MY SOUL AWAY.	246	THE MARROW	9
--AND CLOSE UP THAT CHAPTER OF KIERKEGAARD.	272	DUET	8
CLOSE-AT-HAND			
FAR AWAY, CLOSE-AT-HAND, HIS CALL FLOATING OVER THE ON-COMING TRAFFIC,	234	ALL MORNING	3
CLOSED			
I CLOSED MY EYES, AND SAW SMALL FIGURES DANCING,	163	I'M HERE	65
CLOSELY			
HE CLOSELY RESEMBLES--BUT I CAN'T TELL YOU!	180	THE GNU	2
CLOSER			
CROUCHED CLOSER TO THE FLOOR,	47	THE RETURN	3
EVERYTHING'S CLOSER. IS THIS A CAGE?	77	BRING THE DAY!	17
GHOST, COME CLOSER.	87	PRAISE TO END!	78
AND TREES CAME CLOSER WITH A DENSER SHADE.	133	THE PURE FURY	21
FAR THINGS DRAW CLOSER IN.	148	THE SMALL	10
SOMEWHAT CLOSER, THE TRUCKS COMING	158	FIRST MEDITATN	32

	PAGE	TITLE	LINE
CLOSER (CONTINUED)			
AND THE GROUND-CHILL COMES CLOSER TO US,	162	I'M HERE	55
THERE ARE TIMES WHEN REALITY COMES CLOSER:	166	HER BECOMING	44
THEN A RUNNEL BEHIND ME, CREEPING CLOSER,	190	AT OYSTER RIVER	4
FOR I HAVE MOVED CLOSER TO DEATH, LIVED WITH DEATH;	220	THE ABYSS	37
COMING CLOSER AND CLOSER UPON EACH OTHER;	230	THE STORM	12
COMING CLOSER AND CLOSER UPON EACH OTHER;	230	THE STORM	12
THE LAST WATCHER INDOORS, MOVING THE CARDPLAYERS CLOSER	230	THE STORM	26
WE LIE CLOSER ON THE GRITTY PILLOW,	231	THE STORM	38
WE'RE GETTING CLOSER TO IT ALL THE TIME."	274	SUPPR W LINDSAY	45
CLOSET			
--AND AN ATTIC OF HORRORS, A CLOSET OF FEARS.	32	SALE	4
CLOSING			
OPENING, CLOSING.	226	THE LIZARD	26
CLOTHES			
THE ASPECT OF HIS FLESHY CLOTHES,--	19	EPIDERM MACABRE	2
WITH THE RAGS AND ROTTING CLOTHES,	47	THE RETURN	11
WHEN I TOOK OFF MY CLOTHES	64	SHAPE OF FIRE	24
MUST PULL OFF CLOTHES	65	SHAPE OF FIRE	49
I SHED MY CLOTHES TO SLOW MY DAEMON DOWN.	166	HER BECOMING	59
CLOUD			
THE RAIN STAYED IN ITS CLOUD; FULL DARK CAME NEAR;	6	INTERLUDE	9
THE WINDLESS PERPETUAL MORNING ABOVE A SEPTEMBER CLOUD.	43	CARNATIONS	7
COME OUT OF A CLOUD, ANGEL WITH SEVERAL FACES,	48	LAST WORDS	8
THE FINE RAIN COILED IN A CLOUD	50	THE CYCLE	7
TODAY I SAW A BEARD IN A CLOUD,	76	I NEED, I NEED	48
ENOUGH TO PLEASE A CLOUD!	98	O, THOU OPENING	50
A CLOUD MOVED CLOSE. THE BULK OF THE WIND SHIFTED.	100	THE VISITANT	1
A SHAPE CRIED FROM A CLOUD,	147	THE EXORCISM	7
AND THE SUN COMES OUT OF A BLUE CLOUD OVER THE TETONS,	194	JOURNY INTERIOR	40
HOW THEY FILLED THE ORIOLE'S ELM, A TWITTERING RESTLESS CLOUD, ALL ONE MORNING,	199	THE FAR FIELD	28
AROUND A CLOUD,	219	THE ABYSS	14
A SMALL VOICE CALLING FROM A DRIFTING CLOUD.	248	THE TREE, BIRD	4
SHE'S COME TO PIERCE A CLOUD!	261	THE CHANGELING	56
TO PIERCE A CLOUD.	261	THE CHANGELING	57
A CLOUD.	261	THE CHANGELING	58
SPINNING THROUGH THE LORDLY CLOUD.	266	FOR STEVENS	4
I SAW A FIGURE IN A CLOUD,	268	SAGINAW SONG	56
CLOUDS			
BEFORE OBLIVION CLOUDS THE BRAIN.	8	PRAYER	4
BLEAK CLOUDS ACROSS THE HEAVY SKY,	15	COMING OF COLD	50
CLOUDS GLOW LIKE COALS JUST FRESH FROM FIRE, A FLARE	17	UNEXTINGUISHED	1
A FEW WHITE CLOUDS ALL RUSHING EASTWARD,	43	CHILD ON GRNHSE	5
WHAT A SMALL SONG. WHAT SLOW CLOUDS. WHAT DARK WATER.	56	THE LOST SON	83
WHAT DO THE CLOUDS SAY?	56	THE LOST SON	117
THERE WERE CLOUDS MAKING A ROUT OF SHAPES CROSSING A WINDBREAK OF CEDARS,	63	FIELD OF LIGHT	48
OR BEATING AGAINST THE BLACK CLOUDS OF THE STORM,	209	HER LONGING	22
IN A PLACE OF MOTTLED CLOUDS, A THIN MIST MORNING AND EVENING.	221	THE ABYSS	77
DO THESE ANALOGIES PERPLEX? A SKY WITH CLOUDS,	235	MANIFESTATION	6
CLOUD'S			
THE NAKED FIELDS THE CLOUD'S IMMACULATE FOLDS	5	TO MY SISTER	4
CLOUD-SHAPE			
THE MOON RETREATING INTO A VAGUE CLOUD-SHAPE	202	THE ROSE	18
CLOVER			
CROSS MARSHLAND INTO CLOVER.	7	ORDERS FOR DAY	14
WHEN CLOVER SCENTS DIMINISHED WIND.	14	COMING OF COLD	4
BEYOND THE CLOVER, THE RAGGED HAY,	203	THE ROSE	46
CLUB			
THE FANG AND THE CLAW, THE CLUB AND THE KNOUT, THE IRRATIONAL EDICT,	170	FOURTH MEDITATN	67
CLUE			
CAN FEATHERS EAT ME? THERE'S NO CLUE IN THE SILT.	60	THE LONG ALLEY	32
CLUMP			
EACH CLUMP IN THE SHAPE OF A POT;	43	FLOWER DUMP	9
CLUMSY			
HIS CLUMSY FINGERS BRUISE	7	ORDERS FOR DAY	6
WHEN I SAW THAT CLUMSY CROW	49	NIGHT CROW	1
DO WHAT THE CLUMSY PARTNER WANTS TO DO!	106	SIR JOHN DAVIES	42
I AM THE CLUMSY MAN	154	THE DYING MAN	24

	PAGE	TITLE	LINE
CLUTCHING			
AND FELL IN THE STREAM STILL CLUTCHING A PLANK, ...	117	LADY AND BEAR	27
COAL			
AND POKES THE CRUMBLED COAL THE ASHES HID, ...	17	UNEXTINGUISHED	11
(I FOUND IT LYING AMONG THE RUBBLE OF AN OLD COAL BIN) ...	199	THE FAR FIELD	20
COALS			
CLOUDS GLOW LIKE COALS JUST FRESH FROM FIRE, A FLARE	17	UNEXTINGUISHED	1
COARSE			
WHO SPOKE FIRST IN THE COARSE SHORT-HAND OF THE SUBLIMINAL			
DEPTHS, ...	170	FOURTH MEDITATN	71
DYING BRIGHTLY UNDER THE STREET LIGHTS SUNK IN COARSE			
CONCRETE, ...	193	JOURNY INTERIOR	29
NOT FEELING THE COARSE SHALE	265	HARSH COUNTRY	7
THAT PRICKLES MY COARSE SKIN.	271	THE REPLY	4
COAT			
"ONE COAT OF PRIDE, PERHAPS A BIT THREADBARE;	21	THE AUCTION	5
A COAT OF UNESSENTIAL SKIN, ...	24	BEFORE STUDY	4
COAXING			
BUT STILL THE DELICATE SLIPS KEEP COAXING UP WATER;	37	CUTTINGS	3
COCKALORUM			
ROAR 'EM, WHORE 'EM, COCKALORUM, ...	266	FOR STEVENS	17
COCKROACH			
OLDER THAN I, OR THE COCKROACH.	226	THE LIZARD	31
COCKROACHES			
FETOR OF COCKROACHES, DEAD FISH, PETROLEUM, ...	187	THE LONGING	3
COFFEE			
WITH COLD ROAST BEEF AND COFFEE FOR DESSERT--	274	SUPPR W LINDSAY	33
COGS			
THEY PRAYED THE COGS WOULD CREEP;	46	PICKLE BELT	2
COHERE			
WHERE ELEMENTS COHERE	50	THE CYCLE	10
COILED			
COILED GREEN AND THICK, LIKE DRIPPING SMILAX, ...	39	WEED PULLER	8
THE FINE RAIN COILED IN A CLOUD	50	THE CYCLE	7
THE CHILD'S HAND REACHING INTO THE COILED SMILAX, ...	221	THE ABYSS	65
COILING			
IN COILING OOZE	65	SHAPE OF FIRE	46
COILS			
ALL THE COILS, LOOPS, AND WHORLS.	44	FRAU BAUMAN	24
COLD			
IN RIVULETS; THE COLD ROOTS STIR BELOW.	11	LIGHT BRIGHTER	12
THE COMING OF THE COLD	14	COMING OF COLD	T
BUT SOON COLD RAIN AND FROST COME IN	14	COMING OF COLD	18
THE BUDS DRAW IN BEFORE THE COLD.	15	COMING OF COLD	37
COLD, COLD ACROSS THE FLESH	31	LULL	2
COLD, COLD ACROSS THE FLESH	31	LULL	2
THEY TEASED OUT THE SEED THAT THE COLD KEPT ASLEEP,--	44	FRAU BAUMAN	23
NOW, WHEN I'M ALONE AND COLD IN MY BED, ...	44	FRAU BAUMAN	30
A COLD KEY LET ME IN	47	THE RETURN	8
IN THAT COLD, GRANITIC SLIME, ...	49	RIVER INCIDENT	10
SLEEPERS, NUMB NUDGERS IN COLD DIMENSIONS, ...	50	THE MINIMAL	2
I'M COLD. I'M COLD ALL OVER. RUB ME IN FATHER AND MOTHER.	56	THE LOST SON	85
I'M COLD. I'M COLD ALL OVER. RUB ME IN FATHER AND MOTHER.	56	THE LOST SON	85
THAT COLD MORNING.	56	THE LOST SON	95
NOWHERE IS OUT. I SAW THE COLD.	73	WHERE KNOCK IS	71
IT'S A COLD SCRAPE IN A LOW PLACE.	80	GIVE WAY, GATES	47
THE COLD KNOWS WHEN TO COME.	80	GIVE WAY, GATES	56
IS IT YOU, COLD FATHER? FATHER, ...	90	UNFOLD! UNFOLD!	51
IN THE COLD AIR, ...	104	OLD LADY'S WRDS	63
EYE LEARNED FROM EYE, COLD LIP FROM SENSUAL LIP.	119	THE DREAM	4
WHAT'S HELL BUT A COLD HEART?	122	ALL EARTH, AIR	28
COLD EVIL TWINKLED TIGHTER THAN A STRING; A FIRE	143	SHIMMER OF EVIL	8
A COLD GOD-FURIOUS MAN	147	THE EXORCISM	21
COLD, IN MY OWN DEAD SALT.	147	THE EXORCISM	28
THE COLD SLIME COME INTO BEING, ...	151	SLUG	11
NERVOUS AND COLD, BIRD-FURTIVE, WHISKERY, ...	157	FIRST MEDITATN	16
A COLD WIND COMES OVER STONES;	160	FIRST MEDITATN	92
I KNOW THE COLD FLESHLESS KISS OF CONTRARIES, ...	166	HER BECOMING	40
MUTILATED SOULS IN COLD MORGUES OF OBLIGATION.	166	HER BECOMING	43
AND THEN CAUGHT COLD AND UP AND DIED?	178	THE CEILING	2
A COLD AIR BROUGHT ITS RAIN, ...	212	LIGHT LISTENED	21
THE RUSH OF SMELLS STRIKES LIKE A COLD FIRE, THE THROAT			
FREEZES, ...	220	THE ABYSS	47

	PAGE	TITLE	LINE
COLD (CONTINUED)			
THE SLIPPERY COLD HEIGHTS,	221	THE ABYSS	51
I WARM MYSELF WITH COLD.	259	SONG (3)	33
WITH COLD ROAST BEEF AND COFFEE FOR DESSERT--	274	SUPPR W LINDSAY	33
COLDER			
WHEEL OF THE STARS, THE GREAT BEAR GLITTERING COLDER THAN SNOW,	47	DOUBLE FEATURE	11
FAR FROM THE COLDER SOURCE	50	THE CYCLE	9
COLLAPSE			
IN MY LEFT EAR I HEAR THE LOUD SOUND OF A MINOR COLLAPSE.	165	HER BECOMING	29
COLLAPSES			
YOUR BED COLLAPSES FROM IMAGINED SINS.	25	DIM-WIT COUSIN	6
THE SUDDEN SHUDDER AS THE JUTTING SEA-CLIFF COLLAPSES,	231	THE STORM	42
COLLECTIVE			
TO SPOIL COLLECTIVE LIFE.	31	LULL	6
COLLECTOR			
I MET A COLLECTOR OF STRING, A SHEPHERD OF SLOW FORMS.	90	UNFOLD! UNFOLD!	30
COLLECTORS			
TERROR OF COPS, BILL COLLECTORS, BETRAYERS OF THE POOR,--	223	ELEGY (2)	18
COLLEGE			
"WHO CALLED ME POET OF THE COLLEGE YELL?	274	SUPPR W LINDSAY	40
COLLOPED			
AND COLLOPED ROUND WITH FERN.	145	THE BEAST	9
COLONY			
IT WASN'T THE COLONY; IT WASN'T THE STORK;	111	SQUEEZE-BOX	8
COLOR			
A COLOR PURE, O PURE AS GOLD,	269	GOB MUSIC	26
A COLOR WITHOUT FLAW,	269	GOB MUSIC	27
A COLOR WITHOUT FLAW, FLAW, FLAW,	269	GOB MUSIC	28
A COLOR WITHOUT FLAW.	269	GOB MUSIC	29
THE COLOR, MY DEARS, WAS GUINNESS BROWN,	270	GOB MUSIC	39
COLUMN			
REVOLVING ON HIS SPINAL COLUMN.	24	BEFORE STUDY	8
COMBINE			
OR WHEN TWO RIVERS COMBINE, THE BLUE GLACIAL TORRENT	200	THE FAR FIELD	61
COME			
WHAT WE HAD HOPED FOR HAD NOT COME TO PASS.	6	INTERLUDE	12
AS KNOWN PARTICULARS COME WHEELING BY,	8	THE SIGNALS	3
BUT SOON COLD RAIN AND FROST COME IN	14	COMING OF COLD	18
THE RATS SOON WILL BE LEAVING, THE SNOW WILL COME IN."	27	CLAIRVOY WIDOW	16
HIS OYSTER WORLD WAS EASILY COME BY;	28	THE FAVORITE	3
THE GULLS RIDE ON THE WATER, THE GULLS HAVE COME AND GONE,	28	CLAIRVOY WIDOW	23
COME OUT OF A CLOUD, ANGEL WITH SEVERAL FACES,	48	LAST WORDS	8
I SAID: ON ALL THESE, DEATH, WITH GENTLENESS, COME DOWN.	48	JUDGE NOT	10
VOICE, COME OUT OF THE SILENCE.	54	THE LOST SON	20
COULD IT COME IN THE HOUSE	54	THE LOST SON	52
IT WILL COME AGAIN.	58	THE LOST SON	171
COME TO ME, MILK-NOSE. I NEED A LOAN OF THE QUICK.	59	THE LONG ALLEY	25
BUT THEY DON'T COME	60	THE LONG ALLEY	53
COME LITTLEST, COME TENDEREST,	61	THE LONG ALLEY	66
COME LITTLEST, COME TENDEREST,	61	THE LONG ALLEY	66
COME WHISPERING OVER THE SMALL WATERS,	61	THE LONG ALLEY	67
COME, COME OUT OF THE SHADE, THE COOL WAYS,	61	THE LONG ALLEY	69
COME, COME OUT OF THE SHADE, THE COOL WAYS,	61	THE LONG ALLEY	69
SPIRIT, COME NEAR. THIS IS ONLY THE EDGE OF WHITENESS.	64	SHAPE OF FIRE	12
HAVE YOU COME TO UNHINGE MY SHADOW?	65	SHAPE OF FIRE	33
KISSES COME BACK,	73	WHERE KNOCK IS	76
HAVE I COME TO ALWAYS? NOT YET.	74	WHERE KNOCK IS	86
THE COLD KNOWS WHEN TO COME.	80	GIVE WAY, GATES	56
COMMODITIES, HERE WE COME!	81	SENSIBILITY! LA	20
SUCH OWLY PLEASURES! FISH COME FIRST, SWEET BIRD.	87	PRAISE TO END!	71
GHOST, COME CLOSER.	87	PRAISE TO END!	78
WASPS COME WHEN I ASK FOR PIGEONS.	92	I CRY, LOVE!	2
MOUSE, MOUSE, COME OUT OF THE FERNS,	92	I CRY, LOVE!	22
I SING THE GREEN, AND THINGS TO COME,	99	O, THOU OPENING	56
COME.	99	O, THOU OPENING	80
WHEN THEY COME, DAZEDLY, TO THE PRETTY PASS	113	TO A LADY ED	11
A LIVELY THING CAN COME TO LIFE AGAIN.	129	SHE	12
OR COME TO LOVE ALONE?	130	THE OTHER	14
COME RUNNING FROM THE LEAVES,	147	THE EXORCISM	15
ACROSS MY LAWN THE SOFT-BACKED CREATURES COME;	149	IN LATE SUMMER	3
THE COLD SLIME COME INTO BEING,	151	SLUG	11
"WHAT'S DONE IS YET TO COME;	153	THE DYING MAN	6

	PAGE	TITLE	LINE
COME (CONTINUED)			
WHO'S COME CAN WAIT.	154	THE DYING MAN	35
BY DYING DAILY, I HAVE COME TO BE.	155	THE DYING MAN	71
THE LIGHTS TILTING UP, SKYWARD, AS WE COME OVER A LITTLE RISE,	158	FIRST MEDITATN	24
LONGING FOR ABSOLUTES THAT NEVER COME.	171	WHAT TELL BONES	13
TO WHAT MORE VAST PERMISSION HAVE I COME?	173	WHAT TELL BONES	72
--ALL BEGINNINGS COME.	188	THE LONGING	38
COME THE FIRST TIDE-RIPPLES, MOVING, ALMOST WITHOUT SOUND, TOWARD ME,	190	AT OYSTER RIVER	2
I HAVE COME HERE WITHOUT COURTING SILENCE,	197	THE LONG WATERS	44
FOR TO COME UPON WARBLERS IN EARLY MAY	199	THE FAR FIELD	26
I HAVE COME TO A STILL, BUT NOT A DEEP CENTER,	201	THE FAR FIELD	71
WHAT'S TO COME? WHAT'S TO COME?	211	SONG (1)	8
WHAT'S TO COME? WHAT'S TO COME?	211	SONG (1)	8
WHO SHOULD COME UP RIGHT THEN,	213	THE HAPPY THREE	17
WHEN I COME CLOSE TO HIM?	227	MEADOW MOUSE	18
WE COME TO SOMETHING WITHOUT KNOWING WHY.	235	MANIFESTATION	11
PERIPHERAL DIPPERS COME TO REST ON THE SHORT GRASS,	235	ALL MORNING	34
AND IN BROAD DAY THE MIDNIGHT COME AGAIN!	239	IN A DARK TIME	15
I'VE COME TO LOVE. A VIREO WHETS ITS BILL.	244	INFIRMITY	26
ETERNITY'S NOT EASILY COME BY.	244	INFIRMITY	32
WHEN OPPOSITES COME SUDDENLY IN PLACE,	244	INFIRMITY	33
I'VE COME TO BE.	261	THE CHANGELING	42
SHE'S COME TO PIERCE A CLOUD!	261	THE CHANGELING	56
COME OFF IT MUCH LESS NEAT.	267	SAGINAW SONG	12
TILL YOU COME TO THE LAND OF KINGDOM COME	272	DUET	20
TILL YOU COME TO THE LAND OF KINGDOM COME	272	DUET	20
SHOULD DAME ANXIETY EVER COME NEAR	272	DUET	24
COME EASY TO THE SILL, THINGS LOST FROM FAR AWAY.	273	SUPPR W LINDSAY	4
BUT COME TO THINK, THEY SAY THE SAME OF ME."	273	SUPPR W LINDSAY	23
COMELY			
MY NOSE DEFILES A COMELY HEAD;	8	PRAYER	6
FROM ONE COMELY HEAD.	215	HIS FOREBODING	5
COMES			
THE LIGHT COMES BRIGHTER	11	LIGHT BRIGHTER	T
THE LIGHT COMES BRIGHTER FROM THE EAST; THE CAW	11	LIGHT BRIGHTER	1
THE FEUD WE KEPT WITH SPACE COMES TO AN END.	13	PRAISE PRAIRIE	12
BUT MORNING LIGHT COMES TAPPING AT THE LID,	17	UNEXTINGUISHED	9
THE GREEN COMES UP FOREVER IN THE FIELDS OF OUR COUNTRY."	28	CLAIRVOY WIDOW	26
SO THEIR MUSKY SMELL COMES EVEN STRONGER,	39	ORCHIDS	12
WITH BUCK STILL TIED TO THE LOG, ON COMES THE LIGHT.	47	DOUBLE FEATURE	1
TRICKSY COMES AND TRICKSY GOES	60	THE LONG ALLEY	39
THE WARM COMES WITHOUT SOUND.	64	SHAPE OF FIRE	19
AN EYE COMES OUT OF THE WAVE.	66	SHAPE OF FIRE	60
THE REDEEMER COMES A DARK WAY.	66	SHAPE OF FIRE	63
A SHAPE COMES TO STAY:	81	SENSIBILITY! LA	21
A LIGHT SONG COMES FROM THE LEAVES.	90	UNFOLD! UNFOLD!	48
A DRY CRY COMES FROM MY OWN DESERT;	93	I CRY, LOVE!	31
I THOUGHT THAT ONCE, AND THOUGHT COMES ROUND AGAIN;	107	SIR JOHN DAVIES	87
COMES A TREMULOUS CRY	123	WORDS FOR WIND	28
SHE MOVES AS WATER MOVES, AND COMES TO ME,	129	SHE	15
AS THE THICK SHADE OF THE LONG NIGHT COMES ON.	134	THE PURE FURY	28
A GHOST COMES OUT OF THE UNCONSCIOUS MIND	154	THE DYING MAN	36
OUT OF HER PLACE SHE COMES, A DOLPHIN ONE,	156	THE DYING MAN	80
A COLD WIND COMES OVER STONES;	160	FIRST MEDITATN	92
AND THE GROUND-CHILL COMES CLOSER TO US,	162	I'M HERE	55
THERE ARE TIMES WHEN REALITY COMES CLOSER:	166	HER BECOMING	44
BUT A TIME COMES WHEN THE VAGUE LIFE OF THE MOUTH NO LONGER SUFFICES;	168	FOURTH MEDITATN	18
I DRINK MY TEARS IN A PLACE WHERE ALL LIGHT COMES.	170	FOURTH MEDITATN	78
HE COMES CALLING WITHOUT WIPING HIS SHOES!	183	THE WAGTAIL	8
AND THE SUN COMES OUT OF A BLUE CLOUD OVER THE TETONS,	194	JOURNY INTERIOR	40
A SINGLE WAVE COMES IN LIKE THE NECK OF A GREAT SWAN	197	THE LONG WATERS	52
AND OUR BREATH COMES MORE EASY,--	230	THE STORM	22
HOW SLOWLY DARK COMES DOWN ON WHAT WE DO.	240	IN EVEING AIR	24
AND, PRAISING CHANGE AS THE SLOW NIGHT COMES ON,	250	THE RIGHT THING	16
AND EVERYTHING COMES TO ONE,	251	ONCE MORE, RND	11
COMETH			
FROM WHENCE COMETH SONG?--	236	SONG (2)	1
COMFORT			
YOU WILL FIND NO COMFORT HERE,	54	THE LOST SON	32
THESE FLOWERS ARE ALL FANGS. COMFORT ME, FURY.	64	SHAPE OF FIRE	9

	PAGE	TITLE	LINE
COMING			
THE COMING OF THE COLD	14	COMING OF COLD	T
COMING OUT, SOFT AND DECEPTIVE,	39	ORCHIDS	4
PAPA IS COMING!	57	THE LOST SON	143
COMING DOWN ON THE FLOWERHEADS,	67	SHAPE OF FIRE	80
I HEAR THE OWLS, THE SOFT CALLERS, COMING DOWN FROM THE HEMLOCKS.	93	I CRY, LOVE!	40
SLOW AS A FISH COMING FORWARD,	100	THE VISITANT	11
COMING BEHIND HER FOR HER PRETTY SAKE	127	I KNEW A WOMAN	13
THAT DOVE'S ELABORATE WAY OF COMING NEAR	149	IN LATE SUMMER	23
SOMEWHAT CLOSER, THE TRUCKS COMING	158	FIRST MEDITATN	32
COMING ACROSS SNOW IN EARLY EVENING?	161	I'M HERE	5
I THINK HIS FORWARD'S COMING BACK!	182	THE HIPPO	2
AND WITH WATER: THE WAVES COMING FORWARD, WITHOUT CESSATION,	191	AT OYSTER RIVER	31
THE SUN A BALL OF FIRE COMING DOWN OVER THE WATER,	202	THE ROSE	16
AND THE DEEP CHORUS OF HORNS COMING UP FROM THE STREETS IN EARLY MORNING.	204	THE ROSE	72
I, ON COMING TO LOVE,	207	THE YOUNG GIRL	3
COMING DOWN FROM THE MOUNTAIN,	230	THE STORM	4
COMING CLOSER AND CLOSER UPON EACH OTHER;	230	THE STORM	12
THE FLAT-ROOFED HOUSES, COMING DOWN IN GUSTS, BEATING	230	THE STORM	24
COMING DOWN ON A PATCH OF LAWN:	235	ALL MORNING	38
AND ON THE COMING OF THE OUTRAGEOUS DAWN,	241	THE SEQUEL	15
SHE'S COMING NEAR!	261	THE CHANGELING	44
WHENEVER I FEEL IT COMING ON	269	GOB MUSIC	10
COMING-OUT			
IN THE SLOW COMING-OUT OF SLEEP,	162	I'M HERE	51
COMMA			
RITUAL OF MULTIGRAPH, PAPER-CLIP, COMMA,	46	DOLOR	7
COMMAND			
AND KNEW HOW TO COMMAND;	268	SAGINAW SONG	53
COMMINGLED			
WE PLAYED A MEASURE WITH COMMINGLED FEET:	106	SIR JOHN DAVIES	31
COMMITTED			
AS IF I HAD COMMITTED, AGAINST THE WHOLE SCHEME OF LIFE, A DESECRATION.	40	MOSS-GATHERING	13
COMMODIOUS			
AND GOT A MOST COMMODIOUS TUBA;	115	THE SERPENT	16
COMMODITIES			
COMMODITIES, HERE WE COME!	81	SENSIBILITY! LA	20
COMMON			
MOVED INTO COMMON DAY,	50	THE CYCLE	4
I FEEL HER PRESENCE IN THE COMMON DAY,	129	SHE	13
THE SELF-DESTRUCTIVE SHAKE THE COMMON WALL;	250	THE RIGHT THING	14
REACHES OF COMMON DAY,	263	FOLLIES OF ADAM	25
COMMOTION			
WITHOUT COMMOTION.	163	I'M HERE	81
COMPANY			
I AM BENIGN IN MY OWN COMPANY.	167	HER BECOMING	87
COMPLEMENT			
TO BUILD A COMPLEMENT TO RAGE,	22	SILENCE	12
COMPLETE			
AND YET HIS HAPPINESS WAS NOT COMPLETE;	28	THE FAVORITE	11
THE IMPULSE TO MAKE SOMEONE ELSE COMPLETE?	105	SIR JOHN DAVIES	27
DESTRUCTION IS COMPLETE.	267	SAGINAW SONG	6
COMPREHENSIVE			
HOW COMPREHENSIVE THAT FELICITY!	188	THE LONGING	26
COMPRESSION			
COMPRESSION CANNOT BREAK	9	THE ADAMANT	9
CONCLUDE			
I CONCLUDE! I CONCLUDE!	86	PRAISE TO END!	43
I CONCLUDE! I CONCLUDE!	86	PRAISE TO END!	43
CONCRETE			
UNDER THE CONCRETE BENCHES,	39	WEED PULLER	1
DYING BRIGHTLY UNDER THE STREET LIGHTS SUNK IN COARSE CONCRETE,	193	JOURNY INTERIOR	29
CONCRETENESS			
THAT ANGUISH OF CONCRETENESS!--	92	I CRY, LOVE!	25
CONDEMN			
CONDEMN THE FORTITUDE	20	REPL TO CENSURE	7
CONDITION			
I PROCLAIM ONCE MORE A CONDITION OF JOY.	92	I CRY, LOVE!	28
I'M KING OF ANOTHER CONDITION,	99	O, THOU OPENING	57

	PAGE	TITLE	LINE
CONDITION (CONTINUED)			
ANOTHER CONDITION.	162	I'M HERE	38
DO WE MOVE TOWARD GOD, OR MERELY ANOTHER CONDITION?	221	THE ABYSS	75
CONDONES			
THINGS LOLL AND LOITER. WHO CONDONES THE LOST?	106	SIR JOHN DAVIES	43
CONDONING			
PROFESSORS ARE CONDONING THE CULTURAL LAG.	27	CLAIRVOY WIDOW	12
CONDOR			
OR RISE WITH THE GAR-EAGLE, THE GREAT-WINGED CONDOR.	209	HER LONGING	16
CONDUCTING			
CONDUCTING HIS LONG WARS WITH THE NEIGHBORHOOD CATS,	234	ALL MORNING	16
CONFINE			
IN THAT LAST WHILE, ETERNITY'S CONFINE,	120	THE DREAM	31
I HEARD A BIRD STIR IN ITS TRUE CONFINE;	241	THE SEQUEL	11
CONFLAGRATION			
TO CONFLAGRATION IN THE UPPER AIR.	17	UNEXTINGUISHED	3
CONFLICTING			
AND STEEL RIPS THROUGH CONFLICTING STEEL.	33	HIGHWAY: MICH	17
CONFORM			
THUS I CONFORM TO MY DIVINITY	244	INFIRMITY	11
CONFUSING			
CONFUSING THEM ONCE FLYING STRAIGHT INTO THE SUN	232	THE THING	7
CONFUSION			
AND FLUNG THEM IN CONFUSION ON THE LAND.	6	INTERLUDE	3
AND ALL THE RUBBISH OF CONFUSION SOLD.	21	THE AUCTION	16
NOW IN THE MISERY OF BED-SITTING ROOM CONFUSION,	29	THE REMINDER	9
THAT MAKES AN OLD CONFUSION WORSE.	257	SANITARIUM	2
CONFUSION'S			
CONFUSION'S CORE SET DEEP WITHIN	22	SILENCE	13
PRICKLING PURE WISHES WITH CONFUSION'S IRE;	143	SHIMMER OF EVIL	12
CONGEALED			
A CENTER SO CONGEALED;	9	THE ADAMANT	10
CONGRESS			
AND WHAT A CONGRESS OF STINKS!--	38	ROOT CELLAR	6
A CONGRESS OF TREE-SHREWS AND RATS,	163	I'M HERE	66
CONNOISSEUR			
I AM A CONNOISSEUR OF MIDNIGHT EYES.	149	IN LATE SUMMER	6
CONSIDERED			
I HAVE CONSIDERED AND FOUND	137	LOVE'S PROGRESS	3
CONSOLE			
THE SIDES OF WET STONES CANNOT CONSOLE ME,	102	ELEGY FOR JANE	16
CONSTANCY			
I LOVE MYSELF: THAT'S MY ONE CONSTANCY.	244	INFIRMITY	5
CONSTANT			
IT'S NECESSARY AMONG THE FLIES AND BANANAS, TO KEEP A CONSTANT VIGIL,	86	PRAISE TO END!	24
IN PUREST SONG ONE PLAYS THE CONSTANT FOOL	244	INFIRMITY	1
ENOUGH TO MERIT CONSTANT THOUGHT.	257	SANITARIUM	8
CONSTRICTED			
CONSTRICTED BY MY TORTURED THOUGHT,	24	BEFORE STUDY	1
CONSTRICTION			
THE NERVELESS CONSTRICTION OF SURFACES--	166	HER BECOMING	41
CONSUME			
THE SPIRIT KNOWS THE FLESH IT MUST CONSUME.	131	SENTENTIOUS MAN	10
CONSUMED			
ECHO ITSELF CONSUMED;	167	HER BECOMING	67
CONTAIN			
THE SHAPES A BRIGHT CONTAINER CAN CONTAIN!	127	I KNEW A WOMAN	4
THE WILD STREAM, THE SEA ITSELF CANNOT CONTAIN ME:	209	HER LONGING	12
CONTAINED			
STILL HOLDING AND FEEDING THE STEM OF THE CONTAINED FLOWER.	67	SHAPE OF FIRE	95
TO BE CONTAINED, TO BE A VESSEL?	169	FOURTH MEDITATN	28
WITH A ROUND VIREO'S EYE, QUIET AND CONTAINED,	234	ALL MORNING	13
CONTAINER			
THE SHAPES A BRIGHT CONTAINER CAN CONTAIN!	127	I KNEW A WOMAN	4
CONTEMPLATION			
WHEN CONTEMPLATION DAZZLES ALL I SEE;	246	THE MARROW	8
CONTENDING			
THE WIND FROM THE SEA AND THE WIND FROM THE MOUNTAIN CONTENDING,	230	THE STORM	15
CONTENT			
MY SOURCES DRAINED OF ALL CONTENT,	19	AGNST DISASTER	3
WE SIT IN THE PORCH SWING, CONTENT AND HALF ASLEEP.	33	IDYLL	8

	PAGE	TITLE	LINE
CORNERS			
IT IS HARD TO CARE ABOUT CORNERS,	104	OLD LADY'S WRDS	59
--HOW NEEDLES AND CORNERS PERPLEX ME!	161	I'M HERE	12
CORRECT			
OR HAPPY, CORRECT AS A HAT?	98	O, THOU OPENING	46
CORRESPONDENCES			
A STEADY STORM OF CORRESPONDENCES!	239	IN A DARK TIME	13
CORRIDOR			
IN THE DARKENING CORRIDOR,	47	THE RETURN	2
CORRIDORS			
BUT DOWN LONG CORRIDORS,	147	THE EXORCISM	10
CORRUPTION			
CORRUPTION REAPS THE YOUNG; YOU DREAD	4	FEUD	1
CORTISONE			
AND PUMPED A SHOULDER FULL OF CORTISONE;	244	INFIRMITY	10
COSMOS			
CARNATIONS, VERBENAS, COSMOS,	43	FLOWER DUMP	4
COST			
THE COST OF FOLLY IS FOREVER MOUNTING;	25	DIM-WIT COUSIN	5
COTTONWOODS			
WHIPPING THE LINE OF WHITE LAUNDRY, BENDING THE COTTONWOODS APART,	194	JOURNY INTERIOR	44
COUGH			
THE GENERALS COUGH AND SHIFT	31	LULL	11
COULD			
UNTIL I COULD THINK THERE WERE WAVES ROLLING HIGH AS MY BEDROOM FLOOR;	12	MID-CNTRY BLOW	2
HIS INSOLENCE COULD WEAR NO PATIENCE THIN.	28	THE FAVORITE	7
HOW HE COULD FLICK AND PICK	42	OLD FLORIST	4
COULD MAKE A SMALL BOY DIZZY;	45	MY PAPA'S WALTZ	2
COULD NOT UNFROWN ITSELF.	45	MY PAPA'S WALTZ	8
IN MIST THAT SUN COULD SEIZE.	50	THE CYCLE	6
COULD IT COME IN THE HOUSE	54	THE LOST SON	52
THIS AIR COULD FLESH A DEAD STICK. SWEET JESUS, MAKE ME SWEAT.	61	THE LONG ALLEY	63
I COULD FEEL THE MARE'S NOSE.	63	THE LONG ALLEY	32
I COULD WATCH! I COULD WATCH!	63	FIELD OF LIGHT	44
I COULD WATCH! I COULD WATCH!	63	FIELD OF LIGHT	44
I COULD LOVE A DUCK.	79	GIVE WAY, GATES	3
I COULD MELT DOWN A STONE,--	79	GIVE WAY, GATES	17
I COULD SAY HELLO TO THINGS;	84	O LULL ME, LULL	38
I COULD TALK TO A SNAIL;	84	O LULL ME, LULL	39
THIS TOAD COULD WALTZ ON A DRUM;	92	I CRY, LOVE!	11
SIMPLICITY'S SWEET THING, EITHER. A LEAF COULD DRAG YOU.	98	O, THOU OPENING	29
SO ALIVE I COULD DIE!	99	O, THOU OPENING	58
EVEN A FATHER COULD NOT FIND HER:	102	ELEGY FOR JANE	11
IF ONLY I COULD NUDGE YOU FROM THIS SLEEP,	102	ELEGY FOR JANE	18
IF ONLY I COULD REMEMBER	103	OLD LADY'S WRDS	19
I COULD ROLL IN THE DUST OF A FINE RAGE.	104	OLD LADY'S WRDS	50
THAT MADE HIM THINK THE UNIVERSE COULD HUM?	105	SIR JOHN DAVIES	2
RAPT, WE LEANED FORTH WITH WHAT WE COULD NOT SEE.	107	SIR JOHN DAVIES	88
--BUT HOW SHE COULD BURN UP THE MONEY!	111	SQUEEZE-BOX	16
FOR WHENEVER I COULD, I DEALT THEM ALL IN	112	SQUEEZE-BOX	32
HER SEVERAL PARTS COULD KEEP A PURE REPOSE,	127	I KNEW A WOMAN	19
AND FOUND OUT ALL I COULD OF ALL DESIRE;	132	SENTENTIOUS MAN	32
COULD BRING ME TO MY GOD?	139	PLAINT	8
MY DARLING DOES WHAT I COULD NEVER DO:	140	THE SWAN	6
THAT CHRIST, SECURELY BOUND, COULD BEAR.	144	ELEGY (1)	8
GOD COULD BELIEVE: I AM HERE TO FEAR.	144	ELEGY (1)	12
YOU COULD SAY I WAS MAD.	146	THE SONG	21
THE WORST SURPRISE A CORNER COULD HAVE,	161	I'M HERE	14
ONCE I COULD TOUCH MY SHADOW, AND BE HAPPY;	168	FOURTH MEDITATN	14
THE BEST HE COULD DO WAS JIGGLE HIS BLUBBER.	178	THE WHALE	4
SHE COULD GROWL LIKE A BEAR,--	179	MYRTLE	4
WHY I COULD DO BETTER	179	MYRTLE	10
IF I THOUGHT YOU COULD HEAR IN A HUSH."	182	BOY AND BUSH	5
WHO'D THINK THE MOON COULD PARE ITSELF SO THIN?	188	THE LONGING	30
A SOUND SO THIN IT COULD NOT WOO A BIRD,	204	THE ROSE	77
IF I COULD SEND HIM ONLY	209	HER RETICENCE	1
O WHAT COULD BE MORE NICE	212	LIGHT LISTENED	1
WHO'D LOOK WHEN HE COULD FEEL?	212	LIGHT LISTENED	5
HIS HAND COULD FIT INTO A WOMAN'S GLOVE,	224	OTTO	12
NOR COULD I PUT THAT SOUND OUT OF MY MIND,	245	THE DECISION	5

	PAGE	TITLE	LINE
COULD (CONTINUED)			
THAT ONCE COULD MELT THE DARK WITH ITS SMALL BREATH.	246	THE MARROW	16
I COULD NOT BEAR ITS SONG, THAT ALTERING	248	THE TREE, BIRD	14
I MET A WOMAN WHO COULD BREAK WIND	268	SAGINAW SONG	41
COULDLY			
COULDLY.	74	I NEED, I NEED	7
COULDN'T			
HE COULDN'T FIND A PROPER WIFE;	115	THE SERPENT	6
IF I WERE A FISH I JUST COULDN'T RESIST	117	LADY AND BEAR	23
WHAT HER FRIENDS COULDN'T EAT AT THOSE LUNCHES!	179	MYRTLE'S COUSIN	10
COUNSEL			
IN TEMPTATION, I RARELY SEEK COUNSEL;	173	WHAT TELL BONES	78
I HAVE TAKEN COUNSEL OF THE CRAB AND THE SEA-URCHIN,	222	THE ABYSS	92
COUNT			
BUT WHO WOULD COUNT ETERNITY IN DAYS?	127	I KNEW A WOMAN	26
BUT I COUNT UP TO ONE,	182	PHILANDER	3
COUNTED			
WE COUNTED SEVERAL FLAMES IN ONE SMALL FIRE.	237	THE TRANCED	1
COUNTENANCE			
MY MOTHER'S COUNTENANCE	45	MY PAPA'S WALTZ	7
COUNTER-TURN			
SHE TAUGHT ME TURN, AND COUNTER-TURN, AND STAND;	127	I KNEW A WOMAN	9
COUNTING			
HAPPY ALONE IN HIS BEDROOM COUNTING HIS PULSE.	24	POETASTER	3
COUNTING THE WISPS OF FLAME, AND I WATCH HOW	240	IN EVEING AIR	20
AND THAT MAKES THREE, COUNTING HIS FACE AS ONE.	273	SUPPR W LINDSAY	9
COUNTRY			
AS YOU LOOK ACROSS MY CITY, IN GOD'S COUNTRY?"	27	CLAIRVOY WIDOW	4
THE GREEN COMES UP FOREVER IN THE FIELDS OF OUR COUNTRY."	28	CLAIRVOY WIDOW	26
IN A COUNTRY OF BLEAK STONE,	146	THE SONG	9
ALONE, ON A BUS THROUGH WESTERN COUNTRY.	158	FIRST MEDITATN	21
IN THE COUNTRY OF FEW LAKES, IN THE TALL BUFFALO GRASS AT THE BASE OF THE CLAY BUTTES,	189	THE LONGING	53
A COUNTRY OF BAYS AND INLETS, AND SMALL STREAMS FLOWING SEAWARD.	196	THE LONG WATERS	19
IN A COUNTRY HALF-LAND, HALF-WATER.	201	THE FAR FIELD	76
THE STUNNED COUNTRY OF OURSELVES.	258	SONG (3)	21
THE HARSH COUNTRY	265	HARSH COUNTRY	T
IN THE COUNTRY OF OURSELVES,	265	HARSH COUNTRY	15
IN A COUNTRY OF BRIGHT STONE.	265	HARSH COUNTRY	16
COURSE			
SWEET ALICE S. MORRIS, I AM PLEASED, OF COURSE,	113	TO A LADY ED	1
--OF COURSE, IT'S DIRTY DINKY.	114	DINKY	8
AND SO, OF COURSE, HE HAD TO SING,	115	THE SERPENT	9
HE'S PART OF ONE, AS A MATTER OF COURSE.	264	THREE EPIGRAMS	12
COURSING			
IS THERE NO WAY OUT OF THAT COURSING BLOOD?	140	THE SWAN	4
COURTESY			
TO LIVE BY COURTESY OF THE SHRIKE, THE SNAKE, THE TOM-CAT.	227	MEADOW MOUSE	25
COURTHOUSES			
THEIR WOODEN STORES OF SILVERY PINE AND WEATHER-BEATEN RED COURTHOUSES,	193	JOURNY INTERIOR	31
COURTING			
I HAVE COME HERE WITHOUT COURTING SILENCE.	197	THE LONG WATERS	44
WREN-SONG IN TRELLIS: A LIGHT ECSTASY OF BUTTERFLIES COURTING,	255	LIGHT POEM	1
COUSIN			
BY DAY THE BAT IS COUSIN TO THE MOUSE.	16	THE BAT	1
MY DIM-WIT COUSIN	25	DIM-WIT COUSIN	T
MY DIM-WIT COUSIN, SAVED BY A DEATH-BED QUAVER,	25	DIM-WIT COUSIN	1
IN MY WAY, CLOSE COUSIN	151	SLUG	5
MYRTLE'S COUSIN	179	MYRTLE'S COUSIN	T
AND THEN THERE WAS MYRTLE'S COUSIN,	179	MYRTLE'S COUSIN	1
OH THAT COUSIN! HER MANNERS! AT LUNCHES!	179	MYRTLE'S COUSIN	5
COVE			
THE SOFTEST COVE	62	FIELD OF LIGHT	9
UNTIL, OUT FROM A DARK COVE,	233	THE PIKE	14
COVER			
THE SPIRIT'S TENDER COVER.	7	ORDERS FOR DAY	7
RUNS TO COVER:	210	HER TIME	24
COVERLET			
RUNNING OVER THE COVERLET, DOWN UNDER THE IRON BEDSTEAD.	231	THE STORM	35

	PAGE	TITLE	LINE
COW			
THE COW	114	THE COW	T
THERE ONCE WAS A COW WITH A DOUBLE UDDER.	114	THE COW	1
COWARD			
DIFFUSE THE OUTPOURINGS OF THE SPIRITUAL COWARD,	5	PROGNOSIS	1
COWS			
THE COWS AND BRIARS	55	THE LOST SON	81
UNTIL THE COWS	71	WHERE KNOCK IS	7
COW'S			
A COW'S A CARE AND WHO'S A COO?--	86	PRAISE TO END!	33
COZ			
POOR MYRTLE WOULD SIGH, "SWEET MY COZ,	180	GOO-GIRL	1
CRAB			
AND THE CRAB, THE QUIET BREATHER.	100	THE VISITANT	9
THE OLD HOUSE OF A CRAB;	146	THE SONG	16
AND ONE CRAB, TENTATIVE, HUNCHES HIMSELF BEFORE MOVING ALONG THE BOTTOM,	159	FIRST MEDITATN	62
I HAVE TAKEN COUNSEL OF THE CRAB AND THE SEA-URCHIN,	222	THE ABYSS	92
CRABS			
AND THE LITTLE CRABS SLIPPED INTO SILVERY CRATERS.	66	SHAPE OF FIRE	67
ALIVE WITH TINY STRIPED FISH, AND YOUNG CRABS CLIMBING IN AND OUT OF THE WATER.	190	AT OYSTER RIVER	5
AND THE CRABS BASK NEAR THE EDGE,	200	THE FAR FIELD	69
WITH ITS THICK GRASSY SCUM AND CRABS SCUTTLING BACK INTO THEIR GLISTENING CRATERS.	203	THE ROSE	50
THE CRABS TILT AND EAT, LEISURELY,	233	THE PIKE	5
LITTLE CRABS SLIPPING INTO WATERY CRATERS--	255	LIGHT POEM	4
CRACK			
A CANNON CRACK ANNOUNCE AN EARLY THAW.	11	LIGHT BRIGHTER	4
THEN A CRACK OF THUNDER, AND THE BLACK RAIN RUNS OVER US, OVER	230	THE STORM	23
CRACKED			
A CRACKED POD CALLS.	64	SHAPE OF FIRE	6
THE SKY CRACKED OPEN	87	PRAISE TO END!	59
CRACKING			
CRACKING SO MUCH THIN GLASS	41	BIG WIND	18
AND THE MIDCHANNEL BEGINS CRACKING AND HEAVING FROM THE PRESSURE BENEATH,	191	AT OYSTER RIVER	49
THE ARROYO CRACKING THE ROAD, THE WIND-BITTEN BUTTES, THE CANYONS,	193	JOURNY INTERIOR	7
CRACKLES			
UNTIL THOUGHT CRACKLES WHITE ACROSS THE BRAIN.	17	UNEXTINGUISHED	12
THE SALT-SOAKED WOOD OF A FIRE CRACKLES;	190	AT OYSTER RIVER	21
CRACKLING			
MY FEET CRACKLING SPLINTERS OF GLASS AND DRIED PUTTY,	43	CHILD ON GRNHSE	2
CRADLE			
IN THE CRADLE OF ALL THAT IS,	191	AT OYSTER RIVER	59
CRADLED			
CRADLED IN MY HAND,	227	MEADOW MOUSE	5
CRADLES			
DRIFTING DOWN FROM THEIR MOSSY CRADLES:	39	ORCHIDS	13
CRAGS			
ETERNITY HOWLS IN THE LAST CRAGS,	89	UNFOLD! UNFOLD!	6
CRANE			
AND, STALKING LIKE A CRANE,	7	ORDERS FOR DAY	13
CRANED			
THE CRANED NECKS, THE MOURNERS' ANONYMOUS FACES,	22	ROAD TO WDLAWN	7
CRASH			
CUT BY THE SEA-SLIME, FAR FROM THE CRASH	205	THE ROSE	92
CRASS			
HEARING A CRASS BABBLE OF BIRDS.	258	SONG (3)	9
CRATER			
I CAN'T LAUGH FROM A CRATER OF BURNING PITCH,	166	HER BECOMING	36
CRATERS			
AND THE LITTLE CRABS SLIPPED INTO SILVERY CRATERS.	66	SHAPE OF FIRE	67
WITH ITS THICK GRASSY SCUM AND CRABS SCUTTLING BACK INTO THEIR GLISTENING CRATERS.	203	THE ROSE	50
LITTLE CRABS SLIPPING INTO WATERY CRATERS--	255	LIGHT POEM	4
CRATES			
LOLLING OBSCENELY FROM MILDEWED CRATES,	38	ROOT CELLAR	4
CRAVENS			
WHEN CRAVENS CRY THEM DOWN,	20	REPL TO CENSURE	10

	PAGE	TITLE	LINE
CRAWL			
WATCHING SHADOWS CRAWL,	53	THE LOST SON	17
I CAN'T CRAWL BACK THROUGH THOSE VEINS,	89	UNFOLD! UNFOLD!	3
CRAWLED			
I'VE CRAWLED FROM THE MIRE, ALERT AS A SAINT OR A DOG;	88	PRAISE TO END!	81
CRAWLING			
CRAWLING ON ALL FOURS,	39	WEED PULLER	15
THE SHADOWS CRAWLING DOWN A SUNNY WALL.	171	WHAT TELL BONES	17
CRAWLS			
A FURRED CATERPILLAR CRAWLS DOWN A STRING.	220	THE ABYSS	35
CRAZED			
I'M CRAZED AND GRACELESS,	83	O LULL ME, LULL	27
CRAZILY			
THE LAST TRICYCLE RUNS CRAZILY TO THE END OF THE WALK.	33	IDYLL	4
CRAZY			
HE LOOPS IN CRAZY FIGURES HALF THE NIGHT	16	THE BAT	5
THE GRANDEUR OF A CRAZY ONE ALONE!--	167	HER BECOMING	90
FROM A CRAZY OLD JACK-DAW BIRD	183	THE WAGTAIL	7
CREAK			
UNTIL THEY CREAK THEIR KNEES:	60	THE LONG ALLEY	36
CREAKED			
WHO CREAKED ON THE GREENHOUSE LADDERS,	44	FRAU BAUMAN	2
(DRIED-OUT, SHE CREAKED LIKE A TULIP.)	228	THE GERANIUM	14
CREAKING			
THE DRIVERS CREAKING THE SEATS OF THE BAROQUE HEARSES,	22	ROAD TO WDLAWN	2
CREAKING THE CYPRESS WINDOW-FRAMES,	41	BIG WIND	17
CREAKING THEIR THIN SPINES,	42	TRANSPLANTING	16
THE LADEN WHEELBARROWS CREAKING AND SWAYING,	158	FIRST MEDITATN	46
GLEAMING, FREEZING HARD AGAIN, CREAKING AT MIDNIGHT--	191	AT OYSTER RIVER	51
WINGS WITHOUT FEATHERS CREAKING IN THE SUN,	243	THE MOTION	19
CREAKS			
THE WIND CREAKS SLOWLY BY;	123	WORDS FOR WIND	26
MY BACK CREAKS WITH THE DAWN.	170	FOURTH MEDITATN	84
CREAM			
THE SUDDEN LIGHT SPILLED ON THE FLOOR LIKE CREAM	273	SUPPR W LINDSAY	12
CORNBREAD AND MILK, ICE CREAM AND MORE ICE CREAM,	274	SUPPR W LINDSAY	32
CORNBREAD AND MILK, ICE CREAM AND MORE ICE CREAM,	274	SUPPR W LINDSAY	32
MOSTLY I REMEMBER THE ICE CREAM.	274	SUPPR W LINDSAY	34
CREATE			
HOPE, LOVE, CREATE, OR DRINK AND DIE:	18	LONG LIVE WEEDS	11
CREATED			
CREATED WHAT'S TO BE.	238	THE MOMENT	12
CREATION			
KEEPING CREATION AT EASE;	44	FRAU BAUMAN	20
A TERRIBLE VIOLENCE OF CREATION,	221	THE ABYSS	55
CREATURE			
THESE SHAPE THE CREATURE THAT IS I.	18	LONG LIVE WEEDS	12
A SELF-DELIGHTING CREATURE,	103	OLD LADY'S WRDS	40
CREATURELY CREATURE, SHE!--	126	WORDS FOR WIND	97
WHEN WILL THAT CREATURE GIVE ME BACK MY BREATH?	134	THE PURE FURY	25
SHOULD EVERY CREATURE BE AS I HAVE BEEN,	144	ELEGY (1)	1
CREATURELY			
CREATURELY CREATURE, SHE!--	126	WORDS FOR WIND	97
CREATURES			
THE MINNOWS LOVE ME, AND THE HUMPED AND SPITTING CREATURES.	88	PRAISE TO END!	89
SING, SING, YOU SYMBOLS! ALL SIMPLE CREATURES,	90	UNFOLD! UNFOLD!	45
ACROSS MY LAWN THE SOFT-BACKED CREATURES COME;	149	IN LATE SUMMER	3
THOSE CAT-LIKE IMMACULATE CREATURES	169	FOURTH MEDITATN	48
IN WHICH ALL CREATURES SHARE, AND THEREBY LIVE,	243	THE MOTION	18
CREEK			
THE SPIKEY PURPLE BUSHES IN THE WINDING DRY CREEK BED--	194	JOURNY INTERIOR	37
WHERE THE SLOW CREEK WINDS DOWN TO THE BLACK SAND OF THE SHORE	203	THE ROSE	49
THAT SOME HAVE CALLED SWAN CREEK;	267	SAGINAW SONG	8
CREEKS			
CREEKS SWOLLEN IN MIDSUMMER FROM THE FLASH-FLOOD ROARING INTO THE NARROW VALLEY.	193	JOURNY INTERIOR	8
CREEP			
THEY PRAYED THE COGS WOULD CREEP;	46	PICKLE BELT	2
WE CREEP TO OUR BED, AND ITS STRAW MATTRESS.	231	THE STORM	28
CREEPERS			
AND BACTERIAL CREEPERS	50	THE MINIMAL	6
BEND DOWN, SMALL BREATHERS, CREEPERS AND WINDERS;	61	THE LONG ALLEY	71

	PAGE	TITLE	LINE
CREEPING			
CREEPING AND HEALING.	50	THE MINIMAL	11
CREEPING SLOWLY OVER THE WET GRASS,	151	SLUG	13
THEN A RUNNEL BEHIND ME, CREEPING CLOSER,	190	AT OYSTER RIVER	4
THE TONGUES OF WATER, CREEPING IN, QUIETLY.	191	AT OYSTER RIVER	35
CREEPS			
AS DARKNESS CREEPS UP ON THE WELL-GROOMED SUBURBAN TOWN,	33	IDYLL	5
CREPT			
I'VE CREPT FROM A CRY.	99	O, THOU OPENING	53
O WHAT LEWD MUSIC CREPT INTO OUR EARS!	106	SIR JOHN DAVIES	46
CRETIN			
SO WHEN THAT SNUFFLING CRETIN OF A MAID	228	THE GERANIUM	22
CREVICE			
A BIT OF WATER CAUGHT IN A WRINKLED CREVICE,	168	FOURTH MEDITATN	8
READY FOR ANY CREVICE,	187	THE LONGING	22
CRICKET-VOICE			
THE CRICKET-VOICE DEEP IN THE MIDNIGHT FIELD,	196	THE LONG WATERS	27
CRIED			
UNTIL HE CRIED AT ENEMIES UNDONE	28	THE FAVORITE	13
THE SNAKES CRIED,	55	THE LOST SON	80
CRIED FOR SOUND.	62	FIELD OF LIGHT	10
THE GROUND CRIED MY NAME:	76	I NEED, I NEED	49
THE SPIRIT AND THE FLESH CRIED OUT FOR MORE.	106	SIR JOHN DAVIES	52
THE WAVES BROKE EASY, CRIED TO ME IN WHITE;	107	SIR JOHN DAVIES	83
I CRIED, AND THE BIRDS CAME DOWN	123	WORDS FOR WIND	15
CRIED OUT THEIR LIVES AN INSTANT AND WERE FREE.	143	SHIMMER OF EVIL	14
I CRIED, AND BACKED AWAY.	146	THE SONG	5
A SHAPE CRIED FROM A CLOUD,	147	THE EXORCISM	7
CRIED TO MY FLESH OUT LOUD.	147	THE EXORCISM	8
TO THESE I CRIED MY LIFE--	166	HER BECOMING	63
THE KITTY-CAT BIRD, HE MOPED AND HE CRIED.	177	KITTY-CAT BIRD	13
CRIED THE SOUL	249	THE RESTORED	11
"WHAT MOON?" HE CRIED, HALF-TURNING IN MOCK FURY.	273	SUPPR W LINDSAY	10
CRIES			
SHE CRIES TO THE HEN,	60	THE LONG ALLEY	51
AND THE GROUND CRIES.	83	O LULL ME, LULL	26
SHE CRIES OUT LOUD THE SOUL'S OWN SECRET JOY;	129	SHE	9
GHOST CRIES OUT TO GHOST--	138	THE SURLY ONE	5
FLESH CRIES TO FLESH; AND BONE CRIES OUT TO BONE;	155	THE DYING MAN	58
FLESH CRIES TO FLESH; AND BONE CRIES OUT TO BONE;	155	THE DYING MAN	58
A BEAST CRIES OUT AS IF ITS FLESH WERE TORN,	156	THE DYING MAN	82
MINDFUL OF CRIES,	162	I'M HERE	32
THE LIGHT CRIES OUT, AND I AM THERE TO HEAR--	188	THE LONGING	32
CRIES OF THE SANDPIPER.	191	AT OYSTER RIVER	62
AFTER THE MIDNIGHT CRIES.	194	JOURNY INTERIOR	64
FOR THE SLEEPY CRIES OF THE TOWHEE,	202	THE ROSE	13
TO THE CRIES OF THE OWL, THE EERIE WHOOPER.	202	THE ROSE	19
CRIES, "I'M OLD ENOUGH TO LIVE	208	HER WORDS	3
SHE CRIES TO HER TRUE LOVE.	208	HER WORDS	9
RISING, WHEELING AWAY WITH HARSH CRIES,	235	ALL MORNING	37
CRIME			
OH, IT WASN'T A CRIME, IT WASN'T A SIN,	112	SQUEEZE-BOX	30
CRISP			
A CRISP HYACINTHINE COOLNESS,	43	CARNATIONS	5
CRITIC			
BEHOLD THE CRITIC, PITCHED LIKE THE CASTRATI,	264	THREE EPIGRAMS	1
CROCUSES			
THOUGH THE CROCUSES POKE UP THEIR HEADS IN THE USUAL PLACES,	24	VERNAL SENTIMNT	1
CRONES			
THESE ANCIENT LEATHERY CRONES,	44	FRAU BAUMAN	32
CRONE'S			
I NEED AN OLD CRONE'S KNOWING.	157	FIRST MEDITATN	19
CROOKS			
FROM THE TOWN'S BIGGEST CROOKS.	267	SAGINAW SONG	36
CROONS			
SHE CROONS, LIKE A CAT TO ITS CLAWS;	208	HER WORDS	2
CROSS			
CROSS MARSHLAND INTO CLOVER.	7	ORDERS FOR DAY	14
ALL CROSS MY LINE OF SIGHT,	34	NIGHT JOURNEY	9
CROSS-BAR			
ONLY TO FLY OVER TO HIS FAVORITE PERCH, THE CROSS-BAR OF A TELEPHONE POLE;	234	ALL MORNING	9

	PAGE	TITLE	LINE
CROSSING			
THERE WERE CLOUDS MAKING A ROUT OF SHAPES CROSSING A WINDBREAK OF CEDARS.	63	FIELD OF LIGHT	48
IT'S A SOUL'S CROSSING TIME.	89	UNFOLD! UNFOLD!	8
AS I WAS CROSSING A HOT HOT PLAIN,	114	DINKY	9
THE LAST GEESE CROSSING AGAINST THE REFLECTED AFTERLIGHT,	202	THE ROSE	17
CROSSING-TENDER'S			
I REMEMBER THE CROSSING-TENDER'S GERANIUM BORDER	29	THE REMINDER	1
CROSS-WINDS			
TOPPED BY CROSS-WINDS, TUGGED AT BY SINUOUS UNDERCURRENTS	191	AT OYSTER RIVER	33
SWIMMING SLOWLY, ITS BACK RUFFLED BY THE LIGHT CROSS-WINDS,	197	THE LONG WATERS	53
CROUCHED			
CROUCHED CLOSER TO THE FLOOR,	47	THE RETURN	3
CROW			
NIGHT CROW	49	NIGHT CROW	T
WHEN I SAW THAT CLUMSY CROW	49	NIGHT CROW	1
THE DEAD CROW DRIES ON A POLE.	80	GIVE WAY, GATES	48
FROM A BURNT PINE THE SHARP SPEECH OF A CROW	246	THE MARROW	3
CROWN			
THE DILL BEARS UP ITS ACRID CROWN;	14	COMING OF COLD	14
TO A TREE LYING FLAT, ITS CROWN HALF BROKEN.	197	THE LONG WATERS	54
WAS IT HERE I WORE A CROWN OF BIRDS FOR A MOMENT	202	THE ROSE	26
WHAT ARE SCEPTER AND CROWN?	262	FOLLIES OF ADAM	8
WITH MORE THAN HALF A CROWN.	269	GOB MUSIC	23
CROWS			
OF RESTIVE CROWS IS SHARPER ON THE EAR.	11	LIGHT BRIGHTER	2
AND THE GULLS CRY AGAINST THE CROWS	202	THE ROSE	7
CRUCIFIXION			
AGONY OF CRUCIFIXION ON BARSTOOLS.	187	THE LONGING	6
CRUMBLED			
AND POKES THE CRUMBLED COAL THE ASHES HID,	17	UNEXTINGUISHED	11
CRUMBLED AND FLOWED AWAY,	49	RIVER INCIDENT	8
RINGED ROUND WITH CRUMBLED CLAY:	146	THE SONG	15
CRUMBLES			
WHAT'S BEYOND NEVER CRUMBLES LIKE AN EMBANKMENT,	159	FIRST MEDITATN	76
CRUMBLING			
THE CRUMBLING SMALL HOLLOW STICKS ON THE UNDERSIDE MIXED WITH ROOTS,	40	MOSS-GATHERING	4
I HAVE MYSELF ONE CRUMBLING SKIN TO SHOW;	144	ELEGY (1)	11
WITH ITS LIMESTONE CRUMBLING INTO FINE GREYISH DUST,	226	THE LIZARD	28
CRUSH			
THOUGHT DOES NOT CRUSH TO STONE.	9	THE ADAMANT	1
CRUST			
BREAKS UP THE CRUST OF CINDERS THAT REMAIN,	17	UNEXTINGUISHED	10
CRUSTS			
PECKING AT CRUSTS AND PEANUTS, THEIR GREEN NECKS GLITTERING;	234	ALL MORNING	28
CRY			
MY SECRETS CRY ALOUD.	3	OPEN HOUSE	1
RAGE WARPS MY CLEAREST CRY	3	OPEN HOUSE	17
THOUGH THE DEVOURING MOTHER CRY, ""ESCAPE ME? NEVER--""	5	PROGNOSIS	13
WHEN CRAVENS CRY THEM DOWN,	20	REPL TO CENSURE	10
AT WOODLAWN I HEARD THE DEAD CRY:	53	THE LOST SON	1
I CRY, LOVE! LOVE!	92	I CRY, LOVE!	T
I CARE FOR A CAT'S CRY AND THE HUGS, LIVE AS WATER.	92	I CRY, LOVE!	16
NOW THE GILLS ARE BEGINNING TO CRY.	92	I CRY, LOVE!	18
A DRY CRY COMES FROM MY OWN DESERT;	93	I CRY, LOVE!	31
I'VE CREPT FROM A CRY.	99	O, THOU OPENING	53
WHAT SHAPE LEAPED FORWARD AT THE SENSUAL CRY?--	107	SIR JOHN DAVIES	67
COMES A TREMULOUS CRY	123	WORDS FOR WIND	28
I CRY DELIGHT: I KNOW	124	WORDS FOR WIND	49
THE ROOT, THE CORE OF A CRY.	124	WORDS FOR WIND	50
BY LISTENING TO THE SPIRIT'S SMALLEST CRY;	131	SENTENTIOUS MAN	15
AND THAT CRY TAKES ME BACK WHERE I WAS BORN.	156	THE DYING MAN	83
I NO LONGER CRY FOR GREEN IN THE MIDST OF CINDERS,	173	WHAT TELL BONES	74
AND THE GULLS CRY AGAINST THE CROWS	202	THE ROSE	7
AND THAT THIN CRY, LIKE A NEEDLE PIERCING THE EAR, THE INSISTENT CICADA,	204	THE ROSE	67
FROM THE QUARRY'S WEAK CRY.	236	SONG (2)	4
I HEAR A CRY AND LOSE IT ON THE WIND.	243	THE MOTION	10
WHICH IS THE WAY? I CRY TO THE DREAD BLACK,	245	THE DECISION	9
HOW DEEP THE MOTHER-ROOT OF THAT STILL CRY!	248	THE TREE, BIRD	17
I DO NOT LAUGH; I DO NOT CRY;	256	IN HYDROTHERAPY	9

	PAGE	TITLE	LINE
CRYING			
THE SPIRIT CRYING IN A CAGE	22	SILENCE	11
WATER RECEDES TO THE CRYING OF SPIDERS.	64	SHAPE OF FIRE	4
CRYING SOFTLY.	171	WHAT TELL BONES	33
CRYPTIC			
AS CRYPTIC AS A RUNE,	271	THE REPLY	7
CRYSTAL			
A HAMMER ON THE CRYSTAL WALLS	22	SILENCE	5
CUBA			
THEY SENT,--YOU ALWAYS SEND,--TO CUBA	115	THE SERPENT	15
CUD			
THE RUMINANT, REASON, CHEWS A POISONED CUD.	5	PROGNOSIS	8
CUE			
THE LIVING ALL ASSEMBLE! WHAT'S THE CUE?--	106	SIR JOHN DAVIES	41
CULTURAL			
PROFESSORS ARE CONDONING THE CULTURAL LAG.	27	CLAIRVOY WIDOW	12
CULVERT			
THE SUDDEN SUCKING ROAR AS THE CULVERT LOOSENS ITS DEBRIS OF BRANCHES AND STICKS,	191	AT OYSTER RIVER	53
WHERE THE TURF DROPS OFF INTO A GRASS-HIDDEN CULVERT,	199	THE FAR FIELD	14
CUNNING			
THE LAWYERS ALL ARE CUNNING, THE BUSINESS MEN ARE FAT,	27	CLAIRVOY WIDOW	7
THE HUMMINGBIRD'S SURETY, THE KINGFISHER'S CUNNING--	191	AT OYSTER RIVER	40
CUP			
THE WASP DRINKING AT THE EDGE OF MY CUP;	163	I'M HERE	87
BOILED EGGS FROM A CUP,--	179	MYRTLE'S COUSIN	4
CUPID			
DAN CUPID, I TELL YOU'S A BRAW LADDIE-BUCK;	113	TO A LADY ED	5
CUR			
FROM THE CUR AT MY FEET.	236	SONG (2)	8
CURB			
I TEETER, HEELS HOOKED ON THE CURB, SCRAPE A TOE;	47	DOUBLE FEATURE	7
OVER THE WORN CURB OF THE TERRACE,	226	THE LIZARD	8
I'LL SPIT OVER MY CHIN AND BEYOND THE CURB,	272	DUET	7
CURIOUS			
WE UNDID CHAOS TO A CURIOUS SOUND:	107	SIR JOHN DAVIES	82
CURLED			
THE LEAVES CURLED BACK IN ELABORATE CORINTHIAN SCROLLS;	43	CARNATIONS	2
ENDING CURLED AROUND AND OVER AGAIN,	226	THE LIZARD	11
HIS TAIL CURLED UNDER HIM, HIS BELLY BIG	227	MEADOW MOUSE	14
CURLEW'S			
THE CURLEW'S SLOW NIGHT SONG CAME ON THE WATER.	216	THE SHY MAN	9
CURLING			
I IMAGINED THE UNBORN, STARVING IN WOMBS, CURLING;	48	JUDGE NOT	5
CURRENT			
SLIDING THROUGH THE WHITE CURRENT,	59	THE LONG ALLEY	3
TAIL AROUND, NOSING IN AND OUT OF THE CURRENT,	101	LIGHT BREATHER	9
AS A CHIP OR SHELL, FLOATING LAZILY WITH A SLOW CURRENT,	168	FOURTH MEDITATN	6
YOUNGLINGS, THE SMALL FISH KEEP HEADING INTO THE CURRENT.	170	FOURTH MEDITATN	75
I REMEMBER A STONE BREAKING THE EDDYING CURRENT,	197	THE LONG WATERS	55
A POINT OUTSIDE THE GLITTERING CURRENT;	201	THE FAR FIELD	72
CURRENTS			
INTO THE DARKENING CURRENTS,	202	THE ROSE	23
CURSE			
YOU CURSE THE LEGACY OF PAIN;	4	FEUD	6
ALL THINGS UNHOLY, MARRED BY CURSE,	18	LONG LIVE WEEDS	5
DID I EVER CURSE THE SUN?	62	FIELD OF LIGHT	20
TOUCH AND AROUSE. SUCK AND SOB. CURSE AND MOURN.	80	GIVE WAY, GATES	46
SELF-CONTEMPLATION IS A CURSE	257	SANITARIUM	1
CURSED			
O CURSED BE THE WORK THAT GETS HONORABLE MENTION!	29	THE GENTLE	9
CURTAIN			
OR A MOTH BEATING THE CURTAIN.	54	THE LOST SON	23
AS A BLIND MAN, LIFTING A CURTAIN, KNOWS IT IS MORNING,	195	JOURNY INTERIOR	74
CURVE			
THE STRAINING AT A CURVE;	34	NIGHT JOURNEY	13
CURVED			
IN THE CURVED HARBORS,	202	THE ROSE	8
CURVES			
AND WE RIDE, WE RIDE, TAKING THE CURVES	158	FIRST MEDITATN	31
CURVING			
HIS THOUGHT IS TIED, THE CURVING PROW	4	DEATH PIECE	5

	PAGE	TITLE	LINE
CUSHION			
EACH CUSHION FOUND ITSELF A FIELD OF PINS,	143	SHIMMER OF EVIL	11
CUSHIONY			
THICK AND CUSHIONY, LIKE AN OLD-FASHIONED DOORMAT,	40	MOSS-GATHERING	3
CUT			
CUT STEMS STRUGGLING TO PUT DOWN FEET,	37	CUTTINGS (LATE)	2
AND THEN HE CUT LOOSE WITH A HORRIBLE NOTE	115	THE SERPENT	21
CUT BY THE SEA-SLIME, FAR FROM THE CRASH	205	THE ROSE	92
HAD SLAUGHTERED GAME, AND CUT YOUNG FIR TREES DOWN.	224	OTTO	21
THAT CUT LIKE RAZORS,	265	HARSH COUNTRY	8
CUTS			
THE SUN CUTS DEEP INTO THE HEAVY DRIFT,	11	LIGHT BRIGHTER	5
CUTTINGS			
CUTTINGS	37	CUTTINGS	T
CUTTINGS (LATER)	37	CUTTINGS (LATE)	T
CYCLAMEN			
GREAT CANNAS OR DELICATE CYCLAMEN TIPS,--	38	FORCING HOUSE	4
LILIES, PALE-PINK CYCLAMEN, ROSES,	39	WEED PULLER	12
CYCLAMEN DRIPPING AND LILIES.	61	THE LONG ALLEY	73
TO SEE CYCLAMEN VEINS BECOME CLEARER IN EARLY SUNLIGHT,	67	SHAPE OF FIRE	86
AND THE CYCLAMEN LEAVES GLISTEN LIKE THE BACKS OF BABY TURTLES.	260	THE CHANGELING	15
CYCLE			
THE CYCLE	50	THE CYCLE	T
CYPRESS			
CREAKING THE CYPRESS WINDOW-FRAMES,	41	BIG WIND	17
DABBLE			
I DABBLE MY TOES IN THE BRACKISH FOAM SLIDING FORWARD,	190	AT OYSTER RIVER	15
DAEMON			
I SHED MY CLOTHES TO SLOW MY DAEMON DOWN.	166	HER BECOMING	59
DAFT			
BUT SWEETLY DAFT.	172	WHAT TELL BONES	58
DAH			
OOOMPH DAH DOODLE DAH	269	GOB MUSIC	7
OOOMPH DAH DOODLE DAH	269	GOB MUSIC	7
OOOMPH DAH DOODLE DAH	269	GOB MUSIC	8
OOOMPH DAH DOODLE DAH	269	GOB MUSIC	8
OOOMPH DAH DOODLE DAH DO.	269	GOB MUSIC	9
OOOMPH DAH DOODLE DAH DO.	269	GOB MUSIC	9
DAILY			
IS HUMAN NATURE'S DAILY FOOD.	25	VERSE W ALLUSNS	8
BY DYING DAILY, I HAVE COME TO BE.	155	THE DYING MAN	71
DAISIES			
OF DAISIES WAVED;	51	THE WAKING (1)	14
DAKOTAS			
ON THE BULLHEAD, IN THE DAKOTAS, WHERE THE EAGLES EAT WELL,	188	THE LONGING	52
AND THE TICKING OF SNOW AROUND OIL DRUMS IN THE DAKOTAS,	204	THE ROSE	68
DALLIANCE			
IT'S NO DALLIANCE.	261	THE CHANGELING	36
DALLY			
DALLY AT SHOP WINDOWS, STILL RELUCTANT TO GO;	47	DOUBLE FEATURE	6
DAME			
SHOULD DAME ANXIETY EVER COME NEAR	272	DUET	24
DAMES			
THE DUMB DAMES SHRIEKING HALF THE NIGHT	228	THE GERANIUM	16
DAMP			
LIMP AND DAMP, DELICATE AS A YOUNG BIRD'S TONGUE;	39	ORCHIDS	5
I REMEMBER THE NECKCURLS, LIMP AND DAMP AS TENDRILS;	102	ELEGY FOR JANE	1
OVER THIS DAMP GRAVE I SPEAK THE WORDS OF MY LOVE:	102	ELEGY FOR JANE	20
THE STENCH OF THEIR DAMP FUR DRYING IN THE SUN,	189	THE LONGING	55
THE MOTTLED TIGER, BEST IN THE CORNER OF A DAMP PLACE,	197	THE LONG WATERS	40
DAN			
DAN CUPID, I TELL YOU'S A BRAW LADDIE-BUCK;	113	TO A LADY ED	5
DANCE			
WAKE ME, WITCH, WE'LL DO THE DANCE OF ROTTEN STICKS.	64	SHAPE OF FIRE	10
BUMPKIN, HE CAN DANCE ALONE.	85	PRAISE TO END!	7
CARES ABOUT THE DANCE OF DEAD UNDERWEAR, OR THE SAD WALTZ OF PAPER	98	O, THOU OPENING	26
THE DANCE	105	SIR JOHN DAVIES	ST
IS THAT DANCE SLOWING IN THE MIND OF MAN	105	SIR JOHN DAVIES	1
I KNOW A DANCE THE ELEPHANTS BELIEVE.	106	SIR JOHN DAVIES	40
I HEAR MY BEING DANCE FROM EAR TO EAR.	108	THE WAKING (2)	5
--AS I DANCE TO MY POEM CALLED POEM.	113	TO A LADY ED	16

	PAGE	TITLE	LINE
DANCE (CONTINUED)			
AND I DANCE ROUND AND ROUND,	126	WORDS FOR WIND	102
ALL WOMEN LOVED DANCE IN A DYING LIGHT--	156	THE DYING MAN	78
THE DANCE OF NATURAL OBJECTS IN THE MIND,	171	WHAT TELL BONES	15
I'M RELEASED FROM THE DREARY DANCE OF OPPOSITES.	173	WHAT TELL BONES	80
I DANCE TO THE RIGHT, TO THE LEFT;	208	HER WORDS	6
AND I DANCE WITH WILLIAM BLAKE	251	ONCE MORE, RND	9
AS WE DANCE ON, DANCE ON, DANCE ON.	251	ONCE MORE, RND	12
AS WE DANCE ON, DANCE ON, DANCE ON.	251	ONCE MORE, RND	12
AS WE DANCE ON, DANCE ON, DANCE ON.	251	ONCE MORE, RND	12
DANCED			
MARROW-SOFT, DANCED IN THE SAND.	63	FIELD OF LIGHT	30
LATER, I DID AND I DANCED IN THE SIMPLE WOOD.	90	UNFOLD! UNFOLD!	34
WHEN GLORY FAILED, WE DANCED UPON A PIN.	106	SIR JOHN DAVIES	58
WE DANCED TO SHINING; MOCKED BEFORE THE BLACK	107	SIR JOHN DAVIES	89
THE BUSHES AND THE STONES DANCED ON AND ON;	119	THE DREAM	12
SUBJECT AND OBJECT SANG AND DANCED AS ONE;	237	THE TRANCED	17
WE DANCED, WE DANCED, UNDER A DANCING MOON;	241	THE SEQUEL	14
WE DANCED, WE DANCED, UNDER A DANCING MOON;	241	THE SEQUEL	14
WE DANCED TOGETHER, WE DANCED ON AND ON.	241	THE SEQUEL	16
WE DANCED TOGETHER, WE DANCED ON AND ON.	241	THE SEQUEL	16
DANCED MY OWN SOUL,	249	THE RESTORED	2
AND DANCED, AT HIGH NOON.	249	THE RESTORED	17
DANCES			
SHE DANCES, AND THE GROUND BEARS HER AWAY.	129	SHE	10
NOT EVEN THE SOOT DANCES.	187	THE LONGING	18
AND THE FIRE DANCES	221	THE ABYSS	72
DANCING			
ARE THE RATS DANCING? THE CATS ARE.	79	GIVE WAY, GATES	8
THOUGH DANCING NEEDS A MASTER, I HAD NONE	105	SIR JOHN DAVIES	15
BUT WHAT I LEARNED THERE, DANCING ALL ALONE,	105	SIR JOHN DAVIES	17
ALL SENSUAL LOVE'S BUT DANCING ON A GRAVE.	154	THE DYING MAN	47
I CLOSED MY EYES, AND SAW SMALL FIGURES DANCING,	163	I'M HERE	65
THE CHILDREN DANCING, THE FLOWERS WIDENING.	188	THE LONGING	40
REJOICE IN THE LANGUAGE OF SMELLS AND DANCING.	196	THE LONG WATERS	4
I SAW A BODY DANCING IN THE WIND,	241	THE SEQUEL	9
WE DANCED, WE DANCED, UNDER A DANCING MOON;	241	THE SEQUEL	14
THE CLOSE DIRT DANCING ON A SUNLESS STONE	243	THE MOTION	20
WHERE'S THE BRIDGE OF DANCING CHILDREN?	258	SONG (3)	24
DANCING-MAD			
YES, I WAS DANCING-MAD, AND HOW	105	SIR JOHN DAVIES	23
DANCING-ROOM			
I NEED A PLACE TO SING, AND DANCING-ROOM,	105	SIR JOHN DAVIES	4
DANDELION			
OR THEY SIT SIDEWAYS ON LIMBER DANDELION STEMS,	152	THE SISKINS	10
DANDY			
MY BLUE ORIGINAL DANDY, NUMB WITH SUGAR?	86	PRAISE TO END!	18
HERE'S A MENSCH BUT CAN SING DANDY.	266	FOR STEVENS	14
DANGER			
HOW GRACEFUL THE SMALL BEFORE DANGER!	192	AT OYSTER RIVER	67
DANGEROUS			
THE DANGEROUS FLOODED PLAIN	7	ORDERS FOR DAY	11
FINER THAN FLOUR, ALIVE, MORE DANGEROUS THAN SILICA,	46	DOLOR	10
WHERE'S THE GREAT RAGE OF A ROCKING HEART, THE HIGH RARE TRUE DANGEROUS	98	O, THOU OPENING	30
ALL EXULTATION IS A DANGEROUS THING.	155	THE DYING MAN	72
OR LIVE THE DANGEROUS LIFE OF AN INSECT.	166	HER BECOMING	37
WATCHING FOR DANGEROUS DOWN-HILL PLACES, WHERE THE WHEELS WHINED BEYOND EIGHTY--	193	JOURNY INTERIOR	19
I HAVE TAKEN, TOO OFTEN, THE DANGEROUS PATH,	220	THE ABYSS	21
DANGEROUSLY			
WHERE THE SHALE SLIDES DANGEROUSLY	193	JOURNY INTERIOR	3
DANGLED			
SHOOTS DANGLED AND DROOPED,	38	ROOT CELLAR	3
DANK			
THE DANK BARK DRIES BENEATH THE SUN,	14	COMING OF COLD	32
THE WORM, THOUGH DANK, IS SENSITIVE:	23	AMOROUS LADY	7
NOTHING WOULD SLEEP IN THAT CELLAR, DANK AS A DITCH,	38	ROOT CELLAR	1
DANTE			
DANTE ATTAINED THE PURGATORIAL HILL,	107	SIR JOHN DAVIES	73
DID BEATRICE DENY WHAT DANTE SAW?	107	SIR JOHN DAVIES	76
DANTE HIMSELF ENDURED,	216	HER WRATH	1

	PAGE	TITLE	LINE
DAPPLED			
IN THE RICH WEATHER OF A DAPPLED WOOD	107	SIR JOHN DAVIES	65
THE DEER CAME DOWN, OUT OF THE DAPPLED WOOD.	120	THE DREAM	20
DARE			
DOESN'T DARE	117	LADY AND BEAR	12
DOESN'T DARE	117	LADY AND BEAR	13
DOESN'T DARE	117	LADY AND BEAR	14
THE POSSIBLES WE DARE!	137	LOVE'S PROGRESS	1
I BARE A WOUND, AND DARE MYSELF TO BLEED.	155	THE DYING MAN	69
DARE I SHRINK TO A HAG,	161	I'M HERE	13
DARE I EMBRACE A GHOST FROM MY OWN BREAST?	165	HER BECOMING	21
DARE I SPEAK, ONCE MORE, IN THE MONOTONY OF GREAT PRAISE,	166	HER BECOMING	32
I DARE CARESS THE STONES, THE FIELD MY FRIEND;	167	HER BECOMING	94
DARE I BLAZE LIKE A TREE?	171	WHAT TELL BONES	9
DARE I GRIEVE? DARE I MOURN?	208	THE APPARITION	11
DARE I GRIEVE? DARE I MOURN?	208	THE APPARITION	11
I DARE EMBRACE. BY STRIDING, I REMAIN.	243	THE MOTION	12
DARED			
WE DARED THE DARK TO REACH THE WHITE AND WARM.	107	SIR JOHN DAVIES	92
I DARED TO QUESTION ALL,	154	THE DYING MAN	32
YET DARED TO FIX HIS VISION ANYWHERE.	155	THE DYING MAN	65
DARES			
DARES FACE THE THING HE IS?)	147	THE EXORCISM	4
IN THIS LAST PLACE OF LIGHT: HE DARES TO LIVE	156	THE DYING MAN	99
EXISTENCE DARES PERPETUATE A SOUL,	173	WHAT TELL BONES	67
DARK			
THE MEANING OF THE DAY; DARK FORMS	4	FEUD	14
RECALL THE GRADUAL DARK THE SNOW'S UNMEASURED FALL	5	TO MY SISTER	3
THE RAIN STAYED IN ITS CLOUD; FULL DARK CAME NEAR;	6	INTERLUDE	9
OR WHEN DARK FOLLOWS DARK IN LIGHTNING RIFT.	8	THE SIGNALS	6
OR WHEN DARK FOLLOWS DARK IN LIGHTNING RIFT.	8	THE SIGNALS	6
THE SKY TURNS DARK, THE YEAR GROWS OLD,	15	COMING OF COLD	36
ACCEPT CARESSES IN THE DARK;	23	AMOROUS LADY	2
FROM DARK TO BLAZING BRIGHT;	34	NIGHT JOURNEY	17
BULBS BROKE OUT OF BOXES HUNTING FOR CHINKS IN THE DARK,	38	ROOT CELLAR	2
IN THE DARK, IN THE ROLLING WATER.	49	RIVER INCIDENT	11
DARK WATER, UNDERGROUND,	50	THE CYCLE	1
DARK HOLLOWS SAID, LEE TO THE WIND,	54	THE LOST SON	28
WHAT A SMALL SONG. WHAT SLOW CLOUDS. WHAT DARK WATER.	56	THE LOST SON	83
KISS ME, ASHES, I'M FALLING THROUGH A DARK SWIRL.	57	THE LOST SON	121
THE WAY TO THE BOILER WAS DARK,	57	THE LOST SON	122
DARK ALL THE WAY,	57	THE LOST SON	123
THE ROSES KEPT BREATHING IN THE DARK.	57	THE LOST SON	126
THE DARK FLOWS ON ITSELF. A DEAD MOUTH SINGS UNDER AN OLD TREE.	59	THE LONG ALLEY	6
THE REDEEMER COMES A DARK WAY.	66	SHAPE OF FIRE	63
DARK CAME EARLY.	73	WHERE KNOCK IS	67
MAMMA! PUT ON YOUR DARK HOOD;	82	SENSIBILITY! LA	37
HAS THE DARK A DOOR?	82	SENSIBILITY! LA	47
IT'S DARK IN THIS WOOD, SOFT MOCKER.	85	PRAISE TO END!	1
THE DARK SHOWED ME A FACE.	88	PRAISE TO END!	99
THE DARK HAIR SIGHED.	93	I CRY, LOVE!	56
THE DARK HAS ITS OWN LIGHT.	98	O, THOU OPENING	32
IN THE SOFT DARK OF EARLY EVENING,	100	THE VISITANT	17
IN THAT DARK WORLD WHERE GODS HAVE LOST THEIR WAY.	106	SIR JOHN DAVIES	48
WE PLAYED WITH DARK AND LIGHT AS CHILDREN SHOULD.	107	SIR JOHN DAVIES	66
WE DARED THE DARK TO REACH THE WHITE AND WARM.	107	SIR JOHN DAVIES	92
ONE WITH THE SULLEN DARK.	122	ALL EARTH, AIR	27
IN THAT SLOW DARK THAT WIDENS EVERY EYE.	129	SHE	14
DARK HANGS UPON THE WATERS OF THE SOUL;	135	THE RENEWAL	8
I PAW THE DARK, THE SHIFTING MIDNIGHT AIR.	135	THE RENEWAL	16
THE CLOSE DARK HUGS ME HARD,	138	LOVE'S PROGRESS	21
I STUDY OUT A DARK SIMILITUDE:	140	THE SWAN	1
IN A DARK WOOD I SAW--	147	THE EXORCISM	13
WHEN I SLIP, JUST SLIGHTLY, IN THE DARK,	151	SLUG	8
ONLY TO LOSE MYSELF IN THIS SMALL DARK.	154	THE DYING MAN	41
I BREATHE ALONE UNTIL MY DARK IS BRIGHT.	155	THE DYING MAN	51
WHEN THERE'S A DAZZLING DARK BEHIND THE SUN?	155	THE DYING MAN	53
A MAD HEN IN A FAR CORNER OF THE DARK,	165	HER BECOMING	5
WE START FROM THE DARK. PAIN TEACHES US LITTLE.	166	HER BECOMING	35
ON A DARK DAY I WALK STRAIGHT TOWARD THE RAIN.	170	FOURTH MEDITATN	80
I ROCK IN MY OWN DARK,	172	WHAT TELL BONES	62
WHAT DREAM'S ENOUGH TO BREATHE IN? A DARK DREAM.	188	THE LONGING	28

	PAGE	TITLE	LINE
DARK (CONTINUED)			
AND THE DARK BE FORGOTTEN.	188	THE LONGING	50
IN THE DARK AND LIGHT OF A DRY PLACE,	194	JOURNY INTERIOR	60
AND THE DEAD BEGIN FROM THEIR DARK TO SING IN MY SLEEP.	195	JOURNY INTERIOR	79
THE FIRST SNOW OF THE YEAR IN THE DARK FIR.	197	THE LONG WATERS	31
FLOWERING OUT OF THE DARK,	203	THE ROSE	42
I ROCK BETWEEN DARK AND DARK,	221	THE ABYSS	78
I ROCK BETWEEN DARK AND DARK,	221	THE ABYSS	78
WITH THE DARK HEARSE, AND ENOUGH FLOWERS FOR AN ALDERMAN, --	223	ELEGY (2)	2
UNTIL, OUT FROM A DARK COVE,	233	THE PIKE	14
AND CAME TO A DARK RAVINE,	238	THE MOMENT	2
IN A DARK TIME	239	IN A DARK TIME	T
IN A DARK TIME, THE EYE BEGINS TO SEE,	239	IN A DARK TIME	1
DARK, DARK MY LIGHT, AND DARKER MY DESIRE.	239	IN A DARK TIME	19
DARK, DARK MY LIGHT, AND DARKER MY DESIRE.	239	IN A DARK TIME	19
A DARK THEME KEEPS ME HERE,	240	IN EVEING AIR	1
AND I BEHOLD THE DARK SIDE OF A TREE	240	IN EVEING AIR	14
HOW SLOWLY DARK COMES DOWN ON WHAT WE DO.	240	IN EVEING AIR	24
TO THE DARK BEGINNINGS OF ANOTHER DAY.	241	THE SEQUEL	24
THE CHANGE FROM DARK TO LIGHT OF THE SLOW MOON,	244	INFIRMITY	22
THAT ONCE COULD MELT THE DARK WITH ITS SMALL BREATH.	246	THE MARROW	16
PART OF A TREE STILL DARK, STILL, DEATHLY STILL,	248	THE TREE, BIRD	9
CHILD OF THE DARK, HE CAN OUT LEAP THE SUN,	250	THE RIGHT THING	10
THE DARK HEART OF SOME ANCIENT THING	260	THE CHANGELING	4
IN THE DARK OF AN OULD SPITTOON;	269	GOB MUSIC	21
DARKEN			
UNTIL THE HEADLIGHTS DARKEN.	199	THE FAR FIELD	12
DARKENED			
AND THE BLUE AIR DARKENED.	232	THE THING	23
DARKENING			
IN THE DARKENING CORRIDOR,	47	THE RETURN	2
WE TWO, TOGETHER, ON A DARKENING DAY	106	SIR JOHN DAVIES	53
THE SWAN'S DREAD OF THE DARKENING SHORE,	171	WHAT TELL BONES	25
THE THICKETS DARKENING,	193	JOURNY INTERIOR	16
WHERE IMPULSE NO LONGER DICTATES, NOR THE DARKENING SHADOW,	197	THE LONG WATERS	57
INTO THE DARKENING CURRENTS,	202	THE ROSE	23
THE DOLPHIN RISING FROM THE DARKENING WAVES;	205	THE ROSE	110
I SNIFF THE DARKENING AIR	215	HIS FOREBODING	17
DARKER			
I KNOW IT'S AN OWL. HE'S MAKING IT DARKER.	72	WHERE KNOCK IS	39
DARK, DARK MY LIGHT, AND DARKER MY DESIRE.	239	IN A DARK TIME	19
DARKEST			
THE MOLE MAKING ITS WAY THROUGH DARKEST GROUND,	235	MANIFESTATION	4
DARK-GREEN			
AND LIFT UP A PATCH, DARK-GREEN, THE KIND FOR LINING CEMETERY BASKETS,	40	MOSS-GATHERING	2
DARKNESS			
AS DARKNESS CREEPS UP ON THE WELL-GROOMED SUBURBAN TOWN,	33	IDYLL	5
THE DARKNESS OF FALLING HAIR, THE WARNINGS FROM LINT AND SPIDERS,	159	FIRST MEDITATN	80
WHO TOOK THE DARKNESS FROM THE AIR?	173	WHAT TELL BONES	94
FLICKING THE FOAM FROM THE WHITECAPS STRAIGHT UPWARD INTO THE DARKNESS.	230	THE STORM	16
DARLING			
DARLING OF AN INFECTED BROOD,	4	FEUD	7
MY MAIMED DARLING, MY SKITTERY PIGEON.	102	ELEGY FOR JANE	19
MY DARLING, MY DEAREST, MOST-HONEST-ALIVE,	113	TO A LADY ED	13
AT TIMES MY DARLING SQUEAKS IN PURE PLATO.	133	THE PURE FURY	14
MY DARLING DOES WHAT I COULD NEVER DO:	140	THE SWAN	6
INSIDE, MY DARLING WIFE	213	THE HAPPY THREE	1
MY EX-EXISTENTIALIST DARLING DEAR,	272	DUET	23
DART			
THEY DART ACROSS A CORNER OF THE EYE.	8	THE SIGNALS	4
DAUGHTER			
AS I WALKED BESIDE HER, THE O'CONNELL'S DAUGHTER,	216	THE SHY MAN	11
FOR HERE CLOSE BESIDE ME IS O'CONNELL'S DAUGHTER,	216	THE SHY MAN	20
DAVIES			
FOUR FOR SIR JOHN DAVIES	105	SIR JOHN DAVIES	T
DAWDLE			
I DAWDLE WITH GROUPS NEAR THE RICKETY POP-CORN STAND;	47	DOUBLE FEATURE	5
DAWDLES			
AND A FISHERMAN DAWDLES OVER A WOODEN BRIDGE,	197	THE LONG WATERS	37

	PAGE	TITLE	LINE
DAWN			
THE SECOND DAWN I WOULD NOT HAVE BELIEVED:	12	MID-CNTRY BLOW	5
THE LOOSE VINE DROOPS WITH HOAR AT DAWN,	14	COMING OF COLD	20
LEANING ACROSS A SILL TO GREET THE DAWN?	154	THE DYING MAN	44
DAWN'S WHERE THE WHITE IS. WHO WOULD KNOW THE DAWN	155	THE DYING MAN	52
MAY THEIR EYES GLEAM WITH THE FIRST DAWN;	169	FOURTH MEDITATN	59
MY BACK CREAKS WITH THE DAWN.	170	FOURTH MEDITATN	84
THEN SLOWLY BREAKING WHITER IN THE DAWN;	225	OTTO	37
AND ON THE COMING OF THE OUTRAGEOUS DAWN,	241	THE SEQUEL	15
DAWN'S			
DAWN'S WHERE THE WHITE IS. WHO WOULD KNOW THE DAWN	155	THE DYING MAN	52
DAY			
THE MEANING OF THE DAY: DARK FORMS	4	FEUD	14
ORDERS FOR THE DAY	7	ORDERS FOR DAY	T
ALL NIGHT AND ALL DAY THE WIND ROARED IN THE TREES,	12	MID-CNTRY BLOW	1
BY DAY THE BAT IS COUSIN TO THE MOUSE.	16	THE BAT	1
RIDES BY, FOR AT THE END OF DAY	33	HIGHWAY: MICH	4
TUGGING ALL DAY AT PERVERSE LIFE:	39	WEED PULLER	9
THE FRUIT ROLLED BY ALL DAY.	46	PICKLE BELT	1
MOVED INTO COMMON DAY,	50	THE CYCLE	4
THAT SUMMER DAY.	51	THE WAKING (1)	28
I SANG I SANG ALL DAY.	72	WHERE KNOCK IS	38
A DOVE SAID DOVE ALL DAY.	75	I NEED, I NEED	20
BRING THE DAY!	77	BRING THE DAY!	T
IT'S A GREAT DAY FOR THE MICE.	85	PRAISE TO END!	5
ON A PLAIN DAY.	98	O, THOU OPENING	37
BUT THE BRIGHT DAY HAD NO ANSWER.	101	THE VISITANT	25
THE GOOD DAY HAS GONE:	103	OLD LADY'S WRDS	25
WE TWO, TOGETHER, ON A DARKENING DAY	106	SIR JOHN DAVIES	53
OUR SOULS LOOKED FORTH, AND THE GREAT DAY STOOD STILL.	106	SIR JOHN DAVIES	60
MAKES AN INTENSER DAY	124	WORDS FOR WIND	56
LIKE ANY SUMMER DAY.	128	THE VOICE	24
I FEEL HER PRESENCE IN THE COMMON DAY,	129	SHE	13
DAY AFTER SOMBER DAY,	139	PLAINT	1
DAY AFTER SOMBER DAY,	139	PLAINT	1
THIS WHOLE SEPTEMBER DAY.	148	THE SMALL	6
THE LONG DAY DIES; I WALKED THE WOODS ALONE;	150	IN LATE SUMMER	29
ON LOVE'S WORST UGLY DAY.	157	FIRST MEDITATN	1
AND ANOTHER, OUTSIDE, IN THE BRIGHT DAY,	158	FIRST MEDITATN	41
AND THERE I STAYED UNTIL THE DAY BURNED DOWN.	166	HER BECOMING	52
THE LIGHT AIR SLOWED: IT WAS NOT NIGHT OR DAY.	166	HER BECOMING	56
ON A DARK DAY I WALK STRAIGHT TOWARD THE RAIN.	170	FOURTH MEDITATN	80
A THIN HARSH SONG. THE DAY DIES IN A CHILD.	171	WHAT TELL BONES	19
I WOULDN'T BE YOU FOR EVEN A DAY,	177	KITTY-CAT BIRD	11
ONE DAY HUGH WALKED UP TO A BEAR	181	MONOTONY SONG	5
AND YOU CAN SING IT ALL DAY LONG--	181	MONOTONY SONG	22
HE STARTS TO YAWN--IT TAKES ALL DAY--	182	THE HIPPO	4
I THIRST BY DAY. I WATCH BY NIGHT.	222	THE ABYSS	89
HER FACE LIKE A RAIN-BEATEN STONE ON THE DAY SHE ROLLED OFF	223	ELEGY (2)	1
GOING, WE STAYED; AND NIGHT TURNED INTO DAY;	237	THE TRANCED	12
AND IN BROAD DAY THE MIDNIGHT COME AGAIN!	239	IN A DARK TIME	15
TO THE DARK BEGINNINGS OF ANOTHER DAY.	241	THE SEQUEL	24
GOD'S NIGHT AND DAY: DOWN THIS SPACE HE HAS SMILED,	243	THE MOTION	21
HOPE HAS ITS HUSH: WE MOVE THROUGH ITS BROAD DAY,--	243	THE MOTION	22
THE GREAT DAY BALANCES UPON THE LEAVES;	244	INFIRMITY	27
LORD, HEAR ME OUT, AND HEAR ME OUT THIS DAY:	246	THE MARROW	17
HOW PURE THE MOTION OF THE RISING DAY,	248	THE TREE, BIRD	19
SIX HOURS A DAY I LAY ME DOWN	256	IN HYDROTHERAPY	1
THAT DAY WE TOOK FROM THE ANGELS:	258	SONG (3)	13
I CAN HEAR LIGHT ON A DRY DAY.	260	THE CHANGELING	20
YOU LARKS ALL DAY, YOU ROBINS RIGHT,	260	THE CHANGELING	22
REACHES OF COMMON DAY,	263	FOLLIES OF ADAM	25
I RAN BEHIND HIM EVERY DAY	268	SAGINAW SONG	54
DAYS			
DAYS OF ANOTHER SUMMER.	6	THE PREMONITION	2
READY FOR THE LONG DAYS UNDER THE SLOPED GLASS:	42	TRANSPLANTING	13
BUT WHO WOULD COUNT ETERNITY IN DAYS?	127	I KNEW A WOMAN	26
OF LATE NOVEMBER DAYS.	139	PLAINT	12
HOW CAN I REST IN THE DAYS OF MY SLOWNESS?	157	FIRST MEDITATN	14
DAY'S			
AT ODDS WITH CIRCUMSTANCE? THE DAY'S ON FIRE!	239	IN A DARK TIME	8
DAYTIME			
LIKE BATS IN DAYTIME,	152	THE SISKINS	4

	PAGE	TITLE	LINE
DAZEDLY			
WHEN THEY COME, DAZEDLY, TO THE PRETTY PASS	113	TO A LADY ED	11
DAZZLE			
DAZZLE ME, DIZZY APHORIST.	97	O, THOU OPENING	5
TOO MUCH REALITY CAN BE A DAZZLE, A SURFEIT;	220	THE ABYSS	44
I DAZZLED IN THE DAZZLE OF A STONE.	247	I WAITED	13
DAZZLED			
MY EYES, THEY DAZZLED AT HER FLOWING KNEES;	127	I KNEW A WOMAN	18
I DAZZLED IN THE DAZZLE OF A STONE.	247	I WAITED	13
DAZZLES			
WHEN CONTEMPLATION DAZZLES ALL I SEE;	246	THE MARROW	8
DAZZLING			
WHEN THERE'S A DAZZLING DARK BEHIND THE SUN?	155	THE DYING MAN	53
DEAD			
THE DEAD LEAP AT THE THROAT, DESTROY	4	FEUD	13
UNTIL THE DEAD HAVE BEEN SUBDUED.	4	FEUD	20
MY TONGUE IS GENERATIONS DEAD,	8	PRAYER	5
THAT LATE AUTUMNAL BLOOM, IS DEAD.	15	COMING OF COLD	41
HIS PULSE BEAT IS SO SLOW WE THINK HIM DEAD.	16	THE BAT	4
BUT IN THIS FOREST OF THE DEAD	17	NO BIRD	7
PRETENDS HIS DEAD BUNION GIVES EXQUISITE PAIN.	29	THE GENTLE	4
LIPS NEITHER DEAD NOR ALIVE,	39	ORCHIDS	16
MOLDS, WEEDS, DEAD LEAVES,	43	FLOWER DUMP	5
OVER THE DYING, THE NEWLY DEAD.	43	FLOWER DUMP	13
AT WOODLAWN I HEARD THE DEAD CRY:	53	THE LOST SON	1
THE DARK FLOWS ON ITSELF. A DEAD MOUTH SINGS UNDER AN OLD TREE.	59	THE LONG ALLEY	6
LET'S NOT HURRY. THE DEAD DON'T HURRY.	59	THE LONG ALLEY	18
A WAITING GHOST WARMS UP THE DEAD	60	THE LONG ALLEY	35
THIS AIR COULD FLESH A DEAD STICK. SWEET JESUS, MAKE ME SWEAT.	61	THE LONG ALLEY	63
CAME TO LAKES; CAME TO DEAD WATER,	62	FIELD OF LIGHT	1
DO THE DEAD BITE?	74	I NEED, I NEED	18
DEAD IN A WALL.	79	GIVE WAY, GATES	32
THE DEAD CROW DRIES ON A POLE.	80	GIVE WAY, GATES	48
ARCH MY BACK, PRETTY-BONES, I'M DEAD AT BOTH ENDS.	85	PRAISE TO END!	9
I'VE BEEN ASLEEP IN A BOWER OF DEAD SKIN.	86	PRAISE TO END!	47
THE DEAD SLEPT IN MY SLEEVE;	87	PRAISE TO END!	64
THE DEAD SPEAK NOISE.	89	UNFOLD! UNFOLD!	9
I HEAR A DEAD TONGUE HALLOO.	90	UNFOLD! UNFOLD!	44
THE DEAD THRASH.	91	UNFOLD! UNFOLD!	66
THE DEVIL ISN'T DEAD; HE'S JUST AWAY.	97	O, THOU OPENING	16
CARES ABOUT THE DANCE OF DEAD UNDERWEAR, OR THE SAD WALTZ OF PAPER	98	O, THOU OPENING	26
THE LIVELY DEAD HAD TAUGHT US TO BE FOND.	106	SIR JOHN DAVIES	32
LAY ALL THE LONELY PASTURES OF THE DEAD;	106	SIR JOHN DAVIES	51
IT WAS DEAD MAN'S CORNER, IT WAS KELLY'S STABLE;	112	SQUEEZE-BOX	34
WHERE ARE THE DEAD? BEFORE ME	122	ALL EARTH, AIR	22
WHAT DO THE GREAT DEAD SAY?	123	WORDS FOR WIND	10
I THINK THE DEAD ARE TENDER. SHALL WE KISS?--	129	SHE	1
I FEEL WE'RE BREATHING WITH THE DEAD;	136	THE SENSUALISTS	5
COLD, IN MY OWN DEAD SALT.	147	THE EXORCISM	28
THE DEAD WILL NOT LIE STILL,	148	THE SMALL	22
THE SMALL DEAD PIECES STICKING UNDER AN INSTEP;	151	SLUG	20
PLACES GREAT WITH THEIR DEAD,	154	THE DYING MAN	21
WHEN WE BROOD ON THE DEAD OR THE BELOVED;	156	THE DYING MAN	97
THE DEAD MAKE MORE IMPOSSIBLE DEMANDS FROM THEIR SILENCE;	168	FOURTH MEDITATN	19
I'M IN LOVE WITH THE DEAD! MY WHOLE FOREHEAD'S A NOISE!	170	FOURTH MEDITATN	79
NEAR THE GRAVES OF THE GREAT DEAD,	170	FOURTH MEDITATN	87
THE DEAD LOVE THE UNBORN.	172	WHAT TELL BONES	64
OR DREAM OF THE DEAD, AND THEIR HOLES.	173	WHAT TELL BONES	75
FETOR OF COCKROACHES, DEAD FISH, PETROLEUM,	187	THE LONGING	3
IN THE SUMMER HEAT, I CAN SMELL THE DEAD BUFFALO,	189	THE LONGING	54
RUNNING ALONG THE NARROW FURROWS OF THE SHORE, THE ROWS OF DEAD CLAM SHELLS;	190	AT OYSTER RIVER	3
A FISH RAVEN TURNS ON ITS PERCH (A DEAD TREE IN THE RIVERMOUTH),	190	AT OYSTER RIVER	22
THE DEAD SNAKES AND MUSKRATS, THE TURTLES GASPING IN THE RUBBLE,	194	JOURNY INTERIOR	36
AND THE DEAD BEGIN FROM THEIR DARK TO SING IN MY SLEEP.	195	JOURNY INTERIOR	79
AND THE BRONZE OF A DEAD BURDOCK AT THE EDGE OF A PRAIRIE LAKE,	197	THE LONG WATERS	42
NEITHER WHITE NOR RED, IN THE DEAD MIDDLE WAY,	197	THE LONG WATERS	56

		PAGE	TITLE	LINE
DEAD (CONTINUED)				
AS A FIRE, SEEMINGLY LONG DEAD, FLARES UP FROM A DOWNDRAFT OF AIR IN A CHIMNEY,	....	198	THE LONG WATERS	63
AND IN THE SHRUNKEN FACE OF A DEAD RAT, EATEN BY RAIN AND GROUND-BEETLES	....	199	THE FAR FIELD	19
AND THE FLICKER DRUMMED FROM HIS DEAD TREE IN THE CHICKEN-YARD.	....	200	THE FAR FIELD	37
MY DEAD SELVES SINGING.	....	221	THE ABYSS	80
WHO SAT WITH THE DEAD WHEN THE RELATIVES LEFT,	....	223	ELEGY (2)	8
SOME ARE IN PRISON; SOME ARE DEAD;	....	225	THE CHUMS	1
SO LONG ON GIN, BOBBIE PINS, HALF-SMOKED CIGARS, DEAD BEER,	....	228	THE GERANIUM	10
AND THE HURRICANE DRIVES THE DEAD STRAW INTO THE LIVING PINE-TREE.	....	231	THE STORM	43
MAKING A RACKET TO WAKE THE DEAD,	....	234	ALL MORNING	18
AND THOSE BIRDS FOREVER DEAD,	....	235	ALL MORNING	43
DEAD TO MYSELF, AND ALL I HOLD MOST DEAR,	....	244	INFIRMITY	23
"THE OTHER'S GONE DEAD,"	....	249	THE RESTORED	8
DO THE DEAD WAKE IN THEIR OWN WAY?	....	259	SONG (3)	32
HE LOVES HIMSELF, AND THE ILLUSTRIOUS DEAD;	....	264	THREE EPIGRAMS	4
BY ONE WHO ROSE UP FROM THE DEAD.	....	264	THREE EPIGRAMS	10
AND ONE EYE GAZED ASKEW. "WHY, BLAKE, HE'S DEAD,--	....	273	SUPPR W LINDSAY	22
DEAD-WHITE				
PACING A ROOM, A ROOM WITH DEAD-WHITE WALLS;	....	242	THE SEQUEL	30
DEAL				
I DEAL IN WISDOM, NOT IN DRY DESIRE.	....	273	SUPPR W LINDSAY	1
DEALT				
FOR WHENEVER I COULD, I DEALT THEM ALL IN	....	112	SQUEEZE-BOX	32
DEAR				
HELLO, HELLO. MY NERVES KNEW YOU, DEAR BOY.	....	65	SHAPE OF FIRE	32
IT'S A DEAR LIFE I CAN TOUCH.	....	76	I NEED, I NEED	58
MY DEAREST DEAR MY FAIREST FAIR,	....	86	PRAISE TO END!	35
O PRINT IT, MY DEAR, DO PUBLISH IT, YES,	....	113	TO A LADY ED	9
TELL ME, DEAR BEAR THERE BY THE STREAM,	....	117	LADY AND BEAR	3
ME, AND DEAR MARIANNE--	....	214	THE HAPPY THREE	34
NIGHT I EMBRACE, A DEAR PROXIMITY.	....	240	IN EVEING AIR	18
DEAD TO MYSELF, AND ALL I HOLD MOST DEAR,	....	244	INFIRMITY	23
DEAR SPARROWS OF THIS ALLEY,	....	261	THE CHANGELING	37
NEVER MET HIM, DUTCHMAN DEAR;	....	266	FOR STEVENS	10
I'LL SING WITH DEAR TOM MOORE,	....	268	SAGINAW SONG	48
--IN FEAR AND TREMBLING, DEAR KIERKEGAARD.	....	272	DUET	17
--FAR BEYOND, O BEYOND! DEAR KIERKEGAARD.	....	272	DUET	21
MY EX-EXISTENTIALIST DARLING DEAR,	....	272	DUET	23
DEAREST				
BUT YOU, MY DEAREST, HAVE A SOUL	....	23	AMOROUS LADY	9
MY DEAREST DEAR MY FAIREST FAIR,	....	86	PRAISE TO END!	35
MY DEAREST DUST, I CAN'T STAY HERE.	....	86	PRAISE TO END!	44
DEAREST TREE, I SAID, MAY I REST HERE?	....	100	THE VISITANT	5
MY DARLING, MY DEAREST, MOST-HONEST-ALIVE,	....	113	TO A LADY ED	13
DEARIE				
DEARIE, DELIGHT ME NOW.	....	259	SONG (3)	44
DEARLY				
HOLD TO ADVANTAGE DEARLY WON.	....	33	HIGHWAY: MICH	9
DEARS				
THE COLOR, MY DEARS, WAS GUINNESS BROWN,	....	270	GOB MUSIC	39
DEATH				
DEATH PIECE	....	4	DEATH PIECE	T
REASON EMBRACES DEATH,	....	31	LULL	19
THEY TOY WITH DEATH AND TRAFFIC FINES.	....	33	HIGHWAY: MICH	10
BUT I HUNG ON LIKE DEATH:	....	45	MY PAPA'S WALTZ	3
I SAID: ON ALL THESE, DEATH, WITH GENTLENESS, COME DOWN.	....	48	JUDGE NOT	10
DEATH WAS NOT. I LIVED IN A SIMPLE DROWSE:	....	66	SHAPE OF FIRE	73
DREAM OF A WOMAN, AND A DREAM OF DEATH:	....	134	THE PURE FURY	22
WRAPPED IN THE TATTERED ROBE OF DEATH,	....	136	THE SENSUALISTS	19
DEATH IS A DEEPER SLEEP,	....	139	PLAINT	17
EACH WILLS HIS DEATH: I AM CONVINCED OF THAT;	....	144	ELEGY (1)	5
LAY WITH THE DROSS OF DEATH.	....	147	THE EXORCISM	24
I SHALL UNDO ALL DYING BY MY DEATH.	....	155	THE DYING MAN	77
THE STAND AT THE STRETCH IN THE FACE OF DEATH,	....	194	JOURNY INTERIOR	66
BLASTED TO DEATH BY THE NIGHT WATCHMAN.	....	199	THE FAR FIELD	23
WAS TO FORGET TIME AND DEATH:	....	199	THE FAR FIELD	27
I AM RENEWED BY DEATH, THOUGHT OF MY DEATH,	....	201	THE FAR FIELD	77
I AM RENEWED BY DEATH, THOUGHT OF MY DEATH,	....	201	THE FAR FIELD	77
FOR I HAVE MOVED CLOSER TO DEATH, LIVED WITH DEATH;	....	220	THE ABYSS	37

	PAGE	TITLE	LINE
DEATH (CONTINUED)			
FOR I HAVE MOVED CLOSER TO DEATH, LIVED WITH DEATH;	220	THE ABYSS	37
WHENCE, DEATH?	236	SONG (2)	9
DEATH OF THE SELF IN A LONG, TEARLESS NIGHT,	239	IN A DARK TIME	17
OF GRIEF I DIED, BUT NO ONE KNEW MY DEATH.	241	THE SEQUEL	8
THIS REACH BEYOND THIS DEATH, THIS ACT OF LOVE	243	THE MOTION	17
I'M SON AND FATHER OF MY ONLY DEATH.	244	INFIRMITY	18
FATHER AND SON OF THIS DEATH,	263	FOLLIES OF ADAM	22
DEATH-BED			
MY DIM-WIT COUSIN, SAVED BY A DEATH-BED QUAVER,	25	DIM-WIT COUSIN	1
DEATHLY			
PART OF A TREE STILL DARK, STILL, DEATHLY STILL,	248	THE TREE, BIRD	9
DEATH'S			
DEATH'S POSSIBILITIES;	153	THE DYING MAN	12
IN SLEEP, AFRAID. DEATH'S FACE RISES AFRESH,	190	AT OYSTER RIVER	25
DEBRIS			
THE SUDDEN SUCKING ROAR AS THE CULVERT LOOSENS ITS DEBRIS OF BRANCHES AND STICKS,	191	AT OYSTER RIVER	53
DECAY			
--AND A FUME OF DECAY THAT CLINGS FAST TO THE WOOD.	32	SALE	16
I'M DYING PIECEMEAL, FERVENT IN DECAY;	149	IN LATE SUMMER	15
DECEIVES			
MY SLEEP DECEIVES ME.	82	SENSIBILITY! LA	46
DECEMBER			
THE SUN LOOSENING THE FROST ON DECEMBER WINDOWS,	161	I'M HERE	2
DECENTLY			
AND YOU REFUSE TO DIE DECENTLY!--	151	SLUG	15
DECEPTIVE			
COMING OUT, SOFT AND DECEPTIVE,	39	ORCHIDS	4
DECIDED			
LET THE GESTURES FREEZE; OUR DOOM IS ALREADY DECIDED.	56	THE LOST SON	105
DECISION			
THE DECISION	245	THE DECISION	T
DECISION'S			
DECISION'S SMOKING FUSE;	7	ORDERS FOR DAY	4
DECLARE			
SUMMON A VISION AND DECLARE IT PURE.	107	SIR JOHN DAVIES	78
DECLARED			
THEY HAVE DECLARED THEMSELVES,	220	THE ABYSS	27
DECLARES			
THE SUN DECLARES THE EARTH;	124	WORDS FOR WIND	33
THE SPIRIT DECLARES ITSELF TO THESE ROCKS.	172	WHAT TELL BONES	46
DECREASED			
DECREASED BENEATH AN UNDIVIDED SKY.	6	INTERLUDE	6
DEED			
THE DEED WILL SPEAK THE TRUTH	3	OPEN HOUSE	14
DEE-DEEING			
PITCHING LIGHTLY OVER THE HIGH HEDGEROWS, DEE-DEEING,	234	ALL MORNING	25
DEEP			
THE SUN CUTS DEEP INTO THE HEAVY DRIFT,	11	LIGHT BRIGHTER	5
NOW LIGHT IS LESS; NOON SKIES ARE WIDE AND DEEP;	12	SLOW SEASON	1
CONFUSION'S CORE SET DEEP WITHIN	22	SILENCE	13
THE SLEEP WAS NOT DEEP, BUT THE WAKING IS SLOW.	29	THE GENTLE	12
DEEP IN THE BRAIN, FAR BACK.	49	NIGHT CROW	8
IN THE DEEP GRASS AT THE EDGE OF FIELD,	62	FIELD OF LIGHT	25
A DEEP DISH. LUMPS IN IT.	74	I NEED, I NEED	1
THE DEEP STREAM REMEMBERS:	80	GIVE WAY, GATES	59
DEEP IN THE BELLY OF A THING TO BE.	97	O, THOU OPENING	15
WITH ITS DEEP SHADE, AND BIRDS.	103	OLD LADY'S WRDS	28
IN THE DEEP MIDDLE OF OURSELVES WE LAY;	106	SIR JOHN DAVIES	57
A SHAPE FROM DEEP IN THE EYE--	123	WORDS FOR WIND	30
IN THE DEEP CENTER OF THE VOICE AND FIRE.	132	SENTENTIOUS MAN	34
I LIVED WITH DEEP ROOTS ONCE:	139	PLAINT	13
OR STAY BY YOURSELF DOWN DEEP IN THE WOOD,	177	KITTY-CAT BIRD	7
WHEN YOU HIT THE DEEP PIT AT THE BOTTOM OF THE SWALE,	193	JOURNY INTERIOR	20
THE TOWNS WITH THEIR HIGH PITTED ROAD-CROWNS AND DEEP GUTTERS,	193	JOURNY INTERIOR	30
THE CRICKET-VOICE DEEP IN THE MIDNIGHT FIELD,	196	THE LONG WATERS	27
OF FLYING LIKE A BAT DEEP INTO A NARROWING TUNNEL,	199	THE FAR FIELD	2
I HAVE COME TO A STILL, BUT NOT A DEEP CENTER,	201	THE FAR FIELD	71
AND THE DEEP CHORUS OF HORNS COMING UP FROM THE STREETS IN EARLY MORNING.	204	THE ROSE	72
THE DEEP SHADE GATHERS NIGHT;	212	LIGHT LISTENED	17

	PAGE	TITLE	LINE
DEEP (CONTINUED)			
I THINK OF THE NESTLING FALLEN INTO THE DEEP GRASS,	227	MEADOW MOUSE	26
HIDING DEEP IN THE BLACKBERRY BUSHES--	234	ALL MORNING	20
THE DEEP EYE SEES THE SHIMMER ON THE STONE;	244	INFIRMITY	20
DEEP IN THE GREENS OF SUMMER SING THE LIVES	244	INFIRMITY	25
DEEP IN THE MOW, AND EACH STEP DEEPER DOWN,	247	I WAITED	7
AND WHEN I WALKED, MY FEET SEEMED DEEP IN SAND.	247	I WAITED	16
HOW DEEP THE MOTHER-ROOT OF THAT STILL CRY!	248	THE TREE, BIRD	17
DEEPENED			
HAS DEEPENED TO THE BLACKNESS OF A POOL,	15	THE HERON	2
LIGHT DEEPENED TO A BELL,	212	LIGHT LISTENED	8
DEEPENING			
SILENT, IN THE DEEPENING LIGHT,	190	AT OYSTER RIVER	8
I MEET MY SHADOW IN THE DEEPENING SHADE;	239	IN A DARK TIME	2
I STARE AND STARE INTO A DEEPENING POOL	244	INFIRMITY	3
DEEPENS			
DEW DEEPENS ON THE FRESH-CUT LAWN;	33	IDYLL	7
MIST DEEPENS ON THE PANE;	34	NIGHT JOURNEY	21
DEEPER			
THE MIND REMEMBERS FROM A DEEPER SLEEP:	119	THE DREAM	3
DEATH IS A DEEPER SLEEP,	139	PLAINT	17
DEEP IN THE MOW, AND EACH STEP DEEPER DOWN,	247	I WAITED	7
DEEPEST			
THEY MOCK THE DEEPEST THOUGHT,	20	REPL TO CENSURE	6
I KNOW THE MOTION OF THE DEEPEST STONE.	132	SENTENTIOUS MAN	35
AND SHAKE THE SECRETS FROM MY DEEPEST BONES;	173	WHAT TELL BONES	87
DEEP-HIDDEN			
DEEP-HIDDEN EMBERS, SMOTHERED BY THE SCREEN	17	UNEXTINGUISHED	7
DEEP-THROATED			
HIS DEEP-THROATED COOING PART OF THE EARLY MORNING,	234	ALL MORNING	2
DEER			
THE DEER CAME DOWN, OUT OF THE DAPPLED WOOD.	120	THE DREAM	20
AMONG THE SHY BEASTS, THE DEER AT THE SALT-LICK,	190	AT OYSTER RIVER	26
DEFAMERS			
DEFAMERS OF THE GOOD.	20	REPL TO CENSURE	5
DEFEAT			
AND LONGED TO FEEL THE IMPACT OF DEFEAT.	28	THE FAVORITE	14
DEFEND			
BY SINGING WE DEFEND;	170	FOURTH MEDITATN	82
DEFER			
DEFER THE VICE OF FLESH THE IRREVOCABLE CHOICE	5	TO MY SISTER	8
DEFILES			
MY NOSE DEFILES A COMELY HEAD;	8	PRAYER	6
DEFINED			
ETERNITY DEFINED, AND STREWN WITH STRAW,	156	THE DYING MAN	92
DEIGN			
WALK BOLDLY MY SISTER BUT DO NOT DEIGN TO GIVE	5	TO MY SISTER	10
DELAYED			
I TOUCHED HER SHADOW WHEN THE LIGHT DELAYED;	119	THE DREAM	13
DELIBERATELY			
AND THOSE WHO SUBMERGE THEMSELVES DELIBERATELY IN TRIVIA,	169	FOURTH MEDITATN	38
DELICATE			
THE EAR SO DELICATE AND TRUE	17	NO BIRD	3
DELICATE THE SYLLABLES THAT RELEASE THE REPRESSION;	29	THE GENTLE	1
BUT STILL THE DELICATE SLIPS KEEP COAXING UP WATER;	37	CUTTINGS	3
GREAT CANNAS OR DELICATE CYCLAMEN TIPS,--	38	FORCING HOUSE	4
LIMP AND DAMP, DELICATE AS A YOUNG BIRD'S TONGUE;	39	ORCHIDS	5
DROPPING A FINE FILM ON NAILS AND DELICATE EYEBROWS,	46	DOLOR	12
THAT DELICATE THING	249	THE RESTORED	15
DELIGHT			
DELIGHT ME OTHERLY, WHITE SPIRIT,--	92	I CRY, LOVE!	5
AND SHE BALANCED IN THE DELIGHT OF HER THOUGHT,	102	ELEGY FOR JANE	4
I CRY DELIGHT: I KNOW	124	WORDS FOR WIND	49
I CAN DELIGHT IN MY OWN HARDIHOOD;	132	SENTENTIOUS MAN	26
AND I DELIGHT IN SLEEP.	139	PLAINT	18
STILL TAKING DELIGHT IN NAKEDNESS,	165	HER BECOMING	6
I WOULD DELIGHT IN MY HANDS, THE BRANCH SINGING, ALTERING THE EXCESSIVE BIRD;	188	THE LONGING	44
FEELING, I STILL DELIGHT IN MY LAST FALL.	197	THE LONG WATERS	32
AND DELIGHT IN A LOVER'S PRAISE,	208	HER WORDS	4
DEARIE, DELIGHT ME NOW.	259	SONG (3)	44
DELIGHTED			
THE WORMS WERE DELIGHTED AS WRENS.	63	FIELD OF LIGHT	50

	PAGE	TITLE	LINE
DELIGHTED (CONTINUED)			
ONCE I DELIGHTED IN A SINGLE TREE;	155	THE DYING MAN	54
DELIGHTING			
MY LADY LAUGHS, DELIGHTING IN WHAT IS.	129	SHE	2
THE BODY, DELIGHTING IN THRESHOLDS,	163	I'M HERE	58
A LEAF, I WOULD LOVE THE LEAVES, DELIGHTING IN THE REDOLENT DISORDER OF THIS MORTAL LIFE,	188	THE LONGING	47
DELIGHTING IN SURFACE CHANGE, THE GLITTER OF LIGHT ON WAVES,	195	JOURNY INTERIOR	67
DELIGHTS			
BEING DELIGHTS IN BEING, AND IN TIME.	150	IN LATE SUMMER	31
THE SOUL DELIGHTS IN THAT EXTREMITY.	244	INFIRMITY	16
DELIRIUM			
A DELIRIUM OF BIRDS!	235	ALL MORNING	33
DELIVER			
DELIVER ME, O LORD, FROM ALL	24	BEFORE STUDY	9
DELIVERED			
O TO BE DELIVERED FROM THE RATIONAL INTO THE REALM OF PURE SONG,	172	WHAT TELL BONES	54
DELVE			
LET OTHERS DELVE THAT MYSTERY IF THEY CAN.	250	THE RIGHT THING	6
DEMANDS			
THE DEAD MAKE MORE IMPOSSIBLE DEMANDS FROM THEIR SILENCE;	168	FOURTH MEDITATN	19
DEN			
BEASTS OF THE HILL AND SERPENTS OF THE DEN.	239	IN A DARK TIME	6
DENIED			
WHAT ROOT OF HIS EVER DENIED ITS STEM?	224	OTTO	10
DENIED IN ME, WHO HAS DENIED DESIRE.	242	THE SEQUEL	32
DENIED IN ME, WHO HAS DENIED DESIRE.	242	THE SEQUEL	32
DENIES			
DENIES THE BLESSING OF THE SUN,	4	FEUD	10
THE NEST DENIES.	91	UNFOLD! UNFOLD!	64
DENSE			
DENSE TREES NO LONGER HOLD THE LIGHT,	14	COMING OF COLD	30
DENSE IN THE CENTRAL STONE.	50	THE CYCLE	11
DENSER			
AND TREES CAME CLOSER WITH A DENSER SHADE.	133	THE PURE FURY	21
DENTED			
I STARED INTO THE DENTED HOLE	269	GOB MUSIC	24
DENY			
THEY FEED THE SENSE, DENY THE SOUL,	25	VERSE W ALLUSNS	9
DID BEATRICE DENY WHAT DANTE SAW?	107	SIR JOHN DAVIES	76
DEPARTING			
LACKING THE CANDOR OF DOGS, I KISS THE DEPARTING AIR;	86	PRAISE TO END!	26
DEPTH			
THE DEPTH CALLS TO THE HEIGHT	97	O, THOU OPENING	9
OH, WHEN SHE WAS SAD, SHE CAST HERSELF DOWN INTO SUCH A PURE DEPTH,	102	ELEGY FOR JANE	10
DEPTHS			
CHILL DEPTHS OF THE SPIRIT ARE FLUSHED TO A FEVER,	5	PROGNOSIS	15
WHO SPOKE FIRST IN THE COARSE SHORT-HAND OF THE SUBLIMINAL DEPTHS,	170	FOURTH MEDITATN	71
I, WHO CAME BACK FROM THE DEPTHS LAUGHING TOO LOUDLY,	198	THE LONG WATERS	73
AS IF ANOTHER MAN APPEARED OUT OF THE DEPTHS OF MY BEING,	205	THE ROSE	100
DESCEND			
I ASKED: MAY THE BLESSINGS OF LIFE, O LORD, DESCEND ON THE LIVING.	48	JUDGE NOT	6
DESCEND, O GENTLEST LIGHT, DESCEND, DESCEND.	156	THE DYING MAN	87
DESCEND, O GENTLEST LIGHT, DESCEND, DESCEND.	156	THE DYING MAN	87
DESCEND, O GENTLEST LIGHT, DESCEND, DESCEND.	156	THE DYING MAN	87
DESCENDANTS			
THE DESCENDANTS OF THE PLAYFUL TREE-SHREW THAT SURVIVED THE ARCHAIC KILLERS,	170	FOURTH MEDITATN	66
DESCENDING			
BEFORE DESCENDING TO THE ALLUVIAL PLAIN,	200	THE FAR FIELD	65
DESECRATION			
AS IF I HAD COMMITTED, AGAINST THE WHOLE SCHEME OF LIFE, A DESECRATION.	40	MOSS-GATHERING	13
DESERT			
A DRY CRY COMES FROM MY OWN DESERT;	93	I CRY, LOVE!	31
DESERTS			
THE FLESH DESERTS THE BONE,	153	THE DYING MAN	7
DESIRE			
DESIRE WAS WINTER-CALM,	87	PRAISE TO END!	69

		PAGE	TITLE	LINE
DESIRE (CONTINUED)				
I FIND MYSELF PERPLEXED. WHAT IS DESIRE?--		105	SIR JOHN DAVIES	26
DESIRE EXULTS THE EAR:		128	THE VOICE	19
DESIRE HIDES FROM DESIRE.		130	THE OTHER	22
DESIRE HIDES FROM DESIRE.		130	THE OTHER	22
AND FOUND OUT ALL I COULD OF ALL DESIRE;		132	SENTENTIOUS MAN	32
MY DESIRE FOR THE PEAKS, THE BLACK RAVINES, THE ROLLING MISTS		196	THE LONG WATERS	9
SO THE SEA WIND WAKES DESIRE.		198	THE LONG WATERS	65
BEAUTIFUL MY DESIRE, AND THE PLACE OF MY DESIRE.		204	THE ROSE	78
BEAUTIFUL MY DESIRE, AND THE PLACE OF MY DESIRE.		204	THE ROSE	78
THE BODY MOVES, THOUGH SLOWLY, TOWARD DESIRE.		235	MANIFESTATION	10
DARK, DARK MY LIGHT, AND DARKER MY DESIRE.		239	IN A DARK TIME	19
DENIED IN ME, WHO HAS DENIED DESIRE.		242	THE SEQUEL	32
WHAT BURNS ME NOW? DESIRE, DESIRE, DESIRE.		246	THE MARROW	12
WHAT BURNS ME NOW? DESIRE, DESIRE, DESIRE.		246	THE MARROW	12
WHAT BURNS ME NOW? DESIRE, DESIRE, DESIRE.		246	THE MARROW	12
I DEAL IN WISDOM, NOT IN DRY DESIRE.		273	SUPPR W LINDSAY	1
DESIRES				
ALONE, HIS WIFE IS GRIEVING FOR WHAT HER HEART DESIRES.		27	CLAIRVOY WIDOW	14
DESIRE'S				
MY DESIRE'S A WIND TRAPPED IN A CAVE.		172	WHAT TELL BONES	45
DESOLATE				
THE LAND IS DESOLATE, THE SUN		15	COMING OF COLD	47
DESOLATION				
DESOLATION IN IMMACULATE PUBLIC PLACES,		46	DOLOR	4
THE BULKS CANNOT HIDE US, OR THE BLEAK SHEDS OF OUR DESOLATION,		166	HER BECOMING	39
TO A RICH DESOLATION OF WIND AND WATER,		197	THE LONG WATERS	46
DESPAIR				
THE CLOAK OF EVIL AND DESPAIR,		19	EPIDERM MACABRE	6
I KNOW THE PURITY OF PURE DESPAIR,		239	IN A DARK TIME	9
DESPISE				
THOSE WHO DESPISE THE DOVE.		220	THE ABYSS	28
DESSERT				
WITH COLD ROAST BEEF AND COFFEE FOR DESSERT--		274	SUPPR W LINDSAY	33
DESTROY				
THE DEAD LEAP AT THE THROAT, DESTROY		4	FEUD	13
DESTRUCTION				
DESTRUCTION IS COMPLETE.		267	SAGINAW SONG	6
DETACH				
IF WE DETACH		60	THE LONG ALLEY	55
DETERIORATION'S				
DETERIORATION'S SCRUPULOUS ACCOUNTING		25	DIM-WIT COUSIN	7
DETOUR				
ON THE DUSTY DETOUR.		194	JOURNY INTERIOR	51
DETOURS				
THERE ARE MANY DETOURS, WASHED-OUT INTERRUPTED RAW PLACES		193	JOURNY INTERIOR	2
DEVIL				
THE DEVIL ISN'T DEAD; HE'S JUST AWAY.		97	O, THOU OPENING	16
BUT STEPPED RIGHT UP AND SWUNG AT THE DEVIL;		111	SQUEEZE-BOX	4
INSTEAD OF A DEVIL WITH HORNS, I PREFER A SERPENT WITH SCALES;		173	WHAT TELL BONES	77
DEVIL'S				
MY EARS HAVE BEEN THE VERY DEVIL'S.		8	PRAYER	8
DEVOURED				
WHEN I WAS A WORM, I DEVOURED.		172	WHAT TELL BONES	40
DEVOURING				
THOUGH THE DEVOURING MOTHER CRY, ""ESCAPE ME? NEVER--""		5	PROGNOSIS	13
SO MANY DEVOURING INFANTS!		39	ORCHIDS	14
DEW				
DEW DEEPENS ON THE FRESH-CUT LAWN;		33	IDYLL	7
THE DEW LOOSENED		51	THE WAKING (1)	19
DEW ATE THE FIRE.		76	I NEED, I NEED	66
SNIFFING THE DEW.		87	PRAISE TO END!	62
THE DEW REVIVES ON THE BEACH-GRASS;		190	AT OYSTER RIVER	20
THE DEW DRAWS NEAR.		215	HIS FOREBODING	10
DICTATES				
WHERE IMPULSE NO LONGER DICTATES, NOR THE DARKENING SHADOW,		197	THE LONG WATERS	57
DID				
I DID NOT MOVE TO CLAIM WHAT WAS MY OWN.		21	THE AUCTION	4
FEARLESS AND BOLD, HE DID HIS FELLOWS IN,		28	THE FAVORITE	5
THE LITTLE ONES DID,		51	THE WAKING (1)	10

	PAGE	TITLE	LINE
DID (CONTINUED)			
DID I EVER CURSE THE SUN?	62	FIELD OF LIGHT	20
--OR SAT DOWN AND DID.	89	UNFOLD! UNFOLD!	11
LATER, I DID AND I DANCED IN THE SIMPLE WOOD.	90	UNFOLD! UNFOLD!	34
SHE KISSED ME CLOSE, AND THEN DID SOMETHING ELSE.	106	SIR JOHN DAVIES	35
ATTENDED WHAT WE DID. BEHIND, BEFORE,	106	SIR JOHN DAVIES	50
DID EACH BECOME THE OTHER IN THAT PLAY?	106	SIR JOHN DAVIES	55
DID SPACE SHAKE OFF AN ANGEL WITH A SIGH?	107	SIR JOHN DAVIES	69
DID BEATRICE DENY WHAT DANTE SAW?	107	SIR JOHN DAVIES	76
A PLACE I SURELY DID LIKE TO GO	111	SQUEEZE-BOX	17
AND SING HE DID, LIKE ANYTHING!	115	THE SERPENT	10
SHE WANDERED; I DID NOT:	123	WORDS FOR WIND	20
(BUT WHAT PRODIGIOUS MOWING WE DID MAKE).	127	I KNEW A WOMAN	14
WE DID NOT FLY THE FLESH. WHO DOES, WHEN YOUNG?	131	SENTENTIOUS MAN	7
SOME RAGES SAVE US. DID I RAGE TOO LONG?	131	SENTENTIOUS MAN	9
OF WHAT I DID NOT DO.	154	THE DYING MAN	20
I FOUND MY FATHER WHEN I DID MY WORK,	154	THE DYING MAN	40
DID MY WILL DIE? DID I?	167	HER BECOMING	69
DID MY WILL DIE? DID I?	167	HER BECOMING	69
--DID THE KITTY--THE KITTY-CAT BIRD.	177	KITTY-CAT BIRD	17
WHO ALWAYS DID THINGS BY THE DOZEN;	179	MYRTLE'S COUSIN	2
HOW DID YOU DO THAT?	180	GOO-GIRL	9
I KNEW THAT I DID LOVE HER.	216	THE SHY MAN	12
FOR IF IT DID OCCUR,	268	SAGINAW SONG	39
AND I KNEELED DOWN AND DID PARTAKE	270	GOB MUSIC	34
I DID PARTAKE OF IT, I DID PARTAKE OF IT.	270	GOB MUSIC	43
I DID PARTAKE OF IT, I DID PARTAKE OF IT.	270	GOB MUSIC	43
PAUL BUNYAN IS PART RUSSIAN, DID YOU KNOW?--	274	SUPPR W LINDSAY	44
DIDDLE			
DIDDLE WE CARE	74	I NEED, I NEED	6
DIDN'T			
THEY DIDN'T BOAST; THEY DIDN'T SNIVEL,	111	SQUEEZE-BOX	3
THEY DIDN'T BOAST; THEY DIDN'T SNIVEL,	111	SQUEEZE-BOX	3
HE DIDN'T LIKE HIS KIND OF LIFE;	115	THE SERPENT	5
DIE			
HOPE, LOVE, CREATE, OR DRINK AND DIE:	18	LONG LIVE WEEDS	11
SAID TO ME: DIE.	55	THE LOST SON	82
WENT TO VISIT THE WIND. WHERE THE BIRDS DIE.	73	WHERE KNOCK IS	72
SO ALIVE I COULD DIE!	99	O, THOU OPENING	58
THERE WAS A THICKET WHERE I WENT TO DIE,	132	SENTENTIOUS MAN	21
AND YOU REFUSE TO DIE DECENTLY!--	151	SLUG	15
I DIE INTO THIS LIFE, ALONE YET NOT ALONE.	155	THE DYING MAN	59
WHAT'S WEATHER TO ME? EVEN CARP DIE IN THIS RIVER.	164	I'M HERE	90
DID MY WILL DIE? DID I?	167	HER BECOMING	69
AND IT LIKE TO DIE.	208	THE APPARITION	8
AND WHAT DIED WITH US WAS THE WILL TO DIE.	238	THE TRANCED	25
I'LL MAKE A BROKEN MUSIC, OR I'LL DIE.	240	IN EVEING AIR	6
AND TELL MYSELF MY IMAGE CANNOT DIE.	244	INFIRMITY	4
TELLS ME MY DRINKING BREEDS A WILL TO DIE.	246	THE MARROW	4
I'M LIKE TO DIE,"	249	THE RESTORED	10
I'M SWEATING OUT THE WILL TO DIE.	256	IN HYDROTHERAPY	10
BUT WHEN I DIE--AND THAT WON'T BE SOON--	268	SAGINAW SONG	47
DIED			
AS IF ALL THINGS HAD DIED, AND ROSE AGAIN.	133	THE PURE FURY	6
"AT LAST I'M MYSELF!"--AND HE UP AND DIED	177	KITTY-CAT BIRD	16
AND THEN CAUGHT COLD AND UP AND DIED?	178	THE CEILING	2
AND YET SHE DIED IN AGONY,	223	ELEGY (2)	16
WHEN HATTIE WRIGHT'S ANGORA DIED AS WELL,	224	OTTO	29
AND WHAT DIED WITH US WAS THE WILL TO DIE.	238	THE TRANCED	25
OF GRIEF I DIED, BUT NO ONE KNEW MY DEATH.	241	THE SEQUEL	8
DIES			
THE SMALL BROOK DIES WITHIN ITS BED;	15	COMING OF COLD	38
THE FIRE OF HEAVEN DIES; A FIRE UNSEEN	17	UNEXTINGUISHED	5
THE OUTSIDE DIES WITHIN,	141	MEMORY	3
THE WIND DIES ON THE HILL.	141	MEMORY	7
THE WIND DIES DOWN; MY WILL DIES WITH THE WIND,	149	IN LATE SUMMER	11
THE WIND DIES DOWN; MY WILL DIES WITH THE WIND,	149	IN LATE SUMMER	11
THE LONG DAY DIES; I WALKED THE WOODS ALONE;	150	IN LATE SUMMER	29
"A MAN SEES, AS HE DIES,	153	THE DYING MAN	11
A THIN HARSH SONG. THE DAY DIES IN A CHILD.	171	WHAT TELL BONES	19
HOW SLOWLY PLEASURE DIES!--	197	THE LONG WATERS	29
THE SOUL DIES EVERY NIGHT;	263	FOLLIES OF ADAM	23

	PAGE	TITLE	LINE
DIET			
TODAY I EAT MY USUAL DIET OF SHADOWS.	166	HER BECOMING	31
DIFFICULT			
IT IS DIFFICULT TO SAY ALL THINGS ARE WELL,	172	WHAT TELL BONES	34
DIFFUSE			
DIFFUSE THE OUTPOURINGS OF THE SPIRITUAL COWARD,	5	PROGNOSIS	1
DIGGING			
DIGGING INTO THE SOFT RUBBLE UNDERNEATH,	39	WEED PULLER	4
DIGITS			
AND NOW GRIM DIGITS OF OLD PAIN	30	THE RECKONING	3
DIGNITY			
OF DIGNITY WITHIN,	20	REPL TO CENSURE	15
DILL			
THE DILL BEARS UP ITS ACRID CROWN;	14	COMING OF COLD	14
DIM			
IN THE FAIR NIGHT OF SOME DIM BRAIN,	81	SENSIBILITY! LA	4
DIMENSION			
THE DIRE DIMENSION OF A FINAL THING.	248	THE TREE, BIRD	23
DIMENSIONS			
SLEEPERS, NUMB NUDGERS IN COLD DIMENSIONS,	50	THE MINIMAL	2
AND ALL DIMENSIONS QUIVERED TO ONE THING.	132	SENTENTIOUS MAN	24
DIMINISHED			
WHEN CLOVER SCENTS DIMINISHED WIND.	14	COMING OF COLD	4
THEN, WITH DIMINISHED FORCE,	50	THE CYCLE	13
DIMINISHED, YET STILL HEARD:	128	THE VOICE	10
DIMINISHED BY THE HAZE	139	PLAINT	11
DIMINISHING			
AND I ROSE FROM A LAST DIMINISHING.	240	IN EVEING AIR	12
DIMINUTIVES			
THE LOVELY DIMINUTIVES.	63	FIELD OF LIGHT	43
DIM-WIT			
MY DIM-WIT COUSIN	25	DIM-WIT COUSIN	T
MY DIM-WIT COUSIN, SAVED BY A DEATH-BED QUAVER,	25	DIM-WIT COUSIN	1
DIN			
A FURIOUS, DISSEMBLING DIN.	22	SILENCE	14
DINING			
THE DINING ROOM CARPET DYED BRIGHTER THAN BLOOD,	32	SALE	13
DINKY			
DINKY	114	DINKY	T
--WHY, THERE IS DIRTY DINKY.	114	DINKY	4
--OF COURSE, IT'S DIRTY DINKY.	114	DINKY	8
--IT LOOKED LIKE DIRTY DINKY.	114	DINKY	12
--HE'D GOT IN: DIRTY DINKY.	114	DINKY	16
--YOU MAY BE DIRTY DINKY.	114	DINKY	20
DIOCESE			
IN THIS, THE DIOCESE OF MICE,	83	O LULL ME, LULL	2
DIP			
THE BANK SWALLOWS VEER AND DIP,	152	THE SISKINS	1
DIPPED			
HE DIPPED HIS HAND IN THE SHALLOW:	6	THE PREMONITION	7
QUICKER THAN BIRDS, THEY DIPPED	44	FRAU BAUMAN	13
AND EVERY SNAIL DIPPED TOWARD ME ITS PURE HORN.	248	THE TREE, BIRD	2
DIPPERS			
PERIPHERAL DIPPERS COME TO REST ON THE SHORT GRASS,	235	ALL MORNING	34
DIPPING			
DIPPING AND VEERING CLOSE TO THE MOTIONLESS WATER.	93	I CRY, LOVE!	44
DIPPING UP AND DOWN IN THE RIPPLES,	168	FOURTH MEDITATN	10
THE STERN HIGH, DIPPING LIKE A CHILD'S BOAT IN A POND--	203	THE ROSE	37
I'M NO LONGER A BIRD DIPPING A BEAK INTO RIPPLING WATER	220	THE ABYSS	41
DIPS			
AND THE HUMMINGBIRD DIPS IN AND AROUND THE QUINCE TREE,	234	ALL MORNING	29
DIRE			
FROM DIRE HELL'S MOUTH,	236	SONG (2)	10
THE DIRE DIMENSION OF A FINAL THING.	248	THE TREE, BIRD	23
DIRECTION			
MY INDIRECTION FOUND DIRECTION OUT.	131	SENTENTIOUS MAN	4
DIRECTIONS			
I LIVE IN LIGHT'S EXTREME; I STRETCH IN ALL DIRECTIONS;	173	WHAT TELL BONES	82
DIRT			
IN THE DIRT AND DISORDER I CHERISH ONE SCRAP OF ILLUSION:	29	THE REMINDER	11
EVEN THE DIRT KEPT BREATHING A SMALL BREATH.	38	ROOT CELLAR	11
TAMPING AND STAMPING DIRT INTO POTS,--	42	OLD FLORIST	3
UP AND SIFTED THE DIRT;	44	FRAU BAUMAN	14

	PAGE	TITLE	LINE
DIRT (CONTINUED)			
WITH A PALM CAKED HARD BY DIRT,	45	MY PAPA'S WALTZ	14
WHO STUNNED THE DIRT INTO NOISE?	55	THE LOST SON	66
THE DIRT LEFT MY HAND, VISITOR.	63	FIELD OF LIGHT	31
I CAN'T MARRY THE DIRT.	77	BRING THE DAY!	20
I SAW A VIRGIN WRITHING IN THE DIRT--	131	SENTENTIOUS MAN	2
TO THE DIRT, MY KNEES SCRUBBING	151	SLUG	6
AND THE MEN BENEATH THEM WHEELING IN DIRT TO THE CEMENT BENCHES,	158	FIRST MEDITATN	45
I'M NO MIDGE OF THAT AND THIS. THE DIRT GLITTERS LIKE SALT.	164	I'M HERE	92
FROM THE DIRT IN THE STREET,	236	SONG (2)	6
THE CLOSE DIRT DANCING ON A SUNLESS STONE	243	THE MOTION	20
DIRT'S			
BRING ME A FINGER. THIS DIRT'S LONESOME FOR GRASS.	79	GIVE WAY, GATES	7
DIRTY			
--WHY, THERE IS DIRTY DINKY.	114	DINKY	4
--OF COURSE, IT'S DIRTY DINKY.	114	DINKY	8
--IT LOOKED LIKE DIRTY DINKY.	114	DINKY	12
--HE'D GOT IN: DIRTY DINKY.	114	DINKY	16
--YOU MAY BE DIRTY DINKY.	114	DINKY	20
AND A CHILD'S DIRTY SHIFT BILLOWS UPWARD OUT OF AN ALLEY,	230	THE STORM	18
DISAPPEAR			
ALL PROFITS DISAPPEAR: THE GAIN	30	THE RECKONING	1
HER IMAGE FADES, YET DOES NOT DISAPPEAR--	140	THE SWAN	2
THAT DISAPPEAR INTO A WANING MOON;	173	WHAT TELL BONES	70
CLIFF DISAPPEAR IN A LAST	210	HER TIME	19
DISASTER			
YOU FEEL DISASTER CLIMB THE VEIN.	4	FEUD	8
AGAINST DISASTER	19	AGNST DISASTER	T
DISCIPLINE			
RISING OR FALLING'S ALL ONE DISCIPLINE!	245	THE DECISION	7
DISCOVER			
AND CHARITY DISCOVER	7	ORDERS FOR DAY	19
DISEMBODIED			
DISEMBODIED, UNBLOODY,	209	HER RETICENCE	3
DISENGAGE			
LOVERS DISENGAGE, MOVE SHEEPISHLY TOWARD THE AISLE	47	DOUBLE FEATURE	2
DISGUISE			
MY LOVE, WITH NO DISGUISE.	3	OPEN HOUSE	6
DISH			
WOULD RATHER TAKE THAN DISH IT OUT.	23	AMOROUS LADY	4
WHAT'S THIS? A DISH FOR FAT LIPS.	64	SHAPE OF FIRE	1
A DEEP DISH. LUMPS IN IT.	74	I NEED, I NEED	1
OR LADLE RATTLING IN AN EMPTY DISH?	105	SIR JOHN DAVIES	30
DISK			
HOPE FLUSHED MY CHEEKBONES WITH A SCARLET DISK.	21	THE AUCTION	11
DISMAL			
THE SLACK FACE OF THE DISMAL PURE INANE?	149	IN LATE SUMMER	10
DISMAY			
MADE FROM HIS TERROR AND DISMAY A GRAVE PHILOSOPHICAL LANGUAGE;	170	FOURTH MEDITATN	72
DISMAYED			
MY INWARD WITNESS IS DISMAYED	220	THE ABYSS	19
DISORDER			
IN THE DIRT AND DISORDER I CHERISH ONE SCRAP OF ILLUSION:	29	THE REMINDER	11
A LEAF, I WOULD LOVE THE LEAVES, DELIGHTING IN THE REDOLENT DISORDER OF THIS MORTAL LIFE,	188	THE LONGING	47
DISORDERED			
IN THE WILD DISORDERED LANGUAGE OF THE NATURAL HEART?	166	HER BECOMING	33
DISPENSE			
AND WILLINGLY WOULD I DISPENSE	19	EPIDERM MACABRE	13
DISPERSED			
ALL RANDOM, WASTED, AND DISPERSED,	19	AGNST DISASTER	5
DISPOSITION			
SLOWLY HIS MATCHLESS DISPOSITION SOURED	28	THE FAVORITE	12
DISREPAIR			
WHAT SHAKES MY SKULL TO DISREPAIR	22	SILENCE	19
DISSECTION			
DISSECTION IS A VIRTUE WHEN	257	SANITARIUM	11
DISSEMBLING			
A FURIOUS, DISSEMBLING DIN.	22	SILENCE	14
DISTANCE			
HERE DISTANCE IS FAMILIAR AS A FRIEND.	13	PRAISE PRAIRIE	11

	PAGE	TITLE	LINE
DISTANT			
ALL DISTANT SHAPES TURN BRIGHTER TO THE GAZE.	17	UNEXTINGUISHED	4
DISTENDED			
I CAN SEE THAT BY THE DISTENDED PULSING MIDDLE;	226	THE LIZARD	2
DISTILLS			
DISTILLS A PUNGENCE OF ITS OWN;	14	COMING OF COLD	16
DISTORTIONS			
I WOULD UNLEARN THE LINGO OF EXASPERATION, ALL THE			
DISTORTIONS OF MALICE AND HATRED;	188	THE LONGING	42
DISTRACT			
TO DISTRACT ATTENTION FROM THE SHORT-TAILED RIDICULOUS			
YOUNG ONES	234	ALL MORNING	19
DISTRICT			
HERE IN OUR AGING DISTRICT THE WOOD PIGEON LIVES WITH US,	234	ALL MORNING	1
DISTURB			
(WOULD A CIGARETTE DISTURB HIM?)	226	THE LIZARD	13
DISTURBED			
DISTURBED SOME RHYTHM, OLD AND OF VAST IMPORTANCE, ...	40	MOSS-GATHERING	11
DITCH			
NOTHING WOULD SLEEP IN THAT CELLAR, DANK AS A DITCH, ...	38	ROOT CELLAR	1
LOOK, LOOK, THE DITCH IS RUNNING WHITE!	57	THE LOST SON	119
DITCHES			
INTO THAT MINNOWY WORLD OF WEEDS AND DITCHES, ...	66	SHAPE OF FIRE	65
A CHANCE? PERHAPS. BUT THE ROAD WAS PART OF ME, AND ITS			
DITCHES, ...	193	JOURNY INTERIOR	23
DIVE			
I DIVE WITH THE BLACK HAG, THE CORMORANT, ...	209	HER LONGING	13
DIVERGENT			
DIVERGENT BIRD, ...	261	THE CHANGELING	52
DIVIDE			
I FEEL MY FLESH DIVIDE.	148	THE SMALL	14
DIVIDED			
MY DREAM DIVIDED ON A POINT OF FIRE;	119	THE DREAM	5
WHEN LIGHT DIVIDED ON A STORM-TOSSED TREE.	246	THE MARROW	20
'TWIXT ANIMAL AND MAN DIVIDED, ...	264	THREE EPIGRAMS	13
DIVINE			
I'LL FACE ALL THAT, AND THE DIVINE ABSURD:	272	DUET	5
DIVING			
DIVING DOWN AT MY WINDOWS, ...	152	THE SISKINS	2
THE SMALL THING DIVING DOWN TOWARD A HILL, ...	232	THE THING	10
A FURY OF JAYS, DIVING AND SQUAWKING, ...	234	ALL MORNING	22
ALL THAT DIVING AND PITCHING AND SWOOPING.	255	LIGHT POEM	5
DIVINITY			
DIVINITY ITSELF MALIGN, ABSURD;	237	THE TRANCED	7
THUS I CONFORM TO MY DIVINITY	244	INFIRMITY	11
DIZZY			
COULD MAKE A SMALL BOY DIZZY;	45	MY PAPA'S WALTZ	2
DAZZLE ME, DIZZY APHORIST.	97	O, THOU OPENING	5
DO			
WALK BOLDLY MY SISTER BUT DO NOT DEIGN TO GIVE	5	TO MY SISTER	10
THE HIGHER THINGS IN LIFE DO NOT	25	VERSE W ALLUSNS	5
THE RICH CAN PLAY AT POLO, THE POOR CAN DO THE SHAG, ...	27	CLAIRVOY WIDOW	11
DO YOU SEE ANY SIGN OR SEMBLANCE OF THAT THING CALLED			
"HOPE"?	27	CLAIRVOY WIDOW	18
OUT OF WHAT DOOR DO I GO, ...	54	THE LOST SON	26
WHERE DO THE ROOTS GO?	55	THE LOST SON	62
MY VEINS ARE RUNNING NOWHERE. DO THE BONES CAST OUT THEIR			
FIRE?	56	THE LOST SON	101
WHAT DO THE CLOUDS SAY?	56	THE LOST SON	117
THE FIEND'S FAR AWAY. LORD, WHAT DO YOU REQUIRE?	59	THE LONG ALLEY	21
LOOK WHAT THE LARKS DO.	59	THE LONG ALLEY	28
SO UP AND AWAY AND WHAT DO WE DO	60	THE LONG ALLEY	37
SO UP AND AWAY AND WHAT DO WE DO	60	THE LONG ALLEY	37
WHAT DO WE DO	60	THE LONG ALLEY	57
WHAT DO WE DO	60	THE LONG ALLEY	57
DO WE ROUT THE FISH?	60	THE LONG ALLEY	59
WAKE ME, WITCH, WE'LL DO THE DANCE OF ROTTEN STICKS.	64	SHAPE OF FIRE	10
DO THE DEAD BITE?	74	I NEED, I NEED	18
HOW MANY ANGELS DO YOU KNOW?--	77	BRING THE DAY!	12
LEAVES, DO YOU LIKE ME ANY?	78	BRING THE DAY!	33
THIS DOXIE DOESN'T DO.	83	O LULL ME, LULL	17
WHAT FOOTIE WILL DO WILL BE FINAL.	86	PRAISE TO END!	42
LAY LIKE THE CATS DO	87	PRAISE TO END!	61

	PAGE	TITLE	LINE
DO (CONTINUED)			
DO WHAT THE CLUMSY PARTNER WANTS TO DO!	106	SIR JOHN DAVIES	42
DO WHAT THE CLUMSY PARTNER WANTS TO DO!	106	SIR JOHN DAVIES	42
GREAT NATURE HAS ANOTHER THING TO DO	108	THE WAKING (2)	13
O PRINT IT, MY DEAR, DO PUBLISH IT, YES,	113	TO A LADY ED	9
YOU'D BETTER WATCH THE THINGS YOU DO.	114	DINKY	17
YOU'D BETTER WATCH THE THINGS YOU DO.	114	DINKY	18
I DO NOT LIKE TO BANG OR TOOTLE."	115	THE SERPENT	20
WHAT DO THE GREAT DEAD SAY?	123	WORDS FOR WIND	10
LOVE HAS A THING TO DO.	124	WORDS FOR WIND	53
WHEN I DO WHAT SHE DOES:	126	WORDS FOR WIND	96
MOTION CAN DO NO MORE.	130	THE OTHER	18
IF WE DO THIS AGAIN,"--	136	THE SENSUALISTS	24
MY DARLING DOES WHAT I COULD NEVER DO:	140	THE SWAN	6
OF WHAT I DID NOT DO.	154	THE DYING MAN	20
NOR CAN IMAGINATION DO IT ALL	156	THE DYING MAN	98
MY GERANIUM IS DYING, FOR ALL I CAN DO,	163	I'M HERE	75
A FACE FLOATS IN THE FERNS. DO MAIMED GODS WALK?	165	HER BECOMING	18
WHAT DO THEIR LIVES MEAN,	169	FOURTH MEDITATN	42
WHAT DO THEY NEED?	169	FOURTH MEDITATN	50
DO THESE BONES LIVE? CAN I LIVE WITH THESE BONES?	172	WHAT TELL BONES	52
THE BEST HE COULD DO WAS JIGGLE HIS BLUBBER.	178	THE WHALE	4
WHY I COULD DO BETTER	179	MYRTLE	10
THE THINGS YOU DO, NOBODY DOES:	180	GOO-GIRL	2
HOW DID YOU DO THAT?	180	GOO-GIRL	9
OH WHAT! OH WHAT WHAT CAN I DO?"	182	PHILANDER	5
WHAT DO THEY TELL US, SOUND AND SILENCE?	204	THE ROSE	58
WE LIVE BY WHAT WE DO.	212	LIGHT LISTENED	12
DO WE MOVE TOWARD GOD, OR MERELY ANOTHER CONDITION?	221	THE ABYSS	75
DO I IMAGINE HE NO LONGER TREMBLES	227	MEADOW MOUSE	17
A CAT RUNS FROM THE WIND AS WE DO,	230	THE STORM	19
DO THESE ANALOGIES PERPLEX? A SKY WITH CLOUDS,	235	MANIFESTATION	6
WHAT DOES WHAT IT SHOULD DO NEEDS NOTHING MORE.	235	MANIFESTATION	9
DO WE DO MORE THAN WE KNOW,	237	THE TRANCED	4
DO WE DO MORE THAN WE KNOW,	237	THE TRANCED	4
HOW SLOWLY DARK COMES DOWN ON WHAT WE DO.	240	IN EVEING AIR	24
WHOM DO WE LOVE? I THOUGHT I KNEW THE TRUTH;	241	THE SEQUEL	7
I DO NOT LAUGH; I DO NOT CRY;	256	IN HYDROTHERAPY	9
I DO NOT LAUGH; I DO NOT CRY;	256	IN HYDROTHERAPY	9
DO THE DEAD WAKE IN THEIR OWN WAY?	259	SONG (3)	32
HE DOES WHAT DOVES AND SPARROWS DO--	264	THREE EPIGRAMS	15
I DO NOT HAVE A FIDDLE SO	269	GOB MUSIC	1
OOOMPH DAH DOODLE DAH DO.	269	GOB MUSIC	9
AND DO NOT MIND THE STINK.	269	GOB MUSIC	15
AND WHAT DO YOU THINK I SAW?--	269	GOB MUSIC	25
I STARED AND STARED, AND WHAT DO YOU THINK?	269	GOB MUSIC	30
DOCK			
THE DOCK, SO GARISH TO THE EYE,	14	COMING OF COLD	15
FROM THE RICKETY WOODEN DOCK,	158	FIRST MEDITATN	51
DOCTORS			
THE DOCTORS, THE LAWYERS, THE COPS ARE ALL PAID--	112	SQUEEZE-BOX	42
DOE			
A DOE DRINKS BY A STREAM,	141	MEMORY	9
A DOE AND ITS FAWN.	141	MEMORY	10
THE DOE WITH ITS SLOPED SHOULDERS LOPING ACROSS THE HIGHWAY,	190	AT OYSTER RIVER	27
DOES			
THE SENSE THAT DOES SO FITLY SERVE,	8	PRAYER	20
THOUGHT DOES NOT CRUSH TO STONE.	9	THE ADAMANT	1
WHO ELSE BREATHES HERE? WHAT DOES THE GRAVE SAY?	59	THE LONG ALLEY	19
FILLS AND TREMBLES AT THE EDGE YET DOES NOT FLOW OVER,	67	SHAPE OF FIRE	94
WHAT WATER DOES?	76	I NEED, I NEED	65
WHAT FOOTIE DOES IS FINAL.	86	PRAISE TO END!	34
WHAT FOOTIE DOES IS FINAL.	86	PRAISE TO END!	38
TELL ME, BODY WITHOUT SKIN, DOES A FISH SWEAT?	89	UNFOLD! UNFOLD!	2
A CAGED BEAR RARELY DOES THE SAME THING TWICE	105	SIR JOHN DAVIES	10
WHEN I DO WHAT SHE DOES:	126	WORDS FOR WIND	96
WE DID NOT FLY THE FLESH. WHO DOES, WHEN YOUNG?	131	SENTENTIOUS MAN	7
THE NIGHT WIND RISES. DOES MY FATHER LIVE?	135	THE RENEWAL	7
HER IMAGE FADES, YET DOES NOT DISAPPEAR--	140	THE SWAN	2
MY DARLING DOES WHAT I COULD NEVER DO:	140	THE SWAN	6
ONE FOLLOWS FIRE. ONE DOES.	167	HER BECOMING	80
THE THINGS YOU DO, NOBODY DOES:	180	GOO-GIRL	2
A HEAD OR TAIL--WHICH DOES HE LACK?	182	THE HIPPO	1

	PAGE	TITLE	LINE
DOES (CONTINUED)			
DOES HE POISE IN THE AIR,	183	THE WAGTAIL	4
IN THE MOMENT OF TIME WHEN THE SMALL DROP FORMS, BUT DOES NOT FALL,	194	JOURNY INTERIOR	58
TO FOOLS AND FRAUDS: HE DOES NOT PUT ON AIRS	224	OTTO	3
A FLORIST DOES NOT WOO THE BEAUTIFUL:	224	OTTO	8
TO WHOM DOES THIS TERRACE BELONG?--	226	THE LIZARD	27
WHAT DOES WHAT IT SHOULD DO NEEDS NOTHING MORE.	235	MANIFESTATION	9
HOW BODY FROM SPIRIT SLOWLY DOES UNWIND	244	INFIRMITY	35
A THORN DOES WELL IN THE WIND,	262	FOLLIES OF ADAM	13
THE CENTAUR DOES NOT NEED A HORSE;	264	THREE EPIGRAMS	11
HE DOES WHAT DOVES AND SPARROWS DO--	264	THREE EPIGRAMS	15
WHAT ELSE HE DOES IS UP TO YOU.	264	THREE EPIGRAMS	16
DOESN'T			
THIS DOXIE DOESN'T DO.	83	O LULL ME, LULL	17
DOESN'T DARE	117	LADY AND BEAR	12
DOESN'T DARE	117	LADY AND BEAR	13
DOESN'T DARE	117	LADY AND BEAR	14
DOG			
WE GROW INDIFFERENT TO DOG HOWLS, TO THE NESTLING'S LAST PEEP;	33	IDYLL	6
THEN BRISTLED LIKE A DOG.	47	THE RETURN	4
A TWO-LEGGED DOG HUNTING A NEW HORIZON OF HOWLS.	65	SHAPE OF FIRE	38
YOU ROUND DOG?--	81	SENSIBILITY! LA	17
BE GOOD AS A GOOSE, BE BIG AS A DOG,	86	PRAISE TO END!	40
I'VE CRAWLED FROM THE MIRE, ALERT AS A SAINT OR A DOG;	88	PRAISE TO END!	81
AN OLD DOG	99	O, THOU OPENING	71
I WAITED, ALERT AS A DOG.	100	THE VISITANT	7
THIS JOY OUTLEAPS THE DOG. WHO CARES? WHO CARES?	106	SIR JOHN DAVIES	44
I KEEP A DOG, AND BARK MYSELF.	138	THE SURLY ONE	4
THEREFORE I REJECT THE WORLD OF THE DOG	196	THE LONG WATERS	5
I CAN'T BURY THE BONE OF THIS MISERY LIKE A FASTIDIOUS DOG.	261	THE CHANGELING	31
DOGS			
DOGS OF THE GROIN	55	THE LOST SON	75
CALL OFF THE DOGS, MY PAWS ARE GONE.	61	THE LONG ALLEY	85
I CAN'T LAUGH AT A PROCESSION OF DOGS.	64	SHAPE OF FIRE	13
LACKING THE CANDOR OF DOGS, I KISS THE DEPARTING AIR;	86	PRAISE TO END!	26
HAPPINESS LEFT TO DOGS AND CHILDREN--	187	THE LONGING	9
TO A SCURRY OF SMALL DOGS AND A SHRIEK OF CHILDREN,	193	JOURNY INTERIOR	26
WHEN EVERYTHING--BIRDS, MEN, DOGS--	210	HER TIME	23
IS THIS FARE FOR THE CATS AND DOGS?	261	THE CHANGELING	35
DOING			
I SEE THE TRAFFIC DOING MIRACULOUS FEATS.	27	CLAIRVOY WIDOW	6
BEING, NOT DOING, IS MY FIRST JOY.	222	THE ABYSS	101
DOLOR			
DOLOR	46	DOLOR	T
NEAT IN THEIR BOXES, DOLOR OF PAD AND PAPER-WEIGHT,	46	DOLOR	2
DOLPHIN			
OUT OF HER PLACE SHE COMES, A DOLPHIN ONE,	156	THE DYING MAN	80
THE DOLPHIN RISING FROM THE DARKENING WAVES;	205	THE ROSE	110
DOLPHIN'S			
A DOLPHIN'S AT MY DOOR!	99	O, THOU OPENING	62
DONE			
THE LAST OF HARVESTING IS DONE.	14	COMING OF COLD	33
OF A MAN-TAILORED BLOUSE; THE LIST OF SHOPPING DONE;	29	THE REMINDER	6
A THING IS DONE: A THING	126	WORDS FOR WIND	94
WHAT HAVE I DONE TO YOU?	146	THE SONG	4
AND I GO FASTER IN MY RAGE TO GET DONE WITH IT,	151	SLUG	18
"WHAT'S DONE IS YET TO COME;	153	THE DYING MAN	6
AND THINK I AM DONE!--	182	PHILANDER	4
WALLACE STEVENS, WHAT'S HE DONE?	266	FOR STEVENS	1
DONKEY			
THE DONKEY	178	THE DONKEY	T
I HAD A DONKEY, THAT WAS ALL RIGHT,	178	THE DONKEY	1
YOUR DONKEY IS BETTER BEHAVED, I TRUST.	178	THE DONKEY	4
A DONKEY PATH LED TO A SMALL PLATEAU.	247	I WAITED	21
DONKEY'S			
A DONKEY'S TAIL IS VERY NICE	181	MONOTONY SONG	1
DONNE			
I AM MY FATHER'S SON, I AM JOHN DONNE	140	THE SWAN	13
DON'T			
LET'S NOT HURRY. THE DEAD DON'T HURRY.	59	THE LONG ALLEY	18
BUT THEY DON'T COME	60	THE LONG ALLEY	53

	PAGE	TITLE	LINE
DON'T (CONTINUED)			
I DON'T CARE EITHER.	72	WHERE KNOCK IS	26
I DON'T CARE EITHER.	72	WHERE KNOCK IS	30
DON'T HIT HIM ON THE BOAT, I SAID.	73	WHERE KNOCK IS	59
WHY DON'T YOU, BEGONIA,	74	I NEED, I NEED	13
DON'T TELL MY HANDS.	74	WHERE KNOCK IS	85
YOU AND I DON'T.	75	I NEED, I NEED	41
KEEPER OF HAY. THAT'S A SPRATLING'S PRATTLE. AND DON'T BE THINKING YOU'RE	98	O, THOU OPENING	28
I'VE TRIED I DON'T KNOW HOW MANY TIMES TO REPLANT IT.	163	I'M HERE	77
YOU'D BETTER NOT LAUGH; AND DON'T SAY, "POOH!"	177	KITTY-CAT BIRD	18
DON'T POKE MORE THAN TWICE	183	THE LIZARD	6
BIRD, BIRD DON'T EDGE ME IN;	271	THE REPLY	1
DOODLE			
OOOMPH DAH DOODLE DAH	269	GOB MUSIC	7
OOOMPH DAH DOODLE DAH	269	GOB MUSIC	8
OOOMPH DAH DOODLE DAH DO.	269	GOB MUSIC	9
DOOM			
LET THE GESTURES FREEZE; OUR DOOM IS ALREADY DECIDED.	56	THE LOST SON	105
DOOR			
OFTEN I MEET, ON WALKING FROM A DOOR,	8	THE SIGNALS	1
THE BLUE SPRUCE LASHED LIKE A SURF AT THE DOOR.	12	MID-CNTRY BLOW	4
NEXT DOOR THERE IS A LOVE-NEST OF PLASTER BOARD AND TIN,	27	CLAIRVOY WIDOW	15
OUT OF WHAT DOOR DO I GO,	54	THE LOST SON	26
BY THE CAVE'S DOOR,	55	THE LOST SON	72
HAS THE DARK A DOOR?	82	SENSIBILITY! LA	47
A DOLPHIN'S AT MY DOOR!	99	O, THOU OPENING	62
I CAME TO A GREAT DOOR,	145	THE BEAST	1
TO PREFER A WINDOW TO A DOOR?	169	FOURTH MEDITATN	29
AS WHEN THE DOOR SWINGS OPEN IN A FLORIST'S STOREROOM--	220	THE ABYSS	46
WHERE THE HEAVY DOOR UNLOCKS,	230	THE STORM	21
US, UNDER THE CHAIR-RUNGS, TOWARD THE CELLAR DOOR.	273	SUPPR W LINDSAY	14
DOORMAT			
THICK AND CUSHIONY, LIKE AN OLD-FASHIONED DOORMAT,	40	MOSS-GATHERING	3
UNTIL I'M SCRAPING AND SCRATCHING AT YOU, ON THE DOORMAT,	151	SLUG	19
DOORS			
MY DOORS ARE WIDELY SWUNG.	3	OPEN HOUSE	4
THE DOORS SWINGING OPEN,	103	OLD LADY'S WRDS	21
A THING WE FEEL AT EVENING, AND BY DOORS,	162	I'M HERE	53
DOORSTEPS			
AND PICKED AND PICKLED THE BEST, TO BE LEFT ON RICKETY DOORSTEPS.	223	ELEGY (2)	15
DOTING			
THOSE DOTING AUNTIES NEVER WOULD HAVE BOTHERED.	25	DIM-WIT COUSIN	4
DOUBLE			
ADDS UP A PAIR OF JIGGLING DOUBLE CHINS.	25	DIM-WIT COUSIN	8
THAT RATTLES DOUBLE GLASS.	34	NIGHT JOURNEY	23
DOUBLE FEATURE	47	DOUBLE FEATURE	T
THERE ONCE WAS A COW WITH A DOUBLE UDDER.	114	THE COW	1
ITS SPRAY HOLDING A DOUBLE RAIN-BOW IN EARLY MORNING,	191	AT OYSTER RIVER	45
BEARING ITS LIFE AND MORE, A DOUBLE SOUND,	248	THE TREE, BIRD	11
DOUBT			
ALL WHO REMEMBER, DOUBT. WHO CALLS THAT STRANGE?	120	THE DREAM	21
I DOUBT I'LL USE IT AGAIN.	153	THE DYING MAN	5
DOUGH			
THE DOUGH I SPENT ON CHIPPEWA KATE,	112	SQUEEZE-BOX	39
DOUGHNUTS			
HIM WITH THE PLATITUDES AND RUBBER DOUGHNUTS,	65	SHAPE OF FIRE	30
DOVE			
RAIN SWEETENED THE CAVE AND THE DOVE STILL CALLED;	66	SHAPE OF FIRE	75
A DOVE SAID DOVE ALL DAY.	75	I NEED, I NEED	20
A DOVE SAID DOVE ALL DAY.	75	I NEED, I NEED	20
I'M THICK WITH LEAVES AND TENDER AS A DOVE,	173	WHAT TELL BONES	89
THOSE WHO DESPISE THE DOVE.	220	THE ABYSS	28
DOVE UTTERLY,	261	THE CHANGELING	51
DOVES			
WITH TOWHEES, FINCHES, CHICKADEES, CALIFORNIA QUAIL, WOOD DOVES,	235	ALL MORNING	40
HE DOES WHAT DOVES AND SPARROWS DO--	264	THREE EPIGRAMS	15
DOVE'S			
THE DOVE'S MY WILL TODAY.	124	WORDS FOR WIND	40
THAT DOVE'S ELABORATE WAY OF COMING NEAR	149	IN LATE SUMMER	23

DOWN

	PAGE	TITLE	LINE
THE FEATHER OF THE MILKWEED FLUTTERS DOWN.	12	SLOW SEASON	12
THE YIELD'S HALF DOWN AND HALF IN AIR,	14	COMING OF COLD	8
WHEN CRAVENS CRY THEM DOWN,	20	REPL TO CENSURE	10
WE CANNOT TRACE THE ERROR DOWN.	30	THE RECKONING	8
WHO RAN UP AND DOWN THE BIG CENTER STAIRS	32	SALE	2
CUT STEMS STRUGGLING TO PUT DOWN FEET,	37	CUTTINGS (LATE)	2
HUNG DOWN LONG YELLOW EVIL NECKS, LIKE TROPICAL SNAKES.	38	ROOT CELLAR	5
THE HEAT GOING DOWN	39	ORCHIDS	11
DRIFTING DOWN FROM THEIR MOSSY CRADLES:	39	ORCHIDS	13
ME DOWN IN THAT FETOR OF WEEDS,	39	WEED PULLER	14
SO FAR DOWN THE RIVER	41	BIG WIND	4
A SHAKING DOWN, WHILE THE STEM STAYS STRAIGHT,	42	TRANSPLANTING	10
AND THE AIR COOL, AS IF DRIFTING DOWN FROM WET HEMLOCKS,	43	CARNATIONS	3
AND I LAY DOWN WITH MY LIFE,	47	THE RETURN	10
I SAID: ON ALL THESE, DEATH, WITH GENTLENESS, COME DOWN.	48	JUDGE NOT	10
THE FULL RAIN FELL STRAIGHT DOWN,	50	THE CYCLE	14
DOWN AMONG THE RUBBISH, THE BUG-RIDDLED FOLIAGE,	54	THE LOST SON	41
LOOK DOWN UNDER THE LEAVES.	55	THE LOST SON	63
FELL DREAMILY DOWN?	56	THE LOST SON	91
BEND DOWN, SMALL BREATHERS, CREEPERS AND WINDERS;	61	THE LONG ALLEY	71
SEND DOWN A RUSH OF AIR, O TORRENTIAL,	61	THE LONG ALLEY	83
COMING DOWN ON THE FLOWERHEADS,	67	SHAPE OF FIRE	80
WENT DOWN CELLAR,	74	I NEED, I NEED	8
I COULD MELT DOWN A STONE,--	79	GIVE WAY, GATES	17
FATHER OF TENSIONS, I'M DOWN TO MY SKIN AT LAST.	85	PRAISE TO END!	4
I ROMPED, LITHE AS A CHILD, DOWN THE SUMMERY STREETS OF MY VEINS,	86	PRAISE TO END!	21
--OR SAT DOWN AND DID.	89	UNFOLD! UNFOLD!	11
I HEAR THE OWLS, THE SOFT CALLERS, COMING DOWN FROM THE HEMLOCKS.	93	I CRY, LOVE!	40
OH, WHEN SHE WAS SAD, SHE CAST HERSELF DOWN INTO SUCH A PURE DEPTH,	102	ELEGY FOR JANE	10
DOWN A STEEP HILLSIDE ON A CAKE OF ICE,--	105	SIR JOHN DAVIES	8
IMPALED ON LIGHT, AND WHIRLING SLOWLY DOWN.	107	SIR JOHN DAVIES	72
THEY ALL SAT DOWN LIKE ME AND YOU	111	SQUEEZE-BOX	6
HE GOT NO PLEASURE DOWN HIS HOLE.	115	THE SERPENT	8
THERE, UPSIDE DOWN (UNLIKE A BIRD),	116	THE SLOTH	5
THE DEER CAME DOWN, OUT OF THE DAPPLED WOOD.	120	THE DREAM	20
I CRIED, AND THE BIRDS CAME DOWN	123	WORDS FOR WIND	15
DOWN LONG SEA-CHAMBERS OF THE INNER EAR.	129	SHE	6
IT TIPTOED DOWN THE HALL.	136	THE SENSUALISTS	20
LOST OPPOSITES BEND DOWN--	140	THE SWAN	18
THE WEATHER WEPT, AND ALL THE TREES BENT DOWN;	143	SHIMMER OF EVIL	1
BENT DOWN THEIR BIRDS: THE LIGHT WAVES TOOK THE WAVES;	143	SHIMMER OF EVIL	2
HUNG DOWN: AND I WAS ONLY I.	143	SHIMMER OF EVIL	9
THAT GOD THAT GOD LEANS DOWN HIS HEART TO HEAR.	144	ELEGY (1)	16
I WENT RUNNING DOWN A ROAD,	146	THE SONG	8
DOWN IN THAT WATERY HOLE:	146	THE SONG	19
BUT DOWN LONG CORRIDORS,	147	THE EXORCISM	10
THE MOON GOES SLOWLY DOWN;	148	THE SMALL	8
THE WIND DIES DOWN; MY WILL DIES WITH THE WIND,	149	IN LATE SUMMER	11
DIVING DOWN AT MY WINDOWS,	152	THE SISKINS	2
BENDING THEM DOWN TO THE GROUND;	152	THE SISKINS	11
SCUTTLING DOWN AND AROUND LIKE YOUNG SQUIRRELS,	152	THE SISKINS	17
TOPPLING DOWN AN EMBANKMENT.	157	FIRST MEDITATN	7
THEN DOWN, AS WE ROLL LIKE A BOAT FROM A WAVE-CREST.	158	FIRST MEDITATN	25
DOWN FROM BEHIND THE LAST RANGES,	158	FIRST MEDITATN	33
LUNGING DOWN A HILLSIDE.	159	FIRST MEDITATN	59
AS WHEN SILT DRIFTS AND SIFTS DOWN THROUGH MUDDY POND-WATER,	159	FIRST MEDITATN	60
THE LONG PLAINTIVE NOTES FLOATING DOWN,	159	FIRST MEDITATN	87
I REMEMBER WALKING DOWN A PATH,	162	I'M HERE	45
DOWN WOODEN STEPS TOWARD A WEEDY GARDEN;	162	I'M HERE	46
JUMPING UP AND DOWN ON THEIR HIND FEET,	163	I'M HERE	68
AND THERE I STAYED UNTIL THE DAY BURNED DOWN.	166	HER BECOMING	52
THE MOON, A PURE ISLAMIC SHAPE, LOOKED DOWN.	166	HER BECOMING	55
I SHED MY CLOTHES TO SLOW MY DAEMON DOWN.	166	HER BECOMING	59
DIPPING UP AND DOWN IN THE RIPPLES,	168	FOURTH MEDITATN	10
THE SHADOWS CRAWLING DOWN A SUNNY WALL.	171	WHAT TELL BONES	17
OR STAY BY YOURSELF DOWN DEEP IN THE WOOD,	177	KITTY-CAT BIRD	7
AND THE IVY-BRANCH, CAST TO THE GROUND, PUTS DOWN ROOTS INTO THE SAWDUST,	197	THE LONG WATERS	34
DOWN BY THE MUCK SHRINKING TO THE ALKALINE CENTER.	197	THE LONG WATERS	43

		PAGE	TITLE	LINE
DOWN (CONTINUED)				
BY SMALL STREAMS RUNNING DOWN UNDER FALLEN FIR TREES.	....	197	THE LONG WATERS	48
OR TO SINK DOWN TO THE HIPS IN A MOSSY QUAGMIRE;	....	200	THE FAR FIELD	44
THE SUN A BALL OF FIRE COMING DOWN OVER THE WATER,	....	202	THE ROSE	16
THE PROW PITCHING EASILY UP AND DOWN,	....	203	THE ROSE	35
WHERE THE SLOW CREEK WINDS DOWN TO THE BLACK SAND OF THE				
SHORE	....	203	THE ROSE	49
DOWN IN THE CORNER OF THE GARDEN, AMONG THE RAGGEDY LILACS,		204	THE ROSE	64
"WRITE ALL MY WHISPERS DOWN,"	....	208	HER WORDS	8
DOWN ON THE NEAR SHORE,		210	HER TIME	22
I SANG TO THE ONE STAR THAT LOOKED DOWN AT ME;	....	216	THE SHY MAN	2
THE FULL MOON HAS FALLEN, THE NIGHT WIND IS DOWN	....	216	THE SHY MAN	17
A STEP DOWN THE STAIR."	....	219	THE ABYSS	8
A FURRED CATERPILLAR CRAWLS DOWN A STRING.		220	THE ABYSS	35
WINDING DOWN TO THE STRETCH OF IRREGULAR SAND,		222	THE ABYSS	95
BEARING DOWN, WITH TWO STEADY EYES,	....	223	ELEGY (2)	22
HAD SLAUGHTERED GAME, AND CUT YOUNG FIR TREES DOWN.	....	224	OTTO	21
THEN SLIDES DOWN OVER THE EYE'S SURFACE,	....	226	THE LIZARD	24
COMING DOWN FROM THE MOUNTAIN,	....	230	THE STORM	4
THE FLAT-ROOFED HOUSES, COMING DOWN IN GUSTS, BEATING	....	230	THE STORM	24
BENDING THE TREES HALF-WAY DOWN TO THE GROUND,	....	231	THE STORM	31
A SPIDER EASES HIMSELF DOWN FROM A SWAYING LIGHT-BULB,	...	231	THE STORM	34
RUNNING OVER THE COVERLET, DOWN UNDER THE IRON BEDSTEAD.		231	THE STORM	35
THE SMALL THING DIVING DOWN TOWARD A HILL,	....	232	THE THING	10
AND ONE DROPS DOWN TO THE GARDEN, THE HIGH RHODODENDRON,		234	ALL MORNING	8
AND THE DUCKS NEAR LAKE WASHINGTON WADDLE DOWN THE HIGHWAY				
AFTER A RAIN,	....	234	ALL MORNING	26
COMING DOWN ON A PATCH OF LAWN:	....	235	ALL MORNING	38
I LOOK DOWN THE FAR LIGHT	....	240	IN EVEING AIR	13
FAR DOWN A BILLOWING PLAIN,	....	240	IN EVEING AIR	15
HOW SLOWLY DARK COMES DOWN ON WHAT WE DO.	....	240	IN EVEING AIR	24
BROUGHT ME DOWN TO MY KNEES. O WHO CAN BE		241	THE SEQUEL	5
AN OLD WIND-TATTERED BUTTERFLY FLEW DOWN	....	243	THE MOTION	2
WHAT WE PUT DOWN, MUST WE TAKE UP AGAIN?	....	243	THE MOTION	11
GOD'S NIGHT AND DAY: DOWN THIS SPACE HE HAS SMILED,		243	THE MOTION	21
BREAKS ON ME AS MY MEAGER FLESH BREAKS DOWN--	....	244	INFIRMITY	15
DEEP IN THE MOW, AND EACH STEP DEEPER DOWN,	....	247	I WAITED	7
THEN LOST ITSELF DOWN THROUGH A ROCKY GORGE.	....	247	I WAITED	20
SIX HOURS A DAY I LAY ME DOWN	....	256	IN HYDROTHERAPY	1
MY PAST IS SLIDING DOWN THE DRAIN;	....	256	IN HYDROTHERAPY	11
CAN BRING A GOOD MAN DOWN.		269	GOB MUSIC	19
AND I KNEELED DOWN AND DID PARTAKE	....	270	GOB MUSIC	34
AS I GULPED IT DOWN, AS I GULPED IT DOWN.	....	270	GOB MUSIC	41
AS I GULPED IT DOWN, AS I GULPED IT DOWN.	....	270	GOB MUSIC	41
WILL BRING A GOOD MAN DOWN.	....	270	GOB MUSIC	47
WHEN HE SAID THAT, A SPIDERY SHAPE DROPPED DOWN	....	273	SUPPR W LINDSAY	24
SO WE SAT DOWN AND ATE OURSELVES A MEAL,	....	274	SUPPR W LINDSAY	30
DOWNDRAFT				
AS A FIRE, SEEMINGLY LONG DEAD, FLARES UP FROM A DOWNDRAFT				
OF AIR IN A CHIMNEY,	....	198	THE LONG WATERS	63
DOWN-HILL				
WATCHING FOR DANGEROUS DOWN-HILL PLACES, WHERE THE WHEELS				
WHINED BEYOND EIGHTY--	....	193	JOURNY INTERIOR	19
DOWNWARD				
DOWNWARD AND UPWARD,	....	93	I CRY, LOVE!	43
DOWNY				
WHERE'S SHE NOW, THE MOUNTAIN'S DOWNY GIRL?	....	101	THE VISITANT	24
DOXIE				
THIS DOXIE DOESN'T DO.	....	83	O LULL ME, LULL	17
DOZEN				
WHO ALWAYS DID THINGS BY THE DOZEN;	....	179	MYRTLE'S COUSIN	2
DRAFT				
I'M A DRAFT SLEEPING BY A STICK;	....	97	O, THOU OPENING	7
DRAG				
SIMPLICITY'S SWEET THING, EITHER. A LEAF COULD DRAG YOU.		98	O, THOU OPENING	29
AND THE WAVES FLATTENING OUT WHEN THE FISHERMEN DRAG THEIR				
NETS OVER THE STONES.	....	194	JOURNY INTERIOR	57
DRAGGING				
OR, POISONED, DRAGGING A WHITE SKEIN OF SPITTLE OVER A				
PATH--	....	151	SLUG	21
DRAIN				
(DREAMS DRAIN THE SPIRIT IF WE DREAM TOO LONG.)	....	187	THE LONGING	13
MY PAST IS SLIDING DOWN THE DRAIN;	....	256	IN HYDROTHERAPY	11

		PAGE	TITLE	LINE
DRAINED				
MY SOURCES DRAINED OF ALL CONTENT,		19	AGNST DISASTER	3
SO WE DRAINED THE MANURE-MACHINE		41	BIG WIND	6
HIS LOOK DRAINED THE STONES.		56	THE LOST SON	87
TODAY THEY DRAINED THE FLUID FROM A KNEE		244	INFIRMITY	9
DRAINHOLES				
THOSE LEWD MONKEY-TAILS HANGING FROM DRAINHOLES,--		39	WEED PULLER	3
DRAINPIPES				
WHAT A SCUTTLING AND RAPPING ALONG THE DRAINPIPES,		234	ALL MORNING	21
DRANK				
AND WE DRANK THE DRY HARSH WINE		232	THE THING	20
IF I ATE AND DRANK LIKE HIM,		266	FOR STEVENS	11
DRAW				
THE BUDS DRAW IN BEFORE THE COLD.		15	COMING OF COLD	37
FAR THINGS DRAW CLOSER IN.		148	THE SMALL	10
"ADORE AND DRAW NEAR.		222	THE ABYSS	86
DRAWING				
DRAWING IN THE WARM AIR.		39	ORCHIDS	8
DRAWN				
NOTES FINELY DRAWN.		213	THE HAPPY THREE	32
DRAWS				
THE MOON DRAWS BACK ITS WATERS FROM THE SHORE.		140	THE SWAN	15
BEFORE THE MOON DRAWS BACK,		171	WHAT TELL BONES	8
THE DEW DRAWS NEAR.		215	HIS FOREBODING	10
DREAD				
CORRUPTION REAPS THE YOUNG; YOU DREAD		4	FEUD	1
INCOMPREHENSIBLE GAIETY AND DREAD		106	SIR JOHN DAVIES	49
IN HEAVEN'S PRAISE, I DREAD THE THING I AM.		156	THE DYING MAN	95
THE SWAN'S DREAD OF THE DARKENING SHORE,		171	WHAT TELL BONES	25
THE INCOMMENSURATE DREAD		215	HIS FOREBODING	3
WHICH IS THE WAY? I CRY TO THE DREAD BLACK,		245	THE DECISION	9
DREAM				
OVER THE GULFS OF DREAM		49	NIGHT CROW	4
HANDS AND HAIR MOVED THROUGH A DREAM OF WAKENING BLOSSOMS.		66	SHAPE OF FIRE	74
A GHOULIE IN A DREAM.		71	WHERE KNOCK IS	15
I DREAM OF NOTHING BUT BOARDS;		79	GIVE WAY, GATES	2
I BREATHE INTO A DREAM,		83	O LULL ME, LULL	25
I KNOW THAT DREAM.		103	OLD LADY'S WRDS	2
THE DREAM		119	THE DREAM	T
BEFORE SHE EVER BREATHED, AND IN THAT DREAM		119	THE DREAM	2
MY DREAM DIVIDED ON A POINT OF FIRE;		119	THE DREAM	5
THE FAR STRETCH OF A DREAM,		124	WORDS FOR WIND	36
DREAM OF A WOMAN, AND A DREAM OF DEATH:		134	THE PURE FURY	22
DREAM OF A WOMAN, AND A DREAM OF DEATH:		134	THE PURE FURY	22
IN THE SLOW WORLD OF DREAM,		141	MEMORY	1
A GULL RIDES ON THE RIPPLES OF A DREAM,		149	IN LATE SUMMER	1
I SEE YOU, LOVE, I SEE YOU IN A DREAM;		155	THE DYING MAN	73
OR DREAM OF THE DEAD, AND THEIR HOLES.		173	WHAT TELL BONES	75
(DREAMS DRAIN THE SPIRIT IF WE DREAM TOO LONG.)		187	THE LONGING	13
WHAT DREAM'S ENOUGH TO BREATHE IN? A DARK DREAM.		188	THE LONGING	28
I DREAM OF JOURNEYS REPEATEDLY:		199	THE FAR FIELD	1
HOW CAN I DREAM EXCEPT BEYOND THIS LIFE?		221	THE ABYSS	61
THE FLESH FATHERS A DREAM;		263	FOLLIES OF ADAM	27
DREAMILY				
FELL DREAMILY DOWN?		56	THE LOST SON	91
DREAMING				
I KEEP DREAMING OF BEES.		99	O, THOU OPENING	81
DREAMS				
(DREAMS DRAIN THE SPIRIT IF WE DREAM TOO LONG.)		187	THE LONGING	13
DREAM'S				
THE DREAM'S AN INSTANT THAT CALLS UP HER FACE.		131	SENTENTIOUS MAN	11
WHAT DREAM'S ENOUGH TO BREATHE IN? A DARK DREAM.		188	THE LONGING	28
DREAMT				
I DREAMT I WAS ALL BONES;		87	PRAISE TO END!	63
LAST NIGHT I DREAMT OF A JAUNTIER PRINCIPLE OF ORDER;		165	HER BECOMING	30
DREARILY				
NOT DREARILY BEWITCHED,		172	WHAT TELL BONES	57
DREARY				
REASON? THAT DREARY SHED, THAT HUTCH FOR GRUBBY SCHOOLBOYS!		92	I CRY, LOVE!	14
I'M RELEASED FROM THE DREARY DANCE OF OPPOSITES.		173	WHAT TELL BONES	80
DRESS				
I HATE MY EPIDERMAL DRESS,		19	EPIDERM MACABRE	10
AND MY DRESS CAUGHT ON ROSE-BRIER.		162	I'M HERE	47

		PAGE	TITLE	LINE
DREW				
IT TURNED; IT DREW AWAY;		150	SNAKE	6
DRIED				
MY FEET CRACKLING SPLINTERS OF GLASS AND DRIED PUTTY,		43	CHILD ON GRNHSE	2
A DRIED STRAWBERRY LEAF,		226	THE LIZARD	17
A DRIED STALK IN A WELTER OF SINUOUS GRASSES,		255	LIGHT POEM	8
DRIED-OUT				
(DRIED-OUT, SHE CREAKED LIKE A TULIP.)		228	THE GERANIUM	14
DRIES				
THE DANK BARK DRIES BENEATH THE SUN,		14	COMING OF COLD	32
THEIR INTRICATE STEM-FUR DRIES;		37	CUTTINGS	2
THE DEAD CROW DRIES ON A POLE.		80	GIVE WAY, GATES	48
DRIFT				
THE SUN CUTS DEEP INTO THE HEAVY DRIFT,		11	LIGHT BRIGHTER	5
WE WATCH OPINION DRIFT,		31	LULL	8
OR DRIFT LAZILY IN AND OUT OF THE WEEDS.		233	THE PIKE	7
DRIFTING				
DRIFTING DOWN FROM THEIR MOSSY CRADLES:		39	ORCHIDS	13
AND THE AIR COOL, AS IF DRIFTING DOWN FROM WET HEMLOCKS,		43	CARNATIONS	3
DRIFTING THROUGH LEAVES, OAK AND MAPLE,		159	FIRST MEDITATN	88
A FUME REMINDS ME, DRIFTING ACROSS WET GRAVEL;		160	FIRST MEDITATN	91
DRIFTING WITH THE BLOSSOMS,		168	FOURTH MEDITATN	16
A SMALL VOICE CALLING FROM A DRIFTING CLOUD.		248	THE TREE, BIRD	4
DRIFTS				
THE HAZE OF HARVEST DRIFTS ALONG THE FIELD		12	SLOW SEASON	3
HELD UP, WHILE THE ROWER BREATHES, AND THE SMALL BOAT DRIFTS QUIETLY SHOREWARD;		67	SHAPE OF FIRE	91
AS WHEN SILT DRIFTS AND SIFTS DOWN THROUGH MUDDY POND-WATER,		159	FIRST MEDITATN	60
A WHITE CABBAGE-BUTTERFLY DRIFTS IN,		226	THE LIZARD	20
DRIFTWOOD				
THE WAVES, ALTERED BY SAND-BARS, BEDS OF KELP, MISCELLANEOUS DRIFTWOOD,		191	AT OYSTER RIVER	32
INTO THE SMALL SPILLAGE OF DRIFTWOOD,		202	THE ROSE	24
MOVING WITH THE WAVES, THE UNDULATING DRIFTWOOD,		203	THE ROSE	48
DRINK				
HOPE, LOVE, CREATE, OR DRINK AND DIE:		18	LONG LIVE WEEDS	11
--AND BEGAN TO DRINK UP THE MONEY.		111	SQUEEZE-BOX	7
--WHEN HE TRIED TO DRINK UP THE MONEY.		112	SQUEEZE-BOX	37
I DRINK GOOD LIQUOR WHEN MY LUCK IS GOOD.		132	SENTENTIOUS MAN	28
A DRUNKARD DRINKS, AND BELCHES IN HIS DRINK;		132	SENTENTIOUS MAN	29
I DRINK MY TEARS IN A PLACE WHERE ALL LIGHT COMES.		170	FOURTH MEDITATN	78
YOU DRINK UP IN QUARTS;		180	GOO-GIRL	6
TO DRINK SOME HALF-AND-HALF		213	THE HAPPY THREE	15
I NEED A MORNING DRINK,		269	GOB MUSIC	11
ON THE PERILS OF TOO EARLY DRINK,--		269	GOB MUSIC	17
TOO EARLY DRINK, TOO EARLY DRINK,		269	GOB MUSIC	18
TOO EARLY DRINK, TOO EARLY DRINK,		269	GOB MUSIC	18
MY THIRST CAME ON, AND I HAD TO DRINK.		269	GOB MUSIC	31
ON THE PERILS OF TOO EARLY DRINK,		270	GOB MUSIC	45
TOO EARLY DRINK, TOO EARLY DRINK		270	GOB MUSIC	46
TOO EARLY DRINK, TOO EARLY DRINK		270	GOB MUSIC	46
DRINKERS				
THE RITUALISTS OF THE MIRROR, THE LONELY DRINKERS,		169	FOURTH MEDITATN	36
DRINKING				
AS WE SAT THERE DRINKING THAT BATHTUB GIN		112	SQUEEZE-BOX	24
THE WASP DRINKING AT THE EDGE OF MY CUP;		163	I'M HERE	87
I HEAR THE FLOWERS DRINKING IN THEIR LIGHT,		222	THE ABYSS	91
TELLS ME MY DRINKING BREEDS A WILL TO DIE.		246	THE MARROW	4
DRINKS				
A DRUNKARD DRINKS, AND BELCHES IN HIS DRINK;		132	SENTENTIOUS MAN	29
A RAW GHOST DRINKS THE FLUID IN MY SPINE;		135	THE RENEWAL	14
A DOE DRINKS BY A STREAM,		141	MEMORY	9
DRIP				
THAT DRIP AND SWEAT,		38	FORCING HOUSE	6
SWEAT AND DRIP,		38	FORCING HOUSE	7
A SLOW DRIP OVER STONES,		53	THE LOST SON	3
I HAVE HEARD, IN A DRIP OF LEAVES,		194	JOURNY INTERIOR	62
DRIPPING				
COILED GREEN AND THICK, LIKE DRIPPING SMILAX,		39	WEED PULLER	8
CYCLAMEN DRIPPING AND LILIES.		61	THE LONG ALLEY	73
SALIVA DRIPPING FROM WARM MICROPHONES,		187	THE LONGING	5
DRIPPY				
THE DRIPPY WATER		74	I NEED, I NEED	10

	PAGE	TITLE	LINE
DRIVE			
I REMEMBER HOW IT WAS TO DRIVE IN GRAVEL,	193	JOURNY INTERIOR	18
DRIVER			
ONE DRIVER, PINNED BENEATH THE SEAT,	33	HIGHWAY: MICH	19
DRIVERS			
THE DRIVERS CREAKING THE SEATS OF THE BAROQUE HEARSES,	22	ROAD TO WDLAWN	2
THE DRIVERS FROM PRODUCTION LINES	33	HIGHWAY: MICH	8
DRIVES			
AND THE HURRICANE DRIVES THE DEAD STRAW INTO THE LIVING PINE-TREE.	231	THE STORM	43
DRIVING			
WIND DRIVING WATER	41	BIG WIND	3
OF DRIVING ALONE, WITHOUT LUGGAGE, OUT A LONG PENINSULA,	199	THE FAR FIELD	3
A FINE FUME OF RAIN DRIVING IN FROM THE SEA,	230	THE STORM	13
THE WALLS, THE SLATTED WINDOWS, DRIVING	230	THE STORM	25
DROOP			
STICKS-IN-A-DROWSE DROOP OVER SUGARY LOAM,	37	CUTTINGS	1
DROOPED			
SHOOTS DANGLED AND DROOPED,	38	ROOT CELLAR	3
DROOPS			
THE LOOSE VINE DROOPS WITH HOAR AT DAWN,	14	COMING OF COLD	20
DROP			
A FIVE-FOOT DROP A VALLEY, SO TO SPEAK.	13	PRAISE PRAIRIE	2
A DROP OF THE NIGHT RAIN STILL IN ME,	168	FOURTH MEDITATN	7
IN THE MOMENT OF TIME WHEN THE SMALL DROP FORMS, BUT DOES NOT FALL,	194	JOURNY INTERIOR	58
AND A DROP OF RAIN WATER HANGS AT THE TIP OF A LEAF	204	THE ROSE	86
DROPPED			
THERE IS NO RIVEN TREE, OR LAMB DROPPED BY AN EAGLE.	159	FIRST MEDITATN	82
WHEN GEORGE THE WATCHMAN'S LANTERN DROPPED FROM SIGHT	225	OTTO	38
WHERE THEY DROPPED AGAIN	232	THE THING	11
SHE DROPPED AS IF SHOT.	249	THE RESTORED	6
WHEN HE SAID THAT, A SPIDERY SHAPE DROPPED DOWN	273	SUPPR W LINDSAY	24
DROPPING			
DROPPING A FINE FILM ON NAILS AND DELICATE EYEBROWS,	46	DOLOR	12
DROPPING A FINE YELLOW SILT WHERE THE SUN STAYS;	200	THE FAR FIELD	68
DROPS			
THE GREAT SLEDGE DROPS IN VAIN.	9	THE ADAMANT	2
THE PLUM DROPS PITCH UPON THE GROUND,	14	COMING OF COLD	9
AND A BEE SHAKING DROPS FROM A RAIN-SOAKED HONEYSUCKLE.	63	FIELD OF LIGHT	49
TO FOLLOW THE DROPS SLIDING FROM A LIFTED OAR,	67	SHAPE OF FIRE	90
WHERE THE TURF DROPS OFF INTO A GRASS-HIDDEN CULVERT,	199	THE FAR FIELD	14
AND ONE DROPS DOWN TO THE GARDEN, THE HIGH RHODODENDRON,	234	ALL MORNING	8
DROSS			
LAY WITH THE DROSS OF DEATH.	147	THE EXORCISM	24
DROUGHT			
THE BRIAR BEARS ITS THORN, AND DROUGHT	14	COMING OF COLD	24
DROVE			
DROVE TO THE FAR	41	BIG WIND	14
DROWN			
OR DROWN A BUG IN ONE SPIT OF TOBACCO JUICE,	42	OLD FLORIST	8
FOR I WOULD DROWN IN FIRE.	138	LOVE'S PROGRESS	25
THERE'S TWO MORE TO DROWN	229	ON THE QUAY	5
WITHIN THIS TUB BUT CANNOT DROWN.	256	IN HYDROTHERAPY	2
DROWSE			
IN A WATERY DROWSE.	62	FIELD OF LIGHT	18
DEATH WAS NOT. I LIVED IN A SIMPLE DROWSE:	66	SHAPE OF FIRE	73
THESE WATERS DROWSE ME INTO SLEEP SO KIND	135	THE RENEWAL	11
THE SMALL SHAPES DROWSE: I LIVE	148	THE SMALL	19
DROWSING			
DROWSING IN SOFT LIGHT, PETALS PULSING.	61	THE LONG ALLEY	76
DRUM			
THIS TOAD COULD WALTZ ON A DRUM;	92	I CRY, LOVE!	11
THEY BOUGHT A DRUM. HE WOULDN'T WHACK IT.	115	THE SERPENT	14
DRUMMED			
AND THE FLICKER DRUMMED FROM HIS DEAD TREE IN THE CHICKEN-YARD.	200	THE FAR FIELD	37
A PARTRIDGE DRUMMED; A MINNOW NUDGED ITS STONE;	241	THE SEQUEL	13
DRUMS			
AND THE TICKING OF SNOW AROUND OIL DRUMS IN THE DAKOTAS,	204	THE ROSE	68
DRUNK			
A DRUNK MAN STUMBLES BY, ABSORBED IN SELF-TALK.	33	IDYLL	2

	PAGE	TITLE	LINE
DRUNK (CONTINUED)			
NOW HE'S EATEN HIS THREE KINDS OF CHEESE AND DRUNK FROM HIS BOTTLE-CAP WATERING-TROUGH--	227	MEADOW MOUSE	12
DRUNKARD			
A DRUNKARD DRINKS, AND BELCHES IN HIS DRINK;	132	SENTENTIOUS MAN	29
DRUNKARDS			
YET WHEN I HEARD THE DRUNKARDS HOWLING,	48	JUDGE NOT	7
DRUNKEN			
THE DRUNKEN SOLDIER, THE OLD LADY WITH HER PEPPERMINTS;	158	FIRST MEDITATN	30
I'M OFTEN A DRUNKEN BOOR;	268	SAGINAW SONG	46
DRY			
BUT STILL THE ROAD AND DUSTY FIELD KEPT DRY.	6	INTERLUDE	8
UPON THE FIELD THE SCENT IS DRY:	14	COMING OF COLD	13
THE MOULD UPON THE BRANCH IS DRY.	15	COMING OF COLD	44
THIS URGE, WRESTLE, RESURRECTION OF DRY STICKS,	37	CUTTINGS (LATE)	1
OVER THE DRY SEED-CROWNS,	58	THE LOST SON	156
ALONG THE LOW GROUND DRY ONLY IN AUGUST,--	62	FIELD OF LIGHT	26
A DRY CRY COMES FROM MY OWN DESERT;	93	I CRY, LOVE!	31
HAS SCAMPERED AWAY IN A DRY WIND.	103	OLD LADY'S WRDS	38
BY THE DRY RASP OF THE RECURRING INANE,	104	OLD LADY'S WRDS	57
DRY BONES! DRY BONES! I FIND MY LOVING HEART,	135	THE RENEWAL	19
DRY BONES! DRY BONES! I FIND MY LOVING HEART,	135	THE RENEWAL	19
A DRY SOUL'S WISEST. O, I AM NOT DRY!	140	THE SWAN	5
A DRY SOUL'S WISEST. O, I AM NOT DRY!	140	THE SWAN	5
"MY SOUL'S HUNG OUT TO DRY,	153	THE DYING MAN	3
THOUGH IT REJECT DRY BORDERS OF THE SEEN,	154	THE DYING MAN	42
PLAYS OVER THE DRY PODS,	160	FIRST MEDITATN	94
FROM UNDER THE DRY LEAVES,	162	I'M HERE	56
A VINE LASHING IN DRY FURY,	171	WHAT TELL BONES	30
THE SPIKEY PURPLE BUSHES IN THE WINDING DRY CREEK BED--	194	JOURNY INTERIOR	37
IN THE DARK AND LIGHT OF A DRY PLACE,	194	JOURNY INTERIOR	60
THE DRY BLOOM SPLITTING IN THE WRINKLED VALE,	197	THE LONG WATERS	30
A FINE DRY SNOW TICKING THE WINDSHIELD,	199	THE FAR FIELD	5
THE DRY SCENT OF A DYING GARDEN IN SEPTEMBER,	201	THE FAR FIELD	78
DRY BARK FLEW IN THEIR FACES FROM HIS SHOT,--	224	OTTO	16
AND WE DRANK THE DRY HARSH WINE	232	THE THING	20
I CAN HEAR LIGHT ON A DRY DAY.	260	THE CHANGELING	20
I DEAL IN WISDOM, NOT IN DRY DESIRE.	273	SUPPR W LINDSAY	1
DRYING			
THE STENCH OF THEIR DAMP FUR DRYING IN THE SUN,	189	THE LONGING	55
THE BUFFALO CHIPS DRYING.	189	THE LONGING	56
DUBIOUS			
HORACE THE HIKER ON A DUBIOUS MISSION	29	THE GENTLE	3
THE DUBIOUS SEA-CHANGE, THE HEAVING SANDS, AND MY TENTACLED SEA-COUSINS.	196	THE LONG WATERS	23
DUCK			
A DUCK KNOWS SOMETHING	75	I NEED, I NEED	40
I COULD LOVE A DUCK.	79	GIVE WAY, GATES	3
O MY LOVE'S LIGHT AS A DUCK	83	O LULL ME, LULL	12
DUCKS			
AND THE DUCKS NEAR LAKE WASHINGTON WADDLE DOWN THE HIGHWAY AFTER A RAIN,	234	ALL MORNING	26
THE BOTTOMS OF MIGRATING DUCKS	267	SAGINAW SONG	11
DUET			
DUET	272	DUET	T
DUG			
BUT SOMETHING ALWAYS WENT OUT OF ME WHEN I DUG LOOSE THOSE CARPETS	40	MOSS-GATHERING	7
DUKE			
OOH, OOH, I'M A DUKE OF EELS.	85	PRAISE TO END!	8
DULL			
A THING CARVED OF STONE OR WOOD, WITH THE DULL IRIDESCENCE OF LONG-POLISHED WOOD,	234	ALL MORNING	11
DUMB			
THE DUMB DAMES SHRIEKING HALF THE NIGHT	228	THE GERANIUM	16
DUMP			
FLOWER DUMP	43	FLOWER DUMP	T
DUNES			
TO THE SAND DUNES AND FISH FLIES, HANGING, THICKER THAN MOTHS,	193	JOURNY INTERIOR	28
DUNG			
SHOOTING UP LIME AND DUNG AND GROUND BONES,--	38	FORCING HOUSE	9

	PAGE	TITLE	LINE
DUNK			
SHE'D DUNK AND SHE'D GUBBLE:	179	MYRTLE'S COUSIN	6
DUPLICATE			
GLAZING THE PALE HAIR, THE DUPLICATE GREY STANDARD FACES.	46	DOLOR	13
DUPLICATION			
ENDLESS DUPLICATION OF LIVES AND OBJECTS.	46	DOLOR	8
DURING			
ALL DURING MATING SEASON,	234	ALL MORNING	17
DUSK			
AT DUSK OUR SLOW BREATH THICKENS ON THE AIR.	12	SLOW SEASON	8
MORE HEADY THAN A FIELD AT DUSK	14	COMING OF COLD	3
DUST			
THE RIBS OF LEAVES LIE IN THE DUST,	14	COMING OF COLD	22
OR MAKE THE DUST BUZZ WITH A LIGHT SPRAY,	42	OLD FLORIST	7
AND I HAVE SEEN DUST FROM THE WALLS OF INSTITUTIONS,	46	DOLOR	9
EYES RIMMED WITH PICKLE DUST,	46	PICKLE BELT	10
MAKE THE SEA FLASH IN THE DUST.	61	THE LONG ALLEY	84
WAS IT DUST I WAS KISSING?	63	FIELD OF LIGHT	27
THE DUST, THE LONG DUST, STAYS.	78	BRING THE DAY!	42
THE DUST, THE LONG DUST, STAYS.	78	BRING THE DAY!	42
MY DEAREST DUST, I CAN'T STAY HERE.	86	PRAISE TO END!	44
AND THE FIRST DUST OF SPRING LISTING OVER BACKLOTS,--	92	I CRY, LOVE!	27
I COULD ROLL IN THE DUST OF A FINE RAGE.	104	OLD LADY'S WRDS	50
MY DUST LONGS FOR THE INVISIBLE.	104	OLD LADY'S WRDS	55
DUST IN A CORNER STIRRED,	146	THE SONG	6
THE DUST ROSE AND SPOKE;	147	THE EXORCISM	6
ONLY THE MOTES OF DUST IN THE IMMACULATE HALLWAYS,	159	FIRST MEDITATN	79
AND THE DUST LAY THICK ON MY EYELIDS,--WHO EVER WORE GOGGLES?--	193	JOURNY INTERIOR	24
WITH ITS LIMESTONE CRUMBLING INTO FINE GREYISH DUST,	226	THE LIZARD	28
I WAITED FOR THE WIND TO MOVE THE DUST;	247	I WAITED	1
DUSTY			
BUT STILL THE ROAD AND DUSTY FIELD KEPT DRY.	6	INTERLUDE	8
NOT ON THIS DUSTY ROAD	139	PLAINT	9
THE SCRAGGLY WIND-BREAK OF A DUSTY RANCH-HOUSE.	194	JOURNY INTERIOR	45
ON THE DUSTY DETOUR.	194	JOURNY INTERIOR	51
IN A FLICKER OF FIRE BRISKED BY A DUSTY WIND.	194	JOURNY INTERIOR	61
THE TURTLE GASPING IN THE DUSTY RUBBLE OF THE HIGHWAY,	227	MEADOW MOUSE	27
AND PULSED ITS WINGS UPON THE DUSTY GROUND--	243	THE MOTION	3
SLOWLY I CAME BACK TO THE DUSTY ROAD;	247	I WAITED	15
ON A HOT, DUSTY STONE,	249	THE RESTORED	18
DUTCHMAN			
NEVER MET HIM, DUTCHMAN DEAR;	266	FOR STEVENS	10
DUTIES			
PERFORM YOUR DUTIES WELL,	7	ORDERS FOR DAY	2
DUTY			
O WORM OF DUTY! O SPIRAL KNOWLEDGE!	48	LAST WORDS	6
DYED			
THE DINING ROOM CARPET DYED BRIGHTER THAN BLOOD,	32	SALE	13
DYING			
OVER THE DYING, THE NEWLY DEAD.	43	FLOWER DUMP	13
I'M A TUNE DYING	99	O, THOU OPENING	77
FROM THE DYING EMBER.	103	OLD LADY'S WRDS	32
HER LOOK WAS MORNING IN THE DYING LIGHT.	107	SIR JOHN DAVIES	84
I'M DYING PIECEMEAL, FERVENT IN DECAY;	149	IN LATE SUMMER	15
REMINDS ME I AM DYING WITH THE YEAR.	149	IN LATE SUMMER	24
THE DYING MAN	153	THE DYING MAN	T
I HEARD A DYING MAN	153	THE DYING MAN	1
I KNOW, AS THE DYING KNOW,	153	THE DYING MAN	9
CAUGHT IN THE DYING LIGHT,	154	THE DYING MAN	16
BY DYING DAILY, I HAVE COME TO BE.	155	THE DYING MAN	71
I SHALL UNDO ALL DYING BY MY DEATH.	155	THE DYING MAN	77
ALL WOMEN LOVED DANCE IN A DYING LIGHT--	156	THE DYING MAN	78
SO MUCH OF ADOLESCENCE IS AN ILL-DEFINED DYING,	162	I'M HERE	35
MY GERANIUM IS DYING, FOR ALL I CAN DO,	163	I'M HERE	75
IT'S NOT MY FIRST DYING.	164	I'M HERE	95
THE SELF PERSISTS LIKE A DYING STAR,	190	AT OYSTER RIVER	24
DYING BRIGHTLY UNDER THE STREET LIGHTS SUNK IN COARSE CONCRETE,	193	JOURNY INTERIOR	29
THE DYING OF TIME IN THE WHITE LIGHT OF TOMORROW,	200	THE FAR FIELD	52
THE DRY SCENT OF A DYING GARDEN IN SEPTEMBER,	201	THE FAR FIELD	78
BY DYING INWARD, LIKE AN AGING TREE.	244	INFIRMITY	12

		PAGE	TITLE	LINE
DYNAMITE				
	AND I LONG FOR THE BLAST OF DYNAMITE,	191	AT OYSTER RIVER	52
EACH				
	RECOUNT EACH CHILDHOOD PLEASURE: THE SKIES OF AZURE	5	TO MY SISTER	5
	THE OAK STOOD WITH EACH LEAF STIFF AS A BELL.	12	MID-CNTRY BLOW	6
	OLD NEIGHBORS NUDGED EACH OTHER AT THE FUN.	21	THE AUCTION	12
	MY SPIRITS ROSE EACH TIME THE HAMMER FELL,	21	THE AUCTION	13
	FROM EACH MALIGNANT WISH	31	LULL	5
	NOW EACH MAN STANDS APART.	31	LULL	7
	PALE BLOSSOMS, EACH BALANCED ON A SINGLE JOINTED STEM,	43	CARNATIONS	1
	EACH CLUMP IN THE SHAPE OF A POT;	43	FLOWER DUMP	9
	DID EACH BECOME THE OTHER IN THAT PLAY?	106	SIR JOHN DAVIES	55
	EACH ONE'S HIMSELF, YET EACH ONE'S EVERYONE.	132	SENTENTIOUS MAN	36
	EACH ONE'S HIMSELF, YET EACH ONE'S EVERYONE.	132	SENTENTIOUS MAN	36
	EACH IS AN ANIMAL,"--	136	THE SENSUALISTS	16
	THEN EACH FELL BACK, LIMP AS A SACK,	136	THE SENSUALISTS	25
	EACH SINGLE SUBSTANCE GLIDDERED TO THE STARE;	143	SHIMMER OF EVIL	3
	EACH VISION PURELY, PURELY WAS ITS OWN:	143	SHIMMER OF EVIL	4
	EACH CUSHION FOUND ITSELF A FIELD OF PINS,	143	SHIMMER OF EVIL	11
	EACH WILLS HIS DEATH: I AM CONVINCED OF THAT;	144	ELEGY (1)	5
	IN THE WEAK LIGHT THEY WANDER, EACH ALONE.	149	IN LATE SUMMER	4
	EACH TIME EVER	219	THE ABYSS	9
	WITHOUT HIS RIFLE, AND SLAPPED EACH ONE HARD;	224	OTTO	19
	COMING CLOSER AND CLOSER UPON EACH OTHER;	230	THE STORM	12
	DEEP IN THE MOW, AND EACH STEP DEEPER DOWN,	247	I WAITED	7
	WE'LL GIVE EACH OTHER A BOX ON THE EAR,	272	DUET	25
EAGLE				
	THERE IS NO RIVEN TREE, OR LAMB DROPPED BY AN EAGLE.	159	FIRST MEDITATN	82
	WHAT EAGLE NEEDS A TREE?	263	FOLLIES OF ADAM	26
EAGLES				
	ON THE BULLHEAD, IN THE DAKOTAS, WHERE THE EAGLES EAT WELL,	188	THE LONGING	52
	AND THE EAGLES SAIL LOW OVER THE FIR TREES,	202	THE ROSE	6
EAR				
	TAKE TONGUE AND EAR--ALL ELSE I HAVE--	8	PRAYER	21
	OF RESTIVE CROWS IS SHARPER ON THE EAR.	11	LIGHT BRIGHTER	2
	BUT MY EAR STILL KEPT THE SOUND OF THE SEA LIKE A SHELL.	12	MID-CNTRY BLOW	8
	THE EAR SO DELICATE AND TRUE	17	NO BIRD	3
	SHALL NEVER TOUCH ANOTHER EAR.	22	SILENCE	20
	MY RIGHT EAR SCRAPED A BUCKLE.	45	MY PAPA'S WALTZ	12
	THE EAR HEARS ONLY IN LOW PLACES.	59	THE LONG ALLEY	7
	MOTHER OF QUARTZ, YOUR WORDS WRITHE INTO MY EAR.	65	SHAPE OF FIRE	54
	CAN THE BONES BREATHE? THIS GRAVE HAS AN EAR.	87	PRAISE TO END!	75
	I HEAR MY BEING DANCE FROM EAR TO EAR.	108	THE WAKING (2)	5
	I HEAR MY BEING DANCE FROM EAR TO EAR.	108	THE WAKING (2)	5
	YOU ASK HIM SOMETHING IN HIS EAR,	116	THE SLOTH	2
	DESIRE EXULTS THE EAR:	128	THE VOICE	19
	DOWN LONG SEA-CHAMBERS OF THE INNER EAR.	129	SHE	6
	WITH A CHEEK SOFT AS A HOUND'S EAR.	157	FIRST MEDITATN	17
	IN MY LEFT EAR I HEAR THE LOUD SOUND OF A MINOR COLLAPSE.	165	HER BECOMING	29
	AND THAT THIN CRY, LIKE A NEEDLE PIERCING THE EAR, THE INSISTENT CICADA,	204	THE ROSE	67
	IN YOUR SEA-BURIED EAR,	211	SONG (1)	11
	WE'LL GIVE EACH OTHER A BOX ON THE EAR,	272	DUET	25
EARLY				
	A CANNON CRACK ANNOUNCE AN EARLY THAW.	11	LIGHT BRIGHTER	4
	AN EARLY JOY.	51	THE WAKING (1)	24
	TO SEE CYCLAMEN VEINS BECOME CLEARER IN EARLY SUNLIGHT,	67	SHAPE OF FIRE	86
	DARK CAME EARLY.	73	WHERE KNOCK IS	67
	IN THE SOFT DARK OF EARLY EVENING,	100	THE VISITANT	17
	COMING ACROSS SNOW IN EARLY EVENING?	161	I'M HERE	5
	A VOICE KEEPS RISING IN MY EARLY SLEEP,	165	HER BECOMING	19
	THE YOUNG, BROW-BEATEN EARLY INTO A BALEFUL SILENCE,	169	FOURTH MEDITATN	44
	ITS SPRAY HOLDING A DOUBLE RAIN-BOW IN EARLY MORNING,	191	AT OYSTER RIVER	45
	WHEN THE ICE MELTS ALONG THE EDGES IN EARLY AFTERNOON.	191	AT OYSTER RIVER	48
	IN THE VAPOROUS GREY OF EARLY MORNING,	197	THE LONG WATERS	49
	FOR TO COME UPON WARBLERS IN EARLY MAY	199	THE FAR FIELD	26
	AND THE DEEP CHORUS OF HORNS COMING UP FROM THE STREETS IN EARLY MORNING.	204	THE ROSE	72
	AT THE EDGE OF A RIPENING MEADOW, IN EARLY SUMMER,	204	THE ROSE	80
	A PRUSSIAN WHO LEARNED EARLY TO BE RUDE	224	OTTO	2
	HIS DEEP-THROATED COOING PART OF THE EARLY MORNING,	234	ALL MORNING	2
	ON THE PERILS OF TOO EARLY DRINK,--	269	GOB MUSIC	17
	TOO EARLY DRINK, TOO EARLY DRINK,	269	GOB MUSIC	18

		PAGE	TITLE	LINE
EARLY (CONTINUED)				
TOO EARLY DRINK, TOO EARLY DRINK,	....	269	GOB MUSIC	18
ON THE PERILS OF TOO EARLY DRINK,	....	270	GOB MUSIC	45
TOO EARLY DRINK, TOO EARLY DRINK	....	270	GOB MUSIC	46
TOO EARLY DRINK, TOO EARLY DRINK	....	270	GOB MUSIC	46
EARN				
AND EARN THE RIGHT TO STAND OR SIT,	....	18	LONG LIVE WEEDS	10
EARS				
MY EARS HAVE BEEN THE VERY DEVIL'S.		8	PRAYER	8
MY EARS KNEW	....	51	THE WAKING (1)	23
HIS EARS HAVEN'T TIME.	....	71	WHERE KNOCK IS	9
HEAR ME, SOFT EARS AND ROUNDY STONES!	....	76	I NEED, I NEED	57
FISHING, I CAUGHT MYSELF BEHIND THE EARS.	....	89	UNFOLD! UNFOLD!	23
AND I HAVE MADE A PROMISE TO MY EARS	....	105	SIR JOHN DAVIES	5
O WHAT LEWD MUSIC CREPT INTO OUR EARS!	....	106	SIR JOHN DAVIES	46
OF BEING BORN FAILS ON HIS NAKED EARS.	....	201	THE FAR FIELD	90
AS HIS HEAD; HIS BAT-LIKE EARS	....	227	MEADOW MOUSE	15
MY EARS STILL HEAR THE BIRD WHEN ALL IS STILL;	....	244	INFIRMITY	28
I TEACH MY EYES TO HEAR, MY EARS TO SEE	......	244	INFIRMITY	34
EAR'S				
THE EAR'S NOT HERE	....	64	SHAPE OF FIRE	22
EARTH				
ITS RHYTHM ROCKS THE EARTH,	....	34	NIGHT JOURNEY	2
MY FEET REMEMBERED THE EARTH,	....	104	OLD LADY'S WRDS	44
ALL THE EARTH, ALL THE AIR	....	121	ALL EARTH, AIR	T
THE SUN DECLARES THE EARTH;	....	124	WORDS FOR WIND	33
THE EARTH, THE SOLID AIR--	....	128	THE VOICE	21
A BREATH IS BUT A BREATH: I HAVE THE EARTH;	......	155	THE DYING MAN	76
THE EARTH ITSELF A TUNE.	....	165	HER BECOMING	15
ALWAYS, IN EARTH AND AIR.	....	201	THE FAR FIELD	81
BUT A MOLE WINDING THROUGH EARTH,	....	220	THE ABYSS	42
WHO'S OLD ENOUGH TO LIVE?--A THING OF EARTH	......	243	THE MOTION	14
EARTHLY				
A THING ALL EARTHLY LOVERS UNDERSTAND.	......	149	IN LATE SUMMER	22
THE EARTHLY LIVES IN HER;	....	262	FOLLIES OF ADAM	12
EASE				
OF EASE, THE HOARDED, SECRET SUM;	....	30	THE RECKONING	2
KEEPING CREATION AT EASE;	....	44	FRAU BAUMAN	20
I WORE THE SUN WITH EASE.	....	87	PRAISE TO END!	66
THRUM-THRUM, WHO CAN BE EQUAL TO EASE?	......	97	O, THOU OPENING	13
IN RIVERY AIR, AT EASE,	....	125	WORDS FOR WIND	73
AT EASE AFTER ROCKING THE FLESH TO SLEEP,	......	194	JOURNY INTERIOR	55
WHERE THE SALMON EASE THEIR WAY INTO THE KELP BEDS,	......	205	THE ROSE	96
AMONG THE HALF-DEAD TREES, I CAME UPON THE TRUE EASE OF MYSELF,	....	205	THE ROSE	99
AT EASE WITH JOY, A SELF-ENCHANTED MAN.	......	248	THE TREE, BIRD	6
AT EASE WITH ALL THAT FLOWS.	....	262	FOLLIES OF ADAM	14
EASES				
A SPIDER EASES HIMSELF DOWN FROM A SWAYING LIGHT-BULB,	...	231	THE STORM	34
EASILY				
HIS OYSTER WORLD WAS EASILY COME BY;	....	28	THE FAVORITE	3
EASILY MADDENS	....	65	SHAPE OF FIRE	43
A SINGLE WAVE STARTS LIGHTLY AND EASILY SHOREWARD,	......	93	I CRY, LOVE!	46
THE PROW PITCHING EASILY UP AND DOWN,	......	203	THE ROSE	35
ETERNITY'S NOT EASILY COME BY.	....	244	INFIRMITY	32
EAST				
THE LIGHT COMES BRIGHTER FROM THE EAST; THE CAW	......	11	LIGHT BRIGHTER	1
AND EAST ST. LOUIS AND MONONGAHELA	....	111	SQUEEZE-BOX	19
WHERE IT LEANS, TILTED EAST, A PERCH FOR THE OSPREY,	......	197	THE LONG WATERS	36
EASTWARD				
A FEW WHITE CLOUDS ALL RUSHING EASTWARD,	......	43	CHILD ON GRNHSE	5
EASY				
SUCH WALTZING WAS NOT EASY.	....	45	MY PAPA'S WALTZ	4
FOREVER IS EASY, SHE SAID.	....	77	BRING THE DAY!	11
EASY THE LIFE OF THE MOUTH. WHAT A LUST FOR RIPENESS!	....	90	UNFOLD! UNFOLD!	39
THE WAVES BROKE EASY, CRIED TO ME IN WHITE;	......	107	SIR JOHN DAVIES	83
WHEN, EASY AS A BEAST,	....	121	ALL EARTH, AIR	13
ROSE, EASY ON A STEM,	....	124	WORDS FOR WIND	42
THE THRUSH SINGING ALONE, THAT EASY BIRD,	......	204	THE ROSE	61
AND OUR BREATH COMES MORE EASY,--	....	230	THE STORM	22
COME EASY TO THE SILL, THINGS LOST FROM FAR AWAY.	......	273	SUPPR W LINDSAY	4
EAT				
CAN FEATHERS EAT ME? THERE'S NO CLUE IN THE SILT.	......	60	THE LONG ALLEY	32

	PAGE	TITLE	LINE
EAT (CONTINUED)			
THE EDGE CANNOT EAT THE CENTER.	66	SHAPE OF FIRE	57
EAT WHERE YOU'RE AT. I'M NOT A MOUSE.	72	WHERE KNOCK IS	40
--TO HELP ME EAT UP HER MONEY.	112	SQUEEZE-BOX	45
WHILE ANIMALS EAT TO THE NORTH,	157	FIRST MEDITATN	9
TODAY I EAT MY USUAL DIET OF SHADOWS.	166	HER BECOMING	31
A PRISONER OF SMELLS, I WOULD RATHER EAT THAN PRAY.	173	WHAT TELL BONES	79
SHE WOULD EAT AT ONE GLUP	179	MYRTLE'S COUSIN	3
WHAT HER FRIENDS COULDN'T EAT AT THOSE LUNCHES!	179	MYRTLE'S COUSIN	10
ON THE BULLHEAD, IN THE DAKOTAS, WHERE THE EAGLES EAT WELL,	188	THE LONGING	52
WILL THE HEART EAT THE HEART?	211	SONG (1)	7
IF THEY LET YOU EAT AND SWEAR	228	IN VIOLENT WARD	4
THE CRABS TILT AND EAT, LEISURELY,	233	THE PIKE	5
I SEEMED TO EAT THE AIR;	247	I WAITED	3
AND IF YOU EAT MORE THAN YOU SHOULD,	267	SAGINAW SONG	5
"LET'S EAT!" SAID LINDSAY. "HERE WE'VE GOT THE MOON,	273	SUPPR W LINDSAY	15
"SURE, WE STILL EAT," I SAID. "ENOUGH! OR TOO MUCH."	273	SUPPR W LINDSAY	17
LET'S EAT BEFORE THE MOONLIGHT ALL RUNS OUT."	273	SUPPR W LINDSAY	29
EATEN			
AND IN THE SHRUNKEN FACE OF A DEAD RAT, EATEN BY RAIN AND GROUND-BEETLES	199	THE FAR FIELD	19
HE TOO HAS EATEN WELL--	226	THE LIZARD	1
NOW HE'S EATEN HIS THREE KINDS OF CHEESE AND DRUNK FROM HIS BOTTLE-CAP WATERING-TROUGH--	227	MEADOW MOUSE	12
EATING			
EATING THE HEART OUT OF MY GARDEN.	151	SLUG	14
EATS			
MY MEAT EATS ME. WHO WAITS AT THE GATE?	65	SHAPE OF FIRE	53
MY HOE EATS LIKE A GOAT.	76	I NEED, I NEED	60
THE BLEAK WIND EATS AT THE WEAK PLATEAU,	157	FIRST MEDITATN	11
EAVES			
WE WAITED FOR THE FIRST RAIN IN THE EAVES.	6	INTERLUDE	4
OUTSIDE, THE SAME SPARROWS BICKER IN THE EAVES.	161	I'M HERE	6
EBBED			
THE RIVER EBBED AND FLOWED:	87	PRAISE TO END!	68
ECHO			
ECHO ITSELF CONSUMED;	167	HER BECOMING	67
BEYOND MY OWN ECHO,	195	JOURNY INTERIOR	71
I HEAR MY ECHO IN THE ECHOING WOOD--	239	IN A DARK TIME	3
ECHOING			
A FAR-OFF TRAIN BLOWS ITS ECHOING WHISTLE ONCE;	33	IDYLL	10
I HEAR MY ECHO IN THE ECHOING WOOD--	239	IN A DARK TIME	3
ECORSE			
IN ECORSE, TOLEDO, AND WYANDOTTE	111	SQUEEZE-BOX	11
ECSTASY			
WREN-SONG IN TRELLIS: A LIGHT ECSTASY OF BUTTERFLIES COURTING,	255	LIGHT POEM	1
EDDYING			
I REMEMBER A STONE BREAKING THE EDDYING CURRENT,	197	THE LONG WATERS	55
EDGE			
A WALKER AT THE RIVER'S EDGE MAY HEAR	11	LIGHT BRIGHTER	3
HERE FROM THE FIELD'S EDGE WE SURVEY	33	HIGHWAY: MICH	1
WE GO TO OUR BEDS IN A HOUSE AT THE EDGE OF A MEADOW,	33	IDYLL	11
IN THE DEEP GRASS AT THE EDGE OF FIELD,	62	FIELD OF LIGHT	25
SPIRIT, COME NEAR. THIS IS ONLY THE EDGE OF WHITENESS.	64	SHAPE OF FIRE	12
THE EDGE CANNOT EAT THE CENTER.	66	SHAPE OF FIRE	57
FILLS AND TREMBLES AT THE EDGE YET DOES NOT FLOW OVER,	67	SHAPE OF FIRE	94
BY THE LAKE'S EDGE, I SEE A SILVER SWAN,	140	THE SWAN	16
AT THE EDGE OF A RAW FIELD.	146	THE SONG	13
WALKING THE EDGE, LOQUACIOUS, UNAFRAID.	155	THE DYING MAN	63
THE WEEDS HISS AT THE EDGE OF THE FIELD,	157	FIRST MEDITATN	2
BEHIND THE EYE; THE LOST ACRES AT THE EDGE OF SMOKY CITIES.	159	FIRST MEDITATN	75
AT THE STREAM'S EDGE, TRAILING A VAGUE FINGER;	162	I'M HERE	26
OR WHEN WE STAND AT THE EDGE OF A THICKET	162	I'M HERE	54
THE WASP DRINKING AT THE EDGE OF MY CUP;	163	I'M HERE	87
AT THE EDGE OF THE FIELD WAITING FOR THE PURE MOMENT;	168	FOURTH MEDITATN	3
THE SLAG-HEAPS FUME AT THE EDGE OF THE RAW CITIES:	187	THE LONGING	15
AND THE BACK WHEELS HANG ALMOST OVER THE EDGE	193	JOURNY INTERIOR	4
TO THE CHARRED EDGE OF THE SEA	196	THE LONG WATERS	14
AND THE BRONZE OF A DEAD BURDOCK AT THE EDGE OF A PRAIRIE LAKE,	197	THE LONG WATERS	42
AND THE CRABS BASK NEAR THE EDGE,	200	THE FAR FIELD	69
THE WEEDY EDGE, ALIVE WITH SMALL SNAKES AND BLOODSUCKERS,--	200	THE FAR FIELD	70

	PAGE	TITLE	LINE
EDGE (CONTINUED)			
AT THE EDGE OF A RIPENING MEADOW, IN EARLY SUMMER,	204	THE ROSE	80
WHEN THE SLOW FREIGHT WINDS ALONG THE EDGE OF THE RAVAGED HILLSIDE,	204	THE ROSE	83
MY WRATH, WHERE'S THE EDGE	211	SONG (1)	1
THE EDGE OF ALL THE LAND, THE FINAL SEA?	221	THE ABYSS	63
THE EDGE OF HEAVEN WAS SHARPER THAN A SWORD;	237	THE TRANCED	6
OR WINDING PATH? THE EDGE IS WHAT I HAVE.	239	IN A DARK TIME	12
THE EDGE IS WHAT WE HAVE.	258	SONG (3)	25
I LEAN MY HEAD NEAR THE BRIMMING EDGE	269	GOB MUSIC	14
BIRD, BIRD DON'T EDGE ME IN;	271	THE REPLY	1
EDGES			
THE EDGES OF THE SUMMIT STILL APPALL	156	THE DYING MAN	96
I SANG TO THE EDGES OF FLAME,	162	I'M HERE	42
WHEN THE ICE MELTS ALONG THE EDGES IN EARLY AFTERNOON.	191	AT OYSTER RIVER	48
EDGES, THEIR HOLES	205	THE ROSE	91
EDIBLE			
A BUG-EYED EDIBLE ONE,	209	HER LONGING	8
EDICT			
THE FANG AND THE CLAW, THE CLUB AND THE KNOUT, THE IRRATIONAL EDICT,	170	FOURTH MEDITATN	67
EDITOR			
REPLY TO A LADY EDITOR	113	TO A LADY ED	T
EEL			
THE MOON SAID, BACK OF AN EEL,	54	THE LOST SON	29
AND THE BACK OF AN EEL,	55	THE LOST SON	55
LIKE PIECES OF SMOKED EEL OR RAW OYSTER,	151	SLUG	17
EELS			
LIKE A SLITHER OF EELS	56	THE LOST SON	96
OOH, OOH, I'M A DUKE OF EELS.	85	PRAISE TO END!	8
I NEED A POND WITH SMALL EELS. AND A WINDY ORCHARD.	164	I'M HERE	91
EERIE			
TO THE CRIES OF THE OWL, THE EERIE WHOOPER.	202	THE ROSE	19
EFFLORESCENCE			
FROM THE SLOW SINKING OF THE ISLAND PENINSULA, THE CORAL EFFLORESCENCE,	196	THE LONG WATERS	22
EGG			
PUTTING EGG IN YOUR SHOE	180	GOO-GIRL	3
EGGS			
BOILED EGGS FROM A CUP,--	179	MYRTLE'S COUSIN	4
EIGHT-LEGGED			
AMONG MY EIGHT-LEGGED FRIENDS,	209	HER LONGING	5
EIGHTY			
WATCHING FOR DANGEROUS DOWN-HILL PLACES, WHERE THE WHEELS WHINED BEYOND EIGHTY--	193	JOURNY INTERIOR	19
EITHER (7)			
ELABORATE			
THE LEAVES CURLED BACK IN ELABORATE CORINTHIAN SCROLLS;	43	CARNATIONS	2
THAT DOVE'S ELABORATE WAY OF COMING NEAR	149	IN LATE SUMMER	23
THEIR GAIT FORMAL AND ELABORATE, THEIR HAIR A GLORY,	170	FOURTH MEDITATN	64
LIFTING ME HIGH OVER THE FOUR-FOOT STEMS, THE MRS. RUSSELLS, AND HIS OWN ELABORATE HYBRIDS,	203	THE ROSE	54
ELBOWS			
OF GREEN, OR PLUNGED TO MY ELBOWS IN THE SPONGY YELLOWISH MOSS OF THE MARSHES:	40	MOSS-GATHERING	8
ELEGY			
ELEGY FOR JANE	102	ELEGY FOR JANE	T
ELEGY	144	ELEGY (1)	T
ELEGY	223	ELEGY (2)	T
ELEMENT			
THE ELEMENT OF AIR WAS OUT OF HAND.	6	INTERLUDE	1
NOW I AM OUT OF ELEMENT	19	AGNST DISASTER	1
WITHIN THIS PRIMAL ELEMENT	256	IN HYDROTHERAPY	7
ELEMENTAL			
THIS ELEMENTAL FORCE	18	GENESIS	1
ELEMENTS			
THE ELEMENTS I KEPT WARM	49	RIVER INCIDENT	7
WHERE ELEMENTS COHERE	50	THE CYCLE	10
ELEPHANT-COLORED			
OVER THE LOW, BARNACLED, ELEPHANT-COLORED ROCKS,	190	AT OYSTER RIVER	1
ELEPHANTS			
I KNOW A DANCE THE ELEPHANTS BELIEVE.	106	SIR JOHN DAVIES	40

		PAGE	TITLE	LINE
ELF				
	SMALL AS AN ELF,	249	THE RESTORED	3
ELM				
	WHEN I STOOD AT THE WINDOW, AN ELM BOUGH SWEPT TO MY KNEES;	12	MID-CNTRY BLOW	3
	THE ELM TREE IS OUR HIGHEST MOUNTAIN PEAK;	13	PRAISE PRAIRIE	1
	NOW AS FROM MAPLE TO ELM THE FLITTERMICE SKITTER AND TWIRL,	33	IDYLL	1
	THE GREAT ELM FILLED WITH BIRDS.	63	FIELD OF LIGHT	36
	ELM SWINGING AROUND	103	OLD LADY'S WRDS	27
	THE CERULEAN, HIGH IN THE ELM,	159	FIRST MEDITATN	84
	HOW THEY FILLED THE ORIOLE'S ELM, A TWITTERING RESTLESS CLOUD, ALL ONE MORNING,	199	THE FAR FIELD	28
	THE MOON LOLLING IN THE CLOSE ELM, A SHIMMER OF SILVER,	204	THE ROSE	81
ELMS				
	A LINE OF ELMS PLUNGING AND TOSSING LIKE HORSES,	43	CHILD ON GRNHSE	6
	THE THREE ELMS,	54	THE LOST SON	36
ELM-TREE				
	UNDER THE EYE OF THE GREAT OWL WATCHING FROM THE ELM-TREE,	227	MEADOW MOUSE	24
ELMTREES				
	TO THE CLAY BANKS, AND THE WILD GRAPES HANGING FROM THE ELMTREES.	200	THE FAR FIELD	66
ELSE				
	TAKE TONGUE AND EAR--ALL ELSE I HAVE--	8	PRAYER	21
	WANTS SINGLENESS OF SPIRIT ABOVE ALL ELSE:	24	POETASTER	2
	THOUGH HOME IS NOT HAPPY, WHERE ELSE CAN HE GO?	29	THE GENTLE	10
	THESE NURSES OF NOBODY ELSE.	44	FRAU BAUMAN	12
	AND REMEMBER THERE WAS SOMETHING ELSE I WAS HOPING FOR.	47	DOUBLE FEATURE	12
	WHO ELSE BREATHES HERE? WHAT DOES THE GRAVE SAY?	59	THE LONG ALLEY	19
	BELIEVE ME, THERE'S NO ONE ELSE, KITTEN-LIMP SISTER.	59	THE LONG ALLEY	23
	STAY CLOSE. MUST I KILL SOMETHING ELSE?	60	THE LONG ALLEY	31
	NUTS ARE MONEY: WHEREFORE AND WHAT ELSE?	61	THE LONG ALLEY	82
	GOD'S SOMEWHERE ELSE,	74	WHERE KNOCK IS	80
	I'M SOMEBODY ELSE NOW.	74	WHERE KNOCK IS	84
	WHO ELSE KNOWS	76	I NEED, I NEED	64
	I'M THE SERPENT OF SOMEBODY ELSE.	81	SENSIBILITY! LA	1
	IT'S A LONG WAY TO SOMEWHERE ELSE.	82	SENSIBILITY! LA	38
	I'M SOMEWHERE ELSE,--	82	SENSIBILITY! LA	48
	I HAVE BEEN SOMEWHERE ELSE; I REMEMBER THE SEA-FACED UNCLES.	88	PRAISE TO END!	93
	I WAS FAR BACK, FARTHER THAN ANYBODY ELSE.	89	UNFOLD! UNFOLD!	21
	WHAT ELSE HAS THE VINE LOOSENED?	90	UNFOLD! UNFOLD!	43
	THE STALKS ASK SOMETHING ELSE.	91	UNFOLD! UNFOLD!	62
	WHAT ELSE CAN BEFALL?	92	I CRY, LOVE!	4
	THE HEDGEWREN'S SONG SAYS SOMETHING ELSE.	92	I CRY, LOVE!	15
	THE IMPULSE TO MAKE SOMEONE ELSE COMPLETE?	105	SIR JOHN DAVIES	27
	SHE KISSED ME CLOSE, AND THEN DID SOMETHING ELSE.	106	SIR JOHN DAVIES	35
	WHAT ELSE CAN I STEAL FROM SLEEP?	166	HER BECOMING	34
	WHO ELSE SWEATS LIGHT FROM A STONE?	170	FOURTH MEDITATN	81
	WHAT ELSE TO SAY?	238	THE MOMENT	13
	OH, TO BE SOMETHING ELSE, YET STILL TO BE!	244	INFIRMITY	6
	HOW ELSE, MEADOW-SHAPE?	258	SONG (3)	12
	SAD THE SOUL'S JOY. LOVED HEART, WHAT ELSE CAN I SAY	261	THE CHANGELING	28
	WHAT ELSE HE DOES IS UP TO YOU.	264	THREE EPIGRAMS	16
ELSEWHERE				
	ELSEWHERE, IN HOUSES, EVEN PAILS CAN BE SAD;	157	FIRST MEDITATN	4
	AND I ROAM ELSEWHERE, MY BODY THINKING,	195	JOURNY INTERIOR	68
ELUSIVE				
	MOVING, ELUSIVE AS FISH, FEARLESS,	199	THE FAR FIELD	31
ELVERS				
	LIKE ELVERS IN PONDS,	50	THE MINIMAL	8
'EM				
	ROAR 'EM, WHORE 'EM, COCKALORUM,	266	FOR STEVENS	17
	ROAR 'EM, WHORE 'EM, COCKALORUM,	266	FOR STEVENS	17
EMBANKMENT				
	TOPPLING DOWN AN EMBANKMENT.	157	FIRST MEDITATN	7
	SWERVING UP A STEEP EMBANKMENT.	158	FIRST MEDITATN	55
	WHAT'S BEYOND NEVER CRUMBLES LIKE AN EMBANKMENT,	159	FIRST MEDITATN	76
EMBANKMENTS				
	STANDING, SILENT, ON SANDY BEACHES OR WALKING ALONG GREEN EMBANKMENTS;	168	FOURTH MEDITATN	4
EMBER				
	FROM THE DYING EMBER.	103	OLD LADY'S WRDS	32
EMBERS				
	DEEP-HIDDEN EMBERS, SMOTHERED BY THE SCREEN	17	UNEXTINGUISHED	7

	PAGE	TITLE	LINE
EMBRACE			
WHO CAN EMBRACE THE BODY OF HIS FATE?	106	SIR JOHN DAVIES	33
THOSE WHO EMBRACE, BELIEVE.	125	WORDS FOR WIND	69
THE GRADUAL EMBRACE	139	PLAINT	15
DARE I EMBRACE A GHOST FROM MY OWN BREAST?	165	HER BECOMING	21
I EMBRACE THE WORLD.	198	THE LONG WATERS	78
A SINGLE WILD ROSE, STRUGGLING OUT OF THE WHITE EMBRACE OF			
THE MORNING-GLORY,	203	THE ROSE	44
AS WE EMBRACE BY THE HIGH SEA-WALL.	216	THE SHY MAN	23
AND I EMBRACE THIS CALM--	221	THE ABYSS	81
NIGHT I EMBRACE, A DEAR PROXIMITY.	240	IN EVEING AIR	18
I DARE EMBRACE. BY STRIDING, I REMAIN.	243	THE MOTION	12
EMBRACED			
SMALL ENOUGH TO BE TAKEN IN, EMBRACED, BY TWO ARMS,--	191	AT OYSTER RIVER	46
EMBRACES			
REASON EMBRACES DEATH,	31	LULL	19
EMBRACING			
TAKING AND EMBRACING ITS SURROUNDINGS,	101	LIGHT BREATHER	13
EMINENCE			
A MAN'S HEAD IS AN EMINENCE UPON	13	PRAISE PRAIRIE	3
EMPTINESS			
AGAINST THE IMMENSE IMMEASURABLE EMPTINESS OF THINGS.	156	THE DYING MAN	101
HOW TO TRANSCEND THIS SENSUAL EMPTINESS?	187	THE LONGING	12
EMPTY			
SAT IN AN EMPTY HOUSE	53	THE LOST SON	16
THE SHADOWS ARE EMPTY, THE SLIDING EXTERNALS.	104	OLD LADY'S WRDS	51
OR LADLE RATTLING IN AN EMPTY DISH?	105	SIR JOHN DAVIES	30
I LOVE A WOMAN WITH AN EMPTY FACE.	133	THE PURE FURY	9
BUT THIS MORNING THE SHOE-BOX HOUSE ON THE BACK PORCH IS			
EMPTY.	227	MEADOW MOUSE	20
ENCIRCLED			
A SHAPE OF CHANGE, ENCIRCLED BY ITS FIRE.	119	THE DREAM	10
ENCOMPASSING			
ENCOMPASSING FISH, FLESH, AND FOWL.	23	AMOROUS LADY	10
ENCRUSTED			
ALL THE RINGS AND THE RELICS ENCRUSTED WITH SIN	32	SALE	19
END			
THE FEUD WE KEPT WITH SPACE COMES TO AN END.	13	PRAISE PRAIRIE	12
THE LAST TRICYCLE RUNS CRAZILY TO THE END OF THE WALK.	33	IDYLL	4
RIDES BY, FOR AT THE END OF DAY	33	HIGHWAY: MICH	4
END OF THE ROSE-HOUSE,	41	BIG WIND	15
END WITH WATER.	77	BRING THE DAY!	31
PRAISE TO THE END!	85	PRAISE TO END!	T
AS THE BIRDS FLEW OFF TO THE END OF NEXT WEEK.	115	THE SERPENT	26
NOT EVEN THE END OF HIS CLAW, CLAW, CLAW,	117	LADY AND BEAR	17
NOT EVEN THE END OF HIS CLAW.	117	LADY AND BEAR	18
EXISTENCE MOVES TOWARD A CERTAIN END--	149	IN LATE SUMMER	21
LOOK AT THE FAR TREES AT THE END OF THE GARDEN.	163	I'M HERE	82
--OR YOU'LL END LIKE THE KITTY-CAT BIRD.	177	KITTY-CAT BIRD	21
AT THE FIELD'S END, IN THE CORNER MISSED BY THE MOWER,	199	THE FAR FIELD	13
HANGING, BUNCHED LIKE YOUNG FRUIT, BENDING THE END BRANCHES,	199	THE FAR FIELD	32
HE IS THE END OF THINGS, THE FINAL MAN.	201	THE FAR FIELD	93
WHO KNOWS THE END OF IT ALL?	215	HIS FOREBODING	8
THE LONG PIPES KNOCKED: IT WAS THE END OF NIGHT.	225	OTTO	39
NEAR THE END, SHE SEEMED ALMOST TO HEAR ME--	228	THE GERANIUM	20
FROM BEYOND THE END OF A MOSSY LOG,	233	THE PIKE	15
WE END IN JOY.	238	THE MOMENT	14
UNTIL WE ARE PURE SPIRIT AT THE END.	244	INFIRMITY	36
ENDING			
ENDING AT LAST IN A HOPELESS SAND-RUT,	199	THE FAR FIELD	9
ENDING CURLED AROUND AND OVER AGAIN,	226	THE LIZARD	11
ENDLESS			
ENDLESS DUPLICATION OF LIVES AND OBJECTS.	46	DOLOR	8
THE CLIMBING, THE ENDLESS TURNING,	221	THE ABYSS	53
ENDS			
ARCH MY BACK, PRETTY-BONES, I'M DEAD AT BOTH ENDS.	85	PRAISE TO END!	9
SHE WAKES THE ENDS OF LIFE.	125	WORDS FOR WIND	89
ENDURE			
THE ANGER WILL ENDURE,	3	OPEN HOUSE	13
ALL LOVERS LIVE BY LONGING, AND ENDURE:	107	SIR JOHN DAVIES	77
YET, LIKE A TREE, ENDURE THE SHIFT OF THINGS.	135	THE RENEWAL	6
A SLOW GROWTH IS A HARD THING TO ENDURE.	154	THE DYING MAN	45
THUS I ENDURE THIS LAST PURE STRETCH OF JOY,	248	THE TREE, BIRD	22

	PAGE	TITLE	LINE
ENDURED			
DANTE HIMSELF ENDURED,	216	HER WRATH	1
THE THINGS SHE ENDURED!--	228	THE GERANIUM	15
ENDURING			
A PRINCE OF SMALL BEGINNINGS, ENDURING THE SLOW STRETCHES OF CHANGE,	170	FOURTH MEDITATN	70
ENEMIES			
FROM ENEMIES THAT WHISPER TO THE BLOOD;	5	PROGNOSIS	6
UNTIL HE CRIED AT ENEMIES UNDONE	28	THE FAVORITE	13
YOU ENEMIES OF SKIN,--	99	O, THOU OPENING	61
MY ENEMIES RENEW ME, AND MY BLOOD	155	THE DYING MAN	67
ENGLISH			
OR ENGLISH POETS WHO GREW UP ON GREEK	127	I KNEW A WOMAN	6
ENORMOUS			
LIKE AN ENORMOUS BEACON,	265	HARSH COUNTRY	10
ENOUGH			
YOUR TEARS ARE NOT ENOUGH PRAISE,	54	THE LOST SON	31
ONE FATHER IS ENOUGH.	74	WHERE KNOCK IS	87
BUT NOT ENOUGH.	76	I NEED, I NEED	52
IT'S QUEER ENOUGH HERE, PERHAPS.	81	SENSIBILITY! LA	12
IT'S STILL ENOUGH FOR THE KNOCK OF A WORM.	87	PRAISE TO END!	76
WHAT GRACE I HAVE IS ENOUGH.	91	UNFOLD! UNFOLD!	60
THERE'S TIME ENOUGH.	93	I CRY, LOVE!	37
ENOUGH TO PLEASE A CLOUD!	98	O, THOU OPENING	50
PASSION'S ENOUGH TO GIVE	124	WORDS FOR WIND	47
IS IT ENOUGH?--	161	I'M HERE	1
WHO, STRANGELY ENOUGH, WAS A TURTLE:	179	MYRTLE	2
WHAT DREAM'S ENOUGH TO BREATHE IN? A DARK DREAM.	188	THE LONGING	28
SMALL ENOUGH TO BE TAKEN IN, EMBRACED, BY TWO ARMS,--	191	AT OYSTER RIVER	46
CRIES, "I'M OLD ENOUGH TO LIVE	208	HER WORDS	3
WITH THE DARK HEARSE, AND ENOUGH FLOWERS FOR AN ALDERMAN,--	223	ELEGY (2)	2
WHO'S OLD ENOUGH TO LIVE?--A THING OF EARTH	243	THE MOTION	14
ENOUGH TO MERIT CONSTANT THOUGHT.	257	SANITARIUM	8
BUT THAT'S ENOUGH FOR ANY MAN	267	SAGINAW SONG	29
I'VE HAD ENOUGH TODAY	271	THE REPLY	2
"SURE, WE STILL EAT," I SAID. "ENOUGH! OR TOO MUCH."	273	SUPPR W LINDSAY	17
ENSHROUD			
ENSHROUD ME WITH LIGHT! O WHIRLING! O TERRIBLE LOVE!	48	LAST WORDS	10
ENTER			
WE NEVER ENTER	93	I CRY, LOVE!	57
ENTERED			
THE WALL HAS ENTERED: I MUST LOVE THE WALL,	155	THE DYING MAN	48
ENTERS			
AND GENTLY THE LIGHT ENTERS THE SLEEPING SOUL,	204	THE ROSE	76
AND NOT-KNOWING ENTERS, SILENT,	221	THE ABYSS	70
THE MIND ENTERS ITSELF, AND GOD THE MIND,	239	IN A DARK TIME	23
ENTERTAINED			
ONCE ENTERTAINED YOU.	58	THE LOST SON	170
ENTIRE			
NAKED AND ENTIRE.	82	SENSIBILITY! LA	33
ENTITIES			
AND SCORN THE ABSTRACT ENTITIES.	25	VERSE W ALLUSNS	4
ENTRAILS			
ARE THE ENTRAILS CLEAR, IMMACULATE CABBAGE?	89	UNFOLD! UNFOLD!	19
ITS ENTRAILS STREWN OVER THE HALF-GROWN FLOWERS,	199	THE FAR FIELD	22
ENTRANCES			
SMELLED THE CARRION AT ENTRANCES,	48	JUDGE NOT	8
ENVY			
I ENVY THE TENDRILS, THEIR EYELESS SEEKING,	221	THE ABYSS	64
ENVY'S			
OF ENVY'S MEAN GAZE;	217	WISH YOUNG WIFE	5
EPIC			
AN EPIC OF THE EYES	3	OPEN HOUSE	5
EPIDERMAL			
EPIDERMAL MACABRE	19	EPIDERM MACABRE	T
I HATE MY EPIDERMAL DRESS,	19	EPIDERM MACABRE	10
EPIGRAMS			
THREE EPIGRAMS	264	THREE EPIGRAMS	T
EPILEPTIC			
WHO FED AND TENDED THE INFIRM, THE MAD, THE EPILEPTIC,	223	ELEGY (2)	9
EQUAL			
THRUM-THRUM, WHO CAN BE EQUAL TO EASE?	97	O, THOU OPENING	13
SKIN, A THING YOU CANNOT SAY TO WHISPER AND EQUAL A WOUND?	98	O, THOU OPENING	24

		PAGE	TITLE	LINE
EQUALLY				
	THE MEDITERRANEAN SUN SHINING ON US, EQUALLY,	226	THE LIZARD	4
EQUIPPED				
	THE BEAR, EQUIPPED WITH PAW AND SNOUT,	23	AMOROUS LADY	3
ER				
	WALLACE, WALLACE, WO IST ER?	266	FOR STEVENS	9
	ER IST NIEMALS AUSGEPOOPEN,	266	FOR STEVENS	15
ERNEST				
	IT WASN'T ERNEST; IT WASN'T SCOTT--	111	SQUEEZE-BOX	1
ERRAND				
	SOME ERRAND, OBSCURE AS THE WIND'S CIRCUIT,	92	I CRY, LOVE!	6
ERRANT				
	HER FULL LIPS PURSED, THE ERRANT NOTE TO SEIZE;	127	I KNEW A WOMAN	16
ERRATIC				
	FLYING UPWARD IN LITTLE SKIPS AND ERRATIC LEAPS;	152	THE SISKINS	9
	ROSE UP AND FELL LIKE AN ERRATIC WIND.	237	THE TRANCED	10
ERROR				
	WE CANNOT TRACE THE ERROR DOWN.	30	THE RECKONING	8
ERRORS				
	AND LEADS TO ERRORS IN THE MIND.	257	SANITARIUM	4
ESCAPE				
	THOUGH THE DEVOURING MOTHER CRY, ""ESCAPE ME? NEVER--""	5	PROGNOSIS	13
ESCAPED				
	HAVING ESCAPED HER PEN,	213	THE HAPPY THREE	19
ESCAPES				
	THE WATER STORED IN NARROW POOLS ESCAPES	11	LIGHT BRIGHTER	11
	ESCAPES FROM THE MACHINE AT LAST.	33	HIGHWAY: MICH	20
	HOW FAST THE WINSOME ESCAPES!	258	SONG (3)	19
ESSENTIAL				
	THE LIGHT ESSENTIAL TO YOUR NEED.	4	FEUD	11
	THERE WOULD BE REASON FOR ESSENTIAL SIN;	144	ELEGY (1)	2
ESTUARY				
	AND THE PINE, WHOLE WITH ITS ROOTS, SINKS INTO THE ESTUARY,	197	THE LONG WATERS	35
ETERNAL				
	IS THE ETERNAL NEAR, FONDLING?	87	PRAISE TO END!	73
	I KNOW THE BACK-STREAM'S JOY, AND THE STONE'S ETERNAL PULSELESS LONGING.	88	PRAISE TO END!	82
	SEEKING IN MY OWN WAY, ETERNAL PURPOSE;	168	FOURTH MEDITATN	2
	THE ETERNAL ONE, THE CHILD, THE SWAYING VINE BRANCH,	198	THE LONG WATERS	69
	ONE LEARNED OF THE ETERNAL;	199	THE FAR FIELD	18
	WAS I TOO GLIB ABOUT ETERNAL THINGS,	241	THE SEQUEL	1
	THE ETERNAL SEEKS, AND FINDS, THE TEMPORAL,	244	INFIRMITY	21
ETERNITY				
	LIKE THAT CLEAR AUTUMNAL WEATHER OF ETERNITY,	43	CARNATIONS	6
	ETERNITY HOWLS IN THE LAST CRAGS,	89	UNFOLD! UNFOLD!	6
	WHAT'S FREEDOM FOR? TO KNOW ETERNITY.	127	I KNEW A WOMAN	24
	BUT WHO WOULD COUNT ETERNITY IN DAYS?	127	I KNEW A WOMAN	26
	SUCH ARDOR TAMES ETERNITY, I THINK.	132	SENTENTIOUS MAN	30
	WHERE'S MY ETERNITY	139	PLAINT	4
	MY MOMENTS LINGER--THAT'S ETERNITY.	149	IN LATE SUMMER	16
	ETERNITY IS NOW.	153	THE DYING MAN	10
	ETERNITY DEFINED, AND STREWN WITH STRAW,	156	THE DYING MAN	92
	PART OF ETERNITY,	238	THE TRANCED	24
	ONE TOE IN ETERNITY;	262	FOLLIES OF ADAM	18
ETERNITY'S				
	IN THAT LAST WHILE, ETERNITY'S CONFINE,	120	THE DREAM	31
	ETERNITY'S NOT EASILY COME BY.	244	INFIRMITY	32
EURIPIDES				
	READ ME EURIPIDES,	262	FOLLIES OF ADAM	1
EVEN				
	EVEN THE DIRT KEPT BREATHING A SMALL BREATH.	38	ROOT CELLAR	11
	SO THEIR MUSKY SMELL COMES EVEN STRONGER,	39	ORCHIDS	12
	UNDER EVEN THE ROCK-SHUT GROUND,	50	THE CYCLE	16
	NOT EVEN THE MINNOWS CAME.	53	THE LOST SON	15
	EVEN THE HUSHED FORMS, THE BENT YELLOWY WEEDS	57	THE LOST SON	147
	IT WASN'T EVEN AS	71	WHERE KNOCK IS	14
	EVEN STEVEN ALL IS LESS:	75	I NEED, I NEED	23
	EVEN THREAD HAD A SPEECH.	90	UNFOLD! UNFOLD!	33
	ALL OPENINGS PRAISE US, EVEN OILY HOLES.	90	UNFOLD! UNFOLD!	40
	EVEN A FATHER COULD NOT FIND HER:	102	ELEGY FOR JANE	11
	AND EVEN THE BOYS TURNED OUT TO BE MEN	112	SQUEEZE-BOX	23
	NOT EVEN THE END OF HIS CLAW, CLAW, CLAW,	117	LADY AND BEAR	17
	NOT EVEN THE END OF HIS CLAW.	117	LADY AND BEAR	18

		PAGE	TITLE	LINE
EVEN (CONTINUED)				
ALL'S EVEN WITH THE ODD,	....	123	WORDS FOR WIND	7
EVEN THE CATERPILLAR I CAN LOVE, AND THE VARIOUS VERMIN.		151	SLUG	27
ELSEWHERE, IN HOUSES, EVEN PAILS CAN BE SAD;	....	157	FIRST MEDITATN	4
WHAT'S WEATHER TO ME? EVEN CARP DIE IN THIS RIVER.	....	164	I'M HERE	90
EVEN THE STONES SPEAK.		170	FOURTH MEDITATN	88
I WOULDN'T BE YOU FOR EVEN A DAY,	....	177	KITTY-CAT BIRD	11
AND THEN WITHOUT EVEN A SPOON,		179	MYRTLE'S COUSIN	8
NOT EVEN THE SOOT DANCES.	....	187	THE LONGING	18
EVEN THE GULLS QUIET ON THE FAR ROCKS,		190	AT OYSTER RIVER	7
THE WAVES NOT YET HIGH, BUT EVEN,	....	230	THE STORM	11
NOT EVEN FEATHERS FROM SO FAR AWAY.		232	THE THING	17
NOT EVEN OUT OF BREATH?		262	FOLLIES OF ADAM	7
LINDSAY'S I MEAN: TWO MOONS, OR EVEN THREE,		273	SUPPR W LINDSAY	7
HIS NOSE LOOKED EVEN BIGGER THAN IT WAS,	....	273	SUPPR W LINDSAY	21
EVENING				
THE EVENING CAME		74	WHERE KNOCK IS	82
IN THE SOFT DARK OF EARLY EVENING,		100	THE VISITANT	17
THE EVENING WRAPS ME, STEADY AS A FLAME.	....	150	IN LATE SUMMER	32
THERE ARE STILL TIMES, MORNING AND EVENING:		159	FIRST MEDITATN	83
COMING ACROSS SNOW IN EARLY EVENING?	....	161	I'M HERE	5
A THING WE FEEL AT EVENING, AND BY DOORS,	....	162	I'M HERE	53
AS LIGHT REFLECTS FROM A LAKE, IN LATE EVENING,	....	198	THE LONG WATERS	60
IN A PLACE OF MOTTLED CLOUDS, A THIN MIST MORNING AND				
EVENING.		221	THE ABYSS	77
IN EVENING AIR	....	240	IN EVEING AIR	T
I SEE, IN EVENING AIR,	....	240	IN EVEING AIR	23
EVER				
IF I SHOULD EVER SEEK RELIEF	....	22	SILENCE	15
I REJOICE IN THE SPRING, AS THOUGH NO SPRING EVER HAD BEEN.		24	VERNAL SENTIMNT	8
DID I EVER CURSE THE SUN?	....	62	FIELD OF LIGHT	20
BAGS? WHO EVER SAID GOD SANG IN YOUR FAT SHAPE? YOU'RE NOT				
THE ONLY	....	98	O, THOU OPENING	27
BEFORE SHE EVER BREATHED, AND IN THAT DREAM	....	119	THE DREAM	2
HAVE THEY SEEN, EVER, THE SHARP BONES OF THE POOR?		169	FOURTH MEDITATN	46
YOU HARDLY EVER THINK IT'S THERE.	....	178	THE CHAIR	2
AND THE DUST LAY THICK ON MY EYELIDS,--WHO EVER WORE				
GOGGLES?--	....	193	JOURNY INTERIOR	24
AND YOUR HAIR EVER BLAZE,	....	217	WISH YOUNG WIFE	8
EACH TIME EVER	....	219	THE ABYSS	9
WHAT ROOT OF HIS EVER DENIED ITS STEM?	....	224	OTTO	10
A LARK-SWEET LOVER IF EVER THERE WAS.	....	258	SONG (3)	3
NOT EVER FARTHER.	....	265	HARSH COUNTRY	12
THE ONLY THING I EVER LEARNED	....	267	SAGINAW SONG	27
SHOULD DAME ANXIETY EVER COME NEAR	....	272	DUET	24
EVER-CHANGING				
NOT TOO FAR AWAY FROM THE EVER-CHANGING FLOWER-DUMP,	.....	199	THE FAR FIELD	16
EVERY				
THE HIVE THAT HUMMED IN EVERY CELL	....	4	DEATH PIECE	3
UPON WHOM EVERY GIFT AND THRILL WERE SHOWERED,	....	28	THE FAVORITE	10
I WAKE IN EVERY NERVE.	....	34	NIGHT JOURNEY	15
AT EVERY STEP YOU MISSED		45	MY PAPA'S WALTZ	11
IN THAT SLOW DARK THAT WIDENS EVERY EYE.		129	SHE	14
I FIND HER EVERY PLACE;		130	THE OTHER	9
FOR EVERY MEANING HAD GROWN MEANINGLESS.		133	THE PURE FURY	4
YET WHISTLE BACK AT EVERY WHISTLING BIRD.		140	THE SWAN	11
SHOULD EVERY CREATURE BE AS I HAVE BEEN,	....	144	ELEGY (1)	1
EVERY TIME I LET HIM, THE STRING WOULD BUST.	....	178	THE DONKEY	3
CHANGING WITH EVERY TWIST OF WIND,	....	196	THE LONG WATERS	10
KILLED EVERY CAT THAT NEARED THEIR PHEASANT RUNS;	....	224	OTTO	28
AND EVERY SNAIL DIPPED TOWARD ME ITS PURE HORN.		248	THE TREE, BIRD	2
WITH EVERY SHIFT OF AIR, THOSE BEATING WINGS,	....	248	THE TREE, BIRD	15
THE SOUL DIES EVERY NIGHT;		263	FOLLIES OF ADAM	23
THERE'S BEANS ON EVERY PLATE,	....	267	SAGINAW SONG	4
I RAN BEHIND HIM EVERY DAY	....	268	SAGINAW SONG	54
SHAKES EVERY SENSE. I'M FIVE	....	271	THE REPLY	13
EVERYONE				
THE STETHOSCOPE TELLS WHAT EVERYONE FEARS:	....	23	ACADEMIC	1
THE TABLE WHERE EVERYONE ATE AS HE SHOULD,	....	32	SALE	14
AND EVERYONE, EVERYONE POINTING UP AND SHOUTING!	....	43	CHILD ON GRNHSE	7
AND EVERYONE, EVERYONE POINTING UP AND SHOUTING!	....	43	CHILD ON GRNHSE	7
IS HE A BIRD OR A TREE? NOT EVERYONE CAN TELL.	....	64	SHAPE OF FIRE	3
EACH ONE'S HIMSELF, YET EACH ONE'S EVERYONE.	....	132	SENTENTIOUS MAN	36

		PAGE	TITLE	LINE
EVERYTHING				
	WITH EVERYTHING BLOOMING ABOVE ME,	39	WEED PULLER	11
	EVERYTHING LIMP	43	FLOWER DUMP	10
	EVERYTHING HAS BEEN TWICE.	72	WHERE KNOCK IS	20
	BY MIDNIGHT I LOVE EVERYTHING ALIVE.	173	WHAT TELL BONES	93
	WHEN EVERYTHING--BIRDS, MEN, DOGS--	210	HER TIME	23
	AND EVERYTHING COMES TO ONE,	251	ONCE MORE, RND	11
EVERYTHING'S				
	EVERYTHING'S CLOSER. IS THIS A CAGE?	77	BRING THE DAY!	17
	THOUGH EVERYTHING'S ASTONISHMENT AT LAST,	107	SIR JOHN DAVIES	79
EVERYWHERE				
	I FIND THAT LOVE, AND I AM EVERYWHERE.	135	THE RENEWAL	24
EVIL				
	THE CLOAK OF EVIL AND DESPAIR,	19	EPIDERM MACABRE	6
	I MOVE BENEATH AN EVIL SKY.	19	AGNST DISASTER	8
	HUNG DOWN LONG YELLOW EVIL NECKS, LIKE TROPICAL SNAKES.	38	ROOT CELLAR	5
	"THE SHIMMER OF EVIL"	143	SHIMMER OF EVIL	T
	COLD EVIL TWINKLED TIGHTER THAN A STRING; A FIRE	143	SHIMMER OF EVIL	8
EVILS				
	FOR HEARKENING TO CARNAL EVILS	8	PRAYER	7
EXACT				
	AN EXACT FALL OF WATERS HAS RENDERED ME IMPOTENT.	86	PRAISE TO END!	46
EXACTIOUS				
	A MOST, MOST EXACTIOUS LAW	117	LADY AND BEAR	10
EXALTED				
	EXALTED? YES,--	82	SENSIBILITY! LA	34
EXAMPLES				
	AM I REDUCED TO THE INDIGNITY OF EXAMPLES?	259	SONG (3)	40
EX-AS-PER-AT-ING				
	A MOST EX-AS-PER-AT-ING LUG.	116	THE SLOTH	7
EXASPERATION				
	I WOULD UNLEARN THE LINGO OF EXASPERATION, ALL THE			
	DISTORTIONS OF MALICE AND HATRED;	188	THE LONGING	42
EXCEED				
	NOW THE WATER'S LOW. THE WEEDS EXCEED ME.	86	PRAISE TO END!	23
EXCEEDS				
	THE ROSE EXCEEDS, THE ROSE EXCEEDS US ALL.	188	THE LONGING	29
	THE ROSE EXCEEDS, THE ROSE EXCEEDS US ALL.	188	THE LONGING	29
EXCEPT				
	HOW CAN I DREAM EXCEPT BEYOND THIS LIFE?	221	THE ABYSS	61
EXCESSES				
	I'M UNTRUE TO MY OWN EXCESSES.	86	PRAISE TO END!	27
EXCESSIVE				
	I WOULD DELIGHT IN MY HANDS, THE BRANCH SINGING, ALTERING			
	THE EXCESSIVE BIRD;	188	THE LONGING	44
	MY GRIEF WAS NOT EXCESSIVE.	199	THE FAR FIELD	25
EXCHANGING				
	AND AFTER EXCHANGING A PUNCH OR TWO,	111	SQUEEZE-BOX	5
EX-EXISTENTIALIST				
	MY EX-EXISTENTIALIST DARLING DEAR,	272	DUET	23
EXHAUSTED				
	EXHAUSTED FATHERS THINNED THE BLOOD,	4	FEUD	5
EXHAUSTION				
	TOO CLOSE IMMEDIACY AN EXHAUSTION:	220	THE ABYSS	45
EXISTENCE				
	EXISTENCE MOVES TOWARD A CERTAIN END--	149	IN LATE SUMMER	21
	EXISTENCE DARES PERPETUATE A SOUL,	173	WHAT TELL BONES	67
EXIT				
	A HUTCH BY THE EXIT HIS ROOM WITH A VIEW.	29	THE GENTLE	8
EXORCISM				
	THE EXORCISM	147	THE EXORCISM	T
EXPENSIVE				
	I'M A ROARING GIRL, AN EXPENSIVE WENCH,	272	DUET	15
EXPLODES				
	EXPLODES LIKE A ROSE, OR THRUSTS WINGS OVER THE CARIBBEAN.	159	FIRST MEDITATN	77
EXPLORERS				
	OLD MEN SHOULD BE EXPLORERS?	189	THE LONGING	57
EXQUISITE				
	PRETENDS HIS DEAD BUNION GIVES EXQUISITE PAIN.	29	THE GENTLE	4
EXTEND				
	MY EYES EXTEND BEYOND THE FARTHEST BLOOM OF THE WAVES;	198	THE LONG WATERS	75

	PAGE	TITLE	LINE
EXTENDED			
GROTESQUE, AWKWARD, HIS EXTENDED EYES LOOKING AT NOTHING IN PARTICULAR,	159	FIRST MEDITATN	63
WHEN FLOWERS GREW, THEIR BLOOM EXTENDED HIM.	224	OTTO	11
EXTENDING			
THE BLOSSOMS EXTENDING	42	TRANSPLANTING	19
THE WHOLE FLOWER EXTENDING OUTWARD,	42	TRANSPLANTING	21
THE BIRD, THE BEATING BIRD, EXTENDING WINGS--.	248	THE TREE, BIRD	21
EXTENT			
TO THIS EXTENT I'M A STALK.	188	THE LONGING	35
TO THIS EXTENT I'M A STALK.	261	THE CHANGELING	38
EXTERNALS			
THE SHADOWS ARE EMPTY, THE SLIDING EXTERNALS.	104	OLD LADY'S WRDS	51
EXTREME			
I LIVE IN LIGHT'S EXTREME; I STRETCH IN ALL DIRECTIONS;	173	WHAT TELL BONES	82
LIGHT ON ITS ROUNDS, A PURE EXTREME OF LIGHT	244	INFIRMITY	14
BY LIGHT'S EXTREME,	261	THE CHANGELING	40
EXTREMEST			
AS WATER TEACHES STONE. BELIEVE ME, EXTREMEST ORIOLE,	260	THE CHANGELING	19
EXTREMITY			
THE SOUL DELIGHTS IN THAT EXTREMITY.	244	INFIRMITY	16
EXULTATION			
AN EXULTATION TAKES US OUTSIDE LIFE:	132	SENTENTIOUS MAN	25
ALL EXULTATION IS A DANGEROUS THING.	155	THE DYING MAN	72
EXULTING			
THE EXULTING	155	THE DYING MAN	ST
EXULTS			
DESIRE EXULTS THE EAR:	128	THE VOICE	19
EYE			
THEY DART ACROSS A CORNER OF THE EYE.	8	THE SIGNALS	4
AND SOME HAVE HELD THE EYE TO BE	8	PRAYER	9
THE THINGS THE EYE OR HAND CANNOT POSSESS.	8	THE SIGNALS	10
WHEN I LOOKED AT THE ALTERED SCENE, MY EYE WAS UNDECEIVED,	12	MID-CNTRY BLOW	7
HORIZONS HAVE NO STRANGENESS TO THE EYE.	13	PRAISE PRAIRIE	5
THE DOCK, SO GARISH TO THE EYE,	14	COMING OF COLD	15
THE LONG EYE NOTES THE MINNOW'S HIDING PLACE.	15	THE HERON	7
CARESSES OF THE HAND AND EYE.	19	EPIDERM MACABRE	8
REPULSE THE STARING EYE,	20	REPL TO CENSURE	1
"CLAIRVOYANT WIDOW LADY, WITH AN EYE LIKE A TELESCOPE,	27	CLAIRVOY WIDOW	17
A KNAVE WHO SCAMPERED THROUGH THE NEEDLE'S EYE,	28	THE FAVORITE	1
AN EYE TILTED.	62	FIELD OF LIGHT	6
WHERE'S THE EYE?	64	SHAPE OF FIRE	20
AN EYE COMES OUT OF THE WAVE.	66	SHAPE OF FIRE	60
A MOON LOOSENED FROM A STAG'S EYE,	79	GIVE WAY, GATES	10
MAY I LOOK TOO, LOVED EYE?	79	GIVE WAY, GATES	19
THE EYE PERISHES IN THE SMALL VISION.	90	UNFOLD! UNFOLD!	42
BEHOLD, IN THE LOUT'S EYE,	93	I CRY, LOVE!	38
AN EYE SAYS,	99	O, THOU OPENING	79
AND LEAP OVER MY EYE,	103	OLD LADY'S WRDS	16
EYE LEARNED FROM EYE, COLD LIP FROM SENSUAL LIP.	119	THE DREAM	4
EYE LEARNED FROM EYE, COLD LIP FROM SENSUAL LIP.	119	THE DREAM	4
A SHAPE FROM DEEP IN THE EYE--	123	WORDS FOR WIND	30
IN THAT SLOW DARK THAT WIDENS EVERY EYE.	129	SHE	14
WITH THEIR HARD SNOW; LEANED ON THE LONELY EYE;	143	SHIMMER OF EVIL	7
A LATE ROSE RAVAGES THE CASUAL EYE,	149	IN LATE SUMMER	17
WHAT SENSUAL EYE CAN KEEP AN IMAGE PURE,	154	THE DYING MAN	43
OR AFTER-IMAGE OF THE INNER EYE.	155	THE DYING MAN	57
BEHIND THE EYE; THE LOST ACRES AT THE EDGE OF SMOKY CITIES.	159	FIRST MEDITATN	75
IN MY GRANDMOTHER'S INNER EYE,	163	I'M HERE	71
THE ONLY THING ALIVE IN HEAVEN'S EYE,	166	HER BECOMING	58
IN THE LONG FIELDS, I LEAVE MY FATHER'S EYE;	173	WHAT TELL BONES	86
I WOULD BELIEVE MY PAIN: AND THE EYE QUIET ON THE GROWING ROSE;	188	THE LONGING	43
SLIDING AWAY FROM THE TRAVELER'S EYE,	203	THE ROSE	34
LIKE THE EYE OF A NEW-CAUGHT FISH.	204	THE ROSE	88
WITH A TILT OF HIS EYE,	208	THE APPARITION	6
IN MY MIND'S EYE I SEE THOSE FIELDS OF GLASS,	225	OTTO	34
HIS RIGHT EYE STARING STRAIGHT AT ME,	226	THE LIZARD	6
ONE ROUND EYE STILL TOWARD ME.	226	THE LIZARD	19
BUT THE EYE OF THE TINY LIZARD STAYS WITH ME.	226	THE LIZARD	22
UNDER THE EYE OF THE GREAT OWL WATCHING FROM THE ELM-TREE,	227	MEADOW MOUSE	24
LEAVING A PLACE FOR THE EYE TO REST,	233	THE PIKE	2
AND THE HALF-SUNKEN BRANCH BENDS AWAY FROM THE GAZER'S EYE.	233	THE PIKE	9

		PAGE	TITLE	LINE
EYE (CONTINUED)				
MY EYE ALWAYS BEYOND THE SURFACE REFLECTION;	....	233	THE PIKE	12
WITH A ROUND VIREO'S EYE, QUIET AND CONTAINED,	....	234	ALL MORNING	13
IN A DARK TIME, THE EYE BEGINS TO SEE,	....	239	IN A DARK TIME	1
THOUGH SUMMER BLAZES IN THE VIREO'S EYE.	....	240	IN EVEING AIR	2
AS CHANGES SHIMMER IN THE INNER EYE.	....	244	INFIRMITY	2
THE INSTANT AGES ON THE LIVING EYE;	....	244	INFIRMITY	13
THE DEEP EYE SEES THE SHIMMER ON THE STONE;	....	244	INFIRMITY	20
WHAT SHAKES THE EYE BUT THE INVISIBLE?	....	245	THE DECISION	1
AND THE EYE ALTERING ALL;	....	251	ONCE MORE, RND	8
AND ONE EYE GAZED ASKEW. "WHY, BLAKE, HE'S DEAD,--	....	273	SUPPR W LINDSAY	22
EYEBROWS				
DROPPING A FINE FILM ON NAILS AND DELICATE EYEBROWS,	.....	46	DOLOR	12
EYELESS				
AN EYELESS STARER.	....	187	THE LONGING	23
I ENVY THE TENDRILS, THEIR EYELESS SEEKING,	....	221	THE ABYSS	64
EYELIDS				
SAW WOMEN, THEIR EYELIDS LIKE LITTLE RAGS,	....	48	JUDGE NOT	9
AND THE DUST LAY THICK ON MY EYELIDS,--WHO EVER WORE GOGGLES?--	....	193	JOURNY INTERIOR	24
EYES				
AN EPIC OF THE EYES		3	OPEN HOUSE	5
THE MENACE OF ANCESTRAL EYES;		4	FEUD	2
CHERISH THE EYES THE PROUD INCREDIBLE POISE	....	5	TO MY SISTER	9
EYES, STARING PAST ANOTHER	....	7	ORDERS FOR DAY	15
UNTIL CLEAR EYES PUT ON THE LOOK OF SLEEP.	....	12	SLOW SEASON	4
WE ARE AFRAID OF WHAT OUR EYES HAVE SEEN:	....	16	THE BAT	8
--AND THE EYES, STILL VIVID, LOOKING UP FROM A SUNKEN ROOM.		22	ROAD TO WDLAWN	8
WHILE OUT OF FRIGHTENED EYES		31	LULL	20
--AND SOME WATERY EYES IN A COPLEY HEAD.	....	32	SALE	12
EYES RIMMED WITH PICKLE DUST,	....	46	PICKLE BELT	10
THEIR EYES, RICH AS PLUMS, STARING FROM NEWSPRINT,--	.....	48	JUDGE NOT	3
HER EYES WENT KISSING AWAY	....	72	WHERE KNOCK IS	36
MY EYES HAVE FORGOTTEN.		103	OLD LADY'S WRDS	4
MY EYES, THEY DAZZLED AT HER FLOWING KNEES;		127	I KNEW A WOMAN	18
UNTIL MY EYES LOOK AT A BRIGHTER SUN		134	THE PURE FURY	27
UNTIL IT BROODS IN HER EYES.	....	137	LOVE'S PROGRESS	12
THE GREAT ROUND EYES HAD GONE.	....	145	THE BEAST	17
I TRIED TO MEET HIS EYES.	....	146	THE SONG	3
I AM A CONNOISSEUR OF MIDNIGHT EYES.	....	149	IN LATE SUMMER	6
AS MY EYES FOLLOW AFTER	....	152	THE SISKINS	23
GROTESQUE, AWKWARD, HIS EXTENDED EYES LOOKING AT NOTHING IN PARTICULAR,	....	159	FIRST MEDITATN	63
ON THE SILL OF THE EYES, SOMETHING FLUTTERS,		162	I'M HERE	52
I CLOSED MY EYES, AND SAW SMALL FIGURES DANCING,	....	163	I'M HERE	65
THE EYES REJOICE IN THE ACT OF SEEING AND THE FRESH AFTER-IMAGE;	....	163	I'M HERE	79
TO GAZE AT A FACE WITH THE FIXED EYES OF A SPANIEL?	......	169	FOURTH MEDITATN	34
MAY THEIR EYES GLEAM WITH THE FIRST DAWN;		169	FOURTH MEDITATN	59
HANDS ACTIVE, EYES CHERISHED;		187	THE LONGING	8
WHO MAGNIFIES THE MORNING WITH HER EYES,	....	196	THE LONG WATERS	25
MY EYES EXTEND BEYOND THE FARTHEST BLOOM OF THE WAVES;	...	198	THE LONG WATERS	75
AND I WATCHED AND WATCHED TILL MY EYES BLURRED FROM THE BIRD SHAPES,--		199	THE FAR FIELD	29
MY EYES STARE AT THE BOTTOM OF A RIVER,	....	201	THE FAR FIELD	73
MY EYES NEITHER HERE NOR THERE,	....	207	THE YOUNG GIRL	9
BUT NEVER THE FULL LOOK OF MY EYES,	....	209	HER RETICENCE	6
MAY THE EYES IN YOUR FACE	....	217	WISH YOUNG WIFE	3
BEARING DOWN, WITH TWO STEADY EYES,	....	223	ELEGY (2)	22
ONLY TO FIND, WITH THEIR LONG TERRIBLE EYES		232	THE THING	9
OUR EYES FIXED ON A POINT OF LIGHT SO FINE		237	THE TRANCED	16
I TEACH MY EYES TO HEAR, MY EARS TO SEE	....	244	INFIRMITY	34
I WOULD BE NEAR; I SHUT MY EYES TO SEE;		246	THE MARROW	22
THE SLOW LONG RIPPLES WINKING IN MY EYES.	....	247	I WAITED	9
THE LONELY BUZZ BEHIND MY MIDNIGHT EYES;--	....	248	THE TREE, BIRD	16
EYE'S				
THE PAGEANTRY OF WINGS THE EYE'S BRIGHT TREASURE.		5	TO MY SISTER	6
IN TRUTH, THE EYE'S THE ABETTOR OF	....	8	PRAYER	15
THE EYE'S IN THE STY.	....	64	SHAPE OF FIRE	21
THEN SLIDES DOWN OVER THE EYE'S SURFACE,	....	226	THE LIZARD	24
FABRIC				
THE FLYING FABRIC STITCHED ON BONE,	....	19	EPIDERM MACABRE	3

		PAGE	TITLE	LINE
FACE				
BUT WHEN HE STOOD UP, THAT FACE		6	THE PREMONITION	12
AMONG THE TREES THAT FACE THE CORNER LIGHT.		16	THE BAT	6
WHEN MICE WITH WINGS CAN WEAR A HUMAN FACE.		16	THE BAT	10
SWAYING CLOSE TO THE FACE,		39	ORCHIDS	3
BRICKS FLAKE BEFORE MY FACE. MASTER OF WATER, THAT'S TREES AWAY.		61	THE LONG ALLEY	80
PUT YOUR FINGER IN YOUR FACE,		75	I NEED, I NEED	25
THE DARK SHOWED ME A FACE.		88	PRAISE TO END!	99
THE SHINE ON THE FACE OF THE LAKE		93	I CRY, LOVE!	50
I'VE SEEN MY FATHER'S FACE BEFORE		97	O, THOU OPENING	14
I TURNED MY FACE AWAY, AND YET SHE STAYED.		119	THE DREAM	14
BUT WHO, FACED WITH HER FACE,		122	ALL EARTH, AIR	29
IS THIS MY FINAL FACE?		130	THE OTHER	8
THE DREAM'S AN INSTANT THAT CALLS UP HER FACE.		131	SENTENTIOUS MAN	11
AND THERE I THRASHED, MY THIGHS AND FACE AFLAME.		132	SENTENTIOUS MAN	22
I LOVE A WOMAN WITH AN EMPTY FACE.		133	THE PURE FURY	9
I WALK AS IF MY FACE WOULD KISS THE WIND.		135	THE RENEWAL	12
AND THE SWEAT POURED FROM MY FACE,		146	THE SONG	23
DARES FACE THE THING HE IS?)		147	THE EXORCISM	4
THE SLACK FACE OF THE DISMAL PURE INANE?		149	IN LATE SUMMER	10
HE TURNED HIS FACE: THERE WAS ANOTHER MAN,		155	THE DYING MAN	62
A FACE FLOATS IN THE FERNS. DO MAIMED GODS WALK?		165	HER BECOMING	18
TO GAZE AT A FACE WITH THE FIXED EYES OF A SPANIEL?		169	FOURTH MEDITATN	34
MY FACE ON FIRE, CLOSE TO THE POINTS OF A STAR,		172	WHAT TELL BONES	55
IN SLEEP, AFRAID. DEATH'S FACE RISES AFRESH,		190	AT OYSTER RIVER	25
THE STAND AT THE STRETCH IN THE FACE OF DEATH,		194	JOURNY INTERIOR	66
AND IN THE SHRUNKEN FACE OF A DEAD RAT, EATEN BY RAIN AND GROUND-BEETLES		199	THE FAR FIELD	19
WIDENING AT HIGH NOON, FACE UPWARD,		203	THE ROSE	43
FLIES AWAY FROM MY FACE		210	HER TIME	15
MAY THE EYES IN YOUR FACE		217	WISH YOUNG WIFE	3
HER FACE LIKE A RAIN-BEATEN STONE ON THE DAY SHE ROLLED OFF		223	ELEGY (2)	1
AS A MAN TURNS TO FACE ON-COMING SNOW.		245	THE DECISION	12
ONE WHITE FACE SHIMMERS BRIGHTER THAN THE SUN		246	THE MARROW	7
SPEAK IT FROM THE FACE OUT CLEARLY:		266	FOR STEVENS	13
I'LL FACE ALL THAT, AND THE DIVINE ABSURD:		272	DUET	5
I'D SAY MY FACE IS JUST AS ROUND AS HIS,		273	SUPPR W LINDSAY	8
AND THAT MAKES THREE, COUNTING HIS FACE AS ONE.		273	SUPPR W LINDSAY	9
FACED				
BUT WHO, FACED WITH HER FACE,		122	ALL EARTH, AIR	29
A MAN FACED WITH HIS OWN IMMENSITY		201	THE FAR FIELD	87
FACED UP TO THE WORST.		223	ELEGY (2)	11
FACES				
THE CRANED NECKS, THE MOURNERS' ANONYMOUS FACES,		22	ROAD TO WDLAWN	7
AND BOYS MOON AT GIRLS WITH LAST YEAR'S FATUOUS FACES,		24	VERNAL SENTIMNT	3
GLAZING THE PALE HAIR, THE DUPLICATE GREY STANDARD FACES.		46	DOLOR	13
FACES GREYING FASTER THAN LOAM-CRUMBS ON A HARROW;		48	JUDGE NOT	1
COME OUT OF A CLOUD, ANGEL WITH SEVERAL FACES,		48	LAST WORDS	8
I AM MY FACES,		99	O, THOU OPENING	67
THERE ARE NO PURSUING FORMS, FACES ON WALLS:		159	FIRST MEDITATN	78
DRY BARK FLEW IN THEIR FACES FROM HIS SHOT,--		224	OTTO	16
FADE				
IT WAS FADE ME ANOTHER AND STICK OUT YOUR CAN;		112	SQUEEZE-BOX	27
FADED				
ON THE FADED CARPET, THE STALE		228	THE GERANIUM	12
FADES				
HER IMAGE FADES, YET DOES NOT DISAPPEAR--		140	THE SWAN	2
FAIL				
ALL WATERS WAVER, AND ALL FIRES FAIL.		242	THE SEQUEL	26
I FEEL THE AUTUMN FAIL--ALL THAT SLOW FIRE		242	THE SEQUEL	31
FAILED				
WHEN GLORY FAILED, WE DANCED UPON A PIN.		106	SIR JOHN DAVIES	58
AND MY REASON FAILED.		249	THE RESTORED	14
FAILS				
AND THE SPIRIT FAILS TO MOVE FORWARD,		187	THE LONGING	19
OF BEING BORN FAILS ON HIS NAKED EARS.		201	THE FAR FIELD	90
FAILURE				
FROZEN BY A FATHER'S LIP, A MOTHER'S FAILURE TO ANSWER.		169	FOURTH MEDITATN	45
NOON OF FAILURE,		219	THE ABYSS	11
FAINT				
THE FAINT MOON FALLING THROUGH WHITEWASHED GLASS,		39	ORCHIDS	10
ONCE, TWICE, AND A FAINT THIRD THUMP,--		42	TRANSPLANTING	11

		PAGE	TITLE	LINE
FAINTLY				
THE CLOSE AIR FAINTLY STIRRED.	....	212	LIGHT LISTENED	7
FAIR				
IN THE FAIR NIGHT OF SOME DIM BRAIN,	....	81	SENSIBILITY! LA	4
MY DEAREST DEAR MY FAIREST FAIR,	....	86	PRAISE TO END!	35
THE FAIR HOUSE, THE HIGH	....	103	OLD LADY'S WRDS	26
A FAIR THING GROWS MORE FAIR;	....	124	WORDS FOR WIND	54
A FAIR THING GROWS MORE FAIR;	....	124	WORDS FOR WIND	54
HAS HE GRUBS FOR HIS FAIR?--	....	183	THE WAGTAIL	3
THIS FAIR PARCEL OF SUMMER'S	....	258	SONG (3)	1
FAIREST				
MY DEAREST DEAR MY FAIREST FAIR,	....	86	PRAISE TO END!	35
FAITH				
KEEP FAITH WITH PRESENT JOYS REFUSE TO CHOOSE	....	5	TO MY SISTER	7
AWAY FROM SIMPLE FAITH	....	31	LULL	16
FAKE				
YOU'RE A FAKE, YOUR'RE A FRAUD, YOU'RE A HOR-RID PRETENSE!		177	KITTY-CAT BIRD	3
FALL				
RECALL THE GRADUAL DARK THE SNOW'S UNMEASURED FALL	....	5	TO MY SISTER	3
FALL.	....	85	PRAISE TO END!	16
AN EXACT FALL OF WATERS HAS RENDERED ME IMPOTENT.	....	86	PRAISE TO END!	46
THIS FROG'S HAD ANOTHER FALL.	....	99	O, THOU OPENING	51
THE FALL OF THE LAST ASH	....	103	OLD LADY'S WRDS	31
I FALL, MORE AND MORE,	....	104	OLD LADY'S WRDS	61
WHO RISE FROM FLESH TO SPIRIT KNOW THE FALL:	....	107	SIR JOHN DAVIES	95
THIS JOY'S MY FALL. I AM!--	....	121	ALL EARTH, AIR	6
WHAT FALLS AWAY WILL FALL;	....	125	WORDS FOR WIND	80
PRIDE IN FINE LINEAMENTS PRECEDES A FALL	....	131	SENTENTIOUS MAN	5
A MAN ALIVE, FROM ALL LIGHT I MUST FALL.	....	140	THE SWAN	12
ROSE BUT TO LURCH AND FALL,	....	145	THE BEAST	13
AND SO HE HAD A HORRID FALL.	....	181	MONOTONY SONG	15
I RISE AND FALL IN THE SLOW SEA OF A GRASSY PLAIN,	....	194	JOURNY INTERIOR	42
I RISE AND FALL, AND TIME FOLDS	....	194	JOURNY INTERIOR	46
IN THE MOMENT OF TIME WHEN THE SMALL DROP FORMS, BUT DOES NOT FALL,	....	194	JOURNY INTERIOR	58
FEELING, I STILL DELIGHT IN MY LAST FALL.	....	197	THE LONG WATERS	32
FALLEN				
WHEN THE SUN HAS FALLEN BEHIND A WOODED ISLAND;	....	67	SHAPE OF FIRE	89
BEGUILE ME, CHANGE. WHAT HAVE I FALLEN FROM?	....	170	FOURTH MEDITATN	77
THE WAY BLOCKED AT LAST BY A FALLEN FIR-TREE,	....	193	JOURNY INTERIOR	15
BY SMALL STREAMS RUNNING DOWN UNDER FALLEN FIR TREES.	....	197	THE LONG WATERS	48
THE FULL MOON HAS FALLEN, THE NIGHT WIND IS DOWN	....	216	THE SHY MAN	17
HOW SHE KEPT THE WIZENED, THE FALLEN, THE MISSHAPEN FOR HERSELF,	....	223	ELEGY (2)	14
I THINK OF THE NESTLING FALLEN INTO THE DEEP GRASS,	....	227	MEADOW MOUSE	26
A FALLEN MAN, I CLIMB OUT OF MY FEAR.	....	239	IN A DARK TIME	22
ME HANDKERCHEE HAD FALLEN IN	....	269	GOB MUSIC	22
FALLING				
THE FAINT MOON FALLING THROUGH WHITEWASHED GLASS,	....	39	ORCHIDS	10
MUTTONY TEARS FALLING ON FIGURED LINOLEUM,	....	48	LAST WORDS	3
KISS ME, ASHES, I'M FALLING THROUGH A DARK SWIRL.	....	57	THE LOST SON	121
THE DARKNESS OF FALLING HAIR, THE WARNINGS FROM LINT AND SPIDERS,	....	159	FIRST MEDITATN	80
LIGHT AS A PETAL FALLING UPON STONE.	....	165	HER BECOMING	12
SOFT, SOFT, THE SNOW'S NOT FALLING. WHAT'S A SEED?	....	165	HER BECOMING	17
BETTER TO HUG CLOSE, WARY OF RUBBLE AND FALLING STONES.	....	193	JOURNY INTERIOR	6
I RECALL THE FALLING OF SMALL WATERS,	....	222	THE ABYSS	93
HER SHRIVELED PETALS FALLING	....	228	THE GERANIUM	11
FALLING'S				
RISING OR FALLING'S ALL ONE DISCIPLINE!	....	245	THE DECISION	7
FALLS				
TO KNOW THAT LIGHT FALLS AND FILLS, OFTEN WITHOUT OUR KNOWING,	....	67	SHAPE OF FIRE	92
WHAT FALLS AWAY IS ALWAYS. AND IS NEAR.	....	108	THE WAKING (2)	17
WHAT FALLS AWAY WILL FALL;	....	125	WORDS FOR WIND	80
FALLS BACK, A SLUG, A LOOSE WORM	....	187	THE LONGING	21
THE PRESENT FALLS, THE PRESENT FALLS AWAY;	....	248	THE TREE, BIRD	18
THE PRESENT FALLS, THE PRESENT FALLS AWAY;	....	248	THE TREE, BIRD	18
FALSE				
WITH FALSE ACCOUTERMENTS OF SENSE,	....	19	EPIDERM MACABRE	14
FOR THE ATTACKS OF FALSE HUMILITY TAKE SUDDEN TURNS FOR THE WORSE.	....	86	PRAISE TO END!	25

	PAGE	TITLE	LINE
FALTERED			
FALTERED; ROSE UP AGAIN;	145	THE BEAST	12
FAMILIAR			
ONCE MORE THE TREES ASSUME FAMILIAR SHAPES,	11	LIGHT BRIGHTER	9
HERE DISTANCE IS FAMILIAR AS A FRIEND.	13	PRAISE PRAIRIE	11
I NEVER AM BORED, HOWEVER FAMILIAR THE SCENE.	24	VERNAL SENTIMNT	4
FAN			
OR FAN LIFE INTO WILTED SWEET-PEAS WITH HIS HAT,	42	OLD FLORIST	9
HAND ME A FEATHER, I'LL FAN YOU WARM,	60	THE LONG ALLEY	45
FANCIES			
FANCIES SWAY AWAY	210	HER TIME	3
FANCY'S			
MY FANCY'S WHITE!	99	O, THOU OPENING	66
FANG			
WITH A STUMP OF SCRAGGY FANG	47	THE RETURN	12
THE FANG AND THE CLAW, THE CLUB AND THE KNOUT, THE IRRATIONAL EDICT,	170	FOURTH MEDITATN	67
FANGS			
THESE FLOWERS ARE ALL FANGS. COMFORT ME, FURY.	64	SHAPE OF FIRE	9
A BEAST WITH FANGS, AND OUT FOR HIS OWN BLOOD	133	THE PURE FURY	18
FANNING			
THE WIND SLACKENS, LIGHT AS A MOTH FANNING A STONE:	190	AT OYSTER RIVER	17
THE WIND FANNING THE ASH OF A LOW FIRE.	201	THE FAR FIELD	79
FAR			
WE WALK AWARE OF WHAT IS FAR AND CLOSE.	13	PRAISE PRAIRIE	10
AND FAR FROM ANYTHING MY OWN,	19	AGNST DISASTER	2
YOUR PALM IS MOIST, YOUR MANNER FAR TOO JOLLY	25	DIM-WIT COUSIN	9
SO FAR DOWN THE RIVER	41	BIG WIND	4
DROVE TO THE FAR	41	BIG WIND	14
OR RISING OUT OF FERNS NOT FAR FROM WATER,	43	CARNATIONS	4
DEEP IN THE BRAIN, FAR BACK.	49	NIGHT CROW	8
FAR FROM THE COLDER SOURCE	50	THE CYCLE	9
FAR IN THE WOOD	51	THE WAKING (1)	17
FROST MELTED ON FAR PANES;	57	THE LOST SON	145
THE FIEND'S FAR AWAY. LORD, WHAT DO YOU REQUIRE?	59	THE LONG ALLEY	21
A SIGH CAME FAR.	63	FIELD OF LIGHT	28
THE FAR LEAVES WERE FOR IT.	77	BRING THE DAY!	10
I WAS FAR BACK, FARTHER THAN ANYBODY ELSE.	89	UNFOLD! UNFOLD!	21
THE FAR STRETCH OF A DREAM,	124	WORDS FOR WIND	36
FATHER, I'M FAR FROM HOME,	137	LOVE'S PROGRESS	19
FAR FROM THE MIRRORS ALL THE BUSHES RANG	143	SHIMMER OF EVIL	6
CLOSE, AND YET FAR AWAY.	146	THE SONG	27
FAR THINGS DRAW CLOSER IN.	148	THE SMALL	10
O SWEET FIELD FAR AHEAD, I HEAR YOUR BIRDS,	156	THE DYING MAN	88
AND THE FAR PHOEBE, SINGING,	159	FIRST MEDITATN	86
LOOK AT THE FAR TREES AT THE END OF THE GARDEN.	163	I'M HERE	82
I'M NOT FAR FROM A STREAM.	164	I'M HERE	94
A MAD HEN IN A FAR CORNER OF THE DARK,	165	HER BECOMING	5
IS FAR FROM BECOMING GOD.	172	WHAT TELL BONES	60
THE BEAR SAID, SIR, YOU GO TOO FAR,	181	MONOTONY SONG	9
WHO SIGHS FROM FAR AWAY?	188	THE LONGING	41
EVEN THE GULLS QUIET ON THE FAR ROCKS,	190	AT OYSTER RIVER	7
THE FAR FIELD	199	THE FAR FIELD	T
NOT TOO FAR AWAY FROM THE EVER-CHANGING FLOWER-DUMP,	199	THE FAR FIELD	16
THE FAR FIELD, THE WINDY CLIFFS OF FOREVER,	200	THE FAR FIELD	51
WHILE ON A FAR POINT OF THE ROCKS	202	THE ROSE	27
CUT BY THE SEA-SLIME, FAR FROM THE CRASH	205	THE ROSE	92
OF LIGHT ON THE FAR	210	HER TIME	18
PHOEBE NOT FAR AWAY	213	THE HAPPY THREE	30
O WORLD SO FAR AWAY! O MY LOST WORLD!	225	OTTO	42
NOT EVEN FEATHERS FROM SO FAR AWAY.	232	THE THING	17
FAR AWAY, CLOSE-AT-HAND, HIS CALL FLOATING OVER THE ON-COMING TRAFFIC,	234	ALL MORNING	3
THE GULLS, THE GULLS FAR FROM THEIR WAVES	235	ALL MORNING	36
FROM THE TEAR, FAR AWAY,	236	SONG (2)	2
A MAN GOES FAR TO FIND OUT WHAT HE IS--	239	IN A DARK TIME	16
I LOOK DOWN THE FAR LIGHT	240	IN EVEING AIR	13
FAR DOWN A BILLOWING PLAIN,	240	IN EVEING AIR	15
--FAR BEYOND, O BEYOND! DEAR KIERKEGAARD.	272	DUET	21
COME EASY TO THE SILL, THINGS LOST FROM FAR AWAY.	273	SUPPR W LINDSAY	4
FARE			
WHAT WE ARE SEEKING IS A FARE	30	THE RECKONING	9
IS THIS FARE FOR THE CATS AND DOGS?	261	THE CHANGELING	35

	PAGE	TITLE	LINE
FAREWELL			
THE ARBOR IS COOLER. FAREWELL, FAREWELL, FOND WORM.	64	SHAPE OF FIRE	18
THE ARBOR IS COOLER. FAREWELL, FAREWELL, FOND WORM.	64	SHAPE OF FIRE	18
I SAID FAREWELL TO SIGHS,	167	HER BECOMING	70
I GAVE HER BODY FULL AND GRAVE FAREWELL.	241	THE SEQUEL	21
FARING-FORTH			
WHO BUT THE LOVED KNOW LOVE'S A FARING-FORTH?	243	THE MOTION	13
FAR-OFF			
A FAR-OFF TRAIN BLOWS ITS ECHOING WHISTLE ONCE;	33	IDYLL	10
FART			
THERE'S NEVER A HOUSEHOLD FART,	268	SAGINAW SONG	38
FARTHER			
I WAS FAR BACK, FARTHER THAN ANYBODY ELSE.	89	UNFOLD! UNFOLD!	21
WHILE, FARTHER AWAY, THE HEAT-LIGHTNING FLASHES.	194	JOURNY INTERIOR	41
THE WHITE SEA WIDENING ON A FARTHER SHORE.	248	THE TREE, BIRD	20
NOT EVER FARTHER.	265	HARSH COUNTRY	12
FARTHEST			
MY EYES EXTEND BEYOND THE FARTHEST BLOOM OF THE WAVES;	198	THE LONG WATERS	75
FAST			
--AND A FUME OF DECAY THAT CLINGS FAST TO THE WOOD.	32	SALE.	16
HOW FAST THE WINSOME ESCAPES!	258	SONG (3)	19
FASTER			
THEY FLICKER FASTER THAN A BLUE-TAILED SWIFT,	8	THE SIGNALS	5
THE HEART BEAT FASTER AS THE FAT WORDS ROLLED.	21	THE AUCTION	14
FACES GREYING FASTER THAN LOAM-CRUMBS ON A HARROW;	48	JUDGE NOT	1
AND I GO FASTER IN MY RAGE TO GET DONE WITH IT,	151	SLUG	18
FASTIDIOUS			
I CAN'T BURY THE BONE OF THIS MISERY LIKE A FASTIDIOUS DOG.	261	THE CHANGELING	31
FAT			
THE HEART BEAT FASTER AS THE FAT WORDS ROLLED.	21	THE AUCTION	14
THE LAWYERS ALL ARE CUNNING, THE BUSINESS MEN ARE FAT,	27	CLAIRVOY WIDOW	7
ON FAT LEAVES;	62	FIELD OF LIGHT	16
THE FAT LARK SANG IN THE FIELD;	63	FIELD OF LIGHT	38
WHAT'S THIS? A DISH FOR FAT LIPS.	64	SHAPE OF FIRE	1
MAMMA, SHE'S A SAD FAT.	74	I NEED, I NEED	19
THIS FAT CAN'T LAUGH.	91	UNFOLD! UNFOLD!	57
BAGS? WHO EVER SAID GOD SANG IN YOUR FAT SHAPE? YOU'RE NOT THE ONLY	98	O, THOU OPENING	27
YOU FAT UNNECESSARY HAGS,	99	O, THOU OPENING	60
A FAT, FIVE-INCH APPENDAGE	151	SLUG	12
AND THAT GRAVY AND FAT	180	GOO-GIRL	7
WHAT THE FAT LEAVES HAVE,--	258	SONG (3)	11
ONE OF THOSE FAT ONES WINDING THROUGH A ROSE.	273	SUPPR W LINDSAY	27
FATAL			
IT IS FATAL TO WOO YOURSELF,	172	WHAT TELL BONES	36
FATE			
OF FATE, YOU BLUBBER IN SURPRISE.	4	FEUD	4
O SEE THE FATE OF HIM WHOSE GUARD WAS LOWERED!--	5	PROGNOSIS	3
WHO CAN EMBRACE THE BODY OF HIS FATE?	106	SIR JOHN DAVIES	33
I FEEL MY FATE IN WHAT I CANNOT FEAR.	108	THE WAKING (2)	2
YOU WERE TOO LONELY FOR ANOTHER FATE.	144	ELEGY (1)	6
SCARS, TEMPESTS, FLOODS, THE MOTION OF MAN'S FATE;	144	ELEGY (1)	14
FATES			
SOME FATES ARE WORSE.	161	I'M HERE	16
FATHER			
CLOSE TO THE HEELS OF MY FATHER,	6	THE PREMONITION	4
HATH THE RAIN A FATHER? ALL THE CAVES ARE ICE. ONLY THE SNOW'S HERE.	56	THE LOST SON	84
I'M COLD. I'M COLD ALL OVER. RUB ME IN FATHER AND MOTHER.	56	THE LOST SON	85
FEAR WAS MY FATHER, FATHER FEAR.	56	THE LOST SON	86
FEAR WAS MY FATHER, FATHER FEAR.	56	THE LOST SON	86
MY FATHER IS A FISH.	72	WHERE KNOCK IS	22
ONE FATHER IS ENOUGH.	74	WHERE KNOCK IS	87
FATHER OF TENSIONS, I'M DOWN TO MY SKIN AT LAST.	85	PRAISE TO END!	4
FATHER, FORGIVE MY HANDS.	85	PRAISE TO END!	12
YOUR FATHER TOSSED A CAT IN AIR,	86	PRAISE TO END!	36
IS IT YOU, COLD FATHER? FATHER,	90	UNFOLD! UNFOLD!	51
IS IT YOU, COLD FATHER? FATHER,	90	UNFOLD! UNFOLD!	51
EVEN A FATHER COULD NOT FIND HER:	102	ELEGY FOR JANE	11
NEITHER FATHER NOR LOVER.	102	ELEGY FOR JANE	22
(IT TURNED OUT SHE HADN'T A FATHER AT ALL)	111	SQUEEZE-BOX	15
THE NIGHT WIND RISES. DOES MY FATHER LIVE?	135	THE RENEWAL	7
FATHER, I'M FAR FROM HOME,	137	LOVE'S PROGRESS	19

	PAGE	TITLE	LINE
FATHER (CONTINUED)			
(FATHER OF FLOWERS, WHO	147	THE EXORCISM	3
I FOUND MY FATHER WHEN I DID MY WORK,	154	THE DYING MAN	40
I SAW MY FATHER SHRINKING IN HIS SKIN;	155	THE DYING MAN	61
AND MY FATHER STANDING ASTRIDE THE CEMENT BENCHES,	203	THE ROSE	53
MY FATHER TOOK IT TO HER, BY THE TAIL.	224	OTTO	30
I'M SON AND FATHER OF MY ONLY DEATH.	244	INFIRMITY	18
FATHER AND SON OF THIS DEATH,	263	FOLLIES OF ADAM	22
BROTHER, HE'S OUR FATHER!	266	FOR STEVENS	20
MY FATHER NEVER USED A STICK,	268	SAGINAW SONG	50
--IN HONOR OF FATHER KIERKEGAARD.	272	DUET	26
FATHERS			
EXHAUSTED FATHERS THINNED THE BLOOD,	4	FEUD	5
A SON HAS MANY FATHERS.	98	O, THOU OPENING	33
THE FLESH FATHERS A DREAM;	263	FOLLIES OF ADAM	27
FATHER'S			
AND THE HONEYMOON BE SPOILED BY A FATHER'S GHOST,	5	PROGNOSIS	14
I'VE SEEN MY FATHER'S FACE BEFORE	97	O, THOU OPENING	14
I AM MY FATHER'S SON, I AM JOHN DONNE	140	THE SWAN	13
FROZEN BY A FATHER'S LIP, A MOTHER'S FAILURE TO ANSWER.	169	FOURTH MEDITATN	45
IN THE LONG FIELDS, I LEAVE MY FATHER'S EYE;	173	WHAT TELL BONES	86
BUT GOODNESS ME, HER FATHER'S RICH!	181	MONOTONY SONG	19
WATCHING THE WAKING OF MY FATHER'S WORLD.--	225	OTTO	41
FATIGUES			
LUST FATIGUES THE SOUL.	187	THE LONGING	11
FATTENS			
LIGHT FATTENS THE ROCK.	83	O LULL ME, LULL	19
FATUOUS			
AND BOYS MOON AT GIRLS WITH LAST YEAR'S FATUOUS FACES,	24	VERNAL SENTIMNT	3
FAUCET			
TALKED TO A FAUCET;	74	I NEED, I NEED	9
FAUCETS			
ALL THE FAUCETS STOPPED?--	41	BIG WIND	5
FAVOR			
BUT FOR AN UNCLE YOU WERE THOUGHT TO FAVOR,	25	DIM-WIT COUSIN	3
FAVORITE			
THE FAVORITE	28	THE FAVORITE	T
O HE WAS FORTUNE'S CHILD, A FAVORITE SON	28	THE FAVORITE	9
ONLY TO FLY OVER TO HIS FAVORITE PERCH, THE CROSS-BAR OF A TELEPHONE POLE;	234	ALL MORNING	9
FAWN			
A DOE AND ITS FAWN.	141	MEMORY	10
FAWTHER'S			
IT WAS "WOULD YOU BELIEVE IT--FAWTHER'S TALL!"	111	SQUEEZE-BOX	14
FEAR			
THE VEINS WITHIN OUR HANDS BETRAYED OUR FEAR.	6	INTERLUDE	11
SOME ITEMS, MISCELLANEOUS, MARKED "FEAR";	21	THE AUCTION	7
FEAR WAS MY FATHER, FATHER FEAR.	56	THE LOST SON	86
FEAR WAS MY FATHER, FATHER FEAR.	56	THE LOST SON	86
BOLD IN FEAR THEREFORE;	60	THE LONG ALLEY	40
I FEEL MY FATE IN WHAT I CANNOT FEAR.	108	THE WAKING (2)	2
I FEAR THOSE SHADOWS MOST	138	THE SURLY ONE	7
I FEAR FOR MY OWN JOY;	138	LOVE'S PROGRESS	23
I FEAR MYSELF IN THE FIELD,	138	LOVE'S PROGRESS	24
GOD COULD BELIEVE: I AM HERE TO FEAR.	144	ELEGY (1)	12
I LEARNED NOT TO FEAR INFINITY.	200	THE FAR FIELD	50
A FALLEN MAN, I CLIMB OUT OF MY FEAR.	239	IN A DARK TIME	22
--IN FEAR AND TREMBLING, DEAR KIERKEGAARD.	272	DUET	17
FEARFUL			
ONCE I READ NOTHING THROUGH A FEARFUL NIGHT,	133	THE PURE FURY	3
TO WOO THE FEARFUL SMALL;	148	THE SMALL	20
FEARFUL OF HIGH PLACES, IN LOVE WITH HORSES;	162	I'M HERE	28
A FEARFUL IGNORANCE.	171	WHAT TELL BONES	7
YET IF WE WAIT, UNAFRAID, BEYOND THE FEARFUL INSTANT,	221	THE ABYSS	57
FEARLESS			
FEARLESS AND BOLD, HE DID HIS FELLOWS IN,	28	THE FAVORITE	5
MOVING, ELUSIVE AS FISH, FEARLESS,	199	THE FAR FIELD	31
FEARS			
THE STETHOSCOPE TELLS WHAT EVERYONE FEARS:	23	ACADEMIC	1
--AND AN ATTIC OF HORRORS, A CLOSET OF FEARS.	32	SALE	4
FEATHER			
THE FEATHER OF THE MILKWEED FLUTTERS DOWN.	12	SLOW SEASON	12
HAND ME A FEATHER, I'LL FAN YOU WARM,	60	THE LONG ALLEY	45

		PAGE	TITLE	LINE
FEATHER (CONTINUED)				
ONE FEATHER IS A BIRD,		128	THE VOICE	1
FEATHERINESS				
HER PURE-WHITE FEATHERINESS		213	THE HAPPY THREE	23
FEATHERS				
CAN FEATHERS EAT ME? THERE'S NO CLUE IN THE SILT.		60	THE LONG ALLEY	32
THE ANIMAL'S CANDID GAZE, A SHADE LESS THAN FEATHERS,				
LIGHT'S BROKEN		98	O, THOU OPENING	22
FEATHERS OF THE LONG SWELL, BURNISHED, ALMOST OILY--		197	THE LONG WATERS	51
NOT EVEN FEATHERS FROM SO FAR AWAY.		232	THE THING	17
WINGS WITHOUT FEATHERS CREAKING IN THE SUN,		243	THE MOTION	19
FEATHERY				
OVER THE THIN, FEATHERY RIPPLES BREAKING LIGHTLY AGAINST				
THE IRREGULAR SHORELINE--		197	THE LONG WATERS	50
FEATS				
I SEE THE TRAFFIC DOING MIRACULOUS FEATS.		27	CLAIRVOY WIDOW	6
FEATURE				
DOUBLE FEATURE		47	DOUBLE FEATURE	T
FEBRILE				
WANES TO THE FEBRILE SMOLDERING OF SLEEP;		17	UNEXTINGUISHED	6
FED				
WHO FED AND TENDED THE INFIRM, THE MAD, THE EPILEPTIC,		223	ELEGY (2)	9
FEED				
THEY FEED THE SENSE, DENY THE SOUL,		25	VERSE W ALLUSNS	9
I'LL FEED THE GHOST ALONE.		85	PRAISE TO END!	11
FISH FEED ON FISH, ACCORDING TO THEIR NEED:		155	THE DYING MAN	66
WHEN THE LADIES' GUILD PUTS ON A FEED,		267	SAGINAW SONG	3
FEEDING				
STILL HOLDING AND FEEDING THE STEM OF THE CONTAINED FLOWER.		67	SHAPE OF FIRE	95
FEEL				
YOU FEEL DISASTER CLIMB THE VEIN.		4	FEUD	8
AND LONGED TO FEEL THE IMPACT OF DEFEAT.		28	THE FAVORITE	14
FULL ON MY NECK I FEEL		34	NIGHT JOURNEY	12
IN MY VEINS, IN MY BONES I FEEL IT,--		37	CUTTINGS (LATE)	6
THAT'S THE WAY IT WOULD FEEL.		55	THE LOST SON	57
I FEEL THE SLIME OF A WET NEST.		55	THE LOST SON	68
I COULD FEEL THE MARE'S NOSE.		63	THE LONG ALLEY	32
I FEEL MORE THAN A FISH.		87	PRAISE TO END!	77
I FEEL MY FATE IN WHAT I CANNOT FEAR.		108	THE WAKING (2)	2
HAD THE RED-HOT SPOTS WHERE YOU FEEL A		111	SQUEEZE-BOX	20
I FEEL HER PRESENCE IN THE COMMON DAY,		129	SHE	13
I FEEL WE'RE BREATHING WITH THE DEAD;		136	THE SENSUALISTS	5
I FEEL MY FLESH DIVIDE.		148	THE SMALL	14
A THING WE FEEL AT EVENING, AND BY DOORS,		162	I'M HERE	53
THEY FEEL NEITHER THE TEARING IRON		169	FOURTH MEDITATN	53
I FEEL A WEIGHTLESS CHANGE, A MOVING FORWARD		200	THE FAR FIELD	58
WHO'D LOOK WHEN HE COULD FEEL?		212	LIGHT LISTENED	5
I FEEL THE AUTUMN FAIL--ALL THAT SLOW FIRE		242	THE SEQUEL	31
WHENEVER I FEEL IT COMING ON		269	GOB MUSIC	10
FEELING				
WE THINK BY FEELING. WHAT IS THERE TO KNOW?		108	THE WAKING (2)	4
TO FIND OUT HOW THE CEILING'S FEELING.		178	THE CEILING	6
FEELING, I STILL DELIGHT IN MY LAST FALL.		197	THE LONG WATERS	32
NOT FEELING THE COARSE SHALE		265	HARSH COUNTRY	7
FEELS				
MY NOSE FEELS FOR MY TOE;		130	THE OTHER	11
FEET				
FEET, BEAR THE THIN BONES OVER		7	ORDERS FOR DAY	8
OUR FEET ARE SOMETIMES LEVEL WITH THE SKY,		13	PRAISE PRAIRIE	6
THE GREAT FEET BREAK THE RIDGES OF THE SAND,		15	THE HERON	6
CUT STEMS STRUGGLING TO PUT DOWN FEET,		37	CUTTINGS (LATE)	2
OR STAND ALL NIGHT WATERING ROSES, HIS FEET BLUE IN RUBBER				
BOOTS.		42	OLD FLORIST	10
MY FEET CRACKLING SPLINTERS OF GLASS AND DRIED PUTTY,		43	CHILD ON GRNHSE	2
BITE WITH HIS FEET;		71	WHERE KNOCK IS	2
HER FEET SAID YES.		76	I NEED, I NEED	61
FEET RUN OVER THE SIMPLE STONES,		93	I CRY, LOVE!	36
MY FEET REMEMBERED THE EARTH,		104	OLD LADY'S WRDS	44
WE PLAYED A MEASURE WITH COMMINGLED FEET:		106	SIR JOHN DAVIES	31
IT WAS STAND ON YOUR FEET AS LONG AS YOU'RE ABLE,		112	SQUEEZE-BOX	35
THAT START FROM MY OWN FEET.		138	THE SURLY ONE	8
ON FEET THAT MAKE NO SOUND		148	THE SMALL	17
JUMPING UP AND DOWN ON THEIR HIND FEET,		163	I'M HERE	68

	PAGE	TITLE	LINE
FEET (CONTINUED)			
AND THE IVY ADVANCE WITH ITS WHITE LIZARD FEET--	194	JOURNY INTERIOR	49
AN OLD MAN WITH HIS FEET BEFORE THE FIRE,	201	THE FAR FIELD	85
AND LISTEN TO MY OWN FEET.	215	HIS FOREBODING	18
BUT WHEN I SLOWED MY FEET,	225	THE CHUMS	6
HIS FEET LIKE SMALL LEAVES,	227	MEADOW MOUSE	8
FROM THE CUR AT MY FEET.	236	SONG (2)	8
AND WHEN I WALKED, MY FEET SEEMED DEEP IN SAND.	247	I WAITED	16
THE WIND BLOWS UP YOUR FEET,	267	SAGINAW SONG	2
AND MOSSY FILTHY FEET;	267	SAGINAW SONG	10
FELICITY			
FELICITY I CANNOT HOARD.	88	PRAISE TO END!	83
HOW COMPREHENSIVE THAT FELICITY!	188	THE LONGING	26
FELL			
THE BARGAINS FELL TO BIDDERS, ONE BY ONE.	21	THE AUCTION	10
MY SPIRITS ROSE EACH TIME THE HAMMER FELL,	21	THE AUCTION	13
THE FULL RAIN FELL STRAIGHT DOWN,	50	THE CYCLE	14
FELL DREAMILY DOWN?	56	THE LOST SON	91
A FINE RAIN FELL	62	FIELD OF LIGHT	15
THAT WAS BEFORE. I FELL! I FELL!	73	WHERE KNOCK IS	68
THAT WAS BEFORE. I FELL! I FELL!	73	WHERE KNOCK IS	68
AND FELL IN THE STREAM STILL CLUTCHING A PLANK,	117	LADY AND BEAR	27
I STAYED, AND LIGHT FELL	123	WORDS FOR WIND	21
THEN EACH FELL BACK, LIMP AS A SACK,	136	THE SENSUALISTS	25
THEY SAW THAT I FELL MORE THAN TWICE.	225	THE CHUMS	10
ROSE UP AND FELL LIKE AN ERRATIC WIND.	237	THE TRANCED	10
FELLOWS			
FEARLESS AND BOLD, HE DID HIS FELLOWS IN,	28	THE FAVORITE	5
FELLOWSHIP			
HONORED, ON MY RETURN, BY THE ANCIENT FELLOWSHIP OF ROTTEN STEMS.	89	UNFOLD! UNFOLD!	26
FELT			
AND AFTERWARDS I ALWAYS FELT MEAN, JOGGING BACK OVER THE LOGGING ROAD,	40	MOSS-GATHERING	9
STARING AT A TREE, I FELT THE PULSE OF A STONE.	101	THE VISITANT	22
I FELT MY SLOW BLOOD WARM.	150	SNAKE	9
FEMALE			
WHEN OUR SPAYED FEMALE CAT YAWNS AND STRETCHES OUT IN THE SUNSHINE--	234	ALL MORNING	23
FENCE			
THE KITTY-CAT BIRD, HE SAT ON A FENCE.	177	KITTY-CAT BIRD	1
FENCEPOST			
THE BOBOLINK SKIRRING FROM A BROKEN FENCEPOST,	204	THE ROSE	65
FERN			
WAITING LIKE A FERN, MAKING A SPINY SHADOW.	102	ELEGY FOR JANE	15
AND COLLOPED ROUND WITH FERN.	145	THE BEAST	9
WITH THE SAXIFRAGE AND FERN	146	THE SONG	12
WHAT RUSTLES IN THE FERN?	148	THE SMALL	13
FERNS			
OR RISING OUT OF FERNS NOT FAR FROM WATER,	43	CARNATIONS	4
THE FERNS HAD THEIR WAYS, AND THE PULSING LIZARDS,	63	FIELD OF LIGHT	41
AMONG THE UNWRINKLING FERNS	80	GIVE WAY, GATES	41
MOUSE, MOUSE, COME OUT OF THE FERNS,	92	I CRY, LOVE!	22
SOMEWHERE, AMONG THE FERNS AND BIRDS,	103	OLD LADY'S WRDS	12
A FACE FLOATS IN THE FERNS. DO MAIMED GODS WALK?	165	HER BECOMING	18
MAY THEY SLEEP IN ROBES OF GREEN, AMONG THE ANCIENT FERNS;	169	FOURTH MEDITATN	58
FERN-SHAPES			
OR YANKING TOUGH FERN-SHAPES,	39	WEED PULLER	7
FERNY			
BELOW, ON THE FERNY GROUND,	125	WORDS FOR WIND	72
FERVENT			
I'M DYING PIECEMEAL, FERVENT IN DECAY;	149	IN LATE SUMMER	15
FETOR			
ME DOWN IN THAT FETOR OF WEEDS,	39	WEED PULLER	14
FETOR OF COCKROACHES, DEAD FISH, PETROLEUM,	187	THE LONGING	3
FEUD			
FEUD	4	FEUD	T
INFLAME WITH HATE. THIS ANCIENT FEUD	4	FEUD	18
THE FEUD WE KEPT WITH SPACE COMES TO AN END.	13	PRAISE PRAIRIE	12
FEVER			
CHILL DEPTHS OF THE SPIRIT ARE FLUSHED TO A FEVER,	5	PROGNOSIS	15
FEW			
A FEW WHITE CLOUDS ALL RUSHING EASTWARD,	43	CHILD ON GRNHSE	5

	PAGE	TITLE	LINE
FEW (CONTINUED)			
LIFTING A FEW TWIGS AND FLOATING LEAVES,	93	I CRY, LOVE!	48
THE MOVEMENT IS FORWARD, AFTER A FEW WAVERS,	158	FIRST MEDITATN	27
ONLY A FEW BUBBLES LOOSENING FROM THE ILL-MATCHED TENTACLES,	159	FIRST MEDITATN	64
IS THERE A WISDOM IN OBJECTS? FEW OBJECTS PRAISE THE LORD.	166	HER BECOMING	38
IN THE COUNTRY OF FEW LAKES, IN THE TALL BUFFALO GRASS AT THE BASE OF THE CLAY BUTTES.	189	THE LONGING	53
HE HEAPS FEW HONORS ON A LIVING HEAD;	264	THREE EPIGRAMS	3
FIDDLE			
I DO NOT HAVE A FIDDLE SO	269	GOB MUSIC	1
FIDDLED			
HAVE TOSSED MY HEART AND FIDDLED THROUGH MY BRAIN.	105	SIR JOHN DAVIES	22
FIELD			
WALKING THIS FIELD I REMEMBER	6	THE PREMONITION	1
BUT STILL THE ROAD AND DUSTY FIELD KEPT DRY.	6	INTERLUDE	8
THE RIVER OVERFLOWS THE LEVEL FIELD.	11	LIGHT BRIGHTER	8
SOON FIELD AND WOOD WILL WEAR AN APRIL LOOK,	11	LIGHT BRIGHTER	13
THE HAZE OF HARVEST DRIFTS ALONG THE FIELD	12	SLOW SEASON	3
A FIELD OF BARLEY SPREAD BENEATH THE SUN.	13	PRAISE PRAIRIE	4
MORE HEADY THAN A FIELD AT DUSK	14	COMING OF COLD	3
UPON THE FIELD THE SCENT IS DRY:	14	COMING OF COLD	13
HAS LEFT ITS RAVAGE ON THE FIELD.	14	COMING OF COLD	25
AN OPEN FIELD;	51	THE WAKING (1)	2
THE SHEEP STREWN ON A FIELD,	54	THE LOST SON	37
THE LIGHT MOVED SLOWLY OVER THE FROZEN FIELD,	58	THE LOST SON	155
LIGHT TRAVELED OVER THE WIDE FIELD;	58	THE LOST SON	159
A FIELD OF LIGHT	62	FIELD OF LIGHT	T
IN THE DEEP GRASS AT THE EDGE OF FIELD,	62	FIELD OF LIGHT	25
THE FAT LARK SANG IN THE FIELD;	63	FIELD OF LIGHT	38
SHALE LOOSENS. MARL REACHES INTO THE FIELD. SMALL BIRDS PASS OVER WATER.	64	SHAPE OF FIRE	11
THE FIELD IS NO LONGER SIMPLE:	89	UNFOLD! UNFOLD!	7
A HOUSE FOR WISDOM; A FIELD FOR REVELATION.	90	UNFOLD! UNFOLD!	53
I CAN LEAP, TRUE TO THE FIELD,	98	O, THOU OPENING	42
SHE TURNED THE FIELD INTO A GLITTERING SEA;	120	THE DREAM	27
A FIELD RECEDES IN SLEEP.	122	ALL EARTH, AIR	21
THE FIELD IS MINE! IS MINE!	122	ALL EARTH, AIR	25
A FIELD BREAKS LIKE THE SEA;	124	WORDS FOR WIND	37
I FEAR MYSELF IN THE FIELD,	138	LOVE'S PROGRESS	24
EACH CUSHION FOUND ITSELF A FIELD OF PINS,	143	SHIMMER OF EVIL	11
AT THE EDGE OF A RAW FIELD.	146	THE SONG	13
O SWEET FIELD FAR AHEAD, I HEAR YOUR BIRDS,	156	THE DYING MAN	88
THE WEEDS HISS AT THE EDGE OF THE FIELD,	157	FIRST MEDITATN	2
MOVES OVER THE FIELD.	160	FIRST MEDITATN	96
IN THE RAIN, SLACKENING ON A SUMMER FIELD;	165	HER BECOMING	8
IN A FIELD, IN THE ACTUAL AIR,	166	HER BECOMING	45
ACROSS A FIELD, INTO A LITTLE WOOD.	166	HER BECOMING	51
I DARE CARESS THE STONES, THE FIELD MY FRIEND;	167	HER BECOMING	94
AT THE EDGE OF THE FIELD WAITING FOR THE PURE MOMENT;	168	FOURTH MEDITATN	3
THE CRICKET-VOICE DEEP IN THE MIDNIGHT FIELD.	196	THE LONG WATERS	27
THE FAR FIELD	199	THE FAR FIELD	T
THE FAR FIELD, THE WINDY CLIFFS OF FOREVER,	200	THE FAR FIELD	51
I ROSE, A HEAVY BULK, ABOVE THE FIELD.	247	I WAITED	5
FIELD-MOUSE			
HAUNT OF THE CAT-BIRD, NESTING-PLACE OF THE FIELD-MOUSE,	199	THE FAR FIELD	15
FIELDS			
THE NAKED FIELDS THE CLOUD'S IMMACULATE FOLDS	5	TO MY SISTER	4
THE FIELDS STRETCH OUT IN LONG, UNBROKEN ROWS.	13	PRAISE PRAIRIE	9
THE FIELDS ARE HARSH AND BARE, THE ROCKS	15	COMING OF COLD	45
THE GREEN COMES UP FOREVER IN THE FIELDS OF OUR COUNTRY."	28	CLAIRVOY WIDOW	26
WHOLE FIELDS LOVELY AND INVIOLATE,--	39	WEED PULLER	13
IN THE LONG FIELDS, I LEAVE MY FATHER'S EYE;	173	WHAT TELL BONES	86
THE UNSINGING FIELDS WHERE NO LUNGS BREATHE,	196	THE LONG WATERS	11
IN MY MIND'S EYE I SEE THOSE FIELDS OF GLASS,	225	OTTO	34
UPROSE, UPROSE, THE STONY FIELDS UPROSE,	248	THE TREE, BIRD	1
FIELD'S			
HERE FROM THE FIELD'S EDGE WE SURVEY	33	HIGHWAY: MICH	1
AT THE FIELD'S END, IN THE CORNER MISSED BY THE MOWER,	199	THE FAR FIELD	13
SWAYS ME AWAKE. WHAT HO, AND THE FIELD'S MY FRIEND,	260	THE CHANGELING	14
FIEND'S			
THE FIEND'S FAR AWAY. LORD, WHAT DO YOU REQUIRE?	59	THE LONG ALLEY	21
FIFTY			
FIFTY SUMMERS IN MOTION AT ONCE,	38	FORCING HOUSE	10

		PAGE	TITLE	LINE
FIGURE				
	THE GHOSTLY FIGURE SUCKED ITS BREATH,	136	THE SENSUALISTS	17
	THE FIGURE AT MY BACK IS NOT MY FRIEND;	154	THE DYING MAN	38
	OR HE SITS STILL, A SOLID FIGURE WHEN	250	THE RIGHT THING	13
	I SAW A FIGURE IN A CLOUD,	268	SAGINAW SONG	56
FIGURED				
	MUTTONY TEARS FALLING ON FIGURED LINOLEUM,	48	LAST WORDS	3
FIGURES				
	HE LOOPS IN CRAZY FIGURES HALF THE NIGHT	16	THE BAT	5
	WHEN FIGURES OUT OF OBSCURE SHADOW RAVE,	154	THE DYING MAN	46
	I CLOSED MY EYES, AND SAW SMALL FIGURES DANCING,	163	I'M HERE	65
	I SEE THEM AS FIGURES WALKING IN A GREENY GARDEN,	170	FOURTH MEDITAT'N	63
FILLED				
	THE GREAT ELM FILLED WITH BIRDS.	63	FIELD OF LIGHT	36
	HOW THEY FILLED THE ORIOLE'S ELM, A TWITTERING RESTLESS CLOUD, ALL ONE MORNING,	199	THE FAR FIELD	28
FILLS				
	TO KNOW THAT LIGHT FALLS AND FILLS, OFTEN WITHOUT OUR KNOWING,	67	SHAPE OF FIRE	92
	AS AN OPAQUE VASE FILLS TO THE BRIM FROM A QUICK POURING,	67	SHAPE OF FIRE	93
	FILLS AND TREMBLES AT THE EDGE YET DOES NOT FLOW OVER,	67	SHAPE OF FIRE	94
FILM				
	DROPPING A FINE FILM ON NAILS AND DELICATE EYEBROWS,	46	DOLOR	12
FILMY				
	THEIR FILMY FRINGES OF GREEN, THEIR HARSH	205	THE ROSE	90
FILTH				
	THERE'S NO FILTH ON A PLATEAU OF CINDERS.	59	THE LONG ALLEY	15
FILTHY				
	AND MOSSY FILTHY FEET;	267	SAGINAW SONG	10
FINAL				
	WHAT FOOTIE DOES IS FINAL.	86	PRAISE TO END!	34
	WHAT FOOTIE DOES IS FINAL.	86	PRAISE TO END!	38
	WHAT FOOTIE WILL DO WILL BE FINAL.	86	PRAISE TO END!	42
	IS THIS MY FINAL FACE?	130	THE OTHER	8
	I AM THAT FINAL THING,	153	THE DYING MAN	14
	AND FINAL.	173	WHAT TELL BONES	101
	HE IS THE END OF THINGS, THE FINAL MAN.	201	THE FAR FIELD	93
	SHE SANG A FINAL SONG;	212	LIGHT LISTENED	23
	THE EDGE OF ALL THE LAND, THE FINAL SEA?	221	THE ABYSS	63
	UNTIL THEY REACH THIS FINAL CERTITUDE,	243	THE MOTION	16
	THE DIRE DIMENSION OF A FINAL THING.	248	THE TREE, BIRD	23
FINALLY				
	FINALLY VEERING, WEARING THEMSELVES OUT, MERELY	41	BIG WIND	30
	FOR SHE FINALLY LEFT TOWN ON THE BAY CITY FREIGHT	112	SQUEEZE-BOX	40
FINCHES				
	AND THE FINCHES PITCH THROUGH THE AIR, TWITTERING;	152	THE SISKINS	7
	LIGHTER THAN FINCHES,	200	THE FAR FIELD	35
	THE MORNING BIRDS GONE, THE TWITTERING FINCHES,	202	THE ROSE	14
	WITH TOWHEES, FINCHES, CHICKADEES, CALIFORNIA QUAIL, WOOD DOVES,	235	ALL MORNING	40
FIND				
	YOU WILL FIND NO COMFORT HERE,	54	THE LOST SON	32
	TO FIND A NOSE,	64	SHAPE OF FIRE	25
	WHEN YOU FIND THE WIND	89	UNFOLD! UNFOLD!	16
	EVEN A FATHER COULD NOT FIND HER:	102	ELEGY FOR JANE	11
	I FIND MYSELF PERPLEXED. WHAT IS DESIRE?--	105	SIR JOHN DAVIES	26
	WE WOKE TO FIND THE MOONLIGHT ON OUR TOES.	106	SIR JOHN DAVIES	64
	HE COULDN'T FIND A PROPER WIFE;	115	THE SERPENT	6
	I FIND HER EVERY PLACE;	130	THE OTHER	9
	DRY BONES! DRY BONES! I FIND MY LOVING HEART,	135	THE RENEWAL	19
	I FIND THAT LOVE, AND I AM EVERYWHERE.	135	THE RENEWAL	24
	TO FIND OUT HOW THE CEILING'S FEELING.	178	THE CEILING	6
	YOU'LL FIND I'M EITHER RIGHT OR WRONG	181	MONOTONY SONG	23
	I LOSE AND FIND MYSELF IN THE LONG WATER;	198	THE LONG WATERS	76
	ONLY TO FIND, WITH THEIR LONG TERRIBLE EYES	232	THE THING	9
	A MAN GOES FAR TO FIND OUT WHAT HE IS--	239	IN A DARK TIME	16
	TO FIND THAT, LIKE A FISH,	258	SONG (3)	10
FINDS				
	UNTIL HE FINDS THE THING HE ALMOST WAS	133	THE PURE FURY	19
	THE ETERNAL SEEKS, AND FINDS, THE TEMPORAL,	244	INFIRMITY	21
FINE				
	WINDS BRING A FINE AND BITTER SNOW.	15	COMING OF COLD	52
	THE SUN WARMING THE FINE LOAM,	42	TRANSPLANTING	14

	PAGE	TITLE	LINE
FINE (CONTINUED)			
TWINED LIKE FINE HAIR,	43	FLOWER DUMP	8
DROPPING A FINE FILM ON NAILS AND DELICATE EYEBROWS,	46	DOLOR	12
THAT FINE FUMING STINK OF PARTICULAR KETTLES,	48	LAST WORDS	2
THE FINE RAIN COILED IN A CLOUD	50	THE CYCLE	7
A FINE HAZE MOVED OFF THE LEAVES;	57	THE LOST SON	144
A FINE RAIN FELL	62	FIELD OF LIGHT	15
I COULD ROLL IN THE DUST OF A FINE RAGE.	104	OLD LADY'S WRDS	50
THE FINE SOOT SIFTING THROUGH MY SOUTH WINDOWS.	104	OLD LADY'S WRDS	58
PRIDE IN FINE LINEAMENTS PRECEDES A FALL;	131	SENTENTIOUS MAN	5
THE VINES GRAYING TO A FINE POWDER.	159	FIRST MEDITATN	81
A FINE DRY SNOW TICKING THE WINDSHIELD,	199	THE FAR FIELD	5
DROPPING A FINE YELLOW SILT WHERE THE SUN STAYS;	200	THE FAR FIELD	68
OF THE FINE SHAPELY THOUGHT	211	SONG (1)	2
WITH ITS LIMESTONE CRUMBLING INTO FINE GREYISH DUST,	226	THE LIZARD	28
A FINE FUME OF RAIN DRIVING IN FROM THE SEA,	230	THE STORM	13
OUR EYES FIXED ON A POINT OF LIGHT SO FINE	237	THE TRANCED	16
YET FINE AS MAIDENHAIR,	271	THE REPLY	12
FINE-HONED			
OF YOUR FINE-HONED LAY	271	THE REPLY	3
FINELY			
NOTES FINELY DRAWN.	213	THE HAPPY THREE	32
FINER			
THE HAND-PAINTED WALL-PAPER, FINER THAN SKIN,	32	SALE	17
FINER THAN FLOUR, ALIVE, MORE DANGEROUS THAN SILICA,	46	DOLOR	10
FINES			
THEY TOY WITH DEATH AND TRAFFIC FINES.	33	HIGHWAY: MICH	10
FINGER			
PUT YOUR FINGER IN YOUR FACE,	75	I NEED, I NEED	25
BRING ME A FINGER. THIS DIRT'S LONESOME FOR GRASS.	79	GIVE WAY, GATES	7
ITS SHADOWS LOOSE, A WATERY FINGER;	101	LIGHT BREATHER	10
AT THE STREAM'S EDGE, TRAILING A VAGUE FINGER;	162	I'M HERE	26
I WAS A FINGER POINTING AT THE MOON,	248	THE TREE, BIRD	5
FINGERING			
FINGERING A SHELL,	200	THE FAR FIELD	40
FINGERS			
HIS CLUMSY FINGERS BRUISE	7	ORDERS FOR DAY	6
THEY SLIP BETWEEN THE FINGERS OF MY SIGHT.	8	THE SIGNALS	7
HIS FINGERS MAKE A HAT ABOUT HIS HEAD.	16	THE BAT	3
WHO WANT NO MORE THAN FINGERS SEIZE,	25	VERSE W ALLUSNS	3
SOFT LUMINESCENT FINGERS,	39	ORCHIDS	15
TO LOOSEN WITH ALL TEN FINGERS HELD WIDE AND LIMBER	40	MOSS-GATHERING	1
LIFTING THE YOUNG PLANTS WITH TWO FINGERS,	42	TRANSPLANTING	3
FINGER-TIPS			
A SURGEON GUIDES A SCALPEL WITH THUMB AND FINGER-TIPS.	28	CLAIRVOY WIDOW	20
FINITE			
ALL FINITE THINGS REVEAL INFINITUDE:	201	THE FAR FIELD	94
FINN			
AND NOBODY SLIPPED ME A MICKEY FINN,	112	SQUEEZE-BOX	31
FIR			
THE FIRST SNOW OF THE YEAR IN THE DARK FIR.	197	THE LONG WATERS	31
BY SMALL STREAMS RUNNING DOWN UNDER FALLEN FIR TREES.	197	THE LONG WATERS	48
AND THE EAGLES SAIL LOW OVER THE FIR TREES,	202	THE ROSE	6
HAD SLAUGHTERED GAME, AND CUT YOUNG FIR TREES DOWN.	224	OTTO	21
FIRE			
CLOUDS GLOW LIKE COALS JUST FRESH FROM FIRE, A FLARE	17	UNEXTINGUISHED	1
THE FIRE OF HEAVEN DIES; A FIRE UNSEEN	17	UNEXTINGUISHED	5
THE FIRE OF HEAVEN DIES; A FIRE UNSEEN	17	UNEXTINGUISHED	5
MY VEINS ARE RUNNING NOWHERE. DO THE BONES CAST OUT THEIR FIRE?	56	THE LOST SON	101
I'LL TAKE THE FIRE.	61	THE LONG ALLEY	89
THE SHAPE OF THE FIRE	64	SHAPE OF FIRE	T
IN THE FIRE.	72	WHERE KNOCK IS	34
DEW ATE THE FIRE.	76	I NEED, I NEED	66
I KNOW ANOTHER FIRE.	76	I NEED, I NEED	67
--LOOK FOR THE WHITE FIRE.	89	UNFOLD! UNFOLD!	17
THAT WOMAN WOULD SET SODDEN STRAW ON FIRE.	105	SIR JOHN DAVIES	28
MY DREAM DIVIDED ON A POINT OF FIRE;	119	THE DREAM	5
A SHAPE OF CHANGE, ENCIRCLED BY ITS FIRE.	119	THE DREAM	10
A CHILD STARES PAST A FIRE	130	THE OTHER	19
A FIRE LEAPS ON ITSELF: I KNOW THAT FLAME.	131	SENTENTIOUS MAN	8
SHE CHANGED ME ICE TO FIRE, AND FIRE TO ICE.	131	SENTENTIOUS MAN	12
SHE CHANGED ME ICE TO FIRE, AND FIRE TO ICE.	131	SENTENTIOUS MAN	12

	PAGE	TITLE	LINE
FIRE (CONTINUED)			
IN THE DEEP CENTER OF THE VOICE AND FIRE.	132	SENTENTIOUS MAN	34
FOR I WOULD DROWN IN FIRE.	138	LOVE'S PROGRESS	25
COLD EVIL TWINKLED TIGHTER THAN A STRING; A FIRE	143	SHIMMER OF EVIL	8
ROMPING AROUND A FIRE,	163	I'M HERE	67
ONE FOLLOWS FIRE. ONE DOES.	167	HER BECOMING	80
MY FACE ON FIRE, CLOSE TO THE POINTS OF A STAR,	172	WHAT TELL BONES	55
THE SALT-SOAKED WOOD OF A FIRE CRACKLES;	190	AT OYSTER RIVER	21
IN A FLICKER OF FIRE BRISKED BY A DUSTY WIND.	194	JOURNY INTERIOR	61
I RETURN WHERE FIRE HAS BEEN,	196	THE LONG WATERS	13
AS A FIRE, SEEMINGLY LONG DEAD, FLARES UP FROM A DOWNDRAFT OF AIR IN A CHIMNEY,	198	THE LONG WATERS	63
THE WIND FANNING THE ASH OF A LOW FIRE.	201	THE FAR FIELD	79
AN OLD MAN WITH HIS FEET BEFORE THE FIRE,	201	THE FAR FIELD	85
WAKES ALL THE WAVES, ALL THEIR LOOSE WANDERING FIRE.	201	THE FAR FIELD	88
THE SUN A BALL OF FIRE COMING DOWN OVER THE WATER,	202	THE ROSE	16
I, WHO RENEW THE FIRE,	216	HER WRATH	3
THE RUSH OF SMELLS STRIKES LIKE A COLD FIRE, THE THROAT FREEZES,	220	THE ABYSS	47
STRIKE LIKE A FIRE,	221	THE ABYSS	54
THE FIRE SUBSIDES INTO RINGS OF WATER,	221	THE ABYSS	59
AND THE FIRE DANCES	221	THE ABYSS	72
WE COUNTED SEVERAL FLAMES IN ONE SMALL FIRE.	237	THE TRANCED	1
AT ODDS WITH CIRCUMSTANCE? THE DAY'S ON FIRE!	239	IN A DARK TIME	8
I STAND BY A LOW FIRE	240	IN EVEING AIR	19
I FEEL THE AUTUMN FAIL--ALL THAT SLOW FIRE	242	THE SEQUEL	31
I MOVE BEYOND THE REACH OF WIND AND FIRE.	244	INFIRMITY	24
PAIN WANDERS THROUGH MY BONES LIKE A LOST FIRE;	246	THE MARROW	11
FIREMAN			
WHERE THE FIREMAN PULLED OUT ROSES,	57	THE LOST SON	132
FIRE-PIT			
SWINGING BY THE FIRE-PIT,	57	THE LOST SON	131
FIRES			
I SEE A BANKER'S MANSION WITH TWENTY WOOD-GRATE FIRES,	27	CLAIRVOY WIDOW	13
ALL WATERS WAVER, AND ALL FIRES FAIL.	242	THE SEQUEL	26
FIRMNESS			
A THREAD-LIKE FIRMNESS.	226	THE LIZARD	12
FIRST			
WE WAITED FOR THE FIRST RAIN IN THE EAVES.	6	INTERLUDE	4
AND THEIR SNUFF-LADEN BREATH BLOWING LIGHTLY OVER ME IN MY FIRST SLEEP.	44	FRAU BAUMAN	35
AND MY INTENT STRETCHED OVER THE BUDS AT THEIR FIRST TREMBLING.	66	SHAPE OF FIRE	69
STILL AS A CHILD IN ITS FIRST LONELINESS;	67	SHAPE OF FIRE	85
SUCH OWLY PLEASURES! FISH COME FIRST, SWEET BIRD.	87	PRAISE TO END!	71
AT FIRST THE VISIBLE OBSCURES:	90	UNFOLD! UNFOLD!	55
AND THE FIRST DUST OF SPRING LISTING OVER BACKLOTS,--	92	I CRY, LOVE!	27
I WOKE IN THE FIRST OF MORNING,	101	THE VISITANT	21
WHEN THE PURE FURY FIRST RAGED IN HIS HEAD	133	THE PURE FURY	20
I LOOK AT THE FIRST STAR:	148	THE SMALL	4
FIRST MEDITATION	157	FIRST MEDITATN	T
THE GLITTER OF WET IN THE FIRST OF MORNING?	161	I'M HERE	3
SINGS IN THE FIRST	163	I'M HERE	61
IT'S NOT MY FIRST DYING.	164	I'M HERE	95
MAY THEIR EYES GLEAM WITH THE FIRST DAWN;	169	FOURTH MEDITATN	59
WHO SPOKE FIRST IN THE COARSE SHORT-HAND OF THE SUBLIMINAL DEPTHS,	170	FOURTH MEDITATN	71
THE FIRST AND LAST OF ALL THINGS.	170	FOURTH MEDITATN	86
COME THE FIRST TIDE-RIPPLES, MOVING, ALMOST WITHOUT SOUND, TOWARD ME,	190	AT OYSTER RIVER	2
IN THIS FIRST HEAVEN OF KNOWING,	191	AT OYSTER RIVER	37
OF THE FIRST TREMBLING OF A MICHIGAN BROOK IN APRIL,	191	AT OYSTER RIVER	42
IN THE FIRST OF THE MOON,	192	AT OYSTER RIVER	68
THE FIRST SNOW OF THE YEAR IN THE DARK FIR.	197	THE LONG WATERS	31
AT FIRST A SWIFT RIPPLING BETWEEN ROCKS,	200	THE FAR FIELD	63
THE FIRST RAIN GATHERED?	202	THE ROSE	30
BEING, NOT DOING, IS MY FIRST JOY.	222	THE ABYSS	101
AT THE FIRST SCRATCH OF THE MATCH	226	THE LIZARD	14
THEN THE FIRST BIRD	232	THE THING	13
FIR-TREE			
THE WAY BLOCKED AT LAST BY A FALLEN FIR-TREE,	193	JOURNY INTERIOR	15

	PAGE	TITLE	LINE
FIR-TREES			
THEY SIT, THREE OR FOUR, HIGH IN THE FIR-TREES BACK OF THE HOUSE,	234	ALL MORNING	6
FISH			
ENCOMPASSING FISH, FLESH, AND FOWL.	23	AMOROUS LADY	10
SLIPPERY AS FISH,	37	CUTTINGS (LATE)	10
NIBBLE AGAIN, FISH NERVES.	55	THE LOST SON	70
A FISH FLOATS BELLY UPWARD,	59	THE LONG ALLEY	2
DO WE ROUT THE FISH?	60	THE LONG ALLEY	59
THIS WIND BRINGS MANY FISH;	61	THE LONG ALLEY	86
THE SILVER FISH RAN IN AND OUT OF MY SPECIAL BINDINGS;	65	SHAPE OF FIRE	35
MY FATHER IS A FISH.	72	WHERE KNOCK IS	22
FISH ME OUT.	72	WHERE KNOCK IS	47
I WAS SAD FOR A FISH.	73	WHERE KNOCK IS	58
ROCKING WITH SMALL FISH,	84	O LULL ME, LULL	34
SUCH OWLY PLEASURES! FISH COME FIRST, SWEET BIRD.	87	PRAISE TO END!	71
I FEEL MORE THAN A FISH.	87	PRAISE TO END!	77
WHEREFORE, O BIRDS AND SMALL FISH, SURROUND ME.	88	PRAISE TO END!	97
TELL ME, BODY WITHOUT SKIN, DOES A FISH SWEAT?	89	UNFOLD! UNFOLD!	2
A SECRET TO JERK FROM THE LIPS OF A FISH.	92	I CRY, LOVE!	7
A FISH JUMPS, SHAKING OUT FLAKES OF MOONLIGHT.	93	I CRY, LOVE!	45
SLOW, SLOW AS A FISH SHE CAME,	100	THE VISITANT	10
SLOW AS A FISH COMING FORWARD,	100	THE VISITANT	11
YES, A BEAR HAS TO FISH WITH HIS PAW, PAW, PAW.	117	LADY AND BEAR	19
A BEAR HAS TO FISH WITH HIS PAW."	117	LADY AND BEAR	20
YOU CAN FISH OUT A FISH, OUT A FISH, OUT A FISH,	117	LADY AND BEAR	22
YOU CAN FISH OUT A FISH, OUT A FISH, OUT A FISH,	117	LADY AND BEAR	22
YOU CAN FISH OUT A FISH, OUT A FISH, OUT A FISH,	117	LADY AND BEAR	22
YOU CAN FISH OUT A FISH, OUT A FISH, OUT A FISH,	117	LADY AND BEAR	22
IF I WERE A FISH I JUST COULDN'T RESIST	117	LADY AND BEAR	23
SAY THE STONES, SAY THE FISH.	121	ALL EARTH, AIR	20
FISH FEED ON FISH, ACCORDING TO THEIR NEED:	155	THE DYING MAN	66
FISH FEED ON FISH, ACCORDING TO THEIR NEED:	155	THE DYING MAN	66
BY SWOOPS OF BIRD, BY LEAPS OF FISH, I LIVE.	167	HER BECOMING	91
YOUNGLINGS, THE SMALL FISH KEEP HEADING INTO THE CURRENT.	170	FOURTH MEDITATN	75
FETOR OF COCKROACHES, DEAD FISH, PETROLEUM,	187	THE LONGING	3
I WOULD WITH THE FISH, THE BLACKENING SALMON, AND THE MAD LEMMINGS,	188	THE LONGING	39
ALIVE WITH TINY STRIPED FISH, AND YOUNG CRABS CLIMBING IN AND OUT OF THE WATER.	190	AT OYSTER RIVER	5
A FISH RAVEN TURNS ON ITS PERCH (A DEAD TREE IN THE RIVERMOUTH),	190	AT OYSTER RIVER	22
TO THE SAND DUNES AND FISH FLIES, HANGING, THICKER THAN MOTHS,	193	JOURNY INTERIOR	28
THE HELIOTROPE, VEINED LIKE A FISH, THE PERSISTENT MORNING-GLORY,	197	THE LONG WATERS	41
MOVING, ELUSIVE AS FISH, FEARLESS,	199	THE FAR FIELD	31
THE WAVES LESS THAN THE RIPPLES MADE BY RISING FISH,	203	THE ROSE	32
LIKE THE EYE OF A NEW-CAUGHT FISH.	204	THE ROSE	88
I LIVED SERENE AS A FISH,	209	HER LONGING	2
AND THE SMALL FISH LIE, WITHOUT SHADOW, MOTIONLESS,	233	THE PIKE	6
WITH THE FISH, THE QUESTING SNAIL,	251	ONCE MORE, RND	7
TO FIND THAT, LIKE A FISH,	258	SONG (3)	10
THE WAVE BENDS WITH THE FISH. I'M TAUGHT	260	THE CHANGELING	18
FISHED			
FISHED IN AN OLD WOUND,	53	THE LOST SON	12
ONCE I FISHED FROM THE BANKS, LEAF-LIGHT AND HAPPY:	86	PRAISE TO END!	19
FISHERMAN			
AND A FISHERMAN DAWDLES OVER A WOODEN BRIDGE,	197	THE LONG WATERS	37
FISHERMEN			
AND THE WAVES FLATTENING OUT WHEN THE FISHERMEN DRAG THEIR NETS OVER THE STONES.	194	JOURNY INTERIOR	57
FISHES			
BEETLES IN CAVES, NEWTS, STONE-DEAF FISHES,	50	THE MINIMAL	3
AND YOU, CAT AFTER GREAT MILK AND VASTY FISHES,	79	GIVE WAY, GATES	9
I'VE PLAYED WITH THE FISHES	80	GIVE WAY, GATES	40
THE LITTLE FISHES MOVE.	121	ALL EARTH, AIR	4
THE BIRDS AND FISHES MOVE	125	WORDS FOR WIND	62
YOU FISHES, BE MORE FOND.	261	THE CHANGELING	48
FISHING			
FISHING, I CAUGHT MYSELF BEHIND THE EARS.	89	UNFOLD! UNFOLD!	23
"O WHY ARE YOU FISHING THAT WAY?	117	LADY AND BEAR	2
WHY ARE YOU FISHING THAT WAY?"	117	LADY AND BEAR	4

	PAGE	TITLE	LINE
FISHING (CONTINUED)			
THAT'S WHY I'M FISHING THIS WAY.	117	LADY AND BEAR	6
AND SO,--I'M FISHING THIS WAY.	117	LADY AND BEAR	8
YOU, WHEN YOU ARE FISHING THAT WAY, THAT WAY,	117	LADY AND BEAR	24
WHEN YOU ARE FISHING THAT WAY."	117	LADY AND BEAR	25
AS HE WENT ON FISHING HIS WAY, HIS WAY,	117	LADY AND BEAR	29
AS HE WENT ON FISHING HIS WAY.	117	LADY AND BEAR	30
FOR THE HERON'S HIERATIC FISHING,	202	THE ROSE	12
BRINGING ME HOME FROM THE TWILIGHT FISHING.	221	THE ABYSS	67
I WENT FISHING WITH A PIN	269	GOB MUSIC	20
FISH-WAYS			
WHAT FISH-WAYS YOU HAVE, LITTLEST FLOWERS,	61	THE LONG ALLEY	74
FISSURE			
I STARED AT A FISSURE OF GROUND	146	THE SONG	14
FIT			
HIS HAND COULD FIT INTO A WOMAN'S GLOVE,	224	OTTO	12
FITFULLY			
RUNS FITFULLY ALONG THE STUBBLE,	160	FIRST MEDITATN	95
FITLY			
THE SENSE THAT DOES SO FITLY SERVE,	8	PRAYER	20
FIVE			
WHICH OF THE FIVE I SHALL RETAIN	8	PRAYER	3
I WALK THE NIGHT TO KEEP MY FIVE WITS WARM.	135	THE RENEWAL	18
SHAKES EVERY SENSE. I'M FIVE	271	THE REPLY	13
TIMES FIVE A MAN; I BREATHE	271	THE REPLY	14
FIVE-FOOT			
A FIVE-FOOT DROP A VALLEY, SO TO SPEAK.	13	PRAISE PRAIRIE	2
FIVE-INCH			
A FAT, FIVE-INCH APPENDAGE	151	SLUG	12
FIX			
YET DARED TO FIX HIS VISION ANYWHERE.	155	THE DYING MAN	65
FIXED			
WAS IT THE STONES I HEARD? I STARED AT THE FIXED STARS.	166	HER BECOMING	54
TO GAZE AT A FACE WITH THE FIXED EYES OF A SPANIEL?	169	FOURTH MEDITATN	34
OUR EYES FIXED ON A POINT OF LIGHT SO FINE	237	THE TRANCED	16
FLAILING			
FLAILING HER SIDES WITH SPRAY,	41	BIG WIND	28
FLAKE			
THE TOOL CAN CHIP NO FLAKE:	9	THE ADAMANT	11
BRICKS FLAKE BEFORE MY FACE. MASTER OF WATER, THAT'S TREES AWAY.	61	THE LONG ALLEY	80
FLAKES			
A FISH JUMPS, SHAKING OUT FLAKES OF MOONLIGHT.	93	I CRY, LOVE!	45
FLAME			
THE GROUND'S BEATING LIKE FLAME!	99	O, THOU OPENING	59
I PLAYED IN FLAME AND WATER LIKE A BOY	120	THE DREAM	28
LIKE A WET LOG, I SANG WITHIN A FLAME.	120	THE DREAM	30
A FIRE LEAPS ON ITSELF: I KNOW THAT FLAME.	131	SENTENTIOUS MAN	8
A LOG SINGS IN ITS FLAME.	137	LOVE'S PROGRESS	18
MY BODY HALF IN FLAME.	147	THE EXORCISM	2
THE EVENING WRAPS ME, STEADY AS A FLAME.	150	IN LATE SUMMER	32
A FLAME, INTENSE, VISIBLE,	160	FIRST MEDITATN	93
I SANG TO THE EDGES OF FLAME,	162	I'M HERE	42
A SMALL PLACE ALL IN FLAME.	167	HER BECOMING	77
MAY THEY FLAME INTO BEING!--	169	FOURTH MEDITATN	62
A LION OF FLAME, PRESSED TO THE POINT OF LOVE,	170	FOURTH MEDITATN	73
A GREAT FLAME RISES FROM THE SUNLESS SEA;	188	THE LONGING	31
WHERE SHADOW CAN CHANGE INTO FLAME,	188	THE LONGING	49
MY BODY SHIMMERS WITH A LIGHT FLAME.	198	THE LONG WATERS	66
COUNTING THE WISPS OF FLAME, AND I WATCH HOW	240	IN EVEING AIR	20
BOTH MOTH AND FLAME? THE WEAK MOTH BLUNDERING BY.	241	THE SEQUEL	6
THIS SINGLE TREE TURNS INTO PUREST FLAME.	242	THE SEQUEL	28
FLAMES			
WE COUNTED SEVERAL FLAMES IN ONE SMALL FIRE.	237	THE TRANCED	1
FLAP			
THE WIDE WINGS FLAP BUT ONCE TO LIFT HIM UP.	15	THE HERON	11
FLAP FROM A WASTED TREE,	49	NIGHT CROW	2
FLAPPING			
A THIN WHINE OF WIRES, A RATTLING AND FLAPPING OF LEAVES,	230	THE STORM	6
FLAPPING AWAY HEAVILY WHEN A CAR BLASTS TOO CLOSE,	234	ALL MORNING	7
FLARE			
CLOUDS GLOW LIKE COALS JUST FRESH FROM FIRE, A FLARE	17	UNEXTINGUISHED	1

	PAGE	TITLE	LINE
FLARES			
AS A FIRE, SEEMINGLY LONG DEAD, FLARES UP FROM A DOWNDRAFT OF AIR IN A CHIMNEY,	198	THE LONG WATERS	63
FLASH			
A FLASH OF OBJECTS NEVER SEEN BEFORE.	8	THE SIGNALS	2
MAKE THE SEA FLASH IN THE DUST.	61	THE LONG ALLEY	84
THE GREAT SWAMPS FLASH.	103	OLD LADY'S WRDS	13
BUT STILL THE FLASH OF THE KINGFISHER, THE WINGBEAT OF THE SCOTER,	202	THE ROSE	15
A FLASH INTO THE BURNING HEART OF THE ABOMINABLE;	221	THE ABYSS	56
FLASH ME TO MERCY AND A WHOLE HEART!	259	SONG (3)	42
FLASHED			
FLASHED WITH THE SUN IN THE RIPPLE.	6	THE PREMONITION	11
FLASHES			
MY PALM-SWEAT FLASHES GOLD;	88	PRAISE TO END!	87
WHILE, FARTHER AWAY, THE HEAT-LIGHTNING FLASHES.	194	JOURNY INTERIOR	41
FLASH-FLOOD			
CREEKS SWOLLEN IN MIDSUMMER FROM THE FLASH-FLOOD ROARING INTO THE NARROW VALLEY.	193	JOURNY INTERIOR	8
FLASHING			
UP THROUGH THE STREAKED GLASS, FLASHING WITH SUNLIGHT,	43	CHILD ON GRNHSE	4
FLASHING BETWEEN GOLD LEVELS OF THE LATE SUN,	232	THE THING	5
FLAT			
THIS FLAT LAND HAS BECOME A PIT	19	AGNST DISASTER	9
PAST THE PASTURE OF FLAT STONES,	54	THE LOST SON	35
LET THE KISSES RESOUND, FLAT LIKE A BUTCHER'S PALM;	56	THE LOST SON	104
THIS TAIL HATES A FLAT PATH.	79	GIVE WAY, GATES	15
THE FLAT BRANCH OF THAT HEMLOCK HOLDS THE LAST OF THE SUN,	163	I'M HERE	83
REEDS BEATEN FLAT BY WIND AND RAIN,	193	JOURNY INTERIOR	9
TO A TREE LYING FLAT, ITS CROWN HALF BROKEN.	197	THE LONG WATERS	54
THEN A LONG RUNNING OVER FLAT STONES	200	THE FAR FIELD	64
THE FLAT BOOM ON THE BEACH OF THE TOWERING SEA-SWELL,	231	THE STORM	41
FLAT-BOX			
INTO THE FLAT-BOX IT GOES,	42	TRANSPLANTING	12
FLAT-HEADED			
TIME FOR THE FLAT-HEADED MAN. I RECOGNIZE THAT LISTENER,	65	SHAPE OF FIRE	29
FLAT-ROOFED			
THE FLAT-ROOFED HOUSES, COMING DOWN IN GUSTS, BEATING	230	THE STORM	24
FLATTENING			
AND THE WAVES FLATTENING OUT WHEN THE FISHERMEN DRAG THEIR NETS OVER THE STONES.	194	JOURNY INTERIOR	57
FLATTENING THE LIMBER CARNATIONS.	231	THE STORM	33
FLAVOR			
BUT IT HAD A FLAVOR ALL ITS OWN,	270	GOB MUSIC	40
FLAW			
TREMBLED AT HIDDEN VIRTUE WITHOUT FLAW,	107	SIR JOHN DAVIES	74
A COLOR WITHOUT FLAW,	269	GOB MUSIC	27
A COLOR WITHOUT FLAW, FLAW, FLAW,	269	GOB MUSIC	28
A COLOR WITHOUT FLAW, FLAW, FLAW,	269	GOB MUSIC	28
A COLOR WITHOUT FLAW, FLAW, FLAW,	269	GOB MUSIC	28
A COLOR WITHOUT FLAW.	269	GOB MUSIC	29
FLEAS			
CHIRPING WITH FLEAS IN THE SAND,	165	HER BECOMING	3
FLEDGLING			
THEIR FLUTTERY FLEDGLING LIPS	39	ORCHIDS	6
FLEE			
I WOULD PUT OFF MYSELF AND FLEE	24	BEFORE STUDY	5
WHO FLEE IN WHAT THEIR HANDS HAVE MADE.	33	HIGHWAY: MICH	15
FLESH			
FLESH BEHIND STEEL AND GLASS IS UNPROTECTED	5	PROGNOSIS	5
DEFER THE VICE OF FLESH THE IRREVOCABLE CHOICE	5	TO MY SISTER	8
OF FLESH, BURN BACKWARD TO A BLACKENED HEAP.	17	UNEXTINGUISHED	8
ENCOMPASSING FISH, FLESH, AND FOWL.	23	AMOROUS LADY	10
COLD, COLD ACROSS THE FLESH	31	LULL	2
BY PULLING OFF FLESH FROM THE LIVING PLANET;	40	MOSS-GATHERING	12
THE FRUIT AND FLESH SMELLS MIXED.	46	PICKLE BELT	6
FLESH, YOU OFFEND THIS METAL. HOW LONG NEED THE BONES MOURN?	59	THE LONG ALLEY	12
THIS AIR COULD FLESH A DEAD STICK. SWEET JESUS, MAKE ME SWEAT.	61	THE LONG ALLEY	63
THE JOURNEY FROM FLESH IS LONGEST.	66	SHAPE OF FIRE	61
THE LONG FLESH.	81	SENSIBILITY! LA	22
THIS FLESH HAS AIRY BONES.	99	O, THOU OPENING	82
THE SPIRIT AND THE FLESH CRIED OUT FOR MORE.	106	SIR JOHN DAVIES	52

	PAGE	TITLE	LINE
FLESH (CONTINUED)			
THE FLESH CAN MAKE THE SPIRIT VISIBLE;	106	SIR JOHN DAVIES	63
WHO RISE FROM FLESH TO SPIRIT KNOW THE FALL:	107	SIR JOHN DAVIES	95
TRUE LECHERS LOVE THE FLESH, AND THAT IS ALL.	131	SENTENTIOUS MAN	6
WE DID NOT FLY THE FLESH. WHO DOES, WHEN YOUNG?	131	SENTENTIOUS MAN	7
THE SPIRIT KNOWS THE FLESH IT MUST CONSUME.	131	SENTENTIOUS MAN	10
MY FLESH IS BREATHING SLOWER THAN A WALL.	135	THE RENEWAL	9
CRIED TO MY FLESH OUT LOUD.	147	THE EXORCISM	8
I FEEL MY FLESH DIVIDE.	148	THE SMALL	14
THE FLESH DESERTS THE BONE,	153	THE DYING MAN	7
I BURNED THE FLESH AWAY,	154	THE DYING MAN	26
FLESH CRIES TO FLESH; AND BONE CRIES OUT TO BONE;	155	THE DYING MAN	58
FLESH CRIES TO FLESH; AND BONE CRIES OUT TO BONE;	155	THE DYING MAN	58
A BEAST CRIES OUT AS IF ITS FLESH WERE TORN,	156	THE DYING MAN	82
I'VE BECOME A STRANGE PIECE OF FLESH,	157	FIRST MEDITATN	15
THE FLESH TAKES ON THE PURE POISE OF THE SPIRIT,	191	AT OYSTER RIVER	38
AT EASE AFTER ROCKING THE FLESH TO SLEEP,	194	JOURNY INTERIOR	55
BETWEEN THE SPIRIT AND THE FLESH,--WHAT WAR?	223	ELEGY (2)	5
BREAKS ON ME AS MY MEAGER FLESH BREAKS DOWN--	244	INFIRMITY	15
THE FLESH IS WILLING TO REPENT.	256	IN HYDROTHERAPY	8
GROWS SICK IN FLESH AND SPIRIT BOTH.	257	SANITARIUM	10
STAYS IN HER FLESH;	260	THE CHANGELING	5
THE FLESH FATHERS A DREAM;	263	FOLLIES OF ADAM	27
FLESH-AWKWARD			
FLESH-AWKWARD, HALF-ALIVE,	162	I'M HERE	27
FLESH-BOUND			
THE FLESH-BOUND SIGHING LOVER,	7	ORDERS FOR DAY	5
FLESHLESS			
I KNOW THE COLD FLESHLESS KISS OF CONTRARIES,	166	HER BECOMING	40
FLESHY			
THE ASPECT OF HIS FLESHY CLOTHES,--	19	EPIDERM MACABRE	2
FLEW			
LIKE WITCHES THEY FLEW ALONG ROWS	44	FRAU BAUMAN	19
FLEW A TREMENDOUS BIRD	49	NIGHT CROW	5
AS THE BIRDS FLEW OFF TO THE END OF NEXT WEEK.	115	THE SERPENT	26
A SMALL BIRD FLEW IN CIRCLES WHERE WE STOOD;	120	THE DREAM	19
THE SWALLOWS FLEW IN AND OUT OF THE SMOKELESS CHIMNEYS.	162	I'M HERE	41
DRY BARK FLEW IN THEIR FACES FROM HIS SHOT,--	224	OTTO	16
AN OLD WIND-TATTERED BUTTERFLY FLEW DOWN	243	THE MOTION	2
FLICK			
HOW HE COULD FLICK AND PICK	42	OLD FLORIST	4
"O IT'S WONDERFUL HOW WITH A FLICK OF YOUR WRIST,	117	LADY AND BEAR	21
FLICK OVER THE CLOSE WHITECAPS,	210	HER TIME	11
FLICKER			
THEY FLICKER FASTER THAN A BLUE-TAILED SWIFT,	8	THE SIGNALS	5
IN A FLICKER OF FIRE BRISKED BY A DUSTY WIND.	194	JOURNY INTERIOR	61
AND THE FLICKER DRUMMED FROM HIS DEAD TREE IN THE CHICKEN-YARD.	200	THE FAR FIELD	37
AND FLICKER NEAR OUR LEGS LIKE KEROSENE	274	SUPPR W LINDSAY	36
FLICKERS			
WITH WRENS, SPARROWS, JUNCOS, CEDAR WAXWINGS, FLICKERS,	235	ALL MORNING	41
FLICKER'S			
THAT AIR AND SHINE: AND THE FLICKER'S LOUD SUMMER CALL:	66	SHAPE OF FIRE	70
FLICKING			
FLICKING THE FOAM FROM THE WHITECAPS STRAIGHT UPWARD INTO THE DARKNESS.	230	THE STORM	16
FLIES			
IT'S NECESSARY AMONG THE FLIES AND BANANAS, TO KEEP A CONSTANT VIGIL,	86	PRAISE TO END!	24
SHE TRIES TO THINK, AND IT FLIES LOOSE AGAIN.	133	THE PURE FURY	11
TO THE SAND DUNES AND FISH FLIES, HANGING, THICKER THAN MOTHS,	193	JOURNY INTERIOR	28
WITH ALL THE AIR TO GREET HIM AS HE FLIES,	205	THE ROSE	109
FLIES AWAY FROM MY FACE	210	HER TIME	15
AND MY THOUGHT FLIES TO THE PLACE BY THE BO-TREE.	222	THE ABYSS	100
THE MIST ABOVE ME SINGS WITH ITS SMALL FLIES.	246	THE MARROW	2
THE BIRD FLIES OUT, THE BIRD FLIES BACK AGAIN;	250	THE RIGHT THING	4
THE BIRD FLIES OUT, THE BIRD FLIES BACK AGAIN;	250	THE RIGHT THING	4
FLIGHT			
THE FLIGHT	53	THE LOST SON	ST
FLING			
THE CLIFFS! THE CLIFFS! THEY FLING ME BACK.	89	UNFOLD! UNFOLD!	5
FLING ME A PRECEPT.	97	O, THOU OPENING	6

	PAGE	TITLE	LINE
FLING (CONTINUED)			
I TRIED TO FLING MY SHADOW AT THE MOON,	105	SIR JOHN DAVIES	13
OR THEY FLING THEMSELVES AGAINST TREE TRUNKS,	152	THE SISKINS	16
THE WORLD IS WHERE WE FLING IT; I'M LEAVING WHERE I AM.	260	THE CHANGELING	21
FLINGING			
FLINGING LONG STRINGS OF WET ACROSS THE ROOF-TOP,	41	BIG WIND	29
FLIP-FLAP			
I'M UNDONE BY THE FLIP-FLAP OF ODIOUS PILLOWS.	86	PRAISE TO END!	45
FLIT			
AND THE SMALL MAD SISKINS FLIT BY,	152	THE SISKINS	8
FLITTER-FLAD			
HE CAN PLAY THE FLITTER-FLAD;	266	FOR STEVENS	2
FLITTERMICE			
NOW AS FROM MAPLE TO ELM THE FLITTERMICE SKITTER AND TWIRL,	33	IDYLL	1
FLOATED			
A LONG WEED FLOATED UPWARD;	62	FIELD OF LIGHT	5
WHEN THE HERONS FLOATED HIGH OVER THE WHITE HOUSES,	66	SHAPE OF FIRE	66
OR FLOATED ON THE SURFACE OF A POND,	247	I WAITED	8
FLOATING			
PONDS WITH MOSS AND LEAVES FLOATING,	62	FIELD OF LIGHT	2
THE BULB UNRAVELS. WHO'S FLOATING? NOT ME.	90	UNFOLD! UNFOLD!	41
LIFTING A FEW TWIGS AND FLOATING LEAVES,	93	I CRY, LOVE!	48
THE LONG PLAINTIVE NOTES FLOATING DOWN,	159	FIRST MEDITATN	87
AS A CHIP OR SHELL, FLOATING LAZILY WITH A SLOW CURRENT,	168	FOURTH MEDITATN	6
THE FLOATING HAWKS, THE JACKRABBITS, THE GRAZING CATTLE--	194	JOURNY INTERIOR	38
THE MARE'S TAIL, THE FLOATING FROGBIT,	209	HER LONGING	4
FLOATING OVER THE MOUNTAINS,	209	HER LONGING	17
FAR AWAY, CLOSE-AT-HAND, HIS CALL FLOATING OVER THE ON-COMING TRAFFIC,	234	ALL MORNING	3
FLOATS			
A FISH FLOATS BELLY UPWARD,	59	THE LONG ALLEY	2
FLOATS A SINGLE STAR.	122	ALL EARTH, AIR	23
A FACE FLOATS IN THE FERNS. DO MAIMED GODS WALK?	165	HER BECOMING	18
FLOODED			
THE DANGEROUS FLOODED PLAIN	7	ORDERS FOR DAY	11
FLOODS			
THIS WISDOM FLOODS THE MIND,	18	GENESIS	5
SCARS, TEMPESTS, FLOODS, THE MOTION OF MAN'S FATE;	144	ELEGY (1)	14
FLOOR			
UNTIL I COULD THINK THERE WERE WAVES ROLLING HIGH AS MY BEDROOM FLOOR;	12	MID-CNTRY BLOW	2
CROUCHED CLOSER TO THE FLOOR,	47	THE RETURN	3
WITH JOTS AND JOGS AND CINDERS ON THE FLOOR:	79	GIVE WAY, GATES	27
THE SUDDEN LIGHT SPILLED ON THE FLOOR LIKE CREAM	273	SUPPR W LINDSAY	12
FLORAL			
THE HIGH-PILED FLORAL OFFERINGS WITH SENTIMENTAL VERSES,	22	ROAD TO WDLAWN	3
FLORIST			
OLD FLORIST	42	OLD FLORIST	T
A FLORIST DOES NOT WOO THE BEAUTIFUL:	224	OTTO	8
FLORIST'S			
AS WHEN THE DOOR SWINGS OPEN IN A FLORIST'S STOREROOM--	220	THE ABYSS	46
FLOUR			
FINER THAN FLOUR, ALIVE, MORE DANGEROUS THAN SILICA,	46	DOLOR	10
FLOURISHING			
OR SCOOP OUT A WEED CLOSE TO FLOURISHING ROOTS,	42	OLD FLORIST	6
FLOW			
FILLS AND TREMBLES AT THE EDGE YET DOES NOT FLOW OVER,	67	SHAPE OF FIRE	94
AND HOW THOSE FLOWERHEADS SEEMED TO FLOW TOWARD ME, TO BECKON ME, ONLY A CHILD, OUT OF MYSELF.	203	THE ROSE	55
AND WATCHED THE WEATHER FLOW.	212	LIGHT LISTENED	11
FLOWED			
CRUMBLED AND FLOWED AWAY,	49	RIVER INCIDENT	8
THE RIVER EBBED AND FLOWED:	87	PRAISE TO END!	68
ALL FLOWED: WITHOUT, WITHIN;	238	THE MOMENT	10
FLOWER			
THE WHOLE FLOWER EXTENDING OUTWARD,	42	TRANSPLANTING	21
FLOWER DUMP	43	FLOWER DUMP	T
STILL HOLDING AND FEEDING THE STEM OF THE CONTAINED FLOWER.	67	SHAPE OF FIRE	95
ARE FLOWER AND SEED THE SAME?	123	WORDS FOR WIND	9
MAY THE HIGH FLOWER OF THE HAY CLIMB INTO THEIR HEARTS;	169	FOURTH MEDITATN	56
I SEE THE FLOWER OF ALL WATER, ABOVE AND BELOW ME, THE NEVER RECEDING,	194	JOURNY INTERIOR	52
THE NUMINOUS RING AROUND THE OPENING FLOWER,	198	THE LONG WATERS	70

	PAGE	TITLE	LINE

FLOWER (CONTINUED)
WHILE I POKED WITH A STICK AT A STONE NEAR A FOUR-PRONGED
FLOWER, ... 232 THE THING 21
FLOWER-CROWNS
OR PERCH AND PECK AT LARGER FLOWER-CROWNS, ... 152 THE SISKINS 12
MY THIGHS BRUSHING AGAINST FLOWER-CROWNS; ... 161 I'M HERE 22
FLOWER-DUMP
NOT TOO FAR AWAY FROM THE EVER-CHANGING FLOWER-DUMP, ... 199 THE FAR FIELD 16
FLOWERHEADS
COMING DOWN ON THE FLOWERHEADS, ... 67 SHAPE OF FIRE 80
AND HOW THOSE FLOWERHEADS SEEMED TO FLOW TOWARD ME, TO
BECKON ME, ONLY A CHILD, OUT OF MYSELF. ... 203 THE ROSE 55
FLOWERING
FLOWERING OUT OF THE DARK, ... 203 THE ROSE 42
FLOWERS
AND FLOWERS JUMPED ... 51 THE WAKING (1) 11
ARE THE FLOWERS HERE? THE BIRDS ARE. ... 61 THE LONG ALLEY 64
SHALL I CALL THE FLOWERS? ... 61 THE LONG ALLEY 65
WHAT FISH-WAYS YOU HAVE, LITTLEST FLOWERS, ... 61 THE LONG ALLEY 74
THESE FLOWERS ARE ALL FANGS. COMFORT ME, FURY. ... 64 SHAPE OF FIRE 9
THE FLOWERS LEANED ON THEMSELVES, THE FLOWERS IN HOLLOWS; ... 66 SHAPE OF FIRE 76
THE FLOWERS LEANED ON THEMSELVES, THE FLOWERS IN HOLLOWS; ... 66 SHAPE OF FIRE 76
GOD, GIVE ME A NEAR. I HEAR FLOWERS. ... 73 WHERE KNOCK IS 49
(FATHER OF FLOWERS, WHO ... 147 THE EXORCISM 3
THE CHILDREN DANCING, THE FLOWERS WIDENING. ... 188 THE LONGING 40
THESE WAVES, IN THE SUN, REMIND ME OF FLOWERS: ... 197 THE LONG WATERS 38
ITS ENTRAILS STREWN OVER THE HALF-GROWN FLOWERS, ... 199 THE FAR FIELD 22
I HEAR THE FLOWERS DRINKING IN THEIR LIGHT, ... 222 THE ABYSS 91
WITH THE DARK HEARSE, AND ENOUGH FLOWERS FOR AN ALDERMAN,-- ... 223 ELEGY (2) 2
WHEN FLOWERS GREW, THEIR BLOOM EXTENDED HIM. ... 224 OTTO 11
A HOUSE FOR FLOWERS! HOUSE UPON HOUSE THEY BUILT, ... 224 OTTO 23
FLOWING
I SAW SUBSTANCE FLOWING ... 56 THE LOST SON 94
SHE CAME TOWARD ME IN THE FLOWING AIR, ... 119 THE DREAM 9
MY EYES, THEY DAZZLED AT HER FLOWING KNEES; ... 127 I KNEW A WOMAN 18
THE GARDEN IS A RIVER FLOWING SOUTH. ... 129 SHE 8
AND ONCE TO MY FLOWING THIGHS. ... 167 HER BECOMING 73
A COUNTRY OF BAYS AND INLETS, AND SMALL STREAMS FLOWING
SEAWARD. ... 196 THE LONG WATERS 19
FLOWING. ... 221 THE ABYSS 74
A NIGHT FLOWING WITH BIRDS, A RAGGED MOON, ... 239 IN A DARK TIME 14
FLOWS
THE DARK FLOWS ON ITSELF. A DEAD MOUTH SINGS UNDER AN OLD
TREE. ... 59 THE LONG ALLEY 6
AND ALL FLOWS PAST-- ... 194 JOURNY INTERIOR 34
AT EASE WITH ALL THAT FLOWS. ... 262 FOLLIES OF ADAM 14
FLUID
A RAW GHOST DRINKS THE FLUID IN MY SPINE; ... 135 THE RENEWAL 14
TODAY THEY DRAINED THE FLUID FROM A KNEE ... 244 INFIRMITY 9
FLUNG
AND FLUNG THEM IN CONFUSION ON THE LAND. ... 6 INTERLUDE 3
SEA-BEAST OR BIRD FLUNG TOWARD THE RAVAGED SHORE? ... 107 SIR JOHN DAVIES 68
THEN SUDDENLY FLUNG UP AND OVER, ... 226 THE LIZARD 10
I WAS FLUNG BACK FROM SUFFERING AND LOVE ... 246 THE MARROW 19
FLUSHED
CHILL DEPTHS OF THE SPIRIT ARE FLUSHED TO A FEVER, ... 5 PROGNOSIS 15
HOPE FLUSHED MY CHEEKBONES WITH A SCARLET DISK. ... 21 THE AUCTION 11
FLUTE
THEY GOT A HORN, THEY GOT A FLUTE, ... 115 THE SERPENT 17
FLUTTER
FLUTTER OF WINGS AND SEEDS QUAKING, ... 255 LIGHT POEM 3
FLUTTERS
THE FEATHER OF THE MILKWEED FLUTTERS DOWN. ... 12 SLOW SEASON 12
ON THE SILL OF THE EYES, SOMETHING FLUTTERS, ... 162 I'M HERE 52
FLUTTERY
THEIR FLUTTERY FLEDGLING LIPS ... 39 ORCHIDS 6
FLY
THERE WAS ONE FLY. ... 53 THE LOST SON 19
WE DID NOT FLY THE FLESH. WHO DOES, WHEN YOUNG? ... 131 SENTENTIOUS MAN 7
THUS I; AND SHOULD THESE REASONS FLY APART, ... 144 ELEGY (1) 9
A RAIN-DRENCHED FLY OR SPIDER. ... 151 SLUG 24
I THINK A BIRD, AND IT BEGINS TO FLY. ... 155 THE DYING MAN 70
BUT HE ALWAYS WANTED TO FLY MY KITE; ... 178 THE DONKEY 2

	PAGE	TITLE	LINE

FLY (CONTINUED)

THE YOUNG SNAKE, POISED IN GREEN LEAVES, WAITING FOR ITS
    FLY, ...   190   AT OYSTER RIVER   28
WHEN BATS FLY, CLOSE TO SLIGHTLY TILTING BROWNISH WATER,   198   THE LONG WATERS   61
AND TWO SCOTERS FLY LOW, ...   210   HER TIME   12
ONLY TO FLY OVER TO HIS FAVORITE PERCH, THE CROSS-BAR OF A
    TELEPHONE POLE;   234   ALL MORNING   9
MY SOUL, LIKE SOME HEAT-MADDENED SUMMER FLY, ...   239   IN A DARK TIME   20
"I'M MAIMED; I CAN'T FLY;   249   THE RESTORED   9

FLYING

THE FLYING FABRIC STITCHED ON BONE, ...   19   EPIDERM MACABRE   3
FLYING UPWARD THROUGH THE KNIVES OF MY LAWNMOWER   151   SLUG   16
THEN FLYING ALMOST STRAIGHT UPWARD, ...   152   THE SISKINS   3
FLYING UPWARD IN LITTLE SKIPS AND ERRATIC LEAPS;   152   THE SISKINS   9
OF FLYING LIKE A BAT DEEP INTO A NARROWING TUNNEL, ...   199   THE FAR FIELD   2
SUDDENLY THEY CAME FLYING, LIKE A LONG SCARF OF SMOKE, . . .   232   THE THING   1
CONFUSING THEM ONCE FLYING STRAIGHT INTO THE SUN   232   THE THING   7

FOAM

I DABBLE MY TOES IN THE BRACKISH FOAM SLIDING FORWARD, . . .   190   AT OYSTER RIVER   15
FLICKING THE FOAM FROM THE WHITECAPS STRAIGHT UPWARD INTO
    THE DARKNESS.   230   THE STORM   16

FOAMED

FROM A KNOCKED OVER CHURN, AND FOAMED AROUND   273   SUPPR W LINDSAY   13

FOLD

ALL THINGS ARE BROUGHT TO BARN AND FOLD.   15   COMING OF COLD   34

FOLDERS

ALL THE MISERY OF MANILLA FOLDERS AND MUCILAGE, ...   46   DOLOR   3

FOLDS

THE NAKED FIELDS THE CLOUD'S IMMACULATE FOLDS   5   TO MY SISTER   4
WILL THE SEA GIVE THE WIND SUCK? A TOAD FOLDS INTO A STONE.   64   SHAPE OF FIRE   8
FROM THE FOLDS OF MY SKIN, I SING, ...   165   HER BECOMING   13
IN ITS SMALL FOLDS, STIRRING SLUGGISHLY, ...   171   WHAT TELL BONES   4
I RISE AND FALL, AND TIME FOLDS   194   JOURNY INTERIOR   46

FOLIAGE

DOWN AMONG THE RUBBISH, THE BUG-RIDDLED FOLIAGE, ...   54   THE LOST SON   41

FOLLIES

THE FOLLIES OF ADAM   262   FOLLIES OF ADAM   T

FOLLOW

MORNING-FAIR, FOLLOW ME FURTHER BACK   66   SHAPE OF FIRE   64
TO FOLLOW THE DROPS SLIDING FROM A LIFTED OAR, ...   67   SHAPE OF FIRE   90
WHEN I FOLLOW AFTER THEM, ...   141   MEMORY   11
AS MY EYES FOLLOW AFTER   152   THE SISKINS   23
I'M ONE TO FOLLOW, ...   210   HER TIME   25
TO FOLLOW.   210   HER TIME   26

FOLLOWING

HIS IMAGE KEPT FOLLOWING AFTER,--   6   THE PREMONITION   10

FOLLOWS

OR WHEN DARK FOLLOWS DARK IN LIGHTNING RIFT.   8   THE SIGNALS   6
ONE FOLLOWS FIRE. ONE DOES.   167   HER BECOMING   80

FOLLY

THE COST OF FOLLY IS FOREVER MOUNTING;   25   DIM-WIT COUSIN   5

FOND

THE ARBOR IS COOLER. FAREWELL, FAREWELL, FOND WORM. . . .   64   SHAPE OF FIRE   18
WHEN I SAY THINGS FOND, ...   83   O LULL ME, LULL   10
THE LIVELY DEAD HAD TAUGHT US TO BE FOND.   106   SIR JOHN DAVIES   32
A FOND AND FOOLISH MAN, ...   126   WORDS FOR WIND   103
YOU FISHES, BE MORE FOND.   261   THE CHANGELING   48

FONDLING

REACH ME A PEACH, FONDLING, THE HILLS ARE THERE.   61   THE LONG ALLEY   81
IS THE ETERNAL NEAR, FONDLING?   87   PRAISE TO END!   73

FONDLING'S

RICH ME CHERRIES A FONDLING'S KISS, ...   60   THE LONG ALLEY   43

FOOD

IS HUMAN NATURE'S DAILY FOOD.   25   VERSE W ALLUSNS   8
WE'VE GOT THE LIVING LIGHT, BUT WHERE'S THE FOOD?"   273   SUPPR W LINDSAY   16

FOOL

A FOOL CAN PLAY AT BEING SOLEMN   24   BEFORE STUDY   7
IN PUREST SONG ONE PLAYS THE CONSTANT FOOL   244   INFIRMITY   1
WHAT'S NOT A PROPER FOOL.   267   SAGINAW SONG   30
AND WHAT FOOL WOULDN'T, WHEN THINGS FROM SLEEP   273   SUPPR W LINDSAY   3

FOOLISH

REVEALS A FOOLISH MOTHER, ...   7   ORDERS FOR DAY   17
A FOND AND FOOLISH MAN, ...   126   WORDS FOR WIND   103

	PAGE	TITLE	LINE
FOOLISH (CONTINUED)			
SO FOOLISH AND TRUSTING, LIKE A SICK POODLE,	228	THE GERANIUM	3
FOOLISHNESS			
AND I ACKNOWLEDGE MY FOOLISHNESS WITH GOD,	196	THE LONG WATERS	8
FOOLS			
FOOLS WHO WILL NEVER LEARN;	31	LULL	18
TO FOOLS AND FRAUDS: HE DOES NOT PUT ON AIRS	224	OTTO	3
FOOL'S			
PLATITUDES GARNISHED BEYOND A FOOL'S GAINSAYING;	5	PROGNOSIS	9
FOOT			
THE WALKER'S FOOT HAS SCARCELY ROOM	14	COMING OF COLD	5
A LOG TURNED AT THE TOUCH OF A FOOT;	62	FIELD OF LIGHT	4
I'M STILL WAITING FOR A FOOT.	84	O LULL ME, LULL	30
THE OYSTER'S WEEPING FOOT,	125	WORDS FOR WIND	86
AND THE UP-SPRING OF THE PLANK WHEN A FOOT LEFT THE RUNWAY.	158	FIRST MEDITATN	47
ONE LEAF-LIKE FOOT HUNG LAXLY	226	THE LIZARD	7
AND THEN A JACKASS BRAYED. A LIZARD LEAPED MY FOOT.	247	I WAITED	14
ME STARING PAST MY FOOT,	262	FOLLIES OF ADAM	17
FOOTIE			
WHAT FOOTIE DOES IS FINAL.	86	PRAISE TO END!	34
WHAT FOOTIE DOES IS FINAL.	86	PRAISE TO END!	38
WHAT FOOTIE WILL DO WILL BE FINAL.	86	PRAISE TO END!	42
FOOTMAN			
THE SIDEBOARD BESIDE WHICH A TALL FOOTMAN STOOD	32	SALE	15
FOOTSTEP			
NOR THE SOUND OF ANOTHER FOOTSTEP--	169	FOURTH MEDITATN	54
FOR (180)			
FORCE			
THIS ELEMENTAL FORCE	18	GENESIS	1
THAT FORCE THE SON OF MAN TO TOIL;	18	LONG LIVE WEEDS	4
THEN, WITH DIMINISHED FORCE,	50	THE CYCLE	13
FORCING			
FORCING HOUSE	38	FORCING HOUSE	T
FOREBODING			
HIS FOREBODING	215	HIS FOREBODING	T
FOREHEAD'S			
I'M IN LOVE WITH THE DEAD! MY WHOLE FOREHEAD'S A NOISE!	170	FOURTH MEDITATN	79
FOREKNOWN			
MY TRUTHS ARE ALL FOREKNOWN,	3	OPEN HOUSE	7
FOREPAWS			
THEIR FOREPAWS JOINED TOGETHER, LIKE HANDS--	163	I'M HERE	69
FOREST			
BUT IN THIS FOREST OF THE DEAD	17	NO BIRD	7
THE BURNING LAKE TURNS INTO A FOREST POOL,	221	THE ABYSS	58
FOREVER			
THE COST OF FOLLY IS FOREVER MOUNTING;	25	DIM-WIT COUSIN	5
THE GREEN COMES UP FOREVER IN THE FIELDS OF OUR COUNTRY."	28	CLAIRVOY WIDOW	26
FOREVER IS EASY, SHE SAID.	77	BRING THE DAY!	11
THE FAR FIELD, THE WINDY CLIFFS OF FOREVER,	200	THE FAR FIELD	51
AND THOSE BIRDS FOREVER DEAD,	235	ALL MORNING	43
FOREVER'S			
WHAT'S SEEN RECEDES; FOREVER'S WHAT WE KNOW!--	156	THE DYING MAN	91
FORGET			
LET'S PLAY BEFORE WE FORGET!	83	O LULL ME, LULL	20
WAS TO FORGET TIME AND DEATH:	199	THE FAR FIELD	27
FORGIVE			
FATHER, FORGIVE MY HANDS.	85	PRAISE TO END!	12
FORGIVE ME A MINUTE, NYMPH.	97	O, THOU OPENING	18
FORGOTTEN			
THE SCRATCH FORGOTTEN IS THE SCRATCH INFECTED;	5	PROGNOSIS	7
MY EYES HAVE FORGOTTEN.	103	OLD LADY'S WRDS	4
HAVE I FORGOTTEN THEIR WAYS--	139	PLAINT	14
AND THE DARK BE FORGOTTEN.	188	THE LONGING	50
ALL BIRDS REMEMBERED, O NEVER FORGOTTEN!	235	ALL MORNING	45
FORK			
A CAT IN THE FORK OF A TREE,	121	ALL EARTH, AIR	8
FORM			
SLOWED IN MY HUMAN FORM;	49	RIVER INCIDENT	5
APPEAR IN THE FORM OF A SPIDER	54	THE LOST SON	22
ALIVE AT NOON, I PERISHED IN HER FORM.	107	SIR JOHN DAVIES	94
WILL THE SELF, LOST, BE FOUND AGAIN? IN FORM?	135	THE RENEWAL	17
THE PURE, SENSUOUS FORM.	150	SNAKE	11
I LONG FOR THE IMPERISHABLE QUIET AT THE HEART OF FORM;	188	THE LONGING	45

	PAGE	TITLE	LINE
FORMAL			
THE BRONZE WHEAT ARRANGED IN STRICT AND FORMAL ORDER;	29	THE REMINDER	3
THEIR GAIT FORMAL AND ELABORATE, THEIR HAIR A GLORY, ...	170	FOURTH MEDITATN	64
FORMS			
THE MEANING OF THE DAY; DARK FORMS	4	FEUD	14
EVEN THE HUSHED FORMS, THE BENT YELLOWY WEEDS	57	THE LOST SON	147
I MET A COLLECTOR OF STRING, A SHEPHERD OF SLOW FORMS. ...	90	UNFOLD! UNFOLD!	30
FORMS OF HIS SECRET LIFE	147	THE EXORCISM	23
THERE ARE NO PURSUING FORMS, FACES ON WALLS:	159	FIRST MEDITATN	78
IN THE MOMENT OF TIME WHEN THE SMALL DROP FORMS, BUT DOES NOT FALL, ...	194	JOURNY INTERIOR	58
FORNICATES			
--FORNICATES ON THE STOVE.	99	O, THOU OPENING	70
FORSAKEN			
ALL THINGS INNOCENT, HAPLESS, FORSAKEN.	227	MEADOW MOUSE	29
FORTH			
OUR SOULS LOOKED FORTH, AND THE GREAT DAY STOOD STILL. ...	106	SIR JOHN DAVIES	60
RAPT, WE LEANED FORTH WITH WHAT WE COULD NOT SEE.	107	SIR JOHN DAVIES	88
LEAVES, LEAVES, LEAN FORTH AND TELL ME WHAT I AM;	242	THE SEQUEL	27
FORTITUDE			
CONDEMN THE FORTITUDE	20	REPL TO CENSURE	7
FORTUNATE			
O FORTUNATE HE WHOSE MAMMA PAYS THE BILLS!	24	POETASTER	4
FORTUNE'S			
O HE WAS FORTUNE'S CHILD, A FAVORITE SON	28	THE FAVORITE	9
FORTY			
IMPERIOUS YOUNGLING, THOUGH APPROACHING FORTY;	264	THREE EPIGRAMS	2
FORWARD			
SNAIL, SNAIL, GLISTER ME FORWARD, ...	53	THE LOST SON	8
TILTS, BACKWARD AND FORWARD.	93	I CRY, LOVE!	51
SLOW AS A FISH COMING FORWARD, ...	100	THE VISITANT	11
WHAT SHAPE LEAPED FORWARD AT THE SENSUAL CRY?--	107	SIR JOHN DAVIES	67
AND I SEEM TO LEAN FORWARD, ...	152	THE SISKINS	22
THE MOVEMENT IS FORWARD, AFTER A FEW WAVERS, ...	158	FIRST MEDITATN	27
THEN THEY LURCH FORWARD, ...	159	FIRST MEDITATN	58
STILL SWIMMING FORWARD--	159	FIRST MEDITATN	72
AND THE SPIRIT FAILS TO MOVE FORWARD, ...	187	THE LONGING	19
I DABBLE MY TOES IN THE BRACKISH FOAM SLIDING FORWARD, ...	190	AT OYSTER RIVER	15
AND WITH WATER: THE WAVES COMING FORWARD, WITHOUT CESSATION,	191	AT OYSTER RIVER	31
AND THE WHOLE RIVER BEGINS TO MOVE FORWARD, ITS BRIDGES SHAKING.	191	AT OYSTER RIVER	56
NEITHER FORWARD NOR BACKWARD, ...	195	JOURNY INTERIOR	72
I FEEL A WEIGHTLESS CHANGE, A MOVING FORWARD	200	THE FAR FIELD	58
NEITHER FORWARD NOR BACK, ...	210	HER TIME	7
FORWARD'S			
I THINK HIS FORWARD'S COMING BACK!	182	THE HIPPO	2
FOUND			
THE PLACE WHERE BUTTERNUTS ARE FOUND.	14	COMING OF COLD	11
I FOUND MY CHOICE POSSESSIONS ON THE LAWN.	21	THE AUCTION	2
WISDOM, WHERE IS IT FOUND?--	125	WORDS FOR WIND	68
MY INDIRECTION FOUND DIRECTION OUT.	131	SENTENTIOUS MAN	4
AND FOUND OUT ALL I COULD OF ALL DESIRE;	132	SENTENTIOUS MAN	32
WILL THE SELF, LOST, BE FOUND AGAIN? IN FORM?	135	THE RENEWAL	17
I HAVE CONSIDERED AND FOUND	137	LOVE'S PROGRESS	3
EACH CUSHION FOUND ITSELF A FIELD OF PINS, ...	143	SHIMMER OF EVIL	11
I FOUND MY FATHER WHEN I DID MY WORK, ...	154	THE DYING MAN	40
BUT FOUND HE WASN'T THERE AT ALL, ...	181	MONOTONY SONG	14
(I FOUND IT LYING AMONG THE RUBBLE OF AN OLD COAL BIN) ...	199	THE FAR FIELD	20
SLEEPS THE BABY MOUSE I FOUND IN THE MEADOW, ...	227	MEADOW MOUSE	2
FOUNTAIN			
THE FOUNTAIN	258	SONG (3)	4
FOUR			
FOUR FOR SIR JOHN DAVIES	105	SIR JOHN DAVIES	T
THEIR FOUR WINGS BEATING TOGETHER, ...	210	HER TIME	13
THEY SIT, THREE OR FOUR, HIGH IN THE FIR-TREES BACK OF THE HOUSE, ...	234	ALL MORNING	6
FOUR-FOOT			
LIFTING ME HIGH OVER THE FOUR-FOOT STEMS, THE MRS. RUSSELLS, AND HIS OWN ELABORATE HYBRIDS,	203	THE ROSE	54
FOUR-POSTER			
THE BECHSTEIN PIANO, THE FOUR-POSTER BED, ...	32	SALE	10

	PAGE	TITLE	LINE
FOUR-PRONGED			
WHILE I POKED WITH A STICK AT A STONE NEAR A FOUR-PRONGED FLOWER,	232	THE THING	21
FOURS			
CRAWLING ON ALL FOURS,	39	WEED PULLER	15
FOURTH			
FOURTH MEDITATION	168	FOURTH MEDITATN	T
FOWL			
ENCOMPASSING FISH, FLESH, AND FOWL.	23	AMOROUS LADY	10
FOX			
THE LOVED FOX, AND THE WREN.	166	HER BECOMING	64
FOX-HUNTING			
A STABLE AND PADDOCK, SOME FOX-HUNTING LAND,	32	SALE	6
FRAGRANCE			
TO PRESS PURE FRAGRANCE TO THE SOIL;	14	COMING OF COLD	19
FRAU			
FRAU BAUMAN, FRAU SCHMIDT, AND FRAU SCHWARTZE	44	FRAU BAUMAN	T
FRAU BAUMAN, FRAU SCHMIDT, AND FRAU SCHWARTZE	44	FRAU BAUMAN	T
FRAU BAUMAN, FRAU SCHMIDT, AND FRAU SCHWARTZE	44	FRAU BAUMAN	T
FRAUD			
YOU'RE A FAKE, YOUR'RE A FRAUD, YOU'RE A HOR-RID PRETENSE!	177	KITTY-CAT BIRD	3
FRAUDS			
TO FOOLS AND FRAUDS: HE DOES NOT PUT ON AIRS	224	OTTO	3
FRAYED			
UNTIL THE TOUGHEST NERVES ARE FRAYED.	33	HIGHWAY: MICH	13
FREE			
CRIED OUT THEIR LIVES AN INSTANT AND WERE FREE.	143	SHIMMER OF EVIL	14
--HOW FREE; HOW ALL ALONE.	188	THE LONGING	36
AND ONE IS ONE, FREE IN THE TEARING WIND.	239	IN A DARK TIME	24
HOW FREE! HOW ALL ALONE!	261	THE CHANGELING	39
FREEDOM			
WHAT'S FREEDOM FOR? TO KNOW ETERNITY.	127	I KNEW A WOMAN	24
FREEZE			
LET THE GESTURES FREEZE; OUR DOOM IS ALREADY DECIDED.	56	THE LOST SON	105
FREEZES			
THE RUSH OF SMELLS STRIKES LIKE A COLD FIRE, THE THROAT FREEZES,	220	THE ABYSS	47
FREEZING			
GLEAMING, FREEZING HARD AGAIN, CREAKING AT MIDNIGHT--	191	AT OYSTER RIVER	51
FREIGHT			
FOR SHE FINALLY LEFT TOWN ON THE BAY CITY FREIGHT	112	SQUEEZE-BOX	40
WHEN THE SLOW FREIGHT WINDS ALONG THE EDGE OF THE RAVAGED HILLSIDE,	204	THE ROSE	83
FRENCH			
--AND PISSOIR FRENCH?	272	DUET	14
FRENCHMEN			
OR FRENCHMEN KILLED A HUNDRED YEARS AGO,	224	OTTO	26
FREQUENTLY			
WOULD FREQUENTLY TALK TO A BUSH,	182	BOY AND BUSH	2
FRESH			
CLOUDS GLOW LIKE COALS JUST FRESH FROM FIRE, A FLARE	17	UNEXTINGUISHED	1
ONLY TO GAIN FRESH TRIUMPHS AND APPLAUSE.	28	THE FAVORITE	6
SIFTING IN A PALM-FULL OF FRESH LOAM,--	42	TRANSPLANTING	4
THE EYES REJOICE IN THE ACT OF SEEING AND THE FRESH AFTER-IMAGE;	163	I'M HERE	79
WHERE THE FRESH AND SALT WATERS MEET,	196	THE LONG WATERS	17
BUT THIS PLACE, WHERE SEA AND FRESH WATER MEET,	202	THE ROSE	2
AND FRESH AS SALT-DRENCHED SKIN.	271	THE REPLY	9
FRESH-CUT			
DEW DEEPENS ON THE FRESH-CUT LAWN;	33	IDYLL	7
FRESHENED			
TO A LANDLOCKED BAY, WHERE THE SALT WATER IS FRESHENED	197	THE LONG WATERS	47
FRESHLY			
LIKE THE BLUE SHINE ON FRESHLY FROZEN SNOW,	201	THE FAR FIELD	96
FRESH-SALTED			
LIKE A FRESH-SALTED SKIN;	153	THE DYING MAN	4
FRIDAY			
TOMORROW IS FRIDAY.	75	I NEED, I NEED	42
FRIEND			
HERE DISTANCE IS FAMILIAR AS A FRIEND.	13	PRAISE PRAIRIE	11
MY FRIEND, THE RAT IN THE WALL, BRINGS ME THE CLEAREST MESSAGES;	88	PRAISE TO END!	84
BUT ME AND A GIRL FRIEND LEARNED A LOT	111	SQUEEZE-BOX	10

	PAGE	TITLE	LINE
FRIEND (CONTINUED)			
THE FIGURE AT MY BACK IS NOT MY FRIEND;	154	THE DYING MAN	38
I DARE CARESS THE STONES, THE FIELD MY FRIEND;	167	HER BECOMING	94
THE FRIEND THAT RUNS BEFORE ME ON THE WINDY HEADLANDS,	198	THE LONG WATERS	71
SWAYS ME AWAKE. WHAT HO, AND THE FIELD'S MY FRIEND,	260	THE CHANGELING	14
FRIENDS			
FOR THEY ARE ALL MY FRIENDS: I SAW ONE SLIDE	105	SIR JOHN DAVIES	7
MY FRIENDS BECOME MORE CHRISTIAN, YEAR BY YEAR.	132	SENTENTIOUS MAN	38
WHAT HER FRIENDS COULDN'T EAT AT THOSE LUNCHES!	179	MYRTLE'S COUSIN	10
AND YOUR FRIENDS,--HOW THEY STARE!	180	GOO-GIRL	13
AMONG MY EIGHT-LEGGED FRIENDS,	209	HER LONGING	5
FRIGHTENED			
WHILE OUT OF FRIGHTENED EYES	31	LULL	20
SAGGED LIKE A FRIGHTENED LIP.	47	THE RETURN	7
FRIGHTFUL			
WE'LL SAIL AWAY FROM THE FRIGHTFUL SHORE	272	DUET	9
FRIGIDAIRES			
FRIGIDAIRES SNORING THE SLEEP OF PLENTY,	48	LAST WORDS	4
FRINGE			
A RAGGED FRINGE	51	THE WAKING (1)	13
FRINGES			
THEIR FILMY FRINGES OF GREEN, THEIR HARSH	205	THE ROSE	90
FRISK			
WHO'S READY FOR PINK AND FRISK?	76	I NEED, I NEED	59
AND THE WRENS SCOLD, AND THE CHICKADEES FRISK AND FROLIC,	234	ALL MORNING	24
FRISKS			
HE FRISKS AND WHISKS, HE CAN.	182	THE LAMB	2
FRO			
MY THIN ARMS TO AND FRO,	207	THE YOUNG GIRL	10
FROG			
HE JERKS A FROG ACROSS HIS BONY LIP,	15	THE HERON	9
THE FROG SCUM APPEAR ON THE POND WITH THE SAME FROTH OF GREEN,	24	VERNAL SENTIMNT	2
TO JERK LIKE A FROG	65	SHAPE OF FIRE	50
ONE, HIS NOSE HAD A FROG,	73	WHERE KNOCK IS	56
A WINTER-LEAPING FROG.	83	O LULL ME, LULL	28
BE LARGE AS AN OWL, BE SLICK AS A FROG,	86	PRAISE TO END!	39
BY SNAILS, BY LEAPS OF FROG, I CAME HERE, SPIRIT.	89	UNFOLD! UNFOLD!	1
ONCE TO THE FROG,	167	HER BECOMING	72
FROGBIT			
THE MARE'S TAIL, THE FLOATING FROGBIT,	209	HER LONGING	4
FROGS			
THE SHRILLEST FROGS;	79	GIVE WAY, GATES	30
FROG'S			
THIS FROG'S HAD ANOTHER FALL.	99	O, THOU OPENING	51
FROLIC			
AND THE WRENS SCOLD, AND THE CHICKADEES FRISK AND FROLIC,	234	ALL MORNING	24
FROLICKS			
SHE FROLICKS LIKE A BEAST;	126	WORDS FOR WIND	101
FROM (219)			
FRONT			
THEY THROW YOU THROUGH THE FRONT PLATE GLASS	267	SAGINAW SONG	17
FROST			
THE FROST BE GONE, FOR GREEN IS BREAKING NOW;	11	LIGHT BRIGHTER	14
BUT SOON COLD RAIN AND FROST COME IN	14	COMING OF COLD	18
THE BEAK OF FROST HAS PICKED THE BOUGH,	14	COMING OF COLD	23
AND FROST IS MARROW-COLD, AND SOON	15	COMING OF COLD	51
FROST MELTED ON FAR PANES;	57	THE LOST SON	145
THE SUN LOOSENING THE FROST ON DECEMBER WINDOWS,	161	I'M HERE	2
AND ROBERT FROST. THEY MIGHT REMEMBER ME."	274	SUPPR W LINDSAY	49
FROSTED			
BLASTING THE FROSTED WINDOWS,	158	FIRST MEDITATN	36
FROSTY			
SPEAK TO ME, FROSTY BEARD.	86	PRAISE TO END!	29
FROTH			
THE FROG SCUM APPEAR ON THE POND WITH THE SAME FROTH OF GREEN,	24	VERNAL SENTIMNT	2
FROWN			
SHE FROWNED HER FROWN.	213	THE HAPPY THREE	8
FROWNED			
SHE FROWNED HER FROWN.	213	THE HAPPY THREE	8
FROZEN			
THE LIGHT MOVED SLOWLY OVER THE FROZEN FIELD,	58	THE LOST SON	155

	PAGE	TITLE	LINE
FROZEN (CONTINUED)			
FROZEN BY A FATHER'S LIP, A MOTHER'S FAILURE TO ANSWER.	169	FOURTH MEDITATN	45
LIKE THE BLUE SHINE ON FRESHLY FROZEN SNOW,	201	THE FAR FIELD	96
FRUIT			
THE YOUNG FRUIT SWELL UPON THE PEAR-TREE BOUGH.	11	LIGHT BRIGHTER	16
AND BATTERED FRUIT HAS CHOKED THE GRASS.	14	COMING OF COLD	7
LATE AUTUMN FRUIT IS ROTTED NOW.	14	COMING OF COLD	27
TO BURST THE FRUIT OF GOOD.	18	GENESIS	8
THE FRUIT ROLLED BY ALL DAY.	46	PICKLE BELT	1
THE FRUIT AND FLESH SMELLS MIXED.	46	PICKLE BELT	6
HANGING, BUNCHED LIKE YOUNG FRUIT, BENDING THE END BRANCHES,	199	THE FAR FIELD	32
FULL			
THE RAIN STAYED IN ITS CLOUD; FULL DARK CAME NEAR;	6	INTERLUDE	9
FULL ON MY NECK I FEEL	34	NIGHT JOURNEY	12
CARRYING HER FULL CARGO OF ROSES.	41	BIG WIND	33
THE FULL RAIN FELL STRAIGHT DOWN,	50	THE CYCLE	14
THE LIGHT, THE FULL SUN	67	SHAPE OF FIRE	79
FULL MERRY, A GLEAM	103	OLD LADY'S WRDS	9
I'M ODD AND FULL OF LOVE.	125	WORDS FOR WIND	67
HER FULL LIPS PURSED, THE ERRANT NOTE TO SEIZE;	127	I KNEW A WOMAN	16
THE MOON GOES TO THE FULL;	148	THE SMALL	7
THE TRICK WAS TO THROW THE CAR SIDEWAYS AND CHARGE OVER THE HILL, FULL OF THE THROTTLE.	193	JOURNY INTERIOR	21
BUT NEVER THE FULL LOOK OF MY EYES,	209	HER RETICENCE	6
THE FULL MOON WAS SHINING UPON THE BROAD SEA;	216	THE SHY MAN	1
THE FULL MOON HAS FALLEN, THE NIGHT WIND IS DOWN	216	THE SHY MAN	17
I GAVE HER BODY FULL AND GRAVE FAREWELL.	241	THE SEQUEL	21
AND PUMPED A SHOULDER FULL OF CORTISONE;	244	INFIRMITY	10
FUME			
THE ARBOR IS ALIVE WITH FUME	14	COMING OF COLD	2
--AND A FUME OF DECAY THAT CLINGS FAST TO THE WOOD.	32	SALE	16
A FUME REMINDS ME, DRIFTING ACROSS WET GRAVEL;	160	FIRST MEDITATN	91
THE SLAG-HEAPS FUME AT THE EDGE OF THE RAW CITIES:	187	THE LONGING	15
A FINE FUME OF RAIN DRIVING IN FROM THE SEA,	230	THE STORM	13
FUMING			
THAT FINE FUMING STINK OF PARTICULAR KETTLES,	48	LAST WORDS	2
FUN			
OLD NEIGHBORS NUDGED EACH OTHER AT THE FUN.	21	THE AUCTION	12
FUNERAL			
THEMSELVES, THEIR PARLORS MUSTY AS A FUNERAL HOME.	5	PROGNOSIS	12
FUNGUS			
I WAS PRIVY TO OILY FUNGUS AND THE ALGAE OF STANDING WATER;	89	UNFOLD! UNFOLD!	25
FUNNIER			
THE FUNNIER THAN THAT,--	71	WHERE KNOCK IS	18
FUNNY			
I WISH I WAS A FUNNY	75	I NEED, I NEED	36
A FUNNY THING ABOUT A CHAIR:	178	THE CHAIR	1
FUR			
THE GARMENT NEITHER FUR NOR HAIR,	19	EPIDERM MACABRE	5
THE STENCH OF THEIR DAMP FUR DRYING IN THE SUN,	189	THE LONGING	55
FURIOUS			
A FURIOUS, DISSEMBLING DIN.	22	SILENCE	14
BIRDS FURIOUS AS BEES.	152	THE SISKINS	18
FURLED			
THE LEAFY MIND, THAT LONG WAS TIGHTLY FURLED,	11	LIGHT BRIGHTER	18
FURNISHED			
THE SCHEME WITHOUT PURPOSE; PRIDE IN A FURNISHED ROOM;	5	PROGNOSIS	10
FURNITURE			
THE FURNITURE POLISHED AND POLISHED SO GRAND,	32	SALE	5
FURRED			
A FURRED CATERPILLAR CRAWLS DOWN A STRING.	220	THE ABYSS	35
A FURRED, A ROCKY POOL,	233	THE PIKE	3
FURROWS			
RUNNING ALONG THE NARROW FURROWS OF THE SHORE, THE ROWS OF DEAD CLAM SHELLS;	190	AT OYSTER RIVER	3
FURTHER			
FURTHER AND FURTHER AWAY	49	NIGHT CROW	6
FURTHER AND FURTHER AWAY	49	NIGHT CROW	6
MORNING-FAIR, FOLLOW ME FURTHER BACK	66	SHAPE OF FIRE	64
FURTIVE			
MORE FURTIVE THAN THE HAND IN LOW	8	PRAYER	11
FURY			
TO THE CANT AND FURY OF	31	LULL	17

	PAGE	TITLE	LINE
FURY (CONTINUED)			
THESE FLOWERS ARE ALL FANGS. COMFORT ME, FURY.	64	SHAPE OF FIRE	9
THE PURE FURY	133	THE PURE FURY	T
WHEN THE PURE FURY FIRST RAGED IN HIS HEAD	133	THE PURE FURY	20
THE FURY OF THE SLUG BENEATH THE STONE.	156	THE DYING MAN	93
THE FURY OF THE HATE-DRIVEN ZEALOT, THE MEANNESS OF THE			
HUMAN WEASEL;	170	FOURTH MEDITATN	68
FURY OF WIND, AND NO APPARENT WIND, ...	171	WHAT TELL BONES	28
A VINE LASHING IN DRY FURY, ...	171	WHAT TELL BONES	30
A FURY OF JAYS, DIVING AND SQUAWKING, ...	234	ALL MORNING	22
I'M A SOCRATES OF SMALL FURY.	260	THE CHANGELING	17
"WHAT MOON?" HE CRIED, HALF-TURNING IN MOCK FURY.	273	SUPPR W LINDSAY	10
FUSE			
DECISION'S SMOKING FUSE;	7	ORDERS FOR DAY	4
FUTILE			
HE SAID, "LOOK, BIRDS, ALL THIS IS FUTILE:	115	THE SERPENT	19
FUZZY			
STEAK GREASE STUCK TO HER FUZZY LEAVES.	228	THE GERANIUM	13
GABBED			
PAST ALDER LANE, AND WE GABBED THERE A WHILE.	274	SUPPR W LINDSAY	47
GAIETY			
INCOMPREHENSIBLE GAIETY AND DREAD	106	SIR JOHN DAVIES	49
GAIN			
ONLY TO GAIN FRESH TRIUMPHS AND APPLAUSE.	28	THE FAVORITE	6
ALL PROFITS DISAPPEAR: THE GAIN	30	THE RECKONING	1
GAINSAYING			
PLATITUDES GARNISHED BEYOND A FOOL'S GAINSAYING;	5	PROGNOSIS	9
GAIT			
THEIR GAIT FORMAL AND ELABORATE, THEIR HAIR A GLORY, ...	170	FOURTH MEDITATN	64
GAME			
HAD SLAUGHTERED GAME, AND CUT YOUNG FIR TREES DOWN.	224	OTTO	21
GANDER			
LOVE LIKES A GANDER, AND ADORES A GOOSE:	127	I KNEW A WOMAN	15
THE LIKELIEST GANDER ALIVE.	258	SONG (3)	18
GARBAGE			
THE GULLS WHEEL OVER THEIR SINGULAR GARBAGE;	187	THE LONGING	16
WHEN I PUT HER OUT, ONCE, BY THE GARBAGE PAIL, ...	228	THE GERANIUM	1
GARDEN			
THE GARDEN SPIDER WEAVES A SILKEN PEAR	12	SLOW SEASON	5
POKING ALONE IN MY GARDEN.	103	OLD LADY'S WRDS	34
I STARED, AND A GARDEN STONE	123	WORDS FOR WIND	23
THE GARDEN IS A RIVER FLOWING SOUTH.	129	SHE	8
EATING THE HEART OUT OF MY GARDEN.	151	SLUG	14
DOWN WOODEN STEPS TOWARD A WEEDY GARDEN;	162	I'M HERE	46
LOOK AT THE FAR TREES AT THE END OF THE GARDEN.	163	I'M HERE	82
I SEE THEM AS FIGURES WALKING IN A GREENY GARDEN, ...	170	FOURTH MEDITATN	63
THE DRY SCENT OF A DYING GARDEN IN SEPTEMBER, ...	201	THE FAR FIELD	78
DOWN IN THE CORNER OF THE GARDEN, AMONG THE RAGGEDY LILACS, . .	204	THE ROSE	64
AND ONE DROPS DOWN TO THE GARDEN, THE HIGH RHODODENDRON, . . .	234	ALL MORNING	8
GAR-EAGLE			
OR RISE WITH THE GAR-EAGLE, THE GREAT-WINGED CONDOR.	209	HER LONGING	16
GARISH			
THE DOCK, SO GARISH TO THE EYE, ...	14	COMING OF COLD	15
GARMENT			
THE GARMENT NEITHER FUR NOR HAIR, ...	19	EPIDERM MACABRE	5
GARMENTS			
IN ROBES OF GREEN, IN GARMENTS OF ADIEU.	201	THE FAR FIELD	86
GARNISHED			
PLATITUDES GARNISHED BEYOND A FOOL'S GAINSAYING;	5	PROGNOSIS	9
GARTER			
BUT SNAKES, BOTH POISONOUS AND GARTER, ...	23	AMOROUS LADY	5
GASPING			
THE DEAD SNAKES AND MUSKRATS, THE TURTLES GASPING IN THE			
RUBBLE, ...	194	JOURNY INTERIOR	36
THE TURTLE GASPING IN THE DUSTY RUBBLE OF THE HIGHWAY, . . .	227	MEADOW MOUSE	27
GATE			
MY MEAT EATS ME. WHO WAITS AT THE GATE?	65	SHAPE OF FIRE	53
I SAID TO THE GATE, ...	76	I NEED, I NEED	63
WHAT'S BEATING AT THE GATE?	154	THE DYING MAN	34
THE TICKET MISLAID OR LOST, THE GATE	158	FIRST MEDITATN	49
I WALKED HIM THROUGH THE GRILL AND OUT THE GATE	274	SUPPR W LINDSAY	46
GATES			
MY GATES ARE ALL CAVES.	59	THE LONG ALLEY	20

	PAGE	TITLE	LINE
GATES (CONTINUED)			
GIVE WAY, YE GATES	79	GIVE WAY, GATES	T
GATHER			
WINDS GATHER IN THE NORTH AND BLOW	15	COMING OF COLD	49
WHERE THE WINDS GATHER, ...	103	OLD LADY'S WRDS	15
GATHERED			
LONG SINCE, BRONZE WHEAT WAS GATHERED INTO SHEAVES.	12	SLOW SEASON	10
SAY TO HIS GATHERED KIN, ...	153	THE DYING MAN	2
I AM GATHERED TOGETHER ONCE MORE;	198	THE LONG WATERS	77
THE FIRST RAIN GATHERED?	202	THE ROSE	30
GATHERING			
GATHERING TO ITSELF SOUND AND SILENCE--	205	THE ROSE	113
GATHERS			
THE DEEP SHADE GATHERS NIGHT;	212	LIGHT LISTENED	17
THE INSTANT GATHERS.	258	SONG (3)	27
GAUGE			
WATCHING THE PRESSURE GAUGE	41	BIG WIND	10
GAVE			
I GAVE HER KISSES BACK, AND WOKE A GHOST.	106	SIR JOHN DAVIES	45
HE SIMPLY GAVE UP SERPENTING.	115	THE SERPENT	3
FOR SHE ASKED NO QUARTER AND GAVE NONE, ...	223	ELEGY (2)	7
THEIR SISTERS GAVE ME, ONCE OR TWICE;	225	THE CHUMS	5
I GAVE HER BODY FULL AND GRAVE FAREWELL.	241	THE SEQUEL	21
GAY			
MY GHOSTS ARE ALL GAY.	88	PRAISE TO END!	100
THIS ANIMAL REMEMBERING TO BE GAY.	105	SIR JOHN DAVIES	12
GAZE			
ALL DISTANT SHAPES TURN BRIGHTER TO THE GAZE.	17	UNEXTINGUISHED	4
THE HOSTILE GAZE OF HATE, ...	20	REPL TO CENSURE	2
RETURN THE GAZE OF A POND.	59	THE LONG ALLEY	30
THY SOFT ALBINO GAZE	81	SENSIBILITY! LA	10
THE ANIMAL'S CANDID GAZE, A SHADE LESS THAN FEATHERS, LIGHT'S BROKEN	98	O, THOU OPENING	22
WITH THE SAME ABSENT GAZE:	130	THE OTHER	20
SWAYING, I TOOK ITS GAZE;	145	THE BEAST	11
TO GAZE AT A FACE WITH THE FIXED EYES OF A SPANIEL?	169	FOURTH MEDITATN	34
OF ENVY'S MEAN GAZE;	217	WISH YOUNG WIFE	5
GAZED			
CLIMBED TO HER ATTIC WINDOW AND GAZED ACROSS THE SILL. ...	27	CLAIRVOY WIDOW	2
AND ONE EYE GAZED ASKEW. "WHY, BLAKE, HE'S DEAD,--	273	SUPPR W LINDSAY	22
GAZER'S			
AND THE HALF-SUNKEN BRANCH BENDS AWAY FROM THE GAZER'S EYE.	233	THE PIKE	9
GAZING			
LONG GAZING AT THE CEILING WILL	257	SANITARIUM	5
GEARS			
THE TEETH OF KNITTED GEARS	9	THE ADAMANT	5
GEESE			
THE LAST GEESE CROSSING AGAINST THE REFLECTED AFTERLIGHT,	202	THE ROSE	17
GENERALS			
THE GENERALS COUGH AND SHIFT	31	LULL	11
GENERATIONS			
MY TONGUE IS GENERATIONS DEAD, ...	8	PRAYER	5
GENESIS			
GENESIS	18	GENESIS	T
GENIUS			
O, I'M THE GENIUS OF THE WORLD,--	268	SAGINAW SONG	43
GENTLE			
ITS RAPE IS GENTLE, NEVER MORE	8	PRAYER	13
THE GENTLE	29	THE GENTLE	T
THE GENTLE AND BEAUTIFUL STILL-TO-BE-BORN;	170	FOURTH MEDITATN	65
GENTLENESS			
I SAID: ON ALL THESE, DEATH, WITH GENTLENESS, COME DOWN.	48	JUDGE NOT	10
GENTLES			
THAT GENTLES ON A SUNNY BLUE PLATEAU.	201	THE FAR FIELD	92
GENTLEST			
DESCEND, O GENTLEST LIGHT, DESCEND, DESCEND.	156	THE DYING MAN	87
GENTLY			
GENTLY ROCKING.	93	I CRY, LOVE!	53
STILL SWAYING GENTLY BY HIS TOES, ...	116	THE SLOTH	11
YET MOVES GENTLY AMONG THE BIRDS.	170	FOURTH MEDITATN	74
AND GENTLY THE LIGHT ENTERS THE SLEEPING SOUL, ...	204	THE ROSE	76
GEORGE			
WHEN GEORGE THE WATCHMAN'S LANTERN DROPPED FROM SIGHT	225	OTTO	38

	PAGE	TITLE	LINE
GERANIUM			
I REMEMBER THE CROSSING-TENDER'S GERANIUM BORDER	29	THE REMINDER	1
MY GERANIUM IS DYING, FOR ALL I CAN DO,	163	I'M HERE	75
THE GERANIUM	228	THE GERANIUM	T
GESTURES			
LET THE GESTURES FREEZE; OUR DOOM IS ALREADY DECIDED.	56	THE LOST SON	105
GET			
SO I'VE GOT TO GET ME A RICH UGLY OLD MAID	112	SQUEEZE-BOX	43
I GET A STEP BEYOND	125	WORDS FOR WIND	65
AND I GO FASTER IN MY RAGE TO GET DONE WITH IT,	151	SLUG	18
I GET MYSELF A STICK,	269	GOB MUSIC	2
I GET A STOOL AND SIT AND STARE	269	GOB MUSIC	12
GETS			
O CURSED BE THE WORK THAT GETS HONORABLE MENTION!	29	THE GENTLE	9
GETTING			
--ABOUT GETTING RID OF OUR MONEY.	111	SQUEEZE-BOX	12
WE'RE GETTING CLOSER TO IT ALL THE TIME."	274	SUPPR W LINDSAY	45
GHOST			
AND THE HONEYMOON BE SPOILED BY A FATHER'S GHOST,	5	PROGNOSIS	14
INCARNADINE AND CARNAL GHOST.	19	EPIDERM MACABRE	16
A WAITING GHOST WARMS UP THE DEAD	60	THE LONG ALLEY	35
A GHOST CAN'T WHISTLE.	73	WHERE KNOCK IS	50
AND THE GHOST OF SOME GREAT HOWL	79	GIVE WAY, GATES	31
THERE'S A GHOST LOOSE IN THE LONG GRASS!	82	SENSIBILITY! LA	27
I'LL FEED THE GHOST ALONE.	85	PRAISE TO END!	11
GHOST, COME CLOSER.	87	PRAISE TO END!	78
I GAVE HER KISSES BACK, AND WOKE A GHOST.	106	SIR JOHN DAVIES	45
THAT GHOST WAS MY OWN CHOICE,	128	THE VOICE	13
A RAW GHOST DRINKS THE FLUID IN MY SPINE;	135	THE RENEWAL	14
GHOST CRIES OUT TO GHOST--	138	THE SURLY ONE	5
GHOST CRIES OUT TO GHOST--	138	THE SURLY ONE	5
A GHOST COMES OUT OF THE UNCONSCIOUS MIND	154	THE DYING MAN	36
DARE I EMBRACE A GHOST FROM MY OWN BREAST?	165	HER BECOMING	21
A GHOST FROM THE SOUL'S HOUSE?	165	HER BECOMING	24
FROM THE GHOST WITHOUT BREATH,	236	SONG (2)	11
GHOSTLY			
A CHEAP CLOCK TICKING IN GHOSTLY CICADA VOICE.	29	THE REMINDER	12
LOOSE GHOSTLY MOUTHS	39	ORCHIDS	17
SPEECH REVIVED, A GHOSTLY GOING OF TAME BEARS, A BRIGHT MOON ON GLEAMING	98	O, THOU OPENING	23
BIRD, GIRL, AND GHOSTLY TREE,	128	THE VOICE	20
THE GHOSTLY FIGURE SUCKED ITS BREATH,	136	THE SENSUALISTS	17
GHOSTS			
MY GHOSTS ARE ALL GAY.	88	PRAISE TO END!	100
GHOULIE			
A GHOULIE IN A DREAM.	71	WHERE KNOCK IS	15
GIBBER			
THE GIBBER	55	THE LOST SON	ST
GIFT			
UPON WHOM EVERY GIFT AND THRILL WERE SHOWERED,	28	THE FAVORITE	10
A YOUNG MOUTH LAUGHS AT A GIFT.	208	HER WORDS	1
GILD			
MAY THE SUN GILD THEM A WORM;	169	FOURTH MEDITATN	60
GILDS			
NO LONGER GILDS THE SCENE AT NOON;	15	COMING OF COLD	48
GILLIFLOWER			
GILLIFLOWER HA,	60	THE LONG ALLEY	47
GILLIFLOWER HO,	60	THE LONG ALLEY	48
GILLS			
NOW THE GILLS ARE BEGINNING TO CRY.	92	I CRY, LOVE!	18
GIN			
AS WE SAT THERE DRINKING THAT BATHTUB GIN	112	SQUEEZE-BOX	24
THE GIN AND CIGARETTES,	136	THE SENSUALISTS	8
SO LONG ON GIN, BOBBIE PINS, HALF-SMOKED CIGARS, DEAD BEER,	228	THE GERANIUM	10
GIRL			
WHERE'S SHE NOW, THE MOUNTAIN'S DOWNY GIRL?	101	THE VISITANT	24
BUT ME AND A GIRL FRIEND LEARNED A LOT	111	SQUEEZE-BOX	10
BIRD, GIRL, AND GHOSTLY TREE,	128	THE VOICE	20
A RAW TUMULTUOUS GIRL	166	HER BECOMING	47
A LEARNED NIMBLE GIRL,	172	WHAT TELL BONES	56
THERE ONCE WAS A GIRL NAMED MYRTLE	179	MYRTLE	1
THE YOUNG GIRL	207	THE YOUNG GIRL	T
THE ROSE LEAPS TO THIS GIRL;	262	FOLLIES OF ADAM	11

	PAGE	TITLE	LINE
GIRL (CONTINUED)			
I'M A ROARING GIRL, AN EXPENSIVE WENCH,	272	DUET	15
GIRLS			
AND BOYS MOON AT GIRLS WITH LAST YEAR'S FATUOUS FACES,	24	VERNAL SENTIMNT	3
GIVE			
WALK BOLDLY MY SISTER BUT DO NOT DEIGN TO GIVE	5	TO MY SISTER	10
HIS NOBLE NATURE BIDS HIM GIVE.	23	AMOROUS LADY	8
NOTHING WOULD GIVE UP LIFE:	38	ROOT CELLAR	10
GIVE ME MY HANDS:	61	THE LONG ALLEY	88
WILL THE SEA GIVE THE WIND SUCK? A TOAD FOLDS INTO A STONE.	64	SHAPE OF FIRE	8
GOD, GIVE ME A NEAR. I HEAR FLOWERS.	73	WHERE KNOCK IS	49
GIVE WAY, YE GATES	79	GIVE WAY, GATES	T
I TAKE IT, AND I GIVE IT BACK AGAIN:	105	SIR JOHN DAVIES	20
HE'LL SIGH AND GIVE HIS BRANCH A HUG;	116	THE SLOTH	9
PASSION'S ENOUGH TO GIVE	124	WORDS FOR WIND	47
WHEN WILL THAT CREATURE GIVE ME BACK MY BREATH?	134	THE PURE FURY	25
I GIVE THE CAT A KICK.	269	GOB MUSIC	6
WE'LL GIVE EACH OTHER A BOX ON THE EAR,	272	DUET	25
GIVES			
PRETENDS HIS DEAD BUNION GIVES EXQUISITE PAIN.	29	THE GENTLE	4
THIS WIND GIVES ME SCALES. HAVE MERCY, GRISTLE:	60	THE LONG ALLEY	33
GIVING			
FROM THE HOUND GIVING TONGUE,	236	SONG (2)	3
GIZZARD			
AT AN INTIMATE PLACE LIKE HIS GIZZARD.	183	THE LIZARD	7
GLACIAL			
OR WHEN TWO RIVERS COMBINE, THE BLUE GLACIAL TORRENT	200	THE FAR FIELD	61
GLAD			
THE GLAD HEN ON THE HILL; AND THE TRELLIS HUMMING.	66	SHAPE OF FIRE	72
MY BROTHER THE VINE IS GLAD.	123	WORDS FOR WIND	8
AND ALL THE WINDS CAME TOWARD ME. I WAS GLAD.	247	I WAITED	23
GLANCE			
I CANNOT PUT MY GLANCE UPON THEM TIGHT.	8	THE SIGNALS	8
GLASS			
FLESH BEHIND STEEL AND GLASS IS UNPROTECTED	5	PROGNOSIS	5
THAT RATTLES DOUBLE GLASS.	34	NIGHT JOURNEY	23
THE FAINT MOON FALLING THROUGH WHITEWASHED GLASS,	39	ORCHIDS	10
CRACKING SO MUCH THIN GLASS	41	BIG WIND	18
READY FOR THE LONG DAYS UNDER THE SLOPED GLASS:	42	TRANSPLANTING	13
MY FEET CRACKLING SPLINTERS OF GLASS AND DRIED PUTTY,	43	CHILD ON GRNHSE	2
UP THROUGH THE STREAKED GLASS, FLASHING WITH SUNLIGHT,	43	CHILD ON GRNHSE	4
THE SONGS TUMBLING OVER AND UNDER THE GLASS,	158	FIRST MEDITATN	44
IN MY MIND'S EYE I SEE THOSE FIELDS OF GLASS,	225	OTTO	34
THEY THROW YOU THROUGH THE FRONT PLATE GLASS	267	SAGINAW SONG	17
GLASSY			
THE POND LAPSES BACK INTO A GLASSY SILENCE.	172	WHAT TELL BONES	50
PETALS AND REFLECTIONS OF PETALS MIXED ON THE SURFACE OF A GLASSY POOL,	194	JOURNY INTERIOR	56
GLAZED			
THE ROAD CHANGING FROM GLAZED TARFACE TO A RUBBLE OF STONE,	199	THE FAR FIELD	8
GLAZING			
GLAZING THE PALE HAIR, THE DUPLICATE GREY STANDARD FACES.	46	DOLOR	13
GLEAM			
GLEAM SHARPLY ON THE NARROW SIGHT.	15	COMING OF COLD	46
FULL MERRY, A GLEAM	103	OLD LADY'S WRDS	9
MAY THEIR EYES GLEAM WITH THE FIRST DAWN;	169	FOURTH MEDITATN	59
GLEAMING			
SPEECH REVIVED, A GHOSTLY GOING OF TAME BEARS, A BRIGHT MOON ON GLEAMING	98	O, THOU OPENING	23
GLEAMING, FREEZING HARD AGAIN, CREAKING AT MIDNIGHT--	191	AT OYSTER RIVER	51
GLIB			
WAS I TOO GLIB ABOUT ETERNAL THINGS,	241	THE SEQUEL	1
GLIDDERED			
EACH SINGLE SUBSTANCE GLIDDERED TO THE STARE;	143	SHIMMER OF EVIL	3
GLIDE			
I SAW A YOUNG SNAKE GLIDE	150	SNAKE	1
GLIDES			
A RIVER GLIDES OUT OF THE GRASS. A RIVER OR A SERPENT.	59	THE LONG ALLEY	1
A TREE GLIDES WITH THE MOON.	122	ALL EARTH, AIR	24
GLIDING			
WHAT GLIDING SHAPE	56	THE LOST SON	88
GLINT			
ITS WINGS CATCHING A LAST GLINT OF THE REFLECTED SUNLIGHT.	190	AT OYSTER RIVER	23

	PAGE	TITLE	LINE
GLINT (CONTINUED)			
GLINT OF THE SUN, BEFORE	210	HER TIME	20
GLINTED			
WHEN THE SUN FOR ME GLINTED THE SIDES OF A SAND GRAIN,	66	SHAPE OF FIRE	68
GLISTEN			
AND THE CYCLAMEN LEAVES GLISTEN LIKE THE BACKS OF BABY TURTLES.	260	THE CHANGELING	15
GLISTENING			
WITH ITS THICK GRASSY SCUM AND CRABS SCUTTLING BACK INTO THEIR GLISTENING CRATERS.	203	THE ROSE	50
GLISTENS			
THE GRAPE GLISTENS.	66	SHAPE OF FIRE	58
GLISTER			
SNAIL, SNAIL, GLISTER ME FORWARD,	53	THE LOST SON	8
GLITTER			
TO STARE INTO THE AFTER-LIGHT, THE GLITTER LEFT ON THE LAKE'S SURFACE,	67	SHAPE OF FIRE	88
THE GLITTER OF WET IN THE FIRST OF MORNING?	161	I'M HERE	3
DELIGHTING IN SURFACE CHANGE, THE GLITTER OF LIGHT ON WAVES,	195	JOURNY INTERIOR	67
GLITTER OF BASALT AND MICA,	265	HARSH COUNTRY	3
GLITTERED			
THE SUN GLITTERED ON A SMALL RAPIDS.	63	FIELD OF LIGHT	34
GLITTERING			
WHEEL OF THE STARS, THE GREAT BEAR GLITTERING COLDER THAN SNOW,	47	DOUBLE FEATURE	11
SHE TURNED THE FIELD INTO A GLITTERING SEA;	120	THE DREAM	27
A POINT OUTSIDE THE GLITTERING CURRENT;	201	THE FAR FIELD	72
PECKING AT CRUSTS AND PEANUTS, THEIR GREEN NECKS GLITTERING;	234	ALL MORNING	28
GLITTERS			
I'M NO MIDGE OF THAT AND THIS. THE DIRT GLITTERS LIKE SALT.	164	I'M HERE	92
GLORIES			
WHAT GLORIES WOULD WE? MOTIONS OF THE SOUL?	135	THE RENEWAL	1
GLORY			
THIS SMOKE'S FROM THE GLORY OF GOD.	59	THE LONG ALLEY	16
GLORY TO SEIZE, I SAY.	81	SENSIBILITY! LA	3
WHEN GLORY FAILED, WE DANCED UPON A PIN.	106	SIR JOHN DAVIES	58
YET REMAIN ONLY HALF AWARE OF THE INTRANSIENT GLORY?	169	FOURTH MEDITATN	32
THEIR GAIT FORMAL AND ELABORATE, THEIR HAIR A GLORY,	170	FOURTH MEDITATN	64
AN UNCERTAIN GLORY,	265	HARSH COUNTRY	2
GLOVE			
HIS HAND COULD FIT INTO A WOMAN'S GLOVE,	224	OTTO	12
GLOW			
CLOUDS GLOW LIKE COALS JUST FRESH FROM FIRE, A FLARE	17	UNEXTINGUISHED	1
GLUP			
SHE WOULD EAT AT ONE GLUP	179	MYRTLE'S COUSIN	3
GLUTTONY			
MUCH LOGIC IN THEIR GLUTTONY.	25	VERSE W ALLUSNS	12
GNU			
THE PENSIVE GNU, THE STAID AARDVARK,	23	AMOROUS LADY	1
THE GNU	180	THE GNU	T
THERE'S THIS TO REMEMBER ABOUT THE GNU:	180	THE GNU	1
GO			
YOU'RE LIKELY TO GO ON LIVING FOR YEARS,	23	ACADEMIC	2
THEIR WIVES GO OUT ON SUNDAY BENEATH THE LATEST HAT.	27	CLAIRVOY WIDOW	8
THOUGH HOME IS NOT HAPPY, WHERE ELSE CAN HE GO?	29	THE GENTLE	10
THE LIGHTS IN THE KITCHENS GO OUT; MOTH WINGS UNFURL;	33	IDYLL	3
WE GO TO OUR BEDS IN A HOUSE AT THE EDGE OF A MEADOW,	33	IDYLL	11
DALLY AT SHOP WINDOWS, STILL RELUCTANT TO GO;	47	DOUBLE FEATURE	6
OUT OF WHAT DOOR DO I GO,	54	THE LOST SON	26
WHERE DO THE ROOTS GO?	55	THE LOST SON	62
GO PLAY WITH YOUR NOSE.	75	I NEED, I NEED	44
BUT I CAN'T GO LEAPING ALONE.	84	O LULL ME, LULL	32
GO WHERE LIGHT IS.	90	UNFOLD! UNFOLD!	56
IS THAT THE PLACE TO GO?	99	O, THOU OPENING	76
I LEARN BY GOING WHERE I HAVE TO GO.	108	THE WAKING (2)	3
AND LEARN BY GOING WHERE I HAVE TO GO.	108	THE WAKING (2)	9
AND, LOVELY, LEARN BY GOING WHERE TO GO.	108	THE WAKING (2)	15
I LEARN BY GOING WHERE I HAVE TO GO.	108	THE WAKING (2)	19
A PLACE I SURELY DID LIKE TO GO	111	SQUEEZE-BOX	17
SHE TURNS, AS IF TO GO,	141	MEMORY	5
OR BROKE, BUT WOULD NOT GO.	147	THE EXORCISM	18
AND I GO FASTER IN MY RAGE TO GET DONE WITH IT,	151	SLUG	18
AND I SEEM TO GO BACKWARD,	158	FIRST MEDITATN	37

	PAGE	TITLE	LINE
GO (CONTINUED)			
THE WIDE STREAMS GO THEIR WAY,	172	WHAT TELL BONES	49
YOU SOMETIMES HAVE TO GO AND SIT.	178	THE CHAIR	4
AND GO HUMPING OFF, YICKETTY-YAK.	178	THE YAK	5
WHEN YOU SLURP AND GO, POOF!	180	GOO-GIRL	10
THE BEAR SAID, SIR, YOU GO TOO FAR,	181	MONOTONY SONG	9
A TIME TO GO HOME!--	230	THE STORM	17
WHEN WE ABIDE YET GO	237	THE TRANCED	3
WHICH IS THE WAY? I ASK, AND TURN TO GO,	245	THE DECISION	11
BURNING IN SAND. "IT LOOKS LIKE I SHOULD GO,"--	274	SUPPR W LINDSAY	37
GOAT			
MY HOE EATS LIKE A GOAT.	76	I NEED, I NEED	60
GOATS			
LIKE SMALL GOATS.	51	THE WAKING (1)	12
GOAT'S			
WILL THE GOAT'S MOUTH	60	THE LONG ALLEY	60
GOB			
GOB MUSIC	269	GOB MUSIC	T
GOD			
THIS SMOKE'S FROM THE GLORY OF GOD.	59	THE LONG ALLEY	16
LUMINOUS ONE, SHALL WE MEET ON THE BOSOM OF GOD?	59	THE LONG ALLEY	29
GOD, GIVE ME A NEAR. I HEAR FLOWERS.	73	WHERE KNOCK IS	49
MAYBE GOD HAS A HOUSE.	74	WHERE KNOCK IS	88
BAGS? WHO EVER SAID GOD SANG IN YOUR FAT SHAPE? YOU'RE NOT THE ONLY	98	O, THOU OPENING	27
THE MARROW OF GOD, TALKING,	103	OLD LADY'S WRDS	8
GOD PITY THOSE BUT WANTON TO THE KNEES,--	106	SIR JOHN DAVIES	62
GOD BLESS THE GROUND! I SHALL WALK SOFTLY THERE,	108	THE WAKING (2)	8
COULD BRING ME TO MY GOD?	139	PLAINT	8
OR LISTEN INTO SILENCE, LIKE A GOD.	140	THE SWAN	20
THAT GOD HIMSELF CAN SCARCELY BEAR.	144	ELEGY (1)	4
GOD COULD BELIEVE: I AM HERE TO FEAR.	144	ELEGY (1)	12
THAT GOD THAT GOD LEANS DOWN HIS HEART TO HEAR.	144	ELEGY (1)	16
THAT GOD THAT GOD LEANS DOWN HIS HEART TO HEAR.	144	ELEGY (1)	16
WAS IT A GOD HIS SUFFERING RENEWED?--	155	THE DYING MAN	60
IN SUCH TIMES, LACKING A GOD,	160	FIRST MEDITATN	98
THE CAUSE OF GOD IN ME--HAS IT GONE?	172	WHAT TELL BONES	51
TO TRY TO BECOME LIKE GOD	172	WHAT TELL BONES	59
IS FAR FROM BECOMING GOD.	172	WHAT TELL BONES	60
THINKING, GOD HAS NEED OF ME.	172	WHAT TELL BONES	63
AND I ACKNOWLEDGE MY FOOLISHNESS WITH GOD,	196	THE LONG WATERS	8
DO WE MOVE TOWARD GOD, OR MERELY ANOTHER CONDITION?	221	THE ABYSS	75
THE LORD GOD HAS TAKEN MY HEAVINESS AWAY;	222	THE ABYSS	98
THE MIND ENTERS ITSELF, AND GOD THE MIND,	239	IN A DARK TIME	23
BROODING ON GOD, I MAY BECOME A MAN.	246	THE MARROW	10
GODHEAD ABOVE MY GOD, ARE YOU THERE STILL?	246	THE MARROW	13
UPON THAT GOD WHO KNOWS WHAT I WOULD KNOW.	246	THE MARROW	24
GOD BLESS THE ROOTS!--BODY AND SOUL ARE ONE!	250	THE RIGHT THING	7
GOD-FURIOUS			
A COLD GOD-FURIOUS MAN	147	THE EXORCISM	21
GODHEAD			
GODHEAD ABOVE MY GOD, ARE YOU THERE STILL?	246	THE MARROW	13
GODS			
YOU ALL-OF-A-SUDDEN GODS,	82	SENSIBILITY! LA	26
IN THAT DARK WORLD WHERE GODS HAVE LOST THEIR WAY.	106	SIR JOHN DAVIES	48
OF HER CHOICE VIRTUES ONLY GODS SHOULD SPEAK,	127	I KNEW A WOMAN	5
THE GREAT GODS ARCH MY BONES.	137	LOVE'S PROGRESS	5
A FACE FLOATS IN THE FERNS. DO MAIMED GODS WALK?	165	HER BECOMING	18
GOD'S			
AS YOU LOOK ACROSS MY CITY, IN GOD'S COUNTRY?"	27	CLAIRVOY WIDOW	4
GOD'S SOMEWHERE ELSE,	74	WHERE KNOCK IS	80
GOD'S IN THAT STONE, OR I AM NOT A MAN!	149	IN LATE SUMMER	12
GOD'S NIGHT AND DAY: DOWN THIS SPACE HE HAS SMILED,	243	THE MOTION	21
RUNNING FROM GOD'S THE LONGEST RACE OF ALL.	245	THE DECISION	2
GOES			
INTO THE FLAT-BOX IT GOES,	42	TRANSPLANTING	12
IT USUALLY GOES.	54	THE LOST SON	49
IT USUALLY GOES.	55	THE LOST SON	61
TRICKSY COMES AND TRICKSY GOES	60	THE LONG ALLEY	39
A CAT GOES WIDER.	92	I CRY, LOVE!	9
THEN OFF AGAIN TO SLEEP HE GOES,	116	THE SLOTH	10
THE MOON GOES TO THE FULL;	148	THE SMALL	7
THE MOON GOES SLOWLY DOWN;	148	THE SMALL	8

	PAGE	TITLE	LINE
GOES (CONTINUED)			
BUT IT GOES NOWHERE."	219	THE ABYSS	4
THE BULB GOES ON AND OFF, WEAKLY.	231	THE STORM	36
A MAN GOES FAR TO FIND OUT WHAT HE IS--	239	IN A DARK TIME	16
GOGGLES			
AND THE DUST LAY THICK ON MY EYELIDS,--WHO EVER WORE GOGGLES?--	193	JOURNY INTERIOR	24
GOING			
THE HEAT GOING DOWN	39	ORCHIDS	11
WHERE WERE THE GREENHOUSES GOING,	41	BIG WIND	1
GOODBYE, GOODBYE, OLD STONES, THE TIME-ORDER IS GOING,	56	THE LOST SON	108
SPEECH REVIVED, A GHOSTLY GOING OF TAME BEARS, A BRIGHT MOON ON GLEAMING	98	O, THOU OPENING	23
GOING IS KNOWING.	99	O, THOU OPENING	83
I LEARN BY GOING WHERE I HAVE TO GO.	108	THE WAKING (2)	3
AND LEARN BY GOING WHERE I HAVE TO GO.	108	THE WAKING (2)	9
AND, LOVELY, LEARN BY GOING WHERE TO GO.	108	THE WAKING (2)	15
I LEARN BY GOING WHERE I HAVE TO GO.	108	THE WAKING (2)	19
I THOUGHT I WAS GOING TO SMOTHER.	162	I'M HERE	50
WHERE WAS I GOING? WHERE?	166	HER BECOMING	61
GOING, WE STAYED; AND NIGHT TURNED INTO DAY;	237	THE TRANCED	12
GOLD			
MY PALM-SWEAT FLASHES GOLD;	88	PRAISE TO END!	87
FLASHING BETWEEN GOLD LEVELS OF THE LATE SUN,	232	THE THING	5
A COLOR PURE, O PURE AS GOLD,	269	GOB MUSIC	26
GOLDEN			
HOW SLOW THE CHANGES OF A GOLDEN MEAN:	133	THE PURE FURY	12
WAS CALLED THE GOLDEN RHULE,--	267	SAGINAW SONG	28
GOLDY			
ROMPED UPON THE GOLDY GRASS,	87	PRAISE TO END!	57
GONE			
THE FROST BE GONE, FOR GREEN IS BREAKING NOW;	11	LIGHT BRIGHTER	14
THE GULLS RIDE ON THE WATER, THE GULLS HAVE COME AND GONE,	28	CLAIRVOY WIDOW	23
GONE THE THREE ANCIENT LADIES	44	FRAU BAUMAN	1
CALL OFF THE DOGS, MY PAWS ARE GONE.	61	THE LONG ALLEY	85
HE'S GONE FOR ALWAYS,	72	WHERE KNOCK IS	25
THE CHILL'S GONE FROM THE MOON.	77	BRING THE DAY!	18
THE RINGS HAVE GONE FROM THE POND.	85	PRAISE TO END!	13
THE GOOD DAY HAS GONE:	103	OLD LADY'S WRDS	25
GONE TO BOLSTER A ROAD.	103	OLD LADY'S WRDS	36
AND I HAVE GONE NOWHERE.	137	LOVE'S PROGRESS	20
THE GREAT ROUND EYES HAD GONE.	145	THE BEAST	17
IT QUICKENED, AND WAS GONE.	150	SNAKE	8
I HAVE GONE INTO THE WASTE LONELY PLACES	159	FIRST MEDITATN	74
THE CAUSE OF GOD IN ME--HAS IT GONE?	172	WHAT TELL BONES	51
YEA, I HAVE GONE AND STAYED.	173	WHAT TELL BONES	96
THAT HE WAS GONE, WOULD BE THE ROOF;	178	THE CEILING	4
THE MORNING BIRDS GONE, THE TWITTERING FINCHES,	202	THE ROSE	14
WHERE HE HAS GONE,	208	THE APPARITION	2
THAT I WAS GONE.	213	THE HAPPY THREE	4
ALL RAGE WAS GONE.	213	THE HAPPY THREE	28
WHERE HAS HE GONE, MY MEADOW MOUSE,	227	MEADOW MOUSE	21
WHERE HAVE THE PEOPLE GONE?	230	THE STORM	8
"THE OTHER'S GONE DEAD,"	249	THE RESTORED	8
"THE SPIDER'S GONE," HE SAID BEMUSEDLY.	274	SUPPR W LINDSAY	39
GONG			
THE GONG OF MIDNIGHT STRUCK	238	THE MOMENT	7
GOO			
AND THEN MAKING GOO,	180	GOO-GIRL	4
A MAN NAMED PHILANDER S. GOO	182	PHILANDER	1
GOOD			
TO BURST THE FRUIT OF GOOD.	18	GENESIS	8
DEFAMERS OF THE GOOD.	20	REPL TO CENSURE	5
THEIR ONLY NOTION OF THE GOOD	25	VERSE W ALLUSNS	7
WHATEVER HE SMELLED WAS GOOD:	46	PICKLE BELT	5
BE GOOD AS A GOOSE, BE BIG AS A DOG,	86	PRAISE TO END!	40
THE GOOD DAY HAS GONE:	103	OLD LADY'S WRDS	25
I DRINK GOOD LIQUOR WHEN MY LUCK IS GOOD.	132	SENTENTIOUS MAN	28
I DRINK GOOD LIQUOR WHEN MY LUCK IS GOOD.	132	SENTENTIOUS MAN	28
YOU'VE TOO MANY TUNES, AND NONE OF THEM GOOD:	177	KITTY-CAT BIRD	5
NOW THAT'S A PIECE OF GOOD ADVICE	181	MONOTONY SONG	3
REFITS ME FOR THE TRUE AND GOOD.	256	IN HYDROTHERAPY	6
CAN BRING A GOOD MAN DOWN.	269	GOB MUSIC	19

	PAGE	TITLE	LINE
GOOD (CONTINUED)			
WILL BRING A GOOD MAN DOWN.	270	GOB MUSIC	47
GOODBYE			
GOODBYE, GOODBYE, OLD STONES, THE TIME-ORDER IS GOING,	56	THE LOST SON	108
GOODBYE, GOODBYE, OLD STONES, THE TIME-ORDER IS GOING,	56	THE LOST SON	108
GOOD-BYE			
GOOD-BYE FOR BEING WRONG.	76	I NEED, I NEED	50
GOODNESS			
BUT GOODNESS ME, HER FATHER'S RICH!	181	MONOTONY SONG	19
GOO-GIRL			
GOO-GIRL	180	GOO-GIRL	T
GOOSE			
SHE WAVES TO THE GOOSE,	60	THE LONG ALLEY	52
IT WASN'T A GOOSE,	77	BRING THE DAY!	15
BE GOOD AS A GOOSE, BE BIG AS A DOG,	86	PRAISE TO END!	40
LOVE LIKES A GANDER, AND ADORES A GOOSE:	127	I KNEW A WOMAN	15
BUT OUR GOOSE, MARIANNE,	213	THE HAPPY THREE	18
GORGE			
THEN LOST ITSELF DOWN THROUGH A ROCKY GORGE.	247	I WAITED	20
GOSSAMER			
STRAIGHT FROM THE OAK, THE GOSSAMER IS HUNG.	12	SLOW SEASON	7
GOT			
I KNOW WHO'S GOT HIM,	72	WHERE KNOCK IS	27
SO I'VE GOT TO GET ME A RICH UGLY OLD MAID	112	SQUEEZE-BOX	43
--HE'D GOT IN: DIRTY DINKY.	114	DINKY	16
HE GOT NO PLEASURE DOWN HIS HOLE.	115	THE SERPENT	8
AND GOT A MOST COMMODIOUS TUBA;	115	THE SERPENT	16
THEY GOT A HORN, THEY GOT A FLUTE,	115	THE SERPENT	17
THEY GOT A HORN, THEY GOT A FLUTE,	115	THE SERPENT	17
THE WHOLE PLACE SHOOK WHENEVER I GOT A CHILL--	163	I'M HERE	64
AND WHEN HE GOT TO THE SHORE,	263	FOLLIES OF ADAM	34
"LET'S EAT!" SAID LINDSAY. "HERE WE'VE GOT THE MOON,	273	SUPPR W LINDSAY	15
WE'VE GOT THE LIVING LIGHT, BUT WHERE'S THE FOOD?"	273	SUPPR W LINDSAY	16
GRACE			
HE WALKS THE SHALLOW WITH AN ANTIC GRACE.	15	THE HERON	5
WAY TO ANOTHER GRACE!--	83	O LULL ME, LULL	23
WHAT GRACE I HAVE IS ENOUGH.	91	UNFOLD! UNFOLD!	60
GRACEFUL			
HOWEVER GRACEFUL THE POSTURE.	172	WHAT TELL BONES	37
HOW GRACEFUL THE SMALL BEFORE DANGER!	192	AT OYSTER RIVER	67
GRACELESS			
I'M CRAZED AND GRACELESS,	83	O LULL ME, LULL	27
GRACIOUS			
GRACIOUS AND BLAND,	103	OLD LADY'S WRDS	10
GRADUAL			
RECALL THE GRADUAL DARK THE SNOW'S UNMEASURED FALL	5	TO MY SISTER	3
THE GRADUAL EMBRACE	139	PLAINT	15
GRAIN			
WITH ANKLES BRUISED FROM STUBBLE OF THE GRAIN.	13	PRAISE PRAIRIE	8
AROUND A CENTRAL GRAIN	18	GENESIS	11
WHEN THE SUN FOR ME GLINTED THE SIDES OF A SAND GRAIN,	66	SHAPE OF FIRE	68
GRAINS			
THE TIGHT GRAINS PARTING AT LAST.	37	CUTTINGS (LATE)	8
GRAMMAR			
SHE KNEW THE GRAMMAR OF LEAST MOTION, SHE	120	THE DREAM	23
GRAND			
THE FURNITURE POLISHED AND POLISHED SO GRAND,	32	SALE	5
GRANDEUR			
THE GRANDEUR OF A CRAZY ONE ALONE!--	167	HER BECOMING	90
GRANDFATHER'S			
--AND GRANDFATHER'S SINISTER HOVERING HAND.	32	SALE	8
GRANDMOTHER'S			
IN MY GRANDMOTHER'S INNER EYE,	163	I'M HERE	71
GRANDPA			
I SEE GRANDPA SURVIVING A SERIES OF SEVEN STROKES,	28	CLAIRVOY WIDOW	21
GRANDPA'S			
--ON THAT CHUNK OF GRANDPA'S MONEY.	112	SQUEEZE-BOX	33
GRANITE			
THE VALLEY ROCKED BENEATH THE GRANITE HILL;	106	SIR JOHN DAVIES	59
GRANITIC			
IN THAT COLD, GRANITIC SLIME,	49	RIVER INCIDENT	10
GRAPE			
REACHED FOR A GRAPE	62	FIELD OF LIGHT	11

	PAGE	TITLE	LINE
GRAPE (CONTINUED)			
THE GRAPE GLISTENS.	66	SHAPE OF FIRE	58
GRAPES			
TO THE CLAY BANKS, AND THE WILD GRAPES HANGING FROM THE ELMTREES.	200	THE FAR FIELD	66
GRASS			
THE WIND LAY MOTIONLESS IN THE LONG GRASS.	6	INTERLUDE	10
AND BATTERED FRUIT HAS CHOKED THE GRASS.	14	COMING OF COLD	7
OF MARSH GRASS HEAPED ABOVE A MUSK-RAT HOLE.	15	THE HERON	4
HOW COOL THE GRASS IS.	56	THE LOST SON	113
A RIVER GLIDES OUT OF THE GRASS. A RIVER OR A SERPENT.	59	THE LONG ALLEY	1
IN THE DEEP GRASS AT THE EDGE OF FIELD,	62	FIELD OF LIGHT	25
THE GRASS SAYS WHAT THE WIND SAYS:	77	BRING THE DAY!	29
BRING ME A FINGER. THIS DIRT'S LONESOME FOR GRASS.	79	GIVE WAY, GATES	7
THERE'S A GHOST LOOSE IN THE LONG GRASS!	82	SENSIBILITY! LA	27
ROMPED UPON THE GOLDY GRASS,	87	PRAISE TO END!	57
A LAPFUL OF APPLES SLEEPS IN THIS GRASS.	92	I CRY, LOVE!	24
THE LIVE GRASS WHIRLS WITH THE SUN,	93	I CRY, LOVE!	35
THE WHITE GRASS BENDING AWAY,	103	OLD LADY'S WRDS	20
LET SEED BE GRASS, AND GRASS TURN INTO HAY:	127	I KNEW A WOMAN	22
LET SEED BE GRASS, AND GRASS TURN INTO HAY:	127	I KNEW A WOMAN	22
THE GRASS CHANGES TO STONE.	141	MEMORY	12
THE LONG LUSH GRASS LAY STILL;	145	THE BEAST	18
A WIND MOVES THROUGH THE GRASS,	148	THE SMALL	11
WHAT MOVES IN GRASS I LOVE--	148	THE SMALL	21
CREEPING SLOWLY OVER THE WET GRASS,	151	SLUG	13
RACE OVER THE THICK GRASS;	152	THE SISKINS	6
IN THE COUNTRY OF FEW LAKES, IN THE TALL BUFFALO GRASS AT THE BASE OF THE CLAY BUTTES,	189	THE LONGING	53
WHERE THE YELLOWISH PRONGS OF GRASS POKE THROUGH THE BLACKENED ASH,	196	THE LONG WATERS	15
AND THE TIDE RISES UP AGAINST THE GRASS	202	THE ROSE	9
I THINK OF THE NESTLING FALLEN INTO THE DEEP GRASS,	227	MEADOW MOUSE	26
PERIPHERAL DIPPERS COME TO REST ON THE SHORT GRASS,	235	ALL MORNING	34
GRASSES			
THE GRASSES WHITELY STIR;	17	NO BIRD	6
MY HEART LIFTED UP WITH THE GREAT GRASSES;	63	FIELD OF LIGHT	46
THE GREEN GRASSES,--WOULD THEY?	77	BRING THE DAY!	6
THE GREEN GRASSES?--	77	BRING THE DAY!	7
RUNNING THROUGH HIGH GRASSES,	161	I'M HERE	21
A DRIED STALK IN A WELTER OF SINUOUS GRASSES,	255	LIGHT POEM	8
GRASS-HIDDEN			
WHERE THE TURF DROPS OFF INTO A GRASS-HIDDEN CULVERT,	199	THE FAR FIELD	14
GRASSY			
I RISE AND FALL IN THE SLOW SEA OF A GRASSY PLAIN,	194	JOURNY INTERIOR	42
WITH ITS THICK GRASSY SCUM AND CRABS SCUTTLING BACK INTO THEIR GLISTENING CRATERS.	203	THE ROSE	50
GRATE			
YOU MEW LIKE A CAT, YOU GRATE LIKE A JAY:	177	KITTY-CAT BIRD	9
GRATEFUL			
I'M GRATEFUL FOR THAT.	225	THE CHUMS	11
GRAVE			
LET LIGHT ATTEND ME TO THE GRAVE!	8	PRAYER	22
ALIVE, IN A SLIPPERY GRAVE.	39	WEED PULLER	16
WHO ELSE BREATHES HERE? WHAT DOES THE GRAVE SAY?	59	THE LONG ALLEY	19
CAN THE BONES BREATHE? THIS GRAVE HAS AN EAR.	87	PRAISE TO END!	75
WHAT THE GRAVE SAYS,	91	UNFOLD! UNFOLD!	63
OVER THIS DAMP GRAVE I SPEAK THE WORDS OF MY LOVE:	102	ELEGY FOR JANE	20
ALL SENSUAL LOVE'S BUT DANCING ON A GRAVE.	154	THE DYING MAN	47
MADE FROM HIS TERROR AND DISMAY A GRAVE PHILOSOPHICAL LANGUAGE;	170	FOURTH MEDITATN	72
GRAVE, HIERATIC, A PIECE OF ASSYRIAN SCULPTURE,	234	ALL MORNING	10
I GAVE HER BODY FULL AND GRAVE FAREWELL.	241	THE SEQUEL	21
GRAVEL			
IN THE SPARROW, HAPPY ON GRAVEL;	88	PRAISE TO END!	91
THE GRAVEL, MY NOSE WETTER THAN HIS.	151	SLUG	7
A FUME REMINDS ME, DRIFTING ACROSS WET GRAVEL;	160	FIRST MEDITATN	91
I REMEMBER HOW IT WAS TO DRIVE IN GRAVEL,	193	JOURNY INTERIOR	18
GRAVES			
NEAR THE GRAVES OF THE GREAT DEAD,	170	FOURTH MEDITATN	87
GRAVY			
AND THAT GRAVY AND FAT	180	GOO-GIRL	7

	PAGE	TITLE	LINE
GRAY			
I LOOK ON WHITE, AND IT TURNS INTO GRAY--	134	THE PURE FURY	24
GRAYING			
THE VINES GRAYING TO A FINE POWDER.	159	FIRST MEDITATN	81
GRAZED			
I SANG TO THE WHITE HORSE THAT GRAZED ON THE QUAY,--	216	THE SHY MAN	3
GRAZING			
THE FLOATING HAWKS, THE JACKRABBITS, THE GRAZING CATTLE--	194	JOURNY INTERIOR	38
GREASE			
THEN ROLL THEM IN GREASE,--	55	THE LOST SON	56
STEAK GREASE STUCK TO HER FUZZY LEAVES.	228	THE GERANIUM	13
GREAT			
THE GREAT SLEDGE DROPS IN VAIN.	9	THE ADAMANT	2
THE GREAT FEET BREAK THE RIDGES OF THE SAND,	15	THE HERON	6
GREAT CANNAS OR DELICATE CYCLAMEN TIPS,--	38	FORCING HOUSE	4
WHEEL OF THE STARS, THE GREAT BEAR GLITTERING COLDER THAN SNOW,	47	DOUBLE FEATURE	11
THE GREAT ELM FILLED WITH BIRDS.	63	FIELD OF LIGHT	36
MY HEART LIFTED UP WITH THE GREAT GRASSES;	63	FIELD OF LIGHT	46
AND YOU, CAT AFTER GREAT MILK AND VASTY FISHES,	79	GIVE WAY, GATES	9
THE SEA WILL BE THERE, THE GREAT SQUASHY SHADOWS,	79	GIVE WAY, GATES	28
AND THE GHOST OF SOME GREAT HOWL	79	GIVE WAY, GATES	31
WE'LL STRETCH WITH THE GREAT STEMS.	80	GIVE WAY, GATES	35
TELL ME, GREAT LORDS OF STING,	83	O LULL ME, LULL	8
SOOTHE ME, GREAT GROANS OF UNDERNEATH,	84	O LULL ME, LULL	29
IT'S A GREAT DAY FOR THE MICE.	85	PRAISE TO END!	5
WHERE'S THE GREAT RAGE OF A ROCKING HEART, THE HIGH RARE TRUE DANGEROUS	98	O, THOU OPENING	30
THE GREAT SWAMPS FLASH.	103	OLD LADY'S WRDS	13
THE GREAT WHEEL TURNS ITS AXLE WHEN IT CAN;	105	SIR JOHN DAVIES	3
OUR SOULS LOOKED FORTH, AND THE GREAT DAY STOOD STILL.	106	SIR JOHN DAVIES	60
GREAT NATURE HAS ANOTHER THING TO DO	108	THE WAKING (2)	13
WHAT DO THE GREAT DEAD SAY?	123	WORDS FOR WIND	10
GREAT BOEHME ROOTED ALL IN YES AND NO;	133	THE PURE FURY	13
THE GREAT GODS ARCH MY BONES.	137	LOVE'S PROGRESS	5
I CAME TO A GREAT DOOR,	145	THE BEAST	1
AND THERE A GREAT BEAST PLAYED,	145	THE BEAST	6
THE GREAT ROUND EYES HAD GONE.	145	THE BEAST	17
PLACES GREAT WITH THEIR DEAD,	154	THE DYING MAN	21
A GREAT WOODEN SLEIGH CAREENING BEHIND THEM,	158	FIRST MEDITATN	54
DARE I SPEAK, ONCE MORE, IN THE MONOTONY OF GREAT PRAISE,	166	HER BECOMING	32
NEAR THE GRAVES OF THE GREAT DEAD,	170	FOURTH MEDITATN	87
WHEN HE TRIED TO SPOUT, THAT GREAT BIG LUBBER,	178	THE WHALE	3
AND THEY'LL SOON STAY AWAY IN GREAT BUNCHES!"	180	GOO-GIRL	16
THE GREAT TREES NO LONGER SHIMMER;	187	THE LONGING	17
A GREAT FLAME RISES FROM THE SUNLESS SEA;	188	THE LONGING	31
I WOULD BE A STREAM, WINDING BETWEEN GREAT STRIATED ROCKS IN LATE SUMMER;	188	THE LONGING	46
A SINGLE WAVE COMES IN LIKE THE NECK OF A GREAT SWAN	197	THE LONG WATERS	52
THE GREAT LOGS PILED LIKE MATCHSTICKS.	222	THE ABYSS	96
UNDER THE EYE OF THE GREAT OWL WATCHING FROM THE ELM-TREE,	227	MEADOW MOUSE	24
FOR THE GREAT LAST LEAP OF THE WAVE OVER THE BREAKWATER,	231	THE STORM	40
THE PASSENGER PIGEON, THE GREAT AUK, THE CAROLINA PARAQUET,	235	ALL MORNING	44
THE GREAT DAY BALANCES UPON THE LEAVES;	244	INFIRMITY	27
THE SMALL BECOME THE GREAT, THE GREAT THE SMALL;	250	THE RIGHT THING	8
THE SMALL BECOME THE GREAT, THE GREAT THE SMALL;	250	THE RIGHT THING	8
AND THE GREAT LEAVES CANCEL THEIR STEMS;	259	SONG (3)	50
GREATER			
WHAT'S GREATER, PEBBLE OR POND?	251	ONCE MORE, RND	1
GREAT-WINGED			
OR RISE WITH THE GAR-EAGLE, THE GREAT-WINGED CONDOR.	209	HER LONGING	16
GREEK			
OR ENGLISH POETS WHO GREW UP ON GREEK	127	I KNEW A WOMAN	6
GREEN			
THE FROST BE GONE, FOR GREEN IS BREAKING NOW;	11	LIGHT BRIGHTER	14
WILL TURN ITS PRIVATE SUBSTANCE INTO GREEN,	11	LIGHT BRIGHTER	19
ALL SUMMER GREEN IS NOW UNDONE:	15	COMING OF COLD	42
THE FROG SCUM APPEAR ON THE POND WITH THE SAME FROTH OF GREEN,	24	VERNAL SENTIMNT	2
THE GREEN COMES UP FOREVER IN THE FIELDS OF OUR COUNTRY."	28	CLAIRVOY WIDOW	26
AND PULLED THE GREEN SHADE AGAINST MORNING SUN.	29	THE REMINDER	8
COILED GREEN AND THICK, LIKE DRIPPING SMILAX,	39	WEED PULLER	8

	PAGE	TITLE	LINE
GREEN (CONTINUED)			
OF GREEN, OR PLUNGED TO MY ELBOWS IN THE SPONGY YELLOWISH MOSS OF THE MARSHES:	40	MOSS-GATHERING	8
BEHIND THE GREEN VISCID TRELLIS,	62	FIELD OF LIGHT	24
THE GREEN GRASSES,--WOULD THEY?	77	BRING THE DAY!	6
THE GREEN GRASSES?--	77	BRING THE DAY!	7
IN THE GREEN OF MY SLEEP,	79	GIVE WAY, GATES	12
IN THE GREEN.	79	GIVE WAY, GATES	13
THE LAKE TURNED GREEN;	87	PRAISE TO END!	56
I SING THE GREEN, AND THINGS TO COME,	99	O, THOU OPENING	56
YOU GREEN THING IN MY WAY!"	123	WORDS FOR WIND	14
THE GREEN, THE SPRINGING GREEN	124	WORDS FOR WIND	55
THE GREEN, THE SPRINGING GREEN	124	WORDS FOR WIND	55
THE GREEN, THE ALTERED LEAF,	125	WORDS FOR WIND	85
A MEADOW, LUSH AND GREEN.	145	THE BEAST	5
STANDING, SILENT, ON SANDY BEACHES OR WALKING ALONG GREEN EMBANKMENTS;	168	FOURTH MEDITATN	4
MAY THEY SLEEP IN ROBES OF GREEN, AMONG THE ANCIENT FERNS;	169	FOURTH MEDITATN	58
I NO LONGER CRY FOR GREEN IN THE MIDST OF CINDERS,	173	WHAT TELL BONES	74
THE YOUNG SNAKE, POISED IN GREEN LEAVES, WAITING FOR ITS FLY,	190	AT OYSTER RIVER	28
IN ROBES OF GREEN, IN GARMENTS OF ADIEU.	201	THE FAR FIELD	86
THEIR FILMY FRINGES OF GREEN, THEIR HARSH	205	THE ROSE	90
A GREEN THING LOVES THE GREEN	212	LIGHT LISTENED	15
A GREEN THING LOVES THE GREEN	212	LIGHT LISTENED	15
SURVIVE THE GREEN ICE	217	WISH YOUNG WIFE	4
PECKING AT CRUSTS AND PEANUTS, THEIR GREEN NECKS GLITTERING;	234	ALL MORNING	28
GREEN, A BIRD TIPPING THE TOPMOST BOUGH,	235	MANIFESTATION	2
GREENEST			
MAX LAURISCH HAD THE GREENEST THUMB OF ALL.	224	OTTO	7
GREENHOUSE			
CHILD ON TOP OF A GREENHOUSE	43	CHILD ON GRNHSE	T
WHO CREAKED ON THE GREENHOUSE LADDERS,	44	FRAU BAUMAN	2
THROUGH THE LONG GREENHOUSE.	57	THE LOST SON	125
TWO SONG SPARROWS, ONE WITHIN A GREENHOUSE,	158	FIRST MEDITATN	39
HE WALKED OUR GREENHOUSE LAND.	268	SAGINAW SONG	55
GREENHOUSES			
WHERE WERE THE GREENHOUSES GOING,	41	BIG WIND	1
WHITE AND RED, IN THE WIDE SIX-HUNDRED-FOOT GREENHOUSES,	203	THE ROSE	52
GREENISH			
ONE GREENISH LID LIFTS A BIT HIGHER,	226	THE LIZARD	23
GREENS			
DEEP IN THE GREENS OF SUMMER SING THE LIVES	244	INFIRMITY	25
GREENY			
I SEE THEM AS FIGURES WALKING IN A GREENY GARDEN,	170	FOURTH MEDITATN	63
GREET			
LEANING ACROSS A SILL TO GREET THE DAWN?	154	THE DYING MAN	44
WITH ALL THE AIR TO GREET HIM AS HE FLIES,	205	THE ROSE	109
GREW			
THE CHAOS GREW AS HOUR BY HOUR THE LIGHT	6	INTERLUDE	5
THE AIR GREW LOOSE AND LOUD.	50	THE CYCLE	12
I GREW TIRED OF THE RITUAL OF NAMES AND THE ASSISTANT KEEPER OF THE MOLLUSKS:	65	SHAPE OF FIRE	36
OR ENGLISH POETS WHO GREW UP ON GREEK	127	I KNEW A WOMAN	6
MY BREATH GREW LESS. I LISTENED LIKE A BEAST.	166	HER BECOMING	53
WHO TURNED A CORNER IN TIME, WHEN AT LAST HE GREW A THUMB;	170	FOURTH MEDITATN	69
WHEN FLOWERS GREW, THEIR BLOOM EXTENDED HIM.	224	OTTO	11
THE WAY GREW STEEPER BETWEEN STONY WALLS,	247	I WAITED	19
THE WILLOW WITH ITS BIRD GREW LOUD, GREW LOUDER STILL.	248	THE TREE, BIRD	13
THE WILLOW WITH ITS BIRD GREW LOUD, GREW LOUDER STILL.	248	THE TREE, BIRD	13
GREW BACK A NEW WING,	249	THE RESTORED	16
GREY			
THE HILLS ARE GREY, THE TREES ARE BARE,	15	COMING OF COLD	43
GLAZING THE PALE HAIR, THE DUPLICATE GREY STANDARD FACES.	46	DOLOR	13
I NOTICE A TREE, ARSENICAL GREY IN THE LIGHT, OR THE SLOW	47	DOUBLE FEATURE	10
THE GREY SHEEP CAME. I RAN,	147	THE EXORCISM	1
GREY FROM THE LONG WINTER, BURNT AT THE BASE IN LATE SUMMER.	193	JOURNY INTERIOR	10
IN THE VAPOROUS GREY OF EARLY MORNING,	197	THE LONG WATERS	49
HIS TAIL GREY WITH THE GROUND NOW,	226	THE LIZARD	18
IN THE GREY OTHERWISE,	258	SONG (3)	26
GREYING			
FACES GREYING FASTER THAN LOAM-CRUMBS ON A HARROW;	48	JUDGE NOT	1

	PAGE	TITLE	LINE
GREYISH			
WITH ITS LIMESTONE CRUMBLING INTO FINE GREYISH DUST, ...	226	THE LIZARD	28
GRIEF			
FROM THAT MONOTONY OF GRIEF, ...	22	SILENCE	16
MY GRIEF WAS NOT EXCESSIVE.	199	THE FAR FIELD	25
WITHOUT HATE, WITHOUT GRIEF, ...	217	WISH YOUNG WIFE	7
OF GRIEF I DIED, BUT NO ONE KNEW MY DEATH.	241	THE SEQUEL	8
GRIEVE			
DARE I GRIEVE? DARE I MOURN?	208	THE APPARITION	11
AND GRIEVE INTO THE CERTAINTY OF LOVE.	243	THE MOTION	6
GRIEVING			
ALONE, HIS WIFE IS GRIEVING FOR WHAT HER HEART DESIRES.	27	CLAIRVOY WIDOW	14
GRILL			
I WALKED HIM THROUGH THE GRILL AND OUT THE GATE	274	SUPPR W LINDSAY	46
GRIM			
AND NOW GRIM DIGITS OF OLD PAIN	30	THE RECKONING	3
GRIMACES			
THE UNDERTAKER'S OBSEQUIOUS GRIMACES, ...	22	ROAD TO WDLAWN	6
GRIND			
THE WHEELS OF CIRCUMSTANCE THAT GRIND	22	SILENCE	9
GRINDING			
GRINDING UP AND OVER THE NARROW ROAD, SPITTING AND ROARING.	193	JOURNY INTERIOR	22
GRISTLE			
THIS WIND GIVES ME SCALES. HAVE MERCY, GRISTLE:	60	THE LONG ALLEY	33
BELIEVE ME, KNOT OF GRISTLE, I BLEED LIKE A TREE;	79	GIVE WAY, GATES	1
WHERE ARE YOU NOW, MY BONNY BEATING GRISTLE,	86	PRAISE TO END!	17
GRITTY			
HARD, ON THE GRITTY SILL, ...	145	THE BEAST	14
WE LIE CLOSER ON THE GRITTY PILLOW, ...	231	THE STORM	38
GROANING			
BUT WHY AM I GROANING HERE, ...	262	FOLLIES OF ADAM	6
GROANS			
SOOTHE ME, GREAT GROANS OF UNDERNEATH, ...	84	O LULL ME, LULL	29
GROIN			
DOGS OF THE GROIN	55	THE LOST SON	75
GROOVE			
FROM THE BOLT, STUCK IN ITS GROOVE, ...	236	SONG (2)	7
GROPE			
TO GROPE MY SILL: IT MOANS TO BE REBORN!	154	THE DYING MAN	37
GROTESQUE			
GROTESQUE, AWKWARD, HIS EXTENDED EYES LOOKING AT NOTHING IN PARTICULAR, ...	159	FIRST MEDITATN	63
GROUND			
THE PLUM DROPS PITCH UPON THE GROUND, ...	14	COMING OF COLD	9
IS PRESSED TO NOISELESS GROUND.	17	NO BIRD	4
SHOOTING UP LIME AND DUNG AND GROUND BONES,--	38	FORCING HOUSE	9
UNDER EVEN THE ROCK-SHUT GROUND, ...	50	THE CYCLE	16
RUNNING LIGHTLY OVER SPONGY GROUND, ...	54	THE LOST SON	34
IS THIS THE STORM'S HEART? THE GROUND IS UNSTILLING ITSELF.	56	THE LOST SON	100
ALONG THE LOW GROUND DRY ONLY IN AUGUST,--	62	FIELD OF LIGHT	26
I TOUCHED THE GROUND, THE GROUND WARMED BY THE KILLDEER,	63	FIELD OF LIGHT	39
I TOUCHED THE GROUND, THE GROUND WARMED BY THE KILLDEER,	63	FIELD OF LIGHT	39
PLEASURE ON GROUND	65	SHAPE OF FIRE	41
THE GROUND CRIED MY NAME: ....:	76	I NEED, I NEED	49
WE'RE KING AND QUEEN OF THE RIGHT GROUND.	79	GIVE WAY, GATES	22
AND THE GROUND CRIES.	83	O LULL ME, LULL	26
THOSE CLOSE TO THE GROUND	97	O, THOU OPENING	11
LIGHT ALTERED LIGHT ALONG THE LIVING GROUND.	106	SIR JOHN DAVIES	34
GOD BLESS THE GROUND! I SHALL WALK SOFTLY THERE, ...,...	108	THE WAKING (2)	8
THE GROUND NEEDS THE ABYSS, ...	121	ALL EARTH, AIR	19
BELOW, ON THE FERNY GROUND, ...	125	WORDS FOR WIND	72
ALOFT, AND ON THE GROUND.	128	THE VOICE	12
SHE DANCES, AND THE GROUND BEARS HER AWAY.	129	SHE	10
I STARED AT A FISSURE OF GROUND	146	THE SONG	14
A TOWHEE PECKS THE GROUND;	148	THE SMALL	3
OVER THE SODDEN GROUND.	148	THE SMALL	18
BENDING THEM DOWN TO THE GROUND;	152	THE SISKINS	11
THE AIR STILL, THE GROUND ALIVE, ...	165	HER BECOMING	14
AND THE IVY-BRANCH, CAST TO THE GROUND, PUTS DOWN ROOTS INTO THE SAWDUST,	197	THE LONG WATERS	34
AND LOVES THE LIVING GROUND.	212	LIGHT LISTENED	16
HIS TAIL GREY WITH THE GROUND NOW, ...	226	THE LIZARD	18
BENDING THE TREES HALF-WAY DOWN TO THE GROUND, ...	231	THE STORM	31

	PAGE	TITLE	LINE
GROUND (CONTINUED)			
THE MOLE MAKING ITS WAY THROUGH DARKEST GROUND,	235	MANIFESTATION	4
WE PACED THE LIVING GROUND;	237	THE TRANCED	13
AND PULSED ITS WINGS UPON THE DUSTY GROUND--	243	THE MOTION	3
GROUND-BEETLES			
AND IN THE SHRUNKEN FACE OF A DEAD RAT, EATEN BY RAIN AND GROUND-BEETLES	199	THE FAR FIELD	19
GROUND-CHILL			
AND THE GROUND-CHILL COMES CLOSER TO US,	162	I'M HERE	55
GROUND'S			
THE GROUND'S BEATING LIKE FLAME!	99	O, THOU OPENING	59
GROUPS			
I DAWDLE WITH GROUPS NEAR THE RICKETY POP-CORN STAND;	47	DOUBLE FEATURE	5
MAKES THEM HUDDLE IN GROUPS,--	180	GOO-GIRL	15
GROVE			
THE HEDGE AND ORCHARD GROVE ARE THINNED.	14	COMING OF COLD	31
IN A GROVE OF APPLES.	51	THE WAKING (1)	16
NEAR THIS ROSE, IN THIS GROVE OF SUN-PARCHED, WIND-WARPED MADRONAS,	205	THE ROSE	98
GROW			
THOUGH IT ALL HAPPENED BEFORE, I CANNOT GROW BITTER:	24	VERNAL SENTIMNT	7
SOME LEARN THE ART OF THIEVING, AND SOME GROW UP TO BEG;	27	CLAIRVOY WIDOW	10
INTRICATE PHOBIAS GROW	31	LULL	4
WE GROW INDIFFERENT TO DOG HOWLS, TO THE NESTLING'S LAST PEEP;	33	IDYLL	6
(AND SOME GROW OUT OF SHAPE, THEIR SEED IMPURE;)	225	OTTO	32
GROWING			
AND THE STYLE OF YOUR PROSE GROWING LIMPER AND LIMPER.	23	ACADEMIC	4
I WAS CARELESS IN GROWING.	104	OLD LADY'S WRDS	48
I WOULD BELIEVE MY PAIN: AND THE EYE QUIET ON THE GROWING ROSE;	188	THE LONGING	43
THE LINE OF MY HORIZON'S GROWING THIN!	245	THE DECISION	8
GROWL			
SHE COULD GROWL LIKE A BEAR,--	179	MYRTLE	4
GROWN			
FOR EVERY MEANING HAD GROWN MEANINGLESS.	133	THE PURE FURY	4
GROWS			
THE SKY TURNS DARK, THE YEAR GROWS OLD,	15	COMING OF COLD	36
NEW MEANING GROWS IMMENSE.	18	GENESIS	12
A FAIR THING GROWS MORE FAIR;	124	WORDS FOR WIND	54
GROWS SICK IN FLESH AND SPIRIT BOTH.	257	SANITARIUM	10
GROWTH			
ONE NUB OF GROWTH	37	CUTTINGS	5
A SLOW GROWTH IS A HARD THING TO ENDURE.	154	THE DYING MAN	45
THE ROAD LINED WITH SNOW-LADEN SECOND GROWTH,	199	THE FAR FIELD	4
GRRR			
TO MAKE REMARKS ABOUT MY--GRRR!	181	MONOTONY SONG	11
GRUBBY			
REASON? THAT DREARY SHED, THAT HUTCH FOR GRUBBY SCHOOLBOYS!	92	I CRY, LOVE!	14
GRUBS			
GRUBS AND SNAILS AND SHARP STICKS,	39	WEED PULLER	6
HAS HE GRUBS FOR HIS FAIR?--	183	THE WAGTAIL	3
GUARD			
O SEE THE FATE OF HIM WHOSE GUARD WAS LOWERED!--	5	PROGNOSIS	3
GUARDED			
THOUGH STILL THE GUARDED SNOW IS WINTER-SEALED,	11	LIGHT BRIGHTER	6
GUBBLE			
SHE'D DUNK AND SHE'D GUBBLE:	179	MYRTLE'S COUSIN	6
GUESS			
SOMETIMES THE BLOOD IS PRIVILEGED TO GUESS	8	THE SIGNALS	9
AS YOU CAN SEE I GUESS I GUESS.	75	I NEED, I NEED	34
AS YOU CAN SEE I GUESS I GUESS.	75	I NEED, I NEED	34
THE MORAL IS, I GUESS YOU KEEP	181	MONOTONY SONG	25
GUIDES			
A SURGEON GUIDES A SCALPEL WITH THUMB AND FINGER-TIPS.	28	CLAIRVOY WIDOW	20
GUILD			
WHEN THE LADIES' GUILD PUTS ON A FEED,	267	SAGINAW SONG	3
GUILT			
WHETHER FOR LOVE OR OUT OF OBSCURE GUILT	224	OTTO	24
GUINNESS			
THE COLOR, MY DEARS, WAS GUINNESS BROWN,	270	GOB MUSIC	39
GULFS			
OVER THE GULFS OF DREAM	49	NIGHT CROW	4

	PAGE	TITLE	LINE
GULL			
A GULL RIDES ON THE RIPPLES OF A DREAM,	149	IN LATE SUMMER	1
GULLIES			
AND GULLIES WASHED WITH LIGHT.	34	NIGHT JOURNEY	19
GULLS			
THE GULLS RIDE ON THE WATER, THE GULLS HAVE COME AND GONE,	28	CLAIRVOY WIDOW	23
THE GULLS RIDE ON THE WATER, THE GULLS HAVE COME AND GONE,	28	CLAIRVOY WIDOW	23
THE GULLS WHEEL OVER THEIR SINGULAR GARBAGE;	187	THE LONGING	16
EVEN THE GULLS QUIET ON THE FAR ROCKS,	190	AT OYSTER RIVER	7
AND THE GULLS CRY AGAINST THE CROWS	202	THE ROSE	7
THE GULLS, THE GULLS FAR FROM THEIR WAVES	235	ALL MORNING	36
THE GULLS, THE GULLS FAR FROM THEIR WAVES	235	ALL MORNING	36
GULPED			
AS I GULPED IT DOWN, AS I GULPED IT DOWN.	270	GOB MUSIC	41
AS I GULPED IT DOWN, AS I GULPED IT DOWN.	270	GOB MUSIC	41
GUMPTION			
A BOY WHO HAD GUMPTION AND PUSH	182	BOY AND BUSH	1
GUNS			
UNMINDFUL OF TERROR AND HEADLINES, OF SPEECHES AND GUNS.	33	IDYLL	12
THEY STOOD THERE WITH THEIR GUNS; HE WALKED TOWARD,	224	OTTO	18
AND YET STILL VIOLENT MEN, WHOSE STACKED-UP GUNS	224	OTTO	27
GURGLE			
I AM UNDONE BY THE GURGLE OF BABIES AND PITCHERS,	255	LIGHT POEM	7
GUST			
A GUST BLOWING THE LEAVES SUDDENLY UPWARD,	171	WHAT TELL BONES	29
GUSTS			
THE FLAT-ROOFED HOUSES, COMING DOWN IN GUSTS, BEATING	230	THE STORM	24
GUTTERS			
THE TOWNS WITH THEIR HIGH PITTED ROAD-CROWNS AND DEEP GUTTERS,	193	JOURNY INTERIOR	30
HA			
THE SUMMER BUMPS OF HA:	60	THE LONG ALLEY	44
GILLIFLOWER HA,	60	THE LONG ALLEY	47
HACKING			
HACKING AT BLACK HAIRY ROOTS,--	39	WEED PULLER	2
HAD (45)			
HADN'T			
(IT TURNED OUT SHE HADN'T A FATHER AT ALL)	111	SQUEEZE-BOX	15
HAG			
DARE I SHRINK TO A HAG,	161	I'M HERE	13
I DIVE WITH THE BLACK HAG, THE CORMORANT,	209	HER LONGING	13
BUT I SACKED THE PRESUMPTUOUS HAG THE NEXT WEEK,	228	THE GERANIUM	25
HAGS			
YOU FAT UNNECESSARY HAGS,	99	O, THOU OPENING	60
HAIR			
HAIR ON A NARROW WRIST BONE;	6	THE PREMONITION	9
THE GARMENT NEITHER FUR NOR HAIR,	19	EPIDERM MACABRE	5
TODAY, WHILE SCRAPING HAIR BEFORE THE MIRROR,	25	DIM-WIT COUSIN	10
TWINED LIKE FINE HAIR,	43	FLOWER DUMP	8
GLAZING THE PALE HAIR, THE DUPLICATE GREY STANDARD FACES.	46	DOLOR	13
BENEATH THE HAIR.	64	SHAPE OF FIRE	23
HANDS AND HAIR MOVED THROUGH A DREAM OF WAKENING BLOSSOMS.	66	SHAPE OF FIRE	74
HAIR HAD KISSES.	90	UNFOLD! UNFOLD!	38
THE DARK HAIR SIGHED.	93	I CRY, LOVE!	56
THE WIND IN HER HAIR,	100	THE VISITANT	19
MY HAIR BETWEEN ME AND THE SUN,	104	OLD LADY'S WRDS	42
WHEN SHE SHAKES OUT HER HAIR.	121	ALL EARTH, AIR	9
MUST I STAY TANGLED IN THAT LIVELY HAIR?	140	THE SWAN	3
AND A WIND WOKE IN MY HAIR,	146	THE SONG	22
THE DARKNESS OF FALLING HAIR, THE WARNINGS FROM LINT AND SPIDERS,	159	FIRST MEDITATN	80
THEIR GAIT FORMAL AND ELABORATE, THEIR HAIR A GLORY,	170	FOURTH MEDITATN	64
AND SAID, OLD BOY, YOU'RE SHEDDING HAIR,	181	MONOTONY SONG	6
AND MY SALT-LADEN HAIR	210	HER TIME	14
AND YOUR HAIR EVER BLAZE,	217	WISH YOUNG WIFE	8
HANGS BY ITS HAIR;	258	SONG (3)	5
HAIR'S			
MY HAIR'S ALL TANGLED ON YOUR HEAD,	136	THE SENSUALISTS	3
HAIRY			
HACKING AT BLACK HAIRY ROOTS,--	39	WEED PULLER	2
HALE			
ONCE ON RETURNING HOME, PURSE-PROUD AND HALE,	21	THE AUCTION	1

	PAGE	TITLE	LINE
HALF			
THE YIELD'S HALF DOWN AND HALF IN AIR,	14	COMING OF COLD	8
THE YIELD'S HALF DOWN AND HALF IN AIR,	14	COMING OF COLD	8
HE LOOPS IN CRAZY FIGURES HALF THE NIGHT	16	THE BAT	5
WE SIT IN THE PORCH SWING, CONTENT AND HALF ASLEEP.	33	IDYLL	8
I STAY UP HALF THE NIGHT	34	NIGHT JOURNEY	26
SHE SWAYS, HALF IN THE SUN:	124	WORDS FOR WIND	41
SHE BREAKS MY BREATH IN HALF;	126	WORDS FOR WIND	100
WHEN TRUE LOVE BROKE MY HEART IN HALF,	138	THE SURLY ONE	1
MY BODY HALF IN FLAME.	147	THE EXORCISM	2
ITS SHADOW BENT IN HALF;	150	SNAKE	7
YET REMAIN ONLY HALF AWARE OF THE INTRANSIENT GLORY?	169	FOURTH MEDITATN	32
TO A TREE LYING FLAT, ITS CROWN HALF BROKEN.	197	THE LONG WATERS	54
THE DUMB DAMES SHRIEKING HALF THE NIGHT	228	THE GERANIUM	16
WHO WOULD BE HALF POSSESSED	240	IN EVEING AIR	3
AND THE SUN TOUCHES THE LIZARD'S THROAT, ITS TAIL HALF IN SHADOW.	261	THE CHANGELING	34
WITH MORE THAN HALF A CROWN.	269	GOB MUSIC	23
HALF SIDEWAYS IN THE SHIFTING LIGHT,	273	SUPPR W LINDSAY	20
HALF-ALIVE			
FLESH-AWKWARD, HALF-ALIVE,	162	I'M HERE	27
HALF-AND-HALF			
TO DRINK SOME HALF-AND-HALF	213	THE HAPPY THREE	15
HALF-ANIMAL			
HALF-BIRD, HALF-ANIMAL.	141	MEMORY	6
HALF-BIRD			
HALF-BIRD, HALF-ANIMAL.	141	MEMORY	6
HALF-DEAD			
LIKE THE HALF-DEAD, I HUG MY LAST SECRETS.	103	OLD LADY'S WRDS	5
AMONG THE HALF-DEAD TREES, I CAME UPON THE TRUE EASE OF MYSELF,	205	THE ROSE	99
HALF-DEATH			
TO SLEEP IS ALL MY LIFE. IN SLEEP'S HALF-DEATH,	246	THE MARROW	14
HALF-FLIGHT			
THEN PITCHING AWAY IN HALF-FLIGHT,	200	THE FAR FIELD	34
HALF-GREEN			
WHILE THE WRENS BICKERED AND SANG IN THE HALF-GREEN HEDGEROWS,	200	THE FAR FIELD	36
HALF-GROWN			
THE HALF-GROWN CHRYSANTHEMUMS STARING UP LIKE ACCUSERS,	43	CHILD ON GRNHSE	3
ITS ENTRAILS STREWN OVER THE HALF-GROWN FLOWERS,	199	THE FAR FIELD	22
HALF-LAND			
IN A COUNTRY HALF-LAND, HALF-WATER.	201	THE FAR FIELD	76
HALF-LIFE			
BUT SHRINKS INTO A HALF-LIFE, LESS THAN ITSELF,	187	THE LONGING	20
HALF-OPENED			
THE SCENT OF THE HALF-OPENED BUDS CAME UP OVER ME.	162	I'M HERE	49
HALF-REST			
IN THIS, MY HALF-REST,	221	THE ABYSS	68
HALF-SLEEP			
I'M LULLED INTO HALF-SLEEP	191	AT OYSTER RIVER	60
HALF-SMOKED			
SO LONG ON GIN, BOBBIE PINS, HALF-SMOKED CIGARS, DEAD BEER,	228	THE GERANIUM	10
HALF-STEPS			
MATCHING HIS STRIDE WITH HALF-STEPS	6	THE PREMONITION	5
HALF-SUNKEN			
AND THE HALF-SUNKEN BRANCH BENDS AWAY FROM THE GAZER'S EYE.	233	THE PIKE	9
HALF-TURNING			
"WHAT MOON?" HE CRIED, HALF-TURNING IN MOCK FURY.	273	SUPPR W LINDSAY	10
HALF-UNDRESSED			
AND SHE WAS HALF-UNDRESSED,	268	SAGINAW SONG	59
WHEN THEY ARE HALF-UNDRESSED.	268	SAGINAW SONG	61
HALF-WATER			
IN A COUNTRY HALF-LAND, HALF-WATER.	201	THE FAR FIELD	76
HALF-WAY			
RETIRING TO NUDGE HIS NECK HALF-WAY UNDER	226	THE LIZARD	16
BENDING THE TREES HALF-WAY DOWN TO THE GROUND,	231	THE STORM	31
A SWAYING LIGHT-CORD, THEN RAN HALF-WAY BACK.	273	SUPPR W LINDSAY	25
HALL			
IT TIPTOED DOWN THE HALL.	136	THE SENSUALISTS	20
HALLOO			
I HEAR A DEAD TONGUE HALLOO.	90	UNFOLD! UNFOLD!	44

	PAGE	TITLE	LINE
HALLS			
BECKONING THROUGH HALLS,	56	THE LOST SON	89
HALLWAYS			
ONLY THE MOTES OF DUST IN THE IMMACULATE HALLWAYS,	159	FIRST MEDITATN	79
HAMMER			
MY SPIRITS ROSE EACH TIME THE HAMMER FELL,	21	THE AUCTION	13
A HAMMER ON THE CRYSTAL WALLS	22	SILENCE	5
HAMMER'S			
THE HAMMER'S WEIGHT.	9	THE ADAMANT	8
HAND			
THE ELEMENT OF AIR WAS OUT OF HAND.	6	INTERLUDE	1
HE DIPPED HIS HAND IN THE SHALLOW:	6	THE PREMONITION	7
THE THINGS THE EYE OR HAND CANNOT POSSESS.	8	THE SIGNALS	10
MORE FURTIVE THAN THE HAND IN LOW	8	PRAYER	11
HIS BEAK IS QUICKER THAN A HUMAN HAND.	15	THE HERON	8
CARESSES OF THE HAND AND EYE.	19	EPIDERM MACABRE	8
BY THE CIRCUMFERENCE OF HAND,	25	VERSE W ALLUSNS	2
MY SHAVING HAND JERKED BACK IN SUDDEN TERROR:	25	DIM-WIT COUSIN	11
--AND GRANDFATHER'S SINISTER HOVERING HAND.	32	SALE	8
THE HAND THAT HELD MY WRIST	45	MY PAPA'S WALTZ	9
OR SEND OFF A CAR WITH VAGUE LIFTS OF A HAND.	47	DOUBLE FEATURE	8
HAND ME A FEATHER, I'LL FAN YOU WARM,	60	THE LONG ALLEY	45
THE DIRT LEFT MY HAND, VISITOR.	63	FIELD OF LIGHT	31
LIGHT AS A HAND AMONG BLOSSOMS,	78	BRING THE DAY!	39
THE MOUTH ASKS. THE HAND TAKES.	80	GIVE WAY, GATES	51
I NIBBLED MEEKLY FROM HER PROFFERED HAND;	127	I KNEW A WOMAN	11
THE HAND UPON MY SHOULDER TURNS TO HORN.	154	THE DYING MAN	39
WHAT I LOVE IS NEAR AT HAND,	201	THE FAR FIELD	80
ONE SLEEVE WITH MY HAND IN IT,	209	HER RETICENCE	2
THE CHILD'S HAND REACHING INTO THE COILED SMILAX,	221	THE ABYSS	65
HIS HAND COULD FIT INTO A WOMAN'S GLOVE,	224	OTTO	12
HE THREW HIS RIFLE OVER WITH ONE HAND;	224	OTTO	15
CRADLED IN MY HAND,	227	MEADOW MOUSE	5
IN A HAND LIKE A BOWL	249	THE RESTORED	1
FROM MY HAND LIKE A BOWL.	249	THE RESTORED	12
HE SLAPPED ME WITH HIS HAND;	268	SAGINAW SONG	51
HE SHOOK MY HAND. "TELL WILLIAMS I'VE BEEN HERE,	274	SUPPR W LINDSAY	48
HANDKERCHEE			
ME HANDKERCHEE HAD FALLEN IN	269	GOB MUSIC	22
HANDKERCHIEF			
THE HANDKERCHIEF TUCKED IN THE LEFT-HAND POCKET	29	THE REMINDER	5
HAND-PAINTED			
THE HAND-PAINTED WALL-PAPER, FINER THAN SKIN,	32	SALE	17
HANDS			
THE VEINS WITHIN OUR HANDS BETRAYED OUR FEAR.	6	INTERLUDE	11
HANDS, HARD AND VEINED ALL OVER,	7	ORDERS FOR DAY	1
WHO FLEE IN WHAT THEIR HANDS HAVE MADE.	33	HIGHWAY: MICH	15
WATCHING HANDS TRANSPLANTING,	42	TRANSPLANTING	1
THEIR HANDS TWINKLING WITH WET;	44	FRAU BAUMAN	18
I HAVE MARRIED MY HANDS TO PERPETUAL AGITATION,	56	THE LOST SON	109
GIVE ME MY HANDS:	61	THE LONG ALLEY	88
HANDS AND HAIR MOVED THROUGH A DREAM OF WAKENING BLOSSOMS.	66	SHAPE OF FIRE	74
HELLO HAPPY HANDS.	73	WHERE KNOCK IS	52
DON'T TELL MY HANDS.	74	WHERE KNOCK IS	85
FATHER, FORGIVE MY HANDS.	85	PRAISE TO END!	12
I HEAR THE SOUND OF HANDS.	87	PRAISE TO END!	74
MY HANDS TURN INTO HOOVES.	154	THE DYING MAN	18
THEIR FOREPAWS JOINED TOGETHER, LIKE HANDS--	163	I'M HERE	69
HANDS ACTIVE, EYES CHERISHED;	187	THE LONGING	8
I WOULD DELIGHT IN MY HANDS, THE BRANCH SINGING, ALTERING THE EXCESSIVE BIRD;	188	THE LONGING	44
WATCHING MY HANDS, WARY.	220	THE ABYSS	39
THINGS WITHOUT HANDS TAKE HANDS: THERE IS NO CHOICE,--	244	INFIRMITY	31
THINGS WITHOUT HANDS TAKE HANDS: THERE IS NO CHOICE,--	244	INFIRMITY	31
HANG			
AND HANG, LIMP ON A STONE:	150	SNAKE	3
AND THE BACK WHEELS HANG ALMOST OVER THE EDGE	193	JOURNY INTERIOR	4
HANGING			
THOSE LEWD MONKEY-TAILS HANGING FROM DRAINHOLES,--	39	WEED PULLER	3
TO THE SAND DUNES AND FISH FLIES, HANGING, THICKER THAN MOTHS,	193	JOURNY INTERIOR	28
HANGING, BUNCHED LIKE YOUNG FRUIT, BENDING THE END BRANCHES,	199	THE FAR FIELD	32

	PAGE	TITLE	LINE
HANGING (CONTINUED)			
TO THE CLAY BANKS, AND THE WILD GRAPES HANGING FROM THE ELMTREES.	200	THE FAR FIELD	66
HANGS			
A WAVE OF TIME HANGS MOTIONLESS ON THIS PARTICULAR SHORE.	47	DOUBLE FEATURE	9
DARK HANGS UPON THE WATERS OF THE SOUL;	135	THE RENEWAL	8
AND A DROP OF RAIN WATER HANGS AT THE TIP OF A LEAF	204	THE ROSE	86
HANGS BY ITS HAIR;	258	SONG (3)	5
HAPLESS			
ALL THINGS INNOCENT, HAPLESS, FORSAKEN.	227	MEADOW MOUSE	29
HAPPENED			
THOUGH IT ALL HAPPENED BEFORE, I CANNOT GROW BITTER:	24	VERNAL SENTIMNT	7
IT HAPPENED O, IN BOFIN TOWN,	270	GOB MUSIC	38
HAPPENS			
SHE HAPPENS, TIME ON TIME--	130	THE OTHER	10
THE RIGHT THING HAPPENS TO THE HAPPY MAN.	250	THE RIGHT THING	3
THE RIGHT THING HAPPENS TO THE HAPPY MAN.	250	THE RIGHT THING	9
THE RIGHT THING HAPPENS TO THE HAPPY MAN.	250	THE RIGHT THING	12
THE RIGHT THING HAPPENS TO THE HAPPY MAN.	250	THE RIGHT THING	19
HAPPINESS			
AND YET HIS HAPPINESS WAS NOT COMPLETE;	28	THE FAVORITE	11
HAPPINESS LEFT TO DOGS AND CHILDREN--	187	THE LONGING	9
HAPPY			
HAPPY ALONE IN HIS BEDROOM COUNTING HIS PULSE.	24	POETASTER	3
THRICE HAPPY THEY WHOSE WORLD IS SPANNED	25	VERSE W ALLUSNS	1
THOUGH HOME IS NOT HAPPY, WHERE ELSE CAN HE GO?	29	THE GENTLE	10
HEAT WAS HAPPY.	51	THE WAKING (1)	4
I'M HAPPY WITH MY PAWS.	60	THE LONG ALLEY	46
THE LAKES WILL BE HAPPY:	61	THE LONG ALLEY	87
HELLO HAPPY HANDS.	73	WHERE KNOCK IS	52
ONCE I FISHED FROM THE BANKS, LEAF-LIGHT AND HAPPY:	86	PRAISE TO END!	19
IN THE SPARROW, HAPPY ON GRAVEL;	88	PRAISE TO END!	91
A MOUSE TAUGHT ME HOW, I WAS A HAPPY ASKER.	90	UNFOLD! UNFOLD!	35
OR HAPPY, CORRECT AS A HAT?	98	O, THOU OPENING	46
I'M TRUE TO SOUP, AND HAPPY TO ASK:	99	O, THOU OPENING	55
A WREN, HAPPY, TAIL INTO THE WIND,	102	ELEGY FOR JANE	5
I AM STILL HAPPY.	160	FIRST MEDITATN	99
THEY SEEMED VERY HAPPY.	163	I'M HERE	70
ONCE I COULD TOUCH MY SHADOW, AND BE HAPPY;	168	FOURTH MEDITATN	14
THE HAPPY THREE	213	THE HAPPY THREE	T
MORNING'S A MOTION IN A HAPPY MIND:	241	THE SEQUEL	17
THE RIGHT THING HAPPENS TO THE HAPPY MAN.	250	THE RIGHT THING	3
THE RIGHT THING HAPPENS TO THE HAPPY MAN.	250	THE RIGHT THING	9
THE RIGHT THING HAPPENS TO THE HAPPY MAN.	250	THE RIGHT THING	12
THE RIGHT THING HAPPENS TO THE HAPPY MAN.	250	THE RIGHT THING	19
HAR			
MNETHA, MOTHER OF HAR, PROTECT ME	196	THE LONG WATERS	20
HARBOR			
"I SEE THE RIVER HARBOR, ALIVE WITH MEN AND SHIPS,	28	CLAIRVOY WIDOW	19
HARBORS			
IN THE CURVED HARBORS,	202	THE ROSE	8
HARD			
HANDS, HARD AND VEINED ALL OVER,	7	ORDERS FOR DAY	1
WITH A PALM CAKED HARD BY DIRT,	45	MY PAPA'S WALTZ	14
THIS IS MY HARD TIME.	53	THE LOST SON	11
IT IS HARD TO CARE ABOUT CORNERS,	104	OLD LADY'S WRDS	59
AND BREATHING HARD, AS THAT MAN RODE	136	THE SENSUALISTS	11
THE CLOSE DARK HUGS ME HARD,	138	LOVE'S PROGRESS	21
WITH THEIR HARD SNOW; LEANED ON THE LONELY EYE;	143	SHIMMER OF EVIL	7
HARD, ON THE GRITTY SILL,	145	THE BEAST	14
A SLOW GROWTH IS A HARD THING TO ENDURE.	154	THE DYING MAN	45
GLEAMING, FREEZING HARD AGAIN, CREAKING AT MIDNIGHT--	191	AT OYSTER RIVER	51
WITHOUT HIS RIFLE, AND SLAPPED EACH ONE HARD;	224	OTTO	19
HARDENED			
LIGHT HARDENED ON THE WATER WHERE WE WERE;	119	THE DREAM	6
HARDENS			
HARDENS.	104	OLD LADY'S WRDS	65
HARDER			
FROM A SHELL HARDER THAN HORN.	81	SENSIBILITY! LA	9
SHE WITH HER THIGHS HARDER THAN HOOVES,	260	THE CHANGELING	1
HARDEST			
I SIT ABOVE THE BACK WHEELS, WHERE THE JOLTS ARE HARDEST,	158	FIRST MEDITATN	22

	PAGE	TITLE	LINE
HARDIHOOD			
I CAN DELIGHT IN MY OWN HARDIHOOD;	132	SENTENTIOUS MAN	26
HARDLY			
HARDLY ANY OLD ANGELS ARE AROUND ANY MORE.	78	BRING THE DAY!	40
YOU HARDLY EVER THINK IT'S THERE.	178	THE CHAIR	2
HARDNESS			
THERE WAS A HARDNESS OF STONE,	265	HARSH COUNTRY	1
HARE			
SHE WAS MAD AS A HARE,	179	MYRTLE	3
HARM			
WHEREIN I AM BESET BY HARM,	19	AGNST DISASTER	10
HARP			
SEE WHAT THE SWEET HARP SAYS.	99	O, THOU OPENING	73
HARPY			
OR THAT OLD HARPY SECRETING TOADS IN HER PORTMANTEAU.	82	SENSIBILITY! LA	36
HARRIED			
I RECALL HOW SHE HARRIED THE CHILDREN AWAY ALL THE LATE SUMMER	223	ELEGY (2)	12
HARROW			
FACES GREYING FASTER THAN LOAM-CRUMBS ON A HARROW;	48	JUDGE NOT	1
HARRY			
--HEIGHO, MEET HUGH AND HARRY!	181	MONOTONY SONG	4
--HEIGHO, WE'RE HUGH AND HARRY!	181	MONOTONY SONG	8
--AND THERE WAS ONLY HARRY!	181	MONOTONY SONG	12
THIS HARRY RAN STRAIGHT UP A WALL,	181	MONOTONY SONG	13
--ALAS, ALACK FOR HARRY!	181	MONOTONY SONG	16
--AND I'M NOT HUGH NOR HARRY!	181	MONOTONY SONG	20
--HEIGHO HUGH AND HARRY!	181	MONOTONY SONG	24
--UNLESS YOU'RE HUGH OR HARRY!	181	MONOTONY SONG	28
HARSH			
THE FIELDS ARE HARSH AND BARE, THE ROCKS	15	COMING OF COLD	45
IN THEIR HARSH THICKETS	91	UNFOLD! UNFOLD!	65
ON HARSH STONE.	99	O, THOU OPENING	78
A THIN HARSH SONG. THE DAY DIES IN A CHILD.	171	WHAT TELL BONES	19
THEIR FILMY FRINGES OF GREEN, THEIR HARSH	205	THE ROSE	90
AND, WITH A HARSH RASP OF A LAUGH AT HERSELF,	223	ELEGY (2)	10
AND WE DRANK THE DRY HARSH WINE	232	THE THING	20
RISING, WHEELING AWAY WITH HARSH CRIES,	235	ALL MORNING	37
PROPINQUITY'S A HARSH MASTER;	259	SONG (3)	37
THE HARSH COUNTRY	265	HARSH COUNTRY	T
HARVEST			
THE HAZE OF HARVEST DRIFTS ALONG THE FIELD	12	SLOW SEASON	3
HARVESTING			
THE LAST OF HARVESTING IS DONE.	14	COMING OF COLD	33
HAS (54)			
HAT			
HIS FINGERS MAKE A HAT ABOUT HIS HEAD.	16	THE BAT	3
THEIR WIVES GO OUT ON SUNDAY BENEATH THE LATEST HAT.	27	CLAIRVOY WIDOW	8
OR FAN LIFE INTO WILTED SWEET-PEAS WITH HIS HAT,	42	OLD FLORIST	9
BRING ME MY HAT, MY UMBRELLA AND RUBBERS,	48	LAST WORDS	9
WHO HAD A RUBBER HAT	71	WHERE KNOCK IS	17
A HAT IS A HOUSE.	75	I NEED, I NEED	21
OR HAPPY, CORRECT AS A HAT?	98	O, THOU OPENING	46
ALL OVER YOUR HAT,--	180	GOO-GIRL	8
THE WAY I TIPPED MY HAT.	225	THE CHUMS	8
HATE			
INFLAME WITH HATE. THIS ANCIENT FEUD	4	FEUD	18
REMAIN SECURE FROM PAIN PRESERVE THY HATE THY HEART.	5	TO MY SISTER	11
I HATE MY EPIDERMAL DRESS,	19	EPIDERM MACABRE	10
THE HOSTILE GAZE OF HATE,	20	REPL TO CENSURE	2
I HATE THIS SENSUAL PEN;	136	THE SENSUALISTS	22
WITHOUT HATE, WITHOUT GRIEF,	217	WISH YOUNG WIFE	7
HATED			
HE POTTED PLANTS AS IF HE HATED THEM.	224	OTTO	9
HATE-DRIVEN			
THE FURY OF THE HATE-DRIVEN ZEALOT, THE MEANNESS OF THE HUMAN WEASEL;	170	FOURTH MEDITATN	68
HATES			
THE WHITE WEATHER HATES ME.	77	BRING THE DAY!	22
THIS TAIL HATES A FLAT PATH.	79	GIVE WAY, GATES	15
BUT THE RIND, OFTEN, HATES THE LIFE WITHIN.	157	FIRST MEDITATN	13

	PAGE	TITLE	LINE

HATH
HATH THE RAIN A FATHER? ALL THE CAVES ARE ICE. ONLY THE
    SNOW'S HERE. 56   THE LOST SON   84

HATRED
THE WINDS OF HATRED BLOW 31   LULL   1
I WOULD UNLEARN THE LINGO OF EXASPERATION, ALL THE
    DISTORTIONS OF MALICE AND HATRED; 188   THE LONGING   42

HATRED'S
SKIRT HATRED'S RAGING RIVER, ... 7   ORDERS FOR DAY   10

HATS
I WISH I HAD TEN THOUSAND HATS, ... 75   I NEED, I NEED   37

HATTIE
WHEN HATTIE WRIGHT'S ANGORA DIED AS WELL, ... 224   OTTO   29

HAUNT
HAUNT OF THE CAT-BIRD, NESTING-PLACE OF THE FIELD-MOUSE,   199   THE FAR FIELD   15

HAUNTED
THESE IMAGES HAUNTED ME NOON AND MIDNIGHT. 48   JUDGE NOT   4

HAUNTING
NOR THE SOUL HAUNTING MY BODY, ... 209   HER RETICENCE   8
A BIRD KEPT HAUNTING ME WHEN I WAS YOUNG-- 245   THE DECISION   3

HAVE (102)

HAVEN'T
HIS EARS HAVEN'T TIME. 71   WHERE KNOCK IS   9
I HAVEN'T TIME FOR SUGAR, ... 75   I NEED, I NEED   24

HAVING
ON THE BANKS OF THE TOMBSTONE, THE WIND-HARPS HAVING THEIR
    SAY, ... 204   THE ROSE   60
HAVING ESCAPED HER PEN, ... 213   THE HAPPY THREE   19

HAVOC
FROM THE WORM'S ADVANCE AND RETREAT, FROM THE BUTTERFLY'S
    HAVOC, ... 196   THE LONG WATERS   21

HAWKS
THE FLOATING HAWKS, THE JACKRABBITS, THE GRAZING CATTLE--   194   JOURNY INTERIOR   38
WHERE THE HAWKS SWAY OUT INTO THE WIND, ... 202   THE ROSE   4

HAWK'S
TO RUN UNDER THE HAWK'S WING, ... 227   MEADOW MOUSE   23

HAWTHORN
THEN WHIRRING OFF SIDEWAYS TO THE TOP OF THE HAWTHORN, ... 234   ALL MORNING   31

HAY
THE HAY HOPS IN THE HORSE'S MOUTH, ... 60   THE LONG ALLEY   41
IT WAS ALL HAY. 76   I NEED, I NEED   62
MOTHER OF BLUE AND THE MANY CHANGES OF HAY, ... 79   GIVE WAY, GATES   14
KEEPER OF HAY. THAT'S A SPRATLING'S PRATTLE. AND DON'T BE
    THINKING YOU'RE 98   O, THOU OPENING   28
THE SMELLS, THE MOMENT OF HAY,-- 103   OLD LADY'S WRDS   22
LET SEED BE GRASS, AND GRASS TURN INTO HAY: 127   I KNEW A WOMAN   22
MAY THE HIGH FLOWER OF THE HAY CLIMB INTO THEIR HEARTS;   169   FOURTH MEDITATN   56
YOU SQUEAK LIKE A MOUSE THAT'S LOST IN THE HAY, ... 177   KITTY-CAT BIRD   10
HE LIVES ON CARROTS, LEEKS AND HAY; 182   THE HIPPO   3
BEYOND THE CLOVER, THE RAGGED HAY, ... 203   THE ROSE   46
IT WAS AS IF I TRIED TO WALK IN HAY, ... 247   I WAITED   6

HAZE
THE HAZE OF HARVEST DRIFTS ALONG THE FIELD 12   SLOW SEASON   3
A FINE HAZE MOVED OFF THE LEAVES; 57   THE LOST SON   144
IN THE OBSCURE HAZE, SING! 90   UNFOLD! UNFOLD!   47
DIMINISHED BY THE HAZE 139   PLAINT   11
ABOVE THE BLUE AIR, IN THE SLIGHT HAZE BEYOND, ... 232   THE THING   3
AND SHIMMERING. THE SUN BURNED THROUGH A HAZE, ... 247   I WAITED   11

HE (144)

HEAD
RECOILING FROM THE SERPENT HEAD 4   FEUD   3
MY NOSE DEFILES A COMELY HEAD; 8   PRAYER   6
A MAN'S HEAD IS AN EMINENCE UPON 13   PRAISE PRAIRIE   3
HIS FINGERS MAKE A HAT ABOUT HIS HEAD. 16   THE BAT   3
SLOW SWINGS THE BREEZE ABOVE HER HEAD, ... 17   NO BIRD   5
--AND SOME WATERY EYES IN A COPLEY HEAD. 32   SALE   12
ONE SWAGGERING HEAD 43   FLOWER DUMP   12
YOU BEAT TIME ON MY HEAD 45   MY PAPA'S WALTZ   13
THE HEAD OF A MATCH 60   THE LONG ALLEY   56
WHEN THE PURE FURY FIRST RAGED IN HIS HEAD 133   THE PURE FURY   20
MY HAIR'S ALL TANGLED ON YOUR HEAD, ... 136   THE SENSUALISTS   3
A SNAKE LIFTING ITS HEAD; 163   I'M HERE   88
A HEAD OR TAIL--WHICH DOES HE LACK? 182   THE HIPPO   1

	PAGE	TITLE	LINE
HEAD (CONTINUED)			
O PRIDE, THOU ART A PLUME UPON WHOSE HEAD?	188	THE LONGING	25
FROM ONE COMELY HEAD.	215	HIS FOREBODING	5
HIS HEAD, STIFF AS A SCARAB, TURNED TO ONE SIDE,	226	THE LIZARD	5
HE TURNS HIS HEAD SLIGHTLY,	226	THE LIZARD	15
AS HIS HEAD; HIS BAT-LIKE EARS	227	MEADOW MOUSE	15
LOOKING AT YOU WITHOUT TURNING HIS SMALL HEAD,	234	ALL MORNING	12
VEERING CLOSE TO MY HEAD,	234	ALL MORNING	30
HE HEAPS FEW HONORS ON A LIVING HEAD;	264	THREE EPIGRAMS	3
I LEAN MY HEAD NEAR THE BRIMMING EDGE	269	GOB MUSIC	14
WHEN LINDSAY BENT HIS HEAD	273	SUPPR W LINDSAY	19
HEADED			
AND THE STELLER JAY, RAUCOUS, SOOTY HEADED, LIVES WITH US,	234	ALL MORNING	15
HEADING			
YOUNGLINGS, THE SMALL FISH KEEP HEADING INTO THE CURRENT.	170	FOURTH MEDITATN	75
HEADLANDS			
THE FRIEND THAT RUNS BEFORE ME ON THE WINDY HEADLANDS,	198	THE LONG WATERS	71
THE WATERS SWIRLING PAST THE TINY HEADLANDS.	202	THE ROSE	25
HEADLIGHTS			
UNTIL THE HEADLIGHTS DARKEN.	199	THE FAR FIELD	12
HEADLINES			
UNMINDFUL OF TERROR AND HEADLINES, OF SPEECHES AND GUNS.	33	IDYLL	12
HEADS			
THOUGH THE CROCUSES POKE UP THEIR HEADS IN THE USUAL PLACES,	24	VERNAL SENTIMNT	1
THEIR HEADS JOD-JODDING LIKE PIGEONS;	235	ALL MORNING	35
HEADY			
MORE HEADY THAN A FIELD AT DUSK	14	COMING OF COLD	3
HEALED			
THE RAVAGES OF WIND AND RAIN ARE HEALED.	12	SLOW SEASON	2
HEALING			
CREEPING AND HEALING.	50	THE MINIMAL	11
HEAP			
OF FLESH, BURN BACKWARD TO A BLACKENED HEAP.	17	UNEXTINGUISHED	8
HEAPED			
OF MARSH GRASS HEAPED ABOVE A MUSK-RAT HOLE.	15	THE HERON	4
HEAPS			
HE HEAPS FEW HONORS ON A LIVING HEAD;	264	THREE EPIGRAMS	3
HEAR			
A WALKER AT THE RIVER'S EDGE MAY HEAR	11	LIGHT BRIGHTER	3
I CAN HEAR, UNDERGROUND, THAT SUCKING AND SOBBING,	37	CUTTINGS (LATE)	5
GOD, GIVE ME A NEAR. I HEAR FLOWERS.	73	WHERE KNOCK IS	49
HEAR ME, SOFT EARS AND ROUNDY STONES!	76	I NEED, I NEED	57
I HEAR THE CLAP OF AN OLD WIND.	80	GIVE WAY, GATES	55
I HEAR YOU, ALIEN OF THE MOON.	82	SENSIBILITY! LA	44
I HEAR SINGING.	83	O LULL ME, LULL	11
I HEAR THE SOUND OF HANDS.	87	PRAISE TO END!	74
I HEAR, CLEARLY, THE HEART OF ANOTHER SINGING,	88	PRAISE TO END!	94
I HEAR A DEAD TONGUE HALLOO.	90	UNFOLD! UNFOLD!	44
I HEAR A MOST LOVELY HUZZA:	92	I CRY, LOVE!	12
I HEAR THE OWLS, THE SOFT CALLERS, COMING DOWN FROM THE HEMLOCKS.	93	I CRY, LOVE!	40
I'M TIRED OF ALL THAT, BAG-FOOT. I CAN HEAR SMALL ANGELS ANYTIME. WHO	98	O, THOU OPENING	25
HEAR THE SIGH OF WHAT IS.	98	O, THOU OPENING	35
I HEAR MY BEING DANCE FROM EAR TO EAR.	108	THE WAKING (2)	5
SHE LILTS A LOW SOFT LANGUAGE, AND I HEAR	129	SHE	5
THAT GOD THAT GOD LEANS DOWN HIS HEART TO HEAR.	144	ELEGY (1)	16
THE SMALL! THE SMALL! I HEAR THEM SINGING CLEAR	149	IN LATE SUMMER	7
I HEAR A NOISE OF BEES, A TRELLIS HUM,	155	THE DYING MAN	74
O SWEET FIELD FAR AHEAD, I HEAR YOUR BIRDS,	156	THE DYING MAN	88
IN MY LEFT EAR I HEAR THE LOUD SOUND OF A MINOR COLLAPSE.	165	HER BECOMING	29
I HEAR A BEAT OF BIRDS, THE PLANGENT WINGS	173	WHAT TELL BONES	69
IF I THOUGHT YOU COULD HEAR IN A HUSH."	182	BOY AND BUSH	5
THE LIGHT CRIES OUT, AND I AM THERE TO HEAR--	188	THE LONGING	32
AND I HEAR THE LICHEN SPEAK,	194	JOURNY INTERIOR	48
MINNOWS CAN HEAR, AND BUTTERFLIES, YELLOW AND BLUE,	196	THE LONG WATERS	3
THOUGH HE HEAR A NOTE HIGHER THAN C	196	THE LONG WATERS	6
O LOVE, YOU WHO HEAR	211	SONG (1)	9
AND HEAR MYSELF RETURN	215	HIS FOREBODING	12
I HEAR THE NOISE OF THE WALL.	220	THE ABYSS	26
BY THE SALT WAVES I HEAR A RIVER'S UNDERSONG,	221	THE ABYSS	76
I HEAR THE FLOWERS DRINKING IN THEIR LIGHT,	222	THE ABYSS	91
NEAR THE END, SHE SEEMED ALMOST TO HEAR ME--	228	THE GERANIUM	20

	PAGE	TITLE	LINE

HEAR (CONTINUED)

	PAGE	TITLE	LINE
I HEAR MY ECHO IN THE ECHOING WOOD--	239	IN A DARK TIME	3
I HEAR A CRY AND LOSE IT ON THE WIND.	243	THE MOTION	10
MY EARS STILL HEAR THE BIRD WHEN ALL IS STILL;	244	INFIRMITY	28
I TEACH MY EYES TO HEAR, MY EARS TO SEE	244	INFIRMITY	34
LORD, HEAR ME OUT, AND HEAR ME OUT THIS DAY:	246	THE MARROW	17
LORD, HEAR ME OUT, AND HEAR ME OUT THIS DAY:	246	THE MARROW	17
I CAN HEAR LIGHT ON A DRY DAY.	260	THE CHANGELING	20
I HEAR THEM SINGING!	261	THE CHANGELING	50

HEARD

	PAGE	TITLE	LINE
I HEARD YOUR LAUGHTER RUMBLE FROM MY BELLY.	25	DIM-WIT COUSIN	12
YET WHEN I HEARD THE DRUNKARDS HOWLING,	48	JUDGE NOT	7
AT WOODLAWN I HEARD THE DEAD CRY:	53	THE LOST SON	1
I HAD HEARD BEFORE.	55	THE LOST SON	74
HE WILL ASSUME THAT YOU HAVE HEARD--	116	THE SLOTH	6
IN HER LOW VOICE I HEARD	128	THE VOICE	3
DIMINISHED, YET STILL HEARD:	128	THE VOICE	10
AND IT WAS I WHO HEARD	128	THE VOICE	16
I HEARD; AND ONLY I.	128	THE VOICE	18
WHEN I HEARD, OR THOUGHT I HEARD,	146	THE SONG	24
WHEN I HEARD, OR THOUGHT I HEARD,	146	THE SONG	24
I HEARD A DYING MAN	153	THE DYING MAN	1
WAS IT THE STONES I HEARD? I STARED AT THE FIXED STARS.	166	HER BECOMING	54
BECAUSE NOBODY HEARD,	182	BOY AND BUSH	8
O I'VE HEARD!--	183	THE WAGTAIL	6
I HAVE HEARD, IN A DRIP OF LEAVES,	194	JOURNY INTERIOR	62
BUT HEARD LITTLE.	220	THE ABYSS	18
HEARD IN A VIOLENT WARD	228	IN VIOLENT WARD	T
I HEARD A BIRD STIR IN ITS TRUE CONFINE;	241	THE SEQUEL	11

HEARING

	PAGE	TITLE	LINE
HEARING A CRASS BABBLE OF BIRDS.	258	SONG (3)	9

HEARKENING

	PAGE	TITLE	LINE
FOR HEARKENING TO CARNAL EVILS	8	PRAYER	7

HEARS

	PAGE	TITLE	LINE
THE EAR HEARS ONLY IN LOW PLACES.	59	THE LONG ALLEY	7

HEARSE

	PAGE	TITLE	LINE
WITH THE DARK HEARSE, AND ENOUGH FLOWERS FOR AN ALDERMAN,--	223	ELEGY (2)	2

HEARSES

	PAGE	TITLE	LINE
THE DRIVERS CREAKING THE SEATS OF THE BAROQUE HEARSES,	22	ROAD TO WDLAWN	2

HEART

	PAGE	TITLE	LINE
MY HEART KEEPS OPEN HOUSE,	3	OPEN HOUSE	3
REMAIN SECURE FROM PAIN PRESERVE THY HATE THY HEART.	5	TO MY SISTER	11
THE SECRET HEART OF SOUND.	17	NO BIRD	2
THE HEART MUST RALLY TO MY WIT	19	AGNST DISASTER	11
THE HEART BEAT FASTER AS THE FAT WORDS ROLLED.	21	THE AUCTION	14
ALONE, HIS WIFE IS GRIEVING FOR WHAT HER HEART DESIRES.	27	CLAIRVOY WIDOW	14
AND CHILL THE ANXIOUS HEART;	31	LULL	3
IS THIS THE STORM'S HEART? THE GROUND IS UNSTILLING ITSELF.	56	THE LOST SON	100
MY HEART LIFTED UP WITH THE GREAT GRASSES;	63	FIELD OF LIGHT	46
STOP THE LARKS. CAN I HAVE MY HEART BACK?	76	I NEED, I NEED	47
YOU CHILD WITH A BEAST'S HEART,	80	GIVE WAY, GATES	38
I SEE MY HEART IN THE SEED;	83	O LULL ME, LULL	24
I HEAR, CLEARLY, THE HEART OF ANOTHER SINGING,	88	PRAISE TO END!	94
WHERE'S THE GREAT RAGE OF A ROCKING HEART, THE HIGH RARE TRUE DANGEROUS	98	O, THOU OPENING	30
THE LARK'S MY HEART!	99	O, THOU OPENING	64
HAVE TOSSED MY HEART AND FIDDLED THROUGH MY BRAIN.	105	SIR JOHN DAVIES	22
WHAT'S HELL BUT A COLD HEART?	122	ALL EARTH, AIR	28
WHAT TIME'S MY HEART? I CARE.	125	WORDS FOR WIND	75
HIDDEN IN MY OWN HEART.	128	THE VOICE	6
THE SERPENT'S HEART SUSTAINS THE LOVELESS STONE:	131	SENTENTIOUS MAN	3
DRY BONES! DRY BONES! I FIND MY LOVING HEART,	135	THE RENEWAL	19
MY NECK, IF NOT MY HEART, WILL BREAK	136	THE SENSUALISTS	23
WHEN TRUE LOVE BROKE MY HEART IN HALF,	138	THE SURLY ONE	1
THAT GOD THAT GOD LEANS DOWN HIS HEART TO HEAR.	144	ELEGY (1)	16
MY HEART HELD TO ITS JOY,	148	THE SMALL	5
EATING THE HEART OUT OF MY GARDEN.	151	SLUG	14
MY HEART SWAYS WITH THE WORLD.	153	THE DYING MAN	13
IN THE WILD DISORDERED LANGUAGE OF THE NATURAL HEART?	166	HER BECOMING	33
LOVED HEART, WHAT CAN I SAY?	172	WHAT TELL BONES	38
THE HEART SAYS, I AM LESS;	172	WHAT TELL BONES	42
I LONG FOR THE IMPERISHABLE QUIET AT THE HEART OF FORM;	188	THE LONGING	45
I HAVE KNOWN THE HEART OF THE SUN,--	194	JOURNY INTERIOR	59

	PAGE	TITLE	LINE
HEART (CONTINUED)			
WHO TOOK MY HEART, WHOLE,	208	THE APPARITION	5
NOR THE WHOLE HEART OF MY THOUGHT,	209	HER RETICENCE	7
WILL THE HEART EAT THE HEART?	211	SONG (1)	7
WILL THE HEART EAT THE HEART?	211	SONG (1)	7
THAT TREMBLE OF SWEET NOTES SET MY HEART ASTIR,	216	THE SHY MAN	10
A FLASH INTO THE BURNING HEART OF THE ABOMINABLE;	221	THE ABYSS	56
FLASH ME TO MERCY AND A WHOLE HEART!	259	SONG (3)	42
THE DARK HEART OF SOME ANCIENT THING	260	THE CHANGELING	4
SAD THE SOUL'S JOY. LOVED HEART, WHAT ELSE CAN I SAY	261	THE CHANGELING	28
HEARTS			
MAY THE HIGH FLOWER OF THE HAY CLIMB INTO THEIR HEARTS;	169	FOURTH MEDITATN	56
HEART'S			
ARCH OF AIR, MY HEART'S ORIGINAL KNOCK,	88	PRAISE TO END!	79
LIVING ALL MY HEART'S SUMMER ALONE,	161	I'M HERE	19
WAS NATURE KIND? THE HEART'S CORE TRACTABLE?	242	THE SEQUEL	25
HEAT			
AS THE LIVE HEAT BILLOWS FROM PIPES AND POTS.	38	FORCING HOUSE	11
THE HEAT GOING DOWN	39	ORCHIDS	11
HEAT WAS HAPPY.	51	THE WAKING (1)	4
BY THE SHRUNKEN LAKE, HUNTING, IN THE HEAT OF SUMMER.	54	THE LOST SON	43
BETWEEN SUCH ANIMAL AND HUMAN HEAT	105	SIR JOHN DAVIES	25
WHAT YOU SURVIVED I SHALL BELIEVE: THE HEAT,	144	ELEGY (1)	13
IN THE SUMMER HEAT, I CAN SMELL THE DEAD BUFFALO,	189	THE LONGING	54
AND WE TURN BACK TO THE HEAT OF AUGUST,	220	THE ABYSS	48
HEATED			
THIS WATER, HEATED LIKE MY BLOOD,	256	IN HYDROTHERAPY	5
HEAT-LIGHTNING			
WHILE, FARTHER AWAY, THE HEAT-LIGHTNING FLASHES.	194	JOURNY INTERIOR	41
HEAT-MADDENED			
MY SOUL, LIKE SOME HEAT-MADDENED SUMMER FLY,	239	IN A DARK TIME	20
HEAT-WEARY			
I MOVED LIKE SOME HEAT-WEARY ANIMAL.	247	I WAITED	17
HEAVED			
THE LOAM HEAVED ME	104	OLD LADY'S WRDS	45
AND LINDSAY HEAVED HIMSELF FROM MY OLD CHAIR.	274	SUPPR W LINDSAY	38
HEAVEN			
THE FIRE OF HEAVEN DIES; A FIRE UNSEEN	17	UNEXTINGUISHED	5
MY SPECIAL HEAVEN IS REVERSED,	19	AGNST DISASTER	7
ONE SIGH STRETCHES HEAVEN.	83	O LULL ME, LULL	1
WHO LEAPS TO HEAVEN AT A SINGLE BOUND?	107	SIR JOHN DAVIES	80
IN THIS FIRST HEAVEN OF KNOWING,	191	AT OYSTER RIVER	37
WHAT NEED FOR HEAVEN, THEN,	203	THE ROSE	56
WHAT WEATHER OF HEAVEN IS THIS?"	208	HER WORDS	11
IN HEAVEN, TOO,	228	IN VIOLENT WARD	1
THE EDGE OF HEAVEN WAS SHARPER THAN A SWORD;	237	THE TRANCED	6
HEAVEN'S			
IN HEAVEN'S PRAISE, I DREAD THE THING I AM.	156	THE DYING MAN	95
THE ONLY THING ALIVE IN HEAVEN'S EYE,	166	HER BECOMING	58
A WEDGE OF HEAVEN'S LIGHT, AUTUMNAL SONG.	173	WHAT TELL BONES	68
HEAVEN-SENSE			
HER HEAVEN-SENSE PURE AS A STONE.	260	THE CHANGELING	11
HEAVILY			
BREATHING HEAVILY, HOPING--	231	THE STORM	39
FLAPPING AWAY HEAVILY WHEN A CAR BLASTS TOO CLOSE,	234	ALL MORNING	7
HEAVINESS			
THE LORD GOD HAS TAKEN MY HEAVINESS AWAY;	222	THE ABYSS	98
HEAVING			
AND THE MIDCHANNEL BEGINS CRACKING AND HEAVING FROM THE PRESSURE BENEATH,	191	AT OYSTER RIVER	49
THE DUBIOUS SEA-CHANGE, THE HEAVING SANDS, AND MY TENTACLED SEA-COUSINS.	196	THE LONG WATERS	23
HEAVY			
THE SUN CUTS DEEP INTO THE HEAVY DRIFT,	11	LIGHT BRIGHTER	5
THEN POINTS HIS HEAVY BILL ABOVE THE WOOD.	15	THE HERON	10
BLEAK CLOUDS ACROSS THE HEAVY SKY,	15	COMING OF COLD	50
THE PSYCHE WRITHING AND SQUIRMING IN HEAVY WOOLEN,--	48	LAST WORDS	5
WHERE THE HEAVY DOOR UNLOCKS,	230	THE STORM	21
I ROSE, A HEAVY BULK, ABOVE THE FIELD.	247	I WAITED	5
HE'D			
--HE'D GOT IN: DIRTY DINKY.	114	DINKY	16
"THAT'S NEVER BLAKE," SAID LINDSAY. "HE'D BE A WORM,	273	SUPPR W LINDSAY	26

	PAGE	TITLE	LINE
HEDGE			
THE HEDGE AND ORCHARD GROVE ARE THINNED.	14	COMING OF COLD	31
OUT OF THE BRIARY HEDGE, THE TANGLE OF MATTED UNDERBRUSH,	203	THE ROSE	45
HEDGEROWS			
OLD HEDGEROWS KEEP THE LEAVES; THE PHLOX, ...	15	COMING OF COLD	40
WHILE THE WRENS BICKERED AND SANG IN THE HALF-GREEN			
HEDGEROWS, ...	200	THE FAR FIELD	36
PITCHING LIGHTLY OVER THE HIGH HEDGEROWS, DEE-DEEING, ...	234	ALL MORNING	25
HEDGEWREN'S			
THE HEDGEWREN'S SONG SAYS SOMETHING ELSE.	92	I CRY, LOVE!	15
HEELS			
CLOSE TO THE HEELS OF MY FATHER, ...	6	THE PREMONITION	4
I TEETER, HEELS HOOKED ON THE CURB, SCRAPE A TOE;	47	DOUBLE FEATURE	7
HEIFER			
BE SLEEK AS A HEIFER, BE LONG AS A HOG,--	86	PRAISE TO END!	41
HEIGHO			
--HEIGHO, MEET HUGH AND HARRY!	181	MONOTONY SONG	4
--HEIGHO, WE'RE HUGH AND HARRY!	181	MONOTONY SONG	8
--HEIGHO HUGH AND HARRY!	181	MONOTONY SONG	24
HEIGHT			
THE DEPTH CALLS TO THE HEIGHT	97	O, THOU OPENING	9
HEIGHTENED			
THE LIGHT HEIGHTENED,	202	THE ROSE	28
HEIGHTS			
THE SLIPPERY COLD HEIGHTS, ...	221	THE ABYSS	51
HEIRS			
FOR SALE: BY ORDER OF THE REMAINING HEIRS	32	SALE	1
HELD			
AND SOME HAVE HELD THE EYE TO BE	8	PRAYER	9
TO LOOSEN WITH ALL TEN FINGERS HELD WIDE AND LIMBER	40	MOSS-GATHERING	1
THE HAND THAT HELD MY WRIST	45	MY PAPA'S WALTZ	9
HELD UP, WHILE THE ROWER BREATHES, AND THE SMALL BOAT			
DRIFTS QUIETLY SHOREWARD;	67	SHAPE OF FIRE	91
SHE HELD HER BODY STEADY IN THE WIND;	120	THE DREAM	25
MY HEART HELD TO ITS JOY, ...	148	THE SMALL	5
HELIOTROPE			
THE HELIOTROPE, VEINED LIKE A FISH, THE PERSISTENT			
MORNING-GLORY, ...	197	THE LONG WATERS	41
HELL			
WHAT'S HELL BUT A COLD HEART?	122	ALL EARTH, AIR	28
IN HELL THERE IS NO CHANGE.	139	PLAINT	3
HE'LL			
HE'LL SIGH AND GIVE HIS BRANCH A HUG;	116	THE SLOTH	9
HELLO			
HELLO, HELLO. MY NERVES KNEW YOU, DEAR BOY.	65	SHAPE OF FIRE	32
HELLO, HELLO. MY NERVES KNEW YOU, DEAR BOY.	65	SHAPE OF FIRE	32
HELLO HAPPY HANDS.	73	WHERE KNOCK IS	52
I COULD SAY HELLO TO THINGS;	84	O LULL ME, LULL	38
HELLO, THINGY SPIRIT.	92	I CRY, LOVE!	21
HELL'S			
FROM DIRE HELL'S MOUTH, ...	236	SONG (2)	10
HELP			
THEY HELP.	91	UNFOLD! UNFOLD!	67
--TO HELP ME EAT UP HER MONEY.	112	SQUEEZE-BOX	45
HELPED			
I HELPED OUT WITH THE BOOKS;	267	SAGINAW SONG	32
HELPS			
LOVE HELPS THE SUN.	76	I NEED, I NEED	51
HEMLOCK			
THE FLAT BRANCH OF THAT HEMLOCK HOLDS THE LAST OF THE SUN,	163	I'M HERE	83
OUT HEMLOCK WAY THERE IS A STREAM	267	SAGINAW SONG	7
HEMLOCKS			
AND THE AIR COOL, AS IF DRIFTING DOWN FROM WET HEMLOCKS,	43	CARNATIONS	3
I HEAR THE OWLS, THE SOFT CALLERS, COMING DOWN FROM THE			
HEMLOCKS.	93	I CRY, LOVE!	40
HEN			
SHE CRIES TO THE HEN, ...	60	THE LONG ALLEY	51
THE GLAD HEN ON THE HILL; AND THE TRELLIS HUMMING.	66	SHAPE OF FIRE	72
CAN A CAT MILK A HEN?	81	SENSIBILITY! LA	15
A MAD HEN IN A FAR CORNER OF THE DARK, ...	165	HER BECOMING	5
HER (115)			
HERE			
HERE DISTANCE IS FAMILIAR AS A FRIEND.	13	PRAISE PRAIRIE	11

	PAGE	TITLE	LINE
HERE (CONTINUED)			
NOW HERE IS PEACE FOR ONE WHO KNEW	17	NO BIRD	1
HERE FROM THE FIELD'S EDGE WE SURVEY	33	HIGHWAY: MICH	1
YOU WILL FIND NO COMFORT HERE,	54	THE LOST SON	32
THESE STONES HAVE BEEN HERE TOO LONG.	55	THE LOST SON	65
HATH THE RAIN A FATHER? ALL THE CAVES ARE ICE. ONLY THE SNOW'S HERE.	56	THE LOST SON	84
WHO ELSE BREATHES HERE? WHAT DOES THE GRAVE SAY?	59	THE LONG ALLEY	19
ARE THE FLOWERS HERE? THE BIRDS ARE.	61	THE LONG ALLEY	64
MOTHER ME OUT OF HERE. WHAT MORE WILL THE BONES ALLOW?	64	SHAPE OF FIRE	7
THE EAR'S NOT HERE	64	SHAPE OF FIRE	22
BUT NOT HERE.	74	WHERE KNOCK IS	89
IT'S QUEER ENOUGH HERE, PERHAPS.	81	SENSIBILITY! LA	12
COMMODITIES, HERE WE COME!	81	SENSIBILITY! LA	20
MY DEAREST DUST, I CAN'T STAY HERE.	86	PRAISE TO END!	44
BY SNAILS, BY LEAPS OF FROG, I CAME HERE, SPIRIT.	89	UNFOLD! UNFOLD!	1
DEAREST TREE, I SAID, MAY I REST HERE?	100	THE VISITANT	5
MY SPARROW, YOU ARE NOT HERE,	102	ELEGY FOR JANE	14
GOD COULD BELIEVE: I AM HERE TO FEAR.	144	ELEGY (1)	12
I'M HERE	161	I'M HERE	T
I'M HERE!	164	I'M HERE	100
HERE.	164	I'M HERE	101
AND SHEDDING MORE THAN HERE AND THERE,	181	MONOTONY SONG	7
I HAVE COME HERE WITHOUT COURTING SILENCE,	197	THE LONG WATERS	44
WAS IT HERE I WORE A CROWN OF BIRDS FOR A MOMENT	202	THE ROSE	26
MY EYES NEITHER HERE NOR THERE,	207	THE YOUNG GIRL	9
AND I LIE HERE THINKING IN BLEAK BOFIN TOWN	216	THE SHY MAN	18
I LIE HERE AND THINKING, "I AM NOT ALONE."	216	THE SHY MAN	19
FOR HERE CLOSE BESIDE ME IS O'CONNELL'S DAUGHTER,	216	THE SHY MAN	20
IS THE STAIR HERE?	219	THE ABYSS	1
HERE IN OUR AGING DISTRICT THE WOOD PIGEON LIVES WITH US,	234	ALL MORNING	1
A DARK THEME KEEPS ME HERE,	240	IN EVEING AIR	1
BUT WHY AM I GROANING HERE,	262	FOLLIES OF ADAM	6
BRINGS THE SECRET--RIGHT IN HERE!	266	FOR STEVENS	8
"LET'S EAT!" SAID LINDSAY. "HERE WE'VE GOT THE MOON,	273	SUPPR W LINDSAY	15
JOHN RANSOM SHOULD BE HERE, AND RENE CHAR;	274	SUPPR W LINDSAY	43
HE SHOOK MY HAND. "TELL WILLIAMS I'VE BEEN HERE,	274	SUPPR W LINDSAY	48
HERE'S			
AND HERE'S MORE ADVICE:	183	THE LIZARD	5
HERE'S THE LAST KISS OF MY LUCK:	259	SONG (3)	43
HERE'S A MENSCH BUT CAN SING DANDY.	266	FOR STEVENS	14
HERO			
HERO OF PHANTASIES AND CATCHER OF CHILLS,	24	POETASTER	1
HEROES			
HEROES AND BEARS, AND OLD PHILOSOPHERS--	274	SUPPR W LINDSAY	42
HERON			
THE HERON	15	THE HERON	T
THE HERON STANDS IN WATER WHERE THE SWAMP	15	THE HERON	1
I SEE A HERON PRANCING IN HIS POND;	106	SIR JOHN DAVIES	39
OR WALK THE PEBBLY SHORE WITH THE HUMPBACKED HERON,	209	HER LONGING	14
I LIVE BETWEEN THE HERON AND THE WREN,	239	IN A DARK TIME	5
HERONS			
WHEN THE HERONS FLOATED HIGH OVER THE WHITE HOUSES,	66	SHAPE OF FIRE	66
HERON'S			
FOR THE HERON'S HIERATIC FISHING,	202	THE ROSE	12
HERRINGS			
THE HERRINGS ARE AWAKE.	77	BRING THE DAY!	25
HERS (1)			
HERSELF			
HOW STILL SHE KEEPS HERSELF.	83	O LULL ME, LULL	4
OH, WHEN SHE WAS SAD, SHE CAST HERSELF DOWN INTO SUCH A PURE DEPTH,	102	ELEGY FOR JANE	10
AND, WITH A HARSH RASP OF A LAUGH AT HERSELF,	223	ELEGY (2)	10
HOW SHE KEPT THE WIZENED, THE FALLEN, THE MISSHAPEN FOR HERSELF,	223	ELEGY (2)	14
HE'S			
HE'S GONE FOR ALWAYS,	72	WHERE KNOCK IS	25
I KNOW IT'S AN OWL. HE'S MAKING IT DARKER.	72	WHERE KNOCK IS	39
LOOK AT HIM PUFF. HE'S TRYING TO TALK.	73	WHERE KNOCK IS	60
THE DEVIL ISN'T DEAD; HE'S JUST AWAY.	97	O, THOU OPENING	16
YOU'RE PART OF HIM; HE'S PART OF YOU	114	DINKY	19
NOW HE'S EATEN HIS THREE KINDS OF CHEESE AND DRUNK FROM HIS BOTTLE-CAP WATERING-TROUGH--	227	MEADOW MOUSE	12

	PAGE	TITLE	LINE
HE'S (CONTINUED)			
HE'S PART OF ONE, AS A MATTER OF COURSE.	264	THREE EPIGRAMS	12
HE'S IMAGINATION'S PRINCE:	266	FOR STEVENS	5
BROTHER, HE'S OUR FATHER!	266	FOR STEVENS	20
AND ONE EYE GAZED ASKEW. "WHY, BLAKE, HE'S DEAD,--	273	SUPPR W LINDSAY	22
HID			
AND POKES THE CRUMBLED COAL THE ASHES HID,	17	UNEXTINGUISHED	11
I HID IN HIS.	75	I NEED, I NEED	22
RIDING BENEATH THE MOON, HID FROM THE MOON,	225	OTTO	36
OUR SMALL SOULS HID FROM THEIR SMALL AGONIES,	238	THE TRANCED	21
HIDDEN			
AND SOON A BRANCH, PART OF A HIDDEN SCENE,	11	LIGHT BRIGHTER	17
TREMBLED AT HIDDEN VIRTUE WITHOUT FLAW,	107	SIR JOHN DAVIES	74
HIDDEN IN MY OWN HEART.	128	THE VOICE	6
HIDE			
THE BULKS CANNOT HIDE US, OR THE BLEAK SHEDS OF OUR DESOLATION,	166	HER BECOMING	39
O THE SONGS WE HIDE, SINGING ONLY TO OURSELVES!	168	FOURTH MEDITATN	13
O THE SONGS WE HIDE SINGING TO OURSELVES!--	259	SONG (3)	38
HIDES			
DESIRE HIDES FROM DESIRE.	130	THE OTHER	22
HIDING			
THE LONG EYE NOTES THE MINNOW'S HIDING PLACE.	15	THE HERON	7
HIDING DEEP IN THE BLACKBERRY BUSHES--	234	ALL MORNING	20
HIERATIC			
FOR THE HERON'S HIERATIC FISHING,	202	THE ROSE	12
GRAVE, HIERATIC, A PIECE OF ASSYRIAN SCULPTURE,	234	ALL MORNING	10
HIGH			
UNTIL I COULD THINK THERE WERE WAVES ROLLING HIGH AS MY BEDROOM FLOOR;	12	MID-CNTRY BLOW	2
WHEN THE HERONS FLOATED HIGH OVER THE WHITE HOUSES,	66	SHAPE OF FIRE	66
HOW HIGH IS HAVE?	73	WHERE KNOCK IS	73
WHERE'S THE GREAT RAGE OF A ROCKING HEART, THE HIGH RARE TRUE DANGEROUS	98	O, THOU OPENING	30
I WOULD HOLD HIGH CONVERSE	103	OLD LADY'S WRDS	14
THE FAIR HOUSE, THE HIGH	103	OLD LADY'S WRDS	26
THE HIGH CICADAS CHIRR;	148	THE SMALL	2
THE CERULEAN, HIGH IN THE ELM,	159	FIRST MEDITATN	84
RUNNING THROUGH HIGH GRASSES,	161	I'M HERE	21
FEARFUL OF HIGH PLACES, IN LOVE WITH HORSES;	162	I'M HERE	28
MAY THE HIGH FLOWER OF THE HAY CLIMB INTO THEIR HEARTS;	169	FOURTH MEDITATN	56
THE ICE PILING HIGH AGAINST THE IRON-BOUND SPILES,	191	AT OYSTER RIVER	50
THE TOWNS WITH THEIR HIGH PITTED ROAD-CROWNS AND DEEP GUTTERS,	193	JOURNY INTERIOR	30
THE STERN HIGH, DIPPING LIKE A CHILD'S BOAT IN A POND--	203	THE ROSE	37
WIDENING AT HIGH NOON, FACE UPWARD,	203	THE ROSE	43
LIFTING ME HIGH OVER THE FOUR-FOOT STEMS, THE MRS. RUSSELLS, AND HIS OWN ELABORATE HYBRIDS,	203	THE ROSE	54
AS I WALKED BY THE HIGH SEA-WALL.	216	THE SHY MAN	4
AS I MOPED BY THE HIGH SEA-WALL.	216	THE SHY MAN	8
AS WE WALKED BY THE HIGH SEA-WALL.	216	THE SHY MAN	16
AS WE EMBRACE BY THE HIGH SEA-WALL.	216	THE SHY MAN	23
AS WE KISS BY THE HIGH SEA-WALL.	216	THE SHY MAN	26
AS I LOOKED OUT AT THEM FROM THE HIGH HOUSE,	225	OTTO	35
THE WAVES NOT YET HIGH, BUT EVEN,	230	THE STORM	11
THEY SIT, THREE OR FOUR, HIGH IN THE FIR-TREES BACK OF THE HOUSE,	234	ALL MORNING	6
AND ONE DROPS DOWN TO THE GARDEN, THE HIGH RHODODENDRON,	234	ALL MORNING	8
PITCHING LIGHTLY OVER THE HIGH HEDGEROWS, DEE-DEEING,	234	ALL MORNING	25
AND DANCED, AT HIGH NOON,	249	THE RESTORED	17
THINGS OF HIGH WIT AND CHANGES OF THE MOON.	260	THE CHANGELING	27
HIGHER			
THE HIGHER THINGS IN LIFE DO NOT	25	VERSE W ALLUSNS	5
THEN RETIRE TO A ROCK HIGHER UP ON THE CLIFF-SIDE.	190	AT OYSTER RIVER	16
THOUGH HE HEAR A NOTE HIGHER THAN C	196	THE LONG WATERS	6
ONE GREENISH LID LIFTS A BIT HIGHER,	226	THE LIZARD	23
HIGHEST			
THE ELM TREE IS OUR HIGHEST MOUNTAIN PEAK;	13	PRAISE PRAIRIE	1
HIGH-NOON			
IN THE HIGH-NOON OF THIGHS,	80	GIVE WAY, GATES	33
HIGH-PILED			
THE HIGH-PILED FLORAL OFFERINGS WITH SENTIMENTAL VERSES,	22	ROAD TO WDLAWN	3

	PAGE	TITLE	LINE
HIGHWAY			
HIGHWAY: MICHIGAN	33	HIGHWAY: MICH	T
WALKED ALONG THE HIGHWAY,	87	PRAISE TO END!	53
THE DOE WITH ITS SLOPED SHOULDERS LOPING ACROSS THE HIGHWAY,	190	AT OYSTER RIVER	27
THE HIGHWAY RIBBONING OUT IN A STRAIGHT THRUST TO THE NORTH,	193	JOURNY INTERIOR	27
THE TURTLE GASPING IN THE DUSTY RUBBLE OF THE HIGHWAY,	227	MEADOW MOUSE	27
AND THE DUCKS NEAR LAKE WASHINGTON WADDLE DOWN THE HIGHWAY AFTER A RAIN,	234	ALL MORNING	26
HIKER			
HORACE THE HIKER ON A DUBIOUS MISSION	29	THE GENTLE	3
HILARIOUS			
HER SWART HILARIOUS SKIN;	126	WORDS FOR WIND	99
HILL			
A KINDLY WIDOW LADY, WHO LIVED UPON A HILL,	27	CLAIRVOY WIDOW	1
ARE THOSE HORNS ON TOP OF THE HILL? YESTERDAY HAS A LONG LOOK.	59	THE LONG ALLEY	13
THE SHE-BEAR MOPES UNDER THE HILL.	64	SHAPE OF FIRE	15
THE GLAD HEN ON THE HILL; AND THE TRELLIS HUMMING.	66	SHAPE OF FIRE	72
THE HOLY ROOT WAGS THE TAIL OF A HILL;	99	O, THOU OPENING	54
THE VALLEY ROCKED BENEATH THE GRANITE HILL;	106	SIR JOHN DAVIES	59
DANTE ATTAINED THE PURGATORIAL HILL,	107	SIR JOHN DAVIES	73
THE WIND DIES ON THE HILL.	141	MEMORY	7
THE TRICK WAS TO THROW THE CAR SIDEWAYS AND CHARGE OVER THE HILL, FULL OF THE THROTTLE.	193	JOURNY INTERIOR	21
OR A BREEZE MOVES OVER THE KNEES FROM A LOW HILL,	198	THE LONG WATERS	64
THE SMALL THING DIVING DOWN TOWARD A HILL,	232	THE THING	10
BEASTS OF THE HILL AND SERPENTS OF THE DEN.	239	IN A DARK TIME	6
THE HILL BECOMES THE VALLEY, AND IS STILL;	250	THE RIGHT THING	5
MY TRUE SELF RUNS TOWARD A HILL	251	ONCE MORE, RND	3
FOR A BLOND HILL BECKONED	265	HARSH COUNTRY	9
HILLS			
THE HILLS ARE GREY, THE TREES ARE BARE,	15	COMING OF COLD	43
REACH ME A PEACH, FONDLING, THE HILLS ARE THERE.	61	THE LONG ALLEY	81
HILLSIDE			
DOWN A STEEP HILLSIDE ON A CAKE OF ICE,--	105	SIR JOHN DAVIES	8
WHILE STONES LOOSEN ON THE OBSCURE HILLSIDE,	157	FIRST MEDITATN	5
LUNGING DOWN A HILLSIDE.	159	FIRST MEDITATN	59
WHEN THE SLOW FREIGHT WINDS ALONG THE EDGE OF THE RAVAGED HILLSIDE,	204	THE ROSE	83
HIM (39)			
HIMSELF			
EACH ONE'S HIMSELF, YET EACH ONE'S EVERYONE.	132	SENTENTIOUS MAN	36
THAT GOD HIMSELF CAN SCARCELY BEAR.	144	ELEGY (1)	4
AND ONE CRAB, TENTATIVE, HUNCHES HIMSELF BEFORE MOVING ALONG THE BOTTOM,	159	FIRST MEDITATN	62
DANTE HIMSELF ENDURED.	216	HER WRATH	1
A SPIDER EASES HIMSELF DOWN FROM A SWAYING LIGHT-BULB,	231	THE STORM	34
TAKES TO HIMSELF WHAT MYSTERY HE CAN,	250	THE RIGHT THING	15
HE WHO HIMSELF BEGINS TO LOATHE	257	SANITARIUM	9
BEWILDERS HIMSELF:	259	SONG (3)	46
HE LOVES HIMSELF, AND THE ILLUSTRIOUS DEAD;	264	THREE EPIGRAMS	4
AND LINDSAY HEAVED HIMSELF FROM MY OLD CHAIR.	274	SUPPR W LINDSAY	38
HIND			
JUMPING UP AND DOWN ON THEIR HIND FEET,	163	I'M HERE	68
BUT THE HIND PART OF THE WORM WIGGLES THE MOST,	196	THE LONG WATERS	2
HINT			
WITH NO HINT OF YOUR PRESENCE IN A JUNGLE OF MASCULINE TOYS,	29	THE REMINDER	10
HIP			
OR ONE HIP QUIVER WITH A MOBILE NOSE	127	I KNEW A WOMAN	20
HIPPETY-HOP			
THESE AIRY HIPPETY-HOP SKIPPERS,	152	THE SISKINS	20
HIPPO			
THE HIPPO	182	THE HIPPO	T
HIPS			
OR TO SINK DOWN TO THE HIPS IN A MOSSY QUAGMIRE;	200	THE FAR FIELD	44
HIS (136)			
HISS			
THE WEEDS HISS AT THE EDGE OF THE FIELD,	157	FIRST MEDITATN	2
THE BULLDOZER BACKING AWAY, THE HISS OF THE SANDBLASTER,	204	THE ROSE	71
HISSED			
AS THE SEAMS HISSED	41	BIG WIND	12
HIT			
DON'T HIT HIM ON THE BOAT, I SAID.	73	WHERE KNOCK IS	59

	PAGE	TITLE	LINE
HIT (CONTINUED)			
A PICK LIKES TO HIT ICE.	76	I NEED, I NEED	54
WHEN YOU HIT THE DEEP PIT AT THE BOTTOM OF THE SWALE,	193	JOURNY INTERIOR	20
HITCHED			
WITH THAT HE HITCHED HIS PANTS AND HUMPED AWAY.	274	SUPPR W LINDSAY	50
HITTING			
ITS ALMOST-INVISIBLE WINGS, BUZZING, HITTING THE LOOSE LEAVES INTERMITTENTLY--	234	ALL MORNING	32
HIVE			
THE HIVE THAT HUMMED IN EVERY CELL	4	DEATH PIECE	3
HO			
GILLIFLOWER HO,	60	THE LONG ALLEY	48
SWAYS ME AWAKE. WHAT HO, AND THE FIELD'S MY FRIEND,	260	THE CHANGELING	14
HOAR			
THE LOOSE VINE DROOPS WITH HOAR AT DAWN,	14	COMING OF COLD	20
HOARD			
FELICITY I CANNOT HOARD.	88	PRAISE TO END!	83
HOARDED			
OF EASE, THE HOARDED, SECRET SUM;	30	THE RECKONING	2
HOE			
MY HOE EATS LIKE A GOAT.	76	I NEED, I NEED	60
HOG			
BE SLEEK AS A HEIFER, BE LONG AS A HOG,--	86	PRAISE TO END!	41
HOLD			
DENSE TREES NO LONGER HOLD THE LIGHT,	14	COMING OF COLD	30
HOLD TO ADVANTAGE DEARLY WON.	33	HIGHWAY: MICH	9
I WOULD HOLD HIGH CONVERSE	103	OLD LADY'S WRDS	14
I CAN HOLD THIS VALLEY,	164	I'M HERE	96
DEAD TO MYSELF, AND ALL I HOLD MOST DEAR,	244	INFIRMITY	23
HOLDING			
STILL HOLDING AND FEEDING THE STEM OF THE CONTAINED FLOWER.	67	SHAPE OF FIRE	95
ITS SPRAY HOLDING A DOUBLE RAIN-BOW IN EARLY MORNING,	191	AT OYSTER RIVER	45
HOLDS			
THE STEM THAT HOLDS THE BEE IS PRONE;	15	COMING OF COLD	39
THE FLAT BRANCH OF THAT HEMLOCK HOLDS THE LAST OF THE SUN,	163	I'M HERE	83
HOLE			
OF MARSH GRASS HEAPED ABOVE A MUSK-RAT HOLE.	15	THE HERON	4
I'LL MAKE A HOLE FOR HER.	72	WHERE KNOCK IS	33
OPEN A HOLE AND SEE THE SKY:	75	I NEED, I NEED	39
WHO STANDS IN A HOLE	80	GIVE WAY, GATES	53
HE GOT NO PLEASURE DOWN HIS HOLE.	115	THE SERPENT	8
SMALL WATERS RUN TOWARD A MIRY HOLE--	132	SENTENTIOUS MAN	39
DOWN IN THAT WATERY HOLE:	146	THE SONG	19
I STARED INTO THE DENTED HOLE	269	GOB MUSIC	24
HOLES			
STUFFING THE HOLES WITH BURLAP;	41	BIG WIND	20
ALL OPENINGS PRAISE US, EVEN OILY HOLES.	90	UNFOLD! UNFOLD!	40
OR DREAM OF THE DEAD, AND THEIR HOLES.	173	WHAT TELL BONES	75
THE BLUEBIRD, LOVER OF HOLES IN OLD WOOD, LILTING ITS LIGHT SONG,	204	THE ROSE	66
EDGES, THEIR HOLES	205	THE ROSE	91
HOLIEST			
THE HOLIEST PLATONIC LOVE:	8	PRAYER	16
HOLLOW			
THE CRUMBLING SMALL HOLLOW STICKS ON THE UNDERSIDE MIXED WITH ROOTS,	40	MOSS-GATHERING	4
HOLLOWS			
DARK HOLLOWS SAID, LEE TO THE WIND,	54	THE LOST SON	28
THE FLOWERS LEANED ON THEMSELVES, THE FLOWERS IN HOLLOWS;	66	SHAPE OF FIRE	76
HOLY			
THE HOLY ROOT WAGS THE TAIL OF A HILL;	99	O, THOU OPENING	54
HOPE'S HOLY WRISTS: THE LITTLE BURNING BOYS	143	SHIMMER OF EVIL	13
WOULD BLAKE CALL YOU HOLY?	151	SLUG	29
THE LINE! THE HOLY LINE!	167	HER BECOMING	76
AMONG US, WHO IS HOLY?	220	THE ABYSS	24
HOME			
THEMSELVES, THEIR PARLORS MUSTY AS A FUNERAL HOME.	5	PROGNOSIS	12
ONCE ON RETURNING HOME, PURSE-PROUD AND HALE,	21	THE AUCTION	1
I LEFT MY HOME WITH UNENCUMBERED WILL	21	THE AUCTION	15
THOUGH HOME IS NOT HAPPY, WHERE ELSE CAN HE GO?	29	THE GENTLE	10
RETURN TO LITTER UP OUR HOME.	30	THE RECKONING	4
BIRD, SOFT-SIGH ME HOME,	53	THE LOST SON	9
THE ROUND HOME OF A ROOT,--	99	O, THOU OPENING	75

	PAGE	TITLE	LINE
HOME (CONTINUED)			
FATHER, I'M FAR FROM HOME,	137	LOVE'S PROGRESS	19
I LIVE IN AIR; THE LONG LIGHT IS MY HOME;	167	HER BECOMING	93
BRINGING ME HOME FROM THE TWILIGHT FISHING.	221	THE ABYSS	67
A TIME TO GO HOME!--	230	THE STORM	17
HONEY			
MY JUG, MY HONEY, MY CAN OF BEER,	272	DUET	22
HONEYMOON			
AND THE HONEYMOON BE SPOILED BY A FATHER'S GHOST,	5	PROGNOSIS	14
HONEYSUCKLE			
AND A BEE SHAKING DROPS FROM A RAIN-SOAKED HONEYSUCKLE.	63	FIELD OF LIGHT	49
HONEY-TIGHT			
IS NOW SEALED HONEY-TIGHT.	4	DEATH PIECE	4
HONOR			
THE CHAIR OF HONOR, WITH A MISSING RUNG."	21	THE AUCTION	8
--IN HONOR OF FATHER KIERKEGAARD.	272	DUET	26
HONORABLE			
O CURSED BE THE WORK THAT GETS HONORABLE MENTION!	29	THE GENTLE	9
HONORED			
HONORED, ON MY RETURN, BY THE ANCIENT FELLOWSHIP OF ROTTEN STEMS.	89	UNFOLD! UNFOLD!	26
HONORS			
HE HEAPS FEW HONORS ON A LIVING HEAD;	264	THREE EPIGRAMS	3
HOO			
HOO. I KNOW THE SPOON.	74	I NEED, I NEED	3
HOOD			
MAMMA! PUT ON YOUR DARK HOOD;	82	SENSIBILITY! LA	37
A MUSIC IN A HOOD,	101	LIGHT BREATHER	16
HOOK			
USE A HOOK OR A LINE,	117	LADY AND BEAR	15
HOOKED			
I TEETER, HEELS HOOKED ON THE CURB, SCRAPE A TOE;	47	DOUBLE FEATURE	7
HOORAY			
HOORAY FOR ME AND THE MICE!--	76	I NEED, I NEED	55
HOOVES			
MY HANDS TURN INTO HOOVES.	154	THE DYING MAN	18
SHE WITH HER THIGHS HARDER THAN HOOVES,	260	THE CHANGELING	1
HOPE			
HOPE, LOVE, CREATE, OR DRINK AND DIE:	18	LONG LIVE WEEDS	11
HOPE FLUSHED MY CHEEKBONES WITH A SCARLET DISK.	21	THE AUCTION	11
DO YOU SEE ANY SIGN OR SEMBLANCE OF THAT THING CALLED "HOPE"?	27	CLAIRVOY WIDOW	18
I LIVE NEAR THE ABYSS. I HOPE TO STAY	134	THE PURE FURY	26
HOPE HAS ITS HUSH: WE MOVE THROUGH ITS BROAD DAY,--	243	THE MOTION	22
WITH HOPE, AND NOT ALONE,	265	HARSH COUNTRY	14
HOPED			
WHAT WE HAD HOPED FOR HAD NOT COME TO PASS.	6	INTERLUDE	12
HOPELESS			
ENDING AT LAST IN A HOPELESS SAND-RUT,	199	THE FAR FIELD	9
HOPES			
YOUR HOPES ARE MURDERED AND UNDONE.	4	FEUD	12
HOPE'S			
HOPE'S HOLY WRISTS: THE LITTLE BURNING BOYS	143	SHIMMER OF EVIL	13
HOPING			
AND REMEMBER THERE WAS SOMETHING ELSE I WAS HOPING FOR.	47	DOUBLE FEATURE	12
BREATHING HEAVILY, HOPING--	231	THE STORM	39
HOPPED			
THAT THE KITTY-CAT BIRD JUST HOPPED INSIDE;	177	KITTY-CAT BIRD	15
HOPS			
THE HAY HOPS IN THE HORSE'S MOUTH,	60	THE LONG ALLEY	41
HORACE			
HORACE THE HIKER ON A DUBIOUS MISSION	29	THE GENTLE	3
HORIZON			
A TWO-LEGGED DOG HUNTING A NEW HORIZON OF HOWLS.	65	SHAPE OF FIRE	38
HORIZONS			
HORIZONS HAVE NO STRANGENESS TO THE EYE.	13	PRAISE PRAIRIE	5
HORIZON'S			
THE LINE OF MY HORIZON'S GROWING THIN!	245	THE DECISION	8
HORN			
ITS PALE TENDRILOUS HORN.	37	CUTTINGS	8
FROM A SHELL HARDER THAN HORN.	81	SENSIBILITY! LA	9
THEY GOT A HORN, THEY GOT A FLUTE,	115	THE SERPENT	17
A SHRED OF BONE ITS HORN,	145	THE BEAST	8

	PAGE	TITLE	LINE
HORN (CONTINUED)			
THE HAND UPON MY SHOULDER TURNS TO HORN.	154	THE DYING MAN	39
AND EVERY SNAIL DIPPED TOWARD ME ITS PURE HORN.	248	THE TREE, BIRD	2
HORNS			
THE YOUNG HORNS WINDING AND UNWINDING,	42	TRANSPLANTING	15
ARE THOSE HORNS ON TOP OF THE HILL? YESTERDAY HAS A LONG LOOK.	59	THE LONG ALLEY	13
INSTEAD OF A DEVIL WITH HORNS, I PREFER A SERPENT WITH SCALES;	173	WHAT TELL BONES	77
AND THE DEEP CHORUS OF HORNS COMING UP FROM THE STREETS IN EARLY MORNING.	204	THE ROSE	72
HORRIBLE			
AND THEN HE CUT LOOSE WITH A HORRIBLE NOTE	115	THE SERPENT	21
HORRID			
AND SO HE HAD A HORRID FALL.	181	MONOTONY SONG	15
HOR-RID			
YOU'RE A FAKE, YOUR'RE A FRAUD, YOU'RE A HOR-RID PRETENSE!	177	KITTY-CAT BIRD	3
HORROR			
MELTING AT THE KNEES, A VARICOSE HORROR.	65	SHAPE OF FIRE	31
YOU'RE BECOMING THAT HORROR, A TWO-LEGGED PIG	272	DUET	3
HORRORS			
--AND AN ATTIC OF HORRORS, A CLOSET OF FEARS.	32	SALE	4
HORSE			
THE SOUL RESIDES IN THE HORSE BARN.	59	THE LONG ALLEY	22
I'D SAY IT TO MY HORSE: WE LIVE BEYOND	106	SIR JOHN DAVIES	37
A WITCH WHO SLEEPS WITH HER HORSE?	161	I'M HERE	15
I STEPPED CAREFULLY, LIKE A NEW-SHOD HORSE,	166	HER BECOMING	46
I SANG TO THE WHITE HORSE THAT GRAZED ON THE QUAY,--	216	THE SHY MAN	3
POSEIDON'S ONLY A HORSE,	263	FOLLIES OF ADAM	29
THE CENTAUR DOES NOT NEED A HORSE;	264	THREE EPIGRAMS	11
HORSES			
I MISS THE POLISHED BRASS, THE POWERFUL BLACK HORSES,	22	ROAD TO WDLAWN	1
A LINE OF ELMS PLUNGING AND TOSSING LIKE HORSES,	43	CHILD ON GRNHSE	6
OR TWO HORSES PLUNGING IN SNOW, THEIR LINES TANGLED,	158	FIRST MEDITATN	53
FEARFUL OF HIGH PLACES, IN LOVE WITH HORSES;	162	I'M HERE	28
HORSE'S			
THE HAY HOPS IN THE HORSE'S MOUTH,	60	THE LONG ALLEY	41
HOSTILE			
THE HOSTILE GAZE OF HATE,	20	REPL TO CENSURE	2
HOT			
AS I WAS CROSSING A HOT HOT PLAIN,	114	DINKY	9
AS I WAS CROSSING A HOT HOT PLAIN,	114	DINKY	9
ON A HOT, DUSTY STONE,	249	THE RESTORED	18
HOUND			
FROM THE HOUND GIVING TONGUE,	236	SONG (2)	3
HOUND'S			
WITH A CHEEK SOFT AS A HOUND'S EAR.	157	FIRST MEDITATN	17
HOUR			
THE CHAOS GREW AS HOUR BY HOUR THE LIGHT	6	INTERLUDE	5
THE CHAOS GREW AS HOUR BY HOUR THE LIGHT	6	INTERLUDE	5
IN THE HOUR OF RIPENESS THE TREE IS BARREN.	64	SHAPE OF FIRE	14
IN THIS HOUR,	191	AT OYSTER RIVER	36
HOURS			
SIX HOURS A DAY I LAY ME DOWN	256	IN HYDROTHERAPY	1
HOUSE			
OPEN HOUSE	3	OPEN HOUSE	T
MY HEART KEEPS OPEN HOUSE,	3	OPEN HOUSE	3
HE LIKES THE ATTIC OF AN AGING HOUSE.	16	THE BAT	2
THE SUMMER HOUSE SHAPED LIKE A VILLAGE BAND STAND	32	SALE	7
WE GO TO OUR BEDS IN A HOUSE AT THE EDGE OF A MEADOW,	33	IDYLL	11
FORCING HOUSE	38	FORCING HOUSE	T
SAT IN AN EMPTY HOUSE	53	THE LOST SON	16
COULD IT COME IN THE HOUSE	54	THE LOST SON	52
MAYBE GOD HAS A HOUSE.	74	WHERE KNOCK IS	88
A HAT IS A HOUSE.	75	I NEED, I NEED	21
A HOUSE FOR WISDOM; A FIELD FOR REVELATION.	90	UNFOLD! UNFOLD!	53
THE FAIR HOUSE, THE HIGH	103	OLD LADY'S WRDS	26
THE WIND WANDERS AROUND THE HOUSE	104	OLD LADY'S WRDS	52
A MAN'S A BEAST PROWLING IN HIS OWN HOUSE,	133	THE PURE FURY	17
THE OLD HOUSE OF A CRAB;	146	THE SONG	16
WITH HIS STRIPES OF SILVER AND HIS SMALL HOUSE ON HIS BACK,	151	SLUG	2
A GHOST FROM THE SOUL'S HOUSE?	165	HER BECOMING	24
BACK TO THE HOUSE WE RAN,	214	THE HAPPY THREE	33

		PAGE	TITLE	LINE
HOUSE (CONTINUED)				
PART OF A HOUSE.		219	THE ABYSS	12
A HOUSE FOR FLOWERS! HOUSE UPON HOUSE THEY BUILT,		224	OTTO	23
A HOUSE FOR FLOWERS! HOUSE UPON HOUSE THEY BUILT,		224	OTTO	23
A HOUSE FOR FLOWERS! HOUSE UPON HOUSE THEY BUILT,		224	OTTO	23
AS I LOOKED OUT AT THEM FROM THE HIGH HOUSE,		225	OTTO	35
BUT THIS MORNING THE SHOE-BOX HOUSE ON THE BACK PORCH IS EMPTY.		227	MEADOW MOUSE	20
THEY SIT, THREE OR FOUR, HIGH IN THE FIR-TREES BACK OF THE HOUSE,		234	ALL MORNING	6
HOUSEHOLD				
THERE'S NEVER A HOUSEHOLD FART,		268	SAGINAW SONG	38
HOUSES				
WHEN THE HERONS FLOATED HIGH OVER THE WHITE HOUSES,		66	SHAPE OF FIRE	66
ELSEWHERE, IN HOUSES, EVEN PAILS CAN BE SAD;		157	FIRST MEDITATN	4
THE FLAT-ROOFED HOUSES, COMING DOWN IN GUSTS, BEATING		230	THE STORM	24
HOVE				
SHE HOVE INTO THE TEETH OF IT,		41	BIG WIND	23
HOVER				
WHERE SNAKE AND VULTURE HOVER,		7	ORDERS FOR DAY	12
THEY STILL HOVER OVER ME,		44	FRAU BAUMAN	31
HOVERING				
--AND GRANDFATHER'S SINISTER HOVERING HAND.		32	SALE	8
MY WINGS HOVERING OVER THE SHOREBIRDS,		209	HER LONGING	21
HOW				
HOW HE COULD FLICK AND PICK		42	OLD FLORIST	4
I REMEMBER HOW THEY PICKED ME UP, A SPINDLY KID,		44	FRAU BAUMAN	26
HOW COOL THE GRASS IS.		56	THE LOST SON	113
FLESH, YOU OFFEND THIS METAL. HOW LONG NEED THE BONES MOURN?		59	THE LONG ALLEY	12
A LOW MOUTH LAPS WATER. WEEDS, WEEDS, HOW I LOVE YOU.		64	SHAPE OF FIRE	17
HOW HIGH IS HAVE?		73	WHERE KNOCK IS	73
HOW MANY ANGELS DO YOU KNOW?--		77	BRING THE DAY!	12
WHY IS HOW I LIKE IT.		77	BRING THE DAY!	23
HOW IS IT WITH THE LONG BIRDS?		79	GIVE WAY, GATES	18
HOW STILL SHE KEEPS HERSELF.		83	O LULL ME, LULL	4
A MOUSE TAUGHT ME HOW, I WAS A HAPPY ASKER.		90	UNFOLD! UNFOLD!	35
AND HOW, ONCE STARTLED INTO TALK, THE LIGHT SYLLABLES LEAPED FOR HER,		102	ELEGY FOR JANE	3
YES, I WAS DANCING-MAD, AND HOW		105	SIR JOHN DAVIES	23
THE BODY AND THE SOUL KNOW HOW TO PLAY		106	SIR JOHN DAVIES	47
LIGHT TAKES THE TREE; BUT WHO CAN TELL US HOW?		108	THE WAKING (2)	10
--BUT HOW SHE COULD BURN UP THE MONEY!		111	SQUEEZE-BOX	16
"O IT'S WONDERFUL HOW WITH A FLICK OF YOUR WRIST,		117	LADY AND BEAR	21
HOW WELL HER WISHES WENT! SHE STROKED MY CHIN,		127	I KNEW A WOMAN	8
(I MEASURE TIME BY HOW A BODY SWAYS).		127	I KNEW A WOMAN	28
HOW SLOW THE CHANGES OF A GOLDEN MEAN:		133	THE PURE FURY	12
HOW TERRIBLE THE NEED FOR SOLITUDE:		133	THE PURE FURY	15
HOW I LOVED ONE LIKE YOU WHEN I WAS LITTLE!--		151	SLUG	1
THE MOON'S MY MOTHER: HOW I LOVE THE MOON!		156	THE DYING MAN	79
HOW CAN I REST IN THE DAYS OF MY SLOWNESS?		157	FIRST MEDITATN	14
--HOW NEEDLES AND CORNERS PERPLEX ME!		161	I'M HERE	12
I'VE TRIED I DON'T KNOW HOW MANY TIMES TO REPLANT IT.		163	I'M HERE	77
HOW SWEETLY I ABIDE. AM I A BIRD?		165	HER BECOMING	16
HOW I WISH THEM AWAKE!		169	FOURTH MEDITATN	55
HOW CLOSE WE ARE TO THE SAD ANIMALS!		171	WHAT TELL BONES	20
HOW SLOWLY ALL THINGS ALTER.		173	WHAT TELL BONES	66
TO FIND OUT HOW THE CEILING'S FEELING.		178	THE CEILING	6
HOW DID YOU DO THAT?		180	GOO-GIRL	9
AND YOUR FRIENDS,--HOW THEY STARE!		180	GOO-GIRL	13
WHO KNOWS HOW THE WAG-TAIL WOOS?		183	THE WAGTAIL	1
HOW TO TRANSCEND THIS SENSUAL EMPTINESS?		187	THE LONGING	12
HOW COMPREHENSIVE THAT FELICITY!		188	THE LONGING	26
--HOW FREE; HOW ALL ALONE.		188	THE LONGING	36
--HOW FREE; HOW ALL ALONE:		188	THE LONGING	36
HOW GRACEFUL THE SMALL BEFORE DANGER!		192	AT OYSTER RIVER	67
I REMEMBER HOW IT WAS TO DRIVE IN GRAVEL,		193	JOURNY INTERIOR	18
HOW SLOWLY PLEASURE DIES!--		197	THE LONG WATERS	29
HOW THEY FILLED THE ORIOLE'S ELM, A TWITTERING RESTLESS CLOUD, ALL ONE MORNING,		199	THE FAR FIELD	28
AND HOW THOSE FLOWERHEADS SEEMED TO FLOW TOWARD ME, TO BECKON ME, ONLY A CHILD, OUT OF MYSELF.		203	THE ROSE	55
HOW CAN I DREAM EXCEPT BEYOND THIS LIFE?		221	THE ABYSS	61

	PAGE	TITLE	LINE
HOW (CONTINUED)			
I RECALL HOW SHE HARRIED THE CHILDREN AWAY ALL THE LATE SUMMER	223	ELEGY (2)	12
HOW SHE KEPT THE WIZENED, THE FALLEN, THE MISSHAPEN FOR HERSELF,	223	ELEGY (2)	14
COUNTING THE WISPS OF FLAME, AND I WATCH HOW	240	IN EVEING AIR	20
HOW SLOWLY DARK COMES DOWN ON WHAT WE DO.	240	IN EVEING AIR	24
KNOWING HOW ALL THINGS ALTER IN THE SEED	243	THE MOTION	15
HOW BODY FROM SPIRIT SLOWLY DOES UNWIND	244	INFIRMITY	35
HOW DEEP THE MOTHER-ROOT OF THAT STILL CRY!	248	THE TREE, BIRD	17
HOW PURE THE MOTION OF THE RISING DAY,	248	THE TREE, BIRD	19
HOW ELSE, MEADOW-SHAPE?	258	SONG (3)	12
HOW FAST THE WINSOME ESCAPES!	258	SONG (3)	19
HOW IS IT INSIDE A TREE?	261	THE CHANGELING	30
HOW FREE! HOW ALL ALONE!	261	THE CHANGELING	39
HOW FREE! HOW ALL ALONE!	261	THE CHANGELING	39
AH, HOW SHE LAUGHED TO SEE	262	FOLLIES OF ADAM	16
HOW HE ROLLS THE VOCABLES,	266	FOR STEVENS	7
AND KNEW HOW TO COMMAND;	268	SAGINAW SONG	53
HOWEVER			
I NEVER AM BORED, HOWEVER FAMILIAR THE SCENE.	24	VERNAL SENTIMNT	4
HOWEVER GRACEFUL THE POSTURE.	172	WHAT TELL BONES	37
HOWL			
AND THE GHOST OF SOME GREAT HOWL	79	GIVE WAY, GATES	31
HOWLED			
BARKED AND HOWLED,	55	THE LOST SON	76
HOWLING			
YET WHEN I HEARD THE DRUNKARDS HOWLING,	48	JUDGE NOT	7
HOWLS			
WE GROW INDIFFERENT TO DOG HOWLS, TO THE NESTLING'S LAST PEEP;	33	IDYLL	6
A TWO-LEGGED DOG HUNTING A NEW HORIZON OF HOWLS.	65	SHAPE OF FIRE	38
ETERNITY HOWLS IN THE LAST CRAGS,	89	UNFOLD! UNFOLD!	6
HUDDLE			
MAKES THEM HUDDLE IN GROUPS,--	180	GOO-GIRL	15
HUES			
LOST HUES OF BIRDS THE TREES TAKE AS THEIR OWN.	12	SLOW SEASON	9
HUG			
LIKE THE HALF-DEAD, I HUG MY LAST SECRETS.	103	OLD LADY'S WRDS	5
HE'LL SIGH AND GIVE HIS BRANCH A HUG;	116	THE SLOTH	9
BETTER TO HUG CLOSE, WARY OF RUBBLE AND FALLING STONES.	193	JOURNY INTERIOR	6
HUGH			
--HEIGHO, MEET HUGH AND HARRY!	181	MONOTONY SONG	4
ONE DAY HUGH WALKED UP TO A BEAR	181	MONOTONY SONG	5
--HEIGHO, WE'RE HUGH AND HARRY!	181	MONOTONY SONG	8
--AND I'M NOT HUGH NOR HARRY!	181	MONOTONY SONG	20
--HEIGHO HUGH AND HARRY!	181	MONOTONY SONG	24
--UNLESS YOU'RE HUGH OR HARRY!	181	MONOTONY SONG	28
HUGS			
I CARE FOR A CAT'S CRY AND THE HUGS, LIVE AS WATER.	92	I CRY, LOVE!	16
THE CLOSE DARK HUGS ME HARD,	138	LOVE'S PROGRESS	21
HUM			
THAT MADE HIM THINK THE UNIVERSE COULD HUM?	105	SIR JOHN DAVIES	2
I HEAR A NOISE OF BEES, A TRELLIS HUM,	155	THE DYING MAN	74
I HUM IN PURE VIBRATION, LIKE A SAW.	167	HER BECOMING	89
HUMAN			
HIS BEAK IS QUICKER THAN A HUMAN HAND.	15	THE HERON	8
WHEN MICE WITH WINGS CAN WEAR A HUMAN FACE.	16	THE BAT	10
IS HUMAN NATURE'S DAILY FOOD.	25	VERSE W ALLUSNS	8
SLOWED IN MY HUMAN FORM;	49	RIVER INCIDENT	5
BETWEEN SUCH ANIMAL AND HUMAN HEAT	105	SIR JOHN DAVIES	25
THE FURY OF THE HATE-DRIVEN ZEALOT, THE MEANNESS OF THE HUMAN WEASEL;	170	FOURTH MEDITATN	68
HUMILITY			
FOR THE ATTACKS OF FALSE HUMILITY TAKE SUDDEN TURNS FOR THE WORSE.	86	PRAISE TO END!	25
HUMMED			
THE HIVE THAT HUMMED IN EVERY CELL	4	DEATH PIECE	3
HUMMING			
THE GLAD HEN ON THE HILL; AND THE TRELLIS HUMMING.	66	SHAPE OF FIRE	72
AND THAT SLOW HUMMING RISES INTO SONG.	155	THE DYING MAN	75

	PAGE	TITLE	LINE
HUMMINGBIRD			
THE HUMMINGBIRD, WHIRRING FROM QUINCE-BLOSSOM TO MORNING-GLORY--	190	AT OYSTER RIVER	29
AND THE HUMMINGBIRD DIPS IN AND AROUND THE QUINCE TREE,	234	ALL MORNING	29
HUMMING-BIRD			
LIKE A HUMMING-BIRD,	183	THE WAGTAIL	5
HUMMINGBIRD'S			
THE HUMMINGBIRD'S SURETY, THE KINGFISHER'S CUNNING--	191	AT OYSTER RIVER	40
HUMP			
OR BALANCES WITH ONE LEG ON A HUMP	15	THE HERON	3
THAT HUMP OF A MAN BUNCHING CHRYSANTHEMUMS	42	OLD FLORIST	1
LAUGHED A MASTER OF HUMP AND SNORT;	263	FOLLIES OF ADAM	30
HUMPBACKED			
OR WALK THE PEBBLY SHORE WITH THE HUMPBACKED HERON,	209	HER LONGING	14
HUMPED			
THE MINNOWS LOVE ME, AND THE HUMPED AND SPITTING CREATURES.	88	PRAISE TO END!	89
WITH THAT HE HITCHED HIS PANTS AND HUMPED AWAY.	274	SUPPR W LINDSAY	50
HUMPING			
AND GO HUMPING OFF, YICKETTY-YAK.	178	THE YAK	5
HUNCHES			
AND ONE CRAB, TENTATIVE, HUNCHES HIMSELF BEFORE MOVING ALONG THE BOTTOM,	159	FIRST MEDITATN	62
HUNDRED			
OR FRENCHMEN KILLED A HUNDRED YEARS AGO,	224	OTTO	26
HUNG			
STRAIGHT FROM THE OAK, THE GOSSAMER IS HUNG.	12	SLOW SEASON	7
HUNG DOWN LONG YELLOW EVIL NECKS, LIKE TROPICAL SNAKES.	38	ROOT CELLAR	5
BUT I HUNG ON LIKE DEATH:	45	MY PAPA'S WALTZ	3
WHOSE THIN SONG HUNG IN AIR,	128	THE VOICE	9
HUNG DOWN: AND I WAS ONLY I.	143	SHIMMER OF EVIL	9
"MY SOUL'S HUNG OUT TO DRY,	153	THE DYING MAN	3
ONE LEAF-LIKE FOOT HUNG LAXLY	226	THE LIZARD	7
HUNGER			
OR KNOWN, ONCE, THE SOUL'S AUTHENTIC HUNGER,	169	FOURTH MEDITATN	47
AND THE TERRIBLE HUNGER FOR OBJECTS QUAILS ME:	220	THE ABYSS	32
HUNT			
WE HUNT THE CAUSE OF RUIN, ADD,	30	THE RECKONING	5
HUNTED			
ON THE JACKPINE PLAINS I HUNTED THE BIRD NOBODY KNOWS;	89	UNFOLD! UNFOLD!	22
HUNTER'S			
BARED FOR A HUNTER'S BOOT.	47	THE RETURN	13
HUNTING			
BULBS BROKE OUT OF BOXES HUNTING FOR CHINKS IN THE DARK,	38	ROOT CELLAR	2
HUNTING ALONG THE RIVER,	54	THE LOST SON	40
BY THE SHRUNKEN LAKE, HUNTING, IN THE HEAT OF SUMMER.	54	THE LOST SON	43
A TWO-LEGGED DOG HUNTING A NEW HORIZON OF HOWLS.	65	SHAPE OF FIRE	38
HUNTING THE SUN.	213	THE HAPPY THREE	20
HUNTS			
AND MY THOUGHT HUNTS ANOTHER BODY.	80	GIVE WAY, GATES	44
HURRICANE			
AND THE HURRICANE DRIVES THE DEAD STRAW INTO THE LIVING PINE-TREE.	231	THE STORM	43
HURRY			
LET'S NOT HURRY. THE DEAD DON'T HURRY,	59	THE LONG ALLEY	18
LET'S NOT HURRY. THE DEAD DON'T HURRY.	59	THE LONG ALLEY	18
HURT			
A REAL HURT IS SOFT.	71	WHERE KNOCK IS	11
HUSH			
IF I THOUGHT YOU COULD HEAR IN A HUSH."	182	BOY AND BUSH	5
HOPE HAS ITS HUSH: WE MOVE THROUGH ITS BROAD DAY,--	243	THE MOTION	22
HUSHED			
EVEN THE HUSHED FORMS, THE BENT YELLOWY WEEDS	57	THE LOST SON	147
HUSK			
THE HUSK LIVES ON, ARDENT AS A SEED;	170	FOURTH MEDITATN	83
HUTCH			
A HUTCH BY THE EXIT HIS ROOM WITH A VIEW.	29	THE GENTLE	8
REASON? THAT DREARY SHED, THAT HUTCH FOR GRUBBY SCHOOLBOYS!	92	I CRY, LOVE!	14
HUZZA			
I HEAR A MOST LOVELY HUZZA:	92	I CRY, LOVE!	12
HYACINTHINE			
A CRISP HYACINTHINE COOLNESS,	43	CARNATIONS	5

	PAGE	TITLE	LINE
HYBRIDS			
LIFTING ME HIGH OVER THE FOUR-FOOT STEMS, THE MRS. RUSSELLS, AND HIS OWN ELABORATE HYBRIDS,	203	THE ROSE	54
HYDROTHERAPY			
MEDITATION IN HYDROTHERAPY	256	IN HYDROTHERAPY	T
HYSTERIA			
HYSTERIA MASKS IN THE STUDIED INANE.	29	THE GENTLE	2
I (991)			
ICE			
AT BRIDGEHEADS BUCKLED ICE BEGINS TO SHIFT,	11	LIGHT BRIGHTER	7
HATH THE RAIN A FATHER? ALL THE CAVES ARE ICE. ONLY THE SNOW'S HERE.	56	THE LOST SON	84
A PICK LIKES TO HIT ICE.	76	I NEED, I NEED	54
DOWN A STEEP HILLSIDE ON A CAKE OF ICE,--	105	SIR JOHN DAVIES	8
SHE CHANGED ME ICE TO FIRE, AND FIRE TO ICE.	131	SENTENTIOUS MAN	12
SHE CHANGED ME ICE TO FIRE, AND FIRE TO ICE.	131	SENTENTIOUS MAN	12
WHEN THE ICE MELTS ALONG THE EDGES IN EARLY AFTERNOON.	191	AT OYSTER RIVER	48
THE ICE PILING HIGH AGAINST THE IRON-BOUND SPILES,	191	AT OYSTER RIVER	50
AS THE PILED ICE BREAKS AWAY FROM THE BATTERED SPILES,	191	AT OYSTER RIVER	55
SURVIVE THE GREEN ICE	217	WISH YOUNG WIFE	4
AND WHEN I SLIPPED UPON THE ICE,	225	THE CHUMS	9
WE PASSED THE ICE OF PAIN,	238	THE MOMENT	1
THE ICE CAP AT MY RIGID NECK	256	IN HYDROTHERAPY	3
CORNBREAD AND MILK, ICE CREAM AND MORE ICE CREAM,	274	SUPPR W LINDSAY	32
CORNBREAD AND MILK, ICE CREAM AND MORE ICE CREAM,	274	SUPPR W LINDSAY	32
MOSTLY I REMEMBER THE ICE CREAM.	274	SUPPR W LINDSAY	34
ICE-BURDENED			
THE AFTER-LIGHT UPON ICE-BURDENED PINES;	201	THE FAR FIELD	97
I'D			
I'D SAY IT TO MY HORSE: WE LIVE BEYOND	106	SIR JOHN DAVIES	37
--WHEN SHE THOUGHT I'D RUN OUT OF MONEY.	112	SQUEEZE-BOX	41
(I'D HAVE THEM SING IN CHORUS, CHEEK TO CHEEK).	127	I KNEW A WOMAN	7
I'D LIKE TO TALK BACK,	182	BOY AND BUSH	4
I'D BE BEYOND; I'D BE BEYOND THE MOON,	188	THE LONGING	33
I'D BE BEYOND; I'D BE BEYOND THE MOON,	188	THE LONGING	33
I'D STAND UPON MY BED, A SLEEPLESS CHILD	225	OTTO	40
I'D SAY MY FACE IS JUST AS ROUND AS HIS,	273	SUPPR W LINDSAY	8
IDENTITY			
MANY ASTOUNDS BEFORE, I LOST MY IDENTITY TO A PEBBLE;	88	PRAISE TO END!	88
IDIOT			
AN OLD BRIDGE BELOW WITH A BUCKLED IRON RAILING, BROKEN BY SOME IDIOT PLUNGER;	194	JOURNY INTERIOR	32
IDLING			
IN A TOWER OF WIND, A TREE IDLING IN AIR,	195	JOURNY INTERIOR	70
IDYLL			
IDYLL	33	IDYLL	T
IF			
IF I MUST OF MY SENSES LOSE,	8	PRAYER	1
IF I SHOULD EVER SEEK RELIEF	22	SILENCE	15
AS IF I HAD BROKEN THE NATURAL ORDER OF THINGS IN THAT SWAMPLAND;	40	MOSS-GATHERING	10
AS IF I HAD COMMITTED, AGAINST THE WHOLE SCHEME OF LIFE, A DESECRATION.	40	MOSS-GATHERING	13
AND THE AIR COOL, AS IF DRIFTING DOWN FROM WET HEMLOCKS,	43	CARNATIONS	3
IF WE DETACH	60	THE LONG ALLEY	55
IF ONLY I COULD NUDGE YOU FROM THIS SLEEP,	102	ELEGY FOR JANE	18
IF ONLY I COULD REMEMBER	103	OLD LADY'S WRDS	19
IF I WERE A YOUNG MAN,	104	OLD LADY'S WRDS	49
IF I WERE A FISH I JUST COULDN'T RESIST	117	LADY AND BEAR	23
IF SHE BUT SIGHS, A BIRD PUTS OUT ITS TONGUE.	129	SHE	3
BUT IF I MOVE TOO CLOSE,	130	THE OTHER	5
AS IF A LION KNELT TO KISS A ROSE,	131	SENTENTIOUS MAN	17
AS IF ALL THINGS HAD DIED, AND ROSE AGAIN.	133	THE PURE FURY	6
I WALK AS IF MY FACE WOULD KISS THE WIND.	135	THE RENEWAL	12
AS IF REALITY HAD SPLIT APART	135	THE RENEWAL	22
MY NECK, IF NOT MY HEART, WILL BREAK	136	THE SENSUALISTS	23
IF WE DO THIS AGAIN," --	136	THE SENSUALISTS	24
SHE TURNS, AS IF TO GO,	141	MEMORY	5
AS IF PURE BEING WOKE,	147	THE EXORCISM	5
AS IF OUT OF MY SIDE,	148	THE SMALL	16
A BEAST CRIES OUT AS IF ITS FLESH WERE TORN,	156	THE DYING MAN	82
IF THE WIND MEANS ME,	164	I'M HERE	99
AS IF RELEASED BY A SPIRIT,	173	WHAT TELL BONES	98

I'M

I'M (CONTINUED)

	PAGE	TITLE	LINE
I'M COLD. I'M COLD ALL OVER. RUB ME IN FATHER AND MOTHER.	56	THE LOST SON	85
KISS ME, ASHES, I'M FALLING THROUGH A DARK SWIRL.	57	THE LOST SON	121
I'M HAPPY WITH MY PAWS.	60	THE LONG ALLEY	46
EAT WHERE YOU'RE AT. I'M NOT A MOUSE.	72	WHERE KNOCK IS	40
MAYBE I'M LOST,	72	WHERE KNOCK IS	43
I'M SOMEBODY ELSE NOW.	74	WHERE KNOCK IS	84
I'M A BISCUIT. I'M MELTED ALREADY.	77	BRING THE DAY!	21
I'M A BISCUIT. I'M MELTED ALREADY.	77	BRING THE DAY!	21
WHEN I STAND, I'M ALMOST A TREE.	78	BRING THE DAY!	32
I'M SAD WITH THE LITTLE OWLS.	80	GIVE WAY, GATES	45
I'M THE SERPENT OF SOMEBODY ELSE.	81	SENSIBILITY! LA	1
I'M A TWIG TO TOUCH,	81	SENSIBILITY! LA	24
I'M ALONE WITH MY RIBS;	82	SENSIBILITY! LA	30
I'M SOMEWHERE ELSE,--	82	SENSIBILITY! LA	48
I'M CRAZED AND GRACELESS,	83	O LULL ME, LULL	27
I'M STILL WAITING FOR A FOOT.	84	O LULL ME, LULL	30
I'M AN OTTER WITH ONLY ONE NOSE:	84	O LULL ME, LULL	35
I'M ALL READY TO WHISTLE;	84	O LULL ME, LULL	36
I'M MORE THAN WHEN I WAS BORN!	84	O LULL ME, LULL	37
FATHER OF TENSIONS, I'M DOWN TO MY SKIN AT LAST.	85	PRAISE TO END!	4
OOH, OOH, I'M A DUKE OF EELS.	85	PRAISE TO END!	8
ARCH MY BACK, PRETTY-BONES, I'M DEAD AT BOTH ENDS.	85	PRAISE TO END!	9
I'M UNTRUE TO MY OWN EXCESSES.	86	PRAISE TO END!	27
I'M UNDONE BY THE FLIP-FLAP OF ODIOUS PILLOWS.	86	PRAISE TO END!	45
I'M AWAKE ALL OVER:	88	PRAISE TO END!	80
I'M KING OF THE BOOPS!	92	I CRY, LOVE!	13
BLESS ME AND THE MAZE I'M IN!	92	I CRY, LOVE!	20
I'M A DRAFT SLEEPING BY A STICK;	97	O, THOU OPENING	7
I'M LOST IN WHAT I HAVE.	97	O, THOU OPENING	8
I'M TIRED OF ALL THAT, BAG-FOOT. I CAN HEAR SMALL ANGELS ANYTIME. WHO	98	O, THOU OPENING	25
I'M TRUE TO SOUP, AND HAPPY TO ASK:	99	O, THOU OPENING	55
I'M KING OF ANOTHER CONDITION,	99	O, THOU OPENING	57
I'M TWINKLING LIKE A TWIG!	99	O, THOU OPENING	63
I'M WILD WITH NEWS!	99	O, THOU OPENING	65
I'M A TUNE DYING	99	O, THOU OPENING	77
I'M NEAR.	99	O, THOU OPENING	85
I'M REMINDED TO STAY ALIVE	104	OLD LADY'S WRDS	56
"I'M SERIOUS ABOUT MY SINGING CAREER!"	115	THE SERPENT	24
THAT'S WHY I'M FISHING THIS WAY.	117	LADY AND BEAR	6
AND SO,--I'M FISHING THIS WAY.	117	LADY AND BEAR	8
I'M ODD AND FULL OF LOVE.	125	WORDS FOR WIND	67
I'M MARTYR TO A MOTION NOT MY OWN;	127	I KNEW A WOMAN	23
I WEEP FOR WHAT I'M LIKE WHEN I'M ALONE	132	SENTENTIOUS MAN	33
I WEEP FOR WHAT I'M LIKE WHEN I'M ALONE	132	SENTENTIOUS MAN	33
I'M TIRED OF BROODING ON MY NEIGHBOR'S SOUL;	132	SENTENTIOUS MAN	37
THAT'S NOT A THING I'M SAYING WITH A SNEER--	132	SENTENTIOUS MAN	40
FATHER, I'M FAR FROM HOME,	137	LOVE'S PROGRESS	19
I'M DYING PIECEMEAL, FERVENT IN DECAY;	149	IN LATE SUMMER	15
UNTIL I'M SCRAPING AND SCRATCHING AT YOU, ON THE DOORMAT,	151	SLUG	19
I'M SURE I'VE BEEN A TOAD, ONE TIME OR ANOTHER.	151	SLUG	25
I'M HERE	161	I'M HERE	T
I'M TIRED OF TINY NOISES:	161	I'M HERE	7
I'M NO MIDGE OF THAT AND THIS. THE DIRT GLITTERS LIKE SALT.	164	I'M HERE	92
I'M NOT FAR FROM A STREAM.	164	I'M HERE	94
I'M HERE!	164	I'M HERE	100
I'M WHERE I ALWAYS WAS.	165	HER BECOMING	25
I'M IN LOVE WITH THE DEAD! MY WHOLE FOREHEAD'S A NOISE!	170	FOURTH MEDITATN	79
I'M A SMALL STONE, LOOSE IN THE SHALE.	172	WHAT TELL BONES	47
I'M RELEASED FROM THE DREARY DANCE OF OPPOSITES.	173	WHAT TELL BONES	80
SOMETIMES I THINK I'M SEVERAL.	173	WHAT TELL BONES	83
I'M THICK WITH LEAVES AND TENDER AS A DOVE,	173	WHAT TELL BONES	89
I'M WET WITH ANOTHER LIFE.	173	WHAT TELL BONES	95
"AT LAST I'M MYSELF!"--AND HE UP AND DIED	177	KITTY-CAT BIRD	16
--AND I'M NOT HUGH NOR HARRY!	181	MONOTONY SONG	20
YOU'LL FIND I'M EITHER RIGHT OR WRONG	181	MONOTONY SONG	23
TO THIS EXTENT I'M A STALK.	188	THE LONGING	35
I'M LULLED INTO HALF-SLEEP	191	AT OYSTER RIVER	60
CRIES, "I'M OLD ENOUGH TO LIVE	208	HER WORDS	3
I'M ONE TO FOLLOW,	210	HER TIME	25
I'M NO LONGER A BIRD DIPPING A BEAK INTO RIPPLING WATER	220	THE ABYSS	41
I'M GRATEFUL FOR THAT.	225	THE CHUMS	11

I'M -- IMPORTANT

	PAGE	TITLE	LINE
I'M (CONTINUED)			
I'M SON AND FATHER OF MY ONLY DEATH.	244	INFIRMITY	18
"I'M MAIMED; I CAN'T FLY;	249	THE RESTORED	9
I'M LIKE TO DIE,"	249	THE RESTORED	10
I'M SWEATING OUT THE WILL TO DIE.	256	IN HYDROTHERAPY	10
I'M STILL,	258	SONG (3)	28
I'M STILL SMUDGY FROM SLEEP:	259	SONG (3)	41
I'M A SOCRATES OF SMALL FURY.	260	THE CHANGELING	17
THE WAVE BENDS WITH THE FISH. I'M TAUGHT	260	THE CHANGELING	18
THE WORLD IS WHERE WE FLING IT; I'M LEAVING WHERE I AM.	260	THE CHANGELING	21
TO THIS EXTENT I'M A STALK.	261	THE CHANGELING	38
O, I'M THE GENIUS OF THE WORLD,--	268	SAGINAW SONG	43
I'M OFTEN A DRUNKEN BOOR;	268	SAGINAW SONG	46
I'M NEITHER OUT NOR IN	271	THE REPLY	5
SHAKES EVERY SENSE. I'M FIVE	271	THE REPLY	13
I'M SHANTY IRISH	272	DUET	13
I'M A ROARING GIRL, AN EXPENSIVE WENCH,	272	DUET	15
IMAGE			
HIS IMAGE KEPT FOLLOWING AFTER,--	6	THE PREMONITION	10
I'LL CHANGE THE IMAGE, AND MY SHOES.	97	O, THOU OPENING	19
HER IMAGE FADES, YET DOES NOT DISAPPEAR--	140	THE SWAN	2
WHAT SENSUAL EYE CAN KEEP AN IMAGE PURE,	154	THE DYING MAN	43
AND TELL MYSELF MY IMAGE CANNOT DIE.	244	INFIRMITY	4
IMAGES			
THESE IMAGES HAUNTED ME NOON AND MIDNIGHT.	48	JUDGE NOT	4
IMAGINATION			
NOR CAN IMAGINATION DO IT ALL	156	THE DYING MAN	98
IMAGINATION'S			
HE'S IMAGINATION'S PRINCE:	266	FOR STEVENS	5
IMAGINE			
DO I IMAGINE HE NO LONGER TREMBLES	227	MEADOW MOUSE	17
IMAGINED			
YOUR BED COLLAPSES FROM IMAGINED SINS.	25	DIM-WIT COUSIN	6
I IMAGINED THE UNBORN, STARVING IN WOMBS, CURLING;	48	JUDGE NOT	5
IMAGINING			
WITHIN THE REACH OF MY IMAGINING:	135	THE RENEWAL	3
IMMACULATE			
THE NAKED FIELDS THE CLOUD'S IMMACULATE FOLDS	5	TO MY SISTER	4
DESOLATION IN IMMACULATE PUBLIC PLACES,	46	DOLOR	4
ARE THE ENTRAILS CLEAR, IMMACULATE CABBAGE?	89	UNFOLD! UNFOLD!	19
ONLY THE MOTES OF DUST IN THE IMMACULATE HALLWAYS,	159	FIRST MEDITATN	79
THOSE CAT-LIKE IMMACULATE CREATURES	169	FOURTH MEDITATN	48
IMMEASURABLE			
AGAINST THE IMMENSE IMMEASURABLE EMPTINESS OF THINGS.	156	THE DYING MAN	101
IMMEDIACY			
TOO CLOSE IMMEDIACY AN EXHAUSTION:	220	THE ABYSS	45
IMMEDIATE			
THE SOUL'S IMMEDIATE JOY.	126	WORDS FOR WIND	91
THE IMMEDIATE SHEEN, THE REALITY OF STRAW,	171	WHAT TELL BONES	16
IMMENSE			
NEW MEANING GROWS IMMENSE.	18	GENESIS	12
AGAINST THE IMMENSE IMMEASURABLE EMPTINESS OF THINGS.	156	THE DYING MAN	101
IMMENSITY			
A MAN FACED WITH HIS OWN IMMENSITY	201	THE FAR FIELD	87
IMMODERATELY			
I AM MOST IMMODERATELY MARRIED:	222	THE ABYSS	97
IMMODESTLY			
TO SLEEP IMMODESTLY, A MOST	19	EPIDERM MACABRE	15
IMPACT			
AND LONGED TO FEEL THE IMPACT OF DEFEAT.	28	THE FAVORITE	14
IMPALED			
IMPALED ON LIGHT, AND WHIRLING SLOWLY DOWN.	107	SIR JOHN DAVIES	72
IMPERIOUS			
IMPERIOUS YOUNGLING, THOUGH APPROACHING FORTY;	264	THREE EPIGRAMS	2
IMPERISHABLE			
I LONG FOR THE IMPERISHABLE QUIET AT THE HEART OF FORM;	188	THE LONGING	45
IMPLACABLE			
THEN THROWING ITSELF UP AND AWAY FROM THE IMPLACABLE SWIFT PURSUERS,	232	THE THING	6
IMPORTANCE			
DISTURBED SOME RHYTHM, OLD AND OF VAST IMPORTANCE,	40	MOSS-GATHERING	11
IMPORTANT			
IS IMPORTANT--	202	THE ROSE	3

	PAGE	TITLE	LINE
IMPOSSIBLE			
THE DEAD MAKE MORE IMPOSSIBLE DEMANDS FROM THEIR SILENCE;	168	FOURTH MEDITATN	19
IMPOTENT			
AN EXACT FALL OF WATERS HAS RENDERED ME IMPOTENT.	86	PRAISE TO END!	46
IMPULSE			
THE IMPULSE TO MAKE SOMEONE ELSE COMPLETE?	105	SIR JOHN DAVIES	27
WHERE IMPULSE NO LONGER DICTATES, NOR THE DARKENING SHADOW,	197	THE LONG WATERS	57
IMPURE			
(AND SOME GROW OUT OF SHAPE, THEIR SEED IMPURE;)	225	OTTO	32
IN (738)			
INACCESSIBILITY			
MY INACCESSIBILITY.	24	BEFORE STUDY	6
INACCESSIBLE			
INACCESSIBLE, THE BOAT ALWAYS PULLING OUT	158	FIRST MEDITATN	50
INANE			
HYSTERIA MASKS IN THE STUDIED INANE.	29	THE GENTLE	2
BY THE DRY RASP OF THE RECURRING INANE,	104	OLD LADY'S WRDS	57
THE SLACK FACE OF THE DISMAL PURE INANE?	149	IN LATE SUMMER	10
IN-BETWEEN			
AN IN-BETWEEN TIME,	58	THE LOST SON	150
INCARNADINE			
INCARNADINE AND CARNAL GHOST.	19	EPIDERM MACABRE	16
INCH			
AND THE SHALE SLIDES AN INCH IN THE TALUS,	157	FIRST MEDITATN	10
INCIDENT			
RIVER INCIDENT	49	RIVER INCIDENT	T
INCIPIENT			
AND THE INCIPIENT STAR--	125	WORDS FOR WIND	87
INCLEMENT			
TO KEEP INCLEMENT WEATHER FROM ITS YOUNG.	12	SLOW SEASON	6
INCOMMENSURATE			
THE INCOMMENSURATE DREAD	215	HIS FOREBODING	3
INCOMPREHENSIBLE			
INCOMPREHENSIBLE GAIETY AND DREAD	106	SIR JOHN DAVIES	49
INCREASING			
A STORM'S INCREASING WHERE	215	HIS FOREBODING	19
INCREDIBLE			
CHERISH THE EYES THE PROUD INCREDIBLE POISE	5	TO MY SISTER	9
INDEED			
INDEED I SAW A SHIMMERING LAKE	270	GOB MUSIC	32
INDELICATE			
INDELICATE IS HE WHO LOATHES	19	EPIDERM MACABRE	1
INDIAN			
I'LL BE AN INDIAN.	189	THE LONGING	58
INDIANS			
THE INDIANS LOVED HIM, AND THE POLISH POOR.	225	OTTO	33
INDICATING			
BUT THEY'VE WAYS OF INDICATING WHEN	267	SAGINAW SONG	15
INDICTMENTS			
THE SMALL WINDS MAKE THEIR CHILLY INDICTMENTS.	157	FIRST MEDITATN	3
INDIFFERENT			
WE GROW INDIFFERENT TO DOG HOWLS, TO THE NESTLING'S LAST PEEP;	33	IDYLL	6
INDIGNANT			
STOPPING TRAFFIC, INDIGNANT AS ADDLED OLD LADIES,	234	ALL MORNING	27
INDIGNATION			
INDIGNATION? LET ME PERSUADE MORE SLOWLY:	98	O, THOU OPENING	31
INDIGNITY			
THE INDIGNITY OF IT!--	39	WEED PULLER	10
AM I REDUCED TO THE INDIGNITY OF EXAMPLES?	259	SONG (3)	40
INDIRECTION			
MY INDIRECTION FOUND DIRECTION OUT.	131	SENTENTIOUS MAN	4
INDOORS			
THE LAST WATCHER INDOORS, MOVING THE CARDPLAYERS CLOSER	230	THE STORM	26
INDUCE			
IN TIME INDUCE A MENTAL ILL.	257	SANITARIUM	6
INEXORABLE			
I HAVE KNOWN THE INEXORABLE SADNESS OF PENCILS,	46	DOLOR	1
INFANTS			
SO MANY DEVOURING INFANTS!	39	ORCHIDS	14
INFECTED			
DARLING OF AN INFECTED BROOD,	4	FEUD	7
THE SCRATCH FORGOTTEN IS THE SCRATCH INFECTED;	5	PROGNOSIS	7

	PAGE	TITLE	LINE
INFINITUDE			
ALL FINITE THINGS REVEAL INFINITUDE:	201	THE FAR FIELD	94
INFINITY			
I LEARNED NOT TO FEAR INFINITY,	200	THE FAR FIELD	50
INFIRM			
WHO FED AND TENDED THE INFIRM, THE MAD, THE EPILEPTIC,	223	ELEGY (2)	9
INFIRMITY			
INFIRMITY	244	INFIRMITY	T
SWEET CHRIST, REJOICE IN MY INFIRMITY;	244	INFIRMITY	7
INFLAME			
INFLAME WITH HATE. THIS ANCIENT FEUD	4	FEUD	18
INHERIT			
BLESSED THE MEEK; THEY SHALL INHERIT WRATH;	244	INFIRMITY	17
INLET			
NUDGES INTO A BACK-EDDY, A SANDY INLET,	159	FIRST MEDITATN	69
INLETS			
A COUNTRY OF BAYS AND INLETS, AND SMALL STREAMS FLOWING SEAWARD.	196	THE LONG WATERS	19
INNER			
AND YOUNG SHOOTS SPREAD UPON OUR INNER WORLD.	11	LIGHT BRIGHTER	20
DOWN LONG SEA-CHAMBERS OF THE INNER EAR.	129	SHE	6
I HAVE MYSELF AN INNER WEIGHT OF WOE	144	ELEGY (1)	3
I HAVE MYSELF AN INNER WEIGHT OF WOE	144	ELEGY (1)	7
OR AFTER-IMAGE OF THE INNER EYE.	155	THE DYING MAN	57
IN MY GRANDMOTHER'S INNER EYE,	163	I'M HERE	71
AS CHANGES SHIMMER IN THE INNER EYE.	244	INFIRMITY	2
INNOCENCE			
THE STILE OF INNOCENCE,	7	ORDERS FOR DAY	9
ALL INNOCENCE AND WIT,	121	ALL EARTH, AIR	11
WAS IT YESTERDAY I STRETCHED OUT THE THIN BONES OF MY INNOCENCE?	168	FOURTH MEDITATN	12
INNOCENT			
ALL THINGS INNOCENT, HAPLESS, FORSAKEN.	227	MEADOW MOUSE	29
TO THE LAND WHERE THE INNOCENT STRETCH AND SNORE	272	DUET	11
INSATIATE			
AND ALL WILD LONGINGS OF THE INSATIATE BLOOD	241	THE SEQUEL	4
INSECT			
I SLEPT LIKE AN INSECT.	89	UNFOLD! UNFOLD!	29
OR LIVE THE DANGEROUS LIFE OF AN INSECT.	166	HER BECOMING	37
INSECTS			
OR THESE INSECTS PULSING NEAR MY SKIN,	171	WHAT TELL BONES	26
IN TIME WHEN THE TROUT AND YOUNG SALMON LEAP FOR THE LOW-FLYING INSECTS,	197	THE LONG WATERS	33
THE MEADOW INSECTS MADE A LEVEL NOISE.	247	I WAITED	4
INSENTIENT			
INSENTIENT TO SHOCK.	4	DEATH PIECE	8
INSIDE			
THAT THE KITTY-CAT BIRD JUST HOPPED INSIDE;	177	KITTY-CAT BIRD	15
INSIDE, MY DARLING WIFE	213	THE HAPPY THREE	1
HOW IS IT INSIDE A TREE?	261	THE CHANGELING	30
INSIST			
I INSIST!	82	SENSIBILITY! LA	49
INSISTENCE			
THE APRIL CHEEPING, THE VIREO'S INSISTENCE,	161	I'M HERE	8
INSISTENT			
THIN AND INSISTENT AS A CICADA,	159	FIRST MEDITATN	85
AND THAT THIN CRY, LIKE A NEEDLE PIERCING THE EAR, THE INSISTENT CICADA,	204	THE ROSE	67
INSOLENCE			
HIS INSOLENCE COULD WEAR NO PATIENCE THIN.	28	THE FAVORITE	7
INSOUCIANCE			
ACQUIRES, FOR A TIME, THE SANDPIPER'S INSOUCIANCE,	191	AT OYSTER RIVER	39
INSTANT			
WE'LL SWINGE THE INSTANT!--	79	GIVE WAY, GATES	26
BUT NOW THE INSTANT AGES,	80	GIVE WAY, GATES	43
THE DREAM'S AN INSTANT THAT CALLS UP HER FACE.	131	SENTENTIOUS MAN	11
CRIED OUT THEIR LIVES AN INSTANT AND WERE FREE.	143	SHIMMER OF EVIL	14
THE INSTANT AGES ON.	154	THE DYING MAN	25
YET IF WE WAIT, UNAFRAID, BEYOND THE FEARFUL INSTANT,	221	THE ABYSS	57
THE INSTANT AGES ON THE LIVING EYE;	244	INFIRMITY	13
THE INSTANT GATHERS.	258	SONG (3)	27
INSTEAD			
THE LIBRARY USED AS A CARD ROOM INSTEAD	32	SALE	11

	PAGE	TITLE	LINE
INSTEAD (CONTINUED)			
INSTEAD OF A DEVIL WITH HORNS, I PREFER A SERPENT WITH SCALES;	173	WHAT TELL BONES	77
INSTEP			
THE SMALL DEAD PIECES STICKING UNDER AN INSTEP;	151	SLUG	20
INSTINCT			
LOVE ALTERS ALL. UNBLOOD MY INSTINCT, LOVE.	135	THE RENEWAL	10
INSTITUTIONALIZED			
YOU'D BE INSTITUTIONALIZED.	228	IN VIOLENT WARD	2
INSTITUTIONS			
AND I HAVE SEEN DUST FROM THE WALLS OF INSTITUTIONS,	46	DOLOR	9
INSTRUMENT			
THE INSTRUMENT OF LECHERY,	8	PRAYER	10
INTENSE			
A FLAME, INTENSE, VISIBLE,	160	FIRST MEDITATN	93
INTENSER			
OF WESTERN LIGHT LEAPS WITH INTENSER BLAZE	17	UNEXTINGUISHED	2
MAKES AN INTENSER DAY	124	WORDS FOR WIND	56
INTENT			
AND MY INTENT STRETCHED OVER THE BUDS AT THEIR FIRST TREMBLING.	66	SHAPE OF FIRE	69
INTERIOR			
JOURNEY TO THE INTERIOR	193	JOURNY INTERIOR	T
INTERLUDE			
INTERLUDE	6	INTERLUDE	T
INTERMITTENTLY			
AND THE SPIRIT RUNS, INTERMITTENTLY,	192	AT OYSTER RIVER	64
ITS ALMOST-INVISIBLE WINGS, BUZZING, HITTING THE LOOSE LEAVES INTERMITTENTLY--	234	ALL MORNING	32
INTERRUPTED			
THERE ARE MANY DETOURS, WASHED-OUT INTERRUPTED RAW PLACES	193	JOURNY INTERIOR	2
INTERVAL			
SHE SLOWED TO SIGH, IN THAT LONG INTERVAL.	120	THE DREAM	18
INTERVALS			
OF SENSE AT RAPID INTERVALS.	22	SILENCE	6
THE LUGUBRIOUSLY BEAUTIFUL PLAINT UTTERED AT REGULAR INTERVALS,	234	ALL MORNING	4
I AM A MAN, A MAN AT INTERVALS	242	THE SEQUEL	29
INTIMATE			
AT AN INTIMATE PLACE LIKE HIS GIZZARD.	183	THE LIZARD	7
AN INTIMATE OF AIR AND ALL ITS SONGS?	241	THE SEQUEL	2
INTO			
CROSS MARSHLAND INTO CLOVER.	7	ORDERS FOR DAY	14
THE SUN CUTS DEEP INTO THE HEAVY DRIFT,	11	LIGHT BRIGHTER	5
WILL TURN ITS PRIVATE SUBSTANCE INTO GREEN,	11	LIGHT BRIGHTER	19
LONG SINCE, BRONZE WHEAT WAS GATHERED INTO SHEAVES.	12	SLOW SEASON	10
I STARE INTO THE NIGHT	34	NIGHT JOURNEY	4
WE RUSH INTO A RAIN	34	NIGHT JOURNEY	22
DIGGING INTO THE SOFT RUBBLE UNDERNEATH,	39	WEED PULLER	4
LUNGING INTO THE LASHING	41	BIG WIND	2
INTO THE RUSTY BOILERS,	41	BIG WIND	9
SHE HOVE INTO THE TEETH OF IT,	41	BIG WIND	23
BUCKING INTO THE WIND-WAVES	41	BIG WIND	26
TAMPING AND STAMPING DIRT INTO POTS,--	42	OLD FLORIST	3
OR FAN LIFE INTO WILTED SWEET-PEAS WITH HIS HAT,	42	OLD FLORIST	9
INTO THE FLAT-BOX IT GOES,	42	TRANSPLANTING	12
BREAKING INTO NAKEDNESS,	42	TRANSPLANTING	18
OUT INTO THE SWEET AIR,	42	TRANSPLANTING	20
THEIR SKIRTS BILLOWING OUT WIDE INTO TENTS,	44	FRAU BAUMAN	17
INTO A MOONLESS BLACK,	49	NIGHT CROW	7
MOVED INTO COMMON DAY,	50	THE CYCLE	4
WHO STUNNED THE DIRT INTO NOISE?	55	THE LOST SON	66
WILL THE SEA GIVE THE WIND SUCK? A TOAD FOLDS INTO A STONE.	64	SHAPE OF FIRE	8
SHALE LOOSENS. MARL REACHES INTO THE FIELD. SMALL BIRDS PASS OVER WATER.	64	SHAPE OF FIRE	11
MOTHER OF QUARTZ, YOUR WORDS WRITHE INTO MY EAR.	65	SHAPE OF FIRE	54
INTO THAT MINNOWY WORLD OF WEEDS AND DITCHES,	66	SHAPE OF FIRE	65
AND THE LITTLE CRABS SLIPPED INTO SILVERY CRATERS.	66	SHAPE OF FIRE	67
TO STARE INTO THE AFTER-LIGHT, THE GLITTER LEFT ON THE LAKE'S SURFACE,	67	SHAPE OF FIRE	88
I'VE LISTENED INTO THE LEAST WAVES.	77	BRING THE DAY!	28
THE SPIDERS SAIL INTO SUMMER.	78	BRING THE DAY!	43
I BREATHE INTO A DREAM,	83	O LULL ME, LULL	25

INTO (CONTINUED)

	PAGE	TITLE	LINE
WALK INTO THE WIND, WILLIE!	92	I CRY, LOVE!	29
AND HOW, ONCE STARTLED INTO TALK, THE LIGHT SYLLABLES LEAPED FOR HER,	102	ELEGY FOR JANE	3
A WREN, HAPPY, TAIL INTO THE WIND,	102	ELEGY FOR JANE	5
OH, WHEN SHE WAS SAD, SHE CAST HERSELF DOWN INTO SUCH A PURE DEPTH,	102	ELEGY FOR JANE	10
A BIRD SINGING INTO THE BEYOND,	103	OLD LADY'S WRDS	7
INTO MY OWN SILENCES.	104	OLD LADY'S WRDS	62
O WHAT LEWD MUSIC CREPT INTO OUR EARS!	106	SIR JOHN DAVIES	46
SHE TURNED THE FIELD INTO A GLITTERING SEA;	120	THE DREAM	27
I CAME TO LOVE, I CAME INTO MY OWN.	120	THE DREAM	32
LET SEED BE GRASS, AND GRASS TURN INTO HAY:	127	I KNEW A WOMAN	22
ASTONISHED INTO PASSIONATE REPOSE.	131	SENTENTIOUS MAN	18
BUT MY LEAST MOTION CHANGED INTO A SONG,	132	SENTENTIOUS MAN	23
I LOOK ON WHITE, AND IT TURNS INTO GRAY--	134	THE PURE FURY	24
I TEACH MY SIGHS TO LENGTHEN INTO SONGS,	135	THE RENEWAL	5
THESE WATERS DROWSE ME INTO SLEEP SO KIND	135	THE RENEWAL	11
INTO THE WORLD OF MEN.	136	THE SENSUALISTS	26
OR LISTEN INTO SILENCE, LIKE A GOD.	140	THE SWAN	20
THE COLD SLIME COME INTO BEING,	151	SLUG	11
BACK INTO STRAIGHTNESS;	152	THE SISKINS	15
MY HANDS TURN INTO HOOVES.	154	THE DYING MAN	18
I DIE INTO THIS LIFE, ALONE YET NOT ALONE.	155	THE DYING MAN	59
AND THAT SLOW HUMMING RISES INTO SONG.	155	THE DYING MAN	75
NUDGES INTO A BACK-EDDY, A SANDY INLET,	159	FIRST MEDITATN	69
AROUND, BACK INTO THE TINY MAINCURRENT, THE RUSH OF BROWNISH-WHITE WATER,	159	FIRST MEDITATN	71
I HAVE GONE INTO THE WASTE LONELY PLACES	159	FIRST MEDITATN	74
ACROSS A FIELD, INTO A LITTLE WOOD.	166	HER BECOMING	51
SHAPES STIFFENING INTO METAL,	169	FOURTH MEDITATN	40
THE YOUNG, BROW-BEATEN EARLY INTO A BALEFUL SILENCE,	169	FOURTH MEDITATN	44
MAY THE HIGH FLOWER OF THE HAY CLIMB INTO THEIR HEARTS;	169	FOURTH MEDITATN	56
MAY THEY LEAN INTO LIGHT AND LIVE;	169	FOURTH MEDITATN	57
MAY THEY FLAME INTO BEING!--	169	FOURTH MEDITATN	62
YOUNGLINGS, THE SMALL FISH KEEP HEADING INTO THE CURRENT.	170	FOURTH MEDITATN	75
THE POND LAPSES BACK INTO A GLASSY SILENCE.	172	WHAT TELL BONES	50
O TO BE DELIVERED FROM THE RATIONAL INTO THE REALM OF PURE SONG,	172	WHAT TELL BONES	54
THAT DISAPPEAR INTO A WANING MOON;	173	WHAT TELL BONES	70
BUT SHRINKS INTO A HALF-LIFE, LESS THAN ITSELF,	187	THE LONGING	20
WHERE SHADOW CAN CHANGE INTO FLAME,	188	THE LONGING	49
I'M LULLED INTO HALF-SLEEP	191	AT OYSTER RIVER	60
CREEKS SWOLLEN IN MIDSUMMER FROM THE FLASH-FLOOD ROARING INTO THE NARROW VALLEY.	193	JOURNY INTERIOR	8
INTO A LONG MOMENT;	194	JOURNY INTERIOR	47
AND THE IVY-BRANCH, CAST TO THE GROUND, PUTS DOWN ROOTS INTO THE SAWDUST,	197	THE LONG WATERS	34
AND THE PINE, WHOLE WITH ITS ROOTS, SINKS INTO THE ESTUARY,	197	THE LONG WATERS	35
OF FLYING LIKE A BAT DEEP INTO A NARROWING TUNNEL,	199	THE FAR FIELD	2
WHERE THE TURF DROPS OFF INTO A GRASS-HIDDEN CULVERT,	199	THE FAR FIELD	14
THE TREE RETREATS INTO ITS OWN SHADOW.	200	THE FAR FIELD	57
WHERE THE HAWKS SWAY OUT INTO THE WIND,	202	THE ROSE	4
THE MOON RETREATING INTO A VAGUE CLOUD-SHAPE	202	THE ROSE	18
INTO THE DARKENING CURRENTS,	202	THE ROSE	23
INTO THE SMALL SPILLAGE OF DRIFTWOOD.	202	THE ROSE	24
WITH ITS THICK GRASSY SCUM AND CRABS SCUTTLING BACK INTO THEIR GLISTENING CRATERS.	203	THE ROSE	50
WHERE THE SALMON EASE THEIR WAY INTO THE KELP BEDS,	205	THE ROSE	96
I'M NO LONGER A BIRD DIPPING A BEAK INTO RIPPLING WATER	220	THE ABYSS	41
A FLASH INTO THE BURNING HEART OF THE ABOMINABLE;	221	THE ABYSS	56
THE BURNING LAKE TURNS INTO A FOREST POOL,	221	THE ABYSS	58
THE FIRE SUBSIDES INTO RINGS OF WATER,	221	THE ABYSS	59
THE CHILD'S HAND REACHING INTO THE COILED SMILAX,	221	THE ABYSS	65
HIS HAND COULD FIT INTO A WOMAN'S GLOVE,	224	OTTO	12
WITH ITS LIMESTONE CRUMBLING INTO FINE GREYISH DUST,	226	THE LIZARD	28
I THINK OF THE NESTLING FALLEN INTO THE DEEP GRASS,	227	MEADOW MOUSE	26
THREW HER, POT AND ALL, INTO THE TRASH-CAN,	228	THE GERANIUM	23
FLICKING THE FOAM FROM THE WHITECAPS STRAIGHT UPWARD INTO THE DARKNESS.	230	THE STORM	16
WATER ROARS INTO THE CISTERN.	231	THE STORM	37
AND THE HURRICANE DRIVES THE DEAD STRAW INTO THE LIVING PINE-TREE.	231	THE STORM	43

	PAGE	TITLE	LINE
INTO (CONTINUED)			
CONFUSING THEM ONCE FLYING STRAIGHT INTO THE SUN	232	THE THING	7
AND I LEAN, ALMOST INTO THE WATER,	233	THE PIKE	11
GOING, WE STAYED; AND NIGHT TURNED INTO DAY;	237	THE TRANCED	12
THIS SINGLE TREE TURNS INTO PUREST FLAME.	242	THE SEQUEL	28
AND GRIEVE INTO THE CERTAINTY OF LOVE.	243	THE MOTION	6
I STARE AND STARE INTO A DEEPENING POOL	244	INFIRMITY	3
LITTLE CRABS SLIPPING INTO WATERY CRATERS--	255	LIGHT POEM	4
AS SHE STEPS INTO SUMMER,	260	THE CHANGELING	8
SHE LEANS INTO LIGHT, AND LIVES,	260	THE CHANGELING	10
I STARED INTO THE DENTED HOLE	269	GOB MUSIC	24
INTOLERABLE			
AN INTOLERABLE WAITING,	162	I'M HERE	36
INTRANSIENT			
YET REMAIN ONLY HALF AWARE OF THE INTRANSIENT GLORY?	169	FOURTH MEDITATN	32
INTREPID			
RUNS WITH THE INTREPID SHOREBIRDS--	192	AT OYSTER RIVER	66
THE WORM, INTREPID SCHOLAR OF THE SOIL--	235	MANIFESTATION	5
INTRICATE			
INTRICATE PHOBIAS GROW	31	LULL	4
THEIR INTRICATE STEM-FUR DRIES;	37	CUTTINGS	2
INTUITION			
FOR THE SLEEK CAPTAINS OF INTUITION CANNOT REACH THEM;	169	FOURTH MEDITATN	52
INVADE			
INVADE THEIR PRIVACY OF THOUGHT.	25	VERSE W ALLUSNS	6
INVADES			
INVADES QUIESCENT BLOOD;	18	GENESIS	6
FOR THE WORLD INVADES ME AGAIN,	220	THE ABYSS	30
INVENTED			
THE RAMBLING LIES INVENTED FOR THE SICK.	5	PROGNOSIS	2
INVENTION			
INVENTION SLEEPS WITHIN A SKULL	4	DEATH PIECE	1
NECESSITY STARVES ON THE STOOP OF INVENTION.	29	THE GENTLE	11
INVETERATE			
OF THOSE INVETERATE	20	REPL TO CENSURE	4
INVIOLATE			
WHOLE FIELDS LOVELY AND INVIOLATE,--	39	WEED PULLER	13
INVISIBLE			
SIFT, ALMOST INVISIBLE, THROUGH LONG AFTERNOONS OF TEDIUM,	46	DOLOR	11
MY DUST LONGS FOR THE INVISIBLE.	104	OLD LADY'S WRDS	55
BEFORE THE ALMOST INVISIBLE	210	HER TIME	16
WHAT SHAKES THE EYE BUT THE INVISIBLE?	245	THE DECISION	1
INWARD			
STILL INWARD,	101	LIGHT BREATHER	12
OF INWARD BLESSEDNESS?	139	PLAINT	5
MY INWARD WITNESS IS DISMAYED	220	THE ABYSS	19
BY DYING INWARD, LIKE AN AGING TREE.	244	INFIRMITY	12
INWARDNESS			
STUPOR OF KNOWLEDGE LACKING INWARDNESS--	133	THE PURE FURY	1
IRE			
PRICKLING PURE WISHES WITH CONFUSION'S IRE;	143	SHIMMER OF EVIL	12
AND PURGATORIAL IRE;	216	HER WRATH	2
IRIDESCENCE			
A THING CARVED OF STONE OR WOOD, WITH THE DULL IRIDESCENCE			
OF LONG-POLISHED WOOD,	234	ALL MORNING	11
IRIDESCENT			
AT THE IRREGULAR STONES, IRIDESCENT SANDGRAINS,	201	THE FAR FIELD	74
IRISH			
I'M SHANTY IRISH	272	DUET	13
IRON			
BRIDGES OF IRON LACE,	34	NIGHT JOURNEY	6
I WAS LULLED BY THE SLAMMING OF IRON,	53	THE LOST SON	2
THEY FEEL NEITHER THE TEARING IRON	169	FOURTH MEDITATN	53
AN OLD BRIDGE BELOW WITH A BUCKLED IRON RAILING, BROKEN BY			
SOME IDIOT PLUNGER;	194	JOURNY INTERIOR	32
RUNNING OVER THE COVERLET, DOWN UNDER THE IRON BEDSTEAD.	231	THE STORM	35
IRON-BOUND			
THE ICE PILING HIGH AGAINST THE IRON-BOUND SPILES,	191	AT OYSTER RIVER	50
IROQUOIS			
IROQUOIS.	189	THE LONGING	60
IRRATIONAL			
THE FANG AND THE CLAW, THE CLUB AND THE KNOUT, THE			
IRRATIONAL EDICT,	170	FOURTH MEDITATN	67

	PAGE	TITLE	LINE
IRREGULAR			
OVER THE THIN, FEATHERY RIPPLES BREAKING LIGHTLY AGAINST THE IRREGULAR SHORELINE--	197	THE LONG WATERS	50
AT THE IRREGULAR STONES, IRIDESCENT SANDGRAINS,	201	THE FAR FIELD	74
WINDING DOWN TO THE STRETCH OF IRREGULAR SAND,	222	THE ABYSS	95
THE BOTTOM-STONES SHIMMER BACK THEIR IRREGULAR STRIATIONS,	233	THE PIKE	8
IRREVOCABLE			
DEFER THE VICE OF FLESH THE IRREVOCABLE CHOICE	5	TO MY SISTER	8
IS (264)			
ISLAMIC			
THE MOON, A PURE ISLAMIC SHAPE, LOOKED DOWN.	166	HER BECOMING	55
ISLAND			
WHEN THE SUN HAS FALLEN BEHIND A WOODED ISLAND;	67	SHAPE OF FIRE	89
FROM THE SLOW SINKING OF THE ISLAND PENINSULA, THE CORAL EFFLORESCENCE,	196	THE LONG WATERS	22
ISLANDS			
AND THE SEA REARRANGES ITSELF AMONG THE SMALL ISLANDS.	205	THE ROSE	97
ISN'T			
THE DEVIL ISN'T DEAD; HE'S JUST AWAY.	97	O, THOU OPENING	16
WHO ISN'T UNWILLING, WHO ISN'T AFRAID	112	SQUEEZE-BOX	44
WHO ISN'T UNWILLING, WHO ISN'T AFRAID	112	SQUEEZE-BOX	44
I KNOW IT ISN'T A WET LEAF,	151	SLUG	9
SAID THE WREN, YOUR SONG ISN'T WORTH 10¢.	177	KITTY-CAT BIRD	2
IST			
WALLACE, WALLACE, WO IST ER?	266	FOR STEVENS	9
ER IST NIEMALS AUSGEPOOPEN,	266	FOR STEVENS	15
IT (175)			
ITCH			
IT'S MY LAST WALTZ WITH AN OLD ITCH.	60	THE LONG ALLEY	34
ITCHES			
PRICKLING WITH ALL THE ITCHES	46	PICKLE BELT	11
ITEMS			
SOME ITEMS, MISCELLANEOUS, MARKED "FEAR";	21	THE AUCTION	7
ITS (106)			
IT'S			
IT'S BIGGER THAN THAT.	54	THE LOST SON	45
IT'S LESS THAN A LEG	54	THE LOST SON	46
IT'S SLEEK AS AN OTTER	55	THE LOST SON	58
IT'S MY LAST WALTZ WITH AN OLD ITCH.	60	THE LONG ALLEY	34
I KNOW IT'S AN OWL. HE'S MAKING IT DARKER.	72	WHERE KNOCK IS	39
IT'S A DEAR LIFE I CAN TOUCH.	76	I NEED, I NEED	58
IT'S TIME TO BEGIN!	78	BRING THE DAY!	44
IT'S A WINK BEYOND THE WORLD.	79	GIVE WAY, GATES	20
IT'S A COLD SCRAPE IN A LOW PLACE.	80	GIVE WAY, GATES	47
IT'S QUEER ENOUGH HERE, PERHAPS.	81	SENSIBILITY! LA	12
IT'S A LONG WAY TO SOMEWHERE ELSE.	82	SENSIBILITY! LA	38
IT'S DARK IN THIS WOOD, SOFT MOCKER.	85	PRAISE TO END!	1
IT'S A GREAT DAY FOR THE MICE.	85	PRAISE TO END!	5
IT'S NECESSARY AMONG THE FLIES AND BANANAS, TO KEEP A CONSTANT VIGIL,	86	PRAISE TO END!	24
IT'S A PIECE OF A PRINCE I ATE.	86	PRAISE TO END!	48
IT'S STILL ENOUGH FOR THE KNOCK OF A WORM.	87	PRAISE TO END!	76
IT'S A SOUL'S CROSSING TIME.	89	UNFOLD! UNFOLD!	8
IT'S TIME YOU STOOD UP AND ASKED	89	UNFOLD! UNFOLD!	10
IT'S WINDY THERE, AND RATHER WEIRD,	114	DINKY	2
--OF COURSE, IT'S DIRTY DINKY.	114	DINKY	8
"O IT'S WONDERFUL HOW WITH A FLICK OF YOUR WRIST,	117	LADY AND BEAR	21
FOR WATER MOVES UNTIL IT'S PURIFIED,	132	SENTENTIOUS MAN	41
IT'S MIDNIGHT ON THE MOUSE,	137	LOVE'S PROGRESS	16
IT'S NOT MY FIRST DYING.	164	I'M HERE	95
YOU HARDLY EVER THINK IT'S THERE.	178	THE CHAIR	2
IT'S RIGHT WHERE YOU ARE--	219	THE ABYSS	7
YET IT'S THE NATURE OF ALL LOVE TO RISE:	238	THE TRANCED	22
IT'S LOST UPON THE NIGHT--	240	IN EVEING AIR	17
IT'S NO DALLIANCE	261	THE CHANGELING	36
NOW YOU RUN TO THE MONEY, IT'S JIG, JIG, JIG;	272	DUET	2
MAYBE IT'S WHITMAN'S SPIDER, I CAN'T TELL,	273	SUPPR W LINDSAY	28
ITSELF			
COULD NOT UNFROWN ITSELF.	45	MY PAPA'S WALTZ	8
IS THIS THE STORM'S HEART? THE GROUND IS UNSTILLING ITSELF.	56	THE LOST SON	100
THE DARK FLOWS ON ITSELF. A DEAD MOUTH SINGS UNDER AN OLD TREE.	59	THE LONG ALLEY	6
THE WIND SHARPENED ITSELF ON A ROCK;	65	SHAPE OF FIRE	39

	PAGE	TITLE	LINE
ITSELF (CONTINUED)			
NEVER WISHING ITSELF AWAY,	101	LIGHT BREATHER	14
A FIRE LEAPS ON ITSELF: I KNOW THAT FLAME.	131	SENTENTIOUS MAN	8
"THE BED ITSELF BEGINS TO QUAKE,	136	THE SENSUALISTS	21
EACH CUSHION FOUND ITSELF A FIELD OF PINS,	143	SHIMMER OF EVIL	11
ROCKS IN AND OUT OF ITSELF.	163	I'M HERE	59
THE EARTH ITSELF A TUNE.	165	HER BECOMING	15
ECHO ITSELF CONSUMED;	167	HER BECOMING	67
WAITING, ITSELF A SLOW THING.	168	FOURTH MEDITATN	21
THE SPIRIT DECLARES ITSELF TO THESE ROCKS.	172	WHAT TELL BONES	46
BUT SHRINKS INTO A HALF-LIFE, LESS THAN ITSELF,	187	THE LONGING	20
WHO'D THINK THE MOON COULD PARE ITSELF SO THIN?	188	THE LONGING	30
THE STAR WINKING BEYOND ITSELF,	196	THE LONG WATERS	26
THE WHEEL TURNING AWAY FROM ITSELF,	200	THE FAR FIELD	53
THE RIVER TURNS ON ITSELF,	200	THE FAR FIELD	56
AND THE SEA REARRANGES ITSELF AMONG THE SMALL ISLANDS.	205	THE ROSE	97
GATHERING TO ITSELF SOUND AND SILENCE--	205	THE ROSE	113
THE WILD STREAM, THE SEA ITSELF CANNOT CONTAIN ME:	209	HER LONGING	12
BEARING BEING ITSELF,	221	THE ABYSS	71
THEN THROWING ITSELF UP AND AWAY FROM THE IMPLACABLE SWIFT PURSUERS,	232	THE THING	6
A SEED PUSHING ITSELF BEYOND ITSELF,	235	MANIFESTATION	3
A SEED PUSHING ITSELF BEYOND ITSELF,	235	MANIFESTATION	3
DIVINITY ITSELF MALIGN, ABSURD;	237	THE TRANCED	7
THE MIND ENTERS ITSELF, AND GOD THE MIND,	239	IN A DARK TIME	23
I WATCH A RIVER WIND ITSELF AWAY;	243	THE MOTION	8
THEN LOST ITSELF DOWN THROUGH A ROCKY GORGE.	247	I WAITED	20
ALL BY ITSELF.	249	THE RESTORED	4
I'VE			
I'VE MORE VEINS THAN A TREE!	57	THE LOST SON	120
I'VE LISTENED INTO THE LEAST WAVES.	77	BRING THE DAY!	28
I'VE LET MY NOSE OUT;	79	GIVE WAY, GATES	16
I'VE PLAYED WITH THE FISHES	80	GIVE WAY, GATES	40
I'VE WAKED THE WRONG WIND:	82	SENSIBILITY! LA	29
I'VE BEEN ASLEEP IN A BOWER OF DEAD SKIN.	86	PRAISE TO END!	47
I'VE CRAWLED FROM THE MIRE, ALERT AS A SAINT OR A DOG;	88	PRAISE TO END!	81
I'VE TRACED THESE WORDS IN SAND WITH A VESTIGIAL TAIL;	92	I CRY, LOVE!	17
I'VE SEEN MY FATHER'S FACE BEFORE	97	O, THOU OPENING	14
I'VE CREPT FROM A CRY.	99	O, THOU OPENING	53
I'VE BECOME A SENTRY OF SMALL SEEDS,	103	OLD LADY'S WRDS	33
SO I'VE GOT TO GET ME A RICH UGLY OLD MAID	112	SQUEEZE-BOX	43
I'M SURE I'VE BEEN A TOAD, ONE TIME OR ANOTHER.	151	SLUG	25
I'VE THE LARK'S WORD FOR IT, WHO SINGS ALONE:	156	THE DYING MAN	90
I'VE BECOME A STRANGE PIECE OF FLESH,	157	FIRST MEDITATN	15
I'VE TRIED I DON'T KNOW HOW MANY TIMES TO REPLANT IT.	163	I'M HERE	77
BIRDS ARE AROUND. I'VE ALL THE SINGING I WOULD.	164	I'M HERE	93
O I'VE HEARD!--	183	THE WAGTAIL	6
I'VE COME TO LOVE. A VIREO WHETS ITS BILL.	244	INFIRMITY	26
"I'VE ONLY ONE WING," SHE SAID,	249	THE RESTORED	7
I'VE RECOVERED MY TENDERNESS BY LONG LOOKING;	260	THE CHANGELING	16
I'VE COME TO BE.	261	THE CHANGELING	42
I'VE HAD ENOUGH TODAY	271	THE REPLY	2
HE SHOOK MY HAND. "TELL WILLIAMS I'VE BEEN HERE,	274	SUPPR W LINDSAY	48
IVY			
AND THE IVY ADVANCE WITH ITS WHITE LIZARD FEET--	194	JOURNY INTERIOR	49
IVY-BRANCH			
AND THE IVY-BRANCH, CAST TO THE GROUND, PUTS DOWN ROOTS INTO THE SAWDUST,	197	THE LONG WATERS	34
JACKASS			
AND THEN A JACKASS BRAYED. A LIZARD LEAPED MY FOOT.	247	I WAITED	14
JACK-DAW			
FROM A CRAZY OLD JACK-DAW BIRD	183	THE WAGTAIL	7
JACKPINE			
ON THE JACKPINE PLAINS I HUNTED THE BIRD NOBODY KNOWS;	89	UNFOLD! UNFOLD!	22
JACKRABBITS			
THE FLOATING HAWKS, THE JACKRABBITS, THE GRAZING CATTLE--	194	JOURNY INTERIOR	38
JADED			
THE PROGRESS OF THE JADED. MILE	33	HIGHWAY: MICH	2
JANE			
ELEGY FOR JANE	102	ELEGY FOR JANE	T
JAUNTIER			
LAST NIGHT I DREAMT OF A JAUNTIER PRINCIPLE OF ORDER;	165	HER BECOMING	30

	PAGE	TITLE	LINE
JAY			
YOU MEW LIKE A CAT, YOU GRATE LIKE A JAY:	177	KITTY-CAT BIRD	9
THE BLUE JAY RASPING FROM THE STUNTED PINE.	196	THE LONG WATERS	28
AND THE STELLER JAY, RAUCOUS, SOOTY HEADED, LIVES WITH US,	234	ALL MORNING	15
JAYS			
A FURY OF JAYS, DIVING AND SQUAWKING,	234	ALL MORNING	22
JERK			
THE PISTONS JERK AND SHOVE,	34	NIGHT JOURNEY	25
TO JERK LIKE A FROG	65	SHAPE OF FIRE	50
A SECRET TO JERK FROM THE LIPS OF A FISH.	92	I CRY, LOVE!	7
JERKED			
MY SHAVING HAND JERKED BACK IN SUDDEN TERROR:	25	DIM-WIT COUSIN	11
JERKS			
JERKS SKYWARD AT THE TOUCH OF WIND,	14	COMING OF COLD	29
HE JERKS A FROG ACROSS HIS BONY LIP,	15	THE HERON	9
JESUS			
THIS AIR COULD FLESH A DEAD STICK. SWEET JESUS, MAKE ME SWEAT.	61	THE LONG ALLEY	63
SWEET JESUS TOSSED ME BACK:	87	PRAISE TO END!	65
JESUS-SHIMMER			
AND NOW ARE WE TO HAVE THAT PELLUDIOUS JESUS-SHIMMER OVER ALL THINGS,	98	O, THOU OPENING	21
JIG			
NOW YOU RUN TO THE MONEY, IT'S JIG, JIG, JIG;	272	DUET	2
NOW YOU RUN TO THE MONEY, IT'S JIG, JIG, JIG;	272	DUET	2
NOW YOU RUN TO THE MONEY, IT'S JIG, JIG, JIG;	272	DUET	2
JIGGLE			
THE BEST HE COULD DO WAS JIGGLE HIS BLUBBER.	178	THE WHALE	4
JIGGLING			
ADDS UP A PAIR OF JIGGLING DOUBLE CHINS.	25	DIM-WIT COUSIN	8
JOCKEY			
THEY JOCKEY FOR POSITION ON	33	HIGHWAY: MICH	6
JOCK-WITH-THE-WIND			
WHERE'S ANN? WHERE'S LOU? WHERE'S JOCK-WITH-THE-WIND?	97	O, THOU OPENING	17
JOD-JODDING			
THEIR HEADS JOD-JODDING LIKE PIGEONS;	235	ALL MORNING	35
JOGGING			
AND AFTERWARDS I ALWAYS FELT MEAN, JOGGING BACK OVER THE LOGGING ROAD,	40	MOSS-GATHERING	9
JOGGLES			
WHEN I WALK PAST A VAT, WATER JOGGLES,	173	WHAT TELL BONES	73
JOGS			
WITH JOTS AND JOGS AND CINDERS ON THE FLOOR:	79	GIVE WAY, GATES	27
JOHN			
FOUR FOR SIR JOHN DAVIES	105	SIR JOHN DAVIES	T
I AM MY FATHER'S SON, I AM JOHN DONNE	140	THE SWAN	13
AND THAT SWEET MAN, JOHN CLARE.	228	IN VIOLENT WARD	7
JOHN RANSOM SHOULD BE HERE, AND RENE CHAR;	274	SUPPR W LINDSAY	43
JOHN-OF-THE-THUMB'S			
JOHN-OF-THE-THUMB'S JUMPING;	81	SENSIBILITY! LA	19
JOIN			
ANOTHER JOIN MY SONG	146	THE SONG	25
JOINED			
THEIR FOREPAWS JOINED TOGETHER, LIKE HANDS--	163	I'M HERE	69
JOINTED			
PALE BLOSSOMS, EACH BALANCED ON A SINGLE JOINTED STEM,	43	CARNATIONS	1
STEMS, JOINTED LIKE CORN,	44	FRAU BAUMAN	10
JOINTS			
IT WASN'T THE JOINTS IN NEW YORK, NEW YORK;	111	SQUEEZE-BOX	9
JOKES			
THE UNEMPLOYED AND TELLING STALE UNEMPLOYMENT JOKES.	28	CLAIRVOY WIDOW	22
JOLLY			
YOUR PALM IS MOIST, YOUR MANNER FAR TOO JOLLY	25	DIM-WIT COUSIN	9
JOLTS			
I SIT ABOVE THE BACK WHEELS, WHERE THE JOLTS ARE HARDEST,	158	FIRST MEDITATN	22
JOTS			
WITH JOTS AND JOGS AND CINDERS ON THE FLOOR:	79	GIVE WAY, GATES	27
JOURNEY			
NIGHT JOURNEY	34	NIGHT JOURNEY	T
THE JOURNEY FROM FLESH IS LONGEST.	66	SHAPE OF FIRE	61
JOURNEY AROUND A TREE;	137	LOVE'S PROGRESS	7
MAKING A SLOW JOURNEY AROUND THE WELL-CURB.	151	SLUG	3
JOURNEY WITHIN A JOURNEY:	158	FIRST MEDITATN	48

	PAGE	TITLE	LINE
JOURNEY (CONTINUED)			
JOURNEY WITHIN A JOURNEY:	158	FIRST MEDITATN	48
JOURNEY TO THE INTERIOR	193	JOURNY INTERIOR	T
IN THE LONG JOURNEY OUT OF THE SELF,	193	JOURNY INTERIOR	1
JOURNEYS			
ALL JOURNEYS, I THINK, ARE THE SAME:	158	FIRST MEDITATN	26
SO, I SUPPOSE, THE SPIRIT JOURNEYS.	159	FIRST MEDITATN	73
I DREAM OF JOURNEYS REPEATEDLY:	199	THE FAR FIELD	1
JOY			
AN EARLY JOY.	51	THE WAKING (1)	24
THERE'S NO JOY IN SOFT BONES.	59	THE LONG ALLEY	26
I KNOW THE BACK-STREAM'S JOY, AND THE STONE'S ETERNAL			
PULSELESS LONGING.	88	PRAISE TO END!	82
I PROCLAIM ONCE MORE A CONDITION OF JOY.	92	I CRY, LOVE!	28
THIS JOY OUTLEAPS THE DOG. WHO CARES? WHO CARES?	106	SIR JOHN DAVIES	44
SHAPE TO A RANDOM JOY:	124	WORDS FOR WIND	48
THE BURDEN OF THIS JOY.	124	WORDS FOR WIND	60
THE SOUL'S IMMEDIATE JOY.	126	WORDS FOR WIND	91
SHE CRIES OUT LOUD THE SOUL'S OWN SECRET JOY;	129	SHE	9
I FEAR FOR MY OWN JOY;	138	LOVE'S PROGRESS	23
MY HEART HELD TO ITS JOY,	148	THE SMALL	5
AND THE SUN BRINGS JOY TO SOME.	157	FIRST MEDITATN	12
I PREFER THE STILL JOY:	163	I'M HERE	86
BEING, NOT DOING, IS MY FIRST JOY.	222	THE ABYSS	101
WE END IN JOY.	238	THE MOMENT	14
LOVE BEGETS LOVE. THIS TORMENT IS MY JOY.	243	THE MOTION	7
AT EASE WITH JOY, A SELF-ENCHANTED MAN.	248	THE TREE, BIRD	6
THUS I ENDURE THIS LAST PURE STRETCH OF JOY,	248	THE TREE, BIRD	22
SAD THE SOUL'S JOY. LOVED HEART, WHAT ELSE CAN I SAY	261	THE CHANGELING	28
JOYLESS			
WAS NOT THE JOYLESS MOTION OF A STONE.	105	SIR JOHN DAVIES	18
JOYS			
KEEP FAITH WITH PRESENT JOYS REFUSE TO CHOOSE	5	TO MY SISTER	7
JOY'S			
THIS JOY'S MY FALL. I AM!--	121	ALL EARTH, AIR	6
JUDGE			
JUDGE NOT	48	JUDGE NOT	T
JUG			
--CAN STILL WHISTLE IN A JUG.	89	UNFOLD! UNFOLD!	13
MY JUG, MY HONEY, MY CAN OF BEER,	272	DUET	22
JUGS			
FROM THE MOUTHS OF JUGS	56	THE LOST SON	92
JUICE			
OR DROWN A BUG IN ONE SPIT OF TOBACCO JUICE,	42	OLD FLORIST	8
JUMP			
THEY'LL JUMP ON HIS BELLY,	72	WHERE KNOCK IS	28
TO JUMP OUT OF HIS SKIN.	262	FOLLIES OF ADAM	4
I'LL JUMP ON YOUR BELLY, I'LL KICK YOUR BUM	272	DUET	19
JUMPED			
AND FLOWERS JUMPED	51	THE WAKING (1)	11
I JUMPED IN BUTTER.	90	UNFOLD! UNFOLD!	37
JUMPING			
JOHN-OF-THE-THUMB'S JUMPING;	81	SENSIBILITY! LA	19
JUMPING IN HER SHOES.	103	OLD LADY'S WRDS	18
JUMPING UP AND DOWN ON THEIR HIND FEET,	163	I'M HERE	68
ARE YOU? YOU'RE JUMPING TOO!	182	THE LAMB	4
JUMP-IN-THE-HEDGE			
IT WAS JUMP-IN-THE-HEDGE; IT WAS WAIT-IN-THE-HALL;	111	SQUEEZE-BOX	13
JUMPS			
THE CHIN JUMPS TO THE NOSE.	60	THE LONG ALLEY	42
I SMELL THE JUMPS AHEAD.	81	SENSIBILITY! LA	14
A FISH JUMPS, SHAKING OUT FLAKES OF MOONLIGHT.	93	I CRY, LOVE!	45
HE JUMPS ALL OVER. WHO	182	THE LAMB	3
JUNCOS			
WITH WRENS, SPARROWS, JUNCOS, CEDAR WAXWINGS, FLICKERS,	235	ALL MORNING	41
JUNGLE			
WITH NO HINT OF YOUR PRESENCE IN A JUNGLE OF MASCULINE TOYS,	29	THE REMINDER	10
JUST			
CLOUDS GLOW LIKE COALS JUST FRESH FROM FIRE, A FLARE	17	UNEXTINGUISHED	1
THOUGH JUST MEN ARE REVILED	20	REPL TO CENSURE	9
JUST UNDER THE WATER	54	THE LOST SON	48
JUST UNDER THE WATER	55	THE LOST SON	60
THE DEVIL ISN'T DEAD; HE'S JUST AWAY.	97	O, THOU OPENING	16

	PAGE	TITLE	LINE
JUST (CONTINUED)			
AND SHOULD HE ARRIVE, WHY JUST LEAN YOURSELF BACK	113	TO A LADY ED	7
JUST SEND ME ALONG THAT SWEET SEVENTY-FIVE;	113	TO A LADY ED	14
WHEN I THINK OF IT NOW, I JUST HAVE TO SHUDDER!	114	THE COW	2
AND YOU JUST KNOW HE KNOWS HE KNOWS.	116	THE SLOTH	12
IF I WERE A FISH I JUST COULDN'T RESIST	117	LADY AND BEAR	23
BUT THE BEAR JUST SAT THERE UNTIL SHE SANK;	117	LADY AND BEAR	28
MY BACK IS JUST ONE BRUISE;	136	THE SENSUALISTS	4
WHEN I SLIP, JUST SLIGHTLY, IN THE DARK,	151	SLUG	8
THAT THE KITTY-CAT BIRD JUST HOPPED INSIDE;	177	KITTY-CAT BIRD	15
THE LAMB JUST SAYS, I AM!	182	THE LAMB	1
IS IT A CASE OF JUST PICK AND CHOOSE?	183	THE WAGTAIL	2
IS JUST UNDER HIS CHIN,--	183	THE LIZARD	4
SO MUCH HE JUST LIES IN ONE CORNER,	227	MEADOW MOUSE	13
I'D SAY MY FACE IS JUST AS ROUND AS HIS,	273	SUPPR W LINDSAY	8
JUTTING			
THE SUDDEN SHUDDER AS THE JUTTING SEA-CLIFF COLLAPSES,	231	THE STORM	42
KATE			
THE DOUGH I SPENT ON CHIPPEWA KATE,	112	SQUEEZE-BOX	39
KEEP			
I KEEP THE SPIRIT SPARE.	3	OPEN HOUSE	12
KEEP FAITH WITH PRESENT JOYS REFUSE TO CHOOSE	5	TO MY SISTER	7
TO KEEP INCLEMENT WEATHER FROM ITS YOUNG.	12	SLOW SEASON	6
OLD HEDGEROWS KEEP THE LEAVES; THE PHLOX,	15	COMING OF COLD	40
THAT KEEP THE SPIRIT UNDEFILED.	18	LONG LIVE WEEDS	8
THE BRAVE KEEP UNDEFILED	20	REPL TO CENSURE	11
THE MEN ON RAIL AND ROADWAY KEEP MOVING ON AND ON.	28	CLAIRVOY WIDOW	24
BUT STILL THE DELICATE SLIPS KEEP COAXING UP WATER;	37	CUTTINGS	3
IT'S NECESSARY AMONG THE FLIES AND BANANAS, TO KEEP A CONSTANT VIGIL,	86	PRAISE TO END!	24
I KEEP DREAMING OF BEES.	99	O, THOU OPENING	81
WITH NOTHING ON TO KEEP YOU WARM,	114	DINKY	6
MOTION CAN KEEP ME STILL;	123	WORDS FOR WIND	17
HER SEVERAL PARTS COULD KEEP A PURE REPOSE,	127	I KNEW A WOMAN	19
I WALK THE NIGHT TO KEEP MY FIVE WITS WARM.	135	THE RENEWAL	18
I KEEP A DOG, AND BARK MYSELF.	138	THE SURLY ONE	4
A CASUAL MAN, I KEEP MY CASUAL WORD,	140	THE SWAN	10
WHAT SENSUAL EYE CAN KEEP AN IMAGE PURE,	154	THE DYING MAN	43
YOUNGLINGS, THE SMALL FISH KEEP HEADING INTO THE CURRENT.	170	FOURTH MEDITATN	75
THE MORAL IS, I GUESS YOU KEEP	181	MONOTONY SONG	25
YET KEEP TO MYSELF MY OWN MIND;	208	HER WORDS	5
BY LUST ALONE WE KEEP THE MIND ALIVE,	243	THE MOTION	5
HAS SERVED TO KEEP ME WITH THE QUICK.	256	IN HYDROTHERAPY	4
I'LL KEEP MY BIG MOUTH SHUT.	270	GOB MUSIC	37
KEEPER			
I GREW TIRED OF THE RITUAL OF NAMES AND THE ASSISTANT KEEPER OF THE MOLLUSKS:	65	SHAPE OF FIRE	36
KEEPER OF HAY. THAT'S A SPRATLING'S PRATTLE. AND DON'T BE THINKING YOU'RE	98	O, THOU OPENING	28
KEEPING			
KEEPING CREATION AT EASE;	44	FRAU BAUMAN	20
ROOTED IN STONE, KEEPING THE WHOLE OF LIGHT,	205	THE ROSE	112
KEEPS			
MY HEART KEEPS OPEN HOUSE,	3	OPEN HOUSE	3
THAT KEEPS SUFFICIENT STORE	20	REPL TO CENSURE	14
THE LACK THAT KEEPS US WHAT WE ARE,	30	THE RECKONING	11
A MANIA KEEPS THEM ON THE MOVE	33	HIGHWAY: MICH	12
WHO KEEPS ME LAST?	72	WHERE KNOCK IS	46
HOW STILL SHE KEEPS HERSELF.	83	O LULL ME, LULL	4
THIS SHAKING KEEPS ME STEADY. I SHOULD KNOW.	108	THE WAKING (2)	16
SHE KEEPS MY WISHES WARM;	121	ALL EARTH, AIR	12
KEEPS PACE WHEN I WALK ALONE.	123	WORDS FOR WIND	32
A VOICE KEEPS RISING IN MY EARLY SLEEP,	165	HER BECOMING	19
WHAT LOVER KEEPS HIS SONG?	167	HER BECOMING	82
KEEPS BUZZING AT THE SILL. WHICH I IS I?	239	IN A DARK TIME	21
A DARK THEME KEEPS ME HERE,	240	IN EVEING AIR	1
KELLY'S			
IT WAS DEAD MAN'S CORNER, IT WAS KELLY'S STABLE;	112	SQUEEZE-BOX	34
KELP			
THE WAVES, ALTERED BY SAND-BARS, BEDS OF KELP, MISCELLANEOUS DRIFTWOOD,	191	AT OYSTER RIVER	32
WHERE THE SALMON EASE THEIR WAY INTO THE KELP BEDS,	205	THE ROSE	96

	PAGE	TITLE	LINE
KEPT			
OH THAT WAS LONG AGO! I KEPT	6	THE PREMONITION	3
BUT STILL THE ROAD AND DUSTY FIELD KEPT DRY.	6	INTERLUDE	8
HIS IMAGE KEPT FOLLOWING AFTER,--	6	THE PREMONITION	10
BUT MY EAR STILL KEPT THE SOUND OF THE SEA LIKE A SHELL.	12	MID-CNTRY BLOW	8
THE FEUD WE KEPT WITH SPACE COMES TO AN END.	13	PRAISE PRAIRIE	12
EVEN THE DIRT KEPT BREATHING A SMALL BREATH.	38	ROOT CELLAR	11
THEY TEASED OUT THE SEED THAT THE COLD KEPT ASLEEP,--	44	FRAU BAUMAN	23
THE ELEMENTS I KEPT WARM	49	RIVER INCIDENT	7
THE ROSES KEPT BREATHING IN THE DARK.	57	THE LOST SON	126
THE BONES OF WEEDS KEPT SWINGING IN THE WIND,	58	THE LOST SON	152
HE KEPT IT IN A CAN.	71	WHERE KNOCK IS	19
WHERE'S SHE NOW, I KEPT SAYING.	101	THE VISITANT	23
A BIRD ALWAYS KEPT SINGING.	163	I'M HERE	73
SHE KEPT HER BODY STILL	212	LIGHT LISTENED	10
HOW SHE KEPT THE WIZENED, THE FALLEN, THE MISSHAPEN FOR HERSELF,	223	ELEGY (2)	14
A BIRD KEPT HAUNTING ME WHEN I WAS YOUNG--	245	THE DECISION	3
KEROSENE			
AND FLICKER NEAR OUR LEGS LIKE KEROSENE	274	SUPPR W LINDSAY	36
KETTLES			
THAT FINE FUMING STINK OF PARTICULAR KETTLES,	48	LAST WORDS	2
KEY			
A COLD KEY LET ME IN	47	THE RETURN	8
KICK			
I GIVE THE CAT A KICK.	269	GOB MUSIC	6
I'LL JUMP ON YOUR BELLY, I'LL KICK YOUR BUM	272	DUET	19
KID			
I REMEMBER HOW THEY PICKED ME UP, A SPINDLY KID,	44	FRAU BAUMAN	26
KIDNEYS			
YOU WHISPER OF KIDNEYS,	79	GIVE WAY, GATES	25
KIDS			
THE KIDS PLAY COPS AND ROBBERS, THE KIDS PLAY MUMBLEY-PEG,	27	CLAIRVOY WIDOW	9
THE KIDS PLAY COPS AND ROBBERS, THE KIDS PLAY MUMBLEY-PEG,	27	CLAIRVOY WIDOW	9
KIERKEGAARD			
--IN SPITE OF SOREN KIERKEGAARD.	272	DUET	4
--AND CLOSE UP THAT CHAPTER OF KIERKEGAARD.	272	DUET	8
--WITH NEVER A THOUGHT FOR KIERKEGAARD.	272	DUET	12
--IN FEAR AND TREMBLING, DEAR KIERKEGAARD.	272	DUET	17
--FAR BEYOND, O BEYOND! DEAR KIERKEGAARD.	272	DUET	21
--IN HONOR OF FATHER KIERKEGAARD.	272	DUET	26
KILL			
STAY CLOSE. MUST I KILL SOMETHING ELSE?	60	THE LONG ALLEY	31
KILLDEER			
I TOUCHED THE GROUND, THE GROUND WARMED BY THE KILLDEER,	63	FIELD OF LIGHT	39
THE KILLDEER WHISTLING AWAY FROM ME,	204	THE ROSE	62
KILLED			
OR FRENCHMEN KILLED A HUNDRED YEARS AGO,	224	OTTO	26
KILLED EVERY CAT THAT NEARED THEIR PHEASANT RUNS;	224	OTTO	28
KILLERS			
THE DESCENDANTS OF THE PLAYFUL TREE-SHREW THAT SURVIVED THE ARCHAIC KILLERS,	170	FOURTH MEDITATN	66
KIN			
SAY TO HIS GATHERED KIN,	153	THE DYING MAN	2
AS CLOSE TO HIM AS ANY KITH OR KIN.	224	OTTO	6
KIN TO THE WIND, AND THE BLEAK WHISTLING RAIN.	248	THE TREE, BIRD	12
KIND			
AND LIFT UP A PATCH, DARK-GREEN, THE KIND FOR LINING CEMETERY BASKETS,	40	MOSS-GATHERING	2
HE DIDN'T LIKE HIS KIND OF LIFE;	115	THE SERPENT	5
THESE WATERS DROWSE ME INTO SLEEP SO KIND	135	THE RENEWAL	11
YET LOVE-LONGING OF A KIND	237	THE TRANCED	8
WAS NATURE KIND? THE HEART'S CORE TRACTABLE?	242	THE SEQUEL	25
RIDING THE AIR, A WILLOW WITH ITS KIND,	248	THE TREE, BIRD	10
KINDLY			
A KINDLY WIDOW LADY, WHO LIVED UPON A HILL,	27	CLAIRVOY WIDOW	1
KINDS			
THERE WERE MANY KINDS OF COOL	57	THE LOST SON	137
NOW HE'S EATEN HIS THREE KINDS OF CHEESE AND DRUNK FROM HIS BOTTLE-CAP WATERING-TROUGH--	227	MEADOW MOUSE	12
KING			
WE'RE KING AND QUEEN OF THE RIGHT GROUND.	79	GIVE WAY, GATES	22
I'M KING OF THE BOOPS!	92	I CRY, LOVE!	13

	PAGE	TITLE	LINE
KING (CONTINUED)			
I'M KING OF ANOTHER CONDITION,	99	O, THOU OPENING	57
KINGDOM			
IN THE KINGDOM OF BANG AND BLAB.	54	THE LOST SON	33
A KINGDOM OF STINKS AND SIGHS,	187	THE LONGING	2
TILL YOU COME TO THE LAND OF KINGDOM COME	272	DUET	20
KINGDOMS			
IN THE WHITE KINGDOMS, I WAS LIGHT AS A SEED,	168	FOURTH MEDITATN	15
KINGFISHER			
BUT STILL THE FLASH OF THE KINGFISHER, THE WINGBEAT OF THE SCOTER,	202	THE ROSE	15
KINGFISHER'S			
THE HUMMINGBIRD'S SURETY, THE KINGFISHER'S CUNNING--	191	AT OYSTER RIVER	40
KINSHIP			
WITH BATS, WEASELS, WORMS--I REJOICE IN THE KINSHIP.	151	SLUG	26
KISS			
KISS ME, KISS ME QUICK, MISTRESS OF LOST WISDOM,	48	LAST WORDS	7
KISS ME, KISS ME QUICK, MISTRESS OF LOST WISDOM,	48	LAST WORDS	7
KISS ME, ASHES, I'M FALLING THROUGH A DARK SWIRL.	57	THE LOST SON	121
KISS THE TROUGH, SWINE-ON-FRIDAY.	59	THE LONG ALLEY	24
RICH ME CHERRIES A FONDLING'S KISS,	60	THE LONG ALLEY	43
LACKING THE CANDOR OF DOGS, I KISS THE DEPARTING AIR;	86	PRAISE TO END!	26
SKIN'S THE LEAST OF ME. KISS THIS.	87	PRAISE TO END!	72
I KISS HER MOVING MOUTH,	126	WORDS FOR WIND	98
I THINK THE DEAD ARE TENDER. SHALL WE KISS?--	129	SHE	1
AS IF A LION KNELT TO KISS A ROSE,	131	SENTENTIOUS MAN	17
I TASTE MY SISTER WHEN I KISS MY WIFE;	132	SENTENTIOUS MAN	27
I WALK AS IF MY FACE WOULD KISS THE WIND.	135	THE RENEWAL	12
BUT A KISS WIDENS THE ROSE;	153	THE DYING MAN	8
I KNOW THE COLD FLESHLESS KISS OF CONTRARIES,	166	HER BECOMING	40
"THE STORM, THE STORM OF A KISS."	208	HER WORDS	12
FOR HIM TO KISS OR CARESS	209	HER RETICENCE	4
AS WE KISS BY THE HIGH SEA-WALL.	216	THE SHY MAN	26
SHIFTED WITH OUR SLOW KISS.	238	THE MOMENT	5
HERE'S THE LAST KISS OF MY LUCK:	259	SONG (3)	43
KISSED			
AS MY OWN TONGUE KISSED	56	THE LOST SON	98
ALONE, I KISSED THE SKIN OF A STONE;	63	FIELD OF LIGHT	29
SHE KISSED ME CLOSE, AND THEN DID SOMETHING ELSE.	106	SIR JOHN DAVIES	35
THE LINKS WERE SOFT BETWEEN US; STILL, WE KISSED;	107	SIR JOHN DAVIES	81
SHE KISSED ME OUT OF THOUGHT	123	WORDS FOR WIND	18
SHE KISSED ME MORE THAN TWICE	212	LIGHT LISTENED	3
KISSES			
SOLACE OF KISSES AND COOKIES AND CABBAGE,	48	LAST WORDS	1
LET THE KISSES RESOUND, FLAT LIKE A BUTCHER'S PALM;	56	THE LOST SON	104
KISSES COME BACK,	73	WHERE KNOCK IS	76
HAIR HAD KISSES.	90	UNFOLD! UNFOLD!	38
I GAVE HER KISSES BACK, AND WOKE A GHOST.	106	SIR JOHN DAVIES	45
KISSING			
THEIR WAN MOUTHS KISSING THE WARM SUTURES,	50	THE MINIMAL	9
WAS IT DUST I WAS KISSING?	63	FIELD OF LIGHT	27
HER EYES WENT KISSING AWAY	72	WHERE KNOCK IS	36
IS IT WITH WHISPERS AND KISSING?--	77	BRING THE DAY!	27
ON THE ROCKS SOUTH OF QUIET, IN THE CLOSE REGIONS OF KISSING,	86	PRAISE TO END!	20
KISSING.	98	O, THOU OPENING	39
THE LEAVES, THEIR WHISPERS TURNED TO KISSING;	102	ELEGY FOR JANE	8
KITCHEN			
SLID FROM THE KITCHEN SHELF;	45	MY PAPA'S WALTZ	6
KITCHENS			
THE LIGHTS IN THE KITCHENS GO OUT; MOTH WINGS UNFURL;	33	IDYLL	3
KITE			
BUT HE ALWAYS WANTED TO FLY MY KITE;	178	THE DONKEY	2
KITH			
AS CLOSE TO HIM AS ANY KITH OR KIN.	224	OTTO	6
KITTEN			
A KITTEN CAN	71	WHERE KNOCK IS	1
KITTEN-LIMP			
BELIEVE ME, THERE'S NO ONE ELSE, KITTEN-LIMP SISTER.	59	THE LONG ALLEY	23
KITTENS			
HER NECK HAS KITTENS.	72	WHERE KNOCK IS	32
KITTY			
--DID THE KITTY--THE KITTY-CAT BIRD.	177	KITTY-CAT BIRD	17

	PAGE	TITLE	LINE
KITTY-CAT			
THE KITTY-CAT BIRD	177	KITTY-CAT BIRD	T
THE KITTY-CAT BIRD, HE SAT ON A FENCE.	177	KITTY-CAT BIRD	1
--SAID THE WREN TO THE KITTY-CAT BIRD.	177	KITTY-CAT BIRD	4
--SAID THE WREN TO THE KITTY-CAT BIRD.	177	KITTY-CAT BIRD	8
--SAID THE WREN TO THE KITTY-CAT BIRD.	177	KITTY-CAT BIRD	12
THE KITTY-CAT BIRD, HE MOPED AND HE CRIED.	177	KITTY-CAT BIRD	13
THAT THE KITTY-CAT BIRD JUST HOPPED INSIDE;	177	KITTY-CAT BIRD	15
--DID THE KITTY--THE KITTY-CAT BIRD.	177	KITTY-CAT BIRD	17
--OR YOU'LL END LIKE THE KITTY-CAT BIRD.	177	KITTY-CAT BIRD	21
KNAVE			
A KNAVE WHO SCAMPERED THROUGH THE NEEDLE'S EYE,	28	THE FAVORITE	1
KNEE			
TODAY THEY DRAINED THE FLUID FROM A KNEE	244	INFIRMITY	9
KNEELED			
AND I KNEELED DOWN AND DID PARTAKE	270	GOB MUSIC	34
KNEES			
WHEN I STOOD AT THE WINDOW, AN ELM BOUGH SWEPT TO MY KNEES;	12	MID-CNTRY BLOW	3
AND A LAKE BELOW MY KNEES.	34	NIGHT JOURNEY	11
THAT RIFFLED AROUND MY KNEES.	49	RIVER INCIDENT	3
MY KNEES MADE LITTLE WINDS UNDERNEATH	57	THE LOST SON	128
UNTIL THEY CREAK THEIR KNEES:	60	THE LONG ALLEY	36
MELTING AT THE KNEES, A VARICOSE HORROR.	65	SHAPE OF FIRE	31
GOD PITY THOSE BUT WANTON TO THE KNEES,--	106	SIR JOHN DAVIES	62
MY EYES, THEY DAZZLED AT HER FLOWING KNEES;	127	I KNEW A WOMAN	18
TO THE DIRT, MY KNEES SCRUBBING	151	SLUG	6
SHE WOULD SIT WITH A BOOK ON HER KNEES,--	179	MYRTLE	6
OR A BREEZE MOVES OVER THE KNEES FROM A LOW HILL,	198	THE LONG WATERS	64
OR, WITH SKINNY KNEES, TO SIT ASTRIDE A WET LOG,	200	THE FAR FIELD	45
BROUGHT ME DOWN TO MY KNEES. O WHO CAN BE	241	THE SEQUEL	5
THERE ON MY KNEES, A MAN OF RENOWN,	270	GOB MUSIC	42
KNELT			
AS IF A LION KNELT TO KISS A ROSE,	131	SENTENTIOUS MAN	17
KNEW			
NOW HERE IS PEACE FOR ONE WHO KNEW	17	NO BIRD	1
AND I KNEW I HAD BEEN THERE BEFORE,	49	RIVER INCIDENT	9
MY EARS KNEW	51	THE WAKING (1)	23
HELLO, HELLO. MY NERVES KNEW YOU, DEAR BOY.	65	SHAPE OF FIRE	32
THE WORLD I KNEW;	87	PRAISE TO END!	60
THE BOYS I KNEW WHEN I WENT TO POT;	111	SQUEEZE-BOX	2
SHE KNEW THE GRAMMAR OF LEAST MOTION, SHE	120	THE DREAM	23
I KNEW A WOMAN	127	I KNEW A WOMAN	T
I KNEW A WOMAN, LOVELY IN HER BONES,	127	I KNEW A WOMAN	1
I KNEW THAT I DID LOVE HER.	216	THE SHY MAN	12
SHE NEVER KNEW;	223	ELEGY (2)	6
AND IN A WOOD HE KNEW WHATEVER MOVED;	224	OTTO	13
HE ALWAYS KNEW WHAT HE WAS AIMING AT.	224	OTTO	17
WHOM DO WE LOVE? I THOUGHT I KNEW THE TRUTH;	241	THE SEQUEL	7
OF GRIEF I DIED, BUT NO ONE KNEW MY DEATH.	241	THE SEQUEL	8
AND KNEW HOW TO COMMAND;	268	SAGINAW SONG	53
KNIFE			
PLEASED AS A KNIFE.	81	SENSIBILITY! LA	25
SHARPENED A BUTCHER KNIFE;	213	THE HAPPY THREE	2
KNITTED			
THE TEETH OF KNITTED GEARS	9	THE ADAMANT	5
KNIVES			
FLYING UPWARD THROUGH THE KNIVES OF MY LAWNMOWER	151	SLUG	16
KNOCK			
THAT WAS A CLOSE KNOCK. SEE WHAT THE WILL WANTS.	61	THE LONG ALLEY	62
WHERE KNOCK IS OPEN WIDE	71	WHERE KNOCK IS	T
IT'S STILL ENOUGH FOR THE KNOCK OF A WORM.	87	PRAISE TO END!	76
ARCH OF AIR, MY HEART'S ORIGINAL KNOCK,	88	PRAISE TO END!	79
KNOCKED			
THE LONG PIPES KNOCKED: IT WAS THE END OF NIGHT.	225	OTTO	39
FROM A KNOCKED OVER CHURN, AND FOAMED AROUND	273	SUPPR W LINDSAY	13
KNOCKING			
ALL PULSE WITH THE KNOCKING PIPES	38	FORCING HOUSE	5
KNOCKS			
IN A SODDEN PLACE, ALL RAPS AND KNOCKS APPROVE.	93	I CRY, LOVE!	30
KNOT			
BELIEVE ME, KNOT OF GRISTLE, I BLEED LIKE A TREE;	79	GIVE WAY, GATES	1

	PAGE	TITLE	LINE
KNOUT			
THE FANG AND THE CLAW, THE CLUB AND THE KNOUT, THE			
IRRATIONAL EDICT,	170	FOURTH MEDITATN	67
KNOW			
TO KNOW THAT LIGHT FALLS AND FILLS, OFTEN WITHOUT OUR			
KNOWING,	67	SHAPE OF FIRE	92
I KNOW WHO'S GOT HIM,	72	WHERE KNOCK IS	27
I KNOW HER NOISE.	72	WHERE KNOCK IS	31
I KNOW IT'S AN OWL. HE'S MAKING IT DARKER.	72	WHERE KNOCK IS	39
I KNOW! I KNOW!	73	WHERE KNOCK IS	51
I KNOW! I KNOW!	73	WHERE KNOCK IS	51
HOO. I KNOW THE SPOON.	74	I NEED, I NEED	3
I KNOW WHAT YOU IS:	75	I NEED, I NEED	28
I KNOW YOU ARE MY NEMESIS	75	I NEED, I NEED	31
I KNOW ANOTHER FIRE.	76	I NEED, I NEED	67
HOW MANY ANGELS DO YOU KNOW?--	77	BRING THE DAY!	12
YOU TREE BEGINNING TO KNOW,	79	GIVE WAY, GATES	24
I KNOW THE WAY OUT OF A LAUGH;	81	SENSIBILITY! LA	23
I KNOW MY OWN BONES:	83	O LULL ME, LULL	16
I KNOW THE BACK-STREAM'S JOY, AND THE STONE'S ETERNAL			
PULSELESS LONGING.	88	PRAISE TO END!	82
I KNOW THAT DREAM.	103	OLD LADY'S WRDS	2
THAT CAME TO BE THE BEARS AND YEATS WOULD KNOW.	105	SIR JOHN DAVIES	24
I KNOW A DANCE THE ELEPHANTS BELIEVE.	106	SIR JOHN DAVIES	40
THE BODY AND THE SOUL KNOW HOW TO PLAY	106	SIR JOHN DAVIES	47
WHO RISE FROM FLESH TO SPIRIT KNOW THE FALL:	107	SIR JOHN DAVIES	95
WE THINK BY FEELING. WHAT IS THERE TO KNOW?	108	THE WAKING (2)	4
THIS SHAKING KEEPS ME STEADY. I SHOULD KNOW.	108	THE WAKING (2)	16
AND KNOW THAT TRUE LOVE IS MORE THAN A LIFE-FORCE	113	TO A LADY ED	3
AND YOU JUST KNOW HE KNOWS HE KNOWS.	116	THE SLOTH	12
I CRY DELIGHT: I KNOW	124	WORDS FOR WIND	49
BODY AND SPIRIT KNOW	126	WORDS FOR WIND	95
WHAT'S FREEDOM FOR? TO KNOW ETERNITY.	127	I KNEW A WOMAN	24
NATURE'S TOO MUCH TO KNOW.	130	THE OTHER	12
I KNOW HER CARELESS WAYS!--	130	THE OTHER	21
A FIRE LEAPS ON ITSELF: I KNOW THAT FLAME.	131	SENTENTIOUS MAN	8
I KNOW THE MOTION OF THE DEEPEST STONE.	132	SENTENTIOUS MAN	35
I KNOW I LOVE, YET KNOW NOT WHERE I AM;	135	THE RENEWAL	15
I KNOW I LOVE, YET KNOW NOT WHERE I AM;	135	THE RENEWAL	15
AND I KNOW WHERE SHE IS.	137	LOVE'S PROGRESS	10
LOVE'S ALL. LOVE'S ALL I KNOW.	141	MEMORY	8
I KNOW MYSELF, MY SEASONS, AND I KNOW.	144	ELEGY (1)	10
I KNOW MYSELF, MY SEASONS, AND I KNOW.	144	ELEGY (1)	10
BRING ME THE MEEK, FOR I WOULD KNOW THEIR WAYS;	149	IN LATE SUMMER	5
I KNOW IT ISN'T A WET LEAF,	151	SLUG	9
I KNOW, AS THE DYING KNOW,	153	THE DYING MAN	9
I KNOW, AS THE DYING KNOW,	153	THE DYING MAN	9
DAWN'S WHERE THE WHITE IS. WHO WOULD KNOW THE DAWN	155	THE DYING MAN	52
WHAT'S SEEN RECEDES; FOREVER'S WHAT WE KNOW!--	156	THE DYING MAN	91
I'VE TRIED I DON'T KNOW HOW MANY TIMES TO REPLANT IT.	163	I'M HERE	77
I KNOW THE COLD FLESHLESS KISS OF CONTRARIES,	166	HER BECOMING	40
TO KNOW A CHAIR IS REALLY IT,	178	THE CHAIR	3
SAID, "I KNOW MY LEGS ADD UP TO TWO!	182	PHILANDER	2
I KNOW THIS CHANGE:	195	JOURNY INTERIOR	75
I AM TOLD BY THOSE WHO KNOW,--	207	THE YOUNG GIRL	6
THE LONELIEST THING I KNOW	215	HIS FOREBODING	14
DO WE DO MORE THAN WE KNOW.	237	THE TRANCED	4
I KNOW THE PURITY OF PURE DESPAIR,	239	IN A DARK TIME	9
WHO BUT THE LOVED KNOW LOVE'S A FARING-FORTH?	243	THE MOTION	13
UPON THAT GOD WHO KNOWS WHAT I WOULD KNOW.	246	THE MARROW	24
BUT AT LEAST WE KNOW ONE NEEDN'T BLENCH	272	DUET	16
PAUL BUNYAN IS PART RUSSIAN, DID YOU KNOW?--	274	SUPPR W LINDSAY	44
KNOWING			
TO KNOW THAT LIGHT FALLS AND FILLS, OFTEN WITHOUT OUR			
KNOWING,	67	SHAPE OF FIRE	92
GOING IS KNOWING.	99	O, THOU OPENING	83
I NEED AN OLD CRONE'S KNOWING.	157	FIRST MEDITATN	19
KNOWING THE SINUOUSNESS OF SMALL WATERS:	168	FOURTH MEDITATN	5
IN THIS FIRST HEAVEN OF KNOWING,	191	AT OYSTER RIVER	37
KNOWING SLOWS FOR A MOMENT,	221	THE ABYSS	69
WE COME TO SOMETHING WITHOUT KNOWING WHY.	235	MANIFESTATION	11
KNOWING HOW ALL THINGS ALTER IN THE SEED	243	THE MOTION	15
AND KNOWING THIS, I AM NOT YET UNDONE.	244	INFIRMITY	30

		PAGE	TITLE	LINE
KNOWLEDGE				
O WORM OF DUTY! O SPIRAL KNOWLEDGE!	. . . .	48	LAST WORDS	6
STUPOR OF KNOWLEDGE LACKING INWARDNESS--	. . . .	133	THE PURE FURY	1
WHERE IS THE KNOWLEDGE THAT	. . . .	139	PLAINT	7
KNOWN				
AS KNOWN PARTICULARS COME WHEELING BY,		8	THE SIGNALS	3
IN LOVE ARE NEVER KNOWN TO BARTER;	. . . .	23	AMOROUS LADY	6
I HAVE KNOWN THE INEXORABLE SADNESS OF PENCILS,	. . . .	46	DOLOR	1
"I AM WHAT IS KNOWN AS A BIDDLY BEAR,--	. . . .	117	LADY AND BEAR	5
OR KNOWN, ONCE, THE SOUL'S AUTHENTIC HUNGER,		169	FOURTH MEDITATN	47
I HAVE KNOWN THE HEART OF THE SUN,--		194	JOURNY INTERIOR	59
ALL'S KNOWN, ALL,, ALL AROUND:	. . . .	212	LIGHT LISTENED	13
WHAT CAN BE KNOWN? THE UNKNOWN.		251	ONCE MORE, RND	2
IN THE WIDE WHITE, THE KNOWN	. . . .	263	FOLLIES OF ADAM	24
KNOWS				
ASK THE MOLE, HE KNOWS.	. . . .	55	THE LOST SON	67
A DUCK KNOWS SOMETHING		75	I NEED, I NEED	40
WHO ELSE KNOWS	. . . .	76	I NEED, I NEED	64
THE COLD KNOWS WHEN TO COME.	. . . .	80	GIVE WAY, GATES	56
ON THE JACKPINE PLAINS I HUNTED THE BIRD NOBODY KNOWS;	. . .	89	UNFOLD! UNFOLD!	22
--NEITHER KNOWS IT.		97	O, THOU OPENING	10
THE VISIBLE OBSCURES. BUT WHO KNOWS WHEN?		107	SIR JOHN DAVIES	85
AND YOU JUST KNOW HE KNOWS HE KNOWS.		116	THE SLOTH	12
AND YOU JUST KNOW HE KNOWS HE KNOWS.	. . . .	116	THE SLOTH	12
SHE KNOWS THE SPEECH OF LIGHT, AND MAKES IT PLAIN	. . . . . .	129	SHE	11
THE SPIRIT KNOWS THE FLESH IT MUST CONSUME.		131	SENTENTIOUS MAN	10
AND SHE KNOWS ALL I AM.	. . . .	141	MEMORY	4
THE LILY BROODS. WHO KNOWS		165	HER BECOMING	26
THE SOUL KNOWS NOT WHAT TO BELIEVE,		171	WHAT TELL BONES	3
WHO KNOWS HOW THE WAG-TAIL WOOS?	. . . .	183	THE WAGTAIL	1
AS A BLIND MAN, LIFTING A CURTAIN, KNOWS IT IS MORNING,		195	JOURNY INTERIOR	74
WHO KNOWS THE END OF IT ALL?	. . . .	215	HIS FOREBODING	8
WHO KNOWS THIS--	. . . .	222	THE ABYSS	87
KNOWS ALL."		222	THE ABYSS	88
UPON THAT GOD WHO KNOWS WHAT I WOULD KNOW.		246	THE MARROW	24
KNUCKLE				
WAS BATTERED ON ONE KNUCKLE;	. . . .	45	MY PAPA'S WALTZ	10
LA				
SENSIBILITY! O LA!		81	SENSIBILITY! LA	T
LA, LA,	. . . .	82	SENSIBILITY! LA	41
LA, LA,	. . . .	82	SENSIBILITY! LA	41
LACE				
BRIDGES OF IRON LACE,	. . . .	34	NIGHT JOURNEY	6
LACELIKE				
THE LACELIKE WRINKLES OF THE WAKE WIDENING, THINNING OUT,		203	THE ROSE	33
LACK				
THE LACK THAT KEEPS US WHAT WE ARE,	. . . .	30	THE RECKONING	11
I LACK PLAIN TENDERNESS.	. . . .	139	PLAINT	6
A HEAD OR TAIL--WHICH DOES HE LACK?	. . . .	182	THE HIPPO	1
LACKING				
LACKING THE CANDOR OF DOGS, I KISS THE DEPARTING AIR;	. . . .	86	PRAISE TO END!	26
STUPOR OF KNOWLEDGE LACKING INWARDNESS--	. . . .	133	THE PURE FURY	1
IN SUCH TIMES, LACKING A GOD,	. . . .	160	FIRST MEDITATN	98
LADDERS				
WHO CREAKED ON THE GREENHOUSE LADDERS,	. . . .	44	FRAU BAUMAN	2
LADDIE-BUCK				
DAN CUPID, I TELL YOU'S A BRAW LADDIE-BUCK;	. . . .	113	TO A LADY ED	5
LADEN				
THE LADEN WHEELBARROWS CREAKING AND SWAYING,	. . . .	158	FIRST MEDITATN	46
LADIES				
GONE THE THREE ANCIENT LADIES	. . . .	44	FRAU BAUMAN	1
THAT LADIES THEIR TRUE NATURES NEVER SUPPRESS,		113	TO A LADY ED	10
STOPPING TRAFFIC, INDIGNANT AS ADDLED OLD LADIES,	. . . . . .	234	ALL MORNING	27
LADIES'				
WHEN THE LADIES' GUILD PUTS ON A FEED,	. . . .	267	SAGINAW SONG	3
LADLE				
OR LADLE RATTLING IN AN EMPTY DISH?	. . . .	105	SIR JOHN DAVIES	30
LADY				
FOR AN AMOROUS LADY	. . . .	23	AMOROUS LADY	T
A KINDLY WIDOW LADY, WHO LIVED UPON A HILL,	. . . .	27	CLAIRVOY WIDOW	1
"O TELL ME, WIDOW LADY, WHAT IS IT THAT YOU SEE,		27	CLAIRVOY WIDOW	3
"CLAIRVOYANT WIDOW LADY, WITH AN EYE LIKE A TELESCOPE,	. . .	27	CLAIRVOY WIDOW	17
REPLY TO A LADY EDITOR	. . . .	113	TO A LADY ED	T

	PAGE	TITLE	LINE
LADY (CONTINUED)			
THE LADY AND THE BEAR	117	LADY AND BEAR	T
A LADY CAME TO A BEAR BY A STREAM.	117	LADY AND BEAR	1
AND AT THAT THE LADY SLIPPED FROM THE BANK	117	LADY AND BEAR	26
MY LADY LAUGHS, DELIGHTING IN WHAT IS.	129	SHE	2
THE DRUNKEN SOLDIER. THE OLD LADY WITH HER PEPPERMINTS;	158	FIRST MEDITATN	30
LADY'S			
OLD LADY'S WINTER WORDS	103	OLD LADY'S WRDS	T
LAG			
PROFESSORS ARE CONDONING THE CULTURAL LAG.	27	CLAIRVOY WIDOW	12
LAIR			
THAT SELF-INFECTED LAIR;	47	THE RETURN	9
LAKE			
AND A LAKE BELOW MY KNEES.	34	NIGHT JOURNEY	11
BY THE SHRUNKEN LAKE, HUNTING, IN THE HEAT OF SUMMER.	54	THE LOST SON	43
SEE! SHE'S SLEEPING LIKE A LAKE:	81	SENSIBILITY! LA	2
THE LAKE WASHES ITS STONES.	82	SENSIBILITY! LA	31
THE LAKE TURNED GREEN;	87	PRAISE TO END!	56
THE SHINE ON THE FACE OF THE LAKE	93	I CRY, LOVE!	50
WHAT'S BECOME OF CARE? THIS LAKE BREATHES LIKE A ROSE.	170	FOURTH MEDITATN	76
AND THE BRONZE OF A DEAD BURDOCK AT THE EDGE OF A PRAIRIE LAKE,	197	THE LONG WATERS	42
AS LIGHT REFLECTS FROM A LAKE, IN LATE EVENING,	198	THE LONG WATERS	60
THE BURNING LAKE TURNS INTO A FOREST POOL,	221	THE ABYSS	58
AND THE DUCKS NEAR LAKE WASHINGTON WADDLE DOWN THE HIGHWAY AFTER A RAIN,	234	ALL MORNING	26
INDEED I SAW A SHIMMERING LAKE	270	GOB MUSIC	32
LAKES			
THE LAKES WILL BE HAPPY:	61	THE LONG ALLEY	87
CAME TO LAKES; CAME TO DEAD WATER,	62	FIELD OF LIGHT	1
IN THE COUNTRY OF FEW LAKES, IN THE TALL BUFFALO GRASS AT THE BASE OF THE CLAY BUTTES,	189	THE LONGING	53
LAKE'S			
TO STARE INTO THE AFTER-LIGHT, THE GLITTER LEFT ON THE LAKE'S SURFACE,	67	SHAPE OF FIRE	88
BY THE LAKE'S EDGE, I SEE A SILVER SWAN,	140	THE SWAN	16
LAMB			
THERE IS NO RIVEN TREE, OR LAMB DROPPED BY AN EAGLE.	159	FIRST MEDITATN	82
THE LAMB	182	THE LAMB	T
THE LAMB JUST SAYS, I AM!	182	THE LAMB	1
LAMP			
AND THE SMALL STREET-LAMP SWINGING AND SLAMMING AGAINST THE LAMP POLE.	230	THE STORM	7
LAND			
AND FLUNG THEM IN CONFUSION ON THE LAND.	6	INTERLUDE	3
THE LAND IS DESOLATE, THE SUN	15	COMING OF COLD	47
THIS FLAT LAND HAS BECOME A PIT	19	AGNST DISASTER	9
A STABLE AND PADDOCK, SOME FOX-HUNTING LAND,	32	SALE	6
TO SEE THE LAND I LOVE.	34	NIGHT JOURNEY	27
MOVING, UNMOVING IN A PARCHED LAND, WHITE IN THE MOONLIGHT:	194	JOURNY INTERIOR	53
THE EDGE OF ALL THE LAND, THE FINAL SEA?	221	THE ABYSS	63
ONCE WHEN HE SAW TWO POACHERS ON HIS LAND,	224	OTTO	14
HE WALKED OUR GREENHOUSE LAND.	268	SAGINAW SONG	55
TO THE LAND WHERE THE INNOCENT STRETCH AND SNORE	272	DUET	11
TILL YOU COME TO THE LAND OF KINGDOM COME	272	DUET	20
LANDLOCKED			
TO A LANDLOCKED BAY, WHERE THE SALT WATER IS FRESHENED	197	THE LONG WATERS	47
LANDSCAPE			
THE LANDSCAPE STILL PARTLY BROWN:	58	THE LOST SON	151
PART OF THE LANDSCAPE.	234	ALL MORNING	14
LANE			
BUDS, LONG UNSEALED, OBSCURE THE NARROW LANE.	12	SLOW SEASON	14
PAST ALDER LANE, AND WE GABBED THERE A WHILE.	274	SUPPR W LINDSAY	47
LANES			
THE WOODS IN SPRING THE LEAVES THE SCENTED LANES	5	TO MY SISTER	2
LANGUAGE			
IN LANGUAGE STRICT AND PURE.	3	OPEN HOUSE	15
SHE LILTS A LOW SOFT LANGUAGE, AND I HEAR	129	SHE	5
IN THE WILD DISORDERED LANGUAGE OF THE NATURAL HEART?	166	HER BECOMING	33
MADE FROM HIS TERROR AND DISMAY A GRAVE PHILOSOPHICAL LANGUAGE;	170	FOURTH MEDITATN	72
REJOICE IN THE LANGUAGE OF SMELLS AND DANCING.	196	THE LONG WATERS	4

	PAGE	TITLE	LINE
LANGUISHED			
I LAY; I LANGUISHED THERE.	145	THE BEAST	15
LANTERN			
WHEN GEORGE THE WATCHMAN'S LANTERN DROPPED FROM SIGHT	225	OTTO	38
LAP			
A LAP OF MOUNTAIN MIST	34	NIGHT JOURNEY	8
LOOSE IN MY LAP,	164	I'M HERE	97
LAPFUL			
A LAPFUL OF APPLES SLEEPS IN THIS GRASS.	92	I CRY, LOVE!	24
LAPPING			
BY THE LAPPING OF WATER,	191	AT OYSTER RIVER	61
ONLY AN OMINOUS LAPPING,	230	THE STORM	2
LAPS			
TILL I LAY IN THEIR LAPS, LAUGHING,	44	FRAU BAUMAN	28
A LOW MOUTH LAPS WATER. WEEDS, WEEDS, HOW I LOVE YOU.	64	SHAPE OF FIRE	17
LAPSES			
THE POND LAPSES BACK INTO A GLASSY SILENCE.	172	WHAT TELL BONES	50
LAPSING			
TUNNELED WITH LAPSING SOUND	50	THE CYCLE	15
LARCHY			
SHE WITH HER LARCHY SWEETNESS,	261	THE CHANGELING	54
LARGE			
BE LARGE AS AN OWL, BE SLICK AS A FROG,	86	PRAISE TO END!	39
LARGER			
OR PERCH AND PECK AT LARGER FLOWER-CROWNS,	152	THE SISKINS	12
LARGEST			
THE LARGEST CONTRIBUTIONS CAME	267	SAGINAW SONG	35
LARK			
THE FAT LARK SANG IN THE FIELD;	63	FIELD OF LIGHT	38
THE SHAPE OF A LARK RISES FROM A STONE;	168	FOURTH MEDITATN	25
WHEN I WAS A LARK, I SANG;	172	WHAT TELL BONES	39
TRAILING A THING--WHAT WAS IT?--SMALL AS A LARK	232	THE THING	2
LARKS			
LOOK WHAT THE LARKS DO.	59	THE LONG ALLEY	28
STOP THE LARKS. CAN I HAVE MY HEART BACK?	76	I NEED, I NEED	47
OF VEAL SOAKED IN MARSALA AND LITTLE LARKS ARRANGED ON A LONG PLATTER,	232	THE THING	19
YOU LARKS ALL DAY, YOU ROBINS RIGHT,	260	THE CHANGELING	22
LARK'S			
THE LARK'S MY HEART!	99	O, THOU OPENING	64
I'VE THE LARK'S WORD FOR IT, WHO SINGS ALONE:	156	THE DYING MAN	90
LARK-SWEET			
A LARK-SWEET LOVER IF EVER THERE WAS.	258	SONG (3)	3
LASH			
I WANT THE OLD RAGE, THE LASH OF PRIMORDIAL MILK!	56	THE LOST SON	107
LASHED			
THE BLUE SPRUCE LASHED LIKE A SURF AT THE DOOR.	12	MID-CNTRY BLOW	4
LASHING			
LUNGING INTO THE LASHING	41	BIG WIND	2
A VINE LASHING IN DRY FURY,	171	WHAT TELL BONES	30
LAST			
AS BRANCHES LOOSE LAST VESTIGES OF SNOW.	11	LIGHT BRIGHTER	10
THE LAST OF HARVESTING IS DONE.	14	COMING OF COLD	33
AND BOYS MOON AT GIRLS WITH LAST YEAR'S FATUOUS FACES,	24	VERNAL SENTIMNT	3
THE LAST TRICYCLE RUNS CRAZILY TO THE END OF THE WALK.	33	IDYLL	4
WE GROW INDIFFERENT TO DOG HOWLS, TO THE NESTLING'S LAST PEEP;	33	IDYLL	6
ESCAPES FROM THE MACHINE AT LAST.	33	HIGHWAY: MICH	20
THE TIGHT GRAINS PARTING AT LAST.	37	CUTTINGS (LATE)	8
LAST WORDS	48	LAST WORDS	T
IT'S MY LAST WALTZ WITH AN OLD ITCH.	60	THE LONG ALLEY	34
HAVE THE LAST LAUGH?	60	THE LONG ALLEY	61
LAST NIGHT I SLEPT IN THE PITS OF A TONGUE.	65	SHAPE OF FIRE	34
WHO KEEPS ME LAST?	72	WHERE KNOCK IS	46
FATHER OF TENSIONS, I'M DOWN TO MY SKIN AT LAST.	85	PRAISE TO END!	4
ETERNITY HOWLS IN THE LAST CRAGS,	89	UNFOLD! UNFOLD!	6
THE LAST TIME I NEARLY WHISPERED MYSELF AWAY.	89	UNFOLD! UNFOLD!	20
NOR THE MOSS, WOUND WITH THE LAST LIGHT.	102	ELEGY FOR JANE	17
LIKE THE HALF-DEAD, I HUG MY LAST SECRETS.	103	OLD LADY'S WRDS	5
THE FALL OF THE LAST ASH	103	OLD LADY'S WRDS	31
THOUGH EVERYTHING'S ASTONISHMENT AT LAST,	107	SIR JOHN DAVIES	79
LAST NIGHT YOU LAY A-SLEEPING? NO!	114	DINKY	13
IN THAT LAST WHILE, ETERNITY'S CONFINE,	120	THE DREAM	31

	PAGE	TITLE	LINE
LAST (CONTINUED)			
IN ANOTHER BEING, AT LAST.	126	WORDS FOR WIND	105
WRITHING UNTIL THE LAST	147	THE EXORCISM	22
IN THIS LAST PLACE OF LIGHT: HE DARES TO LIVE	156	THE DYING MAN	99
DOWN FROM BEHIND THE LAST RANGES,	158	FIRST MEDITATN	33
STILL LEANING TOWARD THE LAST PLACE THE SUN WAS.	163	I'M HERE	76
THE FLAT BRANCH OF THAT HEMLOCK HOLDS THE LAST OF THE SUN,	163	I'M HERE	83
LAST NIGHT I DREAMT OF A JAUNTIER PRINCIPLE OF ORDER;	165	HER BECOMING	30
WHO TURNED A CORNER IN TIME, WHEN AT LAST HE GREW A THUMB;	170	FOURTH MEDITATN	69
THE FIRST AND LAST OF ALL THINGS.	170	FOURTH MEDITATN	86
"AT LAST I'M MYSELF!"--AND HE UP AND DIED	177	KITTY-CAT BIRD	16
AT LAST ONE LONG UNDULANT RIPPLE,	190	AT OYSTER RIVER	11
ITS WINGS CATCHING A LAST GLINT OF THE REFLECTED SUNLIGHT.	190	AT OYSTER RIVER	23
THE WAY BLOCKED AT LAST BY A FALLEN FIR-TREE,	193	JOURNY INTERIOR	15
FEELING, I STILL DELIGHT IN MY LAST FALL.	197	THE LONG WATERS	32
ENDING AT LAST IN A HOPELESS SAND-RUT,	199	THE FAR FIELD	9
THE LAST GEESE CROSSING AGAINST THE REFLECTED AFTERLIGHT,	202	THE ROSE	17
CLIFF DISAPPEAR IN A LAST	210	HER TIME	19
HER TONGUE, AT THE LAST, THICK, BLACK AS AN OX'S.	223	ELEGY (2)	17
THE LAST WATCHER INDOORS, MOVING THE CARDPLAYERS CLOSER	230	THE STORM	26
SHAKING LOOSE THE LAST WIZENED ORANGES IN THE ORCHARD,	231	THE STORM	32
FOR THE GREAT LAST LEAP OF THE WAVE OVER THE BREAKWATER,	231	THE STORM	40
MAKE ME, O LORD, A LAST, A SIMPLE THING	240	IN EVEING AIR	8
AND I ROSE FROM A LAST DIMINISHING.	240	IN EVEING AIR	12
THUS I ENDURE THIS LAST PURE STRETCH OF JOY,	248	THE TREE, BIRD	22
OF MY LAST MIDNIGHT.	249	THE RESTORED	20
I SAW IN MY LAST SLEEP	258	SONG (3)	20
HERE'S THE LAST KISS OF MY LUCK:	259	SONG (3)	43
LAST-ABANDONED			
THE LAST-ABANDONED STALK ALWAYS QUIVERING	152	THE SISKINS	14
LATE			
THE LATE PEACH YIELDS A SUBTLE MUSK,	14	COMING OF COLD	1
LATE AUTUMN FRUIT IS ROTTED NOW.	14	COMING OF COLD	27
THAT LATE AUTUMNAL BLOOM, IS DEAD.	15	COMING OF COLD	41
OF LATE NOVEMBER DAYS.	139	PLAINT	12
A WALK IN LATE SUMMER	149	IN LATE SUMMER	T
A LATE ROSE RAVAGES THE CASUAL EYE,	149	IN LATE SUMMER	17
IN A WORLD ALWAYS LATE AFTERNOON,	171	WHAT TELL BONES	10
I WOULD BE A STREAM, WINDING BETWEEN GREAT STRIATED ROCKS IN LATE SUMMER;	188	THE LONGING	46
GREY FROM THE LONG WINTER, BURNT AT THE BASE IN LATE SUMMER.	193	JOURNY INTERIOR	10
AS LIGHT REFLECTS FROM A LAKE, IN LATE EVENING,	198	THE LONG WATERS	60
I RECALL HOW SHE HARRIED THE CHILDREN AWAY ALL THE LATE SUMMER	223	ELEGY (2)	12
OR A WIZENED ASTER IN LATE SEPTEMBER,	228	THE GERANIUM	4
FLASHING BETWEEN GOLD LEVELS OF THE LATE SUN,	232	THE THING	5
LATER			
CUTTINGS (LATER)	37	CUTTINGS (LATE)	T
LATER, I DID AND I DANCED IN THE SIMPLE WOOD.	90	UNFOLD! UNFOLD!	34
LATEST			
THEIR WIVES GO OUT ON SUNDAY BENEATH THE LATEST HAT.	27	CLAIRVOY WIDOW	8
LAUGH			
HAVE THE LAST LAUGH?	60	THE LONG ALLEY	61
I CAN'T LAUGH AT A PROCESSION OF DOGS.	64	SHAPE OF FIRE	13
I KNOW THE WAY OUT OF A LAUGH;	81	SENSIBILITY! LA	23
THIS FAT CAN'T LAUGH.	91	UNFOLD! UNFOLD!	57
I THINK OF THAT, AND LAUGH.	121	ALL EARTH, AIR	10
YET STILL LAUGH IN MY SLEEP.	130	THE OTHER	24
AND TOLD MY NEIGHBORS WHEN TO LAUGH.	138	THE SURLY ONE	3
I CAN'T LAUGH FROM A CRATER OF BURNING PITCH,	166	HER BECOMING	36
YOU'D BETTER NOT LAUGH; AND DON'T SAY, "POOH!"	177	KITTY-CAT BIRD	18
WITH NOT ONE TINY LAUGH	213	THE HAPPY THREE	14
AND, WITH A HARSH RASP OF A LAUGH AT HERSELF,	223	ELEGY (2)	10
I DO NOT LAUGH; I DO NOT CRY;	256	IN HYDROTHERAPY	9
LAUGHED			
THE SALT LAUGHED AND THE STONES;	63	FIELD OF LIGHT	40
SHE LAUGHED ME OUT, AND THEN SHE LAUGHED ME IN;	106	SIR JOHN DAVIES	56
SHE LAUGHED ME OUT, AND THEN SHE LAUGHED ME IN;	106	SIR JOHN DAVIES	56
AH, HOW SHE LAUGHED TO SEE	262	FOLLIES OF ADAM	16
LAUGHED A MASTER OF HUMP AND SNORT:	263	FOLLIES OF ADAM	30
HE LAUGHED, ONCE MORE.	263	FOLLIES OF ADAM	35
LAUGHING			
TILL I LAY IN THEIR LAPS, LAUGHING,	44	FRAU BAUMAN	28

	PAGE	TITLE	LINE
LAUGHING (CONTINUED)			
I, WHO CAME BACK FROM THE DEPTHS LAUGHING TOO LOUDLY, ...	198	THE LONG WATERS	73
LAUGHS			
MY LADY LAUGHS, DELIGHTING IN WHAT IS.	129	SHE	2
A YOUNG MOUTH LAUGHS AT A GIFT.	208	HER WORDS	1
LAUGHTER			
I HEARD YOUR LAUGHTER RUMBLE FROM MY BELLY.	25	DIM-WIT COUSIN	12
HIS LAUGHTER REDUCED THE SING-SONG OF PRATING, ...	29	THE GENTLE	7
LAUNDRY			
WHIPPING THE LINE OF WHITE LAUNDRY, BENDING THE COTTONWOODS APART, ...	194	JOURNY INTERIOR	44
LAURISCH			
MAX LAURISCH HAD THE GREENEST THUMB OF ALL.	224	OTTO	7
LAVATORY			
LONELY RECEPTION ROOM, LAVATORY, SWITCHBOARD, ...	46	DOLOR	5
LAVE			
LAVE ME, ULTIMATE WATERS.	88	PRAISE TO END!	98
LAW			
AND THE PRECISION THAT FOR YOU WAS ULTIMATE LAW:	29	THE REMINDER	4
"AND BESIDES, IT SEEMS THERE'S A LAW:	117	LADY AND BEAR	9
A MOST, MOST EXACTIOUS LAW	117	LADY AND BEAR	10
LAWN			
I FOUND MY CHOICE POSSESSIONS ON THE LAWN.	21	THE AUCTION	2
DEW DEEPENS ON THE FRESH-CUT LAWN;	33	IDYLL	7
ACROSS MY LAWN THE SOFT-BACKED CREATURES COME;	149	IN LATE SUMMER	3
ON THE BACK LAWN.	213	THE HAPPY THREE	16
COMING DOWN ON A PATCH OF LAWN:	235	ALL MORNING	38
LAWNMOWER			
FLYING UPWARD THROUGH THE KNIVES OF MY LAWNMOWER	151	SLUG	16
LAWS			
HE LIVED BEYOND THE TOUCH OF MORTAL LAWS.	28	THE FAVORITE	8
LAWYERS			
THE LAWYERS ALL ARE CUNNING, THE BUSINESS MEN ARE FAT, ...	27	CLAIRVOY WIDOW	7
THE DOCTORS, THE LAWYERS, THE COPS ARE ALL PAID--	112	SQUEEZE-BOX	42
LAXLY			
ONE LEAF-LIKE FOOT HUNG LAXLY	226	THE LIZARD	7
LAY			
THE WIND LAY MOTIONLESS IN THE LONG GRASS.	6	INTERLUDE	10
TILL I LAY IN THEIR LAPS, LAUGHING, ...	44	FRAU BAUMAN	28
AND I LAY DOWN WITH MY LIFE, ...	47	THE RETURN	10
LAY LIKE THE CATS DO	87	PRAISE TO END!	61
LAY ALL THE LONELY PASTURES OF THE DEAD;	106	SIR JOHN DAVIES	51
IN THE DEEP MIDDLE OF OURSELVES WE LAY;	106	SIR JOHN DAVIES	57
LAST NIGHT YOU LAY A-SLEEPING? NO!	114	DINKY	13
AND THE WHOLE MOTION OF THE SOUL LAY BARE:	135	THE RENEWAL	23
I LAY; I LANGUISHED THERE.	145	THE BEAST	15
THE LONG LUSH GRASS LAY STILL;	145	THE BEAST	18
WHEN I STAYED FOR BREATH, I LAY	146	THE SONG	11
LAY WITH THE DROSS OF DEATH.	147	THE EXORCISM	24
AND THE DUST LAY THICK ON MY EYELIDS,--WHO EVER WORE GOGGLES?--	193	JOURNY INTERIOR	24
SIX HOURS A DAY I LAY ME DOWN	256	IN HYDROTHERAPY	1
OF YOUR FINE-HONED LAY	271	THE REPLY	3
LAZILY			
AS A CHIP OR SHELL, FLOATING LAZILY WITH A SLOW CURRENT,	168	FOURTH MEDITATN	6
OR DRIFT LAZILY IN AND OUT OF THE WEEDS.	233	THE PIKE	7
LAZY			
THESE LAZY ASHES.	86	PRAISE TO END!	50
A LAZY NATURAL MAN, ...	130	THE OTHER	15
LEADEN			
I WEAR THE LEADEN WEIGHT	154	THE DYING MAN	19
LEADING			
THE TIGHT NERVES LEADING TO THE THROAT	22	SILENCE	17
UNPERPLEXED, IN A PLACE LEADING NOWHERE.	195	JOURNY INTERIOR	73
LEADS			
AND LEADS TO ERRORS IN THE MIND.	257	SANITARIUM	4
LEAF			
THE OAK STOOD WITH EACH LEAF STIFF AS A BELL.	12	MID-CNTRY BLOW	6
I STUDY THE LIVES ON A LEAF: THE LITTLE	50	THE MINIMAL	1
I WAS PURE AS A WORM ON A LEAF; I CHERISHED THE MOLD'S CHILDREN.	89	UNFOLD! UNFOLD!	27
SIMPLICITY'S SWEET THING, EITHER. A LEAF COULD DRAG YOU.	98	O, THOU OPENING	29
HER SKIRTS NOT TOUCHING A LEAF, ...	100	THE VISITANT	13

	PAGE	TITLE	LINE
LEAF (CONTINUED)			
THE GREEN, THE ALTERED LEAF,	125	WORDS FOR WIND	85
I KNOW IT ISN'T A WET LEAF,	151	SLUG	9
A BIRD, SMALL AS A LEAF,	163	I'M HERE	60
A LEAF, I WOULD LOVE THE LEAVES, DELIGHTING IN THE REDOLENT DISORDER OF THIS MORTAL LIFE,	188	THE LONGING	47
TURNING NOT A LEAF, NOT A RIPPLE.	190	AT OYSTER RIVER	19
AND A DROP OF RAIN WATER HANGS AT THE TIP OF A LEAF	204	THE ROSE	86
A DRIED STRAWBERRY LEAF,	226	THE LIZARD	17
A LIGHT LEAF ON A TREE, SHE SWAYED AWAY	241	THE SEQUEL	23
A LEAF UNALTERED BY THE MIDNIGHT SCENE,	248	THE TREE, BIRD	8
WITH THE BIRD, THE ABIDING LEAF,	251	ONCE MORE, RND	6
LEAF-LIGHT			
ONCE I FISHED FROM THE BANKS, LEAF-LIGHT AND HAPPY:	86	PRAISE TO END!	19
LEAF-LIKE			
ONE LEAF-LIKE FOOT HUNG LAXLY	226	THE LIZARD	7
LEAF-MOLD			
LEAF-MOLD, MANURE, LIME, PILED AGAINST SLIPPERY PLANKS.	38	ROOT CELLAR	9
LEAFY			
THE LEAFY MIND, THAT LONG WAS TIGHTLY FURLED,	11	LIGHT BRIGHTER	18
LEAN			
ALL SHADE IS LEAN, THE ANTIC BRANCH	14	COMING OF COLD	28
I QUAIL, LEAN TO BEGINNINGS, SHEATH-WET.	37	CUTTINGS (LATE)	11
THEY LEAN OVER THE PATH,	39	ORCHIDS	1
LEAN FROM THE TIERS AND BENCHES,	61	THE LONG ALLEY	72
AND SHOULD HE ARRIVE, WHY JUST LEAN YOURSELF BACK	113	TO A LADY ED	7
AND I SEEM TO LEAN FORWARD,	152	THE SISKINS	22
MAY THEY LEAN INTO LIGHT AND LIVE;	169	FOURTH MEDITATN	57
AND I LEAN, ALMOST INTO THE WATER,	233	THE PIKE	11
I LEAN, AND LOVE THESE MANIFOLD SHAPES,	233	THE PIKE	13
LEAVES, LEAVES, LEAN FORTH AND TELL ME WHAT I AM;	242	THE SEQUEL	27
I LEAN MY HEAD NEAR THE BRIMMING EDGE	269	GOB MUSIC	14
LEANED			
THE FLOWERS LEANED ON THEMSELVES, THE FLOWERS IN HOLLOWS;	66	SHAPE OF FIRE	76
RAPT, WE LEANED FORTH WITH WHAT WE COULD NOT SEE.	107	SIR JOHN DAVIES	88
WITH THEIR HARD SNOW; LEANED ON THE LONELY EYE;	143	SHIMMER OF EVIL	7
LEANING			
LEANING OVER A ROCK,	104	OLD LADY'S WRDS	41
LEANING ACROSS A SILL TO GREET THE DAWN?	154	THE DYING MAN	44
AM I BUT NOTHING, LEANING TOWARDS A THING?	156	THE DYING MAN	85
LEANING, OUT OF ALL BREATH,	161	I'M HERE	23
STILL LEANING TOWARD THE LAST PLACE THE SUN WAS.	163	I'M HERE	76
SHE LEANING OUT OF HER POT TOWARD THE WINDOW.	228	THE GERANIUM	19
LEANS			
THAT GOD THAT GOD LEANS DOWN HIS HEART TO HEAR.	144	ELEGY (1)	16
WHERE IT LEANS, TILTED EAST, A PERCH FOR THE OSPREY,	197	THE LONG WATERS	36
SHE LEANS INTO LIGHT, AND LIVES,	260	THE CHANGELING	10
LEAP			
THE DEAD LEAP AT THE THROAT, DESTROY	4	FEUD	13
I CAN LEAP, TRUE TO THE FIELD,	98	O, THOU OPENING	42
AND LEAP OVER MY EYE,	103	OLD LADY'S WRDS	16
THE STONES LEAP IN THE STREAM;	124	WORDS FOR WIND	34
AND SOMETIMES LOOK BEFORE YOU LEAP	181	MONOTONY SONG	27
IN TIME WHEN THE TROUT AND YOUNG SALMON LEAP FOR THE LOW-FLYING INSECTS,	197	THE LONG WATERS	33
FOR THE GREAT LAST LEAP OF THE WAVE OVER THE BREAKWATER,	231	THE STORM	40
CHILD OF THE DARK, HE CAN OUT LEAP THE SUN,	250	THE RIGHT THING	10
LEAPED			
AND HOW, ONCE STARTLED INTO TALK, THE LIGHT SYLLABLES LEAPED FOR HER,	102	ELEGY FOR JANE	3
THE WHILE MY BLOOD LEAPED WITH A WORDLESS SONG.	105	SIR JOHN DAVIES	14
WHAT SHAPE LEAPED FORWARD AT THE SENSUAL CRY?--	107	SIR JOHN DAVIES	67
AND THEN A JACKASS BRAYED. A LIZARD LEAPED MY FOOT.	247	I WAITED	14
LEAPING			
A RIVER'S LEAPING SOURCE	18	GENESIS	3
BUT I CAN'T GO LEAPING ALONE.	84	O LULL ME, LULL	32
THEIR SUNLIT LEAPING.	152	THE SISKINS	24
LEAPS			
OF WESTERN LIGHT LEAPS WITH INTENSER BLAZE	17	UNEXTINGUISHED	2
BY SNAILS, BY LEAPS OF FROG, I CAME HERE, SPIRIT.	89	UNFOLD! UNFOLD!	1
WHO LEAPS TO HEAVEN AT A SINGLE BOUND?	107	SIR JOHN DAVIES	80
A FIRE LEAPS ON ITSELF: I KNOW THAT FLAME.	131	SENTENTIOUS MAN	8
FLYING UPWARD IN LITTLE SKIPS AND ERRATIC LEAPS;	152	THE SISKINS	9

	PAGE	TITLE	LINE
LEAPS (CONTINUED)			
BY SWOOPS OF BIRD, BY LEAPS OF FISH, I LIVE.	167	HER BECOMING	91
THE ROSE LEAPS TO THIS GIRL;	262	FOLLIES OF ADAM	11
LEARN			
SOME LEARN THE ART OF THIEVING, AND SOME GROW UP TO BEG;	27	CLAIRVOY WIDOW	10
FOOLS WHO WILL NEVER LEARN;	31	LULL	18
I LEARN BY GOING WHERE I HAVE TO GO.	108	THE WAKING (2)	3
AND LEARN BY GOING WHERE I HAVE TO GO.	108	THE WAKING (2)	9
AND, LOVELY, LEARN BY GOING WHERE TO GO.	108	THE WAKING (2)	15
I LEARN BY GOING WHERE I HAVE TO GO.	108	THE WAKING (2)	19
THESE OLD BONES LIVE TO LEARN HER WANTON WAYS:	127	I KNEW A WOMAN	27
LEARNED			
BUT WHAT I LEARNED THERE, DANCING ALL ALONE,	105	SIR JOHN DAVIES	17
BUT ME AND A GIRL FRIEND LEARNED A LOT	111	SQUEEZE-BOX	10
EYE LEARNED FROM EYE, COLD LIP FROM SENSUAL LIP.	119	THE DREAM	4
WHAT BOOK, O LEARNED MAN, WILL SET ME RIGHT?	133	THE PURE FURY	2
I HAVE LEARNED TO SIT QUIETLY,	165	HER BECOMING	1
A LEARNED NIMBLE GIRL,	172	WHAT TELL BONES	56
ONE LEARNED OF THE ETERNAL;	199	THE FAR FIELD	18
I LEARNED NOT TO FEAR INFINITY,	200	THE FAR FIELD	50
A PRUSSIAN WHO LEARNED EARLY TO BE RUDE	224	OTTO	2
THE ONLY THING I EVER LEARNED	267	SAGINAW SONG	27
LEARNING			
A MAN LEARNING TO SING."	153	THE DYING MAN	15
LEAST			
A ROSE SWAYS LEAST.	66	SHAPE OF FIRE	62
I'VE LISTENED INTO THE LEAST WAVES.	77	BRING THE DAY!	28
SKIN'S THE LEAST OF ME. KISS THIS.	87	PRAISE TO END!	72
SHE KNEW THE GRAMMAR OF LEAST MOTION, SHE	120	THE DREAM	23
BUT MY LEAST MOTION CHANGED INTO A SONG,	132	SENTENTIOUS MAN	23
IN THE LEAST PLACE OF ITS LIFE,	171	WHAT TELL BONES	5
TWITCHING, TILTING TOWARD THE LEAST SOUND.	227	MEADOW MOUSE	16
BUT AT LEAST WE KNOW ONE NEEDN'T BLENCH	272	DUET	16
LEATHER			
I CIRCLED ON LEATHER PAWS	47	THE RETURN	1
LEATHERY			
THESE ANCIENT LEATHERY CRONES,	44	FRAU BAUMAN	32
LEAVE			
A SINGLE MISSTEP AND WE LEAVE THE QUICK.	5	PROGNOSIS	4
I START TO LEAVE MYSELF.	121	ALL EARTH, AIR	15
A MOUTH I CANNOT LEAVE.	137	LOVE'S PROGRESS	4
IN THE LONG FIELDS, I LEAVE MY FATHER'S EYE;	173	WHAT TELL BONES	86
WE MET TO LEAVE AGAIN	212	LIGHT LISTENED	19
LEAVES			
THE WOODS IN SPRING THE LEAVES THE SCENTED LANES	5	TO MY SISTER	2
THE RUSH OF WIND RIPPED OFF THE TENDER LEAVES	6	INTERLUDE	2
THE WALKER TRUDGES ANKLE-DEEP IN LEAVES;	12	SLOW SEASON	11
THE RIBS OF LEAVES LIE IN THE DUST,	14	COMING OF COLD	22
THE OAK LEAVES STRAIN TO BE UNBOUND,	15	COMING OF COLD	35
OLD HEDGEROWS KEEP THE LEAVES; THE PHLOX,	15	COMING OF COLD	40
AND WINTERGREEN BERRIES AND LEAVES STILL STUCK TO THE TOP,--	40	MOSS-GATHERING	5
ROTTEN LEAVES OR YELLOWY PETALS,	42	OLD FLORIST	5
THE LEAVES CURLED BACK IN ELABORATE CORINTHIAN SCROLLS;	43	CARNATIONS	2
MOLDS, WEEDS, DEAD LEAVES,	43	FLOWER DUMP	5
ALL THE LEAVES STUCK OUT THEIR TONGUES;	53	THE LOST SON	5
LOOK DOWN UNDER THE LEAVES.	55	THE LOST SON	63
A FINE HAZE MOVED OFF THE LEAVES;	57	THE LOST SON	144
THE LEAVES, THE LEAVES BECOME ME!	61	THE LONG ALLEY	78
THE LEAVES, THE LEAVES BECOME ME!	61	THE LONG ALLEY	78
PONDS WITH MOSS AND LEAVES FLOATING,	62	FIELD OF LIGHT	2
AND THE LEAVES CHANGED;	62	FIELD OF LIGHT	12
ON FAT LEAVES;	62	FIELD OF LIGHT	16
UNDER THE BLACKENED LEAVES,	62	FIELD OF LIGHT	23
LEAVES MORE THAN SHOES;	65	SHAPE OF FIRE	48
THE LEAVES LIKED IT.	74	I NEED, I NEED	17
THE FAR LEAVES WERE FOR IT.	77	BRING THE DAY!	10
LEAVES, DO YOU LIKE ME ANY?	78	BRING THE DAY!	33
THE AIR'S QUIET UNDER THE SMALL LEAVES.	78	BRING THE DAY!	41
A LIGHT SONG COMES FROM THE LEAVES.	90	UNFOLD! UNFOLD!	48
LIFTING A FEW TWIGS AND FLOATING LEAVES,	93	I CRY, LOVE!	48
THE LEAVES, THEIR WHISPERS TURNED TO KISSING;	102	ELEGY FOR JANE	8
COME RUNNING FROM THE LEAVES,	147	THE EXORCISM	15
DRIFTING THROUGH LEAVES, OAK AND MAPLE,	159	FIRST MEDITATN	88

	PAGE	TITLE	LINE

LEAVES (CONTINUED)

FROM UNDER THE DRY LEAVES, ... 162 — I'M HERE — 56
A GUST BLOWING THE LEAVES SUDDENLY UPWARD, ... 171 — WHAT TELL BONES — 29
I'M THICK WITH LEAVES AND TENDER AS A DOVE, ... 173 — WHAT TELL BONES — 89
A LEAF, I WOULD LOVE THE LEAVES, DELIGHTING IN THE REDOLENT
    DISORDER OF THIS MORTAL LIFE, ... 188 — THE LONGING — 47
THE YOUNG SNAKE, POISED IN GREEN LEAVES, WAITING FOR ITS
    FLY, ... 190 — AT OYSTER RIVER — 28
I HAVE HEARD, IN A DRIP OF LEAVES, ... 194 — JOURNY INTERIOR — 62
SUCH QUIET UNDER THE SMALL LEAVES!-- . . . . 221 — THE ABYSS — 82
HIS FEET LIKE SMALL LEAVES, ... 227 — MEADOW MOUSE — 8
STEAK GREASE STUCK TO HER FUZZY LEAVES. . . . . 228 — THE GERANIUM — 13
A THIN WHINE OF WIRES, A RATTLING AND FLAPPING OF LEAVES, . . . 230 — THE STORM — 6
ITS ALMOST-INVISIBLE WINGS, BUZZING, HITTING THE LOOSE
    LEAVES INTERMITTENTLY-- . . . . 234 — ALL MORNING — 32
THE LEAVES, THE TREES TURNED OUR TWO SHAPES AROUND. . . . . . 237 — THE TRANCED — 15
SHE STAYED IN LIGHT, AS LEAVES LIVE IN THE WIND, ... 241 — THE SEQUEL — 18
LEAVES, LEAVES, LEAN FORTH AND TELL ME WHAT I AM; . . . . 242 — THE SEQUEL — 27
LEAVES, LEAVES, LEAN FORTH AND TELL ME WHAT I AM; . . . . 242 — THE SEQUEL — 27
THE GREAT DAY BALANCES UPON THE LEAVES; . . . . 244 — INFIRMITY — 27
THE SLEEPY SOUND OF LEAVES IN A LIGHT WIND. . . . . 245 — THE DECISION — 6
WHAT THE FAT LEAVES HAVE, -- . . . . 258 — SONG (3) — 11
AND THE GREAT LEAVES CANCEL THEIR STEMS; . . . . 259 — SONG (3) — 50
AND THE CYCLAMEN LEAVES GLISTEN LIKE THE BACKS OF BABY
    TURTLES. . . . . 260 — THE CHANGELING — 15

LEAVING

THE RATS SOON WILL BE LEAVING, THE SNOW WILL COME IN." . . . 27 — CLAIRVOY WIDOW — 16
IS THE SEED LEAVING THE OLD BED? THESE BUDS ARE LIVE AS
    BIRDS. . . . . 56 — THE LOST SON — 102
LEAVING A PLACE FOR THE EYE TO REST, ... 233 — THE PIKE — 2
LINES UPON LEAVING A SANITARIUM . . . . 257 — SANITARIUM — T
THE WORLD IS WHERE WE FLING IT; I'M LEAVING WHERE I AM. . . . 260 — THE CHANGELING — 21

LECHERS

TRUE LECHERS LOVE THE FLESH, AND THAT IS ALL. . . . . 131 — SENTENTIOUS MAN — 6

LECHERY

THE INSTRUMENT OF LECHERY, ... 8 — PRAYER — 10

LED

A DONKEY PATH LED TO A SMALL PLATEAU. . . . . 247 — I WAITED — 21

LEE

DARK HOLLOWS SAID, LEE TO THE WIND, ... 54 — THE LOST SON — 28

LEECH

THE LEECH CLINGING TO A STONE WAITED; . . . . 100 — THE VISITANT — 8
LIKE A LEECH, LOOPING MYSELF ALONG, ... 209 — HER LONGING — 7

LEEKS

HE LIVES ON CARROTS, LEEKS AND HAY; . . . . 182 — THE HIPPO — 3
MOVING SERENELY AMONG THE LEEKS AND CABBAGES, ... 223 — ELEGY (2) — 20

LEER

"YOU SEE," HE SAID, WITH A SERPENT'S LEER, ... 115 — THE SERPENT — 23

LEFT

HAS LEFT ITS RAVAGE ON THE FIELD. . . . . 14 — COMING OF COLD — 25
I LEFT MY HOME WITH UNENCUMBERED WILL . . . . 21 — THE AUCTION — 15
ALL THE WINDOWS ARE BURNING! WHAT'S LEFT OF MY LIFE? . . . . 56 — THE LOST SON — 106
HAS THE BIRD LEFT? . . . . 56 — THE LOST SON — 114
THE DIRT LEFT MY HAND, VISITOR. . . . . 63 — FIELD OF LIGHT — 31
TO STARE INTO THE AFTER-LIGHT, THE GLITTER LEFT ON THE
    LAKE'S SURFACE, ... 67 — SHAPE OF FIRE — 88
MY LEFT SIDE'S TENDER. . . . . 97 — O, THOU OPENING — 3
FOR SHE FINALLY LEFT TOWN ON THE BAY CITY FREIGHT . . . . . . 112 — SQUEEZE-BOX — 40
WHAT'S LEFT IS LIGHT AS A SEED; . . . . 157 — FIRST MEDITATN — 18
AND THE UP-SPRING OF THE PLANK WHEN A FOOT LEFT THE RUNWAY. . 158 — FIRST MEDITATN — 47
IN MY LEFT EAR I HEAR THE LOUD SOUND OF A MINOR COLLAPSE. . . 165 — HER BECOMING — 29
HAPPINESS LEFT TO DOGS AND CHILDREN-- . . . . 187 — THE LONGING — 9
I HAVE LEFT THE BODY OF THE WHALE, BUT THE MOUTH OF THE
    NIGHT IS STILL WIDE; . . . . 188 — THE LONGING — 51
ALWAYS A SHARP TURN TO THE LEFT PAST A BARN CLOSE TO THE
    ROADSIDE, ... 193 — JOURNY INTERIOR — 25
I DANCE TO THE RIGHT, TO THE LEFT; . . . . 208 — HER WORDS — 6
ONCE WE WERE LEFT ALONE. . . . . 212 — LIGHT LISTENED — 4
WHO SAT WITH THE DEAD WHEN THE RELATIVES LEFT, ... 223 — ELEGY (2) — 8
AND PICKED AND PICKLED THE BEST, TO BE LEFT ON RICKETY
    DOORSTEPS. . . . . 223 — ELEGY (2) — 15
UNTIL THERE WAS NOTHING LEFT, ... 232 — THE THING — 16
SHE LEFT MY BODY, LIGHTER THAN A SEED; . . . . 241 — THE SEQUEL — 20

	PAGE	TITLE	LINE
LEFT (CONTINUED)			
THERE'S LITTLE LEFT I CARE TO CALL MY OWN.	244	INFIRMITY	8
HE LEFT HIS PANTS UPON A CHAIR:	264	THREE EPIGRAMS	7
LEFT-HAND			
THE HANDKERCHIEF TUCKED IN THE LEFT-HAND POCKET	29	THE REMINDER	5
LEG			
OR BALANCES WITH ONE LEG ON A HUMP	15	THE HERON	3
IT'S LESS THAN A LEG	54	THE LOST SON	46
LEGACY			
YOU CURSE THE LEGACY OF PAIN;	4	FEUD	6
LEGS			
THE TAIL AND SMALLER LEGS SLIPPING AND SLIDING SLOWLY BACKWARD--	159	FIRST MEDITATN	65
SAID, "I KNOW MY LEGS ADD UP TO TWO!	182	PHILANDER	2
AND FLICKER NEAR OUR LEGS LIKE KEROSENE	274	SUPPR W LINDSAY	36
LEISURELY			
THE CRABS TILT AND EAT, LEISURELY,	233	THE PIKE	5
LEMMINGS			
I WOULD WITH THE FISH, THE BLACKENING SALMON, AND THE MAD LEMMINGS,	188	THE LONGING	39
LENGTHEN			
I TEACH MY SIGHS TO LENGTHEN INTO SONGS,	135	THE RENEWAL	5
LENGTHS			
THE SEA'S UNEQUAL LENGTHS ANNOUNCED THY BIRTH	81	SENSIBILITY! LA	8
LENT			
LENT ME ONE VIRTUE, AND I LIVE THEREBY.	120	THE DREAM	24
LESS			
NOW LIGHT IS LESS; NOON SKIES ARE WIDE AND DEEP;	12	SLOW SEASON	1
IT'S LESS THAN A LEG	54	THE LOST SON	46
EVEN STEVEN ALL IS LESS:	75	I NEED, I NEED	23
THE ANIMAL'S CANDID GAZE, A SHADE LESS THAN FEATHERS, LIGHT'S BROKEN	98	O, THOU OPENING	22
YOU SHRINK TO SOMETHING LESS,	151	SLUG	23
MY BREATH GREW LESS. I LISTENED LIKE A BEAST.	166	HER BECOMING	53
THE HEART SAYS, I AM LESS;	172	WHAT TELL BONES	42
LESS AND LESS THE ILLUMINATED LIPS,	187	THE LONGING	7
LESS AND LESS THE ILLUMINATED LIPS,	187	THE LONGING	7
BUT SHRINKS INTO A HALF-LIFE, LESS THAN ITSELF,	187	THE LONGING	20
OR PERHAPS WITH ANOTHER MIND, LESS PECULIAR;	200	THE FAR FIELD	43
THE WAVES LESS THAN THE RIPPLES MADE BY RISING FISH,	203	THE ROSE	32
COME OFF IT MUCH LESS NEAT.	267	SAGINAW SONG	12
LESSENING			
THE OLD LOG SUBSIDES WITH THE LESSENING WAVES,	202	THE ROSE	20
LESSER			
OPEN LIKE A POOL, A LESSER PARSNIP,	209	HER LONGING	6
LET			
THEREFORE, O LORD, LET ME PRESERVE	8	PRAYER	19
LET LIGHT ATTEND ME TO THE GRAVE!	8	PRAYER	22
A COLD KEY LET ME IN	47	THE RETURN	8
LET THE KISSES RESOUND, FLAT LIKE A BUTCHER'S PALM;	56	THE LOST SON	104
LET THE GESTURES FREEZE; OUR DOOM IS ALREADY DECIDED.	56	THE LOST SON	105
TO LET HER LOOSE.	60	THE LONG ALLEY	54
TO LET ME IN:	77	BRING THE DAY!	9
I'VE LET MY NOSE OUT;	79	GIVE WAY, GATES	16
INDIGNATION? LET ME PERSUADE MORE SLOWLY:	98	O, THOU OPENING	31
LET SEED BE GRASS, AND GRASS TURN INTO HAY:	127	I KNEW A WOMAN	22
O ANGEL, LET ME LOOSE!"	136	THE SENSUALISTS	6
EVERY TIME I LET HIM, THE STRING WOULD BUST.	178	THE DONKEY	3
IF THEY LET YOU EAT AND SWEAR	228	IN VIOLENT WARD	4
LET OTHERS PROBE THE MYSTERY IF THEY CAN.	250	THE RIGHT THING	1
LET OTHERS DELVE THAT MYSTERY IF THEY CAN.	250	THE RIGHT THING	6
LET'S			
LET'S NOT HURRY. THE DEAD DON'T HURRY.	59	THE LONG ALLEY	18
LET'S PLAY BEFORE WE FORGET!	83	O LULL ME, LULL	20
"LET'S EAT!" SAID LINDSAY. "HERE WE'VE GOT THE MOON,	273	SUPPR W LINDSAY	15
LET'S EAT BEFORE THE MOONLIGHT ALL RUNS OUT."	273	SUPPR W LINDSAY	29
LETTER			
WITH ONLY ONE LETTER,--	179	MYRTLE	11
LEVEL			
THE RIVER OVERFLOWS THE LEVEL FIELD.	11	LIGHT BRIGHTER	8
OUR FEET ARE SOMETIMES LEVEL WITH THE SKY,	13	PRAISE PRAIRIE	6
THE MEADOW INSECTS MADE A LEVEL NOISE.	247	I WAITED	4
BELOW, THE BRIGHT SEA WAS, THE LEVEL WAVES,	247	I WAITED	22

		PAGE	TITLE	LINE
LEVELS				
	FLASHING BETWEEN GOLD LEVELS OF THE LATE SUN,	232	THE THING	5
LEVITY				
	MY SHAPE A LEVITY--YES!--	165	HER BECOMING	4
LEWD				
	THOSE LEWD MONKEY-TAILS HANGING FROM DRAINHOLES,--	39	WEED PULLER	3
	RENEW THE LIGHT, LEWD WHISPER.	65	SHAPE OF FIRE	55
	O WHAT LEWD MUSIC CREPT INTO OUR EARS!	106	SIR JOHN DAVIES	46
	LEWD, TINY, CARELESS LIVES	147	THE EXORCISM	16
LIBERTIES				
	I TAKE THE LIBERTIES A SHORT LIFE PERMITS--	173	WHAT TELL BONES	90
LIBRARY				
	THE LIBRARY USED AS A CARD ROOM INSTEAD	32	SALE	11
LICE				
	LICE TETHERED TO LONG LIMP SUBTERRANEAN WEEDS,	50	THE MINIMAL	4
LICHEN				
	OF LICHEN AROUND STONES?	139	PLAINT	16
	AND I HEAR THE LICHEN SPEAK,	194	JOURNY INTERIOR	48
LICKING				
	THAT BLOSSOMED IN SOOT; A BLACK CAT LICKING ITS PAW;	29	THE REMINDER	2
LID				
	BUT MORNING LIGHT COMES TAPPING AT THE LID,	17	UNEXTINGUISHED	9
	ONE GREENISH LID LIFTS A BIT HIGHER,	226	THE LIZARD	23
LIE				
	THE RIBS OF LEAVES LIE IN THE DUST,	14	COMING OF COLD	22
	THE PARTICLES OF BEING LIE;	19	AGNST DISASTER	6
	THEIR BODIES CANNOT LIE:	121	ALL EARTH, AIR	17
	THE DEAD WILL NOT LIE STILL,	148	THE SMALL	22
	IT LIES UPON US TO UNDO THE LIE	149	IN LATE SUMMER	19
	--OR TO LIE NAKED IN SAND,	200	THE FAR FIELD	38
	AND I LIE HERE THINKING IN BLEAK BOFIN TOWN	216	THE SHY MAN	18
	I LIE HERE AND THINKING, "I AM NOT ALONE."	216	THE SHY MAN	19
	WE LIE CLOSER ON THE GRITTY PILLOW,	231	THE STORM	38
	AND THE SMALL FISH LIE, WITHOUT SHADOW, MOTIONLESS,	233	THE PIKE	6
	YE LITTLES, LIE MORE CLOSE!	240	IN EVEING AIR	7
	TO THE NORTH OF A MOUTH I LIE,	258	SONG (3)	8
LIES				
	THE RAMBLING LIES INVENTED FOR THE SICK.	5	PROGNOSIS	2
	THE CORE LIES SEALED.	9	THE ADAMANT	12
	THE SEASON'S WRECKAGE LIES ABOUT,	14	COMING OF COLD	26
	IT LIES UPON US TO UNDO THE LIE	149	IN LATE SUMMER	19
	SO MUCH HE JUST LIES IN ONE CORNER,	227	MEADOW MOUSE	13
LIFE				
	THE HIGHER THINGS IN LIFE DO NOT	25	VERSE W ALLUSNS	5
	TO SPOIL COLLECTIVE LIFE.	31	LULL	6
	ROSE ON SUCH LOPPED LIMBS TO A NEW LIFE?	37	CUTTINGS (LATE)	4
	NOTHING WOULD GIVE UP LIFE:	38	ROOT CELLAR	10
	TUGGING ALL DAY AT PERVERSE LIFE:	39	WEED PULLER	9
	AS IF I HAD COMMITTED, AGAINST THE WHOLE SCHEME OF LIFE, A DESECRATION.	40	MOSS-GATHERING	13
	OR FAN LIFE INTO WILTED SWEET-PEAS WITH HIS HAT,	42	OLD FLORIST	9
	AND I LAY DOWN WITH MY LIFE,	47	THE RETURN	10
	I ASKED: MAY THE BLESSINGS OF LIFE, O LORD, DESCEND ON THE LIVING.	48	JUDGE NOT	6
	ALL THE WINDOWS ARE BURNING! WHAT'S LEFT OF MY LIFE?	56	THE LOST SON	106
	IT'S A DEAR LIFE I CAN TOUCH.	76	I NEED, I NEED	58
	EASY THE LIFE OF THE MOUTH. WHAT A LUST FOR RIPENESS!	90	UNFOLD! UNFOLD!	39
	SHE WAS TOO MUCH FOR ONE, YOU CAN BET YOUR LIFE:	114	THE COW	3
	HE DIDN'T LIKE HIS KIND OF LIFE;	115	THE SERPENT	5
	SHE WAKES THE ENDS OF LIFE.	125	WORDS FOR WIND	89
	A LIVELY THING CAN COME TO LIFE AGAIN.	129	SHE	12
	AN EXULTATION TAKES US OUTSIDE LIFE:	132	SENTENTIOUS MAN	25
	THAT APPETITE FOR LIFE SO RAVENOUS	133	THE PURE FURY	16
	FORMS OF HIS SECRET LIFE	147	THE EXORCISM	23
	BUT YOU, LOOSE TOE FROM THE OLD LIFE,	151	SLUG	10
	I DIE INTO THIS LIFE, ALONE YET NOT ALONE.	155	THE DYING MAN	59
	BUT THE RIND, OFTEN, HATES THE LIFE WITHIN.	157	FIRST MEDITATN	13
	SO THE SPIRIT TRIES FOR ANOTHER LIFE,	159	FIRST MEDITATN	66
	OR LIVE THE DANGEROUS LIFE OF AN INSECT.	166	HER BECOMING	37
	TO THESE I CRIED MY LIFE--	166	HER BECOMING	63
	BUT A TIME COMES WHEN THE VAGUE LIFE OF THE MOUTH NO LONGER SUFFICES;	168	FOURTH MEDITATN	18
	IN THE LEAST PLACE OF ITS LIFE,	171	WHAT TELL BONES	5

	PAGE	TITLE	LINE
LIFE (CONTINUED)			
I TAKE THE LIBERTIES A SHORT LIFE PERMITS--	173	WHAT TELL BONES	90
I'M WET WITH ANOTHER LIFE.	173	WHAT TELL BONES	95
A LEAF, I WOULD LOVE THE LEAVES, DELIGHTING IN THE REDOLENT DISORDER OF THIS MORTAL LIFE,	188	THE LONGING	47
MAY YOU LIVE OUT YOUR LIFE	217	WISH YOUNG WIFE	6
NEITHER IN NOR OUT OF THIS LIFE.	220	THE ABYSS	23
HOW CAN I DREAM EXCEPT BEYOND THIS LIFE?	221	THE ABYSS	61
WHAT'S THE WORST PORTION IN THIS MORTAL LIFE?	246	THE MARROW	5
TO SLEEP IS ALL MY LIFE. IN SLEEP'S HALF-DEATH,	246	THE MARROW	14
YET WHEN I SIGHED, I STOOD OUTSIDE MY LIFE,	248	THE TREE, BIRD	7
BEARING ITS LIFE AND MORE, A DOUBLE SOUND,	248	THE TREE, BIRD	11
NOW I ADORE MY LIFE	251	ONCE MORE, RND	5
LIFE-FORCE			
AND KNOW THAT TRUE LOVE IS MORE THAN A LIFE-FORCE	113	TO A LADY ED	3
LIFT			
THE WIDE WINGS FLAP BUT ONCE TO LIFT HIM UP.	15	THE HERON	11
AND LIFT UP A PATCH, DARK-GREEN, THE KIND FOR LINING CEMETERY BASKETS,	40	MOSS-GATHERING	2
LIFTED			
MY HEART LIFTED UP WITH THE GREAT GRASSES;	63	FIELD OF LIGHT	46
TO FOLLOW THE DROPS SLIDING FROM A LIFTED OAR,	67	SHAPE OF FIRE	90
LIFTING			
LIFTING THE YOUNG PLANTS WITH TWO FINGERS,	42	TRANSPLANTING	3
AND MIST LIFTING OUT OF THE BROWN CAT-TAILS;	67	SHAPE OF FIRE	87
BY THE LIFTING OF THE TAIL OF A NEIGHBOR'S CAT,	82	SENSIBILITY! LA	35
LIFTING A FEW TWIGS AND FLOATING LEAVES,	93	I CRY, LOVE!	48
LIFTING A NETHER LIP	130	THE OTHER	3
A SNAKE LIFTING ITS HEAD;	163	I'M HERE	88
AS A BLIND MAN, LIFTING A CURTAIN, KNOWS IT IS MORNING,	195	JOURNY INTERIOR	74
LIFTING ME HIGH OVER THE FOUR-FOOT STEMS, THE MRS. RUSSELLS, AND HIS OWN ELABORATE HYBRIDS,	203	THE ROSE	54
LIFTS			
OR SEND OFF A CAR WITH VAGUE LIFTS OF A HAND.	47	DOUBLE FEATURE	8
ONE GREENISH LID LIFTS A BIT HIGHER,	226	THE LIZARD	23
LIGHT			
NO LONGER QUICK WITH LIGHT,	4	DEATH PIECE	2
THE LIGHT ESSENTIAL TO YOUR NEED.	4	FEUD	11
THE CHAOS GREW AS HOUR BY HOUR THE LIGHT	6	INTERLUDE	5
LET LIGHT ATTEND ME TO THE GRAVE!	8	PRAYER	22
THE LIGHT COMES BRIGHTER	11	LIGHT BRIGHTER	T
THE LIGHT COMES BRIGHTER FROM THE EAST; THE CAW	11	LIGHT BRIGHTER	1
NOW LIGHT IS LESS; NOON SKIES ARE WIDE AND DEEP;	12	SLOW SEASON	1
DENSE TREES NO LONGER HOLD THE LIGHT,	14	COMING OF COLD	30
AMONG THE TREES THAT FACE THE CORNER LIGHT.	16	THE BAT	6
OF WESTERN LIGHT LEAPS WITH INTENSER BLAZE	17	UNEXTINGUISHED	2
BUT MORNING LIGHT COMES TAPPING AT THE LID,	17	UNEXTINGUISHED	9
AND GULLIES WASHED WITH LIGHT.	34	NIGHT JOURNEY	19
OR MAKE THE DUST BUZZ WITH A LIGHT SPRAY,	42	OLD FLORIST	7
WITH BUCK STILL TIED TO THE LOG, ON COMES THE LIGHT.	47	DOUBLE FEATURE	1
I NOTICE A TREE, ARSENICAL GREY IN THE LIGHT, OR THE SLOW	47	DOUBLE FEATURE	10
ENSHROUD ME WITH LIGHT! O WHIRLING! O TERRIBLE LOVE!	48	LAST WORDS	10
THESE SWEEPS OF LIGHT UNDO ME.	57	THE LOST SON	118
THERE WAS ALWAYS A SINGLE LIGHT	57	THE LOST SON	130
THE LIGHT IN THE MORNING CAME SLOWLY OVER THE WHITE	57	THE LOST SON	135
THE ROSE, THE CHRYSANTHEMUM TURNED TOWARD THE LIGHT.	57	THE LOST SON	146
THE LIGHT MOVED SLOWLY OVER THE FROZEN FIELD,	58	THE LOST SON	155
LIGHT TRAVELED OVER THE WIDE FIELD;	58	THE LOST SON	159
WAS IT LIGHT?	58	THE LOST SON	164
WAS IT LIGHT WITHIN?	58	THE LOST SON	165
WAS IT LIGHT WITHIN LIGHT?	58	THE LOST SON	166
WAS IT LIGHT WITHIN LIGHT?	58	THE LOST SON	166
DROWSING IN SOFT LIGHT, PETALS PULSING.	61	THE LONG ALLEY	76
LIGHT AIRS! LIGHT AIRS! A PIERCE OF ANGELS!	61	THE LONG ALLEY	77
LIGHT AIRS! LIGHT AIRS! A PIERCE OF ANGELS!	61	THE LONG ALLEY	77
A FIELD OF LIGHT	62	FIELD OF LIGHT	T
AND I WALKED, I WALKED THROUGH THE LIGHT AIR;	63	FIELD OF LIGHT	51
RENEW THE LIGHT, LEWD WHISPER.	65	SHAPE OF FIRE	55
THE LIGHT, THE FULL SUN	67	SHAPE OF FIRE	79
TO KNOW THAT LIGHT FALLS AND FILLS, OFTEN WITHOUT OUR KNOWING,	67	SHAPE OF FIRE	92
LIGHT AS A HAND AMONG BLOSSOMS,	78	BRING THE DAY!	39
THE LIGHT TURNS.	82	SENSIBILITY! LA	42

		PAGE	TITLE	LINE
LIGHT (CONTINUED)				
O MY LOVE'S LIGHT AS A DUCK		83	O LULL ME, LULL	12
LIGHT FATTENS THE ROCK.		83	O LULL ME, LULL	19
THE LIGHT BECOMES ME.		88	PRAISE TO END!	101
A LIGHT SONG COMES FROM THE LEAVES.		90	UNFOLD! UNFOLD!	48
A SLOW SIGH SAYS YES. AND LIGHT SIGHS;		90	UNFOLD! UNFOLD!	49
GO WHERE LIGHT IS.		90	UNFOLD! UNFOLD!	56
THE DARK HAS ITS OWN LIGHT.		98	O, THOU OPENING	32
A LIGHT BREATHER		101	LIGHT BREATHER	T
TURNING IN THE LIGHT WITH ITS TENDRILS;		101	LIGHT BREATHER	6
AND HOW, ONCE STARTLED INTO TALK, THE LIGHT SYLLABLES LEAPED FOR HER,		102	ELEGY FOR JANE	3
NOR THE MOSS, WOUND WITH THE LAST LIGHT.		102	ELEGY FOR JANE	17
ONCE I WAS SWEET WITH THE LIGHT OF MYSELF,		103	OLD LADY'S WRDS	39
LIGHT ALTERED LIGHT ALONG THE LIVING GROUND.		106	SIR JOHN DAVIES	34
LIGHT ALTERED LIGHT ALONG THE LIVING GROUND.		106	SIR JOHN DAVIES	34
WE PLAYED WITH DARK AND LIGHT AS CHILDREN SHOULD.		107	SIR JOHN DAVIES	66
IMPALED ON LIGHT, AND WHIRLING SLOWLY DOWN.		107	SIR JOHN DAVIES	72
HER LOOK WAS MORNING IN THE DYING LIGHT.		107	SIR JOHN DAVIES	84
THE WORD OUTLEAPS THE WORLD, AND LIGHT IS ALL.		107	SIR JOHN DAVIES	96
LIGHT TAKES THE TREE; BUT WHO CAN TELL US HOW?		108	THE WAKING (2)	10
LIGHT HARDENED ON THE WATER WHERE WE WERE;		119	THE DREAM	6
I TOUCHED HER SHADOW WHEN THE LIGHT DELAYED;		119	THE DREAM	13
I STAYED, AND LIGHT FELL		123	WORDS FOR WIND	21
LIGHT, LIGHT, WHERE'S MY REPOSE?		126	WORDS FOR WIND	92
LIGHT, LIGHT, WHERE'S MY REPOSE?		126	WORDS FOR WIND	92
SHE PLAYED IT QUICK, SHE PLAYED IT LIGHT AND LOOSE;		127	I KNEW A WOMAN	17
SHE KNOWS THE SPEECH OF LIGHT, AND MAKES IT PLAIN		129	SHE	11
THE LIGHT AIR TAKES MY BEING'S BREATH AWAY;		134	THE PURE FURY	23
LIGHT STRIDES THE ROSE;		137	LOVE'S PROGRESS	8
LIGHT OF MY SPIRIT, LIGHT		137	LOVE'S PROGRESS	14
LIGHT OF MY SPIRIT, LIGHT		137	LOVE'S PROGRESS	14
OR AFTERNOON OF LIGHT		139	PLAINT	10
A MAN ALIVE, FROM ALL LIGHT I MUST FALL.		140	THE SWAN	12
AND SHE IS WHAT I WOULD. IN THIS LIGHT AIR,		140	THE SWAN	17
BENT DOWN THEIR BIRDS: THE LIGHT WAVES TOOK THE WAVES;		143	SHIMMER OF EVIL	2
--THERE WAS NO LIGHT; THERE WAS NO LIGHT AT ALL:		143	SHIMMER OF EVIL	5
--THERE WAS NO LIGHT; THERE WAS NO LIGHT AT ALL:		143	SHIMMER OF EVIL	5
--THERE WAS NO LIGHT; THERE WAS NO LIGHT AT ALL:		143	SHIMMER OF EVIL	10
--THERE WAS NO LIGHT; THERE WAS NO LIGHT AT ALL:		143	SHIMMER OF EVIL	10
--THERE WAS NO LIGHT; THERE WAS NO LIGHT AT ALL:		143	SHIMMER OF EVIL	15
--THERE WAS NO LIGHT; THERE WAS NO LIGHT AT ALL.		143	SHIMMER OF EVIL	15
AND THINGS THROW LIGHT ON THINGS,		148	THE SMALL	23
IN THE WEAK LIGHT THEY WANDER, EACH ALONE.		149	IN LATE SUMMER	4
IT IS NO TRICK OF CHANGE OR CHANCE OF LIGHT.		150	IN LATE SUMMER	26
LIGHT AS SEED BLOWING OFF THISTLES!		152	THE SISKINS	21
CAUGHT IN THE DYING LIGHT,		154	THE DYING MAN	16
ALL WOMEN LOVED DANCE IN A DYING LIGHT--		156	THE DYING MAN	78
DESCEND, O GENTLEST LIGHT, DESCEND, DESCEND.		156	THE DYING MAN	87
IN THIS LAST PLACE OF LIGHT: HE DARES TO LIVE		156	THE DYING MAN	99
WHAT'S LEFT IS LIGHT AS A SEED;		157	FIRST MEDITATN	18
IN A LIGHT WIND.		163	I'M HERE	85
LIGHT AS A PETAL FALLING UPON STONE.		165	HER BECOMING	12
THE LIGHT AIR SLOWED: IT WAS NOT NIGHT OR DAY.		166	HER BECOMING	56
I LIVE IN AIR; THE LONG LIGHT IS MY HOME;		167	HER BECOMING	93
A LIGHT WIND RISES: I BECOME THE WIND.		167	HER BECOMING	95
IN THE WHITE KINGDOMS, I WAS LIGHT AS A SEED,		168	FOURTH MEDITATN	15
A LIGHT WIND STIRS IN THE PINE NEEDLES.		168	FOURTH MEDITATN	24
MAY THEY LEAN INTO LIGHT AND LIVE;		169	FOURTH MEDITATN	57
I DRINK MY TEARS IN A PLACE WHERE ALL LIGHT COMES.		170	FOURTH MEDITATN	78
WHO ELSE SWEATS LIGHT FROM A STONE?		170	FOURTH MEDITATN	81
A WEDGE OF HEAVEN'S LIGHT, AUTUMNAL SONG.		173	WHAT TELL BONES	68
THE BAREST SPEECH OF LIGHT AMONG THE STONES.		173	WHAT TELL BONES	71
THE LIGHT CRIES OUT, AND I AM THERE TO HEAR--		188	THE LONGING	32
SILENT, IN THE DEEPENING LIGHT,		190	AT OYSTER RIVER	8
THE WIND SLACKENS, LIGHT AS A MOTH FANNING A STONE:		190	AT OYSTER RIVER	17
A TWILIGHT WIND, LIGHT AS A CHILD'S BREATH		190	AT OYSTER RIVER	18
NOW, IN THIS WANING OF LIGHT,		191	AT OYSTER RIVER	57
IN THE DARK AND LIGHT OF A DRY PLACE,		194	JOURNY INTERIOR	60
DELIGHTING IN SURFACE CHANGE, THE GLITTER OF LIGHT ON WAVES,		195	JOURNY INTERIOR	67
TURNING TOWARD THE OTHER SIDE OF LIGHT,		195	JOURNY INTERIOR	69
WHERE LIGHT IS STONE.		196	THE LONG WATERS	12
SWIMMING SLOWLY, ITS BACK RUFFLED BY THE LIGHT CROSS-WINDS,		197	THE LONG WATERS	53

	PAGE	TITLE	LINE
LIGHT (CONTINUED)			
AS LIGHT REFLECTS FROM A LAKE, IN LATE EVENING,	198	THE LONG WATERS	60
MY BODY SHIMMERS WITH A LIGHT FLAME.	198	THE LONG WATERS	66
THE DYING OF TIME IN THE WHITE LIGHT OF TOMORROW,	200	THE FAR FIELD	52
THE LIGHT HEIGHTENED,	202	THE ROSE	28
AS WHEN A SHIP SAILS WITH A LIGHT WIND--	203	THE ROSE	31
THE BLUEBIRD, LOVER OF HOLES IN OLD WOOD, LILTING ITS LIGHT SONG,	204	THE ROSE	66
AND GENTLY THE LIGHT ENTERS THE SLEEPING SOUL,	204	THE ROSE	76
I THINK OF THE ROCK SINGING, AND LIGHT MAKING ITS OWN SILENCE,	204	THE ROSE	79
ROOTED IN STONE, KEEPING THE WHOLE OF LIGHT,	205	THE ROSE	112
OF LIGHT ON THE FAR	210	HER TIME	18
LIGHT LISTENED	212	LIGHT LISTENED	T
LIGHT DEEPENED TO A BELL,	212	LIGHT LISTENED	8
SHE CHANGED WITH CHANGING LIGHT.	212	LIGHT LISTENED	18
LIGHT LISTENED WHEN SHE SANG.	212	LIGHT LISTENED	24
IS SHE THE ALL OF LIGHT?	215	HIS FOREBODING	16
I HEAR THE FLOWERS DRINKING IN THEIR LIGHT,	222	THE ABYSS	91
THERE IS ONE LIGHT ON THE MOUNTAIN.	230	THE STORM	9
THE STONES RANG WITH LIGHT SOUND;	237	THE TRANCED	14
OUR EYES FIXED ON A POINT OF LIGHT SO FINE	237	THE TRANCED	16
OUR BODIES LIGHT, AND LIGHTED BY THE MOON.	237	THE TRANCED	20
ALL NATURAL SHAPES BLAZING UNNATURAL LIGHT.	239	IN A DARK TIME	18
DARK, DARK MY LIGHT, AND DARKER MY DESIRE.	239	IN A DARK TIME	19
I LOOK DOWN THE FAR LIGHT	240	IN EVEING AIR	13
LIGHT SHIFTS UPON THE WALL.	240	IN EVEING AIR	21
SHE STAYED IN LIGHT, AS LEAVES LIVE IN THE WIND,	241	THE SEQUEL	18
A LIGHT LEAF ON A TREE, SHE SWAYED AWAY	241	THE SEQUEL	23
LIGHT ON ITS ROUNDS, A PURE EXTREME OF LIGHT	244	INFIRMITY	14
LIGHT ON ITS ROUNDS, A PURE EXTREME OF LIGHT	244	INFIRMITY	14
THE CHANGE FROM DARK TO LIGHT OF THE SLOW MOON,	244	INFIRMITY	22
THE SLEEPY SOUND OF LEAVES IN A LIGHT WIND.	245	THE DECISION	6
WHEN LIGHT DIVIDED ON A STORM-TOSSED TREE.	246	THE MARROW	20
THE SWEET LIGHT MET ME AS I WALKED TOWARD	248	THE TREE, BIRD	3
IN THE STILL POINT OF LIGHT	249	THE RESTORED	19
LIGHT POEM	255	LIGHT POEM	T
WREN-SONG IN TRELLIS: A LIGHT ECSTASY OF BUTTERFLIES COURTING,	255	LIGHT POEM	1
LIGHT STAYED ALL NIGHT,	258	SONG (3)	14
SHE LEANS INTO LIGHT, AND LIVES,	260	THE CHANGELING	10
I CAN HEAR LIGHT ON A DRY DAY.	260	THE CHANGELING	20
BETWEEN CLIFFS OF LIGHT	265	HARSH COUNTRY	5
THE SUDDEN LIGHT SPILLED ON THE FLOOR LIKE CREAM	273	SUPPR W LINDSAY	12
WE'VE GOT THE LIVING LIGHT, BUT WHERE'S THE FOOD?"	273	SUPPR W LINDSAY	16
HALF SIDEWAYS IN THE SHIFTING LIGHT,	273	SUPPR W LINDSAY	20
AFTER A WHILE THE LIGHT BEGAN TO WANE	274	SUPPR W LINDSAY	35
LIGHT-BULB			
A SPIDER EASES HIMSELF DOWN FROM A SWAYING LIGHT-BULB,	231	THE STORM	34
LIGHT-CORD			
A SWAYING LIGHT-CORD, THEN RAN HALF-WAY BACK.	273	SUPPR W LINDSAY	25
LIGHTED			
BE A BODY LIGHTED WITH LOVE,	98	O, THOU OPENING	44
I SEE A SHAPE, LIGHTED WITH LOVE,	165	HER BECOMING	11
OUR BODIES LIGHT, AND LIGHTED BY THE MOON.	237	THE TRANCED	20
LIGHTER			
LIGHTER THAN BELLS,	88	PRAISE TO END!	95
LIGHTER THAN FINCHES,	200	THE FAR FIELD	35
SHE LEFT MY BODY, LIGHTER THAN A SEED;	241	THE SEQUEL	20
LIGHTLY			
AND THEIR SNUFF-LADEN BREATH BLOWING LIGHTLY OVER ME IN MY FIRST SLEEP.	44	FRAU BAUMAN	35
RUNNING LIGHTLY OVER SPONGY GROUND,	54	THE LOST SON	34
A SINGLE WAVE STARTS LIGHTLY AND EASILY SHOREWARD,	93	I CRY, LOVE!	46
LIGHTLY: SO BUDS UNLEAVE;	130	THE OTHER	4
SLAPPING LIGHTLY AGAINST A SUNKEN LOG.	190	AT OYSTER RIVER	14
OVER THE THIN, FEATHERY RIPPLES BREAKING LIGHTLY AGAINST THE IRREGULAR SHORELINE--	197	THE LONG WATERS	50
PITCHING LIGHTLY OVER THE HIGH HEDGEROWS, DEE-DEEING,	234	ALL MORNING	25
LIGHTNING			
OR WHEN DARK FOLLOWS DARK IN LIGHTNING RIFT.	8	THE SIGNALS	6
LIGHTS			
THE LIGHTS IN THE KITCHENS GO OUT; MOTH WINGS UNFURL;	33	IDYLL	3

	PAGE	TITLE	LINE
LIGHTS (CONTINUED)			
THE LIGHTS TILTING UP, SKYWARD, AS WE COME OVER A LITTLE RISE,	158	FIRST MEDITATN	24
DYING BRIGHTLY UNDER THE STREET LIGHTS SUNK IN COARSE CONCRETE,	193	JOURNY INTERIOR	29
AND NO LIGHTS BEHIND, IN THE BLURRED SIDE-MIRROR,	199	THE FAR FIELD	7
LIGHT'S			
THE ANIMAL'S CANDID GAZE, A SHADE LESS THAN FEATHERS, LIGHT'S BROKEN	98	O, THOU OPENING	22
I LIVE IN LIGHT'S EXTREME; I STRETCH IN ALL DIRECTIONS;	173	WHAT TELL BONES	82
BY LIGHT'S EXTREME,	261	THE CHANGELING	40
LIKE			
AND, STALKING LIKE A CRANE,	7	ORDERS FOR DAY	13
THE BLUE SPRUCE LASHED LIKE A SURF AT THE DOOR.	12	MID-CNTRY BLOW	4
BUT MY EAR STILL KEPT THE SOUND OF THE SEA LIKE A SHELL.	12	MID-CNTRY BLOW	8
CLOUDS GLOW LIKE COALS JUST FRESH FROM FIRE, A FLARE	17	UNEXTINGUISHED	1
"CLAIRVOYANT WIDOW LADY, WITH AN EYE LIKE A TELESCOPE,	27	CLAIRVOY WIDOW	17
THE SUMMER HOUSE SHAPED LIKE A VILLAGE BAND STAND	32	SALE	7
HUNG DOWN LONG YELLOW EVIL NECKS, LIKE TROPICAL SNAKES.	38	ROOT CELLAR	5
COILED GREEN AND THICK, LIKE DRIPPING SMILAX,	39	WEED PULLER	8
THICK AND CUSHIONY, LIKE AN OLD-FASHIONED DOORMAT,	40	MOSS-GATHERING	3
THE HALF-GROWN CHRYSANTHEMUMS STARING UP LIKE ACCUSERS,	43	CHILD ON GRNHSE	3
A LINE OF ELMS PLUNGING AND TOSSING LIKE HORSES,	43	CHILD ON GRNHSE	6
LIKE THAT CLEAR AUTUMNAL WEATHER OF ETERNITY,	43	CARNATIONS	6
TWINED LIKE FINE HAIR,	43	FLOWER DUMP	8
STEMS, JOINTED LIKE CORN,	44	FRAU BAUMAN	10
LIKE WITCHES THEY FLEW ALONG ROWS	44	FRAU BAUMAN	19
BUT I HUNG ON LIKE DEATH:	45	MY PAPA'S WALTZ	3
THEN BRISTLED LIKE A DOG.	47	THE RETURN	4
SAGGED LIKE A FRIGHTENED LIP.	47	THE RETURN	7
CHILDREN, THEIR BELLIES SWOLLEN LIKE BLOWN-UP PAPER BAGS,	48	JUDGE NOT	2
SAW WOMEN, THEIR EYELIDS LIKE LITTLE RAGS,	48	JUDGE NOT	9
LIKE ELVERS IN PONDS,	50	THE MINIMAL	8
LIKE SMALL GOATS.	51	THE WAKING (1)	12
IS IT SOFT LIKE A MOUSE?	54	THE LOST SON	50
LIKE A SLITHER OF EELS	56	THE LOST SON	96
LET THE KISSES RESOUND, FLAT LIKE A BUTCHER'S PALM;	56	THE LOST SON	104
TO JERK LIKE A FROG	65	SHAPE OF FIRE	50
I LIKE SOFT PAWS.	72	WHERE KNOCK IS	42
AND SKIN LIKE PAPER.	73	WHERE KNOCK IS	79
MY HOE EATS LIKE A GOAT.	76	I NEED, I NEED	60
WHY IS HOW I LIKE IT.	77	BRING THE DAY!	23
LEAVES, DO YOU LIKE ME ANY?	78	BRING THE DAY!	33
BELIEVE ME, KNOT OF GRISTLE, I BLEED LIKE A TREE;	79	GIVE WAY, GATES	1
SEE! SHE'S SLEEPING LIKE A LAKE:	81	SENSIBILITY! LA	2
FOR WHOM HAVE I SWELLED LIKE A SEED?	85	PRAISE TO END!	2
MINCING LIKE A CAT.	87	PRAISE TO END!	54
LAY LIKE THE CATS DO	87	PRAISE TO END!	61
I SLEPT LIKE AN INSECT.	89	UNFOLD! UNFOLD!	29
I STRETCHED LIKE A BOARD, ALMOST A TREE.	90	UNFOLD! UNFOLD!	32
A TRUE MOLE WANDERS LIKE A WORM.	97	O, THOU OPENING	20
LIKE A SAPLING TREE,	98	O, THOU OPENING	49
THE GROUND'S BEATING LIKE FLAME!	99	O, THOU OPENING	59
I'M TWINKLING LIKE A TWIG!	99	O, THOU OPENING	63
MOVES, LIKE THE SNAIL,	101	LIGHT BREATHER	11
WAITING LIKE A FERN, MAKING A SPINY SHADOW.	102	ELEGY FOR JANE	15
LIKE THE HALF-DEAD, I HUG MY LAST SECRETS.	103	OLD LADY'S WRDS	5
THEY ALL SAT DOWN LIKE ME AND YOU	111	SQUEEZE-BOX	6
A PLACE I SURELY DID LIKE TO GO	111	SQUEEZE-BOX	17
--LOT LIKE LOSING SOME MONEY.	111	SQUEEZE-BOX	21
--AND SO LIKE MY POEM CALLED POEM.	113	TO A LADY ED	4
--IT LOOKED LIKE DIRTY DINKY.	114	DINKY	12
HE DIDN'T LIKE HIS KIND OF LIFE;	115	THE SERPENT	5
AND SING HE DID, LIKE ANYTHING!	115	THE SERPENT	10
I DO NOT LIKE TO BANG OR TOOTLE."	115	THE SERPENT	20
I PLAYED IN FLAME AND WATER LIKE A BOY	120	THE DREAM	28
LIKE A WET LOG, I SANG WITHIN A FLAME.	120	THE DREAM	30
A FIELD BREAKS LIKE THE SEA;	124	WORDS FOR WIND	37
SHE FROLICKS LIKE A BEAST;	126	WORDS FOR WIND	101
THOSE NOTES WENT, LIKE THE BIRD,	128	THE VOICE	8
LIKE ANY SUMMER DAY.	128	THE VOICE	24
I WEEP FOR WHAT I'M LIKE WHEN I'M ALONE	132	SENTENTIOUS MAN	33
YET, LIKE A TREE, ENDURE THE SHIFT OF THINGS.	135	THE RENEWAL	6

	PAGE	TITLE	LINE
LIKE (CONTINUED)			
OR LISTEN INTO SILENCE, LIKE A GOD.	140	THE SWAN	20
HOW I LOVED ONE LIKE YOU WHEN I WAS LITTLE!--	151	SLUG	1
I LONGED TO BE LIKE HIM, AND WAS,	151	SLUG	4
LIKE PIECES OF SMOKED EEL OR RAW OYSTER,	151	SLUG	17
BEAUTIFUL, IN ITS WAY, LIKE QUICKSILVER--	151	SLUG	22
LIKE BATS IN DAYTIME,	152	THE SISKINS	4
SCUTTLING DOWN AND AROUND LIKE YOUNG SQUIRRELS,	152	THE SISKINS	17
LIKE A FRESH-SALTED SKIN;	153	THE DYING MAN	4
THE LOOSE AIR SENT ME RUNNING LIKE A CHILD--	155	THE DYING MAN	55
HE QUIVERED LIKE A BIRD IN BIRDLESS AIR,	155	THE DYING MAN	64
THEN DOWN, AS WE ROLL LIKE A BOAT FROM A WAVE-CREST.	158	FIRST MEDITATN	25
WHAT'S BEYOND NEVER CRUMBLES LIKE AN EMBANKMENT,	159	FIRST MEDITATN	76
EXPLODES LIKE A ROSE, OR THRUSTS WINGS OVER THE CARIBBEAN.	159	FIRST MEDITATN	77
THEIR FOREPAWS JOINED TOGETHER, LIKE HANDS--	163	I'M HERE	69
WITHOUT STARING LIKE A LOUT, OR A MOPING ADOLESCENT;	163	I'M HERE	80
ROCKING IT, LIKE A SUN-STRUCK POND,	163	I'M HERE	84
I'M NO MIDGE OF THAT AND THIS. THE DIRT GLITTERS LIKE SALT.	164	I'M HERE	92
A SPIRIT PLAYS BEFORE ME LIKE A CHILD,	165	HER BECOMING	22
I STEPPED CAREFULLY, LIKE A NEW-SHOD HORSE,	166	HER BECOMING	46
MY BREATH GREW LESS. I LISTENED LIKE A BEAST.	166	HER BECOMING	53
I HUM IN PURE VIBRATION, LIKE A SAW.	167	HER BECOMING	89
WHAT'S BECOME OF CARE? THIS LAKE BREATHES LIKE A ROSE.	170	FOURTH MEDITATN	76
DARE I BLAZE LIKE A TREE?	171	WHAT TELL BONES	9
TO TRY TO BECOME LIKE GOD	172	WHAT TELL BONES	59
I WISH YOU WOULD ACT LIKE A BIRD REALLY SHOULD,	177	KITTY-CAT BIRD	6
YOU MEW LIKE A CAT, YOU GRATE LIKE A JAY:	177	KITTY-CAT BIRD	9
YOU MEW LIKE A CAT, YOU GRATE LIKE A JAY:	177	KITTY-CAT BIRD	9
YOU SQUEAK LIKE A MOUSE THAT'S LOST IN THE HAY,	177	KITTY-CAT BIRD	10
--OR YOU'LL END LIKE THE KITTY-CAT BIRD.	177	KITTY-CAT BIRD	21
SHE COULD GROWL LIKE A BEAR,--	179	MYRTLE	4
THESE POETS, THEY WRITE LIKE I SNEEZE!"	179	MYRTLE	12
I'D LIKE TO TALK BACK,	182	BOY AND BUSH	4
LIKE A HUMMING-BIRD,	183	THE WAGTAIL	5
AT AN INTIMATE PLACE LIKE HIS GIZZARD.	183	THE LIZARD	7
THE SELF PERSISTS LIKE A DYING STAR,	190	AT OYSTER RIVER	24
THE HELIOTROPE, VEINED LIKE A FISH, THE PERSISTENT MORNING-GLORY,	197	THE LONG WATERS	41
A SINGLE WAVE COMES IN LIKE THE NECK OF A GREAT SWAN	197	THE LONG WATERS	52
OF FLYING LIKE A BAT DEEP INTO A NARROWING TUNNEL,	199	THE FAR FIELD	2
HANGING, BUNCHED LIKE YOUNG FRUIT, BENDING THE END BRANCHES,	199	THE FAR FIELD	32
ONCE I WAS SOMETHING LIKE THIS, MINDLESS,	200	THE FAR FIELD	42
HIS SPIRIT MOVES LIKE MONUMENTAL WIND	201	THE FAR FIELD	91
LIKE THE BLUE SHINE ON FRESHLY FROZEN SNOW,	201	THE FAR FIELD	96
THE STERN HIGH, DIPPING LIKE A CHILD'S BOAT IN A POND--	203	THE ROSE	37
AND THAT THIN CRY, LIKE A NEEDLE PIERCING THE EAR, THE INSISTENT CICADA,	204	THE ROSE	67
LIKE THE EYE OF A NEW-CAUGHT FISH,	204	THE ROSE	88
SHE CROONS, LIKE A CAT TO ITS CLAWS;	208	HER WORDS	2
AND IT LIKE TO DIE.	208	THE APPARITION	8
OPEN LIKE A POOL, A LESSER PARSNIP,	209	HER LONGING	6
LIKE A LEECH, LOOPING MYSELF ALONG,	209	HER LONGING	7
A MOUTH LIKE A STICKLEBACK,--	209	HER LONGING	9
(WHOM I LIKE NONE-THE-LESS),	213	THE HAPPY THREE	22
VANISHED LIKE APRIL SNOW;	213	THE HAPPY THREE	27
LIKE A NURSE HE SAT WITH ME FOR WEEKS, A SLY SURLY ATTENDANT,	220	THE ABYSS	38
THE RUSH OF SMELLS STRIKES LIKE A COLD FIRE, THE THROAT FREEZES,	220	THE ABYSS	47
STRIKE LIKE A FIRE,	221	THE ABYSS	54
THE GREAT LOGS PILED LIKE MATCHSTICKS.	222	THE ABYSS	96
I HAVE MERGED, LIKE THE BIRD, WITH THE BRIGHT AIR,	222	THE ABYSS	99
HER FACE LIKE A RAIN-BEATEN STONE ON THE DAY SHE ROLLED OFF	223	ELEGY (2)	1
HIS ABSURD WHISKERS STICKING OUT LIKE A CARTOON-MOUSE,	227	MEADOW MOUSE	7
HIS FEET LIKE SMALL LEAVES,	227	MEADOW MOUSE	8
WRIGGLING LIKE A MINISCULE PUPPY.	227	MEADOW MOUSE	11
SO FOOLISH AND TRUSTING, LIKE A SICK POODLE,	228	THE GERANIUM	3
(DRIED-OUT, SHE CREAKED LIKE A TULIP.)	228	THE GERANIUM	14
RIDDLING THE SAND, LIKE A WIDE SPRAY OF BUCKSHOT,	230	THE STORM	14
SUDDENLY THEY CAME FLYING, LIKE A LONG SCARF OF SMOKE,	232	THE THING	1
THEIR HEADS JOD-JODDING LIKE PIGEONS;	235	ALL MORNING	35
ROSE UP AND FELL LIKE AN ERRATIC WIND.	237	THE TRANCED	10
MY SOUL, LIKE SOME HEAT-MADDENED SUMMER FLY,	239	IN A DARK TIME	20

		PAGE	TITLE	LINE
LIKE (CONTINUED)				
SWAYING IN AIR, LIKE SOME LONG WATER WEED.		241	THE SEQUEL	19
A WIND CAME CLOSE, LIKE A SHY ANIMAL.		241	THE SEQUEL	22
BY DYING INWARD, LIKE AN AGING TREE.		244	INFIRMITY	12
PAIN WANDERS THROUGH MY BONES LIKE A LOST FIRE;		246	THE MARROW	11
I MOVED LIKE SOME HEAT-WEARY ANIMAL.		247	I WAITED	17
IN A HAND LIKE A BOWL		249	THE RESTORED	1
I'M LIKE TO DIE,"		249	THE RESTORED	10
FROM MY HAND LIKE A BOWL		249	THE RESTORED	12
THIS WATER, HEATED LIKE MY BLOOD,		256	IN HYDROTHERAPY	5
TO FIND THAT, LIKE A FISH,		258	SONG (3)	10
AND THE CYCLAMEN LEAVES GLISTEN LIKE THE BACKS OF BABY TURTLES.		260	THE CHANGELING	15
I CAN'T BURY THE BONE OF THIS MISERY LIKE A FASTIDIOUS DOG.		261	THE CHANGELING	31
BEHOLD THE CRITIC, PITCHED LIKE THE CASTRATI,		264	THREE EPIGRAMS	1
WE STRAYED LIKE CHILDREN,		265	HARSH COUNTRY	6
THAT CUT LIKE RAZORS,		265	HARSH COUNTRY	8
LIKE AN ENORMOUS BEACON,		265	HARSH COUNTRY	10
IF I ATE AND DRANK LIKE HIM,		266	FOR STEVENS	11
AND, LIKE YOU, BIRD, I SING,		271	THE REPLY	16
THE SUDDEN LIGHT SPILLED ON THE FLOOR LIKE CREAM		273	SUPPR W LINDSAY	12
AND FLICKER NEAR OUR LEGS LIKE KEROSENE		274	SUPPR W LINDSAY	36
BURNING IN SAND. "IT LOOKS LIKE I SHOULD GO,"--		274	SUPPR W LINDSAY	37
LIKED				
THE LEAVES LIKED IT.		74	I NEED, I NEED	17
LIKELIEST				
THE LIKELIEST GANDER ALIVE.		258	SONG (3)	18
LIKELY				
YOU'RE LIKELY TO GO ON LIVING FOR YEARS,		23	ACADEMIC	2
A LIKELY THING FOR THEY'RE NO WORSE		267	SAGINAW SONG	21
LIKES				
HE LIKES THE ATTIC OF AN AGING HOUSE.		16	THE BAT	2
A PICK LIKES TO HIT ICE.		76	I NEED, I NEED	54
THE LIKES OF HIM IS BITING WHO,		86	PRAISE TO END!	32
SHE LIKES WHEREVER I AM.		124	WORDS FOR WIND	46
LOVE LIKES A GANDER, AND ADORES A GOOSE:		127	I KNEW A WOMAN	15
WITH THE LIKES OF BLAKE,		228	IN VIOLENT WARD	5
THAN THE LIKES OF YOU OR ME,--		267	SAGINAW SONG	22
A BIT OF THE LIKES OF IT.		270	GOB MUSIC	35
LILAC				
IN THE LILAC CHANGE, THE WHITE REPTILIAN CALM,		205	THE ROSE	107
LILACS				
DOWN IN THE CORNER OF THE GARDEN, AMONG THE RAGGEDY LILACS,		204	THE ROSE	64
LILIES				
LILIES, PALE-PINK CYCLAMEN, ROSES,		39	WEED PULLER	12
CYCLAMEN DRIPPING AND LILIES.		61	THE LONG ALLEY	73
BEES AND LILIES THERE WERE,		77	BRING THE DAY!	1
BEES AND LILIES THERE WERE,		77	BRING THE DAY!	2
BEES AND LILIES WERE THERE.		77	BRING THE DAY!	5
LILTING				
THE BLUEBIRD, LOVER OF HOLES IN OLD WOOD, LILTING ITS LIGHT SONG,		204	THE ROSE	66
LILTS				
SHE LILTS A LOW SOFT LANGUAGE, AND I HEAR		129	SHE	5
LILY				
THE LILY BROODS. WHO KNOWS		165	HER BECOMING	26
IS IT TO BRING THE LILY?		261	THE CHANGELING	45
LILY'S				
IN THE LILY'S SOVEREIGN RIGHT?		98	O, THOU OPENING	43
LOVE, LOVE, A LILY'S MY CARE,		123	WORDS FOR WIND	1
THE LILY'S PIERCING WHITE,		197	THE LONG WATERS	39
LIMBER				
TO LOOSEN WITH ALL TEN FINGERS HELD WIDE AND LIMBER		40	MOSS-GATHERING	1
OR THEY SIT SIDEWAYS ON LIMBER DANDELION STEMS,		152	THE SISKINS	10
FLATTENING THE LIMBER CARNATIONS.		231	THE STORM	33
LIMBS				
ROSE ON SUCH LOPPED LIMBS TO A NEW LIFE?		37	CUTTINGS (LATE)	4
MAY YOUR LIMBS NEVER WITHER,		217	WISH YOUNG WIFE	2
LIME				
LEAF-MOLD, MANURE, LIME, PILED AGAINST SLIPPERY PLANKS.		38	ROOT CELLAR	9
SHOOTING UP LIME AND DUNG AND GROUND BONES,--		38	FORCING HOUSE	9
LIMESTONE				
WITH ITS LIMESTONE CRUMBLING INTO FINE GREYISH DUST,		226	THE LIZARD	28

	PAGE	TITLE	LINE
LIMP			
LIMP AND DAMP, DELICATE AS A YOUNG BIRD'S TONGUE;	39	ORCHIDS	5
EVERYTHING LIMP	43	FLOWER DUMP	10
LICE TETHERED TO LONG LIMP SUBTERRANEAN WEEDS,	50	THE MINIMAL	4
TETHERED TO A LIMP WEED, SWINGING,	101	LIGHT BREATHER	8
I REMEMBER THE NECKCURLS, LIMP AND DAMP AS TENDRILS;	102	ELEGY FOR JANE	1
THEN EACH FELL BACK, LIMP AS A SACK,	136	THE SENSUALISTS	25
AND HANG, LIMP ON A STONE:	150	SNAKE	3
SHE LOOKED SO LIMP AND BEDRAGGLED,	228	THE GERANIUM	2
LIMPER			
AND THE STYLE OF YOUR PROSE GROWING LIMPER AND LIMPER.	23	ACADEMIC	4
AND THE STYLE OF YOUR PROSE GROWING LIMPER AND LIMPER.	23	ACADEMIC	4
LINDSAY			
SUPPER WITH LINDSAY	273	SUPPR W LINDSAY	T
"LET'S EAT!" SAID LINDSAY. "HERE WE'VE GOT THE MOON,	273	SUPPR W LINDSAY	15
WHEN LINDSAY BENT HIS HEAD	273	SUPPR W LINDSAY	19
"THAT'S NEVER BLAKE," SAID LINDSAY. "HE'D BE A WORM,	273	SUPPR W LINDSAY	26
AND LINDSAY HEAVED HIMSELF FROM MY OLD CHAIR.	274	SUPPR W LINDSAY	38
LINDSAY'S			
LINDSAY'S I MEAN: TWO MOONS, OR EVEN THREE,	273	SUPPR W LINDSAY	7
LINE			
ALL CROSS MY LINE OF SIGHT,	34	NIGHT JOURNEY	9
A LINE OF ELMS PLUNGING AND TOSSING LIKE HORSES,	43	CHILD ON GRNHSE	6
NOTHING NIBBLED MY LINE,	53	THE LOST SON	14
USE A HOOK OR A LINE,	117	LADY AND BEAR	15
THE LINE! THE HOLY LINE!	167	HER BECOMING	76
THE LINE! THE HOLY LINE!	167	HER BECOMING	76
WHIPPING THE LINE OF WHITE LAUNDRY, BENDING THE COTTONWOODS APART,	194	JOURNY INTERIOR	44
THE LINE OF MY HORIZON'S GROWING THIN!	245	THE DECISION	8
LINEAMENTS			
PRIDE IN FINE LINEAMENTS PRECEDES A FALL;	131	SENTENTIOUS MAN	5
LINED			
THE ROAD LINED WITH SNOW-LADEN SECOND GROWTH,	199	THE FAR FIELD	4
LINES			
THE DRIVERS FROM PRODUCTION LINES	33	HIGHWAY: MICH	8
OR TWO HORSES PLUNGING IN SNOW, THEIR LINES TANGLED,	158	FIRST MEDITATN	53
LINES UPON LEAVING A SANITARIUM	257	SANITARIUM	T
LINGER			
MY MOMENTS LINGER--THAT'S ETERNITY.	149	IN LATE SUMMER	16
LINGERS			
WHILE THE MOON LINGERS,	204	THE ROSE	85
LINGO			
I WOULD UNLEARN THE LINGO OF EXASPERATION, ALL THE DISTORTIONS OF MALICE AND HATRED;	188	THE LONGING	42
LINING			
AND LIFT UP A PATCH, DARK-GREEN, THE KIND FOR LINING CEMETERY BASKETS,	40	MOSS-GATHERING	2
LINKS			
THE LINKS WERE SOFT BETWEEN US; STILL, WE KISSED;	107	SIR JOHN DAVIES	81
LINOLEUM			
MUTTONY TEARS FALLING ON FIGURED LINOLEUM,	48	LAST WORDS	3
LINT			
THE DARKNESS OF FALLING HAIR, THE WARNINGS FROM LINT AND SPIDERS,	159	FIRST MEDITATN	80
LINTEL			
ITS LINTEL OVERHUNG	145	THE BEAST	2
LION			
AS IF A LION KNELT TO KISS A ROSE,	131	SENTENTIOUS MAN	17
A LION OF FLAME, PRESSED TO THE POINT OF LOVE,	170	FOURTH MEDITATN	73
OR, WITH LUCK, AS A LION.	200	THE FAR FIELD	49
LIP			
LIP, BREAST AND THIGH CANNOT POSSESS	8	PRAYER	17
HE JERKS A FROG ACROSS HIS BONY LIP,	15	THE HERON	9
SAGGED LIKE A FRIGHTENED LIP.	47	THE RETURN	7
EYE LEARNED FROM EYE, COLD LIP FROM SENSUAL LIP.	119	THE DREAM	4
EYE LEARNED FROM EYE, COLD LIP FROM SENSUAL LIP.	119	THE DREAM	4
LIFTING A NETHER LIP	130	THE OTHER	3
FROZEN BY A FATHER'S LIP, A MOTHER'S FAILURE TO ANSWER.	169	FOURTH MEDITATN	45
OVER A LIP OF STONE, THE TINY RIVULET;	191	AT OYSTER RIVER	43
LIPS			
THEIR FLUTTERY FLEDGLING LIPS	39	ORCHIDS	6
LIPS NEITHER DEAD NOR ALIVE,	39	ORCHIDS	16

	PAGE	TITLE	LINE
LIPS (CONTINUED)			
MY LIPS AWAKE.	56	THE LOST SON	99
WHAT'S THIS? A DISH FOR FAT LIPS.	64	SHAPE OF FIRE	1
IS TRAPPED TO THE LIPS,	65	SHAPE OF FIRE	47
A SECRET TO JERK FROM THE LIPS OF A FISH.	92	I CRY, LOVE!	7
HER FULL LIPS PURSED, THE ERRANT NOTE TO SEIZE;	127	I KNEW A WOMAN	16
MY LIPS PRESSED UPON STONE.	146	THE SONG	29
MY OWN, MY SECRET LIPS	147	THE EXORCISM	11
LESS AND LESS THE ILLUMINATED LIPS,	187	THE LONGING	7
BLESSED BY THE LIPS OF A LOW WIND,	197	THE LONG WATERS	45
NOR MY LIPS, MY BREASTS, MY THIGHS	209	HER RETICENCE	9
BUT MY LIPS THEY,	216	THE SHY MAN	5
MY LIPS THEY,	216	THE SHY MAN	6
BUT MY LIPS THEY,	216	THE SHY MAN	13
MY LIPS THEY,	216	THE SHY MAN	14
AND MY LIPS THEY, MY LIPS THEY,	216	THE SHY MAN	21
AND MY LIPS THEY, MY LIPS THEY,	216	THE SHY MAN	21
O! MY LIPS THEY, MY LIPS THEY,	216	THE SHY MAN	24
O! MY LIPS THEY, MY LIPS THEY,	216	THE SHY MAN	24
LIQUESCENT			
A SLOW SNAIL-LIFTING, LIQUESCENT;	67	SHAPE OF FIRE	82
LIQUIDS			
LIQUIDS PURSUE ME, NOTES AND TREMORS:	255	LIGHT POEM	6
LIQUOR			
I DRINK GOOD LIQUOR WHEN MY LUCK IS GOOD.	132	SENTENTIOUS MAN	28
LIST			
OF A MAN-TAILORED BLOUSE; THE LIST OF SHOPPING DONE;	29	THE REMINDER	6
LISTEN			
LISTEN, LOVE,	63	FIELD OF LIGHT	37
TO TEACH MY TOES TO LISTEN TO MY TONGUE.	105	SIR JOHN DAVIES	16
OR LISTEN INTO SILENCE, LIKE A GOD.	140	THE SWAN	20
I LISTEN TO THE WEEDS' VESPERAL WHINE,	171	WHAT TELL BONES	12
AND LISTEN TO MY OWN FEET.	215	HIS FOREBODING	18
WE WAIT; WE LISTEN.	231	THE STORM	29
LISTENED			
I LISTENED TO SOMETHING	55	THE LOST SON	73
I'VE LISTENED INTO THE LEAST WAVES.	77	BRING THE DAY!	28
I HAVE LISTENED CLOSE	103	OLD LADY'S WRDS	29
I TOSSED A STONE, AND LISTENED TO ITS PLUNGE.	120	THE DREAM	22
MY BREATH GREW LESS. I LISTENED LIKE A BEAST.	166	HER BECOMING	53
LIGHT LISTENED	212	LIGHT LISTENED	T
LIGHT LISTENED WHEN SHE SANG.	212	LIGHT LISTENED	24
LISTENER			
TIME FOR THE FLAT-HEADED MAN. I RECOGNIZE THAT LISTENER,	65	SHAPE OF FIRE	29
LISTENING			
BY LISTENING TO THE SPIRIT'S SMALLEST CRY;	131	SENTENTIOUS MAN	15
LISTING			
AND THE FIRST DUST OF SPRING LISTING OVER BACKLOTS,--	92	I CRY, LOVE!	27
LITHE			
I ROMPED, LITHE AS A CHILD, DOWN THE SUMMERY STREETS OF MY VEINS,	86	PRAISE TO END!	21
LITTER			
WHEN FROM UNDER THE BARN THE CAT BRINGS A SIMILAR LITTER,--	24	VERNAL SENTIMNT	5
RETURN TO LITTER UP OUR HOME.	30	THE RECKONING	4
LITTLE			
WITH THESE I MATCH MY LITTLE WIT	18	LONG LIVE WEEDS	9
YOUR LITTLE MANHOOD LONG AGO WAS SMOTHERED.	25	DIM-WIT COUSIN	2
SAW WOMEN, THEIR EYELIDS LIKE LITTLE RAGS,	48	JUDGE NOT	9
I STUDY THE LIVES ON A LEAF: THE LITTLE	50	THE MINIMAL	1
THE LITTLE ONES DID,	51	THE WAKING (1)	10
MY KNEES MADE LITTLE WINDS UNDERNEATH	57	THE LOST SON	128
THE PATH TELLS LITTLE TO THE SERPENT.	66	SHAPE OF FIRE	59
AND THE LITTLE CRABS SLIPPED INTO SILVERY CRATERS.	66	SHAPE OF FIRE	67
I'M SAD WITH THE LITTLE OWLS.	80	GIVE WAY, GATES	45
WENT WEEPING, LITTLE BONES. BUT WHERE?	92	I CRY, LOVE!	1
THE LITTLE FISHES MOVE.	121	ALL EARTH, AIR	4
HOPE'S HOLY WRISTS: THE LITTLE BURNING BOYS	143	SHIMMER OF EVIL	13
HOW I LOVED ONE LIKE YOU WHEN I WAS LITTLE!--	151	SLUG	1
FLYING UPWARD IN LITTLE SKIPS AND ERRATIC LEAPS;	152	THE SISKINS	9
THE LIGHTS TILTING UP, SKYWARD, AS WE COME OVER A LITTLE RISE,	158	FIRST MEDITATN	24
SO SHE TOLD ME WHEN I WAS LITTLE,	163	I'M HERE	72
WE START FROM THE DARK. PAIN TEACHES US LITTLE.	166	HER BECOMING	35

	PAGE	TITLE	LINE
LITTLE (CONTINUED)			
ACROSS A FIELD, INTO A LITTLE WOOD.	166	HER BECOMING	51
BUT HEARD LITTLE.	220	THE ABYSS	18
A LITTLE QUAKER, THE WHOLE BODY OF HIM TREMBLING,	227	MEADOW MOUSE	6
LITTLE LIZARD-FEET,	227	MEADOW MOUSE	9
OF VEAL SOAKED IN MARSALA AND LITTLE LARKS ARRANGED ON A LONG PLATTER,	232	THE THING	19
THERE'S LITTLE LEFT I CARE TO CALL MY OWN.	244	INFIRMITY	8
LITTLE CRABS SLIPPING INTO WATERY CRATERS--	255	LIGHT POEM	4
O WHEN YOU WERE LITTLE, YOU WERE REALLY BIG:	272	DUET	1
LITTLES			
YE LITTLES, LIE MORE CLOSE!	240	IN EVEING AIR	7
LITTLEST			
COME LITTLEST, COME TENDEREST,	61	THE LONG ALLEY	66
WHAT FISH-WAYS YOU HAVE, LITTLEST FLOWERS,	61	THE LONG ALLEY	74
LIVE			
"LONG LIVE THE WEEDS"	18	LONG LIVE WEEDS	T
LONG LIVE THE WEEDS THAT OVERWHELM	18	LONG LIVE WEEDS	1
AS THE LIVE HEAT BILLOWS FROM PIPES AND POTS.	38	FORCING HOUSE	11
AND THE LIVE STEAM	41	BIG WIND	13
IS THE SEED LEAVING THE OLD BED? THESE BUDS ARE LIVE AS BIRDS.	56	THE LOST SON	102
WHERE I LIVE.	74	I NEED, I NEED	15
I CARE FOR A CAT'S CRY AND THE HUGS, LIVE AS WATER.	92	I CRY, LOVE!	16
THE LIVE GRASS WHIRLS WITH THE SUN,	93	I CRY, LOVE!	35
I'D SAY IT TO MY HORSE: WE LIVE BEYOND	106	SIR JOHN DAVIES	37
ALL LOVERS LIVE BY LONGING, AND ENDURE:	107	SIR JOHN DAVIES	77
LENT ME ONE VIRTUE, AND I LIVE THEREBY.	120	THE DREAM	24
THESE OLD BONES LIVE TO LEARN HER WANTON WAYS:	127	I KNEW A WOMAN	27
WHAT IS SHE, WHILE I LIVE?--	130	THE OTHER	1
THE PURE ADMIRE THE PURE, AND LIVE ALONE;	133	THE PURE FURY	8
I LIVE NEAR THE ABYSS. I HOPE TO STAY	134	THE PURE FURY	26
THE NIGHT WIND RISES. DOES MY FATHER LIVE?	135	THE RENEWAL	7
I LIVE, ALIVE AND CERTAIN AS A BULL;	140	THE SWAN	9
THE SMALL SHAPES DROWSE: I LIVE	148	THE SMALL	19
IN THIS LAST PLACE OF LIGHT: HE DARES TO LIVE	156	THE DYING MAN	99
OR LIVE THE DANGEROUS LIFE OF AN INSECT.	166	HER BECOMING	37
BY SWOOPS OF BIRD, BY LEAPS OF FISH, I LIVE.	167	HER BECOMING	91
I LIVE IN AIR; THE LONG LIGHT IS MY HOME;	167	HER BECOMING	93
MAY THEY LEAN INTO LIGHT AND LIVE;	169	FOURTH MEDITATN	57
DO THESE BONES LIVE? CAN I LIVE WITH THESE BONES?	172	WHAT TELL BONES	52
DO THESE BONES LIVE? CAN I LIVE WITH THESE BONES?	172	WHAT TELL BONES	52
I LIVE IN LIGHT'S EXTREME; I STRETCH IN ALL DIRECTIONS;	173	WHAT TELL BONES	82
SOME TIME I THINK I'LL LIVE THAT WAY.	182	THE HIPPO	5
I LIVE WITH THE ROCKS, THEIR WEEDS,	205	THE ROSE	89
CRIES, "I'M OLD ENOUGH TO LIVE	208	HER WORDS	3
WE LIVE BY WHAT WE DO.	212	LIGHT LISTENED	12
MAY YOU LIVE OUT YOUR LIFE	217	WISH YOUNG WIFE	6
TO LIVE BY COURTESY OF THE SHRIKE, THE SNAKE, THE TOM-CAT.	227	MEADOW MOUSE	25
MANY ARRIVALS MAKE US LIVE: THE TREE BECOMING	235	MANIFESTATION	1
I LIVE BETWEEN THE HERON AND THE WREN,	239	IN A DARK TIME	5
SHE STAYED IN LIGHT, AS LEAVES LIVE IN THE WIND,	241	THE SEQUEL	18
WHO'S OLD ENOUGH TO LIVE?--A THING OF EARTH	243	THE MOTION	14
IN WHICH ALL CREATURES SHARE, AND THEREBY LIVE,	243	THE MOTION	18
YEA, I HAVE SLAIN MY WILL, AND STILL I LIVE;	246	THE MARROW	21
LIVED			
A KINDLY WIDOW LADY, WHO LIVED UPON A HILL,	27	CLAIRVOY WIDOW	1
HE LIVED BEYOND THE TOUCH OF MORTAL LAWS.	28	THE FAVORITE	8
DEATH WAS NOT. I LIVED IN A SIMPLE DROWSE:	66	SHAPE OF FIRE	73
WE MET IN A NEST. BEFORE I LIVED.	93	I CRY, LOVE!	55
I LIVED WITH OPEN SOUND,	128	THE VOICE	11
I LIVED WITH DEEP ROOTS ONCE:	139	PLAINT	13
I LIVED SERENE AS A FISH,	209	HER LONGING	2
FOR I HAVE MOVED CLOSER TO DEATH, LIVED WITH DEATH;	220	THE ABYSS	37
WHO LIVED ABOVE A POTTING SHED FOR YEARS.	224	OTTO	4
AT THE TIME: SHE'D LIVED	228	THE GERANIUM	9
LIVELY			
A LIVELY UNDERSTANDABLE SPIRIT	58	THE LOST SON	169
THE LIVELY DEAD HAD TAUGHT US TO BE FOND.	106	SIR JOHN DAVIES	32
TO YOU AND ME; SO TAKE THE LIVELY AIR,	108	THE WAKING (2)	14
A LIVELY THING CAN COME TO LIFE AGAIN.	129	SHE	12
MUST I STAY TANGLED IN THAT LIVELY HAIR?	140	THE SWAN	3
IN LOVE, IN LIVELY MAY.	154	THE DYING MAN	27

	PAGE	TITLE	LINE
LIVELY (CONTINUED)			
MY LIZARD, MY LIVELY WRITHER,	217	WISH YOUNG WIFE	1
LIVES			
ENDLESS DUPLICATION OF LIVES AND OBJECTS.	46	DOLOR	8
I STUDY THE LIVES ON A LEAF: THE LITTLE	50	THE MINIMAL	1
CRIED OUT THEIR LIVES AN INSTANT AND WERE FREE.	143	SHIMMER OF EVIL	14
LEWD, TINY, CARELESS LIVES	147	THE EXORCISM	16
WHAT DO THEIR LIVES MEAN,	169	FOURTH MEDITATN	42
AND THE LIVES OF THEIR CHILDREN?--	169	FOURTH MEDITATN	43
THE HUSK LIVES ON, ARDENT AS A SEED;	170	FOURTH MEDITATN	83
HE LIVES ON CARROTS, LEEKS AND HAY;	182	THE HIPPO	3
HERE IN OUR AGING DISTRICT THE WOOD PIGEON LIVES WITH US,	234	ALL MORNING	1
AND THE STELLER JAY, RAUCOUS, SOOTY HEADED, LIVES WITH US,	234	ALL MORNING	15
DEEP IN THE GREENS OF SUMMER SING THE LIVES	244	INFIRMITY	25
SHE LEANS INTO LIGHT, AND LIVES,	260	THE CHANGELING	10
THE EARTHLY LIVES IN HER;	262	FOLLIES OF ADAM	12
LIVING			
YOU'RE LIKELY TO GO ON LIVING FOR YEARS,	23	ACADEMIC	2
BY PULLING OFF FLESH FROM THE LIVING PLANET;	40	MOSS-GATHERING	12
I ASKED: MAY THE BLESSINGS OF LIFE, O LORD, DESCEND ON THE LIVING.	48	JUDGE NOT	6
LIGHT ALTERED LIGHT ALONG THE LIVING GROUND.	106	SIR JOHN DAVIES	34
THE LIVING ALL ASSEMBLE! WHAT'S THE CUE?--	106	SIR JOHN DAVIES	41
THE WORLD IS FOR THE LIVING. WHO ARE THEY?	107	SIR JOHN DAVIES	91
OF LIVING MERELY IN THE REALM OF TIME.	149	IN LATE SUMMER	20
LIVING ALL MY HEART'S SUMMER ALONE,	161	I'M HERE	19
AND LOVES THE LIVING GROUND.	212	LIGHT LISTENED	16
I, LIVING, STILL ABIDE	215	HIS FOREBODING	2
AND THE HURRICANE DRIVES THE DEAD STRAW INTO THE LIVING PINE-TREE.	231	THE STORM	43
WE PACED THE LIVING GROUND;	237	THE TRANCED	13
THE INSTANT AGES ON THE LIVING EYE;	244	INFIRMITY	13
HE HEAPS FEW HONORS ON A LIVING HEAD;	264	THREE EPIGRAMS	3
WE'VE GOT THE LIVING LIGHT, BUT WHERE'S THE FOOD?"	273	SUPPR W LINDSAY	16
LIZARD			
THE LIZARD	183	THE LIZARD	T
THE TIME TO TICKLE A LIZARD,	183	THE LIZARD	1
AND THE IVY ADVANCE WITH ITS WHITE LIZARD FEET--	194	JOURNY INTERIOR	49
MY LIZARD, MY LIVELY WRITHER,	217	WISH YOUNG WIFE	1
THE LIZARD	226	THE LIZARD	T
BUT THE EYE OF THE TINY LIZARD STAYS WITH ME.	226	THE LIZARD	22
NOT TO ME, BUT THIS LIZARD,	226	THE LIZARD	30
AND THEN A JACKASS BRAYED. A LIZARD LEAPED MY FOOT.	247	I WAITED	14
LIZARD-FEET			
LITTLE LIZARD-FEET,	227	MEADOW MOUSE	9
LIZARDS			
THE FERNS HAD THEIR WAYS, AND THE PULSING LIZARDS,	63	FIELD OF LIGHT	41
LIZARD'S			
AND THE SUN TOUCHES THE LIZARD'S THROAT, ITS TAIL HALF IN SHADOW.	261	THE CHANGELING	34
LOAM			
STICKS-IN-A-DROWSE DROOP OVER SUGARY LOAM,	37	CUTTINGS	1
SIFTING IN A PALM-FULL OF FRESH LOAM,--	42	TRANSPLANTING	4
THE SUN WARMING THE FINE LOAM,	42	TRANSPLANTING	14
REACH ME ROSE, SWEET ONE, STILL MOIST IN THE LOAM,	61	THE LONG ALLEY	68
THE SUN PLAYING ON LOAM,	92	I CRY, LOVE!	26
THE LOAM HEAVED ME	104	OLD LADY'S WRDS	45
LOAM-CRUMBS			
FACES GREYING FASTER THAN LOAM-CRUMBS ON A HARROW;	48	JUDGE NOT	1
LOAN			
COME TO ME, MILK-NOSE. I NEED A LOAN OF THE QUICK.	59	THE LONG ALLEY	25
LOATHE			
HE WHO HIMSELF BEGINS TO LOATHE	257	SANITARIUM	9
LOATHES			
INDELICATE IS HE WHO LOATHES	19	EPIDERM MACABRE	1
LOCKED			
IS LOCKED IN NARROW BONE.	18	GENESIS	4
MY LOVE'S LOCKED IN	60	THE LONG ALLEY	49
LOCKET			
YOU WOUND THE WATCH IN AN OLD-FASHIONED LOCKET	29	THE REMINDER	7
LOG			
WITH BUCK STILL TIED TO THE LOG, ON COMES THE LIGHT.	47	DOUBLE FEATURE	1
A LOG TURNED AT THE TOUCH OF A FOOT;	62	FIELD OF LIGHT	4

	PAGE	TITLE	LINE
LOG (CONTINUED)			
LIKE A WET LOG, I SANG WITHIN A FLAME.	120	THE DREAM	30
A LOG SINGS IN ITS FLAME.	137	LOVE'S PROGRESS	18
SLAPPING LIGHTLY AGAINST A SUNKEN LOG.	190	AT OYSTER RIVER	14
WELTER OF TIN CANS, PAILS, OLD BIRD NESTS, A CHILD'S SHOE RIDING A LOG,	191	AT OYSTER RIVER	54
OR, WITH SKINNY KNEES, TO SIT ASTRIDE A WET LOG,	200	THE FAR FIELD	45
THE OLD LOG SUBSIDES WITH THE LESSENING WAVES,	202	THE ROSE	20
FROM BEYOND THE END OF A MOSSY LOG,	233	THE PIKE	15
LOGGING			
AND AFTERWARDS I ALWAYS FELT MEAN, JOGGING BACK OVER THE LOGGING ROAD,	40	MOSS-GATHERING	9
LOGIC			
MUCH LOGIC IN THEIR GLUTTONY.	25	VERSE W ALLUSNS	12
LOGS			
AND THE BUNCHED LOGS PEEL IN THE AFTERNOON SUNLIGHT,	196	THE LONG WATERS	16
THE STREAM SLIPPING BENEATH THE MOSSY LOGS,	222	THE ABYSS	94
THE GREAT LOGS PILED LIKE MATCHSTICKS.	222	THE ABYSS	96
LOITER			
THINGS LOLL AND LOITER. WHO CONDONES THE LOST?	106	SIR JOHN DAVIES	43
LOLL			
THINGS LOLL AND LOITER. WHO CONDONES THE LOST?	106	SIR JOHN DAVIES	43
I LOLL, I LOLL, ALL TONGUE.	130	THE OTHER	16
I LOLL, I LOLL, ALL TONGUE.	130	THE OTHER	16
LOLLING			
LOLLING OBSCENELY FROM MILDEWED CRATES,	38	ROOT CELLAR	4
THE MOON LOLLING IN THE CLOSE ELM, A SHIMMER OF SILVER,	204	THE ROSE	81
LONELIEST			
THE LONELIEST THING I KNOW	215	HIS FOREBODING	14
LONELINESS			
STILL AS A CHILD IN ITS FIRST LONELINESS;	67	SHAPE OF FIRE	85
LONELY			
LONELY RECEPTION ROOM, LAVATORY, SWITCHBOARD,	46	DOLOR	5
THE BONES ARE LONELY.	93	I CRY, LOVE!	32
LAY ALL THE LONELY PASTURES OF THE DEAD;	106	SIR JOHN DAVIES	51
SHE MAKES SPACE LONELY WITH A LOVELY SONG.	129	SHE	4
WITH THEIR HARD SNOW; LEANED ON THE LONELY EYE;	143	SHIMMER OF EVIL	7
YOU WERE TOO LONELY FOR ANOTHER FATE.	144	ELEGY (1)	6
I HAVE GONE INTO THE WASTE LONELY PLACES	159	FIRST MEDITATN	74
THE SOUL STANDS, LONELY IN ITS CHOICE,	168	FOURTH MEDITATN	20
THE RITUALISTS OF THE MIRROR, THE LONELY DRINKERS,	169	FOURTH MEDITATN	36
OR THAT LONELY TIME BEFORE THE BREAKING OF MORNING	204	THE ROSE	82
I WAS THAT LONELY.	228	THE GERANIUM	26
THE LONELY BUZZ BEHIND MY MIDNIGHT EYES;--	248	THE TREE, BIRD	16
LONESOME			
BRING ME A FINGER. THIS DIRT'S LONESOME FOR GRASS.	79	GIVE WAY, GATES	7
LONG			
OH THAT WAS LONG AGO! I KEPT	6	THE PREMONITION	3
THE WIND LAY MOTIONLESS IN THE LONG GRASS.	6	INTERLUDE	10
THE LEAFY MIND, THAT LONG WAS TIGHTLY FURLED,	11	LIGHT BRIGHTER	18
LONG SINCE, BRONZE WHEAT WAS GATHERED INTO SHEAVES.	12	SLOW SEASON	10
BUDS, LONG UNSEALED, OBSCURE THE NARROW LANE.	12	SLOW SEASON	14
THE FIELDS STRETCH OUT IN LONG, UNBROKEN ROWS.	13	PRAISE-PRAIRIE	9
THE LONG EYE NOTES THE MINNOW'S HIDING PLACE.	15	THE HERON	7
"LONG LIVE THE WEEDS"	18	LONG LIVE WEEDS	T
LONG LIVE THE WEEDS THAT OVERWHELM	18	LONG LIVE WEEDS	1
THE VEIL LONG VIOLATED BY	19	EPIDERM MACABRE	7
YOUR LITTLE MANHOOD LONG AGO WAS SMOTHERED.	25	DIM-WIT COUSIN	2
THE SON OF MISFORTUNE LONG, LONG HAS BEEN WAITING	29	THE GENTLE	5
THE SON OF MISFORTUNE LONG, LONG HAS BEEN WAITING	29	THE GENTLE	5
HUNG DOWN LONG YELLOW EVIL NECKS, LIKE TROPICAL SNAKES.	38	ROOT CELLAR	5
FLINGING LONG STRINGS OF WET ACROSS THE ROOF-TOP,	41	BIG WIND	29
READY FOR THE LONG DAYS UNDER THE SLOPED GLASS:	42	TRANSPLANTING	13
SIFT, ALMOST INVISIBLE, THROUGH LONG AFTERNOONS OF TEDIUM,	46	DOLOR	11
LICE TETHERED TO LONG LIMP SUBTERRANEAN WEEDS,	50	THE MINIMAL	4
THESE STONES HAVE BEEN HERE TOO LONG.	55	THE LOST SON	65
THROUGH THE LONG GREENHOUSE.	57	THE LOST SON	125
THE LONG ALLEY	59	THE LONG ALLEY	T
FLESH, YOU OFFEND THIS METAL. HOW LONG NEED THE BONES MOURN?	59	THE LONG ALLEY	12
ARE THOSE HORNS ON TOP OF THE HILL? YESTERDAY HAS A LONG LOOK.	59	THE LONG ALLEY	13
THE LONG ALLEYS OF STRING AND STEM;	61	THE LONG ALLEY	70
A LONG WEED FLOATED UPWARD;	62	FIELD OF LIGHT	5

	PAGE	TITLE	LINE
LONG (CONTINUED)			
A LONG LONG TIME.	74	WHERE KNOCK IS	83
A LONG LONG TIME.	74	WHERE KNOCK IS	83
THE DUST, THE LONG DUST, STAYS.	78	BRING THE DAY!	42
HOW IS IT WITH THE LONG BIRDS?	79	GIVE WAY, GATES	18
THE LONG FLESH.	81	SENSIBILITY! LA	22
THERE'S A GHOST LOOSE IN THE LONG GRASS!	82	SENSIBILITY! LA	27
IT'S A LONG WAY TO SOMEWHERE ELSE.	82	SENSIBILITY! LA	38
BE SLEEK AS A HEIFER, BE LONG AS A HOG,--	86	PRAISE TO END!	41
SWAYING IN A LONG WAVE;	100	THE VISITANT	12
IT WAS STAND ON YOUR FEET AS LONG AS YOU'RE ABLE,	112	SQUEEZE-BOX	35
SHE SLOWED TO SIGH, IN THAT LONG INTERVAL.	120	THE DREAM	18
THE BREATH OF A LONG ROOT,	125	WORDS FOR WIND	82
THE LONG NOON PULSED AWAY.	128	THE VOICE	23
DOWN LONG SEA-CHAMBERS OF THE INNER EAR.	129	SHE	6
SOME RAGES SAVE US. DID I RAGE TOO LONG?	131	SENTENTIOUS MAN	9
IN THE LONG NIGHT, I REST WITHIN HER NAME--	131	SENTENTIOUS MAN	16
AS THE THICK SHADE OF THE LONG NIGHT COMES ON.	134	THE PURE FURY	28
THE LONG VEINS OF THE VINE	137	LOVE'S PROGRESS	6
WE THINK TOO LONG IN TERMS OF WHAT TO BE;	140	THE SWAN	8
THE LONG LUSH GRASS LAY STILL;	145	THE BEAST	18
BUT DOWN LONG CORRIDORS,	147	THE EXORCISM	10
ON THE LONG BANKS, IN THE SOFT SUMMER AIR.	149	IN LATE SUMMER	8
THE LONG DAY DIES; I WALKED THE WOODS ALONE;	150	IN LATE SUMMER	29
THEN SETTLES BACK TO SHADE AND THE LONG NIGHT.	156	THE DYING MAN	81
THE LONG PLAINTIVE NOTES FLOATING DOWN,	159	FIRST MEDITATN	87
I LIVE IN AIR; THE LONG LIGHT IS MY HOME;	167	HER BECOMING	93
IN THE LONG FIELDS, I LEAVE MY FATHER'S EYE;	173	WHAT TELL BONES	86
I RECOVER MY TENDERNESS BY LONG LOOKING.	173	WHAT TELL BONES	92
AND YOU CAN SING IT ALL DAY LONG--	181	MONOTONY SONG	22
(DREAMS DRAIN THE SPIRIT IF WE DREAM TOO LONG.)	187	THE LONGING	13
I LONG FOR THE IMPERISHABLE QUIET AT THE HEART OF FORM;	188	THE LONGING	45
AT LAST ONE LONG UNDULANT RIPPLE,	190	AT OYSTER RIVER	11
AND I LONG FOR THE BLAST OF DYNAMITE,	191	AT OYSTER RIVER	52
IN THE LONG JOURNEY OUT OF THE SELF,	193	JOURNY INTERIOR	1
GREY FROM THE LONG WINTER, BURNT AT THE BASE IN LATE SUMMER.	193	JOURNY INTERIOR	10
INTO A LONG MOMENT;	194	JOURNY INTERIOR	47
THE LONG WATERS	196	THE LONG WATERS	T
FEATHERS OF THE LONG SWELL, BURNISHED, ALMOST OILY--	197	THE LONG WATERS	51
AS A FIRE, SEEMINGLY LONG DEAD, FLARES UP FROM A DOWNDRAFT OF AIR IN A CHIMNEY,	198	THE LONG WATERS	63
I LOSE AND FIND MYSELF IN THE LONG WATER;	198	THE LONG WATERS	76
OF DRIVING ALONE, WITHOUT LUGGAGE, OUT A LONG PENINSULA,	199	THE FAR FIELD	3
THEN A LONG RUNNING OVER FLAT STONES	200	THE FAR FIELD	64
OF THE LONG SWELL,	205	THE ROSE	93
THE LONG SURF OF THE STORM BOOMS	210	HER TIME	21
THAT I CARRIED SO LONG	211	SONG (1)	3
THE LONG PIPES KNOCKED: IT WAS THE END OF NIGHT.	225	OTTO	39
SO LONG ON GIN, BOBBIE PINS, HALF-SMOKED CIGARS, DEAD BEER,	228	THE GERANIUM	10
SUDDENLY THEY CAME FLYING, LIKE A LONG SCARF OF SMOKE,	232	THE THING	1
ONLY TO FIND, WITH THEIR LONG TERRIBLE EYES	232	THE THING	9
OF VEAL SOAKED IN MARSALA AND LITTLE LARKS ARRANGED ON A LONG PLATTER,	232	THE THING	19
CONDUCTING HIS LONG WARS WITH THE NEIGHBORHOOD CATS,	234	ALL MORNING	16
DEATH OF THE SELF IN A LONG, TEARLESS NIGHT,	239	IN A DARK TIME	17
SWAYING IN AIR, LIKE SOME LONG WATER WEED.	241	THE SEQUEL	19
FROM ME TO THEE'S A LONG AND TERRIBLE WAY.	246	THE MARROW	18
THE SLOW LONG RIPPLES WINKING IN MY EYES.	247	I WAITED	9
LONG GAZING AT THE CEILING WILL	257	SANITARIUM	5
LONG BONES ARE LOVELIEST: I LOVE LONG BONES.	260	THE CHANGELING	12
LONG BONES ARE LOVELIEST: I LOVE LONG BONES.	260	THE CHANGELING	12
I'VE RECOVERED MY TENDERNESS BY LONG LOOKING;	260	THE CHANGELING	16
LONGED			
AND LONGED TO FEEL THE IMPACT OF DEFEAT.	28	THE FAVORITE	14
I LONGED TO BE THAT THING,	150	SNAKE	10
I LONGED TO BE LIKE HIM, AND WAS,	151	SLUG	4
LONGER			
NO LONGER QUICK WITH LIGHT,	4	DEATH PIECE	2
DENSE TREES NO LONGER HOLD THE LIGHT,	14	COMING OF COLD	30
NO LONGER GILDS THE SCENE AT NOON;	15	COMING OF COLD	48
THE FIELD IS NO LONGER SIMPLE:	89	UNFOLD! UNFOLD!	7
I AM NO LONGER YOUNG	125	WORDS FOR WIND	78
THE PRATTLE OF THE YOUNG NO LONGER PLEASES.	161	I'M HERE	9

	PAGE	TITLE	LINE

LONGER (CONTINUED)

BUT A TIME COMES WHEN THE VAGUE LIFE OF THE MOUTH NO LONGER
    SUFFICES;   168   FOURTH MEDITATN   18
I NO LONGER CRY FOR GREEN IN THE MIDST OF CINDERS,   173   WHAT TELL BONES   74
THE GREAT TREES NO LONGER SHIMMER;   187   THE LONGING   17
WHERE IMPULSE NO LONGER DICTATES, NOR THE DARKENING SHADOW,   197   THE LONG WATERS   57
I'M NO LONGER A BIRD DIPPING A BEAK INTO RIPPLING WATER   220   THE ABYSS   41
DO I IMAGINE HE NO LONGER TREMBLES   227   MEADOW MOUSE   17
HE SEEMS NO LONGER TO TREMBLE.   227   MEADOW MOUSE   19

LONGEST
THE JOURNEY FROM FLESH IS LONGEST.   66   SHAPE OF FIRE   61
RUNNING FROM GOD'S THE LONGEST RACE OF ALL.   245   THE DECISION   2

LONGING
I KNOW THE BACK-STREAM'S JOY, AND THE STONE'S ETERNAL
    PULSELESS LONGING.   88   PRAISE TO END!   82
ALL LOVERS LIVE BY LONGING, AND ENDURE: 107   SIR JOHN DAVIES   77
A LONGING FOR ANOTHER PLACE AND TIME,   162   I'M HERE   37
LONGING FOR ABSOLUTES THAT NEVER COME.   171   WHAT TELL BONES   13
THE LONGING   187   THE LONGING   T
HER LONGING   209   HER LONGING   T
BEFORE THIS LONGING,   209   HER LONGING   1

LONGINGS
AND ALL WILD LONGINGS OF THE INSATIATE BLOOD   241   THE SEQUEL   4

LONG-POLISHED
A THING CARVED OF STONE OR WOOD, WITH THE DULL IRIDESCENCE
    OF LONG-POLISHED WOOD,   234   ALL MORNING   11

LONGS
MY DUST LONGS FOR THE INVISIBLE.   104   OLD LADY'S WRDS   55

LOO
LOO, LOO, SAID THE SULPHUROUS WATER,   59   THE LONG ALLEY   14
LOO, LOO, SAID THE SULPHUROUS WATER,   59   THE LONG ALLEY   14

LOOK
WHOSE BOGEY-HAUNTED LOOK   7   ORDERS FOR DAY   16
SOON FIELD AND WOOD WILL WEAR AN APRIL LOOK,   11   LIGHT BRIGHTER   13
UNTIL CLEAR EYES PUT ON THE LOOK OF SLEEP.   12   SLOW SEASON   4
AS YOU LOOK ACROSS MY CITY, IN GOD'S COUNTRY?"   27   CLAIRVOY WIDOW   4
AS I TURNED FOR A BACKWARD LOOK,   47   THE RETURN   5
THE SALT SAID, LOOK BY THE SEA,   54   THE LOST SON   30
LOOK DOWN UNDER THE LEAVES.   55   THE LOST SON   63
HIS LOOK DRAINED THE STONES.   56   THE LOST SON   87
LOOK, LOOK, THE DITCH IS RUNNING WHITE!   57   THE LOST SON   119
LOOK, LOOK, THE DITCH IS RUNNING WHITE!   57   THE LOST SON   119
ARE THOSE HORNS ON TOP OF THE HILL? YESTERDAY HAS A LONG
    LOOK.   59   THE LONG ALLEY   13
LOOK WHAT THE LARKS DO.   59   THE LONG ALLEY   28
LOOK AT HIM PUFF. HE'S TRYING TO TALK.   73   WHERE KNOCK IS   60
MAY I LOOK TOO, LOVED EYE?   79   GIVE WAY, GATES   19
--LOOK FOR THE WHITE FIRE.   89   UNFOLD! UNFOLD!   17
AND HER QUICK LOOK, A SIDELONG PICKEREL SMILE;   102   ELEGY FOR JANE   2
HER LOOK WAS MORNING IN THE DYING LIGHT.   107   SIR JOHN DAVIES   84
HE SAID, "LOOK, BIRDS, ALL THIS IS FUTILE: 115   THE SERPENT   19
I LOOK ON WHITE, AND IT TURNS INTO GRAY--   134   THE PURE FURY   24
UNTIL MY EYES LOOK AT A BRIGHTER SUN   134   THE PURE FURY   27
BEYOND THE LOOK OF LOVE.   137   LOVE'S PROGRESS   15
I LOOK AT THE FIRST STAR: 148   THE SMALL   4
I TURN MY LOOK UPON   154   THE DYING MAN   28
LOOK AT THE FAR TREES AT THE END OF THE GARDEN.   163   I'M HERE   82
AND SOMETIMES LOOK BEFORE YOU LEAP   181   MONOTONY SONG   27
BUT NEVER THE FULL LOOK OF MY EYES,   209   HER RETICENCE   6
WHO'D LOOK WHEN HE COULD FEEL?   212   LIGHT LISTENED   5
I LOOK DOWN THE FAR LIGHT   240   IN EVEING AIR   13
AND WHEN I LOOK AGAIN,   240   IN EVEING AIR   16
ONE LOOK TOO CLOSE CAN TAKE MY SOUL AWAY.   246   THE MARROW   9

LOOKED
WHEN I LOOKED AT THE ALTERED SCENE, MY EYE WAS UNDECEIVED,   12   MID-CNTRY BLOW   7
OUR SOULS LOOKED FORTH, AND THE GREAT DAY STOOD STILL.   106   SIR JOHN DAVIES   60
--IT LOOKED LIKE DIRTY DINKY.   114   DINKY   12
IT LOOKED AT ME; IT STARED.   145   THE BEAST   10
HE LOOKED BEYOND ME WHEN   146   THE SONG   2
THE MOON, A PURE ISLAMIC SHAPE, LOOKED DOWN.   166   HER BECOMING   55
I SANG TO THE ONE STAR THAT LOOKED DOWN AT ME;   216   THE SHY MAN   2
AS I LOOKED OUT AT THEM FROM THE HIGH HOUSE,   225   OTTO   35
SHE LOOKED SO LIMP AND BEDRAGGLED,   228   THE GERANIUM   2

	PAGE	TITLE	LINE
LOOKED (CONTINUED)			
AND I BECAME ALL THAT I LOOKED UPON.	247	I WAITED	12
AND LOOKED AWAY.	262	FOLLIES OF ADAM	21
HIS NOSE LOOKED EVEN BIGGER THAN IT WAS,	273	SUPPR W LINDSAY	21
LOOKING			
--AND THE EYES, STILL VIVID, LOOKING UP FROM A SUNKEN ROOM.	22	ROAD TO WDLAWN	8
LOOKING TOWARD WHAT WE ARE.	80	GIVE WAY, GATES	37
GROTESQUE, AWKWARD, HIS EXTENDED EYES LOOKING AT NOTHING IN PARTICULAR,	159	FIRST MEDITATN	63
BUT THESE ROSES: I CAN WEAR THEM BY LOOKING AWAY.	163	I'M HERE	78
I RECOVER MY TENDERNESS BY LONG LOOKING.	173	WHAT TELL BONES	92
LOOKING AT YOU WITHOUT TURNING HIS SMALL HEAD,	234	ALL MORNING	12
I WENT, NOT LOOKING BACK. I WAS AFRAID.	247	I WAITED	18
I'VE RECOVERED MY TENDERNESS BY LONG LOOKING;	260	THE CHANGELING	16
LOOKS			
TWO YELLOW AND BLACK, AND ONE THAT LOOKS IN BETWEEN,--	24	VERNAL SENTIMNT	6
MY LOOKS HAD A VOICE;	104	OLD LADY'S WRDS	47
AND I REMEMBER LOOKS	225	THE CHUMS	4
MADE WITH THEIR STINGY LOOKS,--	267	SAGINAW SONG	34
BURNING IN SAND. "IT LOOKS LIKE I SHOULD GO,"--	274	SUPPR W LINDSAY	37
LOOPING			
LIKE A LEECH, LOOPING MYSELF ALONG,	209	HER LONGING	7
LOOPS			
HE LOOPS IN CRAZY FIGURES HALF THE NIGHT	16	THE BAT	5
ALL THE COILS, LOOPS, AND WHORLS.	44	FRAU BAUMAN	24
LOOSE			
AS BRANCHES LOOSE LAST VESTIGES OF SNOW.	11	LIGHT BRIGHTER	10
THE LOOSE VINE DROOPS WITH HOAR AT DAWN,	14	COMING OF COLD	20
NUDGES A SAND-CRUMB LOOSE,	37	CUTTINGS	6
LOOSE GHOSTLY MOUTHS	39	ORCHIDS	17
BUT SOMETHING ALWAYS WENT OUT OF ME WHEN I DUG LOOSE THOSE CARPETS	40	MOSS-GATHERING	7
THE AIR GREW LOOSE AND LOUD.	50	THE CYCLE	12
TO LET HER LOOSE.	60	THE LONG ALLEY	54
TUFTY, THE WATER'S LOOSE.	79	GIVE WAY, GATES	6
THERE'S A GHOST LOOSE IN THE LONG GRASS!	82	SENSIBILITY! LA	27
ITS SHADOWS LOOSE, A WATERY FINGER;	101	LIGHT BREATHER	10
AND THEN HE CUT LOOSE WITH A HORRIBLE NOTE	115	THE SERPENT	21
SHE PLAYED IT QUICK, SHE PLAYED IT LIGHT AND LOOSE;	127	I KNEW A WOMAN	17
SHE TRIES TO THINK, AND IT FLIES LOOSE AGAIN.	133	THE PURE FURY	11
O ANGEL, LET ME LOOSE!"	136	THE SENSUALISTS	6
BUT YOU, LOOSE TOE FROM THE OLD LIFE,	151	SLUG	10
THE LOOSE AIR SENT ME RUNNING LIKE A CHILD--	155	THE DYING MAN	55
LOOSE IN MY LAP,	164	I'M HERE	97
I'M A SMALL STONE, LOOSE IN THE SHALE.	172	WHAT TELL BONES	47
FALLS BACK, A SLUG, A LOOSE WORM	187	THE LONGING	21
WAKES ALL THE WAVES, ALL THEIR LOOSE WANDERING FIRE.	201	THE FAR FIELD	88
SHAKING LOOSE THE LAST WIZENED ORANGES IN THE ORCHARD,	231	THE STORM	32
ITS ALMOST-INVISIBLE WINGS, BUZZING, HITTING THE LOOSE LEAVES INTERMITTENTLY--	234	ALL MORNING	32
LOOSEN			
TO LOOSEN WITH ALL TEN FINGERS HELD WIDE AND LIMBER	40	MOSS-GATHERING	1
WHILE STONES LOOSEN ON THE OBSCURE HILLSIDE,	157	FIRST MEDITATN	5
LOOSENED			
THE DEW LOOSENED	51	THE WAKING (1)	19
A MOON LOOSENED FROM A STAG'S EYE,	79	GIVE WAY, GATES	10
WHAT ELSE HAS THE VINE LOOSENED?	90	UNFOLD! UNFOLD!	43
--AND LOOSENED UP WITH OUR MONEY.	112	SQUEEZE-BOX	25
LOOSENING			
ONLY A FEW BUBBLES LOOSENING FROM THE ILL-MATCHED TENTACLES,	159	FIRST MEDITATN	64
THE SUN LOOSENING THE FROST ON DECEMBER WINDOWS,	161	I'M HERE	2
LOOSENS			
SHALE LOOSENS. MARL REACHES INTO THE FIELD. SMALL BIRDS PASS OVER WATER.	64	SHAPE OF FIRE	11
THE SUDDEN SUCKING ROAR AS THE CULVERT LOOSENS ITS DEBRIS OF BRANCHES AND STICKS,	191	AT OYSTER RIVER	53
LOPING			
THE DOE WITH ITS SLOPED SHOULDERS LOPING ACROSS THE HIGHWAY,	190	AT OYSTER RIVER	27
LOPPED			
ROSE ON SUCH LOPPED LIMBS TO A NEW LIFE?	37	CUTTINGS (LATE)	4
LOQUACIOUS			
WALKING THE EDGE, LOQUACIOUS, UNAFRAID.	155	THE DYING MAN	63

	PAGE	TITLE	LINE
LORD			
I PRAY THEE, LORD, THAT I MAY CHOOSE	8	PRAYER	2
THEREFORE, O LORD, LET ME PRESERVE	8	PRAYER	19
DELIVER ME, O LORD, FROM ALL	24	BEFORE STUDY	9
I ASKED: MAY THE BLESSINGS OF LIFE, O LORD, DESCEND ON THE LIVING.	48	JUDGE NOT	6
THE FIEND'S FAR AWAY. LORD, WHAT DO YOU REQUIRE?	59	THE LONG ALLEY	21
IS THERE A WISDOM IN OBJECTS? FEW OBJECTS PRAISE THE LORD.	166	HER BECOMING	38
THE LORD GOD HAS TAKEN MY HEAVINESS AWAY;	222	THE ABYSS	98
A LORD OF NATURE WEEPING TO A TREE.	239	IN A DARK TIME	4
MAKE ME, O LORD, A LAST, A SIMPLE THING	240	IN EVEING AIR	8
LORD, HEAR ME OUT, AND HEAR ME OUT THIS DAY:	246	THE MARROW	17
LORDLY			
SPINNING THROUGH THE LORDLY CLOUD.	266	FOR STEVENS	4
LORDS			
TELL ME, GREAT LORDS OF STING,	83	O LULL ME, LULL	8
LOSE			
IF I MUST OF MY SENSES LOSE,	8	PRAYER	1
ONLY TO LOSE MYSELF IN THIS SMALL DARK.	154	THE DYING MAN	41
I LOSE AND FIND MYSELF IN THE LONG WATER;	198	THE LONG WATERS	76
I HEAR A CRY AND LOSE IT ON THE WIND.	243	THE MOTION	10
LOSING			
--LOT LIKE LOSING SOME MONEY.	111	SQUEEZE-BOX	21
LOST			
THE NIGHTMARE SILENCE IS BROKEN. WE ARE NOT LOST.	5	PROGNOSIS	16
WAS LOST IN A MAZE OF WATER.	6	THE PREMONITION	13
LOST HUES OF BIRDS THE TREES TAKE AS THEIR OWN.	12	SLOW SEASON	9
KISS ME, KISS ME QUICK, MISTRESS OF LOST WISDOM,	48	LAST WORDS	7
THE LOST SON	53	THE LOST SON	T
MAYBE I'M LOST,	72	WHERE KNOCK IS	43
MANY ASTOUNDS BEFORE, I LOST MY IDENTITY TO A PEBBLE;	88	PRAISE TO END!	88
THE LOST HAVE THEIR OWN PACE.	91	UNFOLD! UNFOLD!	61
I'M LOST IN WHAT I HAVE.	97	O, THOU OPENING	8
THINGS LOLL AND LOITER. WHO CONDONES THE LOST?	106	SIR JOHN DAVIES	43
IN THAT DARK WORLD WHERE GODS HAVE LOST THEIR WAY.	106	SIR JOHN DAVIES	48
WILL THE SELF, LOST, BE FOUND AGAIN? IN FORM?	135	THE RENEWAL	17
LOST OPPOSITES BEND DOWN--	140	THE SWAN	18
THINGS LOST IN SLEEP RETURN	148	THE SMALL	15
THE TICKET MISLAID OR LOST, THE GATE	158	FIRST MEDITATN	49
BEHIND THE EYE; THE LOST ACRES AT THE EDGE OF SMOKY CITIES.	159	FIRST MEDITATN	75
TO BECOME LOST IN A LOVE,	169	FOURTH MEDITATN	31
YOU SQUEAK LIKE A MOUSE THAT'S LOST IN THE HAY,	177	KITTY-CAT BIRD	10
THE LOST SELF CHANGES,	201	THE FAR FIELD	82
O WORLD SO FAR AWAY! O MY LOST WORLD!	225	OTTO	42
IT'S LOST UPON THE NIGHT--	240	IN EVEING AIR	17
PAIN WANDERS THROUGH MY BONES LIKE A LOST FIRE;	246	THE MARROW	11
THEN LOST ITSELF DOWN THROUGH A ROCKY GORGE.	247	I WAITED	20
COME EASY TO THE SILL, THINGS LOST FROM FAR AWAY.	273	SUPPR W LINDSAY	4
LOT			
AND MADE A LOT OF MONEY.	75	I NEED, I NEED	38
BUT ME AND A GIRL FRIEND LEARNED A LOT	111	SQUEEZE-BOX	10
--LOT LIKE LOSING SOME MONEY.	111	SQUEEZE-BOX	21
LOU			
WHERE'S ANN? WHERE'S LOU? WHERE'S JOCK-WITH-THE-WIND?	97	O, THOU OPENING	17
LOUD			
THE AIR GREW LOOSE AND LOUD.	50	THE CYCLE	12
THAT AIR AND SHINE: AND THE FLICKER'S LOUD SUMMER CALL:	66	SHAPE OF FIRE	70
SHE CRIES OUT LOUD THE SOUL'S OWN SECRET JOY;	129	SHE	9
CRIED TO MY FLESH OUT LOUD.	147	THE EXORCISM	8
IN MY LEFT EAR I HEAR THE LOUD SOUND OF A MINOR COLLAPSE.	165	HER BECOMING	29
THE WILLOW WITH ITS BIRD GREW LOUD, GREW LOUDER STILL.	248	THE TREE, BIRD	13
LOUDER			
THE WILLOW WITH ITS BIRD GREW LOUD, GREW LOUDER STILL.	248	THE TREE, BIRD	13
LOUDLY			
I, WHO CAME BACK FROM THE DEPTHS LAUGHING TOO LOUDLY,	198	THE LONG WATERS	73
LOUIS			
AND EAST ST. LOUIS AND MONONGAHELA	111	SQUEEZE-BOX	19
LOUT			
WITHOUT STARING LIKE A LOUT, OR A MOPING ADOLESCENT;	163	I'M HERE	80
OR SOME OLD LOUT WHO CAN	262	FOLLIES OF ADAM	2
LOUT'S			
BEHOLD, IN THE LOUT'S EYE,	93	I CRY, LOVE!	38

LOVE

	PAGE	TITLE	LINE
LOVE (CONTINUED)			
FROM WHENCE, LOVE?	236	SONG (2)	5
YET IT'S THE NATURE OF ALL LOVE TO RISE:	238	THE TRANCED	22
WHOM DO WE LOVE? I THOUGHT I KNEW THE TRUTH;	241	THE SEQUEL	7
AND GRIEVE INTO THE CERTAINTY OF LOVE.	243	THE MOTION	6
LOVE BEGETS LOVE. THIS TORMENT IS MY JOY.	243	THE MOTION	7
LOVE BEGETS LOVE. THIS TORMENT IS MY JOY.	243	THE MOTION	7
THIS REACH BEYOND THIS DEATH, THIS ACT OF LOVE	243	THE MOTION	17
I LOVE MYSELF: THAT'S MY ONE CONSTANCY.	244	INFIRMITY	5
I'VE COME TO LOVE. A VIREO WHETS ITS BILL.	244	INFIRMITY	26
I WAS FLUNG BACK FROM SUFFERING AND LOVE	246	THE MARROW	19
FOR LOVE, FOR LOVE'S SAKE;	251	ONCE MORE, RND	10
LOVE.	259	SONG (3)	35
LOVE MAKES ME NAKED;	259	SONG (3)	36
LONG BONES ARE LOVELIEST: I LOVE LONG BONES.	260	THE CHANGELING	12
LOVE-BEAT			
THE LOVE-BEAT OF A BIRD.	212	LIGHT LISTENED	9
LOVED			
MAY I LOOK TOO, LOVED EYE?	79	GIVE WAY, GATES	19
SHE LOVED THE WIND BECAUSE THE WIND LOVED ME.	119	THE DREAM	16
SHE LOVED THE WIND BECAUSE THE WIND LOVED ME.	119	THE DREAM	16
HOW I LOVED ONE LIKE YOU WHEN I WAS LITTLE!--	151	SLUG	1
ALL WOMEN LOVED DANCE IN A DYING LIGHT--	156	THE DYING MAN	78
THE LOVED FOX, AND THE WREN.	166	HER BECOMING	64
LOVED HEART, WHAT CAN I SAY?	172	WHAT TELL BONES	38
FOR ANCESTORS WHO LOVED A WARLIKE SHOW,	224	OTTO	25
THE INDIANS LOVED HIM, AND THE POLISH POOR.	225	OTTO	33
WHO BUT THE LOVED KNOW LOVE'S A FARING-FORTH?	243	THE MOTION	13
SAD THE SOUL'S JOY. LOVED HEART, WHAT ELSE CAN I SAY	261	THE CHANGELING	28
LOVELESS			
THE SERPENT'S HEART SUSTAINS THE LOVELESS STONE:	131	SENTENTIOUS MAN	3
MACHINES, MACHINES, LOVELESS, TEMPORAL;	166	HER BECOMING	42
LOVELIEST			
LONG BONES ARE LOVELIEST: I LOVE LONG BONES.	260	THE CHANGELING	12
LOVE-LONGING			
YET LOVE-LONGING OF A KIND	237	THE TRANCED	8
LOVELY			
WHOLE FIELDS LOVELY AND INVIOLATE,--	39	WEED PULLER	13
THE LOVELY DIMINUTIVES.	63	FIELD OF LIGHT	43
O LOVELY CHINK, O WHITE	83	O LULL ME, LULL	22
I HEAR A MOST LOVELY HUZZA:	92	I CRY, LOVE!	12
AND, LOVELY, LEARN BY GOING WHERE TO GO.	108	THE WAKING (2)	15
AS A LOVELY SUBSTANCE WILL;	123	WORDS FOR WIND	19
I KNEW A WOMAN, LOVELY IN HER BONES,	127	I KNEW A WOMAN	1
SHE MAKES SPACE LONELY WITH A LOVELY SONG.	129	SHE	4
BETWEEN THOSE LOVELY TITS.	136	THE SENSUALISTS	12
WITH THAT LOVELY MAN, TOM MOORE.	268	SAGINAW SONG	49
LOVE-NEST			
NEXT DOOR THERE IS A LOVE-NEST OF PLASTER BOARD AND TIN,	27	CLAIRVOY WIDOW	15
LOVER			
THE FLESH-BOUND SIGHING LOVER,	7	ORDERS FOR DAY	5
NEITHER FATHER NOR LOVER.	102	ELEGY FOR JANE	22
WHAT LOVER KEEPS HIS SONG?	167	HER BECOMING	82
THE BLUEBIRD, LOVER OF HOLES IN OLD WOOD, LILTING ITS LIGHT SONG,	204	THE ROSE	66
A LARK-SWEET LOVER IF EVER THERE WAS.	258	SONG (3)	3
LOVERS			
LOVERS DISENGAGE, MOVE SHEEPISHLY TOWARD THE AISLE	47	DOUBLE FEATURE	2
ALL LOVERS LIVE BY LONGING, AND ENDURE:	107	SIR JOHN DAVIES	77
A THING ALL EARTHLY LOVERS UNDERSTAND.	149	IN LATE SUMMER	22
LOVER'S			
AND DELIGHT IN A LOVER'S PRAISE,	208	HER WORDS	4
LOVES			
A GREEN THING LOVES THE GREEN	212	LIGHT LISTENED	15
AND LOVES THE LIVING GROUND.	212	LIGHT LISTENED	16
WHO LOVES THE SMALL CAN BE BOTH SAINT AND BOOR,	225	OTTO	31
HE LOVES HIMSELF, AND THE ILLUSTRIOUS DEAD;	264	THREE EPIGRAMS	4
LOVE'S			
MY LOVE'S LOCKED IN	60	THE LONG ALLEY	49
O MY LOVE'S LIGHT AS A DUCK	83	O LULL ME, LULL	12
LOVE IS NOT LOVE UNTIL LOVE'S VULNERABLE.	120	THE DREAM	17
LOVE'S PROGRESS	137	LOVE'S PROGRESS	T
LOVE'S ALL. LOVE'S ALL I KNOW.	141	MEMORY	8

	PAGE	TITLE	LINE
LOVE'S (CONTINUED)			
LOVE'S ALL. LOVE'S ALL I KNOW.	141	MEMORY	8
ALL SENSUAL LOVE'S BUT DANCING ON A GRAVE.	154	THE DYING MAN	47
ON LOVE'S WORST UGLY DAY,	157	FIRST MEDITATN	1
WHO BUT THE LOVED KNOW LOVE'S A FARING-FORTH?	243	THE MOTION	13
FOR LOVE, FOR LOVE'S SAKE;	251	ONCE MORE, RND	10
LOVING			
LOVING, I USE THE AIR	123	WORDS FOR WIND	3
DRY BONES! DRY BONES! I FIND MY LOVING HEART,	135	THE RENEWAL	19
LOVINGLY			
MOST LOVINGLY: I BREATHE;	123	WORDS FOR WIND	4
LOW			
MORE FURTIVE THAN THE HAND IN LOW	8	PRAYER	11
THE EAR HEARS ONLY IN LOW PLACES.	59	THE LONG ALLEY	7
ALONG THE LOW GROUND DRY ONLY IN AUGUST,--	62	FIELD OF LIGHT	26
A LOW MOUTH LAPS WATER. WEEDS, WEEDS, HOW I LOVE YOU.	64	SHAPE OF FIRE	17
IT'S A COLD SCRAPE IN A LOW PLACE.	80	GIVE WAY, GATES	47
NOW THE WATER'S LOW. THE WEEDS EXCEED ME.	86	PRAISE TO END!	23
THE SEVERAL SOUNDS WERE LOW;	87	PRAISE TO END!	67
A LOW VOICE, SUMMER-SAD.	90	UNFOLD! UNFOLD!	50
A BIRD SANG LOW; THE MOONLIGHT SIFTED IN;	119	THE DREAM	7
IN HER LOW VOICE I HEARD	128	THE VOICE	3
SHE LILTS A LOW SOFT LANGUAGE, AND I HEAR	129	SHE	5
I WOOED WITH A LOW TUNE;	146	THE SONG	20
I BROKE FROM THAT LOW PLACE	147	THE EXORCISM	26
A MUFFLED VOICE, A LOW SWEET WATERY NOISE.	165	HER BECOMING	20
OVER THE LOW, BARNACLED, ELEPHANT-COLORED ROCKS,	190	AT OYSTER RIVER	1
BLESSED BY THE LIPS OF A LOW WIND,	197	THE LONG WATERS	45
AND THE LOW RIPPLES RUN OVER A PEBBLY SHORELINE,	198	THE LONG WATERS	62
OR A BREEZE MOVES OVER THE KNEES FROM A LOW HILL,	198	THE LONG WATERS	64
THE WIND FANNING THE ASH OF A LOW FIRE.	201	THE FAR FIELD	79
AND THE EAGLES SAIL LOW OVER THE FIR TREES,	202	THE ROSE	6
AND TWO SCOTERS FLY LOW,	210	HER TIME	12
I STAND BY A LOW FIRE	240	IN EVEING AIR	19
LOWERED			
O SEE THE FATE OF HIM WHOSE GUARD WAS LOWERED!--	5	PROGNOSIS	3
LOW-FLYING			
IN TIME WHEN THE TROUT AND YOUNG SALMON LEAP FOR THE LOW-FLYING INSECTS,	197	THE LONG WATERS	33
LOWLY			
THE LOWLY WORM CLIMBS UP A WINDING STAIR;	108	THE WAKING (2)	11
LUBBER			
WHEN HE TRIED TO SPOUT, THAT GREAT BIG LUBBER,	178	THE WHALE	3
LUCIA			
BETWEEN THE WHITENING TREES, UP SANTA LUCIA,	230	THE STORM	20
LUCK			
THE VISIT OF VISION, LUCK YEARS OVERDUE,	29	THE GENTLE	6
A VISIT FROM HIM IS A PIECE OF PURE LUCK,	113	TO A LADY ED	6
I DRINK GOOD LIQUOR WHEN MY LUCK IS GOOD.	132	SENTENTIOUS MAN	28
OR, WITH LUCK, AS A LION.	200	THE FAR FIELD	49
MY LUCK RAISES THE WIND."	208	HER WORDS	7
HERE'S THE LAST KISS OF MY LUCK:	259	SONG (3)	43
LUCK! LUCK! THAT'S WHAT I CARE FOR IN A CAGE	273	SUPPR W LINDSAY	2
LUCK! LUCK! THAT'S WHAT I CARE FOR IN A CAGE	273	SUPPR W LINDSAY	2
LUG			
A MOST EX-AS-PER-AT-ING LUG.	116	THE SLOTH	7
LUGGAGE			
OF DRIVING ALONE, WITHOUT LUGGAGE, OUT A LONG PENINSULA,	199	THE FAR FIELD	3
LUGUBRIOUSLY			
THE LUGUBRIOUSLY BEAUTIFUL PLAINT UTTERED AT REGULAR INTERVALS,	234	ALL MORNING	4
LULL			
LULL	31	LULL	T
O LULL ME, LULL ME	83	O LULL ME, LULL	T
O LULL ME, LULL ME	83	O LULL ME, LULL	T
LULLED			
I WAS LULLED BY THE SLAMMING OF IRON,	53	THE LOST SON	2
I'M LULLED INTO HALF-SLEEP	191	AT OYSTER RIVER	60
LULLS			
THE STORM LULLS OFF, THEN REDOUBLES,	231	THE STORM	30
LUMINESCENT			
SOFT LUMINESCENT FINGERS,	39	ORCHIDS	15

	PAGE	TITLE	LINE
LUMINOUS			
LUMINOUS ONE, SHALL WE MEET ON THE BOSOM OF GOD?	59	THE LONG ALLEY	29
A LUMINOUS STILLNESS.	221	THE ABYSS	84
LUMPS			
A DEEP DISH. LUMPS IN IT.	74	I NEED, I NEED	1
LUNCHES			
OH THAT COUSIN! HER MANNERS! AT LUNCHES!	179	MYRTLE'S COUSIN	5
WHAT HER FRIENDS COULDN'T EAT AT THOSE LUNCHES!	179	MYRTLE'S COUSIN	10
LUNGING			
LUNGING INTO THE LASHING	41	BIG WIND	2
LUNGING DOWN A HILLSIDE.	159	FIRST MEDITATN	59
LUNGS			
THE UNSINGING FIELDS WHERE NO LUNGS BREATHE,	196	THE LONG WATERS	11
LURCH			
ROSE BUT TO LURCH AND FALL,	145	THE BEAST	13
THEN THEY LURCH FORWARD,	159	FIRST MEDITATN	58
LURK			
IN A LURKING-PLACE I LURK,	122	ALL EARTH, AIR	26
LURKING-PLACE			
IN A LURKING-PLACE I LURK,	122	ALL EARTH, AIR	26
LURKS			
LURKS THE BAD ANIMAL.	161	I'M HERE	11
LUSH			
A MEADOW, LUSH AND GREEN.	145	THE BEAST	5
THE LONG LUSH GRASS LAY STILL;	145	THE BEAST	18
LUST			
OF SIXTEEN-YEAR-OLD LUST.	46	PICKLE BELT	12
EASY THE LIFE OF THE MOUTH. WHAT A LUST FOR RIPENESS!	90	UNFOLD! UNFOLD!	39
LUST FATIGUES THE SOUL.	187	THE LONGING	11
BY LUST ALONE WE KEEP THE MIND ALIVE,	243	THE MOTION	5
LYING			
I STOP THE LYING MOUTH:	3	OPEN HOUSE	16
TO A TREE LYING FLAT, ITS CROWN HALF BROKEN.	197	THE LONG WATERS	54
(I FOUND IT LYING AMONG THE RUBBLE OF AN OLD COAL BIN)	199	THE FAR FIELD	20
MA			
MIPS AND MA THE MOOLY MOO,	86	PRAISE TO END!	31
MAC			
AND THE BUSH WOULD SAY, "MAC,	182	BOY AND BUSH	3
MACABRE			
EPIDERMAL MACABRE	19	EPIDERM MACABRE	T
MACHINE			
ESCAPES FROM THE MACHINE AT LAST.	33	HIGHWAY: MICH	20
MACHINERY			
AMONG THE TIN CANS, TIRES, RUSTED PIPES, BROKEN MACHINERY,--	199	THE FAR FIELD	17
MACHINES			
MACHINES, MACHINES, LOVELESS, TEMPORAL;	166	HER BECOMING	42
MACHINES, MACHINES, LOVELESS, TEMPORAL;	166	HER BECOMING	42
MAD			
MAD IN THE WIND I WEAR	123	WORDS FOR WIND	5
YOU COULD SAY I WAS MAD.	146	THE SONG	21
AND THE SMALL MAD SISKINS FLIT BY,	152	THE SISKINS	8
A MAD HEN IN A FAR CORNER OF THE DARK,	165	HER BECOMING	5
SHE WAS MAD AS A HARE,	179	MYRTLE	3
I WOULD WITH THE FISH, THE BLACKENING SALMON, AND THE MAD LEMMINGS,	188	THE LONGING	39
WHO FED AND TENDED THE INFIRM, THE MAD, THE EPILEPTIC,	223	ELEGY (2)	9
MADDENS			
EASILY MADDENS	65	SHAPE OF FIRE	43
MADE			
WHO FLEE IN WHAT THEIR HANDS HAVE MADE.	33	HIGHWAY: MICH	15
MY KNEES MADE LITTLE WINDS UNDERNEATH	57	THE LOST SON	128
FOR WHOM WERE YOU MADE, SWEETNESS I CANNOT TOUCH?	59	THE LONG ALLEY	27
SMALL WINDS MADE	62	FIELD OF LIGHT	7
AND MADE A LOT OF MONEY.	75	I NEED, I NEED	38
A RIPPLE MADE A SOFT REPLY.	100	THE VISITANT	6
THAT MADE HIM THINK THE UNIVERSE COULD HUM?	105	SIR JOHN DAVIES	2
AND I HAVE MADE A PROMISE TO MY EARS	105	SIR JOHN DAVIES	5
AND SHAPELESS NIGHT THAT MADE NO ANSWER BACK.	107	SIR JOHN DAVIES	90
AND MADE MY SONG THEIR OWN.	123	WORDS FOR WIND	16
SING OF THAT NOTHING OF WHICH ALL IS MADE,	140	THE SWAN	19
MADE FROM HIS TERROR AND DISMAY A GRAVE PHILOSOPHICAL LANGUAGE;	170	FOURTH MEDITATN	72
THE WAVES LESS THAN THE RIPPLES MADE BY RISING FISH,	203	THE ROSE	32

	PAGE	TITLE	LINE
MADE (CONTINUED)			
THE MEADOW INSECTS MADE A LEVEL NOISE.	247	I WAITED	4
HER ARMS MADE A SUMMER.	258	SONG (3)	23
MADE WITH THEIR STINGY LOOKS,--	267	SAGINAW SONG	34
MADMAN			
A MADMAN STARING AT PERPETUAL NIGHT,	155	THE DYING MAN	49
MADNESS			
WHAT'S MADNESS BUT NOBILITY OF SOUL	239	IN A DARK TIME	7
MADRONA			
BEYOND THE SEA PINE, THE OAK, THE WIND-TIPPED MADRONA,	203	THE ROSE	47
MADRONAS			
NEAR THIS ROSE, IN THIS GROVE OF SUN-PARCHED, WIND-WARPED MADRONAS,	205	THE ROSE	98
MAGNIFIED			
I SAW ALL THINGS THROUGH WATER, MAGNIFIED,	247	I WAITED	10
MAGNIFIES			
WHO MAGNIFIES THE MORNING WITH HER EYES,	196	THE LONG WATERS	25
MAID			
SO I'VE GOT TO GET ME A RICH UGLY OLD MAID	112	SQUEEZE-BOX	43
SO WHEN THAT SNUFFLING CRETIN OF A MAID	228	THE GERANIUM	22
MAIDENHAIR			
YET FINE AS MAIDENHAIR,	271	THE REPLY	12
MAIMED			
MY MAIMED DARLING, MY SKITTERY PIGEON.	102	ELEGY FOR JANE	19
A FACE FLOATS IN THE FERNS. DO MAIMED GODS WALK?	165	HER BECOMING	18
"I'M MAIMED; I CAN'T FLY;	249	THE RESTORED	9
MAINCURRENT			
AROUND, BACK INTO THE TINY MAINCURRENT, THE RUSH OF BROWNISH-WHITE WATER,	159	FIRST MEDITATN	71
MAKE			
HIS FINGERS MAKE A HAT ABOUT HIS HEAD.	16	THE BAT	3
OR MAKE THE DUST BUZZ WITH A LIGHT SPRAY,	42	OLD FLORIST	7
COULD MAKE A SMALL BOY DIZZY;	45	MY PAPA'S WALTZ	2
THIS AIR COULD FLESH A DEAD STICK. SWEET JESUS, MAKE ME SWEAT.	61	THE LONG ALLEY	63
MAKE THE SEA FLASH IN THE DUST.	61	THE LONG ALLEY	84
I'LL MAKE A HOLE FOR HER.	72	WHERE KNOCK IS	33
MAKE ME A BIRD OR A BEAR!	80	GIVE WAY, GATES	39
I'LL MAKE IT; BUT IT MAY TAKE ME.	97	O, THOU OPENING	1
THE IMPULSE TO MAKE SOMEONE ELSE COMPLETE?	105	SIR JOHN DAVIES	27
THE FLESH CAN MAKE THE SPIRIT VISIBLE;	106	SIR JOHN DAVIES	63
(BUT WHAT PRODIGIOUS MOWING WE DID MAKE).	127	I KNEW A WOMAN	14
ON FEET THAT MAKE NO SOUND	148	THE SMALL	17
THE SMALL WINDS MAKE THEIR CHILLY INDICTMENTS.	157	FIRST MEDITATN	3
THE DEAD MAKE MORE IMPOSSIBLE DEMANDS FROM THEIR SILENCE;	168	FOURTH MEDITATN	19
AND SHAPES MAKE ME AFRAID:	171	WHAT TELL BONES	14
TO MAKE REMARKS ABOUT MY--GRRR!	181	MONOTONY SONG	11
MAKE THAT MY STUDY.	207	THE YOUNG GIRL	4
MANY ARRIVALS MAKE US LIVE: THE TREE BECOMING	235	MANIFESTATION	1
I'LL MAKE A BROKEN MUSIC, OR I'LL DIE.	240	IN EVEING AIR	6
MAKE ME, O LORD, A LAST, A SIMPLE THING	240	IN EVEING AIR	8
SUCH STRETCHINGS OF THE SPIRIT MAKE NO SOUND.	243	THE MOTION	4
MAKER			
BE WITH ME, WHITMAN, MAKER OF CATALOGUES:	220	THE ABYSS	29
MAKES			
MAKES AN INTENSER DAY	124	WORDS FOR WIND	56
SHE MAKES SPACE LONELY WITH A LOVELY SONG.	129	SHE	4
SHE KNOWS THE SPEECH OF LIGHT, AND MAKES IT PLAIN	129	SHE	11
MAKES THEM HUDDLE IN GROUPS,--	180	GOO-GIRL	15
MAKES ALMOST A WAVE OVER A BARRIER OF SMALL STONES,	190	AT OYSTER RIVER	13
THAT MAKES AN OLD CONFUSION WORSE.	257	SANITARIUM	2
LOVE MAKES ME NAKED;	259	SONG (3)	36
AND THAT MAKES THREE, COUNTING HIS FACE AS ONE.	273	SUPPR W LINDSAY	9
MAKING			
THERE WERE CLOUDS MAKING A ROUT OF SHAPES CROSSING A WINDBREAK OF CEDARS,	63	FIELD OF LIGHT	48
I KNOW IT'S AN OWL. HE'S MAKING IT DARKER.	72	WHERE KNOCK IS	39
WAITING LIKE A FERN, MAKING A SPINY SHADOW.	102	ELEGY FOR JANE	15
MAKING A SLOW JOURNEY AROUND THE WELL-CURB.	151	SLUG	3
MAKING IT QUIVER WITH MY BODY;	161	I'M HERE	25
MAKING MY WAY OVER WET STONES.	166	HER BECOMING	48
AND THEN MAKING GOO,	180	GOO-GIRL	4

	PAGE	TITLE	LINE
MAKING (CONTINUED)			
I THINK OF THE ROCK SINGING, AND LIGHT MAKING ITS OWN SILENCE,	204	THE ROSE	79
MAKING A RACKET TO WAKE THE DEAD,	234	ALL MORNING	18
THE MOLE MAKING ITS WAY THROUGH DARKEST GROUND,	235	MANIFESTATION	4
MALICE			
I WOULD UNLEARN THE LINGO OF EXASPERATION, ALL THE DISTORTIONS OF MALICE AND HATRED;	188	THE LONGING	42
MALIGN			
DIVINITY ITSELF MALIGN, ABSURD;	237	THE TRANCED	7
MALIGNANT			
FROM EACH MALIGNANT WISH	31	LULL	5
MAMMA			
O FORTUNATE HE WHOSE MAMMA PAYS THE BILLS!	24	POETASTER	4
PAPA AND MAMMA	71	WHERE KNOCK IS	3
MAMMA, SHE'S A SAD FAT.	74	I NEED, I NEED	19
I SAID TO MAMMA.	74	WHERE KNOCK IS	81
MAMMA! PUT ON YOUR DARK HOOD;	82	SENSIBILITY! LA	37
MAMMALIAN			
AT ONCE MAMMALIAN AND REPTILIAN.	23	AMOROUS LADY	14
MAN			
THAT FORCE THE SON OF MAN TO TOIL;	18	LONG LIVE WEEDS	4
NOW EACH MAN STANDS APART.	31	LULL	7
A DRUNK MAN STUMBLES BY, ABSORBED IN SELF-TALK.	33	IDYLL	2
THAT HUMP OF A MAN BUNCHING CHRYSANTHEMUMS	42	OLD FLORIST	1
TIME FOR THE FLAT-HEADED MAN. I RECOGNIZE THAT LISTENER,	65	SHAPE OF FIRE	29
THE UNEASY MAN.	65	SHAPE OF FIRE	44
THERE WAS A MOOLY MAN	71	WHERE KNOCK IS	16
IF I WERE A YOUNG MAN,	104	OLD LADY'S WRDS	49
IS THAT DANCE SLOWING IN THE MIND OF MAN	105	SIR JOHN DAVIES	1
I TAKE THIS CADENCE FROM A MAN NAMED YEATS;	105	SIR JOHN DAVIES	19
BUT MANY A MAN ROLLED UNDER THE TABLE	112	SQUEEZE-BOX	36
SHE HAD TO BE MILKED BY A MAN AND HIS WIFE.	114	THE COW	4
A MAN RICH AS A CAT,	121	ALL EARTH, AIR	7
I SMILE, NO MINERAL MAN;	124	WORDS FOR WIND	58
A FOND AND FOOLISH MAN,	126	WORDS FOR WIND	103
A LAZY NATURAL MAN,	130	THE OTHER	15
THE SENTENTIOUS MAN	131	SENTENTIOUS MAN	T
WHAT BOOK, O LEARNED MAN, WILL SET ME RIGHT?	133	THE PURE FURY	2
AND BREATHING HARD, AS THAT MAN RODE	136	THE SENSUALISTS	11
A CASUAL MAN, I KEEP MY CASUAL WORD,	140	THE SWAN	10
A MAN ALIVE, FROM ALL LIGHT I MUST FALL.	140	THE SWAN	12
I MET A RAGGED MAN;	146	THE SONG	1
A COLD GOD-FURIOUS MAN	147	THE EXORCISM	21
GOD'S IN THAT STONE, OR I AM NOT A MAN!	149	IN LATE SUMMER	12
THE DYING MAN	153	THE DYING MAN	T
I HEARD A DYING MAN	153	THE DYING MAN	1
"A MAN SEES, AS HE DIES,	153	THE DYING MAN	11
A MAN LEARNING TO SING."	153	THE DYING MAN	15
I AM THE CLUMSY MAN	154	THE DYING MAN	24
HE TURNED HIS FACE: THERE WAS ANOTHER MAN,	155	THE DYING MAN	62
A MAN CHASING A CAT,	171	WHAT TELL BONES	31
A MAN NAMED PHILANDER S. GOO	182	PHILANDER	1
AS A BLIND MAN, LIFTING A CURTAIN, KNOWS IT IS MORNING,	195	JOURNY INTERIOR	74
AN OLD MAN WITH HIS FEET BEFORE THE FIRE,	201	THE FAR FIELD	85
A MAN FACED WITH HIS OWN IMMENSITY	201	THE FAR FIELD	87
HE IS THE END OF THINGS, THE FINAL MAN.	201	THE FAR FIELD	93
THE PURE SERENE OF MEMORY IN ONE MAN,--	201	THE FAR FIELD	101
WITH THAT MAN, AND THOSE ROSES?	203	THE ROSE	57
AS IF ANOTHER MAN APPEARED OUT OF THE DEPTHS OF MY BEING,	205	THE ROSE	100
THAN HER WAYS WITH A MAN?	212	LIGHT LISTENED	2
THE SHY MAN	216	THE SHY MAN	T
AND THAT SWEET MAN, JOHN CLARE.	228	IN VIOLENT WARD	7
A MAN GOES FAR TO FIND OUT WHAT HE IS--	239	IN A DARK TIME	16
A FALLEN MAN, I CLIMB OUT OF MY FEAR.	239	IN A DARK TIME	22
I AM A MAN, A MAN AT INTERVALS	242	THE SEQUEL	29
I AM A MAN, A MAN AT INTERVALS	242	THE SEQUEL	29
AS A MAN TURNS TO FACE ON-COMING SNOW.	245	THE DECISION	12
BROODING ON GOD, I MAY BECOME A MAN.	246	THE MARROW	10
AT EASE WITH JOY, A SELF-ENCHANTED MAN.	248	THE TREE, BIRD	6
THE RIGHT THING HAPPENS TO THE HAPPY MAN.	250	THE RIGHT THING	3
THE RIGHT THING HAPPENS TO THE HAPPY MAN.	250	THE RIGHT THING	9
THE RIGHT THING HAPPENS TO THE HAPPY MAN.	250	THE RIGHT THING	12

	PAGE	TITLE	LINE
MAN (CONTINUED)			
THE RIGHT THING HAPPENS TO THE HAPPY MAN.	250	THE RIGHT THING	19
TAKE NOTICE OF THIS MAN!	260	THE CHANGELING	24
'TWIXT ANIMAL AND MAN DIVIDED,	264	THREE EPIGRAMS	13
BUT THAT'S ENOUGH FOR ANY MAN	267	SAGINAW SONG	29
WITH THAT LOVELY MAN, TOM MOORE.	268	SAGINAW SONG	49
CAN BRING A GOOD MAN DOWN.	269	GOB MUSIC	19
THERE ON MY KNEES, A MAN OF RENOWN,	270	GOB MUSIC	42
WILL BRING A GOOD MAN DOWN.	270	GOB MUSIC	47
TIMES FIVE A MAN; I BREATHE	271	THE REPLY	14
A MAN, A MAN ALIVE.	271	THE REPLY	17
A MAN, A MAN ALIVE.	271	THE REPLY	17
MANAGER'S			
WITH MOTHERS, SLEEP-HEAVY CHILDREN, STALE PERFUME, PAST THE MANAGER'S SMILE	47	DOUBLE FEATURE	3
MANHOOD			
YOUR LITTLE MANHOOD LONG AGO WAS SMOTHERED.	25	DIM-WIT COUSIN	2
MANIA			
A MANIA KEEPS THEM ON THE MOVE	33	HIGHWAY: MICH	12
MANIFEST			
O MOST MANIFEST.	260	THE CHANGELING	9
MANIFESTATION			
THE MANIFESTATION	235	MANIFESTATION	T
MANIFOLD			
I LEAN, AND LOVE THESE MANIFOLD SHAPES,	233	THE PIKE	13
MANILLA			
ALL THE MISERY OF MANILLA FOLDERS AND MUCILAGE,	46	DOLOR	3
MANNER			
YOUR PALM IS MOIST, YOUR MANNER FAR TOO JOLLY	25	DIM-WIT COUSIN	9
BUT SHOULD YOU CALL HIS MANNER SMUG,	116	THE SLOTH	8
MANNERS			
OH THAT COUSIN! HER MANNERS! AT LUNCHES!	179	MYRTLE'S COUSIN	5
MAN'S			
A MAN'S HEAD IS AN EMINENCE UPON	13	PRAISE PRAIRIE	3
IT WAS DEAD MAN'S CORNER, IT WAS KELLY'S STABLE;	112	SQUEEZE-BOX	34
A MAN'S A BEAST PROWLING IN HIS OWN HOUSE,	133	THE PURE FURY	17
SCARS, TEMPESTS, FLOODS, THE MOTION OF MAN'S FATE;	144	ELEGY (1)	14
MANSION			
I SEE A BANKER'S MANSION WITH TWENTY WOOD-GRATE FIRES,	27	CLAIRVOY WIDOW	13
MAN-TAILORED			
OF A MAN-TAILORED BLOUSE: THE LIST OF SHOPPING DONE;	29	THE REMINDER	6
MANURE			
LEAF-MOLD, MANURE, LIME, PILED AGAINST SLIPPERY PLANKS.	38	ROOT CELLAR	9
MANURE-MACHINE			
SO WE DRAINED THE MANURE-MACHINE	41	BIG WIND	6
MANY			
SO MANY DEVOURING INFANTS!	39	ORCHIDS	14
PERCHED ON MANY SHELVES,	56	THE LOST SON	93
THEY HAD MANY MOUTHS TO BREATHE WITH.	57	THE LOST SON	127
THERE WERE MANY KINDS OF COOL	57	THE LOST SON	137
THIS WIND BRINGS MANY FISH;	61	THE LONG ALLEY	86
HOW MANY ANGELS DO YOU KNOW?--	77	BRING THE DAY!	12
MOTHER OF BLUE AND THE MANY CHANGES OF HAY,	79	GIVE WAY, GATES	14
THE SEA HAS MANY STREETS;	83	O LULL ME, LULL	14
MANY ASTOUNDS BEFORE, I LOST MY IDENTITY TO A PEBBLE;	88	PRAISE TO END!	88
QUITE-BY-CHANCE BROUGHT ME MANY COOKIES.	90	UNFOLD! UNFOLD!	36
A SON HAS MANY FATHERS.	98	O, THOU OPENING	33
BUT MANY A MAN ROLLED UNDER THE TABLE	112	SQUEEZE-BOX	36
AND THE WOODS RESOUNDED WITH MANY A SHRIEK	115	THE SERPENT	25
I'VE TRIED I DON'T KNOW HOW MANY TIMES TO REPLANT IT.	163	I'M HERE	77
MERCY HAS MANY ARMS.	173	WHAT TELL BONES	76
YOU'VE TOO MANY TUNES, AND NONE OF THEM GOOD:	177	KITTY-CAT BIRD	5
THERE ARE MANY DETOURS, WASHED-OUT INTERRUPTED RAW PLACES	193	JOURNY INTERIOR	2
SAY MANY A WORD,	216	THE SHY MAN	22
SAY MANY A WORD,	216	THE SHY MAN	25
MANY ARRIVALS MAKE US LIVE: THE TREE BECOMING	235	MANIFESTATION	1
THE SOUL HAS MANY MOTIONS, BODY ONE.	243	THE MOTION	1
MAPLE			
NOW AS FROM MAPLE TO ELM THE FLITTERMICE SKITTER AND TWIRL,	33	IDYLL	1
DRIFTING THROUGH LEAVES, OAK AND MAPLE,	159	FIRST MEDITATN	88
MARE'S			
I COULD FEEL THE MARE'S NOSE.	63	THE LONG ALLEY	32
THE MARE'S TAIL, THE FLOATING FROGBIT,	209	HER LONGING	4

	PAGE	TITLE	LINE
MARIANNE			
BUT OUR GOOSE, MARIANNE,	213	THE HAPPY THREE	18
ME, AND DEAR MARIANNE--	214	THE HAPPY THREE	34
MARKED			
SOME ITEMS, MISCELLANEOUS, MARKED "FEAR";	21	THE AUCTION	7
MARL			
SHALE LOOSENS. MARL REACHES INTO THE FIELD. SMALL BIRDS PASS OVER WATER.	64	SHAPE OF FIRE	11
MARMOREAN-BORN			
THOU WERT MARMOREAN-BORN.	81	SENSIBILITY! LA	5
MARRED			
ALL THINGS UNHOLY, MARRED BY CURSE,	18	LONG LIVE WEEDS	5
MARRIED			
I HAVE MARRIED MY HANDS TO PERPETUAL AGITATION,	56	THE LOST SON	109
I AM MOST IMMODERATELY MARRIED:	222	THE ABYSS	97
MARROW			
THE MARROW OF GOD, TALKING,	103	OLD LADY'S WRDS	8
MY MARROW BEAT AS WILDLY AS MY PULSE.	106	SIR JOHN DAVIES	36
THE MARROW	246	THE MARROW	T
I BLEED MY BONES, THEIR MARROW TO BESTOW	246	THE MARROW	23
MARROW-COLD			
AND FROST IS MARROW-COLD, AND SOON	15	COMING OF COLD	51
MARROW-SOFT			
MARROW-SOFT, DANCED IN THE SAND.	63	FIELD OF LIGHT	30
MARRY			
I CAN'T MARRY THE DIRT.	77	BRING THE DAY!	20
MARSALA			
OF VEAL SOAKED IN MARSALA AND LITTLE LARKS ARRANGED ON A LONG PLATTER,	232	THE THING	19
MARSH			
OF MARSH GRASS HEAPED ABOVE A MUSK-RAT HOLE.	15	THE HERON	4
MARSHES			
OF GREEN, OR PLUNGED TO MY ELBOWS IN THE SPONGY YELLOWISH MOSS OF THE MARSHES:	40	MOSS-GATHERING	8
MARSHLAND			
CROSS MARSHLAND INTO CLOVER.	7	ORDERS FOR DAY	14
MARTYR			
I'M MARTYR TO A MOTION NOT MY OWN;	127	I KNEW A WOMAN	23
MASCULINE			
WITH NO HINT OF YOUR PRESENCE IN A JUNGLE OF MASCULINE TOYS,	29	THE REMINDER	10
MASKS			
HYSTERIA MASKS IN THE STUDIED INANE.	29	THE GENTLE	2
MASTER			
BRICKS FLAKE BEFORE MY FACE. MASTER OF WATER, THAT'S TREES AWAY.	61	THE LONG ALLEY	80
THOUGH DANCING NEEDS A MASTER, I HAD NONE	105	SIR JOHN DAVIES	15
PROPINQUITY'S A HARSH MASTER;	259	SONG (3)	37
LAUGHED A MASTER OF HUMP AND SNORT;	263	FOLLIES OF ADAM	30
MATCH			
THE OVENBIRD WILL MATCH THE VOCAL BROOK.	11	LIGHT BRIGHTER	15
WITH THESE I MATCH MY LITTLE WIT	18	LONG LIVE WEEDS	9
THE HEAD OF A MATCH	60	THE LONG ALLEY	56
AT THE FIRST SCRATCH OF THE MATCH	226	THE LIZARD	14
MATCHING			
MATCHING HIS STRIDE WITH HALF-STEPS	6	THE PREMONITION	5
MATCHLESS			
SLOWLY HIS MATCHLESS DISPOSITION SOURED	28	THE FAVORITE	12
MATCH-MAKERS			
MATCH-MAKERS, ARRANGERS OF PICNICS--	169	FOURTH MEDITATN	41
MATCHSTICKS			
THE GREAT LOGS PILED LIKE MATCHSTICKS.	222	THE ABYSS	96
MATING			
ALL DURING MATING SEASON,	234	ALL MORNING	17
MATTED			
OUT OF THE BRIARY HEDGE, THE TANGLE OF MATTED UNDERBRUSH,	203	THE ROSE	45
MATTER			
I, WITH NO RIGHTS IN THIS MATTER,	102	ELEGY FOR JANE	21
NO MATTER WHICH ONE IS BENEATH,	136	THE SENSUALISTS	15
HE'S PART OF ONE, AS A MATTER OF COURSE.	264	THREE EPIGRAMS	12
MATTERS			
(MATTERS ONLY A SAINT MENTIONS!)	187	THE LONGING	10
ARE THESE MATTERS ONLY A SAINT MENTIONS?	259	SONG (3)	39

	PAGE	TITLE	LINE
MATTRESS			
WE CREEP TO OUR BED, AND ITS STRAW MATTRESS.	231	THE STORM	28
MATUNA			
IT WAS SAMOOTS MATUNA AND BUGS MORAN;	112	SQUEEZE-BOX	26
MAX			
MAX LAURISCH HAD THE GREENEST THUMB OF ALL.	224	OTTO	7
MAY			
I PRAY THEE, LORD, THAT I MAY CHOOSE	8	PRAYER	2
A WALKER AT THE RIVER'S EDGE MAY HEAR	11	LIGHT BRIGHTER	3
I ASKED: MAY THE BLESSINGS OF LIFE, O LORD, DESCEND ON THE LIVING.	48	JUDGE NOT	6
MAY I LOOK TOO, LOVED EYE?	79	GIVE WAY, GATES	19
I'LL MAKE IT; BUT IT MAY TAKE ME.	97	O, THOU OPENING	1
DEAREST TREE, I SAID, MAY I REST HERE?	100	THE VISITANT	5
TO SOME IT MAY SEEM A SAD THING TO RELATE,	112	SQUEEZE-BOX	38
--YOU MAY BE DIRTY DINKY.	114	DINKY	20
AND I MAY BE, SOME TIME.	150	SNAKE	12
IN LOVE, IN LIVELY MAY.	154	THE DYING MAN	27
MAY THE HIGH FLOWER OF THE HAY CLIMB INTO THEIR HEARTS;	169	FOURTH MEDITATN	56
MAY THEY LEAN INTO LIGHT AND LIVE;	169	FOURTH MEDITATN	57
MAY THEY SLEEP IN ROBES OF GREEN, AMONG THE ANCIENT FERNS;	169	FOURTH MEDITATN	58
MAY THEIR EYES GLEAM WITH THE FIRST DAWN;	169	FOURTH MEDITATN	59
MAY THE SUN GILD THEM A WORM;	169	FOURTH MEDITATN	60
MAY THEY BE TAKEN BY THE TRUE BURNING;	169	FOURTH MEDITATN	61
MAY THEY FLAME INTO BEING!--	169	FOURTH MEDITATN	62
FOR TO COME UPON WARBLERS IN EARLY MAY	199	THE FAR FIELD	26
CAPE MAY, BLACKBURNIAN, CERULEAN,--	199	THE FAR FIELD	30
MAY YOUR LIMBS NEVER WITHER,	217	WISH YOUNG WIFE	2
MAY THE EYES IN YOUR FACE	217	WISH YOUNG WIFE	3
MAY YOU LIVE OUT YOUR LIFE	217	WISH YOUNG WIFE	6
BROODING ON GOD, I MAY BECOME A MAN.	246	THE MARROW	10
MAYBE			
MAYBE I'M LOST,	72	WHERE KNOCK IS	43
MAYBE GOD HAS A HOUSE.	74	WHERE KNOCK IS	88
MAYBE IT'S WHITMAN'S SPIDER, I CAN'T TELL,	273	SUPPR W LINDSAY	28
MAZE			
WAS LOST IN A MAZE OF WATER.	6	THE PREMONITION	13
BLESS ME AND THE MAZE I'M IN!	92	I CRY, LOVE!	20
ME (244)			
MEADOW			
WE GO TO OUR BEDS IN A HOUSE AT THE EDGE OF A MEADOW,	33	IDYLL	11
A MEADOW, LUSH AND GREEN.	145	THE BEAST	5
AT THE EDGE OF A RIPENING MEADOW, IN EARLY SUMMER,	204	THE ROSE	80
THE MEADOW MOUSE	227	MEADOW MOUSE	T
SLEEPS THE BABY MOUSE I FOUND IN THE MEADOW,	227	MEADOW MOUSE	2
WHERE HAS HE GONE, MY MEADOW MOUSE,	227	MEADOW MOUSE	21
THE MEADOW INSECTS MADE A LEVEL NOISE.	247	I WAITED	4
MEADOW-SHAPE			
HOW ELSE, MEADOW-SHAPE?	258	SONG (3)	12
MEAGER			
BREAKS ON ME AS MY MEAGER FLESH BREAKS DOWN--	244	INFIRMITY	15
MEAL			
TO BE A MOUTH, A MEAL OF MEAT?	169	FOURTH MEDITATN	33
SO WE SAT DOWN AND ATE OURSELVES A MEAL,	274	SUPPR W LINDSAY	30
MEAN			
AND AFTERWARDS I ALWAYS FELT MEAN, JOGGING BACK OVER THE LOGGING ROAD,	40	MOSS-GATHERING	9
YOU MEAN?--	98	O, THOU OPENING	41
HOW SLOW THE CHANGES OF A GOLDEN MEAN:	133	THE PURE FURY	12
WHAT DO THEIR LIVES MEAN,	169	FOURTH MEDITATN	42
OF ENVY'S MEAN GAZE;	217	WISH YOUNG WIFE	5
LINDSAY'S I MEAN: TWO MOONS, OR EVEN THREE,	273	SUPPR W LINDSAY	7
MEANING			
THE MEANING OF THE DAY; DARK FORMS	4	FEUD	14
NEW MEANING GROWS IMMENSE.	18	GENESIS	12
FOR EVERY MEANING HAD GROWN MEANINGLESS.	133	THE PURE FURY	4
MEANINGFUL			
THE MEANINGFUL WHISPER,	162	I'M HERE	33
MEANINGLESS			
FOR EVERY MEANING HAD GROWN MEANINGLESS.	133	THE PURE FURY	4
MEANNESS			
THE FURY OF THE HATE-DRIVEN ZEALOT, THE MEANNESS OF THE HUMAN WEASEL;	170	FOURTH MEDITATN	68

	PAGE	TITLE	LINE
MEANS			
IF THE WIND MEANS ME,	164	I'M HERE	99
--"THAT MEANS BLAKE, TOO?"	273	SUPPR W LINDSAY	18
MEASURE			
WE PLAYED A MEASURE WITH COMMINGLED FEET:	106	SIR JOHN DAVIES	31
(I MEASURE TIME BY HOW A BODY SWAYS).	127	I KNEW A WOMAN	28
MEASURED			
IN ACCENTS MEASURED BY THE BLOOD.	22	SILENCE	3
MEASURES			
AND VARIOUS MEASURES PROPOUNDED	115	THE SERPENT	12
MEAT			
MY MEAT EATS ME. WHO WAITS AT THE GATE?	65	SHAPE OF FIRE	53
TO BE A MOUTH, A MEAL OF MEAT?	169	FOURTH MEDITATN	33
MEDIOCRE			
THE MEDIOCRE BUSY AT BETRAYING	5	PROGNOSIS	11
MEDITATE			
YOU MEDITATE UPON THE NERVES,	4	FEUD	17
MEDITATION			
FIRST MEDITATION	157	FIRST MEDITATN	T
FOURTH MEDITATION	168	FOURTH MEDITATN	T
MEDITATION AT OYSTER RIVER	190	AT OYSTER RIVER	T
MEDITATION IN HYDROTHERAPY	256	IN HYDROTHERAPY	T
MEDITERRANEAN			
THE MEDITERRANEAN SUN SHINING ON US, EQUALLY,	226	THE LIZARD	4
MEEK			
BRING ME THE MEEK, FOR I WOULD KNOW THEIR WAYS;	149	IN LATE SUMMER	5
BLESSED THE MEEK; THEY SHALL INHERIT WRATH;	244	INFIRMITY	17
MEEKLY			
I NIBBLED MEEKLY FROM HER PROFFERED HAND;	127	I KNEW A WOMAN	11
MEEKNESS			
I'LL SEEK MY OWN MEEKNESS.	91	UNFOLD! UNFOLD!	59
I SEEK MY OWN MEEKNESS;	173	WHAT TELL BONES	91
MEET			
OFTEN I MEET, ON WALKING FROM A DOOR,	8	THE SIGNALS	1
THE PAVEMENT SMOKES WHEN TWO CARS MEET	33	HIGHWAY: MICH	16
LUMINOUS ONE, SHALL WE MEET ON THE BOSOM OF GOD?	59	THE LONG ALLEY	29
WE ROSE TO MEET THE MOON, AND SAW NO MORE.	107	SIR JOHN DAVIES	70
AND PLEASED TO MEET THE MOON.	124	WORDS FOR WIND	45
I TRIED TO MEET HIS EYES.	146	THE SONG	3
--HEIGHO, MEET HUGH AND HARRY!	181	MONOTONY SONG	4
WHERE THE FRESH AND SALT WATERS MEET,	196	THE LONG WATERS	17
BUT THIS PLACE, WHERE SEA AND FRESH WATER MEET,	202	THE ROSE	2
THE WINDS AND WATERS MEET.	215	HIS FOREBODING	20
I MEET MY SHADOW IN THE DEEPENING SHADE;	239	IN A DARK TIME	2
TO MEET THE WORLD, I RISE UP IN MY MIND;	243	THE MOTION	9
MELLOWED			
THE SHOOTS OF SPRING HAVE MELLOWED WITH THE YEAR.	12	SLOW SEASON	13
MELT			
I COULD MELT DOWN A STONE,--	79	GIVE WAY, GATES	17
THAT ONCE COULD MELT THE DARK WITH ITS SMALL BREATH.	246	THE MARROW	16
MELTED			
FROST MELTED ON FAR PANES;	57	THE LOST SON	145
I'M A BISCUIT. I'M MELTED ALREADY.	77	BRING THE DAY!	21
MELTING			
MELTING AT THE KNEES, A VARICOSE HORROR.	65	SHAPE OF FIRE	31
MELTS			
WHEN THE ICE MELTS ALONG THE EDGES IN EARLY AFTERNOON.	191	AT OYSTER RIVER	48
MEMBERS			
THE STINGY MEMBERS WHEN THEY SIGNED	267	SAGINAW SONG	33
MEMORY			
MEMORY	141	MEMORY	T
THE PURE SERENE OF MEMORY IN ONE MAN,--	201	THE FAR FIELD	101
MEN			
THOUGH JUST MEN ARE REVILED	20	REPL TO CENSURE	9
THE LAWYERS ALL ARE CUNNING, THE BUSINESS MEN ARE FAT,	27	CLAIRVOY WIDOW	7
"I SEE THE RIVER HARBOR, ALIVE WITH MEN AND SHIPS,	28	CLAIRVOY WIDOW	19
THE MEN ON RAIL AND ROADWAY KEEP MOVING ON AND ON.	28	CLAIRVOY WIDOW	24
AND EVEN THE BOYS TURNED OUT TO BE MEN	112	SQUEEZE-BOX	23
INTO THE WORLD OF MEN.	136	THE SENSUALISTS	26
AND THE MEN BENEATH THEM WHEELING IN DIRT TO THE CEMENT BENCHES,	158	FIRST MEDITATN	45
OLD MEN SHOULD BE EXPLORERS?	189	THE LONGING	57
WHEN EVERYTHING--BIRDS, MEN, DOGS--	210	HER TIME	23

		PAGE	TITLE	LINE
MEN (CONTINUED)				
I THINK OF HIM, AND I THINK OF HIS MEN,	....	224	OTTO	5
IT WAS NO RANDOM ACT, FOR THOSE TWO MEN		224	OTTO	20
AND YET STILL VIOLENT MEN, WHOSE STACKED-UP GUNS		224	OTTO	27
IT OPERATES ON OTHER MEN.	....	257	SANITARIUM	12
MENACE				
THE MENACE OF ANCESTRAL EYES;	....	4	FEUD	2
MENSCH				
HERE'S A MENSCH BUT CAN SING DANDY.	....	266	FOR STEVENS	14
MENTAL				
IN TIME INDUCE A MENTAL ILL.		257	SANITARIUM	6
MENTION				
O CURSED BE THE WORK THAT GETS HONORABLE MENTION!	....	29	THE GENTLE	9
THE MERE MENTION OF SOUPS	....	180	GOO-GIRL	14
MENTIONS				
(MATTERS ONLY A SAINT MENTIONS!)	....	187	THE LONGING	10
ARE THESE MATTERS ONLY A SAINT MENTIONS?	....	259	SONG (3)	39
MERCY				
THIS WIND GIVES ME SCALES. HAVE MERCY, GRISTLE:	....	60	THE LONG ALLEY	33
MERCY HAS MANY ARMS.	....	173	WHAT TELL BONES	76
FLASH ME TO MERCY AND A WHOLE HEART!	....	259	SONG (3)	42
MERE				
THE MERE MENTION OF SOUPS	....	180	GOO-GIRL	14
MERELY				
FINALLY VEERING, WEARING THEMSELVES OUT, MERELY	....	41	BIG WIND	30
OF LIVING MERELY IN THE REALM OF TIME.	....	149	IN LATE SUMMER	20
DO WE MOVE TOWARD GOD, OR MERELY ANOTHER CONDITION?	......	221	THE ABYSS	75
MERGED				
I HAVE MERGED, LIKE THE BIRD, WITH THE BRIGHT AIR,	....	222	THE ABYSS	99
MERIT				
ENOUGH TO MERIT CONSTANT THOUGHT.	....	257	SANITARIUM	8
MERRY				
FULL MERRY, A GLEAM	....	103	OLD LADY'S WRDS	9
ONE TO BE MERRY WITH,	....	124	WORDS FOR WIND	44
MESSAGES				
MY FRIEND, THE RAT IN THE WALL, BRINGS ME THE CLEAREST MESSAGES;	....	88	PRAISE TO END!	84
MET				
I MET A COLLECTOR OF STRING, A SHEPHERD OF SLOW FORMS.	...	90	UNFOLD! UNFOLD!	30
WE MET IN A NEST. BEFORE I LIVED.	....	93	I CRY, LOVE!	55
I MET HER AS A BLOSSOM ON A STEM	....	119	THE DREAM	1
OUR SHADOWS MET, AND SLOWLY SWUNG AROUND;	....	120	THE DREAM	26
I MET A RAGGED MAN;	....	146	THE SONG	1
WE MET TO LEAVE AGAIN		212	LIGHT LISTENED	19
BODY MET BODY, WE	....	238	THE MOMENT	11
THE SWEET LIGHT MET ME AS I WALKED TOWARD		248	THE TREE, BIRD	3
NEVER MET HIM, DUTCHMAN DEAR;	....	266	FOR STEVENS	10
I MET A WOMAN WHO COULD BREAK WIND	....	268	SAGINAW SONG	41
METAL				
THIS SLAG RUNS SLOW. WHAT BLEEDS WHEN METAL BREAKS?	......	59	THE LONG ALLEY	11
FLESH, YOU OFFEND THIS METAL. HOW LONG NEED THE BONES MOURN?		59	THE LONG ALLEY	12
SHAPES STIFFENING INTO METAL,	....	169	FOURTH MEDITATN	40
METAPHOR				
VIOLENT THAN A METAPHOR.	....	8	PRAYER	14
METER				
AND IF THE METER NEEDS A CHANGE	....	269	GOB MUSIC	5
MEW				
YOU MEW LIKE A CAT, YOU GRATE LIKE A JAY:	....	177	KITTY-CAT BIRD	9
MICA				
GLITTER OF BASALT AND MICA,	....	265	HARSH COUNTRY	3
MICE				
WHEN MICE WITH WINGS CAN WEAR A HUMAN FACE.	....	16	THE BAT	10
HOORAY FOR ME AND THE MICE!--	....	76	I NEED, I NEED	55
IN THIS, THE DIOCESE OF MICE,	....	83	O LULL ME, LULL	2
IT'S A GREAT DAY FOR THE MICE.	....	85	PRAISE TO END!	5
ASK ALL THE MICE WHO CAPER IN THE STRAW--	....	167	HER BECOMING	86
MICHIGAN				
HIGHWAY: MICHIGAN	....	33	HIGHWAY: MICH	T
OF THE FIRST TREMBLING OF A MICHIGAN BROOK IN APRIL,	......	191	AT OYSTER RIVER	42
THE THIN WHINE OF TELEPHONE WIRES IN THE WIND OF A MICHIGAN WINTER,	....	204	THE ROSE	69
WITH BALTIMORE ORIOLES, MICHIGAN BOBOLINKS,	....	235	ALL MORNING	42

		PAGE	TITLE	LINE
MICKEY				
AND NOBODY SLIPPED ME A MICKEY FINN,	....	112	SQUEEZE-BOX	31
MICROPHONES				
SALIVA DRIPPING FROM WARM MICROPHONES,	....	187	THE LONGING	5
MIDCHANNEL				
AND THE MIDCHANNEL BEGINS CRACKING AND HEAVING FROM THE				
PRESSURE BENEATH,	....	191	AT OYSTER RIVER	49
MID-COUNTRY				
MID-COUNTRY BLOW	....	12	MID-CNTRY BLOW	T
MIDDLE				
IN THE DEEP MIDDLE OF OURSELVES WE LAY;	....	106	SIR JOHN DAVIES	57
THE CEMETERY WITH TWO SCRUBBY TREES IN THE MIDDLE OF THE				
PRAIRIE,	....	194	JOURNY INTERIOR	35
AND THE THRUSH STOPPED IN THE MIDDLE OF HIS SONG.	....	196	THE LONG WATERS	7
NEITHER WHITE NOR RED, IN THE DEAD MIDDLE WAY,	....	197	THE LONG WATERS	56
IN THE MIDDLE OF,	....	219	THE ABYSS	13
I CAN SEE THAT BY THE DISTENDED PULSING MIDDLE;	....	226	THE LIZARD	2
MIDGE				
I'M NO MIDGE OF THAT AND THIS. THE DIRT GLITTERS LIKE SALT.		164	I'M HERE	92
MIDGES				
THE RIVER MOVES, WRINKLED BY MIDGES,	....	168	FOURTH MEDITATN	23
MIDNIGHT				
THESE IMAGES HAUNTED ME NOON AND MIDNIGHT.	....	48	JUDGE NOT	4
I PAW THE DARK, THE SHIFTING MIDNIGHT AIR.	....	135	THE RENEWAL	16
IT'S MIDNIGHT ON THE MOUSE,	....	137	LOVE'S PROGRESS	16
I AM A CONNOISSEUR OF MIDNIGHT EYES.	....	149	IN LATE SUMMER	6
AND WE BOUNCE AND SWAY ALONG TOWARD THE MIDNIGHT,	....	158	FIRST MEDITATN	23
BY MIDNIGHT I LOVE EVERYTHING ALIVE.	....	173	WHAT TELL BONES	93
GLEAMING, FREEZING HARD AGAIN, CREAKING AT MIDNIGHT--	....	191	AT OYSTER RIVER	51
AFTER THE MIDNIGHT CRIES.	....	194	JOURNY INTERIOR	64
THE CRICKET-VOICE DEEP IN THE MIDNIGHT FIELD,	....	196	THE LONG WATERS	27
THE GONG OF MIDNIGHT STRUCK	....	238	THE MOMENT	7
AND IN BROAD DAY THE MIDNIGHT COME AGAIN!	....	239	IN A DARK TIME	15
A LEAF UNALTERED BY THE MIDNIGHT SCENE,	....	248	THE TREE, BIRD	8
THE LONELY BUZZ BEHIND MY MIDNIGHT EYES;--	....	248	THE TREE, BIRD	16
OF MY LAST MIDNIGHT.	....	249	THE RESTORED	20
MIDST				
I NO LONGER CRY FOR GREEN IN THE MIDST OF CINDERS,	....	173	WHAT TELL BONES	74
MIDSUMMER				
CREEKS SWOLLEN IN MIDSUMMER FROM THE FLASH-FLOOD ROARING				
INTO THE NARROW VALLEY.	....	193	JOURNY INTERIOR	8
MIGHT				
WE'LL BE AT THE BUSINESS OF WHAT MIGHT BE	....	80	GIVE WAY, GATES	36
AND ROBERT FROST. THEY MIGHT REMEMBER ME."	....	274	SUPPR W LINDSAY	49
MIGHTY				
SHOOK WITH A MIGHTY POWER BEYOND HIS WILL,--	....	107	SIR JOHN DAVIES	75
MIGRATING				
THE BOTTOMS OF MIGRATING DUCKS	....	267	SAGINAW SONG	11
MILDEW				
BEWARE MOTHER MILDEW.	....	55	THE LOST SON	69
MILDEWED				
LOLLING OBSCENELY FROM MILDEWED CRATES,	....	38	ROOT CELLAR	4
MILDEWS				
SCUMS, MILDEWS, SMUTS ALONG STEMS,	....	38	FORCING HOUSE	3
MILE				
THE PROGRESS OF THE JADED. MILE	....	33	HIGHWAY: MICH	2
ON MILE OF TRAFFIC FROM THE TOWN	....	33	HIGHWAY: MICH	3
MILK				
I WANT THE OLD RAGE, THE LASH OF PRIMORDIAL MILK!	....	56	THE LOST SON	107
AND YOU, CAT AFTER GREAT MILK AND VASTY FISHES,	....	79	GIVE WAY, GATES	9
CAN A CAT MILK A HEN?	....	81	SENSIBILITY! LA	15
CORNBREAD AND MILK, ICE CREAM AND MORE ICE CREAM,	....	274	SUPPR W LINDSAY	32
MILKED				
SHE HAD TO BE MILKED BY A MAN AND HIS WIFE.	....	114	THE COW	4
MILK-NOSE				
COME TO ME, MILK-NOSE. I NEED A LOAN OF THE QUICK.	....	59	THE LONG ALLEY	25
MILKWEED				
THE FEATHER OF THE MILKWEED FLUTTERS DOWN.	....	12	SLOW SEASON	12
MILLION				
YOU ARE, IN TRUTH, ONE IN A MILLION,	....	23	AMOROUS LADY	13
"I SEE TEN MILLION WINDOWS, I SEE TEN THOUSAND STREETS,		27	CLAIRVOY WIDOW	5
MIMETIC				
THE MIMETIC CHORTLING OF THE CATBIRD	....	204	THE ROSE	63

	PAGE	TITLE	LINE
MINCING			
MINCING LIKE A CAT.	87	PRAISE TO END!	54
MIND			
THE LEAFY MIND, THAT LONG WAS TIGHTLY FURLED,	11	LIGHT BRIGHTER	18
THIS WISDOM FLOODS THE MIND,	18	GENESIS	5
SO TERRIBLY WITHIN THE MIND,	22	SILENCE	10
THE MIND IS QUICK TO TURN	31	LULL	15
A SHAPE IN THE MIND ROSE UP:	49	NIGHT CROW	3
THE MIND MOVED, NOT ALONE,	58	THE LOST SON	162
IS THAT DANCE SLOWING IN THE MIND OF MAN	105	SIR JOHN DAVIES	1
THE MIND REMEMBERS FROM A DEEPER SLEEP:	119	THE DREAM	3
A GHOST COMES OUT OF THE UNCONSCIOUS MIND	154	THE DYING MAN	36
WHO THOUGHT LOVE BUT A MOTION IN THE MIND?	156	THE DYING MAN	84
IN THE BACK OF MY MIND, RUNNING WITH THE ROLLING WATER,	165	HER BECOMING	9
THE DANCE OF NATURAL OBJECTS IN THE MIND,	171	WHAT TELL BONES	15
OR PERHAPS WITH ANOTHER MIND, LESS PECULIAR;	200	THE FAR FIELD	43
MY MIND MOVES IN MORE THAN ONE PLACE,	201	THE FAR FIELD	75
WHEN THE MIND REMEMBERS ALL,	204	THE ROSE	75
YET KEEP TO MYSELF MY OWN MIND;	208	HER WORDS	5
IS MY OWN MIND AT PLAY.	215	HIS FOREBODING	15
ROSE UP WITHIN THE MIND,	237	THE TRANCED	9
THE MIND ENTERS ITSELF, AND GOD THE MIND,	239	IN A DARK TIME	23
THE MIND ENTERS ITSELF, AND GOD THE MIND,	239	IN A DARK TIME	23
A SHAPE CALLED UP OUT OF MY NATURAL MIND;	241	THE SEQUEL	10
MORNING'S A MOTION IN A HAPPY MIND:	241	THE SEQUEL	17
BY LUST ALONE WE KEEP THE MIND ALIVE,	243	THE MOTION	5
TO MEET THE WORLD, I RISE UP IN MY MIND;	243	THE MOTION	9
A MIND TOO ACTIVE IS NO MIND AT ALL;	244	INFIRMITY	19
A MIND TOO ACTIVE IS NO MIND AT ALL;	244	INFIRMITY	19
NOR COULD I PUT THAT SOUND OUT OF MY MIND,	245	THE DECISION	5
AND LEADS TO ERRORS IN THE MIND.	257	SANITARIUM	4
AND DO NOT MIND THE STINK.	269	GOB MUSIC	15
MINDFUL			
MINDFUL OF CRIES,	162	I'M HERE	32
MINDLESS			
ONCE I WAS SOMETHING LIKE THIS, MINDLESS,	200	THE FAR FIELD	42
MIND'S			
SMALL WAVES REPEAT THE MIND'S SLOW SENSUAL PLAY.	131	SENTENTIOUS MAN	13
IN MY MIND'S EYE I SEE THOSE FIELDS OF GLASS,	225	OTTO	34
MINE			
THE FIELD IS MINE! IS MINE!	122	ALL EARTH, AIR	25
THE FIELD IS MINE! IS MINE!	122	ALL EARTH, AIR	25
MINE AND THE SEA-WIND'S.	205	THE ROSE	114
AND HIS WORLD AND MINE ARE THE SAME,	226	THE LIZARD	3
A NESTLING SIGHED--I CALLED THAT NESTLING MINE;	241	THE SEQUEL	12
MINERAL			
I SMILE, NO MINERAL MAN;	124	WORDS FOR WIND	58
MINIMAL			
THE MINIMAL	50	THE MINIMAL	T
MINIONS			
THE MINIONS OF BENZEDRINE AND PARALDEHYDE,	169	FOURTH MEDITATN	37
MINISCULE			
WRIGGLING LIKE A MINISCULE PUPPY.	227	MEADOW MOUSE	11
MINK			
WORSE THAN CASTOREUM OF MINK OR WEASELS,	187	THE LONGING	4
MINNOW			
PLAYS AS A MINNOW PLAYS,	101	LIGHT BREATHER	7
A PARTRIDGE DRUMMED; A MINNOW NUDGED ITS STONE;	241	THE SEQUEL	13
MINNOWS			
NOT EVEN THE MINNOWS CAME.	53	THE LOST SON	15
THE MINNOWS LOVE ME, AND THE HUMPED AND SPITTING CREATURES.	88	PRAISE TO END!	89
MY MISSION BECAME THE SALVATION OF MINNOWS.	90	UNFOLD! UNFOLD!	31
FOR WHOM THE MINNOWS SANG?	90	UNFOLD! UNFOLD!	52
THINNER THAN MINNOWS.	93	I CRY, LOVE!	34
MINNOWS CAN HEAR, AND BUTTERFLIES, YELLOW AND BLUE,	196	THE LONG WATERS	3
MINNOW'S			
THE LONG EYE NOTES THE MINNOW'S HIDING PLACE.	15	THE HERON	7
MINNOWY			
INTO THAT MINNOWY WORLD OF WEEDS AND DITCHES,	66	SHAPE OF FIRE	65
MINOR			
THEY SING, THEY SING, BUT STILL IN MINOR THIRDS.	156	THE DYING MAN	89
IN MY LEFT EAR I HEAR THE LOUD SOUND OF A MINOR COLLAPSE.	165	HER BECOMING	29

	PAGE	TITLE	LINE
MINSTREL			
O FOR SOME MINSTREL OF WHAT'S TO BE,	103	OLD LADY'S WRDS	6
MINUTE			
FORGIVE ME A MINUTE, NYMPH.	97	O, THOU OPENING	18
SO THEY CIRCLED AIMLESSLY FOR ALMOST A MINUTE,	232	THE THING	8
MINUTES			
AND MINUTES BURST UPON A BROW	4	DEATH PIECE	7
MIPS			
MIPS AND MA THE MOOLY MOO,	86	PRAISE TO END!	31
MIRACULOUS			
I SEE THE TRAFFIC DOING MIRACULOUS FEATS.	27	CLAIRVOY WIDOW	6
MIRE			
I'VE CRAWLED FROM THE MIRE, ALERT AS A SAINT OR A DOG;	88	PRAISE TO END!	81
THE MIRE, THE SODDEN WOOD,	154	THE DYING MAN	22
MIRROR			
TODAY, WHILE SCRAPING HAIR BEFORE THE MIRROR,	25	DIM-WIT COUSIN	10
THE RITUALISTS OF THE MIRROR, THE LONELY DRINKERS,	169	FOURTH MEDITATN	36
THE MIRROR TELLS SOME TRUTH, BUT NOT	257	SANITARIUM	7
MIRRORS			
FAR FROM THE MIRRORS ALL THE BUSHES RANG	143	SHIMMER OF EVIL	6
MIRY			
SMALL WATERS RUN TOWARD A MIRY HOLE--	132	SENTENTIOUS MAN	39
MISCELLANEOUS			
SOME ITEMS, MISCELLANEOUS, MARKED "FEAR";	21	THE AUCTION	7
THE WAVES, ALTERED BY SAND-BARS, BEDS OF KELP, MISCELLANEOUS DRIFTWOOD,	191	AT OYSTER RIVER	32
MISERY			
NOW IN THE MISERY OF BED-SITTING ROOM CONFUSION,	29	THE REMINDER	9
ALL THE MISERY OF MANILLA FOLDERS AND MUCILAGE,	46	DOLOR	3
AFTER THE BLINDING MISERY,	221	THE ABYSS	52
I CAN'T BURY THE BONE OF THIS MISERY LIKE A FASTIDIOUS DOG.	261	THE CHANGELING	31
MISFORTUNE			
THE SON OF MISFORTUNE LONG, LONG HAS BEEN WAITING	29	THE GENTLE	5
MISLAID			
THE TICKET MISLAID OR LOST, THE GATE	158	FIRST MEDITATN	49
MISS			
I MISS THE POLISHED BRASS, THE POWERFUL BLACK HORSES,	22	ROAD TO WDLAWN	1
I MISS THE PALLBEARERS MOMENTOUSLY TAKING THEIR PLACES,	22	ROAD TO WDLAWN	5
"THE ABYSS YOU CAN'T MISS:	219	THE ABYSS	6
MISSED			
AT EVERY STEP YOU MISSED	45	MY PAPA'S WALTZ	11
AT THE FIELD'S END, IN THE CORNER MISSED BY THE MOWER,	199	THE FAR FIELD	13
MISSHAPEN			
HOW SHE KEPT THE WIZENED, THE FALLEN, THE MISSHAPEN FOR HERSELF,	223	ELEGY (2)	14
MISSING			
THE CHAIR OF HONOR, WITH A MISSING RUNG."	21	THE AUCTION	8
MISSION			
HORACE THE HIKER ON A DUBIOUS MISSION	29	THE GENTLE	3
MY MISSION BECAME THE SALVATION OF MINNOWS.	90	UNFOLD! UNFOLD!	31
MISSTEP			
A SINGLE MISSTEP AND WE LEAVE THE QUICK.	5	PROGNOSIS	4
MIST			
A LAP OF MOUNTAIN MIST	34	NIGHT JOURNEY	8
MIST DEEPENS ON THE PANE;	34	NIGHT JOURNEY	21
IN MIST THAT SUN COULD SEIZE.	50	THE CYCLE	6
AND MIST LIFTING OUT OF THE BROWN CAT-TAILS;	67	SHAPE OF FIRE	87
MIST ALTERS THE ROCKS. WHAT CAN I TELL MY BONES?	172	WHAT TELL BONES	44
AND BELOW, IN A MIST OUT OF NOWHERE,	202	THE ROSE	29
IN A PLACE OF MOTTLED CLOUDS, A THIN MIST MORNING AND EVENING.	221	THE ABYSS	77
THE MIST ABOVE ME SINGS WITH ITS SMALL FLIES.	246	THE MARROW	2
MISTAKE			
THE MISTAKE	264	THREE EPIGRAMS	ST
MISTRESS			
KISS ME, KISS ME QUICK, MISTRESS OF LOST WISDOM,	48	LAST WORDS	7
A PENSIVE MISTRESS, AND A YELPING WIFE.	246	THE MARROW	6
A MISTRESS OF ZEN, I'LL BITE YOUR THUMB,	272	DUET	18
MISTS			
MY DESIRE FOR THE PEAKS, THE BLACK RAVINES, THE ROLLING MISTS	196	THE LONG WATERS	9

	PAGE	TITLE	LINE
MIXED			
THE CRUMBLING SMALL HOLLOW STICKS ON THE UNDERSIDE MIXED WITH ROOTS,	40	MOSS-GATHERING	4
THE FRUIT AND FLESH SMELLS MIXED.	46	PICKLE BELT	6
THE SOUND OF VOICES, YOUNG VOICES, MIXED WITH SLEIGHBELLS,	161	I'M HERE	4
PETALS AND REFLECTIONS OF PETALS MIXED ON THE SURFACE OF A GLASSY POOL,	194	JOURNY INTERIOR	56
MIXES			
WE NEED A BREED THAT MIXES BLAKE AND ME,	274	SUPPR W LINDSAY	41
MIXTURE			
PUMPING THE STALE MIXTURE	41	BIG WIND	8
MNETHA			
MNETHA, MOTHER OF HAR, PROTECT ME	196	THE LONG WATERS	20
MOANS			
TO GROPE MY SILL: IT MOANS TO BE REBORN!	154	THE DYING MAN	37
MOBILE			
OR ONE HIP QUIVER WITH A MOBILE NOSE	127	I KNEW A WOMAN	20
MOCK			
THEY MOCK THE DEEPEST THOUGHT,	20	REPL TO CENSURE	6
"WHAT MOON?" HE CRIED, HALF-TURNING IN MOCK FURY.	273	SUPPR W LINDSAY	10
MOCKED			
WE DANCED TO SHINING; MOCKED BEFORE THE BLACK	107	SIR JOHN DAVIES	89
NOW NOBODY SNIGGERED AND MOCKED	182	BOY AND BUSH	6
MOCKER			
IT'S DARK IN THIS WOOD, SOFT MOCKER.	85	PRAISE TO END!	1
MOIST			
YOUR PALM IS MOIST, YOUR MANNER FAR TOO JOLLY	25	DIM-WIT COUSIN	9
REACH ME ROSE, SWEET ONE, STILL MOIST IN THE LOAM,	61	THE LONG ALLEY	68
MOLD			
AND THE MOLD SANG IN THE BLEACHED VALLEYS UNDER THE ROSE.	102	ELEGY FOR JANE	9
MOLDS			
MOLDS, WEEDS, DEAD LEAVES,	43	FLOWER DUMP	5
MOLD'S			
I WAS PURE AS A WORM ON A LEAF; I CHERISHED THE MOLD'S CHILDREN.	89	UNFOLD! UNFOLD!	27
MOLE			
ASK THE MOLE, HE KNOWS.	55	THE LOST SON	67
A TRUE MOLE WANDERS LIKE A WORM.	97	O, THOU OPENING	20
BUT A MOLE WINDING THROUGH EARTH,	220	THE ABYSS	42
THE MOLE MAKING ITS WAY THROUGH DARKEST GROUND,	235	MANIFESTATION	4
MOLLUSKS			
I GREW TIRED OF THE RITUAL OF NAMES AND THE ASSISTANT KEEPER OF THE MOLLUSKS:	65	SHAPE OF FIRE	36
MOMENT			
THE SMELLS, THE MOMENT OF HAY,--	103	OLD LADY'S WRDS	22
FOR A MOMENT THEY STAND ABOVE ME,	158	FIRST MEDITATN	56
AT THE EDGE OF THE FIELD WAITING FOR THE PURE MOMENT;	168	FOURTH MEDITATN	3
AT THE SUDDEN VEERING, THE MOMENT OF TURNING.	193	JOURNY INTERIOR	5
INTO A LONG MOMENT;	194	JOURNY INTERIOR	47
IN THE MOMENT OF TIME WHEN THE SMALL DROP FORMS, BUT DOES NOT FALL,	194	JOURNY INTERIOR	58
STILL FOR A MOMENT,	200	THE FAR FIELD	33
WAS IT HERE I WORE A CROWN OF BIRDS FOR A MOMENT	202	THE ROSE	26
KNOWING SLOWS FOR A MOMENT,	221	THE ABYSS	69
THE MOMENT	238	THE MOMENT	T
MOMENTOUSLY			
I MISS THE PALLBEARERS MOMENTOUSLY TAKING THEIR PLACES,	22	ROAD TO WDLAWN	5
MOMENTS			
MY MOMENTS LINGER--THAT'S ETERNITY.	149	IN LATE SUMMER	16
MONEY			
I RUN, I RUN TO THE WHISTLE OF MONEY.	56	THE LOST SON	110
MONEY MONEY MONEY	56	THE LOST SON	111
MONEY MONEY MONEY	56	THE LOST SON	111
MONEY MONEY MONEY	56	THE LOST SON	111
NUTS ARE MONEY: WHEREFORE AND WHAT ELSE?	61	THE LONG ALLEY	82
AND MADE A LOT OF MONEY.	75	I NEED, I NEED	38
--AND BEGAN TO DRINK UP THE MONEY.	111	SQUEEZE-BOX	7
--ABOUT GETTING RID OF OUR MONEY.	111	SQUEEZE-BOX	12
--BUT HOW SHE COULD BURN UP THE MONEY!	111	SQUEEZE-BOX	16
--LOT LIKE LOSING SOME MONEY.	111	SQUEEZE-BOX	21
--AND LOOSENED UP WITH OUR MONEY.	112	SQUEEZE-BOX	25
--FOR YOU NEVER WON WITH THAT MONEY.	112	SQUEEZE-BOX	29
--ON THAT CHUNK OF GRANDPA'S MONEY.	112	SQUEEZE-BOX	33

	PAGE	TITLE	LINE
MONEY (CONTINUED)			
--WHEN HE TRIED TO DRINK UP THE MONEY.	112	SQUEEZE-BOX	37
--WHEN SHE THOUGHT I'D RUN OUT OF MONEY.	112	SQUEEZE-BOX	41
--TO HELP ME EAT UP HER MONEY.	112	SQUEEZE-BOX	45
NOW YOU RUN TO THE MONEY, IT'S JIG, JIG, JIG;	272	DUET	2
MONKEY-TAILS			
THOSE LEWD MONKEY-TAILS HANGING FROM DRAINHOLES, --	39	WEED PULLER	3
MONONGAHELA			
AND EAST ST. LOUIS AND MONONGAHELA	111	SQUEEZE-BOX	19
MONOTONY			
FROM THAT MONOTONY OF GRIEF,	22	SILENCE	16
DARE I SPEAK, ONCE MORE, IN THE MONOTONY OF GREAT PRAISE,	166	HER BECOMING	32
THE MONOTONY SONG	181	MONOTONY SONG	T
MONSTROUS			
THERE WAS A MOST MONSTROUS WHALE:	178	THE WHALE	1
MONUMENTAL			
HIS SPIRIT MOVES LIKE MONUMENTAL WIND	201	THE FAR FIELD	91
MOO			
MIPS AND MA THE MOOLY MOO,	86	PRAISE TO END!	31
MOOLY			
THERE WAS A MOOLY MAN	71	WHERE KNOCK IS	16
MIPS AND MA THE MOOLY MOO,	86	PRAISE TO END!	31
MOON			
AND BOYS MOON AT GIRLS WITH LAST YEAR'S FATUOUS FACES,	24	VERNAL SENTIMNT	3
THE FAINT MOON FALLING THROUGH WHITEWASHED GLASS,	39	ORCHIDS	10
THE MOON SAID, BACK OF AN EEL,	54	THE LOST SON	29
THE MOON WOULD NOT HAVE ME.	55	THE LOST SON	78
THE CHILL'S GONE FROM THE MOON.	77	BRING THE DAY!	18
A MOON LOOSENED FROM A STAG'S EYE,	79	GIVE WAY, GATES	10
THE MOON STILL ABIDES.	82	SENSIBILITY! LA	43
I HEAR YOU, ALIEN OF THE MOON.	82	SENSIBILITY! LA	44
A MOON AWAY.	87	PRAISE TO END!	70
SPEECH REVIVED, A GHOSTLY GOING OF TAME BEARS, A BRIGHT MOON ON GLEAMING	98	O, THOU OPENING	23
THE MOON BEGINNING.	100	THE VISITANT	20
I TRIED TO FLING MY SHADOW AT THE MOON,	105	SIR JOHN DAVIES	13
WE ROSE TO MEET THE MOON, AND SAW NO MORE.	107	SIR JOHN DAVIES	70
I WATCHED HER THERE, BETWEEN ME AND THE MOON;	119	THE DREAM	11
A TREE GLIDES WITH THE MOON.	122	ALL EARTH, AIR	24
SLOWLY BECAME THE MOON.	123	WORDS FOR WIND	24
AND PLEASED TO MEET THE MOON.	124	WORDS FOR WIND	45
UNDER THE RISING MOON;	124	WORDS FOR WIND	57
THE MOON DRAWS BACK ITS WATERS FROM THE SHORE.	140	THE SWAN	15
THE MOON GOES TO THE FULL;	148	THE SMALL	7
THE MOON GOES SLOWLY DOWN;	148	THE SMALL	8
THE MOON'S MY MOTHER: HOW I LOVE THE MOON!	156	THE DYING MAN	79
THE MOON, A PURE ISLAMIC SHAPE, LOOKED DOWN.	166	HER BECOMING	55
WHO CAN BELIEVE THE MOON?	167	HER BECOMING	74
BEFORE THE MOON DRAWS BACK,	171	WHAT TELL BONES	8
THAT DISAPPEAR INTO A WANING MOON;	173	WHAT TELL BONES	70
AND THE TIME RIPE FOR RUNNING TO THE MOON!	173	WHAT TELL BONES	85
WHO'D THINK THE MOON COULD PARE ITSELF SO THIN?	188	THE LONGING	30
I'D BE BEYOND; I'D BE BEYOND THE MOON,	188	THE LONGING	33
IN THE FIRST OF THE MOON,	192	AT OYSTER RIVER	68
THE MOON RETREATING INTO A VAGUE CLOUD-SHAPE	202	THE ROSE	18
THE MOON LOLLING IN THE CLOSE ELM, A SHIMMER OF SILVER,	204	THE ROSE	81
WHILE THE MOON LINGERS,	204	THE ROSE	85
"I BELIEVE, I BELIEVE, IN THE MOON!--	208	HER WORDS	10
THE FULL MOON WAS SHINING UPON THE BROAD SEA;	216	THE SHY MAN	1
THE FULL MOON HAS FALLEN, THE NIGHT WIND IS DOWN	216	THE SHY MAN	17
RIDING BENEATH THE MOON, HID FROM THE MOON,	225	OTTO	36
RIDING BENEATH THE MOON, HID FROM THE MOON,	225	OTTO	36
THE MOTION OF THE MOON, AND WAVES AT PLAY,	235	MANIFESTATION	7
OUR BODIES LIGHT, AND LIGHTED BY THE MOON.	237	THE TRANCED	20
A NIGHT FLOWING WITH BIRDS, A RAGGED MOON,	239	IN A DARK TIME	14
WE DANCED, WE DANCED, UNDER A DANCING MOON;	241	THE SEQUEL	14
THE CHANGE FROM DARK TO LIGHT OF THE SLOW MOON,	244	INFIRMITY	22
I WAS A FINGER POINTING AT THE MOON,	248	THE TREE, BIRD	5
THINGS OF HIGH WIT AND CHANGES OF THE MOON.	260	THE CHANGELING	27
AS ROUND AND PURE AS THE MOON,	271	THE REPLY	8
BEHOLD, THE MOON!--	273	SUPPR W LINDSAY	5
"WHAT MOON?" HE CRIED, HALF-TURNING IN MOCK FURY.	273	SUPPR W LINDSAY	10
"LET'S EAT!" SAID LINDSAY. "HERE WE'VE GOT THE MOON,	273	SUPPR W LINDSAY	15

	PAGE	TITLE	LINE
MOON-FORGOTTEN			
ON A MOON-FORGOTTEN WAVE!	83	O LULL ME, LULL	13
MOONLESS			
INTO A MOONLESS BLACK,	49	NIGHT CROW	7
MOONLIGHT			
A FISH JUMPS, SHAKING OUT FLAKES OF MOONLIGHT.	93	I CRY, LOVE!	45
WE WOKE TO FIND THE MOONLIGHT ON OUR TOES.	106	SIR JOHN DAVIES	64
A BIRD SANG LOW; THE MOONLIGHT SIFTED IN;	119	THE DREAM	7
MOVING, UNMOVING IN A PARCHED LAND, WHITE IN THE MOONLIGHT:	194	JOURNY INTERIOR	53
LET'S EAT BEFORE THE MOONLIGHT ALL RUNS OUT."	273	SUPPR W LINDSAY	29
MOONS			
LINDSAY'S I MEAN: TWO MOONS, OR EVEN THREE,	273	SUPPR W LINDSAY	7
MOON'S			
THE MOON'S MY MOTHER: HOW I LOVE THE MOON!	156	THE DYING MAN	79
MOORE			
I'LL SING WITH DEAR TOM MOORE,	268	SAGINAW SONG	48
WITH THAT LOVELY MAN, TOM MOORE.	268	SAGINAW SONG	49
MOORED			
OF MOTION MOORED TO ROCK;	4	DEATH PIECE	6
MOPED			
THE KITTY-CAT BIRD, HE MOPED AND HE CRIED.	177	KITTY-CAT BIRD	13
AS I MOPED BY THE HIGH SEA-WALL.	216	THE SHY MAN	8
MOPES			
THE SHE-BEAR MOPES UNDER THE HILL.	64	SHAPE OF FIRE	15
MOPING			
WITHOUT STARING LIKE A LOUT, OR A MOPING ADOLESCENT;	163	I'M HERE	80
MORAL			
THE MORAL IS, I GUESS YOU KEEP	181	MONOTONY SONG	25
MORAN			
IT WAS SAMOOTS MATUNA AND BUGS MORAN;	112	SQUEEZE-BOX	26
MORE			
MORE FURTIVE THAN THE HAND IN LOW	8	PRAYER	11
ITS RAPE IS GENTLE, NEVER MORE	8	PRAYER	13
ONCE MORE THE TREES ASSUME FAMILIAR SHAPES,	11	LIGHT BRIGHTER	9
MORE HEADY THAN A FIELD AT DUSK	14	COMING OF COLD	3
WHO WANT NO MORE THAN FINGERS SEIZE,	25	VERSE W ALLUSNS	3
THEY TRELLISED THE SUN; THEY PLOTTED FOR MORE THAN THEMSELVES.	44	FRAU BAUMAN	25
FINER THAN FLOUR, ALIVE, MORE DANGEROUS THAN SILICA,	46	DOLOR	10
AND MORE THAN A NOSE,	54	THE LOST SON	47
I'VE MORE VEINS THAN A TREE!	57	THE LOST SON	120
MOTHER ME OUT OF HERE. WHAT MORE WILL THE BONES ALLOW?	64	SHAPE OF FIRE	7
LEAVES MORE THAN SHOES;	65	SHAPE OF FIRE	48
HAVE MORE TEETH.	71	WHERE KNOCK IS	4
HARDLY ANY OLD ANGELS ARE AROUND ANY MORE.	78	BRING THE DAY!	40
I'M MORE THAN WHEN I WAS BORN;	84	O LULL ME, LULL	37
I FEEL MORE THAN A FISH.	87	PRAISE TO END!	77
I PROCLAIM ONCE MORE A CONDITION OF JOY.	92	I CRY, LOVE!	28
INDIGNATION? LET ME PERSUADE MORE SLOWLY:	98	O, THOU OPENING	31
I FALL, MORE AND MORE,	104	OLD LADY'S WRDS	61
I FALL, MORE AND MORE,	104	OLD LADY'S WRDS	61
THE SPIRIT AND THE FLESH CRIED OUT FOR MORE.	106	SIR JOHN DAVIES	52
WE ROSE TO MEET THE MOON, AND SAW NO MORE.	107	SIR JOHN DAVIES	70
AND KNOW THAT TRUE LOVE IS MORE THAN A LIFE-FORCE	113	TO A LADY ED	3
A FAIR THING GROWS MORE FAIR;	124	WORDS FOR WIND	54
AH, WHEN SHE MOVED, SHE MOVED MORE WAYS THAN ONE:	127	I KNEW A WOMAN	3
MORE THAN A MORTAL SHOULD;	128	THE VOICE	4
MOTION CAN DO NO MORE.	130	THE OTHER	18
MY FRIENDS BECOME MORE CHRISTIAN, YEAR BY YEAR.	132	SENTENTIOUS MAN	38
WHEN I RAISED MYSELF ONCE MORE,	145	THE BEAST	16
I LOVE THE WORLD; I WANT MORE THAN THE WORLD,	155	THE DYING MAN	56
DARE I SPEAK, ONCE MORE, IN THE MONOTONY OF GREAT PRAISE,	166	HER BECOMING	32
MY BREATH IS MORE THAN YOURS.	167	HER BECOMING	81
THE DEAD MAKE MORE IMPOSSIBLE DEMANDS FROM THEIR SILENCE;	168	FOURTH MEDITATN	19
O MORE THAN A ROARING BOY,	169	FOURTH MEDITATN	51
TO WHAT VAST PERMISSION HAVE I COME?	173	WHAT TELL BONES	72
YOU MUSTN'T PULL IT MORE THAN TWICE,	181	MONOTONY SONG	2
AND SHEDDING MORE THAN HERE AND THERE,	181	MONOTONY SONG	7
AND HERE'S MORE ADVICE:	183	THE LIZARD	5
DON'T POKE MORE THAN TWICE	183	THE LIZARD	6
I AM GATHERED TOGETHER ONCE MORE;	198	THE LONG WATERS	77
MY MIND MOVES IN MORE THAN ONE PLACE,	201	THE FAR FIELD	75
WE ARE ONE, AND YET WE ARE MORE,	207	THE YOUNG GIRL	5

	PAGE	TITLE	LINE
MORE (CONTINUED)			
O WHAT COULD BE MORE NICE	212	LIGHT LISTENED	1
SHE KISSED ME MORE THAN TWICE	212	LIGHT LISTENED	3
SHE'D MORE SIDES THAN A SEAL.	212	LIGHT LISTENED	6
SHIVER, AND MORE THAN TWICE,	216	HER WRATH	4
AND ONCE MORE THE TONGUES BEGIN BABBLING.	220	THE ABYSS	31
I WAS NO MORE THAN SEVEN AT THE TIME.	224	OTTO	22
THEY SAW THAT I FELL MORE THAN TWICE.	225	THE CHUMS	10
THERE'S TWO MORE TO DROWN	229	ON THE QUAY	5
AND OUR BREATH COMES MORE EASY,--	230	THE STORM	22
WHAT DOES WHAT IT SHOULD DO NEEDS NOTHING MORE.	235	MANIFESTATION	9
DO WE DO MORE THAN WE KNOW,	237	THE TRANCED	4
YE LITTLES, LIE MORE CLOSE!	240	IN EVEING AIR	7
BEARING ITS LIFE AND MORE, A DOUBLE SOUND,	248	THE TREE, BIRD	11
TILL MYSTERY IS NO MORE: NO MORE HE CAN.	250	THE RIGHT THING	18
TILL MYSTERY IS NO MORE: NO MORE HE CAN.	250	THE RIGHT THING	18
ONCE MORE, THE ROUND	251	ONCE MORE, RND	T
MORE! O MORE! VISIBLE.	251	ONCE MORE, RND	4
MORE! O MORE! VISIBLE.	251	ONCE MORE, RND	4
YOU FISHES, BE MORE FOND.	261	THE CHANGELING	48
NO MORE THAN WHAT IS RAISED	262	FOLLIES OF ADAM	9
HE LAUGHED, ONCE MORE.	263	FOLLIES OF ADAM	35
AND IF YOU EAT MORE THAN YOU SHOULD,	267	SAGINAW SONG	5
WITH MORE THAN HALF A CROWN.	269	GOB MUSIC	23
CORNBREAD AND MILK, ICE CREAM AND MORE ICE CREAM,	274	SUPPR W LINDSAY	32
MORGUES			
MUTILATED SOULS IN COLD MORGUES OF OBLIGATION.	166	HER BECOMING	43
MORLEYS			
THE MORLEYS AND THE BURROWS ARE	267	SAGINAW SONG	19
MORNING			
BUT MORNING LIGHT COMES TAPPING AT THE LID,	17	UNEXTINGUISHED	9
AND PULLED THE GREEN SHADE AGAINST MORNING SUN.	29	THE REMINDER	8
SHE SAILED UNTIL THE CALM MORNING,	41	BIG WIND	32
THE WINDLESS PERPETUAL MORNING ABOVE A SEPTEMBER CLOUD.	43	CARNATIONS	7
ITS MORNING SMELLS.	51	THE WAKING (1)	20
THAT COLD MORNING.	56	THE LOST SON	95
THE LIGHT IN THE MORNING CAME SLOWLY OVER THE WHITE	57	THE LOST SON	135
SOME MORNING THING CAME, BEATING ITS WINGS.	63	FIELD OF LIGHT	35
I MOVED WITH THE MORNING.	63	FIELD OF LIGHT	52
I WOKE IN THE FIRST OF MORNING.	101	THE VISITANT	21
HER LOOK WAS MORNING IN THE DYING LIGHT.	107	SIR JOHN DAVIES	84
MORNING, I SAW THE WORLD WITH SECOND SIGHT,	133	THE PURE FURY	5
THERE ARE STILL TIMES, MORNING AND EVENING:	159	FIRST MEDITATN	83
THE GLITTER OF WET IN THE FIRST OF MORNING?	161	I'M HERE	3
ITS SPRAY HOLDING A DOUBLE RAIN-BOW IN EARLY MORNING,	191	AT OYSTER RIVER	45
I ROCK WITH THE MOTION OF MORNING;	191	AT OYSTER RIVER	58
AS A BLIND MAN, LIFTING A CURTAIN, KNOWS IT IS MORNING,	195	JOURNY INTERIOR	74
WHO MAGNIFIES THE MORNING WITH HER EYES,	196	THE LONG WATERS	25
IN THE VAPOROUS GREY OF EARLY MORNING,	197	THE LONG WATERS	49
HOW THEY FILLED THE ORIOLE'S ELM, A TWITTERING RESTLESS CLOUD, ALL ONE MORNING,	199	THE FAR FIELD	28
THE MORNING BIRDS GONE, THE TWITTERING FINCHES,	202	THE ROSE	14
AND THE DEEP CHORUS OF HORNS COMING UP FROM THE STREETS IN EARLY MORNING.	204	THE ROSE	72
OR THAT LONELY TIME BEFORE THE BREAKING OF MORNING	204	THE ROSE	82
SHAKING OUT MY CATCH IN THE MORNING SUNLIGHT,	209	HER LONGING	15
IN A PLACE OF MOTTLED CLOUDS, A THIN MIST MORNING AND EVENING.	221	THE ABYSS	77
BUT THIS MORNING THE SHOE-BOX HOUSE ON THE BACK PORCH IS EMPTY.	227	MEADOW MOUSE	20
ALL MORNING	234	ALL MORNING	T
HIS DEEP-THROATED COOING PART OF THE EARLY MORNING,	234	ALL MORNING	2
ALL MORNING! ALL MORNING!	235	ALL MORNING	47
ALL MORNING! ALL MORNING!	235	ALL MORNING	47
I NEED A MORNING DRINK,	269	GOB MUSIC	11
MORNING-FAIR			
MORNING-FAIR, FOLLOW ME FURTHER BACK	66	SHAPE OF FIRE	64
MORNING-GLORY			
THE HUMMINGBIRD, WHIRRING FROM QUINCE-BLOSSOM TO MORNING-GLORY--	190	AT OYSTER RIVER	29
THE HELIOTROPE, VEINED LIKE A FISH, THE PERSISTENT MORNING-GLORY,	197	THE LONG WATERS	41

	PAGE	TITLE	LINE
MORNING-GLORY (CONTINUED)			
A SINGLE WILD ROSE, STRUGGLING OUT OF THE WHITE EMBRACE OF THE MORNING-GLORY,	203	THE ROSE	44
MORNING'S			
MORNING'S A MOTION IN A HAPPY MIND:	241	THE SEQUEL	17
MORRIS			
SWEET ALICE S. MORRIS, I AM PLEASED, OF COURSE,	113	TO A LADY ED	1
MORTAL			
HE LIVED BEYOND THE TOUCH OF MORTAL LAWS.	28	THE FAVORITE	8
MORE THAN A MORTAL SHOULD;	128	THE VOICE	4
A LEAF, I WOULD LOVE THE LEAVES, DELIGHTING IN THE REDOLENT DISORDER OF THIS MORTAL LIFE,	188	THE LONGING	47
WHAT'S THE WORST PORTION IN THIS MORTAL LIFE?	246	THE MARROW	5
MOSS			
OF GREEN, OR PLUNGED TO MY ELBOWS IN THE SPONGY YELLOWISH MOSS OF THE MARSHES:	40	MOSS-GATHERING	8
WHO PUT THE MOSS THERE?	55	THE LOST SON	64
PONDS WITH MOSS AND LEAVES FLOATING,	62	FIELD OF LIGHT	2
NOR THE MOSS, WOUND WITH THE LAST LIGHT.	102	ELEGY FOR JANE	17
MOSS-GATHERING			
MOSS-GATHERING	40	MOSS-GATHERING	T
THAT WAS MOSS-GATHERING.	40	MOSS-GATHERING	6
MOSSY			
DRIFTING DOWN FROM THEIR MOSSY CRADLES:	39	ORCHIDS	13
ROSE FROM A MOSSY MOUND	50	THE CYCLE	5
OR TO SINK DOWN TO THE HIPS IN A MOSSY QUAGMIRE;	200	THE FAR FIELD	44
THE STREAM SLIPPING BENEATH THE MOSSY LOGS,	222	THE ABYSS	94
FROM BEYOND THE END OF A MOSSY LOG,	233	THE PIKE	15
AND MOSSY FILTHY FEET;	267	SAGINAW SONG	10
MOST			
TO SLEEP IMMODESTLY, A MOST	19	EPIDERM MACABRE	15
I HEAR A MOST LOVELY HUZZA:	92	I CRY, LOVE!	12
AND GOT A MOST COMMODIOUS TUBA;	115	THE SERPENT	16
A MOST EX-AS-PER-AT-ING LUG.	116	THE SLOTH	7
A MOST, MOST EXACTIOUS LAW	117	LADY AND BEAR	10
A MOST, MOST EXACTIOUS LAW	117	LADY AND BEAR	10
MOST LOVINGLY: I BREATHE;	123	WORDS FOR WIND	4
I FEAR THOSE SHADOWS MOST	138	THE SURLY ONE	7
BUT AS FOR YOU, MOST ODIOUS--	151	SLUG	28
THERE WAS A MOST ODIOUS YAK	178	THE YAK	1
THERE WAS A MOST MONSTROUS WHALE:	178	THE WHALE	1
I THINK IT WOULD BE MOST REVEALING	178	THE CEILING	5
BUT THE HIND PART OF THE WORM WIGGLES THE MOST,	196	THE LONG WATERS	2
I AM MOST IMMODERATELY MARRIED:	222	THE ABYSS	97
DEAD TO MYSELF, AND ALL I HOLD MOST DEAR,	244	INFIRMITY	23
O MOST MANIFEST.	260	THE CHANGELING	9
MOST-HONEST-ALIVE			
MY DARLING, MY DEAREST, MOST-HONEST-ALIVE,	113	TO A LADY ED	13
MOSTLY			
MOSTLY I REMEMBER THE ICE CREAM.	274	SUPPR W LINDSAY	34
MOTES			
ONLY THE MOTES OF DUST IN THE IMMACULATE HALLWAYS,	159	FIRST MEDITATN	79
MOTH			
THE LIGHTS IN THE KITCHENS GO OUT; MOTH WINGS UNFURL;	33	IDYLL	3
OR A MOTH BEATING THE CURTAIN.	54	THE LOST SON	23
THE WIND SLACKENS, LIGHT AS A MOTH FANNING A STONE:	190	AT OYSTER RIVER	17
BOTH MOTH AND FLAME? THE WEAK MOTH BLUNDERING BY.	241	THE SEQUEL	6
BOTH MOTH AND FLAME? THE WEAK MOTH BLUNDERING BY.	241	THE SEQUEL	6
MOTHER			
THOUGH THE DEVOURING MOTHER CRY, ""ESCAPE ME? NEVER--""	5	PROGNOSIS	13
REVEALS A FOOLISH MOTHER,	7	ORDERS FOR DAY	17
BEWARE MOTHER MILDEW.	55	THE LOST SON	69
I'M COLD. I'M COLD ALL OVER. RUB ME IN FATHER AND MOTHER.	56	THE LOST SON	85
MOTHER ME OUT OF HERE. WHAT MORE WILL THE BONES ALLOW?	64	SHAPE OF FIRE	7
MOTHER, MOTHER, STIR FROM YOUR CAVE OF SORROW.	64	SHAPE OF FIRE	16
MOTHER, MOTHER, STIR FROM YOUR CAVE OF SORROW.	64	SHAPE OF FIRE	16
MOTHER OF QUARTZ, YOUR WORDS WRITHE INTO MY EAR.	65	SHAPE OF FIRE	54
I CAN'T TASTE MY MOTHER.	74	I NEED, I NEED	2
MOTHER OF BLUE AND THE MANY CHANGES OF HAY,	79	GIVE WAY, GATES	14
THE MOON'S MY MOTHER: HOW I LOVE THE MOON!	156	THE DYING MAN	79
MOTHER, MOTHER OF US ALL, TELL ME WHERE I AM!	172	WHAT TELL BONES	53
MOTHER, MOTHER OF US ALL, TELL ME WHERE I AM!	172	WHAT TELL BONES	53
MNETHA, MOTHER OF HAR, PROTECT ME	196	THE LONG WATERS	20

	PAGE	TITLE	LINE
MOTHER (CONTINUED)			
AND IT WAS O, MY MOTHER O,	268	SAGINAW SONG	58
MOTHER-ROOT			
HOW DEEP THE MOTHER-ROOT OF THAT STILL CRY!	248	THE TREE, BIRD	17
MOTHERS			
WITH MOTHERS, SLEEP-HEAVY CHILDREN, STALE PERFUME, PAST THE MANAGER'S SMILE	47	DOUBLE FEATURE	3
MOTHER'S			
MY MOTHER'S COUNTENANCE	45	MY PAPA'S WALTZ	7
FROZEN BY A FATHER'S LIP, A MOTHER'S FAILURE TO ANSWER.	169	FOURTH MEDITATN	45
MOTHS			
TO THE SAND DUNES AND FISH FLIES, HANGING, THICKER THAN MOTHS,	193	JOURNY INTERIOR	28
MOTION			
OF MOTION MOORED TO ROCK;	4	DEATH PIECE	6
FIFTY SUMMERS IN MOTION AT ONCE,	38	FORCING HOUSE	10
WAS NOT THE JOYLESS MOTION OF A STONE.	105	SIR JOHN DAVIES	18
SHE KNEW THE GRAMMAR OF LEAST MOTION, SHE	120	THE DREAM	23
MOTION CAN KEEP ME STILL:	123	WORDS FOR WIND	17
I'M MARTYR TO A MOTION NOT MY OWN;	127	I KNEW A WOMAN	23
MOTION CAN DO NO MORE.	130	THE OTHER	18
THOUGH ALL'S IN MOTION, WHO IS PASSING BY?	132	SENTENTIOUS MAN	19
BUT MY LEAST MOTION CHANGED INTO A SONG,	132	SENTENTIOUS MAN	23
I KNOW THE MOTION OF THE DEEPEST STONE.	132	SENTENTIOUS MAN	35
AND THE WHOLE MOTION OF THE SOUL LAY BARE:	135	THE RENEWAL	23
SCARS, TEMPESTS, FLOODS, THE MOTION OF MAN'S FATE;	144	ELEGY (1)	14
WHO THOUGHT LOVE BUT A MOTION IN THE MIND?	156	THE DYING MAN	84
WITH A WIND FROM THE WEST AND THE TREES ALL IN MOTION.	158	FIRST MEDITATN	42
A BODY WITH THE MOTION OF A SOUL.	188	THE LONGING	27
I ROCK WITH THE MOTION OF MORNING;	191	AT OYSTER RIVER	58
OUR MOTION CONTINUES.	203	THE ROSE	38
THE MOTION OF THE MOON, AND WAVES AT PLAY,	235	MANIFESTATION	7
OR IS THE BODY BUT A MOTION IN A SHOE?	237	THE TRANCED	5
MORNING'S A MOTION IN A HAPPY MIND:	241	THE SEQUEL	17
THE MOTION	243	THE MOTION	T
O, MOTION O, OUR CHANCE IS STILL TO BE!	243	THE MOTION	24
HOW PURE THE MOTION OF THE RISING DAY,	248	THE TREE, BIRD	19
MOTIONLESS			
THE WIND LAY MOTIONLESS IN THE LONG GRASS.	6	INTERLUDE	10
A WAVE OF TIME HANGS MOTIONLESS ON THIS PARTICULAR SHORE.	47	DOUBLE FEATURE	9
DIPPING AND VEERING CLOSE TO THE MOTIONLESS WATER.	93	I CRY, LOVE!	44
AND THE SMALL FISH LIE, WITHOUT SHADOW, MOTIONLESS,	233	THE PIKE	6
MOTIONS			
WHAT GLORIES WOULD WE? MOTIONS OF THE SOUL?	135	THE RENEWAL	1
THE SOUL HAS MANY MOTIONS, BODY ONE.	243	THE MOTION	1
MOTTLED			
OUT OF THE MOTTLED SHADE	150	SNAKE	2
THE MOTTLED TIGER, BEST IN THE CORNER OF A DAMP PLACE,	197	THE LONG WATERS	40
IN A PLACE OF MOTTLED CLOUDS, A THIN MIST MORNING AND EVENING.	221	THE ABYSS	77
MOULD			
THE MOULD UPON THE BRANCH IS DRY,	15	COMING OF COLD	44
MOUND			
ROSE FROM A MOSSY MOUND	50	THE CYCLE	5
MOUNTAIN			
THE ELM TREE IS OUR HIGHEST MOUNTAIN PEAK;	13	PRAISE PRAIRIE	1
A LAP OF MOUNTAIN MIST	34	NIGHT JOURNEY	8
BEYOND THE MOUNTAIN PASS	34	NIGHT JOURNEY	20
THE MOUNTAIN WITH ITS SINGULAR BRIGHT SHADE	201	THE FAR FIELD	95
COMING DOWN FROM THE MOUNTAIN,	230	THE STORM	4
THERE IS ONE LIGHT ON THE MOUNTAIN.	230	THE STORM	9
THE WIND FROM THE SEA AND THE WIND FROM THE MOUNTAIN CONTENDING,	230	THE STORM	15
MOUNTAINS			
FLOATING OVER THE MOUNTAINS,	209	HER LONGING	17
MOUNTAIN'S			
WHERE'S SHE NOW, THE MOUNTAIN'S DOWNY GIRL?	101	THE VISITANT	24
MOUNTAIN-SLOPE			
ODOR OF BASSWOOD ON A MOUNTAIN-SLOPE,	201	THE FAR FIELD	98
MOUNTAINY			
AND THE YELLOWISH-GREEN FROM THE MOUNTAINY UPLAND,--	200	THE FAR FIELD	62
MOUNTING			
THE COST OF FOLLY IS FOREVER MOUNTING;	25	DIM-WIT COUSIN	5

	PAGE	TITLE	LINE
MOURN			
FLESH, YOU OFFEND THIS METAL. HOW LONG NEED THE BONES MOURN?	59	THE LONG ALLEY	12
TOUCH AND AROUSE. SUCK AND SOB. CURSE AND MOURN.	80	GIVE WAY, GATES	46
DARE I GRIEVE? DARE I MOURN?	208	THE APPARITION	11
MOURNERS'			
THE CRANED NECKS, THE MOURNERS' ANONYMOUS FACES,	22	ROAD TO WDLAWN	7
MOUSE			
BY DAY THE BAT IS COUSIN TO THE MOUSE.	16	THE BAT	1
IS IT SOFT LIKE A MOUSE?	54	THE LOST SON	50
EAT WHERE YOU'RE AT. I'M NOT A MOUSE.	72	WHERE KNOCK IS	40
A MOUSE TAUGHT ME HOW, I WAS A HAPPY ASKER.	90	UNFOLD! UNFOLD!	35
MOUSE, MOUSE, COME OUT OF THE FERNS,	92	I CRY, LOVE!	22
MOUSE, MOUSE, COME OUT OF THE FERNS,	92	I CRY, LOVE!	22
IT'S MIDNIGHT ON THE MOUSE,	137	LOVE'S PROGRESS	16
YOU SQUEAK LIKE A MOUSE THAT'S LOST IN THE HAY,	177	KITTY-CAT BIRD	10
THE MEADOW MOUSE	227	MEADOW MOUSE	T
SLEEPS THE BABY MOUSE I FOUND IN THE MEADOW,	227	MEADOW MOUSE	2
WHERE HAS HE GONE, MY MEADOW MOUSE,	227	MEADOW MOUSE	21
MOUSE-WARY			
TURNS, MOUSE-WARY,--	260	THE CHANGELING	2
MOUTH			
I STOP THE LYING MOUTH:	3	OPEN HOUSE	16
AT THE WOOD'S MOUTH,	55	THE LOST SON	71
THE DARK FLOWS ON ITSELF. A DEAD MOUTH SINGS UNDER AN OLD TREE.	59	THE LONG ALLEY	6
THE HAY HOPS IN THE HORSE'S MOUTH,	60	THE LONG ALLEY	41
WILL THE GOAT'S MOUTH	60	THE LONG ALLEY	60
A LOW MOUTH LAPS WATER. WEEDS, WEEDS, HOW I LOVE YOU.	64	SHAPE OF FIRE	17
A WORM HAS A MOUTH.	72	WHERE KNOCK IS	45
SIT IN MY MOUTH.	74	I NEED, I NEED	4
THE MOUTH ASKS. THE HAND TAKES.	80	GIVE WAY, GATES	51
EASY THE LIFE OF THE MOUTH. WHAT A LUST FOR RIPENESS!	90	UNFOLD! UNFOLD!	39
I KISS HER MOVING MOUTH,	126	WORDS FOR WIND	98
WE SING TOGETHER; WE SING MOUTH TO MOUTH.	129	SHE	7
WE SING TOGETHER; WE SING MOUTH TO MOUTH.	129	SHE	7
A MOUTH I CANNOT LEAVE.	137	LOVE'S PROGRESS	4
MOUTH UPON MOUTH, WE SANG,	146	THE SONG	28
MOUTH UPON MOUTH, WE SANG,	146	THE SONG	28
A THIN MOUTH, AND A TONGUE	150	SNAKE	4
BUT A TIME COMES WHEN THE VAGUE LIFE OF THE MOUTH NO LONGER SUFFICES;	168	FOURTH MEDITATN	18
TO BE A MOUTH, A MEAL OF MEAT?	169	FOURTH MEDITATN	33
THEN A REAL CAT CAME WITH A MOUTH SO WIDE,	177	KITTY-CAT BIRD	14
I HAVE LEFT THE BODY OF THE WHALE, BUT THE MOUTH OF THE NIGHT IS STILL WIDE;	188	THE LONGING	51
A YOUNG MOUTH LAUGHS AT A GIFT.	208	HER WORDS	1
A MOUTH LIKE A STICKLEBACK,--	209	HER LONGING	9
BY MY UNGUARDED MOUTH.	220	THE ABYSS	20
FROM DIRE HELL'S MOUTH,	236	SONG (2)	10
TO THE NORTH OF A MOUTH I LIE,	258	SONG (3)	8
I'LL KEEP MY BIG MOUTH SHUT.	270	GOB MUSIC	37
MOUTHS			
LOOSE GHOSTLY MOUTHS	39	ORCHIDS	17
THEIR WAN MOUTHS KISSING THE WARM SUTURES,	50	THE MINIMAL	9
FROM THE MOUTHS OF JUGS	56	THE LOST SON	92
THEY HAD MANY MOUTHS TO BREATHE WITH.	57	THE LOST SON	127
AND SMALL MOUTHS, STAY YOUR AIMLESS CHEEPING:	92	I CRY, LOVE!	23
MOVE			
I MOVE BENEATH AN EVIL SKY.	19	AGNST DISASTER	8
I DID NOT MOVE TO CLAIM WHAT WAS MY OWN.	21	THE AUCTION	4
A MANIA KEEPS THEM ON THE MOVE	33	HIGHWAY: MICH	12
MY MUSCLES MOVE WITH STEEL,	34	NIGHT JOURNEY	14
MOVE SLOWLY,	39	ORCHIDS	7
LOVERS DISENGAGE, MOVE SHEEPISHLY TOWARD THE AISLE	47	DOUBLE FEATURE	2
MOVE ABOUT.	83	O LULL ME, LULL	7
THE LITTLE FISHES MOVE.	121	ALL EARTH, AIR	4
THE BIRDS AND FISHES MOVE	125	WORDS FOR WIND	62
BUT IF I MOVE TOO CLOSE,	130	THE OTHER	5
NOW THEY MOVE ALL TOGETHER!--	152	THE SISKINS	19
AND THE SPIRIT FAILS TO MOVE FORWARD,	187	THE LONGING	19
AND THE WHOLE RIVER BEGINS TO MOVE FORWARD, ITS BRIDGES SHAKING.	191	AT OYSTER RIVER	56
AND THE SEA-WINDS MOVE THROUGH THE PINE TREES,	196	THE LONG WATERS	18

	PAGE	TITLE	LINE
MOVE (CONTINUED)			
DO WE MOVE TOWARD GOD, OR MERELY ANOTHER CONDITION?	221	THE ABYSS	75
HOPE HAS ITS HUSH: WE MOVE THROUGH ITS BROAD DAY,--	243	THE MOTION	22
I MOVE BEYOND THE REACH OF WIND AND FIRE.	244	INFIRMITY	24
I WAITED FOR THE WIND TO MOVE THE DUST;	247	I WAITED	1
MOVED			
MOVED INTO COMMON DAY,	50	THE CYCLE	4
A FINE HAZE MOVED OFF THE LEAVES;	57	THE LOST SON	144
MOVED IN A SLOW UP-SWAY.	57	THE LOST SON	148
THE LIGHT MOVED SLOWLY OVER THE FROZEN FIELD,	58	THE LOST SON	155
THE MIND MOVED, NOT ALONE,	58	THE LOST SON	162
I MOVED WITH THE MORNING.	63	FIELD OF LIGHT	52
HANDS AND HAIR MOVED THROUGH A DREAM OF WAKENING BLOSSOMS.	66	SHAPE OF FIRE	74
THE WORM HAS MOVED AWAY.	73	WHERE KNOCK IS	69
A CLOUD MOVED CLOSE. THE BULK OF THE WIND SHIFTED.	100	THE VISITANT	1
AH, WHEN SHE MOVED, SHE MOVED MORE WAYS THAN ONE:	127	I KNEW A WOMAN	3
AH, WHEN SHE MOVED, SHE MOVED MORE WAYS THAN ONE:	127	I KNEW A WOMAN	3
(SHE MOVED IN CIRCLES, AND THOSE CIRCLES MOVED).	127	I KNEW A WOMAN	21
(SHE MOVED IN CIRCLES, AND THOSE CIRCLES MOVED).	127	I KNEW A WOMAN	21
FOR I HAVE MOVED CLOSER TO DEATH, LIVED WITH DEATH;	220	THE ABYSS	37
AND IN A WOOD HE KNEW WHATEVER MOVED;	224	OTTO	13
SLOWLY WE MOVED BETWEEN	237	THE TRANCED	18
I MOVED LIKE SOME HEAT-WEARY ANIMAL.	247	I WAITED	17
MOVEMENT			
ONE SWIFT MOVEMENT,--	42	TRANSPLANTING	5
THE MOVEMENT IS FORWARD, AFTER A FEW WAVERS,	158	FIRST MEDITATN	27
MOVES			
OUR VERNAL WISDOM MOVES THROUGH RIPE TO SERE.	12	SLOW SEASON	16
THE SPIRIT MOVES,	101	LIGHT BREATHER	1
MOVES, LIKE THE SNAIL,	101	LIGHT BREATHER	11
SHE MOVES WHEN TIME IS SHY:	124	WORDS FOR WIND	52
SHE MOVES AS WATER MOVES, AND COMES TO ME,	129	SHE	15
SHE MOVES AS WATER MOVES, AND COMES TO ME,	129	SHE	15
SHE MOVES, AND I ADORE:	130	THE OTHER	17
FOR WATER MOVES UNTIL IT'S PURIFIED,	132	SENTENTIOUS MAN	41
A WIND MOVES THROUGH THE GRASS,	148	THE SMALL	11
WHAT MOVES IN GRASS I LOVE--	148	THE SMALL	21
EXISTENCE MOVES TOWARD A CERTAIN END--	149	IN LATE SUMMER	21
THE VISION MOVES, AND YET REMAINS THE SAME.	156	THE DYING MAN	94
THE SPIRIT MOVES, BUT NOT ALWAYS UPWARD,	157	FIRST MEDITATN	8
MOVES OVER THE FIELD,	160	FIRST MEDITATN	96
THE RIVER MOVES, WRINKLED BY MIDGES,	168	FOURTH MEDITATN	23
YET MOVES GENTLY AMONG THE BIRDS.	170	FOURTH MEDITATN	74
OR A BREEZE MOVES OVER THE KNEES FROM A LOW HILL,	198	THE LONG WATERS	64
MY MIND MOVES IN MORE THAN ONE PLACE,	201	THE FAR FIELD	75
HIS SPIRIT MOVES LIKE MONUMENTAL WIND	201	THE FAR FIELD	91
WHEN THE TIDE MOVES	210	HER TIME	6
THE BODY MOVES, THOUGH SLOWLY, TOWARD DESIRE.	235	MANIFESTATION	10
MOVING			
THE MEN ON RAIL AND ROADWAY KEEP MOVING ON AND ON.	28	CLAIRVOY WIDOW	24
I KISS HER MOVING MOUTH,	126	WORDS FOR WIND	98
AND ONE CRAB, TENTATIVE, HUNCHES HIMSELF BEFORE MOVING ALONG THE BOTTOM,	159	FIRST MEDITATN	62
OR A SALMON, TIRED, MOVING UP A SHALLOW STREAM,	159	FIRST MEDITATN	68
COME THE FIRST TIDE-RIPPLES, MOVING, ALMOST WITHOUT SOUND, TOWARD ME,	190	AT OYSTER RIVER	2
I AM NOT MOVING BUT THEY ARE,	194	JOURNY INTERIOR	39
MOVING, UNMOVING IN A PARCHED LAND, WHITE IN THE MOONLIGHT:	194	JOURNY INTERIOR	53
MOVING, ELUSIVE AS FISH, FEARLESS,	199	THE FAR FIELD	31
I FEEL A WEIGHTLESS CHANGE, A MOVING FORWARD	200	THE FAR FIELD	58
MOVING WITH THE WAVES, THE UNDULATING DRIFTWOOD,	203	THE ROSE	48
MOVING SERENELY AMONG THE LEEKS AND CABBAGES,	223	ELEGY (2)	20
THE LAST WATCHER INDOORS, MOVING THE CARDPLAYERS CLOSER	230	THE STORM	26
MOVING-SLOW			
IN MOVING-SLOW HE HAS NO PEER.	116	THE SLOTH	1
MOW			
DEEP IN THE MOW, AND EACH STEP DEEPER DOWN,	247	I WAITED	7
MOWER			
AT THE FIELD'S END, IN THE CORNER MISSED BY THE MOWER,	199	THE FAR FIELD	13
I SUFFERED FOR BIRDS, FOR YOUNG RABBITS CAUGHT IN THE MOWER,	199	THE FAR FIELD	24
MOWING			
(BUT WHAT PRODIGIOUS MOWING WE DID MAKE).	127	I KNEW A WOMAN	14

	PAGE	TITLE	LINE
MR			
WHAT A WHELM OF PROVERBS, MR. PINCH!	89	UNFOLD! UNFOLD!	18
MRS			
LIFTING ME HIGH OVER THE FOUR-FOOT STEMS, THE MRS.			
RUSSELLS, AND HIS OWN ELABORATE HYBRIDS,	203	THE ROSE	54
MUCH			
MUCH LOGIC IN THEIR GLUTTONY.	25	VERSE W ALLUSNS	12
WHAT SAINT STRAINED SO MUCH,	37	CUTTINGS (LATE)	3
CRACKING SO MUCH THIN GLASS	41	BIG WIND	18
SHE WAS TOO MUCH FOR ONE, YOU CAN BET YOUR LIFE:	114	THE COW	3
NATURE'S TOO MUCH TO KNOW.	130	THE OTHER	12
SO MUCH OF ADOLESCENCE IS AN ILL-DEFINED DYING,	162	I'M HERE	35
SHE WAS SO MUCH TROUBLE;	179	MYRTLE'S COUSIN	7
TOO MUCH REALITY CAN BE A DAZZLE, A SURFEIT;	220	THE ABYSS	44
SO MUCH HE JUST LIES IN ONE CORNER,	227	MEADOW MOUSE	13
HE CARED SO MUCH FOR THE SPORT,	263	FOLLIES OF ADAM	31
COME OFF IT MUCH LESS NEAT.	267	SAGINAW SONG	12
"SURE, WE STILL EAT," I SAID. "ENOUGH! OR TOO MUCH."	273	SUPPR W LINDSAY	17
MUCILAGE			
ALL THE MISERY OF MANILLA FOLDERS AND MUCILAGE,	46	DOLOR	3
MUCK			
DOWN BY THE MUCK SHRINKING TO THE ALKALINE CENTER.	197	THE LONG WATERS	43
MUDDLE			
SHE'D MUDDLE THE WHOLE AFTERNOON	179	MYRTLE'S COUSIN	9
MUDDY			
BY THE MUDDY POND-EDGE, BY THE BOG-HOLES,	54	THE LOST SON	42
AS WHEN SILT DRIFTS AND SIFTS DOWN THROUGH MUDDY POND-WATER,	159	FIRST MEDITATN	60
AND WHY MUDDY SHOES	213	THE HAPPY THREE	10
MUFFLED			
A MUFFLED VOICE, A LOW SWEET WATERY NOISE.	165	HER BECOMING	20
MULTIGRAPH			
RITUAL OF MULTIGRAPH, PAPER-CLIP, COMMA,	46	DOLOR	7
MULTIPLE			
OF MULTIPLE CHOICE AND EITHER/OR	272	DUET	10
MUMBLEY-PEG			
THE KIDS PLAY COPS AND ROBBERS, THE KIDS PLAY MUMBLEY-PEG,	27	CLAIRVOY WIDOW	9
MURDERED			
YOUR HOPES ARE MURDERED AND UNDONE.	4	FEUD	12
MURMUR			
THE MURMUR OF THE ABSOLUTE, THE WHY	201	THE FAR FIELD	89
MUSCLES			
MY MUSCLES MOVE WITH STEEL,	34	NIGHT JOURNEY	14
THE MUSCLES IN ONE THIGH	47	THE RETURN	6
MUSES			
THE MUSES, THEY MUST ALL ADORE HIM,	266	FOR STEVENS	18
MUSIC			
SUCH MUSIC IN A SKIN!	79	GIVE WAY, GATES	4
A MUSIC IN A HOOD,	101	LIGHT BREATHER	16
O WHAT LEWD MUSIC CREPT INTO OUR EARS!	106	SIR JOHN DAVIES	46
A SNAIL'S MUSIC.	163	I'M HERE	89
I'LL MAKE A BROKEN MUSIC, OR I'LL DIE.	240	IN EVEING AIR	6
GOB MUSIC	269	GOB MUSIC	T
MUSK			
THE LATE PEACH YIELDS A SUBTLE MUSK,	14	COMING OF COLD	1
MUSK-RAT			
OF MARSH GRASS HEAPED ABOVE A MUSK-RAT HOLE.	15	THE HERON	4
MUSKRATS			
THE DEAD SNAKES AND MUSKRATS, THE TURTLES GASPING IN THE			
RUBBLE,	194	JOURNY INTERIOR	36
MUSKY			
SO THEIR MUSKY SMELL COMES EVEN STRONGER,	39	ORCHIDS	12
MUST			
IF I MUST OF MY SENSES LOSE,	8	PRAYER	1
THE HEART MUST RALLY TO MY WIT	19	AGNST DISASTER	11
STAY CLOSE. MUST I KILL SOMETHING ELSE?	60	THE LONG ALLEY	31
MUST PULL OFF CLOTHES	65	SHAPE OF FIRE	49
THE SPIRIT KNOWS THE FLESH IT MUST CONSUME.	131	SENTENTIOUS MAN	10
MUST I STAY TANGLED IN THAT LIVELY HAIR?	140	THE SWAN	3
A MAN ALIVE, FROM ALL LIGHT I MUST FALL.	140	THE SWAN	12
THE WALL HAS ENTERED: I MUST LOVE THE WALL,	155	THE DYING MAN	48
WHAT WE PUT DOWN, MUST WE TAKE UP AGAIN?	243	THE MOTION	11
MY SPEECH MUST BE:	260	THE CHANGELING	25
THE MUSES, THEY MUST ALL ADORE HIM,	266	FOR STEVENS	18

		PAGE	TITLE	LINE
MUSTN'T				
	YOU MUSTN'T PULL IT MORE THAN TWICE,	181	MONOTONY SONG	2
MUSTY				
	THEMSELVES, THEIR PARLORS MUSTY AS A FUNERAL HOME.	5	PROGNOSIS	12
	POKES THROUGH A MUSTY SHEATH	37	CUTTINGS	7
MUTILATED				
	MUTILATED SOULS IN COLD MORGUES OF OBLIGATION.	166	HER BECOMING	43
MUTTONY				
	MUTTONY TEARS FALLING ON FIGURED LINOLEUM,	48	LAST WORDS	3
MY (548)				
MYRTLE				
	MYRTLE	179	MYRTLE	T
	THERE ONCE WAS A GIRL NAMED MYRTLE	179	MYRTLE	1
	O NOBODY UNDERSTOOD MYRTLE!	179	MYRTLE	5
	POOR MYRTLE WOULD SIGH, "SWEET MY COZ,	180	GOO-GIRL	1
MYRTLE'S				
	MYRTLE'S COUSIN	179	MYRTLE'S COUSIN	T
	AND THEN THERE WAS MYRTLE'S COUSIN,	179	MYRTLE'S COUSIN	1
MYSELF				
	MYSELF IS WHAT I WEAR:	3	OPEN HOUSE	11
	I WOULD PUT OFF MYSELF AND FLEE	24	BEFORE STUDY	5
	THE LAST TIME I NEARLY WHISPERED MYSELF AWAY.	89	UNFOLD! UNFOLD!	20
	FISHING, I CAUGHT MYSELF BEHIND THE EARS.	89	UNFOLD! UNFOLD!	23
	ONCE I WAS SWEET WITH THE LIGHT OF MYSELF,	103	OLD LADY'S WRDS	39
	I FIND MYSELF PERPLEXED. WHAT IS DESIRE?--	105	SIR JOHN DAVIES	26
	I START TO LEAVE MYSELF.	121	ALL EARTH, AIR	15
	MYSELF AS I SHOULD BE,	123	WORDS FOR WIND	6
	BEING MYSELF, I SING	126	WORDS FOR WIND	90
	AND SEE AND SUFFER MYSELF	126	WORDS FOR WIND	104
	I KEEP A DOG, AND BARK MYSELF.	138	THE SURLY ONE	4
	I FEAR MYSELF IN THE FIELD,	138	LOVE'S PROGRESS	24
	I HAVE MYSELF AN INNER WEIGHT OF WOE	144	ELEGY (1)	3
	I HAVE MYSELF AN INNER WEIGHT OF WOE	144	ELEGY (1)	7
	I KNOW MYSELF, MY SEASONS, AND I KNOW.	144	ELEGY (1)	10
	I HAVE MYSELF ONE CRUMBLING SKIN TO SHOW;	144	ELEGY (1)	11
	I HAVE MYSELF, AND BEAR ITS WEIGHT OF WOE	144	ELEGY (1)	15
	WHEN I RAISED MYSELF ONCE MORE,	145	THE BEAST	16
	I WAS MYSELF, ALONE.	147	THE EXORCISM	25
	I THOUGHT MYSELF REBORN.	154	THE DYING MAN	17
	ONLY TO LOSE MYSELF IN THIS SMALL DARK.	154	THE DYING MAN	41
	I BARE A WOUND, AND DARE MYSELF TO BLEED.	155	THE DYING MAN	69
	I'LL SCARE MYSELF WITH SIGHING, OR I'LL SING;	156	THE DYING MAN	86
	OFTEN I THINK OF MYSELF AS RIDING--	158	FIRST MEDITATN	20
	WHEN I BENT TO UNTANGLE MYSELF,	162	I'M HERE	48
	RAN AHEAD OF MYSELF,	166	HER BECOMING	50
	"AT LAST I'M MYSELF!"--AND HE UP AND DIED	177	KITTY-CAT BIRD	16
	I REHEARSE MYSELF FOR THIS:	194	JOURNY INTERIOR	65
	I LOSE AND FIND MYSELF IN THE LONG WATER;	198	THE LONG WATERS	76
	I SWAY OUTSIDE MYSELF	202	THE ROSE	22
	AND HOW THOSE FLOWERHEADS SEEMED TO FLOW TOWARD ME, TO BECKON ME, ONLY A CHILD, OUT OF MYSELF.	203	THE ROSE	55
	AMONG THE HALF-DEAD TREES, I CAME UPON THE TRUE EASE OF MYSELF,	205	THE ROSE	99
	AND I STOOD OUTSIDE MYSELF,	205	THE ROSE	101
	YET KEEP TO MYSELF MY OWN MIND;	208	HER WORDS	5
	LIKE A LEECH, LOOPING MYSELF ALONG,	209	HER LONGING	7
	PERPETUALLY RISING OUT OF MYSELF,	209	HER LONGING	20
	SO I BETOOK MYSELF	213	THE HAPPY THREE	13
	AND HEAR MYSELF RETURN	215	HIS FOREBODING	12
	AND TELL MYSELF MY IMAGE CANNOT DIE.	244	INFIRMITY	4
	I LOVE MYSELF: THAT'S MY ONE CONSTANCY.	244	INFIRMITY	5
	DEAD TO MYSELF, AND ALL I HOLD MOST DEAR,	244	INFIRMITY	23
	I SOON WILL BE MYSELF AGAIN.	256	IN HYDROTHERAPY	12
	I WARM MYSELF WITH COLD.	259	SONG (3)	33
	TO THE BEST OF MYSELF I SING,	261	THE CHANGELING	32
	I GET MYSELF A STICK,	269	GOB MUSIC	2
MYSTERIOUS				
	TO YOU ARBUTUS CALM, MYSTERIOUS AS A STONE?	261	THE CHANGELING	29
MYSTERY				
	LET OTHERS PROBE THE MYSTERY IF THEY CAN.	250	THE RIGHT THING	1
	LET OTHERS DELVE THAT MYSTERY IF THEY CAN.	250	THE RIGHT THING	6
	TAKES TO HIMSELF WHAT MYSTERY HE CAN,	250	THE RIGHT THING	15
	TILL MYSTERY IS NO MORE: NO MORE HE CAN.	250	THE RIGHT THING	18

	PAGE	TITLE	LINE
NATURE (CONTINUED)			
WAS NATURE KIND? THE HEART'S CORE TRACTABLE?	242	THE SEQUEL	25
NATURES			
THAT LADIES THEIR TRUE NATURES NEVER SUPPRESS,	113	TO A LADY ED	10
NATURE'S			
IS HUMAN NATURE'S DAILY FOOD.	25	VERSE W ALLUSNS	8
NATURE'S TOO MUCH TO KNOW.	130	THE OTHER	12
NEAR			
THE RAIN STAYED IN ITS CLOUD; FULL DARK CAME NEAR;	6	INTERLUDE	9
I DAWDLE WITH GROUPS NEAR THE RICKETY POP-CORN STAND;	47	DOUBLE FEATURE	5
SPIRIT, COME NEAR. THIS IS ONLY THE EDGE OF WHITENESS.	64	SHAPE OF FIRE	12
GOD, GIVE ME A NEAR. I HEAR FLOWERS.	73	WHERE KNOCK IS	49
IS THE ETERNAL NEAR, FONDLING?	87	PRAISE TO END!	73
I'M NEAR.	99	O, THOU OPENING	85
THE WAVES RIPPLING NEAR ME.	104	OLD LADY'S WRDS	43
WHAT FALLS AWAY IS ALWAYS. AND IS NEAR.	108	THE WAKING (2)	17
I LIVE NEAR THE ABYSS. I HOPE TO STAY	134	THE PURE FURY	26
THAT DOVE'S ELABORATE WAY OF COMING NEAR	149	IN LATE SUMMER	23
NEAR THE GRAVES OF THE GREAT DEAD,	170	FOURTH MEDITATN	87
OR THESE INSECTS PULSING NEAR MY SKIN,	171	WHAT TELL BONES	26
AND THE TOM-CAT, CAUGHT NEAR THE PHEASANT-RUN,	199	THE FAR FIELD	21
AND THE CRABS BASK NEAR THE EDGE,	200	THE FAR FIELD	69
WHAT I LOVE IS NEAR AT HAND,	201	THE FAR FIELD	80
NEAR THIS ROSE, IN THIS GROVE OF SUN-PARCHED, WIND-WARPED MADRONAS,	205	THE ROSE	98
DOWN ON THE NEAR SHORE,	210	HER TIME	22
THE DEW DRAWS NEAR.	215	HIS FOREBODING	10
NEAR THE STEM, WHITER AT ROOT,	221	THE ABYSS	83
"ADORE AND DRAW NEAR.	222	THE ABYSS	86
NEAR THE END, SHE SEEMED ALMOST TO HEAR ME--	228	THE GERANIUM	20
WHILE I POKED WITH A STICK AT A STONE NEAR A FOUR-PRONGED FLOWER,	232	THE THING	21
AND THE DUCKS NEAR LAKE WASHINGTON WADDLE DOWN THE HIGHWAY AFTER A RAIN,	234	ALL MORNING	26
I WOULD BE NEAR; I SHUT MY EYES TO SEE;	246	THE MARROW	22
SHE'S COMING NEAR!	261	THE CHANGELING	44
I LEAN MY HEAD NEAR THE BRIMMING EDGE	269	GOB MUSIC	14
SHOULD DAME ANXIETY EVER COME NEAR	272	DUET	24
AND FLICKER NEAR OUR LEGS LIKE KEROSENE	274	SUPPR W LINDSAY	36
NEARED			
KILLED EVERY CAT THAT NEARED THEIR PHEASANT RUNS;	224	OTTO	28
NEARLY			
THE LAST TIME I NEARLY WHISPERED MYSELF AWAY.	89	UNFOLD! UNFOLD!	20
MY SOUL NEARLY MY OWN,	221	THE ABYSS	79
NEAT			
NEAT IN THEIR BOXES, DOLOR OF PAD AND PAPER-WEIGHT,	46	DOLOR	2
COME OFF IT MUCH LESS NEAT.	267	SAGINAW SONG	12
NECESSARY			
IT'S NECESSARY AMONG THE FLIES AND BANANAS, TO KEEP A CONSTANT VIGIL,	86	PRAISE TO END!	24
NECESSITY			
NECESSITY STARVES ON THE STOOP OF INVENTION.	29	THE GENTLE	11
NECK			
FULL ON MY NECK I FEEL	34	NIGHT JOURNEY	12
HER NECK HAS KITTENS.	72	WHERE KNOCK IS	32
MY NECK, IF NOT MY HEART, WILL BREAK	136	THE SENSUALISTS	23
A SINGLE WAVE COMES IN LIKE THE NECK OF A GREAT SWAN	197	THE LONG WATERS	52
RETIRING TO NUDGE HIS NECK HALF-WAY UNDER	226	THE LIZARD	16
THE ICE CAP AT MY RIGID NECK	256	IN HYDROTHERAPY	3
IN THE SOFT SLACK OF A NECK I SLEPT.	258	SONG (3)	22
NECKCURLS			
I REMEMBER THE NECKCURLS, LIMP AND DAMP AS TENDRILS;	102	ELEGY FOR JANE	1
NECKS			
THE CRANED NECKS, THE MOURNERS' ANONYMOUS FACES,	22	ROAD TO WDLAWN	7
HUNG DOWN LONG YELLOW EVIL NECKS, LIKE TROPICAL SNAKES.	38	ROOT CELLAR	5
PECKING AT CRUSTS AND PEANUTS, THEIR GREEN NECKS GLITTERING;	234	ALL MORNING	28
NEED			
I HAVE NO NEED FOR TONGUE.	3	OPEN HOUSE	2
THE LIGHT ESSENTIAL TO YOUR NEED.	4	FEUD	11
ACCELERATION IS THEIR NEED:	33	HIGHWAY: MICH	11
FLESH, YOU OFFEND THIS METAL. HOW LONG NEED THE BONES MOURN?	59	THE LONG ALLEY	12
COME TO ME, MILK-NOSE. I NEED A LOAN OF THE QUICK.	59	THE LONG ALLEY	25
I NEED, I NEED	74	I NEED, I NEED	T

	PAGE	TITLE	LINE
NEED (CONTINUED)			
I NEED, I NEED	74	I NEED, I NEED	T
NOT YOU I NEED.	75	I NEED, I NEED	43
I NEED A PLACE TO SING, AND DANCING-ROOM, ...	105	SIR JOHN DAVIES	4
HOW TERRIBLE THE NEED FOR SOLITUDE:	133	THE PURE FURY	15
FISH FEED ON FISH, ACCORDING TO THEIR NEED:	155	THE DYING MAN	66
I NEED AN OLD CRONE'S KNOWING.	157	FIRST MEDITATN	19
I NEED A POND WITH SMALL EELS. AND A WINDY ORCHARD.	164	I'M HERE	91
WHAT DO THEY NEED?	169	FOURTH MEDITATN	50
I NEED A POOL; I NEED A PUDDLE'S CALM.	171	WHAT TELL BONES	21
I NEED A POOL; I NEED A PUDDLE'S CALM.	171	WHAT TELL BONES	21
THINKING, GOD HAS NEED OF ME.	172	WHAT TELL BONES	63
WHAT NEED FOR HEAVEN, THEN, ...	203	THE ROSE	56
THE CENTAUR DOES NOT NEED A HORSE;	264	THREE EPIGRAMS	11
I NEED A MORNING DRINK, ...	269	GOB MUSIC	11
WE NEED A BREED THAT MIXES BLAKE AND ME, ...	274	SUPPR W LINDSAY	41
NEEDLE			
WITH A TENDRIL FOR NEEDLE	44	FRAU BAUMAN	21
AND THAT THIN CRY, LIKE A NEEDLE PIERCING THE EAR, THE			
INSISTENT CICADA, ...	204	THE ROSE	67
NEEDLES			
--HOW NEEDLES AND CORNERS PERPLEX ME!	161	I'M HERE	12
A LIGHT WIND STIRS IN THE PINE NEEDLES.	168	FOURTH MEDITATN	24
NEEDLE'S			
A KNAVE WHO SCAMPERED THROUGH THE NEEDLE'S EYE, ...	28	THE FAVORITE	1
NEEDN'T			
BUT AT LEAST WE KNOW ONE NEEDN'T BLENCH	272	DUET	16
NEEDS			
A SWAN NEEDS A POND.	78	BRING THE DAY!	34
THOUGH DANCING NEEDS A MASTER, I HAD NONE	105	SIR JOHN DAVIES	15
THE GROUND NEEDS THE ABYSS, ...	121	ALL EARTH, AIR	19
A WRETCH NEEDS HIS WRETCHEDNESS. YES.	188	THE LONGING	24
WHAT DOES WHAT IT SHOULD DO NEEDS NOTHING MORE.	235	MANIFESTATION	9
A WRETCH NEEDS HIS WRETCHEDNESS. YES. BUT THIS SHAPE	260	THE CHANGELING	13
WHAT EAGLE NEEDS A TREE?	263	FOLLIES OF ADAM	26
AND IF THE METER NEEDS A CHANGE	269	GOB MUSIC	5
NEIGHBORHOOD			
CONDUCTING HIS LONG WARS WITH THE NEIGHBORHOOD CATS, ...	234	ALL MORNING	16
NEIGHBORS			
OLD NEIGHBORS NUDGED EACH OTHER AT THE FUN.	21	THE AUCTION	12
AND TOLD MY NEIGHBORS WHEN TO LAUGH.	138	THE SURLY ONE	3
I THINK MY NEIGHBORS STRANGE;	139	PLAINT	2
NEIGHBOR'S			
BY THE LIFTING OF THE TAIL OF A NEIGHBOR'S CAT, ...	82	SENSIBILITY! LA	35
I'M TIRED OF BROODING ON MY NEIGHBOR'S SOUL;	132	SENTENTIOUS MAN	37
NEITHER (14)			
NEMESIS			
I KNOW YOU ARE MY NEMESIS	75	I NEED, I NEED	31
NERVE			
I WAKE IN EVERY NERVE.	34	NIGHT JOURNEY	15
NERVELESS			
THE NERVELESS CONSTRICTION OF SURFACES--	166	HER BECOMING	41
NERVES			
YOU MEDITATE UPON THE NERVES, ...	4	FEUD	17
THE TIGHT NERVES LEADING TO THE THROAT	22	SILENCE	17
UNTIL THE TOUGHEST NERVES ARE FRAYED.	33	HIGHWAY: MICH	13
NIBBLE AGAIN, FISH NERVES.	55	THE LOST SON	70
HELLO, HELLO. MY NERVES KNEW YOU, DEAR BOY.	65	SHAPE OF FIRE	32
NERVOUS			
NERVOUS AND COLD, BIRD-FURTIVE, WHISKERY, ...	157	FIRST MEDITATN	16
NEST			
I FEEL THE SLIME OF A WET NEST.	55	THE LOST SON	68
THESE WINGS ARE FROM THE WRONG NEST.	80	GIVE WAY, GATES	52
THE NEST DENIES.	91	UNFOLD! UNFOLD!	64
WE MET IN A NEST. BEFORE I LIVED.	93	I CRY, LOVE!	55
NESTING			
THE WEEDS BELIEVED ME, AND THE NESTING BIRDS.	63	FIELD OF LIGHT	47
NESTING-PLACE			
HAUNT OF THE CAT-BIRD, NESTING-PLACE OF THE FIELD-MOUSE,	199	THE FAR FIELD	15
NESTLING			
A NESTLING SIGHED;	51	THE WAKING (1)	18
I THINK OF THE NESTLING FALLEN INTO THE DEEP GRASS, ...	227	MEADOW MOUSE	26
A NESTLING SIGHED--I CALLED THAT NESTLING MINE;	241	THE SEQUEL	12

	PAGE	TITLE	LINE
NESTLING (CONTINUED)			
A NESTLING SIGHED--I CALLED THAT NESTLING MINE;	241	THE SEQUEL	12
NESTLING'S			
WE GROW INDIFFERENT TO DOG HOWLS, TO THE NESTLING'S LAST PEEP;	33	IDYLL	6
OUT OF A NESTLING'S BEAK	123	WORDS FOR WIND	27
NESTS			
WELTER OF TIN CANS, PAILS, OLD BIRD NESTS, A CHILD'S SHOE RIDING A LOG, ...	191	AT OYSTER RIVER	54
NETHER			
LIFTING A NETHER LIP	130	THE OTHER	3
NETS			
AND THE WAVES FLATTENING OUT WHEN THE FISHERMEN DRAG THEIR NETS OVER THE STONES.	194	JOURNY INTERIOR	57
NEVER			
THOUGH THE DEVOURING MOTHER CRY, ""ESCAPE ME? NEVER--""	5	PROGNOSIS	13
A FLASH OF OBJECTS NEVER SEEN BEFORE.	8	THE SIGNALS	2
ITS RAPE IS GENTLE, NEVER MORE	8	PRAYER	13
TRUTH NEVER IS UNDONE;	9	THE ADAMANT	3
SHALL NEVER TOUCH ANOTHER EAR.	22	SILENCE	20
IN LOVE ARE NEVER KNOWN TO BARTER;	23	AMOROUS LADY	6
I NEVER AM BORED, HOWEVER FAMILIAR THE SCENE.	24	VERNAL SENTIMNT	4
THOSE DOTING AUNTIES NEVER WOULD HAVE BOTHERED.	25	DIM-WIT COUSIN	4
HE NEVER TREMBLED AT A VEILED REMARK.	28	THE FAVORITE	2
FOOLS WHO WILL NEVER LEARN;	31	LULL	18
THE ROOM THAT THE CHILDREN HAD NEVER BEEN IN, ...	32	SALE	18
NEVER SPILLS.	80	GIVE WAY, GATES	54
WE NEVER ENTER	93	I CRY, LOVE!	57
NEVER WISHING ITSELF AWAY, ...	101	LIGHT BREATHER	14
--FOR YOU NEVER WON WITH THAT MONEY.	112	SQUEEZE-BOX	29
THAT LADIES THEIR TRUE NATURES NEVER SUPPRESS, ...	113	TO A LADY ED	10
THE AFTER-IMAGE NEVER STAYS THE SAME.	132	SENTENTIOUS MAN	20
MY DARLING DOES WHAT I COULD NEVER DO:	140	THE SWAN	6
WHAT'S BEYOND NEVER CRUMBLES LIKE AN EMBANKMENT, ...	159	FIRST MEDITATN	76
LONGING FOR ABSOLUTES THAT NEVER COME.	171	WHAT TELL BONES	13
I SEE THE FLOWER OF ALL WATER, ABOVE AND BELOW ME, THE NEVER RECEDING, ...	194	JOURNY INTERIOR	52
BUT NEVER THE FULL LOOK OF MY EYES, ...	209	HER RETICENCE	6
SAID NEVER A WORD, ...	216	THE SHY MAN	7
SAID NEVER A WORD, ...	216	THE SHY MAN	15
MAY YOUR LIMBS NEVER WITHER, ...	217	WISH YOUNG WIFE	2
SHE NEVER KNEW;	223	ELEGY (2)	6
ALL BIRDS REMEMBERED, O NEVER FORGOTTEN!	235	ALL MORNING	45
HIS SEX-LIFE NEVER IS ONE-SIDED.	264	THREE EPIGRAMS	14
NEVER MET HIM, DUTCHMAN DEAR;	266	FOR STEVENS	10
THERE'S NEVER A HOUSEHOLD FART, ...	268	SAGINAW SONG	38
MY FATHER NEVER USED A STICK, ...	268	SAGINAW SONG	50
--WITH NEVER A THOUGHT FOR KIERKEGAARD.	272	DUET	12
"THAT'S NEVER BLAKE," SAID LINDSAY. "HE'D BE A WORM, ...	273	SUPPR W LINDSAY	26
NEW			
NEW MEANING GROWS IMMENSE.	18	GENESIS	12
ROSE ON SUCH LOPPED LIMBS TO A NEW LIFE?	37	CUTTINGS (LATE)	4
AND THE NEW PLANTS, STILL AWKWARD IN THEIR SOIL, ...	63	FIELD OF LIGHT	42
A TWO-LEGGED DOG HUNTING A NEW HORIZON OF HOWLS.	65	SHAPE OF FIRE	38
SOME RARE NEW TEDIUM'S TAKING SHAPE:	81	SENSIBILITY! LA	13
IT WASN'T THE JOINTS IN NEW YORK, NEW YORK;	111	SQUEEZE-BOX	9
IT WASN'T THE JOINTS IN NEW YORK, NEW YORK;	111	SQUEEZE-BOX	9
FOR A NEW ROUTINE--	228	THE GERANIUM	6
THE WIND FROM OFF THE SEA SAYS NOTHING NEW.	246	THE MARROW	1
GREW BACK A NEW WING, ...	249	THE RESTORED	16
NEW-CAUGHT			
LIKE THE EYE OF A NEW-CAUGHT FISH.	204	THE ROSE	88
NEWLY			
OVER THE DYING, THE NEWLY DEAD.	43	FLOWER DUMP	13
NEWS			
I'M WILD WITH NEWS!	99	O, THOU OPENING	65
NEW-SHOD			
I STEPPED CAREFULLY, LIKE A NEW-SHOD HORSE, ...	166	HER BECOMING	46
NEWSMEN			
THE NEWSMEN SUCK THEIR THUMBS.	31	LULL	14
NEWSPRINT			
THEIR EYES, RICH AS PLUMS, STARING FROM NEWSPRINT,--	48	JUDGE NOT	3

		PAGE	TITLE	LINE
NEWTS				
BEETLES IN CAVES, NEWTS, STONE-DEAF FISHES,	....	50	THE MINIMAL	3
NEXT				
NEXT DOOR THERE IS A LOVE-NEST OF PLASTER BOARD AND TIN,		27	CLAIRVOY WIDOW	15
AS THE BIRDS FLEW OFF TO THE END OF NEXT WEEK.	....	115	THE SERPENT	26
BUT I SACKED THE PRESUMPTUOUS HAG THE NEXT WEEK,	....	228	THE GERANIUM	25
NIBBLE				
NIBBLE AGAIN, FISH NERVES.	....	55	THE LOST SON	70
NIBBLED				
NOTHING NIBBLED MY LINE,	....	53	THE LOST SON	14
I NIBBLED MEEKLY FROM HER PROFFERED HAND;	....	127	I KNEW A WOMAN	11
NIBBLED BY SHEEP AND RABBITS.	....	202	THE ROSE	10
NICE				
YOU'RE NOT VERY NICE,--	....	75	I NEED, I NEED	29
A DONKEY'S TAIL IS VERY NICE	....	181	MONOTONY SONG	1
O WHAT COULD BE MORE NICE	....	212	LIGHT LISTENED	1
THEY TAUGHT ME NOT TO BE TOO NICE	....	225	THE CHUMS	7
NICELY				
TWICED ME NICELY,--		79	GIVE WAY, GATES	11
NIEMALS				
ER IST NIEMALS AUSGEPOOPEN,	....	266	FOR STEVENS	15
NIGHT				
OUR PUPILS WIDENED WITH UNNATURAL NIGHT,	....	6	INTERLUDE	7
TURN SLOWLY THROUGH THE NIGHT,	....	9	THE ADAMANT	6
ALL NIGHT AND ALL DAY THE WIND ROARED IN THE TREES,	......	12	MID-CNTRY BLOW	1
HE LOOPS IN CRAZY FIGURES HALF THE NIGHT	....	16	THE BAT	5
NIGHT JOURNEY	....	34	NIGHT JOURNEY	T
I STARE INTO THE NIGHT	....	34	NIGHT JOURNEY	4
I STAY UP HALF THE NIGHT	....	34	NIGHT JOURNEY	26
AND AT NIGHT,	....	39	ORCHIDS	9
WE STAYED ALL NIGHT,	....	41	BIG WIND	19
OR STAND ALL NIGHT WATERING ROSES, HIS FEET BLUE IN RUBBER BOOTS.	....	42	OLD FLORIST	10
OUT THROUGH THE VELVETY CHAINS TO THE COOL AIR OF NIGHT.		47	DOUBLE FEATURE	4
NIGHT CROW		49	NIGHT CROW	T
ONCE I STAYED ALL NIGHT.	....	57	THE LOST SON	134
LAST NIGHT I SLEPT IN THE PITS OF A TONGUE.	....	65	SHAPE OF FIRE	34
IN THE FAIR NIGHT OF SOME DIM BRAIN,	....	81	SENSIBILITY! LA	4
AND SHAPELESS NIGHT THAT MADE NO ANSWER BACK.	....	107	SIR JOHN DAVIES	90
LAST NIGHT YOU LAY A-SLEEPING? NO!	....	114	DINKY	13
IN THE LONG NIGHT, I REST WITHIN HER NAME--	....	131	SENTENTIOUS MAN	16
ONCE I READ NOTHING THROUGH A FEARFUL NIGHT,	....	133	THE PURE FURY	3
AS THE THICK SHADE OF THE LONG NIGHT COMES ON.	....	134	THE PURE FURY	28
THE NIGHT WIND RISES. DOES MY FATHER LIVE?	....	135	THE RENEWAL	7
I WALK THE NIGHT TO KEEP MY FIVE WITS WARM.	....	135	THE RENEWAL	18
IN THE WORST NIGHT OF MY WILL,	....	154	THE DYING MAN	31
A MADMAN STARING AT PERPETUAL NIGHT,	....	155	THE DYING MAN	49
THEN SETTLES BACK TO SHADE AND THE LONG NIGHT.	....	156	THE DYING MAN	81
LAST NIGHT I DREAMT OF A JAUNTIER PRINCIPLE OF ORDER;	....	165	HER BECOMING	30
THE LIGHT AIR SLOWED: IT WAS NOT NIGHT OR DAY.	....	166	HER BECOMING	56
A DROP OF THE NIGHT RAIN STILL IN ME,	....	168	FOURTH MEDITATN	7
I HAVE LEFT THE BODY OF THE WHALE, BUT THE MOUTH OF THE NIGHT IS STILL WIDE;	....	188	THE LONGING	51
BLASTED TO DEATH BY THE NIGHT WATCHMAN.	....	199	THE FAR FIELD	23
THE DEEP SHADE GATHERS NIGHT;	....	212	LIGHT LISTENED	17
THE CURLEW'S SLOW NIGHT SONG CAME ON THE WATER.	....	216	THE SHY MAN	9
THE FULL MOON HAS FALLEN, THE NIGHT WIND IS DOWN	....	216	THE SHY MAN	17
I THIRST BY DAY. I WATCH BY NIGHT.	....	222	THE ABYSS	89
THE LONG PIPES KNOCKED: IT WAS THE END OF NIGHT.	....	225	OTTO	39
THE DUMB DAMES SHRIEKING HALF THE NIGHT	....	228	THE GERANIUM	16
GOING, WE STAYED; AND NIGHT TURNED INTO DAY;	....	237	THE TRANCED	12
A NIGHT FLOWING WITH BIRDS, A RAGGED MOON,	....	239	IN A DARK TIME	14
DEATH OF THE SELF IN A LONG, TEARLESS NIGHT,	....	239	IN A DARK TIME	17
IT'S LOST UPON THE NIGHT--	....	240	IN EVEING AIR	17
NIGHT I EMBRACE, A DEAR PROXIMITY.	....	240	IN EVEING AIR	18
GOD'S NIGHT AND DAY: DOWN THIS SPACE HE HAS SMILED,	....	243	THE MOTION	21
AND, PRAISING CHANGE AS THE SLOW NIGHT COMES ON,	....	250	THE RIGHT THING	16
LIGHT STAYED ALL NIGHT,	....	258	SONG (3)	14
THE SOUL DIES EVERY NIGHT;	....	263	FOLLIES OF ADAM	23
HE RODE ALL NIGHT, AND CAME	....	263	FOLLIES OF ADAM	32
NIGHT-FISHING				
A NIGHT-FISHING OTTER.	....	220	THE ABYSS	43

	PAGE	TITLE	LINE
NIGHTMARE			
THE NIGHTMARE SILENCE IS BROKEN. WE ARE NOT LOST.	5	PROGNOSIS	16
NIGHTS			
THERE WERE NO NIGHTS OF SLEEPING IN THE PARK.	28	THE FAVORITE	4
NIMBLE			
A LEARNED NIMBLE GIRL,	172	WHAT TELL BONES	56
NIPPY			
STRICT AS A SEED, NIPPY AND TWIGGY.	86	PRAISE TO END!	22
NO (84)			
NOBILITY			
WHAT'S MADNESS BUT NOBILITY OF SOUL	239	IN A DARK TIME	7
NOBLE			
HIS NOBLE NATURE BIDS HIM GIVE.	23	AMOROUS LADY	8
NOBODY			
THESE NURSES OF NOBODY ELSE.	44	FRAU BAUMAN	12
ON THE JACKPINE PLAINS I HUNTED THE BIRD NOBODY KNOWS;	89	UNFOLD! UNFOLD!	22
AND NOBODY SLIPPED ME A MICKEY FINN,	112	SQUEEZE-BOX	31
O NOBODY UNDERSTOOD MYRTLE!	179	MYRTLE	5
THE THINGS YOU DO, NOBODY DOES:	180	GOO-GIRL	2
NOW NOBODY SNIGGERED AND MOCKED	182	BOY AND BUSH	6
BECAUSE NOBODY HEARD,	182	BOY AND BUSH	8
NOISE			
THERE IS A NOISE WITHIN THE BROW	22	SILENCE	1
WHO STUNNED THE DIRT INTO NOISE?	55	THE LOST SON	66
A CHILLY NOISE;	62	FIELD OF LIGHT	8
I KNOW HER NOISE.	72	WHERE KNOCK IS	31
THE DEAD SPEAK NOISE.	89	UNFOLD! UNFOLD!	9
SUCH A SWEET NOISE: I CAN'T SLEEP FOR IT.	92	I CRY, LOVE!	19
I HEAR A NOISE OF BEES, A TRELLIS HUM,	155	THE DYING MAN	74
A MUFFLED VOICE, A LOW SWEET WATERY NOISE.	165	HER BECOMING	20
I'M IN LOVE WITH THE DEAD! MY WHOLE FOREHEAD'S A NOISE!	170	FOURTH MEDITATN	79
I HEAR THE NOISE OF THE WALL.	220	THE ABYSS	26
THE MEADOW INSECTS MADE A LEVEL NOISE.	247	I WAITED	4
NOISELESS			
IS PRESSED TO NOISELESS GROUND.	17	NO BIRD	4
NOISES			
I'M TIRED OF TINY NOISES:	161	I'M HERE	7
NONE			
THOUGH DANCING NEEDS A MASTER, I HAD NONE	105	SIR JOHN DAVIES	15
A SHAPE WITHOUT A SHADE, OR ALMOST NONE,	167	HER BECOMING	88
YOU'VE TOO MANY TUNES, AND NONE OF THEM GOOD:	177	KITTY-CAT BIRD	5
FOR SHE ASKED NO QUARTER AND GAVE NONE,	223	ELEGY (2)	7
AND NONE HAS READ MY BOOKS,	225	THE CHUMS	2
NONE-THE-LESS			
(WHOM I LIKE NONE-THE-LESS),	213	THE HAPPY THREE	22
NOON			
NOW LIGHT IS LESS; NOON SKIES ARE WIDE AND DEEP;	12	SLOW SEASON	1
NO LONGER GILDS THE SCENE AT NOON;	15	COMING OF COLD	48
THESE IMAGES HAUNTED ME NOON AND MIDNIGHT.	48	JUDGE NOT	4
ALIVE AT NOON, I PERISHED IN HER FORM.	107	SIR JOHN DAVIES	94
THE LONG NOON PULSED AWAY,	128	THE VOICE	23
THE BATS TWITTERED AT NOON.	162	I'M HERE	40
WIDENING AT HIGH NOON, FACE UPWARD,	203	THE ROSE	43
NOON OF FAILURE,	219	THE ABYSS	11
AND DANCED, AT HIGH NOON,	249	THE RESTORED	17
NOR (21)			
NORTH			
WINDS GATHER IN THE NORTH AND BLOW	15	COMING OF COLD	49
NORTH, IN A SINGLE STREAM;	125	WORDS FOR WIND	63
WHILE ANIMALS EAT TO THE NORTH,	157	FIRST MEDITATN	9
THE HIGHWAY RIBBONING OUT IN A STRAIGHT THRUST TO THE NORTH,	193	JOURNY INTERIOR	27
TO THE NORTH OF A MOUTH I LIE,	258	SONG (3)	8
NOSE			
MY NOSE DEFILES A COMELY HEAD;	8	PRAYER	6
AND MORE THAN A NOSE,	54	THE LOST SON	47
CAN IT WRINKLE ITS NOSE?	54	THE LOST SON	51
THE CHIN JUMPS TO THE NOSE.	60	THE LONG ALLEY	42
I COULD FEEL THE MARE'S NOSE.	63	THE LONG ALLEY	32
TO FIND A NOSE,	64	SHAPE OF FIRE	25
ON BELLY AND NOSE	65	SHAPE OF FIRE	51
ONE, HIS NOSE HAD A FROG,	73	WHERE KNOCK IS	56
GO PLAY WITH YOUR NOSE.	75	I NEED, I NEED	44
I'VE LET MY NOSE OUT;	79	GIVE WAY, GATES	16

	PAGE	TITLE	LINE
NOSE (CONTINUED)			
I'M AN OTTER WITH ONLY ONE NOSE:	84	O LULL ME, LULL	35
OR ONE HIP QUIVER WITH A MOBILE NOSE	127	I KNEW A WOMAN	20
WHO BUSKS ME ON THE NOSE?	130	THE OTHER	6
MY NOSE FEELS FOR MY TOE;	130	THE OTHER	11
THE GRAVEL, MY NOSE WETTER THAN HIS.	151	SLUG	7
RUBBING MY NOSE IN THE WOOL OF BLANKETS;	162	I'M HERE	30
HE PIPES, HE SQUEAKS, HE QUIVERS THROUGH HIS NOSE,--	264	THREE EPIGRAMS	5
HIS NOSE LOOKED EVEN BIGGER THAN IT WAS,	273	SUPPR W LINDSAY	21
NOSES			
AND YOU SHOULD SEE HER NOSES TWITCH,--	181	MONOTONY SONG	18
NOSING			
TAIL AROUND, NOSING IN AND OUT OF THE CURRENT,	101	LIGHT BREATHER	9
NOSTRILS			
AND NOSTRILS WIDEN AS THEY PASS	14	COMING OF COLD	10
NOT (111)			
NOTE			
WOULD NOT RELEASE ONE RIVEN NOTE:	22	SILENCE	18
AND THEN HE CUT LOOSE WITH A HORRIBLE NOTE	115	THE SERPENT	21
HER FULL LIPS PURSED, THE ERRANT NOTE TO SEIZE;	127	I KNEW A WOMAN	16
THOUGH HE HEAR A NOTE HIGHER THAN C	196	THE LONG WATERS	6
NOTES			
THE LONG EYE NOTES THE MINNOW'S HIDING PLACE.	15	THE HERON	7
THOSE NOTES WENT, LIKE THE BIRD,	128	THE VOICE	8
THE LONG PLAINTIVE NOTES FLOATING DOWN,	159	FIRST MEDITATN	87
NOTES FINELY DRAWN.	213	THE HAPPY THREE	32
THAT TREMBLE OF SWEET NOTES SET MY HEART ASTIR,	216	THE SHY MAN	10
LIQUIDS PURSUE ME, NOTES AND TREMORS:	255	LIGHT POEM	6
NOTHING			
NOTHING WOULD SLEEP IN THAT CELLAR, DANK AS A DITCH,	38	ROOT CELLAR	1
NOTHING WOULD GIVE UP LIFE:	38	ROOT CELLAR	10
NOTHING NIBBLED MY LINE,	53	THE LOST SON	14
HAD NOTHING TO SAY.	74	I NEED, I NEED	11
I DREAM OF NOTHING BUT BOARDS;	79	GIVE WAY, GATES	2
WITH NOTHING ON TO KEEP YOU WARM,	114	DINKY	6
BUT NOTHING WOULD SUIT.	115	THE SERPENT	18
ONCE I READ NOTHING THROUGH A FEARFUL NIGHT,	133	THE PURE FURY	3
WHENEVER I SEE HER WITH NOTHING ON.	140	THE SWAN	14
SING OF THAT NOTHING OF WHICH ALL IS MADE,	140	THE SWAN	19
AM I BUT NOTHING, LEANING TOWARDS A THING?	156	THE DYING MAN	85
GROTESQUE, AWKWARD, HIS EXTENDED EYES LOOKING AT NOTHING IN PARTICULAR,	159	FIRST MEDITATN	63
THE SPIRIT SAYS, YOU ARE NOTHING.	172	WHAT TELL BONES	43
I SAID NOTHING.	228	THE GERANIUM	24
UNTIL THERE WAS NOTHING LEFT,	232	THE THING	16
WHAT DOES WHAT IT SHOULD DO NEEDS NOTHING MORE.	235	MANIFESTATION	9
THE WIND FROM OFF THE SEA SAYS NOTHING NEW.	246	THE MARROW	1
NOTHINGNESS			
PARMENIDES PUT NOTHINGNESS IN PLACE;	133	THE PURE FURY	10
A PULSE BEYOND NOTHINGNESS,	171	WHAT TELL BONES	6
TO NOTHINGNESS, ALONE.	215	HIS FOREBODING	13
NOTHINGS			
OUT OF THESE NOTHINGS	188	THE LONGING	37
NOTICE			
I NOTICE A TREE, ARSENICAL GREY IN THE LIGHT, OR THE SLOW	47	DOUBLE FEATURE	10
TAKE NOTICE OF THIS MAN!	260	THE CHANGELING	24
NOTION			
THEIR ONLY NOTION OF THE GOOD	25	VERSE W ALLUSNS	7
NOT-KNOWING			
AND NOT-KNOWING ENTERS, SILENT,	221	THE ABYSS	70
NOVEMBER			
OF LATE NOVEMBER DAYS.	139	PLAINT	12
NOW			
IS NOW SEALED HONEY-TIGHT.	4	DEATH PIECE	4
THE FROST BE GONE, FOR GREEN IS BREAKING NOW;	11	LIGHT BRIGHTER	14
NOW LIGHT IS LESS; NOON SKIES ARE WIDE AND DEEP;	12	SLOW SEASON	1
LATE AUTUMN FRUIT IS ROTTED NOW.	14	COMING OF COLD	27
ALL SUMMER GREEN IS NOW UNDONE:	15	COMING OF COLD	42
NOW HERE IS PEACE FOR ONE WHO KNEW	17	NO BIRD	1
NOW I AM OUT OF ELEMENT	19	AGNST DISASTER	1
THAT PULSES UNDIMINISHED NOW	22	SILENCE	2
NOW IN THE MISERY OF BED-SITTING ROOM CONFUSION,	29	THE REMINDER	9
AND NOW GRIM DIGITS OF OLD PAIN	30	THE RECKONING	3

		PAGE	TITLE	LINE
NOW (CONTINUED)				
NOW EACH MAN STANDS APART.		31	LULL	7
NOW AS FROM MAPLE TO ELM THE FLITTERMICE SKITTER AND TWIRL,		33	IDYLL	1
NOW AS THE TRAIN BEARS WEST,		34	NIGHT JOURNEY	1
NOW, WHEN I'M ALONE AND COLD IN MY BED,		44	FRAU BAUMAN	30
I'M SOMEBODY ELSE NOW.		74	WHERE KNOCK IS	84
BUT NOW THE INSTANT AGES,		80	GIVE WAY, GATES	43
WHERE ARE YOU NOW, MY BONNY BEATING GRISTLE,		86	PRAISE TO END!	17
NOW THE WATER'S LOW. THE WEEDS EXCEED ME.		86	PRAISE TO END!	23
NOW THE GILLS ARE BEGINNING TO CRY.		92	I CRY, LOVE!	18
WHO UNTIED THE TREE? I REMEMBER NOW.		93	I CRY, LOVE!	54
AND NOW ARE WE TO HAVE THAT PELLUDIOUS JESUS-SHIMMER OVER ALL THINGS,		98	O, THOU OPENING	21
WHERE'S SHE NOW, I KEPT SAYING.		101	THE VISITANT	23
WHERE'S SHE NOW, THE MOUNTAIN'S DOWNY GIRL?		101	THE VISITANT	24
NOW MY ARDORS SLEEP IN A SLEEVE.		103	OLD LADY'S WRDS	3
WHEN I THINK OF IT NOW, I JUST HAVE TO SHUDDER!		114	THE COW	2
NOW THEY MOVE ALL TOGETHER!--		152	THE SISKINS	19
ETERNITY IS NOW.		153	THE DYING MAN	10
WHAT NOW?		154	THE DYING MAN	ST
NOW, AS THE CASEMENT BLURS.		154	THE DYING MAN	30
WHAT CAME TO ME VAGUELY IS NOW CLEAR,		173	WHAT TELL BONES	97
NOW THAT'S A PIECE OF GOOD ADVICE		181	MONOTONY SONG	3
NOW NOBODY SNIGGERED AND MOCKED		182	BOY AND BUSH	6
NOW THE PLACE TO BEGIN		183	THE LIZARD	3
NOW, IN THIS WANING OF LIGHT,		191	AT OYSTER RIVER	57
BUT NOW--		209	HER LONGING	11
TELL ME NOW, TELL ME NOW.		211	SONG (1)	12
TELL ME NOW, TELL ME NOW.		211	SONG (1)	12
HIS TAIL GREY WITH THE GROUND NOW,		226	THE LIZARD	18
NOW HE'S EATEN HIS THREE KINDS OF CHEESE AND DRUNK FROM HIS BOTTLE-CAP WATERING-TROUGH--		227	MEADOW MOUSE	12
WHAT BURNS ME NOW? DESIRE, DESIRE, DESIRE.		246	THE MARROW	12
NOW I ADORE MY LIFE		251	ONCE MORE, RND	5
DEARIE, DELIGHT ME NOW.		259	SONG (3)	44
NOW YOU RUN TO THE MONEY, IT'S JIG, JIG, JIG;		272	DUET	2
NOWHERE				
MY VEINS ARE RUNNING NOWHERE. DO THE BONES CAST OUT THEIR FIRE?		56	THE LOST SON	101
NOWHERE IS OUT. I SAW THE COLD.		73	WHERE KNOCK IS	71
AND I HAVE GONE NOWHERE.		137	LOVE'S PROGRESS	20
UNPERPLEXED, IN A PLACE LEADING NOWHERE.		195	JOURNY INTERIOR	73
AND BELOW, IN A MIST OUT OF NOWHERE,		202	THE ROSE	29
BUT IT GOES NOWHERE."		219	THE ABYSS	4
NUB				
ONE NUB OF GROWTH		37	CUTTINGS	5
NUDGE				
THE SALMON CLIMB THE RIVERS, THE RIVERS NUDGE THE SEA,		28	CLAIRVOY WIDOW	25
IF ONLY I COULD NUDGE YOU FROM THIS SLEEP,		102	ELEGY FOR JANE	18
RETIRING TO NUDGE HIS NECK HALF-WAY UNDER		226	THE LIZARD	16
NUDGED				
OLD NEIGHBORS NUDGED EACH OTHER AT THE FUN.		21	THE AUCTION	12
AND A BLACK BULL NUDGED AT A WALL IN THE VALLEY BELOW,		232	THE THING	22
A PARTRIDGE DRUMMED; A MINNOW NUDGED ITS STONE;		241	THE SEQUEL	13
NUDGERS				
SLEEPERS, NUMB NUDGERS IN COLD DIMENSIONS,		50	THE MINIMAL	2
NUDGES				
NUDGES A SAND-CRUMB LOOSE,		37	CUTTINGS	6
NUDGES INTO A BACK-EDDY, A SANDY INLET,		159	FIRST MEDITATN	69
NUDGING				
NUDGING AND TICKLING OF ANTS AND SPIDERS,		255	LIGHT POEM	2
NUMB				
SLEEPERS, NUMB NUDGERS IN COLD DIMENSIONS,		50	THE MINIMAL	2
MY BLUE ORIGINAL DANDY, NUMB WITH SUGAR?		86	PRAISE TO END!	18
NUMINOUS				
THE NUMINOUS RING AROUND THE OPENING FLOWER,		198	THE LONG WATERS	70
NURSE				
LIKE A NURSE HE SAT WITH ME FOR WEEKS, A SLY SURLY ATTENDANT,		220	THE ABYSS	38
NURSE-MAID				
WITH A NURSE-MAID WADDLE AND A SHOP-GIRL SIMPER,		23	ACADEMIC	3
NURSES				
THESE NURSES OF NOBODY ELSE.		44	FRAU BAUMAN	12

	PAGE	TITLE	LINE

NUTS

NUTS ARE MONEY: WHEREFORE AND WHAT ELSE? .... 61 THE LONG ALLEY 82

NUZZLED

MY THUMB OF A CHILD THAT NUZZLED IN MY PALM?-- .... 227 MEADOW MOUSE 22

NYLON

IN A SHOE BOX STUFFED IN AN OLD NYLON STOCKING .... 227 MEADOW MOUSE 1

NYMPH

FORGIVE ME A MINUTE, NYMPH. .... 97 O, THOU OPENING 18

O

O MY SISTER REMEMBER THE STARS THE TEARS THE TRAINS ...... 5 TO MY SISTER 1
O SEE THE FATE OF HIM WHOSE GUARD WAS LOWERED!-- .... 5 PROGNOSIS 3
THEREFORE, O LORD, LET ME PRESERVE .... 8 PRAYER 19
O FORTUNATE HE WHOSE MAMMA PAYS THE BILLS! .... 24 POETASTER 4
DELIVER ME, O LORD, FROM ALL .... 24 BEFORE STUDY 9
"O TELL ME, WIDOW LADY, WHAT IS IT THAT YOU SEE, ... 27 CLAIRVOY WIDOW 3
O HE WAS FORTUNE'S CHILD, A FAVORITE SON .... 28 THE FAVORITE 9
O CURSED BE THE WORK THAT GETS HONORABLE MENTION! ...... 29 THE GENTLE 9
O WORM OF DUTY! O SPIRAL KNOWLEDGE! .... 48 LAST WORDS 6
O WORM OF DUTY! O SPIRAL KNOWLEDGE! .... 48 LAST WORDS 6
I ASKED: MAY THE BLESSINGS OF LIFE, O LORD, DESCEND ON THE
    LIVING. .... 48 JUDGE NOT 6
ENSHROUD ME WITH LIGHT! O WHIRLING! O TERRIBLE LOVE! ..... 48 LAST WORDS 10
ENSHROUD ME WITH LIGHT! O WHIRLING! O TERRIBLE LOVE! ..... 48 LAST WORDS 10
SEND DOWN A RUSH OF AIR, O TORRENTIAL, ... 61 THE LONG ALLEY 83
O SMALL BIRD WAKENING, ... 78 BRING THE DAY! 38
SENSIBILITY! O LA! .... 81 SENSIBILITY! LA T
O LULL ME, LULL ME .... 83 O LULL ME, LULL T
O MY LOVE'S LIGHT AS A DUCK .... 83 O LULL ME, LULL 12
O LOVELY CHINK, O WHITE .... 83 O LULL ME, LULL 22
O LOVELY CHINK, O WHITE .... 83 O LULL ME, LULL 22
WHEREFORE, O BIRDS AND SMALL FISH, SURROUND ME. .... 88 PRAISE TO END! 97
O, THOU OPENING, O .... 97 O, THOU OPENING T
O, THOU OPENING, O .... 97 O, THOU OPENING T
O FOR SOME MINSTREL OF WHAT'S TO BE, ... 103 OLD LADY'S WRDS 6
IN THE SAME WAY: O WATCH HIS BODY SWAY!-- .... 105 SIR JOHN DAVIES 11
O WHAT LEWD MUSIC CREPT INTO OUR EARS! .... 106 SIR JOHN DAVIES 46
O PRINT IT, MY DEAR, DO PUBLISH IT, YES, ... 113 TO A LADY ED 9
O WHAT'S THE WEATHER IN A BEARD? .... 114 DINKY 1
"O WHY ARE YOU FISHING THAT WAY? .... 117 LADY AND BEAR 2
"O IT'S WONDERFUL HOW WITH A FLICK OF YOUR WRIST, ... 117 LADY AND BEAR 21
"O LOVE ME WHILE I AM, ... 123 WORDS FOR WIND 13
WHAT BOOK, O LEARNED MAN, WILL SET ME RIGHT? .... 133 THE PURE FURY 2
O ANGEL, LET ME LOOSE!" .... 136 THE SENSUALISTS 6
O RARE PROPINQUITY!-- .... 137 LOVE'S PROGRESS 2
A DRY SOUL'S WISEST. O, I AM NOT DRY! .... 140 THE SWAN 5
DESCEND, O GENTLEST LIGHT, DESCEND, DESCEND. .... 156 THE DYING MAN 87
O SWEET FIELD FAR AHEAD, I HEAR YOUR BIRDS, ... 156 THE DYING MAN 88
O THE SONGS WE HIDE, SINGING ONLY TO OURSELVES! .... 168 FOURTH MEDITATN 13
O MORE THAN A ROARING BOY, ... 169 FOURTH MEDITATN 51
O MY BONES, ... 171 WHAT TELL BONES 22
O TO BE DELIVERED FROM THE RATIONAL INTO THE REALM OF PURE
    SONG, ... 172 WHAT TELL BONES 54
O, BUT I SEEK AND CARE! .... 172 WHAT TELL BONES 61
O NOBODY UNDERSTOOD MYRTLE! .... 179 MYRTLE 5
O I'VE HEARD!-- .... 183 THE WAGTAIL 6
O PRIDE, THOU ART A PLUME UPON WHOSE HEAD? .... 188 THE LONGING 25
O LOVE, YOU WHO HEAR .... 211 SONG (1) 9
O WHAT COULD BE MORE NICE .... 212 LIGHT LISTENED 1
O! MY LIPS THEY, MY LIPS THEY, ... 216 THE SHY MAN 24
O WORLD SO FAR AWAY! O MY LOST WORLD! .... 225 OTTO 42
O WORLD SO FAR AWAY! O MY LOST WORLD! .... 225 OTTO 42
ALL BIRDS REMEMBERED, O NEVER FORGOTTEN! .... 235 ALL MORNING 45
MAKE ME, O LORD, A LAST, A SIMPLE THING .... 240 IN EVEING AIR 8
BROUGHT ME DOWN TO MY KNEES. O WHO CAN BE .... 241 THE SEQUEL 5
O WHO WOULD TAKE THE VISION FROM THE CHILD?-- .... 243 THE MOTION 23
O, MOTION O, OUR CHANCE IS STILL TO BE! .... 243 THE MOTION 24
O, MOTION O, OUR CHANCE IS STILL TO BE! .... 243 THE MOTION 24
MORE! O MORE! VISIBLE. .... 251 ONCE MORE, RND 4
O THE SONGS WE HIDE SINGING TO OURSELVES!-- .... 259 SONG (3) 38
O MOST MANIFEST. .... 260 THE CHANGELING 9
O, I'M THE GENIUS OF THE WORLD,-- .... 268 SAGINAW SONG 43
AND IT WAS O, MY MOTHER O, ... 268 SAGINAW SONG 58
AND IT WAS O, MY MOTHER O, ... 268 SAGINAW SONG 58

	PAGE	TITLE	LINE
O (CONTINUED)			
ALL WOMEN, O, ARE BEAUTIFUL	268	SAGINAW SONG	60
A COLOR PURE, O PURE AS GOLD,	269	GOB MUSIC	26
IT HAPPENED O, IN BOFIN TOWN,	270	GOB MUSIC	38
O WHEN YOU WERE LITTLE, YOU WERE REALLY BIG:	272	DUET	1
--FAR BEYOND, O BEYOND! DEAR KIERKEGAARD.	272	DUET	21
OAK			
THE OAK STOOD WITH EACH LEAF STIFF AS A BELL.	12	MID-CNTRY BLOW	6
STRAIGHT FROM THE OAK, THE GOSSAMER IS HUNG.	12	SLOW SEASON	7
THE OAK LEAVES STRAIN TO BE UNBOUND,	15	COMING OF COLD	35
DRIFTING THROUGH LEAVES, OAK AND MAPLE,	159	FIRST MEDITATN	88
BEYOND THE SEA PINE, THE OAK, THE WIND-TIPPED MADRONA,	203	THE ROSE	47
OAR			
TO FOLLOW THE DROPS SLIDING FROM A LIFTED OAR,	67	SHAPE OF FIRE	90
OATS			
THE OATS ARE ALL RIGHT.	76	I NEED, I NEED	56
OBEY			
AND I OBEY THE WIND AT MY BACK	221	THE ABYSS	66
OBJECT			
SUBJECT AND OBJECT SANG AND DANCED AS ONE;	237	THE TRANCED	17
OBJECTS			
A FLASH OF OBJECTS NEVER SEEN BEFORE.	8	THE SIGNALS	2
ENDLESS DUPLICATION OF LIVES AND OBJECTS.	46	DOLOR	8
IS THERE A WISDOM IN OBJECTS? FEW OBJECTS PRAISE THE LORD.	166	HER BECOMING	38
IS THERE A WISDOM IN OBJECTS? FEW OBJECTS PRAISE THE LORD.	166	HER BECOMING	38
THE DANCE OF NATURAL OBJECTS IN THE MIND,	171	WHAT TELL BONES	15
AND THE TERRIBLE HUNGER FOR OBJECTS QUAILS ME:	220	THE ABYSS	32
OBLIGATION			
MUTILATED SOULS IN COLD MORGUES OF OBLIGATION.	166	HER BECOMING	43
OBLIVION			
BEFORE OBLIVION CLOUDS THE BRAIN.	8	PRAYER	4
OBSCENE			
WORDS SKIRTING THE OBSCENE--	213	THE HAPPY THREE	7
OBSCENELY			
LOLLING OBSCENELY FROM MILDEWED CRATES,	38	ROOT CELLAR	4
OBSCENITY			
THE SAVAGE BLOOD'S OBSCENITY,	19	EPIDERM MACABRE	11
OBSCURE			
BUDS, LONG UNSEALED, OBSCURE THE NARROW LANE.	12	SLOW SEASON	14
IN THE OBSCURE HAZE, SING!	90	UNFOLD! UNFOLD!	47
SOME ERRAND, OBSCURE AS THE WIND'S CIRCUIT,	92	I CRY, LOVE!	6
WHEN FIGURES OUT OF OBSCURE SHADOW RAVE,	154	THE DYING MAN	46
WHILE STONES LOOSEN ON THE OBSCURE HILLSIDE,	157	FIRST MEDITATN	5
WHETHER FOR LOVE OR OUT OF OBSCURE GUILT	224	OTTO	24
OBSCURES			
AT FIRST THE VISIBLE OBSCURES:	90	UNFOLD! UNFOLD!	55
THE VISIBLE OBSCURES. BUT WHO KNOWS WHEN?	107	SIR JOHN DAVIES	85
A TREE THINNED BY THE WIND OBSCURES MY SIGHT.	150	IN LATE SUMMER	28
OBSCURITY			
TOOK ARMS AGAINST OUR OWN OBSCURITY.	106	SIR JOHN DAVIES	54
OBSEQUIOUS			
THE UNDERTAKER'S OBSEQUIOUS GRIMACES,	22	ROAD TO WDLAWN	6
OBVIOUS			
BUSY, OBVIOUS WITH OURSELVES,	158	FIRST MEDITATN	29
OCCUR			
FOR IF IT DID OCCUR,	268	SAGINAW SONG	39
O'CONNELL'S			
AS I WALKED BESIDE HER, THE O'CONNELL'S DAUGHTER,	216	THE SHY MAN	11
FOR HERE CLOSE BESIDE ME IS O'CONNELL'S DAUGHTER,	216	THE SHY MAN	20
ODD			
ALL'S EVEN WITH THE ODD,	123	WORDS FOR WIND	7
I'M ODD AND FULL OF LOVE.	125	WORDS FOR WIND	67
ODDS			
AT ODDS WITH CIRCUMSTANCE? THE DAY'S ON FIRE!	239	IN A DARK TIME	8
ODIOUS			
I'M UNDONE BY THE FLIP-FLAP OF ODIOUS PILLOWS.	86	PRAISE TO END!	45
BUT AS FOR YOU, MOST ODIOUS--	151	SLUG	28
THERE WAS A MOST ODIOUS YAK	178	THE YAK	1
ODOR			
ODOR OF BASSWOOD ON A MOUNTAIN-SLOPE,	201	THE FAR FIELD	98
OF (1006)			
OFF			
THE RUSH OF WIND RIPPED OFF THE TENDER LEAVES	6	INTERLUDE	2

	PAGE	TITLE	LINE
OFF (CONTINUED)			
I WOULD PUT OFF MYSELF AND FLEE	24	BEFORE STUDY	5
BY PULLING OFF FLESH FROM THE LIVING PLANET;	40	MOSS-GATHERING	12
THEN WALTZED ME OFF TO BED	45	MY PAPA'S WALTZ	15
OR SEND OFF A CAR WITH VAGUE LIFTS OF A HAND.	47	DOUBLE FEATURE	8
A FINE HAZE MOVED OFF THE LEAVES;	57	THE LOST SON	144
CALL OFF THE DOGS, MY PAWS ARE GONE.	61	THE LONG ALLEY	85
WHEN I TOOK OFF MY CLOTHES	64	SHAPE OF FIRE	24
MUST PULL OFF CLOTHES	65	SHAPE OF FIRE	49
DID SPACE SHAKE OFF AN ANGEL WITH A SIGH?	107	SIR JOHN DAVIES	69
AS THE BIRDS FLEW OFF TO THE END OF NEXT WEEK.	115	THE SERPENT	26
THEN OFF AGAIN TO SLEEP HE GOES,	116	THE SLOTH	10
LIGHT AS SEED BLOWING OFF THISTLES!	152	THE SISKINS	21
AND GO HUMPING OFF, YICKETTY-YAK.	178	THE YAK	5
WHERE THE TURF DROPS OFF INTO A GRASS-HIDDEN CULVERT,	199	THE FAR FIELD	14
HER FACE LIKE A RAIN-BEATEN STONE ON THE DAY SHE ROLLED OFF	223	ELEGY (2)	1
THE STORM LULLS OFF, THEN REDOUBLES,	231	THE STORM	30
THE BULB GOES ON AND OFF, WEAKLY.	231	THE STORM	36
THEN WHIRRING OFF SIDEWAYS TO THE TOP OF THE HAWTHORN,	234	ALL MORNING	31
THE WIND FROM OFF THE SEA SAYS NOTHING NEW.	246	THE MARROW	1
COME OFF IT MUCH LESS NEAT.	267	SAGINAW SONG	12
OFFEND			
FLESH, YOU OFFEND THIS METAL. HOW LONG NEED THE BONES MOURN?	59	THE LONG ALLEY	12
OFFERINGS			
THE HIGH-PILED FLORAL OFFERINGS WITH SENTIMENTAL VERSES,	22	ROAD TO WDLAWN	3
OFTEN			
OFTEN I MEET, ON WALKING FROM A DOOR,	8	THE SIGNALS	1
TO KNOW THAT LIGHT FALLS AND FILLS, OFTEN WITHOUT OUR KNOWING,	67	SHAPE OF FIRE	92
BUT THE RIND, OFTEN, HATES THE LIFE WITHIN.	157	FIRST MEDITATN	13
OFTEN I THINK OF MYSELF AS RIDING--	158	FIRST MEDITATN	20
I HAVE TAKEN, TOO OFTEN, THE DANGEROUS PATH,	220	THE ABYSS	21
I'M OFTEN A DRUNKEN BOOR;	268	SAGINAW SONG	46
OGALALA			
OGALALA?	189	THE LONGING	59
OH			
OH THAT WAS LONG AGO! I KEPT	6	THE PREMONITION	3
OH, WHAT A WEBBY WONDER I AM!	98	O, THOU OPENING	47
OH, WHEN SHE WAS SAD, SHE CAST HERSELF DOWN INTO SUCH A PURE DEPTH,	102	ELEGY FOR JANE	10
OH, THE SYNCO SEPTET PLAYED FOR US THEN,	112	SQUEEZE-BOX	22
OH, IT WASN'T A CRIME, IT WASN'T A SIN,	112	SQUEEZE-BOX	30
OH THAT COUSIN! HER MANNERS! AT LUNCHES!	179	MYRTLE'S COUSIN	5
OH WHAT! OH WHAT WHAT CAN I DO?"	182	PHILANDER	5
OH WHAT! OH WHAT WHAT CAN I DO?"	182	PHILANDER	5
OH, TO BE SOMETHING ELSE, YET STILL TO BE!	244	INFIRMITY	6
OH, THE SLOP-PAIL IS THE PLACE TO THINK	269	GOB MUSIC	16
AND IT REMINDED ME--BUT OH!	270	GOB MUSIC	36
OH, THE SLOP-PAIL IS THE PLACE TO THINK	270	GOB MUSIC	44
OIL			
AND PUMPKINS SWEAT A BITTER OIL.	14	COMING OF COLD	17
AND THE TICKING OF SNOW AROUND OIL DRUMS IN THE DAKOTAS,	204	THE ROSE	68
OILY			
I WAS PRIVY TO OILY FUNGUS AND THE ALGAE OF STANDING WATER;	89	UNFOLD! UNFOLD!	25
ALL OPENINGS PRAISE US, EVEN OILY HOLES.	90	UNFOLD! UNFOLD!	40
FEATHERS OF THE LONG SWELL, BURNISHED, ALMOST OILY--	197	THE LONG WATERS	51
THE OILY, TAR-LADEN WALLS	205	THE ROSE	94
OLD			
OLD SECRETS TO AMORPHOUS SWARMS.	4	FEUD	16
BREATH, TURN THE OLD BLOOD OVER.	7	ORDERS FOR DAY	21
THE SKY TURNS DARK, THE YEAR GROWS OLD,	15	COMING OF COLD	36
OLD HEDGEROWS KEEP THE LEAVES; THE PHLOX,	15	COMING OF COLD	40
OLD NEIGHBORS NUDGED EACH OTHER AT THE FUN.	21	THE AUCTION	12
AND NOW GRIM DIGITS OF OLD PAIN	30	THE RECKONING	3
ROOTS RIPE AS OLD BAIT,	38	ROOT CELLAR	7
DISTURBED SOME RHYTHM, OLD AND OF VAST IMPORTANCE,	40	MOSS-GATHERING	11
THAT OLD ROSE-HOUSE,	41	BIG WIND	22
OLD FLORIST	42	OLD FLORIST	T
FISHED IN AN OLD WOUND,	53	THE LOST SON	12
IS THE SEED LEAVING THE OLD BED? THESE BUDS ARE LIVE AS BIRDS.	56	THE LOST SON	102
I WANT THE OLD RAGE, THE LASH OF PRIMORDIAL MILK!	56	THE LOST SON	107
GOODBYE, GOODBYE, OLD STONES, THE TIME-ORDER IS GOING,	56	THE LOST SON	108

	PAGE	TITLE	LINE
OLD (CONTINUED)			
THE DARK FLOWS ON ITSELF. A DEAD MOUTH SINGS UNDER AN OLD TREE.	59	THE LONG ALLEY	6
REMEMBER AN OLD SOUND.	59	THE LONG ALLEY	8
IT'S MY LAST WALTZ WITH AN OLD ITCH.	60	THE LONG ALLEY	34
THE OLD SILO.	60	THE LONG ALLEY	50
AN OLD SCOW BUMPS OVER BLACK ROCKS.	64	SHAPE OF FIRE	5
HARDLY ANY OLD ANGELS ARE AROUND ANY MORE.	78	BRING THE DAY!	40
I HEAR THE CLAP OF AN OLD WIND.	80	GIVE WAY, GATES	55
OR THAT OLD HARPY SECRETING TOADS IN HER PORTMANTEAU.	82	SENSIBILITY! LA	36
--WHO CARES? THE OLD OWL?	89	UNFOLD! UNFOLD!	15
THE OLD STALK STILL HAS A PULSE;	99	O, THOU OPENING	52
AN OLD DOG	99	O, THOU OPENING	71
OLD LADY'S WINTER WORDS	103	OLD LADY'S WRDS	T
AN OLD WOMAN	103	OLD LADY'S WRDS	17
SO I'VE GOT TO GET ME A RICH UGLY OLD MAID	112	SQUEEZE-BOX	43
OR AN OLD PIECE OF TWINE,	117	LADY AND BEAR	16
THESE OLD BONES LIVE TO LEARN HER WANTON WAYS:	127	I KNEW A WOMAN	27
THE OLD HOUSE OF A CRAB;	146	THE SONG	16
BUT YOU, LOOSE TOE FROM THE OLD LIFE,	151	SLUG	10
I NEED AN OLD CRONE'S KNOWING.	157	FIRST MEDITATN	19
THE DRUNKEN SOLDIER, THE OLD LADY WITH HER PEPPERMINTS;	158	FIRST MEDITATN	30
AND SAID, OLD BOY, YOU'RE SHEDDING HAIR,	181	MONOTONY SONG	6
FROM A CRAZY OLD JACK-DAW BIRD	183	THE WAGTAIL	7
OLD MEN SHOULD BE EXPLORERS?	189	THE LONGING	57
WELTER OF TIN CANS, PAILS, OLD BIRD NESTS, A CHILD'S SHOE RIDING A LOG,	191	AT OYSTER RIVER	54
AN OLD BRIDGE BELOW WITH A BUCKLED IRON RAILING, BROKEN BY SOME IDIOT PLUNGER;	194	JOURNY INTERIOR	32
(I FOUND IT LYING AMONG THE RUBBLE OF AN OLD COAL BIN)	199	THE FAR FIELD	20
AN OLD MAN WITH HIS FEET BEFORE THE FIRE,	201	THE FAR FIELD	85
THE OLD LOG SUBSIDES WITH THE LESSENING WAVES,	202	THE ROSE	20
THE BLUEBIRD, LOVER OF HOLES IN OLD WOOD, LILTING ITS LIGHT SONG,	204	THE ROSE	66
THE SHRIEK OF NAILS AS OLD SHINGLES ARE RIPPED FROM THE TOP OF A ROOF,	204	THE ROSE	70
CRIES, "I'M OLD ENOUGH TO LIVE	208	HER WORDS	3
IN A SHOE BOX STUFFED IN AN OLD NYLON STOCKING	227	MEADOW MOUSE	1
STOPPING TRAFFIC, INDIGNANT AS ADDLED OLD LADIES,	234	ALL MORNING	27
AN OLD WIND-TATTERED BUTTERFLY FLEW DOWN	243	THE MOTION	2
WHO'S OLD ENOUGH TO LIVE?--A THING OF EARTH	243	THE MOTION	14
WANTING THE QUIET OF OLD WOOD OR STONE WITHOUT WATER.	255	LIGHT POEM	9
THAT MAKES AN OLD CONFUSION WORSE.	257	SANITARIUM	2
OR SOME OLD LOUT WHO CAN	262	FOLLIES OF ADAM	2
AND LINDSAY HEAVED HIMSELF FROM MY OLD CHAIR.	274	SUPPR W LINDSAY	38
HEROES AND BEARS, AND OLD PHILOSOPHERS--	274	SUPPR W LINDSAY	42
OLDER			
OLDER THAN I, OR THE COCKROACH.	226	THE LIZARD	31
OLD-FASHIONED			
YOU WOUND THE WATCH IN AN OLD-FASHIONED LOCKET	29	THE REMINDER	7
THICK AND CUSHIONY, LIKE AN OLD-FASHIONED DOORMAT,	40	MOSS-GATHERING	3
OMINOUS			
ONLY AN OMINOUS LAPPING,	230	THE STORM	2
ON (258)			
ONCE			
ONCE MORE THE TREES ASSUME FAMILIAR SHAPES,	11	LIGHT BRIGHTER	9
THE WIDE WINGS FLAP BUT ONCE TO LIFT HIM UP.	15	THE HERON	11
ONCE ON RETURNING HOME, PURSE-PROUD AND HALE,	21	THE AUCTION	1
AT ONCE MAMMALIAN AND REPTILIAN.	23	AMOROUS LADY	14
A FAR-OFF TRAIN BLOWS ITS ECHOING WHISTLE ONCE;	33	IDYLL	10
FIFTY SUMMERS IN MOTION AT ONCE,	38	FORCING HOUSE	10
ONCE, TWICE, AND A FAINT THIRD THUMP,--	42	TRANSPLANTING	11
ONCE I STAYED ALL NIGHT.	57	THE LOST SON	134
ONCE ENTERTAINED YOU.	58	THE LOST SON	170
ONCE UPON A TREE	71	WHERE KNOCK IS	12
ONCE I WAS A POND.	80	GIVE WAY, GATES	60
ONCE I FISHED FROM THE BANKS, LEAF-LIGHT AND HAPPY:	86	PRAISE TO END!	19
I PROCLAIM ONCE MORE A CONDITION OF JOY.	92	I CRY, LOVE!	28
AND HOW, ONCE STARTLED INTO TALK, THE LIGHT SYLLABLES LEAPED FOR HER,	102	ELEGY FOR JANE	3
ONCE I WAS SWEET WITH THE LIGHT OF MYSELF,	103	OLD LADY'S WRDS	39
I THOUGHT THAT ONCE, AND THOUGHT COMES ROUND AGAIN;	107	SIR JOHN DAVIES	87
THERE ONCE WAS A COW WITH A DOUBLE UDDER.	114	THE COW	1

	PAGE	TITLE	LINE
ONCE (CONTINUED)			
ONCE I READ NOTHING THROUGH A FEARFUL NIGHT,	133	THE PURE FURY	3
I LIVED WITH DEEP ROOTS ONCE:	139	PLAINT	13
WHEN I RAISED MYSELF ONCE MORE,	145	THE BEAST	16
ONCE I DELIGHTED IN A SINGLE TREE;	155	THE DYING MAN	54
DARE I SPEAK, ONCE MORE, IN THE MONOTONY OF GREAT PRAISE,	166	HER BECOMING	32
ONCE TO THE TOAD,	167	HER BECOMING	71
ONCE TO THE FROG,	167	HER BECOMING	72
AND ONCE TO MY FLOWING THIGHS.	167	HER BECOMING	73
ONCE I COULD TOUCH MY SHADOW, AND BE HAPPY;	168	FOURTH MEDITATN	14
OR KNOWN, ONCE, THE SOUL'S AUTHENTIC HUNGER,	169	FOURTH MEDITATN	47
THERE ONCE WAS A GIRL NAMED MYRTLE	179	MYRTLE	1
I AM GATHERED TOGETHER ONCE MORE;	198	THE LONG WATERS	77
ONCE I WAS SOMETHING LIKE THIS, MINDLESS,	200	THE FAR FIELD	42
ONCE WE WERE LEFT ALONE.	212	LIGHT LISTENED	4
AND ONCE MORE THE TONGUES BEGIN BABBLING.	220	THE ABYSS	31
ONCE WHEN HE SAW TWO POACHERS ON HIS LAND,	224	OTTO	14
THEIR SISTERS GAVE ME, ONCE OR TWICE;	225	THE CHUMS	5
WHEN I PUT HER OUT, ONCE, BY THE GARBAGE PAIL,	228	THE GERANIUM	1
CONFUSING THEM ONCE FLYING STRAIGHT INTO THE SUN	232	THE THING	7
ONCE I TRANSCENDED TIME:	240	IN EVEING AIR	10
THAT ONCE COULD MELT THE DARK WITH ITS SMALL BREATH.	246	THE MARROW	16
ONCE MORE, THE ROUND	251	ONCE MORE, RND	T
HE LAUGHED, ONCE MORE.	263	FOLLIES OF ADAM	35
ON-COMING			
ALTERNATE SNOW AND SLEET, NO ON-COMING TRAFFIC,	199	THE FAR FIELD	6
THE ON-COMING WATER.	200	THE FAR FIELD	55
FAR AWAY, CLOSE-AT-HAND, HIS CALL FLOATING OVER THE ON-COMING TRAFFIC,	234	ALL MORNING	3
AS A MAN TURNS TO FACE ON-COMING SNOW.	245	THE DECISION	12
ONE			
OR BALANCES WITH ONE LEG ON A HUMP	15	THE HERON	3
NOW HERE IS PEACE FOR ONE WHO KNEW	17	NO BIRD	1
"ONE COAT OF PRIDE, PERHAPS A BIT THREADBARE;	21	THE AUCTION	5
THE BARGAINS FELL TO BIDDERS, ONE BY ONE.	21	THE AUCTION	10
THE BARGAINS FELL TO BIDDERS, ONE BY ONE.	21	THE AUCTION	10
WOULD NOT RELEASE ONE RIVEN NOTE:	22	SILENCE	18
YOU ARE, IN TRUTH, ONE IN A MILLION,	23	AMOROUS LADY	13
TWO YELLOW AND BLACK, AND ONE THAT LOOKS IN BETWEEN,--	24	VERNAL SENTIMNT	6
IN THE DIRT AND DISORDER I CHERISH ONE SCRAP OF ILLUSION:	29	THE REMINDER	11
ONE WAY, A CHANCE TO BE SECURE:	30	THE RECKONING	10
ONE DRIVER, PINNED BENEATH THE SEAT,	33	HIGHWAY: MICH	19
ONE NUB OF GROWTH	37	CUTTINGS	5
ONE SWIFT MOVEMENT,--	42	TRANSPLANTING	5
ALL IN ONE,	42	TRANSPLANTING	8
OR DROWN A BUG IN ONE SPIT OF TOBACCO JUICE,	42	OLD FLORIST	8
BUT ONE TULIP ON TOP,	43	FLOWER DUMP	11
ONE SWAGGERING HEAD	43	FLOWER DUMP	12
WAS BATTERED ON ONE KNUCKLE;	45	MY PAPA'S WALTZ	10
THE MUSCLES IN ONE THIGH	47	THE RETURN	6
THERE WAS ONE FLY.	53	THE LOST SON	19
BELIEVE ME, THERE'S NO ONE ELSE, KITTEN-LIMP SISTER.	59	THE LONG ALLEY	23
LUMINOUS ONE, SHALL WE MEET ON THE BOSOM OF GOD?	59	THE LONG ALLEY	29
REACH ME ROSE, SWEET ONE, STILL MOIST IN THE LOAM,	61	THE LONG ALLEY	68
THERE WAS ONLY ONE SHOE	64	SHAPE OF FIRE	26
ONE, HIS NOSE HAD A FROG,	73	WHERE KNOCK IS	56
ONE FATHER IS ENOUGH.	74	WHERE KNOCK IS	87
A ONE IS A TWO IS	75	I NEED, I NEED	27
ONE SIGH STRETCHES HEAVEN.	83	O LULL ME, LULL	1
I'M AN OTTER WITH ONLY ONE NOSE:	84	O LULL ME, LULL	35
FOR THEY ARE ALL MY FRIENDS: I SAW ONE SLIDE	105	SIR JOHN DAVIES	7
SHE WAS TOO MUCH FOR ONE, YOU CAN BET YOUR LIFE:	114	THE COW	3
LENT ME ONE VIRTUE, AND I LIVE THEREBY.	120	THE DREAM	24
ONE WITH THE SULLEN DARK.	122	ALL EARTH, AIR	27
ONE WITH THE SIGHING VINE,	124	WORDS FOR WIND	43
ONE TO BE MERRY WITH,	124	WORDS FOR WIND	44
AH, WHEN SHE MOVED, SHE MOVED MORE WAYS THAN ONE:	127	I KNEW A WOMAN	3
OR ONE HIP QUIVER WITH A MOBILE NOSE	127	I KNEW A WOMAN	20
ONE FEATHER IS A BIRD,	128	THE VOICE	1
I CLAIM; ONE TREE, A WOOD;	128	THE VOICE	2
SPIRIT AND NATURE BEAT IN ONE BREAST-BONE--	131	SENTENTIOUS MAN	1
AND ALL DIMENSIONS QUIVERED TO ONE THING.	132	SENTENTIOUS MAN	24
MY BACK IS JUST ONE BRUISE;	136	THE SENSUALISTS	4

	PAGE	TITLE	LINE
ONE (CONTINUED)			
NO MATTER WHICH ONE IS BENEATH,	136	THE SENSUALISTS	15
THE SURLY ONE	138	THE SURLY ONE	T
I HAVE MYSELF ONE CRUMBLING SKIN TO SHOW;	144	ELEGY (1)	11
A SPORTIVE, AIMLESS ONE,	145	THE BEAST	7
BEYOND THE RIDGE TWO WOOD THRUSH SING AS ONE.	150	IN LATE SUMMER	30
HOW I LOVED ONE LIKE YOU WHEN I WAS LITTLE!--	151	SLUG	1
I'M SURE I'VE BEEN A TOAD, ONE TIME OR ANOTHER.	151	SLUG	25
SPRINGING, ONE TO ANOTHER,	152	THE SISKINS	13
OUT OF HER PLACE SHE COMES, A DOLPHIN ONE,	156	THE DYING MAN	80
TWO SONG SPARROWS, ONE WITHIN A GREENHOUSE,	158	FIRST MEDITATN	39
ONE SANG, THEN THE OTHER,	158	FIRST MEDITATN	43
AND ONE CRAB, TENTATIVE, HUNCHES HIMSELF BEFORE MOVING ALONG THE BOTTOM,	159	FIRST MEDITATN	62
ONE FOLLOWS FIRE. ONE DOES.	167	HER BECOMING	80
ONE FOLLOWS FIRE. ONE DOES.	167	HER BECOMING	80
THE GRANDEUR OF A CRAZY ONE ALONE!--	167	HER BECOMING	90
I WAS ALWAYS ONE FOR BEING ALONE,	168	FOURTH MEDITATN	1
SHE WOULD EAT AT ONE GLUP	179	MYRTLE'S COUSIN	3
WITH ONLY ONE LETTER,--	179	MYRTLE	11
ONE DAY HUGH WALKED UP TO A BEAR	181	MONOTONY SONG	5
BUT I COUNT UP TO ONE,	182	PHILANDER	3
AT LAST ONE LONG UNDULANT RIPPLE,	190	AT OYSTER RIVER	11
ON ONE SIDE OF SILENCE THERE IS NO SMILE;	195	JOURNY INTERIOR	76
THE ETERNAL ONE, THE CHILD, THE SWAYING VINE BRANCH,	198	THE LONG WATERS	69
ONE LEARNED OF THE ETERNAL;	199	THE FAR FIELD	18
HOW THEY FILLED THE ORIOLE'S ELM, A TWITTERING RESTLESS CLOUD, ALL ONE MORNING,	199	THE FAR FIELD	28
MY MIND MOVES IN MORE THAN ONE PLACE,	201	THE FAR FIELD	75
THE PURE SERENE OF MEMORY IN ONE MAN,--	201	THE FAR FIELD	101
IN THE BIRD BEYOND THE BOUGH, THE SINGLE ONE	205	THE ROSE	108
WE ARE ONE, AND YET WE ARE MORE,	207	THE YOUNG GIRL	5
THE SOFT-FOOTED ONE	208	THE APPARITION	3
ONE SLEEVE WITH MY HAND IN IT,	209	HER RETICENCE	2
AT ONE WITH THE PLANTS IN THE POND,	209	HER LONGING	3
A BUG-EYED EDIBLE ONE,	209	HER LONGING	8
I'M ONE TO FOLLOW,	210	HER TIME	25
WITH NOT ONE TINY LAUGH	213	THE HAPPY THREE	14
FROM ONE COMELY HEAD.	215	HIS FOREBODING	5
I SANG TO THE ONE STAR THAT LOOKED DOWN AT ME;	216	THE SHY MAN	2
WHEN I AM NO ONE.	217	WISH YOUNG WIFE	11
FROM THE ONE BEAUTIFUL THING IN HER YARD, THE PEACHTREE;	223	ELEGY (2)	13
HE THREW HIS RIFLE OVER WITH ONE HAND;	224	OTTO	15
WITHOUT HIS RIFLE, AND SLAPPED EACH ONE HARD;	224	OTTO	19
HIS HEAD, STIFF AS A SCARAB, TURNED TO ONE SIDE,	226	THE LIZARD	5
ONE LEAF-LIKE FOOT HUNG LAXLY	226	THE LIZARD	7
ONE ROUND EYE STILL TOWARD ME.	226	THE LIZARD	19
ONE GREENISH LID LIFTS A BIT HIGHER,	226	THE LIZARD	23
SO MUCH HE JUST LIES IN ONE CORNER,	227	MEADOW MOUSE	13
THERE IS ONE LIGHT ON THE MOUNTAIN.	230	THE STORM	9
IN ONE STREAK OF PURSUIT.	232	THE THING	12
WITH ONE SINUOUS RIPPLE. THEN A RUSH,	233	THE PIKE	16
AND ONE DROPS DOWN TO THE GARDEN, THE HIGH RHODODENDRON,	234	ALL MORNING	8
WE COUNTED SEVERAL FLAMES IN ONE SMALL FIRE.	237	THE TRANCED	1
SUBJECT AND OBJECT SANG AND DANCED AS ONE;	237	THE TRANCED	17
SOUND, SILENCE SANG AS ONE.	238	THE MOMENT	9
AND ONE IS ONE, FREE IN THE TEARING WIND.	239	IN A DARK TIME	24
AND ONE IS ONE, FREE IN THE TEARING WIND.	239	IN A DARK TIME	24
OF GRIEF I DIED, BUT NO ONE KNEW MY DEATH.	241	THE SEQUEL	8
THE SOUL HAS MANY MOTIONS, BODY ONE.	243	THE MOTION	1
IN PUREST SONG ONE PLAYS THE CONSTANT FOOL	244	INFIRMITY	1
I LOVE MYSELF: THAT'S MY ONE CONSTANCY.	244	INFIRMITY	5
RISING OR FALLING'S ALL ONE DISCIPLINE!	245	THE DECISION	7
ONE WHITE FACE SHIMMERS BRIGHTER THAN THE SUN	246	THE MARROW	7
ONE LOOK TOO CLOSE CAN TAKE MY SOUL AWAY.	246	THE MARROW	9
"I'VE ONLY ONE WING," SHE SAID,	249	THE RESTORED	7
GOD BLESS THE ROOTS!--BODY AND SOUL ARE ONE!	250	THE RIGHT THING	7
AND EVERYTHING COMES TO ONE.	251	ONCE MORE, RND	11
ONE TOE IN ETERNITY;	262	FOLLIES OF ADAM	18
SOME CANNOT PRAISE HIM: I AM ONE OF THOSE.	264	THREE EPIGRAMS	6
BY ONE WHO ROSE UP FROM THE DEAD.	264	THREE EPIGRAMS	10
HE'S PART OF ONE, AS A MATTER OF COURSE.	264	THREE EPIGRAMS	12
A PICTURE WINDOW'S ONE YOU CAN'T	267	SAGINAW SONG	23

		PAGE	TITLE	LINE
ONE (CONTINUED)				
BUT AT LEAST WE KNOW ONE NEEDN'T BLENCH		272	DUET	16
AND THAT MAKES THREE, COUNTING HIS FACE AS ONE.		273	SUPPR W LINDSAY	9
AND ONE EYE GAZED ASKEW. "WHY, BLAKE, HE'S DEAD,--		273	SUPPR W LINDSAY	22
ONE OF THOSE FAT ONES WINDING THROUGH A ROSE.		273	SUPPR W LINDSAY	27
ONES				
THE LITTLE ONES DID,		51	THE WAKING (1)	10
TO DISTRACT ATTENTION FROM THE SHORT-TAILED RIDICULOUS YOUNG ONES		234	ALL MORNING	19
ONE OF THOSE FAT ONES WINDING THROUGH A ROSE.		273	SUPPR W LINDSAY	27
ONE'S				
EACH ONE'S HIMSELF, YET EACH ONE'S EVERYONE.		132	SENTENTIOUS ·MAN	36
EACH ONE'S HIMSELF, YET EACH ONE'S EVERYONE.		132	SENTENTIOUS MAN	36
ONE-SIDED				
HIS SEX-LIFE NEVER IS ONE-SIDED.		264	THREE EPIGRAMS	14
ONLY				
THEIR ONLY NOTION OF THE GOOD		25	VERSE W ALLUSNS	7
ONLY TO GAIN FRESH TRIUMPHS AND APPLAUSE.		28	THE FAVORITE	6
THE STRIP RESERVED FOR PASSING ONLY.		33	HIGHWAY: MICH	7
HATH THE RAIN A FATHER? ALL THE CAVES ARE ICE. ONLY THE SNOW'S HERE.		56	THE LOST SON	84
THE EAR HEARS ONLY IN LOW PLACES.		59	THE LONG ALLEY	7
ALONG THE LOW GROUND DRY ONLY IN AUGUST,--		62	FIELD OF LIGHT	26
SPIRIT. COME NEAR. THIS IS ONLY THE EDGE OF WHITENESS.		64	SHAPE OF FIRE	12
THERE WAS ONLY ONE SHOE		64	SHAPE OF FIRE	26
ONLY THE WOODS ARE ALIVE.		77	BRING THE DAY!	19
I'M AN OTTER WITH ONLY ONE NOSE:		84	O LULL ME, LULL	35
ONLY MY SALT HAS A CHANCE.		91	UNFOLD! UNFOLD!	58
--ONLY STAY OUT OF THE WIND.		97	O, THOU OPENING	12
BAGS? WHO EVER SAID GOD SANG IN YOUR FAT SHAPE? YOU'RE NOT THE ONLY		98	O, THOU OPENING	27
IF ONLY I COULD NUDGE YOU FROM THIS SLEEP,		102	ELEGY FOR JANE	18
IF ONLY I COULD REMEMBER		103	OLD LADY'S WRDS	19
OF HER CHOICE VIRTUES ONLY GODS SHOULD SPEAK,		127	I KNEW A WOMAN	5
I HEARD; AND ONLY I.		128	THE VOICE	18
HUNG DOWN: AND I WAS ONLY I.		143	SHIMMER OF EVIL	9
ONLY TO LOSE MYSELF IN THIS SMALL DARK.		154	THE DYING MAN	41
ONLY A FEW BUBBLES LOOSENING FROM THE ILL-MATCHED TENTACLES,		159	FIRST MEDITATN	64
ONLY THE MOTES OF DUST IN THE IMMACULATE HALLWAYS,		159	FIRST MEDITATN	79
THE ONLY THING ALIVE IN HEAVEN'S EYE,		166	HER BECOMING	58
O THE SONGS WE HIDE, SINGING ONLY TO OURSELVES!		168	FOURTH MEDITATN	13
YET REMAIN ONLY HALF AWARE OF THE INTRANSIENT GLORY?		169	FOURTH MEDITATN	32
WHO TOOK ONLY TOADS ON HIS BACK:		178	THE YAK	2
THE ONLY THING WE'D HAVE FOR PROOF		178	THE CEILING	3
WITH ONLY ONE LETTER,--		179	MYRTLE	11
--AND THERE WAS ONLY HARRY!		181	MONOTONY SONG	12
(MATTERS ONLY A SAINT MENTIONS!)		187	THE LONGING	10
AND HOW THOSE FLOWERHEADS SEEMED TO FLOW TOWARD ME, TO BECKON ME, ONLY A CHILD, OUT OF MYSELF.		203	THE ROSE	55
IF I COULD SEND HIM ONLY		209	HER RETICENCE	1
ONLY AN OMINOUS LAPPING,		230	THE STORM	2
ONLY TO FIND, WITH THEIR LONG TERRIBLE EYES		232	THE THING	9
ONLY TO FLY OVER TO HIS FAVORITE PERCH, THE CROSS-BAR OF A TELEPHONE POLE;		234	ALL MORNING	9
I'M SON AND FATHER OF MY ONLY DEATH.		244	INFIRMITY	18
"I'VE ONLY ONE WING," SHE SAID,		249	THE RESTORED	7
ARE THESE MATTERS ONLY A SAINT MENTIONS?		259	SONG (3)	39
POSEIDON'S ONLY A HORSE,		263	FOLLIES OF ADAM	29
THE ONLY THING I EVER LEARNED		267	SAGINAW SONG	27
OOH				
OOH, OOH, I'M A DUKE OF EELS.		85	PRAISE TO END!	8
OOH, OOH, I'M A DUKE OF EELS.		85	PRAISE TO END!	8
OOOMPH				
OOOMPH DAH DOODLE DAH		269	GOB MUSIC	7
OOOMPH DAH DOODLE DAH		269	GOB MUSIC	8
OOOMPH DAH DOODLE DAH DO.		269	GOB MUSIC	9
OOZE				
IN COILING OOZE		65	SHAPE OF FIRE	46
OPAQUE				
AS AN OPAQUE VASE FILLS TO THE BRIM FROM A QUICK POURING,		67	SHAPE OF FIRE	93
OPEN				
OPEN HOUSE		3	OPEN HOUSE	T
MY HEART KEEPS OPEN HOUSE,		3	OPEN HOUSE	3

		PAGE	TITLE	LINE
OPEN (CONTINUED)				
AN OPEN FIELD;		51	THE WAKING (1)	2
WHERE KNOCK IS OPEN WIDE		71	WHERE KNOCK IS	T
OPEN A HOLE AND SEE THE SKY:		75	I NEED, I NEED	39
THE SKY CRACKED OPEN		87	PRAISE TO END!	59
THE DOORS SWINGING OPEN,		103	OLD LADY'S WRDS	21
I LIVED WITH OPEN SOUND,		128	THE VOICE	11
OPEN LIKE A POOL, A LESSER PARSNIP,		209	HER LONGING	6
AS WHEN THE DOOR SWINGS OPEN IN A FLORIST'S STOREROOM--		220	THE ABYSS	46
OPENING				
O, THOU OPENING, O		97	O, THOU OPENING	T
THE NUMINOUS RING AROUND THE OPENING FLOWER,		198	THE LONG WATERS	70
OPENING, CLOSING.		226	THE LIZARD	26
OPENINGS				
ALL OPENINGS PRAISE US, EVEN OILY HOLES.		90	UNFOLD! UNFOLD!	40
OPERATES				
IT OPERATES ON OTHER MEN.		257	SANITARIUM	12
OPINION				
WE WATCH OPINION DRIFT,		31	LULL	8
OPPOSITES				
LOST OPPOSITES BEND DOWN--		140	THE SWAN	18
I'M RELEASED FROM THE DREARY DANCE OF OPPOSITES.		173	WHAT TELL BONES	80
WHEN OPPOSITES COME SUDDENLY IN PLACE,		244	INFIRMITY	33
OR (125)				
ORANGES				
SHAKING LOOSE THE LAST WIZENED ORANGES IN THE ORCHARD,		231	THE STORM	32
ORCHARD				
UPON THE ORCHARD PATH, FOR SKINNED		14	COMING OF COLD	6
THE HEDGE AND ORCHARD GROVE ARE THINNED.		14	COMING OF COLD	31
I NEED A POND WITH SMALL EELS. AND A WINDY ORCHARD.		164	I'M HERE	91
SHAKING LOOSE THE LAST WIZENED ORANGES IN THE ORCHARD,		231	THE STORM	32
ORCHIDS				
ORCHIDS		39	ORCHIDS	T
ORDER				
THE BRONZE WHEAT ARRANGED IN STRICT AND FORMAL ORDER;		29	THE REMINDER	3
FOR SALE: BY ORDER OF THE REMAINING HEIRS		32	SALE	1
AS IF I HAD BROKEN THE NATURAL ORDER OF THINGS IN THAT SWAMPLAND;		40	MOSS-GATHERING	10
LAST NIGHT I DREAMT OF A JAUNTIER PRINCIPLE OF ORDER;		165	HER BECOMING	30
ORDERS				
ORDERS FOR THE DAY		7	ORDERS FOR DAY	T
ORDNUNG				
ORDNUNG! ORDNUNG!		57	THE LOST SON	142
ORDNUNG! ORDNUNG!		57	THE LOST SON	142
ORIGINAL				
MY BLUE ORIGINAL DANDY, NUMB WITH SUGAR?		86	PRAISE TO END!	18
ARCH OF AIR, MY HEART'S ORIGINAL KNOCK,		88	PRAISE TO END!	79
ORIOLE				
AS WATER TEACHES STONE. BELIEVE ME, EXTREMEST ORIOLE,		260	THE CHANGELING	19
ORIOLES				
WITH BALTIMORE ORIOLES, MICHIGAN BOBOLINKS,		235	ALL MORNING	42
ORIOLE'S				
HOW THEY FILLED THE ORIOLE'S ELM, A TWITTERING RESTLESS CLOUD, ALL ONE MORNING,		199	THE FAR FIELD	28
OSPREY				
WHERE IT LEANS, TILTED EAST, A PERCH FOR THE OSPREY,		197	THE LONG WATERS	36
OTHER				
OLD NEIGHBORS NUDGED EACH OTHER AT THE FUN.		21	THE AUCTION	12
EITHER TO OTHER,		51	THE WAKING (1)	7
EITHER TO OTHER,--		77	BRING THE DAY!	3
FOR OTHER TUNES AND OTHER WANTON BEATS		105	SIR JOHN DAVIES	21
FOR OTHER TUNES AND OTHER WANTON BEATS		105	SIR JOHN DAVIES	21
DID EACH BECOME THE OTHER IN THAT PLAY?		106	SIR JOHN DAVIES	55
THE OTHER		130	THE OTHER	T
ONE SANG, THEN THE OTHER.		158	FIRST MEDITATN	43
TURNING TOWARD THE OTHER SIDE OF LIGHT,		195	JOURNY INTERIOR	69
A SOMETHING WHOLLY OTHER,		205	THE ROSE	103
COMING CLOSER AND CLOSER UPON EACH OTHER;		230	THE STORM	12
IT OPERATES ON OTHER MEN.		257	SANITARIUM	12
WE'LL GIVE EACH OTHER A BOX ON THE EAR,		272	DUET	25
OTHERLY				
DELIGHT ME OTHERLY, WHITE SPIRIT,--		92	I CRY, LOVE!	5

	PAGE	TITLE	LINE
OTHERS			
WHILE OTHERS TAKE THEIR REST.	34	NIGHT JOURNEY	5
LET OTHERS PROBE THE MYSTERY IF THEY CAN.	250	THE RIGHT THING	1
LET OTHERS DELVE THAT MYSTERY IF THEY CAN.	250	THE RIGHT THING	6
OTHER'S			
"THE OTHER'S GONE DEAD,"	249	THE RESTORED	8
OTHERWISE			
IN THE GREY OTHERWISE,	258	SONG (3)	26
OTTER			
IT'S SLEEK AS AN OTTER	55	THE LOST SON	58
I'M AN OTTER WITH ONLY ONE NOSE:	84	O LULL ME. LULL	35
A NIGHT-FISHING OTTER.	220	THE ABYSS	43
OTTO			
OTTO	224	OTTO	T
OULD			
IN THE DARK OF AN OULD SPITTOON;	269	GOB MUSIC	21
OUR (41)			
OURSELVES			
SUBTRACT, AND PUT OURSELVES IN PAWN;	30	THE RECKONING	6
IN THE DEEP MIDDLE OF OURSELVES WE LAY;	106	SIR JOHN DAVIES	57
BUSY. OBVIOUS WITH OURSELVES,	158	FIRST MEDITATN	29
O THE SONGS WE HIDE, SINGING ONLY TO OURSELVES!	168	FOURTH MEDITATN	13
THE STUNNED COUNTRY OF OURSELVES.	258	SONG (3)	21
O THE SONGS WE HIDE SINGING TO OURSELVES!--	259	SONG (3)	38
IN THE COUNTRY OF OURSELVES,	265	HARSH COUNTRY	15
SO WE SAT DOWN AND ATE OURSELVES A MEAL,	274	SUPPR W LINDSAY	30
OUT			
THE ELEMENT OF AIR WAS OUT OF HAND.	6	INTERLUDE	1
THE FIELDS STRETCH OUT IN LONG, UNBROKEN ROWS.	13	PRAISE PRAIRIE	9
THE WIND SHAKES OUT THE SCENT OF PEAR.	14	COMING OF COLD	12
FOR SOMETHING IS AMISS OR OUT OF PLACE	16	THE BAT	9
NOW I AM OUT OF ELEMENT	19	AGNST DISASTER	1
WOULD RATHER TAKE THAN DISH IT OUT.	23	AMOROUS LADY	4
THEIR WIVES GO OUT ON SUNDAY BENEATH THE LATEST HAT.	27	CLAIRVOY WIDOW	8
WHILE OUT OF FRIGHTENED EYES	31	LULL	20
THE LIGHTS IN THE KITCHENS GO OUT; MOTH WINGS UNFURL;	33	IDYLL	3
WHEN SPROUTS BREAK OUT,	37	CUTTINGS (LATE)	9
BULBS BROKE OUT OF BOXES HUNTING FOR CHINKS IN THE DARK,	38	ROOT CELLAR	2
COMING OUT, SOFT AND DECEPTIVE,	39	ORCHIDS	4
BUT SOMETHING ALWAYS WENT OUT OF ME WHEN I DUG LOOSE THOSE CARPETS	40	MOSS-GATHERING	7
BUT SHE RODE IT OUT,	41	BIG WIND	21
FINALLY VEERING, WEARING THEMSELVES OUT, MERELY	41	BIG WIND	30
OR SCOOP OUT A WEED CLOSE TO FLOURISHING ROOTS,	42	OLD FLORIST	6
OUT INTO THE SWEET AIR.	42	TRANSPLANTING	20
THE WIND BILLOWING OUT THE SEAT OF MY BRITCHES,	43	CHILD ON GRNHSE	1
OR RISING OUT OF FERNS NOT FAR FROM WATER,	43	CARNATIONS	4
THEIR SKIRTS BILLOWING OUT WIDE INTO TENTS,	44	FRAU BAUMAN	17
THEY TEASED OUT THE SEED THAT THE COLD KEPT ASLEEP,--	44	FRAU BAUMAN	23
OUT THROUGH THE VELVETY CHAINS TO THE COOL AIR OF NIGHT.	47	DOUBLE FEATURE	4
COME OUT OF A CLOUD, ANGEL WITH SEVERAL FACES,	48	LAST WORDS	8
THE SUN WAS OUT;	51	THE WAKING (1)	3
ALL THE LEAVES STUCK OUT THEIR TONGUES;	53	THE LOST SON	5
VOICE, COME OUT OF THE SILENCE.	54	THE LOST SON	20
OUT OF WHAT DOOR DO I GO,	54	THE LOST SON	26
MY VEINS ARE RUNNING NOWHERE. DO THE BONES CAST OUT THEIR FIRE?	56	THE LOST SON	101
WHERE THE FIREMAN PULLED OUT ROSES,	57	THE LOST SON	132
A RIVER GLIDES OUT OF THE GRASS. A RIVER OR A SERPENT.	59	THE LONG ALLEY	1
COME. COME OUT OF THE SHADE, THE COOL WAYS,	61	THE LONG ALLEY	69
MOTHER ME OUT OF HERE. WHAT MORE WILL THE BONES ALLOW?	64	SHAPE OF FIRE	7
THE SILVER FISH RAN IN AND OUT OF MY SPECIAL BINDINGS;	65	SHAPE OF FIRE	35
AN EYE COMES OUT OF THE WAVE.	66	SHAPE OF FIRE	60
RISING SLOWLY OUT OF ITS BED,	67	SHAPE OF FIRE	84
AND MIST LIFTING OUT OF THE BROWN CAT-TAILS;	67	SHAPE OF FIRE	87
FISH ME OUT.	72	WHERE KNOCK IS	47
BUT HE SLIPPED OUT.	73	WHERE KNOCK IS	57
NOWHERE IS OUT. I SAW THE COLD.	73	WHERE KNOCK IS	71
I'VE LET MY NOSE OUT;	79	GIVE WAY, GATES	16
I KNOW THE WAY OUT OF A LAUGH;	81	SENSIBILITY! LA	23
THE SUN CAME OUT;	87	PRAISE TO END!	55
MOUSE, MOUSE, COME OUT OF THE FERNS,	92	I CRY, LOVE!	22
THE BATS WEAVE IN AND OUT OF THE WILLOWS,	93	I CRY, LOVE!	41

	PAGE	TITLE	LINE
OUT (CONTINUED)			
A FISH JUMPS, SHAKING OUT FLAKES OF MOONLIGHT.	93	I CRY, LOVE!	45
--ONLY STAY OUT OF THE WIND.	97	O, THOU OPENING	12
TAIL AROUND, NOSING IN AND OUT OF THE CURRENT,	101	LIGHT BREATHER	9
THE SPIRIT AND THE FLESH CRIED OUT FOR MORE.	106	SIR JOHN DAVIES	52
SHE LAUGHED ME OUT, AND THEN SHE LAUGHED ME IN;	106	SIR JOHN DAVIES	56
(IT TURNED OUT SHE HADN'T A FATHER AT ALL)	111	SQUEEZE-BOX	15
AND EVEN THE BOYS TURNED OUT TO BE MEN	112	SQUEEZE-BOX	23
IT WAS FADE ME ANOTHER AND STICK OUT YOUR CAN;	112	SQUEEZE-BOX	27
--WHEN SHE THOUGHT I'D RUN OUT OF MONEY.	112	SQUEEZE-BOX	41
SUPPOSE YOU WALK OUT IN A STORM,	114	DINKY	5
YOU CAN FISH OUT A FISH, OUT A FISH, OUT A FISH,	117	LADY AND BEAR	22
YOU CAN FISH OUT A FISH, OUT A FISH, OUT A FISH,	117	LADY AND BEAR	22
YOU CAN FISH OUT A FISH, OUT A FISH, OUT A FISH,	117	LADY AND BEAR	22
THE DEER CAME DOWN, OUT OF THE DAPPLED WOOD.	120	THE DREAM	20
AND I SWAYED OUT BEYOND THE WHITE SEAFOAM;	120	THE DREAM	29
WHEN SHE SHAKES OUT HER HAIR.	121	ALL EARTH, AIR	9
SHE KISSED ME OUT OF THOUGHT	123	WORDS FOR WIND	18
OUT OF A NESTLING'S BEAK	123	WORDS FOR WIND	27
AND YET I ROAMED OUT WHERE	128	THE VOICE	7
IF SHE BUT SIGHS, A BIRD PUTS OUT ITS TONGUE.	129	SHE	3
SHE CRIES OUT LOUD THE SOUL'S OWN SECRET JOY;	129	SHE	9
MY INDIRECTION FOUND DIRECTION OUT.	131	SENTENTIOUS MAN	4
I STAY ALIVE, BOTH IN AND OUT OF TIME,	131	SENTENTIOUS MAN	14
AND FOUND OUT ALL I COULD OF ALL DESIRE;	132	SENTENTIOUS MAN	32
A BEAST WITH FANGS, AND OUT FOR HIS OWN BLOOD	133	THE PURE FURY	18
GHOST CRIES OUT TO GHOST--	138	THE SURLY ONE	5
I STUDY OUT A DARK SIMILITUDE:	140	THE SWAN	1
IS THERE NO WAY OUT OF THAT COURSING BLOOD?	140	THE SWAN	4
CRIED OUT THEIR LIVES AN INSTANT AND WERE FREE.	143	SHIMMER OF EVIL	14
CRIED TO MY FLESH OUT LOUD.	147	THE EXORCISM	8
AS IF OUT OF MY SIDE,	148	THE SMALL	16
OUT OF THE MOTTLED SHADE	150	SNAKE	2
A TREE ALL OUT OF SHAPE FROM WIND AND RAIN,	150	IN LATE SUMMER	27
EATING THE HEART OUT OF MY GARDEN.	151	SLUG	14
"MY SOUL'S HUNG OUT TO DRY,	153	THE DYING MAN	3
A GHOST COMES OUT OF THE UNCONSCIOUS MIND	154	THE DYING MAN	36
WHEN FIGURES OUT OF OBSCURE SHADOW RAVE,	154	THE DYING MAN	46
FLESH CRIES TO FLESH; AND BONE CRIES OUT TO BONE;	155	THE DYING MAN	58
OUT OF HER PLACE SHE COMES, A DOLPHIN ONE,	156	THE DYING MAN	80
A BEAST CRIES OUT AS IF ITS FLESH WERE TORN,	156	THE DYING MAN	82
INACCESSIBLE, THE BOAT ALWAYS PULLING OUT	158	FIRST MEDITATN	50
LEANING, OUT OF ALL BREATH,	161	I'M HERE	23
THE SWALLOWS FLEW IN AND OUT OF THE SMOKELESS CHIMNEYS.	162	I'M HERE	41
ROCKS IN AND OUT OF ITSELF.	163	I'M HERE	59
THE WAY OUT OF A ROSE?	165	HER BECOMING	27
OUT, OUT, YOU SECRET BEASTS,	167	HER BECOMING	78
OUT, OUT, YOU SECRET BEASTS,	167	HER BECOMING	78
WAS IT YESTERDAY I STRETCHED OUT THE THIN BONES OF MY INNOCENCE?	168	FOURTH MEDITATN	12
A BIRD SINGS OUT IN SOLITARINESS	171	WHAT TELL BONES	18
TO FIND OUT HOW THE CEILING'S FEELING.	178	THE CEILING	6
THE LIGHT CRIES OUT, AND I AM THERE TO HEAR--	188	THE LONGING	32
OUT OF THESE NOTHINGS	188	THE LONGING	37
ALIVE WITH TINY STRIPED FISH, AND YOUNG CRABS CLIMBING IN AND OUT OF THE WATER.	190	AT OYSTER RIVER	5
IN AND OUT OF THE SMALL WAVES,	192	AT OYSTER RIVER	65
IN THE LONG JOURNEY OUT OF THE SELF,	193	JOURNY INTERIOR	1
THE HIGHWAY RIBBONING OUT IN A STRAIGHT THRUST TO THE NORTH.	193	JOURNY INTERIOR	27
AND THE SUN COMES OUT OF A BLUE CLOUD OVER THE TETONS,	194	JOURNY INTERIOR	40
AND THE WAVES FLATTENING OUT WHEN THE FISHERMEN DRAG THEIR NETS OVER THE STONES.	194	JOURNY INTERIOR	57
OF DRIVING ALONE, WITHOUT LUGGAGE, OUT A LONG PENINSULA,	199	THE FAR FIELD	3
WHERE THE HAWKS SWAY OUT INTO THE WIND,	202	THE ROSE	4
AND BELOW, IN A MIST OUT OF NOWHERE,	202	THE ROSE	29
THE LACELIKE WRINKLES OF THE WAKE WIDENING, THINNING OUT,	203	THE ROSE	33
FLOWERING OUT OF THE DARK,	203	THE ROSE	42
A SINGLE WILD ROSE, STRUGGLING OUT OF THE WHITE EMBRACE OF THE MORNING-GLORY,	203	THE ROSE	44
OUT OF THE BRIARY HEDGE, THE TANGLE OF MATTED UNDERBRUSH,	203	THE ROSE	45
AND HOW THOSE FLOWERHEADS SEEMED TO FLOW TOWARD ME, TO BECKON ME, ONLY A CHILD, OUT OF MYSELF.	203	THE ROSE	55
AS IF ANOTHER MAN APPEARED OUT OF THE DEPTHS OF MY BEING,	205	THE ROSE	100

	PAGE	TITLE	LINE
OUT (CONTINUED)			
AS IF I SWAYED OUT ON THE WILDEST WAVE ALIVE,	205	THE ROSE	104
SHAKING OUT MY CATCH IN THE MORNING SUNLIGHT,	209	HER LONGING	15
PERPETUALLY RISING OUT OF MYSELF,	209	HER LONGING	20
SIGHED OUT HER PURE RELIEF	213	THE HAPPY THREE	3
SANG OUT AUDACIOUSLY	213	THE HAPPY THREE	31
THEN WE ROMPED OUT AGAIN,	214	THE HAPPY THREE	35
OUT AGAIN,	214	THE HAPPY THREE	36
OUT AGAIN,	214	THE HAPPY THREE	37
MAY YOU LIVE OUT YOUR LIFE	217	WISH YOUNG WIFE	6
NEITHER IN NOR OUT OF THIS LIFE.	220	THE ABYSS	23
WHETHER FOR LOVE OR OUT OF OBSCURE GUILT	224	OTTO	24
(AND SOME GROW OUT OF SHAPE, THEIR SEED IMPURE;)	225	OTTO	32
AS I LOOKED OUT AT THEM FROM THE HIGH HOUSE,	225	OTTO	35
HIS ABSURD WHISKERS STICKING OUT LIKE A CARTOON-MOUSE,	227	MEADOW MOUSE	7
WHEN I PUT HER OUT, ONCE, BY THE GARBAGE PAIL,	228	THE GERANIUM	1
SHE LEANING OUT OF HER POT TOWARD THE WINDOW.	228	THE GERANIUM	19
AND A CHILD'S DIRTY SHIFT BILLOWS UPWARD OUT OF AN ALLEY,	230	THE STORM	18
A THING IN AND OUT OF SIGHT,	232	THE THING	4
OR DRIFT LAZILY IN AND OUT OF THE WEEDS.	233	THE PIKE	7
UNTIL, OUT FROM A DARK COVE,	233	THE PIKE	14
WHEN OUR SPAYED FEMALE CAT YAWNS AND STRETCHES OUT IN THE SUNSHINE--	234	ALL MORNING	23
WE STRUGGLED OUT OF SENSUALITY;	237	THE TRANCED	11
A MAN GOES FAR TO FIND OUT WHAT HE IS--	239	IN A DARK TIME	16
A FALLEN MAN, I CLIMB OUT OF MY FEAR.	239	IN A DARK TIME	22
A SHAPE CALLED UP OUT OF MY NATURAL MIND;	241	THE SEQUEL	10
NOR COULD I PUT THAT SOUND OUT OF MY MIND,	245	THE DECISION	5
LORD, HEAR ME OUT, AND HEAR ME OUT THIS DAY:	246	THE MARROW	17
LORD, HEAR ME OUT, AND HEAR ME OUT THIS DAY:	246	THE MARROW	17
THE BIRD FLIES OUT, THE BIRD FLIES BACK AGAIN;	250	THE RIGHT THING	4
CHILD OF THE DARK, HE CAN OUT LEAP THE SUN,	250	THE RIGHT THING	10
I'M SWEATING OUT THE WILL TO DIE.	256	IN HYDROTHERAPY	10
TO JUMP OUT OF HIS SKIN.	262	FOLLIES OF ADAM	4
NOT EVEN OUT OF BREATH?	262	FOLLIES OF ADAM	7
SPEAK IT FROM THE FACE OUT CLEARLY:	266	FOR STEVENS	13
OUT HEMLOCK WAY THERE IS A STREAM	267	SAGINAW SONG	7
I HELPED OUT WITH THE BOOKS;	267	SAGINAW SONG	32
I'M NEITHER OUT NOR IN	271	THE REPLY	5
LET'S EAT BEFORE THE MOONLIGHT ALL RUNS OUT."	273	SUPPR W LINDSAY	29
I WALKED HIM THROUGH THE GRILL AND OUT THE GATE	274	SUPPR W LINDSAY	46
OUTER			
OUR OUTER SKIN. WHO'S WHISTLING UP MY SLEEVE?	106	SIR JOHN DAVIES	38
OUTLEAP			
CAN I OUTLEAP THE SEA--	221	THE ABYSS	62
OUTLEAPS			
THIS JOY OUTLEAPS THE DOG. WHO CARES? WHO CARES?	106	SIR JOHN DAVIES	44
THE WORD OUTLEAPS THE WORLD, AND LIGHT IS ALL.	107	SIR JOHN DAVIES	96
OUTPOURINGS			
DIFFUSE THE OUTPOURINGS OF THE SPIRITUAL COWARD,	5	PROGNOSIS	1
OUTRAGEOUS			
AND ON THE COMING OF THE OUTRAGEOUS DAWN,	241	THE SEQUEL	15
OUTSIDE			
AN EXULTATION TAKES US OUTSIDE LIFE:	132	SENTENTIOUS MAN	25
THE OUTSIDE DIES WITHIN,	141	MEMORY	3
AND ANOTHER, OUTSIDE, IN THE BRIGHT DAY,	158	FIRST MEDITATN	41
OUTSIDE, THE SAME SPARROWS BICKER IN THE EAVES.	161	I'M HERE	6
OR AGENCY OUTSIDE ME.	173	WHAT TELL BONES	99
SUPPOSE THE CEILING WENT OUTSIDE	178	THE CEILING	1
A POINT OUTSIDE THE GLITTERING CURRENT;	201	THE FAR FIELD	72
I SWAY OUTSIDE MYSELF	202	THE ROSE	22
AND I STOOD OUTSIDE MYSELF,	205	THE ROSE	101
YET WHEN I SIGHED, I STOOD OUTSIDE MY LIFE,	248	THE TREE, BIRD	7
OUTWARD			
THE WHOLE FLOWER EXTENDING OUTWARD,	42	TRANSPLANTING	21
OVENBIRD			
THE OVENBIRD WILL MATCH THE VOCAL BROOK,	11	LIGHT BRIGHTER	15
OVER			
WATER RAN OVER AND UNDER	6	THE PREMONITION	8
HANDS, HARD AND VEINED ALL OVER,	7	ORDERS FOR DAY	1
FEET, BEAR THE THIN BONES OVER	7	ORDERS FOR DAY	8
BREATH, TURN THE OLD BLOOD OVER.	7	ORDERS FOR DAY	21
STICKS-IN-A-DROWSE DROOP OVER SUGARY LOAM,	37	CUTTINGS	1

		PAGE	TITLE	LINE
OVER (CONTINUED)				
THEY LEAN OVER THE PATH,		39	ORCHIDS	1
AND AFTERWARDS I ALWAYS FELT MEAN, JOGGING BACK OVER THE LOGGING ROAD,		40	MOSS-GATHERING	9
WAVER OVER TO RED,		41	BIG WIND	11
THAT BROKE OVER THE WHOLE OF HER,		41	BIG WIND	27
OVER THE DYING, THE NEWLY DEAD.		43	FLOWER DUMP	13
THEY STILL HOVER OVER ME,		44	FRAU BAUMAN	31
AND THEIR SNUFF-LADEN BREATH BLOWING LIGHTLY OVER ME IN MY FIRST SLEEP.		44	FRAU BAUMAN	35
OVER THE GULFS OF DREAM		49	NIGHT CROW	4
RAN OVER STONES:		51	THE WAKING (1)	22
A SLOW DRIP OVER STONES,		53	THE LOST SON	3
RUNNING LIGHTLY OVER SPONGY GROUND,		54	THE LOST SON	34
OVER A RICKETY BRIDGE		54	THE LOST SON	38
I'M COLD. I'M COLD ALL OVER. RUB ME IN FATHER AND MOTHER.		56	THE LOST SON	85
OVER SLIPPERY CINDERS		57	THE LOST SON	124
THE LIGHT IN THE MORNING CAME SLOWLY OVER THE WHITE		57	THE LOST SON	135
SCURRY OF WARM OVER SMALL PLANTS.		57	THE LOST SON	141
THE LIGHT MOVED SLOWLY OVER THE FROZEN FIELD,		58	THE LOST SON	155
OVER THE DRY SEED-CROWNS,		58	THE LOST SON	156
LIGHT TRAVELED OVER THE WIDE FIELD;		58	THE LOST SON	159
COME WHISPERING OVER THE SMALL WATERS,		61	THE LONG ALLEY	67
SWAYING OVER THE WALKS, IN THE WATERY AIR,		61	THE LONG ALLEY	75
AN OLD SCOW BUMPS OVER BLACK ROCKS.		64	SHAPE OF FIRE	5
SHALE LOOSENS. MARL REACHES INTO THE FIELD. SMALL BIRDS PASS OVER WATER.		64	SHAPE OF FIRE	11
UP OVER A VIADUCT I CAME, TO THE SNAKES AND STICKS OF ANOTHER WINTER,		65	SHAPE OF FIRE	37
WHEN THE HERONS FLOATED HIGH OVER THE WHITE HOUSES,		66	SHAPE OF FIRE	66
AND MY INTENT STRETCHED OVER THE BUDS AT THEIR FIRST TREMBLING.		66	SHAPE OF FIRE	69
FILLS AND TREMBLES AT THE EDGE YET DOES NOT FLOW OVER,		67	SHAPE OF FIRE	94
STEPPED IN WET. OVER STONES.		73	WHERE KNOCK IS	55
WHISPER ME OVER,		74	I NEED, I NEED	12
AND OVER BY ALGY'S		77	BRING THE DAY!	13
I'M AWAKE ALL OVER:		88	PRAISE TO END!	80
YOU'RE BLISTERED ALL OVER		89	UNFOLD! UNFOLD!	14
AND THE FIRST DUST OF SPRING LISTING OVER BACKLOTS,--		92	I CRY, LOVE!	27
FEET RUN OVER THE SIMPLE STONES,		93	I CRY, LOVE!	36
THEN WASHING UP OVER SMALL STONES.		93	I CRY, LOVE!	49
AND NOW ARE WE TO HAVE THAT PELLUDIOUS JESUS-SHIMMER OVER ALL THINGS,		98	O, THOU OPENING	21
A TREE SWAYED OVER WATER.		100	THE VISITANT	2
OVER THIS DAMP GRAVE I SPEAK THE WORDS OF MY LOVE:		102	ELEGY FOR JANE	20
AND LEAP OVER MY EYE,		103	OLD LADY'S WRDS	16
LEANING OVER A ROCK,		104	OLD LADY'S WRDS	41
THE CINDERY SNOW TICKS OVER STUBBLE.		104	OLD LADY'S WRDS	54
OVER THE SODDEN GROUND.		148	THE SMALL	18
CREEPING SLOWLY OVER THE WET GRASS,		151	SLUG	13
OR, POISONED, DRAGGING A WHITE SKEIN OF SPITTLE OVER A PATH--		151	SLUG	21
RACE OVER THE THICK GRASS;		152	THE SISKINS	6
THE LIGHTS TILTING UP, SKYWARD, AS WE COME OVER A LITTLE RISE,		158	FIRST MEDITATN	24
THE SONGS TUMBLING OVER AND UNDER THE GLASS,		158	FIRST MEDITATN	44
EXPLODES LIKE A ROSE, OR THRUSTS WINGS OVER THE CARIBBEAN.		159	FIRST MEDITATN	77
A COLD WIND COMES OVER STONES;		160	FIRST MEDITATN	92
PLAYS OVER THE DRY PODS,		160	FIRST MEDITATN	94
MOVES OVER THE FIELD.		160	FIRST MEDITATN	96
THE SCENT OF THE HALF-OPENED BUDS CAME UP OVER ME.		162	I'M HERE	49
MAKING MY WAY OVER WET STONES.		166	HER BECOMING	48
ALL OVER YOUR HAT,--		180	GOO-GIRL	8
HE JUMPS ALL OVER. WHO		182	THE LAMB	3
THE GULLS WHEEL OVER THEIR SINGULAR GARBAGE;		187	THE LONGING	16
OVER THE LOW, BARNACLED, ELEPHANT-COLORED ROCKS,		190	AT OYSTER RIVER	1
THEIR CAT-MEWING OVER,		190	AT OYSTER RIVER	9
MAKES ALMOST A WAVE OVER A BARRIER OF SMALL STONES,		190	AT OYSTER RIVER	13
OVER A LIP OF STONE, THE TINY RIVULET;		191	AT OYSTER RIVER	43
AND THE BACK WHEELS HANG ALMOST OVER THE EDGE		193	JOURNY INTERIOR	4
THE TRICK WAS TO THROW THE CAR SIDEWAYS AND CHARGE OVER THE HILL, FULL OF THE THROTTLE,		193	JOURNY INTERIOR	21
GRINDING UP AND OVER THE NARROW ROAD, SPITTING AND ROARING.		193	JOURNY INTERIOR	22

	PAGE	TITLE	LINE
OVER (CONTINUED)			
AND THE SUN COMES OUT OF A BLUE CLOUD OVER THE TETONS, ...	194	JOURNY INTERIOR	40
AND THE WAVES FLATTENING OUT WHEN THE FISHERMEN DRAG THEIR NETS OVER THE STONES.	194	JOURNY INTERIOR	57
AND A FISHERMAN DAWDLES OVER A WOODEN BRIDGE,	197	THE LONG WATERS	37
OVER THE THIN, FEATHERY RIPPLES BREAKING LIGHTLY AGAINST THE IRREGULAR SHORELINE--	197	THE LONG WATERS	50
AND THE LOW RIPPLES RUN OVER A PEBBLY SHORELINE,	198	THE LONG WATERS	62
OR A BREEZE MOVES OVER THE KNEES FROM A LOW HILL,	198	THE LONG WATERS	64
ITS ENTRAILS STREWN OVER THE HALF-GROWN FLOWERS,	199	THE FAR FIELD	22
THEN A LONG RUNNING OVER FLAT STONES	200	THE FAR FIELD	64
AND THE EAGLES SAIL LOW OVER THE FIR TREES,	202	THE ROSE	6
THE SUN A BALL OF FIRE COMING DOWN OVER THE WATER.	202	THE ROSE	16
LIFTING ME HIGH OVER THE FOUR-FOOT STEMS, THE MRS. RUSSELLS, AND HIS OWN ELABORATE HYBRIDS,	203	THE ROSE	54
FLOATING OVER THE MOUNTAINS,	209	HER LONGING	17
MY WINGS HOVERING OVER THE SHOREBIRDS,	209	HER LONGING	21
FLICK OVER THE CLOSE WHITECAPS,	210	HER TIME	11
HE THREW HIS RIFLE OVER WITH ONE HAND;	224	OTTO	15
OVER THE WORN CURB OF THE TERRACE,	226	THE LIZARD	8
THEN SUDDENLY FLUNG UP AND OVER,	226	THE LIZARD	10
ENDING CURLED AROUND AND OVER AGAIN,	226	THE LIZARD	11
THEN SLIDES DOWN OVER THE EYE'S SURFACE,	226	THE LIZARD	24
THEN A CRACK OF THUNDER, AND THE BLACK RAIN RUNS OVER US, OVER	230	THE STORM	23
THEN A CRACK OF THUNDER, AND THE BLACK RAIN RUNS OVER US, OVER	230	THE STORM	23
RUNNING OVER THE COVERLET, DOWN UNDER THE IRON BEDSTEAD.	231	THE STORM	35
FOR THE GREAT LAST LEAP OF THE WAVE OVER THE BREAKWATER,	231	THE STORM	40
FAR AWAY, CLOSE-AT-HAND, HIS CALL FLOATING OVER THE ON-COMING TRAFFIC,	234	ALL MORNING	3
ONLY TO FLY OVER TO HIS FAVORITE PERCH, THE CROSS-BAR OF A TELEPHONE POLE;	234	ALL MORNING	9
PITCHING LIGHTLY OVER THE HIGH HEDGEROWS, DEE-DEEING,	234	ALL MORNING	25
I'LL SPIT OVER MY CHIN AND BEYOND THE CURB,	272	DUET	7
FROM A KNOCKED OVER CHURN, AND FOAMED AROUND	273	SUPPR W LINDSAY	13
OVERDUE			
THE VISIT OF VISION, LUCK YEARS OVERDUE,	29	THE GENTLE	6
OVERFLOWS			
THE RIVER OVERFLOWS THE LEVEL FIELD.	11	LIGHT BRIGHTER	8
OVERHEAD			
WHILE THE WIND WHINES OVERHEAD,	230	THE STORM	3
OVERHUNG			
ITS LINTEL OVERHUNG	145	THE BEAST	2
OVERWHELM			
LONG LIVE THE WEEDS THAT OVERWHELM	18	LONG LIVE WEEDS	1
TIME CANNOT OVERWHELM.	240	IN EVEING AIR	9
OWED			
WHATEVER I OWED TO TIME	49	RIVER INCIDENT	4
OWL			
I KNOW IT'S AN OWL. HE'S MAKING IT DARKER.	72	WHERE KNOCK IS	39
BE LARGE AS AN OWL, BE SLICK AS A FROG,	86	PRAISE TO END!	39
--WHO CARES? THE OLD OWL?	89	UNFOLD! UNFOLD!	15
TO THE CRIES OF THE OWL, THE EERIE WHOOPER.	202	THE ROSE	19
UNDER THE EYE OF THE GREAT OWL WATCHING FROM THE ELM-TREE.	227	MEADOW MOUSE	24
OWLS			
I'M SAD WITH THE LITTLE OWLS.	80	GIVE WAY, GATES	45
I HEAR THE OWLS, THE SOFT CALLERS, COMING DOWN FROM THE HEMLOCKS.	93	I CRY, LOVE!	40
OWLY			
SUCH OWLY PLEASURES! FISH COME FIRST, SWEET BIRD.	87	PRAISE TO END!	71
OWN			
LOST HUES OF BIRDS THE TREES TAKE AS THEIR OWN.	12	SLOW SEASON	9
DISTILLS A PUNGENCE OF ITS OWN;	14	COMING OF COLD	16
AND FAR FROM ANYTHING MY OWN,	19	AGNST DISASTER	2
A WISDOM OF THEIR OWN.	20	REPL TO CENSURE	12
I DID NOT MOVE TO CLAIM WHAT WAS MY OWN.	21	THE AUCTION	4
THE TIME OF WORKERS IS THEIR OWN.	33	HIGHWAY: MICH	5
AS MY OWN TONGUE KISSED	56	THE LOST SON	98
I KNOW MY OWN BONES:	83	O LULL ME, LULL	16
I'M UNTRUE TO MY OWN EXCESSES.	86	PRAISE TO END!	27
I'LL SEEK MY OWN MEEKNESS.	91	UNFOLD! UNFOLD!	59
THE LOST HAVE THEIR OWN PACE.	91	UNFOLD! UNFOLD!	61

	PAGE	TITLE	LINE
OWN (CONTINUED)			
A DRY CRY COMES FROM MY OWN DESERT;	93	I CRY, LOVE!	31
THE DARK HAS ITS OWN LIGHT.	98	O, THOU OPENING	32
INTO MY OWN SILENCES.	104	OLD LADY'S WRDS	62
TOOK ARMS AGAINST OUR OWN OBSCURITY.	106	SIR JOHN DAVIES	54
I CAME TO LOVE, I CAME INTO MY OWN.	120	THE DREAM	32
AND MADE MY SONG THEIR OWN.	123	WORDS FOR WIND	16
I'M MARTYR TO A MOTION NOT MY OWN;	127	I KNEW A WOMAN	23
HIDDEN IN MY OWN HEART.	128	THE VOICE	6
THAT GHOST WAS MY OWN CHOICE,	128	THE VOICE	13
SHE CRIES OUT LOUD THE SOUL'S OWN SECRET JOY;	129	SHE	9
I CAN DELIGHT IN MY OWN HARDIHOOD;	132	SENTENTIOUS MAN	26
I TOUCHED THE STONES, AND THEY HAD MY OWN SKIN.	133	THE PURE FURY	7
A MAN'S A BEAST PROWLING IN HIS OWN HOUSE,	133	THE PURE FURY	17
A BEAST WITH FANGS, AND OUT FOR HIS OWN BLOOD	133	THE PURE FURY	18
THAT START FROM MY OWN FEET.	138	THE SURLY ONE	8
I FEAR FOR MY OWN JOY;	138	LOVE'S PROGRESS	23
EACH VISION PURELY, PURELY WAS ITS OWN:	143	SHIMMER OF EVIL	4
MY OWN, MY SECRET LIPS	147	THE EXORCISM	11
COLD, IN MY OWN DEAD SALT.	147	THE EXORCISM	28
DARE I EMBRACE A GHOST FROM MY OWN BREAST?	165	HER BECOMING	21
I AM BENIGN IN MY OWN COMPANY.	167	HER BECOMING	87
SEEKING IN MY OWN WAY, ETERNAL PURPOSE;	168	FOURTH MEDITATN	2
I ROCK IN MY OWN DARK,	172	WHAT TELL BONES	62
I SEEK MY OWN MEEKNESS;	173	WHAT TELL BONES	91
BEYOND MY OWN ECHO,	195	JOURNY INTERIOR	71
THE TREE RETREATS INTO ITS OWN SHADOW.	200	THE FAR FIELD	57
A MAN FACED WITH HIS OWN IMMENSITY	201	THE FAR FIELD	87
LIFTING ME HIGH OVER THE FOUR-FOOT STEMS, THE MRS. RUSSELLS, AND HIS OWN ELABORATE HYBRIDS,	203	THE ROSE	54
I THINK OF THE ROCK SINGING, AND LIGHT MAKING ITS OWN SILENCE,	204	THE ROSE	79
YET KEEP TO MYSELF MY OWN MIND;	208	HER WORDS	5
IS MY OWN MIND AT PLAY.	215	HIS FOREBODING	15
AND LISTEN TO MY OWN FEET.	215	HIS FOREBODING	18
MY SOUL NEARLY MY OWN,	221	THE ABYSS	79
BY HIS OWN NAKEDNESS?	240	IN EVEING AIR	4
THERE'S LITTLE LEFT I CARE TO CALL MY OWN.	244	INFIRMITY	8
DANCED MY OWN SOUL,	249	THE RESTORED	2
DO THE DEAD WAKE IN THEIR OWN WAY?	259	SONG (3)	32
THE SOUL HAS ITS OWN SHINE AND SHAPE;	259	SONG (3)	48
BUT IT HAD A FLAVOR ALL ITS OWN,	270	GOB MUSIC	40
OX'S			
HER TONGUE, AT THE LAST, THICK, BLACK AS AN OX'S.	223	ELEGY (2)	17
OYSTER			
HIS OYSTER WORLD WAS EASILY COME BY;	28	THE FAVORITE	3
LIKE PIECES OF SMOKED EEL OR RAW OYSTER.	151	SLUG	17
MEDITATION AT OYSTER RIVER	190	AT OYSTER RIVER	T
OYSTER'S			
THE OYSTER'S WEEPING FOOT,	125	WORDS FOR WIND	86
PACE			
THE LOST HAVE THEIR OWN PACE.	91	UNFOLD! UNFOLD!	61
KEEPS PACE WHEN I WALK ALONE.	123	WORDS FOR WIND	32
PACED			
WE PACED THE LIVING GROUND;	237	THE TRANCED	13
PACING			
PACING A ROOM, A ROOM WITH DEAD-WHITE WALLS;	242	THE SEQUEL	30
PAD			
FOR ALL OUR SCRATCHING ON THE PAD,	30	THE RECKONING	7
NEAT IN THEIR BOXES, DOLOR OF PAD AND PAPER-WEIGHT,	46	DOLOR	2
PADDOCK			
A STABLE AND PADDOCK, SOME FOX-HUNTING LAND,	32	SALE	6
PAGEANTRY			
THE PAGEANTRY OF WINGS THE EYE'S BRIGHT TREASURE.	5	TO MY SISTER	6
PAID			
THE DOCTORS, THE LAWYERS, THE COPS ARE ALL PAID--	112	SQUEEZE-BOX	42
PAIL			
WHEN I PUT HER OUT, ONCE, BY THE GARBAGE PAIL,	228	THE GERANIUM	1
PAILS			
ELSEWHERE, IN HOUSES, EVEN PAILS CAN BE SAD;	157	FIRST MEDITATN	4
WELTER OF TIN CANS, PAILS, OLD BIRD NESTS, A CHILD'S SHOE RIDING A LOG,	191	AT OYSTER RIVER	54

		PAGE	TITLE	LINE
PAIN				
	YOU CURSE THE LEGACY OF PAIN;	4	FEUD	6
	REMAIN SECURE FROM PAIN PRESERVE THY HATE THY HEART.	5	TO MY SISTER	11
	PRETENDS HIS DEAD BUNION GIVES EXQUISITE PAIN.	29	THE GENTLE	4
	AND NOW GRIM DIGITS OF OLD PAIN	30	THE RECKONING	3
	I SAW A SIGHT THAT CAUSED ME PAIN,	114	DINKY	10
	IS PAIN A PROMISE? I WAS SCHOOLED IN PAIN,	132	SENTENTIOUS MAN	31
	IS PAIN A PROMISE? I WAS SCHOOLED IN PAIN,	132	SENTENTIOUS MAN	31
	WE START FROM THE DARK. PAIN TEACHES US LITTLE.	166	HER BECOMING	35
	I WOULD BELIEVE MY PAIN: AND THE EYE QUIET ON THE GROWING ROSE;	188	THE LONGING	43
	WE PASSED THE ICE OF PAIN,	238	THE MOMENT	1
	PAIN WANDERS THROUGH MY BONES LIKE A LOST FIRE;	246	THE MARROW	11
PAINTED				
	PLAYING WITH PAINTED PINS.	31	LULL	12
PAIR				
	ADDS UP A PAIR OF JIGGLING DOUBLE CHINS.	25	DIM-WIT COUSIN	8
PALE				
	ITS PALE TENDRILOUS HORN.	37	CUTTINGS	8
	PALE BLOSSOMS, EACH BALANCED ON A SINGLE JOINTED STEM,	43	CARNATIONS	1
	GLAZING THE PALE HAIR, THE DUPLICATE GREY STANDARD FACES.	46	DOLOR	13
PALE-PINK				
	LILIES, PALE-PINK CYCLAMEN, ROSES,	39	WEED PULLER	12
PALLBEARERS				
	I MISS THE PALLBEARERS MOMENTOUSLY TAKING THEIR PLACES,	22	ROAD TO WDLAWN	5
PALM				
	YOUR PALM IS MOIST, YOUR MANNER FAR TOO JOLLY	25	DIM-WIT COUSIN	9
	WITH A PALM CAKED HARD BY DIRT,	45	MY PAPA'S WALTZ	14
	LET THE KISSES RESOUND, FLAT LIKE A BUTCHER'S PALM;	56	THE LOST SON	104
	MY THUMB OF A CHILD THAT NUZZLED IN MY PALM?--	227	MEADOW MOUSE	22
PALM-FULL				
	SIFTING IN A PALM-FULL OF FRESH LOAM,--	42	TRANSPLANTING	4
PALM-SWEAT				
	MY PALM-SWEAT FLASHES GOLD;	88	PRAISE TO END!	87
PANE				
	MIST DEEPENS ON THE PANE;	34	NIGHT JOURNEY	21
PANES				
	FROST MELTED ON FAR PANES;	57	THE LOST SON	145
PANS				
	WE ROMPED UNTIL THE PANS	45	MY PAPA'S WALTZ	5
PANTS				
	HE LEFT HIS PANTS UPON A CHAIR:	264	THREE EPIGRAMS	7
	WITH THAT HE HITCHED HIS PANTS AND HUMPED AWAY.	274	SUPPR W LINDSAY	50
PAPA				
	PAPA IS COMING!	57	THE LOST SON	143
	PAPA AND MAMMA	71	WHERE KNOCK IS	3
	PAPA THREW HIM BACK.	73	WHERE KNOCK IS	61
	I SAID TO PAPA;	73	WHERE KNOCK IS	77
PAPA'S				
	MY PAPA'S WALTZ	45	MY PAPA'S WALTZ	T
PAPA-SEED				
	WHAT'S THE TIME, PAPA-SEED?	72	WHERE KNOCK IS	20
PAPER				
	CHILDREN, THEIR BELLIES SWOLLEN LIKE BLOWN-UP PAPER BAGS,	48	JUDGE NOT	2
	AND SKIN LIKE PAPER.	73	WHERE KNOCK IS	79
	CARES ABOUT THE DANCE OF DEAD UNDERWEAR, OR THE SAD WALTZ OF PAPER	98	O, THOU OPENING	26
	AND THE SOUND OF PAPER TEARING.	104	OLD LADY'S WRDS	60
PAPER-CLIP				
	RITUAL OF MULTIGRAPH, PAPER-CLIP, COMMA,	46	DOLOR	7
PAPERS				
	MY PAPERS UP, BETWEEN	213	THE HAPPY THREE	6
PAPER-WEIGHT				
	NEAT IN THEIR BOXES, DOLOR OF PAD AND PAPER-WEIGHT,	46	DOLOR	2
PARALDEHYDE				
	THE MINIONS OF BENZEDRINE AND PARALDEHYDE,	169	FOURTH MEDITATN	37
PARALYTIC				
	THE PARALYTIC STUNNED IN THE TUB, AND THE WATER RISING,--	227	MEADOW MOUSE	28
PARAQUET				
	THE PASSENGER PIGEON, THE GREAT AUK, THE CAROLINA PARAQUET,	235	ALL MORNING	44
PARCEL				
	THIS FAIR PARCEL OF SUMMER'S	258	SONG (3)	1

	PAGE	TITLE	LINE
PARCHED			
MOVING, UNMOVING IN A PARCHED LAND, WHITE IN THE MOONLIGHT:	194	JOURNY INTERIOR	53
PARE			
WHO'D THINK THE MOON COULD PARE ITSELF SO THIN?	188	THE LONGING	30
PARK			
THERE WERE NO NIGHTS OF SLEEPING IN THE PARK.	28	THE FAVORITE	4
PARLORS			
THEMSELVES, THEIR PARLORS MUSTY AS A FUNERAL HOME.	5	PROGNOSIS	12
PARMENIDES			
PARMENIDES PUT NOTHINGNESS IN PLACE;	133	THE PURE FURY	10
PARSNIP			
OPEN LIKE A POOL, A LESSER PARSNIP,	209	HER LONGING	6
PART			
AND SOON A BRANCH, PART OF A HIDDEN SCENE,	11	LIGHT BRIGHTER	17
YOU'RE PART OF HIM; HE'S PART OF YOU	114	DINKY	19
YOU'RE PART OF HIM; HE'S PART OF YOU	114	DINKY	19
ARE PART OF WHAT SHE IS.	125	WORDS FOR WIND	88
A CHANCE? PERHAPS. BUT THE ROAD WAS PART OF ME, AND ITS DITCHES,	193	JOURNY INTERIOR	23
BUT THE HIND PART OF THE WORM WIGGLES THE MOST,	196	THE LONG WATERS	2
PART OF A HOUSE.	219	THE ABYSS	12
HIS DEEP-THROATED COOING PART OF THE EARLY MORNING,	234	ALL MORNING	2
PART OF THE LANDSCAPE.	234	ALL MORNING	14
PART OF ETERNITY,	238	THE TRANCED	24
PART OF A TREE STILL DARK, STILL, DEATHLY STILL,	248	THE TREE, BIRD	9
HE'S PART OF ONE, AS A MATTER OF COURSE.	264	THREE EPIGRAMS	12
PAUL BUNYAN IS PART RUSSIAN, DID YOU KNOW?--	274	SUPPR W LINDSAY	44
PARTAKE			
AND I KNEELED DOWN AND DID PARTAKE	270	GOB MUSIC	34
I DID PARTAKE OF IT, I DID PARTAKE OF IT.	270	GOB MUSIC	43
I DID PARTAKE OF IT, I DID PARTAKE OF IT.	270	GOB MUSIC	43
PARTICLES			
THE PARTICLES OF BEING LIE;	19	AGNST DISASTER	6
PARTICULAR			
A WAVE OF TIME HANGS MOTIONLESS ON THIS PARTICULAR SHORE.	47	DOUBLE FEATURE	9
THAT FINE FUMING STINK OF PARTICULAR KETTLES,	48	LAST WORDS	2
GROTESQUE, AWKWARD, HIS EXTENDED EYES LOOKING AT NOTHING IN PARTICULAR,	159	FIRST MEDITATN	63
PARTICULARS			
AS KNOWN PARTICULARS COME WHEELING BY,	8	THE SIGNALS	3
PARTING			
THE TIGHT GRAINS PARTING AT LAST.	37	CUTTINGS (LATE)	8
PARTLY			
THE LANDSCAPE STILL PARTLY BROWN:	58	THE LOST SON	151
PARTNER			
THE PARTNER	105	SIR JOHN DAVIES	ST
DO WHAT THE CLUMSY PARTNER WANTS TO DO!	106	SIR JOHN DAVIES	42
PARTRIDGE			
A PARTRIDGE DRUMMED; A MINNOW NUDGED ITS STONE;	241	THE SEQUEL	13
PARTS			
HER SEVERAL PARTS COULD KEEP A PURE REPOSE,	127	I KNEW A WOMAN	19
PASS			
WHAT WE HAD HOPED FOR HAD NOT COME TO PASS.	6	INTERLUDE	12
AND NOSTRILS WIDEN AS THEY PASS	14	COMING OF COLD	10
BEYOND THE MOUNTAIN PASS	34	NIGHT JOURNEY	20
SHALE LOOSENS. MARL REACHES INTO THE FIELD. SMALL BIRDS PASS OVER WATER.	64	SHAPE OF FIRE	11
WHEN THEY COME, DAZEDLY, TO THE PRETTY PASS	113	TO A LADY ED	11
PASSED			
SPEECH PASSED BETWEEN SMALL BIRDS;	167	HER BECOMING	65
WHO PASSED BY, ALONE.	208	THE APPARITION	4
WE PASSED THE ICE OF PAIN,	238	THE MOMENT	1
PASSENGER			
THE PASSENGER PIGEON, THE GREAT AUK, THE CAROLINA PARAQUET,	235	ALL MORNING	44
PASSING			
THE STRIP RESERVED FOR PASSING ONLY.	33	HIGHWAY: MICH	7
THOUGH ALL'S IN MOTION, WHO IS PASSING BY?	132	SENTENTIOUS MAN	19
PASSIONATE			
ASTONISHED INTO PASSIONATE REPOSE.	131	SENTENTIOUS MAN	18
PASSION'S			
PASSION'S ENOUGH TO GIVE	124	WORDS FOR WIND	47
PAST			
EYES, STARING PAST ANOTHER	7	ORDERS FOR DAY	15

		PAGE	TITLE	LINE
PAST (CONTINUED)				
WITH MOTHERS, SLEEP-HEAVY CHILDREN, STALE PERFUME, PAST THE MANAGER'S SMILE		47	DOUBLE FEATURE	3
PAST THE PASTURE OF FLAT STONES,		54	THE LOST SON	35
A CHILD STARES PAST A FIRE		130	THE OTHER	19
THEIR BLACK SHAPES BREAKING PAST;		158	FIRST MEDITATN	34
WHEN I WALK PAST A VAT, WATER JOGGLES,		173	WHAT TELL BONES	73
ALWAYS A SHARP TURN TO THE LEFT PAST A BARN CLOSE TO THE ROADSIDE,		193	JOURNY INTERIOR	25
AND ALL FLOWS PAST--		194	JOURNY INTERIOR	34
THE WATERS SWIRLING PAST THE TINY HEADLANDS.		202	THE ROSE	25
A PROTEST FROM THE PAST, A REMINDER.		234	ALL MORNING	5
MY PAST IS SLIDING DOWN THE DRAIN;		256	IN HYDROTHERAPY	11
ME STARING PAST MY FOOT,		262	FOLLIES OF ADAM	17
PAST ALDER LANE, AND WE GABBED THERE A WHILE.		274	SUPPR W LINDSAY	47
PASTURE				
PAST THE PASTURE OF FLAT STONES,		54	THE LOST SON	35
ON ITS WAY TO THE BACK PASTURE.		104	OLD LADY'S WRDS	53
PASTURES				
LAY ALL THE LONELY PASTURES OF THE DEAD;		106	SIR JOHN DAVIES	51
PATCH				
AND LIFT UP A PATCH, DARK-GREEN, THE KIND FOR LINING CEMETERY BASKETS,		40	MOSS-GATHERING	2
COMING DOWN ON A PATCH OF LAWN:		235	ALL MORNING	38
PATH				
UPON THE ORCHARD PATH, FOR SKINNED		14	COMING OF COLD	6
THEY LEAN OVER THE PATH,		39	ORCHIDS	1
A PATH WENT WALKING.		63	THE LONG ALLEY	33
THE PATH TELLS LITTLE TO THE SERPENT.		66	SHAPE OF FIRE	59
THIS TAIL HATES A FLAT PATH.		79	GIVE WAY, GATES	15
OR, POISONED, DRAGGING A WHITE SKEIN OF SPITTLE OVER A PATH--		151	SLUG	21
I REMEMBER WALKING DOWN A PATH,		162	I'M HERE	45
--OR THE PATH NARROWING,		193	JOURNY INTERIOR	11
I HAVE TAKEN, TOO OFTEN, THE DANGEROUS PATH,		220	THE ABYSS	21
OR WINDING PATH? THE EDGE IS WHAT I HAVE.		239	IN A DARK TIME	12
A DONKEY PATH LED TO A SMALL PLATEAU.		247	I WAITED	21
PATHOS				
THE UNALTERABLE PATHOS OF BASIN AND PITCHER,		46	DOLOR	6
PATIENCE				
HIS INSOLENCE COULD WEAR NO PATIENCE THIN.		28	THE FAVORITE	7
PAUL				
PAUL BUNYAN IS PART RUSSIAN, DID YOU KNOW?--		274	SUPPR W LINDSAY	44
PAUSE				
WHEN I PAUSE TO TALK TO A STONE,		215	HIS FOREBODING	9
PAUSED				
SHE PAUSED TO PREEN;		213	THE HAPPY THREE	24
PAUSING				
A SEA-WIND PAUSING IN A SUMMER TREE.		235	MANIFESTATION	8
PAVEMENT				
THE PAVEMENT SMOKES WHEN TWO CARS MEET		33	HIGHWAY: MICH	16
PAW				
THE BEAR, EQUIPPED WITH PAW AND SNOUT,		23	AMOROUS LADY	3
THAT BLOSSOMED IN SOOT; A BLACK CAT LICKING ITS PAW;		29	THE REMINDER	2
YES, A BEAR HAS TO FISH WITH HIS PAW, PAW, PAW.		117	LADY AND BEAR	19
YES, A BEAR HAS TO FISH WITH HIS PAW, PAW, PAW.		117	LADY AND BEAR	19
YES, A BEAR HAS TO FISH WITH HIS PAW, PAW, PAW.		117	LADY AND BEAR	19
A BEAR HAS TO FISH WITH HIS PAW."		117	LADY AND BEAR	20
I PAW THE DARK, THE SHIFTING MIDNIGHT AIR.		135	THE RENEWAL	16
PAWN				
SUBTRACT, AND PUT OURSELVES IN PAWN;		30	THE RECKONING	6
PAWS				
I CIRCLED ON LEATHER PAWS		47	THE RETURN	1
I'M HAPPY WITH MY PAWS.		60	THE LONG ALLEY	46
CALL OFF THE DOGS, MY PAWS ARE GONE.		61	THE LONG ALLEY	85
I LIKE SOFT PAWS.		72	WHERE KNOCK IS	42
--SHOULD SLEEP ON HIS PAWS.		99	O, THOU OPENING	72
PAY				
THEY THOUGHT ABOUT SATURDAY PAY,		46	PICKLE BELT	3
PAYS				
O FORTUNATE HE WHOSE MAMMA PAYS THE BILLS!		24	POETASTER	4
PEACE				
NOW HERE IS PEACE FOR ONE WHO KNEW		17	NO BIRD	1

	PAGE	TITLE	LINE
PEACH			
THE LATE PEACH YIELDS A SUBTLE MUSK,	14	COMING OF COLD	1
REACH ME A PEACH, FONDLING, THE HILLS ARE THERE.	61	THE LONG ALLEY	81
PEACHTREE			
FROM THE ONE BEAUTIFUL THING IN HER YARD, THE PEACHTREE;	223	ELEGY (2)	13
PEAK			
THE ELM TREE IS OUR HIGHEST MOUNTAIN PEAK;	13	PRAISE PRAIRIE	1
PEAKS			
MY DESIRE FOR THE PEAKS, THE BLACK RAVINES, THE ROLLING MISTS	196	THE LONG WATERS	9
PEANUTS			
PECKING AT CRUSTS AND PEANUTS, THEIR GREEN NECKS GLITTERING;	234	ALL MORNING	28
PEAR			
THE GARDEN SPIDER WEAVES A SILKEN PEAR	12	SLOW SEASON	5
THE WIND SHAKES OUT THE SCENT OF PEAR.	14	COMING OF COLD	12
PEARL			
A PEARL WITHIN THE BRAIN,	18	GENESIS	9
PEAR-TREE			
THE YOUNG FRUIT SWELL UPON THE PEAR-TREE BOUGH.	11	LIGHT BRIGHTER	16
PEBBLE			
SO BIBBLE WHERE THE PEBBLE IS.	75	I NEED, I NEED	32
MANY ASTOUNDS BEFORE, I LOST MY IDENTITY TO A PEBBLE;	88	PRAISE TO END!	88
WHAT'S GREATER, PEBBLE OR POND?	251	ONCE MORE, RND	1
PEBBLY			
AND THE LOW RIPPLES RUN OVER A PEBBLY SHORELINE,	198	THE LONG WATERS	62
OR WALK THE PEBBLY SHORE WITH THE HUMPBACKED HERON,	209	HER LONGING	14
PECK			
OR PERCH AND PECK AT LARGER FLOWER-CROWNS,	152	THE SISKINS	12
PECKED			
BUT WHEN SHE PECKED MY TOE,	213	THE HAPPY THREE	25
PECKING			
PECKING AT CRUSTS AND PEANUTS, THEIR GREEN NECKS GLITTERING;	234	ALL MORNING	28
PECKS			
A TOWHEE PECKS THE GROUND;	148	THE SMALL	3
PECULIAR			
WHAT'S THAT PECULIAR SMELL?	136	THE SENSUALISTS	14
OR PERHAPS WITH ANOTHER MIND, LESS PECULIAR;	200	THE FAR FIELD	43
PEDANTRY			
AND CHECK THE PEDANTRY	20	REPL TO CENSURE	3
PEE			
RAISE UP WHEN YOU WOULD PEE.	267	SAGINAW SONG	24
PEE-CULIAR			
WE BIDDLY'S ARE PEE-CULIAR BEARS.	117	LADY AND BEAR	7
PEEL			
AND THE BUNCHED LOGS PEEL IN THE AFTERNOON SUNLIGHT,	196	THE LONG WATERS	16
PEEP			
WE GROW INDIFFERENT TO DOG HOWLS, TO THE NESTLING'S LAST PEEP;	33	IDYLL	6
PEER			
IN MOVING-SLOW HE HAS NO PEER.	116	THE SLOTH	1
PELLUDIOUS			
AND NOW ARE WE TO HAVE THAT PELLUDIOUS JESUS-SHIMMER OVER ALL THINGS,	98	O, THOU OPENING	21
PEN			
I HATE THIS SENSUAL PEN;	136	THE SENSUALISTS	22
HAVING ESCAPED HER PEN,	213	THE HAPPY THREE	19
PENCILS			
I HAVE KNOWN THE INEXORABLE SADNESS OF PENCILS,	46	DOLOR	1
PENINSULA			
FROM THE SLOW SINKING OF THE ISLAND PENINSULA, THE CORAL EFFLORESCENCE,	196	THE LONG WATERS	22
OF DRIVING ALONE, WITHOUT LUGGAGE, OUT A LONG PENINSULA,	199	THE FAR FIELD	3
PENNY			
THE PENNY THAT USURPS THE POOR.	30	THE RECKONING	12
PENSIVE			
THE PENSIVE GNU, THE STAID AARDVARK,	23	AMOROUS LADY	1
A PENSIVE PETAL.	168	FOURTH MEDITATN	17
A PENSIVE MISTRESS, AND A YELPING WIFE.	246	THE MARROW	6
PEOPLE			
WHERE HAVE THE PEOPLE GONE?	230	THE STORM	8
PEPPERMINTS			
THE DRUNKEN SOLDIER, THE OLD LADY WITH HER PEPPERMINTS;	158	FIRST MEDITATN	30

		PAGE	TITLE	LINE
PERCH				
	OR PERCH AND PECK AT LARGER FLOWER-CROWNS,	152	THE SISKINS	12
	A FISH RAVEN TURNS ON ITS PERCH (A DEAD TREE IN THE RIVERMOUTH),	190	AT OYSTER RIVER	22
	WHERE IT LEANS, TILTED EAST, A PERCH FOR THE OSPREY,	197	THE LONG WATERS	36
	ONLY TO FLY OVER TO HIS FAVORITE PERCH, THE CROSS-BAR OF A TELEPHONE POLE;	234	ALL MORNING	9
PERCHED				
	PERCHED ON MANY SHELVES,	56	THE LOST SON	93
	SHUTTLING ITS THROAT WHILE PERCHED ON A WIND-VENT,	158	FIRST MEDITATN	40
PERFORM				
	PERFORM YOUR DUTIES WELL,	7	ORDERS FOR DAY	2
PERFUME				
	THE CARRIAGES REEKING WITH VARNISH AND STALE PERFUME.	22	ROAD TO WDLAWN	4
	WITH MOTHERS, SLEEP-HEAVY CHILDREN, STALE PERFUME, PAST THE MANAGER'S SMILE	47	DOUBLE FEATURE	3
PERHAPS				
	"ONE COAT OF PRIDE, PERHAPS A BIT THREADBARE;	21	THE AUCTION	5
	BITING THEMSELVES PERHAPS;	79	GIVE WAY, GATES	29
	IT'S QUEER ENOUGH HERE, PERHAPS.	81	SENSIBILITY! LA	12
	A CHANCE? PERHAPS. BUT THE ROAD WAS PART OF ME, AND ITS DITCHES,	193	JOURNY INTERIOR	23
	OR PERHAPS WITH ANOTHER MIND, LESS PECULIAR;	200	THE FAR FIELD	43
PERILS				
	ON THE PERILS OF TOO EARLY DRINK,--	269	GOB MUSIC	17
	ON THE PERILS OF TOO EARLY DRINK,	270	GOB MUSIC	45
PERIMETER				
	THE SHY PERIMETER	125	WORDS FOR WIND	83
PERIPHERAL				
	PERIPHERAL DIPPERS COME TO REST ON THE SHORT GRASS,	235	ALL MORNING	34
PERISHED				
	ALIVE AT NOON, I PERISHED IN HER FORM.	107	SIR JOHN DAVIES	94
PERISHES				
	THE EYE PERISHES IN THE SMALL VISION.	90	UNFOLD! UNFOLD!	42
PERISHING				
	BEYOND BECOMING AND PERISHING,	205	THE ROSE	102
PERMISSION				
	TO WHAT MORE VAST PERMISSION HAVE I COME?	173	WHAT TELL BONES	72
PERMITS				
	I TAKE THE LIBERTIES A SHORT LIFE PERMITS--	173	WHAT TELL BONES	90
PERPETUAL				
	THE WINDLESS PERPETUAL MORNING ABOVE A SEPTEMBER CLOUD.	43	CARNATIONS	7
	I HAVE MARRIED MY HANDS TO PERPETUAL AGITATION,	56	THE LOST SON	109
	SUCH AFFIRMATIONS ARE PERPETUAL.	135	THE RENEWAL	4
	A MADMAN STARING AT PERPETUAL NIGHT,	155	THE DYING MAN	49
	PERPETUAL BEGINNER,	171	WHAT TELL BONES	2
	BEWARE THOSE PERPETUAL BEGINNINGS,	171	WHAT TELL BONES	23
	ALL IN MY YARD, OF A PERPETUAL SUNDAY,	235	ALL MORNING	46
PERPETUALLY				
	PERPETUALLY RISING OUT OF MYSELF,	209	HER LONGING	20
PERPETUATE				
	EXISTENCE DARES PERPETUATE A SOUL,	173	WHAT TELL BONES	67
PERPLEX				
	--HOW NEEDLES AND CORNERS PERPLEX ME!	161	I'M HERE	12
	DO THESE ANALOGIES PERPLEX? A SKY WITH CLOUDS,	235	MANIFESTATION	6
PERPLEXED				
	AND HE, PERPLEXED;	46	PICKLE BELT	8
	I FIND MYSELF PERPLEXED. WHAT IS DESIRE?--	105	SIR JOHN DAVIES	26
PERSISTENT				
	THE HELIOTROPE, VEINED LIKE A FISH, THE PERSISTENT MORNING-GLORY,	197	THE LONG WATERS	41
PERSISTS				
	THE SELF PERSISTS LIKE A DYING STAR,	190	AT OYSTER RIVER	24
PERSUADE				
	INDIGNATION? LET ME PERSUADE MORE SLOWLY:	98	O, THOU OPENING	31
PERVERSE				
	TUGGING ALL DAY AT PERVERSE LIFE:	39	WEED PULLER	9
PETAL				
	LIGHT AS A PETAL FALLING UPON STONE.	165	HER BECOMING	12
	A PENSIVE PETAL.	168	FOURTH MEDITATN	17
PETALS				
	ROTTEN LEAVES OR YELLOWY PETALS,	42	OLD FLORIST	5
	DROWSING IN SOFT LIGHT, PETALS PULSING.	61	THE LONG ALLEY	76

	PAGE	TITLE	LINE
PETALS (CONTINUED)			
PETALS AND REFLECTIONS OF PETALS MIXED ON THE SURFACE OF A			
GLASSY POOL,	194	JOURNY INTERIOR	56
PETALS AND REFLECTIONS OF PETALS MIXED ON THE SURFACE OF A			
GLASSY POOL,	194	JOURNY INTERIOR	56
HER SHRIVELED PETALS FALLING	228	THE GERANIUM	11
PETROLEUM			
FETOR OF COCKROACHES, DEAD FISH, PETROLEUM,	187	THE LONGING	3
PHANTASIES			
HERO OF PHANTASIES AND CATCHER OF CHILLS,	24	POETASTER	1
PHASE			
THE RAT'S MY PHASE.	97	O, THOU OPENING	2
PHEASANT			
KILLED EVERY CAT THAT NEARED THEIR PHEASANT RUNS;	224	OTTO	28
PHEASANT-RUN			
AND THE TOM-CAT, CAUGHT NEAR THE PHEASANT-RUN,	199	THE FAR FIELD	21
PHILANDER			
PHILANDER	182	PHILANDER	T
A MAN NAMED PHILANDER S. GOO	182	PHILANDER	1
PHILOSOPHERS			
HEROES AND BEARS, AND OLD PHILOSOPHERS--	274	SUPPR W LINDSAY	42
PHILOSOPHICAL			
MADE FROM HIS TERROR AND DISMAY A GRAVE PHILOSOPHICAL			
LANGUAGE;	170	FOURTH MEDITATN	72
PHLOX			
OLD HEDGEROWS KEEP THE LEAVES; THE PHLOX,	15	COMING OF COLD	40
PHOBIAS			
INTRICATE PHOBIAS GROW	31	LULL	4
PHOEBE			
SWEET PHOEBE, SHE'S MY THEME:	123	WORDS FOR WIND	11
AND THE FAR PHOEBE, SINGING,	159	FIRST MEDITATN	86
PHOEBE NOT FAR AWAY	213	THE HAPPY THREE	30
PHOEBE'S			
THE PHOEBE'S SLOW RETREATING FROM ITS SONG,	245	THE DECISION	4
PHOENIX			
A PHOENIX, SURE OF MY BODY,	209	HER LONGING	19
PIANO			
THE BECHSTEIN PIANO, THE FOUR-POSTER BED,	32	SALE	10
PICK			
HOW HE COULD FLICK AND PICK	42	OLD FLORIST	4
A PICK LIKES TO HIT ICE.	76	I NEED, I NEED	54
IS IT A CASE OF JUST PICK AND CHOOSE?	183	THE WAGTAIL	2
PICKED			
THE BEAK OF FROST HAS PICKED THE BOUGH,	14	COMING OF COLD	23
I REMEMBER HOW THEY PICKED ME UP, A SPINDLY KID,	44	FRAU BAUMAN	26
AND PICKED AND PICKLED THE BEST, TO BE LEFT ON RICKETY			
DOORSTEPS.	223	ELEGY (2)	15
PICKEREL			
AND HER QUICK LOOK, A SIDELONG PICKEREL SMILE;	102	ELEGY FOR JANE	2
PICKLE			
PICKLE BELT	46	PICKLE BELT	T
EYES RIMMED WITH PICKLE DUST,	46	PICKLE BELT	10
PICKLED			
AND PICKED AND PICKLED THE BEST, TO BE LEFT ON RICKETY			
DOORSTEPS.	223	ELEGY (2)	15
PICNIC			
AND WE TURNED TO OUR PICNIC	232	THE THING	18
PICNICS			
MATCH-MAKERS, ARRANGERS OF PICNICS--	169	FOURTH MEDITATN	41
PICTURE			
A PICTURE WINDOW'S ONE YOU CAN'T	267	SAGINAW SONG	23
PIECE			
DEATH PIECE	4	DEATH PIECE	T
IT'S A PIECE OF A PRINCE I ATE.	86	PRAISE TO END!	48
A VISIT FROM HIM IS A PIECE OF PURE LUCK,	113	TO A LADY ED	6
OR AN OLD PIECE OF TWINE,	117	LADY AND BEAR	16
I'VE BECOME A STRANGE PIECE OF FLESH,	157	FIRST MEDITATN	15
NOW THAT'S A PIECE OF GOOD ADVICE	181	MONOTONY SONG	3
GRAVE, HIERATIC, A PIECE OF ASSYRIAN SCULPTURE,	234	ALL MORNING	10
PIECEMEAL			
I'M DYING PIECEMEAL, FERVENT IN DECAY;	149	IN LATE SUMMER	15
PIECES			
THE PIECES OF MY SPIRIT STREWN.	19	AGNST DISASTER	4

	PAGE	TITLE	LINE
PIECES (CONTINUED)			
LIKE PIECES OF SMOKED EEL OR RAW OYSTER,	151	SLUG	17
THE SMALL DEAD PIECES STICKING UNDER AN INSTEP;	151	SLUG	20
PIERCE			
LIGHT AIRS! LIGHT AIRS! A PIERCE OF ANGELS!	61	THE LONG ALLEY	77
SHE'S COME TO PIERCE A CLOUD!	261	THE CHANGELING	56
TO PIERCE A CLOUD.	261	THE CHANGELING	57
PIERCING			
THE LILY'S PIERCING WHITE,	197	THE LONG WATERS	39
AND THAT THIN CRY, LIKE A NEEDLE PIERCING THE EAR, THE INSISTENT CICADA,	204	THE ROSE	67
PIFFLEBOB			
I WISH I WAS A PIFFLEBOB	75	I NEED, I NEED	35
PIG			
YOU'RE BECOMING THAT HORROR, A TWO-LEGGED PIG	272	DUET	3
PIGEON			
MY MAIMED DARLING, MY SKITTERY PIGEON.	102	ELEGY FOR JANE	19
HERE IN OUR AGING DISTRICT THE WOOD PIGEON LIVES WITH US,	234	ALL MORNING	1
THE PASSENGER PIGEON, THE GREAT AUK, THE CAROLINA PARAQUET,	235	ALL MORNING	44
PIGEONS			
WASPS COME WHEN I ASK FOR PIGEONS.	92	I CRY, LOVE!	2
THEIR HEADS JOD-JODDING LIKE PIGEONS;	235	ALL MORNING	35
PIKE			
THE PIKE	233	THE PIKE	T
THE PIKE STRIKES.	233	THE PIKE	18
PILE			
WHOLE BEDS OF BLOOM PITCHED ON A PILE,	43	FLOWER DUMP	3
PILED			
LEAF-MOLD, MANURE, LIME, PILED AGAINST SLIPPERY PLANKS.	38	ROOT CELLAR	9
AS THE PILED ICE BREAKS AWAY FROM THE BATTERED SPILES,	191	AT OYSTER RIVER	55
THE GREAT LOGS PILED LIKE MATCHSTICKS.	222	THE ABYSS	96
PILING			
THE ICE PILING HIGH AGAINST THE IRON-BOUND SPILES,	191	AT OYSTER RIVER	50
PILLOW			
MY PILLOW WON'T TELL ME	208	THE APPARITION	1
WE LIE CLOSER ON THE GRITTY PILLOW,	231	THE STORM	38
PILLOWS			
I'M UNDONE BY THE FLIP-FLAP OF ODIOUS PILLOWS.	86	PRAISE TO END!	45
PIN			
WHEN GLORY FAILED, WE DANCED UPON A PIN.	106	SIR JOHN DAVIES	58
THE SCENE SHRANK TO A PIN.	167	HER BECOMING	68
I WENT FISHING WITH A PIN	269	GOB MUSIC	20
PINCH			
THE PINCH OF WHERE.	64	SHAPE OF FIRE	28
WHAT A WHELM OF PROVERBS, MR. PINCH!	89	UNFOLD! UNFOLD!	18
PINCHING			
PINCHING AND POKING MY THIN RIBS	44	FRAU BAUMAN	27
PINCHING-BACK			
OR PINCHING-BACK ASTERS, OR PLANTING AZALEAS,	42	OLD FLORIST	2
PINE			
A LIGHT WIND STIRS IN THE PINE NEEDLES.	168	FOURTH MEDITATN	24
THEIR WOODEN STORES OF SILVERY PINE AND WEATHER-BEATEN RED COURTHOUSES,	193	JOURNY INTERIOR	31
AND THE SEA-WINDS MOVE THROUGH THE PINE TREES,	196	THE LONG WATERS	18
THE BLUE JAY RASPING FROM THE STUNTED PINE.	196	THE LONG WATERS	28
AND THE PINE, WHOLE WITH ITS ROOTS, SINKS INTO THE ESTUARY,	197	THE LONG WATERS	35
BEYOND THE SEA PINE, THE OAK, THE WIND-TIPPED MADRONA,	203	THE ROSE	47
FROM A BURNT PINE THE SHARP SPEECH OF A CROW	246	THE MARROW	3
PINES			
THE AFTER-LIGHT UPON ICE-BURDENED PINES;	201	THE FAR FIELD	97
PINE-TREE			
AND THE HURRICANE DRIVES THE DEAD STRAW INTO THE LIVING PINE-TREE.	231	THE STORM	43
PINK			
WHO'S READY FOR PINK AND FRISK?	76	I NEED, I NEED	59
PINNED			
ONE DRIVER, PINNED BENEATH THE SEAT,	33	HIGHWAY: MICH	19
"YOU HAVE ME PINNED SO CLOSE;	136	THE SENSUALISTS	2
MY SHADOW PINNED AGAINST A SWEATING WALL.	239	IN A DARK TIME	10
PINS			
PLAYING WITH PAINTED PINS.	31	LULL	12
EACH CUSHION FOUND ITSELF A FIELD OF PINS,	143	SHIMMER OF EVIL	11
SO LONG ON GIN, BOBBIE PINS, HALF-SMOKED CIGARS, DEAD BEER,	228	THE GERANIUM	10

	PAGE	TITLE	LINE
PIPE-KNOCK			
PIPE-KNOCK.	57	THE LOST SON	140
PIPES			
ALL PULSE WITH THE KNOCKING PIPES	38	FORCING HOUSE	5
AS THE LIVE HEAT BILLOWS FROM PIPES AND POTS.	38	FORCING HOUSE	11
THEY STOOD ASTRIDE PIPES,	44	FRAU BAUMAN	16
AMONG THE TIN CANS, TIRES, RUSTED PIPES, BROKEN MACHINERY,--	199	THE FAR FIELD	17
THE LONG PIPES KNOCKED: IT WAS THE END OF NIGHT.	225	OTTO	39
HE PIPES, HE SQUEAKS, HE QUIVERS THROUGH HIS NOSE,--	264	THREE EPIGRAMS	5
PIPLING			
PIPLING	264	THREE EPIGRAMS	ST
PISSOIR			
--AND PISSOIR FRENCH?	272	DUET	14
PISTONS			
THE PISTONS JERK AND SHOVE,	34	NIGHT JOURNEY	25
PIT			
THIS FLAT LAND HAS BECOME A PIT	19	AGNST DISASTER	9
THE PIT	55	THE LOST SON	ST
WHEN YOU HIT THE DEEP PIT AT THE BOTTOM OF THE SWALE,	193	JOURNY INTERIOR	20
PITCH			
THE PLUM DROPS PITCH UPON THE GROUND,	14	COMING OF COLD	9
ILLUMINATION BROUGHT TO SUCH A PITCH	135	THE RENEWAL	20
AND THE FINCHES PITCH THROUGH THE AIR, TWITTERING;	152	THE SISKINS	7
I CAN'T LAUGH FROM A CRATER OF BURNING PITCH,	166	HER BECOMING	36
PITCHED			
WHOLE BEDS OF BLOOM PITCHED ON A PILE,	43	FLOWER DUMP	3
BEHOLD THE CRITIC, PITCHED LIKE THE CASTRATI,	264	THREE EPIGRAMS	1
PITCHER			
THE UNALTERABLE PATHOS OF BASIN AND PITCHER,	46	DOLOR	6
PITCHERS			
I AM UNDONE BY THE GURGLE OF BABIES AND PITCHERS,	255	LIGHT POEM	7
PITCHING			
THEN PITCHING AWAY IN HALF-FLIGHT,	200	THE FAR FIELD	34
THE PROW PITCHING EASILY UP AND DOWN,	203	THE ROSE	35
PITCHING LIGHTLY OVER THE HIGH HEDGEROWS, DEE-DEEING,	234	ALL MORNING	25
ALL THAT DIVING AND PITCHING AND SWOOPING.	255	LIGHT POEM	5
PITH			
THE CORE AND PITH OF THAT UGLY STORM,	41	BIG WIND	24
PITS			
LAST NIGHT I SLEPT IN THE PITS OF A TONGUE.	65	SHAPE OF FIRE	34
PITTED			
THE TOWNS WITH THEIR HIGH PITTED ROAD-CROWNS AND DEEP GUTTERS,	193	JOURNY INTERIOR	30
PITTING			
PITTING MY BREAST AGAINST THE RUSHING AIR,	209	HER LONGING	18
PITY			
GOD PITY THOSE BUT WANTON TO THE KNEES,--	106	SIR JOHN DAVIES	62
PLACE			
THE PLACE WHERE BUTTERNUTS ARE FOUND.	14	COMING OF COLD	11
THE LONG EYE NOTES THE MINNOW'S HIDING PLACE.	15	THE HERON	7
FOR SOMETHING IS AMISS OR OUT OF PLACE	16	THE BAT	9
THEN A BLEAK WASTED PLACE,	34	NIGHT JOURNEY	10
IT'S A COLD SCRAPE IN A LOW PLACE.	80	GIVE WAY, GATES	47
IN A SODDEN PLACE, ALL RAPS AND KNOCKS APPROVE.	93	I CRY, LOVE!	30
IS THAT THE PLACE TO GO?	99	O, THOU OPENING	76
I NEED A PLACE TO SING, AND DANCING-ROOM,	105	SIR JOHN DAVIES	4
A PLACE I SURELY DID LIKE TO GO	111	SQUEEZE-BOX	17
IT WAS PLACE AND SHOW AND ALSO RAN	112	SQUEEZE-BOX	28
I FIND HER EVERY PLACE;	130	THE OTHER	9
PARMENIDES PUT NOTHINGNESS IN PLACE;	133	THE PURE FURY	10
"THERE IS NO PLACE TO TURN," SHE SAID,	136	THE SENSUALISTS	1
I BROKE FROM THAT LOW PLACE	147	THE EXORCISM	26
OUT OF HER PLACE SHE COMES, A DOLPHIN ONE,	156	THE DYING MAN	80
IN THIS LAST PLACE OF LIGHT: HE DARES TO LIVE	156	THE DYING MAN	99
ANOTHER WAY AND PLACE IN WHICH TO CONTINUE;	159	FIRST MEDITATN	67
A LONGING FOR ANOTHER PLACE AND TIME,	162	I'M HERE	37
THE WHOLE PLACE SHOOK WHENEVER I GOT A CHILL--	163	I'M HERE	64
STILL LEANING TOWARD THE LAST PLACE THE SUN WAS.	163	I'M HERE	76
A SMALL PLACE ALL IN FLAME.	167	HER BECOMING	77
I DRINK MY TEARS IN A PLACE WHERE ALL LIGHT COMES,	170	FOURTH MEDITATN	78
IN THE LEAST PLACE OF ITS LIFE,	171	WHAT TELL BONES	5
NOW THE PLACE TO BEGIN	183	THE LIZARD	3
AT AN INTIMATE PLACE LIKE HIS GIZZARD.	183	THE LIZARD	7

	PAGE	TITLE	LINE
PLACE (CONTINUED)			
IN THE DARK AND LIGHT OF A DRY PLACE,	194	JOURNY INTERIOR	60
UNPERPLEXED, IN A PLACE LEADING NOWHERE.	195	JOURNY INTERIOR	73
THE MOTTLED TIGER, BEST IN THE CORNER OF A DAMP PLACE,	197	THE LONG WATERS	40
A VULNERABLE PLACE,	197	THE LONG WATERS	58
MY MIND MOVES IN MORE THAN ONE PLACE,	201	THE FAR FIELD	75
THERE ARE THOSE TO WHOM PLACE IS UNIMPORTANT,	202	THE ROSE	1
BUT THIS PLACE, WHERE SEA AND FRESH WATER MEET,	202	THE ROSE	2
STAYS IN ITS TRUE PLACE,	203	THE ROSE	41
BEAUTIFUL MY DESIRE, AND THE PLACE OF MY DESIRE.	204	THE ROSE	78
IN A PLACE OF MOTTLED CLOUDS, A THIN MIST MORNING AND EVENING.	221	THE ABYSS	77
AND MY THOUGHT FLIES TO THE PLACE BY THE BO-TREE.	222	THE ABYSS	100
LEAVING A PLACE FOR THE EYE TO REST,	233	THE PIKE	2
THAT PLACE AMONG THE ROCKS--IS IT A CAVE,	239	IN A DARK TIME	11
WHEN OPPOSITES COME SUDDENLY IN PLACE,	244	INFIRMITY	33
IN THE PLACE OF BEAUTIFUL STONES.	258	SONG (3)	7
IT WOULD BLOW THE PLACE APART,--	268	SAGINAW SONG	40
OH, THE SLOP-PAIL IS THE PLACE TO THINK	269	GOB MUSIC	16
OH, THE SLOP-PAIL IS THE PLACE TO THINK	270	GOB MUSIC	44
PLACES			
I MISS THE PALLBEARERS MOMENTOUSLY TAKING THEIR PLACES,	22	ROAD TO WDLAWN	5
THOUGH THE CROCUSES POKE UP THEIR HEADS IN THE USUAL PLACES,	24	VERNAL SENTIMNT	1
DESOLATION IN IMMACULATE PUBLIC PLACES,	46	DOLOR	4
THE EAR HEARS ONLY IN LOW PLACES.	59	THE LONG ALLEY	7
PLACES GREAT WITH THEIR DEAD,	154	THE DYING MAN	21
I HAVE GONE INTO THE WASTE LONELY PLACES	159	FIRST MEDITATN	74
FEARFUL OF HIGH PLACES, IN LOVE WITH HORSES;	162	I'M HERE	28
THERE ARE MANY DETOURS, WASHED-OUT INTERRUPTED RAW PLACES	193	JOURNY INTERIOR	2
WATCHING FOR DANGEROUS DOWN-HILL PLACES, WHERE THE WHEELS WHINED BEYOND EIGHTY--	193	JOURNY INTERIOR	19
PLAGUES			
WHO PLAGUES ME WITH HER SHAPE,	130	THE OTHER	2
PLAIN			
THE DANGEROUS FLOODED PLAIN	7	ORDERS FOR DAY	11
WHEN WE ARE WALKING ON A TREELESS PLAIN,	13	PRAISE PRAIRIE	7
ON A PLAIN DAY.	98	O, THOU OPENING	37
AS I WAS CROSSING A HOT HOT PLAIN,	114	DINKY	9
ON A WIDE PLAIN, BEYOND	124	WORDS FOR WIND	35
SHE KNOWS THE SPEECH OF LIGHT, AND MAKES IT PLAIN	129	SHE	11
I LACK PLAIN TENDERNESS.	139	PLAINT	6
A TREE ARISES ON A CENTRAL PLAIN--	150	IN LATE SUMMER	25
I RISE AND FALL IN THE SLOW SEA OF A GRASSY PLAIN,	194	JOURNY INTERIOR	42
BEFORE DESCENDING TO THE ALLUVIAL PLAIN,	200	THE FAR FIELD	65
FAR DOWN A BILLOWING PLAIN,	240	IN EVEING AIR	15
PLAINS			
ON THE JACKPINE PLAINS I HUNTED THE BIRD NOBODY KNOWS;	89	UNFOLD! UNFOLD!	22
PLAINT			
PLAINT	139	PLAINT	T
THE LUGUBRIOUSLY BEAUTIFUL PLAINT UTTERED AT REGULAR INTERVALS,	234	ALL MORNING	4
PLAINTIVE			
THE LONG PLAINTIVE NOTES FLOATING DOWN,	159	FIRST MEDITATN	87
PLANET			
BY PULLING OFF FLESH FROM THE LIVING PLANET;	40	MOSS-GATHERING	12
PLANGENT			
I HEAR A BEAT OF BIRDS, THE PLANGENT WINGS	173	WHAT TELL BONES	69
PLANK			
AND FELL IN THE STREAM STILL CLUTCHING A PLANK,	117	LADY AND BEAR	27
AND THE UP-SPRING OF THE PLANK WHEN A FOOT LEFT THE RUNWAY.	158	FIRST MEDITATN	47
PLANKS			
LEAF-MOLD, MANURE, LIME, PILED AGAINST SLIPPERY PLANKS.	38	ROOT CELLAR	9
PLANKS SUNK IN THE SAND.	62	FIELD OF LIGHT	3
PLANT			
FOR THE STEAM PLANT,	41	BIG WIND	7
WHEN YOU PLANT, SPIT IN THE POT.	76	I NEED, I NEED	53
PLANTING			
OR PINCHING-BACK ASTERS, OR PLANTING AZALEAS,	42	OLD FLORIST	2
PLANTS			
LIFTING THE YOUNG PLANTS WITH TWO FINGERS,	42	TRANSPLANTING	3
SCURRY OF WARM OVER SMALL PLANTS.	57	THE LOST SON	141
AND THE NEW PLANTS, STILL AWKWARD IN THEIR SOIL,	63	FIELD OF LIGHT	42
THE PLANTS WAVE ME IN, AND THE SUMMER APPLES;	88	PRAISE TO END!	86

	PAGE	TITLE	LINE
PLANTS (CONTINUED)			
AT ONE WITH THE PLANTS IN THE POND,	209	HER LONGING	3
HE POTTED PLANTS AS IF HE HATED THEM.	224	OTTO	9
PLASTER			
NEXT DOOR THERE IS A LOVE-NEST OF PLASTER BOARD AND TIN,	27	CLAIRVOY WIDOW	15
PLATE			
THERE'S BEANS ON EVERY PLATE,	267	SAGINAW SONG	4
THEY THROW YOU THROUGH THE FRONT PLATE GLASS	267	SAGINAW SONG	17
PLATEAU			
THERE'S NO FILTH ON A PLATEAU OF CINDERS.	59	THE LONG ALLEY	15
THE BLEAK WIND EATS AT THE WEAK PLATEAU,	157	FIRST MEDITATN	11
THAT GENTLES ON A SUNNY BLUE PLATEAU.	201	THE FAR FIELD	92
A DONKEY PATH LED TO A SMALL PLATEAU.	247	I WAITED	21
PLATITUDES			
PLATITUDES GARNISHED BEYOND A FOOL'S GAINSAYING;	5	PROGNOSIS	9
HIM WITH THE PLATITUDES AND RUBBER DOUGHNUTS,	65	SHAPE OF FIRE	30
PLATO			
AT TIMES MY DARLING SQUEAKS IN PURE PLATO.	133	THE PURE FURY	14
PLATONIC			
THE HOLIEST PLATONIC LOVE:	8	PRAYER	16
PLATTER			
OF VEAL SOAKED IN MARSALA AND LITTLE LARKS ARRANGED ON A LONG PLATTER,	232	THE THING	19
PLAY			
A FOOL CAN PLAY AT BEING SOLEMN	24	BEFORE STUDY	7
THE KIDS PLAY COPS AND ROBBERS, THE KIDS PLAY MUMBLEY-PEG,	27	CLAIRVOY WIDOW	9
THE KIDS PLAY COPS AND ROBBERS, THE KIDS PLAY MUMBLEY-PEG,	27	CLAIRVOY WIDOW	9
THE RICH CAN PLAY AT POLO, THE POOR CAN DO THE SHAG,	27	CLAIRVOY WIDOW	11
SIT AND PLAY	71	WHERE KNOCK IS	5
GO PLAY WITH YOUR NOSE.	75	I NEED, I NEED	44
LET'S PLAY BEFORE WE FORGET!	83	O LULL ME, LULL	20
THE BODY AND THE SOUL KNOW HOW TO PLAY	106	SIR JOHN DAVIES	47
DID EACH BECOME THE OTHER IN THAT PLAY?	106	SIR JOHN DAVIES	55
SMALL WAVES REPEAT THE MIND'S SLOW SENSUAL PLAY.	131	SENTENTIOUS MAN	13
A CHILD AT PLAY, A WIND-EXCITED BIRD.	165	HER BECOMING	23
IS MY OWN MIND AT PLAY.	215	HIS FOREBODING	15
THE MOTION OF THE MOON, AND WAVES AT PLAY,	235	MANIFESTATION	7
HE CAN PLAY THE FLITTER-FLAD;	266	FOR STEVENS	2
PLAYED			
I'VE PLAYED WITH THE FISHES	80	GIVE WAY, GATES	40
WE PLAYED A MEASURE WITH COMMINGLED FEET:	106	SIR JOHN DAVIES	31
WE PLAYED WITH DARK AND LIGHT AS CHILDREN SHOULD.	107	SIR JOHN DAVIES	66
OH, THE SYNCO SEPTET PLAYED FOR US THEN,	112	SQUEEZE-BOX	22
I PLAYED IN FLAME AND WATER LIKE A BOY	120	THE DREAM	28
SHE PLAYED IT QUICK, SHE PLAYED IT LIGHT AND LOOSE;	127	I KNEW A WOMAN	17
SHE PLAYED IT QUICK, SHE PLAYED IT LIGHT AND LOOSE;	127	I KNEW A WOMAN	17
AND THERE A GREAT BEAST PLAYED,	145	THE BEAST	6
PLAYFUL			
THE DESCENDANTS OF THE PLAYFUL TREE-SHREW THAT SURVIVED THE ARCHAIC KILLERS,	170	FOURTH MEDITATN	66
PLAYING			
PLAYING WITH PAINTED PINS.	31	LULL	12
THE SUN PLAYING ON LOAM,	92	I CRY, LOVE!	26
PLAYS			
PLAYS AS A MINNOW PLAYS,	101	LIGHT BREATHER	7
PLAYS AS A MINNOW PLAYS,	101	LIGHT BREATHER	7
PLAYS OVER THE DRY PODS,	160	FIRST MEDITATN	94
A SPIRIT PLAYS BEFORE ME LIKE A CHILD,	165	HER BECOMING	22
IN PUREST SONG ONE PLAYS THE CONSTANT FOOL	244	INFIRMITY	1
PLEASE			
SING ME A SLEEP-SONG, PLEASE.	71	WHERE KNOCK IS	10
PLEASE.	72	WHERE KNOCK IS	48
ENOUGH TO PLEASE A CLOUD!	98	O, THOU OPENING	50
MY POETRY-BOOK, IF YOU PLEASE,--	179	MYRTLE	7
PLEASED			
PLEASED AS A KNIFE.	81	SENSIBILITY! LA	25
BE A PLEASED ROCK	98	O, THOU OPENING	36
SWEET ALICE S. MORRIS, I AM PLEASED, OF COURSE,	113	TO A LADY ED	1
AND PLEASED TO MEET THE MOON.	124	WORDS FOR WIND	45
BEMUSED; PLEASED TO BE;	162	I'M HERE	31
PLEASES			
THE PRATTLE OF THE YOUNG NO LONGER PLEASES.	161	I'M HERE	9

	PAGE	TITLE	LINE
PLEASURE			
RECOUNT EACH CHILDHOOD PLEASURE: THE SKIES OF AZURE	5	TO MY SISTER	5
YOU CAN, WITH PLEASURE, BILL OR COO.	23	AMOROUS LADY	12
PLEASURE ON GROUND	65	SHAPE OF FIRE	41
HE GOT NO PLEASURE DOWN HIS HOLE.	115	THE SERPENT	8
HOW SLOWLY PLEASURE DIES!--	197	THE LONG WATERS	29
PLEASURES			
SUCH OWLY PLEASURES! FISH COME FIRST, SWEET BIRD.	87	PRAISE TO END!	71
PLEDGE			
I TOOK THE PLEDGE CARDS ON MY BIKE;	267	SAGINAW SONG	31
PLENTY			
FRIGIDAIRES SNORING THE SLEEP OF PLENTY,	48	LAST WORDS	4
PLINK			
HE CAN PLINK THE SKITTER-BUM;	266	FOR STEVENS	6
PLOTTED			
THEY TRELLISED THE SUN: THEY PLOTTED FOR MORE THAN THEMSELVES.	44	FRAU BAUMAN	25
PLOUGHING			
PLOUGHING WITH HER STIFF PROW,	41	BIG WIND	25
PLUM			
THE PLUM DROPS PITCH UPON THE GROUND,	14	COMING OF COLD	9
PLUME			
O PRIDE, THOU ART A PLUME UPON WHOSE HEAD?	188	THE LONGING	25
PLUMPING			
THEN PLUMPING IN THE BUNCHED ROOTS,	42	TRANSPLANTING	6
PLUMS			
THEIR EYES, RICH AS PLUMS, STARING FROM NEWSPRINT,--	48	JUDGE NOT	3
PLUNGE			
I TOSSED A STONE, AND LISTENED TO ITS PLUNGE.	120	THE DREAM	22
PLUNGED			
OF GREEN, OR PLUNGED TO MY ELBOWS IN THE SPONGY YELLOWISH MOSS OF THE MARSHES:	40	MOSS-GATHERING	8
PLUNGER			
AN OLD BRIDGE BELOW WITH A BUCKLED IRON RAILING, BROKEN BY SOME IDIOT PLUNGER;	194	JOURNY INTERIOR	32
PLUNGING			
A LINE OF ELMS PLUNGING AND TOSSING LIKE HORSES,	43	CHILD ON GRNHSE	6
OR TWO HORSES PLUNGING IN SNOW, THEIR LINES TANGLED,	158	FIRST MEDITATN	53
POACHERS			
ONCE WHEN HE SAW TWO POACHERS ON HIS LAND,	224	OTTO	14
POCKET			
THE HANDKERCHIEF TUCKED IN THE LEFT-HAND POCKET	29	THE REMINDER	5
POD			
A CRACKED POD CALLS.	64	SHAPE OF FIRE	6
PODS			
PLAYS OVER THE DRY PODS,	160	FIRST MEDITATN	94
POEM			
--AND SO LIKE MY POEM CALLED POEM.	113	TO A LADY ED	4
--AND SO LIKE MY POEM CALLED POEM.	113	TO A LADY ED	4
--AND RECITE HIM MY POEM CALLED POEM.	113	TO A LADY ED	8
--AND RECITE HIM MY POEM CALLED POEM.	113	TO A LADY ED	8
--OF ACTING MY POEM CALLED POEM.	113	TO A LADY ED	12
--OF ACTING MY POEM CALLED POEM.	113	TO A LADY ED	12
--AS I DANCE TO MY POEM CALLED POEM.	113	TO A LADY ED	16
--AS I DANCE TO MY POEM CALLED POEM.	113	TO A LADY ED	16
LIGHT POEM	255	LIGHT POEM	T
POET			
"WHO CALLED ME POET OF THE COLLEGE YELL?	274	SUPPR W LINDSAY	40
POETASTER			
POETASTER	24	POETASTER	T
POETESS			
NAMED FOR A POETESS,	213	THE HAPPY THREE	21
POETRY-BOOK			
MY POETRY-BOOK, IF YOU PLEASE,--	179	MYRTLE	7
POETS			
OR ENGLISH POETS WHO GREW UP ON GREEK	127	I KNEW A WOMAN	6
THESE POETS, THEY WRITE LIKE I SNEEZE!"	179	MYRTLE	12
POINT			
MY DREAM DIVIDED ON A POINT OF FIRE;	119	THE DREAM	5
A LION OF FLAME, PRESSED TO THE POINT OF LOVE,	170	FOURTH MEDITATN	73
A POINT OUTSIDE THE GLITTERING CURRENT;	201	THE FAR FIELD	72
WHILE ON A FAR POINT OF THE ROCKS	202	THE ROSE	27
OUR EYES FIXED ON A POINT OF LIGHT SO FINE	237	THE TRANCED	16

	PAGE	TITLE	LINE
POINT (CONTINUED)			
IN THE STILL POINT OF LIGHT	249	THE RESTORED	19
POINTING			
AND EVERYONE, EVERYONE POINTING UP AND SHOUTING!	43	CHILD ON GRNHSE	7
I WAS A FINGER POINTING AT THE MOON,	248	THE TREE, BIRD	5
POINTS			
THEN POINTS HIS HEAVY BILL ABOVE THE WOOD.	15	THE HERON	10
MY FACE ON FIRE, CLOSE TO THE POINTS OF A STAR,	172	WHAT TELL BONES	55
POISE			
CHERISH THE EYES THE PROUD INCREDIBLE POISE	5	TO MY SISTER	9
DOES HE POISE IN THE AIR,	183	THE WAGTAIL	4
THE FLESH TAKES ON THE PURE POISE OF THE SPIRIT,	191	AT OYSTER RIVER	38
POISED			
STOOD POISED ON THE STAIR,	56	THE LOST SON	90
THE YOUNG SNAKE, POISED IN GREEN LEAVES, WAITING FOR ITS FLY,	190	AT OYSTER RIVER	28
POISONED			
THE RUMINANT, REASON, CHEWS A POISONED CUD.	5	PROGNOSIS	8
OR, POISONED, DRAGGING A WHITE SKEIN OF SPITTLE OVER A PATH--	151	SLUG	21
POISONOUS			
BUT SNAKES, BOTH POISONOUS AND GARTER,	23	AMOROUS LADY	5
POKE			
THOUGH THE CROCUSES POKE UP THEIR HEADS IN THE USUAL PLACES,	24	VERNAL SENTIMNT	1
THE POKE OF THE WIND'S CLOSE,	84	O LULL ME, LULL	31
DON'T POKE MORE THAN TWICE	183	THE LIZARD	6
WHERE THE YELLOWISH PRONGS OF GRASS POKE THROUGH THE BLACKENED ASH,	196	THE LONG WATERS	15
POKED			
WHILE I POKED WITH A STICK AT A STONE NEAR A FOUR-PRONGED FLOWER,	232	THE THING	21
POKES			
AND POKES THE CRUMBLED COAL THE ASHES HID,	17	UNEXTINGUISHED	11
POKES THROUGH A MUSTY SHEATH	37	CUTTINGS	7
POKING			
PINCHING AND POKING MY THIN RIBS	44	FRAU BAUMAN	27
POKING ALONE IN MY GARDEN.	103	OLD LADY'S WRDS	34
POLE			
THE DEAD CROW DRIES ON A POLE.	80	GIVE WAY, GATES	48
AND THE SMALL STREET-LAMP SWINGING AND SLAMMING AGAINST THE LAMP POLE.	230	THE STORM	7
ONLY TO FLY OVER TO HIS FAVORITE PERCH, THE CROSS-BAR OF A TELEPHONE POLE;	234	ALL MORNING	9
POLISH			
THE INDIANS LOVED HIM, AND THE POLISH POOR.	225	OTTO	33
POLISHED			
I MISS THE POLISHED BRASS, THE POWERFUL BLACK HORSES,	22	ROAD TO WDLAWN	1
THE FURNITURE POLISHED AND POLISHED SO GRAND,	32	SALE	5
THE FURNITURE POLISHED AND POLISHED SO GRAND,	32	SALE	5
POLO			
THE RICH CAN PLAY AT POLO, THE POOR CAN DO THE SHAG,	27	CLAIRVOY WIDOW	11
POND			
THE FROG SCUM APPEAR ON THE POND WITH THE SAME FROTH OF GREEN,	24	VERNAL SENTIMNT	2
THE SOFT POND OF REPOSE;	53	THE LOST SON	13
RETURN THE GAZE OF A POND.	59	THE LONG ALLEY	30
A SWAN NEEDS A POND.	78	BRING THE DAY!	34
ONCE I WAS A POND.	80	GIVE WAY, GATES	60
FOR YOU, MY POND.	84	O LULL ME, LULL	33
THE RINGS HAVE GONE FROM THE POND.	85	PRAISE TO END!	13
I SEE A HERON PRANCING IN HIS POND;	106	SIR JOHN DAVIES	39
A RIPPLE WAKES THE POND.	121	ALL EARTH, AIR	5
ROCKING IT, LIKE A SUN-STRUCK POND,	163	I'M HERE	84
I NEED A POND WITH SMALL EELS. AND A WINDY ORCHARD.	164	I'M HERE	91
THE POND LAPSES BACK INTO A GLASSY SILENCE.	172	WHAT TELL BONES	50
THE STERN HIGH, DIPPING LIKE A CHILD'S BOAT IN A POND--	203	THE ROSE	37
AT ONE WITH THE PLANTS IN THE POND,	209	HER LONGING	3
OR FLOATED ON THE SURFACE OF A POND,	247	I WAITED	8
WHAT'S GREATER, PEBBLE OR POND?	251	ONCE MORE, RND	1
POND-EDGE			
BY THE MUDDY POND-EDGE, BY THE BOG-HOLES,	54	THE LOST SON	42
PONDS			
LIKE ELVERS IN PONDS,	50	THE MINIMAL	8

		PAGE	TITLE	LINE
PONDS (CONTINUED)				
PONDS WITH MOSS AND LEAVES FLOATING,	....	62	FIELD OF LIGHT	2
POND-WATER				
AS WHEN SILT DRIFTS AND SIFTS DOWN THROUGH MUDDY POND-WATER,		159	FIRST MEDITATN	60
POODLE				
IT WASN'T A POODLE.	....	77	BRING THE DAY!	16
SO FOOLISH AND TRUSTING, LIKE A SICK POODLE,	....	228	THE GERANIUM	3
POOF				
WHEN YOU SLURP AND GO, POOF!	....	180	GOO-GIRL	10
POOH				
YOU'D BETTER NOT LAUGH; AND DON'T SAY, "POOH!"	....	177	KITTY-CAT BIRD	18
POOL				
HAS DEEPENED TO THE BLACKNESS OF A POOL,	....	15	THE HERON	2
A POOL RIDING AND SHINING WITH THE RIVER,	....	168	FOURTH MEDITATN	9
A POOL TO A RIVER?	....	169	FOURTH MEDITATN	30
I NEED A POOL; I NEED A PUDDLE'S CALM.	....	171	WHAT TELL BONES	21
PETALS AND REFLECTIONS OF PETALS MIXED ON THE SURFACE OF A				
GLASSY POOL,	....	194	JOURNY INTERIOR	56
OPEN LIKE A POOL, A LESSER PARSNIP,	....	209	HER LONGING	6
THE BURNING LAKE TURNS INTO A FOREST POOL,	....	221	THE ABYSS	58
A FURRED, A ROCKY POOL,	....	233	THE PIKE	3
A THRASHING-UP OF THE WHOLE POOL,	....	233	THE PIKE	17
I STARE AND STARE INTO A DEEPENING POOL	....	244	INFIRMITY	3
POOLS				
THE WATER STORED IN NARROW POOLS ESCAPES	....	11	LIGHT BRIGHTER	11
POOR				
THE RICH CAN PLAY AT POLO, THE POOR CAN DO THE SHAG,	.....	27	CLAIRVOY WIDOW	11
THE PENNY THAT USURPS THE POOR.	....	30	THE RECKONING	12
SHE WAS THE SICKLE; I, POOR I, THE RAKE,	....	127	I KNEW A WOMAN	12
HAVE THEY SEEN, EVER, THE SHARP BONES OF THE POOR?	....	169	FOURTH MEDITATN	46
POOR MYRTLE WOULD SIGH, "SWEET MY COZ,	....	180	GOO-GIRL	1
TERROR OF COPS, BILL COLLECTORS, BETRAYERS OF THE POOR,--		223	ELEGY (2)	18
THE INDIANS LOVED HIM, AND THE POLISH POOR.	....	225	OTTO	33
POP-CORN				
I DAWDLE WITH GROUPS NEAR THE RICKETY POP-CORN STAND;	....	47	DOUBLE FEATURE	5
PORCH				
WE SIT IN THE PORCH SWING, CONTENT AND HALF ASLEEP.	......	33	IDYLL	8
BUT THIS MORNING THE SHOE-BOX HOUSE ON THE BACK PORCH IS				
EMPTY.	....	227	MEADOW MOUSE	20
PORTION				
WHAT'S THE WORST PORTION IN THIS MORTAL LIFE?	....	246	THE MARROW	5
PORTMANTEAU				
OR THAT OLD HARPY SECRETING TOADS IN HER PORTMANTEAU.	....	82	SENSIBILITY! LA	36
POSEIDON'S				
POSEIDON'S ONLY A HORSE,	....	263	FOLLIES OF ADAM	29
POSITION				
THEY JOCKEY FOR POSITION ON	....	33	HIGHWAY: MICH	6
POSSESS				
THE THINGS THE EYE OR HAND CANNOT POSSESS.	....	8	THE SIGNALS	10
LIP, BREAST AND THIGH CANNOT POSSESS	....	8	PRAYER	17
POSSESSED				
WHO WOULD BE HALF POSSESSED	....	240	IN EVEING AIR	3
POSSESSIONS				
I FOUND MY CHOICE POSSESSIONS ON THE LAWN.	....	21	THE AUCTION	2
WOMEN WHO BECOME THEIR POSSESSIONS,	....	169	FOURTH MEDITATN	39
POSSIBILITIES				
DEATH'S POSSIBILITIES;	....	153	THE DYING MAN	12
POSSIBLES				
THE POSSIBLES WE DARE!	....	137	LOVE'S PROGRESS	1
POSTURE				
HOWEVER GRACEFUL THE POSTURE.	....	172	WHAT TELL BONES	37
POT				
EACH CLUMP IN THE SHAPE OF A POT;	....	43	FLOWER DUMP	9
WHEN YOU PLANT, SPIT IN THE POT.	....	76	I NEED, I NEED	53
THE BOYS I KNEW WHEN I WENT TO POT;	....	111	SQUEEZE-BOX	2
SHE LEANING OUT OF HER POT TOWARD THE WINDOW.		228	THE GERANIUM	19
THREW HER, POT AND ALL, INTO THE TRASH-CAN,	....	228	THE GERANIUM	23
POTS				
AS THE LIVE HEAT BILLOWS FROM PIPES AND POTS.		38	FORCING HOUSE	11
TAMPING AND STAMPING DIRT INTO POTS,--	....	42	OLD FLORIST	3
POTTED				
HE POTTED PLANTS AS IF HE HATED THEM.	....	224	OTTO	9

	PAGE	TITLE	LINE
POTTING			
WHO LIVED ABOVE A POTTING SHED FOR YEARS.	224	OTTO	4
POUND			
OR POUND UPON A BRICK;	269	GOB MUSIC	4
POURED			
AND THE SWEAT POURED FROM MY FACE,	146	THE SONG	23
POURING			
AS AN OPAQUE VASE FILLS TO THE BRIM FROM A QUICK POURING,	67	SHAPE OF FIRE	93
POWDER			
THE VINES GRAYING TO A FINE POWDER.	159	FIRST MEDITATN	81
POWER			
SHOOK WITH A MIGHTY POWER BEYOND HIS WILL,--	107	SIR JOHN DAVIES	75
POWERFUL			
I MISS THE POLISHED BRASS, THE POWERFUL BLACK HORSES,	22	ROAD TO WDLAWN	1
PRACTICALLY			
THAT PRACTICALLY SPLIT THE TOP OF HIS THROAT.	115	THE SERPENT	22
PRAIRIE			
IN PRAISE OF PRAIRIE	13	PRAISE PRAIRIE	T
THE CEMETERY WITH TWO SCRUBBY TREES IN THE MIDDLE OF THE PRAIRIE,	194	JOURNY INTERIOR	35
AND THE BRONZE OF A DEAD BURDOCK AT THE EDGE OF A PRAIRIE LAKE,	197	THE LONG WATERS	42
PRAISE			
IN PRAISE OF PRAIRIE	13	PRAISE PRAIRIE	T
YOUR TEARS ARE NOT ENOUGH PRAISE,	54	THE LOST SON	31
PRAISE TO THE END!	85	PRAISE TO END!	T
ALL OPENINGS PRAISE US, EVEN OILY HOLES.	90	UNFOLD! UNFOLD!	40
IN HEAVEN'S PRAISE, I DREAD THE THING I AM.	156	THE DYING MAN	95
DARE I SPEAK, ONCE MORE, IN THE MONOTONY OF GREAT PRAISE,	166	HER BECOMING	32
IS THERE A WISDOM IN OBJECTS? FEW OBJECTS PRAISE THE LORD.	166	HER BECOMING	38
AND DELIGHT IN A LOVER'S PRAISE,	208	HER WORDS	4
SOME CANNOT PRAISE HIM: I AM ONE OF THOSE.	264	THREE EPIGRAMS	6
PRAISING			
AND, PRAISING CHANGE AS THE SLOW NIGHT COMES ON,	250	THE RIGHT THING	16
PRANCING			
I SEE A HERON PRANCING IN HIS POND;	106	SIR JOHN DAVIES	39
PRATING			
HIS LAUGHTER REDUCED THE SING-SONG OF PRATING,	29	THE GENTLE	7
PRATTLE			
KEEPER OF HAY. THAT'S A SPRATLING'S PRATTLE. AND DON'T BE THINKING YOU'RE	98	O, THOU OPENING	28
THE PRATTLE OF THE YOUNG NO LONGER PLEASES.	161	I'M HERE	9
PRAY			
I PRAY THEE, LORD, THAT I MAY CHOOSE	8	PRAYER	2
A PRISONER OF SMELLS, I WOULD RATHER EAT THAN PRAY.	173	WHAT TELL BONES	79
PRAYED			
THEY PRAYED THE COGS WOULD CREEP;	46	PICKLE BELT	2
PRAYER			
PRAYER	8	PRAYER	T
PRAYER BEFORE STUDY	24	BEFORE STUDY	T
PRECEDES			
PRIDE IN FINE LINEAMENTS PRECEDES A FALL;	131	SENTENTIOUS MAN	5
PRECEPT			
FLING ME A PRECEPT.	97	O, THOU OPENING	6
PRECISION			
AND THE PRECISION THAT FOR YOU WAS ULTIMATE LAW:	29	THE REMINDER	4
PREEN			
SHE PAUSED TO PREEN;	213	THE HAPPY THREE	24
PREFER			
I PREFER THE STILL JOY:	163	I'M HERE	86
TO PREFER A WINDOW TO A DOOR?	169	FOURTH MEDITATN	29
INSTEAD OF A DEVIL WITH HORNS, I PREFER A SERPENT WITH SCALES;	173	WHAT TELL BONES	77
PREMONITION			
THE PREMONITION	6	THE PREMONITION	T
PRESENCE			
WITH NO HINT OF YOUR PRESENCE IN A JUNGLE OF MASCULINE TOYS,	29	THE REMINDER	10
I FEEL HER PRESENCE IN THE COMMON DAY,	129	SHE	13
PRESENT			
KEEP FAITH WITH PRESENT JOYS REFUSE TO CHOOSE	5	TO MY SISTER	7
THE PRESENT FALLS, THE PRESENT FALLS AWAY;	248	THE TREE, BIRD	18
THE PRESENT FALLS, THE PRESENT FALLS AWAY;	248	THE TREE, BIRD	18

	PAGE	TITLE	LINE
PRESERVE			
REMAIN SECURE FROM PAIN PRESERVE THY HATE THY HEART.	5	TO MY SISTER	11
THEREFORE, O LORD, LET ME PRESERVE	8	PRAYER	19
PRESS			
TO PRESS PURE FRAGRANCE TO THE SOIL;	14	COMING OF COLD	19
PRESSED			
IS PRESSED TO NOISELESS GROUND.	17	NO BIRD	4
MY LIPS PRESSED UPON STONE.	146	THE SONG	29
A LION OF FLAME, PRESSED TO THE POINT OF LOVE,	170	FOURTH MEDITATN	73
PRESSURE			
WATCHING THE PRESSURE GAUGE	41	BIG WIND	10
AND THE MIDCHANNEL BEGINS CRACKING AND HEAVING FROM THE PRESSURE BENEATH,	191	AT OYSTER RIVER	49
PRESUMPTUOUS			
BUT I SACKED THE PRESUMPTUOUS HAG THE NEXT WEEK,	228	THE GERANIUM	25
PRETENDS			
PRETENDS HIS DEAD BUNION GIVES EXQUISITE PAIN.	29	THE GENTLE	4
PRETENSE			
YOU'RE A FAKE, YOUR'RE A FRAUD, YOU'RE A HOR-RID PRETENSE!	177	KITTY-CAT BIRD	3
PRETTY			
WHEN THEY COME, DAZEDLY, TO THE PRETTY PASS	113	TO A LADY ED	11
COMING BEHIND HER FOR HER PRETTY SAKE	127	I KNEW A WOMAN	13
PRETTY-BONES			
ARCH MY BACK, PRETTY-BONES, I'M DEAD AT BOTH ENDS.	85	PRAISE TO END!	9
PRICKLE-ME			
PRICKLE-ME, TICKLE-ME, CLOSE STEMS.	85	PRAISE TO END!	6
PRICKLES			
THAT PRICKLES MY COARSE SKIN.	271	THE REPLY	4
PRICKLING			
PRICKLING WITH ALL THE ITCHES	46	PICKLE BELT	11
PRICKLING PURE WISHES WITH CONFUSION'S IRE;	143	SHIMMER OF EVIL	12
PRIDE			
THE SCHEME WITHOUT PURPOSE; PRIDE IN A FURNISHED ROOM;	5	PROGNOSIS	10
"ONE COAT OF PRIDE, PERHAPS A BIT THREADBARE;	21	THE AUCTION	5
OR WAS THAT IN A BOOK? I THINK WITH PRIDE:	105	SIR JOHN DAVIES	9
PRIDE IN FINE LINEAMENTS PRECEDES A FALL;	131	SENTENTIOUS MAN	5
O PRIDE, THOU ART A PLUME UPON WHOSE HEAD?	188	THE LONGING	25
PRIMAL			
WITHIN THIS PRIMAL ELEMENT	256	IN HYDROTHERAPY	7
PRIMEVAL			
UNDER PRIMEVAL STONE.	50	THE CYCLE	18
PRIMORDIAL			
I WANT THE OLD RAGE, THE LASH OF PRIMORDIAL MILK!	56	THE LOST SON	107
PRINCE			
YOU'VE SEEN ME, PRINCE OF STINKS,	82	SENSIBILITY! LA	32
IT'S A PIECE OF A PRINCE I ATE.	86	PRAISE TO END!	48
A PRINCE OF SMALL BEGINNINGS, ENDURING THE SLOW STRETCHES OF CHANGE,	170	FOURTH MEDITATN	70
HE'S IMAGINATION'S PRINCE:	266	FOR STEVENS	5
PRINCIPLE			
LAST NIGHT I DREAMT OF A JAUNTIER PRINCIPLE OF ORDER;	165	HER BECOMING	30
PRINT			
O PRINT IT, MY DEAR, DO PUBLISH IT, YES,	113	TO A LADY ED	9
PRISON			
SOME ARE IN PRISON; SOME ARE DEAD;	225	THE CHUMS	1
PRISONER			
A PRISONER OF SMELLS, I WOULD RATHER EAT THAN PRAY.	173	WHAT TELL BONES	79
PRISONERS			
THEY ARE THE PRISONERS OF SPEED	33	HIGHWAY: MICH	14
TIME-HARRIED PRISONERS OF SHALL AND WILL--	250	THE RIGHT THING	2
PRIVACY			
INVADE THEIR PRIVACY OF THOUGHT.	25	VERSE W ALLUSNS	6
PRIVATE			
WILL TURN ITS PRIVATE SUBSTANCE INTO GREEN,	11	LIGHT BRIGHTER	19
PRIVILEGE			
THE SOUL'S PRIVILEGE?	211	SONG (1)	6
PRIVILEGED			
SOMETIMES THE BLOOD IS PRIVILEGED TO GUESS	8	THE SIGNALS	9
PRIVY			
I WAS PRIVY TO OILY FUNGUS AND THE ALGAE OF STANDING WATER;	89	UNFOLD! UNFOLD!	25
PROBE			
LET OTHERS PROBE THE MYSTERY IF THEY CAN.	250	THE RIGHT THING	1

		PAGE	TITLE	LINE
PROBING				
PROBING THE SQUASH,	....	223	ELEGY (2)	21
PROCESSION				
I CAN'T LAUGH AT A PROCESSION OF DOGS.	....	64	SHAPE OF FIRE	13
PROCLAIM				
I PROCLAIM ONCE MORE A CONDITION OF JOY.	....	92	I CRY, LOVE!	28
PRODIGIOUS				
(BUT WHAT PRODIGIOUS MOWING WE DID MAKE).	....	127	I KNEW A WOMAN	14
PRODUCTION				
THE DRIVERS FROM PRODUCTION LINES	....	33	HIGHWAY: MICH	8
PROFESSORS				
PROFESSORS ARE CONDONING THE CULTURAL LAG.	....	27	CLAIRVOY WIDOW	12
PROFFERED				
I NIBBLED MEEKLY FROM HER PROFFERED HAND;	....	127	I KNEW A WOMAN	11
PROFITS				
ALL PROFITS DISAPPEAR: THE GAIN	....	30	THE RECKONING	1
PROGNOSIS				
PROGNOSIS	....	5	PROGNOSIS	T
PROGRESS				
THE PROGRESS OF THE JADED. MILE	....	33	HIGHWAY: MICH	2
LOVE'S PROGRESS	....	137	LOVE'S PROGRESS	T
PROMISE				
AND I HAVE MADE A PROMISE TO MY EARS	....	105	SIR JOHN DAVIES	5
IS PAIN A PROMISE? I WAS SCHOOLED IN PAIN,	....	132	SENTENTIOUS MAN	31
PRONE				
THE STEM THAT HOLDS THE BEE IS PRONE;	....	15	COMING OF COLD	39
PRONGS				
WHERE THE YELLOWISH PRONGS OF GRASS POKE THROUGH THE				
BLACKENED ASH,	....	196	THE LONG WATERS	15
PROOF				
THE ONLY THING WE'D HAVE FOR PROOF	....	178	THE CEILING	3
PROPER				
HE COULDN'T FIND A PROPER WIFE;	....	115	THE SERPENT	6
WHAT'S NOT A PROPER FOOL.	....	267	SAGINAW SONG	30
PROPINQUITY				
O RARE PROPINQUITY!--	....	137	LOVE'S PROGRESS	2
PROPINQUITY'S				
PROPINQUITY'S A HARSH MASTER;	....	259	SONG (3)	37
PROPOUNDED				
AND VARIOUS MEASURES PROPOUNDED	....	115	THE SERPENT	12
PROSE				
AND THE STYLE OF YOUR PROSE GROWING LIMPER AND LIMPER.	...	23	ACADEMIC	4
PROTECT				
MNETHA, MOTHER OF HAR, PROTECT ME	....	196	THE LONG WATERS	20
PROTECTING				
PROTECTING THE SEA-CLIFFS.	....	209	HER LONGING	23
PROTEST				
A PROTEST FROM THE PAST, A REMINDER.	....	234	ALL MORNING	5
PROUD				
CHERISH THE EYES THE PROUD INCREDIBLE POISE	......	5	TO MY SISTER	9
PROVERBS				
WHAT A WHELM OF PROVERBS, MR. PINCH!	....	89	UNFOLD! UNFOLD!	18
PROVIDES				
PROVIDES.	....	80	GIVE WAY, GATES	62
THE AIR, THE AIR PROVIDES.	....	83	O LULL ME, LULL	18
PROW				
HIS THOUGHT IS TIED, THE CURVING PROW	....	4	DEATH PIECE	5
PLOUGHING WITH HER STIFF PROW,	....	41	BIG WIND	25
THE PROW PITCHING EASILY UP AND DOWN,	....	203	THE ROSE	35
PROWLING				
A MAN'S A BEAST PROWLING IN HIS OWN HOUSE,	....	133	THE PURE FURY	17
PROXIMITY				
NIGHT I EMBRACE, A DEAR PROXIMITY.	....	240	IN EVEING AIR	18
PRUSSIAN				
A PRUSSIAN WHO LEARNED EARLY TO BE RUDE	....	224	OTTO	2
HE WAS A PRUSSIAN THROUGH AND THROUGH	....	268	SAGINAW SONG	52
PSYCHE				
THE PSYCHE WRITHING AND SQUIRMING IN HEAVY WOOLEN,--	.....	48	LAST WORDS	5
PUBLIC				
DESOLATION IN IMMACULATE PUBLIC PLACES,	....	46	DOLOR	4
PUBLISH				
O PRINT IT, MY DEAR, DO PUBLISH IT. YES.	....	113	TO A LADY ED	9

	PAGE	TITLE	LINE
PUDDLE'S			
I NEED A POOL; I NEED A PUDDLE'S CALM.	171	WHAT TELL BONES	21
PUFF			
LOOK AT HIM PUFF. HE'S TRYING TO TALK.	73	WHERE KNOCK IS	60
PULL			
MUST PULL OFF CLOTHES	65	SHAPE OF FIRE	49
YOU MUSTN'T PULL IT MORE THAN TWICE,	181	MONOTONY SONG	2
PULLED			
AND PULLED THE GREEN SHADE AGAINST MORNING SUN.	29	THE REMINDER	8
WHERE THE FIREMAN PULLED OUT ROSES,	57	THE LOST SON	132
STAYED BY WHAT WAS, AND PULLED BY WHAT WOULD BE.	129	SHE	16
PULLER			
WEED PULLER	39	WEED PULLER	T
PULLING			
BY PULLING OFF FLESH FROM THE LIVING PLANET;	40	MOSS-GATHERING	12
INACCESSIBLE, THE BOAT ALWAYS PULLING OUT	158	FIRST MEDITATN	50
PULLMAN			
AND FROM MY PULLMAN BERTH	34	NIGHT JOURNEY	3
PULPY			
PULPY STEMS, RANK, SILO-RICH,	38	ROOT CELLAR	8
PULSE			
HIS PULSE BEAT IS SO SLOW WE THINK HIM DEAD.	16	THE BAT	4
HAPPY ALONE IN HIS BEDROOM COUNTING HIS PULSE.	24	POETASTER	3
ALL PULSE WITH THE KNOCKING PIPES	38	FORCING HOUSE	5
THE OLD STALK STILL HAS A PULSE;	99	O, THOU OPENING	52
STARING AT A TREE, I FELT THE PULSE OF A STONE.	101	THE VISITANT	22
MY MARROW BEAT AS WILDLY AS MY PULSE.	106	SIR JOHN DAVIES	36
A PULSE BEYOND NOTHINGNESS,	171	WHAT TELL BONES	6
PULSED			
THE LONG NOON PULSED AWAY,	128	THE VOICE	23
AND PULSED ITS WINGS UPON THE DUSTY GROUND--	243	THE MOTION	3
PULSELESS			
I KNOW THE BACK-STREAM'S JOY, AND THE STONE'S ETERNAL PULSELESS LONGING.	88	PRAISE TO END!	82
PULSES			
THAT PULSES UNDIMINISHED NOW	22	SILENCE	2
PULSING			
DROWSING IN SOFT LIGHT, PETALS PULSING.	61	THE LONG ALLEY	76
THE FERNS HAD THEIR WAYS, AND THE PULSING LIZARDS,	63	FIELD OF LIGHT	41
IN THE WINTER-WASP, PULSING ITS WINGS IN THE SUNLIGHT;	88	PRAISE TO END!	92
ACROSS HER PULSING THROAT;	123	WORDS FOR WIND	22
OR THESE INSECTS PULSING NEAR MY SKIN,	171	WHAT TELL BONES	26
I CAN SEE THAT BY THE DISTENDED PULSING MIDDLE;	226	THE LIZARD	2
PUMPED			
AND PUMPED A SHOULDER FULL OF CORTISONE;	244	INFIRMITY	10
PUMPING			
PUMPING THE STALE MIXTURE	41	BIG WIND	8
PUMPKINS			
AND PUMPKINS SWEAT A BITTER OIL.	14	COMING OF COLD	17
PUNCH			
AND AFTER EXCHANGING A PUNCH OR TWO,	111	SQUEEZE-BOX	5
PUNGENCE			
DISTILLS A PUNGENCE OF ITS OWN;	14	COMING OF COLD	16
PUPILS			
OUR PUPILS WIDENED WITH UNNATURAL NIGHT,	6	INTERLUDE	7
PUPPIES			
ALL HAVE PUPPIES.	71	WHERE KNOCK IS	8
PUPPY			
WRIGGLING LIKE A MINISCULE PUPPY.	227	MEADOW MOUSE	11
PURE			
IN LANGUAGE STRICT AND PURE.	3	OPEN HOUSE	15
TO PRESS PURE FRAGRANCE TO THE SOIL;	14	COMING OF COLD	19
I WAS PURE AS A WORM ON A LEAF; I CHERISHED THE MOLD'S CHILDREN.	89	UNFOLD! UNFOLD!	27
OH, WHEN SHE WAS SAD, SHE CAST HERSELF DOWN INTO SUCH A PURE DEPTH,	102	ELEGY FOR JANE	10
SUMMON A VISION AND DECLARE IT PURE.	107	SIR JOHN DAVIES	78
A VISIT FROM HIM IS A PIECE OF PURE LUCK,	113	TO A LADY ED	6
HER SEVERAL PARTS COULD KEEP A PURE REPOSE,	127	I KNEW A WOMAN	19
THE PURE FURY	133	THE PURE FURY	T
THE PURE ADMIRE THE PURE, AND LIVE ALONE;	133	THE PURE FURY	8
THE PURE ADMIRE THE PURE, AND LIVE ALONE;	133	THE PURE FURY	8
AT TIMES MY DARLING SQUEAKS IN PURE PLATO.	133	THE PURE FURY	14

	PAGE	TITLE	LINE
PURE (CONTINUED)			
WHEN THE PURE FURY FIRST RAGED IN HIS HEAD	133	THE PURE FURY	20
A WOMAN STOOD, PURE AS A BRIDE,	136	THE SENSUALISTS	9
PRICKLING PURE WISHES WITH CONFUSION'S IRE;	143	SHIMMER OF EVIL	12
AS IF PURE BEING WOKE,	147	THE EXORCISM	5
THE SLACK FACE OF THE DISMAL PURE INANE?	149	IN LATE SUMMER	10
THE PURE, SENSUOUS FORM.	150	SNAKE	11
WHAT SENSUAL EYE CAN KEEP AN IMAGE PURE,	154	THE DYING MAN	43
THE MOON, A PURE ISLAMIC SHAPE, LOOKED DOWN.	166	HER BECOMING	55
I HUM IN PURE VIBRATION, LIKE A SAW.	167	HER BECOMING	89
AT THE EDGE OF THE FIELD WAITING FOR THE PURE MOMENT;	168	FOURTH MEDITATN	3
O TO BE DELIVERED FROM THE RATIONAL INTO THE REALM OF PURE SONG,	172	WHAT TELL BONES	54
THE FLESH TAKES ON THE PURE POISE OF THE SPIRIT,	191	AT OYSTER RIVER	38
THE PURE SERENE OF MEMORY IN ONE MAN,--	201	THE FAR FIELD	101
SIGHED OUT HER PURE RELIEF	213	THE HAPPY THREE	3
I KNOW THE PURITY OF PURE DESPAIR,	239	IN A DARK TIME	9
PURE AIMLESSNESS PURSUED AND YET PURSUED	241	THE SEQUEL	3
LIGHT ON ITS ROUNDS, A PURE EXTREME OF LIGHT	244	INFIRMITY	14
UNTIL WE ARE PURE SPIRIT AT THE END.	244	INFIRMITY	36
AND EVERY SNAIL DIPPED TOWARD ME ITS PURE HORN.	248	THE TREE, BIRD	2
HOW PURE THE MOTION OF THE RISING DAY,	248	THE TREE, BIRD	19
THUS I ENDURE THIS LAST PURE STRETCH OF JOY,	248	THE TREE, BIRD	22
HER HEAVEN-SENSE PURE AS A STONE.	260	THE CHANGELING	11
A COLOR PURE, O PURE AS GOLD,	269	GOB MUSIC	26
A COLOR PURE, O PURE AS GOLD,	269	GOB MUSIC	26
AS ROUND AND PURE AS THE MOON,	271	THE REPLY	8
PURELY			
EACH VISION PURELY, PURELY WAS ITS OWN:	143	SHIMMER OF EVIL	4
EACH VISION PURELY, PURELY WAS ITS OWN:	143	SHIMMER OF EVIL	4
PUREST			
THIS SINGLE TREE TURNS INTO PUREST FLAME.	242	THE SEQUEL	28
IN PUREST SONG ONE PLAYS THE CONSTANT FOOL	244	INFIRMITY	1
PURE-WHITE			
HER PURE-WHITE FEATHERINESS	213	THE HAPPY THREE	23
PURGATORIAL			
DANTE ATTAINED THE PURGATORIAL HILL,	107	SIR JOHN DAVIES	73
AND PURGATORIAL IRE;	216	HER WRATH	2
PURIFIED			
FOR WATER MOVES UNTIL IT'S PURIFIED,	132	SENTENTIOUS MAN	41
PURITY			
I KNOW THE PURITY OF PURE DESPAIR,	239	IN A DARK TIME	9
PURPLE			
THE SPIKEY PURPLE BUSHES IN THE WINDING DRY CREEK BED--	194	JOURNY INTERIOR	37
PURPOSE			
THE SCHEME WITHOUT PURPOSE; PRIDE IN A FURNISHED ROOM;	5	PROGNOSIS	10
SEEKING IN MY OWN WAY, ETERNAL PURPOSE;	168	FOURTH MEDITATN	2
PURSED			
HER FULL LIPS PURSED, THE ERRANT NOTE TO SEIZE;	127	I KNEW A WOMAN	16
PURSE-PROUD			
ONCE ON RETURNING HOME, PURSE-PROUD AND HALE,	21	THE AUCTION	1
PURSUE			
WHEN AMOROUS ARTS WE WOULD PURSUE,	23	AMOROUS LADY	11
LIQUIDS PURSUE ME, NOTES AND TREMORS:	255	LIGHT POEM	6
PURSUED			
PURE AIMLESSNESS PURSUED AND YET PURSUED	241	THE SEQUEL	3
PURE AIMLESSNESS PURSUED AND YET PURSUED	241	THE SEQUEL	3
PURSUERS			
THEN THROWING ITSELF UP AND AWAY FROM THE IMPLACABLE SWIFT PURSUERS,	232	THE THING	6
PURSUING			
THERE ARE NO PURSUING FORMS, FACES ON WALLS:	159	FIRST MEDITATN	78
PURSUIT			
IN ONE STREAK OF PURSUIT.	232	THE THING	12
PUSH			
A BOY WHO HAD GUMPTION AND PUSH	182	BOY AND BUSH	1
PUSHING			
A SEED PUSHING ITSELF BEYOND ITSELF,	235	MANIFESTATION	3
PUT			
I CANNOT PUT MY GLANCE UPON THEM TIGHT.	8	THE SIGNALS	8
UNTIL CLEAR EYES PUT ON THE LOOK OF SLEEP.	12	SLOW SEASON	4
I WOULD PUT OFF MYSELF AND FLEE	24	BEFORE STUDY	5
SUBTRACT, AND PUT OURSELVES IN PAWN;	30	THE RECKONING	6

	PAGE	TITLE	LINE
PUT (CONTINUED)			
CUT STEMS STRUGGLING TO PUT DOWN FEET,	37	CUTTINGS (LATE)	2
WHO PUT THE MOSS THERE?	55	THE LOST SON	64
PUT YOUR FINGER IN YOUR FACE,	75	I NEED, I NEED	25
MAMMA! PUT ON YOUR DARK HOOD;	82	SENSIBILITY! LA	37
PARMENIDES PUT NOTHINGNESS IN PLACE;	133	THE PURE FURY	10
TO FOOLS AND FRAUDS: HE DOES NOT PUT ON AIRS	224	OTTO	3
WHEN I PUT HER OUT, ONCE, BY THE GARBAGE PAIL,	228	THE GERANIUM	1
WHAT WE PUT DOWN, MUST WE TAKE UP AGAIN?	243	THE MOTION	11
NOR COULD I PUT THAT SOUND OUT OF MY MIND,	245	THE DECISION	5
PUTS			
IF SHE BUT SIGHS, A BIRD PUTS OUT ITS TONGUE.	129	SHE	3
AND THE IVY-BRANCH, CAST TO THE GROUND, PUTS DOWN ROOTS INTO THE SAWDUST,	197	THE LONG WATERS	34
WHEN THE LADIES' GUILD PUTS ON A FEED,	267	SAGINAW SONG	3
PUTTING			
PUTTING EGG IN YOUR SHOE	180	GOO-GIRL	3
PUTTY			
MY FEET CRACKLING SPLINTERS OF GLASS AND DRIED PUTTY,	43	CHILD ON GRNHSE	2
QUAGMIRE			
OR TO SINK DOWN TO THE HIPS IN A MOSSY QUAGMIRE;	200	THE FAR FIELD	44
QUAIL			
I QUAIL, LEAN TO BEGINNINGS, SHEATH-WET.	37	CUTTINGS (LATE)	11
WITH TOWHEES, FINCHES, CHICKADEES, CALIFORNIA QUAIL, WOOD DOVES,	235	ALL MORNING	40
QUAILS			
AND THE TERRIBLE HUNGER FOR OBJECTS QUAILS ME:	220	THE ABYSS	32
QUAKE			
"THE BED ITSELF BEGINS TO QUAKE,	136	THE SENSUALISTS	21
QUAKER			
A LITTLE QUAKER, THE WHOLE BODY OF HIM TREMBLING,	227	MEADOW MOUSE	6
QUAKING			
ON THE QUAKING BUTCHER.	223	ELEGY (2)	23
FLUTTER OF WINGS AND SEEDS QUAKING,	255	LIGHT POEM	3
QUARRY'S			
FROM THE QUARRY'S WEAK CRY.	236	SONG (2)	4
QUARTER			
FOR SHE ASKED NO QUARTER AND GAVE NONE,	223	ELEGY (2)	7
QUARTS			
YOU DRINK UP IN QUARTS:	180	GOO-GIRL	6
QUARTZ			
MOTHER OF QUARTZ, YOUR WORDS WRITHE INTO MY EAR.	65	SHAPE OF FIRE	54
QUAVER			
MY DIM-WIT COUSIN, SAVED BY A DEATH-BED QUAVER,	25	DIM-WIT COUSIN	1
QUAY			
I SANG TO THE WHITE HORSE THAT GRAZED ON THE QUAY,--	216	THE SHY MAN	3
ON THE QUAY	229	ON THE QUAY	T
WHAT THEY SAY ON THE QUAY IS,	229	ON THE QUAY	1
QUEEN			
WE'RE KING AND QUEEN OF THE RIGHT GROUND.	79	GIVE WAY, GATES	22
I WAS QUEEN OF THE VALE--	161	I'M HERE	17
QUEER			
IT'S QUEER ENOUGH HERE, PERHAPS.	81	SENSIBILITY! LA	12
QUESTING			
WITH THE FISH, THE QUESTING SNAIL,	251	ONCE MORE, RND	7
QUESTION			
I DARED TO QUESTION ALL,	154	THE DYING MAN	32
THE QUESTION WAS, WHERE WAS THE QUESTIONER?--	237	THE TRANCED	2
QUESTIONER			
THE QUESTION WAS, WHERE WAS THE QUESTIONER?--	237	THE TRANCED	2
QUICK			
NO LONGER QUICK WITH LIGHT,	4	DEATH PIECE	2
A SINGLE MISSTEP AND WE LEAVE THE QUICK.	5	PROGNOSIS	4
THE MIND IS QUICK TO TURN	31	LULL	15
QUICK ON THE WOODEN BENCH,	42	TRANSPLANTING	9
KISS ME, KISS ME QUICK, MISTRESS OF LOST WISDOM,	48	LAST WORDS	7
COME TO ME, MILK-NOSE. I NEED A LOAN OF THE QUICK.	59	THE LONG ALLEY	25
AS AN OPAQUE VASE FILLS TO THE BRIM FROM A QUICK POURING,	67	SHAPE OF FIRE	93
AND HER QUICK LOOK, A SIDELONG PICKEREL SMILE;	102	ELEGY FOR JANE	2
SHE PLAYED IT QUICK, SHE PLAYED IT LIGHT AND LOOSE;	127	I KNEW A WOMAN	17
AND THE QUICK WINDS	210	HER TIME	10
HAS SERVED TO KEEP ME WITH THE QUICK.	256	IN HYDROTHERAPY	4

	PAGE	TITLE	LINE
QUICKENED			
IT QUICKENED, AND WAS GONE.	150	SNAKE	8
QUICKENING			
AS OF WATER QUICKENING BEFORE A NARROWING CHANNEL	200	THE FAR FIELD	59
QUICKER			
HIS BEAK IS QUICKER THAN A HUMAN HAND.	15	THE HERON	8
QUICKER THAN BIRDS, THEY DIPPED	44	FRAU BAUMAN	13
QUICKSAND			
THROUGH THE SWAMP ALIVE WITH QUICKSAND,	193	JOURNY INTERIOR	14
QUICKSILVER			
BEAUTIFUL, IN ITS WAY, LIKE QUICKSILVER--	151	SLUG	22
QUICK-WATER			
TOWARD THE QUICK-WATER, WRINKLING AND RIPPLING.	54	THE LOST SON	39
QUIESCENT			
INVADES QUIESCENT BLOOD;	18	GENESIS	6
A THING QUIESCENT!	209	HER LONGING	10
QUIET			
AND QUIET AT THE CORE.	20	REPL TO CENSURE	16
THE AIR'S QUIET UNDER THE SMALL LEAVES.	78	BRING THE DAY!	41
ON THE ROCKS SOUTH OF QUIET, IN THE CLOSE REGIONS OF KISSING,	86	PRAISE TO END!	20
AND THE CRAB, THE QUIET BREATHER.	100	THE VISITANT	9
I WOULD BELIEVE MY PAIN: AND THE EYE QUIET ON THE GROWING ROSE;	188	THE LONGING	43
I LONG FOR THE IMPERISHABLE QUIET AT THE HEART OF FORM;	188	THE LONGING	45
EVEN THE GULLS QUIET ON THE FAR ROCKS,	190	AT OYSTER RIVER	7
SUCH QUIET UNDER THE SMALL LEAVES!--	221	THE ABYSS	82
WITH A ROUND VIREO'S EYE, QUIET AND CONTAINED,	234	ALL MORNING	13
WANTING THE QUIET OF OLD WOOD OR STONE WITHOUT WATER.	255	LIGHT POEM	9
QUIETLY			
HELD UP, WHILE THE ROWER BREATHES, AND THE SMALL BOAT DRIFTS QUIETLY SHOREWARD;	67	SHAPE OF FIRE	91
I HAVE LEARNED TO SIT QUIETLY,	165	HER BECOMING	1
AS THOSE TWO QUIETLY TALKED,	182	BOY AND BUSH	7
THE TONGUES OF WATER, CREEPING IN, QUIETLY.	191	AT OYSTER RIVER	35
QUINCE			
AND THE HUMMINGBIRD DIPS IN AND AROUND THE QUINCE TREE,	234	ALL MORNING	29
QUINCE-BLOSSOM			
THE HUMMINGBIRD, WHIRRING FROM QUINCE-BLOSSOM TO MORNING-GLORY--	190	AT OYSTER RIVER	29
QUITE			
BUT WHAT WE ATE I CAN'T REMEMBER QUITE:	274	SUPPR W LINDSAY	31
QUITE-BY-CHANCE			
QUITE-BY-CHANCE BROUGHT ME MANY COOKIES.	90	UNFOLD! UNFOLD!	36
QUIVER			
OR ONE HIP QUIVER WITH A MOBILE NOSE	127	I KNEW A WOMAN	20
MAKING IT QUIVER WITH MY BODY;	161	I'M HERE	25
QUIVERED			
AND ALL DIMENSIONS QUIVERED TO ONE THING.	132	SENTENTIOUS MAN	24
HE QUIVERED LIKE A BIRD IN BIRDLESS AIR,	155	THE DYING MAN	64
QUIVERING			
THE LAST-ABANDONED STALK ALWAYS QUIVERING	152	THE SISKINS	14
QUIVERS			
HE PIPES, HE SQUEAKS, HE QUIVERS THROUGH HIS NOSE,--	264	THREE EPIGRAMS	5
RABBIT			
THE RABBIT, AND THE WREN;	137	LOVE'S PROGRESS	17
RABBITS			
I SUFFERED FOR BIRDS, FOR YOUNG RABBITS CAUGHT IN THE MOWER,	199	THE FAR FIELD	24
NIBBLED BY SHEEP AND RABBITS.	202	THE ROSE	10
RACE			
RACE OVER THE THICK GRASS;	152	THE SISKINS	6
RUNNING FROM GOD'S THE LONGEST RACE OF ALL.	245	THE DECISION	2
RACKET			
TO STOP THE SERPENT'S AWFUL RACKET:	115	THE SERPENT	13
MAKING A RACKET TO WAKE THE DEAD,	234	ALL MORNING	18
RAGE			
RAGE WARPS MY CLEAREST CRY	3	OPEN HOUSE	17
TO BUILD A COMPLEMENT TO RAGE,	22	SILENCE	12
I WANT THE OLD RAGE, THE LASH OF PRIMORDIAL MILK!	56	THE LOST SON	107
WHERE'S THE GREAT RAGE OF A ROCKING HEART, THE HIGH RARE TRUE DANGEROUS	98	O, THOU OPENING	30
I COULD ROLL IN THE DUST OF A FINE RAGE.	104	OLD LADY'S WRDS	50
SOME RAGES SAVE US. DID I RAGE TOO LONG?	131	SENTENTIOUS MAN	9

	PAGE	TITLE	LINE
RAGE (CONTINUED)			
AND I GO FASTER IN MY RAGE TO GET DONE WITH IT,	151	SLUG	18
MY RAGE, WHAT'S TO BE	211	SONG (1)	5
ALL RAGE WAS GONE.	213	THE HAPPY THREE	28
RAGED			
WHEN THE PURE FURY FIRST RAGED IN HIS HEAD	133	THE PURE FURY	20
WHEN I RAGED, WHEN I WAILED,	249	THE RESTORED	13
RAGES			
SOME RAGES SAVE US. DID I RAGE TOO LONG?	131	SENTENTIOUS MAN	9
RAGGED			
A RAGGED FRINGE	51	THE WAKING (1)	13
I MET A RAGGED MAN;	146	THE SONG	1
AND SHOCKS OF RAGGED CORN;	146	THE SONG	10
BEYOND THE CLOVER, THE RAGGED HAY,	203	THE ROSE	46
A NIGHT FLOWING WITH BIRDS, A RAGGED MOON,	239	IN A DARK TIME	14
RAGGEDY			
DOWN IN THE CORNER OF THE GARDEN, AMONG THE RAGGEDY LILACS,	204	THE ROSE	64
RAGING			
SKIRT HATRED'S RAGING RIVER,	7	ORDERS FOR DAY	10
A SPIRIT RAGING AT THE VISIBLE.	155	THE DYING MAN	50
RAGS			
THE RAGS OF MY ANATOMY,	19	EPIDERM MACABRE	12
WITH THE RAGS AND ROTTING CLOTHES,	47	THE RETURN	11
SAW WOMEN, THEIR EYELIDS LIKE LITTLE RAGS,	48	JUDGE NOT	9
RAIL			
THE MEN ON RAIL AND ROADWAY KEEP MOVING ON AND ON.	28	CLAIRVOY WIDOW	24
RAILING			
AN OLD BRIDGE BELOW WITH A BUCKLED IRON RAILING, BROKEN BY SOME IDIOT PLUNGER;	194	JOURNY INTERIOR	32
RAIN			
WE WAITED FOR THE FIRST RAIN IN THE EAVES.	6	INTERLUDE	4
THE RAIN STAYED IN ITS CLOUD; FULL DARK CAME NEAR;	6	INTERLUDE	9
THE RAVAGES OF WIND AND RAIN ARE HEALED.	12	SLOW SEASON	2
BUT SOON COLD RAIN AND FROST COME IN	14	COMING OF COLD	18
WE RUSH INTO A RAIN	34	NIGHT JOURNEY	22
THE FINE RAIN COILED IN A CLOUD	50	THE CYCLE	7
THE FULL RAIN FELL STRAIGHT DOWN,	50	THE CYCLE	14
HATH THE RAIN A FATHER? ALL THE CAVES ARE ICE. ONLY THE SNOW'S HERE.	56	THE LOST SON	84
A FINE RAIN FELL	62	FIELD OF LIGHT	15
RAIN SWEETENED THE CAVE AND THE DOVE STILL CALLED;	66	SHAPE OF FIRE	75
RAIN.	78	BRING THE DAY!	37
IN THE SLOW RAIN, WHO'S AFRAID?	79	GIVE WAY, GATES	21
A TREE ALL OUT OF SHAPE FROM WIND AND RAIN,	150	IN LATE SUMMER	27
IN THE RAIN, SLACKENING ON A SUMMER FIELD;	165	HER BECOMING	8
A DROP OF THE NIGHT RAIN STILL IN ME,	168	FOURTH MEDITATN	7
ON A DARK DAY I WALK STRAIGHT TOWARD THE RAIN.	170	FOURTH MEDITATN	80
THE WIND ROCKS WITH MY WISH; THE RAIN SHIELDS ME;	173	WHAT TELL BONES	81
IN A BLEAK TIME, WHEN A WEEK OF RAIN IS A YEAR,	187	THE LONGING	14
REEDS BEATEN FLAT BY WIND AND RAIN,	193	JOURNY INTERIOR	9
AND IN THE SHRUNKEN FACE OF A DEAD RAT, EATEN BY RAIN AND GROUND-BEETLES	199	THE FAR FIELD	19
THE FIRST RAIN GATHERED?	202	THE ROSE	30
AND A DROP OF RAIN WATER HANGS AT THE TIP OF A LEAF	204	THE ROSE	86
A COLD AIR BROUGHT ITS RAIN,	212	LIGHT LISTENED	21
A FINE FUME OF RAIN DRIVING IN FROM THE SEA,	230	THE STORM	13
THEN A CRACK OF THUNDER, AND THE BLACK RAIN RUNS OVER US, OVER	230	THE STORM	23
AND THE DUCKS NEAR LAKE WASHINGTON WADDLE DOWN THE HIGHWAY AFTER A RAIN,	234	ALL MORNING	26
KIN TO THE WIND, AND THE BLEAK WHISTLING RAIN.	248	THE TREE, BIRD	12
RAIN-BEATEN			
HER FACE LIKE A RAIN-BEATEN STONE ON THE DAY SHE ROLLED OFF	223	ELEGY (2)	1
RAINBOW			
HIS THUMB HAD A RAINBOW.	73	WHERE KNOCK IS	65
RAIN-BOW			
ITS SPRAY HOLDING A DOUBLE RAIN-BOW IN EARLY MORNING,	191	AT OYSTER RIVER	45
RAIN-DRENCHED			
A RAIN-DRENCHED FLY OR SPIDER.	151	SLUG	24
RAIN-SOAKED			
AND A BEE SHAKING DROPS FROM A RAIN-SOAKED HONEYSUCKLE.	63	FIELD OF LIGHT	49
RAISE			
RAISE UP WHEN YOU WOULD PEE.	267	SAGINAW SONG	24

	PAGE	TITLE	LINE
RAISED			
WHEN I RAISED MYSELF ONCE MORE,	145	THE BEAST	16
NO MORE THAN WHAT IS RAISED	262	FOLLIES OF ADAM	9
RAISES			
MY LUCK RAISES THE WIND."	208	HER WORDS	7
RAKE			
SHE WAS THE SICKLE; I, POOR I, THE RAKE,	127	I KNEW A WOMAN	12
RALLY			
THE HEART MUST RALLY TO MY WIT	19	AGNST DISASTER	11
RAMBLING			
THE RAMBLING LIES INVENTED FOR THE SICK.	5	PROGNOSIS	2
RAN			
WATER RAN OVER AND UNDER	6	THE PREMONITION	8
THE SPIEL RAN ON; THE SALE WAS BRIEF AND BRISK;	21	THE AUCTION	9
WHO RAN UP AND DOWN THE BIG CENTER STAIRS	32	SALE	2
RAN OVER STONES:	51	THE WAKING (1)	22
THE SILVER FISH RAN IN AND OUT OF MY SPECIAL BINDINGS;	65	SHAPE OF FIRE	35
IT WAS PLACE AND SHOW AND ALSO RAN	112	SQUEEZE-BOX	28
THE GREY SHEEP CAME. I RAN,	147	THE EXORCISM	1
AND THEN I RAN--	166	HER BECOMING	49
RAN AHEAD OF MYSELF,	166	HER BECOMING	50
AND THEN I RAN AGAIN.	166	HER BECOMING	60
THIS HARRY RAN STRAIGHT UP A WALL,	181	MONOTONY SONG	13
BACK TO THE HOUSE WE RAN,	214	THE HAPPY THREE	33
I RAN BEHIND HIM EVERY DAY	268	SAGINAW SONG	54
A SWAYING LIGHT-CORD, THEN RAN HALF-WAY BACK.	273	SUPPR W LINDSAY	25
RANCH-HOUSE			
THE SCRAGGLY WIND-BREAK OF A DUSTY RANCH-HOUSE.	194	JOURNY INTERIOR	45
RANDOM			
ALL RANDOM, WASTED, AND DISPERSED,	19	AGNST DISASTER	5
SHAPE TO A RANDOM JOY:	124	WORDS FOR WIND	48
IT WAS NO RANDOM ACT, FOR THOSE TWO MEN	224	OTTO	20
THIS SUDDEN RANDOM SONG,	271	THE REPLY	15
RANG			
FAR FROM THE MIRRORS ALL THE BUSHES RANG	143	SHIMMER OF EVIL	6
THE STONES RANG WITH LIGHT SOUND;	237	THE TRANCED	14
RANGES			
DOWN FROM BEHIND THE LAST RANGES,	158	FIRST MEDITATN	33
RANK			
PULPY STEMS, RANK, SILO-RICH,	38	ROOT CELLAR	8
RANSOM			
JOHN RANSOM SHOULD BE HERE, AND RENE CHAR;	274	SUPPR W LINDSAY	43
RANT			
SHE'D RANT AND SHE'D ROAR:	179	MYRTLE	8
RAPE			
ITS RAPE IS GENTLE, NEVER MORE	8	PRAYER	13
RAPID			
OF SENSE AT RAPID INTERVALS.	22	SILENCE	6
RAPIDS			
THE SUN GLITTERED ON A SMALL RAPIDS.	63	FIELD OF LIGHT	34
RAPPING			
WHAT A SCUTTLING AND RAPPING ALONG THE DRAINPIPES,	234	ALL MORNING	21
RAPS			
IN A SODDEN PLACE, ALL RAPS AND KNOCKS APPROVE.	93	I CRY, LOVE!	30
RAPT			
RAPT, WE LEANED FORTH WITH WHAT WE COULD NOT SEE.	107	SIR JOHN DAVIES	88
A RAPT THING WITH A NAME.	167	HER BECOMING	85
RARE			
SOME RARE NEW TEDIUM'S TAKING SHAPE:	81	SENSIBILITY! LA	13
WHERE'S THE GREAT RAGE OF A ROCKING HEART, THE HIGH RARE TRUE DANGEROUS	98	O, THOU OPENING	30
O RARE PROPINQUITY!--	137	LOVE'S PROGRESS	2
RARELY			
A CAGED BEAR RARELY DOES THE SAME THING TWICE	105	SIR JOHN DAVIES	10
IN TEMPTATION, I RARELY SEEK COUNSEL;	173	WHAT TELL BONES	78
RASP			
BY THE DRY RASP OF THE RECURRING INANE,	104	OLD LADY'S WRDS	57
AND, WITH A HARSH RASP OF A LAUGH AT HERSELF,	223	ELEGY (2)	10
RASPING			
THE BLUE JAY RASPING FROM THE STUNTED PINE.	196	THE LONG WATERS	28
RAT			
THE SHAPE OF A RAT?	54	THE LOST SON	44

	PAGE	TITLE	LINE
RAT (CONTINUED)			
MY FRIEND, THE RAT IN THE WALL, BRINGS ME THE CLEAREST			
MESSAGES;	88	PRAISE TO END!	84
AND IN THE SHRUNKEN FACE OF A DEAD RAT, EATEN BY RAIN AND			
GROUND-BEETLES	199	THE FAR FIELD	19
RATHER			
WOULD RATHER TAKE THAN DISH IT OUT.	23	AMOROUS LADY	4
WHICH WOULD YOU RATHER?	77	BRING THE DAY!	4
IT'S WINDY THERE, AND RATHER WEIRD.	114	DINKY	2
A PRISONER OF SMELLS, I WOULD RATHER EAT THAN PRAY.	173	WHAT TELL BONES	79
RATIONAL			
O TO BE DELIVERED FROM THE RATIONAL INTO THE REALM OF PURE			
SONG,	172	WHAT TELL BONES	54
RATS			
THE RATS SOON WILL BE LEAVING, THE SNOW WILL COME IN."	27	CLAIRVOY WIDOW	16
ARE THE RATS DANCING? THE CATS ARE.	79	GIVE WAY, GATES	8
A CONGRESS OF TREE-SHREWS AND RATS,	163	I'M HERE	66
RAT'S			
THE RAT'S MY PHASE.	97	O, THOU OPENING	2
RATTLES			
THAT RATTLES DOUBLE GLASS.	34	NIGHT JOURNEY	23
RATTLING			
OR LADLE RATTLING IN AN EMPTY DISH?	105	SIR JOHN DAVIES	30
A THIN WHINE OF WIRES, A RATTLING AND FLAPPING OF LEAVES,	230	THE STORM	6
RAUCOUS			
AS A SNAKE OR A RAUCOUS BIRD,	200	THE FAR FIELD	48
AND THE STELLER JAY, RAUCOUS, SOOTY HEADED, LIVES WITH US,	234	ALL MORNING	15
RAVAGE			
HAS LEFT ITS RAVAGE ON THE FIELD.	14	COMING OF COLD	25
RAVAGED			
SEA-BEAST OR BIRD FLUNG TOWARD THE RAVAGED SHORE?	107	SIR JOHN DAVIES	68
WHEN THE SLOW FREIGHT WINDS ALONG THE EDGE OF THE RAVAGED			
HILLSIDE,	204	THE ROSE	83
RAVAGES			
THE RAVAGES OF WIND AND RAIN ARE HEALED.	12	SLOW SEASON	2
A LATE ROSE RAVAGES THE CASUAL EYE,	149	IN LATE SUMMER	17
RAVE			
WHEN FIGURES OUT OF OBSCURE SHADOW RAVE,	154	THE DYING MAN	46
RAVEN			
A FISH RAVEN TURNS ON ITS PERCH (A DEAD TREE IN THE			
RIVERMOUTH),	190	AT OYSTER RIVER	22
RAVENOUS			
THAT APPETITE FOR LIFE SO RAVENOUS	133	THE PURE FURY	16
RAVENS			
AND THE SHEEN OF RAVENS.	265	HARSH COUNTRY	4
RAVINE			
AND CAME TO A DARK RAVINE,	238	THE MOMENT	2
RAVINES			
WE THUNDER THROUGH RAVINES	34	NIGHT JOURNEY	18
THE RAVINES UGLY.	193	JOURNY INTERIOR	17
MY DESIRE FOR THE PEAKS, THE BLACK RAVINES, THE ROLLING			
MISTS	196	THE LONG WATERS	9
RAW			
A RAW GHOST DRINKS THE FLUID IN MY SPINE;	135	THE RENEWAL	14
AT THE EDGE OF A RAW FIELD.	146	THE SONG	13
LIKE PIECES OF SMOKED EEL OR RAW OYSTER,	151	SLUG	17
A RAW TUMULTUOUS GIRL	166	HER BECOMING	47
THE SLAG-HEAPS FUME AT THE EDGE OF THE RAW CITIES:	187	THE LONGING	15
THERE ARE MANY DETOURS, WASHED-OUT INTERRUPTED RAW PLACES	193	JOURNY INTERIOR	2
RAZORS			
THAT CUT LIKE RAZORS,	265	HARSH COUNTRY	8
REACH			
REACH ME ROSE, SWEET ONE, STILL MOIST IN THE LOAM,	61	THE LONG ALLEY	68
REACH ME A PEACH, FONDLING, THE HILLS ARE THERE.	61	THE LONG ALLEY	81
WE DARED THE DARK TO REACH THE WHITE AND WARM.	107	SIR JOHN DAVIES	92
WITHIN THE REACH OF MY IMAGINING:	135	THE RENEWAL	3
FOR THE SLEEK CAPTAINS OF INTUITION CANNOT REACH THEM;	169	FOURTH MEDITATN	52
UNTIL THEY REACH THIS FINAL CERTITUDE.	243	THE MOTION	16
THIS REACH BEYOND THIS DEATH, THIS ACT OF LOVE	243	THE MOTION	17
I MOVE BEYOND THE REACH OF WIND AND FIRE.	244	INFIRMITY	24
REACHED			
REACHED FOR A GRAPE	62	FIELD OF LIGHT	11

		PAGE	TITLE	LINE
REACHES				
SHALE LOOSENS. MARL REACHES INTO THE FIELD. SMALL BIRDS PASS OVER WATER.	......	64	SHAPE OF FIRE	11
REACHES OF COMMON DAY,	......	263	FOLLIES OF ADAM	25
REACHING				
STRETCHING AND REACHING.	......	42	TRANSPLANTING	22
REACHING UP WHITE STRINGS	......	44	FRAU BAUMAN	3
HER WHITE ARMS REACHING TOWARDS ME.	......	100	THE VISITANT	14
THE CHILD'S HAND REACHING INTO THE COILED SMILAX,	......	221	THE ABYSS	65
READ				
READ ME THE STREAM.	......	97	O, THOU OPENING	4
YOU TAKE THE TIMES SUPPLEMENT, AND READ ITS VERSE,	......	113	TO A LADY ED	2
ONCE I READ NOTHING THROUGH A FEARFUL NIGHT,	......	133	THE PURE FURY	3
AND NONE HAS READ MY BOOKS,	......	225	THE CHUMS	2
READ ME EURIPIDES,	......	262	FOLLIES OF ADAM	1
READS				
WHO READS IN BED	......	99	O, THOU OPENING	69
READY				
READY FOR THE LONG DAYS UNDER THE SLOPED GLASS:	......	42	TRANSPLANTING	13
WHO'S READY FOR PINK AND FRISK?	......	76	I NEED, I NEED	59
I'M ALL READY TO WHISTLE;	......	84	O LULL ME, LULL	36
READY FOR ANY CREVICE,	......	187	THE LONGING	22
MY BIRD-BLOOD READY.	......	207	THE YOUNG GIRL	12
REAL				
A REAL HURT IS SOFT.	......	71	WHERE KNOCK IS	11
THEN A REAL CAT CAME WITH A MOUTH SO WIDE,	......	177	KITTY-CAT BIRD	14
REALITY				
AS IF REALITY HAD SPLIT APART	......	135	THE RENEWAL	22
THERE ARE TIMES WHEN REALITY COMES CLOSER:	......	166	HER BECOMING	44
THE IMMEDIATE SHEEN, THE REALITY OF STRAW,	......	171	WHAT TELL BONES	16
TOO MUCH REALITY CAN BE A DAZZLE, A SURFEIT;	......	220	THE ABYSS	44
REALLY				
I WISH YOU WOULD ACT LIKE A BIRD REALLY SHOULD,	......	177	KITTY-CAT BIRD	6
TO KNOW A CHAIR IS REALLY IT,	......	178	THE CHAIR	3
O WHEN YOU WERE LITTLE, YOU WERE REALLY BIG:	......	272	DUET	1
REALM				
MY NARROW VEGETABLE REALM!	......	18	LONG LIVE WEEDS	2
OF LIVING MERELY IN THE REALM OF TIME.	......	149	IN LATE SUMMER	20
O TO BE DELIVERED FROM THE RATIONAL INTO THE REALM OF PURE SONG,	......	172	WHAT TELL BONES	54
REAPS				
CORRUPTION REAPS THE YOUNG; YOU DREAD	......	4	FEUD	1
REARRANGES				
AND THE SEA REARRANGES ITSELF AMONG THE SMALL ISLANDS.	...	205	THE ROSE	97
REASON				
THE RUMINANT, REASON, CHEWS A POISONED CUD.	......	5	PROGNOSIS	8
REASON EMBRACES DEATH,	......	31	LULL	19
REASON? THAT DREARY SHED, THAT HUTCH FOR GRUBBY SCHOOLBOYS!	......	92	I CRY, LOVE!	14
THERE WOULD BE REASON FOR ESSENTIAL SIN;	......	144	ELEGY (1)	2
AND MY REASON FAILED,	......	249	THE RESTORED	14
REASONS				
THUS I; AND SHOULD THESE REASONS FLY APART.	......	144	ELEGY (1)	9
REBORN				
I THOUGHT MYSELF REBORN.	......	154	THE DYING MAN	17
TO GROPE MY SILL: IT MOANS TO BE REBORN!	......	154	THE DYING MAN	37
RECALL				
RECALL THE GRADUAL DARK THE SNOW'S UNMEASURED FALL	......	5	TO MY SISTER	3
I RECALL THE FALLING OF SMALL WATERS,	......	222	THE ABYSS	93
I RECALL HOW SHE HARRIED THE CHILDREN AWAY ALL THE LATE SUMMER	......	223	ELEGY (2)	12
RECEDES				
THE WORLD RECEDES IN THE BLACK REVOLVING SHADOW;	......	33	IDYLL	9
WATER RECEDES TO THE CRYING OF SPIDERS.	......	64	SHAPE OF FIRE	4
THE WATER RECEDES SLOWLY,	......	93	I CRY, LOVE!	52
A FIELD RECEDES IN SLEEP.	......	122	ALL EARTH, AIR	21
WHAT'S SEEN RECEDES; FOREVER'S WHAT WE KNOW!--	......	156	THE DYING MAN	91
RECEDING				
I SEE THE FLOWER OF ALL WATER, ABOVE AND BELOW ME, THE NEVER RECEDING,	......	194	JOURNY INTERIOR	52
RECEIVE				
I RECEIVE! I HAVE BEEN RECEIVED!	......	222	THE ABYSS	90
RECEIVED				
I RECEIVE! I HAVE BEEN RECEIVED!	......	222	THE ABYSS	90

	PAGE	TITLE	LINE
RECEPTION			
LONELY RECEPTION ROOM, LAVATORY, SWITCHBOARD, ...	46	DOLOR	5
RECITE			
--AND RECITE HIM MY POEM CALLED POEM.	113	TO A LADY ED	8
RECKONING			
THE RECKONING	30	THE RECKONING	T
RECOGNIZE			
TIME FOR THE FLAT-HEADED MAN. I RECOGNIZE THAT LISTENER,	65	SHAPE OF FIRE	29
RECOILING			
RECOILING FROM THE SERPENT HEAD	4	FEUD	3
RECOUNT			
RECOUNT EACH CHILDHOOD PLEASURE: THE SKIES OF AZURE	5	TO MY SISTER	5
RECOVER			
I RECOVER MY TENDERNESS BY LONG LOOKING.	173	WHAT TELL BONES	92
RECOVERED			
I'VE RECOVERED MY TENDERNESS BY LONG LOOKING;	260	THE CHANGELING	16
RECUMBENCY			
RECUMBENCY IS UNREFINED	257	SANITARIUM	3
RECURRING			
BY THE DRY RASP OF THE RECURRING INANE, ...	104	OLD LADY'S WRDS	57
RED			
THE ANTIMACASSAR FOR THE SOFA IN RED, ...	32	SALE	9
WAVER OVER TO RED, ...	41	BIG WIND	11
CARNATIONS, RED	44	FRAU BAUMAN	8
THEIR WOODEN STORES OF SILVERY PINE AND WEATHER-BEATEN RED			
COURTHOUSES,	193	JOURNY INTERIOR	31
NEITHER WHITE NOR RED, IN THE DEAD MIDDLE WAY, ...	197	THE LONG WATERS	56
WHITE AND RED, IN THE WIDE SIX-HUNDRED-FOOT GREENHOUSES,	203	THE ROSE	52
REDEEM			
REDEEM THIS TEACHER, ...	259	SONG (3)	34
REDEEMER			
THE REDEEMER COMES A DARK WAY.	66	SHAPE OF FIRE	63
RED-HOT			
HAD THE RED-HOT SPOTS WHERE YOU FEEL A	111	SQUEEZE-BOX	20
REDOLENT			
A LEAF, I WOULD LOVE THE LEAVES, DELIGHTING IN THE REDOLENT			
DISORDER OF THIS MORTAL LIFE, ...	188	THE LONGING	47
REDOUBLES			
THE STORM LULLS OFF, THEN REDOUBLES, ...	231	THE STORM	30
REDUCED			
HIS LAUGHTER REDUCED THE SING-SONG OF PRATING, ...	29	THE GENTLE	7
AM I REDUCED TO THE INDIGNITY OF EXAMPLES?	259	SONG (3)	40
REEDS			
WRINKLING BETWEEN REEDS IN SHALLOWER WATER, ...	93	I CRY, LOVE!	47
REEDS BEATEN FLAT BY WIND AND RAIN, ...	193	JOURNY INTERIOR	9
REEKING			
THE CARRIAGES REEKING WITH VARNISH AND STALE PERFUME.	22	ROAD TO WDLAWN	4
REFITS			
REFITS ME FOR THE TRUE AND GOOD.	256	IN HYDROTHERAPY	6
REFLECTED			
ITS WINGS CATCHING A LAST GLINT OF THE REFLECTED SUNLIGHT.	190	AT OYSTER RIVER	23
THE LAST GEESE CROSSING AGAINST THE REFLECTED AFTERLIGHT,	202	THE ROSE	17
REFLECTION			
MY EYE ALWAYS BEYOND THE SURFACE REFLECTION;	233	THE PIKE	12
REFLECTIONS			
PETALS AND REFLECTIONS OF PETALS MIXED ON THE SURFACE OF A			
GLASSY POOL, ...	194	JOURNY INTERIOR	56
REFLECTS			
AS LIGHT REFLECTS FROM A LAKE, IN LATE EVENING, ...	198	THE LONG WATERS	60
REFUSE			
KEEP FAITH WITH PRESENT JOYS REFUSE TO CHOOSE	5	TO MY SISTER	7
AND YOU REFUSE TO DIE DECENTLY!--	151	SLUG	15
REGIONS			
ON THE ROCKS SOUTH OF QUIET, IN THE CLOSE REGIONS OF			
KISSING, ...	86	PRAISE TO END!	20
REGULAR			
THE LUGUBRIOUSLY BEAUTIFUL PLAINT UTTERED AT REGULAR			
INTERVALS, ...	234	ALL MORNING	4
REHEARSE			
I REHEARSE MYSELF FOR THIS:	194	JOURNY INTERIOR	65
REJECT			
THOUGH IT REJECT DRY BORDERS OF THE SEEN, ...	154	THE DYING MAN	42
THEREFORE I REJECT THE WORLD OF THE DOG	196	THE LONG WATERS	5

	PAGE	TITLE	LINE
REJOICE			
I REJOICE IN THE SPRING, AS THOUGH NO SPRING EVER HAD BEEN.	24	VERNAL SENTIMNT	8
WOULD NOT REJOICE?	122	ALL EARTH, AIR	30
WITH BATS, WEASELS, WORMS--I REJOICE IN THE KINSHIP.	151	SLUG	26
THE EYES REJOICE IN THE ACT OF SEEING AND THE FRESH AFTER-IMAGE;	163	I'M HERE	79
REJOICE IN THE LANGUAGE OF SMELLS AND DANCING.	196	THE LONG WATERS	4
SWEET CHRIST, REJOICE IN MY INFIRMITY;	244	INFIRMITY	7
REJOICED			
AND I REJOICED IN BEING WHAT I WAS:	205	THE ROSE	106
RELATE			
TO SOME IT MAY SEEM A SAD THING TO RELATE,	112	SQUEEZE-BOX	38
RELATIVES			
WHO SAT WITH THE DEAD WHEN THE RELATIVES LEFT,	223	ELEGY (2)	8
RELEASE			
WOULD NOT RELEASE ONE RIVEN NOTE:	22	SILENCE	18
DELICATE THE SYLLABLES THAT RELEASE THE REPRESSION;	29	THE GENTLE	1
RELEASED			
I'M RELEASED FROM THE DREARY DANCE OF OPPOSITES.	173	WHAT TELL BONES	80
AS IF RELEASED BY A SPIRIT,	173	WHAT TELL BONES	98
RELICS			
ALL THE RINGS AND THE RELICS ENCRUSTED WITH SIN	32	SALE	19
RELIEF			
IF I SHOULD EVER SEEK RELIEF	22	SILENCE	15
SIGHED OUT HER PURE RELIEF	213	THE HAPPY THREE	3
RELUCTANT			
DALLY AT SHOP WINDOWS, STILL RELUCTANT TO GO;	47	DOUBLE FEATURE	6
REMAIN			
REMAIN SECURE FROM PAIN PRESERVE THY HATE THY HEART.	5	TO MY SISTER	11
ITS SHAFTS REMAIN.	9	THE ADAMANT	4
BREAKS UP THE CRUST OF CINDERS THAT REMAIN,	17	UNEXTINGUISHED	10
YET REMAIN ONLY HALF AWARE OF THE INTRANSIENT GLORY?	169	FOURTH MEDITATN	32
I DARE EMBRACE. BY STRIDING, I REMAIN.	243	THE MOTION	12
REMAINING			
FOR SALE: BY ORDER OF THE REMAINING HEIRS	32	SALE	1
REMAINS			
THE VISION MOVES, AND YET REMAINS THE SAME.	156	THE DYING MAN	94
REMARK			
HE NEVER TREMBLED AT A VEILED REMARK.	28	THE FAVORITE	2
REMARKS			
TO MAKE REMARKS ABOUT MY--GRRR!	181	MONOTONY SONG	11
REMEMBER			
O MY SISTER REMEMBER THE STARS THE TEARS THE TRAINS	5	TO MY SISTER	1
WALKING THIS FIELD I REMEMBER	6	THE PREMONITION	1
I REMEMBER THE CROSSING-TENDER'S GERANIUM BORDER	29	THE REMINDER	1
I REMEMBER HOW THEY PICKED ME UP, A SPINDLY KID,	44	FRAU BAUMAN	26
AND REMEMBER THERE WAS SOMETHING ELSE I WAS HOPING FOR.	47	DOUBLE FEATURE	12
REMEMBER AN OLD SOUND.	59	THE LONG ALLEY	8
REMEMBER	59	THE LONG ALLEY	9
I HAVE BEEN SOMEWHERE ELSE; I REMEMBER THE SEA-FACED UNCLES.	88	PRAISE TO END!	93
WHO UNTIED THE TREE? I REMEMBER NOW.	93	I CRY, LOVE!	54
I REMEMBER THE NECKCURLS, LIMP AND DAMP AS TENDRILS;	102	ELEGY FOR JANE	1
IF ONLY I COULD REMEMBER	103	OLD LADY'S WRDS	19
ALL WHO REMEMBER, DOUBT. WHO CALLS THAT STRANGE?	120	THE DREAM	21
I REMEMBER WALKING DOWN A PATH,	162	I'M HERE	45
THERE'S THIS TO REMEMBER ABOUT THE GNU:	180	THE GNU	1
I REMEMBER HOW IT WAS TO DRIVE IN GRAVEL,	193	JOURNY INTERIOR	18
I REMEMBER A STONE BREAKING THE EDDYING CURRENT,	197	THE LONG WATERS	55
AND I REMEMBER LOOKS	225	THE CHUMS	4
REMEMBER WHAT IT WAS	262	FOLLIES OF ADAM	3
BUT WHAT WE ATE I CAN'T REMEMBER QUITE:	274	SUPPR W LINDSAY	31
MOSTLY I REMEMBER THE ICE CREAM.	274	SUPPR W LINDSAY	34
AND ROBERT FROST. THEY MIGHT REMEMBER ME."	274	SUPPR W LINDSAY	49
REMEMBERED			
MY FEET REMEMBERED THE EARTH,	104	OLD LADY'S WRDS	44
ALL BIRDS REMEMBERED, O NEVER FORGOTTEN!	235	ALL MORNING	45
REMEMBERING			
THIS ANIMAL REMEMBERING TO BE GAY.	105	SIR JOHN DAVIES	12
REMEMBERS			
THE DEEP STREAM REMEMBERS:	80	GIVE WAY, GATES	59
THE MIND REMEMBERS FROM A DEEPER SLEEP:	119	THE DREAM	3
WHEN THE MIND REMEMBERS ALL,	204	THE ROSE	75

	PAGE	TITLE	LINE
REMIND			
REMIND ME TO STAY ALIVE.	154	THE DYING MAN	23
THESE WAVES, IN THE SUN, REMIND ME OF FLOWERS:	197	THE LONG WATERS	38
REMINDED			
I'M REMINDED TO STAY ALIVE	104	OLD LADY'S WRDS	56
BY WHAT REMINDED?	260	THE CHANGELING	3
AND IT REMINDED ME--BUT OH!	270	GOB MUSIC	36
REMINDER			
THE REMINDER	29	THE REMINDER	T
A PROTEST FROM THE PAST, A REMINDER.	234	ALL MORNING	5
REMINDS			
REMINDS ME I AM DYING WITH THE YEAR.	149	IN LATE SUMMER	24
A FUME REMINDS ME, DRIFTING ACROSS WET GRAVEL;	160	FIRST MEDITATN	91
RENDERED			
AN EXACT FALL OF WATERS HAS RENDERED ME IMPOTENT.	86	PRAISE TO END!	46
RENE			
JOHN RANSOM SHOULD BE HERE, AND RENE CHAR;	274	SUPPR W LINDSAY	43
RENEW			
RENEW THE LIGHT, LEWD WHISPER.	65	SHAPE OF FIRE	55
MY ENEMIES RENEW ME, AND MY BLOOD	155	THE DYING MAN	67
I, WHO RENEW THE FIRE,	216	HER WRATH	3
RENEWAL			
THE RENEWAL	135	THE RENEWAL	T
SUDDEN RENEWAL OF THE SELF--FROM WHERE?	135	THE RENEWAL	13
RENEWED			
WAS IT A GOD HIS SUFFERING RENEWED?--	155	THE DYING MAN	60
I AM RENEWED BY DEATH, THOUGHT OF MY DEATH,	201	THE FAR FIELD	77
RENOWN			
THERE ON MY KNEES, A MAN OF RENOWN,	270	GOB MUSIC	42
REPEAT			
SMALL WAVES REPEAT THE MIND'S SLOW SENSUAL PLAY.	131	SENTENTIOUS MAN	13
REPEATEDLY			
I DREAM OF JOURNEYS REPEATEDLY:	199	THE FAR FIELD	1
REPENT			
THE FLESH IS WILLING TO REPENT.	256	IN HYDROTHERAPY	8
REPLANT			
I'VE TRIED I DON'T KNOW HOW MANY TIMES TO REPLANT IT.	163	I'M HERE	77
REPLIED			
BUT WHEN THE ROOT REPLIED,	262	FOLLIES OF ADAM	19
REPLY			
REPLY TO CENSURE	20	REPL TO CENSURE	T
A RIPPLE MADE A SOFT REPLY.	100	THE VISITANT	6
REPLY TO A LADY EDITOR	113	TO A LADY ED	T
A SLIGHT VOICE REPLY;	128	THE VOICE	17
THE REPLY	271	THE REPLY	T
REPOSE			
THE SOFT POND OF REPOSE;	53	THE LOST SON	13
LIGHT, LIGHT, WHERE'S MY REPOSE?	126	WORDS FOR WIND	92
HER SEVERAL PARTS COULD KEEP A PURE REPOSE,	127	I KNEW A WOMAN	19
ASTONISHED INTO PASSIONATE REPOSE.	131	SENTENTIOUS MAN	18
REPRESSION			
DELICATE THE SYLLABLES THAT RELEASE THE REPRESSION;	29	THE GENTLE	1
REPTILIAN			
AT ONCE MAMMALIAN AND REPTILIAN.	23	AMOROUS LADY	14
IN THE LILAC CHANGE, THE WHITE REPTILIAN CALM,	205	THE ROSE	107
REPULSE			
REPULSE THE STARING EYE,	20	REPL TO CENSURE	1
REQUIRE			
THE FIEND'S FAR AWAY. LORD, WHAT DO YOU REQUIRE?	59	THE LONG ALLEY	21
RESEMBLES			
HE CLOSELY RESEMBLES--BUT I CAN'T TELL YOU!	180	THE GNU	2
RESERVED			
THE STRIP RESERVED FOR PASSING ONLY.	33	HIGHWAY: MICH	7
RESIDES			
THE SOUL RESIDES IN THE HORSE BARN.	59	THE LONG ALLEY	22
RESIST			
IF I WERE A FISH I JUST COULDN'T RESIST	117	LADY AND BEAR	23
RESOUND			
LET THE KISSES RESOUND, FLAT LIKE A BUTCHER'S PALM;	56	THE LOST SON	104
RESOUNDED			
AND THE WOODS RESOUNDED WITH MANY A SHRIEK	115	THE SERPENT	25
REST			
WHILE OTHERS TAKE THEIR REST.	34	NIGHT JOURNEY	5

		PAGE	TITLE	LINE
REST (CONTINUED)				
DEAREST TREE, I SAID, MAY I REST HERE?	....	100	THE VISITANT	5
IN THE LONG NIGHT, I REST WITHIN HER NAME--	....	131	SENTENTIOUS MAN	16
HOW CAN I REST IN THE DAYS OF MY SLOWNESS?	....	157	FIRST MEDITATN	14
LEAVING A PLACE FOR THE EYE TO REST,	....	233	THE PIKE	2
PERIPHERAL DIPPERS COME TO REST ON THE SHORT GRASS,	......	235	ALL MORNING	34
RESTIVE				
OF RESTIVE CROWS IS SHARPER ON THE EAR.	....	11	LIGHT BRIGHTER	2
RESTLESS				
HOW THEY FILLED THE ORIOLE'S ELM, A TWITTERING RESTLESS				
CLOUD, ALL ONE MORNING,	....	199	THE FAR FIELD	28
RESTORED				
THE RESTORED	....	249	THE RESTORED	T
RESURRECTION				
THIS URGE, WRESTLE, RESURRECTION OF DRY STICKS,	....	37	CUTTINGS (LATE)	1
RETAIN				
WHICH OF THE FIVE I SHALL RETAIN	....	8	PRAYER	3
RETICENCE				
HER RETICENCE	....	209	HER RETICENCE	T
RETIRE				
THEN RETIRE TO A ROCK HIGHER UP ON THE CLIFF-SIDE.	....	190	AT OYSTER RIVER	16
RETIRING				
RETIRING TO NUDGE HIS NECK HALF-WAY UNDER	....	226	THE LIZARD	16
RETREAT				
FROM THE WORM'S ADVANCE AND RETREAT, FROM THE BUTTERFLY'S				
HAVOC,	....	196	THE LONG WATERS	21
RETREATING				
I SEE IN THE ADVANCING AND RETREATING WATERS	....	198	THE LONG WATERS	67
THE MOON RETREATING INTO A VAGUE CLOUD-SHAPE	....	202	THE ROSE	18
THE PHOEBE'S SLOW RETREATING FROM ITS SONG,	....	245	THE DECISION	4
RETREATS				
THE TREE RETREATS INTO ITS OWN SHADOW.	....	200	THE FAR FIELD	57
RETURN				
RETURN TO LITTER UP OUR HOME.	....	30	THE RECKONING	4
THE RETURN	....	47	THE RETURN	T
THE RETURN	....	57	THE LOST SON	ST
RETURN THE GAZE OF A POND.	....	59	THE LONG ALLEY	30
HONORED, ON MY RETURN, BY THE ANCIENT FELLOWSHIP OF ROTTEN				
STEMS.	....	89	UNFOLD! UNFOLD!	26
THINGS LOST IN SLEEP RETURN	....	148	THE SMALL	15
I RETURN WHERE FIRE HAS BEEN,	....	196	THE LONG WATERS	13
I'LL RETURN AGAIN,	....	200	THE FAR FIELD	47
I RETURN TO THE TWITTERING OF SWALLOWS ABOVE WATER,	....	204	THE ROSE	73
AND HEAR MYSELF RETURN	....	215	HIS FOREBODING	12
RETURNING				
ONCE ON RETURNING HOME, PURSE-PROUD AND HALE,	....	21	THE AUCTION	1
REVEAL				
ALL FINITE THINGS REVEAL INFINITUDE:	....	201	THE FAR FIELD	94
REVEALING				
I THINK IT WOULD BE MOST REVEALING	....	178	THE CEILING	5
REVEALS				
REVEALS A FOOLISH MOTHER,	....	7	ORDERS FOR DAY	17
REVELATION				
A HOUSE FOR WISDOM; A FIELD FOR REVELATION.	....	90	UNFOLD! UNFOLD!	53
REVERSED				
MY SPECIAL HEAVEN IS REVERSED,	....	19	AGNST DISASTER	7
REVILED				
THOUGH JUST MEN ARE REVILED	....	20	REPL TO CENSURE	9
REVIVED				
SPEECH REVIVED, A GHOSTLY GOING OF TAME BEARS, A BRIGHT				
MOON ON GLEAMING	....	98	O, THOU OPENING	23
REVIVES				
THE DEW REVIVES ON THE BEACH-GRASS;	....	190	AT OYSTER RIVER	20
REVOLVING				
REVOLVING ON HIS SPINAL COLUMN.	....	24	BEFORE STUDY	8
THE WORLD RECEDES IN THE BLACK REVOLVING SHADOW;	....	33	IDYLL	9
TURNED BY REVOLVING AIR	....	50	THE CYCLE	8
RHODODENDRON				
AND ONE DROPS DOWN TO THE GARDEN, THE HIGH RHODODENDRON,		234	ALL MORNING	8
RHULE				
WAS CALLED THE GOLDEN RHULE,--	....	267	SAGINAW SONG	28
RHYTHM				
ITS RHYTHM ROCKS THE EARTH,	....	34	NIGHT JOURNEY	2

	PAGE	TITLE	LINE
RHYTHM (CONTINUED)			
DISTURBED SOME RHYTHM, OLD AND OF VAST IMPORTANCE,	40	MOSS-GATHERING	11
RIBBONING			
THE HIGHWAY RIBBONING OUT IN A STRAIGHT THRUST TO THE NORTH,	193	JOURNY INTERIOR	27
RIBS			
THE RIBS OF LEAVES LIE IN THE DUST,	14	COMING OF COLD	22
PINCHING AND POKING MY THIN RIBS	44	FRAU BAUMAN	27
I'M ALONE WITH MY RIBS;	82	SENSIBILITY! LA	30
RICH			
THE RICH CAN PLAY AT POLO, THE POOR CAN DO THE SHAG,	27	CLAIRVOY WIDOW	11
THEIR EYES, RICH AS PLUMS, STARING FROM NEWSPRINT,--	48	JUDGE NOT	3
RICH ME CHERRIES A FONDLING'S KISS,	60	THE LONG ALLEY	43
IN THE RICH WEATHER OF A DAPPLED WOOD	107	SIR JOHN DAVIÈS	65
SO I'VE GOT TO GET ME A RICH UGLY OLD MAID	112	SQUEEZE-BOX	43
A MAN RICH AS A CAT,	121	ALL EARTH, AIR	7
BUT GOODNESS ME, HER FATHER'S RICH!	181	MONOTONY SONG	19
TO A RICH DESOLATION OF WIND AND WATER,	197	THE LONG WATERS	46
RICHES			
THE RICHES OF THE AIR BLOW THIN.	14	COMING OF COLD	21
RICKETY			
I DAWDLE WITH GROUPS NEAR THE RICKETY POP-CORN STAND;	47	DOUBLE FEATURE	5
OVER A RICKETY BRIDGE	54	THE LOST SON	38
FROM THE RICKETY WOODEN DOCK,	158	FIRST MEDITATN	51
AND PICKED AND PICKLED THE BEST, TO BE LEFT ON RICKETY DOORSTEPS.	223	ELEGY (2)	15
ITS BEVY OF BEES, AND ITS WIND-BEATEN RICKETY SUN-CHAIRS.	226	THE LIZARD	29
RID			
--ABOUT GETTING RID OF OUR MONEY.	111	SQUEEZE-BOX	12
RIDDLING			
RIDDLING THE SAND, LIKE A WIDE SPRAY OF BUCKSHOT,	230	THE STORM	14
RIDE			
THE GULLS RIDE ON THE WATER, THE GULLS HAVE COME AND GONE,	28	CLAIRVOY WIDOW	23
AND WE RIDE, WE RIDE, TAKING THE CURVES	158	FIRST MEDITATN	31
AND WE RIDE, WE RIDE, TAKING THE CURVES	158	FIRST MEDITATN	31
IF YOU ASKED FOR A RIDE,	178	THE YAK	3
RIDES			
RIDES BY, FOR AT THE END OF DAY	33	HIGHWAY: MICH	4
A GULL RIDES ON THE RIPPLES OF A DREAM,	149	IN LATE SUMMER	1
RIDGE			
BEYOND THE RIDGE TWO WOOD THRUSH SING AS ONE.	150	IN LATE SUMMER	30
RIDGES			
THE GREAT FEET BREAK THE RIDGES OF THE SAND,	15	THE HERON	6
OR THE WHIPPOORWILL, ALONG THE SMOKY RIDGES,	160	FIRST MEDITATN	89
THE TIDE RUSTLING IN, SLIDING BETWEEN THE RIDGES OF STONE,	191	AT OYSTER RIVER	34
RIDICULOUS			
TO DISTRACT ATTENTION FROM THE SHORT-TAILED RIDICULOUS YOUNG ONES	234	ALL MORNING	19
RIDING			
OFTEN I THINK OF MYSELF AS RIDING--	158	FIRST MEDITATN	20
A POOL RIDING AND SHINING WITH THE RIVER,	168	FOURTH MEDITATN	9
WELTER OF TIN CANS, PAILS, OLD BIRD NESTS, A CHILD'S SHOE RIDING A LOG,	191	AT OYSTER RIVER	54
RIDING BENEATH THE MOON, HID FROM THE MOON,	225	OTTO	36
RIDING THE AIR, A WILLOW WITH ITS KIND,	248	THE TREE, BIRD	10
RIFFLE			
WATCHING THE WIND RIFFLE THE BACKS OF SMALL BIRDS,	165	HER BECOMING	2
RIFFLED			
THAT RIFFLED AROUND MY KNEES.	49	RIVER INCIDENT	3
RIFLE			
HE THREW HIS RIFLE OVER WITH ONE HAND;	224	OTTO	15
WITHOUT HIS RIFLE, AND SLAPPED EACH ONE HARD;	224	OTTO	19
RIFT			
OR WHEN DARK FOLLOWS DARK IN LIGHTNING RIFT.	8	THE SIGNALS	6
RIGHT			
AND EARN THE RIGHT TO STAND OR SIT,	18	LONG LIVE WEEDS	10
MY RIGHT EAR SCRAPED A BUCKLE.	45	MY PAPA'S WALTZ	12
THE OATS ARE ALL RIGHT.	76	I NEED, I NEED	56
WE'RE KING AND QUEEN OF THE RIGHT GROUND.	79	GIVE WAY, GATES	22
IN THE LILY'S SOVEREIGN RIGHT?	98	O, THOU OPENING	43
BUT STEPPED RIGHT UP AND SWUNG AT THE DEVIL;	111	SQUEEZE-BOX	4
WHAT BOOK, O LEARNED MAN, WILL SET ME RIGHT?	133	THE PURE FURY	2
AND SHE WAS RIGHT, FOR THERE BESIDE	136	THE SENSUALISTS	7
I HAD A DONKEY, THAT WAS ALL RIGHT,	178	THE DONKEY	1

		PAGE	TITLE	LINE
RIGHT (CONTINUED)				
YOU'LL FIND I'M EITHER RIGHT OR WRONG	....	181	MONOTONY SONG	23
IS BEFORE, OR RIGHT AFTER, A BLIZZARD.	....	183	THE LIZARD	2
THE WIND VEERING THE CAR SLIGHTLY TO THE RIGHT.	....	194	JOURNY INTERIOR	43
I DANCE TO THE RIGHT, TO THE LEFT;	....	208	HER WORDS	6
WHO SHOULD COME UP RIGHT THEN,	....	213	THE HAPPY THREE	17
"THE STAIR'S RIGHT THERE,	....	219	THE ABYSS	3
IT'S RIGHT WHERE YOU ARE--	....	219	THE ABYSS	7
HIS RIGHT EYE STARING STRAIGHT AT ME,	....	226	THE LIZARD	6
BUT THAT'S ALL RIGHT,--	....	228	IN VIOLENT WARD	3
THE RIGHT THING	....	250	THE RIGHT THING	T
THE RIGHT THING HAPPENS TO THE HAPPY MAN.	....	250	THE RIGHT THING	3
THE RIGHT THING HAPPENS TO THE HAPPY MAN.	....	250	THE RIGHT THING	9
THE RIGHT THING HAPPENS TO THE HAPPY MAN.	....	250	THE RIGHT THING	12
THE RIGHT THING HAPPENS TO THE HAPPY MAN.	....	250	THE RIGHT THING	19
YOU LARKS ALL DAY, YOU ROBINS RIGHT,	....	260	THE CHANGELING	22
BRINGS THE SECRET--RIGHT IN HERE!	....	266	FOR STEVENS	8
RIGHTS				
I, WITH NO RIGHTS IN THIS MATTER,	....	102	ELEGY FOR JANE	21
RIGID				
THE ICE CAP AT MY RIGID NECK	....	256	IN HYDROTHERAPY	3
RIMMED				
EYES RIMMED WITH PICKLE DUST,	....	46	PICKLE BELT	10
RIND				
A SEED THAT SWELLS THE RIND	....	18	GENESIS	7
BUT THE RIND, OFTEN, HATES THE LIFE WITHIN.	....	157	FIRST MEDITATN	13
RING				
IT IS THE UNMELODIC RING	....	22	SILENCE	7
THE NUMINOUS RING AROUND THE OPENING FLOWER,	......	198	THE LONG WATERS	70
RINGED				
RINGED ROUND WITH CRUMBLED CLAY:	....	146	THE SONG	15
RINGS				
ALL THE RINGS AND THE RELICS ENCRUSTED WITH SIN	....	32	SALE	19
THE RINGS HAVE GONE FROM THE POND.	....	85	PRAISE TO END!	13
THE FIRE SUBSIDES INTO RINGS OF WATER,	....	221	THE ABYSS	59
RIPE				
OUR VERNAL WISDOM MOVES THROUGH RIPE TO SERE.	......	12	SLOW SEASON	16
ROOTS RIPE AS OLD BAIT,	....	38	ROOT CELLAR	7
AND THE TIME RIPE FOR RUNNING TO THE MOON!	....	173	WHAT TELL BONES	85
RIPENESS				
IN THE HOUR OF RIPENESS THE TREE IS BARREN.	....	64	SHAPE OF FIRE	14
EASY THE LIFE OF THE MOUTH. WHAT A LUST FOR RIPENESS!	....	90	UNFOLD! UNFOLD!	39
RIPENING				
AT THE EDGE OF A RIPENING MEADOW, IN EARLY SUMMER,	....	204	THE ROSE	80
RIPPED				
THE RUSH OF WIND RIPPED OFF THE TENDER LEAVES	....	6	INTERLUDE	2
THE SHRIEK OF NAILS AS OLD SHINGLES ARE RIPPED FROM THE TOP				
OF A ROOF,	....	204	THE ROSE	70
RIPPLE				
FLASHED WITH THE SUN IN THE RIPPLE.	....	6	THE PREMONITION	11
A SINGLE RIPPLE STARTS FROM WHERE HE STOOD.	....	15	THE HERON	12
A RIPPLE MADE A SOFT REPLY.	....	100	THE VISITANT	6
A RIPPLE WAKES THE POND.	....	121	ALL EARTH, AIR	5
AT LAST ONE LONG UNDULANT RIPPLE,	....	190	AT OYSTER RIVER	11
TURNING NOT A LEAF, NOT A RIPPLE.	....	190	AT OYSTER RIVER	19
A RIPPLE WIDENING FROM A SINGLE STONE	....	201	THE FAR FIELD	102
WITH ONE SINUOUS RIPPLE, THEN A RUSH,	....	233	THE PIKE	16
RIPPLED				
THE WATER RIPPLED, AND SHE RIPPLED ON.	....	119	THE DREAM	8
THE WATER RIPPLED, AND SHE RIPPLED ON.	....	119	THE DREAM	8
RIPPLES				
A GULL RIDES ON THE RIPPLES OF A DREAM,	....	149	IN LATE SUMMER	1
DIPPING UP AND DOWN IN THE RIPPLES,	....	168	FOURTH MEDITATN	10
OVER THE THIN, FEATHERY RIPPLES BREAKING LIGHTLY AGAINST				
THE IRREGULAR SHORELINE--		197	THE LONG WATERS	50
AND THE LOW RIPPLES RUN OVER A PEBBLY SHORELINE,	....	198	THE LONG WATERS	62
THE WAVES LESS THAN THE RIPPLES MADE BY RISING FISH,	.....	203	THE ROSE	32
THE SLOW LONG RIPPLES WINKING IN MY EYES.	....	247	I WAITED	9
RIPPLING				
TOWARD THE QUICK-WATER, WRINKLING AND RIPPLING.	....	54	THE LOST SON	39
THE WAVES RIPPLING NEAR ME.	....	104	OLD LADY'S WRDS	43
AT FIRST A SWIFT RIPPLING BETWEEN ROCKS,	....	200	THE FAR FIELD	63
I'M NO LONGER A BIRD DIPPING A BEAK INTO RIPPLING WATER		220	THE ABYSS	41

	PAGE	TITLE	LINE
RIPS			
AND STEEL RIPS THROUGH CONFLICTING STEEL.	33	HIGHWAY: MICH	17
RISE			
WHO RISE FROM FLESH TO SPIRIT KNOW THE FALL:	107	SIR JOHN DAVIES	95
THE LIGHTS TILTING UP, SKYWARD, AS WE COME OVER A LITTLE RISE,	158	FIRST MEDITATN	24
I RISE AND FALL IN THE SLOW SEA OF A GRASSY PLAIN,	194	JOURNY INTERIOR	42
I RISE AND FALL, AND TIME FOLDS	194	JOURNY INTERIOR	46
OR RISE WITH THE GAR-EAGLE, THE GREAT-WINGED CONDOR.	209	HER LONGING	16
YET IT'S THE NATURE OF ALL LOVE TO RISE:	238	THE TRANCED	22
TO MEET THE WORLD, I RISE UP IN MY MIND;	243	THE MOTION	9
RISES			
THE BEACH RISES WITH THE WAVES.	83	O LULL ME, LULL	15
THE NIGHT WIND RISES. DOES MY FATHER LIVE?	135	THE RENEWAL	7
AND THAT SLOW HUMMING RISES INTO SONG.	155	THE DYING MAN	75
A LIGHT WIND RISES: I BECOME THE WIND.	167	HER BECOMING	95
THE SHAPE OF A LARK RISES FROM A STONE;	168	FOURTH MEDITATN	25
MY SPIRIT RISES WITH THE RISING WIND;	173	WHAT TELL BONES	88
A GREAT FLAME RISES FROM THE SUNLESS SEA;	188	THE LONGING	31
IN SLEEP, AFRAID. DEATH'S FACE RISES AFRESH,	190	AT OYSTER RIVER	25
AND THE TIDE RISES UP AGAINST THE GRASS	202	THE ROSE	9
RISING			
OR RISING OUT OF FERNS NOT FAR FROM WATER,	43	CARNATIONS	4
RISING SLOWLY OUT OF ITS BED,	67	SHAPE OF FIRE	84
UNDER THE RISING MOON;	124	WORDS FOR WIND	57
A VOICE KEEPS RISING IN MY EARLY SLEEP,	165	HER BECOMING	19
MY SPIRIT RISES WITH THE RISING WIND;	173	WHAT TELL BONES	88
THE WAVES LESS THAN THE RIPPLES MADE BY RISING FISH,	203	THE ROSE	32
THE DOLPHIN RISING FROM THE DARKENING WAVES;	205	THE ROSE	110
PERPETUALLY RISING OUT OF MYSELF,	209	HER LONGING	20
BEGIN RISING WHITELY,	210	HER TIME	9
RISING AGAIN, SLOWLY,	226	THE LIZARD	25
THE PARALYTIC STUNNED IN THE TUB, AND THE WATER RISING,--	227	MEADOW MOUSE	28
RISING, WHEELING AWAY WITH HARSH CRIES,	235	ALL MORNING	37
RISING OR FALLING'S ALL ONE DISCIPLINE!	245	THE DECISION	7
HOW PURE THE MOTION OF THE RISING DAY,	248	THE TREE, BIRD	19
RISINGS			
ALL RISINGS	85	PRAISE TO END!	15
RISK			
I'LL RISK THE WINTER FOR YOU.	79	GIVE WAY, GATES	23
RITUAL			
RITUAL OF MULTIGRAPH, PAPER-CLIP, COMMA,	46	DOLOR	7
I GREW TIRED OF THE RITUAL OF NAMES AND THE ASSISTANT KEEPER OF THE MOLLUSKS:	65	SHAPE OF FIRE	36
RITUALISTS			
THE RITUALISTS OF THE MIRROR, THE LONELY DRINKERS,	169	FOURTH MEDITATN	36
RIVEN			
WOULD NOT RELEASE ONE RIVEN NOTE:	22	SILENCE	18
THERE IS NO RIVEN TREE, OR LAMB DROPPED BY AN EAGLE.	159	FIRST MEDITATN	82
RIVER			
UNTIL WE CAME TO A RIVER.	6	THE PREMONITION	6
SKIRT HATRED'S RAGING RIVER,	7	ORDERS FOR DAY	10
THE RIVER OVERFLOWS THE LEVEL FIELD.	11	LIGHT BRIGHTER	8
"I SEE THE RIVER HARBOR, ALIVE WITH MEN AND SHIPS,	28	CLAIRVOY WIDOW	19
SO FAR DOWN THE RIVER	41	BIG WIND	4
RIVER INCIDENT	49	RIVER INCIDENT	T
I CAME WHERE THE RIVER	51	THE WAKING (1)	21
HUNTING ALONG THE RIVER,	54	THE LOST SON	40
A RIVER GLIDES OUT OF THE GRASS. A RIVER OR A SERPENT.	59	THE LONG ALLEY	1
A RIVER GLIDES OUT OF THE GRASS. A RIVER OR A SERPENT.	59	THE LONG ALLEY	1
WE WENT BY THE RIVER.	73	WHERE KNOCK IS	53
THE RIVER EBBED AND FLOWED:	87	PRAISE TO END!	68
THE GARDEN IS A RIVER FLOWING SOUTH.	129	SHE	8
WHAT'S WEATHER TO ME? EVEN CARP DIE IN THIS RIVER.	164	I'M HERE	90
A POOL RIDING AND SHINING WITH THE RIVER,	168	FOURTH MEDITATN	9
THE RIVER MOVES, WRINKLED BY MIDGES,	168	FOURTH MEDITATN	23
A POOL TO A RIVER?	169	FOURTH MEDITATN	30
MEDITATION AT OYSTER RIVER	190	AT OYSTER RIVER	T
AND THE WHOLE RIVER BEGINS TO MOVE FORWARD, ITS BRIDGES SHAKING.	191	AT OYSTER RIVER	56
IN THE SILTED SHALLOWS OF A SLOW RIVER,	200	THE FAR FIELD	39
THE RIVER TURNS ON ITSELF,	200	THE FAR FIELD	56
WHEN BANKS CONVERGE, AND THE WIDE RIVER WHITENS;	200	THE FAR FIELD	60

	PAGE	TITLE	LINE
RIVER (CONTINUED)			
MY EYES STARE AT THE BOTTOM OF A RIVER,	201	THE FAR FIELD	73
THE RIVER TURNS,	233	THE PIKE	1
I WATCH A RIVER WIND ITSELF AWAY;	243	THE MOTION	8
RIVERMOUTH			
A FISH RAVEN TURNS ON ITS PERCH (A DEAD TREE IN THE RIVERMOUTH),	190	AT OYSTER RIVER	22
RIVERS			
THE SALMON CLIMB THE RIVERS, THE RIVERS NUDGE THE SEA,	28	CLAIRVOY WIDOW	25
THE SALMON CLIMB THE RIVERS, THE RIVERS NUDGE THE SEA,	28	CLAIRVOY WIDOW	25
OR WHEN TWO RIVERS COMBINE, THE BLUE GLACIAL TORRENT	200	THE FAR FIELD	61
RIVER'S			
A WALKER AT THE RIVER'S EDGE MAY HEAR	11	LIGHT BRIGHTER	3
A RIVER'S LEAPING SOURCE	18	GENESIS	3
UNDER A RIVER'S SOURCE,	50	THE CYCLE	17
THE RIVER'S ALONE WITH ITS WATER.	85	PRAISE TO END!	14
BY THE SALT WAVES I HEAR A RIVER'S UNDERSONG,	221	THE ABYSS	76
RIVERY			
IN RIVERY AIR, AT EASE,	125	WORDS FOR WIND	73
RIVULET			
OVER A LIP OF STONE, THE TINY RIVULET;	191	AT OYSTER RIVER	43
RIVULETS			
IN RIVULETS; THE COLD ROOTS STIR BELOW.	11	LIGHT BRIGHTER	12
ROAD			
BUT STILL THE ROAD AND DUSTY FIELD KEPT DRY.	6	INTERLUDE	8
ON THE ROAD TO WOODLAWN	22	ROAD TO WDLAWN	T
AND AFTERWARDS I ALWAYS FELT MEAN, JOGGING BACK OVER THE LOGGING ROAD,	40	MOSS-GATHERING	9
GONE TO BOLSTER A ROAD.	103	OLD LADY'S WRDS	36
NOT ON THIS DUSTY ROAD	139	PLAINT	9
I WENT RUNNING DOWN A ROAD,	146	THE SONG	8
THE ARROYO CRACKING THE ROAD, THE WIND-BITTEN BUTTES, THE CANYONS,	193	JOURNY INTERIOR	7
GRINDING UP AND OVER THE NARROW ROAD, SPITTING AND ROARING.	193	JOURNY INTERIOR	22
A CHANCE? PERHAPS. BUT THE ROAD WAS PART OF ME, AND ITS DITCHES,	193	JOURNY INTERIOR	23
ON THE SHIMMERING ROAD,	194	JOURNY INTERIOR	50
THE ROAD LINED WITH SNOW-LADEN SECOND GROWTH,	199	THE FAR FIELD	4
THE ROAD CHANGING FROM GLAZED TARFACE TO A RUBBLE OF STONE,	199	THE FAR FIELD	8
SLOWLY I CAME BACK TO THE DUSTY ROAD;	247	I WAITED	15
ROADBED			
WHEELS SHAKE THE ROADBED STONE,	34	NIGHT JOURNEY	24
ROAD-CROWNS			
THE TOWNS WITH THEIR HIGH PITTED ROAD-CROWNS AND DEEP GUTTERS,	193	JOURNY INTERIOR	30
ROADSIDE			
ALWAYS A SHARP TURN TO THE LEFT PAST A BARN CLOSE TO THE ROADSIDE,	193	JOURNY INTERIOR	25
ROADWAY			
THE MEN ON RAIL AND ROADWAY KEEP MOVING ON AND ON.	28	CLAIRVOY WIDOW	24
ROAM			
AND I ROAM ELSEWHERE, MY BODY THINKING,	195	JOURNY INTERIOR	68
ROAMED			
AND YET I ROAMED OUT WHERE	128	THE VOICE	7
ROAR			
SHE'D RANT AND SHE'D ROAR:	179	MYRTLE	8
THE SUDDEN SUCKING ROAR AS THE CULVERT LOOSENS ITS DEBRIS OF BRANCHES AND STICKS,	191	AT OYSTER RIVER	53
ROAR 'EM, WHORE 'EM, COCKALORUM,	266	FOR STEVENS	17
ROARED			
ALL NIGHT AND ALL DAY THE WIND ROARED IN THE TREES,	12	MID-CNTRY BLOW	1
ROARING			
O MORE THAN A ROARING BOY,	169	FOURTH MEDITATN	51
CREEKS SWOLLEN IN MIDSUMMER FROM THE FLASH-FLOOD ROARING INTO THE NARROW VALLEY.	193	JOURNY INTERIOR	8
GRINDING UP AND OVER THE NARROW ROAD, SPITTING AND ROARING.	193	JOURNY INTERIOR	22
I'M A ROARING GIRL, AN EXPENSIVE WENCH,	272	DUET	15
ROARS			
WATER ROARS INTO THE CISTERN.	231	THE STORM	37
ROAST			
WITH COLD ROAST BEEF AND COFFEE FOR DESSERT--	274	SUPPR W LINDSAY	33
ROBBERS			
THE KIDS PLAY COPS AND ROBBERS, THE KIDS PLAY MUMBLEY-PEG,	27	CLAIRVOY WIDOW	9

	PAGE	TITLE	LINE
ROBE			
WRAPPED IN THE TATTERED ROBE OF DEATH,	136	THE SENSUALISTS	19
ROBERT			
AND ROBERT FROST. THEY MIGHT REMEMBER ME."	274	SUPPR W LINDSAY	49
ROBES			
MAY THEY SLEEP IN ROBES OF GREEN, AMONG THE ANCIENT FERNS;	169	FOURTH MEDITATN	58
IN ROBES OF GREEN, IN GARMENTS OF ADIEU.	201	THE FAR FIELD	86
ROBINS			
YOU LARKS ALL DAY, YOU ROBINS RIGHT,	260	THE CHANGELING	22
ROCK			
OF MOTION MOORED TO ROCK;	4	DEATH PIECE	6
THE BITTER ROCK, THE BARREN SOIL	18	LONG LIVE WEEDS	3
BENEATH THE ROCK AND CLAY,	50	THE CYCLE	2
THE WIND SHARPENED ITSELF ON A ROCK;	65	SHAPE OF FIRE	39
BEGIN WITH THE ROCK;	77	BRING THE DAY!	30
LIGHT FATTENS THE ROCK.	83	O LULL ME, LULL	19
ROCK ME TO SLEEP, THE WEATHER'S WRONG.	86	PRAISE TO END!	28
BE A PLEASED ROCK	98	O, THOU OPENING	36
LEANING OVER A ROCK,	104	OLD LADY'S WRDS	41
I ROCK IN MY OWN DARK,	172	WHAT TELL BONES	62
THEN RETIRE TO A ROCK HIGHER UP ON THE CLIFF-SIDE.	190	AT OYSTER RIVER	16
I SHIFT ON MY ROCK, AND I THINK:	191	AT OYSTER RIVER	41
AND THAT WRIST-THICK CASCADE TUMBLING FROM A CLEFT ROCK,	191	AT OYSTER RIVER	44
I ROCK WITH THE MOTION OF MORNING;	191	AT OYSTER RIVER	58
I THINK OF THE ROCK SINGING, AND LIGHT MAKING ITS OWN SILENCE,	204	THE ROSE	79
I ROCK BETWEEN DARK AND DARK,	221	THE ABYSS	78
ROCKED			
THE VALLEY ROCKED BENEATH THE GRANITE HILL;	106	SIR JOHN DAVIES	59
ROCKER			
UNDER THE ROCKER	71	WHERE KNOCK IS	6
ROCKING			
ROCKING WITH SMALL FISH,	84	O LULL ME, LULL	34
GENTLY ROCKING.	93	I CRY, LOVE!	53
WHERE'S THE GREAT RAGE OF A ROCKING HEART, THE HIGH RARE TRUE DANGEROUS	98	O, THOU OPENING	30
ROCKING IT, LIKE A SUN-STRUCK POND,	163	I'M HERE	84
AT EASE AFTER ROCKING THE FLESH TO SLEEP,	194	JOURNY INTERIOR	55
ROCKING THE BLOSSOMS;	258	SONG (3)	15
ROCKS			
THE FIELDS ARE HARSH AND BARE, THE ROCKS	15	COMING OF COLD	45
ITS RHYTHM ROCKS THE EARTH,	34	NIGHT JOURNEY	2
AN OLD SCOW BUMPS OVER BLACK ROCKS.	64	SHAPE OF FIRE	5
ON THE ROCKS SOUTH OF QUIET, IN THE CLOSE REGIONS OF KISSING,	86	PRAISE TO END!	20
ROCKS IN AND OUT OF ITSELF.	163	I'M HERE	59
MIST ALTERS THE ROCKS. WHAT CAN I TELL MY BONES?	172	WHAT TELL BONES	44
THE SPIRIT DECLARES ITSELF TO THESE ROCKS.	172	WHAT TELL BONES	46
THE WIND ROCKS WITH MY WISH; THE RAIN SHIELDS ME;	173	WHAT TELL BONES	81
I WOULD BE A STREAM, WINDING BETWEEN GREAT STRIATED ROCKS IN LATE SUMMER;	188	THE LONGING	46
OVER THE LOW, BARNACLED, ELEPHANT-COLORED ROCKS,	190	AT OYSTER RIVER	1
EVEN THE GULLS QUIET ON THE FAR ROCKS,	190	AT OYSTER RIVER	7
AT FIRST A SWIFT RIPPLING BETWEEN ROCKS,	200	THE FAR FIELD	63
WHILE ON A FAR POINT OF THE ROCKS	202	THE ROSE	27
I LIVE WITH THE ROCKS, THEIR WEEDS,	205	THE ROSE	89
THE SHOAL ROCKS WITH THE SEA.	215	HIS FOREBODING	1
THAT PLACE AMONG THE ROCKS--IS IT A CAVE,	239	IN A DARK TIME	11
ROCK-SEAMS			
WHILE THE ROCK-SEAMS SWELL WITH THE SEA,	261	THE CHANGELING	33
ROCK-SHUT			
UNDER EVEN THE ROCK-SHUT GROUND,	50	THE CYCLE	16
ROCKY			
A FURRED, A ROCKY POOL,	233	THE PIKE	3
THEN LOST ITSELF DOWN THROUGH A ROCKY GORGE.	247	I WAITED	20
RODE			
BUT SHE RODE IT OUT,	41	BIG WIND	21
AND BREATHING HARD, AS THAT MAN RODE	136	THE SENSUALISTS	11
HE RODE ALL NIGHT, AND CAME	263	FOLLIES OF ADAM	32
ROLL			
THEN ROLL THEM IN GREASE,--	55	THE LOST SON	56
I COULD ROLL IN THE DUST OF A FINE RAGE.	104	OLD LADY'S WRDS	50
THEN DOWN, AS WE ROLL LIKE A BOAT FROM A WAVE-CREST.	158	FIRST MEDITATN	25

	PAGE	TITLE	LINE
ROLLED			
THE HEART BEAT FASTER AS THE FAT WORDS ROLLED.	21	THE AUCTION	14
THE FRUIT ROLLED BY ALL DAY.	46	PICKLE BELT	1
BUT MANY A MAN ROLLED UNDER THE TABLE	112	SQUEEZE-BOX	36
HER FACE LIKE A RAIN-BEATEN STONE ON THE DAY SHE ROLLED OFF	223	ELEGY (2)	1
ROLLING			
UNTIL I COULD THINK THERE WERE WAVES ROLLING HIGH AS MY BEDROOM FLOOR;	12	MID-CNTRY BLOW	2
IN THE DARK, IN THE ROLLING WATER.	49	RIVER INCIDENT	11
IN THE BACK OF MY MIND, RUNNING WITH THE ROLLING WATER,	165	HER BECOMING	9
MY DESIRE FOR THE PEAKS, THE BLACK RAVINES, THE ROLLING MISTS	196	THE LONG WATERS	9
THE WHOLE SHIP ROLLING SLIGHTLY SIDEWAYS,	203	THE ROSE	36
ROLLS			
HOW HE ROLLS THE VOCABLES,	266	FOR STEVENS	7
ROMP			
THE CENTAUR AND THE SIBYL ROMP AND SING	135	THE RENEWAL	2
ROMPED			
WE ROMPED UNTIL THE PANS	45	MY PAPA'S WALTZ	5
I ROMPED, LITHE AS A CHILD, DOWN THE SUMMERY STREETS OF MY VEINS,	86	PRAISE TO END!	21
ROMPED UPON THE GOLDY GRASS,	87	PRAISE TO END!	57
THEN WE ROMPED OUT AGAIN,	214	THE HAPPY THREE	35
ROMPING			
I'LL SING AND WHISTLE ROMPING WITH THE BEARS.	105	SIR JOHN DAVIES	6
ROMPING AROUND A FIRE,	163	I'M HERE	67
ROOF			
THAT HE WAS GONE, WOULD BE THE ROOF;	178	THE CEILING	4
THE CAT RUNS FOR A ROOF	180	GOO-GIRL	11
THE SHRIEK OF NAILS AS OLD SHINGLES ARE RIPPED FROM THE TOP OF A ROOF,	204	THE ROSE	70
ROOF-TOP			
FLINGING LONG STRINGS OF WET ACROSS THE ROOF-TOP,	41	BIG WIND	29
ROOM			
THE SCHEME WITHOUT PURPOSE; PRIDE IN A FURNISHED ROOM;	5	PROGNOSIS	10
THE WALKER'S FOOT HAS SCARCELY ROOM	14	COMING OF COLD	5
--AND THE EYES, STILL VIVID, LOOKING UP FROM A SUNKEN ROOM.	22	ROAD TO WDLAWN	8
A HUTCH BY THE EXIT HIS ROOM WITH A VIEW.	29	THE GENTLE	8
NOW IN THE MISERY OF BED-SITTING ROOM CONFUSION,	29	THE REMINDER	9
THE LIBRARY USED AS A CARD ROOM INSTEAD	32	SALE	11
THE DINING ROOM CARPET DYED BRIGHTER THAN BLOOD,	32	SALE	13
THE ROOM THAT THE CHILDREN HAD NEVER BEEN IN,	32	SALE	18
LONELY RECEPTION ROOM, LAVATORY, SWITCHBOARD,	46	DOLOR	5
THE ROOM WAS THIRTY-FIVE BELOW;	114	DINKY	14
PACING A ROOM, A ROOM WITH DEAD-WHITE WALLS;	242	THE SEQUEL	30
PACING A ROOM, A ROOM WITH DEAD-WHITE WALLS;	242	THE SEQUEL	30
AND IT STEPPED IN THE ROOM, UNDER HIS ARM,--	273	SUPPR W LINDSAY	6
ROOT			
THERE'S CANKER AT THE ROOT, YOUR SEED	4	FEUD	9
ROOT CELLAR	38	ROOT CELLAR	T
THE HOLY ROOT WAGS THE TAIL OF A HILL;	99	O, THOU OPENING	54
THE ROUND HOME OF A ROOT,--	99	O, THOU OPENING	75
THE ROOT, THE CORE OF A CRY.	124	WORDS FOR WIND	50
THE BREATH OF A LONG ROOT,	125	WORDS FOR WIND	82
NEAR THE STEM, WHITER AT ROOT,	221	THE ABYSS	83
WHAT ROOT OF HIS EVER DENIED ITS STEM?	224	OTTO	10
I TALKED TO A SHRUNKEN ROOT;	262	FOLLIES OF ADAM	15
BUT WHEN THE ROOT REPLIED,	262	FOLLIES OF ADAM	19
ROOTED			
GREAT BOEHME ROOTED ALL IN YES AND NO;	133	THE PURE FURY	13
ROOTED IN STONE, KEEPING THE WHOLE OF LIGHT,	205	THE ROSE	112
ROOTS			
IN RIVULETS; THE COLD ROOTS STIR BELOW.	11	LIGHT BRIGHTER	12
ROOTS RIPE AS OLD BAIT,	38	ROOT CELLAR	7
SWELLING THE ROOTS WITH STEAM AND STENCH,	38	FORCING HOUSE	8
HACKING AT BLACK HAIRY ROOTS,--	39	WEED PULLER	2
THE CRUMBLING SMALL HOLLOW STICKS ON THE UNDERSIDE MIXED WITH ROOTS,	40	MOSS-GATHERING	4
OR SCOOP OUT A WEED CLOSE TO FLOURISHING ROOTS,	42	OLD FLORIST	6
THEN PLUMPING IN THE BUNCHED ROOTS,	42	TRANSPLANTING	6
TURNED-OVER ROOTS	43	FLOWER DUMP	6
BENEATH THE ROOTS OF TREES,	50	THE CYCLE	3
WHERE DO THE ROOTS GO?	55	THE LOST SON	62

	PAGE	TITLE	LINE
ROOTS (CONTINUED)			
HAS ROOTS.	76	I NEED, I NEED	68
I LIVED WITH DEEP ROOTS ONCE:	139	PLAINT	13
AND A TREE TILTS FROM ITS ROOTS,	157	FIRST MEDITATN	6
AND THE IVY-BRANCH, CAST TO THE GROUND, PUTS DOWN ROOTS INTO THE SAWDUST,	197	THE LONG WATERS	34
AND THE PINE, WHOLE WITH ITS ROOTS, SINKS INTO THE ESTUARY,	197	THE LONG WATERS	35
GOD BLESS THE ROOTS!--BODY AND SOUL ARE ONE!	250	THE RIGHT THING	7
ROSE			
MY SPIRITS ROSE EACH TIME THE HAMMER FELL,	21	THE AUCTION	13
ROSE ON SUCH LOPPED LIMBS TO A NEW LIFE?	37	CUTTINGS (LATE)	4
A SHAPE IN THE MIND ROSE UP:	49	NIGHT CROW	3
ROSE FROM A MOSSY MOUND	50	THE CYCLE	5
THE ROSE, THE CHRYSANTHEMUM TURNED TOWARD THE LIGHT.	57	THE LOST SON	146
REACH ME ROSE, SWEET ONE, STILL MOIST IN THE LOAM,	61	THE LONG ALLEY	68
A ROSE SWAYS LEAST.	66	SHAPE OF FIRE	62
TO BE BY THE ROSE	67	SHAPE OF FIRE	83
THE WORM AND THE ROSE	78	BRING THE DAY!	35
AND THE MOLD SANG IN THE BLEACHED VALLEYS UNDER THE ROSE.	102	ELEGY FOR JANE	9
WE ROSE TO MEET THE MOON, AND SAW NO MORE.	107	SIR JOHN DAVIES	70
ROSE, EASY ON A STEM,	124	WORDS FOR WIND	42
OF THE UNFOLDING ROSE,	125	WORDS FOR WIND	84
AS IF A LION KNELT TO KISS A ROSE,	131	SENTENTIOUS MAN	17
AS IF ALL THINGS HAD DIED, AND ROSE AGAIN.	133	THE PURE FURY	6
LIGHT STRIDES THE ROSE;	137	LOVE'S PROGRESS	8
FALTERED; ROSE UP AGAIN;	145	THE BEAST	12
ROSE BUT TO LURCH AND FALL,	145	THE BEAST	13
THE DUST ROSE AND SPOKE;	147	THE EXORCISM	6
A LATE ROSE RAVAGES THE CASUAL EYE,	149	IN LATE SUMMER	17
BUT A KISS WIDENS THE ROSE;	153	THE DYING MAN	8
EXPLODES LIKE A ROSE, OR THRUSTS WINGS OVER THE CARIBBEAN.	159	FIRST MEDITATN	77
THE WAY OUT OF A ROSE?	165	HER BECOMING	27
WHAT'S BECOME OF CARE? THIS LAKE BREATHES LIKE A ROSE.	170	FOURTH MEDITATN	76
THE ROSE EXCEEDS, THE ROSE EXCEEDS US ALL.	188	THE LONGING	29
THE ROSE EXCEEDS, THE ROSE EXCEEDS US ALL.	188	THE LONGING	29
I WOULD BELIEVE MY PAIN: AND THE EYE QUIET ON THE GROWING ROSE;	188	THE LONGING	43
THE ROSE	202	THE ROSE	T
BUT THIS ROSE, THIS ROSE IN THE SEA-WIND,	203	THE ROSE	39
BUT THIS ROSE, THIS ROSE IN THE SEA-WIND,	203	THE ROSE	39
A SINGLE WILD ROSE, STRUGGLING OUT OF THE WHITE EMBRACE OF THE MORNING-GLORY,	203	THE ROSE	44
NEAR THIS ROSE, IN THIS GROVE OF SUN-PARCHED, WIND-WARPED MADRONAS,	205	THE ROSE	98
AND IN THIS ROSE, THIS ROSE IN THE SEA-WIND,	205	THE ROSE	111
AND IN THIS ROSE, THIS ROSE IN THE SEA-WIND,	205	THE ROSE	111
ROSE UP WITHIN THE MIND,	237	THE TRANCED	9
ROSE UP AND FELL LIKE AN ERRATIC WIND.	237	THE TRANCED	10
A BUD BROKE TO A ROSE,	240	IN EVEING AIR	11
AND I ROSE FROM A LAST DIMINISHING.	240	IN EVEING AIR	12
I ROSE, A HEAVY BULK, ABOVE THE FIELD.	247	I WAITED	5
THE ROSE LEAPS TO THIS GIRL;	262	FOLLIES OF ADAM	11
BY ONE WHO ROSE UP FROM THE DEAD.	264	THREE EPIGRAMS	10
ONE OF THOSE FAT ONES WINDING THROUGH A ROSE.	273	SUPPR W LINDSAY	27
ROSE-BRIER			
AND MY DRESS CAUGHT ON ROSE-BRIER.	162	I'M HERE	47
ROSE-HOUSE			
END OF THE ROSE-HOUSE,	41	BIG WIND	15
THAT OLD ROSE-HOUSE,	41	BIG WIND	22
ROSES			
LILIES, PALE-PINK CYCLAMEN, ROSES,	39	WEED PULLER	12
CARRYING HER FULL CARGO OF ROSES.	41	BIG WIND	33
OR STAND ALL NIGHT WATERING ROSES, HIS FEET BLUE IN RUBBER BOOTS.	42	OLD FLORIST	10
ROSES, TO STRAIGHTEN	44	FRAU BAUMAN	7
THE ROSES KEPT BREATHING IN THE DARK.	57	THE LOST SON	126
WHERE THE FIREMAN PULLED OUT ROSES,	57	THE LOST SON	132
THE BIG ROSES, THE BIG BLOODY CLINKERS.	57	THE LOST SON	133
HE WATERED THE ROSES.	73	WHERE KNOCK IS	64
BUT THESE ROSES: I CAN WEAR THEM BY LOOKING AWAY.	163	I'M HERE	78
AND I THINK OF ROSES, ROSES,	203	THE ROSE	51
AND I THINK OF ROSES, ROSES,	203	THE ROSE	51
WITH THAT MAN, AND THOSE ROSES?	203	THE ROSE	57

	PAGE	TITLE	LINE
ROTTED			
LATE AUTUMN FRUIT IS ROTTED NOW.	14	COMING OF COLD	27
ROTTEN			
ROTTEN LEAVES OR YELLOWY PETALS,	42	OLD FLORIST	5
WAKE ME, WITCH, WE'LL DO THE DANCE OF ROTTEN STICKS.	64	SHAPE OF FIRE	10
HONORED, ON MY RETURN, BY THE ANCIENT FELLOWSHIP OF ROTTEN STEMS.	89	UNFOLD! UNFOLD!	26
ROTTING			
WITH THE RAGS AND ROTTING CLOTHES,	47	THE RETURN	11
ROUGH			
THE ROUGH, THE WICKED, AND THE WILD	18	LONG LIVE WEEDS	7
ROUND			
YOU ROUND DOG?--	81	SENSIBILITY! LA	17
THE ROUND HOME OF A ROOT,--	99	O, THOU OPENING	75
I THOUGHT THAT ONCE, AND THOUGHT COMES ROUND AGAIN;	107	SIR JOHN DAVIES	87
A WIND WREATHES ROUND A TREE.	126	WORDS FOR WIND	93
AND I DANCE ROUND AND ROUND,	126	WORDS FOR WIND	102
AND I DANCE ROUND AND ROUND,	126	WORDS FOR WIND	102
AND COLLOPED ROUND WITH FERN.	145	THE BEAST	9
THE GREAT ROUND EYES HAD GONE.	145	THE BEAST	17
RINGED ROUND WITH CRUMBLED CLAY:	146	THE SONG	15
ONE ROUND EYE STILL TOWARD ME.	226	THE LIZARD	19
WITH A ROUND VIREO'S EYE, QUIET AND CONTAINED,	234	ALL MORNING	13
ONCE MORE, THE ROUND	251	ONCE MORE, RND	T
AS ROUND AND PURE AS THE MOON,	271	THE REPLY	8
I'D SAY MY FACE IS JUST AS ROUND AS HIS,	273	SUPPR W LINDSAY	8
ROUNDS			
LIGHT ON ITS ROUNDS, A PURE EXTREME OF LIGHT	244	INFIRMITY	14
ROUNDY			
HEAR ME, SOFT EARS AND ROUNDY STONES!	76	I NEED, I NEED	57
ROUSE			
A ROUSE FOR STEVENS	266	FOR STEVENS	T
ROUT			
AND ROUT THE SPECTER OF ALARM.	19	AGNST DISASTER	12
DO WE ROUT THE FISH?	60	THE LONG ALLEY	59
THERE WERE CLOUDS MAKING A ROUT OF SHAPES CROSSING A WINDBREAK OF CEDARS,	63	FIELD OF LIGHT	48
ROUTINE			
FOR A NEW ROUTINE--	228	THE GERANIUM	6
ROWER			
HELD UP, WHILE THE ROWER BREATHES, AND THE SMALL BOAT DRIFTS QUIETLY SHOREWARD;	67	SHAPE OF FIRE	91
ROWS			
THE FIELDS STRETCH OUT IN LONG, UNBROKEN ROWS.	13	PRAISE PRAIRIE	9
LIKE WITCHES THEY FLEW ALONG ROWS	44	FRAU BAUMAN	19
RUNNING ALONG THE NARROW FURROWS OF THE SHORE, THE ROWS OF DEAD CLAM SHELLS;	190	AT OYSTER RIVER	3
RUB			
I'M COLD. I'M COLD ALL OVER. RUB ME IN FATHER AND MOTHER.	56	THE LOST SON	85
RUBBER			
OR STAND ALL NIGHT WATERING ROSES, HIS FEET BLUE IN RUBBER BOOTS.	42	OLD FLORIST	10
HIM WITH THE PLATITUDES AND RUBBER DOUGHNUTS,	65	SHAPE OF FIRE	30
WHO HAD A RUBBER HAT	71	WHERE KNOCK IS	17
RUBBERS			
BRING ME MY HAT, MY UMBRELLA AND RUBBERS,	48	LAST WORDS	9
RUBBERY			
AND RUBBERY SHOOTS,	38	FORCING HOUSE	2
RUBBING			
RUBBING MY NOSE IN THE WOOL OF BLANKETS;	162	I'M HERE	30
RUBBISH			
AND ALL THE RUBBISH OF CONFUSION SOLD.	21	THE AUCTION	16
DOWN AMONG THE RUBBISH, THE BUG-RIDDLED FOLIAGE,	54	THE LOST SON	41
RUBBLE			
DIGGING INTO THE SOFT RUBBLE UNDERNEATH,	39	WEED PULLER	4
BETTER TO HUG CLOSE, WARY OF RUBBLE AND FALLING STONES.	193	JOURNY INTERIOR	6
THE DEAD SNAKES AND MUSKRATS, THE TURTLES GASPING IN THE RUBBLE,	194	JOURNY INTERIOR	36
THE ROAD CHANGING FROM GLAZED TARFACE TO A RUBBLE OF STONE,	199	THE FAR FIELD	8
(I FOUND IT LYING AMONG THE RUBBLE OF AN OLD COAL BIN)	199	THE FAR FIELD	20
THE TURTLE GASPING IN THE DUSTY RUBBLE OF THE HIGHWAY,	227	MEADOW MOUSE	27
RUBBLESTONES			
I SEE THE RUBBLESTONES BEGIN TO STRETCH	135	THE RENEWAL	21

	PAGE	TITLE	LINE
RUDE			
A PRUSSIAN WHO LEARNED EARLY TO BE RUDE	224	OTTO	2
RUFFLED			
SWIMMING SLOWLY, ITS BACK RUFFLED BY THE LIGHT CROSS-WINDS,	197	THE LONG WATERS	53
RUIN			
WE HUNT THE CAUSE OF RUIN, ADD,	30	THE RECKONING	5
RUMBLE			
I HEARD YOUR LAUGHTER RUMBLE FROM MY BELLY.	25	DIM-WIT COUSIN	12
RUMINANT			
THE RUMINANT, REASON, CHEWS A POISONED CUD.	5	PROGNOSIS	8
RUN			
I RUN, I RUN TO THE WHISTLE OF MONEY.	56	THE LOST SON	110
I RUN, I RUN TO THE WHISTLE OF MONEY.	56	THE LOST SON	110
FEET RUN OVER THE SIMPLE STONES,	93	I CRY, LOVE!	36
--WHEN SHE THOUGHT I'D RUN OUT OF MONEY.	112	SQUEEZE-BOX	41
SMALL WATERS RUN TOWARD A MIRY HOLE--	132	SENTENTIOUS MAN	39
AND THE LOW RIPPLES RUN OVER A PEBBLY SHORELINE,	198	THE LONG WATERS	62
TO RUN UNDER THE HAWK'S WING,	227	MEADOW MOUSE	23
NOW YOU RUN TO THE MONEY, IT'S JIG, JIG, JIG;	272	DUET	2
RUNE			
AS CRYPTIC AS A RUNE,	271	THE REPLY	7
RUNG			
THE CHAIR OF HONOR, WITH A MISSING RUNG."	21	THE AUCTION	8
RUNNEL			
THEN A RUNNEL BEHIND ME, CREEPING CLOSER,	190	AT OYSTER RIVER	4
RUNNING			
--AND THE TAINT IN A BLOOD THAT WAS RUNNING TOO THIN.	32	SALE	20
RUNNING LIGHTLY OVER SPONGY GROUND,	54	THE LOST SON	34
MY VEINS ARE RUNNING NOWHERE. DO THE BONES CAST OUT THEIR FIRE?	56	THE LOST SON	101
LOOK, LOOK, THE DITCH IS RUNNING WHITE!	57	THE LOST SON	119
I WENT RUNNING DOWN A ROAD,	146	THE SONG	8
COME RUNNING FROM THE LEAVES,	147	THE EXORCISM	15
THE LOOSE AIR SENT ME RUNNING LIKE A CHILD--	155	THE DYING MAN	55
RUNNING THROUGH HIGH GRASSES,	161	I'M HERE	21
IN THE BACK OF MY MIND, RUNNING WITH THE ROLLING WATER,	165	HER BECOMING	9
WHAT WAS I RUNNING FROM?	166	HER BECOMING	62
AND THE TIME RIPE FOR RUNNING TO THE MOON!	173	WHAT TELL BONES	85
RUNNING ALONG THE NARROW FURROWS OF THE SHORE, THE ROWS OF DEAD CLAM SHELLS;	190	AT OYSTER RIVER	3
UNDERNEATH, THE SLUGGISH WATER RUNNING BETWEEN WEEDS, BROKEN WHEELS, TIRES, STONES.	194	JOURNY INTERIOR	33
BY SMALL STREAMS RUNNING DOWN UNDER FALLEN FIR TREES.	197	THE LONG WATERS	48
THEN A LONG RUNNING OVER FLAT STONES	200	THE FAR FIELD	64
RUNNING OVER THE COVERLET, DOWN UNDER THE IRON BEDSTEAD.	231	THE STORM	35
RUNNING FROM GOD'S THE LONGEST RACE OF ALL.	245	THE DECISION	2
RUNS			
THE LAST TRICYCLE RUNS CRAZILY TO THE END OF THE WALK.	33	IDYLL	4
THIS SLAG RUNS SLOW. WHAT BLEEDS WHEN METAL BREAKS?	59	THE LONG ALLEY	11
THE SHALLOW STREAM RUNS SLACK;	123	WORDS FOR WIND	25
RUNS FITFULLY ALONG THE STUBBLE,	160	FIRST MEDITATN	95
THE CAT RUNS FOR A ROOF	180	GOO-GIRL	11
AND THE SPIRIT RUNS, INTERMITTENTLY,	192	AT OYSTER RIVER	64
RUNS WITH THE INTREPID SHOREBIRDS--	192	AT OYSTER RIVER	66
THE FRIEND THAT RUNS BEFORE ME ON THE WINDY HEADLANDS,	198	THE LONG WATERS	71
RUNS TO COVER:	210	HER TIME	24
KILLED EVERY CAT THAT NEARED THEIR PHEASANT RUNS;	224	OTTO	28
A CAT RUNS FROM THE WIND AS WE DO,	230	THE STORM	19
THEN A CRACK OF THUNDER, AND THE BLACK RAIN RUNS OVER US, OVER	230	THE STORM	23
MY TRUE SELF RUNS TOWARD A HILL	251	ONCE MORE, RND	3
LET'S EAT BEFORE THE MOONLIGHT ALL RUNS OUT."	273	SUPPR W LINDSAY	29
RUNWAY			
AND THE UP-SPRING OF THE PLANK WHEN A FOOT LEFT THE RUNWAY.	158	FIRST MEDITATN	47
RUSH			
THE RUSH OF WIND RIPPED OFF THE TENDER LEAVES	6	INTERLUDE	2
WE RUSH INTO A RAIN	34	NIGHT JOURNEY	22
SEND DOWN A RUSH OF AIR, O TORRENTIAL,	61	THE LONG ALLEY	83
AROUND, BACK INTO THE TINY MAINCURRENT, THE RUSH OF BROWNISH-WHITE WATER,	159	FIRST MEDITATN	71
THE RUSH OF SMELLS STRIKES LIKE A COLD FIRE, THE THROAT FREEZES,	220	THE ABYSS	47
WITH ONE SINUOUS RIPPLE, THEN A RUSH,	233	THE PIKE	16

	PAGE	TITLE	LINE
RUSHING			
A FEW WHITE CLOUDS ALL RUSHING EASTWARD,	43	CHILD ON GRNHSE	5
PITTING MY BREAST AGAINST THE RUSHING AIR,	209	HER LONGING	18
RUSSELLS			
LIFTING ME HIGH OVER THE FOUR-FOOT STEMS, THE MRS.			
RUSSELLS, AND HIS OWN ELABORATE HYBRIDS,	203	THE ROSE	54
RUSSIAN			
PAUL BUNYAN IS PART RUSSIAN, DID YOU KNOW?--	274	SUPPR W LINDSAY	44
RUSTED			
AMONG THE TIN CANS, TIRES, RUSTED PIPES, BROKEN MACHINERY,--	199	THE FAR FIELD	17
RUSTLES			
WHAT RUSTLES IN THE FERN?	148	THE SMALL	13
RUSTLING			
THE TIDE RUSTLING IN, SLIDING BETWEEN THE RIDGES OF STONE,	191	AT OYSTER RIVER	34
RUSTY			
INTO THE RUSTY BOILERS,	41	BIG WIND	9
S			
SWEET ALICE S. MORRIS, I AM PLEASED, OF COURSE,	113	TO A LADY ED	1
A MAN NAMED PHILANDER S. GOO	182	PHILANDER	1
SACK			
THEN EACH FELL BACK, LIMP AS A SACK,	136	THE SENSUALISTS	25
SACKED			
BUT I SACKED THE PRESUMPTUOUS HAG THE NEXT WEEK,	228	THE GERANIUM	25
SAD			
I WAS SAD FOR A FISH.	73	WHERE KNOCK IS	58
MAMMA, SHE'S A SAD FAT.	74	I NEED, I NEED	19
I'M SAD WITH THE LITTLE OWLS.	80	GIVE WAY, GATES	45
CARES ABOUT THE DANCE OF DEAD UNDERWEAR, OR THE SAD WALTZ			
OF PAPER	98	O, THOU OPENING	26
SAD, IN A SINGING-TIME?	98	O, THOU OPENING	45
OH, WHEN SHE WAS SAD, SHE CAST HERSELF DOWN INTO SUCH A			
PURE DEPTH,	102	ELEGY FOR JANE	10
TO SOME IT MAY SEEM A SAD THING TO RELATE,	112	SQUEEZE-BOX	38
ELSEWHERE, IN HOUSES, EVEN PAILS CAN BE SAD;	157	FIRST MEDITATN	4
HOW CLOSE WE ARE TO THE SAD ANIMALS!	171	WHAT TELL BONES	20
UNTIL YOU HAVE THOUGHT THIS SAD TALE THROUGH:	177	KITTY-CAT BIRD	19
SAD THE SOUL'S JOY. LOVED HEART, WHAT ELSE CAN I SAY	261	THE CHANGELING	28
SADNESS			
I HAVE KNOWN THE INEXORABLE SADNESS OF PENCILS,	46	DOLOR	1
SAGGED			
SAGGED LIKE A FRIGHTENED LIP.	47	THE RETURN	7
SAGINAW			
THE SAGINAW SONG	267	SAGINAW SONG	T
IN SAGINAW, IN SAGINAW,	267	SAGINAW SONG	1
IN SAGINAW, IN SAGINAW,	267	SAGINAW SONG	1
IN SAGINAW, IN SAGINAW,	267	SAGINAW SONG	13
IN SAGINAW, IN SAGINAW,	267	SAGINAW SONG	13
IN SAGINAW, IN SAGINAW,	268	SAGINAW SONG	37
IN SAGINAW, IN SAGINAW,	268	SAGINAW SONG	37
SAID			
I SAID: ON ALL THESE, DEATH, WITH GENTLENESS, COME DOWN.	48	JUDGE NOT	10
DARK HOLLOWS SAID, LEE TO THE WIND,	54	THE LOST SON	28
THE MOON SAID, BACK OF AN EEL,	54	THE LOST SON	29
THE SALT SAID, LOOK BY THE SEA,	54	THE LOST SON	30
SAID TO ME: DIE.	55	THE LOST SON	82
LOO, LOO, SAID THE SULPHUROUS WATER,	59	THE LONG ALLEY	14
DON'T HIT HIM ON THE BOAT, I SAID.	73	WHERE KNOCK IS	59
THE STEMS SAID, THANK YOU.	73	WHERE KNOCK IS	66
I SAID TO PAPA;	73	WHERE KNOCK IS	77
I SAID TO MAMMA.	74	WHERE KNOCK IS	81
A DOVE SAID DOVE ALL DAY.	75	I NEED, I NEED	20
HER FEET SAID YES.	76	I NEED, I NEED	61
I SAID TO THE GATE,	76	I NEED, I NEED	63
FOREVER IS EASY, SHE SAID.	77	BRING THE DAY!	11
BAGS? WHO EVER SAID GOD SANG IN YOUR FAT SHAPE? YOU'RE NOT			
THE ONLY	98	O, THOU OPENING	27
A VOICE SAID:	100	THE VISITANT	3
DEAREST TREE, I SAID, MAY I REST HERE?	100	THE VISITANT	5
HE SAID, "LOOK, BIRDS, ALL THIS IS FUTILE:	115	THE SERPENT	19
"YOU SEE," HE SAID, WITH A SERPENT'S LEER,	115	THE SERPENT	23
"THERE IS NO PLACE TO TURN," SHE SAID,	136	THE SENSUALISTS	1
I SAID FAREWELL TO SIGHS,	167	HER BECOMING	70
SAID THE WREN, YOUR SONG ISN'T WORTH 10¢.	177	KITTY-CAT BIRD	2

	PAGE	TITLE	LINE
SAID (CONTINUED)			
--SAID THE WREN TO THE KITTY-CAT BIRD.	177	KITTY-CAT BIRD	4
--SAID THE WREN TO THE KITTY-CAT BIRD.	177	KITTY-CAT BIRD	8
--SAID THE WREN TO THE KITTY-CAT BIRD.	177	KITTY-CAT BIRD	12
AND SAID, OLD BOY, YOU'RE SHEDDING HAIR,	181	MONOTONY SONG	6
THE BEAR SAID, SIR, YOU GO TOO FAR,	181	MONOTONY SONG	9
SAID, "I KNOW MY LEGS ADD UP TO TWO!"	182	PHILANDER	2
SAID NEVER A WORD,	216	THE SHY MAN	7
SAID NEVER A WORD,	216	THE SHY MAN	15
I SAID NOTHING.	228	THE GERANIUM	24
"I'VE ONLY ONE WING," SHE SAID,	249	THE RESTORED	7
SHE WAS A WIDOW, SO SHE SAID:	264	THREE EPIGRAMS	8
"LET'S EAT!" SAID LINDSAY. "HERE WE'VE GOT THE MOON,	273	SUPPR W LINDSAY	15
"SURE, WE STILL EAT," I SAID. "ENOUGH! OR TOO MUCH."	273	SUPPR W LINDSAY	17
WHEN HE SAID THAT, A SPIDERY SHAPE DROPPED DOWN	273	SUPPR W LINDSAY	24
"THAT'S NEVER BLAKE," SAID LINDSAY. "HE'D BE A WORM,	273	SUPPR W LINDSAY	26
"THE SPIDER'S GONE," HE SAID BEMUSEDLY.	274	SUPPR W LINDSAY	39
SAIL			
THE SPIDERS SAIL INTO SUMMER.	78	BRING THE DAY!	43
AND THE EAGLES SAIL LOW OVER THE FIR TREES,	202	THE ROSE	6
WE'LL SAIL AWAY FROM THE FRIGHTFUL SHORE	272	DUET	9
SAILED			
SHE SAILED UNTIL THE CALM MORNING,	41	BIG WIND	32
SAILS			
AS WHEN A SHIP SAILS WITH A LIGHT WIND--	203	THE ROSE	31
SAINT			
WHAT SAINT STRAINED SO MUCH,	37	CUTTINGS (LATE)	3
I'VE CRAWLED FROM THE MIRE, ALERT AS A SAINT OR A DOG;	88	PRAISE TO END!	81
(MATTERS ONLY A SAINT MENTIONS!)	187	THE LONGING	10
WHO LOVES THE SMALL CAN BE BOTH SAINT AND BOOR,	225	OTTO	31
ARE THESE MATTERS ONLY A SAINT MENTIONS?	259	SONG (3)	39
SAKE			
COMING BEHIND HER FOR HER PRETTY SAKE	127	I KNEW A WOMAN	13
FOR LOVE, FOR LOVE'S SAKE;	251	ONCE MORE, RND	10
SALE			
AN AUCTIONEER WAS WHIPPING UP A SALE.	21	THE AUCTION	3
THE SPIEL RAN ON; THE SALE WAS BRIEF AND BRISK;	21	THE AUCTION	9
SALE	32	SALE	T
FOR SALE: BY ORDER OF THE REMAINING HEIRS	32	SALE	1
SALIVA			
SALIVA DRIPPING FROM WARM MICROPHONES,	187	THE LONGING	5
SALMON			
THE SALMON CLIMB THE RIVERS, THE RIVERS NUDGE THE SEA,	28	CLAIRVOY WIDOW	25
OR A SALMON, TIRED, MOVING UP A SHALLOW STREAM,	159	FIRST MEDITATN	68
I WOULD WITH THE FISH, THE BLACKENING SALMON, AND THE MAD LEMMINGS,	188	THE LONGING	39
IN TIME WHEN THE TROUT AND YOUNG SALMON LEAP FOR THE LOW-FLYING INSECTS,	197	THE LONG WATERS	33
WHERE THE SALMON EASE THEIR WAY INTO THE KELP BEDS,	205	THE ROSE	96
SALT			
THE SALT SAID, LOOK BY THE SEA,	54	THE LOST SON	30
THE SALT LAUGHED AND THE STONES;	63	FIELD OF LIGHT	40
THIS SALT CAN'T WARM A STONE.	86	PRAISE TO END!	49
ONLY MY SALT HAS A CHANCE.	91	UNFOLD! UNFOLD!	58
COLD, IN MY OWN DEAD SALT.	147	THE EXORCISM	28
I'M NO MIDGE OF THAT AND THIS. THE DIRT GLITTERS LIKE SALT.	164	I'M HERE	92
WHERE THE FRESH AND SALT WATERS MEET,	196	THE LONG WATERS	17
TO A LANDLOCKED BAY, WHERE THE SALT WATER IS FRESHENED	197	THE LONG WATERS	47
BY THE SALT WAVES I HEAR A RIVER'S UNDERSONG,	221	THE ABYSS	76
SALT-DRENCHED			
AND FRESH AS SALT-DRENCHED SKIN.	271	THE REPLY	9
SALT-LADEN			
AND MY SALT-LADEN HAIR	210	HER TIME	14
SALT-LICK			
AMONG THE SHY BEASTS, THE DEER AT THE SALT-LICK,	190	AT OYSTER RIVER	26
SALT-SOAKED			
THE SALT-SOAKED WOOD OF A FIRE CRACKLES;	190	AT OYSTER RIVER	21
SALVATION			
MY MISSION BECAME THE SALVATION OF MINNOWS.	90	UNFOLD! UNFOLD!	31
SAME			
THE FROG SCUM APPEAR ON THE POND WITH THE SAME FROTH OF GREEN,	24	VERNAL SENTIMNT	2
A CAGED BEAR RARELY DOES THE SAME THING TWICE	105	SIR JOHN DAVIES	10

	PAGE	TITLE	LINE
SAME (CONTINUED)			
IN THE SAME WAY: O WATCH HIS BODY SWAY!--	105	SIR JOHN DAVIES	11
ARE FLOWER AND SEED THE SAME?	123	WORDS FOR WIND	9
WITH THE SAME ABSENT GAZE:	130	THE OTHER	20
THE AFTER-IMAGE NEVER STAYS THE SAME.	132	SENTENTIOUS MAN	20
AND WOULD THE SAME AGAIN.	154	THE DYING MAN	33
THE VISION MOVES, AND YET REMAINS THE SAME.	156	THE DYING MAN	94
ALL JOURNEYS, I THINK, ARE THE SAME:	158	FIRST MEDITATN	26
OUTSIDE, THE SAME SPARROWS BICKER IN THE EAVES.	161	I'M HERE	6
AND HIS WORLD AND MINE ARE THE SAME,	226	THE LIZARD	3
BUT COME TO THINK, THEY SAY THE SAME OF ME."	273	SUPPR W LINDSAY	23
SAMOOTS			
IT WAS SAMOOTS MATUNA AND BUGS MORAN;	112	SQUEEZE-BOX	26
SAND			
THE GREAT FEET BREAK THE RIDGES OF THE SAND,	15	THE HERON	6
PLANKS SUNK IN THE SAND.	62	FIELD OF LIGHT	3
MARROW-SOFT, DANCED IN THE SAND.	63	FIELD OF LIGHT	30
WHEN THE SUN FOR ME GLINTED THE SIDES OF A SAND GRAIN,	66	SHAPE OF FIRE	68
I'VE TRACED THESE WORDS IN SAND WITH A VESTIGIAL TAIL;	92	I CRY, LOVE!	17
CHIRPING WITH FLEAS IN THE SAND,	165	HER BECOMING	3
TO THE SAND DUNES AND FISH FLIES, HANGING, THICKER THAN MOTHS,	193	JOURNY INTERIOR	28
SURROUNDED BY SAND, BROKEN SHELLS, THE WRECKAGE OF WATER.	197	THE LONG WATERS	59
--OR TO LIE NAKED IN SAND,	200	THE FAR FIELD	38
WHERE THE SLOW CREEK WINDS DOWN TO THE BLACK SAND OF THE SHORE	203	THE ROSE	49
WINDING DOWN TO THE STRETCH OF IRREGULAR SAND,	222	THE ABYSS	95
RIDDLING THE SAND, LIKE A WIDE SPRAY OF BUCKSHOT,	230	THE STORM	14
AND WHEN I WALKED, MY FEET SEEMED DEEP IN SAND.	247	I WAITED	16
BURNING IN SAND. "IT LOOKS LIKE I SHOULD GO,"--	274	SUPPR W LINDSAY	37
SAND-BARS			
THE WAVES, ALTERED BY SAND-BARS, BEDS OF KELP, MISCELLANEOUS DRIFTWOOD,	191	AT OYSTER RIVER	32
SANDBLASTER			
THE BULLDOZER BACKING AWAY, THE HISS OF THE SANDBLASTER,	204	THE ROSE	71
SAND-CRUMB			
NUDGES A SAND-CRUMB LOOSE.	37	CUTTINGS	6
SANDGRAINS			
AT THE IRREGULAR STONES, IRIDESCENT SANDGRAINS,	201	THE FAR FIELD	74
SANDPIPER			
CRIES OF THE SANDPIPER.	191	AT OYSTER RIVER	62
SANDPIPER'S			
ACQUIRES, FOR A TIME, THE SANDPIPER'S INSOUCIANCE,	191	AT OYSTER RIVER	39
SAND-RUT			
ENDING AT LAST IN A HOPELESS SAND-RUT,	199	THE FAR FIELD	9
SANDS			
THE SISTER SANDS, THEY SLIPPER SOFT AWAY.	92	I CRY, LOVE!	3
THE DUBIOUS SEA-CHANGE, THE HEAVING SANDS, AND MY TENTACLED SEA-COUSINS.	196	THE LONG WATERS	23
SANDY			
NUDGES INTO A BACK-EDDY, A SANDY INLET,	159	FIRST MEDITATN	69
STANDING, SILENT, ON SANDY BEACHES OR WALKING ALONG GREEN EMBANKMENTS;	168	FOURTH MEDITATN	4
SANG			
THE BLOSSOMS SANG.	51	THE WAKING (1)	8
THE STONES SANG,	51	THE WAKING (1)	9
SANG IN MY VEINS	51	THE WAKING (1)	27
THE FAT LARK SANG IN THE FIELD;	63	FIELD OF LIGHT	38
A VOICE SANG:	65	SHAPE OF FIRE	40
AND LOVE, LOVE SANG TOWARD.	66	SHAPE OF FIRE	77
WINKIE WILL YELLOW I SANG.	72	WHERE KNOCK IS	35
I SANG I SANG ALL DAY.	72	WHERE KNOCK IS	38
I SANG I SANG ALL DAY.	72	WHERE KNOCK IS	38
FOR WHOM THE MINNOWS SANG?	90	UNFOLD! UNFOLD!	52
BAGS? WHO EVER SAID GOD SANG IN YOUR FAT SHAPE? YOU'RE NOT THE ONLY	98	O, THOU OPENING	27
THE SHADE SANG WITH HER;	102	ELEGY FOR JANE	7
AND THE MOLD SANG IN THE BLEACHED VALLEYS UNDER THE ROSE.	102	ELEGY FOR JANE	9
A BIRD SANG LOW; THE MOONLIGHT SIFTED IN;	119	THE DREAM	7
A BIRD SANG FROM THE CENTER OF A TREE;	119	THE DREAM	15
LIKE A WET LOG, I SANG WITHIN A FLAME.	120	THE DREAM	30
IT SANG WITH HER TRUE VOICE,	128	THE VOICE	15
THEIR SLOW SONG SANG IN ME;	128	THE VOICE	22

	PAGE	TITLE	LINE
SANG (CONTINUED)			
I SANG TO WHATEVER HAD BEEN	146	THE SONG	18
MOUTH UPON MOUTH, WE SANG,	146	THE SONG	28
ONE SANG, THEN THE OTHER,	158	FIRST MEDITATN	43
I SANG TO THE EDGES OF FLAME,	162	I'M HERE	42
WHEN I WAS A LARK, I SANG;	172	WHAT TELL BONES	39
WHILE THE WRENS BICKERED AND SANG IN THE HALF-GREEN HEDGEROWS,	200	THE FAR FIELD	36
SHE SANG A FINAL SONG;	212	LIGHT LISTENED	23
LIGHT LISTENED WHEN SHE SANG.	212	LIGHT LISTENED	24
SANG OUT AUDACIOUSLY	213	THE HAPPY THREE	31
I SANG TO THE ONE STAR THAT LOOKED DOWN AT ME;	216	THE SHY MAN	2
I SANG TO THE WHITE HORSE THAT GRAZED ON THE QUAY,--	216	THE SHY MAN	3
SUBJECT AND OBJECT SANG AND DANCED AS ONE;	237	THE TRANCED	17
AND THERE WE SANG WITH THE SEA:	238	THE MOMENT	3
SOUND, SILENCE SANG AS ONE.	238	THE MOMENT	9
I SANG, TO THE STRAW,	258	SONG (3)	17
SANITARIUM			
LINES UPON LEAVING A SANITARIUM	257	SANITARIUM	T
SANK			
BUT THE BEAR JUST SAT THERE UNTIL SHE SANK;	117	LADY AND BEAR	28
SANTA			
BETWEEN THE WHITENING TREES, UP SANTA LUCIA,	230	THE STORM	20
SAPLING			
LIKE A SAPLING TREE,	98	O, THOU OPENING	49
BRACING MY BACK AGAINST A SAPLING,	161	I'M HERE	24
SAT			
SAT IN AN EMPTY HOUSE	53	THE LOST SON	16
--OR SAT DOWN AND DID.	89	UNFOLD! UNFOLD!	11
THEY ALL SAT DOWN LIKE ME AND YOU	111	SQUEEZE-BOX	6
AS WE SAT THERE DRINKING THAT BATHTUB GIN	112	SQUEEZE-BOX	24
BUT THE BEAR JUST SAT THERE UNTIL SHE SANK;	117	LADY AND BEAR	28
THE KITTY-CAT BIRD, HE SAT ON A FENCE.	177	KITTY-CAT BIRD	1
LIKE A NURSE HE SAT WITH ME FOR WEEKS, A SLY SURLY ATTENDANT,	220	THE ABYSS	38
WHO SAT WITH THE DEAD WHEN THE RELATIVES LEFT,	223	ELEGY (2)	8
SO WE SAT DOWN AND ATE OURSELVES A MEAL,	274	SUPPR W LINDSAY	30
SATURDAY			
THEY THOUGHT ABOUT SATURDAY PAY,	46	PICKLE BELT	3
SAVAGE			
THE SAVAGE BLOOD'S OBSCENITY,	19	EPIDERM MACABRE	11
SAVE			
SOME RAGES SAVE US. DID I RAGE TOO LONG?	131	SENTENTIOUS MAN	9
SAVED			
MY DIM-WIT COUSIN, SAVED BY A DEATH-BED QUAVER,	25	DIM-WIT COUSIN	1
SAVES			
SAVES.	259	SONG (3)	52
SAW			
SAW WOMEN, THEIR EYELIDS LIKE LITTLE RAGS,	48	JUDGE NOT	9
WHEN I SAW THAT CLUMSY CROW	49	NIGHT CROW	1
I SAW SUBSTANCE FLOWING	56	THE LOST SON	94
I SAW THE SEPARATENESS OF ALL THINGS!	63	FIELD OF LIGHT	45
NOWHERE IS OUT. I SAW THE COLD.	73	WHERE KNOCK IS	71
TODAY I SAW A BEARD IN A CLOUD.	76	I NEED, I NEED	48
FOR THEY ARE ALL MY FRIENDS: I SAW ONE SLIDE	105	SIR JOHN DAVIES	7
WE ROSE TO MEET THE MOON, AND SAW NO MORE.	107	SIR JOHN DAVIES	70
DID BEATRICE DENY WHAT DANTE SAW?	107	SIR JOHN DAVIES	76
I SAW A SIGHT THAT CAUSED ME PAIN,	114	DINKY	10
THAT WOMAN I SAW IN A STONE--	123	WORDS FOR WIND	31
I SAW A VIRGIN WRITHING IN THE DIRT--	131	SENTENTIOUS MAN	2
MORNING, I SAW THE WORLD WITH SECOND SIGHT,	133	THE PURE FURY	5
AND WHEN IT SWUNG, I SAW	145	THE BEAST	4
IN A DARK WOOD I SAW--	147	THE EXORCISM	13
I SAW MY SEVERAL SELVES	147	THE EXORCISM	14
I SAW A YOUNG SNAKE GLIDE	150	SNAKE	1
I SAW MY FATHER SHRINKING IN HIS SKIN;	155	THE DYING MAN	61
I CLOSED MY EYES, AND SAW SMALL FIGURES DANCING,	163	I'M HERE	65
I HUM IN PURE VIBRATION, LIKE A SAW.	167	HER BECOMING	89
ONCE WHEN HE SAW TWO POACHERS ON HIS LAND,	224	OTTO	14
THEY SAW THAT I FELL MORE THAN TWICE.	225	THE CHUMS	10
I SAW A BODY DANCING IN THE WIND,	241	THE SEQUEL	9
I SAW ALL THINGS THROUGH WATER, MAGNIFIED,	247	I WAITED	10
I SAW IN MY LAST SLEEP	258	SONG (3)	20

	PAGE	TITLE	LINE
SAW (CONTINUED)			
I SAW A FIGURE IN A CLOUD,	268	SAGINAW SONG	56
AND WHAT DO YOU THINK I SAW?--	269	GOB MUSIC	25
INDEED I SAW A SHIMMERING LAKE	270	GOB MUSIC	32
SAWDUST			
AND THE IVY-BRANCH, CAST TO THE GROUND, PUTS DOWN ROOTS INTO THE SAWDUST,	197	THE LONG WATERS	34
SAXIFRAGE			
WITH THE SAXIFRAGE AND FERN	146	THE SONG	12
SAY			
SAY SOMETHING.	54	THE LOST SON	21
WHAT DO THE CLOUDS SAY?	56	THE LOST SON	117
WHO ELSE BREATHES HERE? WHAT DOES THE GRAVE SAY?	59	THE LONG ALLEY	19
HAD NOTHING TO SAY.	74	I NEED, I NEED	11
GLORY TO SEIZE, I SAY.	81	SENSIBILITY! LA	3
WHEN I SAY THINGS FOND,	83	O LULL ME, LULL	10
I COULD SAY HELLO TO THINGS;	84	O LULL ME, LULL	38
SKIN, A THING YOU CANNOT SAY TO WHISPER AND EQUAL A WOUND?	98	O, THOU OPENING	24
I'D SAY IT TO MY HORSE: WE LIVE BEYOND	106	SIR JOHN DAVIES	37
SAY THE STONES, SAY THE FISH.	121	ALL EARTH, AIR	20
SAY THE STONES, SAY THE FISH.	121	ALL EARTH, AIR	20
WHAT DO THE GREAT DEAD SAY?	123	WORDS FOR WIND	10
YOU COULD SAY I WAS MAD.	146	THE SONG	21
SAY TO HIS GATHERED KIN,	153	THE DYING MAN	2
IT IS DIFFICULT TO SAY ALL THINGS ARE WELL,	172	WHAT TELL BONES	34
LOVED HEART, WHAT CAN I SAY?	172	WHAT TELL BONES	38
YOU'D BETTER NOT LAUGH; AND DON'T SAY, "POOH!"	177	KITTY-CAT BIRD	18
AND THE BUSH WOULD SAY, "MAC,	182	BOY AND BUSH	3
WHETHER THE BEES HAVE THOUGHTS, WE CANNOT SAY,	196	THE LONG WATERS	1
ON THE BANKS OF THE TOMBSTONE, THE WIND-HARPS HAVING THEIR SAY,	204	THE ROSE	60
SAY MANY A WORD,	216	THE SHY MAN	22
SAY MANY A WORD,	216	THE SHY MAN	25
WHAT THEY SAY ON THE QUAY IS,	229	ON THE QUAY	1
WHAT ELSE TO SAY?	238	THE MOMENT	13
SAD THE SOUL'S JOY. LOVED HEART, WHAT ELSE CAN I SAY	261	THE CHANGELING	28
I'D SAY MY FACE IS JUST AS ROUND AS HIS,	273	SUPPR W LINDSAY	8
BUT COME TO THINK, THEY SAY THE SAME OF ME."	273	SUPPR W LINDSAY	23
SAYING			
SAYING,	53	THE LOST SON	7
WHERE'S SHE NOW, I KEPT SAYING.	101	THE VISITANT	23
THAT'S NOT A THING I'M SAYING WITH A SNEER--	132	SENTENTIOUS MAN	40
SAYS			
WHO SAYS? A NAMELESS STRANGER.	64	SHAPE OF FIRE	2
THE GRASS SAYS WHAT THE WIND SAYS:	77	BRING THE DAY!	29
THE GRASS SAYS WHAT THE WIND SAYS:	77	BRING THE DAY!	29
THE SHADE SAYS: LOVE THE SUN.	82	SENSIBILITY! LA	39
A SLOW SIGH SAYS YES. AND LIGHT SIGHS;	90	UNFOLD! UNFOLD!	49
WHAT THE GRAVE SAYS,	91	UNFOLD! UNFOLD!	63
THE HEDGEWREN'S SONG SAYS SOMETHING ELSE.	92	I CRY, LOVE!	15
SEE WHAT THE SWEET HARP SAYS.	99	O, THOU OPENING	73
AN EYE SAYS,	99	O, THOU OPENING	79
AND, THEN, BEFORE HE SAYS A WORD	116	THE SLOTH	4
SAYS A BEAR	117	LADY AND BEAR	11
SAYS A SONG TIED TO A TREE.	125	WORDS FOR WIND	71
THE SELF SAYS, I AM;	172	WHAT TELL BONES	41
THE HEART SAYS, I AM LESS;	172	WHAT TELL BONES	42
THE SPIRIT SAYS, YOU ARE NOTHING.	172	WHAT TELL BONES	43
THE LAMB JUST SAYS, I AM!	182	THE LAMB	1
SIGHS, SIGHS, WHO SAYS THEY HAVE SEQUENCE?	223	ELEGY (2)	4
THE WIND FROM OFF THE SEA SAYS NOTHING NEW.	246	THE MARROW	1
SCALED			
HAVE SCALED YOUR WALLS, AND SPIES BETRAY	4	FEUD	15
SCALES			
THIS WIND GIVES ME SCALES. HAVE MERCY, GRISTLE:	60	THE LONG ALLEY	33
INSTEAD OF A DEVIL WITH HORNS, I PREFER A SERPENT WITH SCALES;	173	WHAT TELL BONES	77
SCALPEL			
A SURGEON GUIDES A SCALPEL WITH THUMB AND FINGER-TIPS.	28	CLAIRVOY WIDOW	20
SCAMPERED			
A KNAVE WHO SCAMPERED THROUGH THE NEEDLE'S EYE,	28	THE FAVORITE	1
HAS SCAMPERED AWAY IN A DRY WIND.	103	OLD LADY'S WRDS	38

	PAGE	TITLE	LINE
SCARAB			
HIS HEAD, STIFF AS A SCARAB, TURNED TO ONE SIDE, ...	226	THE LIZARD	5
SCARCELY			
THE WALKER'S FOOT HAS SCARCELY ROOM	14	COMING OF COLD	5
THAT GOD HIMSELF CAN SCARCELY BEAR.	144	ELEGY (1)	4
SCARE			
I'LL SCARE MYSELF WITH SIGHING, OR I'LL SING;	156	THE DYING MAN	86
SCARF			
SUDDENLY THEY CAME FLYING, LIKE A LONG SCARF OF SMOKE, ...	232	THE THING	1
SCARLET			
HOPE FLUSHED MY CHEEKBONES WITH A SCARLET DISK.	21	THE AUCTION	11
SCARS			
SCARS, TEMPESTS, FLOODS, THE MOTION OF MAN'S FATE;	144	ELEGY (1)	14
SCARY			
AND THAT WAS SCARY--	228	THE GERANIUM	21
SCATTERING			
ALL'S A SCATTERING, ...	192	AT OYSTER RIVER	69
SCENE			
AND SOON A BRANCH, PART OF A HIDDEN SCENE, ...	11	LIGHT BRIGHTER	17
WHEN I LOOKED AT THE ALTERED SCENE, MY EYE WAS UNDECEIVED,	12	MID-CNTRY BLOW	7
NO LONGER GILDS THE SCENE AT NOON;	15	COMING OF COLD	48
I NEVER AM BORED, HOWEVER FAMILIAR THE SCENE.	24	VERNAL SENTIMNT	4
THE SCENE SHRANK TO A PIN.	167	HER BECOMING	68
A SCENE FOR THE SELF TO ABJURE!--	233	THE PIKE	10
A LEAF UNALTERED BY THE MIDNIGHT SCENE, ...	248	THE TREE, BIRD	8
SCENT			
THE WIND SHAKES OUT THE SCENT OF PEAR.	14	COMING OF COLD	12
UPON THE FIELD THE SCENT IS DRY:	14	COMING OF COLD	13
THE SCENT OF THE HALF-OPENED BUDS CAME UP OVER ME.	162	I'M HERE	49
THE DRY SCENT OF A DYING GARDEN IN SEPTEMBER, ...	201	THE FAR FIELD	78
A SCENT BELOVED OF BEES;	201	THE FAR FIELD	99
SCENTED			
THE WOODS IN SPRING THE LEAVES THE SCENTED LANES	5	TO MY SISTER	2
SCENTS			
WHEN CLOVER SCENTS DIMINISHED WIND.	14	COMING OF COLD	4
SCEPTER			
WHAT ARE SCEPTER AND CROWN?	262	FOLLIES OF ADAM	8
SCHEME			
THE SCHEME WITHOUT PURPOSE; PRIDE IN A FURNISHED ROOM; ...	5	PROGNOSIS	10
AS IF I HAD COMMITTED, AGAINST THE WHOLE SCHEME OF LIFE, A			
DESECRATION.	40	MOSS-GATHERING	13
SCHMIDT			
FRAU BAUMAN, FRAU SCHMIDT, AND FRAU SCHWARTZE	44	FRAU BAUMAN	T
SCHOLAR			
THE WORM, INTREPID SCHOLAR OF THE SOIL--	235	MANIFESTATION	5
SCHOOLBOYS			
REASON? THAT DREARY SHED, THAT HUTCH FOR GRUBBY SCHOOLBOYS!	92	I CRY, LOVE!	14
SCHOOLED			
IS PAIN A PROMISE? I WAS SCHOOLED IN PAIN, ...	132	SENTENTIOUS MAN	31
SCHWARTZE			
FRAU BAUMAN, FRAU SCHMIDT, AND FRAU SCHWARTZE	44	FRAU BAUMAN	T
SCOLD			
AND THE WRENS SCOLD, AND THE CHICKADEES FRISK AND FROLIC,	234	ALL MORNING	24
SCOOP			
OR SCOOP OUT A WEED CLOSE TO FLOURISHING ROOTS, ...	42	OLD FLORIST	6
SCORN			
AND SCORN THE ABSTRACT ENTITIES.	25	VERSE W ALLUSNS	4
SCOTER			
BUT STILL THE FLASH OF THE KINGFISHER, THE WINGBEAT OF THE			
SCOTER, ...	202	THE ROSE	15
SCOTERS			
AND TWO SCOTERS FLY LOW, ...	210	HER TIME	12
SCOTT			
IT WASN'T ERNEST; IT WASN'T SCOTT--	111	SQUEEZE-BOX	1
SCOW			
AN OLD SCOW BUMPS OVER BLACK ROCKS.	64	SHAPE OF FIRE	5
SCRAGGLY			
THE SCRAGGLY WIND-BREAK OF A DUSTY RANCH-HOUSE.	194	JOURNY INTERIOR	45
SCRAGGY			
WITH A STUMP OF SCRAGGY FANG	47	THE RETURN	12
SCRAP			
IN THE DIRT AND DISORDER I CHERISH ONE SCRAP OF ILLUSION:	29	THE REMINDER	11

		PAGE	TITLE	LINE
SCRAPE				
I TEETER, HEELS HOOKED ON THE CURB, SCRAPE A TOE;	....	47	DOUBLE FEATURE	7
IT'S A COLD SCRAPE IN A LOW PLACE.	....	80	GIVE WAY, GATES	47
SCRAPED				
MY RIGHT EAR SCRAPED A BUCKLE.	....	45	MY PAPA'S WALTZ	12
SCRAPING				
TODAY, WHILE SCRAPING HAIR BEFORE THE MIRROR,	....	25	DIM-WIT COUSIN	10
SCRAPING HER CHEEK AGAINST STRAW;		102	ELEGY FOR JANE	12
UNTIL I'M SCRAPING AND SCRATCHING AT YOU, ON THE DOORMAT,		151	SLUG	19
SCRATCH				
THE SCRATCH FORGOTTEN IS THE SCRATCH INFECTED;	....	5	PROGNOSIS	7
THE SCRATCH FORGOTTEN IS THE SCRATCH INFECTED;	....	5	PROGNOSIS	7
AT THE FIRST SCRATCH OF THE MATCH	....	226	THE LIZARD	14
SCRATCHED				
SCRATCHED THE WIND WITH A STICK.	....	74	I NEED, I NEED	16
SCRATCHING				
FOR ALL OUR SCRATCHING ON THE PAD,	....	30	THE RECKONING	7
SCRATCHING.	....	53	THE LOST SON	18
UNTIL I'M SCRAPING AND SCRATCHING AT YOU, ON THE DOORMAT,		151	SLUG	19
SCREEN				
BUT WHEN HE BRUSHES UP AGAINST A SCREEN,	....	16	THE BAT	7
DEEP-HIDDEN EMBERS, SMOTHERED BY THE SCREEN	....	17	UNEXTINGUISHED	7
SCROLLS				
THE LEAVES CURLED BACK IN ELABORATE CORINTHIAN SCROLLS;		43	CARNATIONS	2
SCRUBBING				
TO THE DIRT, MY KNEES SCRUBBING	....	151	SLUG	6
SCRUBBY				
THE CEMETERY WITH TWO SCRUBBY TREES IN THE MIDDLE OF THE PRAIRIE,	....	194	JOURNY INTERIOR	35
SCRUPULOUS				
DETERIORATION'S SCRUPULOUS ACCOUNTING	....	25	DIM-WIT COUSIN	7
SCULPTURE				
GRAVE, HIERATIC, A PIECE OF ASSYRIAN SCULPTURE,	....	234	ALL MORNING	10
SCUM				
THE FROG SCUM APPEAR ON THE POND WITH THE SAME FROTH OF GREEN,	....	24	VERNAL SENTIMNT	2
WITH ITS THICK GRASSY SCUM AND CRABS SCUTTLING BACK INTO THEIR GLISTENING CRATERS.		203	THE ROSE	50
SCUMS				
SCUMS, MILDEWS, SMUTS ALONG STEMS,	....	38	FORCING HOUSE	3
SCURRY				
SCURRY OF WARM OVER SMALL PLANTS.	....	57	THE LOST SON	141
TO A SCURRY OF SMALL DOGS AND A SHRIEK OF CHILDREN,	......	193	JOURNY INTERIOR	26
SCUTTLED				
THAT SCUTTLED UNDER STONES,	....	147	THE EXORCISM	17
SCUTTLING				
SCUTTLING DOWN AND AROUND LIKE YOUNG SQUIRRELS,	....	152	THE SISKINS	17
WITH ITS THICK GRASSY SCUM AND CRABS SCUTTLING BACK INTO THEIR GLISTENING CRATERS.	....	203	THE ROSE	50
WHAT A SCUTTLING AND RAPPING ALONG THE DRAINPIPES,	....	234	ALL MORNING	21
SEA				
BUT MY EAR STILL KEPT THE SOUND OF THE SEA LIKE A SHELL.		12	MID-CNTRY BLOW	8
THE SALMON CLIMB THE RIVERS, THE RIVERS NUDGE THE SEA,	...	28	CLAIRVOY WIDOW	25
SEA WATER STOOD IN MY VEINS,		49	RIVER INCIDENT	6
THE SALT SAID, LOOK BY THE SEA,	....	54	THE LOST SON	30
MAKE THE SEA FLASH IN THE DUST.	....	61	THE LONG ALLEY	84
WILL THE SEA GIVE THE WIND SUCK? A TOAD FOLDS INTO A STONE.		64	SHAPE OF FIRE	8
THE SEA WILL BE THERE, THE GREAT SQUASHY SHADOWS,	....	79	GIVE WAY, GATES	28
THE SEA HAS MANY STREETS;	....	83	O LULL ME, LULL	14
WHEN I WENT TO SEA IN A SIGH,	....	103	OLD LADY'S WRDS	23
SHE TURNED THE FIELD INTO A GLITTERING SEA;	....	120	THE DREAM	27
A FIELD BREAKS LIKE THE SEA;	....	124	WORDS FOR WIND	37
IS IT THE SEA WE WISH? THE SLEEP OF THE CHANGELESS?	......	165	HER BECOMING	28
A GREAT FLAME RISES FROM THE SUNLESS SEA;		188	THE LONGING	31
I RISE AND FALL IN THE SLOW SEA OF A GRASSY PLAIN,	....	194	JOURNY INTERIOR	42
TO THE CHARRED EDGE OF THE SEA		196	THE LONG WATERS	14
SO THE SEA WIND WAKES DESIRE.	....	198	THE LONG WATERS	65
TURNING TOWARD THE SEA,	....	201	THE FAR FIELD	83
BUT THIS PLACE, WHERE SEA AND FRESH WATER MEET,	....	202	THE ROSE	2
BEYOND THE SEA PINE, THE OAK, THE WIND-TIPPED MADRONA,	...	203	THE ROSE	47
AND THE SEA REARRANGES ITSELF AMONG THE SMALL ISLANDS.	...	205	THE ROSE	97
THE WILD STREAM, THE SEA ITSELF CANNOT CONTAIN ME:	....	209	HER LONGING	12
THE SHOAL ROCKS WITH THE SEA.	....	215	HIS FOREBODING	1

	PAGE	TITLE	LINE
SEA (CONTINUED)			
THE FULL MOON WAS SHINING UPON THE BROAD SEA;	216	THE SHY MAN	1
CAN I OUTLEAP THE SEA--	221	THE ABYSS	62
THE EDGE OF ALL THE LAND, THE FINAL SEA?	221	THE ABYSS	63
A FINE FUME OF RAIN DRIVING IN FROM THE SEA, ...	230	THE STORM	13
THE WIND FROM THE SEA AND THE WIND FROM THE MOUNTAIN			
CONTENDING, ...	230	THE STORM	15
AND THERE WE SANG WITH THE SEA:	238	THE MOMENT	3
THE WIND FROM OFF THE SEA SAYS NOTHING NEW.	246	THE MARROW	1
BELOW, THE BRIGHT SEA WAS, THE LEVEL WAVES, ...	247	I WAITED	22
THE WHITE SEA WIDENING ON A FARTHER SHORE.	248	THE TREE, BIRD	20
THE SEA BARKED IN ITS CAVES.	258	SONG (3)	16
WHILE THE ROCK-SEAMS SWELL WITH THE SEA, ...	261	THE CHANGELING	33
SHIFTING IN SEA CHANGE, ...	265	HARSH COUNTRY	11
SEA-BEAST			
SEA-BEAST OR BIRD FLUNG TOWARD THE RAVAGED SHORE?	107	SIR JOHN DAVIES	68
SEA-BURIED			
IN YOUR SEA-BURIED EAR, ...	211	SONG (1)	11
SEA-CHAMBERS			
DOWN LONG SEA-CHAMBERS OF THE INNER EAR.	129	SHE	6
SEA-CHANGE			
THE DUBIOUS SEA-CHANGE, THE HEAVING SANDS, AND MY TENTACLED			
SEA-COUSINS.	196	THE LONG WATERS	23
SEA-CLIFF			
THE SUDDEN SHUDDER AS THE JUTTING SEA-CLIFF COLLAPSES, ...	231	THE STORM	42
SEA-CLIFFS			
PROTECTING THE SEA-CLIFFS.	209	HER LONGING	23
SEA-COUSINS			
THE DUBIOUS SEA-CHANGE, THE HEAVING SANDS, AND MY TENTACLED			
SEA-COUSINS.	196	THE LONG WATERS	23
SEA-FACED			
I HAVE BEEN SOMEWHERE ELSE; I REMEMBER THE SEA-FACED UNCLES.	88	PRAISE TO END!	93
SEAFOAM			
AND I SWAYED OUT BEYOND THE WHITE SEAFOAM;	120	THE DREAM	29
SEA-FOAM			
BACK ON THE SEA-FOAM;	263	FOLLIES OF ADAM	33
SEAL			
SHE'D MORE SIDES THAN A SEAL.	212	LIGHT LISTENED	6
SEALED			
IS NOW SEALED HONEY-TIGHT.	4	DEATH PIECE	4
THE CORE LIES SEALED.	9	THE ADAMANT	12
SEAMS			
AS THE SEAMS HISSED	41	BIG WIND	12
SEA'S			
THE SEA'S UNEQUAL LENGTHS ANNOUNCED THY BIRTH	81	SENSIBILITY! LA	8
FROM ME, IN THE SEA'S SILENCE;	210	HER TIME	4
OR THE SEA'S BANTER,--	229	ON THE QUAY	4
SEA-SHAPE			
A SEA-SHAPE TURNING AROUND,--	201	THE FAR FIELD	84
SEA-SLIME			
CUT BY THE SEA-SLIME, FAR FROM THE CRASH	205	THE ROSE	92
SEASON			
SLOW SEASON	12	SLOW SEASON	T
ALL DURING MATING SEASON, ...	234	ALL MORNING	17
SEASONS			
I KNOW MYSELF, MY SEASONS, AND I KNOW.	144	ELEGY (1)	10
SEASON'S			
THE SEASON'S WRECKAGE LIES ABOUT, ...	14	COMING OF COLD	26
SEA-SWELL			
THE FLAT BOOM ON THE BEACH OF THE TOWERING SEA-SWELL, ...	231	THE STORM	41
SEAT			
ONE DRIVER, PINNED BENEATH THE SEAT, ...	33	HIGHWAY: MICH	19
THE WIND BILLOWING OUT THE SEAT OF MY BRITCHES, ...	43	CHILD ON GRNHSE	1
SEATS			
THE DRIVERS CREAKING THE SEATS OF THE BAROQUE HEARSES, ...	22	ROAD TO WDLAWN	2
SEA-URCHIN			
I HAVE TAKEN COUNSEL OF THE CRAB AND THE SEA-URCHIN, ...	222	THE ABYSS	92
SEA-WALL			
AS I WALKED BY THE HIGH SEA-WALL.	216	THE SHY MAN	4
AS I MOPED BY THE HIGH SEA-WALL.	216	THE SHY MAN	8
AS WE WALKED BY THE HIGH SEA-WALL.	216	THE SHY MAN	16
AS WE EMBRACE BY THE HIGH SEA-WALL.	216	THE SHY MAN	23
AS WE KISS BY THE HIGH SEA-WALL.	216	THE SHY MAN	26

	PAGE	TITLE	LINE
SEA-WALL (CONTINUED)			
ALONG THE SEA-WALL, A STEADY SLOSHING OF THE SWELL, ...	230	THE STORM	10
SEAWARD			
A COUNTRY OF BAYS AND INLETS, AND SMALL STREAMS FLOWING SEAWARD.	196	THE LONG WATERS	19
SEA-WIND			
BUT THIS ROSE, THIS ROSE IN THE SEA-WIND, ...	203	THE ROSE	39
AND IN THIS ROSE, THIS ROSE IN THE SEA-WIND, ...	205	THE ROSE	111
A SEA-WIND PAUSING IN A SUMMER TREE.	235	MANIFESTATION	8
SEA-WINDS			
AND THE SEA-WINDS MOVE THROUGH THE PINE TREES, ...	196	THE LONG WATERS	18
SEA-WIND'S			
MINE AND THE SEA-WIND'S.	205	THE ROSE	114
SECOND			
THE SECOND DAWN I WOULD NOT HAVE BELIEVED:	12	MID-CNTRY BLOW	5
MORNING, I SAW THE WORLD WITH SECOND SIGHT, ...	133	THE PURE FURY	5
THE ROAD LINED WITH SNOW-LADEN SECOND GROWTH, ...	199	THE FAR FIELD	4
HE CAN SEE THE SECOND SUN	266	FOR STEVENS	3
SECRET			
THE SECRET HEART OF SOUND.	17	NO BIRD	2
OF EASE, THE HOARDED, SECRET SUM;	30	THE RECKONING	2
A SECRET TO JERK FROM THE LIPS OF A FISH.	92	I CRY, LOVE!	7
SHE CRIES OUT LOUD THE SOUL'S OWN SECRET JOY;	129	SHE	9
MY OWN, MY SECRET LIPS	147	THE EXORCISM	11
FORMS OF HIS SECRET LIFE	147	THE EXORCISM	23
OUT, OUT, YOU SECRET BEASTS, ...	167	HER BECOMING	78
BRINGS THE SECRET--RIGHT IN HERE!	266	FOR STEVENS	8
SECRETING			
OR THAT OLD HARPY SECRETING TOADS IN HER PORTMANTEAU.	82	SENSIBILITY! LA	36
SECRETION			
SECRETION OF THE SENSE;	18	GENESIS	10
SECRETS			
MY SECRETS CRY ALOUD.	3	OPEN HOUSE	1
OLD SECRETS TO AMORPHOUS SWARMS.	4	FEUD	16
LIKE THE HALF-DEAD, I HUG MY LAST SECRETS.	103	OLD LADY'S WRDS	5
AND SHAKE THE SECRETS FROM MY DEEPEST BONES;	173	WHAT TELL BONES	87
SECURE			
REMAIN SECURE FROM PAIN PRESERVE THY HATE THY HEART.	5	TO MY SISTER	11
ONE WAY, A CHANCE TO BE SECURE:	30	THE RECKONING	10
SECURELY			
THAT CHRIST, SECURELY BOUND, COULD BEAR.	144	ELEGY (1)	8
SEE			
O SEE THE FATE OF HIM WHOSE GUARD WAS LOWERED!--	5	PROGNOSIS	3
I, STARVELING YEARNER, SEEM TO SEE	25	VERSE W ALLUSNS	11
"O TELL ME, WIDOW LADY, WHAT IS IT THAT YOU SEE, ...	27	CLAIRVOY WIDOW	3
"I SEE TEN MILLION WINDOWS, I SEE TEN THOUSAND STREETS,	27	CLAIRVOY WIDOW	5
"I SEE TEN MILLION WINDOWS, I SEE TEN THOUSAND STREETS,	27	CLAIRVOY WIDOW	5
I SEE THE TRAFFIC DOING MIRACULOUS FEATS.	27	CLAIRVOY WIDOW	6
I SEE A BANKER'S MANSION WITH TWENTY WOOD-GRATE FIRES, ...	27	CLAIRVOY WIDOW	13
DO YOU SEE ANY SIGN OR SEMBLANCE OF THAT THING CALLED "HOPE"?"	27	CLAIRVOY WIDOW	18
"I SEE THE RIVER HARBOR, ALIVE WITH MEN AND SHIPS,	28	CLAIRVOY WIDOW	19
I SEE GRANDPA SURVIVING A SERIES OF SEVEN STROKES,	28	CLAIRVOY WIDOW	21
TO SEE THE LAND I LOVE.	34	NIGHT JOURNEY	27
THAT WAS A CLOSE KNOCK. SEE WHAT THE WILL WANTS.	61	THE LONG ALLEY	62
TO SEE CYCLAMEN VEINS BECOME CLEARER IN EARLY SUNLIGHT,	67	SHAPE OF FIRE	86
AS YOU CAN SEE I GUESS I GUESS.	75	I NEED, I NEED	34
OPEN A HOLE AND SEE THE SKY:	75	I NEED, I NEED	39
SEE! SHE'S SLEEPING LIKE A LAKE:	81	SENSIBILITY! LA	2
I SEE MY HEART IN THE SEED;	83	O LULL ME, LULL	24
I SEE WHAT SINGS!	84	O LULL ME, LULL	40
SEE WHAT THE SWEET HARP SAYS.	99	O, THOU OPENING	73
I SEE; I SEEK;	99	O, THOU OPENING	84
I SEE A HERON PRANCING IN HIS POND;	106	SIR JOHN DAVIES	39
RAPT, WE LEANED FORTH WITH WHAT WE COULD NOT SEE.	107	SIR JOHN DAVIES	88
"YOU SEE," HE SAID, WITH A SERPENT'S LEER, ...	115	THE SERPENT	23
AND SEE AND SUFFER MYSELF	126	WORDS FOR WIND	104
I SEE THE RUBBLESTONES BEGIN TO STRETCH	135	THE RENEWAL	21
WHENEVER I SEE HER WITH NOTHING ON.	140	THE SWAN	14
BY THE LAKE'S EDGE, I SEE A SILVER SWAN, ...	140	THE SWAN	16
I SEE YOU, LOVE, I SEE YOU IN A DREAM;	155	THE DYING MAN	73
I SEE YOU, LOVE, I SEE YOU IN A DREAM;	155	THE DYING MAN	73
I SEE A SHAPE, LIGHTED WITH LOVE, ...	165	HER BECOMING	11

	PAGE	TITLE	LINE
SEE (CONTINUED)			
I SEE THEM AS FIGURES WALKING IN A GREENY GARDEN, ...	170	FOURTH MEDITATN	63
AND YOU SHOULD SEE HER NOSES TWITCH,--	181	MONOTONY SONG	18
THIS IS, YOU SEE, A SILLY SONG	181	MONOTONY SONG	21
I SEE THE FLOWER OF ALL WATER, ABOVE AND BELOW ME, THE NEVER RECEDING, ...	194	JOURNY INTERIOR	52
I SEE IN THE ADVANCING AND RETREATING WATERS	198	THE LONG WATERS	67
I SEE YOU IN SOME CELESTIAL SUPERMARKET,	223	ELEGY (2)	19
IN MY MIND'S EYE I SEE THOSE FIELDS OF GLASS, ...	225	OTTO	34
I CAN SEE THAT BY THE DISTENDED PULSING MIDDLE;	226	THE LIZARD	2
IN A DARK TIME, THE EYE BEGINS TO SEE, ...	239	IN A DARK TIME	1
I SEE, IN EVENING AIR, ...	240	IN EVEING AIR	23
I TEACH MY EYES TO HEAR, MY EARS TO SEE	244	INFIRMITY	34
WHEN CONTEMPLATION DAZZLES ALL I SEE;	246	THE MARROW	8
I WOULD BE NEAR; I SHUT MY EYES TO SEE;	246	THE MARROW	22
AH, HOW SHE LAUGHED TO SEE	262	FOLLIES OF ADAM	16
HE CAN SEE THE SECOND SUN	266	FOR STEVENS	3
SEED			
THERE'S CANKER AT THE ROOT, YOUR SEED	4	FEUD	9
A SEED THAT SWELLS THE RIND	18	GENESIS	7
THEY TEASED OUT THE SEED THAT THE COLD KEPT ASLEEP,--	44	FRAU BAUMAN	23
IS THE SEED LEAVING THE OLD BED? THESE BUDS ARE LIVE AS BIRDS.	56	THE LOST SON	102
I SEE MY HEART IN THE SEED;	83	O LULL ME, LULL	24
FOR WHOM HAVE I SWELLED LIKE A SEED?	85	PRAISE TO END!	2
STRICT AS A SEED, NIPPY AND TWIGGY.	86	PRAISE TO END!	22
ARE FLOWER AND SEED THE SAME?	123	WORDS FOR WIND	9
LET SEED BE GRASS, AND GRASS TURN INTO HAY:	127	I KNEW A WOMAN	22
LIGHT AS SEED BLOWING OFF THISTLES!	152	THE SISKINS	21
WHAT'S LEFT IS LIGHT AS A SEED;	157	FIRST MEDITATN	18
SOFT, SOFT, THE SNOW'S NOT FALLING. WHAT'S A SEED?	165	HER BECOMING	17
IN THE WHITE KINGDOMS, I WAS LIGHT AS A SEED,	168	FOURTH MEDITATN	15
THE HUSK LIVES ON, ARDENT AS A SEED;	170	FOURTH MEDITATN	83
(AND SOME GROW OUT OF SHAPE, THEIR SEED IMPURE;)	225	OTTO	32
A SEED PUSHING ITSELF BEYOND ITSELF, ...	235	MANIFESTATION	3
SHE LEFT MY BODY, LIGHTER THAN A SEED;	241	THE SEQUEL	20
KNOWING HOW ALL THINGS ALTER IN THE SEED	243	THE MOTION	15
SEED-CROWNS			
OVER THE DRY SEED-CROWNS, ...	58	THE LOST SON	156
SEEDS			
I'VE BECOME A SENTRY OF SMALL SEEDS, ...	103	OLD LADY'S WRDS	33
FLUTTER OF WINGS AND SEEDS QUAKING, ...	255	LIGHT POEM	3
SEEDY			
OR THE TWO OF US, ALONE, BOTH SEEDY, ...	228	THE GERANIUM	17
SEEING			
THE EYES REJOICE IN THE ACT OF SEEING AND THE FRESH AFTER-IMAGE;	163	I'M HERE	79
SEEK			
IF I SHOULD EVER SEEK RELIEF	22	SILENCE	15
I'LL SEEK MY OWN MEEKNESS.	91	UNFOLD! UNFOLD!	59
I SEE; I SEEK;	99	O, THOU OPENING	84
O, BUT I SEEK AND CARE!	172	WHAT TELL BONES	61
IN TEMPTATION, I RARELY SEEK COUNSEL;	173	WHAT TELL BONES	78
I SEEK MY OWN MEEKNESS;	173	WHAT TELL BONES	91
SEEKING			
WHAT WE ARE SEEKING IS A FARE	30	THE RECKONING	9
SEEKING IN MY OWN WAY, ETERNAL PURPOSE;	168	FOURTH MEDITATN	2
I ENVY THE TENDRILS, THEIR EYELESS SEEKING, ...	221	THE ABYSS	64
SEEKS			
THE ETERNAL SEEKS, AND FINDS, THE TEMPORAL, ...	244	INFIRMITY	21
SEEM			
I, STARVELING YEARNER, SEEM TO SEE	25	VERSE W ALLUSNS	11
TO SOME IT MAY SEEM A SAD THING TO RELATE, ...	112	SQUEEZE-BOX	38
AND I SEEM TO LEAN FORWARD, ...	152	THE SISKINS	22
AND I SEEM TO GO BACKWARD, ...	158	FIRST MEDITATN	37
SEEMED			
THEY SEEMED VERY HAPPY.	163	I'M HERE	70
AND HOW THOSE FLOWERHEADS SEEMED TO FLOW TOWARD ME, TO BECKON ME, ONLY A CHILD, OUT OF MYSELF.	203	THE ROSE	55
SUSTENANCE SEEMED SENSIBLE	228	THE GERANIUM	8
NEAR THE END, SHE SEEMED ALMOST TO HEAR ME--	228	THE GERANIUM	20
I SEEMED TO EAT THE AIR;	247	I WAITED	3
AND WHEN I WALKED, MY FEET SEEMED DEEP IN SAND.	247	I WAITED	16

	PAGE	TITLE	LINE

SEEMINGLY
AS A FIRE, SEEMINGLY LONG DEAD, FLARES UP FROM A DOWNDRAFT
    OF AIR IN A CHIMNEY, ... 198 THE LONG WATERS 63

SEEMS
"AND BESIDES, IT SEEMS THERE'S A LAW: .... 117 LADY AND BEAR 9
HE SEEMS NO LONGER TO TREMBLE. .... 227 MEADOW MOUSE 19

SEEN
A FLASH OF OBJECTS NEVER SEEN BEFORE. .... 8 THE SIGNALS 2
WE ARE AFRAID OF WHAT OUR EYES HAVE SEEN: .... 16 THE BAT 8
AND I HAVE SEEN DUST FROM THE WALLS OF INSTITUTIONS, ... 46 DOLOR 9
YOU'VE SEEN ME, PRINCE OF STINKS, ... 82 SENSIBILITY! LA 32
I'VE SEEN MY FATHER'S FACE BEFORE .... 97 O, THOU OPENING 14
THOUGH IT REJECT DRY BORDERS OF THE SEEN, ... 154 THE DYING MAN 42
WHAT'S SEEN RECEDES; FOREVER'S WHAT WE KNOW!-- .... 156 THE DYING MAN 91
I HAVE SEEN! I HAVE SEEN!-- .... 167 HER BECOMING 75
I HAVE SEEN! I HAVE SEEN!-- .... 167 HER BECOMING 75
HAVE THEY SEEN, EVER, THE SHARP BONES OF THE POOR? .... 169 FOURTH MEDITATN 46
THE UNSEEN AND THE SEEN, ... 237 THE TRANCED 19

SEEPING
THE SMALL WATERS SEEPING UPWARD, ... 37 CUTTINGS (LATE) 7

SEES
"A MAN SEES, AS HE DIES, ... 153 THE DYING MAN 11
THE DEEP EYE SEES THE SHIMMER ON THE STONE; .... 244 INFIRMITY 20

SEIZE
WHO WANT NO MORE THAN FINGERS SEIZE, ... 25 VERSE W ALLUSNS 3
IN MIST THAT SUN COULD SEIZE. .... 50 THE CYCLE 6
GLORY TO SEIZE, I SAY. .... 81 SENSIBILITY! LA 3
TO SEIZE, TO SEIZE,-- .... 103 OLD LADY'S WRDS 1
TO SEIZE, TO SEIZE,-- .... 103 OLD LADY'S WRDS 1
HER FULL LIPS PURSED, THE ERRANT NOTE TO SEIZE; .... 127 I KNEW A WOMAN 16

SELDOM
IS SELDOM WON. THE SPIRIT STARVES .... 4 FEUD 19

SELF
SUDDEN RENEWAL OF THE SELF--FROM WHERE? .... 135 THE RENEWAL 13
WILL THE SELF, LOST, BE FOUND AGAIN? IN FORM? .... 135 THE RENEWAL 17
THE SELF SAYS, I AM; .... 172 WHAT TELL BONES 41
THE SELF PERSISTS LIKE A DYING STAR, ... 190 AT OYSTER RIVER 24
IN THE LONG JOURNEY OUT OF THE SELF, ... 193 JOURNY INTERIOR 1
THE LOST SELF CHANGES, ... 201 THE FAR FIELD 82
A SCENE FOR THE SELF TO ABJURE!-- .... 233 THE PIKE 10
DEATH OF THE SELF IN A LONG, TEARLESS NIGHT, ... 239 IN A DARK TIME 17
MY TRUE SELF RUNS TOWARD A HILL .... 251 ONCE MORE, RND 3

SELF-CONTEMPLATION
SELF-CONTEMPLATION IS A CURSE .... 257 SANITARIUM 1

SELF-DELIGHTING
A SELF-DELIGHTING CREATURE, ... 103 OLD LADY'S WRDS 40

SELF-DESTRUCTIVE
THE SELF-DESTRUCTIVE SHAKE THE COMMON WALL; .... 250 THE RIGHT THING 14

SELF-ENCHANTED
AT EASE WITH JOY, A SELF-ENCHANTED MAN. .... 248 THE TREE, BIRD 6

SELF-INFECTED
THAT SELF-INFECTED LAIR; .... 47 THE RETURN 9

SELF-INVOLVED
I THINK OF THE SELF-INVOLVED: .... 169 FOURTH MEDITATN 35

SELF-REVEALED
THIS ANGUISH SELF-REVEALED. .... 3 OPEN HOUSE 8

SELF-TALK
A DRUNK MAN STUMBLES BY, ABSORBED IN SELF-TALK. .... 33 IDYLL 2

SELVES
I SAW MY SEVERAL SELVES .... 147 THE EXORCISM 14
MY DEAD SELVES SINGING. .... 221 THE ABYSS 80

SEMBLANCE
DO YOU SEE ANY SIGN OR SEMBLANCE OF THAT THING CALLED
    "HOPE"? .... 27 CLAIRVOY WIDOW 18

SEND
OR SEND OFF A CAR WITH VAGUE LIFTS OF A HAND. .... 47 DOUBLE FEATURE 8
SEND DOWN A RUSH OF AIR, O TORRENTIAL, ... 61 THE LONG ALLEY 83
JUST SEND ME ALONG THAT SWEET SEVENTY-FIVE; .... 113 TO A LADY ED 14
THEY SENT,--YOU ALWAYS SEND,--TO CUBA .... 115 THE SERPENT 15
IF I COULD SEND HIM ONLY .... 209 HER RETICENCE 1
AND THEN SEND YOU THE BILL. .... 267 SAGINAW SONG 18

SENSE
THE SENSE THAT DOES SO FITLY SERVE, ... 8 PRAYER 20

	PAGE	TITLE	LINE
SENSE (CONTINUED)			
SECRETION OF THE SENSE;	18	GENESIS	10
WITH FALSE ACCOUTERMENTS OF SENSE,	19	EPIDERM MACABRE	14
OF SENSE AT RAPID INTERVALS.	22	SILENCE	6
THEY FEED THE SENSE, DENY THE SOUL,	25	VERSE W ALLUSNS	9
SHAKES EVERY SENSE. I'M FIVE	271	THE REPLY	13
SENSES			
IF I MUST OF MY SENSES LOSE,	8	PRAYER	1
SENSIBILITY			
SENSIBILITY! O LA!	81	SENSIBILITY! LA	T
SENSIBLE			
SUSTENANCE SEEMED SENSIBLE	228	THE GERANIUM	8
SENSITIVE			
THE WORM, THOUGH DANK, IS SENSITIVE:	23	AMOROUS LADY	7
SENSUAL			
WHAT SHAPE LEAPED FORWARD AT THE SENSUAL CRY?--	107	SIR JOHN DAVIES	67
EYE LEARNED FROM EYE, COLD LIP FROM SENSUAL LIP.	119	THE DREAM	4
SMALL WAVES REPEAT THE MIND'S SLOW SENSUAL PLAY.	131	SENTENTIOUS MAN	13
I HATE THIS SENSUAL PEN;	136	THE SENSUALISTS	22
WHAT SENSUAL EYE CAN KEEP AN IMAGE PURE,	154	THE DYING MAN	43
ALL SENSUAL LOVE'S BUT DANCING ON A GRAVE.	154	THE DYING MAN	47
HOW TO TRANSCEND THIS SENSUAL EMPTINESS?	187	THE LONGING	12
SENSUALISTS			
THE SENSUALISTS	136	THE SENSUALISTS	T
SENSUALITY			
WE STRUGGLED OUT OF SENSUALITY;	237	THE TRANCED	11
SENSUOUS			
THE PURE, SENSUOUS FORM.	150	SNAKE	11
SENT			
THEY SENT,--YOU ALWAYS SEND,--TO CUBA	115	THE SERPENT	15
THE LOOSE AIR SENT ME RUNNING LIKE A CHILD--	155	THE DYING MAN	55
WHO SENT HIM AWAY?	220	THE ABYSS	40
SENTENTIOUS			
THE SENTENTIOUS MAN	131	SENTENTIOUS MAN	T
SENTIMENT			
VERNAL SENTIMENT	24	VERNAL SENTIMNT	T
SENTIMENTAL			
THE HIGH-PILED FLORAL OFFERINGS WITH SENTIMENTAL VERSES,	22	ROAD TO WDLAWN	3
SENTRY			
I'VE BECOME A SENTRY OF SMALL SEEDS,	103	OLD LADY'S WRDS	33
SEPARATE			
THINK OF OUR SEPARATE SKINS.	31	LULL	9
SEPARATENESS			
I SAW THE SEPARATENESS OF ALL THINGS!	63	FIELD OF LIGHT	45
SEPTEMBER			
THE WINDLESS PERPETUAL MORNING ABOVE A SEPTEMBER CLOUD.	43	CARNATIONS	7
THIS WHOLE SEPTEMBER DAY.	148	THE SMALL	6
THE DRY SCENT OF A DYING GARDEN IN SEPTEMBER,	201	THE FAR FIELD	78
OR A WIZENED ASTER IN LATE SEPTEMBER,	228	THE GERANIUM	4
SEPTET			
OH, THE SYNCO SEPTET PLAYED FOR US THEN,	112	SQUEEZE-BOX	22
SEQUEL			
THE SEQUEL	241	THE SEQUEL	T
SEQUENCE			
SIGHS, SIGHS, WHO SAYS THEY HAVE SEQUENCE?	223	ELEGY (2)	4
SERE			
OUR VERNAL WISDOM MOVES THROUGH RIPE TO SERE.	12	SLOW SEASON	16
SERENE			
THE PURE SERENE OF MEMORY IN ONE MAN,--	201	THE FAR FIELD	101
I LIVED SERENE AS A FISH,	209	HER LONGING	2
SERENELY			
MOVING SERENELY AMONG THE LEEKS AND CABBAGES,	223	ELEGY (2)	20
SERIES			
I SEE GRANDPA SURVIVING A SERIES OF SEVEN STROKES,	28	CLAIRVOY WIDOW	21
SERIOUS			
"I'M SERIOUS ABOUT MY SINGING CAREER!"	115	THE SERPENT	24
SHE WAS A SERIOUS WOMAN.	163	I'M HERE	74
SERPENT			
RECOILING FROM THE SERPENT HEAD	4	FEUD	3
A RIVER GLIDES OUT OF THE GRASS. A RIVER OR A SERPENT.	59	THE LONG ALLEY	1
THE PATH TELLS LITTLE TO THE SERPENT.	66	SHAPE OF FIRE	59
I'M THE SERPENT OF SOMEBODY ELSE.	81	SENSIBILITY! LA	1
THE SERPENT	115	THE SERPENT	T

	PAGE	TITLE	LINE
SERPENT (CONTINUED)			
THERE WAS A SERPENT WHO HAD TO SING.	115	THE SERPENT	1
HE WAS A SERPENT WITH A SOUL;	115	THE SERPENT	7
INSTEAD OF A DEVIL WITH HORNS, I PREFER A SERPENT WITH SCALES;	173	WHAT TELL BONES	77
SERPENTING			
HE SIMPLY GAVE UP SERPENTING.	115	THE SERPENT	3
SERPENTS			
BEASTS OF THE HILL AND SERPENTS OF THE DEN.	239	IN A DARK TIME	6
SERPENT'S			
TO STOP THE SERPENT'S AWFUL RACKET:	115	THE SERPENT	13
"YOU SEE," HE SAID, WITH A SERPENT'S LEER,	115	THE SERPENT	23
THE SERPENT'S HEART SUSTAINS THE LOVELESS STONE:	131	SENTENTIOUS MAN	3
SERVANT			
WAS I THE SERVANT OF A SOVEREIGN WISH,	105	SIR JOHN DAVIES	29
SERVE			
THE SENSE THAT DOES SO FITLY SERVE,	8	PRAYER	20
SERVED			
HAS SERVED TO KEEP ME WITH THE QUICK.	256	IN HYDROTHERAPY	4
SET			
CONFUSION'S CORE SET DEEP WITHIN	22	SILENCE	13
THAT WOMAN WOULD SET SODDEN STRAW ON FIRE.	105	SIR JOHN DAVIES	28
WHAT BOOK, O LEARNED MAN, WILL SET ME RIGHT?	133	THE PURE FURY	2
THAT TREMBLE OF SWEET NOTES SET MY HEART ASTIR,	216	THE SHY MAN	10
SETTEE			
THE WHAT-NOT, THE SETTEE, THE CHIPPENDALE CHAIRS	32	SALE	3
SETTLES			
THEN SETTLES BACK TO SHADE AND THE LONG NIGHT.	156	THE DYING MAN	81
SETTLING			
SETTLING IN SMALL BEADS AROUND WEEDS AND SUNKEN BRANCHES,	159	FIRST MEDITATN	61
SEVEN			
I SEE GRANDPA SURVIVING A SERIES OF SEVEN STROKES,	28	CLAIRVOY WIDOW	21
I WAS NO MORE THAN SEVEN AT THE TIME.	224	OTTO	22
SEVENTY-FIVE			
JUST SEND ME ALONG THAT SWEET SEVENTY-FIVE;	113	TO A LADY ED	14
SEVERAL			
COME OUT OF A CLOUD, ANGEL WITH SEVERAL FACES,	48	LAST WORDS	8
THE SEVERAL SOUNDS WERE LOW;	87	PRAISE TO END!	67
HER SEVERAL PARTS COULD KEEP A PURE REPOSE,	127	I KNEW A WOMAN	19
I SAW MY SEVERAL SELVES	147	THE EXORCISM	14
SOMETIMES I THINK I'M SEVERAL.	173	WHAT TELL BONES	83
WE COUNTED SEVERAL FLAMES IN ONE SMALL FIRE.	237	THE TRANCED	1
SEWED			
THEY SEWED UP THE AIR WITH A STEM;	44	FRAU BAUMAN	22
SEX-LIFE			
HIS SEX-LIFE NEVER IS ONE-SIDED.	264	THREE EPIGRAMS	14
SHADE			
ALL SHADE IS LEAN, THE ANTIC BRANCH	14	COMING OF COLD	28
AND PULLED THE GREEN SHADE AGAINST MORNING SUN.	29	THE REMINDER	8
COME, COME OUT OF THE SHADE, THE COOL WAYS,	61	THE LONG ALLEY	69
SHAPES IN THE SHADE	80	GIVE WAY, GATES	49
THE SHADE SAYS: LOVE THE SUN.	82	SENSIBILITY! LA	39
BEGINNINGS START WITHOUT SHADE,	93	I CRY, LOVE!	33
THE ANIMAL'S CANDID GAZE, A SHADE LESS THAN FEATHERS, LIGHT'S BROKEN	98	O, THOU OPENING	22
THE SHADE SANG WITH HER;	102	ELEGY FOR JANE	7
WITH ITS DEEP SHADE, AND BIRDS.	103	OLD LADY'S WRDS	28
AND TREES CAME CLOSER WITH A DENSER SHADE.	133	THE PURE FURY	21
AS THE THICK SHADE OF THE LONG NIGHT COMES ON.	134	THE PURE FURY	28
OUT OF THE MOTTLED SHADE	150	SNAKE	2
THEN SETTLES BACK TO SHADE AND THE LONG NIGHT.	156	THE DYING MAN	81
A SHAPE WITHOUT A SHADE, OR ALMOST NONE,	167	HER BECOMING	88
THE MOUNTAIN WITH ITS SINGULAR BRIGHT SHADE	201	THE FAR FIELD	95
THE DEEP SHADE GATHERS NIGHT;	212	LIGHT LISTENED	17
THE SHADE SPEAKS SLOWLY:	222	THE ABYSS	85
I MEET MY SHADOW IN THE DEEPENING SHADE;	239	IN A DARK TIME	2
THE SHIFTING SHADE, THE CINDERS AT MY BACK.	245	THE DECISION	10
SHADOW			
THE WORLD RECEDES IN THE BLACK REVOLVING SHADOW;	33	IDYLL	9
HAS THE WORM A SHADOW?	56	THE LOST SON	116
HAVE YOU COME TO UNHINGE MY SHADOW?	65	SHAPE OF FIRE	33
WAITING LIKE A FERN, MAKING A SPINY SHADOW.	102	ELEGY FOR JANE	15
I TRIED TO FLING MY SHADOW AT THE MOON,	105	SIR JOHN DAVIES	13

	PAGE	TITLE	LINE
SHADOW (CONTINUED)			
I TOUCHED HER SHADOW WHEN THE LIGHT DELAYED;	119	THE DREAM	13
I SWEAR SHE CAST A SHADOW WHITE AS STONE.	127	I KNEW A WOMAN	25
ITS SHADOW BENT IN HALF.	150	SNAKE	7
WHEN FIGURES OUT OF OBSCURE SHADOW RAVE,	154	THE DYING MAN	46
MY SHADOW STEADIES IN A SHIFTING STREAM;	167	HER BECOMING	92
ONCE I COULD TOUCH MY SHADOW, AND BE HAPPY;	168	FOURTH MEDITATN	14
WHERE SHADOW CAN CHANGE INTO FLAME,	188	THE LONGING	49
WHERE IMPULSE NO LONGER DICTATES, NOR THE DARKENING SHADOW,	197	THE LONG WATERS	57
THE TREE RETREATS INTO ITS OWN SHADOW.	200	THE FAR FIELD	57
AND THE SMALL FISH LIE, WITHOUT SHADOW, MOTIONLESS,	233	THE PIKE	6
I MEET MY SHADOW IN THE DEEPENING SHADE;	239	IN A DARK TIME	2
MY SHADOW PINNED AGAINST A SWEATING WALL.	239	IN A DARK TIME	10
AND THE SUN TOUCHES THE LIZARD'S THROAT, ITS TAIL HALF IN SHADOW.	261	THE CHANGELING	34
SHADOWS			
WATCHING SHADOWS CRAWL,	53	THE LOST SON	17
THE SEA WILL BE THERE, THE GREAT SQUASHY SHADOWS,	79	GIVE WAY, GATES	28
ITS SHADOWS LOOSE, A WATERY FINGER;	101	LIGHT BREATHER	10
THE SHADOWS ARE EMPTY, THE SLIDING EXTERNALS.	104	OLD LADY'S WRDS	51
OUR SHADOWS MET, AND SLOWLY SWUNG AROUND;	120	THE DREAM	26
I FEAR THOSE SHADOWS MOST	138	THE SURLY ONE	7
AND THEIR SHADOWS, BIGGER,	152	THE SISKINS	5
TODAY I EAT MY USUAL DIET OF SHADOWS.	166	HER BECOMING	31
THE SHADOWS CRAWLING DOWN A SUNNY WALL.	171	WHAT TELL BONES	17
SHAFTS			
ITS SHAFTS REMAIN.	9	THE ADAMANT	4
SHAG			
THE RICH CAN PLAY AT POLO, THE POOR CAN DO THE SHAG,	27	CLAIRVOY WIDOW	11
SHAGINAW			
IN SHAGINAW, IN SHAGINAW	267	SAGINAW SONG	25
IN SHAGINAW, IN SHAGINAW	267	SAGINAW SONG	25
SHAKE			
WHEELS SHAKE THE ROADBED STONE,	34	NIGHT JOURNEY	24
DID SPACE SHAKE OFF AN ANGEL WITH A SIGH?	107	SIR JOHN DAVIES	69
AND SHAKE THE SECRETS FROM MY DEEPEST BONES;	173	WHAT TELL BONES	87
THE SELF-DESTRUCTIVE SHAKE THE COMMON WALL;	250	THE RIGHT THING	14
SHAKES			
THE WIND SHAKES OUT THE SCENT OF PEAR.	14	COMING OF COLD	12
WHAT SHAKES MY SKULL TO DISREPAIR	22	SILENCE	19
WHEN SHE SHAKES OUT HER HAIR.	121	ALL EARTH, AIR	9
WHAT SHAKES THE EYE BUT THE INVISIBLE?	245	THE DECISION	1
SHAKES EVERY SENSE. I'M FIVE	271	THE REPLY	13
SHAKING			
A SHAKING DOWN, WHILE THE STEM STAYS STRAIGHT,	42	TRANSPLANTING	10
AND A BEE SHAKING DROPS FROM A RAIN-SOAKED HONEYSUCKLE.	63	FIELD OF LIGHT	49
A FISH JUMPS, SHAKING OUT FLAKES OF MOONLIGHT.	93	I CRY, LOVE!	45
THIS SHAKING KEEPS ME STEADY. I SHOULD KNOW.	108	THE WAKING (2)	16
AND THE WHOLE RIVER BEGINS TO MOVE FORWARD, ITS BRIDGES SHAKING.	191	AT OYSTER RIVER	56
SHAKING OUT MY CATCH IN THE MORNING SUNLIGHT,	209	HER LONGING	15
SHAKING LOOSE THE LAST WIZENED ORANGES IN THE ORCHARD,	231	THE STORM	32
SHALE			
SHALE LOOSENS. MARL REACHES INTO THE FIELD. SMALL BIRDS PASS OVER WATER.	64	SHAPE OF FIRE	11
AND THE SHALE SLIDES AN INCH IN THE TALUS,	157	FIRST MEDITATN	10
I'M A SMALL STONE, LOOSE IN THE SHALE.	172	WHAT TELL BONES	47
WHERE THE SHALE SLIDES DANGEROUSLY	193	JOURNY INTERIOR	3
NOT FEELING THE COARSE SHALE	265	HARSH COUNTRY	7
SHALL			
WHICH OF THE FIVE I SHALL RETAIN	8	PRAYER	3
SHALL NEVER TOUCH ANOTHER EAR.	22	SILENCE	20
LUMINOUS ONE, SHALL WE MEET ON THE BOSOM OF GOD?	59	THE LONG ALLEY	29
SHALL I CALL THE FLOWERS?	61	THE LONG ALLEY	65
GOD BLESS THE GROUND! I SHALL WALK SOFTLY THERE,	108	THE WAKING (2)	8
I THINK THE DEAD ARE TENDER. SHALL WE KISS?--	129	SHE	1
WHAT YOU SURVIVED I SHALL BELIEVE: THE HEAT,	144	ELEGY (1)	13
I SHALL UNDO ALL DYING BY MY DEATH.	155	THE DYING MAN	77
BLESSED THE MEEK; THEY SHALL INHERIT WRATH;	244	INFIRMITY	17
TIME-HARRIED PRISONERS OF SHALL AND WILL--	250	THE RIGHT THING	2
SHALLOW			
HE DIPPED HIS HAND IN THE SHALLOW:	6	THE PREMONITION	7
HE WALKS THE SHALLOW WITH AN ANTIC GRACE.	15	THE HERON	5

	PAGE	TITLE	LINE
SHALLOW (CONTINUED)			
THE SHALLOW STREAM RUNS SLACK;	123	WORDS FOR WIND	25
OR A SALMON, TIRED, MOVING UP A SHALLOW STREAM,	159	FIRST MEDITATN	68
SHALLOWER			
WRINKLING BETWEEN REEDS IN SHALLOWER WATER,	93	I CRY, LOVE!	47
SHALLOWS			
IN THE SILTED SHALLOWS OF A SLOW RIVER,	200	THE FAR FIELD	39
SHAME			
IS CIRCULARITY SUCH A SHAME?	92	I CRY, LOVE!	8
SHANTY			
I'M SHANTY IRISH	272	DUET	13
SHAPE			
THESE SHAPE THE CREATURE THAT IS I.	18	LONG LIVE WEEDS	12
EACH CLUMP IN THE SHAPE OF A POT;	43	FLOWER DUMP	9
A SHAPE IN THE MIND ROSE UP:	49	NIGHT CROW	3
THE SHAPE OF A RAT?	54	THE LOST SON	44
WHAT GLIDING SHAPE	56	THE LOST SON	88
A STONE'S SHAPE	62	FIELD OF LIGHT	13
THE SHAPE OF THE FIRE	64	SHAPE OF FIRE	T
SOME RARE NEW TEDIUM'S TAKING SHAPE:	81	SENSIBILITY! LA	13
A SHAPE COMES TO STAY;	81	SENSIBILITY! LA	21
WHAT'S A THICK? TWO-BY-TWO'S A SHAPE.	92	I CRY, LOVE!	10
BAGS? WHO EVER SAID GOD SANG IN YOUR FAT SHAPE? YOU'RE NOT THE ONLY	98	O, THOU OPENING	27
WHAT SHAPE LEAPED FORWARD AT THE SENSUAL CRY?--	107	SIR JOHN DAVIES	67
IT WAS AND WAS NOT SHE, A SHAPE ALONE,	107	SIR JOHN DAVIES	71
A SHAPE OF CHANGE, ENCIRCLED BY ITS FIRE.	119	THE DREAM	10
A SHAPE FROM DEEP IN THE EYE--	123	WORDS FOR WIND	30
SHAPE TO A RANDOM JOY:	124	WORDS FOR WIND	48
WHO PLAGUES ME WITH HER SHAPE,	130	THE OTHER	2
A SHAPE CRIED FROM A CLOUD,	147	THE EXORCISM	7
A TREE ALL OUT OF SHAPE FROM WIND AND RAIN,	150	IN LATE SUMMER	27
ANOTHER SHAPE THAN HERS	154	THE DYING MAN	29
MY SHAPE A LEVITY--YES!--	165	HER BECOMING	4
I SEE A SHAPE, LIGHTED WITH LOVE,	165	HER BECOMING	11
THE MOON, A PURE ISLAMIC SHAPE, LOOKED DOWN.	166	HER BECOMING	55
A SHAPE WITHOUT A SHADE, OR ALMOST NONE,	167	HER BECOMING	88
THE SHAPE OF A LARK RISES FROM A STONE;	168	FOURTH MEDITATN	25
THE SHAPE THAT CAME FROM MY SLEEP, WEEPING:	198	THE LONG WATERS	68
AND THE WIND TRIES THE SHAPE OF A TREE,	204	THE ROSE	84
THE SHAPE OF THINGS TO BE;	212	LIGHT LISTENED	14
(AND SOME GROW OUT OF SHAPE, THEIR SEED IMPURE;)	225	OTTO	32
A SHAPE CALLED UP OUT OF MY NATURAL MIND;	241	THE SEQUEL	10
THE SOUL HAS ITS OWN SHINE AND SHAPE;	259	SONG (3)	48
A WRETCH NEEDS HIS WRETCHEDNESS. YES. BUT THIS SHAPE	260	THE CHANGELING	13
WHEN HE SAID THAT, A SPIDERY SHAPE DROPPED DOWN	273	SUPPR W LINDSAY	24
SHAPED			
THE SUMMER HOUSE SHAPED LIKE A VILLAGE BAND STAND	32	SALE	7
SHAPELESS			
AND SHAPELESS NIGHT THAT MADE NO ANSWER BACK.	107	SIR JOHN DAVIES	90
SHAPELY			
OF THE FINE SHAPELY THOUGHT	211	SONG (1)	2
SHAPES			
ONCE MORE THE TREES ASSUME FAMILIAR SHAPES,	11	LIGHT BRIGHTER	9
ALL DISTANT SHAPES TURN BRIGHTER TO THE GAZE.	17	UNEXTINGUISHED	4
THERE WERE CLOUDS MAKING A ROUT OF SHAPES CROSSING A WINDBREAK OF CEDARS,	63	FIELD OF LIGHT	48
SHAPES IN THE SHADE	80	GIVE WAY, GATES	49
ALL SMALL SHAPES, WILLOW-SHY,	90	UNFOLD! UNFOLD!	46
THE SHAPES A BRIGHT CONTAINER CAN CONTAIN!	127	I KNEW A WOMAN	4
THE SMALL SHAPES DROWSE: I LIVE	148	THE SMALL	19
THEIR BLACK SHAPES BREAKING PAST;	158	FIRST MEDITATN	34
ALL NATURAL SHAPES BECAME SYMBOLICAL.	166	HER BECOMING	57
SHAPES STIFFENING INTO METAL,	169	FOURTH MEDITATN	40
AND SHAPES MAKE ME AFRAID:	171	WHAT TELL BONES	14
AND I WATCHED AND WATCHED TILL MY EYES BLURRED FROM THE BIRD SHAPES,--	199	THE FAR FIELD	29
SPRAY, AND THE SMALL SHAPES	210	HER TIME	17
I LEAN, AND LOVE THESE MANIFOLD SHAPES,	233	THE PIKE	13
THE LEAVES, THE TREES TURNED OUR TWO SHAPES AROUND.	237	THE TRANCED	15
ALL NATURAL SHAPES BLAZING UNNATURAL LIGHT.	239	IN A DARK TIME	18
SHARDS			
THINGS HAVE THEIR THOUGHT: THEY ARE THE SHARDS OF ME;	107	SIR JOHN DAVIES	86

	PAGE	TITLE	LINE
SHARE			
IN WHICH ALL CREATURES SHARE, AND THEREBY LIVE,	243	THE MOTION	18
SHARP			
GRUBS AND SNAILS AND SHARP STICKS,	39	WEED PULLER	6
THE STONES WERE SHARP,	87	PRAISE TO END!	51
THE SHARP STARS SWING AROUND;	125	WORDS FOR WIND	64
HAVE THEY SEEN, EVER, THE SHARP BONES OF THE POOR?	169	FOURTH MEDITATN	46
WINDING UPWARD TOWARD THE STREAM WITH ITS SHARP STONES,	193	JOURNY INTERIOR	12
ALWAYS A SHARP TURN TO THE LEFT PAST A BARN CLOSE TO THE ROADSIDE,	193	JOURNY INTERIOR	25
FROM A BURNT PINE THE SHARP SPEECH OF A CROW	246	THE MARROW	3
SHARPENED			
THE WIND SHARPENED ITSELF ON A ROCK;	65	SHAPE OF FIRE	39
SHARPENED A BUTCHER KNIFE;	213	THE HAPPY THREE	2
SHARPER			
OF RESTIVE CROWS IS SHARPER ON THE EAR.	11	LIGHT BRIGHTER	2
THE EDGE OF HEAVEN WAS SHARPER THAN A SWORD;	237	THE TRANCED	6
SHARPLY			
GLEAM SHARPLY ON THE NARROW SIGHT.	15	COMING OF COLD	46
SHAVING			
MY SHAVING HAND JERKED BACK IN SUDDEN TERROR:	25	DIM-WIT COUSIN	11
SHE (135)			
SHEATH			
POKES THROUGH A MUSTY SHEATH	37	CUTTINGS	7
SHEATH-WET			
I QUAIL, LEAN TO BEGINNINGS, SHEATH-WET.	37	CUTTINGS (LATE)	11
SHEAVES			
LONG SINCE, BRONZE WHEAT WAS GATHERED INTO SHEAVES.	12	SLOW SEASON	10
UNDER, UNDER THE SHEAVES,	62	FIELD OF LIGHT	22
SHE-BEAR			
THE SHE-BEAR MOPES UNDER THE HILL.	64	SHAPE OF FIRE	15
SHED			
REASON? THAT DREARY SHED, THAT HUTCH FOR GRUBBY SCHOOLBOYS!	92	I CRY, LOVE!	14
I SHED MY CLOTHES TO SLOW MY DAEMON DOWN.	166	HER BECOMING	59
WHO LIVED ABOVE A POTTING SHED FOR YEARS.	224	OTTO	4
SHE'D			
SHE'D DUNK AND SHE'D GUBBLE:	179	MYRTLE'S COUSIN	6
SHE'D DUNK AND SHE'D GUBBLE:	179	MYRTLE'S COUSIN	6
SHE'D RANT AND SHE'D ROAR:	179	MYRTLE	8
SHE'D RANT AND SHE'D ROAR:	179	MYRTLE	8
SHE'D MUDDLE THE WHOLE AFTERNOON	179	MYRTLE'S COUSIN	9
SHE'D MORE SIDES THAN A SEAL.	212	LIGHT LISTENED	6
AT THE TIME: SHE'D LIVED	228	THE GERANIUM	9
SHEDDING			
AND SAID, OLD BOY, YOU'RE SHEDDING HAIR,	181	MONOTONY SONG	6
AND SHEDDING MORE THAN HERE AND THERE,	181	MONOTONY SONG	7
SHEDS			
THE BULKS CANNOT HIDE US, OR THE BLEAK SHEDS OF OUR DESOLATION,	166	HER BECOMING	39
SHEEN			
THE IMMEDIATE SHEEN, THE REALITY OF STRAW,	171	WHAT TELL BONES	16
AND THE SHEEN OF RAVENS.	265	HARSH COUNTRY	4
SHEEP			
THE SHEEP STREWN ON A FIELD,	54	THE LOST SON	37
THE GREY SHEEP CAME. I RAN,	147	THE EXORCISM	1
NIBBLED BY SHEEP AND RABBITS.	202	THE ROSE	10
SHEEPISHLY			
LOVERS DISENGAGE, MOVE SHEEPISHLY TOWARD THE AISLE	47	DOUBLE FEATURE	2
SHEETS			
THE SHEETS AND BLANKETS TURNED TO SNOW.	114	DINKY	15
SHELF			
SLID FROM THE KITCHEN SHELF;	45	MY PAPA'S WALTZ	6
I TOOK THE WHISKEY FROM THE SHELF,	138	THE SURLY ONE	2
SHELL			
BUT MY EAR STILL KEPT THE SOUND OF THE SEA LIKE A SHELL.	12	MID-CNTRY BLOW	8
A SHELL ARCHED UNDER MY TOES,	49	RIVER INCIDENT	1
FROM A SHELL HARDER THAN HORN.	81	SENSIBILITY! LA	9
AS A CHIP OR SHELL, FLOATING LAZILY WITH A SLOW CURRENT,	168	FOURTH MEDITATN	6
FINGERING A SHELL,	200	THE FAR FIELD	40
SHELLS			
RUNNING ALONG THE NARROW FURROWS OF THE SHORE, THE ROWS OF DEAD CLAM SHELLS;	190	AT OYSTER RIVER	3
SURROUNDED BY SAND, BROKEN SHELLS, THE WRECKAGE OF WATER.	197	THE LONG WATERS	59

	PAGE	TITLE	LINE
SHELLS (CONTINUED)			
HER NAILS BRIGHTER THAN SHELLS,	261	THE CHANGELING	55
SHELTER			
"THERE'S NO SHELTER	229	ON THE QUAY	2
SHELVES			
PERCHED ON MANY SHELVES,	56	THE LOST SON	93
SHELVES HAVE A SPECIAL USE;	213	THE HAPPY THREE	9
SHEPHERD			
I MET A COLLECTOR OF STRING, A SHEPHERD OF SLOW FORMS.	90	UNFOLD! UNFOLD!	30
SHE'S			
MAMMA, SHE'S A SAD FAT.	74	I NEED, I NEED	19
SEE! SHE'S SLEEPING LIKE A LAKE:	81	SENSIBILITY! LA	2
SHE'S SWEETER THAN A TREE.	123	WORDS FOR WIND	2
SWEET PHOEBE, SHE'S MY THEME:	123	WORDS FOR WIND	11
SHE'S COMING NEAR!	261	THE CHANGELING	44
SHE'S COME TO PIERCE A CLOUD!	261	THE CHANGELING	56
SHIELD			
WITH NAKEDNESS MY SHIELD.	3	OPEN HOUSE	10
SHIELDS			
THE WIND ROCKS WITH MY WISH; THE RAIN SHIELDS ME;	173	WHAT TELL BONES	81
SHIFT			
AT BRIDGEHEADS BUCKLED ICE BEGINS TO SHIFT,	11	LIGHT BRIGHTER	7
THE GENERALS COUGH AND SHIFT	31	LULL	11
YET, LIKE A TREE, ENDURE THE SHIFT OF THINGS.	135	THE RENEWAL	6
I SHIFT ON MY ROCK, AND I THINK:	191	AT OYSTER RIVER	41
AND A CHILD'S DIRTY SHIFT BILLOWS UPWARD OUT OF AN ALLEY,	230	THE STORM	18
WITH EVERY SHIFT OF AIR, THOSE BEATING WINGS,	248	THE TREE, BIRD	15
SHIFTED			
A CLOUD MOVED CLOSE. THE BULK OF THE WIND SHIFTED.	100	THE VISITANT	1
SHIFTED WITH OUR SLOW KISS.	238	THE MOMENT	5
SHIFTING			
I PAW THE DARK, THE SHIFTING MIDNIGHT AIR.	135	THE RENEWAL	16
MY SHADOW STEADIES IN A SHIFTING STREAM;	167	HER BECOMING	92
SHIFTING IN THE WAKENING SUNLIGHT	204	THE ROSE	87
THE WIND SHIFTING SOUTH.	236	SONG (2)	12
THE SHIFTING SHADE, THE CINDERS AT MY BACK.	245	THE DECISION	10
SHIFTING IN SEA CHANGE,	265	HARSH COUNTRY	11
HALF SIDEWAYS IN THE SHIFTING LIGHT,	273	SUPPR W LINDSAY	20
SHIFTS			
LIGHT SHIFTS UPON THE WALL.	240	IN EVEING AIR	21
SHIMMER			
"THE SHIMMER OF EVIL"	143	SHIMMER OF EVIL	T
THE GREAT TREES NO LONGER SHIMMER;	187	THE LONGING	17
THE MOON LOLLING IN THE CLOSE ELM, A SHIMMER OF SILVER,	204	THE ROSE	81
THE BOTTOM-STONES SHIMMER BACK THEIR IRREGULAR STRIATIONS,	233	THE PIKE	8
AS CHANGES SHIMMER IN THE INNER EYE.	244	INFIRMITY	2
THE DEEP EYE SEES THE SHIMMER ON THE STONE;	244	INFIRMITY	20
SHIMMERED			
THE WREN'S THROAT SHIMMERED,	51	THE WAKING (1)	6
SHIMMERING			
ON THE SHIMMERING ROAD,	194	JOURNY INTERIOR	50
AND SHIMMERING. THE SUN BURNED THROUGH A HAZE,	247	I WAITED	11
INDEED I SAW A SHIMMERING LAKE	270	GOB MUSIC	32
SHIMMERS			
MY BODY SHIMMERS WITH A LIGHT FLAME.	198	THE LONG WATERS	66
ONE WHITE FACE SHIMMERS BRIGHTER THAN THE SUN	246	THE MARROW	7
SHINE			
THAT AIR AND SHINE: AND THE FLICKER'S LOUD SUMMER CALL:	66	SHAPE OF FIRE	70
THE SHINE ON THE FACE OF THE LAKE	93	I CRY, LOVE!	50
LIKE THE BLUE SHINE ON FRESHLY FROZEN SNOW,	201	THE FAR FIELD	96
THE SOUL HAS ITS OWN SHINE AND SHAPE;	259	SONG (3)	48
SHINGLES			
THE SHRIEK OF NAILS AS OLD SHINGLES ARE RIPPED FROM THE TOP OF A ROOF,	204	THE ROSE	70
SHINING			
WE DANCED TO SHINING; MOCKED BEFORE THE BLACK	107	SIR JOHN DAVIES	89
A POOL RIDING AND SHINING WITH THE RIVER,	168	FOURTH MEDITATN	9
A SHINING.	192	AT OYSTER RIVER	70
THE FULL MOON WAS SHINING UPON THE BROAD SEA;	216	THE SHY MAN	1
THE MEDITERRANEAN SUN SHINING ON US, EQUALLY,	226	THE LIZARD	4
OF SLIME AND SHINING SPIT,	270	GOB MUSIC	33
SHINY			
CANNAS SHINY AS SLAG,	43	FLOWER DUMP	1

	PAGE	TITLE	LINE
SHIP			
IN THE WAKE OF A SHIP OF WIND;	80	GIVE WAY, GATES	42
AS WHEN A SHIP SAILS WITH A LIGHT WIND--	203	THE ROSE	31
THE WHOLE SHIP ROLLING SLIGHTLY SIDEWAYS,	203	THE ROSE	36
SHIPS			
"I SEE THE RIVER HARBOR, ALIVE WITH MEN AND SHIPS,	28	CLAIRVOY WIDOW	19
SHIRT			
STILL CLINGING TO YOUR SHIRT.	45	MY PAPA'S WALTZ	16
SHIVER			
WE SHIVER AT THE SIREN'S BLAST.	33	HIGHWAY: MICH	18
THAT SHIVER IN THE WIND	209	HER RETICENCE	10
SHIVER, AND MORE THAN TWICE,	216	HER WRATH	4
SHIVERED			
SHE SHIVERED IN HER SKIN,	262	FOLLIES OF ADAM	20
SHIVERS			
THIS SHIVERS ME; I SWEAR	271	THE REPLY	10
SHOAL			
THE SHOAL ROCKS WITH THE SEA.	215	HIS FOREBODING	1
SHOCK			
INSENTIENT TO SHOCK.	4	DEATH PIECE	8
SHOCKS			
AND SHOCKS OF RAGGED CORN;	146	THE SONG	10
SHOE			
THERE WAS ONLY ONE SHOE	64	SHAPE OF FIRE	26
PUTTING EGG IN YOUR SHOE	180	GOO-GIRL	3
WELTER OF TIN CANS, PAILS, OLD BIRD NESTS, A CHILD'S SHOE RIDING A LOG,	191	AT OYSTER RIVER	54
IN A SHOE BOX STUFFED IN AN OLD NYLON STOCKING	227	MEADOW MOUSE	1
OR IS THE BODY BUT A MOTION IN A SHOE?	237	THE TRANCED	5
SHOE-BOX			
BUT THIS MORNING THE SHOE-BOX HOUSE ON THE BACK PORCH IS EMPTY.	227	MEADOW MOUSE	20
SHOES			
LEAVES MORE THAN SHOES;	65	SHAPE OF FIRE	48
I'LL CHANGE THE IMAGE, AND MY SHOES.	97	O, THOU OPENING	19
JUMPING IN HER SHOES.	103	OLD LADY'S WRDS	18
HE COMES CALLING WITHOUT WIPING HIS SHOES!	183	THE WAGTAIL	8
AND WHY MUDDY SHOES	213	THE HAPPY THREE	10
SHOOK			
THEY SPRINKLED AND SHOOK;	44	FRAU BAUMAN	15
I SHOOK THE SOFTENING CHALK OF MY BONES,	53	THE LOST SON	6
SHOOK WITH A MIGHTY POWER BEYOND HIS WILL,--	107	SIR JOHN DAVIES	75
THE WHOLE PLACE SHOOK WHENEVER I GOT A CHILL--	163	I'M HERE	64
WHERE HE TREMBLED AND SHOOK BENEATH A STICK	227	MEADOW MOUSE	3
HE SHOOK MY HAND. "TELL WILLIAMS I'VE BEEN HERE,	274	SUPPR W LINDSAY	48
SHOOTING			
SHOOTING UP LIME AND DUNG AND GROUND BONES,--	38	FORCING HOUSE	9
SHOOTS			
AND YOUNG SHOOTS SPREAD UPON OUR INNER WORLD.	11	LIGHT BRIGHTER	20
THE SHOOTS OF SPRING HAVE MELLOWED WITH THE YEAR.	12	SLOW SEASON	13
AND RUBBERY SHOOTS,	38	FORCING HOUSE	2
SHOOTS DANGLED AND DROOPED,	38	ROOT CELLAR	3
SHOP			
DALLY AT SHOP WINDOWS, STILL RELUCTANT TO GO;	47	DOUBLE FEATURE	6
SHOP-GIRL			
WITH A NURSE-MAID WADDLE AND A SHOP-GIRL SIMPER,	23	ACADEMIC	3
SHOPPING			
OF A MAN-TAILORED BLOUSE; THE LIST OF SHOPPING DONE;	29	THE REMINDER	6
SHORE			
A WAVE OF TIME HANGS MOTIONLESS ON THIS PARTICULAR SHORE..	47	DOUBLE FEATURE	9
SEA-BEAST OR BIRD FLUNG TOWARD THE RAVAGED SHORE?	107	SIR JOHN DAVIES	68
THE MOON DRAWS BACK ITS WATERS FROM THE SHORE.	140	THE SWAN	15
THE SWAN'S DREAD OF THE DARKENING SHORE,	171	WHAT TELL BONES	25
RUNNING ALONG THE NARROW FURROWS OF THE SHORE, THE ROWS OF DEAD CLAM SHELLS;	190	AT OYSTER RIVER	3
WHERE THE SLOW CREEK WINDS DOWN TO THE BLACK SAND OF THE SHORE	203	THE ROSE	49
TODAY I SKIPPED ON THE SHORE,	207	THE YOUNG GIRL	8
OR WALK THE PEBBLY SHORE WITH THE HUMPBACKED HERON,	209	HER LONGING	14
DOWN ON THE NEAR SHORE,	210	HER TIME	22
THE WHITE SEA WIDENING ON A FARTHER SHORE.	248	THE TREE, BIRD	20
AND WHEN HE GOT TO THE SHORE,	263	FOLLIES OF ADAM	34
WE'LL SAIL AWAY FROM THE FRIGHTFUL SHORE	272	DUET	9

	PAGE	TITLE	LINE
SHOREBIRDS			
RUNS WITH THE INTREPID SHOREBIRDS--	192	AT OYSTER RIVER	66
MY WINGS HOVERING OVER THE SHOREBIRDS,	209	HER LONGING	21
SHORELINE			
OVER THE THIN, FEATHERY RIPPLES BREAKING LIGHTLY AGAINST THE IRREGULAR SHORELINE--	197	THE LONG WATERS	50
AND THE LOW RIPPLES RUN OVER A PEBBLY SHORELINE,	198	THE LONG WATERS	62
SHOREWARD			
HELD UP, WHILE THE ROWER BREATHES, AND THE SMALL BOAT DRIFTS QUIETLY SHOREWARD;	67	SHAPE OF FIRE	91
A SINGLE WAVE STARTS LIGHTLY AND EASILY SHOREWARD,	93	I CRY, LOVE!	46
SHORT			
FOR A SHORT WHILE,	161	I'M HERE	18
I TAKE THE LIBERTIES A SHORT LIFE PERMITS--	173	WHAT TELL BONES	90
PERIPHERAL DIPPERS COME TO REST ON THE SHORT GRASS,	235	ALL MORNING	34
SHORT-HAND			
WHO SPOKE FIRST IN THE COARSE SHORT-HAND OF THE SUBLIMINAL DEPTHS,	170	FOURTH MEDITATN	71
SHORT-TAILED			
TO DISTRACT ATTENTION FROM THE SHORT-TAILED RIDICULOUS YOUNG ONES	234	ALL MORNING	19
SHOT			
DRY BARK FLEW IN THEIR FACES FROM HIS SHOT,--	224	OTTO	16
SHE DROPPED AS IF SHOT.	249	THE RESTORED	6
SHOULD			
IF I SHOULD EVER SEEK RELIEF	22	SILENCE	15
THE TABLE WHERE EVERYONE ATE AS HE SHOULD,	32	SALE	14
--SHOULD SLEEP ON HIS PAWS.	99	O, THOU OPENING	72
SHOULD A SONG BREAK A SLEEP?	99	O, THOU OPENING	74
WE PLAYED WITH DARK AND LIGHT AS CHILDREN SHOULD.	107	SIR JOHN DAVIES	66
THIS SHAKING KEEPS ME STEADY. I SHOULD KNOW.	108	THE WAKING (2)	16
AND SHOULD HE ARRIVE, WHY JUST LEAN YOURSELF BACK	113	TO A LADY ED	7
BUT SHOULD YOU CALL HIS MANNER SMUG,	116	THE SLOTH	8
MYSELF AS I SHOULD BE,	123	WORDS FOR WIND	6
OF HER CHOICE VIRTUES ONLY GODS SHOULD SPEAK,	127	I KNEW A WOMAN	5
MORE THAN A MORTAL SHOULD;	128	THE VOICE	4
SHOULD EVERY CREATURE BE AS I HAVE BEEN,	144	ELEGY (1)	1
THUS I; AND SHOULD THESE REASONS FLY APART,	144	ELEGY (1)	9
I WISH YOU WOULD ACT LIKE A BIRD REALLY SHOULD.	177	KITTY-CAT BIRD	6
AND YOU SHOULD SEE HER NOSES TWITCH,--	181	MONOTONY SONG	18
OLD MEN SHOULD BE EXPLORERS?	189	THE LONGING	57
WHO SHOULD COME UP RIGHT THEN,	213	THE HAPPY THREE	17
WHAT DOES WHAT IT SHOULD DO NEEDS NOTHING MORE.	235	MANIFESTATION	9
AND IF YOU EAT MORE THAN YOU SHOULD,	267	SAGINAW SONG	5
SHOULD DAME ANXIETY EVER COME NEAR	272	DUET	24
BURNING IN SAND. "IT LOOKS LIKE I SHOULD GO,"--	274	SUPPR W LINDSAY	37
JOHN RANSOM SHOULD BE HERE, AND RENE CHAR;	274	SUPPR W LINDSAY	43
SHOULDER			
THE HAND UPON MY SHOULDER TURNS TO HORN.	154	THE DYING MAN	39
AND PUMPED A SHOULDER FULL OF CORTISONE;	244	INFIRMITY	10
SHOULDERS			
THE DOE WITH ITS SLOPED SHOULDERS LOPING ACROSS THE HIGHWAY,	190	AT OYSTER RIVER	27
SHOULDER'S			
"MY SHOULDER'S BITTEN FROM YOUR TEETH;	136	THE SENSUALISTS	13
SHOUTING			
AND EVERYONE, EVERYONE POINTING UP AND SHOUTING!	43	CHILD ON GRNHSE	7
SHOVE			
THE PISTONS JERK AND SHOVE,	34	NIGHT JOURNEY	25
SHOW			
IT WAS PLACE AND SHOW AND ALSO RAN	112	SQUEEZE-BOX	28
I HAVE MYSELF ONE CRUMBLING SKIN TO SHOW;	144	ELEGY (1)	11
FOR ANCESTORS WHO LOVED A WARLIKE SHOW,	224	OTTO	25
SHOWED			
THE DARK SHOWED ME A FACE.	88	PRAISE TO END!	99
SHOWERED			
UPON WHOM EVERY GIFT AND THRILL WERE SHOWERED,	28	THE FAVORITE	10
SHRANK			
THE SCENE SHRANK TO A PIN.	167	HER BECOMING	68
SHRED			
A SHRED OF BONE ITS HORN,	145	THE BEAST	8
SHRIEK			
AND THE WOODS RESOUNDED WITH MANY A SHRIEK	115	THE SERPENT	25
TO A SCURRY OF SMALL DOGS AND A SHRIEK OF CHILDREN,	193	JOURNY INTERIOR	26

	PAGE	TITLE	LINE
SHRIEK (CONTINUED)			
THE SHRIEK OF NAILS AS OLD SHINGLES ARE RIPPED FROM THE TOP OF A ROOF,	204	THE ROSE	70
SHRIEKING			
THE DUMB DAMES SHRIEKING HALF THE NIGHT	228	THE GERANIUM	16
SHRIKE			
TO LIVE BY COURTESY OF THE SHRIKE, THE SNAKE, THE TOM-CAT.	227	MEADOW MOUSE	25
SHRILLEST			
THE SHRILLEST FROGS;	79	GIVE WAY, GATES	30
SHRINK			
YOU SHRINK TO SOMETHING LESS,	151	SLUG	23
DARE I SHRINK TO A HAG,	161	I'M HERE	13
SHRINKING			
I SAW MY FATHER SHRINKING IN HIS SKIN;	155	THE DYING MAN	61
DOWN BY THE MUCK SHRINKING TO THE ALKALINE CENTER.	197	THE LONG WATERS	43
SHRINKS			
BUT SHRINKS INTO A HALF-LIFE, LESS THAN ITSELF,	187	THE LONGING	20
SHRIVELED			
HER SHRIVELED PETALS FALLING	228	THE GERANIUM	11
SHRUNKEN			
HE, IN HIS SHRUNKEN BRITCHES,	46	PICKLE BELT	9
BY THE SHRUNKEN LAKE, HUNTING, IN THE HEAT OF SUMMER.	54	THE LOST SON	43
THE SHRUNKEN SOIL	103	OLD LADY'S WRDS	37
AND IN THE SHRUNKEN FACE OF A DEAD RAT, EATEN BY RAIN AND GROUND-BEETLES	199	THE FAR FIELD	19
I TALKED TO A SHRUNKEN ROOT;	262	FOLLIES OF ADAM	15
SHUDDER			
WHEN I THINK OF IT NOW, I JUST HAVE TO SHUDDER!	114	THE COW	2
THE SUDDEN SHUDDER AS THE JUTTING SEA-CLIFF COLLAPSES,	231	THE STORM	42
SHUDDERED			
AND SHUDDERED TOWARD THE WALL;	136	THE SENSUALISTS	18
SHUDDERING			
THEIR BLACK SKINS SHUDDERING:	159	FIRST MEDITATN	57
SHULE			
I WENT TO SHUNDAY SHULE;	267	SAGINAW SONG	26
SHUNDAY			
I WENT TO SHUNDAY SHULE;	267	SAGINAW SONG	26
SHUT			
I WOULD BE NEAR; I SHUT MY EYES TO SEE;	246	THE MARROW	22
I'LL KEEP MY BIG MOUTH SHUT.	270	GOB MUSIC	37
SHUTTLING			
SHUTTLING ITS THROAT WHILE PERCHED ON A WIND-VENT,	158	FIRST MEDITATN	40
SHY			
SHE MOVES WHEN TIME IS SHY:	124	WORDS FOR WIND	52
THE SHY PERIMETER	125	WORDS FOR WIND	83
THE SHY CERULEAN BIRD;	128	THE VOICE	14
AMONG THE SHY BEASTS, THE DEER AT THE SALT-LICK,	190	AT OYSTER RIVER	26
THE SHY MAN	216	THE SHY MAN	T
A WIND CAME CLOSE, LIKE A SHY ANIMAL.	241	THE SEQUEL	22
SIBYL			
THE CENTAUR AND THE SIBYL ROMP AND SING	135	THE RENEWAL	2
SICK			
THE RAMBLING LIES INVENTED FOR THE SICK.	5	PROGNOSIS	2
AND THE TIME I WAS SO SICK--	163	I'M HERE	63
SO FOOLISH AND TRUSTING, LIKE A SICK POODLE,	228	THE GERANIUM	3
GROWS SICK IN FLESH AND SPIRIT BOTH.	257	SANITARIUM	10
SICKLE			
SHE WAS THE SICKLE; I, POOR I, THE RAKE,	127	I KNEW A WOMAN	12
SIDE			
AS IF OUT OF MY SIDE,	148	THE SMALL	16
TURNING TOWARD THE OTHER SIDE OF LIGHT,	195	JOURNY INTERIOR	69
ON ONE SIDE OF SILENCE THERE IS NO SMILE;	195	JOURNY INTERIOR	76
HIS HEAD, STIFF AS A SCARAB, TURNED TO ONE SIDE,	226	THE LIZARD	5
AND I BEHOLD THE DARK SIDE OF A TREE	240	IN EVEING AIR	14
SIDEBOARD			
THE SIDEBOARD BESIDE WHICH A TALL FOOTMAN STOOD	32	SALE	15
SIDELONG			
AND HER QUICK LOOK, A SIDELONG PICKEREL SMILE;	102	ELEGY FOR JANE	2
SIDE-MIRROR			
AND NO LIGHTS BEHIND, IN THE BLURRED SIDE-MIRROR,	199	THE FAR FIELD	7
SIDES			
FLAILING HER SIDES WITH SPRAY,	41	BIG WIND	28
WHEN THE SUN FOR ME GLINTED THE SIDES OF A SAND GRAIN,	66	SHAPE OF FIRE	68

	PAGE	TITLE	LINE
SIDES (CONTINUED)			
THE SIDES OF WET STONES CANNOT CONSOLE ME,	102	ELEGY FOR JANE	16
SHE'D MORE SIDES THAN A SEAL.	212	LIGHT LISTENED	6
SIDE'S			
MY LEFT SIDE'S TENDER.	97	O, THOU OPENING	3
SIDEWAYS			
OR THEY SIT SIDEWAYS ON LIMBER DANDELION STEMS,	152	THE SISKINS	10
THE TRICK WAS TO THROW THE CAR SIDEWAYS AND CHARGE OVER THE HILL, FULL OF THE THROTTLE.	193	JOURNY INTERIOR	21
THE WHOLE SHIP ROLLING SLIGHTLY SIDEWAYS,	203	THE ROSE	36
THEN WHIRRING OFF SIDEWAYS TO THE TOP OF THE HAWTHORN,	234	ALL MORNING	31
HALF SIDEWAYS IN THE SHIFTING LIGHT,	273	SUPPR W LINDSAY	20
SIFT			
SIFT, ALMOST INVISIBLE, THROUGH LONG AFTERNOONS OF TEDIUM,	46	DOLOR	11
SIFTED			
UP AND SIFTED THE DIRT;	44	FRAU BAUMAN	14
A BIRD SANG LOW; THE MOONLIGHT SIFTED IN;	119	THE DREAM	7
SIFTING			
SIFTING IN A PALM-FULL OF FRESH LOAM,--	42	TRANSPLANTING	4
THE FINE SOOT SIFTING THROUGH MY SOUTH WINDOWS.	104	OLD LADY'S WRDS	58
SIFTS			
AS WHEN SILT DRIFTS AND SIFTS DOWN THROUGH MUDDY POND-WATER,	159	FIRST MEDITATN	60
SIGH			
A SIGH CAME FAR.	63	FIELD OF LIGHT	28
ONE SIGH STRETCHES HEAVEN.	83	O LULL ME, LULL	1
A SLOW SIGH SAYS YES. AND LIGHT SIGHS;	90	UNFOLD! UNFOLD!	49
HEAR THE SIGH OF WHAT IS.	98	O, THOU OPENING	35
WHEN I WENT TO SEA IN A SIGH,	103	OLD LADY'S WRDS	23
DID SPACE SHAKE OFF AN ANGEL WITH A SIGH?	107	SIR JOHN DAVIES	69
HE'LL SIGH AND GIVE HIS BRANCH A HUG;	116	THE SLOTH	9
SHE SLOWED TO SIGH, IN THAT LONG INTERVAL.	120	THE DREAM	18
WHEN SMALL BIRDS SIGHED, SHE WOULD SIGH BACK AT THEM;	127	I KNEW A WOMAN	2
I SIGH BEFORE I SING.	167	HER BECOMING	83
POOR MYRTLE WOULD SIGH, "SWEET MY COZ,	180	GOO-GIRL	1
MY BREATH BUT A SIGH.	208	THE APPARITION	10
SIGHED			
A NESTLING SIGHED;	51	THE WAKING (1)	18
THE DARK HAIR SIGHED.	93	I CRY, LOVE!	56
WHEN SMALL BIRDS SIGHED, SHE WOULD SIGH BACK AT THEM;	127	I KNEW A WOMAN	2
SIGHED OUT HER PURE RELIEF	213	THE HAPPY THREE	3
A NESTLING SIGHED--I CALLED THAT NESTLING MINE;	241	THE SEQUEL	12
YET WHEN I SIGHED, I STOOD OUTSIDE MY LIFE,	248	THE TREE, BIRD	7
SIGHING			
THE FLESH-BOUND SIGHING LOVER,	7	ORDERS FOR DAY	5
ONE WITH THE SIGHING VINE,	124	WORDS FOR WIND	43
I'LL SCARE MYSELF WITH SIGHING, OR I'LL SING;	156	THE DYING MAN	86
SIGHS			
A SLOW SIGH SAYS YES. AND LIGHT SIGHS;	90	UNFOLD! UNFOLD!	49
IF SHE BUT SIGHS, A BIRD PUTS OUT ITS TONGUE.	129	SHE	3
I TEACH MY SIGHS TO LENGTHEN INTO SONGS,	135	THE RENEWAL	5
SHE SIGHS ME WHITE, A SOCRATES OF SNOW.	140	THE SWAN	7
I SAID FAREWELL TO SIGHS,	167	HER BECOMING	70
A KINGDOM OF STINKS AND SIGHS,	187	THE LONGING	2
WHO SIGHS FROM FAR AWAY?	188	THE LONGING	41
WHEN THE WIND SIGHS	209	HER RETICENCE	11
SIGHS, SIGHS, WHO SAYS THEY HAVE SEQUENCE?	223	ELEGY (2)	4
SIGHS, SIGHS, WHO SAYS THEY HAVE SEQUENCE?	223	ELEGY (2)	4
SIGHT			
THEY SLIP BETWEEN THE FINGERS OF MY SIGHT.	8	THE SIGNALS	7
GLEAM SHARPLY ON THE NARROW SIGHT.	15	COMING OF COLD	46
ALL CROSS MY LINE OF SIGHT,	34	NIGHT JOURNEY	9
I SAW A SIGHT THAT CAUSED ME PAIN,	114	DINKY	10
MORNING, I SAW THE WORLD WITH SECOND SIGHT,	133	THE PURE FURY	5
A TREE THINNED BY THE WIND OBSCURES MY SIGHT.	150	IN LATE SUMMER	28
WHEN GEORGE THE WATCHMAN'S LANTERN DROPPED FROM SIGHT	225	OTTO	38
A THING IN AND OUT OF SIGHT,	232	THE THING	4
SIGN			
DO YOU SEE ANY SIGN OR SEMBLANCE OF THAT THING CALLED "HOPE"?"	27	CLAIRVOY WIDOW	18
SIGNALS			
THE SIGNALS	8	THE SIGNALS	T
SIGNED			
THE STINGY MEMBERS WHEN THEY SIGNED	267	SAGINAW SONG	33

	PAGE	TITLE	LINE
SILENCE			
THE NIGHTMARE SILENCE IS BROKEN. WE ARE NOT LOST.	5	PROGNOSIS	16
SILENCE	22	SILENCE	T
VOICE, COME OUT OF THE SILENCE.	54	THE LOST SON	20
THROUGH THE CLEAR AIR, IN THE SILENCE.	58	THE LOST SON	163
OR LISTEN INTO SILENCE, LIKE A GOD.	140	THE SWAN	20
SILENCE BECAME A THING;	167	HER BECOMING	66
THE DEAD MAKE MORE IMPOSSIBLE DEMANDS FROM THEIR SILENCE;	168	FOURTH MEDITATN	19
THE YOUNG, BROW-BEATEN EARLY INTO A BALEFUL SILENCE,	169	FOURTH MEDITATN	44
THE POND LAPSES BACK INTO A GLASSY SILENCE.	172	WHAT TELL BONES	50
THIS AMBUSH, THIS SILENCE,	188	THE LONGING	48
ON ONE SIDE OF SILENCE THERE IS NO SMILE;	195	JOURNY INTERIOR	76
I HAVE COME HERE WITHOUT COURTING SILENCE,	197	THE LONG WATERS	44
SILENCE OF WATER ABOVE A SUNKEN TREE:	201	THE FAR FIELD	100
AND THERE IS SILENCE.	202	THE ROSE	21
WHAT DO THEY TELL US, SOUND AND SILENCE?	204	THE ROSE	58
I THINK OF AMERICAN SOUNDS IN THIS SILENCE:	204	THE ROSE	59
I THINK OF THE ROCK SINGING, AND LIGHT MAKING ITS OWN SILENCE,	204	THE ROSE	79
GATHERING TO ITSELF SOUND AND SILENCE--	205	THE ROSE	113
FROM ME, IN THE SEA'S SILENCE;	210	HER TIME	4
A SUNLIT SILENCE.	221	THE ABYSS	60
SOUND, SILENCE SANG AS ONE.	238	THE MOMENT	9
SILENCES			
INTO MY OWN SILENCES.	104	OLD LADY'S WRDS	62
SILENT			
STANDING, SILENT, ON SANDY BEACHES OR WALKING ALONG GREEN EMBANKMENTS;	168	FOURTH MEDITATN	4
SILENT, IN THE DEEPENING LIGHT,	190	AT OYSTER RIVER	8
AND NOT-KNOWING ENTERS, SILENT,	221	THE ABYSS	70
SILICA			
FINER THAN FLOUR, ALIVE, MORE DANGEROUS THAN SILICA,	46	DOLOR	10
SILKEN			
THE GARDEN SPIDER WEAVES A SILKEN PEAR	12	SLOW SEASON	5
SILKS			
IN LOVE WITH STUFFS, SILKS,	162	I'M HERE	29
SILL			
CLIMBED TO HER ATTIC WINDOW AND GAZED ACROSS THE SILL.	27	CLAIRVOY WIDOW	2
HARD, ON THE GRITTY SILL,	145	THE BEAST	14
TO GROPE MY SILL: IT MOANS TO BE REBORN!	154	THE DYING MAN	37
LEANING ACROSS A SILL TO GREET THE DAWN?	154	THE DYING MAN	44
ON THE SILL OF THE EYES, SOMETHING FLUTTERS,	162	I'M HERE	52
THE SILL TREMBLES.	220	THE ABYSS	33
KEEPS BUZZING AT THE SILL. WHICH I IS I?	239	IN A DARK TIME	21
COME EASY TO THE SILL, THINGS LOST FROM FAR AWAY.	273	SUPPR W LINDSAY	4
SILLY			
THIS IS, YOU SEE, A SILLY SONG	181	MONOTONY SONG	21
SILO			
THE OLD SILO.	60	THE LONG ALLEY	50
SILO-RICH			
PULPY STEMS, RANK, SILO-RICH,	38	ROOT CELLAR	8
SILT			
STIRRED UP A WHIRL OF SILT	49	RIVER INCIDENT	2
CAN FEATHERS EAT ME? THERE'S NO CLUE IN THE SILT.	60	THE LONG ALLEY	32
AS WHEN SILT DRIFTS AND SIFTS DOWN THROUGH MUDDY POND-WATER,	159	FIRST MEDITATN	60
DROPPING A FINE YELLOW SILT WHERE THE SUN STAYS;	200	THE FAR FIELD	68
SILTED			
IN THE SILTED SHALLOWS OF A SLOW RIVER,	200	THE FAR FIELD	39
SILVER			
THE SILVER FISH RAN IN AND OUT OF MY SPECIAL BINDINGS;	65	SHAPE OF FIRE	35
BY THE LAKE'S EDGE, I SEE A SILVER SWAN,	140	THE SWAN	16
WITH HIS STRIPES OF SILVER AND HIS SMALL HOUSE ON HIS BACK,	151	SLUG	2
THE MOON LOLLING IN THE CLOSE ELM, A SHIMMER OF SILVER,	204	THE ROSE	81
SILVERY			
AND THE LITTLE CRABS SLIPPED INTO SILVERY CRATERS.	66	SHAPE OF FIRE	67
THEIR WOODEN STORES OF SILVERY PINE AND WEATHER-BEATEN RED COURTHOUSES,	193	JOURNY INTERIOR	31
SIMILAR			
WHEN FROM UNDER THE BARN THE CAT BRINGS A SIMILAR LITTER,--	24	VERNAL SENTIMNT	5
SIMILITUDE			
I STUDY OUT A DARK SIMILITUDE:	140	THE SWAN	1
SIMPER			
WITH A NURSE-MAID WADDLE AND A SHOP-GIRL SIMPER,	23	ACADEMIC	3

	PAGE	TITLE	LINE
SIMPLE			
AWAY FROM SIMPLE FAITH	31	LULL	16
DEATH WAS NOT. I LIVED IN A SIMPLE DROWSE:	66	SHAPE OF FIRE	73
THE FIELD IS NO LONGER SIMPLE:	89	UNFOLD! UNFOLD!	7
LATER, I DID AND I DANCED IN THE SIMPLE WOOD.	90	UNFOLD! UNFOLD!	34
SING, SING, YOU SYMBOLS! ALL SIMPLE CREATURES,	90	UNFOLD! UNFOLD!	45
FEET RUN OVER THE SIMPLE STONES,	93	I CRY, LOVE!	36
MAKE ME, O LORD, A LAST, A SIMPLE THING	240	IN EVEING AIR	8
BEFORE THAT SIMPLE TUNE	271	THE REPLY	6
SIMPLICITY'S			
SIMPLICITY'S SWEET THING, EITHER. A LEAF COULD DRAG YOU.	98	O, THOU OPENING	29
SIMPLY			
HE SIMPLY GAVE UP SERPENTING.	115	THE SERPENT	3
SIN			
ALL THE RINGS AND THE RELICS ENCRUSTED WITH SIN	32	SALE	19
OH, IT WASN'T A CRIME, IT WASN'T A SIN,	112	SQUEEZE-BOX	30
THERE WOULD BE REASON FOR ESSENTIAL SIN;	144	ELEGY (1)	2
SINCE			
LONG SINCE, BRONZE WHEAT WAS GATHERED INTO SHEAVES.	12	SLOW SEASON	10
SING			
SING ME A SLEEP-SONG, PLEASE.	71	WHERE KNOCK IS	10
I SING A SMALL SING,	72	WHERE KNOCK IS	23
I SING A SMALL SING,	72	WHERE KNOCK IS	23
SING THE SNAKE TO SLEEP.	73	WHERE KNOCK IS	75
SING TO ME, SWEET.	86	PRAISE TO END!	30
SING, SING, YOU SYMBOLS! ALL SIMPLE CREATURES,	90	UNFOLD! UNFOLD!	45
SING, SING, YOU SYMBOLS! ALL SIMPLE CREATURES,	90	UNFOLD! UNFOLD!	45
IN THE OBSCURE HAZE, SING!	90	UNFOLD! UNFOLD!	47
I SING THE GREEN, AND THINGS TO COME,	99	O, THOU OPENING	56
I NEED A PLACE TO SING, AND DANCING-ROOM,	105	SIR JOHN DAVIES	4
I'LL SING AND WHISTLE ROMPING WITH THE BEARS.	105	SIR JOHN DAVIES	6
THERE WAS A SERPENT WHO HAD TO SING.	115	THE SERPENT	1
AND SO, OF COURSE, HE HAD TO SING,	115	THE SERPENT	9
AND SING HE DID, LIKE ANYTHING!	115	THE SERPENT	10
BEING MYSELF, I SING	126	WORDS FOR WIND	90
(I'D HAVE THEM SING IN CHORUS, CHEEK TO CHEEK).	127	I KNEW A WOMAN	7
WE SING TOGETHER; WE SING MOUTH TO MOUTH.	129	SHE	7
WE SING TOGETHER; WE SING MOUTH TO MOUTH.	129	SHE	7
THE CENTAUR AND THE SIBYL ROMP AND SING	135	THE RENEWAL	2
SING OF THAT NOTHING OF WHICH ALL IS MADE,	140	THE SWAN	19
STARED, AND BEGAN TO SING.	146	THE SONG	17
BEYOND THE RIDGE TWO WOOD THRUSH SING AS ONE.	150	IN LATE SUMMER	30
A MAN LEARNING TO SING."	153	THE DYING MAN	15
THEY SING, THEY SING	156	THE DYING MAN	ST
THEY SING, THEY SING	156	THE DYING MAN	ST
I'LL SCARE MYSELF WITH SIGHING, OR I'LL SING;	156	THE DYING MAN	86
THEY SING, THEY SING, BUT STILL IN MINOR THIRDS.	156	THE DYING MAN	89
THEY SING, THEY SING, BUT STILL IN MINOR THIRDS.	156	THE DYING MAN	89
FROM THE FOLDS OF MY SKIN, I SING,	165	HER BECOMING	13
I SIGH BEFORE I SING.	167	HER BECOMING	83
AND YOU CAN SING IT ALL DAY LONG--	181	MONOTONY SONG	22
AND THE DEAD BEGIN FROM THEIR DARK TO SING IN MY SLEEP.	195	JOURNY INTERIOR	79
I SING THE WIND AROUND	215	HIS FOREBODING	11
DEEP IN THE GREENS OF SUMMER SING THE LIVES	244	INFIRMITY	25
I'LL SING BEYOND THE WIND	260	THE CHANGELING	26
TO THE BEST OF MYSELF I SING,	261	THE CHANGELING	32
ALL TRUE BONES SING ALONE.	263	FOLLIES OF ADAM	28
HERE'S A MENSCH BUT CAN SING DANDY.	266	FOR STEVENS	14
I'LL SING WITH DEAR TOM MOORE,	268	SAGINAW SONG	48
AND, LIKE YOU, BIRD, I SING,	271	THE REPLY	16
SINGING			
WHAT'S ALL THE SINGING BETWEEN?--	77	BRING THE DAY!	26
I HEAR SINGING.	83	O LULL ME, LULL	11
I HEAR, CLEARLY, THE HEART OF ANOTHER SINGING,	88	PRAISE TO END!	94
SINGING.	101	LIGHT BREATHER	18
A BIRD SINGING INTO THE BEYOND,	103	OLD LADY'S WRDS	7
"I'M SERIOUS ABOUT MY SINGING CAREER!"	115	THE SERPENT	24
THE SMALL! THE SMALL! I HEAR THEM SINGING CLEAR	149	IN LATE SUMMER	7
AND THE FAR PHOEBE, SINGING,	159	FIRST MEDITATN	86
A BIRD ALWAYS KEPT SINGING.	163	I'M HERE	73
BIRDS ARE AROUND. I'VE ALL THE SINGING I WOULD.	164	I'M HERE	93
O THE SONGS WE HIDE, SINGING ONLY TO OURSELVES!	168	FOURTH MEDITATN	13
BY SINGING WE DEFEND;	170	FOURTH MEDITATN	82

	PAGE	TITLE	LINE

SINGING (CONTINUED)
I WOULD DELIGHT IN MY HANDS, THE BRANCH SINGING, ALTERING
    THE EXCESSIVE BIRD; 188   THE LONGING   44
THE THRUSH SINGING ALONE, THAT EASY BIRD, ... 204   THE ROSE   61
I THINK OF THE ROCK SINGING, AND LIGHT MAKING ITS OWN
    SILENCE, ... 204   THE ROSE   79
THE SINGING OF A STEM. 212   LIGHT LISTENED   22
MY DEAD SELVES SINGING. 221   THE ABYSS   80
O THE SONGS WE HIDE SINGING TO OURSELVES!-- 259   SONG (3)   38
I HEAR THEM SINGING! 261   THE CHANGELING   50
SINGING-TIME
SAD, IN A SINGING-TIME? 98   O, THOU OPENING   45
SINGLE
A SINGLE MISSTEP AND WE LEAVE THE QUICK. 5   PROGNOSIS   4
A SINGLE RIPPLE STARTS FROM WHERE HE STOOD. 15   THE HERON   12
A SINGLE TWIST OF THE THUMBS, A TAMPING AND TURNING, ... 42   TRANSPLANTING   7
PALE BLOSSOMS, EACH BALANCED ON A SINGLE JOINTED STEM, ... 43   CARNATIONS   1
THERE WAS ALWAYS A SINGLE LIGHT 57   THE LOST SON   130
A SINGLE WAVE STARTS LIGHTLY AND EASILY SHOREWARD, ... 93   I CRY, LOVE!   46
WHO LEAPS TO HEAVEN AT A SINGLE BOUND? 107   SIR JOHN DAVIES   80
FLOATS A SINGLE STAR. 122   ALL EARTH, AIR   23
NORTH, IN A SINGLE STREAM; 125   WORDS FOR WIND   63
EACH SINGLE SUBSTANCE GLIDDERED TO THE STARE; 143   SHIMMER OF EVIL   3
ONCE I DELIGHTED IN A SINGLE TREE; 155   THE DYING MAN   54
A SINGLE BIRD CALLING AND CALLING; 160   FIRST MEDITATN   90
A SINGLE WAVE COMES IN LIKE THE NECK OF A GREAT SWAN 197   THE LONG WATERS   52
A RIPPLE WIDENING FROM A SINGLE STONE 201   THE FAR FIELD   102
WITHOUT A SINGLE WINGBEAT, ... 202   THE ROSE   5
A SINGLE WILD ROSE, STRUGGLING OUT OF THE WHITE EMBRACE OF
    THE MORNING-GLORY, ... 203   THE ROSE   44
AND THAT SOUND, THAT SINGLE SOUND, ... 204   THE ROSE   74
IN THE BIRD BEYOND THE BOUGH, THE SINGLE ONE 205   THE ROSE   108
THIS SINGLE TREE TURNS INTO PUREST FLAME. 242   THE SEQUEL   28
HIS BEING SINGLE, AND THAT BEING ALL: 250   THE RIGHT THING   11
SINGLENESS
WANTS SINGLENESS OF SPIRIT ABOVE ALL ELSE: 24   POETASTER   2
SINGS
THE DARK FLOWS ON ITSELF. A DEAD MOUTH SINGS UNDER AN OLD
    TREE. 59   THE LONG ALLEY   6
A BIRD SINGS IN THE BUSH OF YOUR BONES. 79   GIVE WAY, GATES   5
I SEE WHAT SINGS! 84   O LULL ME, LULL   40
WHAT SINGS! 84   O LULL ME, LULL   41
A LOG SINGS IN ITS FLAME. 137   LOVE'S PROGRESS   18
I'VE THE LARK'S WORD FOR IT, WHO SINGS ALONE: 156   THE DYING MAN   90
SINGS IN THE FIRST 163   I'M HERE   61
A BIRD SINGS OUT IN SOLITARINESS 171   WHAT TELL BONES   18
THE MIST ABOVE ME SINGS WITH ITS SMALL FLIES. 246   THE MARROW   2
SING-SONG
HIS LAUGHTER REDUCED THE SING-SONG OF PRATING, ... 29   THE GENTLE   7
SINGULAR
SO SINGULAR A BLESSEDNESS. 8   PRAYER   18
THE GULLS WHEEL OVER THEIR SINGULAR GARBAGE; 187   THE LONGING   16
THE MOUNTAIN WITH ITS SINGULAR BRIGHT SHADE 201   THE FAR FIELD   95
SINISTER
--AND GRANDFATHER'S SINISTER HOVERING HAND. 32   SALE   8
SINK
OR TO SINK DOWN TO THE HIPS IN A MOSSY QUAGMIRE; 200   THE FAR FIELD   44
IN THE SLOP-PAIL BY THE SINK; 269   GOB MUSIC   13
SINKING
FROM THE SLOW SINKING OF THE ISLAND PENINSULA, THE CORAL
    EFFLORESCENCE, ... 196   THE LONG WATERS   22
SINKS
AND THE PINE, WHOLE WITH ITS ROOTS, SINKS INTO THE ESTUARY, ... 197   THE LONG WATERS   35
SINS
YOUR BED COLLAPSES FROM IMAGINED SINS. 25   DIM-WIT COUSIN   6
SINUOSITY
AND SINUOSITY 259   SONG (3)   51
SINUOUS
TOPPED BY CROSS-WINDS, TUGGED AT BY SINUOUS UNDERCURRENTS 191   AT OYSTER RIVER   33
WITH ONE SINUOUS RIPPLE, THEN A RUSH, ... 233   THE PIKE   16
A DRIED STALK IN A WELTER OF SINUOUS GRASSES, ... 255   LIGHT POEM   8
SINUOUSNESS
KNOWING THE SINUOUSNESS OF SMALL WATERS: 168   FOURTH MEDITATN   5

	PAGE	TITLE	LINE
SIR			
FOUR FOR SIR JOHN DAVIES	105	SIR JOHN DAVIES	T
THE BEAR SAID, SIR, YOU GO TOO FAR,	181	MONOTONY SONG	9
SIREN'S			
WE SHIVER AT THE SIREN'S BLAST.	33	HIGHWAY: MICH	18
SISKINS			
THE SISKINS	152	THE SISKINS	T
AND THE SMALL MAD SISKINS FLIT BY,	152	THE SISKINS	8
SISTER			
TO MY SISTER	5	TO MY SISTER	T
O MY SISTER REMEMBER THE STARS THE TEARS THE TRAINS	5	TO MY SISTER	1
WALK BOLDLY MY SISTER BUT DO NOT DEIGN TO GIVE	5	TO MY SISTER	10
BELIEVE ME, THERE'S NO ONE ELSE, KITTEN-LIMP SISTER.	59	THE LONG ALLEY	23
THE SISTER SANDS, THEY SLIPPER SOFT AWAY.	92	I CRY, LOVE!	3
I TASTE MY SISTER WHEN I KISS MY WIFE;	132	SENTENTIOUS MAN	27
SISTERS			
THEIR SISTERS GAVE ME, ONCE OR TWICE;	225	THE CHUMS	5
SIT			
AND EARN THE RIGHT TO STAND OR SIT,	18	LONG LIVE WEEDS	10
WE SIT IN THE PORCH SWING, CONTENT AND HALF ASLEEP.	33	IDYLL	8
SIT AND PLAY	71	WHERE KNOCK IS	5
SIT IN MY MOUTH.	74	I NEED, I NEED	4
OR THEY SIT SIDEWAYS ON LIMBER DANDELION STEMS,	152	THE SISKINS	10
I SIT ABOVE THE BACK WHEELS, WHERE THE JOLTS ARE HARDEST,	158	FIRST MEDITATN	22
I HAVE LEARNED TO SIT QUIETLY,	165	HER BECOMING	1
YOU SOMETIMES HAVE TO GO AND SIT.	178	THE CHAIR	4
SHE WOULD SIT WITH A BOOK ON HER KNEES,--	179	MYRTLE	6
OR, WITH SKINNY KNEES, TO SIT ASTRIDE A WET LOG,	200	THE FAR FIELD	45
THEY SIT, THREE OR FOUR, HIGH IN THE FIR-TREES BACK OF THE HOUSE,	234	ALL MORNING	6
I GET A STOOL AND SIT AND STARE	269	GOB MUSIC	12
SITS			
OR HE SITS STILL, A SOLID FIGURE WHEN	250	THE RIGHT THING	13
SITTING			
BLUE-BLACK FROM WHERE I AM SITTING,	190	AT OYSTER RIVER	12
SIX			
SIX HOURS A DAY I LAY ME DOWN	256	IN HYDROTHERAPY	1
SIX-HUNDRED-FOOT			
WHITE AND RED, IN THE WIDE SIX-HUNDRED-FOOT GREENHOUSES,	203	THE ROSE	52
SIXTEEN-YEAR-OLD			
OF SIXTEEN-YEAR-OLD LUST.	46	PICKLE BELT	12
SKEIN			
OR, POISONED, DRAGGING A WHITE SKEIN OF SPITTLE OVER A PATH--	151	SLUG	21
SKELETON			
THE VESTURE OF THE SKELETON,	19	EPIDERM MACABRE	4
SKIES			
RECOUNT EACH CHILDHOOD PLEASURE: THE SKIES OF AZURE	5	TO MY SISTER	5
NOW LIGHT IS LESS; NOON SKIES ARE WIDE AND DEEP;	12	SLOW SEASON	1
SKIN			
THE BOLD WEAR TOUGHENED SKIN	20	REPL TO CENSURE	13
A COAT OF UNESSENTIAL SKIN,	24	BEFORE STUDY	4
THE HAND-PAINTED WALL-PAPER, FINER THAN SKIN,	32	SALE	17
TAKE THE SKIN OF A CAT	55	THE LOST SON	54
ALONE, I KISSED THE SKIN OF A STONE;	63	FIELD OF LIGHT	29
AND SKIN LIKE PAPER.	73	WHERE KNOCK IS	79
SHE ASKED HER SKIN	77	BRING THE DAY!	8
SUCH MUSIC IN A SKIN!	79	GIVE WAY, GATES	4
FATHER OF TENSIONS, I'M DOWN TO MY SKIN AT LAST.	85	PRAISE TO END!	4
I'VE BEEN ASLEEP IN A BOWER OF DEAD SKIN.	86	PRAISE TO END!	47
TELL ME, BODY WITHOUT SKIN, DOES A FISH SWEAT?	89	UNFOLD! UNFOLD!	2
SKIN, A THING YOU CANNOT SAY TO WHISPER AND EQUAL A WOUND?	98	O, THOU OPENING	24
YOU ENEMIES OF SKIN,--	99	O, THOU OPENING	61
SKIN.	99	O, THOU OPENING	87
OUR OUTER SKIN. WHO'S WHISTLING UP MY SLEEVE?	106	SIR JOHN DAVIES	38
HER SWART HILARIOUS SKIN;	126	WORDS FOR WIND	99
SHE TAUGHT ME TOUCH, THAT UNDULANT WHITE SKIN;	127	I KNEW A WOMAN	10
I TOUCHED THE STONES, AND THEY HAD MY OWN SKIN.	133	THE PURE FURY	7
I HAVE MYSELF ONE CRUMBLING SKIN TO SHOW;	144	ELEGY (1)	11
LIKE A FRESH-SALTED SKIN;	153	THE DYING MAN	4
I SAW MY FATHER SHRINKING IN HIS SKIN;	155	THE DYING MAN	61
MY SKIN WHITER IN THE SOFT WEATHER,	162	I'M HERE	43
FROM THE FOLDS OF MY SKIN, I SING,	165	HER BECOMING	13

	PAGE	TITLE	LINE
SKIN (CONTINUED)			
OR THESE INSECTS PULSING NEAR MY SKIN,	171	WHAT TELL BONES	26
HE HAD NO SKIN, HE HAD NO TAIL.	178	THE WHALE	2
ASLEEP IN HER SKIN,	258	SONG (3)	2
TO JUMP OUT OF HIS SKIN.	262	FOLLIES OF ADAM	4
SHE SHIVERED IN HER SKIN,	262	FOLLIES OF ADAM	20
THAT PRICKLES MY COARSE SKIN.	271	THE REPLY	4
AND FRESH AS SALT-DRENCHED SKIN.	271	THE REPLY	9
SKINNED			
UPON THE ORCHARD PATH, FOR SKINNED	14	COMING OF COLD	6
SKINNY			
OR, WITH SKINNY KNEES, TO SIT ASTRIDE A WET LOG,	200	THE FAR FIELD	45
SKINS			
THINK OF OUR SEPARATE SKINS.	31	LULL	9
THEIR BLACK SKINS SHUDDERING:	159	FIRST MEDITATN	57
SKIN'S			
SKIN'S THE LEAST OF ME. KISS THIS.	87	PRAISE TO END!	72
SKIPPED			
TODAY I SKIPPED ON THE SHORE,	207	THE YOUNG GIRL	8
SKIPPERS			
THESE AIRY HIPPETY-HOP SKIPPERS,	152	THE SISKINS	20
SKIPS			
FLYING UPWARD IN LITTLE SKIPS AND ERRATIC LEAPS;	152	THE SISKINS	9
SKIRRING			
THE BOBOLINK SKIRRING FROM A BROKEN FENCEPOST,	204	THE ROSE	65
SKIRT			
SKIRT HATRED'S RAGING RIVER,	7	ORDERS FOR DAY	10
SKIRTING			
WORDS SKIRTING THE OBSCENE--	213	THE HAPPY THREE	7
SKIRTS			
THEIR SKIRTS BILLOWING OUT WIDE INTO TENTS,	44	FRAU BAUMAN	17
HER SKIRTS NOT TOUCHING A LEAF,	100	THE VISITANT	13
SKITTER			
NOW AS FROM MAPLE TO ELM THE FLITTERMICE SKITTER AND TWIRL,	33	IDYLL	1
SKITTER-BUM			
HE CAN PLINK THE SKITTER-BUM;	266	FOR STEVENS	6
SKITTERY			
MY MAIMED DARLING, MY SKITTERY PIGEON.	102	ELEGY FOR JANE	19
SKULL			
INVENTION SLEEPS WITHIN A SKULL	4	DEATH PIECE	1
WHAT SHAKES MY SKULL TO DISREPAIR	22	SILENCE	19
SKY			
DECREASED BENEATH AN UNDIVIDED SKY.	6	INTERLUDE	6
OUR FEET ARE SOMETIMES LEVEL WITH THE SKY,	13	PRAISE PRAIRIE	6
THE SKY TURNS DARK, THE YEAR GROWS OLD,	15	COMING OF COLD	36
BLEAK CLOUDS ACROSS THE HEAVY SKY,	15	COMING OF COLD	50
I MOVE BENEATH AN EVIL SKY.	19	AGNST DISASTER	8
OPEN A HOLE AND SEE THE SKY:	75	I NEED, I NEED	39
THE SKY CRACKED OPEN	87	PRAISE TO END!	59
AND WHEN YOU THINK THE SKY HAS CLEARED	114	DINKY	3
DO THESE ANALOGIES PERPLEX? A SKY WITH CLOUDS,	235	MANIFESTATION	6
SKYWARD			
JERKS SKYWARD AT THE TOUCH OF WIND,	14	COMING OF COLD	29
THE LIGHTS TILTING UP, SKYWARD, AS WE COME OVER A LITTLE RISE,	158	FIRST MEDITATN	24
SLACK			
THE SHALLOW STREAM RUNS SLACK;	123	WORDS FOR WIND	25
THE SLACK FACE OF THE DISMAL PURE INANE?	149	IN LATE SUMMER	10
IN THE SOFT SLACK OF A NECK I SLEPT.	258	SONG (3)	22
SLACKENING			
IN THE RAIN, SLACKENING ON A SUMMER FIELD;	165	HER BECOMING	8
SLACKENS			
THE WIND SLACKENS, LIGHT AS A MOTH FANNING A STONE:	190	AT OYSTER RIVER	17
SLAG			
CANNAS SHINY AS SLAG,	43	FLOWER DUMP	1
THIS SLAG RUNS SLOW. WHAT BLEEDS WHEN METAL BREAKS?	59	THE LONG ALLEY	11
SLAG-HEAPS			
THE SLAG-HEAPS FUME AT THE EDGE OF THE RAW CITIES:	187	THE LONGING	15
SLAIN			
YEA, I HAVE SLAIN MY WILL, AND STILL I LIVE;	246	THE MARROW	21
SLAMMING			
I WAS LULLED BY THE SLAMMING OF IRON,	53	THE LOST SON	2

	PAGE	TITLE	LINE
SLAMMING (CONTINUED)			
AND THE SMALL STREET-LAMP SWINGING AND SLAMMING AGAINST THE LAMP POLE.	230	THE STORM	7
SLAPPED			
WITHOUT HIS RIFLE, AND SLAPPED EACH ONE HARD;	224	OTTO	19
HE SLAPPED ME WITH HIS HAND;	268	SAGINAW SONG	51
SLAPPING			
SLAPPING LIGHTLY AGAINST A SUNKEN LOG.	190	AT OYSTER RIVER	14
SLATTED			
THE WALLS, THE SLATTED WINDOWS, DRIVING	230	THE STORM	25
SLAUGHTERED			
HAD SLAUGHTERED GAME, AND CUT YOUNG FIR TREES DOWN.	224	OTTO	21
SLEDGE			
THE GREAT SLEDGE DROPS IN VAIN.	9	THE ADAMANT	2
SLEEK			
IT'S SLEEK AS AN OTTER	55	THE LOST SON	58
BE SLEEK AS A HEIFER, BE LONG AS A HOG,--	86	PRAISE TO END!	41
FOR THE SLEEK CAPTAINS OF INTUITION CANNOT REACH THEM;	169	FOURTH MEDITATN	52
SLEEP			
UNTIL CLEAR EYES PUT ON THE LOOK OF SLEEP.	12	SLOW SEASON	4
WANES TO THE FEBRILE SMOLDERING OF SLEEP;	17	UNEXTINGUISHED	6
TO SLEEP IMMODESTLY, A MOST	19	EPIDERM MACABRE	15
THE SLEEP WAS NOT DEEP, BUT THE WAKING IS SLOW.	29	THE GENTLE	12
NOTHING WOULD SLEEP IN THAT CELLAR, DANK AS A DITCH,	38	ROOT CELLAR	1
AND THEIR SNUFF-LADEN BREATH BLOWING LIGHTLY OVER ME IN MY FIRST SLEEP.	44	FRAU BAUMAN	35
AND SUNDAY SLEEP.	46	PICKLE BELT	4
FRIGIDAIRES SNORING THE SLEEP OF PLENTY,	48	LAST WORDS	4
SING THE SNAKE TO SLEEP.	73	WHERE KNOCK IS	75
A SNEEZE CAN'T SLEEP.	74	I NEED, I NEED	5
IN THE GREEN OF MY SLEEP,	79	GIVE WAY, GATES	12
MY SLEEP DECEIVES ME.	82	SENSIBILITY! LA	46
ROCK ME TO SLEEP, THE WEATHER'S WRONG.	86	PRAISE TO END!	28
SUCH A SWEET NOISE: I CAN'T SLEEP FOR IT.	92	I CRY, LOVE!	19
--SHOULD SLEEP ON HIS PAWS.	99	O, THOU OPENING	72
SHOULD A SONG BREAK A SLEEP?	99	O, THOU OPENING	74
IF ONLY I COULD NUDGE YOU FROM THIS SLEEP,	102	ELEGY FOR JANE	18
NOW MY ARDORS SLEEP IN A SLEEVE.	103	OLD LADY'S WRDS	3
I WAKE TO SLEEP, AND TAKE MY WAKING SLOW.	108	THE WAKING (2)	1
I WAKE TO SLEEP, AND TAKE MY WAKING SLOW.	108	THE WAKING (2)	6
I WAKE TO SLEEP, AND TAKE MY WAKING SLOW.	108	THE WAKING (2)	12
I WAKE TO SLEEP, AND TAKE MY WAKING SLOW.	108	THE WAKING (2)	18
THEN OFF AGAIN TO SLEEP HE GOES,	116	THE SLOTH	10
THE MIND REMEMBERS FROM A DEEPER SLEEP:	119	THE DREAM	3
A FIELD RECEDES IN SLEEP.	122	ALL EARTH, AIR	21
YET STILL LAUGH IN MY SLEEP.	130	THE OTHER	24
THESE WATERS DROWSE ME INTO SLEEP SO KIND	135	THE RENEWAL	11
DEATH IS A DEEPER SLEEP,	139	PLAINT	17
AND I DELIGHT IN SLEEP.	139	PLAINT	18
THINGS LOST IN SLEEP RETURN	148	THE SMALL	15
IN THE SLOW COMING-OUT OF SLEEP,	162	I'M HERE	51
A VOICE KEEPS RISING IN MY EARLY SLEEP,	165	HER BECOMING	19
IS IT THE SEA WE WISH? THE SLEEP OF THE CHANGELESS?	165	HER BECOMING	28
WHAT ELSE CAN I STEAL FROM SLEEP?	166	HER BECOMING	34
MAY THEY SLEEP IN ROBES OF GREEN, AMONG THE ANCIENT FERNS;	169	FOURTH MEDITATN	58
YOURSELF AWAKE UNTIL YOU SLEEP,	181	MONOTONY SONG	26
IN SLEEP, AFRAID. DEATH'S FACE RISES AFRESH,	190	AT OYSTER RIVER	25
AT EASE AFTER ROCKING THE FLESH TO SLEEP,	194	JOURNY INTERIOR	55
AND THE DEAD BEGIN FROM THEIR DARK TO SING IN MY SLEEP.	195	JOURNY INTERIOR	79
THE SHAPE THAT CAME FROM MY SLEEP, WEEPING:	198	THE LONG WATERS	68
TO SLEEP IS ALL MY LIFE. IN SLEEP'S HALF-DEATH,	246	THE MARROW	14
I SAW IN MY LAST SLEEP	258	SONG (3)	20
I'M STILL SMUDGY FROM SLEEP:	259	SONG (3)	41
AND WHAT FOOL WOULDN'T, WHEN THINGS FROM SLEEP	273	SUPPR W LINDSAY	3
SLEEP-DAZE			
ALONE, IN A SLEEP-DAZE, I STARED AT BILLBOARDS;	89	UNFOLD! UNFOLD!	24
SLEEPERS			
SLEEPERS, NUMB NUDGERS IN COLD DIMENSIONS,	50	THE MINIMAL	2
SLEEP-HEAVY			
WITH MOTHERS, SLEEP-HEAVY CHILDREN, STALE PERFUME, PAST THE MANAGER'S SMILE	47	DOUBLE FEATURE	3
SLEEPING			
THERE WERE NO NIGHTS OF SLEEPING IN THE PARK.	28	THE FAVORITE	4

		PAGE	TITLE	LINE
SLEEPING (CONTINUED)				
SEE! SHE'S SLEEPING LIKE A LAKE:	....	81	SENSIBILITY! LA	2
I'M A DRAFT SLEEPING BY A STICK;	....	97	O, THOU OPENING	7
AND GENTLY THE LIGHT ENTERS THE SLEEPING SOUL,	....	204	THE ROSE	76
SLEEPLESS				
I'D STAND UPON MY BED, A SLEEPLESS CHILD	....	225	OTTO	40
SLEEPS				
INVENTION SLEEPS WITHIN A SKULL	....	4	DEATH PIECE	1
A LAPFUL OF APPLES SLEEPS IN THIS GRASS.	....	92	I CRY, LOVE!	24
A WITCH WHO SLEEPS WITH HER HORSE?	....	161	I'M HERE	15
SLEEPS THE BABY MOUSE I FOUND IN THE MEADOW,	....	227	MEADOW MOUSE	2
SLEEP'S				
TO SLEEP IS ALL MY LIFE. IN SLEEP'S HALF-DEATH,	......	246	THE MARROW	14
SLEEP-SONG				
SING ME A SLEEP-SONG, PLEASE.	....	71	WHERE KNOCK IS	10
SLEEPY				
FOR THE SLEEPY CRIES OF THE TOWHEE,	....	202	THE ROSE	13
THE SLEEPY SOUND OF LEAVES IN A LIGHT WIND.	....	245	THE DECISION	6
SLEET				
ALTERNATE SNOW AND SLEET, NO ON-COMING TRAFFIC,	....	199	THE FAR FIELD	6
SLEEVE				
THE DEAD SLEPT IN MY SLEEVE;	....	87	PRAISE TO END!	64
NOW MY ARDORS SLEEP IN A SLEEVE.	....	103	OLD LADY'S WRDS	3
OUR OUTER SKIN. WHO'S WHISTLING UP MY SLEEVE?	....	106	SIR JOHN DAVIES	38
ONE SLEEVE WITH MY HAND IN IT,	....	209	HER RETICENCE	2
SLEIGH				
A GREAT WOODEN SLEIGH CAREENING BEHIND THEM,	....	158	FIRST MEDITATN	54
SLEIGHBELLS				
THE SOUND OF VOICES, YOUNG VOICES, MIXED WITH SLEIGHBELLS,		161	I'M HERE	4
SLEPT				
WHERE THE WEEDS SLEPT.	....	57	THE LOST SON	129
LAST NIGHT I SLEPT IN THE PITS OF A TONGUE.	....	65	SHAPE OF FIRE	34
THE DEAD SLEPT IN MY SLEEVE;	....	87	PRAISE TO END!	64
I SLEPT LIKE AN INSECT.	....	89	UNFOLD! UNFOLD!	29
IN THE SOFT SLACK OF A NECK I SLEPT.	....	258	SONG (3)	22
SLICK				
BE LARGE AS AN OWL, BE SLICK AS A FROG,	....	86	PRAISE TO END!	39
SLID				
SLID FROM THE KITCHEN SHELF;	....	45	MY PAPA'S WALTZ	6
SLIDE				
FOR THEY ARE ALL MY FRIENDS: I SAW ONE SLIDE	....	105	SIR JOHN DAVIES	7
SLIDES				
WHAT SLIDES AWAY	....	80	GIVE WAY, GATES	61
AND THE SHALE SLIDES AN INCH IN THE TALUS,	....	157	FIRST MEDITATN	10
WHERE THE SHALE SLIDES DANGEROUSLY	....	193	JOURNY INTERIOR	3
THEN SLIDES DOWN OVER THE EYE'S SURFACE,	....	226	THE LIZARD	24
SLIDING				
SLIDING THROUGH THE WHITE CURRENT,	....	59	THE LONG ALLEY	3
TO FOLLOW THE DROPS SLIDING FROM A LIFTED OAR,	....	67	SHAPE OF FIRE	90
THE SHADOWS ARE EMPTY, THE SLIDING EXTERNALS.	....	104	OLD LADY'S WRDS	51
THE TAIL AND SMALLER LEGS SLIPPING AND SLIDING SLOWLY				
BACKWARD--		159	FIRST MEDITATN	65
I DABBLE MY TOES IN THE BRACKISH FOAM SLIDING FORWARD,		190	AT OYSTER RIVER	15
THE TIDE RUSTLING IN, SLIDING BETWEEN THE RIDGES OF STONE,		191	AT OYSTER RIVER	34
SLIDING AWAY FROM THE TRAVELER'S EYE,	....	203	THE ROSE	34
MY PAST IS SLIDING DOWN THE DRAIN;	....	256	IN HYDROTHERAPY	11
SLIGHT				
A SLIGHT VOICE REPLY;	....	128	THE VOICE	17
A SLIGHT SONG,	....	194	JOURNY INTERIOR	63
ABOVE THE BLUE AIR, IN THE SLIGHT HAZE BEYOND,	....	232	THE THING	3
SLIGHTLY				
WHEN I SLIP, JUST SLIGHTLY, IN THE DARK,	....	151	SLUG	8
THE WIND VEERING THE CAR SLIGHTLY TO THE RIGHT,	....	194	JOURNY INTERIOR	43
WHEN BATS FLY, CLOSE TO SLIGHTLY TILTING BROWNISH WATER,		198	THE LONG WATERS	61
THE SLIGHTLY TREMBLING WATER		200	THE FAR FIELD	67
THE WHOLE SHIP ROLLING SLIGHTLY SIDEWAYS,	....	203	THE ROSE	36
HE TURNS HIS HEAD SLIGHTLY,	....	226	THE LIZARD	15
SLIME				
IN THAT COLD, GRANITIC SLIME,	....	49	RIVER INCIDENT	10
I FEEL THE SLIME OF A WET NEST.	....	55	THE LOST SON	68
THE COLD SLIME COME INTO BEING,	....	151	SLUG	11
OF SLIME AND SHINING SPIT,	....	270	GOB MUSIC	33

	PAGE	TITLE	LINE
SLIP			
THEY SLIP BETWEEN THE FINGERS OF MY SIGHT.	8	THE SIGNALS	7
WHEN I SLIP, JUST SLIGHTLY, IN THE DARK,	151	SLUG	8
SLIP-OOZE			
STAY. STAY BY THE SLIP-OOZE. STAY.	100	THE VISITANT	4
SLIPPED			
AND THE LITTLE CRABS SLIPPED INTO SILVERY CRATERS.	66	SHAPE OF FIRE	67
BUT HE SLIPPED OUT.	73	WHERE KNOCK IS	57
AND NOBODY SLIPPED ME A MICKEY FINN,	112	SQUEEZE-BOX	31
AND AT THAT THE LADY SLIPPED FROM THE BANK	117	LADY AND BEAR	26
AND WHEN I SLIPPED UPON THE ICE,	225	THE CHUMS	9
SLIPPER			
THE SISTER SANDS, THEY SLIPPER SOFT AWAY.	92	I CRY, LOVE!	3
SLIPPERY			
SLIPPERY AS FISH,	37	CUTTINGS (LATE)	10
LEAF-MOLD, MANURE, LIME, PILED AGAINST SLIPPERY PLANKS.	38	ROOT CELLAR	9
ALIVE, IN A SLIPPERY GRAVE.	39	WEED PULLER	16
OVER SLIPPERY CINDERS	57	THE LOST SON	124
THE SLIPPERY COLD HEIGHTS,	221	THE ABYSS	51
SLIPPING			
THE TAIL AND SMALLER LEGS SLIPPING AND SLIDING SLOWLY BACKWARD--	159	FIRST MEDITATN	65
THE STREAM SLIPPING BENEATH THE MOSSY LOGS,	222	THE ABYSS	94
LITTLE CRABS SLIPPING INTO WATERY CRATERS--	255	LIGHT POEM	4
SLIPS			
BUT STILL THE DELICATE SLIPS KEEP COAXING UP WATER;	37	CUTTINGS	3
WHO, CARELESS, SLIPS	65	SHAPE OF FIRE	45
SLITHER			
LIKE A SLITHER OF EELS	56	THE LOST SON	96
SLOBBERS			
WHICH, WITH SLOBBERS AND SNORTS,	180	GOO-GIRL	5
SLOPED			
READY FOR THE LONG DAYS UNDER THE SLOPED GLASS:	42	TRANSPLANTING	13
THE DOE WITH ITS SLOPED SHOULDERS LOPING ACROSS THE HIGHWAY,	190	AT OYSTER RIVER	27
SLOP-PAIL			
IN THE SLOP-PAIL BY THE SINK;	269	GOB MUSIC	13
OH, THE SLOP-PAIL IS THE PLACE TO THINK	269	GOB MUSIC	16
OH, THE SLOP-PAIL IS THE PLACE TO THINK	270	GOB MUSIC	44
SLOSHING			
ALONG THE SEA-WALL, A STEADY SLOSHING OF THE SWELL,	230	THE STORM	10
SLOTH			
THE SLOTH	116	THE SLOTH	T
SLOW			
SLOW SEASON	12	SLOW SEASON	T
AT DUSK OUR SLOW BREATH THICKENS ON THE AIR.	12	SLOW SEASON	8
HIS PULSE BEAT IS SO SLOW WE THINK HIM DEAD.	16	THE BAT	4
SLOW SWINGS THE BREEZE ABOVE HER HEAD,	17	NO BIRD	5
THE SLEEP WAS NOT DEEP, BUT THE WAKING IS SLOW.	29	THE GENTLE	12
I NOTICE A TREE, ARSENICAL GREY IN THE LIGHT, OR THE SLOW	47	DOUBLE FEATURE	10
A SLOW DRIP OVER STONES,	53	THE LOST SON	3
WHAT A SMALL SONG. WHAT SLOW CLOUDS. WHAT DARK WATER.	56	THE LOST SON	83
MOVED IN A SLOW UP-SWAY.	57	THE LOST SON	148
THIS SLAG RUNS SLOW. WHAT BLEEDS WHEN METAL BREAKS?	59	THE LONG ALLEY	11
A SLOW SNAIL-LIFTING, LIQUESCENT;	67	SHAPE OF FIRE	82
IN THE SLOW RAIN, WHO'S AFRAID?	79	GIVE WAY, GATES	21
I MET A COLLECTOR OF STRING, A SHEPHERD OF SLOW FORMS.	90	UNFOLD! UNFOLD!	30
A SLOW SIGH SAYS YES. AND LIGHT SIGHS;	90	UNFOLD! UNFOLD!	49
STAND BY A SLOW STREAM:	98	O, THOU OPENING	34
SLOW, SLOW AS A FISH SHE CAME,	100	THE VISITANT	10
SLOW, SLOW AS A FISH SHE CAME,	100	THE VISITANT	10
SLOW AS A FISH COMING FORWARD,	100	THE VISITANT	11
I WAKE TO SLEEP, AND TAKE MY WAKING SLOW.	108	THE WAKING (2)	1
I WAKE TO SLEEP, AND TAKE MY WAKING SLOW.	108	THE WAKING (2)	6
I WAKE TO SLEEP, AND TAKE MY WAKING SLOW.	108	THE WAKING (2)	12
I WAKE TO SLEEP, AND TAKE MY WAKING SLOW.	108	THE WAKING (2)	18
THEIR SLOW SONG SANG IN ME;	128	THE VOICE	22
IN THAT SLOW DARK THAT WIDENS EVERY EYE.	129	SHE	14
SMALL WAVES REPEAT THE MIND'S SLOW SENSUAL PLAY.	131	SENTENTIOUS MAN	13
HOW SLOW THE CHANGES OF A GOLDEN MEAN:	133	THE PURE FURY	12
IN THE SLOW WORLD OF DREAM,	141	MEMORY	1
I FELT MY SLOW BLOOD WARM.	150	SNAKE	9
MAKING A SLOW JOURNEY AROUND THE WELL-CURB.	151	SLUG	3
A SLOW GROWTH IS A HARD THING TO ENDURE.	154	THE DYING MAN	45

	PAGE	TITLE	LINE
SLOW (CONTINUED)			
AND THAT SLOW HUMMING RISES INTO SONG.	155	THE DYING MAN	75
IN THE SLOW COMING-OUT OF SLEEP,	162	I'M HERE	51
I SHED MY CLOTHES TO SLOW MY DAEMON DOWN.	166	HER BECOMING	59
AS A CHIP OR SHELL, FLOATING LAZILY WITH A SLOW CURRENT,	168	FOURTH MEDITATN	6
WAITING, ITSELF A SLOW THING,	168	FOURTH MEDITATN	21
A PRINCE OF SMALL BEGINNINGS, ENDURING THE SLOW STRETCHES OF CHANGE,	170	FOURTH MEDITATN	70
IN THE CIRCULAR SMELLS OF A SLOW WIND,	171	WHAT TELL BONES	11
I RISE AND FALL IN THE SLOW SEA OF A GRASSY PLAIN,	194	JOURNY INTERIOR	42
FROM THE SLOW SINKING OF THE ISLAND PENINSULA, THE CORAL EFFLORESCENCE,	196	THE LONG WATERS	22
IN THE SILTED SHALLOWS OF A SLOW RIVER,	200	THE FAR FIELD	39
WHERE THE SLOW CREEK WINDS DOWN TO THE BLACK SAND OF THE SHORE	203	THE ROSE	49
WHEN THE SLOW FREIGHT WINDS ALONG THE EDGE OF THE RAVAGED HILLSIDE,	204	THE ROSE	83
THE SLOW TICK OF TIME	211	SONG (1)	10
THE CURLEW'S SLOW NIGHT SONG CAME ON THE WATER.	216	THE SHY MAN	9
SHIFTED WITH OUR SLOW KISS.	238	THE MOMENT	5
I FEEL THE AUTUMN FAIL--ALL THAT SLOW FIRE	242	THE SEQUEL	31
THE CHANGE FROM DARK TO LIGHT OF THE SLOW MOON,	244	INFIRMITY	22
THE PHOEBE'S SLOW RETREATING FROM ITS SONG,	245	THE DECISION	4
THE SLOW LONG RIPPLES WINKING IN MY EYES.	247	I WAITED	9
AND, PRAISING CHANGE AS THE SLOW NIGHT COMES ON,	250	THE RIGHT THING	16
SLOWED			
SLOWED IN MY HUMAN FORM;	49	RIVER INCIDENT	5
SHE SLOWED TO SIGH, IN THAT LONG INTERVAL.	120	THE DREAM	18
THE LIGHT AIR SLOWED: IT WAS NOT NIGHT OR DAY.	166	HER BECOMING	56
BUT WHEN I SLOWED MY FEET,	225	THE CHUMS	6
SLOWER			
MY FLESH IS BREATHING SLOWER THAN A WALL.	135	THE RENEWAL	9
BREATHING A SLOWER BREATH,	147	THE EXORCISM	27
BEATS SLOWER IN MY CARELESS SOLITUDE.	155	THE DYING MAN	68
SLOWING			
IS THAT DANCE SLOWING IN THE MIND OF MAN	105	SIR JOHN DAVIES	1
THE WIND'S SLOWING.	219	THE ABYSS	16
SLOWLY			
TURN SLOWLY THROUGH THE NIGHT,	9	THE ADAMANT	6
SLOWLY HIS MATCHLESS DISPOSITION SOURED	28	THE FAVORITE	12
MOVE SLOWLY,	39	ORCHIDS	7
THE LIGHT IN THE MORNING CAME SLOWLY OVER THE WHITE	57	THE LOST SON	135
THE LIGHT MOVED SLOWLY OVER THE FROZEN FIELD,	58	THE LOST SON	155
SLOWLY TURNING,	59	THE LONG ALLEY	4
SLOWLY.	59	THE LONG ALLEY	5
THE TENDRILS TURNING SLOWLY,	67	SHAPE OF FIRE	81
RISING SLOWLY OUT OF ITS BED,	67	SHAPE OF FIRE	84
THE WATER RECEDES SLOWLY,	93	I CRY, LOVE!	52
INDIGNATION? LET ME PERSUADE MORE SLOWLY:	98	O, THOU OPENING	31
SLOWLY UNFOLDING,	101	LIGHT BREATHER	5
IMPALED ON LIGHT, AND WHIRLING SLOWLY DOWN.	107	SIR JOHN DAVIES	72
OUR SHADOWS MET, AND SLOWLY SWUNG AROUND;	120	THE DREAM	26
SLOWLY BECAME THE MOON.	123	WORDS FOR WIND	24
THE WIND CREAKS SLOWLY BY;	123	WORDS FOR WIND	26
THE MOON GOES SLOWLY DOWN;	148	THE SMALL	8
CREEPING SLOWLY OVER THE WET GRASS,	151	SLUG	13
THE TAIL AND SMALLER LEGS SLIPPING AND SLIDING SLOWLY BACKWARD--	159	FIRST MEDITATN	65
HOW SLOWLY ALL THINGS ALTER.	173	WHAT TELL BONES	66
HOW SLOWLY PLEASURE DIES!--	197	THE LONG WATERS	29
SWIMMING SLOWLY, ITS BACK RUFFLED BY THE LIGHT CROSS-WINDS,	197	THE LONG WATERS	53
THE SHADE SPEAKS SLOWLY:	222	THE ABYSS	85
THEN SLOWLY BREAKING WHITER IN THE DAWN;	225	OTTO	37
RISING AGAIN, SLOWLY,	226	THE LIZARD	25
THE BODY MOVES, THOUGH SLOWLY, TOWARD DESIRE.	235	MANIFESTATION	10
SLOWLY WE MOVED BETWEEN	237	THE TRANCED	18
HOW SLOWLY DARK COMES DOWN ON WHAT WE DO.	240	IN EVEING AIR	24
HOW BODY FROM SPIRIT SLOWLY DOES UNWIND	244	INFIRMITY	35
SLOWLY I CAME BACK TO THE DUSTY ROAD;	247	I WAITED	15
SLOWNESS			
HOW CAN I REST IN THE DAYS OF MY SLOWNESS?	157	FIRST MEDITATN	14
SLOWS			
THE BLOOD SLOWS TRANCE-LIKE IN THE ALTERED VEIN;	12	SLOW SEASON	15

	PAGE	TITLE	LINE
SLOWS (CONTINUED)			
KNOWING SLOWS FOR A MOMENT,	221	THE ABYSS	69
SLOW-SETTLING			
WHITE UPON WHITE, SLOW-SETTLING ON A STONE;	149	IN LATE SUMMER	2
SLUG			
SLUG	151	SLUG	T
THE FURY OF THE SLUG BENEATH THE STONE.	156	THE DYING MAN	93
FALLS BACK, A SLUG, A LOOSE WORM	187	THE LONGING	21
SLUGGISH			
UNDERNEATH, THE SLUGGISH WATER RUNNING BETWEEN WEEDS, BROKEN WHEELS, TIRES, STONES.	194	JOURNY INTERIOR	33
SLUGGISHLY			
IN ITS SMALL FOLDS, STIRRING SLUGGISHLY,	171	WHAT TELL BONES	4
SLUG-SOFT			
SLUG-SOFT STEMS,	43	FLOWER DUMP	2
SLURP			
WHEN YOU SLURP AND GO, POOF!	180	GOO-GIRL	10
SLY			
LIKE A NURSE HE SAT WITH ME FOR WEEKS, A SLY SURLY ATTENDANT,	220	THE ABYSS	38
SMALL			
THE SMALL BROOK DIES WITHIN ITS BED;	15	COMING OF COLD	38
THE SMALL CELLS BULGE;	37	CUTTINGS	4
THE SMALL WATERS SEEPING UPWARD,	37	CUTTINGS (LATE)	7
EVEN THE DIRT KEPT BREATHING A SMALL BREATH.	38	ROOT CELLAR	11
THE CRUMBLING SMALL HOLLOW STICKS ON THE UNDERSIDE MIXED WITH ROOTS,	40	MOSS-GATHERING	4
COULD MAKE A SMALL BOY DIZZY;	45	MY PAPA'S WALTZ	2
LIKE SMALL GOATS.	51	THE WAKING (1)	12
WHAT A SMALL SONG. WHAT SLOW CLOUDS. WHAT DARK WATER.	56	THE LOST SON	83
SCURRY OF WARM OVER SMALL PLANTS.	57	THE LOST SON	141
COME WHISPERING OVER THE SMALL WATERS,	61	THE LONG ALLEY	67
BEND DOWN, SMALL BREATHERS, CREEPERS AND WINDERS;	61	THE LONG ALLEY	71
SMALL WINDS MADE	62	FIELD OF LIGHT	7
THE SUN GLITTERED ON A SMALL RAPIDS.	63	FIELD OF LIGHT	34
SHALE LOOSENS. MARL REACHES INTO THE FIELD. SMALL BIRDS PASS OVER WATER.	64	SHAPE OF FIRE	11
HELD UP, WHILE THE ROWER BREATHES, AND THE SMALL BOAT DRIFTS QUIETLY SHOREWARD;	67	SHAPE OF FIRE	91
I SING A SMALL SING,	72	WHERE KNOCK IS	23
O SMALL BIRD WAKENING,	78	BRING THE DAY!	38
THE AIR'S QUIET UNDER THE SMALL LEAVES.	78	BRING THE DAY!	41
ROCKING WITH SMALL FISH,	84	O LULL ME, LULL	34
WHEREFORE, O BIRDS AND SMALL FISH, SURROUND ME.	88	PRAISE TO END!	97
THE EYE PERISHES IN THE SMALL VISION.	90	UNFOLD! UNFOLD!	42
ALL SMALL SHAPES, WILLOW-SHY,	90	UNFOLD! UNFOLD!	46
AND SMALL MOUTHS, STAY YOUR AIMLESS CHEEPING:	92	I CRY, LOVE!	23
THEN WASHING UP OVER SMALL STONES.	93	I CRY, LOVE!	49
I'M TIRED OF ALL THAT, BAG-FOOT. I CAN HEAR SMALL ANGELS ANYTIME. WHO	98	O, THOU OPENING	25
A SMALL THING,	101	LIGHT BREATHER	17
HER SONG TREMBLING THE TWIGS AND SMALL BRANCHES.	102	ELEGY FOR JANE	6
I'VE BECOME A SENTRY OF SMALL SEEDS,	103	OLD LADY'S WRDS	33
A SMALL BIRD FLEW IN CIRCLES WHERE WE STOOD;	120	THE DREAM	19
WHEN SMALL BIRDS SIGHED, SHE WOULD SIGH BACK AT THEM;	127	I KNEW A WOMAN	2
SMALL WAVES REPEAT THE MIND'S SLOW SENSUAL PLAY.	131	SENTENTIOUS MAN	13
SMALL WATERS RUN TOWARD A MIRY HOLE--	132	SENTENTIOUS MAN	39
WITH THE SMALL VOICE OF A CHILD,	146	THE SONG	26
THE SMALL	148	THE SMALL	T
THE SMALL BIRDS SWIRL AROUND;	148	THE SMALL	1
THE SMALL SHAPES DROWSE: I LIVE	148	THE SMALL	19
TO WOO THE FEARFUL SMALL;	148	THE SMALL	20
THE SMALL! THE SMALL! I HEAR THEM SINGING CLEAR	149	IN LATE SUMMER	7
THE SMALL! THE SMALL! I HEAR THEM SINGING CLEAR	149	IN LATE SUMMER	7
WITH HIS STRIPES OF SILVER AND HIS SMALL HOUSE ON HIS BACK,	151	SLUG	2
THE SMALL DEAD PIECES STICKING UNDER AN INSTEP;	151	SLUG	20
AND THE SMALL MAD SISKINS FLIT BY,	152	THE SISKINS	8
ONLY TO LOSE MYSELF IN THIS SMALL DARK.	154	THE DYING MAN	41
THE SMALL WINDS MAKE THEIR CHILLY INDICTMENTS.	157	FIRST MEDITATN	3
SETTLING IN SMALL BEADS AROUND WEEDS AND SUNKEN BRANCHES,	159	FIRST MEDITATN	61
A BIRD, SMALL AS A LEAF,	163	I'M HERE	60
I CLOSED MY EYES, AND SAW SMALL FIGURES DANCING,	163	I'M HERE	65
I NEED A POND WITH SMALL EELS. AND A WINDY ORCHARD.	164	I'M HERE	91

	PAGE	TITLE	LINE
SMALL (CONTINUED)			
WATCHING THE WIND RIFFLE THE BACKS OF SMALL BIRDS,	165	HER BECOMING	2
SPEECH PASSED BETWEEN SMALL BIRDS;	167	HER BECOMING	65
A SMALL PLACE ALL IN FLAME.	167	HER BECOMING	77
KNOWING THE SINUOUSNESS OF SMALL WATERS:	168	FOURTH MEDITATN	5
A PRINCE OF SMALL BEGINNINGS, ENDURING THE SLOW STRETCHES OF CHANGE,	170	FOURTH MEDITATN	70
YOUNGLINGS, THE SMALL FISH KEEP HEADING INTO THE CURRENT.	170	FOURTH MEDITATN	75
IN ITS SMALL FOLDS, STIRRING SLUGGISHLY,	171	WHAT TELL BONES	4
I'M A SMALL STONE, LOOSE IN THE SHALE.	172	WHAT TELL BONES	47
MAKES ALMOST A WAVE OVER A BARRIER OF SMALL STONES,	190	AT OYSTER RIVER	13
SMALL ENOUGH TO BE TAKEN IN, EMBRACED, BY TWO ARMS,--	191	AT OYSTER RIVER	46
IN AND OUT OF THE SMALL WAVES,	192	AT OYSTER RIVER	65
HOW GRACEFUL THE SMALL BEFORE DANGER!	192	AT OYSTER RIVER	67
TO A SCURRY OF SMALL DOGS AND A SHRIEK OF CHILDREN,	193	JOURNY INTERIOR	26
IN THE MOMENT OF TIME WHEN THE SMALL DROP FORMS, BUT DOES NOT FALL,	194	JOURNY INTERIOR	58
A COUNTRY OF BAYS AND INLETS, AND SMALL STREAMS FLOWING SEAWARD.	196	THE LONG WATERS	19
BY SMALL STREAMS RUNNING DOWN UNDER FALLEN FIR TREES.	197	THE LONG WATERS	48
THE WEEDY EDGE, ALIVE WITH SMALL SNAKES AND BLOODSUCKERS,--	200	THE FAR FIELD	70
INTO THE SMALL SPILLAGE OF DRIFTWOOD,	202	THE ROSE	24
AND THE SEA REARRANGES ITSELF AMONG THE SMALL ISLANDS.	205	THE ROSE	97
AND THE SMALL WAVES	210	HER TIME	8
SPRAY, AND THE SMALL SHAPES	210	HER TIME	17
SUCH QUIET UNDER THE SMALL LEAVES!--	221	THE ABYSS	82
I RECALL THE FALLING OF SMALL WATERS.	222	THE ABYSS	93
WHO LOVES THE SMALL CAN BE BOTH SAINT AND BOOR,	225	OTTO	31
HIS FEET LIKE SMALL LEAVES,	227	MEADOW MOUSE	8
AND THE SMALL STREET-LAMP SWINGING AND SLAMMING AGAINST THE LAMP POLE.	230	THE STORM	7
TRAILING A THING--WHAT WAS IT?--SMALL AS A LARK	232	THE THING	2
THE SMALL THING DIVING DOWN TOWARD A HILL,	232	THE THING	10
AND THE SMALL FISH LIE, WITHOUT SHADOW, MOTIONLESS,	233	THE PIKE	6
LOOKING AT YOU WITHOUT TURNING HIS SMALL HEAD,	234	ALL MORNING	12
WE COUNTED SEVERAL FLAMES IN ONE SMALL FIRE.	237	THE TRANCED	1
OUR SMALL SOULS HID FROM THEIR SMALL AGONIES,	238	THE TRANCED	21
OUR SMALL SOULS HID FROM THEIR SMALL AGONIES,	238	THE TRANCED	21
THE MIST ABOVE ME SINGS WITH ITS SMALL FLIES.	246	THE MARROW	2
THAT ONCE COULD MELT THE DARK WITH ITS SMALL BREATH.	246	THE MARROW	16
A DONKEY PATH LED TO A SMALL PLATEAU.	247	I WAITED	21
A SMALL VOICE CALLING FROM A DRIFTING CLOUD.	248	THE TREE, BIRD	4
SMALL AS AN ELF,	249	THE RESTORED	3
THE SMALL BECOME THE GREAT, THE GREAT THE SMALL;	250	THE RIGHT THING	8
THE SMALL BECOME THE GREAT, THE GREAT THE SMALL;	250	THE RIGHT THING	8
THE BIRD IN THE SMALL BUSH	259	SONG (3)	45
I'M A SOCRATES OF SMALL FURY.	260	THE CHANGELING	17
THE SMALL! THE SMALL!	261	THE CHANGELING	49
THE SMALL! THE SMALL!	261	THE CHANGELING	49
SMALLER			
THE TAIL AND SMALLER LEGS SLIPPING AND SLIDING SLOWLY BACKWARD--	159	FIRST MEDITATN	65
SMALLEST			
THE UNDERLEAVES, THE SMALLEST BUDS	42	TRANSPLANTING	17
BY LISTENING TO THE SPIRIT'S SMALLEST CRY;	131	SENTENTIOUS MAN	15
SMART			
AND CHRISTOPHER SMART,	228	IN VIOLENT WARD	6
SMELL			
SO THEIR MUSKY SMELL COMES EVEN STRONGER,	39	ORCHIDS	12
I SMELL THE JUMPS AHEAD.	81	SENSIBILITY! LA	14
WHAT'S THAT PECULIAR SMELL?	136	THE SENSUALISTS	14
IN THE SUMMER HEAT, I CAN SMELL THE DEAD BUFFALO,	189	THE LONGING	54
SMELLED			
WHATEVER HE SMELLED WAS GOOD:	46	PICKLE BELT	5
SMELLED THE CARRION AT ENTRANCES,	48	JUDGE NOT	8
SMELLS			
THE FRUIT AND FLESH SMELLS MIXED.	46	PICKLE BELT	6
ITS MORNING SMELLS.	51	THE WAKING (1)	20
THE SMELLS, THE MOMENT OF HAY,--	103	OLD LADY'S WRDS	22
IN THE CIRCULAR SMELLS OF A SLOW WIND,	171	WHAT TELL BONES	11
A PRISONER OF SMELLS, I WOULD RATHER EAT THAN PRAY.	173	WHAT TELL BONES	79
REJOICE IN THE LANGUAGE OF SMELLS AND DANCING.	196	THE LONG WATERS	4

	PAGE	TITLE	LINE
SMELLS (CONTINUED)			
THE RUSH OF SMELLS STRIKES LIKE A COLD FIRE, THE THROAT FREEZES,	220	THE ABYSS	47
SMILAX			
COILED GREEN AND THICK, LIKE DRIPPING SMILAX,	39	WEED PULLER	8
THE SWEET-PEA TENDRILS, THE SMILAX,	44	FRAU BAUMAN	5
THE CHILD'S HAND REACHING INTO THE COILED SMILAX,	221	THE ABYSS	65
SMILE			
WITH MOTHERS, SLEEP-HEAVY CHILDREN, STALE PERFUME, PAST THE MANAGER'S SMILE	47	DOUBLE FEATURE	3
AND HER QUICK LOOK, A SIDELONG PICKEREL SMILE;	102	ELEGY FOR JANE	2
I SMILE, NO MINERAL MAN;	124	WORDS FOR WIND	58
ON ONE SIDE OF SILENCE THERE IS NO SMILE;	195	JOURNY INTERIOR	76
SMILED			
GOD'S NIGHT AND DAY: DOWN THIS SPACE HE HAS SMILED,	243	THE MOTION	21
SMOKE			
SUDDENLY THEY CAME FLYING, LIKE A LONG SCARF OF SMOKE,	232	THE THING	1
SMOKED			
LIKE PIECES OF SMOKED EEL OR RAW OYSTER,	151	SLUG	17
SMOKELESS			
THE SWALLOWS FLEW IN AND OUT OF THE SMOKELESS CHIMNEYS.	162	I'M HERE	41
SMOKE'S			
THE PAVEMENT SMOKES WHEN TWO CARS MEET	33	HIGHWAY: MICH	16
SMOKE'S			
THIS SMOKE'S FROM THE GLORY OF GOD.	59	THE LONG ALLEY	16
SMOKING			
DECISION'S SMOKING FUSE;	7	ORDERS FOR DAY	4
SMOKY			
BEHIND THE EYE; THE LOST ACRES AT THE EDGE OF SMOKY CITIES.	159	FIRST MEDITATN	75
OR THE WHIPPOORWILL, ALONG THE SMOKY RIDGES,	160	FIRST MEDITATN	89
SMOLDERING			
WANES TO THE FEBRILE SMOLDERING OF SLEEP;	17	UNEXTINGUISHED	6
SMOTHER			
FOR CARELESSNESS CAN SMOTHER	7	ORDERS FOR DAY	3
I THOUGHT I WAS GOING TO SMOTHER.	162	I'M HERE	50
SMOTHERED			
DEEP-HIDDEN EMBERS, SMOTHERED BY THE SCREEN	17	UNEXTINGUISHED	7
YOUR LITTLE MANHOOD LONG AGO WAS SMOTHERED.	25	DIM-WIT COUSIN	2
SMUDGY			
I'M STILL SMUDGY FROM SLEEP:	259	SONG (3)	41
SMUG			
BUT SHOULD YOU CALL HIS MANNER SMUG,	116	THE SLOTH	8
SMUTS			
SCUMS, MILDEWS, SMUTS ALONG STEMS,	38	FORCING HOUSE	3
SNAIL			
SNAIL, SNAIL, GLISTER ME FORWARD,	53	THE LOST SON	8
SNAIL, SNAIL, GLISTER ME FORWARD,	53	THE LOST SON	8
I COULD TALK TO A SNAIL;	84	O LULL ME, LULL	39
MOVES, LIKE THE SNAIL,	101	LIGHT BREATHER	11
AND EVERY SNAIL DIPPED TOWARD ME ITS PURE HORN.	248	THE TREE, BIRD	2
WITH THE FISH, THE QUESTING SNAIL,	251	ONCE MORE, RND	7
SNAIL-LIFTING			
A SLOW SNAIL-LIFTING, LIQUESCENT;	67	SHAPE OF FIRE	82
SNAILS			
GRUBS AND SNAILS AND SHARP STICKS,	39	WEED PULLER	6
BY SNAILS, BY LEAPS OF FROG, I CAME HERE, SPIRIT.	89	UNFOLD! UNFOLD!	1
SNAIL'S			
A SNAIL'S MUSIC.	163	I'M HERE	89
SNAKE			
WHERE SNAKE AND VULTURE HOVER,	7	ORDERS FOR DAY	12
SING THE SNAKE TO SLEEP.	73	WHERE KNOCK IS	75
SNAKE	150	SNAKE	T
I SAW A YOUNG SNAKE GLIDE	150	SNAKE	1
A SNAKE LIFTING ITS HEAD;	163	I'M HERE	88
THE YOUNG SNAKE, POISED IN GREEN LEAVES, WAITING FOR ITS FLY,	190	AT OYSTER RIVER	28
AS A SNAKE OR A RAUCOUS BIRD,	200	THE FAR FIELD	48
TO LIVE BY COURTESY OF THE SHRIKE, THE SNAKE, THE TOM-CAT.	227	MEADOW MOUSE	25
SNAKE-EYES			
SNAKE-EYES.	75	I NEED, I NEED	46
SNAKES			
BUT SNAKES, BOTH POISONOUS AND GARTER,	23	AMOROUS LADY	5
HUNG DOWN LONG YELLOW EVIL NECKS, LIKE TROPICAL SNAKES.	38	ROOT CELLAR	5

	PAGE	TITLE	LINE
SNAKES (CONTINUED)			
THE SNAKES CRIED,	55	THE LOST SON	80
UP OVER A VIADUCT I CAME, TO THE SNAKES AND STICKS OF ANOTHER WINTER,	65	SHAPE OF FIRE	37
THE DEAD SNAKES AND MUSKRATS, THE TURTLES GASPING IN THE RUBBLE,	194	JOURNY INTERIOR	36
THE WEEDY EDGE, ALIVE WITH SMALL SNAKES AND BLOODSUCKERS,--	200	THE FAR FIELD	70
SNEER			
THAT'S NOT A THING I'M SAYING WITH A SNEER--	132	SENTENTIOUS MAN	40
SNEEZE			
A SNEEZE CAN'T SLEEP.	74	I NEED, I NEED	5
THESE POETS, THEY WRITE LIKE I SNEEZE!"	179	MYRTLE	12
SNIDE			
HE WOULD ACT VERY SNIDE,	178	THE YAK	4
SNIFF			
I SNIFF THE DARKENING AIR	215	HIS FOREBODING	17
SNIFFING			
SNIFFING THE DEW.	87	PRAISE TO END!	62
SNIGGERED			
NOW NOBODY SNIGGERED AND MOCKED	182	BOY AND BUSH	6
SNIVEL			
THEY DIDN'T BOAST; THEY DIDN'T SNIVEL,	111	SQUEEZE-BOX	3
SNORE			
TO THE LAND WHERE THE INNOCENT STRETCH AND SNORE	272	DUET	11
SNORING			
FRIGIDAIRES SNORING THE SLEEP OF PLENTY,	48	LAST WORDS	4
SNORT			
LAUGHED A MASTER OF HUMP AND SNORT;	263	FOLLIES OF ADAM	30
SNORTS			
WHICH, WITH SLOBBERS AND SNORTS,	180	GOO-GIRL	5
SNOUT			
THE BEAR, EQUIPPED WITH PAW AND SNOUT,	23	AMOROUS LADY	3
SNOW			
THOUGH STILL THE GUARDED SNOW IS WINTER-SEALED,	11	LIGHT BRIGHTER	6
AS BRANCHES LOOSE LAST VESTIGES OF SNOW.	11	LIGHT BRIGHTER	10
WINDS BRING A FINE AND BITTER SNOW.	15	COMING OF COLD	52
THE RATS SOON WILL BE LEAVING, THE SNOW WILL COME IN."	27	CLAIRVOY WIDOW	16
WHEEL OF THE STARS, THE GREAT BEAR GLITTERING COLDER THAN SNOW,	47	DOUBLE FEATURE	11
SNOW.	57	THE LOST SON	136
ABOVE THE BLUE SNOW.	58	THE LOST SON	153
THE CINDERY SNOW TICKS OVER STUBBLE.	104	OLD LADY'S WRDS	54
THE SHEETS AND BLANKETS TURNED TO SNOW.	114	DINKY	15
SHE SIGHS ME WHITE, A SOCRATES OF SNOW.	140	THE SWAN	7
WITH THEIR HARD SNOW; LEANED ON THE LONELY EYE;	143	SHIMMER OF EVIL	7
OR TWO HORSES PLUNGING IN SNOW, THEIR LINES TANGLED,	158	FIRST MEDITATN	53
COMING ACROSS SNOW IN EARLY EVENING?	161	I'M HERE	5
THE FIRST SNOW OF THE YEAR IN THE DARK FIR.	197	THE LONG WATERS	31
A FINE DRY SNOW TICKING THE WINDSHIELD,	199	THE FAR FIELD	5
ALTERNATE SNOW AND SLEET, NO ON-COMING TRAFFIC,	199	THE FAR FIELD	6
LIKE THE BLUE SHINE ON FRESHLY FROZEN SNOW,	201	THE FAR FIELD	96
AND THE TICKING OF SNOW AROUND OIL DRUMS IN THE DAKOTAS,	204	THE ROSE	68
VANISHED LIKE APRIL SNOW;	213	THE HAPPY THREE	27
AS A MAN TURNS TO FACE ON-COMING SNOW.	245	THE DECISION	12
SNOWDRIFT			
CHURNING IN A SNOWDRIFT	199	THE FAR FIELD	11
SNOW-LADEN			
THE ROAD LINED WITH SNOW-LADEN SECOND GROWTH,	199	THE FAR FIELD	4
SNOW'S			
RECALL THE GRADUAL DARK THE SNOW'S UNMEASURED FALL	5	TO MY SISTER	3
HATH THE RAIN A FATHER? ALL THE CAVES ARE ICE. ONLY THE SNOW'S HERE.	56	THE LOST SON	84
SOFT, SOFT, THE SNOW'S NOT FALLING. WHAT'S A SEED?	165	HER BECOMING	17
SNUFF-LADEN			
AND THEIR SNUFF-LADEN BREATH BLOWING LIGHTLY OVER ME IN MY FIRST SLEEP.	44	FRAU BAUMAN	35
SNUFFLING			
SO WHEN THAT SNUFFLING CRETIN OF A MAID	228	THE GERANIUM	22
SO			
AND VICIOUS VENERY--NOT SO!	8	PRAYER	12
SO SINGULAR A BLESSEDNESS.	8	PRAYER	18
THE SENSE THAT DOES SO FITLY SERVE,	8	PRAYER	20
A CENTER SO CONGEALED;	9	THE ADAMANT	10

	PAGE	TITLE	LINE
SO (CONTINUED)			
A FIVE-FOOT DROP A VALLEY, SO TO SPEAK.	13	PRAISE PRAIRIE	2
THE DOCK, SO GARISH TO THE EYE,	14	COMING OF COLD	15
HIS PULSE BEAT IS SO SLOW WE THINK HIM DEAD.	16	THE BAT	4
THE EAR SO DELICATE AND TRUE	17	NO BIRD	3
SO TERRIBLY WITHIN THE MIND,	22	SILENCE	10
SO CAGED AND CADGED, SO CLOSE WITHIN	24	BEFORE STUDY	3
SO CAGED AND CADGED, SO CLOSE WITHIN	24	BEFORE STUDY	3
THE FURNITURE POLISHED AND POLISHED SO GRAND,	32	SALE	5
WHAT SAINT STRAINED SO MUCH,	37	CUTTINGS (LATE)	3
SO THEIR MUSKY SMELL COMES EVEN STRONGER,	39	ORCHIDS	12
SO MANY DEVOURING INFANTS!	39	ORCHIDS	14
SO FAR DOWN THE RIVER	41	BIG WIND	4
SO WE DRAINED THE MANURE-MACHINE	41	BIG WIND	6
CRACKING SO MUCH THIN GLASS	41	BIG WIND	18
SO UP AND AWAY AND WHAT DO WE DO	60	THE LONG ALLEY	37
SO TOUCH MY TOES TWICE.	75	I NEED, I NEED	30
SO BIBBLE WHERE THE PEBBLE IS.	75	I NEED, I NEED	32
SO ALIVE I COULD DIE!	99	O, THOU OPENING	58
OF THOSE SO CLOSE BESIDE ME, WHICH ARE YOU?	108	THE WAKING (2)	7
TO YOU AND ME; SO TAKE THE LIVELY AIR,	108	THE WAKING (2)	14
SO I'VE GOT TO GET ME A RICH UGLY OLD MAID	112	SQUEEZE-BOX	43
--AND SO LIKE MY POEM CALLED POEM.	113	TO A LADY ED	4
AND SO, OF COURSE, HE HAD TO SING,	115	THE SERPENT	9
AND SO,--I'M FISHING THIS WAY.	117	LADY AND BEAR	8
AND SO I STOOD APART,	128	THE VOICE	5
LIGHTLY: SO BUDS UNLEAVE;	130	THE OTHER	4
THAT APPETITE FOR LIFE SO RAVENOUS	133	THE PURE FURY	16
THESE WATERS DROWSE ME INTO SLEEP SO KIND	135	THE RENEWAL	11
"YOU HAVE ME PINNED SO CLOSE;	136	THE SENSUALISTS	2
SO THE SPIRIT TRIES FOR ANOTHER LIFE,	159	FIRST MEDITATN	66
SO, I SUPPOSE, THE SPIRIT JOURNEYS.	159	FIRST MEDITATN	73
SO MUCH OF ADOLESCENCE IS AN ILL-DEFINED DYING,	162	I'M HERE	35
AND THE TIME I WAS SO SICK--	163	I'M HERE	63
SO SHE TOLD ME WHEN I WAS LITTLE,	163	I'M HERE	72
THEN A REAL CAT CAME WITH A MOUTH SO WIDE,	177	KITTY-CAT BIRD	14
SHE WAS SO MUCH TROUBLE;	179	MYRTLE'S COUSIN	7
AND SO HE HAD A HORRID FALL.	181	MONOTONY SONG	15
SO THEY TALKED AND THEY TALKED AND THEY TALKED.	182	BOY AND BUSH	10
WHO'D THINK THE MOON COULD PARE ITSELF SO THIN?	188	THE LONGING	30
SO THE SEA WIND WAKES DESIRE.	198	THE LONG WATERS	65
A SOUND SO THIN IT COULD NOT WOO A BIRD,	204	THE ROSE	77
THAT I CARRIED SO LONG	211	SONG (1)	3
WHEN SO YOUNG, WHEN SO YOUNG?	211	SONG (1)	4
WHEN SO YOUNG, WHEN SO YOUNG?	211	SONG (1)	4
SO I BETOOK MYSELF	213	THE HAPPY THREE	13
SO THE ABYSS--	221	THE ABYSS	50
AND SO SHE WAS, IN HER WAY, AUNT TILLY.	223	ELEGY (2)	3
O WORLD SO FAR AWAY! O MY LOST WORLD!	225	OTTO	42
SO MUCH HE JUST LIES IN ONE CORNER,	227	MEADOW MOUSE	13
SHE LOOKED SO LIMP AND BEDRAGGLED,	228	THE GERANIUM	2
SO FOOLISH AND TRUSTING, LIKE A SICK POODLE.	228	THE GERANIUM	3
SO LONG ON GIN, BOBBIE PINS, HALF-SMOKED CIGARS, DEAD BEER,	228	THE GERANIUM	10
SO WHEN THAT SNUFFLING CRETIN OF A MAID	228	THE GERANIUM	22
SO THEY CIRCLED AIMLESSLY FOR ALMOST A MINUTE,	232	THE THING	8
NOT EVEN FEATHERS FROM SO FAR AWAY.	232	THE THING	17
OUR EYES FIXED ON A POINT OF LIGHT SO FINE	237	THE TRANCED	16
HE CARED SO MUCH FOR THE SPORT,	263	FOLLIES OF ADAM	31
SHE WAS A WIDOW, SO SHE SAID:	264	THREE EPIGRAMS	8
I DO NOT HAVE A FIDDLE SO	269	GOB MUSIC	1
A TUNE SO BOLD AND BARE,	271	THE REPLY	11
SO WE SAT DOWN AND ATE OURSELVES A MEAL,	274	SUPPR W LINDSAY	30
SOAKED			
OF VEAL SOAKED IN MARSALA AND LITTLE LARKS ARRANGED ON A LONG PLATTER,	232	THE THING	19
SOB			
TOUCH AND AROUSE. SUCK AND SOB. CURSE AND MOURN.	80	GIVE WAY, GATES	46
SOBBING			
I CAN HEAR, UNDERGROUND, THAT SUCKING AND SOBBING,	37	CUTTINGS (LATE)	5
SOCRATES			
SHE SIGHS ME WHITE, A SOCRATES OF SNOW.	140	THE SWAN	7
I'M A SOCRATES OF SMALL FURY.	260	THE CHANGELING	17

	PAGE	TITLE	LINE
SODDEN			
IN A SODDEN PLACE, ALL RAPS AND KNOCKS APPROVE.	93	I CRY, LOVE!	30
THAT WOMAN WOULD SET SODDEN STRAW ON FIRE.	105	SIR JOHN DAVIES	28
OVER THE SODDEN GROUND.	148	THE SMALL	18
THE MIRE, THE SODDEN WOOD,	154	THE DYING MAN	22
SOFA			
THE ANTIMACASSAR FOR THE SOFA IN RED,	32	SALE	9
SOFT			
DIGGING INTO THE SOFT RUBBLE UNDERNEATH,	39	WEED PULLER	4
COMING OUT, SOFT AND DECEPTIVE,	39	ORCHIDS	4
SOFT LUMINESCENT FINGERS,	39	ORCHIDS	15
THE SOFT POND OF REPOSE;	53	THE LOST SON	13
IS IT SOFT LIKE A MOUSE?	54	THE LOST SON	50
THERE'S NO JOY IN SOFT BONES.	59	THE LONG ALLEY	26
DROWSING IN SOFT LIGHT, PETALS PULSING.	61	THE LONG ALLEY	76
A REAL HURT IS SOFT.	71	WHERE KNOCK IS	11
I LIKE SOFT PAWS.	72	WHERE KNOCK IS	42
HEAR ME, SOFT EARS AND ROUNDY STONES!	76	I NEED, I NEED	57
THY SOFT ALBINO GAZE	81	SENSIBILITY! LA	10
IT'S DARK IN THIS WOOD, SOFT MOCKER.	85	PRAISE TO END!	1
THE SISTER SANDS, THEY SLIPPER SOFT AWAY.	92	I CRY, LOVE!	3
I HEAR THE OWLS, THE SOFT CALLERS, COMING DOWN FROM THE HEMLOCKS.	93	I CRY, LOVE!	40
A RIPPLE MADE A SOFT REPLY.	100	THE VISITANT	6
IN THE SOFT DARK OF EARLY EVENING,	100	THE VISITANT	17
THE LINKS WERE SOFT BETWEEN US; STILL, WE KISSED;	107	SIR JOHN DAVIES	81
SHE LILTS A LOW SOFT LANGUAGE, AND I HEAR	129	SHE	5
ON THE LONG BANKS, IN THE SOFT SUMMER AIR.	149	IN LATE SUMMER	8
WITH A CHEEK SOFT AS A HOUND'S EAR.	157	FIRST MEDITATN	17
MY SKIN WHITER IN THE SOFT WEATHER,	162	I'M HERE	43
SOFT, SOFT, THE SNOW'S NOT FALLING. WHAT'S A SEED?	165	HER BECOMING	17
SOFT, SOFT, THE SNOW'S NOT FALLING. WHAT'S A SEED?	165	HER BECOMING	17
IN THE SOFT SLACK OF A NECK I SLEPT.	258	SONG (3)	22
SOFT-BACKED			
ACROSS MY LAWN THE SOFT-BACKED CREATURES COME;	149	IN LATE SUMMER	3
SOFTENING			
I SHOOK THE SOFTENING CHALK OF MY BONES,	53	THE LOST SON	6
SOFTER			
SOFTER THAN WATER.	88	PRAISE TO END!	96
MY VOICE SOFTER.	162	I'M HERE	44
SOFTEST			
THE SOFTEST COVE	62	FIELD OF LIGHT	9
SOFT-FOOTED			
THE SOFT-FOOTED ONE	208	THE APPARITION	3
SOFTLY			
SOFTLY SOFTLY, YOU'LL WAKE THE CLAMS.	85	PRAISE TO END!	10
SOFTLY SOFTLY, YOU'LL WAKE THE CLAMS.	85	PRAISE TO END!	10
GOD BLESS THE GROUND! I SHALL WALK SOFTLY THERE,	108	THE WAKING (2)	8
CRYING SOFTLY.	171	WHAT TELL BONES	33
SOFT-SIGH			
BIRD, SOFT-SIGH ME HOME,	53	THE LOST SON	9
SOIL			
TO PRESS PURE FRAGRANCE TO THE SOIL;	14	COMING OF COLD	19
THE BITTER ROCK, THE BARREN SOIL	18	LONG LIVE WEEDS	3
AND THE NEW PLANTS, STILL AWKWARD IN THEIR SOIL,	63	FIELD OF LIGHT	42
THE SHRUNKEN SOIL	103	OLD LADY'S WRDS	37
THE WORM, INTREPID SCHOLAR OF THE SOIL--	235	MANIFESTATION	5
SOLACE			
SOLACE OF KISSES AND COOKIES AND CABBAGE,	48	LAST WORDS	1
SOLD			
AND ALL THE RUBBISH OF CONFUSION SOLD.	21	THE AUCTION	16
SOLDIER			
THE DRUNKEN SOLDIER, THE OLD LADY WITH HER PEPPERMINTS;	158	FIRST MEDITATN	30
SOLEMN			
A FOOL CAN PLAY AT BEING SOLEMN	24	BEFORE STUDY	7
SOLID			
THE EARTH, THE SOLID AIR--	128	THE VOICE	21
OR HE SITS STILL, A SOLID FIGURE WHEN	250	THE RIGHT THING	13
SOLITARINESS			
A BIRD SINGS OUT IN SOLITARINESS	171	WHAT TELL BONES	18
SOLITUDE			
IT BREAKS UPON MY SOLITUDE--	22	SILENCE	4
HOW TERRIBLE THE NEED FOR SOLITUDE:	133	THE PURE FURY	15

	PAGE	TITLE	LINE
SOLITUDE (CONTINUED)			
BEATS SLOWER IN MY CARELESS SOLITUDE.	155	THE DYING MAN	68
SOMBER			
DAY AFTER SOMBER DAY,	139	PLAINT	1
SOME			
AND SOME HAVE HELD THE EYE TO BE	8	PRAYER	9
SOME ITEMS, MISCELLANEOUS, MARKED "FEAR";	21	THE AUCTION	7
SOME LEARN THE ART OF THIEVING, AND SOME GROW UP TO BEG;	27	CLAIRVOY WIDOW	10
SOME LEARN THE ART OF THIEVING, AND SOME GROW UP TO BEG;	27	CLAIRVOY WIDOW	10
A STABLE AND PADDOCK, SOME FOX-HUNTING LAND,	32	SALE	6
--AND SOME WATERY EYES IN A COPLEY HEAD.	32	SALE	12
DISTURBED SOME RHYTHM, OLD AND OF VAST IMPORTANCE,	40	MOSS-GATHERING	11
SOME MORNING THING CAME, BEATING ITS WINGS.	63	FIELD OF LIGHT	35
SOME STONES ARE STILL WARM.	72	WHERE KNOCK IS	41
AND THE GHOST OF SOME GREAT HOWL	79	GIVE WAY, GATES	31
IN THE FAIR NIGHT OF SOME DIM BRAIN,	81	SENSIBILITY! LA	4
SOME RARE NEW TEDIUM'S TAKING SHAPE:	81	SENSIBILITY! LA	13
SOME ERRAND, OBSCURE AS THE WIND'S CIRCUIT,	92	I CRY, LOVE!	6
O FOR SOME MINSTREL OF WHAT'S TO BE,	103	OLD LADY'S WRDS	6
--LOT LIKE LOSING SOME MONEY.	111	SQUEEZE-BOX	21
TO SOME IT MAY SEEM A SAD THING TO RELATE,	112	SQUEEZE-BOX	38
SOME RAGES SAVE US. DID I RAGE TOO LONG?	131	SENTENTIOUS MAN	9
AND I MAY BE, SOME TIME.	150	SNAKE	12
AND THE SUN BRINGS JOY TO SOME.	157	FIRST MEDITATN	12
SOME FATES ARE WORSE.	161	I'M HERE	16
SOME TIME I THINK I'LL LIVE THAT WAY.	182	THE HIPPO	5
AN OLD BRIDGE BELOW WITH A BUCKLED IRON RAILING, BROKEN BY SOME IDIOT PLUNGER;	194	JOURNY INTERIOR	32
TO DRINK SOME HALF-AND-HALF	213	THE HAPPY THREE	15
I SEE YOU IN SOME CELESTIAL SUPERMARKET,	223	ELEGY (2)	19
SOME ARE IN PRISON; SOME ARE DEAD;	225	THE CHUMS	1
SOME ARE IN PRISON; SOME ARE DEAD;	225	THE CHUMS	1
(AND SOME GROW OUT OF SHAPE, THEIR SEED IMPURE;)	225	OTTO	32
MY SOUL, LIKE SOME HEAT-MADDENED SUMMER FLY,	239	IN A DARK TIME	20
SWAYING IN AIR, LIKE SOME LONG WATER WEED.	241	THE SEQUEL	19
I MOVED LIKE SOME HEAT-WEARY ANIMAL.	247	I WAITED	17
THE MIRROR TELLS SOME TRUTH, BUT NOT	257	SANITARIUM	7
THE DARK HEART OF SOME ANCIENT THING	260	THE CHANGELING	4
OR SOME OLD LOUT WHO CAN	262	FOLLIES OF ADAM	2
SOME CANNOT PRAISE HIM: I AM ONE OF THOSE.	264	THREE EPIGRAMS	6
THAT SOME HAVE CALLED SWAN CREEK;	267	SAGINAW SONG	8
SOMEBODY			
I'M SOMEBODY ELSE NOW.	74	WHERE KNOCK IS	84
I'M THE SERPENT OF SOMEBODY ELSE.	81	SENSIBILITY! LA	1
SOMEONE			
THE IMPULSE TO MAKE SOMEONE ELSE COMPLETE?	105	SIR JOHN DAVIES	27
SOMETHING			
FOR SOMETHING IS AMISS OR OUT OF PLACE	16	THE BAT	9
BUT SOMETHING ALWAYS WENT OUT OF ME WHEN I DUG LOOSE THOSE CARPETS	40	MOSS-GATHERING	7
AND REMEMBER THERE WAS SOMETHING ELSE I WAS HOPING FOR.	47	DOUBLE FEATURE	12
SAY SOMETHING.	54	THE LOST SON	21
I LISTENED TO SOMETHING	55	THE LOST SON	73
STAY CLOSE. MUST I KILL SOMETHING ELSE?	60	THE LONG ALLEY	31
A DUCK KNOWS SOMETHING	75	I NEED, I NEED	40
SOMETHING CAME BY ME,	77	BRING THE DAY!	14
THE STALKS ASK SOMETHING ELSE.	91	UNFOLD! UNFOLD!	62
THE HEDGEWREN'S SONG SAYS SOMETHING ELSE.	92	I CRY, LOVE!	15
SHE KISSED ME CLOSE, AND THEN DID SOMETHING ELSE.	106	SIR JOHN DAVIES	35
YOU ASK HIM SOMETHING IN HIS EAR,	116	THE SLOTH	2
YOU SHRINK TO SOMETHING LESS,	151	SLUG	23
ON THE SILL OF THE EYES, SOMETHING FLUTTERS,	162	I'M HERE	52
ONCE I WAS SOMETHING LIKE THIS, MINDLESS,	200	THE FAR FIELD	42
A SOMETHING WHOLLY OTHER,	205	THE ROSE	103
WE COME TO SOMETHING WITHOUT KNOWING WHY.	235	MANIFESTATION	11
OH, TO BE SOMETHING ELSE, YET STILL TO BE!	244	INFIRMITY	6
SOMETIMES			
SOMETIMES THE BLOOD IS PRIVILEGED TO GUESS	8	THE SIGNALS	9
OUR FEET ARE SOMETIMES LEVEL WITH THE SKY,	13	PRAISE PRAIRIE	6
AGING, I SOMETIMES WEEP,	130	THE OTHER	23
SOMETIMES I THINK I'M SEVERAL.	173	WHAT TELL BONES	83
YOU SOMETIMES HAVE TO GO AND SIT.	178	THE CHAIR	4
AND SOMETIMES LOOK BEFORE YOU LEAP	181	MONOTONY SONG	27

	PAGE	TITLE	LINE
SOMEWHAT			
SOMEWHAT CLOSER, THE TRUCKS COMING	158	FIRST MEDITATN	32
SOMEWHERE			
GOD'S SOMEWHERE ELSE,	74	WHERE KNOCK IS	80
IT'S A LONG WAY TO SOMEWHERE ELSE.	82	SENSIBILITY! LA	38
I'M SOMEWHERE ELSE, --	82	SENSIBILITY! LA	48
I HAVE BEEN SOMEWHERE ELSE; I REMEMBER THE SEA-FACED UNCLES.	88	PRAISE TO END!	93
SOMEWHERE, AMONG THE FERNS AND BIRDS,	103	OLD LADY'S WRDS	12
SON			
THAT FORCE THE SON OF MAN TO TOIL;	18	LONG LIVE WEEDS	4
O HE WAS FORTUNE'S CHILD, A FAVORITE SON	28	THE FAVORITE	9
THE SON OF MISFORTUNE LONG, LONG HAS BEEN WAITING	29	THE GENTLE	5
THE LOST SON	53	THE LOST SON	T
A SON HAS MANY FATHERS.	98	O, THOU OPENING	33
I AM MY FATHER'S SON, I AM JOHN DONNE	140	THE SWAN	13
HE WAS THE YOUNGEST SON OF A STRANGE BROOD,	224	OTTO	1
I'M SON AND FATHER OF MY ONLY DEATH.	244	INFIRMITY	18
MY SOUL IS STILL MY SOUL, AND STILL THE SON,	244	INFIRMITY	29
FATHER AND SON OF THIS DEATH,	263	FOLLIES OF ADAM	22
SONG			
WHAT A SMALL SONG. WHAT SLOW CLOUDS. WHAT DARK WATER.	56	THE LOST SON	83
A TONGUE WITHOUT SONG	89	UNFOLD! UNFOLD!	12
A LIGHT SONG COMES FROM THE LEAVES.	90	UNFOLD! UNFOLD!	48
THE HEDGEWREN'S SONG SAYS SOMETHING ELSE.	92	I CRY, LOVE!	15
SHOULD A SONG BREAK A SLEEP?	99	O, THOU OPENING	74
HER SONG TREMBLING THE TWIGS AND SMALL BRANCHES.	102	ELEGY FOR JANE	6
THE WHILE MY BLOOD LEAPED WITH A WORDLESS SONG.	105	SIR JOHN DAVIES	14
SONG FOR THE SQUEEZE-BOX	111	SQUEEZE-BOX	T
AND MADE MY SONG THEIR OWN.	123	WORDS FOR WIND	16
SAYS A SONG TIED TO A TREE.	125	WORDS FOR WIND	71
WHOSE THIN SONG HUNG IN AIR,	128	THE VOICE	9
THEIR SLOW SONG SANG IN ME;	128	THE VOICE	22
SHE MAKES SPACE LONELY WITH A LOVELY SONG.	129	SHE	4
BUT MY LEAST MOTION CHANGED INTO A SONG,	132	SENTENTIOUS MAN	23
THE SONG	146	THE SONG	T
ANOTHER JOIN MY SONG	146	THE SONG	25
AND THAT SLOW HUMMING RISES INTO SONG.	155	THE DYING MAN	75
TWO SONG SPARROWS, ONE WITHIN A GREENHOUSE,	158	FIRST MEDITATN	39
WHAT LOVER KEEPS HIS SONG?	167	HER BECOMING	82
BUT THERE IS NO SONG.	168	FOURTH MEDITATN	26
A THIN HARSH SONG. THE DAY DIES IN A CHILD.	171	WHAT TELL BONES	19
O TO BE DELIVERED FROM THE RATIONAL INTO THE REALM OF PURE SONG,	172	WHAT TELL BONES	54
A WEDGE OF HEAVEN'S LIGHT, AUTUMNAL SONG.	173	WHAT TELL BONES	68
SAID THE WREN, YOUR SONG ISN'T WORTH 10¢.	177	KITTY-CAT BIRD	2
THE MONOTONY SONG	181	MONOTONY SONG	T
THIS IS, YOU SEE, A SILLY SONG	181	MONOTONY SONG	21
A SLIGHT SONG,	194	JOURNY INTERIOR	63
AND THE THRUSH STOPPED IN THE MIDDLE OF HIS SONG.	196	THE LONG WATERS	7
THE BLUEBIRD, LOVER OF HOLES IN OLD WOOD, LILTING ITS LIGHT SONG,	204	THE ROSE	66
SONG	211	SONG (1)	T
SHE SANG A FINAL SONG;	212	LIGHT LISTENED	23
THE CURLEW'S SLOW NIGHT SONG CAME ON THE WATER.	216	THE SHY MAN	9
SONG	236	SONG (2)	T
FROM WHENCE COMETH SONG?--	236	SONG (2)	1
IN PUREST SONG ONE PLAYS THE CONSTANT FOOL	244	INFIRMITY	1
THE PHOEBE'S SLOW RETREATING FROM ITS SONG,	245	THE DECISION	4
I COULD NOT BEAR ITS SONG, THAT ALTERING	248	THE TREE, BIRD	14
SONG	258	SONG (3)	T
THE SAGINAW SONG	267	SAGINAW SONG	T
THIS SUDDEN RANDOM SONG,	271	THE REPLY	15
SONGS			
I TEACH MY SIGHS TO LENGTHEN INTO SONGS,	135	THE RENEWAL	5
THE SONGS TUMBLING OVER AND UNDER THE GLASS,	158	FIRST MEDITATN	44
O THE SONGS WE HIDE, SINGING ONLY TO OURSELVES!	168	FOURTH MEDITATN	13
THE SONGS FROM A SPIRAL TREE.	171	WHAT TELL BONES	27
AN INTIMATE OF AIR AND ALL ITS SONGS?	241	THE SEQUEL	2
O THE SONGS WE HIDE SINGING TO OURSELVES!--	259	SONG (3)	38
SOON			
SOON FIELD AND WOOD WILL WEAR AN APRIL LOOK,	11	LIGHT BRIGHTER	13
AND SOON A BRANCH, PART OF A HIDDEN SCENE,	11	LIGHT BRIGHTER	17
BUT SOON COLD RAIN AND FROST COME IN	14	COMING OF COLD	18

	PAGE	TITLE	LINE
SOON (CONTINUED)			
AND FROST IS MARROW-COLD, AND SOON	15	COMING OF COLD	51
THE RATS SOON WILL BE LEAVING, THE SNOW WILL COME IN."	27	CLAIRVOY WIDOW	16
AND THEY'LL SOON STAY AWAY IN GREAT BUNCHES!"	180	GOO-GIRL	16
I SOON WILL BE MYSELF AGAIN.	256	IN HYDROTHERAPY	12
BUT WHEN I DIE--AND THAT WON'T BE SOON--	268	SAGINAW SONG	47
SOOT			
THAT BLOSSOMED IN SOOT; A BLACK CAT LICKING ITS PAW;	29	THE REMINDER	2
THE FINE SOOT SIFTING THROUGH MY SOUTH WINDOWS.	104	OLD LADY'S WRDS	58
NOT EVEN THE SOOT DANCES.	187	THE LONGING	18
SOOTHE			
SOOTHE ME, GREAT GROANS OF UNDERNEATH,	84	O LULL ME, LULL	29
SOOTY			
AND THE STELLER JAY, RAUCOUS, SOOTY HEADED, LIVES WITH US,	234	ALL MORNING	15
SOREN			
--IN SPITE OF SOREN KIERKEGAARD.	272	DUET	4
SORES			
THE TURTLES HAVE BLOODSUCKER SORES,	267	SAGINAW SONG	9
SORROW			
MOTHER, MOTHER, STIR FROM YOUR CAVE OF SORROW.	64	SHAPE OF FIRE	16
SOUL			
BUT YOU, MY DEAREST, HAVE A SOUL	23	AMOROUS LADY	9
THEY FEED THE SENSE, DENY THE SOUL,	25	VERSE W ALLUSNS	9
THE SOUL RESIDES IN THE HORSE BARN.	59	THE LONG ALLEY	22
THE BODY AND THE SOUL KNOW HOW TO PLAY	106	SIR JOHN DAVIES	47
HE WAS A SERPENT WITH A SOUL;	115	THE SERPENT	7
I'M TIRED OF BROODING ON MY NEIGHBOR'S SOUL;	132	SENTENTIOUS MAN	37
WHAT GLORIES WOULD WE? MOTIONS OF THE SOUL?	135	THE RENEWAL	1
DARK HANGS UPON THE WATERS OF THE SOUL;	135	THE RENEWAL	8
AND THE WHOLE MOTION OF THE SOUL LAY BARE:	135	THE RENEWAL	23
WHAT IS THERE FOR THE SOUL TO UNDERSTAND?	149	IN LATE SUMMER	9
BODY AND SOUL TRANSCEND APPEARANCES	149	IN LATE SUMMER	13
THE SOUL STANDS, LONELY IN ITS CHOICE,	168	FOURTH MEDITATN	20
THE SOUL KNOWS NOT WHAT TO BELIEVE,	171	WHAT TELL BONES	3
EXISTENCE DARES PERPETUATE A SOUL,	173	WHAT TELL BONES	67
LUST FATIGUES THE SOUL.	187	THE LONGING	11
A BODY WITH THE MOTION OF A SOUL.	188	THE LONGING	27
THE SOUL AT A STILL-STAND,	194	JOURNY INTERIOR	54
AND GENTLY THE LIGHT ENTERS THE SLEEPING SOUL,	204	THE ROSE	76
AND WITH IT, MY SOUL,	208	THE APPARITION	7
NOR THE SOUL HAUNTING MY BODY,	209	HER RETICENCE	8
A BURDEN TO THE SOUL.	215	HIS FOREBODING	7
MY SOUL NEARLY MY OWN,	221	THE ABYSS	79
WHAT'S MADNESS BUT NOBILITY OF SOUL	239	IN A DARK TIME	7
MY SOUL, LIKE SOME HEAT-MADDENED SUMMER FLY,	239	IN A DARK TIME	20
THE SOUL HAS MANY MOTIONS, BODY ONE.	243	THE MOTION	1
THE SOUL DELIGHTS IN THAT EXTREMITY.	244	INFIRMITY	16
MY SOUL IS STILL MY SOUL, AND STILL THE SON,	244	INFIRMITY	29
MY SOUL IS STILL MY SOUL, AND STILL THE SON,	244	INFIRMITY	29
ONE LOOK TOO CLOSE CAN TAKE MY SOUL AWAY.	246	THE MARROW	9
MY BODY ALTERS, ALTERING THE SOUL	246	THE MARROW	15
DANCED MY OWN SOUL,	249	THE RESTORED	2
CRIED THE SOUL	249	THE RESTORED	11
GOD BLESS THE ROOTS!--BODY AND SOUL ARE ONE!	250	THE RIGHT THING	7
THE SOUL HAS ITS OWN SHINE AND SHAPE;	259	SONG (3)	48
THE SOUL DIES EVERY NIGHT;	263	FOLLIES OF ADAM	23
SOULS			
OUR SOULS LOOKED FORTH, AND THE GREAT DAY STOOD STILL.	106	SIR JOHN DAVIES	60
MUTILATED SOULS IN COLD MORGUES OF OBLIGATION.	166	HER BECOMING	43
OUR SMALL SOULS HID FROM THEIR SMALL AGONIES,	238	THE TRANCED	21
SOUL'S			
IT'S A SOUL'S CROSSING TIME.	89	UNFOLD! UNFOLD!	8
THE SOUL'S IMMEDIATE JOY.	126	WORDS FOR WIND	91
SHE CRIES OUT LOUD THE SOUL'S OWN SECRET JOY;	129	SHE	9
A DRY SOUL'S WISEST. O, I AM NOT DRY!	140	THE SWAN	5
"MY SOUL'S HUNG OUT TO DRY,	153	THE DYING MAN	3
A GHOST FROM THE SOUL'S HOUSE?	165	HER BECOMING	24
OR KNOWN, ONCE, THE SOUL'S AUTHENTIC HUNGER,	169	FOURTH MEDITATN	47
THINNING THE SOUL'S SUBSTANCE;	171	WHAT TELL BONES	24
THE SOUL'S PRIVILEGE?	211	SONG (1)	6
SAD THE SOUL'S JOY. LOVED HEART, WHAT ELSE CAN I SAY	261	THE CHANGELING	28
SOUND			
BUT MY EAR STILL KEPT THE SOUND OF THE SEA LIKE A SHELL.	12	MID-CNTRY BLOW	8

	PAGE	TITLE	LINE
SOUND (CONTINUED)			
THE SECRET HEART OF SOUND.	17	NO BIRD	2
TUNNELED WITH LAPSING SOUND	50	THE CYCLE	15
REMEMBER AN OLD SOUND.	59	THE LONG ALLEY	8
CRIED FOR SOUND.	62	FIELD OF LIGHT	10
THE WARM COMES WITHOUT SOUND.	64	SHAPE OF FIRE	19
HAS NO SOUND,	65	SHAPE OF FIRE	42
I HEAR THE SOUND OF HANDS.	87	PRAISE TO END!	74
SHE CAME WITHOUT SOUND,	100	THE VISITANT	15
FOR THE THIN SOUND IN THE WINDY CHIMNEY,	103	OLD LADY'S WRDS	30
AND THE SOUND OF PAPER TEARING.	104	OLD LADY'S WRDS	60
WE UNDID CHAOS TO A CURIOUS SOUND:	107	SIR JOHN DAVIES	82
I LIVED WITH OPEN SOUND,	128	THE VOICE	11
ON FEET THAT MAKE NO SOUND	148	THE SMALL	17
THE SOUND OF VOICES, YOUNG VOICES, MIXED WITH SLEIGHBELLS,	161	I'M HERE	4
IN MY LEFT EAR I HEAR THE LOUD SOUND OF A MINOR COLLAPSE.	165	HER BECOMING	29
NOR THE SOUND OF ANOTHER FOOTSTEP--	169	FOURTH MEDITATN	54
COME THE FIRST TIDE-RIPPLES, MOVING, ALMOST WITHOUT SOUND, TOWARD ME,	190	AT OYSTER RIVER	2
NO SOUND FROM THE BAY. NO VIOLENCE.	190	AT OYSTER RIVER	6
WHAT DO THEY TELL US, SOUND AND SILENCE?	204	THE ROSE	58
AND THAT SOUND, THAT SINGLE SOUND,	204	THE ROSE	74
AND THAT SOUND, THAT SINGLE SOUND,	204	THE ROSE	74
A SOUND SO THIN IT COULD NOT WOO A BIRD,	204	THE ROSE	77
GATHERING TO ITSELF SOUND AND SILENCE--	205	THE ROSE	113
TWITCHING, TILTING TOWARD THE LEAST SOUND.	227	MEADOW MOUSE	16
THE STONES RANG WITH LIGHT SOUND;	237	THE TRANCED	14
SOUND, SILENCE SANG AS ONE.	238	THE MOMENT	9
SUCH STRETCHINGS OF THE SPIRIT MAKE NO SOUND.	243	THE MOTION	4
NOR COULD I PUT THAT SOUND OUT OF MY MIND,	245	THE DECISION	5
THE SLEEPY SOUND OF LEAVES IN A LIGHT WIND.	245	THE DECISION	6
BEARING ITS LIFE AND MORE, A DOUBLE SOUND,	248	THE TREE, BIRD	11
SOUNDS			
THE SEVERAL SOUNDS WERE LOW;	87	PRAISE TO END!	67
I THINK OF AMERICAN SOUNDS IN THIS SILENCE:	204	THE ROSE	59
SOUP			
I'M TRUE TO SOUP, AND HAPPY TO ASK:	99	O, THOU OPENING	55
SOUPS			
THE MERE MENTION OF SOUPS	180	GOO-GIRL	14
SOURCE			
A RIVER'S LEAPING SOURCE	18	GENESIS	3
FAR FROM THE COLDER SOURCE	50	THE CYCLE	9
UNDER A RIVER'S SOURCE,	50	THE CYCLE	17
SOURCES			
MY SOURCES DRAINED OF ALL CONTENT,	19	AGNST DISASTER	3
SOURED			
SLOWLY HIS MATCHLESS DISPOSITION SOURED	28	THE FAVORITE	12
SOUTH			
ON THE ROCKS SOUTH OF QUIET, IN THE CLOSE REGIONS OF KISSING,	86	PRAISE TO END!	20
THE FINE SOOT SIFTING THROUGH MY SOUTH WINDOWS.	104	OLD LADY'S WRDS	58
THE GARDEN IS A RIVER FLOWING SOUTH.	129	SHE	8
THE WIND SHIFTING SOUTH.	236	SONG (2)	12
SOUTHERN			
UNDER A SOUTHERN WIND,	125	WORDS FOR WIND	61
SOVEREIGN			
IN THE LILY'S SOVEREIGN RIGHT?	98	O, THOU OPENING	43
WAS I THE SERVANT OF A SOVEREIGN WISH,	105	SIR JOHN DAVIES	29
SPACE			
THE FEUD WE KEPT WITH SPACE COMES TO AN END.	13	PRAISE PRAIRIE	12
DID SPACE SHAKE OFF AN ANGEL WITH A SIGH?	107	SIR JOHN DAVIES	69
SHE MAKES SPACE LONELY WITH A LOVELY SONG.	129	SHE	4
SPACE STRUGGLED WITH TIME;	238	THE MOMENT	6
GOD'S NIGHT AND DAY: DOWN THIS SPACE HE HAS SMILED,	243	THE MOTION	21
SPANIEL			
TO GAZE AT A FACE WITH THE FIXED EYES OF A SPANIEL?	169	FOURTH MEDITATN	34
SPANNED			
THRICE HAPPY THEY WHOSE WORLD IS SPANNED	25	VERSE W ALLUSNS	1
SPARE			
I KEEP THE SPIRIT SPARE.	3	OPEN HOUSE	12
SPARROW			
IN THE SPARROW, HAPPY ON GRAVEL;	88	PRAISE TO END!	91
MY SPARROW, YOU ARE NOT HERE,	102	ELEGY FOR JANE	14

	PAGE	TITLE	LINE
SPARROWS			
TWO SONG SPARROWS, ONE WITHIN A GREENHOUSE,	158	FIRST MEDITATN	39
OUTSIDE, THE SAME SPARROWS BICKER IN THE EAVES.	161	I'M HERE	6
WITH WRENS, SPARROWS, JUNCOS, CEDAR WAXWINGS, FLICKERS,	235	ALL MORNING	41
DEAR SPARROWS OF THIS ALLEY,	261	THE CHANGELING	37
HE DOES WHAT DOVES AND SPARROWS DO--	264	THREE EPIGRAMS	15
SPAYED			
WHEN OUR SPAYED FEMALE CAT YAWNS AND STRETCHES OUT IN THE SUNSHINE--	234	ALL MORNING	23
SPEAK			
THE DEED WILL SPEAK THE TRUTH	3	OPEN HOUSE	14
A FIVE-FOOT DROP A VALLEY, SO TO SPEAK.	13	PRAISE PRAIRIE	2
SPEAK AND ABIDE.	62	FIELD OF LIGHT	21
SPEAK TO ME, FROSTY BEARD.	86	PRAISE TO END!	29
THE DEAD SPEAK NOISE.	89	UNFOLD! UNFOLD!	9
SPEAK TO THE STONES, AND THE STARS ANSWER.	90	UNFOLD! UNFOLD!	54
OVER THIS DAMP GRAVE I SPEAK THE WORDS OF MY LOVE:	102	ELEGY FOR JANE	20
OF HER CHOICE VIRTUES ONLY GODS SHOULD SPEAK,	127	I KNEW A WOMAN	5
DARE I SPEAK, ONCE MORE, IN THE MONOTONY OF GREAT PRAISE,	166	HER BECOMING	32
EVEN THE STONES SPEAK.	170	FOURTH MEDITATN	88
AND I HEAR THE LICHEN SPEAK,	194	JOURNY INTERIOR	48
THINGS SPEAK TO ME, I SWEAR;	262	FOLLIES OF ADAM	5
SPEAK IT FROM THE FACE OUT CLEARLY:	266	FOR STEVENS	13
SPEAKING			
IS MY BODY SPEAKING? I BREATHE WHAT I AM:	170	FOURTH MEDITATN	85
SPEAKS			
THE SHADE SPEAKS SLOWLY:	222	THE ABYSS	85
SPECIAL			
MY SPECIAL HEAVEN IS REVERSED,	19	AGNST DISASTER	7
THE SILVER FISH RAN IN AND OUT OF MY SPECIAL BINDINGS;	65	SHAPE OF FIRE	35
SHELVES HAVE A SPECIAL USE;	213	THE HAPPY THREE	9
SPECTER			
AND ROUT THE SPECTER OF ALARM.	19	AGNST DISASTER	12
SPEECH			
EVEN THREAD HAD A SPEECH.	90	UNFOLD! UNFOLD!	33
SPEECH REVIVED, A GHOSTLY GOING OF TAME BEARS, A BRIGHT MOON ON GLEAMING	98	O, THOU OPENING	23
SHE KNOWS THE SPEECH OF LIGHT, AND MAKES IT PLAIN	129	SHE	11
SPEECH PASSED BETWEEN SMALL BIRDS;	167	HER BECOMING	65
THE BAREST SPEECH OF LIGHT AMONG THE STONES.	173	WHAT TELL BONES	71
WHAT SPEECH ABIDES?	220	THE ABYSS	25
FROM A BURNT PINE THE SHARP SPEECH OF A CROW	246	THE MARROW	3
MY SPEECH MUST BE:	260	THE CHANGELING	25
SPEECHES			
UNMINDFUL OF TERROR AND HEADLINES, OF SPEECHES AND GUNS.	33	IDYLL	12
SPEED			
THEY ARE THE PRISONERS OF SPEED	33	HIGHWAY: MICH	14
SPELL			
THERE WAS A BODY, AND IT CAST A SPELL,--	106	SIR JOHN DAVIES	61
SPENT			
THE DOUGH I SPENT ON CHIPPEWA KATE,	112	SQUEEZE-BOX	39
SPIDER			
THE GARDEN SPIDER WEAVES A SILKEN PEAR	12	SLOW SEASON	5
APPEAR IN THE FORM OF A SPIDER	54	THE LOST SON	22
A RAIN-DRENCHED FLY OR SPIDER.	151	SLUG	24
A SPIDER EASES HIMSELF DOWN FROM A SWAYING LIGHT-BULB,	231	THE STORM	34
MAYBE IT'S WHITMAN'S SPIDER, I CAN'T TELL,	273	SUPPR W LINDSAY	28
SPIDERS			
WATER RECEDES TO THE CRYING OF SPIDERS.	64	SHAPE OF FIRE	4
THE SPIDERS SAIL INTO SUMMER.	78	BRING THE DAY!	43
THE DARKNESS OF FALLING HAIR, THE WARNINGS FROM LINT AND SPIDERS,	159	FIRST MEDITATN	80
NUDGING AND TICKLING OF ANTS AND SPIDERS,	255	LIGHT POEM	2
SPIDER'S			
"THE SPIDER'S GONE," HE SAID BEMUSEDLY.	274	SUPPR W LINDSAY	39
SPIDERY			
WHEN HE SAID THAT, A SPIDERY SHAPE DROPPED DOWN	273	SUPPR W LINDSAY	24
SPIEL			
THE SPIEL RAN ON; THE SALE WAS BRIEF AND BRISK;	21	THE AUCTION	9
SPIES			
HAVE SCALED YOUR WALLS, AND SPIES BETRAY	4	FEUD	15
SPIKEY			
THE SPIKEY PURPLE BUSHES IN THE WINDING DRY CREEK BED--	194	JOURNY INTERIOR	37

	PAGE	TITLE	LINE
SPILES			
THE ICE PILING HIGH AGAINST THE IRON-BOUND SPILES,	191	AT OYSTER RIVER	50
AS THE PILED ICE BREAKS AWAY FROM THE BATTERED SPILES,	191	AT OYSTER RIVER	55
SPILLAGE			
INTO THE SMALL SPILLAGE OF DRIFTWOOD,	202	THE ROSE	24
SPILLED			
AND THEN IT SPILLED:	273	SUPPR W LINDSAY	11
THE SUDDEN LIGHT SPILLED ON THE FLOOR LIKE CREAM	273	SUPPR W LINDSAY	12
SPILLS			
NEVER SPILLS.	80	GIVE WAY, GATES	54
SPINAL			
REVOLVING ON HIS SPINAL COLUMN.	24	BEFORE STUDY	8
SPINDLY			
I REMEMBER HOW THEY PICKED ME UP, A SPINDLY KID,	44	FRAU BAUMAN	26
SPINE			
A RAW GHOST DRINKS THE FLUID IN MY SPINE;	135	THE RENEWAL	14
I TURNED UPON MY SPINE,	147	THE EXORCISM	19
SPINES			
CREAKING THEIR THIN SPINES,	42	TRANSPLANTING	16
SPINNING			
SPINNING THROUGH THE LORDLY CLOUD.	266	FOR STEVENS	4
SPINY			
WAITING LIKE A FERN, MAKING A SPINY SHADOW.	102	ELEGY FOR JANE	15
SPIRAL			
O WORM OF DUTY! O SPIRAL KNOWLEDGE!	48	LAST WORDS	6
THE SONGS FROM A SPIRAL TREE.	171	WHAT TELL BONES	27
SPIRIT			
I KEEP THE SPIRIT SPARE.	3	OPEN HOUSE	12
IS SELDOM WON. THE SPIRIT STARVES	4	FEUD	19
CHILL DEPTHS OF THE SPIRIT ARE FLUSHED TO A FEVER,	5	PROGNOSIS	15
THAT KEEP THE SPIRIT UNDEFILED.	18	LONG LIVE WEEDS	8
THE PIECES OF MY SPIRIT STREWN.	19	AGNST DISASTER	4
THE SPIRIT CRYING IN A CAGE	22	SILENCE	11
WANTS SINGLENESS OF SPIRIT ABOVE ALL ELSE:	24	POETASTER	2
A LIVELY UNDERSTANDABLE SPIRIT	58	THE LOST SON	169
SPIRIT, COME NEAR. THIS IS ONLY THE EDGE OF WHITENESS.	64	SHAPE OF FIRE	12
SPOKE TO MY SPIRIT.	81	SENSIBILITY! LA	11
BY SNAILS, BY LEAPS OF FROG, I CAME HERE, SPIRIT.	89	UNFOLD! UNFOLD!	1
DELIGHT ME OTHERLY, WHITE SPIRIT,--	92	I CRY, LOVE!	5
HELLO, THINGY SPIRIT.	92	I CRY, LOVE!	21
THE SPIRIT MOVES,	101	LIGHT BREATHER	1
THE SPIRIT	104	OLD LADY'S WRDS	64
THE SPIRIT AND THE FLESH CRIED OUT FOR MORE.	106	SIR JOHN DAVIES	52
THE FLESH CAN MAKE THE SPIRIT VISIBLE;	106	SIR JOHN DAVIES	63
WHO RISE FROM FLESH TO SPIRIT KNOW THE FALL:	107	SIR JOHN DAVIES	95
BODY AND SPIRIT KNOW	126	WORDS FOR WIND	95
SPIRIT AND NATURE BEAT IN ONE BREAST-BONE--	131	SENTENTIOUS MAN	1
THE SPIRIT KNOWS THE FLESH IT MUST CONSUME.	131	SENTENTIOUS MAN	10
LIGHT OF MY SPIRIT, LIGHT	137	LOVE'S PROGRESS	14
A SPIRIT RAGING AT THE VISIBLE.	155	THE DYING MAN	50
THE SPIRIT MOVES, BUT NOT ALWAYS UPWARD,	157	FIRST MEDITATN	8
SO THE SPIRIT TRIES FOR ANOTHER LIFE,	159	FIRST MEDITATN	66
SO, I SUPPOSE, THE SPIRIT JOURNEYS.	159	FIRST MEDITATN	73
WARD OF MY SPIRIT,	161	I'M HERE	20
A SPIRIT PLAYS BEFORE ME LIKE A CHILD,	165	HER BECOMING	22
THE SPIRIT SAYS, YOU ARE NOTHING.	172	WHAT TELL BONES	43
THE SPIRIT DECLARES ITSELF TO THESE ROCKS.	172	WHAT TELL BONES	46
MY SPIRIT RISES WITH THE RISING WIND;	173	WHAT TELL BONES	88
AS IF RELEASED BY A SPIRIT,	173	WHAT TELL BONES	98
(DREAMS DRAIN THE SPIRIT IF WE DREAM TOO LONG.)	187	THE LONGING	13
AND THE SPIRIT FAILS TO MOVE FORWARD,	187	THE LONGING	19
THE FLESH TAKES ON THE PURE POISE OF THE SPIRIT,	191	AT OYSTER RIVER	38
AND THE SPIRIT RUNS, INTERMITTENTLY,	192	AT OYSTER RIVER	64
THE SPIRIT OF WRATH BECOMES THE SPIRIT OF BLESSING,	195	JOURNY INTERIOR	78
THE SPIRIT OF WRATH BECOMES THE SPIRIT OF BLESSING,	195	JOURNY INTERIOR	78
HIS SPIRIT MOVES LIKE MONUMENTAL WIND	201	THE FAR FIELD	91
WHAT CAN THE SPIRIT BELIEVE?--	207	THE YOUNG GIRL	1
BETWEEN THE SPIRIT AND THE FLESH,--WHAT WAR?	223	ELEGY (2)	5
SUCH STRETCHINGS OF THE SPIRIT MAKE NO SOUND.	243	THE MOTION	4
HOW BODY FROM SPIRIT SLOWLY DOES UNWIND	244	INFIRMITY	35
UNTIL WE ARE PURE SPIRIT AT THE END.	244	INFIRMITY	36
GROWS SICK IN FLESH AND SPIRIT BOTH.	257	SANITARIUM	10

	PAGE	TITLE	LINE
SPIRITS			
MY SPIRITS ROSE EACH TIME THE HAMMER FELL,	21	THE AUCTION	13
SPIRIT'S			
THE SPIRIT'S TENDER COVER.	7	ORDERS FOR DAY	7
BY LISTENING TO THE SPIRIT'S SMALLEST CRY;	131	SENTENTIOUS MAN	15
SPIRITUAL			
DIFFUSE THE OUTPOURINGS OF THE SPIRITUAL COWARD,	5	PROGNOSIS	1
SPIT			
OR DROWN A BUG IN ONE SPIT OF TOBACCO JUICE,	42	OLD FLORIST	8
WHEN YOU PLANT, SPIT IN THE POT.	76	I NEED, I NEED	53
OF SLIME AND SHINING SPIT.	270	GOB MUSIC	33
I'LL SPIT OVER MY CHIN AND BEYOND THE CURB,	272	DUET	7
SPITE			
--IN SPITE OF SOREN KIERKEGAARD.	272	DUET	4
SPITTING			
THE MINNOWS LOVE ME, AND THE HUMPED AND SPITTING CREATURES.	88	PRAISE TO END!	89
GRINDING UP AND OVER THE NARROW ROAD, SPITTING AND ROARING.	193	JOURNY INTERIOR	22
SPITTLE			
OR. POISONED, DRAGGING A WHITE SKEIN OF SPITTLE OVER A PATH--	151	SLUG	21
SPITTOON			
IN THE DARK OF AN OULD SPITTOON;	269	GOB MUSIC	21
SPLENDID			
ILLUSION'S TRINKETS, SPLENDID FOR THE YOUNG;	21	THE AUCTION	6
SPLINTERS			
MY FEET CRACKLING SPLINTERS OF GLASS AND DRIED PUTTY,	43	CHILD ON GRNHSE	2
SPLIT			
THAT PRACTICALLY SPLIT THE TOP OF HIS THROAT.	115	THE SERPENT	22
AS IF REALITY HAD SPLIT APART	135	THE RENEWAL	22
SPLITTING			
THE DRY BLOOM SPLITTING IN THE WRINKLED VALE,	197	THE LONG WATERS	30
SPOIL			
TO SPOIL COLLECTIVE LIFE.	31	LULL	6
SPOILED			
AND THE HONEYMOON BE SPOILED BY A FATHER'S GHOST,	5	PROGNOSIS	14
SPOKE			
SPOKE TO MY SPIRIT.	81	SENSIBILITY! LA	11
THE DUST ROSE AND SPOKE;	147	THE EXORCISM	6
WHO SPOKE FIRST IN THE COARSE SHORT-HAND OF THE SUBLIMINAL DEPTHS,	170	FOURTH MEDITATN	71
SPOKEN			
I HAVE BEEN SPOKEN TO VARIOUSLY	220	THE ABYSS	17
SPONGY			
OF GREEN, OR PLUNGED TO MY ELBOWS IN THE SPONGY YELLOWISH MOSS OF THE MARSHES:	40	MOSS-GATHERING	8
RUNNING LIGHTLY OVER SPONGY GROUND,	54	THE LOST SON	34
SPOON			
HOO. I KNOW THE SPOON.	74	I NEED, I NEED	3
AND THEN WITHOUT EVEN A SPOON,	179	MYRTLE'S COUSIN	8
SPORT			
HE CARED SO MUCH FOR THE SPORT,	263	FOLLIES OF ADAM	31
SPORTIVE			
A SPORTIVE, AIMLESS ONE,	145	THE BEAST	7
SPOT			
I AM TOO CENTERED ON THIS SPOT.	24	BEFORE STUDY	2
SPOTS			
HAD THE RED-HOT SPOTS WHERE YOU FEEL A	111	SQUEEZE-BOX	20
SPOUT			
WHEN HE TRIED TO SPOUT, THAT GREAT BIG LUBBER,	178	THE WHALE	3
SPRATLING'S			
KEEPER OF HAY. THAT'S A SPRATLING'S PRATTLE. AND DON'T BE THINKING YOU'RE	98	O, THOU OPENING	28
SPRAWL			
THE SPRAWL OF THE WAVE,	200	THE FAR FIELD	54
SPRAY			
FLAILING HER SIDES WITH SPRAY,	41	BIG WIND	28
OR MAKE THE DUST BUZZ WITH A LIGHT SPRAY,	42	OLD FLORIST	7
ITS SPRAY HOLDING A DOUBLE RAIN-BOW IN EARLY MORNING,	191	AT OYSTER RIVER	45
SPRAY, AND THE SMALL SHAPES	210	HER TIME	17
RIDDLING THE SAND, LIKE A WIDE SPRAY OF BUCKSHOT,	230	THE STORM	14
SPREAD			
AND YOUNG SHOOTS SPREAD UPON OUR INNER WORLD.	11	LIGHT BRIGHTER	20
A FIELD OF BARLEY SPREAD BENEATH THE SUN.	13	PRAISE PRAIRIE	4

	PAGE	TITLE	LINE
SPREAD (CONTINUED)			
WHITISH AND SPREAD WIDE WHEN HE TRIED TO STRUGGLE AWAY,	227	MEADOW MOUSE	10
SPRING			
THE WOODS IN SPRING THE LEAVES THE SCENTED LANES	5	TO MY SISTER	2
THE SHOOTS OF SPRING HAVE MELLOWED WITH THE YEAR.	12	SLOW SEASON	13
I REJOICE IN THE SPRING, AS THOUGH NO SPRING EVER HAD BEEN.	24	VERNAL SENTIMNT	8
I REJOICE IN THE SPRING, AS THOUGH NO SPRING EVER HAD BEEN.	24	VERNAL SENTIMNT	8
AND THE FIRST DUST OF SPRING LISTING OVER BACKLOTS,--	92	I CRY, LOVE!	27
OR THE TITTEBAWASEE, IN THE TIME BETWEEN WINTER AND SPRING,	191	AT OYSTER RIVER	47
IT IS NEITHER SPRING NOR SUMMER: IT IS ALWAYS,	235	ALL MORNING	39
SPRINGING			
THE GREEN, THE SPRINGING GREEN	124	WORDS FOR WIND	55
SPRINGING, ONE TO ANOTHER,	152	THE SISKINS	13
SPRINGTIME			
IN THE SPRINGTIME OF STONES,	80	GIVE WAY, GATES	34
SPRINKLED			
THEY SPRINKLED AND SHOOK;	44	FRAU BAUMAN	15
SPROUTS			
WHEN SPROUTS BREAK OUT,	37	CUTTINGS (LATE)	9
SPRUCE			
THE BLUE SPRUCE LASHED LIKE A SURF AT THE DOOR.	12	MID-CNTRY BLOW	4
SQUASH			
PROBING THE SQUASH,	223	ELEGY (2)	21
SQUASHY			
THE SEA WILL BE THERE, THE GREAT SQUASHY SHADOWS,	79	GIVE WAY, GATES	28
SQUAWKING			
A FURY OF JAYS, DIVING AND SQUAWKING,	234	ALL MORNING	22
SQUEAK			
YOU SQUEAK LIKE A MOUSE THAT'S LOST IN THE HAY,	177	KITTY-CAT BIRD	10
SQUEAKS			
AT TIMES MY DARLING SQUEAKS IN PURE PLATO.	133	THE PURE FURY	14
HE PIPES, HE SQUEAKS, HE QUIVERS THROUGH HIS NOSE,--	264	THREE EPIGRAMS	5
SQUEEZE			
BUT BARLEY-BREAK AND SQUEEZE.	60	THE LONG ALLEY	38
SQUEEZE-BOX			
SONG FOR THE SQUEEZE-BOX	111	SQUEEZE-BOX	T
SQUIRMERS			
SQUIRMERS IN BOGS,	50	THE MINIMAL	5
SQUIRMING			
THE PSYCHE WRITHING AND SQUIRMING IN HEAVY WOOLEN,--	48	LAST WORDS	5
SQUIRRELS			
SCUTTLING DOWN AND AROUND LIKE YOUNG SQUIRRELS,	152	THE SISKINS	17
ST			
AND EAST ST. LOUIS AND MONONGAHELA	111	SQUEEZE-BOX	19
STABLE			
A STABLE AND PADDOCK, SOME FOX-HUNTING LAND,	32	SALE	6
IT WAS DEAD MAN'S CORNER, IT WAS KELLY'S STABLE;	112	SQUEEZE-BOX	34
STACKED-UP			
AND YET STILL VIOLENT MEN, WHOSE STACKED-UP GUNS	224	OTTO	27
STAG'S			
A MOON LOOSENED FROM A STAG'S EYE,	79	GIVE WAY, GATES	10
STAID			
THE PENSIVE GNU, THE STAID AARDVARK,	23	AMOROUS LADY	1
STAIR			
STOOD POISED ON THE STAIR,	56	THE LOST SON	90
THE LOWLY WORM CLIMBS UP A WINDING STAIR;	108	THE WAKING (2)	11
IS THE STAIR HERE?	219	THE ABYSS	1
WHERE'S THE STAIR?	219	THE ABYSS	2
A STEP DOWN THE STAIR."	219	THE ABYSS	8
STAIRS			
WHO RAN UP AND DOWN THE BIG CENTER STAIRS	32	SALE	2
STAIR'S			
"THE STAIR'S RIGHT THERE,	219	THE ABYSS	3
STALE			
THE CARRIAGES REEKING WITH VARNISH AND STALE PERFUME.	22	ROAD TO WDLAWN	4
THE UNEMPLOYED AND TELLING STALE UNEMPLOYMENT JOKES.	28	CLAIRVOY WIDOW	22
PUMPING THE STALE MIXTURE	41	BIG WIND	8
WITH MOTHERS, SLEEP-HEAVY CHILDREN, STALE PERFUME, PAST THE MANAGER'S SMILE	47	DOUBLE FEATURE	3
ON THE FADED CARPET, THE STALE	228	THE GERANIUM	12
STALK			
THE STALK STILL SWAYS.	56	THE LOST SON	115
THE OLD STALK STILL HAS A PULSE;	99	O, THOU OPENING	52

	PAGE	TITLE	LINE
STALK (CONTINUED)			
THE LAST-ABANDONED STALK ALWAYS QUIVERING	152	THE SISKINS	14
TO THIS EXTENT I'M A STALK.	188	THE LONGING	35
A DRIED STALK IN A WELTER OF SINUOUS GRASSES,	255	LIGHT POEM	8
TO THIS EXTENT I'M A STALK.	261	THE CHANGELING	38
STALKING			
AND, STALKING LIKE A CRANE,	7	ORDERS FOR DAY	13
STALKS			
THE STALKS ASK SOMETHING ELSE.	91	UNFOLD! UNFOLD!	62
STALLS			
WHERE THE CAR STALLS,	199	THE FAR FIELD	10
STAMPING			
TAMPING AND STAMPING DIRT INTO POTS,--	42	OLD FLORIST	3
STAND			
AND EARN THE RIGHT TO STAND OR SIT,	18	LONG LIVE WEEDS	10
THE SUMMER HOUSE SHAPED LIKE A VILLAGE BAND STAND	32	SALE	7
OR STAND ALL NIGHT WATERING ROSES, HIS FEET BLUE IN RUBBER BOOTS.	42	OLD FLORIST	10
I DAWDLE WITH GROUPS NEAR THE RICKETY POP-CORN STAND;	47	DOUBLE FEATURE	5
WHEN I STAND, I'M ALMOST A TREE.	78	BRING THE DAY!	32
STAND BY A SLOW STREAM:	98	O, THOU OPENING	34
IT WAS STAND ON YOUR FEET AS LONG AS YOU'RE ABLE,	112	SQUEEZE-BOX	35
I STAND WITH STANDING STONES.	121	ALL EARTH, AIR	1
SHE TAUGHT ME TURN, AND COUNTER-TURN, AND STAND;	127	I KNEW A WOMAN	9
FOR A MOMENT THEY STAND ABOVE ME,	158	FIRST MEDITATN	56
OR WHEN WE STAND AT THE EDGE OF A THICKET,	162	I'M HERE	54
THE STAND AT THE STRETCH IN THE FACE OF DEATH,	194	JOURNY INTERIOR	66
I'D STAND UPON MY BED, A SLEEPLESS CHILD	225	OTTO	40
I STAND BY A LOW FIRE	240	IN EVEING AIR	19
STANDARD			
GLAZING THE PALE HAIR, THE DUPLICATE GREY STANDARD FACES.	46	DOLOR	13
STANDING			
I WAS PRIVY TO OILY FUNGUS AND THE ALGAE OF STANDING WATER;	89	UNFOLD! UNFOLD!	25
I STAND WITH STANDING STONES.	121	ALL EARTH, AIR	1
STANDING, SILENT, ON SANDY BEACHES OR WALKING ALONG GREEN EMBANKMENTS;	168	FOURTH MEDITATN	4
AND MY FATHER STANDING ASTRIDE THE CEMENT BENCHES,	203	THE ROSE	53
STANDS			
THE HERON STANDS IN WATER WHERE THE SWAMP	15	THE HERON	1
NOW EACH MAN STANDS APART.	31	LULL	7
WHO STANDS IN A HOLE	80	GIVE WAY, GATES	53
THE SOUL STANDS, LONELY IN ITS CHOICE,	168	FOURTH MEDITATN	20
STAR			
FLOATS A SINGLE STAR.	122	ALL EARTH, AIR	23
AND THE INCIPIENT STAR--	125	WORDS FOR WIND	87
I LOOK AT THE FIRST STAR:	148	THE SMALL	4
MY FACE ON FIRE, CLOSE TO THE POINTS OF A STAR,	172	WHAT TELL BONES	55
THE SELF PERSISTS LIKE A DYING STAR,	190	AT OYSTER RIVER	24
THE STAR WINKING BEYOND ITSELF,	196	THE LONG WATERS	26
I SANG TO THE ONE STAR THAT LOOKED DOWN AT ME;	216	THE SHY MAN	2
STARE			
I STARE INTO THE NIGHT	34	NIGHT JOURNEY	4
TO STARE INTO THE AFTER-LIGHT, THE GLITTER LEFT ON THE LAKE'S SURFACE,	67	SHAPE OF FIRE	88
EACH SINGLE SUBSTANCE GLIDDERED TO THE STARE;	143	SHIMMER OF EVIL	3
AND YOUR FRIENDS,--HOW THEY STARE!	180	GOO-GIRL	13
MY EYES STARE AT THE BOTTOM OF A RIVER,	201	THE FAR FIELD	73
I STARE AND STARE INTO A DEEPENING POOL	244	INFIRMITY	3
I STARE AND STARE INTO A DEEPENING POOL	244	INFIRMITY	3
I GET A STOOL AND SIT AND STARE	269	GOB MUSIC	12
STARED			
ALONE, IN A SLEEP-DAZE, I STARED AT BILLBOARDS;	89	UNFOLD! UNFOLD!	24
I STARED, AND A GARDEN STONE	123	WORDS FOR WIND	23
IT LOOKED AT ME; IT STARED.	145	THE BEAST	10
I STARED AT A FISSURE OF GROUND	146	THE SONG	14
STARED, AND BEGAN TO SING.	146	THE SONG	17
WAS IT THE STONES I HEARD? I STARED AT THE FIXED STARS.	166	HER BECOMING	54
I STARED INTO THE DENTED HOLE	269	GOB MUSIC	24
I STARED AND STARED, AND WHAT DO YOU THINK?	269	GOB MUSIC	30
I STARED AND STARED, AND WHAT DO YOU THINK?	269	GOB MUSIC	30
STARER			
AN EYELESS STARER.	187	THE LONGING	23

	PAGE	TITLE	LINE
STARES			
STILL STARES THE WISH TO LOVE.	31	LULL	21
A CHILD STARES PAST A FIRE	130	THE OTHER	19
STARING			
EYES, STARING PAST ANOTHER	7	ORDERS FOR DAY	15
REPULSE THE STARING EYE,	20	REPL TO CENSURE	1
THE HALF-GROWN CHRYSANTHEMUMS STARING UP LIKE ACCUSERS,	43	CHILD ON GRNHSE	3
THEIR EYES, RICH AS PLUMS, STARING FROM NEWSPRINT,--	48	JUDGE NOT	3
STARING AT A TREE, I FELT THE PULSE OF A STONE.	101	THE VISITANT	22
A MADMAN STARING AT PERPETUAL NIGHT,	155	THE DYING MAN	49
WITHOUT STARING LIKE A LOUT, OR A MOPING ADOLESCENT;	163	I'M HERE	80
HIS RIGHT EYE STARING STRAIGHT AT ME,	226	THE LIZARD	6
ME STARING PAST MY FOOT,	262	FOLLIES OF ADAM	17
STARS			
O MY SISTER REMEMBER THE STARS THE TEARS THE TRAINS	5	TO MY SISTER	1
WHEEL OF THE STARS, THE GREAT BEAR GLITTERING COLDER THAN SNOW,	47	DOUBLE FEATURE	11
SPEAK TO THE STONES, AND THE STARS ANSWER.	90	UNFOLD! UNFOLD!	54
THE SHARP STARS SWING AROUND;	125	WORDS FOR WIND	64
WAS IT THE STONES I HEARD? I STARED AT THE FIXED STARS.	166	HER BECOMING	54
START			
BEGINNINGS START WITHOUT SHADE,	93	I CRY, LOVE!	33
I START TO LEAVE MYSELF.	121	ALL EARTH, AIR	15
THAT START FROM MY OWN FEET.	138	THE SURLY ONE	8
WE START FROM THE DARK. PAIN TEACHES US LITTLE.	166	HER BECOMING	35
STARTLED			
AND HOW, ONCE STARTLED INTO TALK, THE LIGHT SYLLABLES LEAPED FOR HER,	102	ELEGY FOR JANE	3
STARTS			
A SINGLE RIPPLE STARTS FROM WHERE HE STOOD.	15	THE HERON	12
A SINGLE WAVE STARTS LIGHTLY AND EASILY SHOREWARD,	93	I CRY, LOVE!	46
HE STARTS TO YAWN--IT TAKES ALL DAY--	182	THE HIPPO	4
STARVELING			
I, STARVELING YEARNER, SEEM TO SEE	25	VERSE W ALLUSNS	11
STARVES			
IS SELDOM WON. THE SPIRIT STARVES	4	FEUD	19
NECESSITY STARVES ON THE STOOP OF INVENTION.	29	THE GENTLE	11
STARVING			
I IMAGINED THE UNBORN, STARVING IN WOMBS, CURLING;	48	JUDGE NOT	5
STAY			
I STAY UP HALF THE NIGHT	34	NIGHT JOURNEY	26
STAY CLOSE. MUST I KILL SOMETHING ELSE?	60	THE LONG ALLEY	31
STAY IN THE SUN,	75	I NEED, I NEED	45
A SHAPE COMES TO STAY:	81	SENSIBILITY! LA	21
MY DEAREST DUST, I CAN'T STAY HERE.	86	PRAISE TO END!	44
AND SMALL MOUTHS, STAY YOUR AIMLESS CHEEPING:	92	I CRY, LOVE!	23
--ONLY STAY OUT OF THE WIND.	97	O, THOU OPENING	12
STAY. STAY BY THE SLIP-OOZE. STAY.	100	THE VISITANT	4
STAY. STAY BY THE SLIP-OOZE. STAY.	100	THE VISITANT	4
STAY. STAY BY THE SLIP-OOZE. STAY.	100	THE VISITANT	4
I'M REMINDED TO STAY ALIVE	104	OLD LADY'S WRDS	56
THE STONES STAY WHERE THEY ARE.	121	ALL EARTH, AIR	2
I STAY ALIVE, BOTH IN AND OUT OF TIME,	131	SENTENTIOUS MAN	14
I LIVE NEAR THE ABYSS. I HOPE TO STAY	134	THE PURE FURY	26
MUST I STAY TANGLED IN THAT LIVELY HAIR?	140	THE SWAN	3
REMIND ME TO STAY ALIVE.	154	THE DYING MAN	23
OR STAY BY YOURSELF DOWN DEEP IN THE WOOD,	177	KITTY-CAT BIRD	7
AND THEY'LL SOON STAY AWAY IN GREAT BUNCHES!"	180	GOO-GIRL	16
STAYED			
THE RAIN STAYED IN ITS CLOUD; FULL DARK CAME NEAR;	6	INTERLUDE	9
WE STAYED ALL NIGHT,	41	BIG WIND	19
ONCE I STAYED ALL NIGHT.	57	THE LOST SON	134
STAYED.	58	THE LOST SON	160
I TURNED MY FACE AWAY, AND YET SHE STAYED.	119	THE DREAM	14
I STAYED, AND LIGHT FELL	123	WORDS FOR WIND	21
STAYED BY WHAT WAS, AND PULLED BY WHAT WOULD BE.	129	SHE	16
WHEN I STAYED FOR BREATH, I LAY	146	THE SONG	11
STAYED, IN THE STILL AIR.	150	SNAKE	5
I STAYED: A WILLOW TO THE WIND.	162	I'M HERE	39
AND THERE I STAYED UNTIL THE DAY BURNED DOWN.	166	HER BECOMING	52
YEA, I HAVE GONE AND STAYED.	173	WHAT TELL BONES	96
GOING, WE STAYED; AND NIGHT TURNED INTO DAY;	237	THE TRANCED	12
SHE STAYED IN LIGHT, AS LEAVES LIVE IN THE WIND,	241	THE SEQUEL	18

	PAGE	TITLE	LINE
STAYED (CONTINUED)			
LIGHT STAYED ALL NIGHT,	258	SONG (3)	14
STAYS			
A SHAKING DOWN, WHILE THE STEM STAYS STRAIGHT,	42	TRANSPLANTING	10
THE DUST, THE LONG DUST, STAYS.	78	BRING THE DAY!	42
YET STAYS:	101	LIGHT BREATHER	2
THE AFTER-IMAGE NEVER STAYS THE SAME.	132	SENTENTIOUS MAN	20
DROPPING A FINE YELLOW SILT WHERE THE SUN STAYS;	200	THE FAR FIELD	68
STAYS,	203	THE ROSE	40
STAYS IN ITS TRUE PLACE,	203	THE ROSE	41
BUT THE EYE OF THE TINY LIZARD STAYS WITH ME.	226	THE LIZARD	22
STAYS IN HER FLESH;	260	THE CHANGELING	5
STEADIES			
MY SHADOW STEADIES IN A SHIFTING STREAM;	167	HER BECOMING	92
STEADILY			
BUT VIEW THINGS STEADILY AND WHOLE.	25	VERSE W ALLUSNS	10
STEADY			
THIS SHAKING KEEPS ME STEADY. I SHOULD KNOW.	108	THE WAKING (2)	16
SHE HELD HER BODY STEADY IN THE WIND;	120	THE DREAM	25
THE EVENING WRAPS ME, STEADY AS A FLAME.	150	IN LATE SUMMER	32
BEARING DOWN, WITH TWO STEADY EYES,	223	ELEGY (2)	22
ALONG THE SEA-WALL, A STEADY SLOSHING OF THE SWELL,	230	THE STORM	10
A STEADY STORM OF CORRESPONDENCES!	239	IN A DARK TIME	13
STEAK			
STEAK GREASE STUCK TO HER FUZZY LEAVES.	228	THE GERANIUM	13
STEAL			
WHAT ELSE CAN I STEAL FROM SLEEP?	166	HER BECOMING	34
STEAM			
SWELLING THE ROOTS WITH STEAM AND STENCH,	38	FORCING HOUSE	8
FOR THE STEAM PLANT,	41	BIG WIND	7
AND THE LIVE STEAM	41	BIG WIND	13
THEN CAME STEAM.	57	THE LOST SON	139
STEEL			
FLESH BEHIND STEEL AND GLASS IS UNPROTECTED	5	PROGNOSIS	5
AND STEEL RIPS THROUGH CONFLICTING STEEL.	33	HIGHWAY: MICH	17
AND STEEL RIPS THROUGH CONFLICTING STEEL.	33	HIGHWAY: MICH	17
MY MUSCLES MOVE WITH STEEL,	34	NIGHT JOURNEY	14
STEEP			
DOWN A STEEP HILLSIDE ON A CAKE OF ICE,--	105	SIR JOHN DAVIES	8
SWERVING UP A STEEP EMBANKMENT.	158	FIRST MEDITATN	55
STEEPER			
THE WAY GREW STEEPER BETWEEN STONY WALLS,	247	I WAITED	19
STELLER			
AND THE STELLER JAY, RAUCOUS, SOOTY HEADED, LIVES WITH US,	234	ALL MORNING	15
STEM			
THE STEM THAT HOLDS THE BEE IS PRONE;	15	COMING OF COLD	39
A SHAKING DOWN, WHILE THE STEM STAYS STRAIGHT,	42	TRANSPLANTING	10
PALE BLOSSOMS, EACH BALANCED ON A SINGLE JOINTED STEM,	43	CARNATIONS	1
THEY SEWED UP THE AIR WITH A STEM;	44	FRAU BAUMAN	22
THE LONG ALLEYS OF STRING AND STEM;	61	THE LONG ALLEY	70
STILL HOLDING AND FEEDING THE STEM OF THE CONTAINED FLOWER.	67	SHAPE OF FIRE	95
I MET HER AS A BLOSSOM ON A STEM	119	THE DREAM	1
ROSE, EASY ON A STEM,	124	WORDS FOR WIND	42
A BLAZE OF BEING ON A CENTRAL STEM.	149	IN LATE SUMMER	18
THE SINGING OF A STEM.	212	LIGHT LISTENED	22
NEAR THE STEM, WHITER AT ROOT,	221	THE ABYSS	83
WHAT ROOT OF HIS EVER DENIED ITS STEM?	224	OTTO	10
BY A NAKED STEM:	262	FOLLIES OF ADAM	10
STEM-FUR			
THEIR INTRICATE STEM-FUR DRIES;	37	CUTTINGS	2
STEMS			
CUT STEMS STRUGGLING TO PUT DOWN FEET,	37	CUTTINGS (LATE)	2
SCUMS, MILDEWS, SMUTS ALONG STEMS,	38	FORCING HOUSE	3
PULPY STEMS, RANK, SILO-RICH,	38	ROOT CELLAR	8
SLUG-SOFT STEMS,	43	FLOWER DUMP	2
STEMS, JOINTED LIKE CORN,	44	FRAU BAUMAN	10
THE STEMS SAID, THANK YOU.	73	WHERE KNOCK IS	66
WE'LL STRETCH WITH THE GREAT STEMS.	80	GIVE WAY, GATES	35
PRICKLE-ME, TICKLE-ME, CLOSE STEMS.	85	PRAISE TO END!	6
HONORED, ON MY RETURN, BY THE ANCIENT FELLOWSHIP OF ROTTEN STEMS.	89	UNFOLD! UNFOLD!	26
OR THEY SIT SIDEWAYS ON LIMBER DANDELION STEMS,	152	THE SISKINS	10

	PAGE	TITLE	LINE
STEMS (CONTINUED)			
LIFTING ME HIGH OVER THE FOUR-FOOT STEMS, THE MRS.			
RUSSELLS, AND HIS OWN ELABORATE HYBRIDS,	203	THE ROSE	54
AND THE GREAT LEAVES CANCEL THEIR STEMS;	259	SONG (3)	50
STENCH			
SWELLING THE ROOTS WITH STEAM AND STENCH,	38	FORCING HOUSE	8
THE STENCH OF THEIR DAMP FUR DRYING IN THE SUN,	189	THE LONGING	55
STEP			
AT EVERY STEP YOU MISSED	45	MY PAPA'S WALTZ	11
AND THEN STEP BAREFOOT ON A WORM	114	DINKY	7
I GET A STEP BEYOND	125	WORDS FOR WIND	65
A STEP DOWN THE STAIR."	219	THE ABYSS	8
DEEP IN THE MOW, AND EACH STEP DEEPER DOWN,	247	I WAITED	7
STEPPED			
STEPPED IN WET. OVER STONES.	73	WHERE KNOCK IS	55
BUT STEPPED RIGHT UP AND SWUNG AT THE DEVIL;	111	SQUEEZE-BOX	4
I STEPPED CAREFULLY, LIKE A NEW-SHOD HORSE,	166	HER BECOMING	46
AND IT STEPPED IN THE ROOM, UNDER HIS ARM,--	273	SUPPR W LINDSAY	6
STEPS			
SHE STEPS ALONG THE STREET,	121	ALL EARTH, AIR	14
DOWN WOODEN STEPS TOWARD A WEEDY GARDEN;	162	I'M HERE	46
AS SHE STEPS INTO SUMMER,	260	THE CHANGELING	8
STERN			
THE STERN HIGH, DIPPING LIKE A CHILD'S BOAT IN A POND--	203	THE ROSE	37
STETHOSCOPE			
THE STETHOSCOPE TELLS WHAT EVERYONE FEARS:	23	ACADEMIC	1
STEVEN			
EVEN STEVEN ALL IS LESS:	75	I NEED, I NEED	23
STEVENS			
A ROUSE FOR STEVENS	266	FOR STEVENS	T
WALLACE STEVENS, WHAT'S HE DONE?	266	FOR STEVENS	1
WALLACE STEVENS--ARE WE FOR HIM?	266	FOR STEVENS	19
STICK			
THIS AIR COULD FLESH A DEAD STICK. SWEET JESUS, MAKE ME			
SWEAT.	61	THE LONG ALLEY	63
SCRATCHED THE WIND WITH A STICK.	74	I NEED, I NEED	16
I'M A DRAFT SLEEPING BY A STICK;	97	O, THOU OPENING	7
IT WAS FADE ME ANOTHER AND STICK OUT YOUR CAN;	112	SQUEEZE-BOX	27
WHERE HE TREMBLED AND SHOOK BENEATH A STICK	227	MEADOW MOUSE	3
WHILE I POKED WITH A STICK AT A STONE NEAR A FOUR-PRONGED			
FLOWER,	232	THE THING	21
MY FATHER NEVER USED A STICK,	268	SAGINAW SONG	50
I GET MYSELF A STICK,	269	GOB MUSIC	2
STICKING			
THE SMALL DEAD PIECES STICKING UNDER AN INSTEP;	151	SLUG	20
HIS ABSURD WHISKERS STICKING OUT LIKE A CARTOON-MOUSE,	227	MEADOW MOUSE	7
STICKLEBACK			
A MOUTH LIKE A STICKLEBACK,--	209	HER LONGING	9
STICKS			
THIS URGE, WRESTLE, RESURRECTION OF DRY STICKS,	37	CUTTINGS (LATE)	1
GRUBS AND SNAILS AND SHARP STICKS,	39	WEED PULLER	6
THE CRUMBLING SMALL HOLLOW STICKS ON THE UNDERSIDE MIXED			
WITH ROOTS,	40	MOSS-GATHERING	4
WAKE ME, WITCH, WE'LL DO THE DANCE OF ROTTEN STICKS.	64	SHAPE OF FIRE	10
UP OVER A VIADUCT I CAME, TO THE SNAKES AND STICKS OF			
ANOTHER WINTER,	65	SHAPE OF FIRE	37
BUMPING AGAINST STICKS AND BOTTOM-STONES, THEN SWINGING	159	FIRST MEDITATN	70
THE SUDDEN SUCKING ROAR AS THE CULVERT LOOSENS ITS DEBRIS			
OF BRANCHES AND STICKS,	191	AT OYSTER RIVER	53
STICKS-IN-A-DROWSE			
STICKS-IN-A-DROWSE DROOP OVER SUGARY LOAM,	37	CUTTINGS	1
STIFF			
THE OAK STOOD WITH EACH LEAF STIFF AS A BELL.	12	MID-CNTRY BLOW	6
PLOUGHING WITH HER STIFF PROW,	41	BIG WIND	25
CHRYSANTHEMUMS; THE STIFF	44	FRAU BAUMAN	9
HIS HEAD, STIFF AS A SCARAB, TURNED TO ONE SIDE,	226	THE LIZARD	5
STIFFENED			
WITH THEIR BANDANNAS STIFFENED WITH SWEAT,	44	FRAU BAUMAN	33
STIFFENING			
SHAPES STIFFENING INTO METAL,	169	FOURTH MEDITATN	40
STILE			
THE STILE OF INNOCENCE,	7	ORDERS FOR DAY	9

STILL   PAGE   TITLE   LINE

	PAGE	TITLE	LINE
BUT STILL THE ROAD AND DUSTY FIELD KEPT DRY.	6	INTERLUDE	8
THOUGH STILL THE GUARDED SNOW IS WINTER-SEALED.	11	LIGHT BRIGHTER	6
BUT MY EAR STILL KEPT THE SOUND OF THE SEA LIKE A SHELL.	12	MID-CNTRY BLOW	8
--AND THE EYES, STILL VIVID, LOOKING UP FROM A SUNKEN ROOM.	22	ROAD TO WDLAWN	8
STILL STARES THE WISH TO LOVE.	31	LULL	21
BUT STILL THE DELICATE SLIPS KEEP COAXING UP WATER;	37	CUTTINGS	3
AND WINTERGREEN BERRIES AND LEAVES STILL STUCK TO THE TOP,--	40	MOSS-GATHERING	5
THEY STILL HOVER OVER ME.	44	FRAU BAUMAN	31
STILL CLINGING TO YOUR SHIRT.	45	MY PAPA'S WALTZ	16
WITH BUCK STILL TIED TO THE LOG, ON COMES THE LIGHT.	47	DOUBLE FEATURE	1
DALLY AT SHOP WINDOWS, STILL RELUCTANT TO GO;	47	DOUBLE FEATURE	6
THE STALK STILL SWAYS.	56	THE LOST SON	115
THE LANDSCAPE STILL PARTLY BROWN:	58	THE LOST SON	151
YET STILL?	58	THE LOST SON	168
BE STILL.	58	THE LOST SON	172
REACH ME ROSE, SWEET ONE, STILL MOIST IN THE LOAM,	61	THE LONG ALLEY	68
AND THE NEW PLANTS, STILL AWKWARD IN THEIR SOIL.	63	FIELD OF LIGHT	42
RAIN SWEETENED THE CAVE AND THE DOVE STILL CALLED;	66	SHAPE OF FIRE	75
STILL AS A CHILD IN ITS FIRST LONELINESS;	67	SHAPE OF FIRE	85
STILL HOLDING AND FEEDING THE STEM OF THE CONTAINED FLOWER.	67	SHAPE OF FIRE	95
SOME STONES ARE STILL WARM.	72	WHERE KNOCK IS	41
I STILL BEAR.	80	GIVE WAY, GATES	58
MY SWEETHEART'S STILL IN HER CAVE.	82	SENSIBILITY! LA	28
THE MOON STILL ABIDES.	82	SENSIBILITY! LA	43
HOW STILL SHE KEEPS HERSELF.	83	O LULL ME, LULL	4
I'M STILL WAITING FOR A FOOT.	84	O LULL ME, LULL	30
IT'S STILL ENOUGH FOR THE KNOCK OF A WORM.	87	PRAISE TO END!	76
--CAN STILL WHISTLE IN A JUG.	89	UNFOLD! UNFOLD!	13
THE OLD STALK STILL HAS A PULSE;	99	O, THOU OPENING	52
STILL WET FROM ITS BUD-SHEATH,	101	LIGHT BREATHER	4
STILL INWARD,	101	LIGHT BREATHER	12
OUR SOULS LOOKED FORTH, AND THE GREAT DAY STOOD STILL.	106	SIR JOHN DAVIES	60
THE LINKS WERE SOFT BETWEEN US; STILL, WE KISSED;	107	SIR JOHN DAVIES	81
STILL SWAYING GENTLY BY HIS TOES,	116	THE SLOTH	11
AND FELL IN THE STREAM STILL CLUTCHING A PLANK,	117	LADY AND BEAR	27
MOTION CAN KEEP ME STILL:	123	WORDS FOR WIND	17
WHATEVER WAS, STILL IS,	125	WORDS FOR WIND	70
DIMINISHED, YET STILL HEARD:	128	THE VOICE	10
YET STILL LAUGH IN MY SLEEP.	130	THE OTHER	24
THE LONG LUSH GRASS LAY STILL;	145	THE BEAST	18
THE DEAD WILL NOT LIE STILL,	148	THE SMALL	22
STAYED, IN THE STILL AIR.	150	SNAKE	5
THEY SING, THEY SING, BUT STILL IN MINOR THIRDS.	156	THE DYING MAN	89
THE EDGES OF THE SUMMIT STILL APPALL	156	THE DYING MAN	96
STILL SWIMMING FORWARD--	159	FIRST MEDITATN	72
THERE ARE STILL TIMES, MORNING AND EVENING:	159	FIRST MEDITATN	83
I AM STILL HAPPY.	160	FIRST MEDITATN	99
STILL LEANING TOWARD THE LAST PLACE THE SUN WAS.	163	I'M HERE	76
I PREFER THE STILL JOY:	163	I'M HERE	86
STILL TAKING DELIGHT IN NAKEDNESS,	165	HER BECOMING	6
THE AIR STILL, THE GROUND ALIVE,	165	HER BECOMING	14
A DROP OF THE NIGHT RAIN STILL IN ME,	168	FOURTH MEDITATN	7
I HAVE LEFT THE BODY OF THE WHALE, BUT THE MOUTH OF THE NIGHT IS STILL WIDE;	188	THE LONGING	51
FEELING, I STILL DELIGHT IN MY LAST FALL.	197	THE LONG WATERS	32
STILL FOR A MOMENT,	200	THE FAR FIELD	33
I HAVE COME TO A STILL, BUT NOT A DEEP CENTER,	201	THE FAR FIELD	71
BUT STILL THE FLASH OF THE KINGFISHER, THE WINGBEAT OF THE SCOTER,	202	THE ROSE	15
AND YET WAS STILL.	205	THE ROSE	105
SHE KEPT HER BODY STILL	212	LIGHT LISTENED	10
I, LIVING, STILL ABIDE	215	HIS FOREBODING	2
AND YET STILL VIOLENT MEN, WHOSE STACKED-UP GUNS	224	OTTO	27
ONE ROUND EYE STILL TOWARD ME.	226	THE LIZARD	19
I BID STILLNESS BE STILL.	240	IN EVEING AIR	22
O, MOTION O, OUR CHANCE IS STILL TO BE!	243	THE MOTION	24
OH, TO BE SOMETHING ELSE, YET STILL TO BE!	244	INFIRMITY	6
MY EARS STILL HEAR THE BIRD WHEN ALL IS STILL;	244	INFIRMITY	28
MY EARS STILL HEAR THE BIRD WHEN ALL IS STILL;	244	INFIRMITY	28
MY SOUL IS STILL MY SOUL, AND STILL THE SON	244	INFIRMITY	29
MY SOUL IS STILL MY SOUL, AND STILL THE SON,	244	INFIRMITY	29
GODHEAD ABOVE MY GOD, ARE YOU THERE STILL?	246	THE MARROW	13

	PAGE	TITLE	LINE
STILL (CONTINUED)			
YEA, I HAVE SLAIN MY WILL, AND STILL I LIVE;	246	THE MARROW	21
PART OF A TREE STILL DARK, STILL, DEATHLY STILL,	248	THE TREE, BIRD	9
PART OF A TREE STILL DARK, STILL, DEATHLY STILL,	248	THE TREE, BIRD	9
PART OF A TREE STILL DARK, STILL, DEATHLY STILL,	248	THE TREE, BIRD	9
THE WILLOW WITH ITS BIRD GREW LOUD, GREW LOUDER STILL.	248	THE TREE, BIRD	13
HOW DEEP THE MOTHER-ROOT OF THAT STILL CRY!	248	THE TREE, BIRD	17
IN THE STILL POINT OF LIGHT	249	THE RESTORED	19
THE HILL BECOMES THE VALLEY, AND IS STILL;	250	THE RIGHT THING	5
OR HE SITS STILL, A SOLID FIGURE WHEN	250	THE RIGHT THING	13
I'M STILL,	258	SONG (3)	28
STILL AS THE WIND'S CENTER,	258	SONG (3)	29
STILL AS A CLAY SUNK	258	SONG (3)	30
I'M STILL SMUDGY FROM SLEEP:	259	SONG (3)	41
ALL THINGS ARE VULNERABLE, STILL;	259	SONG (3)	47
"SURE, WE STILL EAT," I SAID. "ENOUGH! OR TOO MUCH."	273	SUPPR W LINDSAY	17
STILLNESS			
STILLNESS BECOMING ALIVE,	58	THE LOST SON	167
A LUMINOUS STILLNESS.	221	THE ABYSS	84
I BID STILLNESS BE STILL.	240	IN EVEING AIR	22
STILL-STAND			
THE SOUL AT A STILL-STAND,	194	JOURNY INTERIOR	54
STILL-TO-BE-BORN			
THE GENTLE AND BEAUTIFUL STILL-TO-BE-BORN;	170	FOURTH MEDITATN	65
STING			
TELL ME, GREAT LORDS OF STING,	83	O LULL ME, LULL	8
STINGS			
THE BLOSSOM STINGS THE BEE.	121	ALL EARTH, AIR	18
STINGY			
THE STINGY MEMBERS WHEN THEY SIGNED	267	SAGINAW SONG	33
MADE WITH THEIR STINGY LOOKS,--	267	SAGINAW SONG	34
STINK			
THAT FINE FUMING STINK OF PARTICULAR KETTLES,	48	LAST WORDS	2
AND DO NOT MIND THE STINK.	269	GOB MUSIC	15
STINKS			
AND WHAT A CONGRESS OF STINKS!--	38	ROOT CELLAR	6
YOU'VE SEEN ME, PRINCE OF STINKS,	82	SENSIBILITY! LA	32
A KINGDOM OF STINKS AND SIGHS,	187	THE LONGING	2
STIR			
IN RIVULETS; THE COLD ROOTS STIR BELOW.	11	LIGHT BRIGHTER	12
THE GRASSES WHITELY STIR;	17	NO BIRD	6
MOTHER, MOTHER, STIR FROM YOUR CAVE OF SORROW.	64	SHAPE OF FIRE	16
I HEARD A BIRD STIR IN ITS TRUE CONFINE;	241	THE SEQUEL	11
STIRRED			
STIRRED UP A WHIRL OF SILT	49	RIVER INCIDENT	2
A WIND STIRRED IN A WEB OF APPLEWORMS;	101	THE VISITANT	26
DUST IN A CORNER STIRRED,	146	THE SONG	6
THE CLOSE AIR FAINTLY STIRRED.	212	LIGHT LISTENED	7
STIRRING			
STIRRING THE CLEAREST WATER.	102	ELEGY FOR JANE	13
IN ITS SMALL FOLDS, STIRRING SLUGGISHLY,	171	WHAT TELL BONES	4
STIRS			
STIRS AS A BLOSSOM STIRS,	101	LIGHT BREATHER	3
STIRS AS A BLOSSOM STIRS,	101	LIGHT BREATHER	3
A LIGHT WIND STIRS IN THE PINE NEEDLES.	168	FOURTH MEDITATN	24
STITCHED			
THE FLYING FABRIC STITCHED ON BONE,	19	EPIDERM MACABRE	3
STOCKING			
IN A SHOE BOX STUFFED IN AN OLD NYLON STOCKING	227	MEADOW MOUSE	1
STONE			
THOUGHT DOES NOT CRUSH TO STONE.	9	THE ADAMANT	1
WHEELS SHAKE THE ROADBED STONE,	34	NIGHT JOURNEY	24
DENSE IN THE CENTRAL STONE.	50	THE CYCLE	11
UNDER PRIMEVAL STONE.	50	THE CYCLE	18
ALONE, I KISSED THE SKIN OF A STONE;	63	FIELD OF LIGHT	29
WILL THE SEA GIVE THE WIND SUCK? A TOAD FOLDS INTO A STONE.	64	SHAPE OF FIRE	8
I COULD MELT DOWN A STONE,--	79	GIVE WAY, GATES	17
THIS SALT CAN'T WARM A STONE.	86	PRAISE TO END!	49
ON HARSH STONE.	99	O, THOU OPENING	78
THE LEECH CLINGING TO A STONE WAITED;	100	THE VISITANT	8
STARING AT A TREE, I FELT THE PULSE OF A STONE.	101	THE VISITANT	22
ON A BRIGHT STONE.	103	OLD LADY'S WRDS	11
THE STONE WALKS, WHERE ARE THEY?	103	OLD LADY'S WRDS	35

	PAGE	TITLE	LINE
STONE (CONTINUED)			
WAS NOT THE JOYLESS MOTION OF A STONE.	105	SIR JOHN DAVIES	18
I TOSSED A STONE, AND LISTENED TO ITS PLUNGE.	120	THE DREAM	22
I STARED, AND A GARDEN STONE	123	WORDS FOR WIND	23
THAT WOMAN I SAW IN A STONE--	123	WORDS FOR WIND	31
I SWEAR SHE CAST A SHADOW WHITE AS STONE.	127	I KNEW A WOMAN	25
THE SERPENT'S HEART SUSTAINS THE LOVELESS STONE:	131	SENTENTIOUS MAN	3
I KNOW THE MOTION OF THE DEEPEST STONE.	132	SENTENTIOUS MAN	35
AND ALL THE BIRDS ARE STONE.	138	LOVE'S PROGRESS	22
THE GRASS CHANGES TO STONE.	141	MEMORY	12
IN A COUNTRY OF BLEAK STONE,	146	THE SONG	9
MY LIPS PRESSED UPON STONE.	146	THE SONG	29
WHITE UPON WHITE, SLOW-SETTLING ON A STONE;	149	IN LATE SUMMER	2
GOD'S IN THAT STONE, OR I AM NOT A MAN!	149	IN LATE SUMMER	12
AND HANG, LIMP ON A STONE:	150	SNAKE	3
THE FURY OF THE SLUG BENEATH THE STONE.	156	THE DYING MAN	93
LIGHT AS A PETAL FALLING UPON STONE.	165	HER BECOMING	12
THE SHAPE OF A LARK RISES FROM A STONE;	168	FOURTH MEDITATN	25
WHO ELSE SWEATS LIGHT FROM A STONE?	170	FOURTH MEDITATN	81
I'M A SMALL STONE, LOOSE IN THE SHALE.	172	WHAT TELL BONES	47
THE WIND SLACKENS, LIGHT AS A MOTH FANNING A STONE:	190	AT OYSTER RIVER	17
THE TIDE RUSTLING IN, SLIDING BETWEEN THE RIDGES OF STONE,	191	AT OYSTER RIVER	34
OVER A LIP OF STONE, THE TINY RIVULET;	191	AT OYSTER RIVER	43
WHERE LIGHT IS STONE.	196	THE LONG WATERS	12
I REMEMBER A STONE BREAKING THE EDDYING CURRENT,	197	THE LONG WATERS	55
THE ROAD CHANGING FROM GLAZED TARFACE TO A RUBBLE OF STONE.	199	THE FAR FIELD	8
A RIPPLE WIDENING FROM A SINGLE STONE	201	THE FAR FIELD	102
ROOTED IN STONE, KEEPING THE WHOLE OF LIGHT,	205	THE ROSE	112
WHEN I PAUSE TO TALK TO A STONE,	215	HIS FOREBODING	9
HER FACE LIKE A RAIN-BEATEN STONE ON THE DAY SHE ROLLED OFF	223	ELEGY (2)	1
AGAINST THE STONE BREAKWATER,	230	THE STORM	1
WHILE I POKED WITH A STICK AT A STONE NEAR A FOUR-PRONGED FLOWER,	232	THE THING	21
A THING CARVED OF STONE OR WOOD, WITH THE DULL IRIDESCENCE OF LONG-POLISHED WOOD,	234	ALL MORNING	11
A PARTRIDGE DRUMMED; A MINNOW NUDGED ITS STONE;	241	THE SEQUEL	13
THE CLOSE DIRT DANCING ON A SUNLESS STONE	243	THE MOTION	20
THE DEEP EYE SEES THE SHIMMER ON THE STONE;	244	INFIRMITY	20
I DAZZLED IN THE DAZZLE OF A STONE.	247	I WAITED	13
ON A HOT, DUSTY STONE,	249	THE RESTORED	18
WANTING THE QUIET OF OLD WOOD OR STONE WITHOUT WATER.	255	LIGHT POEM	9
STONE.	258	SONG (3)	31
HER HEAVEN-SENSE PURE AS A STONE.	260	THE CHANGELING	11
AS WATER TEACHES STONE. BELIEVE ME, EXTREMEST ORIOLE,	260	THE CHANGELING	19
TO YOU ARBUTUS CALM, MYSTERIOUS AS A STONE?	261	THE CHANGELING	29
THERE WAS A HARDNESS OF STONE,	265	HARSH COUNTRY	1
IN A COUNTRY OF BRIGHT STONE.	265	HARSH COUNTRY	16
STONE-DEAF			
BEETLES IN CAVES, NEWTS, STONE-DEAF FISHES,	50	THE MINIMAL	3
STONES			
THE STONES SANG,	51	THE WAKING (1)	9
RAN OVER STONES:	51	THE WAKING (1)	22
A SLOW DRIP OVER STONES,	53	THE LOST SON	3
PAST THE PASTURE OF FLAT STONES,	54	THE LOST SON	35
THESE STONES HAVE BEEN HERE TOO LONG.	55	THE LOST SON	65
HIS LOOK DRAINED THE STONES.	56	THE LOST SON	87
GOODBYE, GOODBYE, OLD STONES, THE TIME-ORDER IS GOING,	56	THE LOST SON	108
THE SALT LAUGHED AND THE STONES;	63	FIELD OF LIGHT	40
SOME STONES ARE STILL WARM.	72	WHERE KNOCK IS	41
STEPPED IN WET. OVER STONES.	73	WHERE KNOCK IS	55
HEAR ME, SOFT EARS AND ROUNDY STONES!	76	I NEED, I NEED	57
IN THE SPRINGTIME OF STONES,	80	GIVE WAY, GATES	34
THE LAKE WASHES ITS STONES.	82	SENSIBILITY! LA	31
THE STONES WERE SHARP,	87	PRAISE TO END!	51
SPEAK TO THE STONES, AND THE STARS ANSWER.	90	UNFOLD! UNFOLD!	54
FEET RUN OVER THE SIMPLE STONES,	93	I CRY, LOVE!	36
THEN WASHING UP OVER SMALL STONES.	93	I CRY, LOVE!	49
WITHOUT BRUSHING THE WET STONES,	100	THE VISITANT	16
THE SIDES OF WET STONES CANNOT CONSOLE ME,	102	ELEGY FOR JANE	16
THE BUSHES AND THE STONES DANCED ON AND ON;	119	THE DREAM	12
I STAND WITH STANDING STONES.	121	ALL EARTH, AIR	1
THE STONES STAY WHERE THEY ARE.	121	ALL EARTH, AIR	2
SAY THE STONES, SAY THE FISH.	121	ALL EARTH, AIR	20

	PAGE	TITLE	LINE
STONES (CONTINUED)			
THE STONES LEAP IN THE STREAM;	124	WORDS FOR WIND	34
I TOUCHED THE STONES, AND THEY HAD MY OWN SKIN.	133	THE PURE FURY	7
OF LICHEN AROUND STONES?	139	PLAINT	16
THAT SCUTTLED UNDER STONES,	147	THE EXORCISM	17
AND ALL THE STONES HAVE WINGS.	148	THE SMALL	24
WHILE STONES LOOSEN ON THE OBSCURE HILLSIDE,	157	FIRST MEDITATN	5
A COLD WIND COMES OVER STONES;	160	FIRST MEDITATN	92
MAKING MY WAY OVER WET STONES.	166	HER BECOMING	48
WAS IT THE STONES I HEARD? I STARED AT THE FIXED STARS.	166	HER BECOMING	54
I DARE CARESS THE STONES, THE FIELD MY FRIEND;	167	HER BECOMING	94
EVEN THE STONES SPEAK.	170	FOURTH MEDITATN	88
THE BAREST SPEECH OF LIGHT AMONG THE STONES.	173	WHAT TELL BONES	71
MAKES ALMOST A WAVE OVER A BARRIER OF SMALL STONES,	190	AT OYSTER RIVER	13
BETTER TO HUG CLOSE, WARY OF RUBBLE AND FALLING STONES.	193	JOURNY INTERIOR	6
WINDING UPWARD TOWARD THE STREAM WITH ITS SHARP STONES,	193	JOURNY INTERIOR	12
UNDERNEATH, THE SLUGGISH WATER RUNNING BETWEEN WEEDS, BROKEN WHEELS, TIRES, STONES.	194	JOURNY INTERIOR	33
AND THE WAVES FLATTENING OUT WHEN THE FISHERMEN DRAG THEIR NETS OVER THE STONES.	194	JOURNY INTERIOR	57
THEN A LONG RUNNING OVER FLAT STONES	200	THE FAR FIELD	64
AT THE IRREGULAR STONES, IRIDESCENT SANDGRAINS,	201	THE FAR FIELD	74
THE STONES RANG WITH LIGHT SOUND;	237	THE TRANCED	14
IN THE PLACE OF BEAUTIFUL STONES.	258	SONG (3)	7
STONE'S			
A STONE'S SHAPE	62	FIELD OF LIGHT	13
I KNOW THE BACK-STREAM'S JOY, AND THE STONE'S ETERNAL PULSELESS LONGING.	88	PRAISE TO END!	82
STONY			
THE WAY GREW STEEPER BETWEEN STONY WALLS,	247	I WAITED	19
UPROSE, UPROSE, THE STONY FIELDS UPROSE,	248	THE TREE, BIRD	1
STOOD			
BUT WHEN HE STOOD UP, THAT FACE	6	THE PREMONITION	12
WHEN I STOOD AT THE WINDOW, AN ELM BOUGH SWEPT TO MY KNEES;	12	MID-CNTRY BLOW	3
THE OAK STOOD WITH EACH LEAF STIFF AS A BELL.	12	MID-CNTRY BLOW	6
A SINGLE RIPPLE STARTS FROM WHERE HE STOOD.	15	THE HERON	12
THE SIDEBOARD BESIDE WHICH A TALL FOOTMAN STOOD	32	SALE	15
THEY STOOD ASTRIDE PIPES,	44	FRAU BAUMAN	16
THERE BESIDE HIM SHE STOOD,--	46	PICKLE BELT	7
SEA WATER STOOD IN MY VEINS,	49	RIVER INCIDENT	6
STOOD POISED ON THE STAIR,	56	THE LOST SON	90
IT'S TIME YOU STOOD UP AND ASKED	89	UNFOLD! UNFOLD!	10
OUR SOULS LOOKED FORTH, AND THE GREAT DAY STOOD STILL.	106	SIR JOHN DAVIES	60
A SMALL BIRD FLEW IN CIRCLES WHERE WE STOOD;	120	THE DREAM	19
AND SO I STOOD APART,	128	THE VOICE	5
A WOMAN STOOD, PURE AS A BRIDE,	136	THE SENSUALISTS	9
AND I STOOD OUTSIDE MYSELF,	205	THE ROSE	101
THEY STOOD THERE WITH THEIR GUNS; HE WALKED TOWARD,	224	OTTO	18
YET WHEN I SIGHED, I STOOD OUTSIDE MY LIFE,	248	THE TREE, BIRD	7
STOOL			
I GET A STOOL AND SIT AND STARE	269	GOB MUSIC	12
STOOP			
NECESSITY STARVES ON THE STOOP OF INVENTION.	29	THE GENTLE	11
STOP			
I STOP THE LYING MOUTH:	3	OPEN HOUSE	16
STOP THE LARKS. CAN I HAVE MY HEART BACK?	76	I NEED, I NEED	47
TO STOP THE SERPENT'S AWFUL RACKET:	115	THE SERPENT	13
STOPPED			
ALL THE FAUCETS STOPPED?--	41	BIG WIND	5
THE WEEDS STOPPED SWINGING.	58	THE LOST SON	161
AND THE THRUSH STOPPED IN THE MIDDLE OF HIS SONG.	196	THE LONG WATERS	7
STOPPING			
STOPPING TRAFFIC, INDIGNANT AS ADDLED OLD LADIES,	234	ALL MORNING	27
STOPS			
WHO STOPS BEING A BIRD, YET BEATS HIS WINGS	156	THE DYING MAN	100
STORE			
THAT KEEPS SUFFICIENT STORE	20	REPL TO CENSURE	14
STORED			
THE WATER STORED IN NARROW POOLS ESCAPES	11	LIGHT BRIGHTER	11
STOREROOM			
AS WHEN THE DOOR SWINGS OPEN IN A FLORIST'S STOREROOM--	220	THE ABYSS	46

	PAGE	TITLE	LINE
STORES			
THEIR WOODEN STORES OF SILVERY PINE AND WEATHER-BEATEN RED COURTHOUSES,	193	JOURNY INTERIOR	31
STORK			
IT WASN'T THE COLONY; IT WASN'T THE STORK;	111	SQUEEZE-BOX	8
STORM			
THE CORE AND PITH OF THAT UGLY STORM,	41	BIG WIND	24
SUPPOSE YOU WALK OUT IN A STORM,	114	DINKY	5
"THE STORM, THE STORM OF A KISS."	208	HER WORDS	12
"THE STORM, THE STORM OF A KISS."	208	HER WORDS	12
OR BEATING AGAINST THE BLACK CLOUDS OF THE STORM,	209	HER LONGING	22
THE LONG SURF OF THE STORM BOOMS	210	HER TIME	21
THE STORM	230	THE STORM	T
THE STORM LULLS OFF, THEN REDOUBLES,	231	THE STORM	30
A STEADY STORM OF CORRESPONDENCES!	239	IN A DARK TIME	13
STORM'S			
IS THIS THE STORM'S HEART? THE GROUND IS UNSTILLING ITSELF.	56	THE LOST SON	100
A STORM'S INCREASING WHERE	215	HIS FOREBODING	19
STORM-TOSSED			
WHEN LIGHT DIVIDED ON A STORM-TOSSED TREE.	246	THE MARROW	20
STOVE			
--FORNICATES ON THE STOVE.	99	O, THOU OPENING	70
STRAIGHT			
STRAIGHT FROM THE OAK, THE GOSSAMER IS HUNG.	12	SLOW SEASON	7
A SHAKING DOWN, WHILE THE STEM STAYS STRAIGHT,	42	TRANSPLANTING	10
THE FULL RAIN FELL STRAIGHT DOWN,	50	THE CYCLE	14
THEN FLYING ALMOST STRAIGHT UPWARD,	152	THE SISKINS	3
ON A DARK DAY I WALK STRAIGHT TOWARD THE RAIN.	170	FOURTH MEDITATN	80
THIS HARRY RAN STRAIGHT UP A WALL,	181	MONOTONY SONG	13
THE HIGHWAY RIBBONING OUT IN A STRAIGHT THRUST TO THE NORTH,	193	JOURNY INTERIOR	27
HIS RIGHT EYE STARING STRAIGHT AT ME,	226	THE LIZARD	6
THE TAIL STRAIGHT AS AN AWL,	226	THE LIZARD	9
FLICKING THE FOAM FROM THE WHITECAPS STRAIGHT UPWARD INTO THE DARKNESS,	230	THE STORM	16
CONFUSING THEM ONCE FLYING STRAIGHT INTO THE SUN	232	THE THING	7
STRAIGHTEN			
ROSES, TO STRAIGHTEN	44	FRAU BAUMAN	7
STRAIGHTNESS			
BACK INTO STRAIGHTNESS;	152	THE SISKINS	15
STRAIN			
THE OAK LEAVES STRAIN TO BE UNBOUND,	15	COMING OF COLD	35
STRAINED			
WHAT SAINT STRAINED SO MUCH,	37	CUTTINGS (LATE)	3
STRAINING			
THE STRAINING AT A CURVE;	34	NIGHT JOURNEY	13
STRANGE			
ALL WHO REMEMBER, DOUBT. WHO CALLS THAT STRANGE?	120	THE DREAM	21
I THINK MY NEIGHBORS STRANGE;	139	PLAINT	2
I'VE BECOME A STRANGE PIECE OF FLESH,	157	FIRST MEDITATN	15
HE WAS THE YOUNGEST SON OF A STRANGE BROOD,	224	OTTO	1
STRANGELY			
WHO, STRANGELY ENOUGH, WAS A TURTLE:	179	MYRTLE	2
STRANGENESS			
HORIZONS HAVE NO STRANGENESS TO THE EYE.	13	PRAISE PRAIRIE	5
STRANGER			
WHO SAYS? A NAMELESS STRANGER.	64	SHAPE OF FIRE	2
STRAW			
SCRAPING HER CHEEK AGAINST STRAW;	102	ELEGY FOR JANE	12
THAT WOMAN WOULD SET SODDEN STRAW ON FIRE.	105	SIR JOHN DAVIES	28
ETERNITY DEFINED, AND STREWN WITH STRAW,	156	THE DYING MAN	92
ASK ALL THE MICE WHO CAPER IN THE STRAW--	167	HER BECOMING	86
THE IMMEDIATE SHEEN, THE REALITY OF STRAW,	171	WHAT TELL BONES	16
WE CREEP TO OUR BED, AND ITS STRAW MATTRESS.	231	THE STORM	28
AND THE HURRICANE DRIVES THE DEAD STRAW INTO THE LIVING PINE-TREE.	231	THE STORM	43
I SANG TO THE STRAW,	258	SONG (3)	17
STRAWBERRY			
A DRIED STRAWBERRY LEAF,	226	THE LIZARD	17
STRAYED			
WE STRAYED LIKE CHILDREN,	265	HARSH COUNTRY	6
STREAK			
IN ONE STREAK OF PURSUIT.	232	THE THING	12

	PAGE	TITLE	LINE
STREAKED			
UP THROUGH THE STREAKED GLASS, FLASHING WITH SUNLIGHT, ...	43	CHILD ON GRNHSE	4
STREAM			
THE BEARDED BOARDS IN THE STREAM AND THE ALL OF APPLES;	66	SHAPE OF FIRE	71
THE DEEP STREAM REMEMBERS:	80	GIVE WAY, GATES	59
READ ME THE STREAM.	97	O, THOU OPENING	4
STAND BY A SLOW STREAM:	98	O, THOU OPENING	34
A LADY CAME TO A BEAR BY A STREAM.	117	LADY AND BEAR	1
TELL ME, DEAR BEAR THERE BY THE STREAM, ...	117	LADY AND BEAR	3
AND FELL IN THE STREAM STILL CLUTCHING A PLANK, ...	117	LADY AND BEAR	27
THE SHALLOW STREAM RUNS SLACK;	123	WORDS FOR WIND	25
THE STONES LEAP IN THE STREAM;	124	WORDS FOR WIND	34
NORTH, IN A SINGLE STREAM;	125	WORDS FOR WIND	63
A DOE DRINKS BY A STREAM, ...	141	MEMORY	9
OR A SALMON, TIRED, MOVING UP A SHALLOW STREAM, ...	159	FIRST MEDITATN	68
I'M NOT FAR FROM A STREAM.	164	I'M HERE	94
MY SHADOW STEADIES IN A SHIFTING STREAM;	167	HER BECOMING	92
I WOULD BE A STREAM, WINDING BETWEEN GREAT STRIATED ROCKS IN LATE SUMMER;	188	THE LONGING	46
WINDING UPWARD TOWARD THE STREAM WITH ITS SHARP STONES,	193	JOURNY INTERIOR	12
THE WILD STREAM, THE SEA ITSELF CANNOT CONTAIN ME:	209	HER LONGING	12
THE STREAM SLIPPING BENEATH THE MOSSY LOGS, ...	222	THE ABYSS	94
OUT HEMLOCK WAY THERE IS A STREAM	267	SAGINAW SONG	7
STREAMS			
OF ALL THE STREAMS	51	THE WAKING (1)	26
THE WIDE STREAMS GO THEIR WAY, ...	172	WHAT TELL BONES	49
A COUNTRY OF BAYS AND INLETS, AND SMALL STREAMS FLOWING SEAWARD.	196	THE LONG WATERS	19
BY SMALL STREAMS RUNNING DOWN UNDER FALLEN FIR TREES.	197	THE LONG WATERS	48
STREAM'S			
AT THE STREAM'S EDGE, TRAILING A VAGUE FINGER;	162	I'M HERE	26
TO THE STREAM'S	221	THE ABYSS	73
STREET			
SHE STEPS ALONG THE STREET, ...	121	ALL EARTH, AIR	14
DYING BRIGHTLY UNDER THE STREET LIGHTS SUNK IN COARSE CONCRETE, ...	193	JOURNY INTERIOR	29
FROM THE DIRT IN THE STREET, ...	236	SONG (2)	6
STREET-LAMP			
AND THE SMALL STREET-LAMP SWINGING AND SLAMMING AGAINST THE LAMP POLE.	230	THE STORM	7
STREETS			
"I SEE TEN MILLION WINDOWS, I SEE TEN THOUSAND STREETS,	27	CLAIRVOY WIDOW	5
THE SEA HAS MANY STREETS;	83	O LULL ME, LULL	14
I ROMPED, LITHE AS A CHILD, DOWN THE SUMMERY STREETS OF MY VEINS,	86	PRAISE TO END!	21
AND THE DEEP CHORUS OF HORNS COMING UP FROM THE STREETS IN EARLY MORNING.	204	THE ROSE	72
STRENGTHENS			
AND THE WEAK BRIDEGROOM STRENGTHENS IN HIS BRIDE.	132	SENTENTIOUS MAN	42
STRETCH			
THE FIELDS STRETCH OUT IN LONG, UNBROKEN ROWS.	13	PRAISE PRAIRIE	9
WE'LL STRETCH WITH THE GREAT STEMS.	80	GIVE WAY, GATES	35
THE FAR STRETCH OF A DREAM, ...	124	WORDS FOR WIND	36
I SEE THE RUBBLESTONES BEGIN TO STRETCH · · · · · · · · · · ·	135	THE RENEWAL	21
I LIVE IN LIGHT'S EXTREME; I STRETCH IN ALL DIRECTIONS;	173	WHAT TELL BONES	82
THE STAND AT THE STRETCH IN THE FACE OF DEATH, ...	194	JOURNY INTERIOR	66
WINDING DOWN TO THE STRETCH OF IRREGULAR SAND, ...	222	THE ABYSS	95
THUS I ENDURE THIS LAST PURE STRETCH OF JOY, ...	248	THE TREE, BIRD	22
TO THE LAND WHERE THE INNOCENT STRETCH AND SNORE	272	DUET	11
STRETCHED			
AND MY INTENT STRETCHED OVER THE BUDS AT THEIR FIRST TREMBLING.	66	SHAPE OF FIRE	69
I STRETCHED LIKE A BOARD, ALMOST A TREE.	90	UNFOLD! UNFOLD!	32
AND THE WALLS STRETCHED WIDE.	146	THE SONG	7
WAS IT YESTERDAY I STRETCHED OUT THE THIN BONES OF MY INNOCENCE?	168	FOURTH MEDITATN	12
STRETCHES			
ONE SIGH STRETCHES HEAVEN.	83	O LULL ME, LULL	1
A PRINCE OF SMALL BEGINNINGS, ENDURING THE SLOW STRETCHES OF CHANGE, ...	170	FOURTH MEDITATN	70
WHEN OUR SPAYED FEMALE CAT YAWNS AND STRETCHES OUT IN THE SUNSHINE--	234	ALL MORNING	23

	PAGE	TITLE	LINE
STRETCHING			
STRETCHING AND REACHING.	42	TRANSPLANTING	22
STRETCHINGS			
SUCH STRETCHINGS OF THE SPIRIT MAKE NO SOUND.	243	THE MOTION	4
STREWN			
THE PIECES OF MY SPIRIT STREWN.	19	AGNST DISASTER	4
THE SHEEP STREWN ON A FIELD,	54	THE LOST SON	37
ETERNITY DEFINED, AND STREWN WITH STRAW,	156	THE DYING MAN	92
ITS ENTRAILS STREWN OVER THE HALF-GROWN FLOWERS,	199	THE FAR FIELD	22
STRIATED			
I WOULD BE A STREAM, WINDING BETWEEN GREAT STRIATED ROCKS IN LATE SUMMER;	188	THE LONGING	46
STRIATIONS			
THE BOTTOM-STONES SHIMMER BACK THEIR IRREGULAR STRIATIONS,	233	THE PIKE	8
STRICT			
IN LANGUAGE STRICT AND PURE.	3	OPEN HOUSE	15
THE BRONZE WHEAT ARRANGED IN STRICT AND FORMAL ORDER;	29	THE REMINDER	3
STRICT AS A SEED, NIPPY AND TWIGGY.	86	PRAISE TO END!	22
STRIDE			
MATCHING HIS STRIDE WITH HALF-STEPS	6	THE PREMONITION	5
STRIDES			
LIGHT STRIDES THE ROSE;	137	LOVE'S PROGRESS	8
STRIDING			
I DARE EMBRACE. BY STRIDING, I REMAIN.	243	THE MOTION	12
STRIKE			
STRIKE LIKE A FIRE,	221	THE ABYSS	54
STRIKES			
THE RUSH OF SMELLS STRIKES LIKE A COLD FIRE, THE THROAT FREEZES,	220	THE ABYSS	47
THE PIKE STRIKES.	233	THE PIKE	18
STRING			
BEFORE THE BREAKING OF A STRING,	22	SILENCE	8
THE LONG ALLEYS OF STRING AND STEM;	61	THE LONG ALLEY	70
I MET A COLLECTOR OF STRING, A SHEPHERD OF SLOW FORMS.	90	UNFOLD! UNFOLD!	30
COLD EVIL TWINKLED TIGHTER THAN A STRING; A FIRE	143	SHIMMER OF EVIL	8
EVERY TIME I LET HIM, THE STRING WOULD BUST.	178	THE DONKEY	3
A FURRED CATERPILLAR CRAWLS DOWN A STRING.	220	THE ABYSS	35
STRINGS			
FLINGING LONG STRINGS OF WET ACROSS THE ROOF-TOP,	41	BIG WIND	29
REACHING UP WHITE STRINGS	44	FRAU BAUMAN	3
STRIP			
THE STRIP RESERVED FOR PASSING ONLY.	33	HIGHWAY: MICH	7
STRIPED			
ALIVE WITH TINY STRIPED FISH, AND YOUNG CRABS CLIMBING IN AND OUT OF THE WATER.	190	AT OYSTER RIVER	5
STRIPES			
WITH HIS STRIPES OF SILVER AND HIS SMALL HOUSE ON HIS BACK,	151	SLUG	2
STROKED			
HOW WELL HER WISHES WENT! SHE STROKED MY CHIN,	127	I KNEW A WOMAN	8
STROKES			
I SEE GRANDPA SURVIVING A SERIES OF SEVEN STROKES,	28	CLAIRVOY WIDOW	21
STROLLED			
I STROLLED ACROSS	51	THE WAKING (1)	1
STRONGER			
SO THEIR MUSKY SMELL COMES EVEN STRONGER,	39	ORCHIDS	12
STRUCK			
STRUCK;	232	THE THING	14
THE GONG OF MIDNIGHT STRUCK	238	THE MOMENT	7
STRUGGLE			
WHITISH AND SPREAD WIDE WHEN HE TRIED TO STRUGGLE AWAY,	227	MEADOW MOUSE	10
STRUGGLED			
WE STRUGGLED OUT OF SENSUALITY;	237	THE TRANCED	11
SPACE STRUGGLED WITH TIME;	238	THE MOMENT	6
STRUGGLING			
CUT STEMS STRUGGLING TO PUT DOWN FEET,	37	CUTTINGS (LATE)	2
A SINGLE WILD ROSE, STRUGGLING OUT OF THE WHITE EMBRACE OF THE MORNING-GLORY,	203	THE ROSE	44
STUBBLE			
WITH ANKLES BRUISED FROM STUBBLE OF THE GRAIN.	13	PRAISE PRAIRIE	8
THE CINDERY SNOW TICKS OVER STUBBLE.	104	OLD LADY'S WRDS	54
RUNS FITFULLY ALONG THE STUBBLE,	160	FIRST MEDITATN	95
STUCK			
AND WINTERGREEN BERRIES AND LEAVES STILL STUCK TO THE TOP,--	40	MOSS-GATHERING	5

	PAGE	TITLE	LINE
STUCK (CONTINUED)			
ALL THE LEAVES STUCK OUT THEIR TONGUES;	53	THE LOST SON	5
STEAK GREASE STUCK TO HER FUZZY LEAVES.	228	THE GERANIUM	13
FROM THE BOLT, STUCK IN ITS GROOVE,	236	SONG (2)	7
STUDIED			
HYSTERIA MASKS IN THE STUDIED INANE.	29	THE GENTLE	2
STUDY			
PRAYER BEFORE STUDY	24	BEFORE STUDY	T
I STUDY THE LIVES ON A LEAF: THE LITTLE	50	THE MINIMAL	1
I STUDY OUT A DARK SIMILITUDE:	140	THE SWAN	1
MAKE THAT MY STUDY.	207	THE YOUNG GIRL	4
STUFF			
"THIS STUFF IS A BORE!	179	MYRTLE	9
STUFFED			
IN A SHOE BOX STUFFED IN AN OLD NYLON STOCKING	227	MEADOW MOUSE	1
STUFFING			
STUFFING THE HOLES WITH BURLAP;	41	BIG WIND	20
STUFFS			
IN LOVE WITH STUFFS, SILKS,	162	I'M HERE	29
STUMBLES			
A DRUNK MAN STUMBLES BY, ABSORBED IN SELF-TALK.	33	IDYLL	2
STUMP			
WITH A STUMP OF SCRAGGY FANG	47	THE RETURN	12
STUNNED			
WHO STUNNED THE DIRT INTO NOISE?	55	THE LOST SON	66
THE PARALYTIC STUNNED IN THE TUB, AND THE WATER RISING,--	227	MEADOW MOUSE	28
THE STUNNED COUNTRY OF OURSELVES.	258	SONG (3)	21
STUNTED			
THE BLUE JAY RASPING FROM THE STUNTED PINE.	196	THE LONG WATERS	28
STUPOR			
STUPOR OF KNOWLEDGE LACKING INWARDNESS--	133	THE PURE FURY	1
STY			
THE EYE'S IN THE STY.	64	SHAPE OF FIRE	21
STYLE			
AND THE STYLE OF YOUR PROSE GROWING LIMPER AND LIMPER.	23	ACADEMIC	4
SUBDUED			
UNTIL THE DEAD HAVE BEEN SUBDUED.	4	FEUD	20
SUBJECT			
SUBJECT AND OBJECT SANG AND DANCED AS ONE;	237	THE TRANCED	17
SUBLIMINAL			
WHO SPOKE FIRST IN THE COARSE SHORT-HAND OF THE SUBLIMINAL DEPTHS,	170	FOURTH MEDITATN	71
SUBMERGE			
AND THOSE WHO SUBMERGE THEMSELVES DELIBERATELY IN TRIVIA,	169	FOURTH MEDITATN	38
SUBSIDES			
THE OLD LOG SUBSIDES WITH THE LESSENING WAVES,	202	THE ROSE	20
THE FIRE SUBSIDES INTO RINGS OF WATER,	221	THE ABYSS	59
SUBSTANCE			
BUT THE TRUE SUBSTANCE BEARS	9	THE ADAMANT	7
WILL TURN ITS PRIVATE SUBSTANCE INTO GREEN,	11	LIGHT BRIGHTER	19
I SAW SUBSTANCE FLOWING	56	THE LOST SON	94
AS A LOVELY SUBSTANCE WILL;	123	WORDS FOR WIND	19
EACH SINGLE SUBSTANCE GLIDDERED TO THE STARE;	143	SHIMMER OF EVIL	3
THINNING THE SOUL'S SUBSTANCE;	171	WHAT TELL BONES	24
SUBTERRANEAN			
LICE TETHERED TO LONG LIMP SUBTERRANEAN WEEDS,	50	THE MINIMAL	4
SUBTLE			
THE LATE PEACH YIELDS A SUBTLE MUSK,	14	COMING OF COLD	1
SUBTRACT			
SUBTRACT, AND PUT OURSELVES IN PAWN;	30	THE RECKONING	6
SUBURBAN			
AS DARKNESS CREEPS UP ON THE WELL-GROOMED SUBURBAN TOWN,	33	IDYLL	5
SUCH			
YET SUCH IS MY UNSEEMLINESS:	19	EPIDERM MACABRE	9
ROSE ON SUCH LOPPED LIMBS TO A NEW LIFE?	37	CUTTINGS (LATE)	4
SUCH WALTZING WAS NOT EASY.	45	MY PAPA'S WALTZ	4
SUCH MUSIC IN A SKIN!	79	GIVE WAY, GATES	4
SUCH OWLY PLEASURES! FISH COME FIRST, SWEET BIRD.	87	PRAISE TO END!	71
IS CIRCULARITY SUCH A SHAME?	92	I CRY, LOVE!	8
SUCH A SWEET NOISE: I CAN'T SLEEP FOR IT.	92	I CRY, LOVE!	19
OH, WHEN SHE WAS SAD, SHE CAST HERSELF DOWN INTO SUCH A PURE DEPTH,	102	ELEGY FOR JANE	10
BETWEEN SUCH ANIMAL AND HUMAN HEAT	105	SIR JOHN DAVIES	25

	PAGE	TITLE	LINE
SUCH (CONTINUED)			
SUCH ARDOR TAMES ETERNITY, I THINK.	132	SENTENTIOUS MAN	30
SUCH AFFIRMATIONS ARE PERPETUAL.	135	THE RENEWAL	4
ILLUMINATION BROUGHT TO SUCH A PITCH	135	THE RENEWAL	20
IN SUCH TIMES, LACKING A GOD,	160	FIRST MEDITATN	98
SUCH QUIET UNDER THE SMALL LEAVES!--	221	THE ABYSS	82
SUCH STRETCHINGS OF THE SPIRIT MAKE NO SOUND.	243	THE MOTION	4
SUCK			
THE NEWSMEN SUCK THEIR THUMBS.	31	LULL	14
WILL THE SEA GIVE THE WIND SUCK? A TOAD FOLDS INTO A STONE.	64	SHAPE OF FIRE	8
TOUCH AND AROUSE. SUCK AND SOB. CURSE AND MOURN.	80	GIVE WAY, GATES	46
SUCKED			
THE GHOSTLY FIGURE SUCKED ITS BREATH,	136	THE SENSUALISTS	17
SUCKING			
I CAN HEAR, UNDERGROUND, THAT SUCKING AND SOBBING,	37	CUTTINGS (LATE)	5
FROM THE SUCKING BOG.	65	SHAPE OF FIRE	52
THE SUDDEN SUCKING ROAR AS THE CULVERT LOOSENS ITS DEBRIS OF BRANCHES AND STICKS,	191	AT OYSTER RIVER	53
SUDDEN			
MY SHAVING HAND JERKED BACK IN SUDDEN TERROR:	25	DIM-WIT COUSIN	11
FOR THE ATTACKS OF FALSE HUMILITY TAKE SUDDEN TURNS FOR THE WORSE.	86	PRAISE TO END!	25
SUDDEN RENEWAL OF THE SELF--FROM WHERE?	135	THE RENEWAL	13
THE SUDDEN SUCKING ROAR AS THE CULVERT LOOSENS ITS DEBRIS OF BRANCHES AND STICKS,	191	AT OYSTER RIVER	53
AT THE SUDDEN VEERING, THE MOMENT OF TURNING.	193	JOURNY INTERIOR	5
THE SUDDEN SHUDDER AS THE JUTTING SEA-CLIFF COLLAPSES,	231	THE STORM	42
THIS SUDDEN RANDOM SONG,	271	THE REPLY	15
THE SUDDEN LIGHT SPILLED ON THE FLOOR LIKE CREAM	273	SUPPR W LINDSAY	12
SUDDENLY			
A GUST BLOWING THE LEAVES SUDDENLY UPWARD,	171	WHAT TELL BONES	29
THEN SUDDENLY FLUNG UP AND OVER,	226	THE LIZARD	10
SUDDENLY THEY CAME FLYING, LIKE A LONG SCARF OF SMOKE,	232	THE THING	1
WHEN OPPOSITES COME SUDDENLY IN PLACE,	244	INFIRMITY	33
SUDDENNESS			
A SUDDENNESS OF TREES,	34	NIGHT JOURNEY	7
SUFFER			
AND SEE AND SUFFER MYSELF	126	WORDS FOR WIND	104
SUFFERED			
I SUFFERED FOR BIRDS, FOR YOUNG RABBITS CAUGHT IN THE MOWER,	199	THE FAR FIELD	24
SUFFERING			
WAS IT A GOD HIS SUFFERING RENEWED?--	155	THE DYING MAN	60
I WAS FLUNG BACK FROM SUFFERING AND LOVE	246	THE MARROW	19
SUFFICES			
BUT A TIME COMES WHEN THE VAGUE LIFE OF THE MOUTH NO LONGER SUFFICES:	168	FOURTH MEDITATN	18
SUFFICIENT			
THAT KEEPS SUFFICIENT STORE	20	REPL TO CENSURE	14
SUGAR			
I HAVEN'T TIME FOR SUGAR,	75	I NEED, I NEED	24
MY BLUE ORIGINAL DANDY, NUMB WITH SUGAR?	86	PRAISE TO END!	18
SUGARY			
STICKS-IN-A-DROWSE DROOP OVER SUGARY LOAM,	37	CUTTINGS	1
SUIT			
BUT NOTHING WOULD SUIT.	115	THE SERPENT	18
SULLEN			
ONE WITH THE SULLEN DARK.	122	ALL EARTH, AIR	27
SULPHUROUS			
LOO, LOO, SAID THE SULPHUROUS WATER,	59	THE LONG ALLEY	14
SUM			
OF EASE, THE HOARDED, SECRET SUM;	30	THE RECKONING	2
SUMMER			
DAYS OF ANOTHER SUMMER.	6	THE PREMONITION	2
ALL SUMMER GREEN IS NOW UNDONE:	15	COMING OF COLD	42
THE SUMMER HOUSE SHAPED LIKE A VILLAGE BAND STAND	32	SALE	7
THAT SUMMER DAY.	51	THE WAKING (1)	28
BY THE SHRUNKEN LAKE, HUNTING, IN THE HEAT OF SUMMER.	54	THE LOST SON	43
THE SUMMER BUMPS OF HA:	60	THE LONG ALLEY	44
THAT AIR AND SHINE: AND THE FLICKER'S LOUD SUMMER CALL:	66	SHAPE OF FIRE	70
THE SPIDERS SAIL INTO SUMMER.	78	BRING THE DAY!	43
THE PLANTS WAVE ME IN, AND THE SUMMER APPLES;	88	PRAISE TO END!	86
LIKE ANY SUMMER DAY.	128	THE VOICE	24
A WALK IN LATE SUMMER	149	IN LATE SUMMER	T

	PAGE	TITLE	LINE
SUMMER (CONTINUED)			
ON THE LONG BANKS, IN THE SOFT SUMMER AIR.	149	IN LATE SUMMER	8
LIVING ALL MY HEART'S SUMMER ALONE,	161	I'M HERE	19
IN THE RAIN, SLACKENING ON A SUMMER FIELD;	165	HER BECOMING	8
I WOULD BE A STREAM, WINDING BETWEEN GREAT STRIATED ROCKS IN LATE SUMMER:	188	THE LONGING	46
IN THE SUMMER HEAT, I CAN SMELL THE DEAD BUFFALO,	189	THE LONGING	54
GREY FROM THE LONG WINTER, BURNT AT THE BASE IN LATE SUMMER.	193	JOURNY INTERIOR	10
AT THE EDGE OF A RIPENING MEADOW, IN EARLY SUMMER,	204	THE ROSE	80
I RECALL HOW SHE HARRIED THE CHILDREN AWAY ALL THE LATE SUMMER	223	ELEGY (2)	12
A SEA-WIND PAUSING IN A SUMMER TREE.	235	MANIFESTATION	8
IT IS NEITHER SPRING NOR SUMMER: IT IS ALWAYS,	235	ALL MORNING	39
MY SOUL, LIKE SOME HEAT-MADDENED SUMMER FLY,	239	IN A DARK TIME	20
THOUGH SUMMER BLAZES IN THE VIREO'S EYE.	240	IN EVEING AIR	2
DEEP IN THE GREENS OF SUMMER SING THE LIVES	244	INFIRMITY	25
HER ARMS MADE A SUMMER.	258	SONG (3)	23
AS SHE STEPS INTO SUMMER,	260	THE CHANGELING	8
SUMMERS			
FIFTY SUMMERS IN MOTION AT ONCE,	38	FORCING HOUSE	10
SUMMER'S			
THIS FAIR PARCEL OF SUMMER'S	258	SONG (3)	1
SUMMER-SAD			
A LOW VOICE, SUMMER-SAD.	90	UNFOLD! UNFOLD!	50
SUMMERY			
I ROMPED, LITHE AS A CHILD, DOWN THE SUMMERY STREETS OF MY VEINS,	86	PRAISE TO END!	21
SUMMIT			
THE EDGES OF THE SUMMIT STILL APPALL	156	THE DYING MAN	96
SUMMON			
SUMMON A VISION AND DECLARE IT PURE.	107	SIR JOHN DAVIES	78
SUN			
DENIES THE BLESSING OF THE SUN,	4	FEUD	10
FLASHED WITH THE SUN IN THE RIPPLE.	6	THE PREMONITION	11
THE SUN CUTS DEEP INTO THE HEAVY DRIFT,	11	LIGHT BRIGHTER	5
A FIELD OF BARLEY SPREAD BENEATH THE SUN.	13	PRAISE PRAIRIE	4
THE DANK BARK DRIES BENEATH THE SUN,	14	COMING OF COLD	32
THE LAND IS DESOLATE, THE SUN	15	COMING OF COLD	47
WAS WRESTED FROM THE SUN;	18	GENESIS	2
AND PULLED THE GREEN SHADE AGAINST MORNING SUN.	29	THE REMINDER	8
THE SUN WARMING THE FINE LOAM,	42	TRANSPLANTING	14
THEY TRELLISED THE SUN; THEY PLOTTED FOR MORE THAN THEMSELVES.	44	FRAU BAUMAN	25
IN MIST THAT SUN COULD SEIZE.	50	THE CYCLE	6
THE SUN WAS OUT;	51	THE WAKING (1)	3
THE SUN WAS AGAINST ME,	55	THE LOST SON	77
DID I EVER CURSE THE SUN?	62	FIELD OF LIGHT	20
THE SUN GLITTERED ON A SMALL RAPIDS.	63	FIELD OF LIGHT	34
WHEN THE SUN FOR ME GLINTED THE SIDES OF A SAND GRAIN,	66	SHAPE OF FIRE	68
THE LIGHT, THE FULL SUN	67	SHAPE OF FIRE	79
WHEN THE SUN HAS FALLEN BEHIND A WOODED ISLAND;	67	SHAPE OF FIRE	89
STAY IN THE SUN,	75	I NEED, I NEED	45
LOVE HELPS THE SUN.	76	I NEED, I NEED	51
THE SHADE SAYS: LOVE THE SUN.	82	SENSIBILITY! LA	39
IS THE SUN UNDER MY ARM?	82	SENSIBILITY! LA	45
THE SUN CAME OUT;	87	PRAISE TO END!	55
I WORE THE SUN WITH EASE.	87	PRAISE TO END!	66
THE SUN PLAYING ON LOAM,	92	I CRY, LOVE!	26
THE LIVE GRASS WHIRLS WITH THE SUN,	93	I CRY, LOVE!	35
MY HAIR BETWEEN ME AND THE SUN,	104	OLD LADY'S WRDS	42
THE SUN DECLARES THE EARTH;	124	WORDS FOR WIND	33
SHE SWAYS, HALF IN THE SUN:	124	WORDS FOR WIND	41
UNTIL MY EYES LOOK AT A BRIGHTER SUN	134	THE PURE FURY	27
WHEN THERE'S A DAZZLING DARK BEHIND THE SUN?	155	THE DYING MAN	53
AND THE SUN BRINGS JOY TO SOME.	157	FIRST MEDITATN	12
THE SUN LOOSENING THE FROST ON DECEMBER WINDOWS,	161	I'M HERE	2
STILL LEANING TOWARD THE LAST PLACE THE SUN WAS,	163	I'M HERE	76
THE FLAT BRANCH OF THAT HEMLOCK HOLDS THE LAST OF THE SUN,	163	I'M HERE	83
IN THE SUN, BUSY AT A YOUNG BODY,	165	HER BECOMING	7
MAY THE SUN GILD THEM A WORM;	169	FOURTH MEDITATN	60
THE SUN! THE SUN! AND ALL WE CAN BECOME!	173	WHAT TELL BONES	84
THE SUN! THE SUN! AND ALL WE CAN BECOME!	173	WHAT TELL BONES	84
THE STENCH OF THEIR DAMP FUR DRYING IN THE SUN,	189	THE LONGING	55

	PAGE	TITLE	LINE

SUN (CONTINUED)

AND THE SUN COMES OUT OF A BLUE CLOUD OVER THE TETONS, ...	194	JOURNY INTERIOR	40
I HAVE KNOWN THE HEART OF THE SUN,--	194	JOURNY INTERIOR	59
THESE WAVES, IN THE SUN, REMIND ME OF FLOWERS:	197	THE LONG WATERS	38
DROPPING A FINE YELLOW SILT WHERE THE SUN STAYS;	200	THE FAR FIELD	68
THE SUN A BALL OF FIRE COMING DOWN OVER THE WATER,	202	THE ROSE	16
GLINT OF THE SUN, BEFORE	210	HER TIME	20
HUNTING THE SUN.	213	THE HAPPY THREE	20
THREE IN THE SUN.	214	THE HAPPY THREE	38
IN THE SUN, IN THE SUN,	217	WISH YOUNG WIFE	9
IN THE SUN, IN THE SUN,	217	WISH YOUNG WIFE	9
THE MEDITERRANEAN SUN SHINING ON US, EQUALLY,	226	THE LIZARD	4
FLASHING BETWEEN GOLD LEVELS OF THE LATE SUN,	232	THE THING	5
CONFUSING THEM ONCE FLYING STRAIGHT INTO THE SUN	232	THE THING	7
WINGS WITHOUT FEATHERS CREAKING IN THE SUN,	243	THE MOTION	19
ONE WHITE FACE SHIMMERS BRIGHTER THAN THE SUN	246	THE MARROW	7
AND SHIMMERING. THE SUN BURNED THROUGH A HAZE,	247	I WAITED	11
CHILD OF THE DARK, HE CAN OUT LEAP THE SUN,	250	THE RIGHT THING	10
AND THE SUN TOUCHES THE LIZARD'S THROAT, ITS TAIL HALF IN SHADOW.	261	THE CHANGELING	34
HE CAN SEE THE SECOND SUN	266	FOR STEVENS	3

SUN-CHAIRS

ITS BEVY OF BEES, AND ITS WIND-BEATEN RICKETY SUN-CHAIRS.	226	THE LIZARD	29

SUNDAY

THEIR WIVES GO OUT ON SUNDAY BENEATH THE LATEST HAT.	27	CLAIRVOY WIDOW	8
AND SUNDAY SLEEP.	46	PICKLE BELT	4
ALL IN MY YARD, OF A PERPETUAL SUNDAY,	235	ALL MORNING	46

SUNK

PLANKS SUNK IN THE SAND.	62	FIELD OF LIGHT	3
DYING BRIGHTLY UNDER THE STREET LIGHTS SUNK IN COARSE CONCRETE,	193	JOURNY INTERIOR	29
STILL AS A CLAY SUNK	258	SONG (3)	30

SUNKEN

--AND THE EYES, STILL VIVID, LOOKING UP FROM A SUNKEN ROOM.	22	ROAD TO WDLAWN	8
SETTLING IN SMALL BEADS AROUND WEEDS AND SUNKEN BRANCHES,	159	FIRST MEDITATN	61
SLAPPING LIGHTLY AGAINST A SUNKEN LOG.	190	AT OYSTER RIVER	14
SILENCE OF WATER ABOVE A SUNKEN TREE:	201	THE FAR FIELD	100

SUNLESS

A GREAT FLAME RISES FROM THE SUNLESS SEA;	188	THE LONGING	31
THE CLOSE DIRT DANCING ON A SUNLESS STONE	243	THE MOTION	20

SUNLIGHT

UP THROUGH THE STREAKED GLASS, FLASHING WITH SUNLIGHT, ...	43	CHILD ON GRNHSE	4
TO SEE CYCLAMEN VEINS BECOME CLEARER IN EARLY SUNLIGHT,	67	SHAPE OF FIRE	86
IN THE WINTER-WASP, PULSING ITS WINGS IN THE SUNLIGHT; ...	88	PRAISE TO END!	92
SUNLIGHT.	163	I'M HERE	62
TILTING BACK THE SUNLIGHT.	168	FOURTH MEDITATN	11
ITS WINGS CATCHING A LAST GLINT OF THE REFLECTED SUNLIGHT.	190	AT OYSTER RIVER	23
AND THE BUNCHED LOGS PEEL IN THE AFTERNOON SUNLIGHT,	196	THE LONG WATERS	16
SHIFTING IN THE WAKENING SUNLIGHT	204	THE ROSE	87
SHAKING OUT MY CATCH IN THE MORNING SUNLIGHT,	209	HER LONGING	15

SUNLIT

THEIR SUNLIT LEAPING.	152	THE SISKINS	24
A SUNLIT SILENCE.	221	THE ABYSS	60

SUNNY

THE SHADOWS CRAWLING DOWN A SUNNY WALL.	171	WHAT TELL BONES	17
THAT GENTLES ON A SUNNY BLUE PLATEAU.	201	THE FAR FIELD	92

SUN-PARCHED

NEAR THIS ROSE, IN THIS GROVE OF SUN-PARCHED, WIND-WARPED MADRONAS,	205	THE ROSE	98

SUNSHINE

WHEN OUR SPAYED FEMALE CAT YAWNS AND STRETCHES OUT IN THE SUNSHINE--	234	ALL MORNING	23

SUN-STRUCK

ROCKING IT, LIKE A SUN-STRUCK POND,	163	I'M HERE	84

SUPERMARKET

I SEE YOU IN SOME CELESTIAL SUPERMARKET,	223	ELEGY (2)	19

SUPPER

SUPPER WITH LINDSAY	273	SUPPR W LINDSAY	T

SUPPLEMENT

YOU TAKE THE TIMES SUPPLEMENT, AND READ ITS VERSE,	113	TO A LADY ED	2

SUPPOSE

SUPPOSE YOU WALK OUT IN A STORM,	114	DINKY	5
SO, I SUPPOSE, THE SPIRIT JOURNEYS.	159	FIRST MEDITATN	73

	PAGE	TITLE	LINE
SUPPOSE (CONTINUED)			
SUPPOSE THE CEILING WENT OUTSIDE	178	THE CEILING	1
SUPPRESS			
THAT LADIES THEIR TRUE NATURES NEVER SUPPRESS, ...	113	TO A LADY ED	10
SURE			
WING-CROOKED AND SURE, ...	93	I CRY, LOVE!	42
I'M SURE I'VE BEEN A TOAD, ONE TIME OR ANOTHER.	151	SLUG	25
BE SURE THAT WHATEVER YOU ARE IS YOU	177	KITTY-CAT BIRD	20
A PHOENIX, SURE OF MY BODY, ...	209	HER LONGING	19
OF THAT YOU CAN BE SURE, ...	268	SAGINAW SONG	44
"SURE, WE STILL EAT," I SAID. "ENOUGH! OR TOO MUCH."	273	SUPPR W LINDSAY	17
SURELY			
A PLACE I SURELY DID LIKE TO GO	111	SQUEEZE-BOX	17
SURETY			
THE HUMMINGBIRD'S SURETY, THE KINGFISHER'S CUNNING--	191	AT OYSTER RIVER	40
SURF			
THE BLUE SPRUCE LASHED LIKE A SURF AT THE DOOR.	12	MID-CNTRY BLOW	4
THE LONG SURF OF THE STORM BOOMS	210	HER TIME	21
SURFACE			
TO STARE INTO THE AFTER-LIGHT, THE GLITTER LEFT ON THE LAKE'S SURFACE,	67	SHAPE OF FIRE	88
PETALS AND REFLECTIONS OF PETALS MIXED ON THE SURFACE OF A GLASSY POOL, ...	194	JOURNY INTERIOR	56
DELIGHTING IN SURFACE CHANGE, THE GLITTER OF LIGHT ON WAVES,	195	JOURNY INTERIOR	67
THEN SLIDES DOWN OVER THE EYE'S SURFACE, ...	226	THE LIZARD	24
MY EYE ALWAYS BEYOND THE SURFACE REFLECTION;	233	THE PIKE	12
OR FLOATED ON THE SURFACE OF A POND, ...	247	I WAITED	8
SURFACES			
THE NERVELESS CONSTRICTION OF SURFACES--	166	HER BECOMING	41
SURFEIT			
TOO MUCH REALITY CAN BE A DAZZLE, A SURFEIT;	220	THE ABYSS	44
SURGEON			
A SURGEON GUIDES A SCALPEL WITH THUMB AND FINGER-TIPS. ...	28	CLAIRVOY WIDOW	20
SURLY			
THE SURLY ONE	138	THE SURLY ONE	T
LIKE A NURSE HE SAT WITH ME FOR WEEKS, A SLY SURLY ATTENDANT, ...	220	THE ABYSS	38
SURPRISE			
OF FATE, YOU BLUBBER IN SURPRISE.	4	FEUD	4
WHO CAN SURPRISE A THING	130	THE OTHER	13
THE WORST SURPRISE A CORNER COULD HAVE, ...	161	I'M HERE	14
SURRENDERING			
WILLS WHAT HE WOULD, SURRENDERING HIS WILL	250	THE RIGHT THING	17
SURROUND			
WHEREFORE, O BIRDS AND SMALL FISH, SURROUND ME.	88	PRAISE TO END!	97
SURROUNDED			
SURROUNDED BY SAND, BROKEN SHELLS, THE WRECKAGE OF WATER.	197	THE LONG WATERS	59
SURROUNDINGS			
TAKING AND EMBRACING ITS SURROUNDINGS, ...	101	LIGHT BREATHER	13
SURVEY			
HERE FROM THE FIELD'S EDGE WE SURVEY	33	HIGHWAY: MICH	1
SURVIVE			
SURVIVE THE GREEN ICE	217	WISH YOUNG WIFE	4
SURVIVED			
WHAT YOU SURVIVED I SHALL BELIEVE: THE HEAT, ...	144	ELEGY (1)	13
THE DESCENDANTS OF THE PLAYFUL TREE-SHREW THAT SURVIVED THE ARCHAIC KILLERS, ...	170	FOURTH MEDITATN	66
SURVIVING			
I SEE GRANDPA SURVIVING A SERIES OF SEVEN STROKES, ...	28	CLAIRVOY WIDOW	21
THE BEAUTIFUL SURVIVING BONES	58	THE LOST SON	157
SUSTAINS			
THE SERPENT'S HEART SUSTAINS THE LOVELESS STONE:	131	SENTENTIOUS MAN	3
SUSTENANCE			
SUSTENANCE SEEMED SENSIBLE	228	THE GERANIUM	8
SUTURES			
THEIR WAN MOUTHS KISSING THE WARM SUTURES, ...	50	THE MINIMAL	9
SWAGGERING			
ONE SWAGGERING HEAD	43	FLOWER DUMP	12
SWALE			
WHEN YOU HIT THE DEEP PIT AT THE BOTTOM OF THE SWALE, ...	193	JOURNY INTERIOR	20
SWALLOWS			
THE BANK SWALLOWS VEER AND DIP, ...	152	THE SISKINS	1
THE SWALLOWS FLEW IN AND OUT OF THE SMOKELESS CHIMNEYS.	162	I'M HERE	41

	PAGE	TITLE	LINE
SWALLOWS (CONTINUED)			
I RETURN TO THE TWITTERING OF SWALLOWS ABOVE WATER,	204	THE ROSE	73
SWAMP			
THE HERON STANDS IN WATER WHERE THE SWAMP	15	THE HERON	1
THROUGH THE SWAMP ALIVE WITH QUICKSAND,	193	JOURNY INTERIOR	14
SWAMPLAND			
AS IF I HAD BROKEN THE NATURAL ORDER OF THINGS IN THAT SWAMPLAND;	40	MOSS-GATHERING	10
SWAMPS			
THE GREAT SWAMPS FLASH.	103	OLD LADY'S WRDS	13
SWAN			
A SWAN NEEDS A POND.	78	BRING THE DAY!	34
THE SWAN	140	THE SWAN	T
BY THE LAKE'S EDGE, I SEE A SILVER SWAN,	140	THE SWAN	16
A SINGLE WAVE COMES IN LIKE THE NECK OF A GREAT SWAN	197	THE LONG WATERS	52
THAT SOME HAVE CALLED SWAN CREEK;	267	SAGINAW SONG	8
SWAN-HEART			
SWAN-HEART, ARBUTUS-CALM,	124	WORDS FOR WIND	51
SWAN'S			
THE SWAN'S DREAD OF THE DARKENING SHORE,	171	WHAT TELL BONES	25
SWARMS			
OLD SECRETS TO AMORPHOUS SWARMS.	4	FEUD	16
SWART			
HER SWART HILARIOUS SKIN;	126	WORDS FOR WIND	99
SWAY			
IN THE SAME WAY: O WATCH HIS BODY SWAY!--	105	SIR JOHN DAVIES	11
SHE SWAYS WHENEVER I SWAY.	123	WORDS FOR WIND	12
AND WE BOUNCE AND SWAY ALONG TOWARD THE MIDNIGHT,	158	FIRST MEDITATN	23
WHERE THE HAWKS SWAY OUT INTO THE WIND,	202	THE ROSE	4
I SWAY OUTSIDE MYSELF	202	THE ROSE	22
FANCIES SWAY AWAY	210	HER TIME	3
SWAYED			
A TREE SWAYED OVER WATER.	100	THE VISITANT	2
THE TREE, THE CLOSE WILLOW, SWAYED.	101	THE VISITANT	27
AND I SWAYED OUT BEYOND THE WHITE SEAFOAM;	120	THE DREAM	29
AS IF I SWAYED OUT ON THE WILDEST WAVE ALIVE,	205	THE ROSE	104
A LIGHT LEAF ON A TREE, SHE SWAYED AWAY	241	THE SEQUEL	23
SWAYING			
SWAYING CLOSE TO THE FACE,	39	ORCHIDS	3
SWAYING OVER THE WALKS, IN THE WATERY AIR,	61	THE LONG ALLEY	75
SWAYING, WOULD YOU BELIEVE,	98	O, THOU OPENING	48
SWAYING IN A LONG WAVE;	100	THE VISITANT	12
STILL SWAYING GENTLY BY HIS TOES,	116	THE SLOTH	11
SWAYING, I TOOK ITS GAZE;	145	THE BEAST	11
THE LADEN WHEELBARROWS CREAKING AND SWAYING,	158	FIRST MEDITATN	46
THE ETERNAL ONE, THE CHILD, THE SWAYING VINE BRANCH,	198	THE LONG WATERS	69
A SPIDER EASES HIMSELF DOWN FROM A SWAYING LIGHT-BULB,	231	THE STORM	34
SWAYING IN AIR, LIKE SOME LONG WATER WEED.	241	THE SEQUEL	19
A SWAYING LIGHT-CORD, THEN RAN HALF-WAY BACK.	273	SUPPR W LINDSAY	25
SWAYS			
THE STALK STILL SWAYS.	56	THE LOST SON	115
A ROSE SWAYS LEAST.	66	SHAPE OF FIRE	62
SHE SWAYS WHENEVER I SWAY.	123	WORDS FOR WIND	12
SHE SWAYS, HALF IN THE SUN:	124	WORDS FOR WIND	41
(I MEASURE TIME BY HOW A BODY SWAYS).	127	I KNEW A WOMAN	28
MY HEART SWAYS WITH THE WORLD.	153	THE DYING MAN	13
SWAYS ME AWAKE. WHAT HO, AND THE FIELD'S MY FRIEND,	260	THE CHANGELING	14
SWEAR			
I SWEAR SHE CAST A SHADOW WHITE AS STONE.	127	I KNEW A WOMAN	25
IF THEY LET YOU EAT AND SWEAR	228	IN VIOLENT WARD	4
THINGS SPEAK TO ME, I SWEAR;	262	FOLLIES OF ADAM	5
THIS SHIVERS ME; I SWEAR	271	THE REPLY	10
SWEAT			
AND PUMPKINS SWEAT A BITTER OIL.	14	COMING OF COLD	17
THAT DRIP AND SWEAT,	38	FORCING HOUSE	6
SWEAT AND DRIP,	38	FORCING HOUSE	7
WITH THEIR BANDANNAS STIFFENED WITH SWEAT,	44	FRAU BAUMAN	33
THIS AIR COULD FLESH A DEAD STICK. SWEET JESUS, MAKE ME SWEAT.	61	THE LONG ALLEY	63
TELL ME, BODY WITHOUT SKIN, DOES A FISH SWEAT?	89	UNFOLD! UNFOLD!	2
AND THE SWEAT POURED FROM MY FACE,	146	THE SONG	23
SWEATING			
MY SHADOW PINNED AGAINST A SWEATING WALL.	239	IN A DARK TIME	10

	PAGE	TITLE	LINE
SWEATING (CONTINUED)			
I'M SWEATING OUT THE WILL TO DIE.	256	IN HYDROTHERAPY	10
SWEATS			
WHO ELSE SWEATS LIGHT FROM A STONE?	170	FOURTH MEDITATN	81
SWEEPS			
THESE SWEEPS OF LIGHT UNDO ME.	57	THE LOST SON	118
SWEET			
OUT INTO THE SWEET AIR,	42	TRANSPLANTING	20
THIS AIR COULD FLESH A DEAD STICK. SWEET JESUS, MAKE ME			
SWEAT.	61	THE LONG ALLEY	63
REACH ME ROSE, SWEET ONE, STILL MOIST IN THE LOAM,	61	THE LONG ALLEY	68
SING TO ME, SWEET.	86	PRAISE TO END!	30
SWEET JESUS TOSSED ME BACK:	87	PRAISE TO END!	65
SUCH OWLY PLEASURES! FISH COME FIRST, SWEET BIRD.	87	PRAISE TO END!	71
SUCH A SWEET NOISE: I CAN'T SLEEP FOR IT.	92	I CRY, LOVE!	19
SIMPLICITY'S SWEET THING, EITHER. A LEAF COULD DRAG YOU.	98	O, THOU OPENING	29
SEE WHAT THE SWEET HARP SAYS.	99	O, THOU OPENING	73
ONCE I WAS SWEET WITH THE LIGHT OF MYSELF,	103	OLD LADY'S WRDS	39
SWEET ALICE S. MORRIS, I AM PLEASED, OF COURSE,	113	TO A LADY ED	1
JUST SEND ME ALONG THAT SWEET SEVENTY-FIVE;	113	TO A LADY ED	14
SWEET PHOEBE, SHE'S MY THEME:	123	WORDS FOR WIND	11
O SWEET FIELD FAR AHEAD, I HEAR YOUR BIRDS,	156	THE DYING MAN	88
A MUFFLED VOICE, A LOW SWEET WATERY NOISE.	165	HER BECOMING	20
POOR MYRTLE WOULD SIGH, "SWEET MY COZ,	180	GOO-GIRL	1
THAT TREMBLE OF SWEET NOTES SET MY HEART ASTIR,	216	THE SHY MAN	10
AND THAT SWEET MAN, JOHN CLARE.	228	IN VIOLENT WARD	7
SWEET CHRIST, REJOICE IN MY INFIRMITY;	244	INFIRMITY	7
THE SWEET LIGHT MET ME AS I WALKED TOWARD	248	THE TREE, BIRD	3
SWEETENED			
RAIN SWEETENED THE CAVE AND THE DOVE STILL CALLED;	66	SHAPE OF FIRE	75
BEETLES SWEETENED MY BREATH.	89	UNFOLD! UNFOLD!	28
SWEETER			
SHE'S SWEETER THAN A TREE.	123	WORDS FOR WIND	2
SWEETHEART			
MY SWEETHEART IS A UGLY WITCH,	181	MONOTONY SONG	17
SWEET-HEART			
AND SHE IS MY SWEET-HEART.	268	SAGINAW SONG	42
SWEETHEART'S			
MY SWEETHEART'S STILL IN HER CAVE.	82	SENSIBILITY! LA	28
SWEETLY			
HOW SWEETLY I ABIDE. AM I A BIRD?	165	HER BECOMING	16
BUT SWEETLY DAFT.	172	WHAT TELL BONES	58
SWEETNESS			
FOR WHOM WERE YOU MADE, SWEETNESS I CANNOT TOUCH?	59	THE LONG ALLEY	27
SHE WITH HER LARCHY SWEETNESS,	261	THE CHANGELING	54
SWEET-PEA			
THE SWEET-PEA TENDRILS, THE SMILAX,	44	FRAU BAUMAN	5
SWEET-PEAS			
OR FAN LIFE INTO WILTED SWEET-PEAS WITH HIS HAT,	42	OLD FLORIST	9
SWELL			
THE YOUNG FRUIT SWELL UPON THE PEAR-TREE BOUGH.	11	LIGHT BRIGHTER	16
FEATHERS OF THE LONG SWELL, BURNISHED, ALMOST OILY--	197	THE LONG WATERS	51
OF THE LONG SWELL,	205	THE ROSE	93
ALONG THE SEA-WALL, A STEADY SLOSHING OF THE SWELL,	230	THE STORM	10
WHILE THE ROCK-SEAMS SWELL WITH THE SEA,	261	THE CHANGELING	33
SWELLED			
FOR WHOM HAVE I SWELLED LIKE A SEED?	85	PRAISE TO END!	2
SWELLING			
SWELLING THE ROOTS WITH STEAM AND STENCH,	38	FORCING HOUSE	8
SWELLS			
A SEED THAT SWELLS THE RIND	18	GENESIS	7
SWEPT			
WHEN I STOOD AT THE WINDOW, AN ELM BOUGH SWEPT TO MY KNEES;	12	MID-CNTRY BLOW	3
SWERVING			
SWERVING UP A STEEP EMBANKMENT.	158	FIRST MEDITATN	55
SWIFT			
THEY FLICKER FASTER THAN A BLUE-TAILED SWIFT,	8	THE SIGNALS	5
ONE SWIFT MOVEMENT,--	42	TRANSPLANTING	5
AT FIRST A SWIFT RIPPLING BETWEEN ROCKS,	200	THE FAR FIELD	63
THEN THROWING ITSELF UP AND AWAY FROM THE IMPLACABLE SWIFT			
PURSUERS,	232	THE THING	6
SWIMMING			
STILL SWIMMING FORWARD--	159	FIRST MEDITATN	72

	PAGE	TITLE	LINE
SWIMMING (CONTINUED)			
SWIMMING SLOWLY, ITS BACK RUFFLED BY THE LIGHT CROSS-WINDS,	197	THE LONG WATERS	53
SWINE-ON-FRIDAY			
KISS THE TROUGH, SWINE-ON-FRIDAY.	59	THE LONG ALLEY	24
SWING			
WE SIT IN THE PORCH SWING, CONTENT AND HALF ASLEEP.	33	IDYLL	8
I WATCH A BEACON SWING	34	NIGHT JOURNEY	16
THE SHARP STARS SWING AROUND;	125	WORDS FOR WIND	64
SWINGE			
WE'LL SWINGE THE INSTANT!--	79	GIVE WAY, GATES	26
SWINGING			
SWINGING BY THE FIRE-PIT,	57	THE LOST SON	131
THE BONES OF WEEDS KEPT SWINGING IN THE WIND,	58	THE LOST SON	152
SWINGING IN THE WIND.	58	THE LOST SON	158
THE WEEDS STOPPED SWINGING.	58	THE LOST SON	161
TETHERED TO A LIMP WEED, SWINGING,	101	LIGHT BREATHER	8
THE DOORS SWINGING OPEN,	103	OLD LADY'S WRDS	21
ELM SWINGING AROUND	103	OLD LADY'S WRDS	27
BUMPING AGAINST STICKS AND BOTTOM-STONES, THEN SWINGING	159	FIRST MEDITATN	70
AND THE SMALL STREET-LAMP SWINGING AND SLAMMING AGAINST THE LAMP POLE.	230	THE STORM	7
SWINGS			
SLOW SWINGS THE BREEZE ABOVE HER HEAD,	17	NO BIRD	5
AS WHEN THE DOOR SWINGS OPEN IN A FLORIST'S STOREROOM--	220	THE ABYSS	46
SWIRL			
KISS ME, ASHES, I'M FALLING THROUGH A DARK SWIRL.	57	THE LOST SON	121
THE SMALL BIRDS SWIRL AROUND;	148	THE SMALL	1
SWIRLING			
THE WATERS SWIRLING PAST THE TINY HEADLANDS.	202	THE ROSE	25
SWITCHBOARD			
LONELY RECEPTION ROOM, LAVATORY, SWITCHBOARD.	46	DOLOR	5
SWOLLEN			
CHILDREN, THEIR BELLIES SWOLLEN LIKE BLOWN-UP PAPER BAGS,	48	JUDGE NOT	2
CREEKS SWOLLEN IN MIDSUMMER FROM THE FLASH-FLOOD ROARING INTO THE NARROW VALLEY.	193	JOURNY INTERIOR	8
SWOOPING			
ALL THAT DIVING AND PITCHING AND SWOOPING.	255	LIGHT POEM	5
SWOOPS			
BY SWOOPS OF BIRD, BY LEAPS OF FISH, I LIVE.	167	HER BECOMING	91
SWORD			
THE EDGE OF HEAVEN WAS SHARPER THAN A SWORD;	237	THE TRANCED	6
SWUNG			
MY DOORS ARE WIDELY SWUNG.	3	OPEN HOUSE	4
BUT STEPPED RIGHT UP AND SWUNG AT THE DEVIL;	111	SQUEEZE-BOX	4
OUR SHADOWS MET, AND SLOWLY SWUNG AROUND;	120	THE DREAM	26
AND WHEN IT SWUNG, I SAW	145	THE BEAST	4
SYLLABLES			
DELICATE THE SYLLABLES THAT RELEASE THE REPRESSION;	29	THE GENTLE	1
AND HOW, ONCE STARTLED INTO TALK, THE LIGHT SYLLABLES LEAPED FOR HER,	102	ELEGY FOR JANE	3
SYMBOL			
MY SYMBOL!	220	THE ABYSS	36
SYMBOLICAL			
ALL NATURAL SHAPES BECAME SYMBOLICAL.	166	HER BECOMING	57
SYMBOLS			
SING, SING, YOU SYMBOLS! ALL SIMPLE CREATURES,	90	UNFOLD! UNFOLD!	45
SYNCO			
OH, THE SYNCO SEPTET PLAYED FOR US THEN,	112	SQUEEZE-BOX	22
TABLE			
THE TABLE WHERE EVERYONE ATE AS HE SHOULD,	32	SALE	14
BUT MANY A MAN ROLLED UNDER THE TABLE	112	SQUEEZE-BOX	36
TAIL			
THIS TAIL HATES A FLAT PATH.	79	GIVE WAY, GATES	15
BY THE LIFTING OF THE TAIL OF A NEIGHBOR'S CAT,	82	SENSIBILITY! LA	35
I'VE TRACED THESE WORDS IN SAND WITH A VESTIGIAL TAIL;	92	I CRY, LOVE!	17
THE HOLY ROOT WAGS THE TAIL OF A HILL;	99	O, THOU OPENING	54
TAIL AROUND, NOSING IN AND OUT OF THE CURRENT,	101	LIGHT BREATHER	9
A WREN, HAPPY, TAIL INTO THE WIND,	102	ELEGY FOR JANE	5
THE TAIL AND SMALLER LEGS SLIPPING AND SLIDING SLOWLY BACKWARD--	159	FIRST MEDITATN	65
HE HAD NO SKIN, HE HAD NO TAIL.	178	THE WHALE	2
A DONKEY'S TAIL IS VERY NICE	181	MONOTONY SONG	1
A HEAD OR TAIL--WHICH DOES HE LACK?	182	THE HIPPO	1

	PAGE	TITLE	LINE
TAIL (CONTINUED)			
THE MARE'S TAIL, THE FLOATING FROGBIT,	209	HER LONGING	4
MY FATHER TOOK IT TO HER, BY THE TAIL.	224	OTTO	30
THE TAIL STRAIGHT AS AN AWL,	226	THE LIZARD	9
HIS TAIL GREY WITH THE GROUND NOW,	226	THE LIZARD	18
TILL I CAUGHT HIM UP BY THE TAIL AND BROUGHT HIM IN,	227	MEADOW MOUSE	4
HIS TAIL CURLED UNDER HIM, HIS BELLY BIG	227	MEADOW MOUSE	14
AND THE SUN TOUCHES THE LIZARD'S THROAT, ITS TAIL HALF IN SHADOW.	261	THE CHANGELING	34
TAINT			
--AND THE TAINT IN A BLOOD THAT WAS RUNNING TOO THIN.	32	SALE	20
TAKE			
TAKE TONGUE AND EAR--ALL ELSE I HAVE--	8	PRAYER	21
LOST HUES OF BIRDS THE TREES TAKE AS THEIR OWN.	12	SLOW SEASON	9
WOULD RATHER TAKE THAN DISH IT OUT.	23	AMOROUS LADY	4
WHILE OTHERS TAKE THEIR REST.	34	NIGHT JOURNEY	5
WHICH IS THE WAY I TAKE;	54	THE LOST SON	25
TAKE THE SKIN OF A CAT	55	THE LOST SON	54
I'LL TAKE THE FIRE.	61	THE LONG ALLEY	89
FOR THE ATTACKS OF FALSE HUMILITY TAKE SUDDEN TURNS FOR THE WORSE.	86	PRAISE TO END!	25
I'LL MAKE IT; BUT IT MAY TAKE ME.	97	O, THOU OPENING	1
I TAKE THIS CADENCE FROM A MAN NAMED YEATS;	105	SIR JOHN DAVIES	19
I TAKE IT, AND I GIVE IT BACK AGAIN:	105	SIR JOHN DAVIES	20
I WAKE TO SLEEP, AND TAKE MY WAKING SLOW.	108	THE WAKING (2)	1
I WAKE TO SLEEP, AND TAKE MY WAKING SLOW.	108	THE WAKING (2)	6
I WAKE TO SLEEP, AND TAKE MY WAKING SLOW.	108	THE WAKING (2)	12
TO YOU AND ME; SO TAKE THE LIVELY AIR,	108	THE WAKING (2)	14
I WAKE TO SLEEP, AND TAKE MY WAKING SLOW.	108	THE WAKING (2)	18
YOU TAKE THE TIMES SUPPLEMENT, AND READ ITS VERSE,	113	TO A LADY ED	2
I TAKE THE LIBERTIES A SHORT LIFE PERMITS--	173	WHAT TELL BONES	90
WHAT WE PUT DOWN, MUST WE TAKE UP AGAIN?	243	THE MOTION	11
O WHO WOULD TAKE THE VISION FROM THE CHILD?--	243	THE MOTION	23
THINGS WITHOUT HANDS TAKE HANDS: THERE IS NO CHOICE,--	244	INFIRMITY	31
ONE LOOK TOO CLOSE CAN TAKE MY SOUL AWAY.	246	THE MARROW	9
TAKE NOTICE OF THIS MAN!	260	THE CHANGELING	24
TAKEN			
MAY THEY BE TAKEN BY THE TRUE BURNING;	169	FOURTH MEDITATN	61
SMALL ENOUGH TO BE TAKEN IN, EMBRACED, BY TWO ARMS,--	191	AT OYSTER RIVER	46
I HAVE TAKEN, TOO OFTEN, THE DANGEROUS PATH,	220	THE ABYSS	21
I HAVE TAKEN COUNSEL OF THE CRAB AND THE SEA-URCHIN,	222	THE ABYSS	92
THE LORD GOD HAS TAKEN MY HEAVINESS AWAY;	222	THE ABYSS	98
TAKES			
THE MOUTH ASKS. THE HAND TAKES.	80	GIVE WAY, GATES	51
LIGHT TAKES THE TREE; BUT WHO CAN TELL US HOW?	108	THE WAKING (2)	10
AN EXULTATION TAKES US OUTSIDE LIFE:	132	SENTENTIOUS MAN	25
THE LIGHT AIR TAKES MY BEING'S BREATH AWAY;	134	THE PURE FURY	23
AND THAT CRY TAKES ME BACK WHERE I WAS BORN.	156	THE DYING MAN	83
HE STARTS TO YAWN--IT TAKES ALL DAY--	182	THE HIPPO	4
THE FLESH TAKES ON THE PURE POISE OF THE SPIRIT,	191	AT OYSTER RIVER	38
IT TAKES IN THE WHOLE BODY;	207	THE YOUNG GIRL	2
TAKES TO HIMSELF WHAT MYSTERY HE CAN,	250	THE RIGHT THING	15
TAKING			
I MISS THE PALLBEARERS MOMENTOUSLY TAKING THEIR PLACES,	22	ROAD TO WDLAWN	5
SOME RARE NEW TEDIUM'S TAKING SHAPE:	81	SENSIBILITY! LA	13
TAKING AND EMBRACING ITS SURROUNDINGS,	101	LIGHT BREATHER	13
AND WE RIDE, WE RIDE, TAKING THE CURVES	158	FIRST MEDITATN	31
STILL TAKING DELIGHT IN NAKEDNESS,	165	HER BECOMING	6
TALE			
UNTIL YOU HAVE THOUGHT THIS SAD TALE THROUGH:	177	KITTY-CAT BIRD	19
TALK			
LOOK AT HIM PUFF. HE'S TRYING TO TALK.	73	WHERE KNOCK IS	60
I COULD TALK TO A SNAIL;	84	O LULL ME, LULL	39
AND HOW, ONCE STARTLED INTO TALK, THE LIGHT SYLLABLES LEAPED FOR HER,	102	ELEGY FOR JANE	3
WOULD FREQUENTLY TALK TO A BUSH,	182	BOY AND BUSH	2
I'D LIKE TO TALK BACK,	182	BOY AND BUSH	4
WHEN I PAUSE TO TALK TO A STONE,	215	HIS FOREBODING	9
TALKED			
TALKED TO A FAUCET;	74	I NEED, I NEED	9
AS THOSE TWO QUIETLY TALKED,	182	BOY AND BUSH	7
SO THEY TALKED AND THEY TALKED AND THEY TALKED.	182	BOY AND BUSH	10
SO THEY TALKED AND THEY TALKED AND THEY TALKED.	182	BOY AND BUSH	10

	PAGE	TITLE	LINE
TALKED (CONTINUED)			
SO THEY TALKED AND THEY TALKED AND THEY TALKED.	182	BOY AND BUSH	10
I TALKED TO A SHRUNKEN ROOT;	262	FOLLIES OF ADAM	15
TALKING			
THE MARROW OF GOD, TALKING,	103	OLD LADY'S WRDS	8
TALL			
THE SIDEBOARD BESIDE WHICH A TALL FOOTMAN STOOD	32	SALE	15
IT WAS "WOULD YOU BELIEVE IT--FAWTHER'S TALL!"	111	SQUEEZE-BOX	14
IN THE COUNTRY OF FEW LAKES, IN THE TALL BUFFALO GRASS AT THE BASE OF THE CLAY BUTTES,	189	THE LONGING	53
TALUS			
AND THE SHALE SLIDES AN INCH IN THE TALUS,	157	FIRST MEDITATN	10
TAME			
SPEECH REVIVED, A GHOSTLY GOING OF TAME BEARS, A BRIGHT MOON ON GLEAMING	98	O, THOU OPENING	23
TAMES			
SUCH ARDOR TAMES ETERNITY, I THINK.	132	SENTENTIOUS MAN	30
TAMPING			
TURNING AND TAMPING,	42	TRANSPLANTING	2
TAMPING AND STAMPING DIRT INTO POTS,--	42	OLD FLORIST	3
A SINGLE TWIST OF THE THUMBS, A TAMPING AND TURNING,	42	TRANSPLANTING	7
TANGLE			
OUT OF THE BRIARY HEDGE, THE TANGLE OF MATTED UNDERBRUSH,	203	THE ROSE	45
TANGLED			
MY HAIR'S ALL TANGLED ON YOUR HEAD,	136	THE SENSUALISTS	3
MUST I STAY TANGLED IN THAT LIVELY HAIR?	140	THE SWAN	3
OR TWO HORSES PLUNGING IN SNOW, THEIR LINES TANGLED,	158	FIRST MEDITATN	53
TAPPING			
BUT MORNING LIGHT COMES TAPPING AT THE LID,	17	UNEXTINGUISHED	9
TARFACE			
THE ROAD CHANGING FROM GLAZED TARFACE TO A RUBBLE OF STONE,	199	THE FAR FIELD	8
TAR-LADEN			
THE OILY, TAR-LADEN WALLS	205	THE ROSE	94
TASK			
THINK OF THE TASK OF AIR!--	260	THE CHANGELING	7
TASTE			
I CAN'T TASTE MY MOTHER.	74	I NEED, I NEED	2
I TASTE MY SISTER WHEN I KISS MY WIFE;	132	SENTENTIOUS MAN	27
TATTERED			
WRAPPED IN THE TATTERED ROBE OF DEATH,	136	THE SENSUALISTS	19
TAUGHT			
A MOUSE TAUGHT ME HOW, I WAS A HAPPY ASKER.	90	UNFOLD! UNFOLD!	35
THE LIVELY DEAD HAD TAUGHT US TO BE FOND.	106	SIR JOHN DAVIES	32
SHE TAUGHT ME TURN, AND COUNTER-TURN, AND STAND;	127	I KNEW A WOMAN	9
SHE TAUGHT ME TOUCH, THAT UNDULANT WHITE SKIN;	127	I KNEW A WOMAN	10
THEY TAUGHT ME NOT TO BE TOO NICE	225	THE CHUMS	7
THE WAVE BENDS WITH THE FISH. I'M TAUGHT	260	THE CHANGELING	18
TEACH			
TO TEACH MY TOES TO LISTEN TO MY TONGUE.	105	SIR JOHN DAVIES	16
I TEACH MY SIGHS TO LENGTHEN INTO SONGS,	135	THE RENEWAL	5
I TEACH MY EYES TO HEAR, MY EARS TO SEE	244	INFIRMITY	34
TEACHER			
REDEEM THIS TEACHER,	259	SONG (3)	34
TEACHES			
WE START FROM THE DARK. PAIN TEACHES US LITTLE.	166	HER BECOMING	35
AS WATER TEACHES STONE. BELIEVE ME, EXTREMEST ORIOLE,	260	THE CHANGELING	19
TEAR			
FROM THE TEAR, FAR AWAY,	236	SONG (2)	2
TEARING			
AND THE SOUND OF PAPER TEARING.	104	OLD LADY'S WRDS	60
THEY FEEL NEITHER THE TEARING IRON	169	FOURTH MEDITATN	53
AND ONE IS ONE, FREE IN THE TEARING WIND.	239	IN A DARK TIME	24
TEARLESS			
DEATH OF THE SELF IN A LONG, TEARLESS NIGHT,	239	IN A DARK TIME	17
TEARS			
O MY SISTER REMEMBER THE STARS THE TEARS THE TRAINS	5	TO MY SISTER	1
MUTTONY TEARS FALLING ON FIGURED LINOLEUM,	48	LAST WORDS	3
YOUR TEARS ARE NOT ENOUGH PRAISE,	54	THE LOST SON	31
WHERE, WHERE ARE THE TEARS OF THE WORLD?	56	THE LOST SON	103
MY TEARS ARE TIRED.	73	WHERE KNOCK IS	70
I DRINK MY TEARS IN A PLACE WHERE ALL LIGHT COMES.	170	FOURTH MEDITATN	78
TEASED			
THEY TEASED OUT THE SEED THAT THE COLD KEPT ASLEEP,--	44	FRAU BAUMAN	23

		PAGE	TITLE	LINE
TEDIUM				
	SIFT, ALMOST INVISIBLE, THROUGH LONG AFTERNOONS OF TEDIUM,	46	DOLOR	11
TEDIUM'S				
	SOME RARE NEW TEDIUM'S TAKING SHAPE:	81	SENSIBILITY! LA	13
TEETER				
	I TEETER, HEELS HOOKED ON THE CURB, SCRAPE A TOE;	47	DOUBLE FEATURE	7
TEETH				
	THE TEETH OF KNITTED GEARS	9	THE ADAMANT	5
	SHE HOVE INTO THE TEETH OF IT,	41	BIG WIND	23
	HAVE MORE TEETH.	71	WHERE KNOCK IS	4
	"MY SHOULDER'S BITTEN FROM YOUR TEETH;	136	THE SENSUALISTS	13
TELEPHONE				
	THE THIN WHINE OF TELEPHONE WIRES IN THE WIND OF A MICHIGAN WINTER,	204	THE ROSE	69
	ONLY TO FLY OVER TO HIS FAVORITE PERCH, THE CROSS-BAR OF A TELEPHONE POLE;	234	ALL MORNING	9
TELESCOPE				
	"CLAIRVOYANT WIDOW LADY, WITH AN EYE LIKE A TELESCOPE,	27	CLAIRVOY WIDOW	17
TELL				
	"O TELL ME, WIDOW LADY, WHAT IS IT THAT YOU SEE,	27	CLAIRVOY WIDOW	3
	TELL ME:	54	THE LOST SON	24
	IS HE A BIRD OR A TREE? NOT EVERYONE CAN TELL.	64	SHAPE OF FIRE	3
	DON'T TELL MY HANDS.	74	WHERE KNOCK IS	85
	TELL ME, GREAT LORDS OF STING,	83	O LULL ME, LULL	8
	TELL ME, BODY WITHOUT SKIN, DOES A FISH SWEAT?	89	UNFOLD! UNFOLD!	2
	LIGHT TAKES THE TREE; BUT WHO CAN TELL US HOW?	108	THE WAKING (2)	10
	DAN CUPID, I TELL YOU'S A BRAW LADDIE-BUCK;	113	TO A LADY ED	5
	YOU ASKED ME BEFORE, I'LL TELL YOU AGAIN:	114	DINKY	11
	TELL ME, DEAR BEAR THERE BY THE STREAM,	117	LADY AND BEAR	3
	WHAT CAN I TELL MY BONES?	171	WHAT TELL BONES	T
	MIST ALTERS THE ROCKS. WHAT CAN I TELL MY BONES?	172	WHAT TELL BONES	44
	MOTHER, MOTHER OF US ALL, TELL ME WHERE I AM!	172	WHAT TELL BONES	53
	HE CLOSELY RESEMBLES--BUT I CAN'T TELL YOU!	180	THE GNU	2
	WHAT DO THEY TELL US, SOUND AND SILENCE?	204	THE ROSE	58
	MY PILLOW WON'T TELL ME	208	THE APPARITION	1
	TELL ME NOW, TELL ME NOW.	211	SONG (1)	12
	TELL ME NOW, TELL ME NOW.	211	SONG (1)	12
	LEAVES, LEAVES, LEAN FORTH AND TELL ME WHAT I AM;	242	THE SEQUEL	27
	AND TELL MYSELF MY IMAGE CANNOT DIE.	244	INFIRMITY	4
	MAYBE IT'S WHITMAN'S SPIDER, I CAN'T TELL,	273	SUPPR W LINDSAY	28
	HE SHOOK MY HAND. "TELL WILLIAMS I'VE BEEN HERE,	274	SUPPR W LINDSAY	48
TELLING				
	THE UNEMPLOYED AND TELLING STALE UNEMPLOYMENT JOKES.	28	CLAIRVOY WIDOW	22
TELLS				
	THE STETHOSCOPE TELLS WHAT EVERYONE FEARS:	23	ACADEMIC	1
	THE PATH TELLS LITTLE TO THE SERPENT.	66	SHAPE OF FIRE	59
	TELLS ME MY DRINKING BREEDS A WILL TO DIE.	246	THE MARROW	4
	THE MIRROR TELLS SOME TRUTH, BUT NOT	257	SANITARIUM	7
TEMPESTS				
	SCARS, TEMPESTS, FLOODS, THE MOTION OF MAN'S FATE;	144	ELEGY (1)	14
TEMPORAL				
	HAD OF THE TEMPORAL:	125	WORDS FOR WIND	77
	MACHINES, MACHINES, LOVELESS, TEMPORAL;	166	HER BECOMING	42
	THE ETERNAL SEEKS, AND FINDS, THE TEMPORAL,	244	INFIRMITY	21
TEMPTATION				
	IN TEMPTATION, I RARELY SEEK COUNSEL;	173	WHAT TELL BONES	78
TEN				
	"I SEE TEN MILLION WINDOWS, I SEE TEN THOUSAND STREETS,	27	CLAIRVOY WIDOW	5
	"I SEE TEN MILLION WINDOWS, I SEE TEN THOUSAND STREETS,	27	CLAIRVOY WIDOW	5
	TO LOOSEN WITH ALL TEN FINGERS HELD WIDE AND LIMBER	40	MOSS-GATHERING	1
	I WISH I HAD TEN THOUSAND HATS,	75	I NEED, I NEED	37
TENDED				
	WHO FED AND TENDED THE INFIRM, THE MAD, THE EPILEPTIC,	223	ELEGY (2)	9
TENDER				
	THE RUSH OF WIND RIPPED OFF THE TENDER LEAVES	6	INTERLUDE	2
	THE SPIRIT'S TENDER COVER.	7	ORDERS FOR DAY	7
	IS THE WASP TENDER?	81	SENSIBILITY! LA	18
	MY LEFT SIDE'S TENDER.	97	O, THOU OPENING	3
	I THINK THE DEAD ARE TENDER. SHALL WE KISS?--	129	SHE	1
	I'M THICK WITH LEAVES AND TENDER AS A DOVE,	173	WHAT TELL BONES	89
TENDEREST				
	COME LITTLEST, COME TENDEREST,	61	THE LONG ALLEY	66

	PAGE	TITLE	LINE
TENDERNESS			
I LACK PLAIN TENDERNESS.	139	PLAINT	6
I RECOVER MY TENDERNESS BY LONG LOOKING.	173	WHAT TELL BONES	92
I'VE RECOVERED MY TENDERNESS BY LONG LOOKING;	260	THE CHANGELING	16
TENDRIL			
WITH A TENDRIL FOR NEEDLE	44	FRAU BAUMAN	21
TENDRILOUS			
ITS PALE TENDRILOUS HORN.	37	CUTTINGS	8
TENDRILS			
THE SWEET-PEA TENDRILS, THE SMILAX,	44	FRAU BAUMAN	5
THE TENDRILS HAVE ME!	61	THE LONG ALLEY	79
THE TENDRILS TURNING SLOWLY,	67	SHAPE OF FIRE	81
TURNING IN THE LIGHT WITH ITS TENDRILS;	101	LIGHT BREATHER	6
I REMEMBER THE NECKCURLS, LIMP AND DAMP AS TENDRILS;	102	ELEGY FOR JANE	1
I ENVY THE TENDRILS, THEIR EYELESS SEEKING,	221	THE ABYSS	64
TENSIONS			
FATHER OF TENSIONS, I'M DOWN TO MY SKIN AT LAST.	85	PRAISE TO END!	4
TENTACLED			
THE DUBIOUS SEA-CHANGE, THE HEAVING SANDS, AND MY TENTACLED SEA-COUSINS.	196	THE LONG WATERS	23
TENTACLES			
ONLY A FEW BUBBLES LOOSENING FROM THE ILL-MATCHED TENTACLES,	159	FIRST MEDITATN	64
TENTATIVE			
AND ONE CRAB, TENTATIVE, HUNCHES HIMSELF BEFORE MOVING ALONG THE BOTTOM,	159	FIRST MEDITATN	62
TENTS			
THEIR SKIRTS BILLOWING OUT WIDE INTO TENTS,	44	FRAU BAUMAN	17
TERMS			
WE THINK TOO LONG IN TERMS OF WHAT TO BE;	140	THE SWAN	8
TERRACE			
OVER THE WORN CURB OF THE TERRACE,	226	THE LIZARD	8
TO WHOM DOES THIS TERRACE BELONG?--	226	THE LIZARD	27
TERRACES			
WHISTLING BETWEEN THE ARBORS, THE WINDING TERRACES;	230	THE STORM	5
TERRIBLE			
ENSHROUD ME WITH LIGHT! O WHIRLING! O TERRIBLE LOVE!	48	LAST WORDS	10
HOW TERRIBLE THE NEED FOR SOLITUDE:	133	THE PURE FURY	15
AND THE TERRIBLE HUNGER FOR OBJECTS QUAILS ME:	220	THE ABYSS	32
A TERRIBLE VIOLENCE OF CREATION,	221	THE ABYSS	55
ONLY TO FIND, WITH THEIR LONG TERRIBLE EYES	232	THE THING	9
FROM ME TO THEE'S A LONG AND TERRIBLE WAY.	246	THE MARROW	18
TERRIBLY			
SO TERRIBLY WITHIN THE MIND,	22	SILENCE	10
TERROR			
MY SHAVING HAND JERKED BACK IN SUDDEN TERROR:	25	DIM-WIT COUSIN	11
UNMINDFUL OF TERROR AND HEADLINES, OF SPEECHES AND GUNS.	33	IDYLL	12
MADE FROM HIS TERROR AND DISMAY A GRAVE PHILOSOPHICAL LANGUAGE;	170	FOURTH MEDITATN	72
TERROR OF COPS, BILL COLLECTORS, BETRAYERS OF THE POOR,--	223	ELEGY (2)	18
TETHERED			
LICE TETHERED TO LONG LIMP SUBTERRANEAN WEEDS,	50	THE MINIMAL	4
TETHERED TO A LIMP WEED, SWINGING,	101	LIGHT BREATHER	8
TETONS			
AND THE SUN COMES OUT OF A BLUE CLOUD OVER THE TETONS,	194	JOURNY INTERIOR	40
THAN			
THEY FLICKER FASTER THAN A BLUE-TAILED SWIFT,	8	THE SIGNALS	5
MORE FURTIVE THAN THE HAND IN LOW	8	PRAYER	11
VIOLENT THAN A METAPHOR.	8	PRAYER	14
MORE HEADY THAN A FIELD AT DUSK	14	COMING OF COLD	3
HIS BEAK IS QUICKER THAN A HUMAN HAND.	15	THE HERON	8
WOULD RATHER TAKE THAN DISH IT OUT.	23	AMOROUS LADY	4
WHO WANT NO MORE THAN FINGERS SEIZE,	25	VERSE W ALLUSNS	3
THE DINING ROOM CARPET DYED BRIGHTER THAN BLOOD,	32	SALE	13
THE HAND-PAINTED WALL-PAPER, FINER THAN SKIN,	32	SALE	17
VINES TOUGHER THAN WRISTS	38	FORCING HOUSE	1
QUICKER THAN BIRDS, THEY DIPPED	44	FRAU BAUMAN	13
THEY TRELLISED THE SUN; THEY PLOTTED FOR MORE THAN THEMSELVES.	44	FRAU BAUMAN	25
FINER THAN FLOUR, ALIVE, MORE DANGEROUS THAN SILICA,	46	DOLOR	10
FINER THAN FLOUR, ALIVE, MORE DANGEROUS THAN SILICA,	46	DOLOR	10
WHEEL OF THE STARS, THE GREAT BEAR GLITTERING COLDER THAN SNOW,	47	DOUBLE FEATURE	11
FACES GREYING FASTER THAN LOAM-CRUMBS ON A HARROW;	48	JUDGE NOT	1

	PAGE	TITLE	LINE
THAN (CONTINUED)			
IT'S BIGGER THAN THAT.	54	THE LOST SON	45
IT'S LESS THAN A LEG	54	THE LOST SON	46
AND MORE THAN A NOSE,	54	THE LOST SON	47
I'VE MORE VEINS THAN A TREE!	57	THE LOST SON	120
LEAVES MORE THAN SHOES;	65	SHAPE OF FIRE	48
THE FUNNIER THAN THAT,--	71	WHERE KNOCK IS	18
FROM A SHELL HARDER THAN HORN,	81	SENSIBILITY! LA	9
I'M MORE THAN WHEN I WAS BORN;	84	O LULL ME, LULL	37
I FEEL MORE THAN A FISH.	87	PRAISE TO END!	77
LIGHTER THAN BELLS,	88	PRAISE TO END!	95
SOFTER THAN WATER.	88	PRAISE TO END!	96
I WAS FAR BACK, FARTHER THAN ANYBODY ELSE.	89	UNFOLD! UNFOLD!	21
THINNER THAN MINNOWS.	93	I CRY, LOVE!	34
THE ANIMAL'S CANDID GAZE, A SHADE LESS THAN FEATHERS, LIGHT'S BROKEN	98	O, THOU OPENING	22
AND KNOW THAT TRUE LOVE IS MORE THAN A LIFE-FORCE	113	TO A LADY ED	3
SHE'S SWEETER THAN A TREE.	123	WORDS FOR WIND	2
AH, WHEN SHE MOVED, SHE MOVED MORE WAYS THAN ONE:	127	I KNEW A WOMAN	3
MORE THAN A MORTAL SHOULD;	128	THE VOICE	4
MY FLESH IS BREATHING SLOWER THAN A WALL.	135	THE RENEWAL	9
COLD EVIL TWINKLED TIGHTER THAN A STRING; A FIRE	143	SHIMMER OF EVIL	8
THE GRAVEL, MY NOSE WETTER THAN HIS.	151	SLUG	7
ANOTHER SHAPE THAN HERS	154	THE DYING MAN	29
I LOVE THE WORLD; I WANT MORE THAN THE WORLD,	155	THE DYING MAN	56
MY BREATH IS MORE THAN YOURS.	167	HER BECOMING	81
O MORE THAN A ROARING BOY,	169	FOURTH MEDITATN	51
A PRISONER OF SMELLS, I WOULD RATHER EAT THAN PRAY.	173	WHAT TELL BONES	79
YOU MUSTN'T PULL IT MORE THAN TWICE,	181	MONOTONY SONG	2
AND SHEDDING MORE THAN HERE AND THERE,	181	MONOTONY SONG	7
DON'T POKE MORE THAN TWICE	183	THE LIZARD	6
WORSE THAN CASTOREUM OF MINK OR WEASELS,	187	THE LONGING	4
BUT SHRINKS INTO A HALF-LIFE, LESS THAN ITSELF,	187	THE LONGING	20
TO THE SAND DUNES AND FISH FLIES, HANGING, THICKER THAN MOTHS,	193	JOURNY INTERIOR	28
THOUGH HE HEAR A NOTE HIGHER THAN C	196	THE LONG WATERS	6
LIGHTER THAN FINCHES,	200	THE FAR FIELD	35
MY MIND MOVES IN MORE THAN ONE PLACE,	201	THE FAR FIELD	75
THE WAVES LESS THAN THE RIPPLES MADE BY RISING FISH,	203	THE ROSE	32
THAN HER WAYS WITH A MAN?	212	LIGHT LISTENED	2
SHE KISSED ME MORE THAN TWICE	212	LIGHT LISTENED	3
SHE'D MORE SIDES THAN A SEAL.	212	LIGHT LISTENED	6
SHIVER, AND MORE THAN TWICE,	216	HER WRATH	4
I WAS NO MORE THAN SEVEN AT THE TIME.	224	OTTO	22
THEY SAW THAT I FELL MORE THAN TWICE.	225	THE CHUMS	10
OLDER THAN I, OR THE COCKROACH.	226	THE LIZARD	31
DO WE DO MORE THAN WE KNOW,	237	THE TRANCED	4
THE EDGE OF HEAVEN WAS SHARPER THAN A SWORD;	237	THE TRANCED	6
SHE LEFT MY BODY, LIGHTER THAN A SEED;	241	THE SEQUEL	20
ONE WHITE FACE SHIMMERS BRIGHTER THAN THE SUN	246	THE MARROW	7
SHE WITH HER THIGHS HARDER THAN HOOVES,	260	THE CHANGELING	1
HER NAILS BRIGHTER THAN SHELLS,	261	THE CHANGELING	55
NO MORE THAN WHAT IS RAISED	262	FOLLIES OF ADAM	9
AND IF YOU EAT MORE THAN YOU SHOULD,	267	SAGINAW SONG	5
THAN THE LIKES OF YOU OR ME,--	267	SAGINAW SONG	22
WITH MORE THAN HALF A CROWN.	269	GOB MUSIC	23
HIS NOSE LOOKED EVEN BIGGER THAN IT WAS,	273	SUPPR W LINDSAY	21
THANK			
THE STEMS SAID, THANK YOU.	73	WHERE KNOCK IS	66
THAT (213)			
THAT'S			
THAT'S THE WAY IT WOULD FEEL.	55	THE LOST SON	57
BRICKS FLAKE BEFORE MY FACE. MASTER OF WATER, THAT'S TREES AWAY.	61	THE LONG ALLEY	80
KEEPER OF HAY. THAT'S A SPRATLING'S PRATTLE. AND DON'T BE THINKING YOU'RE	98	O, THOU OPENING	28
THAT'S WHY I'M FISHING THIS WAY.	117	LADY AND BEAR	6
THAT'S NOT A THING I'M SAYING WITH A SNEER--	132	SENTENTIOUS MAN	40
MY MOMENTS LINGER--THAT'S ETERNITY.	149	IN LATE SUMMER	16
YOU SQUEAK LIKE A MOUSE THAT'S LOST IN THE HAY,	177	KITTY-CAT BIRD	10
NOW THAT'S A PIECE OF GOOD ADVICE	181	MONOTONY SONG	3
BUT THAT'S ALL RIGHT,--	228	IN VIOLENT WARD	3
I LOVE MYSELF: THAT'S MY ONE CONSTANCY.	244	INFIRMITY	5

		PAGE	TITLE	LINE
THAT'S (CONTINUED)				
BUT THAT'S ENOUGH FOR ANY MAN		267	SAGINAW SONG	29
LUCK! LUCK! THAT'S WHAT I CARE FOR IN A CAGE		273	SUPPR W LINDSAY	2
"THAT'S NEVER BLAKE," SAID LINDSAY. "HE'D BE A WORM,		273	SUPPR W LINDSAY	26
THAW				
A CANNON CRACK ANNOUNCE AN EARLY THAW.		11	LIGHT BRIGHTER	4
THE (3323)				
THEE				
I PRAY THEE, LORD, THAT I MAY CHOOSE		8	PRAYER	2
I NAME THEE: WENCH OF THINGS,		81	SENSIBILITY! LA	6
THEE'S				
FROM ME TO THEE'S A LONG AND TERRIBLE WAY.		246	THE MARROW	18
THEIR (107)				
THEM (25)				
THEME				
SWEET PHOEBE, SHE'S MY THEME:		123	WORDS FOR WIND	11
A DARK THEME KEEPS ME HERE,		240	IN EVEING AIR	1
THEMSELVES				
THEMSELVES, THEIR PARLORS MUSTY AS A FUNERAL HOME.		5	PROGNOSIS	12
FINALLY VEERING, WEARING THEMSELVES OUT, MERELY		41	BIG WIND	30
THEY TRELLISED THE SUN; THEY PLOTTED FOR MORE THAN THEMSELVES.		44	FRAU BAUMAN	25
THE FLOWERS LEANED ON THEMSELVES, THE FLOWERS IN HOLLOWS;		66	SHAPE OF FIRE	76
BITING THEMSELVES PERHAPS;		79	GIVE WAY, GATES	29
OR THEY FLING THEMSELVES AGAINST TREE TRUNKS,		152	THE SISKINS	16
AND THOSE WHO SUBMERGE THEMSELVES DELIBERATELY IN TRIVIA,		169	FOURTH MEDITATN	38
THEY HAVE DECLARED THEMSELVES,		220	THE ABYSS	27
THEN				
THEN POINTS HIS HEAVY BILL ABOVE THE WOOD.		15	THE HERON	10
THEN A BLEAK WASTED PLACE,		34	NIGHT JOURNEY	10
THEN PLUMPING IN THE BUNCHED ROOTS,		42	TRANSPLANTING	6
THEN WALTZED ME OFF TO BED		45	MY PAPA'S WALTZ	15
THEN BRISTLED LIKE A DOG.		47	THE RETURN	4
THEN, WITH DIMINISHED FORCE,		50	THE CYCLE	13
THEN ROLL THEM IN GREASE,--		55	THE LOST SON	56
THEN CAME STEAM.		57	THE LOST SON	139
THEN WASHING UP OVER SMALL STONES.		93	I CRY, LOVE!	49
SHE KISSED ME CLOSE, AND THEN DID SOMETHING ELSE.		106	SIR JOHN DAVIES	35
SHE LAUGHED ME OUT, AND THEN SHE LAUGHED ME IN;		106	SIR JOHN DAVIES	56
OH, THE SYNCO SEPTET PLAYED FOR US THEN,		112	SQUEEZE-BOX	22
AND THEN STEP BAREFOOT ON A WORM		114	DINKY	7
AND THEN HE CUT LOOSE WITH A HORRIBLE NOTE		115	THE SERPENT	21
AND, THEN, BEFORE HE SAYS A WORD		116	THE SLOTH	4
THEN OFF AGAIN TO SLEEP HE GOES,		116	THE SLOTH	10
THEN EACH FELL BACK, LIMP AS A SACK,		136	THE SENSUALISTS	25
THEN ALL IS AS IT WAS.		148	THE SMALL	12
THEN FLYING ALMOST STRAIGHT UPWARD,		152	THE SISKINS	3
THEN SETTLES BACK TO SHADE AND THE LONG NIGHT.		156	THE DYING MAN	81
THEN DOWN, AS WE ROLL LIKE A BOAT FROM A WAVE-CREST.		158	FIRST MEDITATN	25
ONE SANG, THEN THE OTHER,		158	FIRST MEDITATN	43
THEN THEY LURCH FORWARD,		159	FIRST MEDITATN	58
BUMPING AGAINST STICKS AND BOTTOM-STONES, THEN SWINGING		159	FIRST MEDITATN	70
AND THEN I RAN--		166	HER BECOMING	49
AND THEN I RAN AGAIN.		166	HER BECOMING	60
THEN A REAL CAT CAME WITH A MOUTH SO WIDE,		177	KITTY-CAT BIRD	14
AND THEN CAUGHT COLD AND UP AND DIED?		178	THE CEILING	2
AND THEN THERE WAS MYRTLE'S COUSIN,		179	MYRTLE'S COUSIN	1
AND THEN WITHOUT EVEN A SPOON,		179	MYRTLE'S COUSIN	8
AND THEN MAKING GOO.		180	GOO-GIRL	4
THEN A RUNNEL BEHIND ME, CREEPING CLOSER,		190	AT OYSTER RIVER	4
THEN RETIRE TO A ROCK HIGHER UP ON THE CLIFF-SIDE.		190	AT OYSTER RIVER	16
THEN PITCHING AWAY IN HALF-FLIGHT,		200	THE FAR FIELD	34
THEN A LONG RUNNING OVER FLAT STONES		200	THE FAR FIELD	64
WHAT NEED FOR HEAVEN, THEN,		203	THE ROSE	56
WHO SHOULD COME UP RIGHT THEN,		213	THE HAPPY THREE	17
THEN A CLOSE TOWHEE, A		213	THE HAPPY THREE	29
THEN WE ROMPED OUT AGAIN,		214	THE HAPPY THREE	35
THEN SLOWLY BREAKING WHITER IN THE DAWN;		225	OTTO	37
THEN SUDDENLY FLUNG UP AND OVER,		226	THE LIZARD	10
THEN SLIDES DOWN OVER THE EYE'S SURFACE,		226	THE LIZARD	24
THEN A CRACK OF THUNDER, AND THE BLACK RAIN RUNS OVER US, OVER		230	THE STORM	23
THE STORM LULLS OFF, THEN REDOUBLES,		231	THE STORM	30

	PAGE	TITLE	LINE
THEN (CONTINUED)			
THEN THROWING ITSELF UP AND AWAY FROM THE IMPLACABLE SWIFT			
PURSUERS,	232	THE THING	6
THEN THE FIRST BIRD	232	THE THING	13
THEN ANOTHER, ANOTHER,	232	THE THING	15
WITH ONE SINUOUS RIPPLE, THEN A RUSH,	233	THE PIKE	16
THEN WHIRRING OFF SIDEWAYS TO THE TOP OF THE HAWTHORN,	234	ALL MORNING	31
AND THEN A JACKASS BRAYED. A LIZARD LEAPED MY FOOT.	247	I WAITED	14
THEN LOST ITSELF DOWN THROUGH A ROCKY GORGE.	247	I WAITED	20
AND THEN SEND YOU THE BILL.	267	SAGINAW SONG	18
AND THEN I BEAT UPON A CAN,	269	GOB MUSIC	3
AND THEN IT SPILLED:	273	SUPPR W LINDSAY	11
A SWAYING LIGHT-CORD, THEN RAN HALF-WAY BACK.	273	SUPPR W LINDSAY	25
THERE			
UNTIL I COULD THINK THERE WERE WAVES ROLLING HIGH AS MY			
BEDROOM FLOOR;	12	MID-CNTRY BLOW	2
THERE IS A NOISE WITHIN THE BROW	22	SILENCE	1
NEXT DOOR THERE IS A LOVE-NEST OF PLASTER BOARD AND TIN,	27	CLAIRVOY WIDOW	15
THERE WERE NO NIGHTS OF SLEEPING IN THE PARK.	28	THE FAVORITE	4
THERE BESIDE HIM SHE STOOD,--	46	PICKLE BELT	7
AND REMEMBER THERE WAS SOMETHING ELSE I WAS HOPING FOR.	47	DOUBLE FEATURE	12
AND I KNEW I HAD BEEN THERE BEFORE,	49	RIVER INCIDENT	9
THERE WAS ONE FLY.	53	THE LOST SON	19
WHO PUT THE MOSS THERE?	55	THE LOST SON	64
THERE WAS ALWAYS A SINGLE LIGHT	57	THE LOST SON	130
THERE WERE MANY KINDS OF COOL	57	THE LOST SON	137
REACH ME A PEACH, FONDLING, THE HILLS ARE THERE.	61	THE LONG ALLEY	81
I WAS THERE ALONE	62	FIELD OF LIGHT	17
THERE WERE CLOUDS MAKING A ROUT OF SHAPES CROSSING A			
WINDBREAK OF CEDARS,	63	FIELD OF LIGHT	48
THERE WAS ONLY ONE SHOE	64	SHAPE OF FIRE	26
THERE WAS A MOOLY MAN	71	WHERE KNOCK IS	16
IT WAS AND IT WASN'T HER THERE	72	WHERE KNOCK IS	37
AND THERE WILL BE A BOOGER.	75	I NEED, I NEED	26
BEES AND LILIES THERE WERE,	77	BRING THE DAY!	1
BEES AND LILIES THERE WERE,	77	BRING THE DAY!	2
BEES AND LILIES WERE THERE,	77	BRING THE DAY!	5
THE SEA WILL BE THERE, THE GREAT SQUASHY SHADOWS,	79	GIVE WAY, GATES	28
THOUGH NEITHER YOU NOR I WAS THERE,--	86	PRAISE TO END!	37
BUT WHAT I LEARNED THERE, DANCING ALL ALONE,	105	SIR JOHN DAVIES	17
THERE WAS A BODY, AND IT CAST A SPELL,--	106	SIR JOHN DAVIES	61
WE THINK BY FEELING. WHAT IS THERE TO KNOW?	108	THE WAKING (2)	4
GOD BLESS THE GROUND! I SHALL WALK SOFTLY THERE,	108	THE WAKING (2)	8
AS WE SAT THERE DRINKING THAT BATHTUB GIN	112	SQUEEZE-BOX	24
THERE ONCE WAS A COW WITH A DOUBLE UDDER.	114	THE COW	1
IT'S WINDY THERE, AND RATHER WEIRD,	114	DINKY	2
--WHY, THERE IS DIRTY DINKY.	114	DINKY	4
THERE WAS A SERPENT WHO HAD TO SING.	115	THE SERPENT	1
THERE WAS. THERE WAS.	115	THE SERPENT	2
THERE WAS. THERE WAS.	115	THE SERPENT	2
THERE, UPSIDE DOWN (UNLIKE A BIRD),	116	THE SLOTH	5
TELL ME, DEAR BEAR THERE BY THE STREAM,	117	LADY AND BEAR	3
BUT THE BEAR JUST SAT THERE UNTIL SHE SANK;	117	LADY AND BEAR	28
I WATCHED HER THERE, BETWEEN ME AND THE MOON;	119	THE DREAM	11
THE WIND, AND THERE I AM,	125	WORDS FOR WIND	66
THERE WAS A THICKET WHERE I WENT TO DIE,	132	SENTENTIOUS MAN	21
AND THERE I THRASHED, MY THIGHS AND FACE AFLAME.	132	SENTENTIOUS MAN	22
"THERE IS NO PLACE TO TURN," SHE SAID,	136	THE SENSUALISTS	1
AND SHE WAS RIGHT, FOR THERE BESIDE	136	THE SENSUALISTS	7
IN HELL THERE IS NO CHANGE.	139	PLAINT	3
IS THERE NO WAY OUT OF THAT COURSING BLOOD?	140	THE SWAN	4
--THERE WAS NO LIGHT; THERE WAS NO LIGHT AT ALL:	143	SHIMMER OF EVIL	5
--THERE WAS NO LIGHT; THERE WAS NO LIGHT AT ALL:	143	SHIMMER OF EVIL	5
--THERE WAS NO LIGHT; THERE WAS NO LIGHT AT ALL:	143	SHIMMER OF EVIL	10
--THERE WAS NO LIGHT; THERE WAS NO LIGHT AT ALL:	143	SHIMMER OF EVIL	10
--THERE WAS NO LIGHT; THERE WAS NO LIGHT AT ALL:	143	SHIMMER OF EVIL	15
--THERE WAS NO LIGHT; THERE WAS NO LIGHT AT ALL.	143	SHIMMER OF EVIL	15
THERE WOULD BE REASON FOR ESSENTIAL SIN;	144	ELEGY (1)	2
AND THERE A GREAT BEAST PLAYED,	145	THE BEAST	6
I LAY; I LANGUISHED THERE.	145	THE BEAST	15
AND I WEPT THERE, ALONE.	145	THE BEAST	19
(AND YET I WAS NOT THERE,	147	THE EXORCISM	9
WHAT IS THERE FOR THE SOUL TO UNDERSTAND?	149	IN LATE SUMMER	9

	PAGE	TITLE	LINE
THERE (CONTINUED)			
HE TURNED HIS FACE: THERE WAS ANOTHER MAN,	155	THE DYING MAN	62
THERE ARE NO PURSUING FORMS, FACES ON WALLS:	159	FIRST MEDITATN	78
THERE IS NO RIVEN TREE, OR LAMB DROPPED BY AN EAGLE.	159	FIRST MEDITATN	82
THERE ARE STILL TIMES, MORNING AND EVENING:	159	FIRST MEDITATN	83
IS THERE A WISDOM IN OBJECTS? FEW OBJECTS PRAISE THE LORD.	166	HER BECOMING	38
THERE ARE TIMES WHEN REALITY COMES CLOSER:	166	HER BECOMING	44
AND THERE I STAYED UNTIL THE DAY BURNED DOWN.	166	HER BECOMING	52
BUT THERE IS NO SONG.	168	FOURTH MEDITATN	26
THERE WAS A MOST ODIOUS YAK	178	THE YAK	1
THERE WAS A MOST MONSTROUS WHALE:	178	THE WHALE	1
YOU HARDLY EVER THINK IT'S THERE.	178	THE CHAIR	2
THERE ONCE WAS A GIRL NAMED MYRTLE	179	MYRTLE	1
AND THEN THERE WAS MYRTLE'S COUSIN,	179	MYRTLE'S COUSIN	1
AND SHEDDING MORE THAN HERE AND THERE,	181	MONOTONY SONG	7
--AND THERE WAS ONLY HARRY!	181	MONOTONY SONG	12
BUT FOUND HE WASN'T THERE AT ALL,	181	MONOTONY SONG	14
THE LIGHT CRIES OUT, AND I AM THERE TO HEAR--	188	THE LONGING	32
THERE ARE MANY DETOURS, WASHED-OUT INTERRUPTED RAW PLACES	193	JOURNY INTERIOR	2
ON ONE SIDE OF SILENCE THERE IS NO SMILE;	195	JOURNY INTERIOR	76
THERE ARE THOSE TO WHOM PLACE IS UNIMPORTANT,	202	THE ROSE	1
AND THERE IS SILENCE.	202	THE ROSE	21
MY EYES NEITHER HERE NOR THERE,	207	THE YOUNG GIRL	9
"THE STAIR'S RIGHT THERE,	219	THE ABYSS	3
THERE ALWAYS IS	219	THE ABYSS	10
AND THERE ON THE BLIND	220	THE ABYSS	34
THEY STOOD THERE WITH THEIR GUNS; HE WALKED TOWARD,	224	OTTO	18
THERE IS ONE LIGHT ON THE MOUNTAIN.	230	THE STORM	9
UNTIL THERE WAS NOTHING LEFT,	232	THE THING	16
AND THERE WE SANG WITH THE SEA:	238	THE MOMENT	3
THINGS WITHOUT HANDS TAKE HANDS: THERE IS NO CHOICE,--	244	INFIRMITY	31
GODHEAD ABOVE MY GOD, ARE YOU THERE STILL?	246	THE MARROW	13
A LARK-SWEET LOVER IF EVER THERE WAS.	258	SONG (3)	3
THERE WAS A HARDNESS OF STONE,	265	HARSH COUNTRY	1
OUT HEMLOCK WAY THERE IS A STREAM	267	SAGINAW SONG	7
THERE ON MY KNEES, A MAN OF RENOWN,	270	GOB MUSIC	42
PAST ALDER LANE, AND WE GABBED THERE A WHILE.	274	SUPPR W LINDSAY	47
THEREBY			
LENT ME ONE VIRTUE, AND I LIVE THEREBY.	120	THE DREAM	24
IN WHICH ALL CREATURES SHARE, AND THEREBY LIVE,	243	THE MOTION	18
THEREFORE			
THEREFORE, O LORD, LET ME PRESERVE	8	PRAYER	19
BOLD IN FEAR THEREFORE;	60	THE LONG ALLEY	40
THEREFORE I REJECT THE WORLD OF THE DOG	196	THE LONG WATERS	5
THERE'S			
THERE'S CANKER AT THE ROOT, YOUR SEED	4	FEUD	9
THERE'S NO FILTH ON A PLATEAU OF CINDERS.	59	THE LONG ALLEY	15
BELIEVE ME, THERE'S NO ONE ELSE, KITTEN-LIMP SISTER.	59	THE LONG ALLEY	23
THERE'S NO JOY IN SOFT BONES.	59	THE LONG ALLEY	26
CAN FEATHERS EAT ME? THERE'S NO CLUE IN THE SILT.	60	THE LONG ALLEY	32
THERE'S NO ALAS	74	I NEED, I NEED	14
THERE'S A GHOST LOOSE IN THE LONG GRASS!	82	SENSIBILITY! LA	27
THERE'S TIME ENOUGH.	93	I CRY, LOVE!	37
"AND BESIDES, IT SEEMS THERE'S A LAW:	117	LADY AND BEAR	9
WHEN THERE'S A DAZZLING DARK BEHIND THE SUN?	155	THE DYING MAN	53
THERE'S THIS TO REMEMBER ABOUT THE GNU:	180	THE GNU	1
"THERE'S NO SHELTER	229	ON THE QUAY	2
THERE'S TWO MORE TO DROWN	229	ON THE QUAY	5
THERE'S LITTLE LEFT I CARE TO CALL MY OWN.	244	INFIRMITY	8
THERE'S BEANS ON EVERY PLATE,	267	SAGINAW SONG	4
THERE'S NEVER A HOUSEHOLD FART,	268	SAGINAW SONG	38
THESE (30)			
THEY (106)			
THEY'LL			
THEY'LL JUMP ON HIS BELLY,	72	WHERE KNOCK IS	28
AND THEY'LL SOON STAY AWAY IN GREAT BUNCHES!"	180	GOO-GIRL	16
THEY'RE			
A LIKELY THING FOR THEY'RE NO WORSE	267	SAGINAW SONG	21
THEY'VE			
BUT THEY'VE WAYS OF INDICATING WHEN	267	SAGINAW SONG	15
THICK			
COILED GREEN AND THICK, LIKE DRIPPING SMILAX,	39	WEED PULLER	8
THICK AND CUSHIONY, LIKE AN OLD-FASHIONED DOORMAT,	40	MOSS-GATHERING	3

	PAGE	TITLE	LINE
THICK (CONTINUED)			
WHAT'S A THICK? TWO-BY-TWO'S A SHAPE.	92	I CRY, LOVE!	10
AS THE THICK SHADE OF THE LONG NIGHT COMES ON.	134	THE PURE FURY	28
RACE OVER THE THICK GRASS;	152	THE SISKINS	6
I'M THICK WITH LEAVES AND TENDER AS A DOVE,	173	WHAT TELL BONES	89
AND THE DUST LAY THICK ON MY EYELIDS,--WHO EVER WORE GOGGLES?--	193	JOURNY INTERIOR	24
WITH ITS THICK GRASSY SCUM AND CRABS SCUTTLING BACK INTO THEIR GLISTENING CRATERS.	203	THE ROSE	50
HER TONGUE, AT THE LAST, THICK, BLACK AS AN OX'S.	223	ELEGY (2)	17
THICKENS			
AT DUSK OUR SLOW BREATH THICKENS ON THE AIR.	12	SLOW SEASON	8
THICKER			
TO THE SAND DUNES AND FISH FLIES, HANGING, THICKER THAN MOTHS,	193	JOURNY INTERIOR	28
THICKET			
THERE WAS A THICKET WHERE I WENT TO DIE,	132	SENTENTIOUS MAN	21
OR WHEN WE STAND AT THE EDGE OF A THICKET,	162	I'M HERE	54
THICKETS			
IN THEIR HARSH THICKETS	91	UNFOLD! UNFOLD!	65
THE THICKETS DARKENING,	193	JOURNY INTERIOR	16
THIEVING			
SOME LEARN THE ART OF THIEVING, AND SOME GROW UP TO BEG;	27	CLAIRVOY WIDOW	10
THIGH			
LIP, BREAST AND THIGH CANNOT POSSESS	8	PRAYER	17
THE MUSCLES IN ONE THIGH	47	THE RETURN	6
THIGHS			
IN THE HIGH-NOON OF THIGHS,	80	GIVE WAY, GATES	33
AND THERE I THRASHED, MY THIGHS AND FACE AFLAME.	132	SENTENTIOUS MAN	22
MY THIGHS BRUSHING AGAINST FLOWER-CROWNS;	161	I'M HERE	22
AND ONCE TO MY FLOWING THIGHS.	167	HER BECOMING	73
NOR MY LIPS, MY BREASTS, MY THIGHS	209	HER RETICENCE	9
SHE WITH HER THIGHS HARDER THAN HOOVES,	260	THE CHANGELING	1
THIN			
FEET, BEAR THE THIN BONES OVER	7	ORDERS FOR DAY	8
THE RICHES OF THE AIR BLOW THIN.	14	COMING OF COLD	21
HIS INSOLENCE COULD WEAR NO PATIENCE THIN.	28	THE FAVORITE	7
--AND THE TAINT IN A BLOOD THAT WAS RUNNING TOO THIN.	32	SALE	20
CRACKING SO MUCH THIN GLASS	41	BIG WIND	18
CREAKING THEIR THIN SPINES,	42	TRANSPLANTING	16
PINCHING AND POKING MY THIN RIBS	44	FRAU BAUMAN	27
FOR THE THIN SOUND IN THE WINDY CHIMNEY,	103	OLD LADY'S WRDS	30
WHOSE THIN SONG HUNG IN AIR,	128	THE VOICE	9
A THIN MOUTH, AND A TONGUE	150	SNAKE	4
THIN AND INSISTENT AS A CICADA,	159	FIRST MEDITATN	85
WAS IT YESTERDAY I STRETCHED OUT THE THIN BONES OF MY INNOCENCE?	168	FOURTH MEDITATN	12
A THIN HARSH SONG. THE DAY DIES IN A CHILD.	171	WHAT TELL BONES	19
WHO'D THINK THE MOON COULD PARE ITSELF SO THIN?	188	THE LONGING	30
OVER THE THIN, FEATHERY RIPPLES BREAKING LIGHTLY AGAINST THE IRREGULAR SHORELINE--	197	THE LONG WATERS	50
AND THAT THIN CRY, LIKE A NEEDLE PIERCING THE EAR, THE INSISTENT CICADA,	204	THE ROSE	67
THE THIN WHINE OF TELEPHONE WIRES IN THE WIND OF A MICHIGAN WINTER,	204	THE ROSE	69
A SOUND SO THIN IT COULD NOT WOO A BIRD,	204	THE ROSE	77
MY THIN ARMS TO AND FRO,	207	THE YOUNG GIRL	10
IN A PLACE OF MOTTLED CLOUDS, A THIN MIST MORNING AND EVENING.	221	THE ABYSS	77
A THIN WHINE OF WIRES, A RATTLING AND FLAPPING OF LEAVES,	230	THE STORM	6
THE LINE OF MY HORIZON'S GROWING THIN!	245	THE DECISION	8
THING			
DO YOU SEE ANY SIGN OR SEMBLANCE OF THAT THING CALLED "HOPE"?	27	CLAIRVOY WIDOW	18
SOME MORNING THING CAME, BEATING ITS WINGS.	63	FIELD OF LIGHT	35
DEEP IN THE BELLY OF A THING TO BE.	97	O, THOU OPENING	15
SKIN, A THING YOU CANNOT SAY TO WHISPER AND EQUAL A WOUND?	98	O, THOU OPENING	24
SIMPLICITY'S SWEET THING, EITHER. A LEAF COULD DRAG YOU.	98	O, THOU OPENING	29
A SMALL THING,	101	LIGHT BREATHER	17
A CAGED BEAR RARELY DOES THE SAME THING TWICE	105	SIR JOHN DAVIES	10
GREAT NATURE HAS ANOTHER THING TO DO	108	THE WAKING (2)	13
TO SOME IT MAY SEEM A SAD THING TO RELATE,	112	SQUEEZE-BOX	38
YOU GREEN THING IN MY WAY!"	123	WORDS FOR WIND	14

	PAGE	TITLE	LINE
THING (CONTINUED)			
LOVE HAS A THING TO DO.	124	WORDS FOR WIND	53
A FAIR THING GROWS MORE FAIR;	124	WORDS FOR WIND	54
A THING IS DONE: A THING	126	WORDS FOR WIND	94
A THING IS DONE: A THING	126	WORDS FOR WIND	94
A LIVELY THING CAN COME TO LIFE AGAIN.	129	SHE	12
WHO CAN SURPRISE A THING	130	THE OTHER	13
AND ALL DIMENSIONS QUIVERED TO ONE THING.	132	SENTENTIOUS MAN	24
THAT'S NOT A THING I'M SAYING WITH A SNEER--	132	SENTENTIOUS MAN	40
UNTIL HE FINDS THE THING HE ALMOST WAS	133	THE PURE FURY	19
DARES FACE THE THING HE IS?)	147	THE EXORCISM	4
A THING ALL EARTHLY LOVERS UNDERSTAND.	149	IN LATE SUMMER	22
I LONGED TO BE THAT THING,	150	SNAKE	10
I AM THAT FINAL THING,	153	THE DYING MAN	14
A SLOW GROWTH IS A HARD THING TO ENDURE.	154	THE DYING MAN	45
ALL EXULTATION IS A DANGEROUS THING.	155	THE DYING MAN	72
AM I BUT NOTHING, LEANING TOWARDS A THING?	156	THE DYING MAN	85
IN HEAVEN'S PRAISE, I DREAD THE THING I AM.	156	THE DYING MAN	95
A THING WE FEEL AT EVENING, AND BY DOORS,	162	I'M HERE	53
THE ONLY THING ALIVE IN HEAVEN'S EYE,	166	HER BECOMING	58
SILENCE BECAME A THING;	167	HER BECOMING	66
A RAPT THING WITH A NAME.	167	HER BECOMING	85
WAITING, ITSELF A SLOW THING,	168	FOURTH MEDITATN	21
A FUNNY THING ABOUT A CHAIR:	178	THE CHAIR	1
THE ONLY THING WE'D HAVE FOR PROOF	178	THE CEILING	3
BECOME ANOTHER THING;	198	THE LONG WATERS	74
A THING QUIESCENT!	209	HER LONGING	10
A GREEN THING LOVES THE GREEN	212	LIGHT LISTENED	15
THE LONELIEST THING I KNOW	215	HIS FOREBODING	14
FROM THE ONE BEAUTIFUL THING IN HER YARD, THE PEACHTREE;	223	ELEGY (2)	13
THE THING	232	THE THING	T
TRAILING A THING--WHAT WAS IT?--SMALL AS A LARK	232	THE THING	2
A THING IN AND OUT OF SIGHT,	232	THE THING	4
THE SMALL THING DIVING DOWN TOWARD A HILL,	232	THE THING	10
A THING CARVED OF STONE OR WOOD, WITH THE DULL IRIDESCENCE OF LONG-POLISHED WOOD,	234	ALL MORNING	11
MAKE ME, O LORD, A LAST, A SIMPLE THING	240	IN EVEING AIR	8
WHO'S OLD ENOUGH TO LIVE?--A THING OF EARTH	243	THE MOTION	14
THE DIRE DIMENSION OF A FINAL THING.	248	THE TREE, BIRD	23
THAT DELICATE THING	249	THE RESTORED	15
THE RIGHT THING	250	THE RIGHT THING	T
THE RIGHT THING HAPPENS TO THE HAPPY MAN.	250	THE RIGHT THING	3
THE RIGHT THING HAPPENS TO THE HAPPY MAN.	250	THE RIGHT THING	9
THE RIGHT THING HAPPENS TO THE HAPPY MAN.	250	THE RIGHT THING	12
THE RIGHT THING HAPPENS TO THE HAPPY MAN.	250	THE RIGHT THING	19
THE DARK HEART OF SOME ANCIENT THING	260	THE CHANGELING	4
A LIKELY THING FOR THEY'RE NO WORSE	267	SAGINAW SONG	21
THE ONLY THING I EVER LEARNED	267	SAGINAW SONG	27
THINGS			
THE THINGS THE EYE OR HAND CANNOT POSSESS.	8	THE SIGNALS	10
ALL THINGS ARE BROUGHT TO BARN AND FOLD.	15	COMING OF COLD	34
ALL THINGS UNHOLY, MARRED BY CURSE,	18	LONG LIVE WEEDS	5
THE HIGHER THINGS IN LIFE DO NOT	25	VERSE W ALLUSNS	5
BUT VIEW THINGS STEADILY AND WHOLE.	25	VERSE W ALLUSNS	10
AS IF I HAD BROKEN THE NATURAL ORDER OF THINGS IN THAT SWAMPLAND;	40	MOSS-GATHERING	10
I SAW THE SEPARATENESS OF ALL THINGS!	63	FIELD OF LIGHT	45
I NAME THEE: WENCH OF THINGS,	81	SENSIBILITY! LA	6
WHEN I SAY THINGS FOND,	83	O LULL ME, LULL	10
I COULD SAY HELLO TO THINGS;	84	O LULL ME, LULL	38
AND NOW ARE WE TO HAVE THAT PELLUDIOUS JESUS-SHIMMER OVER ALL THINGS,	98	O, THOU OPENING	21
I SING THE GREEN, AND THINGS TO COME,	99	O, THOU OPENING	56
IN A BOAT OF BEAUTIFUL THINGS.	103	OLD LADY'S WRDS	24
THINGS LOLL AND LOITER. WHO CONDONES THE LOST?	106	SIR JOHN DAVIES	43
THINGS HAVE THEIR THOUGHT: THEY ARE THE SHARDS OF ME;	107	SIR JOHN DAVIES	86
YOU'D BETTER WATCH THE THINGS YOU DO.	114	DINKY	17
YOU'D BETTER WATCH THE THINGS YOU DO.	114	DINKY	18
ALL THINGS BRING ME TO LOVE.	125	WORDS FOR WIND	81
AS IF ALL THINGS HAD DIED, AND ROSE AGAIN.	133	THE PURE FURY	6
YET, LIKE A TREE, ENDURE THE SHIFT OF THINGS.	135	THE RENEWAL	6
FAR THINGS DRAW CLOSER IN.	148	THE SMALL	10
THINGS LOST IN SLEEP RETURN	148	THE SMALL	15

		PAGE	TITLE	LINE
THINKING				
KEEPER OF HAY. THAT'S A SPRATLING'S PRATTLE. AND DON'T BE THINKING YOU'RE		98	O, THOU OPENING	28
THINKING, GOD HAS NEED OF ME.		172	WHAT TELL BONES	63
AND I ROAM ELSEWHERE, MY BODY THINKING,		195	JOURNY INTERIOR	68
THINKING:		200	THE FAR FIELD	41
AND I LIE HERE THINKING IN BLEAK BOFIN TOWN		216	THE SHY MAN	18
I LIE HERE AND THINKING, "I AM NOT ALONE."		216	THE SHY MAN	19
THINKS				
HE THINKS ABOUT IT FOR A YEAR;		116	THE SLOTH	3
THINLY				
WHISTLING THINLY UNDER THE WIND-VENTS;		41	BIG WIND	31
THINNED				
EXHAUSTED FATHERS THINNED THE BLOOD,		4	FEUD	5
THE HEDGE AND ORCHARD GROVE ARE THINNED.		14	COMING OF COLD	31
A TREE THINNED BY THE WIND OBSCURES MY SIGHT.		150	IN LATE SUMMER	28
THINNER				
THINNER THAN MINNOWS.		93	I CRY, LOVE!	34
THINNING				
THINNING THE SOUL'S SUBSTANCE;		171	WHAT TELL BONES	24
THE LACELIKE WRINKLES OF THE WAKE WIDENING, THINNING OUT,		203	THE ROSE	33
THIRD				
ONCE, TWICE, AND A FAINT THIRD THUMP,--		42	TRANSPLANTING	11
THIRDS				
THEY SING, THEY SING, BUT STILL IN MINOR THIRDS.		156	THE DYING MAN	89
THIRST				
I THIRST BY DAY. I WATCH BY NIGHT.		222	THE ABYSS	89
MY THIRST CAME ON, AND I HAD TO DRINK.		269	GOB MUSIC	31
THIRTEEN				
AGED THIRTEEN.		87	PRAISE TO END!	58
THIRTY-FIVE				
THE ROOM WAS THIRTY-FIVE BELOW;		114	DINKY	14
THIS (124)				
THISTLE				
ON TOP A THISTLE		219	THE ABYSS	15
THISTLES				
LIGHT AS SEED BLOWING OFF THISTLES!		152	THE SISKINS	21
THORN				
THE BRIAR BEARS ITS THORN, AND DROUGHT		14	COMING OF COLD	24
WITH BURR, BRAMBLE, AND THORN;		145	THE BEAST	3
A THORN DOES WELL IN THE WIND,		262	FOLLIES OF ADAM	13
THORN-BITTEN				
AND THEIR THORN-BITTEN WRISTS,		44	FRAU BAUMAN	34
THOSE (31)				
THOU				
THOU WERT MARMOREAN-BORN.		81	SENSIBILITY! LA	5
O, THOU OPENING, O		97	O, THOU OPENING	T
O PRIDE, THOU ART A PLUME UPON WHOSE HEAD?		188	THE LONGING	25
THOUGH				
THOUGH THE DEVOURING MOTHER CRY, ""ESCAPE ME? NEVER--""		5	PROGNOSIS	13
THOUGH STILL THE GUARDED SNOW IS WINTER-SEALED,		11	LIGHT BRIGHTER	6
THOUGH JUST MEN ARE REVILED		20	REPL TO CENSURE	9
THE WORM, THOUGH DANK, IS SENSITIVE:		23	AMOROUS LADY	7
THOUGH THE CROCUSES POKE UP THEIR HEADS IN THE USUAL PLACES,		24	VERNAL SENTIMNT	1
THOUGH IT ALL HAPPENED BEFORE, I CANNOT GROW BITTER:		24	VERNAL SENTIMNT	7
I REJOICE IN THE SPRING, AS THOUGH NO SPRING EVER HAD BEEN.		24	VERNAL SENTIMNT	8
THOUGH HOME IS NOT HAPPY, WHERE ELSE CAN HE GO?		29	THE GENTLE	10
THOUGH NEITHER YOU NOR I WAS THERE,--		86	PRAISE TO END!	37
THOUGH DANCING NEEDS A MASTER, I HAD NONE		105	SIR JOHN DAVIES	15
THOUGH EVERYTHING'S ASTONISHMENT AT LAST,		107	SIR JOHN DAVIES	79
THOUGH ALL'S IN MOTION, WHO IS PASSING BY?		132	SENTENTIOUS MAN	19
THOUGH IT REJECT DRY BORDERS OF THE SEEN,		154	THE DYING MAN	42
THOUGH HE HEAR A NOTE HIGHER THAN C		196	THE LONG WATERS	6
THE BODY MOVES, THOUGH SLOWLY, TOWARD DESIRE.		235	MANIFESTATION	10
THOUGH SUMMER BLAZES IN THE VIREO'S EYE.		240	IN EVEING AIR	2
IMPERIOUS YOUNGLING, THOUGH APPROACHING FORTY;		264	THREE EPIGRAMS	2
THOUGHT				
HIS THOUGHT IS TIED. THE CURVING PROW		4	DEATH PIECE	5
THOUGHT DOES NOT CRUSH TO STONE.		9	THE ADAMANT	1
UNTIL THOUGHT CRACKLES WHITE ACROSS THE BRAIN.		17	UNEXTINGUISHED	12
THEY MOCK THE DEEPEST THOUGHT,		20	REPL TO CENSURE	6
CONSTRICTED BY MY TORTURED THOUGHT,		24	BEFORE STUDY	1
BUT FOR AN UNCLE YOU WERE THOUGHT TO FAVOR,		25	DIM-WIT COUSIN	3

	PAGE	TITLE	LINE
THOUGHT (CONTINUED)			
INVADE THEIR PRIVACY OF THOUGHT.	25	VERSE W ALLUSNS	6
THEY THOUGHT ABOUT SATURDAY PAY,	46	PICKLE BELT	3
AND MY THOUGHT HUNTS ANOTHER BODY.	80	GIVE WAY, GATES	44
AND SHE BALANCED IN THE DELIGHT OF HER THOUGHT,	102	ELEGY FOR JANE	4
THINGS HAVE THEIR THOUGHT: THEY ARE THE SHARDS OF ME;	107	SIR JOHN DAVIES	86
I THOUGHT THAT ONCE, AND THOUGHT COMES ROUND AGAIN;	107	SIR JOHN DAVIES	87
I THOUGHT THAT ONCE, AND THOUGHT COMES ROUND AGAIN;	107	SIR JOHN DAVIES	87
--WHEN SHE THOUGHT I'D RUN OUT OF MONEY.	112	SQUEEZE-BOX	41
SHE KISSED ME OUT OF THOUGHT	123	WORDS FOR WIND	18
WHEN I HEARD, OR THOUGHT I HEARD,	146	THE SONG	24
I THOUGHT MYSELF REBORN.	154	THE DYING MAN	17
WHO THOUGHT LOVE BUT A MOTION IN THE MIND?	156	THE DYING MAN	84
I THOUGHT I WAS GOING TO SMOTHER.	162	I'M HERE	50
UNTIL YOU HAVE THOUGHT THIS SAD TALE THROUGH:	177	KITTY-CAT BIRD	19
IF I THOUGHT YOU COULD HEAR IN A HUSH."	182	BOY AND BUSH	5
I AM RENEWED BY DEATH, THOUGHT OF MY DEATH,	201	THE FAR FIELD	77
NOR THE WHOLE HEART OF MY THOUGHT,	209	HER RETICENCE	7
OF THE FINE SHAPELY THOUGHT	211	SONG (1)	2
THOUGHT UPON THOUGHT CAN BE	215	HIS FOREBODING	6
THOUGHT UPON THOUGHT CAN BE	215	HIS FOREBODING	6
AND MY THOUGHT FLIES TO THE PLACE BY THE BO-TREE.	222	THE ABYSS	100
AND YET MY THOUGHT TURNS BACK TO THEM,	225	THE CHUMS	3
WHOM DO WE LOVE? I THOUGHT I KNEW THE TRUTH;	241	THE SEQUEL	7
WHEN SHE THOUGHT I THOUGHT	249	THE RESTORED	5
WHEN SHE THOUGHT I THOUGHT	249	THE RESTORED	5
ENOUGH TO MERIT CONSTANT THOUGHT.	257	SANITARIUM	8
--WITH NEVER A THOUGHT FOR KIERKEGAARD.	272	DUET	12
THOUGHTS			
WHETHER THE BEES HAVE THOUGHTS, WE CANNOT SAY,	196	THE LONG WATERS	1
THOUSAND			
"I SEE TEN MILLION WINDOWS, I SEE TEN THOUSAND STREETS,	27	CLAIRVOY WIDOW	5
I WISH I HAD TEN THOUSAND HATS,	75	I NEED, I NEED	37
THRASH			
THE DEAD THRASH.	91	UNFOLD! UNFOLD!	66
THRASHED			
AND THERE I THRASHED, MY THIGHS AND FACE AFLAME.	132	SENTENTIOUS MAN	22
THRASHING-UP			
A THRASHING-UP OF THE WHOLE POOL,	233	THE PIKE	17
THREAD			
EVEN THREAD HAD A SPEECH.	90	UNFOLD! UNFOLD!	33
THREADBARE			
"ONE COAT OF PRIDE, PERHAPS A BIT THREADBARE;	21	THE AUCTION	5
THREAD-LIKE			
A THREAD-LIKE FIRMNESS.	226	THE LIZARD	12
THREE			
GONE THE THREE ANCIENT LADIES	44	FRAU BAUMAN	1
THE THREE ELMS,	54	THE LOST SON	36
THE HAPPY THREE	213	THE HAPPY THREE	T
THREE IN THE SUN.	214	THE HAPPY THREE	38
NOW HE'S EATEN HIS THREE KINDS OF CHEESE AND DRUNK FROM HIS BOTTLE-CAP WATERING-TROUGH--	227	MEADOW MOUSE	12
THEY SIT, THREE OR FOUR, HIGH IN THE FIR-TREES BACK OF THE HOUSE,	234	ALL MORNING	6
THREE EPIGRAMS	264	THREE EPIGRAMS	T
LINDSAY'S I MEAN: TWO MOONS, OR EVEN THREE,	273	SUPPR W LINDSAY	7
AND THAT MAKES THREE, COUNTING HIS FACE AS ONE.	273	SUPPR W LINDSAY	9
THRESHOLDS			
THE BODY, DELIGHTING IN THRESHOLDS,	163	I'M HERE	58
THREW			
PAPA THREW HIM BACK.	73	WHERE KNOCK IS	61
HE THREW HIS RIFLE OVER WITH ONE HAND;	224	OTTO	15
THREW HER, POT AND ALL, INTO THE TRASH-CAN,	228	THE GERANIUM	23
THRICE			
THRICE HAPPY THEY WHOSE WORLD IS SPANNED	25	VERSE W ALLUSNS	1
THRILL			
UPON WHOM EVERY GIFT AND THRILL WERE SHOWERED,	28	THE FAVORITE	10
THROAT			
THE DEAD LEAP AT THE THROAT, DESTROY	4	FEUD	13
THE TIGHT NERVES LEADING TO THE THROAT	22	SILENCE	17
THE WREN'S THROAT SHIMMERED,	51	THE WAKING (1)	6
THAT PRACTICALLY SPLIT THE TOP OF HIS THROAT.	115	THE SERPENT	22
ACROSS HER PULSING THROAT;	123	WORDS FOR WIND	22

	PAGE	TITLE	LINE
THROAT (CONTINUED)			
SHUTTLING ITS THROAT WHILE PERCHED ON A WIND-VENT,	158	FIRST MEDITATN	40
THE RUSH OF SMELLS STRIKES LIKE A COLD FIRE, THE THROAT FREEZES,	220	THE ABYSS	47
AND THE SUN TOUCHES THE LIZARD'S THROAT, ITS TAIL HALF IN SHADOW.	261	THE CHANGELING	34
THROTTLE			
THE TRICK WAS TO THROW THE CAR SIDEWAYS AND CHARGE OVER THE HILL, FULL OF THE THROTTLE.	193	JOURNY INTERIOR	21
THROUGH (47)			
THROW			
AND THINGS THROW LIGHT ON THINGS,	148	THE SMALL	23
THE TRICK WAS TO THROW THE CAR SIDEWAYS AND CHARGE OVER THE HILL, FULL OF THE THROTTLE.	193	JOURNY INTERIOR	21
THEY THROW YOU THROUGH THE FRONT PLATE GLASS	267	SAGINAW SONG	17
THROWING			
THEN THROWING ITSELF UP AND AWAY FROM THE IMPLACABLE SWIFT PURSUERS,	232	THE THING	6
THRUM-THRUM			
THRUM-THRUM, WHO CAN BE EQUAL TO EASE?	97	O, THOU OPENING	13
THRUSH			
BEYOND THE RIDGE TWO WOOD THRUSH SING AS ONE.	150	IN LATE SUMMER	30
AND THE THRUSH STOPPED IN THE MIDDLE OF HIS SONG.	196	THE LONG WATERS	7
THE THRUSH SINGING ALONE, THAT EASY BIRD,	204	THE ROSE	61
THRUST			
THE HIGHWAY RIBBONING OUT IN A STRAIGHT THRUST TO THE NORTH,	193	JOURNY INTERIOR	27
THRUSTS			
EXPLODES LIKE A ROSE, OR THRUSTS WINGS OVER THE CARIBBEAN.	159	FIRST MEDITATN	77
THUMB			
A SURGEON GUIDES A SCALPEL WITH THUMB AND FINGER-TIPS.	28	CLAIRVOY WIDOW	20
HIS THUMB HAD A RAINBOW.	73	WHERE KNOCK IS	65
WHO TURNED A CORNER IN TIME, WHEN AT LAST HE GREW A THUMB;	170	FOURTH MEDITATN	69
MAX LAURISCH HAD THE GREENEST THUMB OF ALL.	224	OTTO	7
MY THUMB OF A CHILD THAT NUZZLED IN MY PALM?--	227	MEADOW MOUSE	22
A MISTRESS OF ZEN, I'LL BITE YOUR THUMB,	272	DUET	18
THUMBS			
THE NEWSMEN SUCK THEIR THUMBS.	31	LULL	14
A SINGLE TWIST OF THE THUMBS, A TAMPING AND TURNING,	42	TRANSPLANTING	7
THUMP			
ONCE, TWICE, AND A FAINT THIRD THUMP,--	42	TRANSPLANTING	11
THUNDER			
WE THUNDER THROUGH RAVINES	34	NIGHT JOURNEY	18
THEN A CRACK OF THUNDER, AND THE BLACK RAIN RUNS OVER US, OVER	230	THE STORM	23
THUS			
THUS I; AND SHOULD THESE REASONS FLY APART,	144	ELEGY (1)	9
THUS I CONFORM TO MY DIVINITY	244	INFIRMITY	11
THUS I ENDURE THIS LAST PURE STRETCH OF JOY,	248	THE TREE, BIRD	22
THY			
REMAIN SECURE FROM PAIN PRESERVE THY HATE THY HEART.	5	TO MY SISTER	11
REMAIN SECURE FROM PAIN PRESERVE THY HATE THY HEART.	5	TO MY SISTER	11
THE SEA'S UNEQUAL LENGTHS ANNOUNCED THY BIRTH	81	SENSIBILITY! LA	8
THY SOFT ALBINO GAZE	81	SENSIBILITY! LA	10
TICK			
THE SLOW TICK OF TIME	211	SONG (1)	10
TICKET			
THE TICKET MISLAID OR LOST, THE GATE	158	FIRST MEDITATN	49
TICKING			
A CHEAP CLOCK TICKING IN GHOSTLY CICADA VOICE.	29	THE REMINDER	12
A FINE DRY SNOW TICKING THE WINDSHIELD,	199	THE FAR FIELD	5
AND THE TICKING OF SNOW AROUND OIL DRUMS IN THE DAKOTAS,	204	THE ROSE	68
TICKLE			
THE TIME TO TICKLE A LIZARD,	183	THE LIZARD	1
TICKLE-ME			
PRICKLE-ME, TICKLE-ME, CLOSE STEMS.	85	PRAISE TO END!	6
TICKLING			
NUDGING AND TICKLING OF ANTS AND SPIDERS,	255	LIGHT POEM	2
TICKS			
THE CINDERY SNOW TICKS OVER STUBBLE.	104	OLD LADY'S WRDS	54
TIDE			
THE TIDE RUSTLING IN, SLIDING BETWEEN THE RIDGES OF STONE,	191	AT OYSTER RIVER	34
AND THE TIDE RISES UP AGAINST THE GRASS	202	THE ROSE	9
A TIME FOR WATCHING THE TIDE,	202	THE ROSE	11

	PAGE	TITLE	LINE
TIDE (CONTINUED)			
WHEN THE TIDE MOVES	210	HER TIME	6
TIDE-RIPPLES			
COME THE FIRST TIDE-RIPPLES, MOVING, ALMOST WITHOUT SOUND, TOWARD ME,	190	AT OYSTER RIVER	2
TIED			
HIS THOUGHT IS TIED, THE CURVING PROW	4	DEATH PIECE	5
THEY TIED AND TUCKED,--	44	FRAU BAUMAN	11
WITH BUCK STILL TIED TO THE LOG, ON COMES THE LIGHT.	47	DOUBLE FEATURE	1
SAYS A SONG TIED TO A TREE.	125	WORDS FOR WIND	71
TIERS			
LEAN FROM THE TIERS AND BENCHES,	61	THE LONG ALLEY	72
TIGER			
THE MOTTLED TIGER, BEST IN THE CORNER OF A DAMP PLACE,	197	THE LONG WATERS	40
TIGHT			
I CANNOT PUT MY GLANCE UPON THEM TIGHT.	8	THE SIGNALS	8
THE TIGHT NERVES LEADING TO THE THROAT	22	SILENCE	17
THE TIGHT GRAINS PARTING AT LAST.	37	CUTTINGS (LATE)	8
TIGHTER			
COLD EVIL TWINKLED TIGHTER THAN A STRING; A FIRE	143	SHIMMER OF EVIL	8
TIGHTLY			
THE LEAFY MIND, THAT LONG WAS TIGHTLY FURLED,	11	LIGHT BRIGHTER	18
TILL			
TILL I LAY IN THEIR LAPS, LAUGHING,	44	FRAU BAUMAN	28
AND I WATCHED AND WATCHED TILL MY EYES BLURRED FROM THE BIRD SHAPES,--	199	THE FAR FIELD	29
TILL I CAUGHT HIM UP BY THE TAIL AND BROUGHT HIM IN,	227	MEADOW MOUSE	4
TILL MYSTERY IS NO MORE: NO MORE HE CAN.	250	THE RIGHT THING	18
TILL YOU COME TO THE LAND OF KINGDOM COME	272	DUET	20
TILLY			
AND SO SHE WAS, IN HER WAY, AUNT TILLY.	223	ELEGY (2)	3
TILT			
WITH A TILT OF HIS EYE,	208	THE APPARITION	6
THE CRABS TILT AND EAT, LEISURELY,	233	THE PIKE	5
TILTED			
AN EYE TILTED.	62	FIELD OF LIGHT	6
WHERE IT LEANS, TILTED EAST, A PERCH FOR THE OSPREY,	197	THE LONG WATERS	36
TILTING			
THE LIGHTS TILTING UP, SKYWARD, AS WE COME OVER A LITTLE RISE,	158	FIRST MEDITATN	24
TILTING BACK THE SUNLIGHT.	168	FOURTH MEDITATN	11
WHEN BATS FLY, CLOSE TO SLIGHTLY TILTING BROWNISH WATER,	198	THE LONG WATERS	61
TWITCHING, TILTING TOWARD THE LEAST SOUND.	227	MEADOW MOUSE	16
TILTS			
TILTS, BACKWARD AND FORWARD.	93	I CRY, LOVE!	51
AND A TREE TILTS FROM ITS ROOTS,	157	FIRST MEDITATN	6
TIME			
MY SPIRITS ROSE EACH TIME THE HAMMER FELL,	21	THE AUCTION	13
THE TIME OF WORKERS IS THEIR OWN.	33	HIGHWAY: MICH	5
YOU BEAT TIME ON MY HEAD	45	MY PAPA'S WALTZ	13
A WAVE OF TIME HANGS MOTIONLESS ON THIS PARTICULAR SHORE.	47	DOUBLE FEATURE	9
WHATEVER I OWED TO TIME	49	RIVER INCIDENT	4
THIS IS MY HARD TIME.	53	THE LOST SON	11
AN IN-BETWEEN TIME,	58	THE LOST SON	150
TIME FOR THE FLAT-HEADED MAN. I RECOGNIZE THAT LISTENER,	65	SHAPE OF FIRE	29
HIS EARS HAVEN'T TIME.	71	WHERE KNOCK IS	9
I CAME ACROSS A TIME,	71	WHERE KNOCK IS	13
WHAT'S THE TIME, PAPA-SEED?	72	WHERE KNOCK IS	20
A LONG LONG TIME.	74	WHERE KNOCK IS	83
I HAVEN'T TIME FOR SUGAR,	75	I NEED, I NEED	24
IT'S TIME TO BEGIN!	78	BRING THE DAY!	44
IS IT TIME TO THINK?	83	O LULL ME, LULL	9
IT'S A SOUL'S CROSSING TIME.	89	UNFOLD! UNFOLD!	8
IT'S TIME YOU STOOD UP AND ASKED	89	UNFOLD! UNFOLD!	10
THE LAST TIME I NEARLY WHISPERED MYSELF AWAY.	89	UNFOLD! UNFOLD!	20
THERE'S TIME ENOUGH.	93	I CRY, LOVE!	37
SHE MOVES WHEN TIME IS SHY:	124	WORDS FOR WIND	52
(I MEASURE TIME BY HOW A BODY SWAYS).	127	I KNEW A WOMAN	28
SHE HAPPENS, TIME ON TIME--	130	THE OTHER	10
SHE HAPPENS, TIME ON TIME--	130	THE OTHER	10
I STAY ALIVE, BOTH IN AND OUT OF TIME,	131	SENTENTIOUS MAN	14
OF LIVING MERELY IN THE REALM OF TIME.	149	IN LATE SUMMER	20
AND I MAY BE, SOME TIME.	150	SNAKE	12

	PAGE	TITLE	LINE
TIME (CONTINUED)			
BEING DELIGHTS IN BEING, AND IN TIME.	150	IN LATE SUMMER	31
I'M SURE I'VE BEEN A TOAD, ONE TIME OR ANOTHER.	151	SLUG	25
BACKWARD IN TIME:	158	FIRST MEDITATN	38
A LONGING FOR ANOTHER PLACE AND TIME,	162	I'M HERE	37
AND THE TIME I WAS SO SICK--	163	I'M HERE	63
BUT A TIME COMES WHEN THE VAGUE LIFE OF THE MOUTH NO LONGER SUFFICES;	168	FOURTH MEDITATN	18
WHO TURNED A CORNER IN TIME, WHEN AT LAST HE GREW A THUMB;	170	FOURTH MEDITATN	69
AND THE TIME RIPE FOR RUNNING TO THE MOON!	173	WHAT TELL BONES	85
EVERY TIME I LET HIM, THE STRING WOULD BUST.	178	THE DONKEY	3
SOME TIME I THINK I'LL LIVE THAT WAY.	182	THE HIPPO	5
THE TIME TO TICKLE A LIZARD	183	THE LIZARD	1
IN A BLEAK TIME, WHEN A WEEK OF RAIN IS A YEAR,	187	THE LONGING	14
ACQUIRES, FOR A TIME, THE SANDPIPER'S INSOUCIANCE,	191	AT OYSTER RIVER	39
OR THE TITTEBAWASEE, IN THE TIME BETWEEN WINTER AND SPRING,	191	AT OYSTER RIVER	47
I RISE AND FALL, AND TIME FOLDS	194	JOURNY INTERIOR	46
IN THE MOMENT OF TIME WHEN THE SMALL DROP FORMS, BUT DOES NOT FALL,	194	JOURNY INTERIOR	58
IN TIME WHEN THE TROUT AND YOUNG SALMON LEAP FOR THE LOW-FLYING INSECTS,	197	THE LONG WATERS	33
WAS TO FORGET TIME AND DEATH:	199	THE FAR FIELD	27
THE DYING OF TIME IN THE WHITE LIGHT OF TOMORROW,	200	THE FAR FIELD	52
A TIME FOR WATCHING THE TIDE,	202	THE ROSE	11
OR THAT LONELY TIME BEFORE THE BREAKING OF MORNING	204	THE ROSE	82
HER TIME	210	HER TIME	T
IN THE TIME	210	HER TIME	5
THE SLOW TICK OF TIME	211	SONG (1)	10
THE TIME WE BROKE FROM TIME;	212	LIGHT LISTENED	20
THE TIME WE BROKE FROM TIME;	212	LIGHT LISTENED	20
EACH TIME EVER	219	THE ABYSS	9
I WAS NO MORE THAN SEVEN AT THE TIME.	224	OTTO	22
AT THE TIME: SHE'D LIVED	228	THE GERANIUM	9
A TIME TO GO HOME!--	230	THE STORM	17
SPACE STRUGGLED WITH TIME;	238	THE MOMENT	6
IN A DARK TIME	239	IN A DARK TIME	T
IN A DARK TIME, THE EYE BEGINS TO SEE,	239	IN A DARK TIME	1
TIME CANNOT OVERWHELM.	240	IN EVEING AIR	9
ONCE I TRANSCENDED TIME:	240	IN EVEING AIR	10
IN TIME INDUCE A MENTAL ILL.	257	SANITARIUM	6
WE'RE GETTING CLOSER TO IT ALL THE TIME."	274	SUPPR W LINDSAY	45
TIME-HARRIED			
TIME-HARRIED PRISONERS OF SHALL AND WILL--	250	THE RIGHT THING	2
TIME-ORDER			
GOODBYE, GOODBYE, OLD STONES, THE TIME-ORDER IS GOING,	56	THE LOST SON	108
TIMES			
YOU TAKE THE TIMES SUPPLEMENT, AND READ ITS VERSE,	113	TO A LADY ED	2
AT TIMES MY DARLING SQUEAKS IN PURE PLATO.	133	THE PURE FURY	14
THERE ARE STILL TIMES, MORNING AND EVENING:	159	FIRST MEDITATN	83
IN SUCH TIMES, LACKING A GOD,	160	FIRST MEDITATN	98
I'VE TRIED I DON'T KNOW HOW MANY TIMES TO REPLANT IT.	163	I'M HERE	77
THERE ARE TIMES WHEN REALITY COMES CLOSER:	166	HER BECOMING	44
AT TIMES CONTENT TO BE TWO.	207	THE YOUNG GIRL	7
TIMES FIVE A MAN; I BREATHE	271	THE REPLY	14
TIME'S			
WHAT TIME'S MY HEART? I CARE.	125	WORDS FOR WIND	75
TIN			
NEXT DOOR THERE IS A LOVE-NEST OF PLASTER BOARD AND TIN,	27	CLAIRVOY WIDOW	15
WELTER OF TIN CANS, PAILS, OLD BIRD NESTS, A CHILD'S SHOE RIDING A LOG,	191	AT OYSTER RIVER	54
AMONG THE TIN CANS, TIRES, RUSTED PIPES, BROKEN MACHINERY,--	199	THE FAR FIELD	17
TINY			
LEWD, TINY, CARELESS LIVES	147	THE EXORCISM	16
AROUND, BACK INTO THE TINY MAINCURRENT, THE RUSH OF BROWNISH-WHITE WATER,	159	FIRST MEDITATN	71
I'M TIRED OF TINY NOISES:	161	I'M HERE	7
ALIVE WITH TINY STRIPED FISH, AND YOUNG CRABS CLIMBING IN AND OUT OF THE WATER.	190	AT OYSTER RIVER	5
OVER A LIP OF STONE, THE TINY RIVULET;	191	AT OYSTER RIVER	43
THE WATERS SWIRLING PAST THE TINY HEADLANDS.	202	THE ROSE	25
WITH NOT ONE TINY LAUGH	213	THE HAPPY THREE	14
BUT THE EYE OF THE TINY LIZARD STAYS WITH ME.	226	THE LIZARD	22

	PAGE	TITLE	LINE
TIP			
AND A DROP OF RAIN WATER HANGS AT THE TIP OF A LEAF	204	THE ROSE	86
TIPPED			
THE WAY I TIPPED MY HAT.	225	THE CHUMS	8
TIPPING			
GREEN, A BIRD TIPPING THE TOPMOST BOUGH,	235	MANIFESTATION	2
TIPS			
GREAT CANNAS OR DELICATE CYCLAMEN TIPS,--	38	FORCING HOUSE	4
ON THE TIPS OF ITS TOES?	54	THE LOST SON	53
TIPTOED			
IT TIPTOED DOWN THE HALL.	136	THE SENSUALISTS	20
TIRED			
I GREW TIRED OF THE RITUAL OF NAMES AND THE ASSISTANT KEEPER OF THE MOLLUSKS:	65	SHAPE OF FIRE	36
MY TEARS ARE TIRED.	73	WHERE KNOCK IS	70
I'M TIRED OF ALL THAT, BAG-FOOT. I CAN HEAR SMALL ANGELS ANYTIME. WHO	98	O, THOU OPENING	25
I'M TIRED OF BROODING ON MY NEIGHBOR'S SOUL;	132	SENTENTIOUS MAN	37
OR A SALMON, TIRED, MOVING UP A SHALLOW STREAM,	159	FIRST MEDITATN	68
I'M TIRED OF TINY NOISES:	161	I'M HERE	7
TIRES			
UNDERNEATH, THE SLUGGISH WATER RUNNING BETWEEN WEEDS, BROKEN WHEELS, TIRES, STONES.	194	JOURNY INTERIOR	33
AMONG THE TIN CANS, TIRES, RUSTED PIPES, BROKEN MACHINERY,--	199	THE FAR FIELD	17
TITS			
BETWEEN THOSE LOVELY TITS.	136	THE SENSUALISTS	12
TITTEBAWASEE			
OR THE TITTEBAWASEE, IN THE TIME BETWEEN WINTER AND SPRING,	191	AT OYSTER RIVER	47
TO (614)			
TOAD			
WILL THE SEA GIVE THE WIND SUCK? A TOAD FOLDS INTO A STONE.	64	SHAPE OF FIRE	8
THIS TOAD COULD WALTZ ON A DRUM;	92	I CRY, LOVE!	11
I'M SURE I'VE BEEN A TOAD, ONE TIME OR ANOTHER.	151	SLUG	25
ONCE TO THE TOAD,	167	HER BECOMING	71
TOADS			
TOADS BROODING WELLS.	53	THE LOST SON	4
OR THAT OLD HARPY SECRETING TOADS IN HER PORTMANTEAU.	82	SENSIBILITY! LA	36
WHO TOOK ONLY TOADS ON HIS BACK:	178	THE YAK	2
TOBACCO			
OR DROWN A BUG IN ONE SPIT OF TOBACCO JUICE,	42	OLD FLORIST	8
TODAY			
TODAY, WHILE SCRAPING HAIR BEFORE THE MIRROR,	25	DIM-WIT COUSIN	10
TODAY I SAW A BEARD IN A CLOUD.	76	I NEED, I NEED	48
THE DOVE'S MY WILL TODAY.	124	WORDS FOR WIND	40
TODAY I EAT MY USUAL DIET OF SHADOWS.	166	HER BECOMING	31
TODAY I SKIPPED ON THE SHORE,	207	THE YOUNG GIRL	8
TODAY THEY DRAINED THE FLUID FROM A KNEE	244	INFIRMITY	9
I'VE HAD ENOUGH TODAY	271	THE REPLY	2
TOE			
I TEETER, HEELS HOOKED ON THE CURB, SCRAPE A TOE;	47	DOUBLE FEATURE	7
MY NOSE FEELS FOR MY TOE;	130	THE OTHER	11
BUT YOU, LOOSE TOE FROM THE OLD LIFE,	151	SLUG	10
BUT WHEN SHE PECKED MY TOE,	213	THE HAPPY THREE	25
ONE TOE IN ETERNITY;	262	FOLLIES OF ADAM	18
TOES			
A SHELL ARCHED UNDER MY TOES,	49	RIVER INCIDENT	1
ON THE TIPS OF ITS TOES?	54	THE LOST SON	53
WITH WIDE WEBBY TOES	55	THE LOST SON	59
SO TOUCH MY TOES TWICE.	75	I NEED, I NEED	30
TO TEACH MY TOES TO LISTEN TO MY TONGUE.	105	SIR JOHN DAVIES	16
WE WOKE TO FIND THE MOONLIGHT ON OUR TOES.	106	SIR JOHN DAVIES	64
STILL SWAYING GENTLY BY HIS TOES,	116	THE SLOTH	11
I DABBLE MY TOES IN THE BRACKISH FOAM SLIDING FORWARD,	190	AT OYSTER RIVER	15
TOGETHER			
WE TWO, TOGETHER, ON A DARKENING DAY	106	SIR JOHN DAVIES	53
WE SING TOGETHER; WE SING MOUTH TO MOUTH.	129	SHE	7
NOW THEY MOVE ALL TOGETHER!--	152	THE SISKINS	19
THEIR FOREPAWS JOINED TOGETHER, LIKE HANDS--	163	I'M HERE	69
I AM GATHERED TOGETHER ONCE MORE;	198	THE LONG WATERS	77
THEIR FOUR WINGS BEATING TOGETHER,	210	HER TIME	13
WE DANCED TOGETHER, WE DANCED ON AND ON.	241	THE SEQUEL	16
TOIL			
THAT FORCE THE SON OF MAN TO TOIL;	18	LONG LIVE WEEDS	4

	PAGE	TITLE	LINE

TOLD

AND TOLD MY NEIGHBORS WHEN TO LAUGH. .... 138 THE SURLY ONE 3

SO SHE TOLD ME WHEN I WAS LITTLE, ... 163 I'M HERE 72

I AM TOLD BY THOSE WHO KNOW,-- .... 207 THE YOUNG GIRL 6

TOLEDO

IN ECORSE, TOLEDO, AND WYANDOTTE .... 111 SQUEEZE-BOX 11

TOM

I'LL SING WITH DEAR TOM MOORE, ... 268 SAGINAW SONG 48

WITH THAT LOVELY MAN, TOM MOORE. .... 268 SAGINAW SONG 49

TOMBSTONE

ON THE BANKS OF THE TOMBSTONE, THE WIND-HARPS HAVING THEIR
SAY, ... 204 THE ROSE 60

TOM-CAT

AND THE TOM-CAT, CAUGHT NEAR THE PHEASANT-RUN, ... 199 THE FAR FIELD 21

TO LIVE BY COURTESY OF THE SHRIKE, THE SNAKE, THE TOM-CAT. 227 MEADOW MOUSE 25

TOMORROW

TOMORROW IS FRIDAY. .... 75 I NEED, I NEED 42

THE DYING OF TIME IN THE WHITE LIGHT OF TOMORROW, ... 200 THE FAR FIELD 52

TONGUE

I HAVE NO NEED FOR TONGUE. .... 3 OPEN HOUSE 2

MY TONGUE IS GENERATIONS DEAD, ... 8 PRAYER 5

TAKE TONGUE AND EAR--ALL ELSE I HAVE-- .... 8 PRAYER 21

LIMP AND DAMP, DELICATE AS A YOUNG BIRD'S TONGUE; .... 39 ORCHIDS 5

AS MY OWN TONGUE KISSED .... 56 THE LOST SON 98

LAST NIGHT I SLEPT IN THE PITS OF A TONGUE. .... 65 SHAPE OF FIRE 34

A TONGUE WITHOUT SONG .... 89 UNFOLD! UNFOLD! 12

I HEAR A DEAD TONGUE HALLOO. .... 90 UNFOLD! UNFOLD! 44

TO TEACH MY TOES TO LISTEN TO MY TONGUE. .... 105 SIR JOHN DAVIES 16

IF SHE BUT SIGHS, A BIRD PUTS OUT ITS TONGUE. .... 129 SHE 3

I LOLL, I LOLL, ALL TONGUE. .... 130 THE OTHER 16

A THIN MOUTH, AND A TONGUE .... 150 SNAKE 4

HER TONGUE, AT THE LAST, THICK, BLACK AS AN OX'S. .... 223 ELEGY (2) 17

FROM THE HOUND GIVING TONGUE, ... 236 SONG (2) 3

TONGUES

ALL THE LEAVES STUCK OUT THEIR TONGUES; .... 53 THE LOST SON 5

THE TONGUES OF WATER, CREEPING IN, QUIETLY. .... 191 AT OYSTER RIVER 35

AND ONCE MORE THE TONGUES BEGIN BABBLING. .... 220 THE ABYSS 31

TOO

I AM TOO CENTERED ON THIS SPOT. .... 24 BEFORE STUDY 2

YOUR PALM IS MOIST, YOUR MANNER FAR TOO JOLLY . . . 25 DIM-WIT COUSIN 9

--AND THE TAINT IN A BLOOD THAT WAS RUNNING TOO THIN. .... 32 SALE 20

THESE STONES HAVE BEEN HERE TOO LONG. .... 55 THE LOST SON 65

MAY I LOOK TOO, LOVED EYE? .... 79 GIVE WAY, GATES 19

SHE WAS TOO MUCH FOR ONE, YOU CAN BET YOUR LIFE: .... 114 THE COW 3

BUT IF I MOVE TOO CLOSE, ... 130 THE OTHER 5

NATURE'S TOO MUCH TO KNOW. .... 130 THE OTHER 12

SOME RAGES SAVE US. DID I RAGE TOO LONG? .... 131 SENTENTIOUS MAN 9

WE THINK TOO LONG IN TERMS OF WHAT TO BE; .... 140 THE SWAN 8

YOU WERE TOO LONELY FOR ANOTHER FATE. .... 144 ELEGY (1) 6

YOU'VE TOO MANY TUNES, AND NONE OF THEM GOOD: .... 177 KITTY-CAT BIRD 5

THE BEAR SAID, SIR, YOU GO TOO FAR, ... 181 MONOTONY SONG 9

ARE YOU? YOU'RE JUMPING TOO! .... 182 THE LAMB 4

(DREAMS DRAIN THE SPIRIT IF WE DREAM TOO LONG.) .... 187 THE LONGING 13

I, WHO CAME BACK FROM THE DEPTHS LAUGHING TOO LOUDLY, ... 198 THE LONG WATERS 73

NOT TOO FAR AWAY FROM THE EVER-CHANGING FLOWER-DUMP, ... 199 THE FAR FIELD 16

I HAVE TAKEN, TOO OFTEN, THE DANGEROUS PATH, ... 220 THE ABYSS 21

TOO MUCH REALITY CAN BE A DAZZLE, A SURFEIT; .... 220 THE ABYSS 44

TOO CLOSE IMMEDIACY AN EXHAUSTION: .... 220 THE ABYSS 45

THEY TAUGHT ME NOT TO BE TOO NICE .... 225 THE CHUMS 7

HE TOO HAS EATEN WELL-- .... 226 THE LIZARD 1

IN HEAVEN, TOO, ... 228 IN VIOLENT WARD 1

FLAPPING AWAY HEAVILY WHEN A CAR BLASTS TOO CLOSE, ... 234 ALL MORNING 7

WAS I TOO GLIB ABOUT ETERNAL THINGS, ... 241 THE SEQUEL 1

A MIND TOO ACTIVE IS NO MIND AT ALL; .... 244 INFIRMITY 19

ONE LOOK TOO CLOSE CAN TAKE MY SOUL AWAY. .... 246 THE MARROW 9

ON THE PERILS OF TOO EARLY DRINK,-- .... 269 GOB MUSIC 17

TOO EARLY DRINK, TOO EARLY DRINK, ... 269 GOB MUSIC 18

TOO EARLY DRINK, TOO EARLY DRINK, ... 269 GOB MUSIC 18

ON THE PERILS OF TOO EARLY DRINK, ... 270 GOB MUSIC 45

TOO EARLY DRINK, TOO EARLY DRINK, ... 270 GOB MUSIC 46

TOO EARLY DRINK, TOO EARLY DRINK .... 270 GOB MUSIC 46

"SURE, WE STILL EAT," I SAID. "ENOUGH! OR TOO MUCH." ..... 273 SUPPR W LINDSAY 17

--"THAT MEANS BLAKE, TOO?" .... 273 SUPPR W LINDSAY 18

	PAGE	TITLE	LINE
TOOK			
WHEN I TOOK OFF MY CLOTHES	64	SHAPE OF FIRE	24
TOOK ARMS AGAINST OUR OWN OBSCURITY.	106	SIR JOHN DAVIES	54
I TOOK THE WHISKEY FROM THE SHELF, ...	138	THE SURLY ONE	2
BENT DOWN THEIR BIRDS: THE LIGHT WAVES TOOK THE WAVES; ...	143	SHIMMER OF EVIL	2
SWAYING, I TOOK ITS GAZE;	145	THE BEAST	11
WHO TOOK THE DARKNESS FROM THE AIR?	173	WHAT TELL BONES	94
WHO TOOK ONLY TOADS ON HIS BACK:	178	THE YAK	2
WHO TOOK MY HEART, WHOLE, ...	208	THE APPARITION	5
MY FATHER TOOK IT TO HER, BY THE TAIL.	224	OTTO	30
THAT DAY WE TOOK FROM THE ANGELS:	258	SONG (3)	13
I TOOK THE PLEDGE CARDS ON MY BIKE;	267	SAGINAW SONG	31
TOOL			
THE TOOL CAN CHIP NO FLAKE:	9	THE ADAMANT	11
TOOTLE			
I DO NOT LIKE TO BANG OR TOOTLE."	115	THE SERPENT	20
TOP			
AND WINTERGREEN BERRIES AND LEAVES STILL STUCK TO THE TOP,--	40	MOSS-GATHERING	5
CHILD ON TOP OF A GREENHOUSE	43	CHILD ON GRNHSE	T
BUT ONE TULIP ON TOP,	43	FLOWER DUMP	11
ARE THOSE HORNS ON TOP OF THE HILL? YESTERDAY HAS A LONG			
LOOK.	59	THE LONG ALLEY	13
THAT PRACTICALLY SPLIT THE TOP OF HIS THROAT.	115	THE SERPENT	22
THE SHRIEK OF NAILS AS OLD SHINGLES ARE RIPPED FROM THE TOP			
OF A ROOF, ...	204	THE ROSE	70
ON TOP A THISTLE	219	THE ABYSS	15
THEN WHIRRING OFF SIDEWAYS TO THE TOP OF THE HAWTHORN, ...	234	ALL MORNING	31
TOPMOST			
GREEN, A BIRD TIPPING THE TOPMOST BOUGH, ...	235	MANIFESTATION	2
TOPPED			
TOPPED BY CROSS-WINDS, TUGGED AT BY SINUOUS UNDERCURRENTS	191	AT OYSTER RIVER	33
TOPPLING			
TOPPLING DOWN AN EMBANKMENT.	157	FIRST MEDITATN	7
OF THE TOPPLING WAVES, ...	205	THE ROSE	95
TORMENT			
LOVE BEGETS LOVE. THIS TORMENT IS MY JOY.	243	THE MOTION	7
TORN			
A BEAST CRIES OUT AS IF ITS FLESH WERE TORN, ...	156	THE DYING MAN	82
TORPOR			
BLESSED BE TORPOR.	83	O LULL ME, LULL	5
TORRENT			
OR WHEN TWO RIVERS COMBINE, THE BLUE GLACIAL TORRENT	200	THE FAR FIELD	61
TORRENTIAL			
SEND DOWN A RUSH OF AIR, O TORRENTIAL, ...	61	THE LONG ALLEY	83
TORTURED			
CONSTRICTED BY MY TORTURED THOUGHT, ...	24	BEFORE STUDY	1
TOSSED			
YOUR FATHER TOSSED A CAT IN AIR, ...	86	PRAISE TO END!	36
SWEET JESUS TOSSED ME BACK:	87	PRAISE TO END!	65
HAVE TOSSED MY HEART AND FIDDLED THROUGH MY BRAIN.	105	SIR JOHN DAVIES	22
I TOSSED A STONE, AND LISTENED TO ITS PLUNGE.	120	THE DREAM	22
TOSSING			
A LINE OF ELMS PLUNGING AND TOSSING LIKE HORSES, ...	43	CHILD ON GRNHSE	6
TOUCH			
JERKS SKYWARD AT THE TOUCH OF WIND, ...	14	COMING OF COLD	29
SHALL NEVER TOUCH ANOTHER EAR.	22	SILENCE	20
HE LIVED BEYOND THE TOUCH OF MORTAL LAWS.	28	THE FAVORITE	8
FOR WHOM WERE YOU MADE, SWEETNESS I CANNOT TOUCH?	59	THE LONG ALLEY	27
A LOG TURNED AT THE TOUCH OF A FOOT;	62	FIELD OF LIGHT	4
SO TOUCH MY TOES TWICE.	75	I NEED, I NEED	30
IT'S A DEAR LIFE I CAN TOUCH.	76	I NEED, I NEED	58
TOUCH AND AROUSE. SUCK AND SOB. CURSE AND MOURN.	80	GIVE WAY, GATES	46
I'M A TWIG TO TOUCH, ...	81	SENSIBILITY! LA	24
SHE TAUGHT ME TOUCH, THAT UNDULANT WHITE SKIN;	127	I KNEW A WOMAN	10
ONCE I COULD TOUCH MY SHADOW, AND BE HAPPY;	168	FOURTH MEDITATN	14
TOUCHED			
I TOUCHED THE GROUND, THE GROUND WARMED BY THE KILLDEER,	63	FIELD OF LIGHT	39
I TOUCHED HER SHADOW WHEN THE LIGHT DELAYED;	119	THE DREAM	13
I TOUCHED THE STONES, AND THEY HAD MY OWN SKIN.	133	THE PURE FURY	7
TOUCHES			
AND THE SUN TOUCHES THE LIZARD'S THROAT, ITS TAIL HALF IN			
SHADOW.	261	THE CHANGELING	34

	PAGE	TITLE	LINE
TOUCHING			
HER SKIRTS NOT TOUCHING A LEAF,	100	THE VISITANT	13
TOUGH			
OR YANKING TOUGH FERN-SHAPES,	39	WEED PULLER	7
TOUGHENED			
THE BOLD WEAR TOUGHENED SKIN	20	REPL TO CENSURE	13
TOUGHER			
VINES TOUGHER THAN WRISTS	38	FORCING HOUSE	1
TOUGHEST			
UNTIL THE TOUGHEST NERVES ARE FRAYED.	33	HIGHWAY: MICH	13
TOWARD			
LOVERS DISENGAGE, MOVE SHEEPISHLY TOWARD THE AISLE	47	DOUBLE FEATURE	2
TOWARD THE QUICK-WATER, WRINKLING AND RIPPLING.	54	THE LOST SON	39
THE ROSE, THE CHRYSANTHEMUM TURNED TOWARD THE LIGHT.	57	THE LOST SON	146
AND LOVE, LOVE SANG TOWARD.	66	SHAPE OF FIRE	77
LOOKING TOWARD WHAT WE ARE.	80	GIVE WAY, GATES	37
SEA-BEAST OR BIRD FLUNG TOWARD THE RAVAGED SHORE?	107	SIR JOHN DAVIES	68
SHE CAME TOWARD ME IN THE FLOWING AIR,	119	THE DREAM	9
SMALL WATERS RUN TOWARD A MIRY HOLE--	132	SENTENTIOUS MAN	39
AND SHUDDERED TOWARD THE WALL;	136	THE SENSUALISTS	18
EXISTENCE MOVES TOWARD A CERTAIN END--	149	IN LATE SUMMER	21
AND WE BOUNCE AND SWAY ALONG TOWARD THE MIDNIGHT,	158	FIRST MEDITATN	23
DOWN WOODEN STEPS TOWARD A WEEDY GARDEN;	162	I'M HERE	46
STILL LEANING TOWARD THE LAST PLACE THE SUN WAS.	163	I'M HERE	76
ON A DARK DAY I WALK STRAIGHT TOWARD THE RAIN.	170	FOURTH MEDITATN	80
WEEDS TURN TOWARD THE WIND WEED-SKELETONS.	173	WHAT TELL BONES	65
COME THE FIRST TIDE-RIPPLES, MOVING, ALMOST WITHOUT SOUND, TOWARD ME,	190	AT OYSTER RIVER	2
WINDING UPWARD TOWARD THE STREAM WITH ITS SHARP STONES,	193	JOURNY INTERIOR	12
TURNING TOWARD THE OTHER SIDE OF LIGHT,	195	JOURNY INTERIOR	69
TURNING TOWARD THE SEA,	201	THE FAR FIELD	83
AND HOW THOSE FLOWERHEADS SEEMED TO FLOW TOWARD ME, TO BECKON ME, ONLY A CHILD, OUT OF MYSELF.	203	THE ROSE	55
DO WE MOVE TOWARD GOD, OR MERELY ANOTHER CONDITION?	221	THE ABYSS	75
THEY STOOD THERE WITH THEIR GUNS; HE WALKED TOWARD,	224	OTTO	18
ONE ROUND EYE STILL TOWARD ME.	226	THE LIZARD	19
TWITCHING, TILTING TOWARD THE LEAST SOUND.	227	MEADOW MOUSE	16
SHE LEANING OUT OF HER POT TOWARD THE WINDOW.	228	THE GERANIUM	19
THE SMALL THING DIVING DOWN TOWARD A HILL,	232	THE THING	10
THE BODY MOVES, THOUGH SLOWLY, TOWARD DESIRE.	235	MANIFESTATION	10
AND ALL THE WINDS CAME TOWARD ME. I WAS GLAD.	247	I WAITED	23
AND EVERY SNAIL DIPPED TOWARD ME ITS PURE HORN.	248	THE TREE, BIRD	2
THE SWEET LIGHT MET ME AS I WALKED TOWARD	248	THE TREE, BIRD	3
MY TRUE SELF RUNS TOWARD A HILL	251	ONCE MORE, RND	3
US, UNDER THE CHAIR-RUNGS, TOWARD THE CELLAR DOOR.	273	SUPPR W LINDSAY	14
TOWARDS			
HER WHITE ARMS REACHING TOWARDS ME.	100	THE VISITANT	14
AM I BUT NOTHING, LEANING TOWARDS A THING?	156	THE DYING MAN	85
TOWER			
IN A TOWER OF WIND, A TREE IDLING IN AIR,	195	JOURNY INTERIOR	70
TOWERING			
THE FLAT BOOM ON THE BEACH OF THE TOWERING SEA-SWELL,	231	THE STORM	41
TOWHEE			
A TOWHEE PECKS THE GROUND;	148	THE SMALL	3
FOR THE SLEEPY CRIES OF THE TOWHEE,	202	THE ROSE	13
THEN A CLOSE TOWHEE, A	213	THE HAPPY THREE	29
TOWHEES			
WITH TOWHEES, FINCHES, CHICKADEES, CALIFORNIA QUAIL, WOOD DOVES,	235	ALL MORNING	40
TOWN			
ON MILE OF TRAFFIC FROM THE TOWN	33	HIGHWAY: MICH	3
AS DARKNESS CREEPS UP ON THE WELL-GROOMED SUBURBAN TOWN,	33	IDYLL	5
FOR SHE FINALLY LEFT TOWN ON THE BAY CITY FREIGHT	112	SQUEEZE-BOX	40
AND I LIE HERE THINKING IN BLEAK BOFIN TOWN	216	THE SHY MAN	18
IT HAPPENED O, IN BOFIN TOWN,	270	GOB MUSIC	38
TOWNS			
THE TOWNS WITH THEIR HIGH PITTED ROAD-CROWNS AND DEEP GUTTERS,	193	JOURNY INTERIOR	30
TOWN'S			
FROM THE TOWN'S BIGGEST CROOKS.	267	SAGINAW SONG	36
TOY			
THEY TOY WITH DEATH AND TRAFFIC FINES.	33	HIGHWAY: MICH	10

	PAGE	TITLE	LINE
TOYS			
WITH NO HINT OF YOUR PRESENCE IN A JUNGLE OF MASCULINE TOYS,	29	THE REMINDER	10
TRACE			
WE CANNOT TRACE THE ERROR DOWN.	30	THE RECKONING	8
TRACED			
I'VE TRACED THESE WORDS IN SAND WITH A VESTIGIAL TAIL;	92	I CRY, LOVE!	17
TRACTABLE			
WAS NATURE KIND? THE HEART'S CORE TRACTABLE?	242	THE SEQUEL	25
TRAFFIC			
I SEE THE TRAFFIC DOING MIRACULOUS FEATS.	27	CLAIRVOY WIDOW	6
ON MILE OF TRAFFIC FROM THE TOWN	33	HIGHWAY: MICH	3
THEY TOY WITH DEATH AND TRAFFIC FINES.	33	HIGHWAY: MICH	10
ALTERNATE SNOW AND SLEET, NO ON-COMING TRAFFIC,	199	THE FAR FIELD	6
FAR AWAY, CLOSE-AT-HAND, HIS CALL FLOATING OVER THE ON-COMING TRAFFIC,	234	ALL MORNING	3
STOPPING TRAFFIC, INDIGNANT AS ADDLED OLD LADIES,	234	ALL MORNING	27
TRAILING			
AT THE STREAM'S EDGE, TRAILING A VAGUE FINGER;	162	I'M HERE	26
TRAILING A THING--WHAT WAS IT?--SMALL AS A LARK	232	THE THING	2
TRAIN			
A FAR-OFF TRAIN BLOWS ITS ECHOING WHISTLE ONCE;	33	IDYLL	10
NOW AS THE TRAIN BEARS WEST,	34	NIGHT JOURNEY	1
TRAINS			
O MY SISTER REMEMBER THE STARS THE TEARS THE TRAINS	5	TO MY SISTER	1
TRANCED			
THE TRANCED	237	THE TRANCED	T
TRANCE-LIKE			
THE BLOOD SLOWS TRANCE-LIKE IN THE ALTERED VEIN;	12	SLOW SEASON	15
TRANSCEND			
BODY AND SOUL TRANSCEND APPEARANCES	149	IN LATE SUMMER	13
HOW TO TRANSCEND THIS SENSUAL EMPTINESS?	187	THE LONGING	12
TRANSCENDED			
ONCE I TRANSCENDED TIME:	240	IN EVEING AIR	10
TRANSPLANTING			
TRANSPLANTING	42	TRANSPLANTING	T
WATCHING HANDS TRANSPLANTING,	42	TRANSPLANTING	1
TRAPPED			
IS TRAPPED TO THE LIPS,	65	SHAPE OF FIRE	47
MY DESIRE'S A WIND TRAPPED IN A CAVE.	172	WHAT TELL BONES	45
TRASH-CAN			
THREW HER, POT AND ALL, INTO THE TRASH-CAN,	228	THE GERANIUM	23
TRAVELED			
LIGHT TRAVELED OVER THE WIDE FIELD;	58	THE LOST SON	159
TRAVELER'S			
SLIDING AWAY FROM THE TRAVELER'S EYE,	203	THE ROSE	34
TRAVELLED			
YET FOR THIS WE TRAVELLED	265	HARSH COUNTRY	13
TREASURE			
THE PAGEANTRY OF WINGS THE EYE'S BRIGHT TREASURE.	5	TO MY SISTER	6
TREE			
THE ELM TREE IS OUR HIGHEST MOUNTAIN PEAK;	13	PRAISE PRAIRIE	1
I NOTICE A TREE, ARSENICAL GREY IN THE LIGHT, OR THE SLOW	47	DOUBLE FEATURE	10
FLAP FROM A WASTED TREE,	49	NIGHT CROW	2
I'VE MORE VEINS THAN A TREE!	57	THE LOST SON	120
THE DARK FLOWS ON ITSELF. A DEAD MOUTH SINGS UNDER AN OLD TREE.	59	THE LONG ALLEY	6
IS HE A BIRD OR A TREE? NOT EVERYONE CAN TELL.	64	SHAPE OF FIRE	3
IN THE HOUR OF RIPENESS THE TREE IS BARREN.	64	SHAPE OF FIRE	14
ONCE UPON A TREE	71	WHERE KNOCK IS	12
WHEN I STAND, I'M ALMOST A TREE.	78	BRING THE DAY!	32
BELIEVE ME, KNOT OF GRISTLE, I BLEED LIKE A TREE;	79	GIVE WAY, GATES	1
YOU TREE BEGINNING TO KNOW,	79	GIVE WAY, GATES	24
I STRETCHED LIKE A BOARD, ALMOST A TREE.	90	UNFOLD! UNFOLD!	32
WHO UNTIED THE TREE? I REMEMBER NOW.	93	I CRY, LOVE!	54
LIKE A SAPLING TREE,	98	O, THOU OPENING	49
A TREE SWAYED OVER WATER.	100	THE VISITANT	2
DEAREST TREE, I SAID, MAY I REST HERE?	100	THE VISITANT	5
STARING AT A TREE, I FELT THE PULSE OF A STONE.	101	THE VISITANT	22
THE TREE, THE CLOSE WILLOW, SWAYED.	101	THE VISITANT	27
LIGHT TAKES THE TREE; BUT WHO CAN TELL US HOW?	108	THE WAKING (2)	10
A BIRD SANG FROM THE CENTER OF A TREE;	119	THE DREAM	15
A CAT IN THE FORK OF A TREE,	121	ALL EARTH, AIR	8
A TREE GLIDES WITH THE MOON.	122	ALL EARTH, AIR	24

	PAGE	TITLE	LINE
TREE (CONTINUED)			
SHE'S SWEETER THAN A TREE.	123	WORDS FOR WIND	2
SAYS A SONG TIED TO A TREE.	125	WORDS FOR WIND	71
A WIND WREATHES ROUND A TREE.	126	WORDS FOR WIND	93
I CLAIM; ONE TREE, A WOOD;	128	THE VOICE	2
BIRD, GIRL, AND GHOSTLY TREE,	128	THE VOICE	20
YET, LIKE A TREE, ENDURE THE SHIFT OF THINGS.	135	THE RENEWAL	6
JOURNEY AROUND A TREE;	137	LOVE'S PROGRESS	7
A TREE ARISES ON A CENTRAL PLAIN--	150	IN LATE SUMMER	25
A TREE ALL OUT OF SHAPE FROM WIND AND RAIN,	150	IN LATE SUMMER	27
A TREE THINNED BY THE WIND OBSCURES MY SIGHT.	150	IN LATE SUMMER	28
OR THEY FLING THEMSELVES AGAINST TREE TRUNKS,	152	THE SISKINS	16
ONCE I DELIGHTED IN A SINGLE TREE;	155	THE DYING MAN	54
AND A TREE TILTS FROM ITS ROOTS,	157	FIRST MEDITATN	6
THERE IS NO RIVEN TREE, OR LAMB DROPPED BY AN EAGLE.	159	FIRST MEDITATN	82
DARE I BLAZE LIKE A TREE?	171	WHAT TELL BONES	9
THE SONGS FROM A SPIRAL TREE.	171	WHAT TELL BONES	27
A FISH RAVEN TURNS ON ITS PERCH (A DEAD TREE IN THE RIVERMOUTH),	190	AT OYSTER RIVER	22
IN A TOWER OF WIND, A TREE IDLING IN AIR,	195	JOURNY INTERIOR	70
TO A TREE LYING FLAT, ITS CROWN HALF BROKEN.	197	THE LONG WATERS	54
AND THE FLICKER DRUMMED FROM HIS DEAD TREE IN THE CHICKEN-YARD.	200	THE FAR FIELD	37
THE TREE RETREATS INTO ITS OWN SHADOW.	200	THE FAR FIELD	57
SILENCE OF WATER ABOVE A SUNKEN TREE:	201	THE FAR FIELD	100
AND THE WIND TRIES THE SHAPE OF A TREE,	204	THE ROSE	84
AND THE HUMMINGBIRD DIPS IN AND AROUND THE QUINCE TREE,	234	ALL MORNING	29
MANY ARRIVALS MAKE US LIVE: THE TREE BECOMING	235	MANIFESTATION	1
A SEA-WIND PAUSING IN A SUMMER TREE.	235	MANIFESTATION	8
A LORD OF NATURE WEEPING TO A TREE.	239	IN A DARK TIME	4
AND I BEHOLD THE DARK SIDE OF A TREE	240	IN EVEING AIR	14
A LIGHT LEAF ON A TREE, SHE SWAYED AWAY	241	THE SEQUEL	23
THIS SINGLE TREE TURNS INTO PUREST FLAME.	242	THE SEQUEL	28
BY DYING INWARD, LIKE AN AGING TREE.	244	INFIRMITY	12
WHEN LIGHT DIVIDED ON A STORM-TOSSED TREE.	246	THE MARROW	20
THE TREE, THE BIRD	248	THE TREE, BIRD	T
PART OF A TREE STILL DARK, STILL, DEATHLY STILL,	248	THE TREE, BIRD	9
HOW IS IT INSIDE A TREE?	261	THE CHANGELING	30
WHAT EAGLE NEEDS A TREE?	263	FOLLIES OF ADAM	26
TREELESS			
WHEN WE ARE WALKING ON A TREELESS PLAIN,	13	PRAISE PRAIRIE	7
TREES			
ONCE MORE THE TREES ASSUME FAMILIAR SHAPES,	11	LIGHT BRIGHTER	9
ALL NIGHT AND ALL DAY THE WIND ROARED IN THE TREES,	12	MID-CNTRY BLOW	1
LOST HUES OF BIRDS THE TREES TAKE AS THEIR OWN.	12	SLOW SEASON	9
DENSE TREES NO LONGER HOLD THE LIGHT,	14	COMING OF COLD	30
THE HILLS ARE GREY, THE TREES ARE BARE,	15	COMING OF COLD	43
AMONG THE TREES THAT FACE THE CORNER LIGHT.	16	THE BAT	6
A SUDDENNESS OF TREES,	34	NIGHT JOURNEY	7
BENEATH THE ROOTS OF TREES,	50	THE CYCLE	3
BRICKS FLAKE BEFORE MY FACE. MASTER OF WATER, THAT'S TREES AWAY.	61	THE LONG ALLEY	80
AND TREES CAME CLOSER WITH A DENSER SHADE.	133	THE PURE FURY	21
THE WEATHER WEPT, AND ALL THE TREES BENT DOWN;	143	SHIMMER OF EVIL	1
WITH A WIND FROM THE WEST AND THE TREES ALL IN MOTION.	158	FIRST MEDITATN	42
LOOK AT THE FAR TREES AT THE END OF THE GARDEN.	163	I'M HERE	82
THE GREAT TREES NO LONGER SHIMMER;	187	THE LONGING	17
THE CEMETERY WITH TWO SCRUBBY TREES IN THE MIDDLE OF THE PRAIRIE,	194	JOURNY INTERIOR	35
AND THE SEA-WINDS MOVE THROUGH THE PINE TREES,	196	THE LONG WATERS	18
BY SMALL STREAMS RUNNING DOWN UNDER FALLEN FIR TREES.	197	THE LONG WATERS	48
AND THE EAGLES SAIL LOW OVER THE FIR TREES,	202	THE ROSE	6
AMONG THE HALF-DEAD TREES, I CAME UPON THE TRUE EASE OF MYSELF,	205	THE ROSE	99
HAD SLAUGHTERED GAME, AND CUT YOUNG FIR TREES DOWN.	224	OTTO	21
BETWEEN THE WHITENING TREES, UP SANTA LUCIA,	230	THE STORM	20
BENDING THE TREES HALF-WAY DOWN TO THE GROUND,	231	THE STORM	31
THE LEAVES, THE TREES TURNED OUR TWO SHAPES AROUND.	237	THE TRANCED	15
TREE-SHREW			
THE DESCENDANTS OF THE PLAYFUL TREE-SHREW THAT SURVIVED THE ARCHAIC KILLERS,	170	FOURTH MEDITATN	66
TREE-SHREWS			
A CONGRESS OF TREE-SHREWS AND RATS,	163	I'M HERE	66

	PAGE	TITLE	LINE
TRELLIS			
BEHIND THE GREEN VISCID TRELLIS,	62	FIELD OF LIGHT	24
THE GLAD HEN ON THE HILL; AND THE TRELLIS HUMMING.	66	SHAPE OF FIRE	72
I HEAR A NOISE OF BEES, A TRELLIS HUM,	155	THE DYING MAN	74
WREN-SONG IN TRELLIS: A LIGHT ECSTASY OF BUTTERFLIES COURTING,	255	LIGHT POEM	1
TRELLISED			
THEY TRELLISED THE SUN; THEY PLOTTED FOR MORE THAN THEMSELVES.	44	FRAU BAUMAN	25
TREMBLE			
THAT TREMBLE OF SWEET NOTES SET MY HEART ASTIR,	216	THE SHY MAN	10
HE SEEMS NO LONGER TO TREMBLE.	227	MEADOW MOUSE	19
TREMBLED			
HE NEVER TREMBLED AT A VEILED REMARK.	28	THE FAVORITE	2
TREMBLED AT HIDDEN VIRTUE WITHOUT FLAW,	107	SIR JOHN DAVIES	74
WHERE HE TREMBLED AND SHOOK BENEATH A STICK	227	MEADOW MOUSE	3
TREMBLES			
FILLS AND TREMBLES AT THE EDGE YET DOES NOT FLOW OVER,	67	SHAPE OF FIRE	94
THE SILL TREMBLES.	220	THE ABYSS	33
DO I IMAGINE HE NO LONGER TREMBLES	227	MEADOW MOUSE	17
TREMBLING			
AND MY INTENT STRETCHED OVER THE BUDS AT THEIR FIRST TREMBLING.	66	SHAPE OF FIRE	69
HER SONG TREMBLING THE TWIGS AND SMALL BRANCHES.	102	ELEGY FOR JANE	6
OF THE FIRST TREMBLING OF A MICHIGAN BROOK IN APRIL,	191	AT OYSTER RIVER	42
THE SLIGHTLY TREMBLING WATER	200	THE FAR FIELD	67
A LITTLE QUAKER, THE WHOLE BODY OF HIM TREMBLING,	227	MEADOW MOUSE	6
--IN FEAR AND TREMBLING, DEAR KIERKEGAARD.	272	DUET	17
TREMENDOUS			
FLEW A TREMENDOUS BIRD	49	NIGHT CROW	5
TREMORS			
LIQUIDS PURSUE ME, NOTES AND TREMORS:	255	LIGHT POEM	6
TREMULOUS			
COMES A TREMULOUS CRY	123	WORDS FOR WIND	28
TRICK			
IT IS NO TRICK OF CHANGE OR CHANCE OF LIGHT.	150	IN LATE SUMMER	26
THE TRICK WAS TO THROW THE CAR SIDEWAYS AND CHARGE OVER THE HILL, FULL OF THE THROTTLE.	193	JOURNY INTERIOR	21
TRICKSY			
TRICKSY COMES AND TRICKSY GOES	60	THE LONG ALLEY	39
TRICKSY COMES AND TRICKSY GOES	60	THE LONG ALLEY	39
TRICYCLE			
THE LAST TRICYCLE RUNS CRAZILY TO THE END OF THE WALK.	33	IDYLL	4
TRIED			
I TRIED TO FLING MY SHADOW AT THE MOON,	105	SIR JOHN DAVIES	13
--WHEN HE TRIED TO DRINK UP THE MONEY.	112	SQUEEZE-BOX	37
I TRIED TO MEET HIS EYES.	146	THE SONG	3
I'VE TRIED I DON'T KNOW HOW MANY TIMES TO REPLANT IT.	163	I'M HERE	77
WHEN HE TRIED TO SPOUT, THAT GREAT BIG LUBBER,	178	THE WHALE	3
WHEN I HAD TRIED TO CLEAN	213	THE HAPPY THREE	5
WHITISH AND SPREAD WIDE WHEN HE TRIED TO STRUGGLE AWAY,	227	MEADOW MOUSE	10
IT WAS AS IF I TRIED TO WALK IN HAY,	247	I WAITED	6
TRIES			
SHE TRIES TO THINK, AND IT FLIES LOOSE AGAIN.	133	THE PURE FURY	11
SO THE SPIRIT TRIES FOR ANOTHER LIFE,	159	FIRST MEDITATN	66
AND THE WIND TRIES THE SHAPE OF A TREE,	204	THE ROSE	84
TRINKETS			
ILLUSION'S TRINKETS, SPLENDID FOR THE YOUNG;	21	THE AUCTION	6
TRIUMPHS			
ONLY TO GAIN FRESH TRIUMPHS AND APPLAUSE.	28	THE FAVORITE	6
TRIVIA			
AND THOSE WHO SUBMERGE THEMSELVES DELIBERATELY IN TRIVIA,	169	FOURTH MEDITATN	38
TROPICAL			
HUNG DOWN LONG YELLOW EVIL NECKS, LIKE TROPICAL SNAKES.	38	ROOT CELLAR	5
TROUBLE			
THE TROUBLE IS WITH NO AND YES	75	I NEED, I NEED	33
SHE WAS SO MUCH TROUBLE;	179	MYRTLE'S COUSIN	7
TROUGH			
KISS THE TROUGH, SWINE-ON-FRIDAY.	59	THE LONG ALLEY	24
TROUT			
IN TIME WHEN THE TROUT AND YOUNG SALMON LEAP FOR THE LOW-FLYING INSECTS,	197	THE LONG WATERS	33

	PAGE	TITLE	LINE
TRUCKS			
SOMEWHAT CLOSER, THE TRUCKS COMING	158	FIRST MEDITATN	32
TRUDGES			
THE WALKER TRUDGES ANKLE-DEEP IN LEAVES;	12	SLOW SEASON	11
TRUE			
BUT THE TRUE SUBSTANCE BEARS	9	THE ADAMANT	7
THE EAR SO DELICATE AND TRUE	17	NO BIRD	3
WHEREBY TRUE WORK IS WROUGHT.	20	REPL TO CENSURE	8
A TRUE ZEPHYR-HAUNTED WOODIE.	81	SENSIBILITY! LA	7
A TRUE MOLE WANDERS LIKE A WORM.	97	O, THOU OPENING	20
WHERE'S THE GREAT RAGE OF A ROCKING HEART, THE HIGH RARE TRUE DANGEROUS	98	O, THOU OPENING	30
I CAN LEAP, TRUE TO THE FIELD,	98	O, THOU OPENING	42
I'M TRUE TO SOUP, AND HAPPY TO ASK:	99	O, THOU OPENING	55
BE TRUE,	99	O, THOU OPENING	86
AND KNOW THAT TRUE LOVE IS MORE THAN A LIFE-FORCE	113	TO A LADY ED	3
THAT LADIES THEIR TRUE NATURES NEVER SUPPRESS,	113	TO A LADY ED	10
I WALK WITH MY TRUE LOVE.	125	WORDS FOR WIND	74
IT SANG WITH HER TRUE VOICE,	128	THE VOICE	15
TRUE LECHERS LOVE THE FLESH, AND THAT IS ALL.	131	SENTENTIOUS MAN	6
TRUE, SHE CAN THINK A BIRD	137	LOVE'S PROGRESS	11
WHEN TRUE LOVE BROKE MY HEART IN HALF,	138	THE SURLY ONE	1
MAY THEY BE TAKEN BY THE TRUE BURNING;	169	FOURTH MEDITATN	61
STAYS IN ITS TRUE PLACE,	203	THE ROSE	41
AMONG THE HALF-DEAD TREES, I CAME UPON THE TRUE EASE OF MYSELF,	205	THE ROSE	99
SHE CRIES TO HER TRUE LOVE.	208	HER WORDS	9
I HEARD A BIRD STIR IN ITS TRUE CONFINE;	241	THE SEQUEL	11
MY TRUE SELF RUNS TOWARD A HILL	251	ONCE MORE, RND	3
REFITS ME FOR THE TRUE AND GOOD.	256	IN HYDROTHERAPY	6
ALL TRUE BONES SING ALONE.	263	FOLLIES OF ADAM	28
TRULY			
THE TRULY BEAUTIFUL,	121	ALL EARTH, AIR	16
TRUNKS			
OR THEY FLING THEMSELVES AGAINST TREE TRUNKS,	152	THE SISKINS	16
TRUST			
YOUR DONKEY IS BETTER BEHAVED, I TRUST.	178	THE DONKEY	4
TRUSTING			
SO FOOLISH AND TRUSTING, LIKE A SICK POODLE,	228	THE GERANIUM	3
TRUTH			
THE DEED WILL SPEAK THE TRUTH	3	OPEN HOUSE	14
IN TRUTH, THE EYE'S THE ABETTOR OF	8	PRAYER	15
TRUTH NEVER IS UNDONE;	9	THE ADAMANT	3
YOU ARE, IN TRUTH, ONE IN A MILLION,	23	AMOROUS LADY	13
WHOM DO WE LOVE? I THOUGHT I KNEW THE TRUTH;	241	THE SEQUEL	7
THE MIRROR TELLS SOME TRUTH, BUT NOT	257	SANITARIUM	7
TRUTHS			
MY TRUTHS ARE ALL FOREKNOWN,	3	OPEN HOUSE	7
TRY			
TO TRY TO BECOME LIKE GOD	172	WHAT TELL BONES	59
TRYING			
LOOK AT HIM PUFF. HE'S TRYING TO TALK.	73	WHERE KNOCK IS	60
TUB			
THE PARALYTIC STUNNED IN THE TUB, AND THE WATER RISING,--	227	MEADOW MOUSE	28
WITHIN THIS TUB BUT CANNOT DROWN.	256	IN HYDROTHERAPY	2
TUBA			
AND GOT A MOST COMMODIOUS TUBA;	115	THE SERPENT	16
TUCKED			
THE HANDKERCHIEF TUCKED IN THE LEFT-HAND POCKET	29	THE REMINDER	5
THEY TIED AND TUCKED,--	44	FRAU BAUMAN	11
TUFTY			
TUFTY, THE WATER'S LOOSE.	79	GIVE WAY, GATES	6
TUGGED			
TOPPED BY CROSS-WINDS, TUGGED AT BY SINUOUS UNDERCURRENTS	191	AT OYSTER RIVER	33
TUGGING			
TUGGING ALL DAY AT PERVERSE LIFE:	39	WEED PULLER	9
TULIP			
BUT ONE TULIP ON TOP,	43	FLOWER DUMP	11
(DRIED-OUT, SHE CREAKED LIKE A TULIP.)	228	THE GERANIUM	14
TUMBLING			
THE SONGS TUMBLING OVER AND UNDER THE GLASS,	158	FIRST MEDITATN	44
AND THAT WRIST-THICK CASCADE TUMBLING FROM A CLEFT ROCK,	191	AT OYSTER RIVER	44

	PAGE	TITLE	LINE
TUMULTUOUS			
A RAW TUMULTUOUS GIRL	166	HER BECOMING	47
TUNE			
I'M A TUNE DYING	99	O, THOU OPENING	77
I WOOED WITH A LOW TUNE;	146	THE SONG	20
THE EARTH ITSELF A TUNE.	165	HER BECOMING	15
BEFORE THAT SIMPLE TUNE	271	THE REPLY	6
A TUNE SO BOLD AND BARE,	271	THE REPLY	11
TUNES			
FOR OTHER TUNES AND OTHER WANTON BEATS	105	SIR JOHN DAVIES	21
YOU'VE TOO MANY TUNES, AND NONE OF THEM GOOD:	177	KITTY-CAT BIRD	5
TUNNEL			
OF FLYING LIKE A BAT DEEP INTO A NARROWING TUNNEL,	199	THE FAR FIELD	2
TUNNELED			
TUNNELED WITH LAPSING SOUND	50	THE CYCLE	15
TURF			
WHERE THE TURF DROPS OFF INTO A GRASS-HIDDEN CULVERT,	199	THE FAR FIELD	14
TURN			
BREATH, TURN THE OLD BLOOD OVER.	7	ORDERS FOR DAY	21
TURN SLOWLY THROUGH THE NIGHT,	9	THE ADAMANT	6
WILL TURN ITS PRIVATE SUBSTANCE INTO GREEN,	11	LIGHT BRIGHTER	19
ALL DISTANT SHAPES TURN BRIGHTER TO THE GAZE.	17	UNEXTINGUISHED	4
THE MIND IS QUICK TO TURN	31	LULL	15
SHE TAUGHT ME TURN, AND COUNTER-TURN, AND STAND;	127	I KNEW A WOMAN	9
LET SEED BE GRASS, AND GRASS TURN INTO HAY:	127	I KNEW A WOMAN	22
"THERE IS NO PLACE TO TURN," SHE SAID,	136	THE SENSUALISTS	1
MY HANDS TURN INTO HOOVES.	154	THE DYING MAN	18
I TURN MY LOOK UPON	154	THE DYING MAN	28
WEEDS TURN TOWARD THE WIND WEED-SKELETONS.	173	WHAT TELL BONES	65
ALWAYS A SHARP TURN TO THE LEFT PAST A BARN CLOSE TO THE ROADSIDE,	193	JOURNY INTERIOR	25
I TWIST, AND I TURN,	208	THE APPARITION	9
AND WE TURN BACK TO THE HEAT OF AUGUST,	220	THE ABYSS	48
WHICH IS THE WAY? I ASK, AND TURN TO GO,	245	THE DECISION	11
TURNED			
AS I TURNED FOR A BACKWARD LOOK,	47	THE RETURN	5
TURNED BY REVOLVING AIR	50	THE CYCLE	8
THE ROSE, THE CHRYSANTHEMUM TURNED TOWARD THE LIGHT.	57	THE LOST SON	146
A LOG TURNED AT THE TOUCH OF A FOOT;	62	FIELD OF LIGHT	4
THE LAKE TURNED GREEN;	87	PRAISE TO END!	56
THE LEAVES, THEIR WHISPERS TURNED TO KISSING;	102	ELEGY FOR JANE	8
(IT TURNED OUT SHE HADN'T A FATHER AT ALL)	111	SQUEEZE-BOX	15
AND EVEN THE BOYS TURNED OUT TO BE MEN	112	SQUEEZE-BOX	23
THE SHEETS AND BLANKETS TURNED TO SNOW.	114	DINKY	15
I TURNED MY FACE AWAY, AND YET SHE STAYED.	119	THE DREAM	14
SHE TURNED THE FIELD INTO A GLITTERING SEA;	120	THE DREAM	27
I TURNED UPON MY SPINE,	147	THE EXORCISM	19
I TURNED AND TURNED AGAIN,	147	THE EXORCISM	20
I TURNED AND TURNED AGAIN,	147	THE EXORCISM	20
IT TURNED; IT DREW AWAY;	150	SNAKE	6
HE TURNED HIS FACE: THERE WAS ANOTHER MAN,	155	THE DYING MAN	62
WHO TURNED A CORNER IN TIME, WHEN AT LAST HE GREW A THUMB;	170	FOURTH MEDITATN	69
HIS HEAD, STIFF AS A SCARAB, TURNED TO ONE SIDE,	226	THE LIZARD	5
AND WE TURNED TO OUR PICNIC	232	THE THING	18
GOING, WE STAYED; AND NIGHT TURNED INTO DAY;	237	THE TRANCED	12
THE LEAVES, THE TREES TURNED OUR TWO SHAPES AROUND.	237	THE TRANCED	15
TURNED-OVER			
TURNED-OVER ROOTS	43	FLOWER DUMP	6
TURNING			
TURNING AND TAMPING,	42	TRANSPLANTING	2
A SINGLE TWIST OF THE THUMBS, A TAMPING AND TURNING,	42	TRANSPLANTING	7
SLOWLY TURNING,	59	THE LONG ALLEY	4
THE TENDRILS TURNING SLOWLY,	67	SHAPE OF FIRE	81
TURNING IN THE LIGHT WITH ITS TENDRILS;	101	LIGHT BREATHER	6
TURNING NOT A LEAF, NOT A RIPPLE.	190	AT OYSTER RIVER	19
AT THE SUDDEN VEERING, THE MOMENT OF TURNING.	193	JOURNY INTERIOR	5
TURNING TOWARD THE OTHER SIDE OF LIGHT,	195	JOURNY INTERIOR	69
THE WHEEL TURNING AWAY FROM ITSELF,	200	THE FAR FIELD	53
TURNING TOWARD THE SEA,	201	THE FAR FIELD	83
A SEA-SHAPE TURNING AROUND,--	201	THE FAR FIELD	84
THE CLIMBING, THE ENDLESS TURNING,	221	THE ABYSS	53
LOOKING AT YOU WITHOUT TURNING HIS SMALL HEAD,	234	ALL MORNING	12

	PAGE	TITLE	LINE
TURNS			
THE SKY TURNS DARK, THE YEAR GROWS OLD,	15	COMING OF COLD	36
THE LIGHT TURNS.	82	SENSIBILITY! LA	42
FOR THE ATTACKS OF FALSE HUMILITY TAKE SUDDEN TURNS FOR THE WORSE.	86	PRAISE TO END!	25
THE GREAT WHEEL TURNS ITS AXLE WHEN IT CAN;	105	SIR JOHN DAVIES	3
I LOOK ON WHITE, AND IT TURNS INTO GRAY--	134	THE PURE FURY	24
SHE TURNS, AS IF TO GO,	141	MEMORY	5
THE HAND UPON MY SHOULDER TURNS TO HORN.	154	THE DYING MAN	39
A FISH RAVEN TURNS ON ITS PERCH (A DEAD TREE IN THE RIVERMOUTH),	190	AT OYSTER RIVER	22
THE RIVER TURNS ON ITSELF,	200	THE FAR FIELD	56
THE BURNING LAKE TURNS INTO A FOREST POOL,	221	THE ABYSS	58
AND YET MY THOUGHT TURNS BACK TO THEM,	225	THE CHUMS	3
HE TURNS HIS HEAD SLIGHTLY,	226	THE LIZARD	15
THE RIVER TURNS,	233	THE PIKE	1
THIS SINGLE TREE TURNS INTO PUREST FLAME.	242	THE SEQUEL	28
AS A MAN TURNS TO FACE ON-COMING SNOW.	245	THE DECISION	12
TURNS, MOUSE-WARY,--	260	THE CHANGELING	2
TURTLE			
WHO, STRANGELY ENOUGH, WAS A TURTLE:	179	MYRTLE	2
THE TURTLE GASPING IN THE DUSTY RUBBLE OF THE HIGHWAY,	227	MEADOW MOUSE	27
TURTLES			
THE DEAD SNAKES AND MUSKRATS, THE TURTLES GASPING IN THE RUBBLE,	194	JOURNY INTERIOR	36
AND THE CYCLAMEN LEAVES GLISTEN LIKE THE BACKS OF BABY TURTLES.	260	THE CHANGELING	15
THE TURTLES HAVE BLOODSUCKER SORES,	267	SAGINAW SONG	9
TWENTY			
I SEE A BANKER'S MANSION WITH TWENTY WOOD-GRATE FIRES,	27	CLAIRVOY WIDOW	13
TWICE			
ONCE, TWICE, AND A FAINT THIRD THUMP,--	42	TRANSPLANTING	11
EVERYTHING HAS BEEN TWICE.	72	WHERE KNOCK IS	20
SO TOUCH MY TOES TWICE.	75	I NEED, I NEED	30
A CAGED BEAR RARELY DOES THE SAME THING TWICE	105	SIR JOHN DAVIES	10
YOU MUSTN'T PULL IT MORE THAN TWICE,	181	MONOTONY SONG	2
DON'T POKE MORE THAN TWICE	183	THE LIZARD	6
SHE KISSED ME MORE THAN TWICE	212	LIGHT LISTENED	3
SHIVER, AND MORE THAN TWICE,	216	HER WRATH	4
THEIR SISTERS GAVE ME, ONCE OR TWICE;	225	THE CHUMS	5
THEY SAW THAT I FELL MORE THAN TWICE.	225	THE CHUMS	10
TWICED			
TWICED ME NICELY,--	79	GIVE WAY, GATES	11
TWIG			
I'M A TWIG TO TOUCH,	81	SENSIBILITY! LA	24
I'M TWINKLING LIKE A TWIG!	99	O, THOU OPENING	63
TWIGGY			
STRICT AS A SEED, NIPPY AND TWIGGY.	86	PRAISE TO END!	22
TWIGS			
LIFTING A FEW TWIGS AND FLOATING LEAVES,	93	I CRY, LOVE!	48
HER SONG TREMBLING THE TWIGS AND SMALL BRANCHES.	102	ELEGY FOR JANE	6
TWILIGHT			
A TWILIGHT WIND, LIGHT AS A CHILD'S BREATH	190	AT OYSTER RIVER	18
BRINGING ME HOME FROM THE TWILIGHT FISHING.	221	THE ABYSS	67
TWINE			
OR AN OLD PIECE OF TWINE,	117	LADY AND BEAR	16
TWINED			
TWINED LIKE FINE HAIR,	43	FLOWER DUMP	8
TWINKLED			
COLD EVIL TWINKLED TIGHTER THAN A STRING; A FIRE	143	SHIMMER OF EVIL	8
TWINKLING			
THEIR HANDS TWINKLING WITH WET;	44	FRAU BAUMAN	18
I'M TWINKLING LIKE A TWIG!	99	O, THOU OPENING	63
TWINY			
THE TWINY WINDERS WIND;	121	ALL EARTH, AIR	3
TWIRL			
NOW AS FROM MAPLE TO ELM THE FLITTERMICE SKITTER AND TWIRL,	33	IDYLL	1
TWIST			
A SINGLE TWIST OF THE THUMBS, A TAMPING AND TURNING,	42	TRANSPLANTING	7
CHANGING WITH EVERY TWIST OF WIND,	196	THE LONG WATERS	10
I TWIST, AND I TURN,	208	THE APPARITION	9
TWITCH			
AND YOU SHOULD SEE HER NOSES TWITCH,--	181	MONOTONY SONG	18

	PAGE	TITLE	LINE
TWITCHING			
TWITCHING, TILTING TOWARD THE LEAST SOUND.	227	MEADOW MOUSE	16
TWITTERED			
THE BATS TWITTERED AT NOON.	162	I'M HERE	40
TWITTERING			
AND THE FINCHES PITCH THROUGH THE AIR, TWITTERING;	152	THE SISKINS	7
HOW THEY FILLED THE ORIOLE'S ELM, A TWITTERING RESTLESS CLOUD, ALL ONE MORNING,	199	THE FAR FIELD	28
THE MORNING BIRDS GONE, THE TWITTERING FINCHES,	202	THE ROSE	14
I RETURN TO THE TWITTERING OF SWALLOWS ABOVE WATER,	204	THE ROSE	73
'TWIXT			
'TWIXT ANIMAL AND MAN DIVIDED,	264	THREE EPIGRAMS	13
TWO			
TWO YELLOW AND BLACK, AND ONE THAT LOOKS IN BETWEEN,--	24	VERNAL SENTIMNT	6
THE PAVEMENT SMOKES WHEN TWO CARS MEET	33	HIGHWAY: MICH	16
LIFTING THE YOUNG PLANTS WITH TWO FINGERS,	42	TRANSPLANTING	3
A ONE IS A TWO IS	75	I NEED, I NEED	27
WE TWO, TOGETHER, ON A DARKENING DAY	106	SIR JOHN DAVIES	53
AND AFTER EXCHANGING A PUNCH OR TWO,	111	SQUEEZE-BOX	5
BEYOND THE RIDGE TWO WOOD THRUSH SING AS ONE.	150	IN LATE SUMMER	30
TWO SONG SPARROWS, ONE WITHIN A GREENHOUSE,	158	FIRST MEDITATN	39
OR TWO HORSES PLUNGING IN SNOW, THEIR LINES TANGLED,	158	FIRST MEDITATN	53
SAID, "I KNOW MY LEGS ADD UP TO TWO!	182	PHILANDER	2
AS THOSE TWO QUIETLY TALKED,	182	BOY AND BUSH	7
SMALL ENOUGH TO BE TAKEN IN, EMBRACED, BY TWO ARMS,--	191	AT OYSTER RIVER	46
THE CEMETERY WITH TWO SCRUBBY TREES IN THE MIDDLE OF THE PRAIRIE,	194	JOURNY INTERIOR	35
OR WHEN TWO RIVERS COMBINE, THE BLUE GLACIAL TORRENT	200	THE FAR FIELD	61
AT TIMES CONTENT TO BE TWO.	207	THE YOUNG GIRL	7
AND TWO SCOTERS FLY LOW,	210	HER TIME	12
BEARING DOWN, WITH TWO STEADY EYES,	223	ELEGY (2)	22
ONCE WHEN HE SAW TWO POACHERS ON HIS LAND,	224	OTTO	14
IT WAS NO RANDOM ACT, FOR THOSE TWO MEN	224	OTTO	20
OR THE TWO OF US, ALONE, BOTH SEEDY,	228	THE GERANIUM	17
THERE'S TWO MORE TO DROWN	229	ON THE QUAY	5
THE LEAVES, THE TREES TURNED OUR TWO SHAPES AROUND.	237	THE TRANCED	15
LINDSAY'S I MEAN: TWO MOONS, OR EVEN THREE,	273	SUPPR W LINDSAY	7
TWO-BY-TWO'S			
WHAT'S A THICK? TWO-BY-TWO'S A SHAPE.	92	I CRY, LOVE!	10
TWO-LEGGED			
A TWO-LEGGED DOG HUNTING A NEW HORIZON OF HOWLS.	65	SHAPE OF FIRE	38
YOU'RE BECOMING THAT HORROR, A TWO-LEGGED PIG	272	DUET	3
UDDER			
THERE ONCE WAS A COW WITH A DOUBLE UDDER.	114	THE COW	1
UGLY			
THE UGLY OF THE UNIVERSE.	18	LONG LIVE WEEDS	6
THE CORE AND PITH OF THAT UGLY STORM,	41	BIG WIND	24
SO I'VE GOT TO GET ME A RICH UGLY OLD MAID	112	SQUEEZE-BOX	43
ON LOVE'S WORST UGLY DAY,	157	FIRST MEDITATN	1
MY SWEETHEART IS A UGLY WITCH,	181	MONOTONY SONG	17
THE RAVINES UGLY.	193	JOURNY INTERIOR	17
ULTIMATE			
AND THE PRECISION THAT FOR YOU WAS ULTIMATE LAW:	29	THE REMINDER	4
LAVE ME, ULTIMATE WATERS.	88	PRAISE TO END!	98
UMBRELLA			
BRING ME MY HAT, MY UMBRELLA AND RUBBERS,	48	LAST WORDS	9
WITH A BROKEN UMBRELLA,	171	WHAT TELL BONES	32
UNAFRAID			
UNAFRAID OF WHAT IT IS,	101	LIGHT BREATHER	15
WALKING THE EDGE, LOQUACIOUS, UNAFRAID.	155	THE DYING MAN	63
YET IF WE WAIT, UNAFRAID, BEYOND THE FEARFUL INSTANT,	221	THE ABYSS	57
UNALTERABLE			
THE UNALTERABLE PATHOS OF BASIN AND PITCHER,	46	DOLOR	6
UNALTERED			
A LEAF UNALTERED BY THE MIDNIGHT SCENE,	248	THE TREE, BIRD	8
UNBLOOD			
LOVE ALTERS ALL. UNBLOOD MY INSTINCT, LOVE.	135	THE RENEWAL	10
UNBLOODY			
DISEMBODIED, UNBLOODY,	209	HER RETICENCE	3
UNBORN			
I IMAGINED THE UNBORN, STARVING IN WOMBS, CURLING;	48	JUDGE NOT	5
THE DEAD LOVE THE UNBORN.	172	WHAT TELL BONES	64

	PAGE	TITLE	LINE
UNBOUND			
THE OAK LEAVES STRAIN TO BE UNBOUND,	15	COMING OF COLD	35
UNBROKEN			
THE FIELDS STRETCH OUT IN LONG, UNBROKEN ROWS.	13	PRAISE PRAIRIE	9
UNCERTAIN			
AN UNCERTAIN GLORY,	265	HARSH COUNTRY	2
UNCLE			
BUT FOR AN UNCLE YOU WERE THOUGHT TO FAVOR,	25	DIM-WIT COUSIN	3
UNCLES			
I HAVE BEEN SOMEWHERE ELSE; I REMEMBER THE SEA-FACED UNCLES.	88	PRAISE TO END!	93
UNCLE'S			
MY UNCLE'S AWAY,	72	WHERE KNOCK IS	24
UNCONSCIOUS			
A GHOST COMES OUT OF THE UNCONSCIOUS MIND	154	THE DYING MAN	36
UNDECEIVED			
WHEN I LOOKED AT THE ALTERED SCENE, MY EYE WAS UNDECEIVED,	12	MID-CNTRY BLOW	7
UNDEFILED			
THAT KEEP THE SPIRIT UNDEFILED.	18	LONG LIVE WEEDS	8
THE BRAVE KEEP UNDEFILED	20	REPL TO CENSURE	11
UNDER			
WATER RAN OVER AND UNDER	6	THE PREMONITION	8
WHEN FROM UNDER THE BARN THE CAT BRINGS A SIMILAR LITTER,--	24	VERNAL SENTIMNT	5
UNDER THE CONCRETE BENCHES,	39	WEED PULLER	1
WHISTLING THINLY UNDER THE WIND-VENTS;	41	BIG WIND	31
READY FOR THE LONG DAYS UNDER THE SLOPED GLASS:	42	TRANSPLANTING	13
A SHELL ARCHED UNDER MY TOES,	49	RIVER INCIDENT	1
UNDER EVEN THE ROCK-SHUT GROUND,	50	THE CYCLE	16
UNDER A RIVER'S SOURCE,	50	THE CYCLE	17
UNDER PRIMEVAL STONE.	50	THE CYCLE	18
JUST UNDER THE WATER	54	THE LOST SON	48
JUST UNDER THE WATER	55	THE LOST SON	60
LOOK DOWN UNDER THE LEAVES.	55	THE LOST SON	63
THE DARK FLOWS ON ITSELF. A DEAD MOUTH SINGS UNDER AN OLD TREE.	59	THE LONG ALLEY	6
UNDER, UNDER THE SHEAVES,	62	FIELD OF LIGHT	22
UNDER, UNDER THE SHEAVES,	62	FIELD OF LIGHT	22
UNDER THE BLACKENED LEAVES,	62	FIELD OF LIGHT	23
THE SHE-BEAR MOPES UNDER THE HILL.	64	SHAPE OF FIRE	15
UNDER THE ROCKER	71	WHERE KNOCK IS	6
THE AIR'S QUIET UNDER THE SMALL LEAVES.	78	BRING THE DAY!	41
IS THE SUN UNDER MY ARM?	82	SENSIBILITY! LA	45
AND THE MOLD SANG IN THE BLEACHED VALLEYS UNDER THE ROSE.	102	ELEGY FOR JANE	9
BUT MANY A MAN ROLLED UNDER THE TABLE	112	SQUEEZE-BOX	36
UNDER THE RISING MOON;	124	WORDS FOR WIND	57
UNDER A SOUTHERN WIND,	125	WORDS FOR WIND	61
THAT SCUTTLED UNDER STONES,	147	THE EXORCISM	17
THE SMALL DEAD PIECES STICKING UNDER AN INSTEP;	151	SLUG	20
THE SONGS TUMBLING OVER AND UNDER THE GLASS,	158	FIRST MEDITATN	44
FROM UNDER THE DRY LEAVES,	162	I'M HERE	56
CLEAR UNDER THE CHAIR;	180	GOO-GIRL	12
IS JUST UNDER HIS CHIN,--	183	THE LIZARD	4
DYING BRIGHTLY UNDER THE STREET LIGHTS SUNK IN COARSE CONCRETE,	193	JOURNY INTERIOR	29
BY SMALL STREAMS RUNNING DOWN UNDER FALLEN FIR TREES.	197	THE LONG WATERS	48
SUCH QUIET UNDER THE SMALL LEAVES!--	221	THE ABYSS	82
RETIRING TO NUDGE HIS NECK HALF-WAY UNDER	226	THE LIZARD	16
HIS TAIL CURLED UNDER HIM, HIS BELLY BIG	227	MEADOW MOUSE	14
TO RUN FROM THE HAWK'S WING,	227	MEADOW MOUSE	23
UNDER THE EYE OF THE GREAT OWL WATCHING FROM THE ELM-TREE,	227	MEADOW MOUSE	24
RUNNING OVER THE COVERLET, DOWN UNDER THE IRON BEDSTEAD.	231	THE STORM	35
WE DANCED, WE DANCED, UNDER A DANCING MOON;	241	THE SEQUEL	14
AND IT STEPPED IN THE ROOM, UNDER HIS ARM,--	273	SUPPR W LINDSAY	6
US, UNDER THE CHAIR-RUNGS, TOWARD THE CELLAR DOOR.	273	SUPPR W LINDSAY	14
UNDERBELLY			
WAS THE UNDERBELLY OF CICERO;	111	SQUEEZE-BOX	18
UNDERBRUSH			
OUT OF THE BRIARY HEDGE, THE TANGLE OF MATTED UNDERBRUSH,	203	THE ROSE	45
UNDERCLOTHES			
IN WITH YOUR UNDERCLOTHES?	213	THE HAPPY THREE	11
UNDERCURRENTS			
TOPPED BY CROSS-WINDS, TUGGED AT BY SINUOUS UNDERCURRENTS	191	AT OYSTER RIVER	33
UNDERGROUND			
I CAN HEAR, UNDERGROUND, THAT SUCKING AND SOBBING,	37	CUTTINGS (LATE)	5

	PAGE	TITLE	LINE
UNDERGROUND (CONTINUED)			
DARK WATER, UNDERGROUND,	50	THE CYCLE	1
UNDERLEAVES			
THE UNDERLEAVES, THE SMALLEST BUDS	42	TRANSPLANTING	17
UNDERNEATH			
DIGGING INTO THE SOFT RUBBLE UNDERNEATH,	39	WEED PULLER	4
MY KNEES MADE LITTLE WINDS UNDERNEATH	57	THE LOST SON	128
SOOTHE ME, GREAT GROANS OF UNDERNEATH,	84	O LULL ME, LULL	29
UNDERNEATH, THE SLUGGISH WATER RUNNING BETWEEN WEEDS, BROKEN WHEELS, TIRES, STONES.	194	JOURNY INTERIOR	33
UNDERSIDE			
THE CRUMBLING SMALL HOLLOW STICKS ON THE UNDERSIDE MIXED WITH ROOTS,	40	MOSS-GATHERING	4
UNDERSONG			
BY THE SALT WAVES I HEAR A RIVER'S UNDERSONG,	221	THE ABYSS	76
UNDERSTAND			
WHAT IS THERE FOR THE SOUL TO UNDERSTAND?	149	IN LATE SUMMER	9
A THING ALL EARTHLY LOVERS UNDERSTAND.	149	IN LATE SUMMER	22
UNDERSTANDABLE			
A LIVELY UNDERSTANDABLE SPIRIT	58	THE LOST SON	169
UNDERSTOOD			
O NOBODY UNDERSTOOD MYRTLE!	179	MYRTLE	5
UNDERTAKER'S			
THE UNDERTAKER'S OBSEQUIOUS GRIMACES,	22	ROAD TO WDLAWN	6
UNDERWEAR			
CARES ABOUT THE DANCE OF DEAD UNDERWEAR, OR THE SAD WALTZ OF PAPER	98	O, THOU OPENING	26
UNDID			
WE UNDID CHAOS TO A CURIOUS SOUND:	107	SIR JOHN DAVIES	82
UNDIMINISHED			
THAT PULSES UNDIMINISHED NOW	22	SILENCE	2
UNDIVIDED			
DECREASED BENEATH AN UNDIVIDED SKY.	6	INTERLUDE	6
UNDO			
THESE SWEEPS OF LIGHT UNDO ME.	57	THE LOST SON	118
IT LIES UPON US TO UNDO THE LIE	149	IN LATE SUMMER	19
I SHALL UNDO ALL DYING BY MY DEATH.	155	THE DYING MAN	77
UNDONE			
YOUR HOPES ARE MURDERED AND UNDONE.	4	FEUD	12
TRUTH NEVER IS UNDONE;	9	THE ADAMANT	3
ALL SUMMER GREEN IS NOW UNDONE:	15	COMING OF COLD	42
UNTIL HE CRIED AT ENEMIES UNDONE	28	THE FAVORITE	13
I'M UNDONE BY THE FLIP-FLAP OF ODIOUS PILLOWS.	86	PRAISE TO END!	45
WHEN I AM UNDONE,	217	WISH YOUNG WIFE	10
AND KNOWING THIS, I AM NOT YET UNDONE.	244	INFIRMITY	30
I AM UNDONE BY THE GURGLE OF BABIES AND PITCHERS,	255	LIGHT POEM	7
UNDULANT			
SHE TAUGHT ME TOUCH, THAT UNDULANT WHITE SKIN;	127	I KNEW A WOMAN	10
AT LAST ONE LONG UNDULANT RIPPLE,	190	AT OYSTER RIVER	11
UNDULATING			
MOVING WITH THE WAVES, THE UNDULATING DRIFTWOOD,	203	THE ROSE	48
UNEASY			
THE UNEASY MAN.	65	SHAPE OF FIRE	44
UNEMPLOYED			
THE UNEMPLOYED AND TELLING STALE UNEMPLOYMENT JOKES.	28	CLAIRVOY WIDOW	22
UNEMPLOYMENT			
THE UNEMPLOYED AND TELLING STALE UNEMPLOYMENT JOKES.	28	CLAIRVOY WIDOW	22
UNENCUMBERED			
I LEFT MY HOME WITH UNENCUMBERED WILL	21	THE AUCTION	15
UNEQUAL			
THE SEA'S UNEQUAL LENGTHS ANNOUNCED THY BIRTH	81	SENSIBILITY! LA	8
UNESSENTIAL			
A COAT OF UNESSENTIAL SKIN,	24	BEFORE STUDY	4
UNEXTINGUISHED			
THE UNEXTINGUISHED	17	UNEXTINGUISHED	T
UNFOLD			
UNFOLD! UNFOLD!	89	UNFOLD! UNFOLD!	T
UNFOLD! UNFOLD!	89	UNFOLD! UNFOLD!	T
UNFOLDING			
SLOWLY UNFOLDING,	101	LIGHT BREATHER	5
OF THE UNFOLDING ROSE,	125	WORDS FOR WIND	84
UNFROWN			
COULD NOT UNFROWN ITSELF.	45	MY PAPA'S WALTZ	8

	PAGE	TITLE	LINE
UNFURL			
THE LIGHTS IN THE KITCHENS GO OUT; MOTH WINGS UNFURL;	33	IDYLL	3
UNGUARDED			
BY MY UNGUARDED MOUTH.	220	THE ABYSS	20
UNHINGE			
HAVE YOU COME TO UNHINGE MY SHADOW?	65	SHAPE OF FIRE	33
UNHOLY			
ALL THINGS UNHOLY, MARRED BY CURSE,	18	LONG LIVE WEEDS	5
UNIMPORTANT			
THERE ARE THOSE TO WHOM PLACE IS UNIMPORTANT,	202	THE ROSE	1
UNISON			
WE BREATHE IN UNISON.	141	MEMORY	2
UNIVERSE			
THE UGLY OF THE UNIVERSE.	18	LONG LIVE WEEDS	6
THAT MADE HIM THINK THE UNIVERSE COULD HUM?	105	SIR JOHN DAVIES	2
UNKNOWN			
WHAT CAN BE KNOWN? THE UNKNOWN.	251	ONCE MORE, RND	2
UNLEARN			
I WOULD UNLEARN THE LINGO OF EXASPERATION, ALL THE DISTORTIONS OF MALICE AND HATRED;	188	THE LONGING	42
UNLEAVE			
LIGHTLY: SO BUDS UNLEAVE;	130	THE OTHER	4
UNLESS			
--UNLESS YOU'RE HUGH OR HARRY!	181	MONOTONY SONG	28
UNLIKE			
THERE, UPSIDE DOWN (UNLIKE A BIRD),	116	THE SLOTH	5
UNLOCKS			
WHERE THE HEAVY DOOR UNLOCKS,	230	THE STORM	21
UNMEASURED			
RECALL THE GRADUAL DARK THE SNOW'S UNMEASURED FALL	5	TO MY SISTER	3
UNMELODIC			
IT IS THE UNMELODIC RING	22	SILENCE	7
UNMINDFUL			
UNMINDFUL OF TERROR AND HEADLINES, OF SPEECHES AND GUNS.	33	IDYLL	12
UNMOVING			
MOVING, UNMOVING IN A PARCHED LAND, WHITE IN THE MOONLIGHT:	194	JOURNY INTERIOR	53
UNNATURAL			
OUR PUPILS WIDENED WITH UNNATURAL NIGHT,	6	INTERLUDE	7
ALL NATURAL SHAPES BLAZING UNNATURAL LIGHT.	239	IN A DARK TIME	18
UNNECESSARY			
YOU FAT UNNECESSARY HAGS,	99	O, THOU OPENING	60
UNPERPLEXED			
UNPERPLEXED, IN A PLACE LEADING NOWHERE.	195	JOURNY INTERIOR	73
UNPRAYED-FOR			
UNPRAYED-FOR,	173	WHAT TELL BONES	100
UNPROTECTED			
FLESH BEHIND STEEL AND GLASS IS UNPROTECTED	5	PROGNOSIS	5
UNRAVELS			
THE BULB UNRAVELS. WHO'S FLOATING? NOT ME.	90	UNFOLD! UNFOLD!	41
UNREFINED			
RECUMBENCY IS UNREFINED	257	SANITARIUM	3
UNSEALED			
BUDS, LONG UNSEALED, OBSCURE THE NARROW LANE.	12	SLOW SEASON	14
UNSEEMLINESS			
YET SUCH IS MY UNSEEMLINESS:	19	EPIDERM MACABRE	9
UNSEEN			
THE FIRE OF HEAVEN DIES; A FIRE UNSEEN	17	UNEXTINGUISHED	5
THE UNSEEN AND THE SEEN,	237	THE TRANCED	19
UNSINGING			
THE UNSINGING FIELDS WHERE NO LUNGS BREATHE,	196	THE LONG WATERS	11
UNSTILLING			
IS THIS THE STORM'S HEART? THE GROUND IS UNSTILLING ITSELF.	56	THE LOST SON	100
UNTANGLE			
WHEN I BENT TO UNTANGLE MYSELF,	162	I'M HERE	48
UNTIED			
WHO UNTIED THE TREE? I REMEMBER NOW.	93	I CRY, LOVE!	54
UNTIL			
UNTIL THE DEAD HAVE BEEN SUBDUED.	4	FEUD	20
UNTIL WE CAME TO A RIVER.	6	THE PREMONITION	6
UNTIL I COULD THINK THERE WERE WAVES ROLLING HIGH AS MY BEDROOM FLOOR;	12	MID-CNTRY BLOW	2
UNTIL CLEAR EYES PUT ON THE LOOK OF SLEEP.	12	SLOW SEASON	4
UNTIL THOUGHT CRACKLES WHITE ACROSS THE BRAIN.	17	UNEXTINGUISHED	12

	PAGE	TITLE	LINE
UNTIL (CONTINUED)			
UNTIL HE CRIED AT ENEMIES UNDONE	28	THE FAVORITE	13
UNTIL THE TOUGHEST NERVES ARE FRAYED.	33	HIGHWAY: MICH	13
SHE SAILED UNTIL THE CALM MORNING,	41	BIG WIND	32
WE ROMPED UNTIL THE PANS	45	MY PAPA'S WALTZ	5
UNTIL THEY CREAK THEIR KNEES:	60	THE LONG ALLEY	36
UNTIL THE COWS	71	WHERE KNOCK IS	7
BUT THE BEAR JUST SAT THERE UNTIL SHE SANK;	117	LADY AND BEAR	28
LOVE IS NOT LOVE UNTIL LOVE'S VULNERABLE.	120	THE DREAM	17
FOR WATER MOVES UNTIL IT'S PURIFIED,	132	SENTENTIOUS MAN	41
UNTIL HE FINDS THE THING HE ALMOST WAS	133	THE PURE FURY	19
UNTIL MY EYES LOOK AT A BRIGHTER SUN	134	THE PURE FURY	27
UNTIL IT BROODS IN HER EYES.	137	LOVE'S PROGRESS	12
WRITHING UNTIL THE LAST	147	THE EXORCISM	22
UNTIL I'M SCRAPING AND SCRATCHING AT YOU, ON THE DOORMAT,	151	SLUG	19
I BREATHE ALONE UNTIL MY DARK IS BRIGHT.	155	THE DYING MAN	51
AND THERE I STAYED UNTIL THE DAY BURNED DOWN.	166	HER BECOMING	52
UNTIL YOU HAVE THOUGHT THIS SAD TALE THROUGH:	177	KITTY-CAT BIRD	19
YOURSELF AWAKE UNTIL YOU SLEEP,	181	MONOTONY SONG	26
UNTIL THE HEADLIGHTS DARKEN.	199	THE FAR FIELD	12
UNTIL THERE WAS NOTHING LEFT,	232	THE THING	16
UNTIL, OUT FROM A DARK COVE,	233	THE PIKE	14
UNTIL THEY REACH THIS FINAL CERTITUDE,	243	THE MOTION	16
UNTIL WE ARE PURE SPIRIT AT THE END.	244	INFIRMITY	36
UNTRUE			
I'M UNTRUE TO MY OWN EXCESSES.	86	PRAISE TO END!	27
UNWILLING			
WHO ISN'T UNWILLING, WHO ISN'T AFRAID	112	SQUEEZE-BOX	44
UNWIND			
HOW BODY FROM SPIRIT SLOWLY DOES UNWIND	244	INFIRMITY	35
UNWINDING			
THE YOUNG HORNS WINDING AND UNWINDING,	42	TRANSPLANTING	15
UNWRINKLING			
AMONG THE UNWRINKLING FERNS	80	GIVE WAY, GATES	41
UP			
BUT WHEN HE STOOD UP, THAT FACE	6	THE PREMONITION	12
THE DILL BEARS UP ITS ACRID CROWN;	14	COMING OF COLD	14
THE WIDE WINGS FLAP BUT ONCE TO LIFT HIM UP.	15	THE HERON	11
BUT WHEN HE BRUSHES UP AGAINST A SCREEN,	16	THE BAT	7
BREAKS UP THE CRUST OF CINDERS THAT REMAIN,	17	UNEXTINGUISHED	10
AN AUCTIONEER WAS WHIPPING UP A SALE.	21	THE AUCTION	3
--AND THE EYES, STILL VIVID, LOOKING UP FROM A SUNKEN ROOM.	22	ROAD TO WDLAWN	8
THOUGH THE CROCUSES POKE UP THEIR HEADS IN THE USUAL PLACES,	24	VERNAL SENTIMNT	1
ADDS UP A PAIR OF JIGGLING DOUBLE CHINS.	25	DIM-WIT COUSIN	8
SOME LEARN THE ART OF THIEVING, AND SOME GROW UP TO BEG;	27	CLAIRVOY WIDOW	10
THE GREEN COMES UP FOREVER IN THE FIELDS OF OUR COUNTRY."	28	CLAIRVOY WIDOW	26
RETURN TO LITTER UP OUR HOME.	30	THE RECKONING	4
WHO RAN UP AND DOWN THE BIG CENTER STAIRS	32	SALE	2
AS DARKNESS CREEPS UP ON THE WELL-GROOMED SUBURBAN TOWN,	33	IDYLL	5
I STAY UP HALF THE NIGHT	34	NIGHT JOURNEY	26
BUT STILL THE DELICATE SLIPS KEEP COAXING UP WATER;	37	CUTTINGS	3
SHOOTING UP LIME AND DUNG AND GROUND BONES,--	38	FORCING HOUSE	9
NOTHING WOULD GIVE UP LIFE:	38	ROOT CELLAR	10
AND LIFT UP A PATCH, DARK-GREEN, THE KIND FOR LINING CEMETERY BASKETS,	40	MOSS-GATHERING	2
THE HALF-GROWN CHRYSANTHEMUMS STARING UP LIKE ACCUSERS,	43	CHILD ON GRNHSE	3
UP THROUGH THE STREAKED GLASS, FLASHING WITH SUNLIGHT,	43	CHILD ON GRNHSE	4
AND EVERYONE, EVERYONE POINTING UP AND SHOUTING!	43	CHILD ON GRNHSE	7
REACHING UP WHITE STRINGS	44	FRAU BAUMAN	3
UP AND SIFTED THE DIRT;	44	FRAU BAUMAN	14
THEY SEWED UP THE AIR WITH A STEM;	44	FRAU BAUMAN	22
I REMEMBER HOW THEY PICKED ME UP, A SPINDLY KID,	44	FRAU BAUMAN	26
STIRRED UP A WHIRL OF SILT	49	RIVER INCIDENT	2
A SHAPE IN THE MIND ROSE UP:	49	NIGHT CROW	3
A WAITING GHOST WARMS UP THE DEAD	60	THE LONG ALLEY	35
SO UP AND AWAY AND WHAT DO WE DO	60	THE LONG ALLEY	37
MY HEART LIFTED UP WITH THE GREAT GRASSES;	63	FIELD OF LIGHT	46
UP OVER A VIADUCT I CAME, TO THE SNAKES AND STICKS OF ANOTHER WINTER,	65	SHAPE OF FIRE	37
HELD UP, WHILE THE ROWER BREATHES, AND THE SMALL BOAT DRIFTS QUIETLY SHOREWARD;	67	SHAPE OF FIRE	91
IT'S TIME YOU STOOD UP AND ASKED	89	UNFOLD! UNFOLD!	10
THEN WASHING UP OVER SMALL STONES.	93	I CRY, LOVE!	49

		PAGE	TITLE	LINE

UP (CONTINUED)

	PAGE	TITLE	LINE
OUR OUTER SKIN. WHO'S WHISTLING UP MY SLEEVE?	106	SIR JOHN DAVIES	38
THE LOWLY WORM CLIMBS UP A WINDING STAIR;	108	THE WAKING (2)	11
BUT STEPPED RIGHT UP AND SWUNG AT THE DEVIL;	111	SQUEEZE-BOX	4
--AND BEGAN TO DRINK UP THE MONEY.	111	SQUEEZE-BOX	7
--BUT HOW SHE COULD BURN UP THE MONEY!	111	SQUEEZE-BOX	16
--AND LOOSENED UP WITH OUR MONEY.	112	SQUEEZE-BOX	25
--WHEN HE TRIED TO DRINK UP THE MONEY.	112	SQUEEZE-BOX	37
--TO HELP ME EAT UP HER MONEY.	112	SQUEEZE-BOX	45
HE SIMPLY GAVE UP SERPENTING.	115	THE SERPENT	3
OR ENGLISH POETS WHO GREW UP ON GREEK	127	I KNEW A WOMAN	6
THE DREAM'S AN INSTANT THAT CALLS UP HER FACE.	131	SENTENTIOUS MAN	11
FALTERED; ROSE UP AGAIN;	145	THE BEAST	12
THE LIGHTS TILTING UP, SKYWARD, AS WE COME OVER A LITTLE RISE,	158	FIRST MEDITATN	24
SWERVING UP A STEEP EMBANKMENT.	158	FIRST MEDITATN	55
OR A SALMON, TIRED, MOVING UP A SHALLOW STREAM,	159	FIRST MEDITATN	68
THE SCENT OF THE HALF-OPENED BUDS CAME UP OVER ME.	162	I'M HERE	49
JUMPING UP AND DOWN ON THEIR HIND FEET,	163	I'M HERE	68
DIPPING UP AND DOWN IN THE RIPPLES,	168	FOURTH MEDITATN	10
"AT LAST I'M MYSELF!"--AND HE UP AND DIED	177	KITTY-CAT BIRD	16
AND THEN CAUGHT COLD AND UP AND DIED?	178	THE CEILING	2
YOU DRINK UP IN QUARTS;	180	GOO-GIRL	6
ONE DAY HUGH WALKED UP TO A BEAR	181	MONOTONY SONG	5
THIS HARRY RAN STRAIGHT UP A WALL,	181	MONOTONY SONG	13
SAID, "I KNOW MY LEGS ADD UP TO TWO!	182	PHILANDER	2
BUT I COUNT UP TO ONE,	182	PHILANDER	3
THEN RETIRE TO A ROCK HIGHER UP ON THE CLIFF-SIDE.	190	AT OYSTER RIVER	16
GRINDING UP AND OVER THE NARROW ROAD, SPITTING AND ROARING.	193	JOURNY INTERIOR	22
AS A FIRE, SEEMINGLY LONG DEAD, FLARES UP FROM A DOWNDRAFT OF AIR IN A CHIMNEY,	198	THE LONG WATERS	63
AND THE TIDE RISES UP AGAINST THE GRASS	202	THE ROSE	9
THE PROW PITCHING EASILY UP AND DOWN,	203	THE ROSE	35
AND THE DEEP CHORUS OF HORNS COMING UP FROM THE STREETS IN EARLY MORNING.	204	THE ROSE	72
MY PAPERS UP, BETWEEN	213	THE HAPPY THREE	6
WHO SHOULD COME UP RIGHT THEN,	213	THE HAPPY THREE	17
FACED UP TO THE WORST.	223	ELEGY (2)	11
THEN SUDDENLY FLUNG UP AND OVER,	226	THE LIZARD	10
BUMBLING UP AND AROUND THE BAMBOO WINDBREAK;	226	THE LIZARD	21
TILL I CAUGHT HIM UP BY THE TAIL AND BROUGHT HIM IN,	227	MEADOW MOUSE	4
BETWEEN THE WHITENING TREES, UP SANTA LUCIA,	230	THE STORM	20
THEN THROWING ITSELF UP AND AWAY FROM THE IMPLACABLE SWIFT PURSUERS,	232	THE THING	6
ROSE UP WITHIN THE MIND,	237	THE TRANCED	9
ROSE UP AND FELL LIKE AN ERRATIC WIND.	237	THE TRANCED	10
A SHAPE CALLED UP OUT OF MY NATURAL MIND;	241	THE SEQUEL	10
TO MEET THE WORLD, I RISE UP IN MY MIND;	243	THE MOTION	9
WHAT WE PUT DOWN, MUST WE TAKE UP AGAIN?	243	THE MOTION	11
BY ONE WHO ROSE UP FROM THE DEAD.	264	THREE EPIGRAMS	10
WHAT ELSE HE DOES IS UP TO YOU.	264	THREE EPIGRAMS	16
THE WIND BLOWS UP YOUR FEET,	267	SAGINAW SONG	2
RAISE UP WHEN YOU WOULD PEE.	267	SAGINAW SONG	24
--AND CLOSE UP THAT CHAPTER OF KIERKEGAARD.	272	DUET	8

UPLAND

	PAGE	TITLE	LINE
THE UPLAND OF ALDER AND BIRCHTREES,	193	JOURNY INTERIOR	13
AND THE YELLOWISH-GREEN FROM THE MOUNTAINY UPLAND,--	200	THE FAR FIELD	62

UPON

	PAGE	TITLE	LINE
AND MINUTES BURST UPON A BROW	4	DEATH PIECE	7
YOU MEDITATE UPON THE NERVES.	4	FEUD	17
I CANNOT PUT MY GLANCE UPON THEM TIGHT.	8	THE SIGNALS	8
THE YOUNG FRUIT SWELL UPON THE PEAR-TREE BOUGH.	11	LIGHT BRIGHTER	16
AND YOUNG SHOOTS SPREAD UPON OUR INNER WORLD.	11	LIGHT BRIGHTER	20
A MAN'S HEAD IS AN EMINENCE UPON	13	PRAISE PRAIRIE	3
UPON THE ORCHARD PATH, FOR SKINNED	14	COMING OF COLD	6
THE PLUM DROPS PITCH UPON THE GROUND,	14	COMING OF COLD	9
UPON THE FIELD THE SCENT IS DRY:	14	COMING OF COLD	13
THE MOULD UPON THE BRANCH IS DRY,	15	COMING OF COLD	44
IT BREAKS UPON MY SOLITUDE--	22	SILENCE	4
A KINDLY WIDOW LADY, WHO LIVED UPON A HILL,	27	CLAIRVOY WIDOW	1
UPON WHOM EVERY GIFT AND THRILL WERE SHOWERED,	28	THE FAVORITE	10
ONCE UPON A TREE	71	WHERE KNOCK IS	12
ROMPED UPON THE GOLDY GRASS,	87	PRAISE TO END!	57

		PAGE	TITLE	LINE
UPON (CONTINUED)				
WHEN GLORY FAILED, WE DANCED UPON A PIN.		106	SIR JOHN DAVIES	58
DARK HANGS UPON THE WATERS OF THE SOUL;		135	THE RENEWAL	8
MOUTH UPON MOUTH, WE SANG,		146	THE SONG	28
MY LIPS PRESSED UPON STONE.		146	THE SONG	29
I TURNED UPON MY SPINE,		147	THE EXORCISM	19
WHITE UPON WHITE, SLOW-SETTLING ON A STONE;		149	IN LATE SUMMER	2
IT LIES UPON US TO UNDO THE LIE		149	IN LATE SUMMER	19
I TURN MY LOOK UPON		154	THE DYING MAN	28
THE HAND UPON MY SHOULDER TURNS TO HORN.		154	THE DYING MAN	39
LIGHT AS A PETAL FALLING UPON STONE.		165	HER BECOMING	12
O PRIDE, THOU ART A PLUME UPON WHOSE HEAD?		188	THE LONGING	25
FOR TO COME UPON WARBLERS IN EARLY MAY		199	THE FAR FIELD	26
THE AFTER-LIGHT UPON ICE-BURDENED PINES;		201	THE FAR FIELD	97
AMONG THE HALF-DEAD TREES, I CAME UPON THE TRUE EASE OF MYSELF,		205	THE ROSE	99
THOUGHT UPON THOUGHT CAN BE		215	HIS FOREBODING	6
THE FULL MOON WAS SHINING UPON THE BROAD SEA;		216	THE SHY MAN	1
A HOUSE FOR FLOWERS! HOUSE UPON HOUSE THEY BUILT,		224	OTTO	23
AND WHEN I SLIPPED UPON THE ICE,		225	THE CHUMS	9
I'D STAND UPON MY BED, A SLEEPLESS CHILD		225	OTTO	40
COMING CLOSER AND CLOSER UPON EACH OTHER;		230	THE STORM	12
IT'S LOST UPON THE NIGHT--		240	IN EVEING AIR	17
LIGHT SHIFTS UPON THE WALL.		240	IN EVEING AIR	21
AND PULSED ITS WINGS UPON THE DUSTY GROUND--		243	THE MOTION	3
THE GREAT DAY BALANCES UPON THE LEAVES;		244	INFIRMITY	27
UPON THAT GOD WHO KNOWS WHAT I WOULD KNOW.		246	THE MARROW	24
AND I BECAME ALL THAT I LOOKED UPON.		247	I WAITED	12
LINES UPON LEAVING A SANITARIUM		257	SANITARIUM	T
HE LEFT HIS PANTS UPON A CHAIR:		264	THREE EPIGRAMS	7
A CHILD UPON HER BREAST,		268	SAGINAW SONG	57
AND THEN I BEAT UPON A CAN,		269	GOB MUSIC	3
OR POUND UPON A BRICK;		269	GOB MUSIC	4
UPPER				
TO CONFLAGRATION IN THE UPPER AIR.		17	UNEXTINGUISHED	3
UPROSE				
UPROSE, UPROSE, THE STONY FIELDS UPROSE,		248	THE TREE, BIRD	1
UPROSE, UPROSE, THE STONY FIELDS UPROSE,		248	THE TREE, BIRD	1
UPROSE, UPROSE, THE STONY FIELDS UPROSE,		248	THE TREE, BIRD	1
UPSIDE				
THERE, UPSIDE DOWN (UNLIKE A BIRD),		116	THE SLOTH	5
UP-SPRING				
AND THE UP-SPRING OF THE PLANK WHEN A FOOT LEFT THE RUNWAY.		158	FIRST MEDITATN	47
UP-SWAY				
MOVED IN A SLOW UP-SWAY.		57	THE LOST SON	148
UPWARD				
THE SMALL WATERS SEEPING UPWARD,		37	CUTTINGS (LATE)	7
A FISH FLOATS BELLY UPWARD,		59	THE LONG ALLEY	2
A LONG WEED FLOATED UPWARD;		62	FIELD OF LIGHT	5
DOWNWARD AND UPWARD,		93	I CRY, LOVE!	43
FLYING UPWARD THROUGH THE KNIVES OF MY LAWNMOWER		151	SLUG	16
THEN FLYING ALMOST STRAIGHT UPWARD,		152	THE SISKINS	3
FLYING UPWARD IN LITTLE SKIPS AND ERRATIC LEAPS;		152	THE SISKINS	9
THE SPIRIT MOVES, BUT NOT ALWAYS UPWARD,		157	FIRST MEDITATN	8
A GUST BLOWING THE LEAVES SUDDENLY UPWARD,		171	WHAT TELL BONES	29
WINDING UPWARD TOWARD THE STREAM WITH ITS SHARP STONES,		193	JOURNY INTERIOR	12
WIDENING AT HIGH NOON, FACE UPWARD,		203	THE ROSE	43
FLICKING THE FOAM FROM THE WHITECAPS STRAIGHT UPWARD INTO THE DARKNESS.		230	THE STORM	16
AND A CHILD'S DIRTY SHIFT BILLOWS UPWARD OUT OF AN ALLEY,		230	THE STORM	18
URGE				
THIS URGE, WRESTLE, RESURRECTION OF DRY STICKS,		37	CUTTINGS (LATE)	1
URINALS				
BABBLING IN URINALS.)		147	THE EXORCISM	12
US (25)				
USE				
USE A HOOK OR A LINE,		117	LADY AND BEAR	15
LOVING, I USE THE AIR		123	WORDS FOR WIND	3
I DOUBT I'LL USE IT AGAIN.		153	THE DYING MAN	5
SHELVES HAVE A SPECIAL USE;		213	THE HAPPY THREE	9
USED				
THE LIBRARY USED AS A CARD ROOM INSTEAD		32	SALE	11
MY FATHER NEVER USED A STICK,		268	SAGINAW SONG	50

	PAGE	TITLE	LINE
USUAL			
THOUGH THE CROCUSES POKE UP THEIR HEADS IN THE USUAL PLACES,	24	VERNAL SENTIMNT	1
TODAY I EAT MY USUAL DIET OF SHADOWS.	166	HER BECOMING	31
USUALLY			
IT USUALLY GOES.	54	THE LOST SON	49
IT USUALLY GOES.	55	THE LOST SON	61
USURPS			
THE PENNY THAT USURPS THE POOR.	30	THE RECKONING	12
UTTERED			
THE LUGUBRIOUSLY BEAUTIFUL PLAINT UTTERED AT REGULAR INTERVALS,	234	ALL MORNING	4
UTTERLY			
DOVE UTTERLY,	261	THE CHANGELING	51
VAGUE			
OR SEND OFF A CAR WITH VAGUE LIFTS OF A HAND.	47	DOUBLE FEATURE	8
AT THE STREAM'S EDGE, TRAILING A VAGUE FINGER;	162	I'M HERE	26
BUT A TIME COMES WHEN THE VAGUE LIFE OF THE MOUTH NO LONGER SUFFICES;	168	FOURTH MEDITATN	18
THE MOON RETREATING INTO A VAGUE CLOUD-SHAPE	202	THE ROSE	18
THE VAGUE, THE ARID,	220	THE ABYSS	22
VAGUELY			
WHAT CAME TO ME VAGUELY IS NOW CLEAR,	173	WHAT TELL BONES	97
VAIN			
THE GREAT SLEDGE DROPS IN VAIN.	9	THE ADAMANT	2
VALE			
I WAS QUEEN OF THE VALE--	161	I'M HERE	17
THE DRY BLOOM SPLITTING IN THE WRINKLED VALE,	197	THE LONG WATERS	30
VALLEY			
A FIVE-FOOT DROP A VALLEY, SO TO SPEAK.	13	PRAISE PRAIRIE	2
THE VALLEY ROCKED BENEATH THE GRANITE HILL;	106	SIR JOHN DAVIES	59
I CAN HOLD THIS VALLEY	164	I'M HERE	96
CREEKS SWOLLEN IN MIDSUMMER FROM THE FLASH-FLOOD ROARING INTO THE NARROW VALLEY.	193	JOURNY INTERIOR	8
AND A BLACK BULL NUDGED AT A WALL IN THE VALLEY BELOW,	232	THE THING	22
THE HILL BECOMES THE VALLEY, AND IS STILL;	250	THE RIGHT THING	5
VALLEYS			
AND THE MOLD SANG IN THE BLEACHED VALLEYS UNDER THE ROSE.	102	ELEGY FOR JANE	9
VANISHED			
VANISHED LIKE APRIL SNOW;	213	THE HAPPY THREE	27
VAPOROUS			
IN THE VAPOROUS GREY OF EARLY MORNING,	197	THE LONG WATERS	49
VARICOSE			
MELTING AT THE KNEES, A VARICOSE HORROR.	65	SHAPE OF FIRE	31
VARIOUS			
AND VARIOUS MEASURES PROPOUNDED	115	THE SERPENT	12
EVEN THE CATERPILLAR I CAN LOVE, AND THE VARIOUS VERMIN.	151	SLUG	27
VARIOUSLY			
I HAVE BEEN SPOKEN TO VARIOUSLY	220	THE ABYSS	17
VARNISH			
THE CARRIAGES REEKING WITH VARNISH AND STALE PERFUME.	22	ROAD TO WDLAWN	4
VASE			
AS AN OPAQUE VASE FILLS TO THE BRIM FROM A QUICK POURING,	67	SHAPE OF FIRE	93
VAST			
DISTURBED SOME RHYTHM, OLD AND OF VAST IMPORTANCE,	40	MOSS-GATHERING	11
TO WHAT MORE VAST PERMISSION HAVE I COME?	173	WHAT TELL BONES	72
VASTY			
AND YOU, CAT AFTER GREAT MILK AND VASTY FISHES,	79	GIVE WAY, GATES	9
VAT			
WHEN I WALK PAST A VAT, WATER JOGGLES,	173	WHAT TELL BONES	73
VEAL			
OF VEAL SOAKED IN MARSALA AND LITTLE LARKS ARRANGED ON A LONG PLATTER,	232	THE THING	19
VEER			
THE BANK SWALLOWS VEER AND DIP,	152	THE SISKINS	1
VEERING			
FINALLY VEERING, WEARING THEMSELVES OUT, MERELY	41	BIG WIND	30
DIPPING AND VEERING CLOSE TO THE MOTIONLESS WATER.	93	I CRY, LOVE!	44
AT THE SUDDEN VEERING, THE MOMENT OF TURNING.	193	JOURNY INTERIOR	5
THE WIND VEERING THE CAR SLIGHTLY TO THE RIGHT,	194	JOURNY INTERIOR	43
VEERING CLOSE TO MY HEAD,	234	ALL MORNING	30
VEGETABLE			
MY NARROW VEGETABLE REALM!	18	LONG LIVE WEEDS	2

	PAGE	TITLE	LINE
VEIL			
THE VEIL LONG VIOLATED BY	19	EPIDERM MACABRE	7
VEILED			
HE NEVER TREMBLED AT A VEILED REMARK.	28	THE FAVORITE	2
VEIN			
YOU FEEL DISASTER CLIMB THE VEIN.	4	FEUD	8
THE BLOOD SLOWS TRANCE-LIKE IN THE ALTERED VEIN;	12	SLOW SEASON	15
VEINED			
HANDS, HARD AND VEINED ALL OVER,	7	ORDERS FOR DAY	1
THE HELIOTROPE, VEINED LIKE A FISH, THE PERSISTENT MORNING-GLORY,	197	THE LONG WATERS	41
VEINS			
THE VEINS WITHIN OUR HANDS BETRAYED OUR FEAR.	6	INTERLUDE	11
IN MY VEINS, IN MY BONES I FEEL IT,--	37	CUTTINGS (LATE)	6
WITH BLEACHED VEINS	43	FLOWER DUMP	7
SEA WATER STOOD IN MY VEINS,	49	RIVER INCIDENT	6
SANG IN MY VEINS	51	THE WAKING (1)	27
MY VEINS ARE RUNNING NOWHERE. DO THE BONES CAST OUT THEIR FIRE?	56	THE LOST SON	101
I'VE MORE VEINS THAN A TREE!	57	THE LOST SON	120
TO SEE CYCLAMEN VEINS BECOME CLEARER IN EARLY SUNLIGHT,	67	SHAPE OF FIRE	86
I ROMPED, LITHE AS A CHILD, DOWN THE SUMMERY STREETS OF MY VEINS,	86	PRAISE TO END!	21
I CAN'T CRAWL BACK THROUGH THOSE VEINS,	89	UNFOLD! UNFOLD!	3
THE LONG VEINS OF THE VINE	137	LOVE'S PROGRESS	6
VELVETY			
OUT THROUGH THE VELVETY CHAINS TO THE COOL AIR OF NIGHT.	47	DOUBLE FEATURE	4
VENERY			
AND VICIOUS VENERY--NOT SO!	8	PRAYER	12
VERB			
YOU BE AN ADVERB, I'LL BE A VERB,	272	DUET	6
VERBENAS			
CARNATIONS, VERBENAS, COSMOS,	43	FLOWER DUMP	4
VERMIN			
EVEN THE CATERPILLAR I CAN LOVE, AND THE VARIOUS VERMIN.	151	SLUG	27
VERNAL			
OUR VERNAL WISDOM MOVES THROUGH RIPE TO SERE.	12	SLOW SEASON	16
VERNAL SENTIMENT	24	VERNAL SENTIMNT	T
VERSE			
VERSE WITH ALLUSIONS	25	VERSE W ALLUSNS	T
YOU TAKE THE TIMES SUPPLEMENT, AND READ ITS VERSE,	113	TO A LADY ED	2
VERSES			
THE HIGH-PILED FLORAL OFFERINGS WITH SENTIMENTAL VERSES,	22	ROAD TO WDLAWN	3
VERTIGO			
MY BANKED-UP VERTIGO	213	THE HAPPY THREE	26
VERY			
MY EARS HAVE BEEN THE VERY DEVIL'S.	8	PRAYER	8
YOU'RE NOT VERY NICE,--	75	I NEED, I NEED	29
THEY SEEMED VERY HAPPY.	163	I'M HERE	70
HE WOULD ACT VERY SNIDE,	178	THE YAK	4
A DONKEY'S TAIL IS VERY NICE	181	MONOTONY SONG	1
VESPERAL			
I LISTEN TO THE WEEDS' VESPERAL WHINE,	171	WHAT TELL BONES	12
VESSEL			
TO BE CONTAINED, TO BE A VESSEL?	169	FOURTH MEDITATN	28
VESTIGES			
AS BRANCHES LOOSE LAST VESTIGES OF SNOW.	11	LIGHT BRIGHTER	10
VESTIGIAL			
I'VE TRACED THESE WORDS IN SAND WITH A VESTIGIAL TAIL;	92	I CRY, LOVE!	17
VESTURE			
THE VESTURE OF THE SKELETON,	19	EPIDERM MACABRE	4
VIADUCT			
UP OVER A VIADUCT I CAME, TO THE SNAKES AND STICKS OF ANOTHER WINTER,	65	SHAPE OF FIRE	37
VIBRATION			
I HUM IN PURE VIBRATION, LIKE A SAW.	167	HER BECOMING	89
VICE			
DEFER THE VICE OF FLESH THE IRREVOCABLE CHOICE	5	TO MY SISTER	8
VICIOUS			
AND VICIOUS VENERY--NOT SO!	8	PRAYER	12
VIEW			
BUT VIEW THINGS STEADILY AND WHOLE.	25	VERSE W ALLUSNS	10
A HUTCH BY THE EXIT HIS ROOM WITH A VIEW.	29	THE GENTLE	8

		PAGE	TITLE	LINE
VIGIL				
IT'S NECESSARY AMONG THE FLIES AND BANANAS, TO KEEP A CONSTANT VIGIL,		86	PRAISE TO END!	24
THE VIGIL		107	SIR JOHN DAVIES	ST
VILLAGE				
THE SUMMER HOUSE SHAPED LIKE A VILLAGE BAND STAND		32	SALE	7
VINE				
THE LOOSE VINE DROOPS WITH HOAR AT DAWN,		14	COMING OF COLD	20
WHAT ELSE HAS THE VINE LOOSENED?		90	UNFOLD! UNFOLD!	43
MY BROTHER THE VINE IS GLAD.		123	WORDS FOR WIND	8
ONE WITH THE SIGHING VINE,		124	WORDS FOR WIND	43
THE LONG VEINS OF THE VINE		137	LOVE'S PROGRESS	6
A VINE LASHING IN DRY FURY,		171	WHAT TELL BONES	30
THE ETERNAL ONE, THE CHILD, THE SWAYING VINE BRANCH,		198	THE LONG WATERS	69
AND THE VINE CLIMBS;		259	SONG (3)	49
THE VINE WINDS TO ITS WORK;		261	THE CHANGELING	53
VINES				
VINES TOUGHER THAN WRISTS		38	FORCING HOUSE	1
THE VINES GRAYING TO A FINE POWDER.		159	FIRST MEDITATN	81
VIOLATED				
THE VEIL LONG VIOLATED BY		19	EPIDERM MACABRE	7
VIOLENCE				
LOVE ME, MY VIOLENCE,		137	LOVE'S PROGRESS	13
NO SOUND FROM THE BAY. NO VIOLENCE.		190	AT OYSTER RIVER	6
A TERRIBLE VIOLENCE OF CREATION,		221	THE ABYSS	55
VIOLENT				
VIOLENT THAN A METAPHOR.		8	PRAYER	14
AND YET STILL VIOLENT MEN, WHOSE STACKED-UP GUNS		224	OTTO	27
HEARD IN A VIOLENT WARD		228	IN VIOLENT WARD	T
VIREO				
I'VE COME TO LOVE. A VIREO WHETS ITS BILL.		244	INFIRMITY	26
VIREO'S				
THE APRIL CHEEPING, THE VIREO'S INSISTENCE,		161	I'M HERE	8
WITH A ROUND VIREO'S EYE, QUIET AND CONTAINED,		234	ALL MORNING	13
THOUGH SUMMER BLAZES IN THE VIREO'S EYE.		240	IN EVEING AIR	2
VIRGIN				
I SAW A VIRGIN WRITHING IN THE DIRT--		131	SENTENTIOUS MAN	2
VIRTUE				
TREMBLED AT HIDDEN VIRTUE WITHOUT FLAW,		107	SIR JOHN DAVIES	74
LENT ME ONE VIRTUE, AND I LIVE THEREBY.		120	THE DREAM	24
DISSECTION IS A VIRTUE WHEN		257	SANITARIUM	11
VIRTUES				
OF HER CHOICE VIRTUES ONLY GODS SHOULD SPEAK,		127	I KNEW A WOMAN	5
VIRULENT				
AMONG THE VIRULENT.		7	ORDERS FOR DAY	20
VISCID				
BEHIND THE GREEN VISCID TRELLIS,		62	FIELD OF LIGHT	24
VISIBLE				
AT FIRST THE VISIBLE OBSCURES:		90	UNFOLD! UNFOLD!	55
THE FLESH CAN MAKE THE SPIRIT VISIBLE;		106	SIR JOHN DAVIES	63
THE VISIBLE OBSCURES. BUT WHO KNOWS WHEN?		107	SIR JOHN DAVIES	85
A SPIRIT RAGING AT THE VISIBLE.		155	THE DYING MAN	50
A FLAME, INTENSE, VISIBLE,		160	FIRST MEDITATN	93
MORE! O MORE! VISIBLE.		251	ONCE MORE, RND	4
VISION				
THE VISIT OF VISION, LUCK YEARS OVERDUE,		29	THE GENTLE	6
THE EYE PERISHES IN THE SMALL VISION.		90	UNFOLD! UNFOLD!	42
SUMMON A VISION AND DECLARE IT PURE.		107	SIR JOHN DAVIES	78
EACH VISION PURELY, PURELY WAS ITS OWN:		143	SHIMMER OF EVIL	4
YET DARED TO FIX HIS VISION ANYWHERE.		155	THE DYING MAN	65
THE VISION MOVES, AND YET REMAINS THE SAME.		156	THE DYING MAN	94
NEITHER VOICE NOR VISION.		198	THE LONG WATERS	72
O WHO WOULD TAKE THE VISION FROM THE CHILD?--		243	THE MOTION	23
VISIT				
THE VISIT OF VISION, LUCK YEARS OVERDUE,		29	THE GENTLE	6
WENT TO VISIT THE WIND. WHERE THE BIRDS DIE.		73	WHERE KNOCK IS	72
A VISIT FROM HIM IS A PIECE OF PURE LUCK,		113	TO A LADY ED	6
VISITANT				
THE VISITANT		100	THE VISITANT	T
VISITOR				
THE DIRT LEFT MY HAND, VISITOR.		63	FIELD OF LIGHT	31
VITAMINS				
VITAMINS, WATER, AND WHATEVER		228	THE GERANIUM	7

	PAGE	TITLE	LINE
VIVID			
--AND THE EYES, STILL VIVID, LOOKING UP FROM A SUNKEN ROOM.	22	ROAD TO WDLAWN	8
VOCABLES			
HOW HE ROLLS THE VOCABLES,	266	FOR STEVENS	7
VOCAL			
THE OVENBIRD WILL MATCH THE VOCAL BROOK,	11	LIGHT BRIGHTER	15
VOICE			
A CHEAP CLOCK TICKING IN GHOSTLY CICADA VOICE.	29	THE REMINDER	12
VOICE, COME OUT OF THE SILENCE.	54	THE LOST SON	20
A VOICE SANG:	65	SHAPE OF FIRE	40
A LOW VOICE, SUMMER-SAD.	90	UNFOLD! UNFOLD!	50
A VOICE SAID:	100	THE VISITANT	3
MY LOOKS HAD A VOICE;	104	OLD LADY'S WRDS	47
THE VOICE	128	THE VOICE	T
IN HER LOW VOICE I HEARD	128	THE VOICE	3
IT SANG WITH HER TRUE VOICE,	128	THE VOICE	15
A SLIGHT VOICE REPLY;	128	THE VOICE	17
IN THE DEEP CENTER OF THE VOICE AND FIRE.	132	SENTENTIOUS MAN	34
WITH THE SMALL VOICE OF A CHILD,	146	THE SONG	26
MY VOICE SOFTER.	162	I'M HERE	44
A VOICE KEEPS RISING IN MY EARLY SLEEP,	165	HER BECOMING	19
A MUFFLED VOICE, A LOW SWEET WATERY NOISE.	165	HER BECOMING	20
NEITHER VOICE NOR VISION.	198	THE LONG WATERS	72
A SMALL VOICE CALLING FROM A DRIFTING CLOUD.	248	THE TREE, BIRD	4
VOICES			
THE SOUND OF VOICES, YOUNG VOICES, MIXED WITH SLEIGHBELLS,	161	I'M HERE	4
THE SOUND OF VOICES, YOUNG VOICES, MIXED WITH SLEIGHBELLS,	161	I'M HERE	4
VULNERABLE			
LOVE IS NOT LOVE UNTIL LOVE'S VULNERABLE.	120	THE DREAM	17
A VULNERABLE PLACE,	197	THE LONG WATERS	58
ALL THINGS ARE VULNERABLE, STILL;	259	SONG (3)	47
VULTURE			
WHERE SNAKE AND VULTURE HOVER,	7	ORDERS FOR DAY	12
WADDLE			
WITH A NURSE-MAID WADDLE AND A SHOP-GIRL SIMPER,	23	ACADEMIC	3
AND THE DUCKS NEAR LAKE WASHINGTON WADDLE DOWN THE HIGHWAY AFTER A RAIN,	234	ALL MORNING	26
WAGS			
THE HOLY ROOT WAGS THE TAIL OF A HILL;	99	O, THOU OPENING	54
WAGTAIL			
THE WAGTAIL	183	THE WAGTAIL	T
WAG-TAIL			
WHO KNOWS HOW THE WAG-TAIL WOOS?	183	THE WAGTAIL	1
WAILED			
WHEN I RAGED, WHEN I WAILED,	249	THE RESTORED	13
WAIT			
THE ARBITRATORS WAIT;	31	LULL	13
WAIT.	58	THE LOST SON	173
WHO'S COME CAN WAIT.	154	THE DYING MAN	35
YET IF WE WAIT, UNAFRAID, BEYOND THE FEARFUL INSTANT,	221	THE ABYSS	57
WE WAIT; WE LISTEN.	231	THE STORM	29
WAITED			
WE WAITED FOR THE FIRST RAIN IN THE EAVES.	6	INTERLUDE	4
I WAITED, ALERT AS A DOG.	100	THE VISITANT	7
THE LEECH CLINGING TO A STONE WAITED;	100	THE VISITANT	8
I WAITED	247	I WAITED	T
I WAITED FOR THE WIND TO MOVE THE DUST;	247	I WAITED	1
WAITING			
THE SON OF MISFORTUNE LONG, LONG HAS BEEN WAITING	29	THE GENTLE	5
A WAITING GHOST WARMS UP THE DEAD	60	THE LONG ALLEY	35
I'M STILL WAITING FOR A FOOT.	84	O LULL ME, LULL	30
WAITING LIKE A FERN, MAKING A SPINY SHADOW.	102	ELEGY FOR JANE	15
AN INTOLERABLE WAITING,	162	I'M HERE	36
AT THE EDGE OF THE FIELD WAITING FOR THE PURE MOMENT;	168	FOURTH MEDITATN	3
WAITING, ITSELF A SLOW THING,	168	FOURTH MEDITATN	21
THE YOUNG SNAKE, POISED IN GREEN LEAVES, WAITING FOR ITS FLY,	190	AT OYSTER RIVER	28
WAIT-IN-THE-HALL			
IT WAS JUMP-IN-THE-HEDGE; IT WAS WAIT-IN-THE-HALL;	111	SQUEEZE-BOX	13
WAITS			
MY MEAT EATS ME. WHO WAITS AT THE GATE?	65	SHAPE OF FIRE	53
THE WASP WAITS.	66	SHAPE OF FIRE	56

	PAGE	TITLE	LINE
WAKE			
I WAKE IN EVERY NERVE.	34	NIGHT JOURNEY	15
WAKE ME, WITCH, WE'LL DO THE DANCE OF ROTTEN STICKS.	64	SHAPE OF FIRE	10
IN THE WAKE OF A SHIP OF WIND;	80	GIVE WAY, GATES	42
SOFTLY SOFTLY, YOU'LL WAKE THE CLAMS.	85	PRAISE TO END!	10
I WAKE TO SLEEP, AND TAKE MY WAKING SLOW.	108	THE WAKING (2)	1
I WAKE TO SLEEP, AND TAKE MY WAKING SLOW.	108	THE WAKING (2)	6
I WAKE TO SLEEP, AND TAKE MY WAKING SLOW.	108	THE WAKING (2)	12
I WAKE TO SLEEP, AND TAKE MY WAKING SLOW.	108	THE WAKING (2)	18
THE LACELIKE WRINKLES OF THE WAKE WIDENING, THINNING OUT,	203	THE ROSE	33
MAKING A RACKET TO WAKE THE DEAD,	234	ALL MORNING	18
DO THE DEAD WAKE IN THEIR OWN WAY?	259	SONG (3)	32
WAKED			
I'VE WAKED THE WRONG WIND:	82	SENSIBILITY! LA	29
WAKENING			
HANDS AND HAIR MOVED THROUGH A DREAM OF WAKENING BLOSSOMS.	66	SHAPE OF FIRE	74
O SMALL BIRD WAKENING,	78	BRING THE DAY!	38
SHIFTING IN THE WAKENING SUNLIGHT	204	THE ROSE	87
WAKES			
A RIPPLE WAKES THE POND.	121	ALL EARTH, AIR	5
SHE WAKES THE ENDS OF LIFE.	125	WORDS FOR WIND	89
SO THE SEA WIND WAKES DESIRE.	198	THE LONG WATERS	65
WAKES ALL THE WAVES, ALL THEIR LOOSE WANDERING FIRE.	201	THE FAR FIELD	88
WAKING			
THE SLEEP WAS NOT DEEP, BUT THE WAKING IS SLOW.	29	THE GENTLE	12
THE WAKING	51	THE WAKING (1)	T
THE WAKING	108	THE WAKING (2)	T
I WAKE TO SLEEP, AND TAKE MY WAKING SLOW.	108	THE WAKING (2)	1
I WAKE TO SLEEP, AND TAKE MY WAKING SLOW.	108	THE WAKING (2)	6
I WAKE TO SLEEP, AND TAKE MY WAKING SLOW.	108	THE WAKING (2)	12
I WAKE TO SLEEP, AND TAKE MY WAKING SLOW.	108	THE WAKING (2)	18
WATCHING THE WAKING OF MY FATHER'S WORLD.--	225	OTTO	41
WAKING'S			
WAKING'S	98	O, THOU OPENING	38
WAKING'S MY CARE--	240	IN EVEING AIR	5
WALK			
WALK BOLDLY MY SISTER BUT DO NOT DEIGN TO GIVE	5	TO MY SISTER	10
WE WALK AWARE OF WHAT IS FAR AND CLOSE.	13	PRAISE PRAIRIE	10
THE LAST TRICYCLE RUNS CRAZILY TO THE END OF THE WALK.	33	IDYLL	4
WALK INTO THE WIND, WILLIE!	92	I CRY, LOVE!	29
GOD BLESS THE GROUND! I SHALL WALK SOFTLY THERE,	108	THE WAKING (2)	8
SUPPOSE YOU WALK OUT IN A STORM,	114	DINKY	5
KEEPS PACE WHEN I WALK ALONE.	123	WORDS FOR WIND	32
AND I WALK WITH THE WIND.	124	WORDS FOR WIND	39
I WALK WITH MY TRUE LOVE.	125	WORDS FOR WIND	74
I WALK AS IF MY FACE WOULD KISS THE WIND.	135	THE RENEWAL	12
I WALK THE NIGHT TO KEEP MY FIVE WITS WARM.	135	THE RENEWAL	18
A WALK IN LATE SUMMER	149	IN LATE SUMMER	T
A FACE FLOATS IN THE FERNS. DO MAIMED GODS WALK?	165	HER BECOMING	18
ON A DARK DAY I WALK STRAIGHT TOWARD THE RAIN.	170	FOURTH MEDITATN	80
WHEN I WALK PAST A VAT, WATER JOGGLES,	173	WHAT TELL BONES	73
OR WALK THE PEBBLY SHORE WITH THE HUMPBACKED HERON,	209	HER LONGING	14
IT WAS AS IF I TRIED TO WALK IN HAY,	247	I WAITED	6
WALKED			
AND I WALKED, I WALKED THROUGH THE LIGHT AIR;	63	FIELD OF LIGHT	51
AND I WALKED, I WALKED THROUGH THE LIGHT AIR;	63	FIELD OF LIGHT	51
WALKED ALONG THE HIGHWAY,	87	PRAISE TO END!	53
THE LONG DAY DIES; I WALKED THE WOODS ALONE;	150	IN LATE SUMMER	29
ONE DAY HUGH WALKED UP TO A BEAR	181	MONOTONY SONG	5
AS I WALKED BY THE HIGH SEA-WALL.	216	THE SHY MAN	4
AS I WALKED BESIDE HER, THE O'CONNELL'S DAUGHTER,	216	THE SHY MAN	11
AS WE WALKED BY THE HIGH SEA-WALL.	216	THE SHY MAN	16
THEY STOOD THERE WITH THEIR GUNS; HE WALKED TOWARD,	224	OTTO	18
AND WHEN I WALKED, MY FEET SEEMED DEEP IN SAND.	247	I WAITED	16
THE SWEET LIGHT MET ME AS I WALKED TOWARD	248	THE TREE, BIRD	3
HE WALKED OUR GREENHOUSE LAND.	268	SAGINAW SONG	55
I WALKED HIM THROUGH THE GRILL AND OUT THE GATE	274	SUPPR W LINDSAY	46
WALKER			
A WALKER AT THE RIVER'S EDGE MAY HEAR	11	LIGHT BRIGHTER	3
THE WALKER TRUDGES ANKLE-DEEP IN LEAVES;	12	SLOW SEASON	11
WALKER'S			
THE WALKER'S FOOT HAS SCARCELY ROOM	14	COMING OF COLD	5

	PAGE	TITLE	LINE
WALKING			
WALKING THIS FIELD I REMEMBER	6	THE PREMONITION	1
OFTEN I MEET, ON WALKING FROM A DOOR,	8	THE SIGNALS	1
WHEN WE ARE WALKING ON A TREELESS PLAIN,	13	PRAISE PRAIRIE	7
A PATH WENT WALKING.	63	THE LONG ALLEY	33
WALKING THE EDGE, LOQUACIOUS, UNAFRAID.	155	THE DYING MAN	63
I REMEMBER WALKING DOWN A PATH,	162	I'M HERE	45
STANDING, SILENT, ON SANDY BEACHES OR WALKING ALONG GREEN EMBANKMENTS;	168	FOURTH MEDITATN	4
I SEE THEM AS FIGURES WALKING IN A GREENY GARDEN,	170	FOURTH MEDITATN	63
WALKS			
HE WALKS THE SHALLOW WITH AN ANTIC GRACE.	15	THE HERON	5
SWAYING OVER THE WALKS, IN THE WATERY AIR,	61	THE LONG ALLEY	75
THE STONE WALKS, WHERE ARE THEY?	103	OLD LADY'S WRDS	35
HE WALKS BY. HE WALKS BY.	208	THE APPARITION	12
HE WALKS BY. HE WALKS BY.	208	THE APPARITION	12
WALL			
DEAD IN A WALL.	79	GIVE WAY, GATES	32
MY FRIEND, THE RAT IN THE WALL, BRINGS ME THE CLEAREST MESSAGES;	88	PRAISE TO END!	84
MY FLESH IS BREATHING SLOWER THAN A WALL.	135	THE RENEWAL	9
AND SHUDDERED TOWARD THE WALL;	136	THE SENSUALISTS	18
THE WOOD BECOMES A WALL.	148	THE SMALL	9
THE WALL	154	THE DYING MAN	ST
THE WALL HAS ENTERED: I MUST LOVE THE WALL,	155	THE DYING MAN	48
THE WALL HAS ENTERED: I MUST LOVE THE WALL,	155	THE DYING MAN	48
THE SHADOWS CRAWLING DOWN A SUNNY WALL.	171	WHAT TELL BONES	17
THIS HARRY RAN STRAIGHT UP A WALL,	181	MONOTONY SONG	13
I HEAR THE NOISE OF THE WALL.	220	THE ABYSS	26
AND A BLACK BULL NUDGED AT A WALL IN THE VALLEY BELOW,	232	THE THING	22
MY SHADOW PINNED AGAINST A SWEATING WALL.	239	IN A DARK TIME	10
LIGHT SHIFTS UPON THE WALL.	240	IN EVEING AIR	21
THE SELF-DESTRUCTIVE SHAKE THE COMMON WALL;	250	THE RIGHT THING	14
WALLACE			
WALLACE STEVENS, WHAT'S HE DONE?	266	FOR STEVENS	1
WALLACE, WALLACE, WO IST ER?	266	FOR STEVENS	9
WALLACE, WALLACE, WO IST ER?	266	FOR STEVENS	9
WALLACE STEVENS--ARE WE FOR HIM?	266	FOR STEVENS	19
WALL-PAPER			
THE HAND-PAINTED WALL-PAPER, FINER THAN SKIN,	32	SALE	17
WALLS			
HAVE SCALED YOUR WALLS, AND SPIES BETRAY	4	FEUD	15
A HAMMER ON THE CRYSTAL WALLS	22	SILENCE	5
AND I HAVE SEEN DUST FROM THE WALLS OF INSTITUTIONS,	46	DOLOR	9
AND THE WALLS STRETCHED WIDE.	146	THE SONG	7
THERE ARE NO PURSUING FORMS, FACES ON WALLS:	159	FIRST MEDITATN	78
THE OILY, TAR-LADEN WALLS	205	THE ROSE	94
THE WALLS, THE SLATTED WINDOWS, DRIVING	230	THE STORM	25
PACING A ROOM, A ROOM WITH DEAD-WHITE WALLS;	242	THE SEQUEL	30
THE WAY GREW STEEPER BETWEEN STONY WALLS,	247	I WAITED	19
WALTZ			
MY PAPA'S WALTZ	45	MY PAPA'S WALTZ	T
IT'S MY LAST WALTZ WITH AN OLD ITCH.	60	THE LONG ALLEY	34
FOR THE WALTZ OF TO,	64	SHAPE OF FIRE	27
THIS TOAD COULD WALTZ ON A DRUM;	92	I CRY, LOVE!	11
CARES ABOUT THE DANCE OF DEAD UNDERWEAR, OR THE SAD WALTZ OF PAPER	98	O, THOU OPENING	26
WALTZED			
THEN WALTZED ME OFF TO BED	45	MY PAPA'S WALTZ	15
WALTZING			
SUCH WALTZING WAS NOT EASY.	45	MY PAPA'S WALTZ	4
WAN			
THEIR WAN MOUTHS KISSING THE WARM SUTURES,	50	THE MINIMAL	9
WANDER			
IN THE WEAK LIGHT THEY WANDER, EACH ALONE.	149	IN LATE SUMMER	4
WANDERED			
SHE WANDERED; I DID NOT:	123	WORDS FOR WIND	20
WANDERING			
WAKES ALL THE WAVES, ALL THEIR LOOSE WANDERING FIRE.	201	THE FAR FIELD	88
WANDERS			
A TRUE MOLE WANDERS LIKE A WORM.	97	O, THOU OPENING	20
THE WIND WANDERS AROUND THE HOUSE	104	OLD LADY'S WRDS	52
PAIN WANDERS THROUGH MY BONES LIKE A LOST FIRE;	246	THE MARROW	11

	PAGE	TITLE	LINE
WANE			
AFTER A WHILE THE LIGHT BEGAN TO WANE	274	SUPPR W LINDSAY	35
WANES			
WANES TO THE FEBRILE SMOLDERING OF SLEEP;	17	UNEXTINGUISHED	6
WANING			
THAT DISAPPEAR INTO A WANING MOON;	173	WHAT TELL BONES	70
NOW, IN THIS WANING OF LIGHT,	191	AT OYSTER RIVER	57
WANT			
WHO WANT NO MORE THAN FINGERS SEIZE,	25	VERSE W ALLUSNS	3
I WANT THE OLD RAGE, THE LASH OF PRIMORDIAL MILK!	56	THE LOST SON	107
I LOVE THE WORLD; I WANT MORE THAN THE WORLD,	155	THE DYING MAN	56
WANTED			
BUT HE ALWAYS WANTED TO FLY MY KITE;	178	THE DONKEY	2
WANTING			
WANTING THE QUIET OF OLD WOOD OR STONE WITHOUT WATER.	255	LIGHT POEM	9
WANTON			
FOR OTHER TUNES AND OTHER WANTON BEATS	105	SIR JOHN DAVIES	21
GOD PITY THOSE BUT WANTON TO THE KNEES,--	106	SIR JOHN DAVIES	62
THESE OLD BONES LIVE TO LEARN HER WANTON WAYS:	127	I KNEW A WOMAN	27
WANTS			
WANTS SINGLENESS OF SPIRIT ABOVE ALL ELSE:	24	POETASTER	2
THAT WAS A CLOSE KNOCK. SEE WHAT THE WILL WANTS.	61	THE LONG ALLEY	62
DO WHAT THE CLUMSY PARTNER WANTS TO DO!	106	SIR JOHN DAVIES	42
WAR			
BETWEEN THE SPIRIT AND THE FLESH,--WHAT WAR?	223	ELEGY (2)	5
WARBLERS			
FOR TO COME UPON WARBLERS IN EARLY MAY	199	THE FAR FIELD	26
WARD			
WARD OF MY SPIRIT,	161	I'M HERE	20
HEARD IN A VIOLENT WARD	228	IN VIOLENT WARD	T
WARLIKE			
FOR ANCESTORS WHO LOVED A WARLIKE SHOW,	224	OTTO	25
WARM			
DRAWING IN THE WARM AIR.	39	ORCHIDS	8
THE ELEMENTS I KEPT WARM	49	RIVER INCIDENT	7
THEIR WAN MOUTHS KISSING THE WARM SUTURES,	50	THE MINIMAL	9
SCURRY OF WARM OVER SMALL PLANTS.	57	THE LOST SON	141
HAND ME A FEATHER, I'LL FAN YOU WARM,	60	THE LONG ALLEY	45
THE WARM COMES WITHOUT SOUND.	64	SHAPE OF FIRE	19
SOME STONES ARE STILL WARM.	72	WHERE KNOCK IS	41
THIS SALT CAN'T WARM A STONE.	86	PRAISE TO END!	49
WE DARED THE DARK TO REACH THE WHITE AND WARM.	107	SIR JOHN DAVIES	92
WITH NOTHING ON TO KEEP YOU WARM,	114	DINKY	6
SHE KEEPS MY WISHES WARM;	121	ALL EARTH, AIR	12
I WALK THE NIGHT TO KEEP MY FIVE WITS WARM.	135	THE RENEWAL	18
I FELT MY SLOW BLOOD WARM.	150	SNAKE	9
SALIVA DRIPPING FROM WARM MICROPHONES,	187	THE LONGING	5
I WARM MYSELF WITH COLD.	259	SONG (3)	33
WARMED			
I TOUCHED THE GROUND, THE GROUND WARMED BY THE KILLDEER,	63	FIELD OF LIGHT	39
WARMING			
THE SUN WARMING THE FINE LOAM,	42	TRANSPLANTING	14
WARMS			
A WAITING GHOST WARMS UP THE DEAD	60	THE LONG ALLEY	35
WARNINGS			
THE DARKNESS OF FALLING HAIR, THE WARNINGS FROM LINT AND SPIDERS,	159	FIRST MEDITATN	80
WARPS			
RAGE WARPS MY CLEAREST CRY	3	OPEN HOUSE	17
WARS			
CONDUCTING HIS LONG WARS WITH THE NEIGHBORHOOD CATS,	234	ALL MORNING	16
WARY			
BETTER TO HUG CLOSE, WARY OF RUBBLE AND FALLING STONES.	193	JOURNY INTERIOR	6
WATCHING MY HANDS, WARY.	220	THE ABYSS	39
WAS (193)			
WASHED			
AND GULLIES WASHED WITH LIGHT.	34	NIGHT JOURNEY	19
WASHED-OUT			
THERE ARE MANY DETOURS, WASHED-OUT INTERRUPTED RAW PLACES	193	JOURNY INTERIOR	2
WASHES			
THE LAKE WASHES ITS STONES.	82	SENSIBILITY! LA	31
WASHING			
THEN WASHING UP OVER SMALL STONES.	93	I CRY, LOVE!	49

	PAGE	TITLE	LINE
WASHINGTON			
AND THE DUCKS NEAR LAKE WASHINGTON WADDLE DOWN THE HIGHWAY			
AFTER A RAIN,	234	ALL MORNING	26
WASN'T			
I WASN'T ALONE	51	THE WAKING (1)	15
IT WASN'T EVEN AS	71	WHERE KNOCK IS	14
IT WAS AND IT WASN'T HER THERE	72	WHERE KNOCK IS	37
IT WASN'T A GOOSE,	77	BRING THE DAY!	15
IT WASN'T A POODLE.	77	BRING THE DAY!	16
IT WASN'T ERNEST; IT WASN'T SCOTT--	111	SQUEEZE-BOX	1
IT WASN'T ERNEST; IT WASN'T SCOTT--	111	SQUEEZE-BOX	1
IT WASN'T THE COLONY; IT WASN'T THE STORK;	111	SQUEEZE-BOX	8
IT WASN'T THE COLONY; IT WASN'T THE STORK;	111	SQUEEZE-BOX	8
IT WASN'T THE JOINTS IN NEW YORK, NEW YORK;	111	SQUEEZE-BOX	9
OH, IT WASN'T A CRIME, IT WASN'T A SIN,	112	SQUEEZE-BOX	30
OH, IT WASN'T A CRIME, IT WASN'T A SIN,	112	SQUEEZE-BOX	30
BUT FOUND HE WASN'T THERE AT ALL,	181	MONOTONY SONG	14
WASP			
THE WASP WAITS.	66	SHAPE OF FIRE	56
IS THE WASP TENDER?	81	SENSIBILITY! LA	18
THE WASP DRINKING AT THE EDGE OF MY CUP;	163	I'M HERE	87
WASPS			
WASPS COME WHEN I ASK FOR PIGEONS.	92	I CRY, LOVE!	2
WASTE			
I HAVE GONE INTO THE WASTE LONELY PLACES	159	FIRST MEDITATN	74
WASTED			
ALL RANDOM, WASTED, AND DISPERSED,	19	AGNST DISASTER	5
THEN A BLEAK WASTED PLACE,	34	NIGHT JOURNEY	10
FLAP FROM A WASTED TREE,	49	NIGHT CROW	2
WATCH			
YOU WOUND THE WATCH IN AN OLD-FASHIONED LOCKET	29	THE REMINDER	7
WE WATCH OPINION DRIFT,	31	LULL	8
I WATCH A BEACON SWING	34	NIGHT JOURNEY	16
I COULD WATCH! I COULD WATCH!	63	FIELD OF LIGHT	44
I COULD WATCH! I COULD WATCH!	63	FIELD OF LIGHT	44
WATCH.	80	GIVE WAY, GATES	50
IN THE SAME WAY: O WATCH HIS BODY SWAY!--	105	SIR JOHN DAVIES	11
YOU'D BETTER WATCH THE THINGS YOU DO.	114	DINKY	17
YOU'D BETTER WATCH THE THINGS YOU DO.	114	DINKY	18
I THIRST BY DAY. I WATCH BY NIGHT.	222	THE ABYSS	89
COUNTING THE WISPS OF FLAME, AND I WATCH HOW	240	IN EVEING AIR	20
I WATCH A RIVER WIND ITSELF AWAY;	243	THE MOTION	8
WATCHED			
I WATCHED HER THERE, BETWEEN ME AND THE MOON;	119	THE DREAM	11
AND I WATCHED AND WATCHED TILL MY EYES BLURRED FROM THE			
BIRD SHAPES,--	199	THE FAR FIELD	29
AND I WATCHED AND WATCHED TILL MY EYES BLURRED FROM THE			
BIRD SHAPES,--	199	THE FAR FIELD	29
AND WATCHED THE WEATHER FLOW.	212	LIGHT LISTENED	11
WATCHER			
THE LAST WATCHER INDOORS, MOVING THE CARDPLAYERS CLOSER	230	THE STORM	26
WATCHING			
WATCHING THE PRESSURE GAUGE	41	BIG WIND	10
WATCHING HANDS TRANSPLANTING,	42	TRANSPLANTING	1
WATCHING SHADOWS CRAWL,	53	THE LOST SON	17
WATCHING THE WIND RIFFLE THE BACKS OF SMALL BIRDS,	165	HER BECOMING	2
WATCHING FOR DANGEROUS DOWN-HILL PLACES, WHERE THE WHEELS			
WHINED BEYOND EIGHTY--	193	JOURNY INTERIOR	19
A TIME FOR WATCHING THE TIDE,	202	THE ROSE	11
WATCHING MY HANDS, WARY.	220	THE ABYSS	39
WATCHING THE WAKING OF MY FATHER'S WORLD.--	225	OTTO	41
UNDER THE EYE OF THE GREAT OWL WATCHING FROM THE ELM-TREE,	227	MEADOW MOUSE	24
WATCHMAN			
BLASTED TO DEATH BY THE NIGHT WATCHMAN.	199	THE FAR FIELD	23
WATCHMAN'S			
WHEN GEORGE THE WATCHMAN'S LANTERN DROPPED FROM SIGHT	225	OTTO	38
WATER			
WATER RAN OVER AND UNDER	6	THE PREMONITION	8
WAS LOST IN A MAZE OF WATER.	6	THE PREMONITION	13
THE WATER STORED IN NARROW POOLS ESCAPES	11	LIGHT BRIGHTER	11
THE HERON STANDS IN WATER WHERE THE SWAMP	15	THE HERON	1
THE GULLS RIDE ON THE WATER, THE GULLS HAVE COME AND GONE,	28	CLAIRVOY WIDOW	23
BUT STILL THE DELICATE SLIPS KEEP COAXING UP WATER;	37	CUTTINGS	3

	PAGE	TITLE	LINE
WATER (CONTINUED)			
WIND DRIVING WATER	41	BIG WIND	3
OR RISING OUT OF FERNS NOT FAR FROM WATER,	43	CARNATIONS	4
SEA WATER STOOD IN MY VEINS,	49	RIVER INCIDENT	6
IN THE DARK, IN THE ROLLING WATER.	49	RIVER INCIDENT	11
DARK WATER, UNDERGROUND,	50	THE CYCLE	1
JUST UNDER THE WATER	54	THE LOST SON	48
JUST UNDER THE WATER	55	THE LOST SON	60
WHAT A SMALL SONG. WHAT SLOW CLOUDS. WHAT DARK WATER.	56	THE LOST SON	83
WATER WATER WATER	56	THE LOST SON	112
WATER WATER WATER	56	THE LOST SON	112
WATER WATER WATER	56	THE LOST SON	112
WATER.	59	THE LONG ALLEY	10
LOO, LOO, SAID THE SULPHUROUS WATER,	59	THE LONG ALLEY	14
BRICKS FLAKE BEFORE MY FACE. MASTER OF WATER, THAT'S TREES AWAY.	61	THE LONG ALLEY	80
CAME TO LAKES; CAME TO DEAD WATER,	62	FIELD OF LIGHT	1
WATER RECEDES TO THE CRYING OF SPIDERS.	64	SHAPE OF FIRE	4
SHALE LOOSENS. MARL REACHES INTO THE FIELD. SMALL BIRDS PASS OVER WATER.	64	SHAPE OF FIRE	11
A LOW MOUTH LAPS WATER. WEEDS, WEEDS, HOW I LOVE YOU.	64	SHAPE OF FIRE	17
WATER BIRDS WENT CHING. WENT CHING.	73	WHERE KNOCK IS	54
THE DRIPPY WATER	74	I NEED, I NEED	10
WHAT WATER DOES?	76	I NEED, I NEED	65
END WITH WATER.	77	BRING THE DAY!	31
THE RIVER'S ALONE WITH ITS WATER.	85	PRAISE TO END!	14
SOFTER THAN WATER.	88	PRAISE TO END!	96
I WAS PRIVY TO OILY FUNGUS AND THE ALGAE OF STANDING WATER;	89	UNFOLD! UNFOLD!	25
I CARE FOR A CAT'S CRY AND THE HUGS, LIVE AS WATER.	92	I CRY, LOVE!	16
DIPPING AND VEERING CLOSE TO THE MOTIONLESS WATER.	93	I CRY, LOVE!	44
WRINKLING BETWEEN REEDS IN SHALLOWER WATER,	93	I CRY, LOVE!	47
THE WATER RECEDES SLOWLY,	93	I CRY, LOVE!	52
A TREE SWAYED OVER WATER.	100	THE VISITANT	2
STIRRING THE CLEAREST WATER.	102	ELEGY FOR JANE	13
LIGHT HARDENED ON THE WATER WHERE WE WERE;	119	THE DREAM	6
THE WATER RIPPLED, AND SHE RIPPLED ON.	119	THE DREAM	8
I PLAYED IN FLAME AND WATER LIKE A BOY	120	THE DREAM	28
SHE MOVES AS WATER MOVES, AND COMES TO ME,	129	SHE	15
FOR WATER MOVES UNTIL IT'S PURIFIED,	132	SENTENTIOUS MAN	41
A WOMAN'S NAKED IN WATER,	137	LOVE'S PROGRESS	9
AROUND, BACK INTO THE TINY MAINCURRENT, THE RUSH OF BROWNISH-WHITE WATER,	159	FIRST MEDITATN	71
IN THE BACK OF MY MIND, RUNNING WITH THE ROLLING WATER,	165	HER BECOMING	9
A BIT OF WATER CAUGHT IN A WRINKLED CREVICE,	168	FOURTH MEDITATN	8
WHEN I WALK PAST A VAT, WATER JOGGLES,	173	WHAT TELL BONES	73
ALIVE WITH TINY STRIPED FISH, AND YOUNG CRABS CLIMBING IN AND OUT OF THE WATER.	190	AT OYSTER RIVER	5
AND WITH WATER: THE WAVES COMING FORWARD, WITHOUT CESSATION,	191	AT OYSTER RIVER	31
THE TONGUES OF WATER, CREEPING IN, QUIETLY.	191	AT OYSTER RIVER	35
BY THE LAPPING OF WATER,	191	AT OYSTER RIVER	61
UNDERNEATH, THE SLUGGISH WATER RUNNING BETWEEN WEEDS, BROKEN WHEELS, TIRES, STONES.	194	JOURNY INTERIOR	33
I SEE THE FLOWER OF ALL WATER, ABOVE AND BELOW ME, THE NEVER RECEDING,	194	JOURNY INTERIOR	52
TO A RICH DESOLATION OF WIND AND WATER,	197	THE LONG WATERS	46
TO A LANDLOCKED BAY, WHERE THE SALT WATER IS FRESHENED	197	THE LONG WATERS	47
SURROUNDED BY SAND, BROKEN SHELLS, THE WRECKAGE OF WATER.	197	THE LONG WATERS	59
WHEN BATS FLY, CLOSE TO SLIGHTLY TILTING BROWNISH WATER,	198	THE LONG WATERS	61
I LOSE AND FIND MYSELF IN THE LONG WATER;	198	THE LONG WATERS	76
THE ON-COMING WATER.	200	THE FAR FIELD	55
AS OF WATER QUICKENING BEFORE A NARROWING CHANNEL	200	THE FAR FIELD	59
THE SLIGHTLY TREMBLING WATER	200	THE FAR FIELD	67
SILENCE OF WATER ABOVE A SUNKEN TREE:	201	THE FAR FIELD	100
BUT THIS PLACE, WHERE SEA AND FRESH WATER MEET,	202	THE ROSE	2
THE SUN A BALL OF FIRE COMING DOWN OVER THE WATER,	202	THE ROSE	16
I RETURN TO THE TWITTERING OF SWALLOWS ABOVE WATER,	204	THE ROSE	73
AND A DROP OF RAIN WATER HANGS AT THE TIP OF A LEAF	204	THE ROSE	86
THE CURLEW'S SLOW NIGHT SONG CAME ON THE WATER.	216	THE SHY MAN	9
I'M NO LONGER A BIRD DIPPING A BEAK INTO RIPPLING WATER	220	THE ABYSS	41
THE FIRE SUBSIDES INTO RINGS OF WATER,	221	THE ABYSS	59
THE PARALYTIC STUNNED IN THE TUB, AND THE WATER RISING,--	227	MEADOW MOUSE	28
VITAMINS, WATER, AND WHATEVER	228	THE GERANIUM	7
WATER ROARS INTO THE CISTERN.	231	THE STORM	37

		PAGE	TITLE	LINE
WATER (CONTINUED)				
A BOTTOM OF WATER.		233	THE PIKE	4
AND I LEAN, ALMOST INTO THE WATER,		233	THE PIKE	11
SWAYING IN AIR, LIKE SOME LONG WATER WEED.		241	THE SEQUEL	19
I SAW ALL THINGS THROUGH WATER, MAGNIFIED,		247	I WAITED	10
WANTING THE QUIET OF OLD WOOD OR STONE WITHOUT WATER.		255	LIGHT POEM	9
THIS WATER, HEATED LIKE MY BLOOD,		256	IN HYDROTHERAPY	5
THE WATER IS BUSY		258	SONG (3)	6
AS WATER TEACHES STONE. BELIEVE ME, EXTREMEST ORIOLE,		260	THE CHANGELING	19
WATERED				
HE WATERED THE ROSES.		73	WHERE KNOCK IS	64
WATERFALL				
MY WATERFALL		210	HER TIME	2
WATERING				
OR STAND ALL NIGHT WATERING ROSES, HIS FEET BLUE IN RUBBER BOOTS.		42	OLD FLORIST	10
WATERING-TROUGH				
NOW HE'S EATEN HIS THREE KINDS OF CHEESE AND DRUNK FROM HIS BOTTLE-CAP WATERING-TROUGH--		227	MEADOW MOUSE	12
WATERS				
THE SMALL WATERS SEEPING UPWARD,		37	CUTTINGS (LATE)	7
AND ALL THE WATERS		51	THE WAKING (1)	25
COME WHISPERING OVER THE SMALL WATERS,		61	THE LONG ALLEY	67
AN EXACT FALL OF WATERS HAS RENDERED ME IMPOTENT.		86	PRAISE TO END!	46
LAVE ME, ULTIMATE WATERS.		88	PRAISE TO END!	98
BUT THE WINDS AND WATERS ARE;		125	WORDS FOR WIND	79
SMALL WATERS RUN TOWARD A MIRY HOLE--		132	SENTENTIOUS MAN	39
DARK HANGS UPON THE WATERS OF THE SOUL;		135	THE RENEWAL	8
THESE WATERS DROWSE ME INTO SLEEP SO KIND		135	THE RENEWAL	11
THE MOON DRAWS BACK ITS WATERS FROM THE SHORE.		140	THE SWAN	15
KNOWING THE SINUOUSNESS OF SMALL WATERS:		168	FOURTH MEDITATN	5
THE LONG WATERS		196	THE LONG WATERS	T
WHERE THE FRESH AND SALT WATERS MEET,		196	THE LONG WATERS	17
I SEE IN THE ADVANCING AND RETREATING WATERS		198	THE LONG WATERS	67
WINDING AROUND THE WATERS OF THE WORLD.		201	THE FAR FIELD	103
THE WATERS SWIRLING PAST THE TINY HEADLANDS.		202	THE ROSE	25
THE WINDS AND WATERS MEET.		215	HIS FOREBODING	20
I RECALL THE FALLING OF SMALL WATERS,		222	THE ABYSS	93
ALL WATERS WAVER, AND ALL FIRES FAIL.		242	THE SEQUEL	26
WATER'S				
TUFTY, THE WATER'S LOOSE.		79	GIVE WAY, GATES	6
NOW THE WATER'S LOW. THE WEEDS EXCEED ME.		86	PRAISE TO END!	23
WATER'S MY WILL, AND MY WAY,		191	AT OYSTER RIVER	63
WATERY				
--AND SOME WATERY EYES IN A COPLEY HEAD.		32	SALE	12
THAT WATERY CHEEK		56	THE LOST SON	97
SWAYING OVER THE WALKS, IN THE WATERY AIR,		61	THE LONG ALLEY	75
IN A WATERY DROWSE.		62	FIELD OF LIGHT	18
ITS SHADOWS LOOSE, A WATERY FINGER;		101	LIGHT BREATHER	10
DOWN IN THAT WATERY HOLE:		146	THE SONG	19
A MUFFLED VOICE, A LOW SWEET WATERY NOISE.		165	HER BECOMING	20
LITTLE CRABS SLIPPING INTO WATERY CRATERS--		255	LIGHT POEM	4
BIRDS TO THIS WATERY AIR?		261	THE CHANGELING	47
WAVE				
A WAVE OF TIME HANGS MOTIONLESS ON THIS PARTICULAR SHORE.		47	DOUBLE FEATURE	9
AN EYE COMES OUT OF THE WAVE.		66	SHAPE OF FIRE	60
ON A MOON-FORGOTTEN WAVE!		83	O LULL ME, LULL	13
THE PLANTS WAVE ME IN, AND THE SUMMER APPLES;		88	PRAISE TO END!	86
A SINGLE WAVE STARTS LIGHTLY AND EASILY SHOREWARD,		93	I CRY, LOVE!	46
SWAYING IN A LONG WAVE;		100	THE VISITANT	12
MAKES ALMOST A WAVE OVER A BARRIER OF SMALL STONES,		190	AT OYSTER RIVER	13
A SINGLE WAVE COMES IN LIKE THE NECK OF A GREAT SWAN		197	THE LONG WATERS	52
THE SPRAWL OF THE WAVE,		200	THE FAR FIELD	54
AS IF I SWAYED OUT ON THE WILDEST WAVE ALIVE,		205	THE ROSE	104
FOR THE GREAT LAST LEAP OF THE WAVE OVER THE BREAKWATER,		231	THE STORM	40
THE WAVE BENDS WITH THE FISH. I'M TAUGHT		260	THE CHANGELING	18
WAVE-CREST				
THEN DOWN, AS WE ROLL LIKE A BOAT FROM A WAVE-CREST.		158	FIRST MEDITATN	25
WAVED				
OF DAISIES WAVED;		51	THE WAKING (1)	14
WAVER				
WAVER OVER TO RED,		41	BIG WIND	11
ALL WATERS WAVER, AND ALL FIRES FAIL.		242	THE SEQUEL	26

	PAGE	TITLE	LINE
WAVERS			
THE MOVEMENT IS FORWARD, AFTER A FEW WAVERS, ...	158	FIRST MEDITATN	27
WAVES			
UNTIL I COULD THINK THERE WERE WAVES ROLLING HIGH AS MY			
BEDROOM FLOOR;	12	MID-CNTRY BLOW	2
SHE WAVES TO THE GOOSE, ...	60	THE LONG ALLEY	52
I'VE LISTENED INTO THE LEAST WAVES.	77	BRING THE DAY!	28
THE BEACH RISES WITH THE WAVES.	83	O LULL ME, LULL	15
THE WAVES RIPPLING NEAR ME.	104	OLD LADY'S WRDS	43
THE WAVES BROKE EASY, CRIED TO ME IN WHITE;	107	SIR JOHN DAVIES	83
SMALL WAVES REPEAT THE MIND'S SLOW SENSUAL PLAY.	131	SENTENTIOUS MAN	13
BENT DOWN THEIR BIRDS: THE LIGHT WAVES TOOK THE WAVES; ...	143	SHIMMER OF EVIL	2
BENT DOWN THEIR BIRDS: THE LIGHT WAVES TOOK THE WAVES; ...	143	SHIMMER OF EVIL	2
MY BREAST WILD AS THE WAVES.	165	HER BECOMING	10
AND WITH WATER: THE WAVES COMING FORWARD, WITHOUT CESSATION,	191	AT OYSTER RIVER	31
THE WAVES, ALTERED BY SAND-BARS, BEDS OF KELP,			
MISCELLANEOUS DRIFTWOOD,	191	AT OYSTER RIVER	32
IN AND OUT OF THE SMALL WAVES,	192	AT OYSTER RIVER	65
AND THE WAVES FLATTENING OUT WHEN THE FISHERMEN DRAG THEIR			
NETS OVER THE STONES.	194	JOURNY INTERIOR	57
DELIGHTING IN SURFACE CHANGE, THE GLITTER OF LIGHT ON WAVES,	195	JOURNY INTERIOR	67
THESE WAVES, IN THE SUN, REMIND ME OF FLOWERS:	197	THE LONG WATERS	38
MY EYES EXTEND BEYOND THE FARTHEST BLOOM OF THE WAVES; ...	198	THE LONG WATERS	75
WAKES ALL THE WAVES, ALL THEIR LOOSE WANDERING FIRE.	201	THE FAR FIELD	88
THE OLD LOG SUBSIDES WITH THE LESSENING WAVES, ...	202	THE ROSE	20
THE WAVES LESS THAN THE RIPPLES MADE BY RISING FISH, ...	203	THE ROSE	32
MOVING WITH THE WAVES, THE UNDULATING DRIFTWOOD, ...	203	THE ROSE	48
OF THE TOPPLING WAVES, ...	205	THE ROSE	95
THE DOLPHIN RISING FROM THE DARKENING WAVES;	205	THE ROSE	110
AND THE SMALL WAVES	210	HER TIME	8
BY THE SALT WAVES I HEAR A RIVER'S UNDERSONG, ...	221	THE ABYSS	76
THE WAVES NOT YET HIGH, BUT EVEN, ...	230	THE STORM	11
THE MOTION OF THE MOON, AND WAVES AT PLAY, ...	235	MANIFESTATION	7
THE GULLS, THE GULLS FAR FROM THEIR WAVES	235	ALL MORNING	36
BELOW, THE BRIGHT SEA WAS, THE LEVEL WAVES, ...	247	I WAITED	22
WAVING			
THE CHILDREN WAVING;	158	FIRST MEDITATN	52
WAXWINGS			
WITH WRENS, SPARROWS, JUNCOS, CEDAR WAXWINGS, FLICKERS,	235	ALL MORNING	41
WAY			
ONE WAY, A CHANCE TO BE SECURE:	30	THE RECKONING	10
THIS WAY! THIS WAY!	51	THE WAKING (1)	5
THIS WAY! THIS WAY!	51	THE WAKING (1)	5
WHICH IS THE WAY I TAKE;	54	THE LOST SON	25
THAT'S THE WAY IT WOULD FEEL.	55	THE LOST SON	57
THE WAY TO THE BOILER WAS DARK, ...	57	THE LOST SON	122
DARK ALL THE WAY, ...	57	THE LOST SON	123
THE REDEEMER COMES A DARK WAY.	66	SHAPE OF FIRE	63
GIVE WAY, YE GATES	79	GIVE WAY, GATES	T
I KNOW THE WAY OUT OF A LAUGH;	81	SENSIBILITY! LA	23
IT'S A LONG WAY TO SOMEWHERE ELSE.	82	SENSIBILITY! LA	38
WAY TO ANOTHER GRACE!--	83	O LULL ME, LULL	23
THAT WAY AND THIS.	104	OLD LADY'S WRDS	46
ON ITS WAY TO THE BACK PASTURE.	104	OLD LADY'S WRDS	53
IN THE SAME WAY: O WATCH HIS BODY SWAY!--	105	SIR JOHN DAVIES	11
IN THAT DARK WORLD WHERE GODS HAVE LOST THEIR WAY.	106	SIR JOHN DAVIES	48
SHE WAS THE WIND WHEN WIND WAS IN MY WAY;	107	SIR JOHN DAVIES	93
"O WHY ARE YOU FISHING THAT WAY?	117	LADY AND BEAR	2
WHY ARE YOU FISHING THAT WAY?"	117	LADY AND BEAR	4
THAT'S WHY I'M FISHING THIS WAY.	117	LADY AND BEAR	6
AND SO,--I'M FISHING THIS WAY.	117	LADY AND BEAR	8
YOU, WHEN YOU ARE FISHING THAT WAY, THAT WAY, ...	117	LADY AND BEAR	24
YOU, WHEN YOU ARE FISHING THAT WAY, THAT WAY, ...	117	LADY AND BEAR	24
WHEN YOU ARE FISHING THAT WAY."	117	LADY AND BEAR	25
AS HE WENT ON FISHING HIS WAY, HIS WAY, ...	117	LADY AND BEAR	29
AS HE WENT ON FISHING HIS WAY, HIS WAY, ...	117	LADY AND BEAR	29
AS HE WENT ON FISHING HIS WAY.	117	LADY AND BEAR	30
YOU GREEN THING IN MY WAY!"	123	WORDS FOR WIND	14
IS THERE NO WAY OUT OF THAT COURSING BLOOD?	140	THE SWAN	4
THAT DOVE'S ELABORATE WAY OF COMING NEAR	149	IN LATE SUMMER	23
IN MY WAY, CLOSE COUSIN	151	SLUG	5
BEAUTIFUL, IN ITS WAY, LIKE QUICKSILVER--	151	SLUG	22
ANOTHER WAY AND PLACE IN WHICH TO CONTINUE;	159	FIRST MEDITATN	67

		PAGE	TITLE	LINE
WAY (CONTINUED)				
THE WAY OUT OF A ROSE?		165	HER BECOMING	27
MAKING MY WAY OVER WET STONES.		166	HER BECOMING	48
SEEKING IN MY OWN WAY, ETERNAL PURPOSE;		168	FOURTH MEDITATN	2
THE WIDE STREAMS GO THEIR WAY,		172	WHAT TELL BONES	49
SOME TIME I THINK I'LL LIVE THAT WAY.		182	THE HIPPO	5
WATER'S MY WILL, AND MY WAY,		191	AT OYSTER RIVER	63
THE WAY BLOCKED AT LAST BY A FALLEN FIR-TREE,		193	JOURNY INTERIOR	15
NEITHER WHITE NOR RED, IN THE DEAD MIDDLE WAY,		197	THE LONG WATERS	56
WHERE THE SALMON EASE THEIR WAY INTO THE KELP BEDS,		205	THE ROSE	96
AND SO SHE WAS, IN HER WAY, AUNT TILLY.		223	ELEGY (2)	3
THE WAY I TIPPED MY HAT.		225	THE CHUMS	8
THE MOLE MAKING ITS WAY THROUGH DARKEST GROUND,		235	MANIFESTATION	4
WHICH IS THE WAY? I CRY TO THE DREAD BLACK,		245	THE DECISION	9
WHICH IS THE WAY? I ASK, AND TURN TO GO,		245	THE DECISION	11
FROM ME TO THEE'S A LONG AND TERRIBLE WAY.		246	THE MARROW	18
THE WAY GREW STEEPER BETWEEN STONY WALLS,		247	I WAITED	19
DO THE DEAD WAKE IN THEIR OWN WAY?		259	SONG (3)	32
OUT HEMLOCK WAY THERE IS A STREAM		267	SAGINAW SONG	7
WAYS				
COME, COME OUT OF THE SHADE, THE COOL WAYS,		61	THE LONG ALLEY	69
THE FERNS HAD THEIR WAYS, AND THE PULSING LIZARDS,		63	FIELD OF LIGHT	41
AH, WHEN SHE MOVED, SHE MOVED MORE WAYS THAN ONE:		127	I KNEW A WOMAN	3
THESE OLD BONES LIVE TO LEARN HER WANTON WAYS:		127	I KNEW A WOMAN	27
I KNOW HER CARELESS WAYS!--		130	THE OTHER	21
HAVE I FORGOTTEN THEIR WAYS--		139	PLAINT	14
BRING ME THE MEEK, FOR I WOULD KNOW THEIR WAYS;		149	IN LATE SUMMER	5
THAN HER WAYS WITH A MAN?		212	LIGHT LISTENED	2
BUT THEY'VE WAYS OF INDICATING WHEN		267	SAGINAW SONG	15
WE (149)				
WEAK				
WEAK AS A WHIFFET;		44	FRAU BAUMAN	29
AND THE WEAK BRIDEGROOM STRENGTHENS IN HIS BRIDE.		132	SENTENTIOUS MAN	42
IN THE WEAK LIGHT THEY WANDER, EACH ALONE.		149	IN LATE SUMMER	4
THE BLEAK WIND EATS AT THE WEAK PLATEAU,		157	FIRST MEDITATN	11
FROM THE QUARRY'S WEAK CRY.		236	SONG (2)	4
BOTH MOTH AND FLAME? THE WEAK MOTH BLUNDERING BY.		241	THE SEQUEL	6
WEAKLY				
THE BULB GOES ON AND OFF, WEAKLY.		231	THE STORM	36
WEAR				
MYSELF IS WHAT I WEAR:		3	OPEN HOUSE	11
SOON FIELD AND WOOD WILL WEAR AN APRIL LOOK,		11	LIGHT BRIGHTER	13
WHEN MICE WITH WINGS CAN WEAR A HUMAN FACE.		16	THE BAT	10
THE BOLD WEAR TOUGHENED SKIN		20	REPL TO CENSURE	13
HIS INSOLENCE COULD WEAR NO PATIENCE THIN.		28	THE FAVORITE	7
MAD IN THE WIND I WEAR		123	WORDS FOR WIND	5
I WEAR THE LEADEN WEIGHT		154	THE DYING MAN	19
BUT THESE ROSES: I CAN WEAR THEM BY LOOKING AWAY.		163	I'M HERE	78
WEARING				
FINALLY VEERING, WEARING THEMSELVES OUT, MERELY		41	BIG WIND	30
WEASEL				
THE FURY OF THE HATE-DRIVEN ZEALOT, THE MEANNESS OF THE HUMAN WEASEL;		170	FOURTH MEDITATN	68
WEASELS				
WITH BATS, WEASELS, WORMS--I REJOICE IN THE KINSHIP.		151	SLUG	26
WORSE THAN CASTOREUM OF MINK OR WEASELS,		187	THE LONGING	4
WEATHER				
TO KEEP INCLEMENT WEATHER FROM ITS YOUNG.		12	SLOW SEASON	6
LIKE THAT CLEAR AUTUMNAL WEATHER OF ETERNITY,		43	CARNATIONS	6
THE WHITE WEATHER HATES ME.		77	BRING THE DAY!	22
IN THE RICH WEATHER OF A DAPPLED WOOD		107	SIR JOHN DAVIES	65
O WHAT'S THE WEATHER IN A BEARD?		114	DINKY	1
THE WEATHER WEPT, AND ALL THE TREES BENT DOWN;		143	SHIMMER OF EVIL	1
MY SKIN WHITER IN THE SOFT WEATHER,		162	I'M HERE	43
WHAT'S WEATHER TO ME? EVEN CARP DIE IN THIS RIVER.		164	I'M HERE	90
WHAT WEATHER OF HEAVEN IS THIS?"		208	HER WORDS	11
AND WATCHED THE WEATHER FLOW.		212	LIGHT LISTENED	11
WEATHER-BEATEN				
THEIR WOODEN STORES OF SILVERY PINE AND WEATHER-BEATEN RED COURTHOUSES,		193	JOURNY INTERIOR	31
WEATHER'S				
ROCK ME TO SLEEP, THE WEATHER'S WRONG.		86	PRAISE TO END!	28

	PAGE	TITLE	LINE
WEAVE			
THE BATS WEAVE IN AND OUT OF THE WILLOWS, ...	93	I CRY, LOVE!	41
WEAVES			
THE GARDEN SPIDER WEAVES A SILKEN PEAR	12	SLOW SEASON	5
WEB			
A WIND STIRRED IN A WEB OF APPLEWORMS;	101	THE VISITANT	26
WEBBY			
WITH WIDE WEBBY TOES	55	THE LOST SON	59
OH, WHAT A WEBBY WONDER I AM!	98	O, THOU OPENING	47
WEBS			
WEBS AND WEEDS, ...	39	WEED PULLER	5
WE'D			
THE ONLY THING WE'D HAVE FOR PROOF	178	THE CEILING	3
WEDGE			
A WEDGE OF HEAVEN'S LIGHT, AUTUMNAL SONG.	173	WHAT TELL BONES	68
WEED			
WEED PULLER	39	WEED PULLER	T
OR SCOOP OUT A WEED CLOSE TO FLOURISHING ROOTS, ...	42	OLD FLORIST	6
A LONG WEED FLOATED UPWARD;	62	FIELD OF LIGHT	5
TETHERED TO A LIMP WEED, SWINGING, ...	101	LIGHT BREATHER	8
SWAYING IN AIR, LIKE SOME LONG WATER WEED.	241	THE SEQUEL	19
WEEDS			
"LONG LIVE THE WEEDS"	18	LONG LIVE WEEDS	T
LONG LIVE THE WEEDS THAT OVERWHELM	18	LONG LIVE WEEDS	1
WEBS AND WEEDS, ...	39	WEED PULLER	5
ME DOWN IN THAT FETOR OF WEEDS, ...	39	WEED PULLER	14
MOLDS, WEEDS, DEAD LEAVES, ...	43	FLOWER DUMP	5
LICE TETHERED TO LONG LIMP SUBTERRANEAN WEEDS, ...	50	THE MINIMAL	4
THE WEEDS WHINED, ...	55	THE LOST SON	79
WHERE THE WEEDS SLEPT.	57	THE LOST SON	129
EVEN THE HUSHED FORMS, THE BENT YELLOWY WEEDS	57	THE LOST SON	147
THE BONES OF WEEDS KEPT SWINGING IN THE WIND, ...	58	THE LOST SON	152
THE WEEDS STOPPED SWINGING.	58	THE LOST SON	161
THE WEEDS BELIEVED ME, AND THE NESTING BIRDS.	63	FIELD OF LIGHT	47
A LOW MOUTH LAPS WATER. WEEDS, WEEDS, HOW I LOVE YOU.	64	SHAPE OF FIRE	17
A LOW MOUTH LAPS WATER. WEEDS, WEEDS, HOW I LOVE YOU.	64	SHAPE OF FIRE	17
INTO THAT MINNOWY WORLD OF WEEDS AND DITCHES, ...	66	SHAPE OF FIRE	65
NOW THE WATER'S LOW. THE WEEDS EXCEED ME.	86	PRAISE TO END!	23
THE WEEDS HISS AT THE EDGE OF THE FIELD.	157	FIRST MEDITATN	2
SETTLING IN SMALL BEADS AROUND WEEDS AND SUNKEN BRANCHES,	159	FIRST MEDITATN	61
WEEDS TURN TOWARD THE WIND WEED-SKELETONS.	173	WHAT TELL BONES	65
UNDERNEATH, THE SLUGGISH WATER RUNNING BETWEEN WEEDS,			
BROKEN WHEELS, TIRES, STONES.	194	JOURNY INTERIOR	33
I LIVE WITH THE ROCKS, THEIR WEEDS, ...	205	THE ROSE	89
OR DRIFT LAZILY IN AND OUT OF THE WEEDS.	233	THE PIKE	7
WEEDS'			
I LISTEN TO THE WEEDS' VESPERAL WHINE, ...	171	WHAT TELL BONES	12
WEED-SKELETONS			
WEEDS TURN TOWARD THE WIND WEED-SKELETONS.	173	WHAT TELL BONES	65
WEEDY			
DOWN WOODEN STEPS TOWARD A WEEDY GARDEN;	162	I'M HERE	46
THE WEEDY EDGE, ALIVE WITH SMALL SNAKES AND BLOODSUCKERS,--	200	THE FAR FIELD	70
WEEK			
AS THE BIRDS FLEW OFF TO THE END OF NEXT WEEK.	115	THE SERPENT	26
IN A BLEAK TIME, WHEN A WEEK OF RAIN IS A YEAR, ...	187	THE LONGING	14
BUT I SACKED THE PRESUMPTUOUS HAG THE NEXT WEEK, ...	228	THE GERANIUM	25
THE WEEK AFTER."	229	ON THE QUAY	6
WEEKS			
LIKE A NURSE HE SAT WITH ME FOR WEEKS, A SLY SURLY			
ATTENDANT, ...	220	THE ABYSS	38
WEEP			
AGING, I SOMETIMES WEEP, ...	130	THE OTHER	23
I WEEP FOR WHAT I'M LIKE WHEN I'M ALONE	132	SENTENTIOUS MAN	33
WEEPING			
WENT WEEPING, LITTLE BONES. BUT WHERE?	92	I CRY, LOVE!	1
THE OYSTER'S WEEPING FOOT, ...	125	WORDS FOR WIND	86
THE SHAPE THAT CAME FROM MY SLEEP, WEEPING:	198	THE LONG WATERS	68
A LORD OF NATURE WEEPING TO A TREE.	239	IN A DARK TIME	4
WEIGHT			
THE HAMMER'S WEIGHT.	9	THE ADAMANT	8
I HAVE MYSELF AN INNER WEIGHT OF WOE	144	ELEGY (1)	3
I HAVE MYSELF AN INNER WEIGHT OF WOE	144	ELEGY (1)	7
I HAVE MYSELF, AND BEAR ITS WEIGHT OF WOE	144	ELEGY (1)	15

	PAGE	TITLE	LINE
WEIGHT (CONTINUED)			
I WEAR THE LEADEN WEIGHT	154	THE DYING MAN	19
WEIGHTLESS			
I FEEL A WEIGHTLESS CHANGE, A MOVING FORWARD	200	THE FAR FIELD	58
WEIRD			
IT'S WINDY THERE, AND RATHER WEIRD,	114	DINKY	2
WELL			
PERFORM YOUR DUTIES WELL,	7	ORDERS FOR DAY	2
HOW WELL HER WISHES WENT! SHE STROKED MY CHIN,	127	I KNEW A WOMAN	8
IT IS DIFFICULT TO SAY ALL THINGS ARE WELL,	172	WHAT TELL BONES	34
ON THE BULLHEAD, IN THE DAKOTAS, WHERE THE EAGLES EAT WELL,	188	THE LONGING	52
WHEN HATTIE WRIGHT'S ANGORA DIED AS WELL,	224	OTTO	29
HE TOO HAS EATEN WELL--	226	THE LIZARD	1
A THORN DOES WELL IN THE WIND,	262	FOLLIES OF ADAM	13
YOU ARE NOT ACTING WELL:	267	SAGINAW SONG	16
WE'LL			
WAKE ME, WITCH, WE'LL DO THE DANCE OF ROTTEN STICKS.	64	SHAPE OF FIRE	10
WE'LL SWINGE THE INSTANT!--	79	GIVE WAY, GATES	26
WE'LL STRETCH WITH THE GREAT STEMS.	80	GIVE WAY, GATES	35
WE'LL BE AT THE BUSINESS OF WHAT MIGHT BE	80	GIVE WAY, GATES	36
WE'LL SAIL AWAY FROM THE FRIGHTFUL SHORE	272	DUET	9
WE'LL GIVE EACH OTHER A BOX ON THE EAR,	272	DUET	25
WELL-CURB			
MAKING A SLOW JOURNEY AROUND THE WELL-CURB.	151	SLUG	3
WELL-GROOMED			
AS DARKNESS CREEPS UP ON THE WELL-GROOMED SUBURBAN TOWN,	33	IDYLL	5
WELLS			
TOADS BROODING WELLS.	53	THE LOST SON	4
WELL-UPHOLSTERED			
ON WELL-UPHOLSTERED BUMS	31	LULL	10
WELTER			
WELTER OF TIN CANS, PAILS, OLD BIRD NESTS, A CHILD'S SHOE RIDING A LOG,	191	AT OYSTER RIVER	54
A DRIED STALK IN A WELTER OF SINUOUS GRASSES,	255	LIGHT POEM	8
WENCH			
I NAME THEE: WENCH OF THINGS,	81	SENSIBILITY! LA	6
I'M A ROARING GIRL, AN EXPENSIVE WENCH,	272	DUET	15
WENT			
BUT SOMETHING ALWAYS WENT OUT OF ME WHEN I DUG LOOSE THOSE CARPETS	40	MOSS-GATHERING	7
A PATH WENT WALKING.	63	THE LONG ALLEY	33
HER EYES WENT KISSING AWAY	72	WHERE KNOCK IS	36
WE WENT BY THE RIVER.	73	WHERE KNOCK IS	53
WATER BIRDS WENT CHING. WENT CHING.	73	WHERE KNOCK IS	54
WATER BIRDS WENT CHING. WENT CHING.	73	WHERE KNOCK IS	54
WENT TO VISIT THE WIND. WHERE THE BIRDS DIE.	73	WHERE KNOCK IS	72
WENT DOWN CELLAR,	74	I NEED, I NEED	8
WENT WEEPING, LITTLE BONES. BUT WHERE?	92	I CRY, LOVE!	1
WHEN I WENT TO SEA IN A SIGH,	103	OLD LADY'S WRDS	23
THE BOYS I KNEW WHEN I WENT TO POT;	111	SQUEEZE-BOX	2
AS HE WENT ON FISHING HIS WAY, HIS WAY,	117	LADY AND BEAR	29
AS HE WENT ON FISHING HIS WAY.	117	LADY AND BEAR	30
HOW WELL HER WISHES WENT! SHE STROKED MY CHIN,	127	I KNEW A WOMAN	8
THOSE NOTES WENT, LIKE THE BIRD,	128	THE VOICE	8
THERE WAS A THICKET WHERE I WENT TO DIE,	132	SENTENTIOUS MAN	21
I WENT RUNNING DOWN A ROAD,	146	THE SONG	8
SUPPOSE THE CEILING WENT OUTSIDE	178	THE CEILING	1
I WENT, NOT LOOKING BACK. I WAS AFRAID.	247	I WAITED	18
I WENT TO SHUNDAY SHULE;	267	SAGINAW SONG	26
I WENT FISHING WITH A PIN	269	GOB MUSIC	20
WEPT			
THE WEATHER WEPT, AND ALL THE TREES BENT DOWN;	143	SHIMMER OF EVIL	1
AND I WEPT THERE, ALONE.	145	THE BEAST	19
WERE (27.)			
WE'RE			
WE'RE KING AND QUEEN OF THE RIGHT GROUND.	79	GIVE WAY, GATES	22
I FEEL WE'RE BREATHING WITH THE DEAD;	136	THE SENSUALISTS	5
--HEIGHO, WE'RE HUGH AND HARRY!	181	MONOTONY SONG	8
WE'RE GETTING CLOSER TO IT ALL THE TIME."	274	SUPPR W LINDSAY	45
WERT			
THOU WERT MARMOREAN-BORN.	81	SENSIBILITY! LA	5
WEST			
NOW AS THE TRAIN BEARS WEST,	34	NIGHT JOURNEY	1

	PAGE	TITLE	LINE
WEST (CONTINUED)			
WITH A WIND FROM THE WEST AND THE TREES ALL IN MOTION. ...	158	FIRST MEDITATN	42
WESTERN			
OF WESTERN LIGHT LEAPS WITH INTENSER BLAZE	17	UNEXTINGUISHED	2
ALONE, ON A BUS THROUGH WESTERN COUNTRY.	158	FIRST MEDITATN	21
YOU BIRDS, YOU WESTERN BIRDS.	167	HER BECOMING	79
WET			
FLINGING LONG STRINGS OF WET ACROSS THE ROOF-TOP,	41	BIG WIND	29
AND THE AIR COOL, AS IF DRIFTING DOWN FROM WET HEMLOCKS,	43	CARNATIONS	3
THEIR HANDS TWINKLING WITH WET;	44	FRAU BAUMAN	18
I FEEL THE SLIME OF A WET NEST.	55	THE LOST SON	68
STEPPED IN WET. OVER STONES.	73	WHERE KNOCK IS	55
WITHOUT BRUSHING THE WET STONES,	100	THE VISITANT	16
STILL WET FROM ITS BUD-SHEATH,	101	LIGHT BREATHER	4
THE SIDES OF WET STONES CANNOT CONSOLE ME,	102	ELEGY FOR JANE	16
LIKE A WET LOG, I SANG WITHIN A FLAME.	120	THE DREAM	30
I KNOW IT ISN'T A WET LEAF,	151	SLUG	9
CREEPING SLOWLY OVER THE WET GRASS,	151	SLUG	13
A FUME REMINDS ME, DRIFTING ACROSS WET GRAVEL;	160	FIRST MEDITATN	91
THE GLITTER OF WET IN THE FIRST OF MORNING?	161	I'M HERE	3
MAKING MY WAY OVER WET STONES.	166	HER BECOMING	48
I'M WET WITH ANOTHER LIFE.	173	WHAT TELL BONES	95
OR, WITH SKINNY KNEES, TO SIT ASTRIDE A WET LOG,	200	THE FAR FIELD	45
WETNESS			
A BEACHY WETNESS.	162	I'M HERE	57
WETTER			
THE GRAVEL, MY NOSE WETTER THAN HIS.	151	SLUG	7
WE'VE			
"LET'S EAT!" SAID LINDSAY. "HERE WE'VE GOT THE MOON,	273	SUPPR W LINDSAY	15
WE'VE GOT THE LIVING LIGHT, BUT WHERE'S THE FOOD?"	273	SUPPR W LINDSAY	16
WHACK			
THEY BOUGHT A DRUM. HE WOULDN'T WHACK IT.	115	THE SERPENT	14
WHALE			
THE WHALE	178	THE WHALE	T
THERE WAS A MOST MONSTROUS WHALE:	178	THE WHALE	1
I HAVE LEFT THE BODY OF THE WHALE, BUT THE MOUTH OF THE NIGHT IS STILL WIDE;	188	THE LONGING	51
WHAT			
MYSELF IS WHAT I WEAR:	3	OPEN HOUSE	11
WHAT WE HAD HOPED FOR HAD NOT COME TO PASS.	6	INTERLUDE	12
WE WALK AWARE OF WHAT IS FAR AND CLOSE.	13	PRAISE PRAIRIE	10
WE ARE AFRAID OF WHAT OUR EYES HAVE SEEN:	16	THE BAT	8
I DID NOT MOVE TO CLAIM WHAT WAS MY OWN.	21	THE AUCTION	4
WHAT SHAKES MY SKULL TO DISREPAIR	22	SILENCE	19
THE STETHOSCOPE TELLS WHAT EVERYONE FEARS:	23	ACADEMIC	1
"O TELL ME, WIDOW LADY, WHAT IS IT THAT YOU SEE,	27	CLAIRVOY WIDOW	3
ALONE, HIS WIFE IS GRIEVING FOR WHAT HER HEART DESIRES.	27	CLAIRVOY WIDOW	14
WHAT WE ARE SEEKING IS A FARE	30	THE RECKONING	9
THE LACK THAT KEEPS US WHAT WE ARE,	30	THE RECKONING	11
WHO FLEE IN WHAT THEIR HANDS HAVE MADE.	33	HIGHWAY: MICH	15
WHAT SAINT STRAINED SO MUCH,	37	CUTTINGS (LATE)	3
AND WHAT A CONGRESS OF STINKS!--	38	ROOT CELLAR	6
OUT OF WHAT DOOR DO I GO,	54	THE LOST SON	26
WHAT A SMALL SONG. WHAT SLOW CLOUDS. WHAT DARK WATER.	56	THE LOST SON	83
WHAT A SMALL SONG. WHAT SLOW CLOUDS. WHAT DARK WATER.	56	THE LOST SON	83
WHAT A SMALL SONG. WHAT SLOW CLOUDS. WHAT DARK WATER.	56	THE LOST SON	83
WHAT GLIDING SHAPE	56	THE LOST SON	88
WHAT DO THE CLOUDS SAY?	56	THE LOST SON	117
THIS SLAG RUNS SLOW. WHAT BLEEDS WHEN METAL BREAKS?	59	THE LONG ALLEY	11
WHO ELSE BREATHES HERE? WHAT DOES THE GRAVE SAY?	59	THE LONG ALLEY	19
THE FIEND'S FAR AWAY. LORD, WHAT DO YOU REQUIRE?	59	THE LONG ALLEY	21
LOOK WHAT THE LARKS DO.	59	THE LONG ALLEY	28
SO UP AND AWAY AND WHAT DO WE DO	60	THE LONG ALLEY	37
WHAT DO WE DO	60	THE LONG ALLEY	57
THAT WAS A CLOSE KNOCK. SEE WHAT THE WILL WANTS.	61	THE LONG ALLEY	62
WHAT FISH-WAYS YOU HAVE, LITTLEST FLOWERS,	61	THE LONG ALLEY	74
NUTS ARE MONEY: WHEREFORE AND WHAT ELSE?	61	THE LONG ALLEY	82
MOTHER ME OUT OF HERE. WHAT MORE WILL THE BONES ALLOW? ...	64	SHAPE OF FIRE	7
I KNOW WHAT YOU IS:	75	I NEED, I NEED	28
WHAT WATER DOES?	76	I NEED, I NEED	65
THE GRASS SAYS WHAT THE WIND SAYS:	77	BRING THE DAY!	29
WE'LL BE AT THE BUSINESS OF WHAT MIGHT BE	80	GIVE WAY, GATES	36
LOOKING TOWARD WHAT WE ARE.	80	GIVE WAY, GATES	37

		PAGE	TITLE	LINE
WHAT (CONTINUED)				
WHAT BEATS IN ME		80	GIVE WAY, GATES	57
WHAT SLIDES AWAY		80	GIVE WAY, GATES	61
A WHISPER OF WHAT,		81	SENSIBILITY! LA	16
I SEE WHAT SINGS!		84	O LULL ME, LULL	40
WHAT SINGS!		84	O LULL ME, LULL	41
WHAT A BONE-ACHE I HAVE.		85	PRAISE TO END!	3
WHAT FOOTIE DOES IS FINAL.		86	PRAISE TO END!	34
WHAT FOOTIE DOES IS FINAL.		86	PRAISE TO END!	38
WHAT FOOTIE WILL DO WILL BE FINAL.		86	PRAISE TO END!	42
WHAT A WHELM OF PROVERBS, MR. PINCH!		89	UNFOLD! UNFOLD!	18
EASY THE LIFE OF THE MOUTH. WHAT A LUST FOR RIPENESS!		90	UNFOLD! UNFOLD!	39
WHAT ELSE HAS THE VINE LOOSENED?		90	UNFOLD! UNFOLD!	43
WHAT GRACE I HAVE IS ENOUGH.		91	UNFOLD! UNFOLD!	60
WHAT THE GRAVE SAYS,		91	UNFOLD! UNFOLD!	63
WHAT ELSE CAN BEFALL?		92	I CRY, LOVE!	4
I'M LOST IN WHAT I HAVE.		97	O, THOU OPENING	8
HEAR THE SIGH OF WHAT IS.		98	O, THOU OPENING	35
OH, WHAT A WEBBY WONDER I AM!		98	O, THOU OPENING	47
SEE WHAT THE SWEET HARP SAYS.		99	O, THOU OPENING	73
UNAFRAID OF WHAT IT IS,		101	LIGHT BREATHER	15
BUT WHAT I LEARNED THERE, DANCING ALL ALONE,		105	SIR JOHN DAVIES	17
I FIND MYSELF PERPLEXED. WHAT IS DESIRE?--		105	SIR JOHN DAVIES	26
DO WHAT THE CLUMSY PARTNER WANTS TO DO!		106	SIR JOHN DAVIES	42
O WHAT LEWD MUSIC CREPT INTO OUR EARS!		106	SIR JOHN DAVIES	46
ATTENDED WHAT WE DID. BEHIND, BEFORE,		106	SIR JOHN DAVIES	50
WHAT SHAPE LEAPED FORWARD AT THE SENSUAL CRY?--		107	SIR JOHN DAVIES	67
DID BEATRICE DENY WHAT DANTE SAW?		107	SIR JOHN DAVIES	76
RAPT, WE LEANED FORTH WITH WHAT WE COULD NOT SEE.		107	SIR JOHN DAVIES	88
I FEEL MY FATE IN WHAT I CANNOT FEAR.		108	THE WAKING (2)	2
WE THINK BY FEELING. WHAT IS THERE TO KNOW?		108	THE WAKING (2)	4
WHAT FALLS AWAY IS ALWAYS. AND IS NEAR.		108	THE WAKING (2)	17
"I AM WHAT IS KNOWN AS A BIDDLY BEAR,--		117	LADY AND BEAR	5
WHAT DO THE GREAT DEAD SAY?		123	WORDS FOR WIND	10
WHAT TIME'S MY HEART? I CARE.		125	WORDS FOR WIND	75
I CHERISH WHAT I HAVE		125	WORDS FOR WIND	76
WHAT FALLS AWAY WILL FALL;		125	WORDS FOR WIND	80
ARE PART OF WHAT SHE IS.		125	WORDS FOR WIND	88
WHEN I DO WHAT SHE DOES:		126	WORDS FOR WIND	96
(BUT WHAT PRODIGIOUS MOWING WE DID MAKE).		127	I KNEW A WOMAN	14
MY LADY LAUGHS, DELIGHTING IN WHAT IS.		129	SHE	2
STAYED BY WHAT WAS, AND PULLED BY WHAT WOULD BE.		129	SHE	16
STAYED BY WHAT WAS, AND PULLED BY WHAT WOULD BE.		129	SHE	16
WHAT IS SHE, WHILE I LIVE?--		130	THE OTHER	1
IS SHE WHAT I BECOME?		130	THE OTHER	7
I WEEP FOR WHAT I'M LIKE WHEN I'M ALONE		132	SENTENTIOUS MAN	33
WHAT BOOK, O LEARNED MAN, WILL SET ME RIGHT?		133	THE PURE FURY	2
WHAT GLORIES WOULD WE? MOTIONS OF THE SOUL?		135	THE RENEWAL	1
MY DARLING DOES WHAT I COULD NEVER DO:		140	THE SWAN	6
WE THINK TOO LONG IN TERMS OF WHAT TO BE;		140	THE SWAN	8
AND SHE IS WHAT I WOULD. IN THIS LIGHT AIR,		140	THE SWAN	17
WHAT YOU SURVIVED I SHALL BELIEVE: THE HEAT,		144	ELEGY (1)	13
WHAT HAVE I DONE TO YOU?		146	THE SONG	4
WHAT RUSTLES IN THE FERN?		148	THE SMALL	13
WHAT MOVES IN GRASS I LOVE--		148	THE SMALL	21
WHAT IS THERE FOR THE SOUL TO UNDERSTAND?		149	IN LATE SUMMER	9
WHAT NOW?		154	THE DYING MAN	ST
OF WHAT I DID NOT DO.		154	THE DYING MAN	20
WHAT SENSUAL EYE CAN KEEP AN IMAGE PURE,		154	THE DYING MAN	43
WHAT'S SEEN RECEDES; FOREVER'S WHAT WE KNOW!--		156	THE DYING MAN	91
WHAT ELSE CAN I STEAL FROM SLEEP?		166	HER BECOMING	34
WHAT WAS I RUNNING FROM?		166	HER BECOMING	62
WHAT LOVER KEEPS HIS SONG?		167	HER BECOMING	82
WHAT IS IT TO BE A WOMAN?		169	FOURTH MEDITATN	27
WHAT DO THEIR LIVES MEAN,		169	FOURTH MEDITATN	42
WHAT DO THEY NEED?		169	FOURTH MEDITATN	50
BEGUILE ME, CHANGE. WHAT HAVE I FALLEN FROM?		170	FOURTH MEDITATN	77
IS MY BODY SPEAKING? I BREATHE WHAT I AM:		170	FOURTH MEDITATN	85
WHAT CAN I TELL MY BONES?		171	WHAT TELL BONES	T
THE SOUL KNOWS NOT WHAT TO BELIEVE,		171	WHAT TELL BONES	3
LOVED HEART, WHAT CAN I SAY?		172	WHAT TELL BONES	38
MIST ALTERS THE ROCKS. WHAT CAN I TELL MY BONES?		172	WHAT TELL BONES	44
TO WHAT MORE VAST PERMISSION HAVE I COME?		173	WHAT TELL BONES	72

		PAGE	TITLE	LINE
WHAT (CONTINUED)				
WHAT CAME TO ME VAGUELY IS NOW CLEAR,		173	WHAT TELL BONES	97
WHAT HER FRIENDS COULDN'T EAT AT THOSE LUNCHES!		179	MYRTLE'S COUSIN	10
OH WHAT! OH WHAT WHAT CAN I DO?"		182	PHILANDER	5
OH WHAT! OH WHAT WHAT CAN I DO?"		182	PHILANDER	5
OH WHAT! OH WHAT WHAT CAN I DO?"		182	PHILANDER	5
WHAT DREAM'S ENOUGH TO BREATHE IN? A DARK DREAM.		188	THE LONGING	28
BUT WHAT OF HER?--		196	THE LONG WATERS	24
WHAT I LOVE IS NEAR AT HAND,		201	THE FAR FIELD	80
WHAT NEED FOR HEAVEN, THEN,		203	THE ROSE	56
WHAT DO THEY TELL US, SOUND AND SILENCE?		204	THE ROSE	58
AND I REJOICED IN BEING WHAT I WAS:		205	THE ROSE	106
WHAT CAN THE SPIRIT BELIEVE?--		207	THE YOUNG GIRL	1
WHAT WEATHER OF HEAVEN IS THIS?"		208	HER WORDS	11
O WHAT COULD BE MORE NICE		212	LIGHT LISTENED	1
WE LIVE BY WHAT WE DO.		212	LIGHT LISTENED	12
WHAT SPEECH ABIDES?		220	THE ABYSS	25
BETWEEN THE SPIRIT AND THE FLESH,--WHAT WAR?		223	ELEGY (2)	5
WHAT ROOT OF HIS EVER DENIED ITS STEM?		224	OTTO	10
HE ALWAYS KNEW WHAT HE WAS AIMING AT.		224	OTTO	17
WHAT THEY SAY ON THE QUAY IS,		229	ON THE QUAY	1
TRAILING A THING--WHAT WAS IT?--SMALL AS A LARK		232	THE THING	2
WHAT A SCUTTLING AND RAPPING ALONG THE DRAINPIPES,		234	ALL MORNING	21
WHAT DOES WHAT IT SHOULD DO NEEDS NOTHING MORE.		235	MANIFESTATION	9
WHAT DOES WHAT IT SHOULD DO NEEDS NOTHING MORE.		235	MANIFESTATION	9
WHAT ELSE TO SAY?		238	THE MOMENT	13
AND WHAT DIED WITH US WAS THE WILL TO DIE.		238	THE TRANCED	25
OR WINDING PATH? THE EDGE IS WHAT I HAVE.		239	IN A DARK TIME	12
A MAN GOES FAR TO FIND OUT WHAT HE IS--		239	IN A DARK TIME	16
HOW SLOWLY DARK COMES DOWN ON WHAT WE DO.		240	IN EVEING AIR	24
LEAVES, LEAVES, LEAN FORTH AND TELL ME WHAT I AM;		242	THE SEQUEL	27
WHAT WE PUT DOWN, MUST WE TAKE UP AGAIN?		243	THE MOTION	11
WHAT SHAKES THE EYE BUT THE INVISIBLE?		245	THE DECISION	1
WHAT BURNS ME NOW? DESIRE, DESIRE, DESIRE.		246	THE MARROW	12
UPON THAT GOD WHO KNOWS WHAT I WOULD KNOW.		246	THE MARROW	24
TAKES TO HIMSELF WHAT MYSTERY HE CAN,		250	THE RIGHT THING	15
WILLS WHAT HE WOULD, SURRENDERING HIS WILL		250	THE RIGHT THING	17
WHAT CAN BE KNOWN? THE UNKNOWN.		251	ONCE MORE, RND	2
WHAT THE FAT LEAVES HAVE,--		258	SONG (3)	11
THE EDGE IS WHAT WE HAVE.		258	SONG (3)	25
BY WHAT REMINDED?		260	THE CHANGELING	3
SWAYS ME AWAKE. WHAT HO, AND THE FIELD'S MY FRIEND,		260	THE CHANGELING	14
SAD THE SOUL'S JOY. LOVED HEART, WHAT ELSE CAN I SAY		261	THE CHANGELING	28
REMEMBER WHAT IT WAS		262	FOLLIES OF ADAM	3
WHAT ARE SCEPTER AND CROWN?		262	FOLLIES OF ADAM	8
NO MORE THAN WHAT IS RAISED		262	FOLLIES OF ADAM	9
WHAT EAGLE NEEDS A TREE?		263	FOLLIES OF ADAM	26
HE DOES WHAT DOVES AND SPARROWS DO--		264	THREE EPIGRAMS	15
WHAT ELSE HE DOES IS UP TO YOU.		264	THREE EPIGRAMS	16
AND WHAT DO YOU THINK I SAW?--		269	GOB MUSIC	25
I STARED AND STARED, AND WHAT DO YOU THINK?		269	GOB MUSIC	30
LUCK! LUCK! THAT'S WHAT I CARE FOR IN A CAGE		273	SUPPR W LINDSAY	2
AND WHAT FOOL WOULDN'T, WHEN THINGS FROM SLEEP		273	SUPPR W LINDSAY	3
"WHAT MOON?" HE CRIED, HALF-TURNING IN MOCK FURY.		273	SUPPR W LINDSAY	10
BUT WHAT WE ATE I CAN'T REMEMBER QUITE:		274	SUPPR W LINDSAY	31
WHATEVER				
WHATEVER HE SMELLED WAS GOOD:		46	PICKLE BELT	5
WHATEVER I OWED TO TIME		49	RIVER INCIDENT	4
WHATEVER WAS, STILL IS,		125	WORDS FOR WIND	70
I SANG TO WHATEVER HAD BEEN		146	THE SONG	18
BE SURE THAT WHATEVER YOU ARE IS YOU		177	KITTY-CAT BIRD	20
AND IN A WOOD HE KNEW WHATEVER MOVED;		224	OTTO	13
VITAMINS, WATER, AND WHATEVER		228	THE GERANIUM	7
WHAT-NOT				
THE WHAT-NOT, THE SETTEE, THE CHIPPENDALE CHAIRS		32	SALE	3
WHAT'S				
ALL THE WINDOWS ARE BURNING! WHAT'S LEFT OF MY LIFE?		56	THE LOST SON	106
WHAT'S THIS? A DISH FOR FAT LIPS.		64	SHAPE OF FIRE	1
WHAT'S THE TIME, PAPA-SEED?		72	WHERE KNOCK IS	20
WHAT'S ALL THE SINGING BETWEEN?--		77	BRING THE DAY!	26
WHAT'S A THICK? TWO-BY-TWO'S A SHAPE.		92	I CRY, LOVE!	10
O FOR SOME MINSTREL OF WHAT'S TO BE,		103	OLD LADY'S WRDS	6
THE LIVING ALL ASSEMBLE! WHAT'S THE CUE?--		106	SIR JOHN DAVIES	41

	PAGE	TITLE	LINE
WHAT'S (CONTINUED)			
O WHAT'S THE WEATHER IN A BEARD?	114	DINKY	1
WHAT'S HELL BUT A COLD HEART?	122	ALL EARTH, AIR	28
WHAT'S FREEDOM FOR? TO KNOW ETERNITY.	127	I KNEW A WOMAN	24
WHAT'S THAT PECULIAR SMELL?	136	THE SENSUALISTS	14
"WHAT'S DONE IS YET TO COME;	153	THE DYING MAN	6
WHAT'S BEATING AT THE GATE?	154	THE DYING MAN	34
WHAT'S SEEN RECEDES; FOREVER'S WHAT WE KNOW!--	156	THE DYING MAN	91
WHAT'S LEFT IS LIGHT AS A SEED;	157	FIRST MEDITATN	18
WHAT'S BEYOND NEVER CRUMBLES LIKE AN EMBANKMENT,	159	FIRST MEDITATN	76
WHAT'S WEATHER TO ME? EVEN CARP DIE IN THIS RIVER.	164	I'M HERE	90
SOFT, SOFT, THE SNOW'S NOT FALLING. WHAT'S A SEED?	165	HER BECOMING	17
WHAT'S BECOME OF CARE? THIS LAKE BREATHES LIKE A ROSE.	170	FOURTH MEDITATN	76
MY RAGE, WHAT'S TO BE	211	SONG (1)	5
WHAT'S TO COME? WHAT'S TO COME?	211	SONG (1)	8
WHAT'S TO COME? WHAT'S TO COME?	211	SONG (1)	8
CREATED WHAT'S TO BE.	238	THE MOMENT	12
WHAT'S MADNESS BUT NOBILITY OF SOUL	239	IN A DARK TIME	7
WHAT'S THE WORST PORTION IN THIS MORTAL LIFE?	246	THE MARROW	5
WHAT'S GREATER, PEBBLE OR POND?	251	ONCE MORE, RND	1
WALLACE STEVENS, WHAT'S HE DONE?	266	FOR STEVENS	1
WHAT'S NOT A PROPER FOOL.	267	SAGINAW SONG	30
WHEAT			
LONG SINCE, BRONZE WHEAT WAS GATHERED INTO SHEAVES.	12	SLOW SEASON	10
THE BRONZE WHEAT ARRANGED IN STRICT AND FORMAL ORDER;	29	THE REMINDER	3
WHEEL			
WHEEL OF THE STARS, THE GREAT BEAR GLITTERING COLDER THAN SNOW,	47	DOUBLE FEATURE	11
THE GREAT WHEEL TURNS ITS AXLE WHEN IT CAN;	105	SIR JOHN DAVIES	3
THE GULLS WHEEL OVER THEIR SINGULAR GARBAGE;	187	THE LONGING	16
THE WHEEL TURNING AWAY FROM ITSELF,	200	THE FAR FIELD	53
WHEELBARROWS			
THE LADEN WHEELBARROWS CREAKING AND SWAYING,	158	FIRST MEDITATN	46
WHEELING			
AS KNOWN PARTICULARS COME WHEELING BY,	8	THE SIGNALS	3
AND THE MEN BENEATH THEM WHEELING IN DIRT TO THE CEMENT BENCHES,	158	FIRST MEDITATN	45
RISING, WHEELING AWAY WITH HARSH CRIES,	235	ALL MORNING	37
WHEELS			
THE WHEELS OF CIRCUMSTANCE THAT GRIND	22	SILENCE	9
WHEELS SHAKE THE ROADBED STONE,	34	NIGHT JOURNEY	24
I SIT ABOVE THE BACK WHEELS, WHERE THE JOLTS ARE HARDEST,	158	FIRST MEDITATN	22
AND THE BACK WHEELS HANG ALMOST OVER THE EDGE	193	JOURNY INTERIOR	4
WATCHING FOR DANGEROUS DOWN-HILL PLACES, WHERE THE WHEELS WHINED BEYOND EIGHTY--	193	JOURNY INTERIOR	19
UNDERNEATH, THE SLUGGISH WATER RUNNING BETWEEN WEEDS, BROKEN WHEELS, TIRES, STONES.	194	JOURNY INTERIOR	33
WHELM			
WHAT A WHELM OF PROVERBS, MR. PINCH!	89	UNFOLD! UNFOLD!	18
WHEN			
BUT WHEN HE STOOD UP, THAT FACE	6	THE PREMONITION	12
OR WHEN DARK FOLLOWS DARK IN LIGHTNING RIFT.	8	THE SIGNALS	6
WHEN I STOOD AT THE WINDOW, AN ELM BOUGH SWEPT TO MY KNEES;	12	MID-CNTRY BLOW	3
WHEN I LOOKED AT THE ALTERED SCENE, MY EYE WAS UNDECEIVED,	12	MID-CNTRY BLOW	7
WHEN WE ARE WALKING ON A TREELESS PLAIN,	13	PRAISE PRAIRIE	7
WHEN CLOVER SCENTS DIMINISHED WIND.	14	COMING OF COLD	4
BUT WHEN HE BRUSHES UP AGAINST A SCREEN,	16	THE BAT	7
WHEN MICE WITH WINGS CAN WEAR A HUMAN FACE.	16	THE BAT	10
WHEN CRAVENS CRY THEM DOWN,	20	REPL TO CENSURE	10
WHEN AMOROUS ARTS WE WOULD PURSUE,	23	AMOROUS LADY	11
WHEN FROM UNDER THE BARN THE CAT BRINGS A SIMILAR LITTER,--	24	VERNAL SENTIMNT	5
THE PAVEMENT SMOKES WHEN TWO CARS MEET	33	HIGHWAY: MICH	16
WHEN SPROUTS BREAK OUT,	37	CUTTINGS (LATE)	9
BUT SOMETHING ALWAYS WENT OUT OF ME WHEN I DUG LOOSE THOSE CARPETS	40	MOSS-GATHERING	7
NOW, WHEN I'M ALONE AND COLD IN MY BED,	44	FRAU BAUMAN	30
YET WHEN I HEARD THE DRUNKARDS HOWLING,	48	JUDGE NOT	7
WHEN I SAW THAT CLUMSY CROW	49	NIGHT CROW	1
THIS SLAG RUNS SLOW. WHAT BLEEDS WHEN METAL BREAKS?	59	THE LONG ALLEY	11
WHEN I TOOK OFF MY CLOTHES	64	SHAPE OF FIRE	24
WHEN THE HERONS FLOATED HIGH OVER THE WHITE HOUSES,	66	SHAPE OF FIRE	66
WHEN THE SUN FOR ME GLINTED THE SIDES OF A SAND GRAIN,	66	SHAPE OF FIRE	68
WHEN THE SUN HAS FALLEN BEHIND A WOODED ISLAND;	67	SHAPE OF FIRE	89

	PAGE	TITLE	LINE
WHEN (CONTINUED)			
WHEN YOU PLANT, SPIT IN THE POT.	76	I NEED, I NEED	53
WHEN I STAND, I'M ALMOST A TREE.	78	BRING THE DAY!	32
THE COLD KNOWS WHEN TO COME.	80	GIVE WAY, GATES	56
WHEN I SAY THINGS FOND,	83	O LULL ME, LULL	10
I'M MORE THAN WHEN I WAS BORN;	84	O LULL ME, LULL	37
WHEN YOU FIND THE WIND	89	UNFOLD! UNFOLD!	16
WASPS COME WHEN I ASK FOR PIGEONS.	92	I CRY, LOVE!	2
OH, WHEN SHE WAS SAD, SHE CAST HERSELF DOWN INTO SUCH A PURE DEPTH,	102	ELEGY FOR JANE	10
WHEN I WENT TO SEA IN A SIGH,	103	OLD LADY'S WRDS	23
THE GREAT WHEEL TURNS ITS AXLE WHEN IT CAN;	105	SIR JOHN DAVIES	3
WHEN GLORY FAILED, WE DANCED UPON A PIN.	106	SIR JOHN DAVIES	58
THE VISIBLE OBSCURES. BUT WHO KNOWS WHEN?	107	SIR JOHN DAVIES	85
SHE WAS THE WIND WHEN WIND WAS IN MY WAY;	107	SIR JOHN DAVIES	93
THE BOYS I KNEW WHEN I WENT TO POT;	111	SQUEEZE-BOX	2
--WHEN HE TRIED TO DRINK UP THE MONEY.	112	SQUEEZE-BOX	37
--WHEN SHE THOUGHT I'D RUN OUT OF MONEY.	112	SQUEEZE-BOX	41
WHEN THEY COME, DAZEDLY, TO THE PRETTY PASS	113	TO A LADY ED	11
WHEN I THINK OF IT NOW, I JUST HAVE TO SHUDDER!	114	THE COW	2
AND WHEN YOU THINK THE SKY HAS CLEARED	114	DINKY	3
YOU, WHEN YOU ARE FISHING THAT WAY, THAT WAY,	117	LADY AND BEAR	24
WHEN YOU ARE FISHING THAT WAY."	117	LADY AND BEAR	25
I TOUCHED HER SHADOW WHEN THE LIGHT DELAYED;	119	THE DREAM	13
WHEN SHE SHAKES OUT HER HAIR.	121	ALL EARTH, AIR	9
WHEN, EASY AS A BEAST,	121	ALL EARTH, AIR	13
KEEPS PACE WHEN I WALK ALONE.	123	WORDS FOR WIND	32
SHE MOVES WHEN TIME IS SHY:	124	WORDS FOR WIND	52
WHEN I DO WHAT SHE DOES:	126	WORDS FOR WIND	96
WHEN SMALL BIRDS SIGHED, SHE WOULD SIGH BACK AT THEM;	127	I KNEW A WOMAN	2
AH, WHEN SHE MOVED, SHE MOVED MORE WAYS THAN ONE:	127	I KNEW A WOMAN	3
WE DID NOT FLY THE FLESH. WHO DOES, WHEN YOUNG?	131	SENTENTIOUS MAN	7
I TASTE MY SISTER WHEN I KISS MY WIFE;	132	SENTENTIOUS MAN	27
I DRINK GOOD LIQUOR WHEN MY LUCK IS GOOD.	132	SENTENTIOUS MAN	28
I WEEP FOR WHAT I'M LIKE WHEN I'M ALONE	132	SENTENTIOUS MAN	33
WHEN THE PURE FURY FIRST RAGED IN HIS HEAD	133	THE PURE FURY	20
WHEN WILL THAT CREATURE GIVE ME BACK MY BREATH?	134	THE PURE FURY	25
WHEN TRUE LOVE BROKE MY HEART IN HALF,	138	THE SURLY ONE	1
AND TOLD MY NEIGHBORS WHEN TO LAUGH.	138	THE SURLY ONE	3
WHEN I FOLLOW AFTER THEM,	141	MEMORY	11
AND WHEN IT SWUNG, I SAW	145	THE BEAST	4
WHEN I RAISED MYSELF ONCE MORE,	145	THE BEAST	16
HE LOOKED BEYOND ME WHEN	146	THE SONG	2
WHEN I STAYED FOR BREATH, I LAY	146	THE SONG	11
WHEN I HEARD, OR THOUGHT I HEARD,	146	THE SONG	24
HOW I LOVED ONE LIKE YOU WHEN I WAS LITTLE!--	151	SLUG	1
WHEN I SLIP, JUST SLIGHTLY, IN THE DARK,	151	SLUG	8
I FOUND MY FATHER WHEN I DID MY WORK,	154	THE DYING MAN	40
WHEN FIGURES OUT OF OBSCURE SHADOW RAVE,	154	THE DYING MAN	46
WHEN THERE'S A DAZZLING DARK BEHIND THE SUN?	155	THE DYING MAN	53
WHEN WE BROOD ON THE DEAD OR THE BELOVED;	156	THE DYING MAN	97
AND THE UP-SPRING OF THE PLANK WHEN A FOOT LEFT THE RUNWAY.	158	FIRST MEDITATN	47
AS WHEN SILT DRIFTS AND SIFTS DOWN THROUGH MUDDY POND-WATER,	159	FIRST MEDITATN	60
WHEN I BENT TO UNTANGLE MYSELF,	162	I'M HERE	48
OR WHEN WE STAND AT THE EDGE OF A THICKET,	162	I'M HERE	54
SO SHE TOLD ME WHEN I WAS LITTLE,	163	I'M HERE	72
THERE ARE TIMES WHEN REALITY COMES CLOSER:	166	HER BECOMING	44
BUT A TIME COMES WHEN THE VAGUE LIFE OF THE MOUTH NO LONGER SUFFICES;	168	FOURTH MEDITATN	18
WHO TURNED A CORNER IN TIME, WHEN AT LAST HE GREW A THUMB;	170	FOURTH MEDITATN	69
WHEN THE WORST IS ABOUT TO ARRIVE;	172	WHAT TELL BONES	35
WHEN I WAS A LARK, I SANG;	172	WHAT TELL BONES	39
WHEN I WAS A WORM, I DEVOURED.	172	WHAT TELL BONES	40
WHEN I WALK PAST A VAT, WATER JOGGLES,	173	WHAT TELL BONES	73
WHEN HE TRIED TO SPOUT, THAT GREAT BIG LUBBER,	178	THE WHALE	3
WHEN YOU SLURP AND GO, POOF!	180	GOO-GIRL	10
IN A BLEAK TIME, WHEN A WEEK OF RAIN IS A YEAR,	187	THE LONGING	14
WHEN THE ICE MELTS ALONG THE EDGES IN EARLY AFTERNOON.	191	AT OYSTER RIVER	48
WHEN YOU HIT THE DEEP PIT AT THE BOTTOM OF THE SWALE,	193	JOURNY INTERIOR	20
AND THE WAVES FLATTENING OUT WHEN THE FISHERMEN DRAG THEIR NETS OVER THE STONES.	194	JOURNY INTERIOR	57
IN THE MOMENT OF TIME WHEN THE SMALL DROP FORMS, BUT DOES NOT FALL,	194	JOURNY INTERIOR	58

	PAGE	TITLE	LINE
WHEN (CONTINUED)			
BUT WHEN I BREATHE WITH THE BIRDS,	195	JOURNY INTERIOR	77
IN TIME WHEN THE TROUT AND YOUNG SALMON LEAP FOR THE LOW-FLYING INSECTS,	197	THE LONG WATERS	33
WHEN BATS FLY, CLOSE TO SLIGHTLY TILTING BROWNISH WATER,	198	THE LONG WATERS	61
WHEN BANKS CONVERGE, AND THE WIDE RIVER WHITENS;	200	THE FAR FIELD	60
OR WHEN TWO RIVERS COMBINE, THE BLUE GLACIAL TORRENT	200	THE FAR FIELD	61
AS WHEN A SHIP SAILS WITH A LIGHT WIND--	203	THE ROSE	31
WHEN THE MIND REMEMBERS ALL,	204	THE ROSE	75
WHEN THE SLOW FREIGHT WINDS ALONG THE EDGE OF THE RAVAGED HILLSIDE,	204	THE ROSE	83
WHEN THE WIND SIGHS.	209	HER RETICENCE	11
WHEN ALL	210	HER TIME	1
WHEN THE TIDE MOVES	210	HER TIME	6
WHEN EVERYTHING--BIRDS, MEN, DOGS--	210	HER TIME	23
WHEN SO YOUNG, WHEN SO YOUNG?	211	SONG (1)	4
WHEN SO YOUNG, WHEN SO YOUNG?	211	SONG (1)	4
WHO'D LOOK WHEN HE COULD FEEL?	212	LIGHT LISTENED	5
LIGHT LISTENED WHEN SHE SANG.	212	LIGHT LISTENED	24
WHEN I HAD TRIED TO CLEAN	213	THE HAPPY THREE	5
BUT WHEN SHE PECKED MY TOE,	213	THE HAPPY THREE	25
WHEN I PAUSE TO TALK TO A STONE,	215	HIS FOREBODING	9
WHEN I AM UNDONE,	217	WISH YOUNG WIFE	10
WHEN I AM NO ONE.	217	WISH YOUNG WIFE	11
AS WHEN THE DOOR SWINGS OPEN IN A FLORIST'S STOREROOM--	220	THE ABYSS	46
WHO SAT WITH THE DEAD WHEN THE RELATIVES LEFT,	223	ELEGY (2)	8
WHEN FLOWERS GREW, THEIR BLOOM EXTENDED HIM.	224	OTTO	11
ONCE WHEN HE SAW TWO POACHERS ON HIS LAND,	224	OTTO	14
WHEN HATTIE WRIGHT'S ANGORA DIED AS WELL,	224	OTTO	29
BUT WHEN I SLOWED MY FEET,	225	THE CHUMS	6
AND WHEN I SLIPPED UPON THE ICE,	225	THE CHUMS	9
WHEN GEORGE THE WATCHMAN'S LANTERN DROPPED FROM SIGHT	225	OTTO	38
WHITISH AND SPREAD WIDE WHEN HE TRIED TO STRUGGLE AWAY,	227	MEADOW MOUSE	10
WHEN I COME CLOSE TO HIM?	227	MEADOW MOUSE	18
WHEN I PUT HER OUT, ONCE, BY THE GARBAGE PAIL,	228	THE GERANIUM	1
SO WHEN THAT SNUFFLING CRETIN OF A MAID	228	THE GERANIUM	22
FLAPPING AWAY HEAVILY WHEN A CAR BLASTS TOO CLOSE,	234	ALL MORNING	7
WHEN OUR SPAYED FEMALE CAT YAWNS AND STRETCHES OUT IN THE SUNSHINE--	234	ALL MORNING	23
WHEN WE ABIDE YET GO	237	THE TRANCED	3
AND WHEN I LOOK AGAIN,	240	IN EVEING AIR	16
MY EARS STILL HEAR THE BIRD WHEN ALL IS STILL;	244	INFIRMITY	28
WHEN OPPOSITES COME SUDDENLY IN PLACE,	244	INFIRMITY	33
A BIRD KEPT HAUNTING ME WHEN I WAS YOUNG--	245	THE DECISION	3
WHEN CONTEMPLATION DAZZLES ALL I SEE;	246	THE MARROW	8
WHEN LIGHT DIVIDED ON A STORM-TOSSED TREE.	246	THE MARROW	20
AND WHEN I WALKED, MY FEET SEEMED DEEP IN SAND.	247	I WAITED	16
YET WHEN I SIGHED, I STOOD OUTSIDE MY LIFE,	248	THE TREE, BIRD	7
WHEN SHE THOUGHT I THOUGHT	249	THE RESTORED	5
WHEN I RAGED, WHEN I WAILED,	249	THE RESTORED	13
WHEN I RAGED, WHEN I WAILED,	249	THE RESTORED	13
OR HE SITS STILL, A SOLID FIGURE WHEN	250	THE RIGHT THING	13
DISSECTION IS A VIRTUE WHEN	257	SANITARIUM	11
BUT WHEN THE ROOT REPLIED,	262	FOLLIES OF ADAM	19
AND WHEN HE GOT TO THE SHORE,	263	FOLLIES OF ADAM	34
WHEN THE LADIES' GUILD PUTS ON A FEED,	267	SAGINAW SONG	3
BUT THEY'VE WAYS OF INDICATING WHEN	267	SAGINAW SONG	15
RAISE UP WHEN YOU WOULD PEE.	267	SAGINAW SONG	24
THE STINGY MEMBERS WHEN THEY SIGNED	267	SAGINAW SONG	33
BUT WHEN I DIE--AND THAT WON'T BE SOON--	268	SAGINAW SONG	47
WHEN THEY ARE HALF-UNDRESSED.	268	SAGINAW SONG	61
O WHEN YOU WERE LITTLE, YOU WERE REALLY BIG:	272	DUET	1
AND WHAT FOOL WOULDN'T, WHEN THINGS FROM SLEEP	273	SUPPR W LINDSAY	3
WHEN LINDSAY BENT HIS HEAD	273	SUPPR W LINDSAY	19
WHEN HE SAID THAT, A SPIDERY SHAPE DROPPED DOWN	273	SUPPR W LINDSAY	24
WHENCE			
FROM WHENCE COMETH SONG?--	236	SONG (2)	1
FROM WHENCE, LOVE?	236	SONG (2)	5
WHENCE, DEATH?	236	SONG (2)	9
WHENEVER			
FOR WHENEVER I COULD, I DEALT THEM ALL IN	112	SQUEEZE-BOX	32
SHE SWAYS WHENEVER I SWAY.	123	WORDS FOR WIND	12
WHENEVER I SEE HER WITH NOTHING ON.	140	THE SWAN	14

	PAGE	TITLE	LINE
WHENEVER (CONTINUED)			
THE WHOLE PLACE SHOOK WHENEVER I GOT A CHILL--	163	I'M HERE	64
WHENEVER I FEEL IT COMING ON	269	GOB MUSIC	10
WHERE			
WHERE SNAKE AND VULTURE HOVER,	7	ORDERS FOR DAY	12
THE PLACE WHERE BUTTERNUTS ARE FOUND.	14	COMING OF COLD	11
THE HERON STANDS IN WATER WHERE THE SWAMP	15	THE HERON	1
A SINGLE RIPPLE STARTS FROM WHERE HE STOOD.	15	THE HERON	12
THOUGH HOME IS NOT HAPPY, WHERE ELSE CAN HE GO?	29	THE GENTLE	10
THE TABLE WHERE EVERYONE ATE AS HE SHOULD,	32	SALE	14
WHERE WERE THE GREENHOUSES GOING,	41	BIG WIND	1
WHERE THE WORST WIND WAS,	41	BIG WIND	16
WHERE ELEMENTS COHERE	50	THE CYCLE	10
I CAME WHERE THE RIVER	51	THE WAKING (1)	21
WHERE AND TO WHOM?	54	THE LOST SON	27
WHERE DO THE ROOTS GO?	55	THE LOST SON	62
WHERE, WHERE ARE THE TEARS OF THE WORLD?	56	THE LOST SON	103
WHERE, WHERE ARE THE TEARS OF THE WORLD?	56	THE LOST SON	103
WHERE THE WEEDS SLEPT.	57	THE LOST SON	129
WHERE THE FIREMAN PULLED OUT ROSES,	57	THE LOST SON	132
THE PINCH OF WHERE.	64	SHAPE OF FIRE	28
WHERE KNOCK IS OPEN WIDE	71	WHERE KNOCK IS	T
EAT WHERE YOU'RE AT. I'M NOT A MOUSE.	72	WHERE KNOCK IS	40
WENT TO VISIT THE WIND. WHERE THE BIRDS DIE.	73	WHERE KNOCK IS	72
WHERE I LIVE.	74	I NEED, I NEED	15
SO BIBBLE WHERE THE PEBBLE IS.	75	I NEED, I NEED	32
WHERE ARE YOU NOW, MY BONNY BEATING GRISTLE,	86	PRAISE TO END!	17
GO WHERE LIGHT IS.	90	UNFOLD! UNFOLD!	56
WENT WEEPING, LITTLE BONES. BUT WHERE?	92	I CRY, LOVE!	1
WHERE THE WINDS GATHER,	103	OLD LADY'S WRDS	15
THE STONE WALKS, WHERE ARE THEY?	103	OLD LADY'S WRDS	35
IN THAT DARK WORLD WHERE GODS HAVE LOST THEIR WAY.	106	SIR JOHN DAVIES	48
I LEARN BY GOING WHERE I HAVE TO GO.	108	THE WAKING (2)	3
AND LEARN BY GOING WHERE I HAVE TO GO.	108	THE WAKING (2)	9
AND, LOVELY, LEARN BY GOING WHERE TO GO.	108	THE WAKING (2)	15
I LEARN BY GOING WHERE I HAVE TO GO.	108	THE WAKING (2)	19
HAD THE RED-HOT SPOTS WHERE YOU FEEL A	111	SQUEEZE-BOX	20
LIGHT HARDENED ON THE WATER WHERE WE WERE;	119	THE DREAM	6
A SMALL BIRD FLEW IN CIRCLES WHERE WE STOOD;	120	THE DREAM	19
THE STONES STAY WHERE THEY ARE.	121	ALL EARTH, AIR	2
WHERE ARE THE DEAD? BEFORE ME	122	ALL EARTH, AIR	22
WISDOM, WHERE IS IT FOUND?--	125	WORDS FOR WIND	68
AND YET I ROAMED OUT WHERE	128	THE VOICE	7
THERE WAS A THICKET WHERE I WENT TO DIE,	132	SENTENTIOUS MAN	21
SUDDEN RENEWAL OF THE SELF--FROM WHERE?	135	THE RENEWAL	13
I KNOW I LOVE, YET KNOW NOT WHERE I AM;	135	THE RENEWAL	15
AND I KNOW WHERE SHE IS.	137	LOVE'S PROGRESS	10
WHERE IS THE KNOWLEDGE THAT	139	PLAINT	7
DAWN'S WHERE THE WHITE IS. WHO WOULD KNOW THE DAWN	155	THE DYING MAN	52
AND THAT CRY TAKES ME BACK WHERE I WAS BORN.	156	THE DYING MAN	83
I SIT ABOVE THE BACK WHEELS, WHERE THE JOLTS ARE HARDEST,	158	FIRST MEDITATN	22
I'M WHERE I ALWAYS WAS.	165	HER BECOMING	25
WHERE WAS I GOING? WHERE?	166	HER BECOMING	61
WHERE WAS I GOING? WHERE?	166	HER BECOMING	61
I DRINK MY TEARS IN A PLACE WHERE ALL LIGHT COMES.	170	FOURTH MEDITATN	78
MOTHER, MOTHER OF US ALL, TELL ME WHERE I AM!	172	WHAT TELL BONES	53
WHERE SHADOW CAN CHANGE INTO FLAME,	188	THE LONGING	49
ON THE BULLHEAD, IN THE DAKOTAS, WHERE THE EAGLES EAT WELL,	188	THE LONGING	52
BLUE-BLACK FROM WHERE I AM SITTING,	190	AT OYSTER RIVER	12
WHERE THE SHALE SLIDES DANGEROUSLY	193	JOURNY INTERIOR	3
WATCHING FOR DANGEROUS DOWN-HILL PLACES, WHERE THE WHEELS WHINED BEYOND EIGHTY--	193	JOURNY INTERIOR	19
THE UNSINGING FIELDS WHERE NO LUNGS BREATHE,	196	THE LONG WATERS	11
WHERE LIGHT IS STONE.	196	THE LONG WATERS	12
I RETURN WHERE FIRE HAS BEEN,	196	THE LONG WATERS	13
WHERE THE YELLOWISH PRONGS OF GRASS POKE THROUGH THE BLACKENED ASH,	196	THE LONG WATERS	15
WHERE THE FRESH AND SALT WATERS MEET,	196	THE LONG WATERS	17
WHERE IT LEANS, TILTED EAST, A PERCH FOR THE OSPREY,	197	THE LONG WATERS	36
TO A LANDLOCKED BAY, WHERE THE SALT WATER IS FRESHENED	197	THE LONG WATERS	47
WHERE IMPULSE NO LONGER DICTATES, NOR THE DARKENING SHADOW,	197	THE LONG WATERS	57
WHERE THE CAR STALLS,	199	THE FAR FIELD	10
WHERE THE TURF DROPS OFF INTO A GRASS-HIDDEN CULVERT,	199	THE FAR FIELD	14

	PAGE	TITLE	LINE
WHERE (CONTINUED)			
DROPPING A FINE YELLOW SILT WHERE THE SUN STAYS;	200	THE FAR FIELD	68
BUT THIS PLACE, WHERE SEA AND FRESH WATER MEET,	202	THE ROSE	2
WHERE THE HAWKS SWAY OUT INTO THE WIND,	202	THE ROSE	4
WHERE THE SLOW CREEK WINDS DOWN TO THE BLACK SAND OF THE SHORE	203	THE ROSE	49
WHERE THE SALMON EASE THEIR WAY INTO THE KELP BEDS,	205	THE ROSE	96
WHERE HE HAS GONE,	208	THE APPARITION	2
A STORM'S INCREASING WHERE	215	HIS FOREBODING	19
IT'S RIGHT WHERE YOU ARE--	219	THE ABYSS	7
WHERE HE TREMBLED AND SHOOK BENEATH A STICK	227	MEADOW MOUSE	3
WHERE HAS HE GONE, MY MEADOW MOUSE,	227	MEADOW MOUSE	21
WHERE HAVE THE PEOPLE GONE?	230	THE STORM	8
WHERE THE HEAVY DOOR UNLOCKS,	230	THE STORM	21
WHERE THEY DROPPED AGAIN	232	THE THING	11
THE QUESTION WAS, WHERE WAS THE QUESTIONER?--	237	THE TRANCED	2
THE WORLD IS WHERE WE FLING IT; I'M LEAVING WHERE I AM.	260	THE CHANGELING	21
THE WORLD IS WHERE WE FLING IT; I'M LEAVING WHERE I AM.	260	THE CHANGELING	21
TO THE LAND WHERE THE INNOCENT STRETCH AND SNORE	272	DUET	11
WHEREBY			
WHEREBY TRUE WORK IS WROUGHT.	20	REPL TO CENSURE	8
WHEREFORE			
NUTS ARE MONEY: WHEREFORE AND WHAT ELSE?	61	THE LONG ALLEY	82
WHEREFORE, O BIRDS AND SMALL FISH, SURROUND ME.	88	PRAISE TO END!	97
WHEREIN			
WHEREIN I AM BESET BY HARM,	19	AGNST DISASTER	10
WHERE'S			
WHERE'S THE EYE?	64	SHAPE OF FIRE	20
WHERE'S ANN? WHERE'S LOU? WHERE'S JOCK-WITH-THE-WIND?	97	O, THOU OPENING	17
WHERE'S ANN? WHERE'S LOU? WHERE'S JOCK-WITH-THE-WIND?	97	O, THOU OPENING	17
WHERE'S ANN? WHERE'S LOU? WHERE'S JOCK-WITH-THE-WIND?	97	O, THOU OPENING	17
WHERE'S THE GREAT RAGE OF A ROCKING HEART, THE HIGH RARE TRUE DANGEROUS	98	O, THOU OPENING	30
WHERE'S SHE NOW, I KEPT SAYING.	101	THE VISITANT	23
WHERE'S SHE NOW, THE MOUNTAIN'S DOWNY GIRL?	101	THE VISITANT	24
LIGHT, LIGHT, WHERE'S MY REPOSE?	126	WORDS FOR WIND	92
WHERE'S MY ETERNITY	139	PLAINT	4
MY WRATH, WHERE'S THE EDGE	211	SONG (1)	1
WHERE'S THE STAIR?	219	THE ABYSS	2
WHERE'S THE BRIDGE OF DANCING CHILDREN?	258	SONG (3)	24
WE'VE GOT THE LIVING LIGHT, BUT WHERE'S THE FOOD?"	273	SUPPR W LINDSAY	16
WHEREVER			
SHE LIKES WHEREVER I AM.	124	WORDS FOR WIND	46
WHETHER			
WHETHER THE BEES HAVE THOUGHTS, WE CANNOT SAY,	196	THE LONG WATERS	1
WHETHER FOR LOVE OR OUT OF OBSCURE GUILT	224	OTTO	24
WHETS			
I'VE COME TO LOVE. A VIREO WHETS ITS BILL.	244	INFIRMITY	26
WHICH			
WHICH OF THE FIVE I SHALL RETAIN	8	PRAYER	3
THE SIDEBOARD BESIDE WHICH A TALL FOOTMAN STOOD	32	SALE	15
WHICH IS THE WAY I TAKE;	54	THE LOST SON	25
WHICH WOULD YOU RATHER?	77	BRING THE DAY!	4
OF THOSE SO CLOSE BESIDE ME, WHICH ARE YOU?	108	THE WAKING (2)	7
NO MATTER WHICH ONE IS BENEATH,	136	THE SENSUALISTS	15
SING OF THAT NOTHING OF WHICH ALL IS MADE,	140	THE SWAN	19
ANOTHER WAY AND PLACE IN WHICH TO CONTINUE;	159	FIRST MEDITATN	67
WHICH, WITH SLOBBERS AND SNORTS,	180	GOO-GIRL	5
A HEAD OR TAIL--WHICH DOES HE LACK?	182	THE HIPPO	1
KEEPS BUZZING AT THE SILL. WHICH I IS I?	239	IN A DARK TIME	21
IN WHICH ALL CREATURES SHARE, AND THEREBY LIVE,	243	THE MOTION	18
WHICH IS THE WAY? I CRY TO THE DREAD BLACK,	245	THE DECISION	9
WHICH IS THE WAY? I ASK, AND TURN TO GO,	245	THE DECISION	11
WHIFFET			
WEAK AS A WHIFFET;	44	FRAU BAUMAN	29
WHILE			
TODAY, WHILE SCRAPING HAIR BEFORE THE MIRROR,	25	DIM-WIT COUSIN	10
WHILE OUT OF FRIGHTENED EYES	31	LULL	20
WHILE OTHERS TAKE THEIR REST.	34	NIGHT JOURNEY	5
A SHAKING DOWN, WHILE THE STEM STAYS STRAIGHT,	42	TRANSPLANTING	10
HELD UP, WHILE THE ROWER BREATHES, AND THE SMALL BOAT DRIFTS QUIETLY SHOREWARD;	67	SHAPE OF FIRE	91
THE WHILE MY BLOOD LEAPED WITH A WORDLESS SONG.	105	SIR JOHN DAVIES	14

	PAGE	TITLE	LINE
WHILE (CONTINUED)			
IN THAT LAST WHILE, ETERNITY'S CONFINE,	120	THE DREAM	31
"O LOVE ME WHILE I AM,	123	WORDS FOR WIND	13
WHAT IS SHE, WHILE I LIVE?--	130	THE OTHER	1
WHILE STONES LOOSEN ON THE OBSCURE HILLSIDE,	157	FIRST MEDITATN	5
WHILE ANIMALS EAT TO THE NORTH,	157	FIRST MEDITATN	9
AND FOR A WHILE WE ARE ALL ALONE,	158	FIRST MEDITATN	28
SHUTTLING ITS THROAT WHILE PERCHED ON A WIND-VENT,	158	FIRST MEDITATN	40
FOR A SHORT WHILE,	161	I'M HERE	18
WHILE, FARTHER AWAY, THE HEAT-LIGHTNING FLASHES.	194	JOURNY INTERIOR	41
WHILE THE WRENS BICKERED AND SANG IN THE HALF-GREEN HEDGEROWS,	200	THE FAR FIELD	36
WHILE ON A FAR POINT OF THE ROCKS	202	THE ROSE	27
WHILE THE MOON LINGERS,	204	THE ROSE	85
WHILE THE WIND WHINES OVERHEAD,	230	THE STORM	3
WHILE I POKED WITH A STICK AT A STONE NEAR A FOUR-PRONGED FLOWER,	232	THE THING	21
WHILE THE ROCK-SEAMS SWELL WITH THE SEA,	261	THE CHANGELING	33
AFTER A WHILE THE LIGHT BEGAN TO WANE	274	SUPPR W LINDSAY	35
PAST ALDER LANE, AND WE GABBED THERE A WHILE.	274	SUPPR W LINDSAY	47
WHINE			
I LISTEN TO THE WEEDS' VESPERAL WHINE,	171	WHAT TELL BONES	12
THE THIN WHINE OF TELEPHONE WIRES IN THE WIND OF A MICHIGAN WINTER,	204	THE ROSE	69
A THIN WHINE OF WIRES, A RATTLING AND FLAPPING OF LEAVES,	230	THE STORM	6
WHINED			
THE WEEDS WHINED,	55	THE LOST SON	79
WATCHING FOR DANGEROUS DOWN-HILL PLACES, WHERE THE WHEELS WHINED BEYOND EIGHTY--	193	JOURNY INTERIOR	19
WHINES			
WHILE THE WIND WHINES OVERHEAD,	230	THE STORM	3
WHIPPING			
AN AUCTIONEER WAS WHIPPING UP A SALE.	21	THE AUCTION	3
WHIPPING THE LINE OF WHITE LAUNDRY, BENDING THE COTTONWOODS APART,	194	JOURNY INTERIOR	44
WHIPPOORWILL			
OR THE WHIPPOORWILL, ALONG THE SMOKY RIDGES,	160	FIRST MEDITATN	89
WHIRL			
STIRRED UP A WHIRL OF SILT	49	RIVER INCIDENT	2
WHIRLING			
ENSHROUD ME WITH LIGHT! O WHIRLING! O TERRIBLE LOVE!	48	LAST WORDS	10
IMPALED ON LIGHT, AND WHIRLING SLOWLY DOWN.	107	SIR JOHN DAVIES	72
WHIRLS			
THE LIVE GRASS WHIRLS WITH THE SUN,	93	I CRY, LOVE!	35
WHIRRING			
THE HUMMINGBIRD, WHIRRING FROM QUINCE-BLOSSOM TO MORNING-GLORY--	190	AT OYSTER RIVER	29
THEN WHIRRING OFF SIDEWAYS TO THE TOP OF THE HAWTHORN,	234	ALL MORNING	31
WHISKERS			
BULLHEADS HAVE WHISKERS.	73	WHERE KNOCK IS	62
HIS ABSURD WHISKERS STICKING OUT LIKE A CARTOON-MOUSE,	227	MEADOW MOUSE	7
WHISKERY			
NERVOUS AND COLD, BIRD-FURTIVE, WHISKERY,	157	FIRST MEDITATN	16
WHISKEY			
THE WHISKEY ON YOUR BREATH	45	MY PAPA'S WALTZ	1
I TOOK THE WHISKEY FROM THE SHELF,	138	THE SURLY ONE	2
WHISKS			
HE FRISKS AND WHISKS, HE CAN.	182	THE LAMB	2
WHISPER			
FROM ENEMIES THAT WHISPER TO THE BLOOD;	5	PROGNOSIS	6
RENEW THE LIGHT, LEWD WHISPER.	65	SHAPE OF FIRE	55
WHISPER ME OVER,	74	I NEED, I NEED	12
YOU WHISPER OF KIDNEYS,	79	GIVE WAY, GATES	25
A WHISPER OF WHAT,	81	SENSIBILITY! LA	16
SKIN, A THING YOU CANNOT SAY TO WHISPER AND EQUAL A WOUND?	98	O, THOU OPENING	24
THE MEANINGFUL WHISPER,	162	I'M HERE	33
HER CHOICES WHISPER.	260	THE CHANGELING	6
WHISPERED			
THE LAST TIME I NEARLY WHISPERED MYSELF AWAY.	89	UNFOLD! UNFOLD!	20
WHISPERING			
COME WHISPERING OVER THE SMALL WATERS,	61	THE LONG ALLEY	67
WHISPERS			
IS IT WITH WHISPERS AND KISSING?--	77	BRING THE DAY!	27

	PAGE	TITLE	LINE
WHISPERS (CONTINUED)			
THE LEAVES, THEIR WHISPERS TURNED TO KISSING;	102	ELEGY FOR JANE	8
"WRITE ALL MY WHISPERS DOWN,"	208	HER WORDS	8
WHISTLE			
A FAR-OFF TRAIN BLOWS ITS ECHOING WHISTLE ONCE;	33	IDYLL	10
I RUN, I RUN TO THE WHISTLE OF MONEY.	56	THE LOST SON	110
A GHOST CAN'T WHISTLE.	73	WHERE KNOCK IS	50
I'M ALL READY TO WHISTLE;	84	O LULL ME, LULL	36
--CAN STILL WHISTLE IN A JUG.	89	UNFOLD! UNFOLD!	13
I'LL SING AND WHISTLE ROMPING WITH THE BEARS.	105	SIR JOHN DAVIES	6
YET WHISTLE BACK AT EVERY WHISTLING BIRD.	140	THE SWAN	11
WHISTLING			
WHISTLING THINLY UNDER THE WIND-VENTS;	41	BIG WIND	31
OUR OUTER SKIN. WHO'S WHISTLING UP MY SLEEVE?	106	SIR JOHN DAVIES	38
YET WHISTLE BACK AT EVERY WHISTLING BIRD.	140	THE SWAN	11
THE KILLDEER WHISTLING AWAY FROM ME,	204	THE ROSE	62
WHISTLING BETWEEN THE ARBORS, THE WINDING TERRACES;	230	THE STORM	5
KIN TO THE WIND, AND THE BLEAK WHISTLING RAIN.	248	THE TREE, BIRD	12
WHITE			
UNTIL THOUGHT CRACKLES WHITE ACROSS THE BRAIN.	17	UNEXTINGUISHED	12
A FEW WHITE CLOUDS ALL RUSHING EASTWARD,	43	CHILD ON GRNHSE	5
REACHING UP WHITE STRINGS	44	FRAU BAUMAN	3
LOOK, LOOK, THE DITCH IS RUNNING WHITE!	57	THE LOST SON	119
THE LIGHT IN THE MORNING CAME SLOWLY OVER THE WHITE	57	THE LOST SON	135
SLIDING THROUGH THE WHITE CURRENT,	59	THE LONG ALLEY	3
WHEN THE HERONS FLOATED HIGH OVER THE WHITE HOUSES,	66	SHAPE OF FIRE	66
THE WHITE WEATHER HATES ME.	77	BRING THE DAY!	22
O LOVELY CHINK, O WHITE	83	O LULL ME, LULL	22
--LOOK FOR THE WHITE FIRE.	89	UNFOLD! UNFOLD!	17
DELIGHT ME OTHERLY, WHITE SPIRIT,--	92	I CRY, LOVE!	5
MY FANCY'S WHITE!	99	O, THOU OPENING	66
HER WHITE ARMS REACHING TOWARDS ME.	100	THE VISITANT	14
THE WHITE GRASS BENDING AWAY,	103	OLD LADY'S WRDS	20
THE WAVES BROKE EASY, CRIED TO ME IN WHITE;	107	SIR JOHN DAVIES	83
WE DARED THE DARK TO REACH THE WHITE AND WARM.	107	SIR JOHN DAVIES	92
AND I SWAYED OUT BEYOND THE WHITE SEAFOAM;	120	THE DREAM	29
THE WIND'S WHITE WITH HER NAME,	124	WORDS FOR WIND	38
SHE TAUGHT ME TOUCH, THAT UNDULANT WHITE SKIN;	127	I KNEW A WOMAN	10
I SWEAR SHE CAST A SHADOW WHITE AS STONE.	127	I KNEW A WOMAN	25
I LOOK ON WHITE, AND IT TURNS INTO GRAY--	134	THE PURE FURY	24
SHE SIGHS ME WHITE, A SOCRATES OF SNOW.	140	THE SWAN	7
WHITE UPON WHITE, SLOW-SETTLING ON A STONE;	149	IN LATE SUMMER	2
WHITE UPON WHITE, SLOW-SETTLING ON A STONE;	149	IN LATE SUMMER	2
OR, POISONED, DRAGGING A WHITE SKEIN OF SPITTLE OVER A PATH--	151	SLUG	21
DAWN'S WHERE THE WHITE IS. WHO WOULD KNOW THE DAWN	155	THE DYING MAN	52
IN THE WHITE KINGDOMS, I WAS LIGHT AS A SEED,	168	FOURTH MEDITATN	15
WHIPPING THE LINE OF WHITE LAUNDRY, BENDING THE COTTONWOODS APART,	194	JOURNY INTERIOR	44
AND THE IVY ADVANCE WITH ITS WHITE LIZARD FEET--	194	JOURNY INTERIOR	49
MOVING, UNMOVING IN A PARCHED LAND, WHITE IN THE MOONLIGHT:	194	JOURNY INTERIOR	53
THE LILY'S PIERCING WHITE;	197	THE LONG WATERS	39
NEITHER WHITE NOR RED, IN THE DEAD MIDDLE WAY,	197	THE LONG WATERS	56
THE DYING OF TIME IN THE WHITE LIGHT OF TOMORROW,	200	THE FAR FIELD	52
A SINGLE WILD ROSE, STRUGGLING OUT OF THE WHITE EMBRACE OF THE MORNING-GLORY,	203	THE ROSE	44
WHITE AND RED, IN THE WIDE SIX-HUNDRED-FOOT GREENHOUSES,	203	THE ROSE	52
IN THE LILAC CHANGE, THE WHITE REPTILIAN CALM,	205	THE ROSE	107
I SANG TO THE WHITE HORSE THAT GRAZED ON THE QUAY,--	216	THE SHY MAN	3
A WHITE CABBAGE-BUTTERFLY DRIFTS IN,	226	THE LIZARD	20
ONE WHITE FACE SHIMMERS BRIGHTER THAN THE SUN	246	THE MARROW	7
THE WHITE SEA WIDENING ON A FARTHER SHORE.	248	THE TREE, BIRD	20
IN THE WIDE WHITE, THE KNOWN	263	FOLLIES OF ADAM	24
WHITECAPS			
FLICK OVER THE CLOSE WHITECAPS,	210	HER TIME	11
FLICKING THE FOAM FROM THE WHITECAPS STRAIGHT UPWARD INTO THE DARKNESS.	230	THE STORM	16
WHITELY			
THE GRASSES WHITELY STIR;	17	NO BIRD	6
BEGIN RISING WHITELY,	210	HER TIME	9
WHITENESS			
SPIRIT, COME NEAR. THIS IS ONLY THE EDGE OF WHITENESS.	64	SHAPE OF FIRE	12

	PAGE	TITLE	LINE
WHITENING			
BETWEEN THE WHITENING TREES, UP SANTA LUCIA,	230	THE STORM	20
WHITENS			
WHEN BANKS CONVERGE, AND THE WIDE RIVER WHITENS;	200	THE FAR FIELD	60
WHITER			
MY SKIN WHITER IN THE SOFT WEATHER,	162	I'M HERE	43
NEAR THE STEM, WHITER AT ROOT,	221	THE ABYSS	83
THEN SLOWLY BREAKING WHITER IN THE DAWN;	225	OTTO	37
WHITEWASHED			
THE FAINT MOON FALLING THROUGH WHITEWASHED GLASS,	39	ORCHIDS	10
WHITEY			
HE WAS ALL WHITEY BONES	73	WHERE KNOCK IS	78
WHITISH			
WHITISH AND SPREAD WIDE WHEN HE TRIED TO STRUGGLE AWAY,	227	MEADOW MOUSE	10
WHITMAN			
BE WITH ME, WHITMAN, MAKER OF CATALOGUES:	220	THE ABYSS	29
WHITMAN'S			
MAYBE IT'S WHITMAN'S SPIDER, I CAN'T TELL,	273	SUPPR W LINDSAY	28
WHO			
NOW HERE IS PEACE FOR ONE WHO KNEW	17	NO BIRD	1
INDELICATE IS HE WHO LOATHES	19	EPIDERM MACABRE	1
WHO WANT NO MORE THAN FINGERS SEIZE,	25	VERSE W ALLUSNS	3
A KINDLY WIDOW LADY, WHO LIVED UPON A HILL,	27	CLAIRVOY WIDOW	1
A KNAVE WHO SCAMPERED THROUGH THE NEEDLE'S EYE,	28	THE FAVORITE	1
FOOLS WHO WILL NEVER LEARN;	31	LULL	18
WHO RAN UP AND DOWN THE BIG CENTER STAIRS	32	SALE	2
WHO FLEE IN WHAT THEIR HANDS HAVE MADE.	33	HIGHWAY: MICH	15
WHO CREAKED ON THE GREENHOUSE LADDERS,	44	FRAU BAUMAN	2
WHO PUT THE MOSS THERE?	55	THE LOST SON	64
WHO STUNNED THE DIRT INTO NOISE?	55	THE LOST SON	66
WHO ELSE BREATHES HERE? WHAT DOES THE GRAVE SAY?	59	THE LONG ALLEY	19
WHO SAYS? A NAMELESS STRANGER.	64	SHAPE OF FIRE	2
WHO, CARELESS, SLIPS	65	SHAPE OF FIRE	45
MY MEAT EATS ME. WHO WAITS AT THE GATE?	65	SHAPE OF FIRE	53
WHO HAD A RUBBER HAT	71	WHERE KNOCK IS	17
WHO KEEPS ME LAST?	72	WHERE KNOCK IS	46
WHO ELSE KNOWS	76	I NEED, I NEED	64
WHO STANDS IN A HOLE	80	GIVE WAY, GATES	53
THE LIKES OF HIM IS BITING WHO,	86	PRAISE TO END!	32
--WHO CARES? THE OLD OWL?	89	UNFOLD! UNFOLD!	15
WHO UNTIED THE TREE? I REMEMBER NOW.	93	I CRY, LOVE!	54
THRUM-THRUM, WHO CAN BE EQUAL TO EASE?	97	O, THOU OPENING	13
I'M TIRED OF ALL THAT, BAG-FOOT. I CAN HEAR SMALL ANGELS ANYTIME. WHO	98	O, THOU OPENING	25
BAGS? WHO EVER SAID GOD SANG IN YOUR FAT SHAPE? YOU'RE NOT THE ONLY	98	O, THOU OPENING	27
WHO READS IN BED	99	O, THOU OPENING	69
WHO CAN EMBRACE THE BODY OF HIS FATE?	106	SIR JOHN DAVIES	33
THINGS LOLL AND LOITER. WHO CONDONES THE LOST?	106	SIR JOHN DAVIES	43
THIS JOY OUTLEAPS THE DOG. WHO CARES? WHO CARES?	106	SIR JOHN DAVIES	44
THIS JOY OUTLEAPS THE DOG. WHO CARES? WHO CARES?	106	SIR JOHN DAVIES	44
WHO LEAPS TO HEAVEN AT A SINGLE BOUND?	107	SIR JOHN DAVIES	80
THE VISIBLE OBSCURES. BUT WHO KNOWS WHEN?	107	SIR JOHN DAVIES	85
THE WORLD IS FOR THE LIVING. WHO ARE THEY?	107	SIR JOHN DAVIES	91
WHO RISE FROM FLESH TO SPIRIT KNOW THE FALL:	107	SIR JOHN DAVIES	95
LIGHT TAKES THE TREE; BUT WHO CAN TELL US HOW?	108	THE WAKING (2)	10
WHO ISN'T UNWILLING, WHO ISN'T AFRAID	112	SQUEEZE-BOX	44
WHO ISN'T UNWILLING, WHO ISN'T AFRAID	112	SQUEEZE-BOX	44
THERE WAS A SERPENT WHO HAD TO SING.	115	THE SERPENT	1
ALL WHO REMEMBER, DOUBT. WHO CALLS THAT STRANGE?	120	THE DREAM	21
ALL WHO REMEMBER, DOUBT. WHO CALLS THAT STRANGE?	120	THE DREAM	21
BUT WHO, FACED WITH HER FACE,	122	ALL EARTH, AIR	29
THOSE WHO EMBRACE, BELIEVE.	125	WORDS FOR WIND	69
OR ENGLISH POETS WHO GREW UP ON GREEK	127	I KNEW A WOMAN	6
BUT WHO WOULD COUNT ETERNITY IN DAYS?	127	I KNEW A WOMAN	26
AND IT WAS I WHO HEARD	128	THE VOICE	16
WHO PLAGUES ME WITH HER SHAPE,	130	THE OTHER	2
WHO BUSKS ME ON THE NOSE?	130	THE OTHER	6
WHO CAN SURPRISE A THING	130	THE OTHER	13
WE DID NOT FLY THE FLESH. WHO DOES, WHEN YOUNG?	131	SENTENTIOUS MAN	7
THOUGH ALL'S IN MOTION, WHO IS PASSING BY?	132	SENTENTIOUS MAN	19
(FATHER OF FLOWERS, WHO	147	THE EXORCISM	3
DAWN'S WHERE THE WHITE IS. WHO WOULD KNOW THE DAWN	155	THE DYING MAN	52

	PAGE	TITLE	LINE
WHO (CONTINUED)			
WHO THOUGHT LOVE BUT A MOTION IN THE MIND?	156	THE DYING MAN	84
I'VE THE LARK'S WORD FOR IT, WHO SINGS ALONE:	156	THE DYING MAN	90
WHO STOPS BEING A BIRD, YET BEATS HIS WINGS	156	THE DYING MAN	100
A WITCH WHO SLEEPS WITH HER HORSE?	161	I'M HERE	15
THE LILY BROODS. WHO KNOWS	165	HER BECOMING	26
WHO CAN BELIEVE THE MOON?	167	HER BECOMING	74
ASK ALL THE MICE WHO CAPER IN THE STRAW--	167	HER BECOMING	86
AND THOSE WHO SUBMERGE THEMSELVES DELIBERATELY IN TRIVIA,	169	FOURTH MEDITATN	38
WOMEN WHO BECOME THEIR POSSESSIONS,	169	FOURTH MEDITATN	39
WHO TURNED A CORNER IN TIME, WHEN AT LAST HE GREW A THUMB;	170	FOURTH MEDITATN	69
WHO SPOKE FIRST IN THE COARSE SHORT-HAND OF THE SUBLIMINAL DEPTHS,	170	FOURTH MEDITATN	71
WHO ELSE SWEATS LIGHT FROM A STONE?	170	FOURTH MEDITATN	81
WHO TOOK THE DARKNESS FROM THE AIR?	173	WHAT TELL BONES	94
WHO TOOK ONLY TOADS ON HIS BACK:	178	THE YAK	2
WHO, STRANGELY ENOUGH, WAS A TURTLE:	179	MYRTLE	2
WHO ALWAYS DID THINGS BY THE DOZEN;	179	MYRTLE'S COUSIN	2
I WONDER WHO YOU THINK YOU ARE	181	MONOTONY SONG	10
A BOY WHO HAD GUMPTION AND PUSH	182	BOY AND BUSH	1
HE JUMPS ALL OVER. WHO	182	THE LAMB	3
WHO KNOWS HOW THE WAG-TAIL WOOS?	183	THE WAGTAIL	1
WHO SIGHS FROM FAR AWAY?	188	THE LONGING	41
AND THE DUST LAY THICK ON MY EYELIDS,--WHO EVER WORE GOGGLES?--	193	JOURNY INTERIOR	24
WHO MAGNIFIES THE MORNING WITH HER EYES,	196	THE LONG WATERS	25
I, WHO CAME BACK FROM THE DEPTHS LAUGHING TOO LOUDLY,	198	THE LONG WATERS	73
I AM TOLD BY THOSE WHO KNOW,--	207	THE YOUNG GIRL	6
WHO PASSED BY, ALONE.	208	THE APPARITION	4
WHO TOOK MY HEART, WHOLE,	208	THE APPARITION	5
O LOVE, YOU WHO HEAR	211	SONG (1)	9
WHO SHOULD COME UP RIGHT THEN,	213	THE HAPPY THREE	17
WHO KNOWS THE END OF IT ALL?	215	HIS FOREBODING	8
I, WHO RENEW THE FIRE,	216	HER WRATH	3
AMONG US, WHO IS HOLY?	220	THE ABYSS	24
THOSE WHO DESPISE THE DOVE.	220	THE ABYSS	28
WHO SENT HIM AWAY?	220	THE ABYSS	40
WHO KNOWS THIS--	222	THE ABYSS	87
SIGHS, SIGHS, WHO SAYS THEY HAVE SEQUENCE?	223	ELEGY (2)	4
WHO SAT WITH THE DEAD WHEN THE RELATIVES LEFT,	223	ELEGY (2)	8
WHO FED AND TENDED THE INFIRM, THE MAD, THE EPILEPTIC,	223	ELEGY (2)	9
A PRUSSIAN WHO LEARNED EARLY TO BE RUDE	224	OTTO	2
WHO LIVED ABOVE A POTTING SHED FOR YEARS.	224	OTTO	4
FOR ANCESTORS WHO LOVED A WARLIKE SHOW,	224	OTTO	25
WHO LOVES THE SMALL CAN BE BOTH SAINT AND BOOR,	225	OTTO	31
WHO WOULD BE HALF POSSESSED	240	IN EVEING AIR	3
BROUGHT ME DOWN TO MY KNEES. O WHO CAN BE	241	THE SEQUEL	5
DENIED IN ME, WHO HAS DENIED DESIRE.	242	THE SEQUEL	32
WHO BUT THE LOVED KNOW LOVE'S A FARING-FORTH?	243	THE MOTION	13
O WHO WOULD TAKE THE VISION FROM THE CHILD?--	243	THE MOTION	23
UPON THAT GOD WHO KNOWS WHAT I WOULD KNOW.	246	THE MARROW	24
HE WHO HIMSELF BEGINS TO LOATHE	257	SANITARIUM	9
OR SOME OLD LOUT WHO CAN	262	FOLLIES OF ADAM	2
BY ONE WHO ROSE UP FROM THE DEAD.	264	THREE EPIGRAMS	10
I MET A WOMAN WHO COULD BREAK WIND	268	SAGINAW SONG	41
"WHO CALLED ME POET OF THE COLLEGE YELL?	274	SUPPR W LINDSAY	40
WHO'D			
WHO'D THINK THE MOON COULD PARE ITSELF SO THIN?	188	THE LONGING	30
WHO'D LOOK WHEN HE COULD FEEL?	212	LIGHT LISTENED	5
WHOLE			
BUT VIEW THINGS STEADILY AND WHOLE.	25	VERSE W ALLUSNS	10
WHOLE FIELDS LOVELY AND INVIOLATE,--	39	WEED PULLER	13
AS IF I HAD COMMITTED, AGAINST THE WHOLE SCHEME OF LIFE, A DESECRATION.	40	MOSS-GATHERING	13
THAT BROKE OVER THE WHOLE OF HER,	41	BIG WIND	27
THE WHOLE FLOWER EXTENDING OUTWARD,	42	TRANSPLANTING	21
WHOLE BEDS OF BLOOM PITCHED ON A PILE,	43	FLOWER DUMP	3
TO HAVE THE WHOLE AIR!--	67	SHAPE OF FIRE	78
AND THE WHOLE MOTION OF THE SOUL LAY BARE:	135	THE RENEWAL	23
THIS WHOLE SEPTEMBER DAY.	148	THE SMALL	6
THE WHOLE PLACE SHOOK WHENEVER I GOT A CHILL--	163	I'M HERE	64
I'M IN LOVE WITH THE DEAD! MY WHOLE FOREHEAD'S A NOISE!	170	FOURTH MEDITATN	79
SHE'D MUDDLE THE WHOLE AFTERNOON	179	MYRTLE'S COUSIN	9

	PAGE	TITLE	LINE
WHOLE (CONTINUED)			
AND THE WHOLE RIVER BEGINS TO MOVE FORWARD, ITS BRIDGES SHAKING.	191	AT OYSTER RIVER	56
AND THE PINE, WHOLE WITH ITS ROOTS, SINKS INTO THE ESTUARY,	197	THE LONG WATERS	35
THE WHOLE SHIP ROLLING SLIGHTLY SIDEWAYS,	203	THE ROSE	36
ROOTED IN STONE, KEEPING THE WHOLE OF LIGHT,	205	THE ROSE	112
IT TAKES IN THE WHOLE BODY;	207	THE YOUNG GIRL	2
WHO TOOK MY HEART, WHOLE,	208	THE APPARITION	5
NOR THE WHOLE HEART OF MY THOUGHT,	209	HER RETICENCE	7
A LITTLE QUAKER, THE WHOLE BODY OF HIM TREMBLING,	227	MEADOW MOUSE	6
A THRASHING-UP OF THE WHOLE POOL,	233	THE PIKE	17
FLASH ME TO MERCY AND A WHOLE HEART!	259	SONG (3)	42
WHOLLY			
A SOMETHING WHOLLY OTHER,	205	THE ROSE	103
WHOM			
UPON WHOM EVERY GIFT AND THRILL WERE SHOWERED,	28	THE FAVORITE	10
WHERE AND TO WHOM?	54	THE LOST SON	27
FOR WHOM WERE YOU MADE, SWEETNESS I CANNOT TOUCH?	59	THE LONG ALLEY	27
FOR WHOM HAVE I SWELLED LIKE A SEED?	85	PRAISE TO END!	2
FOR WHOM THE MINNOWS SANG?	90	UNFOLD! UNFOLD!	52
FOR WHOM THE WORLD WORKS?	169	FOURTH MEDITATN	49
THERE ARE THOSE TO WHOM PLACE IS UNIMPORTANT,	202	THE ROSE	1
(WHOM I LIKE NONE-THE-LESS),	213	THE HAPPY THREE	22
TO WHOM DOES THIS TERRACE BELONG?--	226	THE LIZARD	27
WHOM DO WE LOVE? I THOUGHT I KNEW THE TRUTH;	241	THE SEQUEL	7
WHOOPER			
TO THE CRIES OF THE OWL, THE EERIE WHOOPER.	202	THE ROSE	19
WHORE			
ROAR 'EM, WHORE 'EM, COCKALORUM,	266	FOR STEVENS	17
WHORLS			
ALL THE COILS, LOOPS, AND WHORLS.	44	FRAU BAUMAN	24
WHO'S			
I KNOW WHO'S GOT HIM,	72	WHERE KNOCK IS	27
WHO'S READY FOR PINK AND FRISK?	76	I NEED, I NEED	59
IN THE SLOW RAIN, WHO'S AFRAID?	79	GIVE WAY, GATES	21
WHO'S BISHOP OF BREATHING?	83	O LULL ME, LULL	3
A COW'S A CARE AND WHO'S A COO?--	86	PRAISE TO END!	33
THE BULB UNRAVELS. WHO'S FLOATING? NOT ME.	90	UNFOLD! UNFOLD!	41
OUR OUTER SKIN. WHO'S WHISTLING UP MY SLEEVE?	106	SIR JOHN DAVIES	38
BUT WHO'S AFRAID OF THAT?	138	THE SURLY ONE	6
WHO'S COME CAN WAIT.	154	THE DYING MAN	35
WHO'S OLD ENOUGH TO LIVE?--A THING OF EARTH	243	THE MOTION	14
WHOSE			
O SEE THE FATE OF HIM WHOSE GUARD WAS LOWERED!--	5	PROGNOSIS	3
WHOSE BOGEY-HAUNTED LOOK	7	ORDERS FOR DAY	16
O FORTUNATE HE WHOSE MAMMA PAYS THE BILLS!	24	POETASTER	4
THRICE HAPPY THEY WHOSE WORLD IS SPANNED	25	VERSE W ALLUSNS	1
WHOSE THIN SONG HUNG IN AIR,	128	THE VOICE	9
O PRIDE, THOU ART A PLUME UPON WHOSE HEAD?	188	THE LONGING	25
AND YET STILL VIOLENT MEN, WHOSE STACKED-UP GUNS	224	OTTO	27
WHY			
WHY DON'T YOU, BEGONIA,	74	I NEED, I NEED	13
WHY IS HOW I LIKE IT.	77	BRING THE DAY!	23
AND SHOULD HE ARRIVE, WHY JUST LEAN YOURSELF BACK	113	TO A LADY ED	7
--WHY, THERE IS DIRTY DINKY.	114	DINKY	4
"O WHY ARE YOU FISHING THAT WAY?	117	LADY AND BEAR	2
WHY ARE YOU FISHING THAT WAY?"	117	LADY AND BEAR	4
THAT'S WHY I'M FISHING THIS WAY.	117	LADY AND BEAR	6
WHY I COULD DO BETTER	179	MYRTLE	10
THE MURMUR OF THE ABSOLUTE, THE WHY	201	THE FAR FIELD	89
AND WHY MUDDY SHOES	213	THE HAPPY THREE	10
WE COME TO SOMETHING WITHOUT KNOWING WHY.	235	MANIFESTATION	11
BUT WHY AM I GROANING HERE,	262	FOLLIES OF ADAM	6
AND ONE EYE GAZED ASKEW. "WHY, BLAKE, HE'S DEAD,--	273	SUPPR W LINDSAY	22
WICKED			
THE ROUGH, THE WICKED, AND THE WILD	18	LONG LIVE WEEDS	7
WIDE			
NOW LIGHT IS LESS; NOON SKIES ARE WIDE AND DEEP;	12	SLOW SEASON	1
THE WIDE WINGS FLAP BUT ONCE TO LIFT HIM UP.	15	THE HERON	11
TO LOOSEN WITH ALL TEN FINGERS HELD WIDE AND LIMBER	40	MOSS-GATHERING	1
THEIR SKIRTS BILLOWING OUT WIDE INTO TENTS,	44	FRAU BAUMAN	17
WITH WIDE WEBBY TOES	55	THE LOST SON	59
LIGHT TRAVELED OVER THE WIDE FIELD;	58	THE LOST SON	159

	PAGE	TITLE	LINE
WIDE (CONTINUED)			
WHERE KNOCK IS OPEN WIDE	71	WHERE KNOCK IS	T
ON A WIDE PLAIN, BEYOND	124	WORDS FOR WIND	35
AND THE WALLS STRETCHED WIDE.	146	THE SONG	7
THE WIDE STREAMS GO THEIR WAY,	172	WHAT TELL BONES	49
THEN A REAL CAT CAME WITH A MOUTH SO WIDE,	177	KITTY-CAT BIRD	14
I HAVE LEFT THE BODY OF THE WHALE, BUT THE MOUTH OF THE NIGHT IS STILL WIDE;	188	THE LONGING	51
WHEN BANKS CONVERGE, AND THE WIDE RIVER WHITENS;	200	THE FAR FIELD	60
WHITE AND RED, IN THE WIDE SIX-HUNDRED-FOOT GREENHOUSES,	203	THE ROSE	52
WHITISH AND SPREAD WIDE WHEN HE TRIED TO STRUGGLE AWAY,	227	MEADOW MOUSE	10
RIDDLING THE SAND, LIKE A WIDE SPRAY OF BUCKSHOT,	230	THE STORM	14
THE WIDE, THE BLEAK ABYSS	238	THE MOMENT	4
IN THE WIDE WHITE, THE KNOWN	263	FOLLIES OF ADAM	24
WIDELY			
MY DOORS ARE WIDELY SWUNG.	3	OPEN HOUSE	4
WIDEN			
AND NOSTRILS WIDEN AS THEY PASS	14	COMING OF COLD	10
WIDENED			
OUR PUPILS WIDENED WITH UNNATURAL NIGHT,	6	INTERLUDE	7
WIDENING			
THE CHILDREN DANCING, THE FLOWERS WIDENING.	188	THE LONGING	40
A RIPPLE WIDENING FROM A SINGLE STONE	201	THE FAR FIELD	102
THE LACELIKE WRINKLES OF THE WAKE WIDENING, THINNING OUT,	203	THE ROSE	33
WIDENING AT HIGH NOON, FACE UPWARD,	203	THE ROSE	43
THE WHITE SEA WIDENING ON A FARTHER SHORE.	248	THE TREE, BIRD	20
WIDENS			
IN THAT SLOW DARK THAT WIDENS EVERY EYE.	129	SHE	14
BUT A KISS WIDENS THE ROSE;	153	THE DYING MAN	8
WIDER			
A CAT GOES WIDER.	92	I CRY, LOVE!	9
WIDOW			
BALLAD OF THE CLAIRVOYANT WIDOW	27	CLAIRVOY WIDOW	T
A KINDLY WIDOW LADY, WHO LIVED UPON A HILL,	27	CLAIRVOY WIDOW	1
"O TELL ME, WIDOW LADY, WHAT IS IT THAT YOU SEE,	27	CLAIRVOY WIDOW	3
"CLAIRVOYANT WIDOW LADY, WITH AN EYE LIKE A TELESCOPE,	27	CLAIRVOY WIDOW	17
SHE WAS A WIDOW, SO SHE SAID:	264	THREE EPIGRAMS	8
WIFE			
ALONE, HIS WIFE IS GRIEVING FOR WHAT HER HEART DESIRES.	27	CLAIRVOY WIDOW	14
SHE HAD TO BE MILKED BY A MAN AND HIS WIFE.	114	THE COW	4
HE COULDN'T FIND A PROPER WIFE;	115	THE SERPENT	6
I TASTE MY SISTER WHEN I KISS MY WIFE;	132	SENTENTIOUS MAN	27
INSIDE, MY DARLING WIFE	213	THE HAPPY THREE	1
WISH FOR A YOUNG WIFE	217	WISH YOUNG WIFE	T
A PENSIVE MISTRESS, AND A YELPING WIFE.	246	THE MARROW	6
WIGGLES			
BUT THE HIND PART OF THE WORM WIGGLES THE MOST,	196	THE LONG WATERS	2
WILD			
THE ROUGH, THE WICKED, AND THE WILD	18	LONG LIVE WEEDS	7
I'M WILD WITH NEWS!	99	O, THOU OPENING	65
MY BREAST WILD AS THE WAVES.	165	HER BECOMING	10
IN THE WILD DISORDERED LANGUAGE OF THE NATURAL HEART?	166	HER BECOMING	33
TO THE CLAY BANKS, AND THE WILD GRAPES HANGING FROM THE ELMTREES,	200	THE FAR FIELD	66
A SINGLE WILD ROSE, STRUGGLING OUT OF THE WHITE EMBRACE OF THE MORNING-GLORY,	203	THE ROSE	44
THE WILD STREAM, THE SEA ITSELF CANNOT CONTAIN ME:	209	HER LONGING	12
AND ALL WILD LONGINGS OF THE INSATIATE BLOOD	241	THE SEQUEL	4
WILDEST			
AS IF I SWAYED OUT ON THE WILDEST WAVE ALIVE,	205	THE ROSE	104
WILDLY			
MY MARROW BEAT AS WILDLY AS MY PULSE.	106	SIR JOHN DAVIES	36
WILL			
THE ANGER WILL ENDURE,	3	OPEN HOUSE	13
THE DEED WILL SPEAK THE TRUTH	3	OPEN HOUSE	14
SOON FIELD AND WOOD WILL WEAR AN APRIL LOOK,	11	LIGHT BRIGHTER	13
THE OVENBIRD WILL MATCH THE VOCAL BROOK,	11	LIGHT BRIGHTER	15
WILL TURN ITS PRIVATE SUBSTANCE INTO GREEN,	11	LIGHT BRIGHTER	19
I LEFT MY HOME WITH UNENCUMBERED WILL	21	THE AUCTION	15
THE RATS SOON WILL BE LEAVING, THE SNOW WILL COME IN."	27	CLAIRVOY WIDOW	16
THE RATS SOON WILL BE LEAVING, THE SNOW WILL COME IN."	27	CLAIRVOY WIDOW	16
FOOLS WHO WILL NEVER LEARN;	31	LULL	18
YOU WILL FIND NO COMFORT HERE,	54	THE LOST SON	32

	PAGE	TITLE	LINE
WILL (CONTINUED)			
IT WILL COME AGAIN.	58	THE LOST SON	171
WILL THE GOAT'S MOUTH	60	THE LONG ALLEY	60
THAT WAS A CLOSE KNOCK. SEE WHAT THE WILL WANTS.	61	THE LONG ALLEY	62
THE LAKES WILL BE HAPPY:	61	THE LONG ALLEY	87
MOTHER ME OUT OF HERE. WHAT MORE WILL THE BONES ALLOW?	64	SHAPE OF FIRE	7
WILL THE SEA GIVE THE WIND SUCK? A TOAD FOLDS INTO A STONE.	64	SHAPE OF FIRE	8
WINKIE WILL YELLOW I SANG.	72	WHERE KNOCK IS	35
AND THERE WILL BE A BOOGER.	75	I NEED, I NEED	26
THE SEA WILL BE THERE, THE GREAT SQUASHY SHADOWS,	79	GIVE WAY, GATES	28
WHAT FOOTIE WILL DO WILL BE FINAL.	86	PRAISE TO END!	42
WHAT FOOTIE WILL DO WILL BE FINAL.	86	PRAISE TO END!	42
SHOOK WITH A MIGHTY POWER BEYOND HIS WILL,--	107	SIR JOHN DAVIES	75
HE WILL ASSUME THAT YOU HAVE HEARD--	116	THE SLOTH	6
AS A LOVELY SUBSTANCE WILL;	123	WORDS FOR WIND	19
THE DOVE'S MY WILL TODAY.	124	WORDS FOR WIND	40
WHAT FALLS AWAY WILL FALL;	125	WORDS FOR WIND	80
WHAT BOOK, O LEARNED MAN, WILL SET ME RIGHT?	133	THE PURE FURY	2
WHEN WILL THAT CREATURE GIVE ME BACK MY BREATH?	134	THE PURE FURY	25
WILL THE SELF, LOST, BE FOUND AGAIN? IN FORM?	135	THE RENEWAL	17
MY NECK, IF NOT MY HEART, WILL BREAK	136	THE SENSUALISTS	23
THE DEAD WILL NOT LIE STILL,	148	THE SMALL	22
THE WIND DIES DOWN; MY WILL DIES WITH THE WIND,	149	IN LATE SUMMER	11
IN THE WORST NIGHT OF MY WILL,	154	THE DYING MAN	31
DID MY WILL DIE? DID I?	167	HER BECOMING	69
WATER'S MY WILL, AND MY WAY,	191	AT OYSTER RIVER	63
WILL THE HEART EAT THE HEART?	211	SONG (1)	7
AND WHAT DIED WITH US WAS THE WILL TO DIE.	238	THE TRANCED	25
TELLS ME MY DRINKING BREEDS A WILL TO DIE.	246	THE MARROW	4
YEA, I HAVE SLAIN MY WILL, AND STILL I LIVE;	246	THE MARROW	21
TIME-HARRIED PRISONERS OF SHALL AND WILL--	250	THE RIGHT THING	2
WILLS WHAT HE WOULD, SURRENDERING HIS WILL	250	THE RIGHT THING	17
I'M SWEATING OUT THE WILL TO DIE.	256	IN HYDROTHERAPY	10
I SOON WILL BE MYSELF AGAIN.	256	IN HYDROTHERAPY	12
LONG GAZING AT THE CEILING WILL	257	SANITARIUM	5
WILL BRING A GOOD MAN DOWN.	270	GOB MUSIC	47
WILLIAM			
AND I DANCE WITH WILLIAM BLAKE	251	ONCE MORE, RND	9
WILLIAMS			
HE SHOOK MY HAND. "TELL WILLIAMS I'VE BEEN HERE,	274	SUPPR W LINDSAY	48
WILLIE			
WALK INTO THE WIND, WILLIE!	92	I CRY, LOVE!	29
WILLING			
THE FLESH IS WILLING TO REPENT.	256	IN HYDROTHERAPY	8
WILLINGLY			
AND WILLINGLY WOULD I DISPENSE	19	EPIDERM MACABRE	13
WILLOW			
THE TREE, THE CLOSE WILLOW, SWAYED.	101	THE VISITANT	27
I STAYED: A WILLOW TO THE WIND.	162	I'M HERE	39
RIDING THE AIR, A WILLOW WITH ITS KIND,	248	THE TREE, BIRD	10
THE WILLOW WITH ITS BIRD GREW LOUD, GREW LOUDER STILL.	248	THE TREE, BIRD	13
WILLOWS			
THE BATS WEAVE IN AND OUT OF THE WILLOWS,	93	I CRY, LOVE!	41
WILLOW-SHY			
ALL SMALL SHAPES, WILLOW-SHY,	90	UNFOLD! UNFOLD!	46
WILLS			
EACH WILLS HIS DEATH: I AM CONVINCED OF THAT;	144	ELEGY (1)	5
WILLS WHAT HE WOULD, SURRENDERING HIS WILL	250	THE RIGHT THING	17
WILTED			
OR FAN LIFE INTO WILTED SWEET-PEAS WITH HIS HAT,	42	OLD FLORIST	9
WIND			
THE RUSH OF WIND RIPPED OFF THE TENDER LEAVES	6	INTERLUDE	2
THE WIND LAY MOTIONLESS IN THE LONG GRASS.	6	INTERLUDE	10
ALL NIGHT AND ALL DAY THE WIND ROARED IN THE TREES,	12	MID-CNTRY BLOW	1
THE RAVAGES OF WIND AND RAIN ARE HEALED.	12	SLOW SEASON	2
WHEN CLOVER SCENTS DIMINISHED WIND.	14	COMING OF COLD	4
THE WIND SHAKES OUT THE SCENT OF PEAR.	14	COMING OF COLD	12
JERKS SKYWARD AT THE TOUCH OF WIND,	14	COMING OF COLD	29
BIG WIND	41	BIG WIND	T
WIND DRIVING WATER	41	BIG WIND	3
WHERE THE WORST WIND WAS,	41	BIG WIND	16
THE WIND BILLOWING OUT THE SEAT OF MY BRITCHES,	43	CHILD ON GRNHSE	1
TO WIND, TO WIND	44	FRAU BAUMAN	4

		PAGE	TITLE	LINE

WIND (CONTINUED)

	PAGE	TITLE	LINE
TO WIND, TO WIND	44	FRAU BAUMAN	4
DARK HOLLOWS SAID, LEE TO THE WIND,	54	THE LOST SON	28
THE BONES OF WEEDS KEPT SWINGING IN THE WIND,	58	THE LOST SON	152
SWINGING IN THE WIND.	58	THE LOST SON	158
THIS WIND GIVES ME SCALES. HAVE MERCY, GRISTLE:	60	THE LONG ALLEY	33
THIS WIND BRINGS MANY FISH;	61	THE LONG ALLEY	86
WILL THE SEA GIVE THE WIND SUCK? A TOAD FOLDS INTO A STONE.	64	SHAPE OF FIRE	8
THE WIND SHARPENED ITSELF ON A ROCK;	65	SHAPE OF FIRE	39
WENT TO VISIT THE WIND. WHERE THE BIRDS DIE.	73	WHERE KNOCK IS	72
SCRATCHED THE WIND WITH A STICK.	74	I NEED, I NEED	16
THE GRASS SAYS WHAT THE WIND SAYS:	77	BRING THE DAY!	29
IN THE WAKE OF A SHIP OF WIND;	80	GIVE WAY, GATES	42
I HEAR THE CLAP OF AN OLD WIND.	80	GIVE WAY, GATES	55
I'VE WAKED THE WRONG WIND:	82	SENSIBILITY! LA	29
THE WIND CAME AT MY BACK;	87	PRAISE TO END!	52
WHEN YOU FIND THE WIND	89	UNFOLD! UNFOLD!	16
WALK INTO THE WIND, WILLIE!	92	I CRY, LOVE!	29
--ONLY STAY OUT OF THE WIND.	97	O, THOU OPENING	12
A CLOUD MOVED CLOSE. THE BULK OF THE WIND SHIFTED.	100	THE VISITANT	1
THE WIND IN HER HAIR,	100	THE VISITANT	19
A WIND STIRRED IN A WEB OF APPLEWORMS;	101	THE VISITANT	26
A WREN, HAPPY, TAIL INTO THE WIND,	102	ELEGY FOR JANE	5
HAS SCAMPERED AWAY IN A DRY WIND.	103	OLD LADY'S WRDS	38
THE WIND WANDERS AROUND THE HOUSE	104	OLD LADY'S WRDS	52
SHE WAS THE WIND WHEN WIND WAS IN MY WAY;	107	SIR JOHN DAVIES	93
SHE WAS THE WIND WHEN WIND WAS IN MY WAY;	107	SIR JOHN DAVIES	93
SHE LOVED THE WIND BECAUSE THE WIND LOVED ME.	119	THE DREAM	16
SHE LOVED THE WIND BECAUSE THE WIND LOVED ME.	119	THE DREAM	16
SHE HELD HER BODY STEADY IN THE WIND;	120	THE DREAM	25
THE TWINY WINDERS WIND;	121	ALL EARTH, AIR	3
WORDS FOR THE WIND	123	WORDS FOR WIND	T
MAD IN THE WIND I WEAR	123	WORDS FOR WIND	5
THE WIND CREAKS SLOWLY BY;	123	WORDS FOR WIND	26
AND I WALK WITH THE WIND.	124	WORDS FOR WIND	39
UNDER A SOUTHERN WIND,	125	WORDS FOR WIND	61
THE WIND, AND THERE I AM,	125	WORDS FOR WIND	66
A WIND WREATHES ROUND A TREE.	126	WORDS FOR WIND	93
THE NIGHT WIND RISES. DOES MY FATHER LIVE?	135	THE RENEWAL	7
I WALK AS IF MY FACE WOULD KISS THE WIND.	135	THE RENEWAL	12
THE WIND DIES ON THE HILL.	141	MEMORY	7
AND A WIND WOKE IN MY HAIR,	146	THE SONG	22
A WIND MOVES THROUGH THE GRASS,	148	THE SMALL	11
THE WIND DIES DOWN; MY WILL DIES WITH THE WIND,	149	IN LATE SUMMER	11
THE WIND DIES DOWN; MY WILL DIES WITH THE WIND,	149	IN LATE SUMMER	11
A TREE ALL OUT OF SHAPE FROM WIND AND RAIN,	150	IN LATE SUMMER	27
A TREE THINNED BY THE WIND OBSCURES MY SIGHT.	150	IN LATE SUMMER	28
THE BLEAK WIND EATS AT THE WEAK PLATEAU,	157	FIRST MEDITATN	11
WITH A WIND FROM THE WEST AND THE TREES ALL IN MOTION.	158	FIRST MEDITATN	42
A COLD WIND COMES OVER STONES;	160	FIRST MEDITATN	92
I STAYED: A WILLOW TO THE WIND.	162	I'M HERE	39
IN A LIGHT WIND.	163	I'M HERE	85
IF THE WIND MEANS ME,	164	I'M HERE	99
WATCHING THE WIND RIFFLE THE BACKS OF SMALL BIRDS,	165	HER BECOMING	2
A LIGHT WIND RISES: I BECOME THE WIND.	167	HER BECOMING	95
A LIGHT WIND RISES: I BECOME THE WIND.	167	HER BECOMING	95
A LIGHT WIND STIRS IN THE PINE NEEDLES.	168	FOURTH MEDITATN	24
IN THE CIRCULAR SMELLS OF A SLOW WIND,	171	WHAT TELL BONES	11
FURY OF WIND, AND NO APPARENT WIND,	171	WHAT TELL BONES	28
FURY OF WIND, AND NO APPARENT WIND,	171	WHAT TELL BONES	28
MY DESIRE'S A WIND TRAPPED IN A CAVE.	172	WHAT TELL BONES	45
WEEDS TURN TOWARD THE WIND WEED-SKELETONS.	173	WHAT TELL BONES	65
THE WIND ROCKS WITH MY WISH; THE RAIN SHIELDS ME;	173	WHAT TELL BONES	81
MY SPIRIT RISES WITH THE RISING WIND;	173	WHAT TELL BONES	88
THE WIND SLACKENS, LIGHT AS A MOTH FANNING A STONE:	190	AT OYSTER RIVER	17
A TWILIGHT WIND, LIGHT AS A CHILD'S BREATH	190	AT OYSTER RIVER	18
REEDS BEATEN FLAT BY WIND AND RAIN,	193	JOURNY INTERIOR	9
THE WIND VEERING THE CAR SLIGHTLY TO THE RIGHT,	194	JOURNY INTERIOR	43
IN A FLICKER OF FIRE BRISKED BY A DUSTY WIND.	194	JOURNY INTERIOR	61
IN A TOWER OF WIND, A TREE IDLING IN AIR,	195	JOURNY INTERIOR	70
CHANGING WITH EVERY TWIST OF WIND,	196	THE LONG WATERS	10
BLESSED BY THE LIPS OF A LOW WIND,	197	THE LONG WATERS	45
TO A RICH DESOLATION OF WIND AND WATER,	197	THE LONG WATERS	46

	PAGE	TITLE	LINE
WIND (CONTINUED)			
SO THE SEA WIND WAKES DESIRE.	198	THE LONG WATERS	65
THE WIND FANNING THE ASH OF A LOW FIRE.	201	THE FAR FIELD	79
HIS SPIRIT MOVES LIKE MONUMENTAL WIND	201	THE FAR FIELD	91
WHERE THE HAWKS SWAY OUT INTO THE WIND,	202	THE ROSE	4
AS WHEN A SHIP SAILS WITH A LIGHT WIND--	203	THE ROSE	31
THE THIN WHINE OF TELEPHONE WIRES IN THE WIND OF A MICHIGAN WINTER,	204	THE ROSE	69
AND THE WIND TRIES THE SHAPE OF A TREE,	204	THE ROSE	84
MY LUCK RAISES THE WIND."	208	HER WORDS	7
THAT SHIVER IN THE WIND	209	HER RETICENCE	10
WHEN THE WIND SIGHS.	209	HER RETICENCE	11
I SING THE WIND AROUND	215	HIS FOREBODING	11
THE FULL MOON HAS FALLEN, THE NIGHT WIND IS DOWN	216	THE SHY MAN	17
AND I OBEY THE WIND AT MY BACK	221	THE ABYSS	66
FROM THE BLOW OF THE WIND,	229	ON THE QUAY	3
WHILE THE WIND WHINES OVERHEAD,	230	THE STORM	3
THE WIND FROM THE SEA AND THE WIND FROM THE MOUNTAIN CONTENDING,	230	THE STORM	15
THE WIND FROM THE SEA AND THE WIND FROM THE MOUNTAIN CONTENDING,	230	THE STORM	15
A CAT RUNS FROM THE WIND AS WE DO,	230	THE STORM	19
THE WIND SHIFTING SOUTH.	236	SONG (2)	12
ROSE UP AND FELL LIKE AN ERRATIC WIND.	237	THE TRANCED	10
AND ONE IS ONE, FREE IN THE TEARING WIND.	239	IN A DARK TIME	24
I SAW A BODY DANCING IN THE WIND,	241	THE SEQUEL	9
SHE STAYED IN LIGHT, AS LEAVES LIVE IN THE WIND,	241	THE SEQUEL	18
A WIND CAME CLOSE, LIKE A SHY ANIMAL.	241	THE SEQUEL	22
I WATCH A RIVER WIND ITSELF AWAY;	243	THE MOTION	8
I HEAR A CRY AND LOSE IT ON THE WIND.	243	THE MOTION	10
I MOVE BEYOND THE REACH OF WIND AND FIRE.	244	INFIRMITY	24
THE SLEEPY SOUND OF LEAVES IN A LIGHT WIND.	245	THE DECISION	6
THE WIND FROM OFF THE SEA SAYS NOTHING NEW.	246	THE MARROW	1
I WAITED FOR THE WIND TO MOVE THE DUST;	247	I WAITED	1
BUT NO WIND CAME.	247	I WAITED	2
KIN TO THE WIND, AND THE BLEAK WHISTLING RAIN.	248	THE TREE, BIRD	12
I'LL SING BEYOND THE WIND	260	THE CHANGELING	26
A THORN DOES WELL IN THE WIND,	262	FOLLIES OF ADAM	13
THE WIND BLOWS UP YOUR FEET,	267	SAGINAW SONG	2
I MET A WOMAN WHO COULD BREAK WIND	268	SAGINAW SONG	41
WIND-BEATEN			
ITS BEVY OF BEES, AND ITS WIND-BEATEN RICKETY SUN-CHAIRS.	226	THE LIZARD	29
WIND-BITTEN			
THE ARROYO CRACKING THE ROAD, THE WIND-BITTEN BUTTES, THE CANYONS,	193	JOURNY INTERIOR	7
WINDBREAK			
THERE WERE CLOUDS MAKING A ROUT OF SHAPES CROSSING A WINDBREAK OF CEDARS,	63	FIELD OF LIGHT	48
BUMBLING UP AND AROUND THE BAMBOO WINDBREAK;	226	THE LIZARD	21
WIND-BREAK			
THE SCRAGGLY WIND-BREAK OF A DUSTY RANCH-HOUSE.	194	JOURNY INTERIOR	45
WINDERS			
BEND DOWN, SMALL BREATHERS, CREEPERS AND WINDERS;	61	THE LONG ALLEY	71
THE TWINY WINDERS WIND;	121	ALL EARTH, AIR	3
WIND-EXCITED			
A CHILD AT PLAY, A WIND-EXCITED BIRD.	165	HER BECOMING	23
WIND-HARPS			
ON THE BANKS OF THE TOMBSTONE, THE WIND-HARPS HAVING THEIR SAY,	204	THE ROSE	60
WINDING			
THE YOUNG HORNS WINDING AND UNWINDING,	42	TRANSPLANTING	15
THE LOWLY WORM CLIMBS UP A WINDING STAIR;	108	THE WAKING (2)	11
I WOULD BE A STREAM, WINDING BETWEEN GREAT STRIATED ROCKS IN LATE SUMMER;	188	THE LONGING	46
WINDING UPWARD TOWARD THE STREAM WITH ITS SHARP STONES,	193	JOURNY INTERIOR	12
THE SPIKEY PURPLE BUSHES IN THE WINDING DRY CREEK BED--	194	JOURNY INTERIOR	37
WINDING AROUND THE WATERS OF THE WORLD.	201	THE FAR FIELD	103
BUT A MOLE WINDING THROUGH EARTH,	220	THE ABYSS	42
WINDING DOWN TO THE STRETCH OF IRREGULAR SAND,	222	THE ABYSS	95
WHISTLING BETWEEN THE ARBORS, THE WINDING TERRACES;	230	THE STORM	5
OR WINDING PATH? THE EDGE IS WHAT I HAVE.	239	IN A DARK TIME	12
ONE OF THOSE FAT ONES WINDING THROUGH A ROSE.	273	SUPPR W LINDSAY	27

	PAGE	TITLE	LINE
WINDLESS			
THE WINDLESS PERPETUAL MORNING ABOVE A SEPTEMBER CLOUD.	43	CARNATIONS	7
WINDOW			
WHEN I STOOD AT THE WINDOW, AN ELM BOUGH SWEPT TO MY KNEES;	12	MID-CNTRY BLOW	3
CLIMBED TO HER ATTIC WINDOW AND GAZED ACROSS THE SILL. ...	27	CLAIRVOY WIDOW	2
TO PREFER A WINDOW TO A DOOR?	169	FOURTH MEDITATN	29
SHE LEANING OUT OF HER POT TOWARD THE WINDOW.	228	THE GERANIUM	19
WINDOW-FRAMES			
CREAKING THE CYPRESS WINDOW-FRAMES,	41	BIG WIND	17
WINDOWS			
"I SEE TEN MILLION WINDOWS, I SEE TEN THOUSAND STREETS,	27	CLAIRVOY WIDOW	5
DALLY AT SHOP WINDOWS, STILL RELUCTANT TO GO;	47	DOUBLE FEATURE	6
ALL THE WINDOWS ARE BURNING! WHAT'S LEFT OF MY LIFE?	56	THE LOST SON	106
THE FINE SOOT SIFTING THROUGH MY SOUTH WINDOWS.	104	OLD LADY'S WRDS	58
DIVING DOWN AT MY WINDOWS,	152	THE SISKINS	2
BLASTING THE FROSTED WINDOWS,	158	FIRST MEDITATN	36
THE SUN LOOSENING THE FROST ON DECEMBER WINDOWS,	161	I'M HERE	2
THE WALLS, THE SLATTED WINDOWS, DRIVING	230	THE STORM	25
WINDOW'S			
A PICTURE WINDOW'S ONE YOU CAN'T	267	SAGINAW SONG	23
WINDS			
WINDS GATHER IN THE NORTH AND BLOW	15	COMING OF COLD	49
WINDS BRING A FINE AND BITTER SNOW.	15	COMING OF COLD	52
THE WINDS OF HATRED BLOW	31	LULL	1
MY KNEES MADE LITTLE WINDS UNDERNEATH	57	THE LOST SON	128
SMALL WINDS MADE	62	FIELD OF LIGHT	7
WHERE THE WINDS GATHER,	103	OLD LADY'S WRDS	15
BUT THE WINDS AND WATERS ARE;	125	WORDS FOR WIND	79
THE SMALL WINDS MAKE THEIR CHILLY INDICTMENTS.	157	FIRST MEDITATN	3
WHERE THE SLOW CREEK WINDS DOWN TO THE BLACK SAND OF THE SHORE	203	THE ROSE	49
WHEN THE SLOW FREIGHT WINDS ALONG THE EDGE OF THE RAVAGED HILLSIDE,	204	THE ROSE	83
AND THE QUICK WINDS	210	HER TIME	10
THE WINDS AND WATERS MEET.	215	HIS FOREBODING	20
AND ALL THE WINDS CAME TOWARD ME. I WAS GLAD.	247	I WAITED	23
THE VINE WINDS TO ITS WORK;	261	THE CHANGELING	53
WIND'S			
THE POKE OF THE WIND'S CLOSE,	84	O LULL ME, LULL	31
SOME ERRAND, OBSCURE AS THE WIND'S CIRCUIT,	92	I CRY, LOVE!	6
THE WIND'S WHITE WITH HER NAME,	124	WORDS FOR WIND	38
THE WIND'S SLOWING.	219	THE ABYSS	16
STILL AS THE WIND'S CENTER,	258	SONG (3)	29
WINDSHIELD			
A FINE DRY SNOW TICKING THE WINDSHIELD,	199	THE FAR FIELD	5
WIND-TATTERED			
AN OLD WIND-TATTERED BUTTERFLY FLEW DOWN	243	THE MOTION	2
WIND-TIPPED			
BEYOND THE SEA PINE, THE OAK, THE WIND-TIPPED MADRONA, ...	203	THE ROSE	47
WIND-VENT			
SHUTTLING ITS THROAT WHILE PERCHED ON A WIND-VENT,	158	FIRST MEDITATN	40
WIND-VENTS			
WHISTLING THINLY UNDER THE WIND-VENTS;	41	BIG WIND	31
WIND-WARPED			
NEAR THIS ROSE, IN THIS GROVE OF SUN-PARCHED, WIND-WARPED MADRONAS,	205	THE ROSE	98
WIND-WAVES			
BUCKING INTO THE WIND-WAVES	41	BIG WIND	26
WINDY			
FOR THE THIN SOUND IN THE WINDY CHIMNEY,	103	OLD LADY'S WRDS	30
IT'S WINDY THERE, AND RATHER WEIRD,	114	DINKY	2
I NEED A POND WITH SMALL EELS. AND A WINDY ORCHARD.	164	I'M HERE	91
THE FRIEND THAT RUNS BEFORE ME ON THE WINDY HEADLANDS, ...	198	THE LONG WATERS	71
THE FAR FIELD, THE WINDY CLIFFS OF FOREVER,	200	THE FAR FIELD	51
WINE			
AND WE DRANK THE DRY HARSH WINE	232	THE THING	20
WING			
TO RUN UNDER THE HAWK'S WING,	227	MEADOW MOUSE	23
"I'VE ONLY ONE WING," SHE SAID,	249	THE RESTORED	7
GREW BACK A NEW WING,	249	THE RESTORED	16
WINGBEAT			
WITHOUT A SINGLE WINGBEAT,	202	THE ROSE	5

	PAGE	TITLE	LINE
WINGBEAT (CONTINUED)			
BUT STILL THE FLASH OF THE KINGFISHER, THE WINGBEAT OF THE SCOTER,	202	THE ROSE	15
WING-CROOKED			
WING-CROOKED AND SURE,	93	I CRY, LOVE!	42
WINGS			
THE PAGEANTRY OF WINGS THE EYE'S BRIGHT TREASURE.	5	TO MY SISTER	6
THE WIDE WINGS FLAP BUT ONCE TO LIFT HIM UP.	15	THE HERON	11
WHEN MICE WITH WINGS CAN WEAR A HUMAN FACE.	16	THE BAT	10
THE LIGHTS IN THE KITCHENS GO OUT; MOTH WINGS UNFURL;	33	IDYLL	3
SOME MORNING THING CAME, BEATING ITS WINGS.	63	FIELD OF LIGHT	35
THESE WINGS ARE FROM THE WRONG NEST.	80	GIVE WAY, GATES	52
IN THE WINTER-WASP, PULSING ITS WINGS IN THE SUNLIGHT;	88	PRAISE TO END!	92
AND ALL THE STONES HAVE WINGS.	148	THE SMALL	24
WHO STOPS BEING A BIRD, YET BEATS HIS WINGS	156	THE DYING MAN	100
EXPLODES LIKE A ROSE, OR THRUSTS WINGS OVER THE CARIBBEAN.	159	FIRST MEDITATN	77
I HEAR A BEAT OF BIRDS, THE PLANGENT WINGS	173	WHAT TELL BONES	69
ITS WINGS CATCHING A LAST GLINT OF THE REFLECTED SUNLIGHT.	190	AT OYSTER RIVER	23
MY WINGS HOVERING OVER THE SHOREBIRDS,	209	HER LONGING	21
THEIR FOUR WINGS BEATING TOGETHER,	210	HER TIME	13
ITS ALMOST-INVISIBLE WINGS, BUZZING, HITTING THE LOOSE LEAVES INTERMITTENTLY--	234	ALL MORNING	32
AND PULSED ITS WINGS UPON THE DUSTY GROUND--	243	THE MOTION	3
WINGS WITHOUT FEATHERS CREAKING IN THE SUN,	243	THE MOTION	19
WITH EVERY SHIFT OF AIR, THOSE BEATING WINGS,	248	THE TREE, BIRD	15
THE BIRD, THE BEATING BIRD, EXTENDING WINGS--.	248	THE TREE, BIRD	21
FLUTTER OF WINGS AND SEEDS QUAKING,	255	LIGHT POEM	3
WINK			
I'LL BE A BITE. YOU BE A WINK.	73	WHERE KNOCK IS	74
IT'S A WINK BEYOND THE WORLD.	79	GIVE WAY, GATES	20
WINKIE			
WINKIE WILL YELLOW I SANG.	72	WHERE KNOCK IS	35
WINKING			
THE STAR WINKING BEYOND ITSELF,	196	THE LONG WATERS	26
THE SLOW LONG RIPPLES WINKING IN MY EYES.	247	I WAITED	9
WINSOME			
HOW FAST THE WINSOME ESCAPES!	258	SONG (3)	19
WINTER			
"IT WAS BEGINNING WINTER"	58	THE LOST SON	ST
IT WAS BEGINNING WINTER,	58	THE LOST SON	149
IT WAS BEGINNING WINTER,	58	THE LOST SON	154
UP OVER A VIADUCT I CAME, TO THE SNAKES AND STICKS OF ANOTHER WINTER,	65	SHAPE OF FIRE	37
I'LL RISK THE WINTER FOR YOU.	79	GIVE WAY, GATES	23
OLD LADY'S WINTER WORDS	103	OLD LADY'S WRDS	T
OR THE TITTEBAWASEE, IN THE TIME BETWEEN WINTER AND SPRING,	191	AT OYSTER RIVER	47
GREY FROM THE LONG WINTER, BURNT AT THE BASE IN LATE SUMMER.	193	JOURNY INTERIOR	10
THE THIN WHINE OF TELEPHONE WIRES IN THE WIND OF A MICHIGAN WINTER,	204	THE ROSE	69
WINTER-CALM			
DESIRE WAS WINTER-CALM,	87	PRAISE TO END!	69
WINTERGREEN			
AND WINTERGREEN BERRIES AND LEAVES STILL STUCK TO THE TOP,--	40	MOSS-GATHERING	5
WINTER-LEAPING			
A WINTER-LEAPING FROG.	83	O LULL ME, LULL	28
WINTER-SEALED			
THOUGH STILL THE GUARDED SNOW IS WINTER-SEALED,	11	LIGHT BRIGHTER	6
WINTER-WASP			
IN THE WINTER-WASP, PULSING ITS WINGS IN THE SUNLIGHT;	88	PRAISE TO END!	92
WIPING			
HE COMES CALLING WITHOUT WIPING HIS SHOES!	183	THE WAGTAIL	8
WIRES			
THE THIN WHINE OF TELEPHONE WIRES IN THE WIND OF A MICHIGAN WINTER,	204	THE ROSE	69
A THIN WHINE OF WIRES, A RATTLING AND FLAPPING OF LEAVES,	230	THE STORM	6
WISDOM			
OUR VERNAL WISDOM MOVES THROUGH RIPE TO SERE.	12	SLOW SEASON	16
THIS WISDOM FLOODS THE MIND,	18	GENESIS	5
A WISDOM OF THEIR OWN.	20	REPL TO CENSURE	12
KISS ME, KISS ME QUICK, MISTRESS OF LOST WISDOM,	48	LAST WORDS	7
A HOUSE FOR WISDOM; A FIELD FOR REVELATION.	90	UNFOLD! UNFOLD!	53
WISDOM, WHERE IS IT FOUND?--	125	WORDS FOR WIND	68
IS THERE A WISDOM IN OBJECTS? FEW OBJECTS PRAISE THE LORD.	166	HER BECOMING	38

		PAGE	TITLE	LINE
WISDOM (CONTINUED)				
I DEAL IN WISDOM, NOT IN DRY DESIRE.		273	SUPPR W LINDSAY	1
WISEST				
A DRY SOUL'S WISEST. O, I AM NOT DRY!		140	THE SWAN	5
WISH				
FROM EACH MALIGNANT WISH		31	LULL	5
STILL STARES THE WISH TO LOVE.		31	LULL	21
TO THE CAT'S WISH?		60	THE LONG ALLEY	58
I WISH I WAS A PIFFLEBOB		75	I NEED, I NEED	35
I WISH I WAS A FUNNY		75	I NEED, I NEED	36
I WISH I HAD TEN THOUSAND HATS,		75	I NEED, I NEED	37
A WISH! A WISH!		83	O LULL ME, LULL	21
A WISH! A WISH!		83	O LULL ME, LULL	21
WAS I THE SERVANT OF A SOVEREIGN WISH,		105	SIR JOHN DAVIES	29
IS IT THE SEA WE WISH? THE SLEEP OF THE CHANGELESS?		165	HER BECOMING	28
HOW I WISH THEM AWAKE!		169	FOURTH MEDITATN	55
THE WIND ROCKS WITH MY WISH; THE RAIN SHIELDS ME;		173	WHAT TELL BONES	81
I WISH YOU WOULD ACT LIKE A BIRD REALLY SHOULD,		177	KITTY-CAT BIRD	6
WISH FOR A YOUNG WIFE		217	WISH YOUNG WIFE	T
WISHES				
SHE KEEPS MY WISHES WARM;		121	ALL EARTH, AIR	12
HOW WELL HER WISHES WENT! SHE STROKED MY CHIN,		127	I KNEW A WOMAN	8
PRICKLING PURE WISHES WITH CONFUSION'S IRE;		143	SHIMMER OF EVIL	12
WISHING				
NEVER WISHING ITSELF AWAY,		101	LIGHT BREATHER	14
WISPS				
COUNTING THE WISPS OF FLAME, AND I WATCH HOW		240	IN EVEING AIR	20
WIT				
WITH THESE I MATCH MY LITTLE WIT		18	LONG LIVE WEEDS	9
THE HEART MUST RALLY TO MY WIT		19	AGNST DISASTER	11
ALL INNOCENCE AND WIT,		121	ALL EARTH, AIR	11
THINGS OF HIGH WIT AND CHANGES OF THE MOON.		260	THE CHANGELING	27
WITCH				
WAKE ME, WITCH, WE'LL DO THE DANCE OF ROTTEN STICKS.		64	SHAPE OF FIRE	10
A WITCH WHO SLEEPS WITH HER HORSE?		161	I'M HERE	15
MY SWEETHEART IS A UGLY WITCH,		181	MONOTONY SONG	17
WITCHES				
LIKE WITCHES THEY FLEW ALONG ROWS		44	FRAU BAUMAN	19
WITH (320)				
WITHER				
MAY YOUR LIMBS NEVER WITHER,		217	WISH YOUNG WIFE	2
WITHIN				
INVENTION SLEEPS WITHIN A SKULL		4	DEATH PIECE	1
THE VEINS WITHIN OUR HANDS BETRAYED OUR FEAR.		6	INTERLUDE	11
THE SMALL BROOK DIES WITHIN ITS BED;		15	COMING OF COLD	38
A PEARL WITHIN THE BRAIN,		18	GENESIS	9
OF DIGNITY WITHIN,		20	REPL TO CENSURE	15
THERE IS A NOISE WITHIN THE BROW		22	SILENCE	1
SO TERRIBLY WITHIN THE MIND,		22	SILENCE	10
CONFUSION'S CORE SET DEEP WITHIN		22	SILENCE	13
SO CAGED AND CADGED, SO CLOSE WITHIN		24	BEFORE STUDY	3
WAS IT LIGHT WITHIN?		58	THE LOST SON	165
WAS IT LIGHT WITHIN LIGHT?		58	THE LOST SON	166
ANGEL WITHIN ME, I ASKED,		62	FIELD OF LIGHT	19
LIKE A WET LOG, I SANG WITHIN A FLAME.		120	THE DREAM	30
IN THE LONG NIGHT, I REST WITHIN HER NAME--		131	SENTENTIOUS MAN	16
WITHIN THE REACH OF MY IMAGINING:		135	THE RENEWAL	3
THE OUTSIDE DIES WITHIN.		141	MEMORY	3
BUT THE RIND, OFTEN, HATES THE LIFE WITHIN.		157	FIRST MEDITATN	13
TWO SONG SPARROWS, ONE WITHIN A GREENHOUSE,		158	FIRST MEDITATN	39
JOURNEY WITHIN A JOURNEY:		158	FIRST MEDITATN	48
ROSE UP WITHIN THE MIND,		237	THE TRANCED	9
ALL FLOWED: WITHOUT, WITHIN;		238	THE MOMENT	10
WITHIN THIS TUB BUT CANNOT DROWN.		256	IN HYDROTHERAPY	2
WITHIN THIS PRIMAL ELEMENT		256	IN HYDROTHERAPY	7
WITHOUT				
THE SCHEME WITHOUT PURPOSE; PRIDE IN A FURNISHED ROOM;		5	PROGNOSIS	10
THE WARM COMES WITHOUT SOUND.		64	SHAPE OF FIRE	19
TO KNOW THAT LIGHT FALLS AND FILLS, OFTEN WITHOUT OUR KNOWING,		67	SHAPE OF FIRE	92
TELL ME, BODY WITHOUT SKIN, DOES A FISH SWEAT?		89	UNFOLD! UNFOLD!	2
A TONGUE WITHOUT SONG		89	UNFOLD! UNFOLD!	12
BEGINNINGS START WITHOUT SHADE,		93	I CRY, LOVE!	33

	PAGE	TITLE	LINE
WITHOUT (CONTINUED)			
SHE CAME WITHOUT SOUND,	100	THE VISITANT	15
WITHOUT BRUSHING THE WET STONES,	100	THE VISITANT	16
TREMBLED AT HIDDEN VIRTUE WITHOUT FLAW,	107	SIR JOHN DAVIES	74
WITHOUT BURNING.	160	FIRST MEDITATN	97
WITHOUT STARING LIKE A LOUT, OR A MOPING ADOLESCENT;	163	I'M HERE	80
WITHOUT COMMOTION.	163	I'M HERE	81
A SHAPE WITHOUT A SHADE, OR ALMOST NONE,	167	HER BECOMING	88
AND THEN WITHOUT EVEN A SPOON,	179	MYRTLE'S COUSIN	8
HE COMES CALLING WITHOUT WIPING HIS SHOES!	183	THE WAGTAIL	8
COME THE FIRST TIDE-RIPPLES, MOVING, ALMOST WITHOUT SOUND, TOWARD ME,	190	AT OYSTER RIVER	2
AND WITH WATER: THE WAVES COMING FORWARD, WITHOUT CESSATION,	191	AT OYSTER RIVER	31
I HAVE COME HERE WITHOUT COURTING SILENCE,	197	THE LONG WATERS	44
OF DRIVING ALONE, WITHOUT LUGGAGE, OUT A LONG PENINSULA,	199	THE FAR FIELD	3
WITHOUT A SINGLE WINGBEAT,	202	THE ROSE	5
WITHOUT HATE, WITHOUT GRIEF,	217	WISH YOUNG WIFE	7
WITHOUT HATE, WITHOUT GRIEF,	217	WISH YOUNG WIFE	7
WITHOUT HIS RIFLE, AND SLAPPED EACH ONE HARD;	224	OTTO	19
AND THE SMALL FISH LIE, WITHOUT SHADOW, MOTIONLESS,	233	THE PIKE	6
LOOKING AT YOU WITHOUT TURNING HIS SMALL HEAD,	234	ALL MORNING	12
WE COME TO SOMETHING WITHOUT KNOWING WHY.	235	MANIFESTATION	11
FROM THE GHOST WITHOUT BREATH,	236	SONG (2)	11
ALL FLOWED: WITHOUT, WITHIN;	238	THE MOMENT	10
WINGS WITHOUT FEATHERS CREAKING IN THE SUN,	243	THE MOTION	19
THINGS WITHOUT HANDS TAKE HANDS: THERE IS NO CHOICE,--	244	INFIRMITY	31
WANTING THE QUIET OF OLD WOOD OR STONE WITHOUT WATER.	255	LIGHT POEM	9
A COLOR WITHOUT FLAW,	269	GOB MUSIC	27
A COLOR WITHOUT FLAW, FLAW, FLAW,	269	GOB MUSIC	28
A COLOR WITHOUT FLAW.	269	GOB MUSIC	29
WITLESS			
TO WITLESS AGONY.	3	OPEN HOUSE	18
WITNESS			
MY INWARD WITNESS IS DISMAYED	220	THE ABYSS	19
WITS			
I WALK THE NIGHT TO KEEP MY FIVE WITS WARM.	135	THE RENEWAL	18
AFFRIGHTED FROM HER WITS,	136	THE SENSUALISTS	10
WIVES			
THEIR WIVES GO OUT ON SUNDAY BENEATH THE LATEST HAT.	27	CLAIRVOY WIDOW	8
WIZENED			
HOW SHE KEPT THE WIZENED, THE FALLEN, THE MISSHAPEN FOR HERSELF,	223	ELEGY (2)	14
OR A WIZENED ASTER IN LATE SEPTEMBER,	228	THE GERANIUM	4
SHAKING LOOSE THE LAST WIZENED ORANGES IN THE ORCHARD,	231	THE STORM	32
WO			
WALLACE, WALLACE, WO IST ER?	266	FOR STEVENS	9
WOE			
I HAVE MYSELF AN INNER WEIGHT OF WOE	144	ELEGY (1)	3
I HAVE MYSELF AN INNER WEIGHT OF WOE	144	ELEGY (1)	7
I HAVE MYSELF, AND BEAR ITS WEIGHT OF WOE	144	ELEGY (1)	15
WOKE			
I WOKE IN THE FIRST OF MORNING.	101	THE VISITANT	21
I GAVE HER KISSES BACK, AND WOKE A GHOST.	106	SIR JOHN DAVIES	45
WE WOKE TO FIND THE MOONLIGHT ON OUR TOES.	106	SIR JOHN DAVIES	64
AND A WIND WOKE IN MY HAIR,	146	THE SONG	22
AS IF PURE BEING WOKE,	147	THE EXORCISM	5
WOMAN			
AN OLD WOMAN	103	OLD LADY'S WRDS	17
THAT WOMAN WOULD SET SODDEN STRAW ON FIRE.	105	SIR JOHN DAVIES	28
THAT WOMAN I SAW IN A STONE--	123	WORDS FOR WIND	31
I KNEW A WOMAN	127	I KNEW A WOMAN	T
I KNEW A WOMAN, LOVELY IN HER BONES,	127	I KNEW A WOMAN	1
I LOVE A WOMAN WITH AN EMPTY FACE.	133	THE PURE FURY	9
DREAM OF A WOMAN, AND A DREAM OF DEATH:	134	THE PURE FURY	22
A WOMAN STOOD, PURE AS A BRIDE,	136	THE SENSUALISTS	9
SHE WAS A SERIOUS WOMAN.	163	I'M HERE	74
WHAT IS IT TO BE A WOMAN?	169	FOURTH MEDITATN	27
SHE ASKED, WOMAN.	213	THE HAPPY THREE	12
I MET A WOMAN WHO COULD BREAK WIND	268	SAGINAW SONG	41
WOMAN'S			
A WOMAN'S NAKED IN WATER,	137	LOVE'S PROGRESS	9
HIS HAND COULD FIT INTO A WOMAN'S GLOVE,	224	OTTO	12

	PAGE	TITLE	LINE
WOMBS			
I IMAGINED THE UNBORN, STARVING IN WOMBS, CURLING;	48	JUDGE NOT	5
WOMEN			
SAW WOMEN, THEIR EYELIDS LIKE LITTLE RAGS,	48	JUDGE NOT	9
ALL WOMEN LOVED DANCE IN A DYING LIGHT--	156	THE DYING MAN	78
WOMEN WHO BECOME THEIR POSSESSIONS,	169	FOURTH MEDITATN	39
ALL WOMEN, O, ARE BEAUTIFUL	268	SAGINAW SONG	60
WON			
IS SELDOM WON. THE SPIRIT STARVES	4	FEUD	19
HOLD TO ADVANTAGE DEARLY WON.	33	HIGHWAY: MICH	9
--FOR YOU NEVER WON WITH THAT MONEY.	112	SQUEEZE-BOX	29
WONDER			
OH, WHAT A WEBBY WONDER I AM!	98	O, THOU OPENING	47
I WONDER WHO YOU THINK YOU ARE	181	MONOTONY SONG	10
WONDERFUL			
"O IT'S WONDERFUL HOW WITH A FLICK OF YOUR WRIST,	117	LADY AND BEAR	21
WON'T			
HE WON'T BE AN ANGEL,	72	WHERE KNOCK IS	29
MY PILLOW WON'T TELL ME	208	THE APPARITION	1
BUT WHEN I DIE--AND THAT WON'T BE SOON--	268	SAGINAW SONG	47
WOO			
TO WOO THE FEARFUL SMALL;	148	THE SMALL	20
IT IS FATAL TO WOO YOURSELF,	172	WHAT TELL BONES	36
A SOUND SO THIN IT COULD NOT WOO A BIRD,	204	THE ROSE	77
A FLORIST DOES NOT WOO THE BEAUTIFUL:	224	OTTO	8
WOOD			
SOON FIELD AND WOOD WILL WEAR AN APRIL LOOK,	11	LIGHT BRIGHTER	13
THEN POINTS HIS HEAVY BILL ABOVE THE WOOD.	15	THE HERON	10
--AND A FUME OF DECAY THAT CLINGS FAST TO THE WOOD.	32	SALE	16
FAR IN THE WOOD	51	THE WAKING (1)	17
IT'S DARK IN THIS WOOD, SOFT MOCKER.	85	PRAISE TO END!	1
LATER, I DID AND I DANCED IN THE SIMPLE WOOD.	90	UNFOLD! UNFOLD!	34
IN THE RICH WEATHER OF A DAPPLED WOOD	107	SIR JOHN DAVIES	65
THE DEER CAME DOWN, OUT OF THE DAPPLED WOOD.	120	THE DREAM	20
I CLAIM; ONE TREE, A WOOD;	128	THE VOICE	2
IN A DARK WOOD I SAW--	147	THE EXORCISM	13
THE WOOD BECOMES A WALL.	148	THE SMALL	9
BEYOND THE RIDGE TWO WOOD THRUSH SING AS ONE.	150	IN LATE SUMMER	30
THE MIRE, THE SODDEN WOOD,	154	THE DYING MAN	22
ACROSS A FIELD, INTO A LITTLE WOOD.	166	HER BECOMING	51
OR STAY BY YOURSELF DOWN DEEP IN THE WOOD,	177	KITTY-CAT BIRD	7
THE SALT-SOAKED WOOD OF A FIRE CRACKLES;	190	AT OYSTER RIVER	21
THE BLUEBIRD, LOVER OF HOLES IN OLD WOOD, LILTING ITS LIGHT SONG,	204	THE ROSE	66
AND IN A WOOD HE KNEW WHATEVER MOVED;	224	OTTO	13
HERE IN OUR AGING DISTRICT THE WOOD PIGEON LIVES WITH US,	234	ALL MORNING	1
A THING CARVED OF STONE OR WOOD, WITH THE DULL IRIDESCENCE OF LONG-POLISHED WOOD,	234	ALL MORNING	11
A THING CARVED OF STONE OR WOOD, WITH THE DULL IRIDESCENCE OF LONG-POLISHED WOOD,	234	ALL MORNING	11
WITH TOWHEES, FINCHES, CHICKADEES, CALIFORNIA QUAIL, WOOD DOVES,	235	ALL MORNING	40
I HEAR MY ECHO IN THE ECHOING WOOD--	239	IN A DARK TIME	3
WANTING THE QUIET OF OLD WOOD OR STONE WITHOUT WATER.	255	LIGHT POEM	9
WOODED			
WHEN THE SUN HAS FALLEN BEHIND A WOODED ISLAND;	67	SHAPE OF FIRE	89
WOODEN			
QUICK ON THE WOODEN BENCH,	42	TRANSPLANTING	9
FROM THE RICKETY WOODEN DOCK,	158	FIRST MEDITATN	51
A GREAT WOODEN SLEIGH CAREENING BEHIND THEM,	158	FIRST MEDITATN	54
DOWN WOODEN STEPS TOWARD A WEEDY GARDEN;	162	I'M HERE	46
THEIR WOODEN STORES OF SILVERY PINE AND WEATHER-BEATEN RED COURTHOUSES,	193	JOURNY INTERIOR	31
AND A FISHERMAN DAWDLES OVER A WOODEN BRIDGE,	197	THE LONG WATERS	37
WOOD-GRATE			
I SEE A BANKER'S MANSION WITH TWENTY WOOD-GRATE FIRES,	27	CLAIRVOY WIDOW	13
WOODIE			
A TRUE ZEPHYR-HAUNTED WOODIE.	81	SENSIBILITY! LA	7
WOODLAWN			
ON THE ROAD TO WOODLAWN	22	ROAD TO WDLAWN	T
AT WOODLAWN I HEARD THE DEAD CRY:	53	THE LOST SON	1
WOODS			
THE WOODS IN SPRING THE LEAVES THE SCENTED LANES	5	TO MY SISTER	2

	PAGE	TITLE	LINE
WOODS (CONTINUED)			
ONLY THE WOODS ARE ALIVE.	77	BRING THE DAY!	19
AND THE WOODS RESOUNDED WITH MANY A SHRIEK	115	THE SERPENT	25
THE LONG DAY DIES; I WALKED THE WOODS ALONE;	150	IN LATE SUMMER	29
WOOD'S			
AT THE WOOD'S MOUTH,	55	THE LOST SON	71
WOOED			
I WOOED WITH A LOW TUNE;	146	THE SONG	20
WOOL			
RUBBING MY NOSE IN THE WOOL OF BLANKETS;	162	I'M HERE	30
WOOLEN			
THE PSYCHE WRITHING AND SQUIRMING IN HEAVY WOOLEN,--	48	LAST WORDS	5
WOOS			
WHO KNOWS HOW THE WAG-TAIL WOOS?	183	THE WAGTAIL	1
WORD			
THE WORD OUTLEAPS THE WORLD, AND LIGHT IS ALL.	107	SIR JOHN DAVIES	96
AND, THEN, BEFORE HE SAYS A WORD	116	THE SLOTH	4
A CASUAL MAN, I KEEP MY CASUAL WORD,	140	THE SWAN	10
I'VE THE LARK'S WORD FOR IT, WHO SINGS ALONE:	156	THE DYING MAN	90
SAID NEVER A WORD,	216	THE SHY MAN	7
SAID NEVER A WORD,	216	THE SHY MAN	15
SAY MANY A WORD,	216	THE SHY MAN	22
SAY MANY A WORD,	216	THE SHY MAN	25
WORDLESS			
THE WHILE MY BLOOD LEAPED WITH A WORDLESS SONG.	105	SIR JOHN DAVIES	14
WORDS			
THE HEART BEAT FASTER AS THE FAT WORDS ROLLED.	21	THE AUCTION	14
LAST WORDS	48	LAST WORDS	T
MOTHER OF QUARTZ, YOUR WORDS WRITHE INTO MY EAR.	65	SHAPE OF FIRE	54
I'VE TRACED THESE WORDS IN SAND WITH A VESTIGIAL TAIL;	92	I CRY, LOVE!	17
OVER THIS DAMP GRAVE I SPEAK THE WORDS OF MY LOVE:	102	ELEGY FOR JANE	20
OLD LADY'S WINTER WORDS	103	OLD LADY'S WRDS	T
WORDS FOR THE WIND	123	WORDS FOR WIND	T
HIS WORDS	153	THE DYING MAN	ST
HER WORDS	208	HER WORDS	T
WORDS SKIRTING THE OBSCENE--	213	THE HAPPY THREE	7
WORE			
I WORE THE SUN WITH EASE.	87	PRAISE TO END!	66
AND THE DUST LAY THICK ON MY EYELIDS,--WHO EVER WORE GOGGLES?--	193	JOURNY INTERIOR	24
WAS IT HERE I WORE A CROWN OF BIRDS FOR A MOMENT	202	THE ROSE	26
WORK			
WHEREBY TRUE WORK IS WROUGHT.	20	REPL TO CENSURE	8
O CURSED BE THE WORK THAT GETS HONORABLE MENTION!	29	THE GENTLE	9
I FOUND MY FATHER WHEN I DID MY WORK,	154	THE DYING MAN	40
THE VINE WINDS TO ITS WORK;	261	THE CHANGELING	53
WORKERS			
THE TIME OF WORKERS IS THEIR OWN.	33	HIGHWAY: MICH	5
WORKS			
FOR WHOM THE WORLD WORKS?	169	FOURTH MEDITATN	49
WORLD			
AND YOUNG SHOOTS SPREAD UPON OUR INNER WORLD.	11	LIGHT BRIGHTER	20
THRICE HAPPY THEY WHOSE WORLD IS SPANNED	25	VERSE W ALLUSNS	1
HIS OYSTER WORLD WAS EASILY COME BY;	28	THE FAVORITE	3
THE WORLD RECEDES IN THE BLACK REVOLVING SHADOW;	33	IDYLL	9
WHERE, WHERE ARE THE TEARS OF THE WORLD?	56	THE LOST SON	103
INTO THAT MINNOWY WORLD OF WEEDS AND DITCHES,	66	SHAPE OF FIRE	65
IT'S A WINK BEYOND THE WORLD.	79	GIVE WAY, GATES	20
THE WORLD I KNEW;	87	PRAISE TO END!	60
IN THAT DARK WORLD WHERE GODS HAVE LOST THEIR WAY.	106	SIR JOHN DAVIES	48
THE WORLD IS FOR THE LIVING. WHO ARE THEY?	107	SIR JOHN DAVIES	91
THE WORD OUTLEAPS THE WORLD, AND LIGHT IS ALL.	107	SIR JOHN DAVIES	96
MORNING, I SAW THE WORLD WITH SECOND SIGHT,	133	THE PURE FURY	5
INTO THE WORLD OF MEN.	136	THE SENSUALISTS	26
IN THE SLOW WORLD OF DREAM,	141	MEMORY	1
MY HEART SWAYS WITH THE WORLD.	153	THE DYING MAN	13
I LOVE THE WORLD; I WANT MORE THAN THE WORLD,	155	THE DYING MAN	56
I LOVE THE WORLD; I WANT MORE THAN THE WORLD,	155	THE DYING MAN	56
FOR WHOM THE WORLD WORKS?	169	FOURTH MEDITATN	49
IN A WORLD ALWAYS LATE AFTERNOON,	171	WHAT TELL BONES	10
THEREFORE I REJECT THE WORLD OF THE DOG	196	THE LONG WATERS	5
I EMBRACE THE WORLD.	198	THE LONG WATERS	78
WINDING AROUND THE WATERS OF THE WORLD.	201	THE FAR FIELD	103

	PAGE	TITLE	LINE
WORLD (CONTINUED)			
FOR THE WORLD INVADES ME AGAIN,	220	THE ABYSS	30
WATCHING THE WAKING OF MY FATHER'S WORLD.--	225	OTTO	41
O WORLD SO FAR AWAY! O MY LOST WORLD!	225	OTTO	42
O WORLD SO FAR AWAY! O MY LOST WORLD!	225	OTTO	42
AND HIS WORLD AND MINE ARE THE SAME,	226	THE LIZARD	3
TO MEET THE WORLD, I RISE UP IN MY MIND;	243	THE MOTION	9
THE WORLD IS WHERE WE FLING IT; I'M LEAVING WHERE I AM.	260	THE CHANGELING	21
O, I'M THE GENIUS OF THE WORLD,--	268	SAGINAW SONG	43
WORM			
THE WORM, THOUGH DANK, IS SENSITIVE:	23	AMOROUS LADY	7
O WORM OF DUTY! O SPIRAL KNOWLEDGE!	48	LAST WORDS	6
WORM, BE WITH ME.	53	THE LOST SON	10
HAS THE WORM A SHADOW?	56	THE LOST SON	116
THE ARBOR IS COOLER. FAREWELL, FAREWELL, FOND WORM.	64	SHAPE OF FIRE	18
A WORM HAS A MOUTH.	72	WHERE KNOCK IS	45
THE WORM HAS MOVED AWAY.	73	WHERE KNOCK IS	69
THE WORM AND THE ROSE	78	BRING THE DAY!	35
IT'S STILL ENOUGH FOR THE KNOCK OF A WORM.	87	PRAISE TO END!	76
I WAS PURE AS A WORM ON A LEAF; I CHERISHED THE MOLD'S CHILDREN.	89	UNFOLD! UNFOLD!	27
A TRUE MOLE WANDERS LIKE A WORM.	97	O, THOU OPENING	20
THE LOWLY WORM CLIMBS UP A WINDING STAIR;	108	THE WAKING (2)	11
AND THEN STEP BAREFOOT ON A WORM	114	DINKY	7
MAY THE SUN GILD THEM A WORM;	169	FOURTH MEDITATN	60
WHEN I WAS A WORM, I DEVOURED.	172	WHAT TELL BONES	40
FALLS BACK, A SLUG, A LOOSE WORM	187	THE LONGING	21
BARE AS A BUD, AND NAKED AS A WORM.	188	THE LONGING	34
BUT THE HIND PART OF THE WORM WIGGLES THE MOST,	196	THE LONG WATERS	2
THE WORM, INTREPID SCHOLAR OF THE SOIL--	235	MANIFESTATION	5
"THAT'S NEVER BLAKE," SAID LINDSAY. "HE'D BE A WORM,	273	SUPPR W LINDSAY	26
WORMS			
THE WORMS WERE DELIGHTED AS WRENS.	63	FIELD OF LIGHT	50
WITH BATS, WEASELS, WORMS--I REJOICE IN THE KINSHIP.	151	SLUG	26
WORM'S			
FROM THE WORM'S ADVANCE AND RETREAT, FROM THE BUTTERFLY'S HAVOC,	196	THE LONG WATERS	21
WORN			
OVER THE WORN CURB OF THE TERRACE,	226	THE LIZARD	8
WORSE			
FOR THE ATTACKS OF FALSE HUMILITY TAKE SUDDEN TURNS FOR THE WORSE.	86	PRAISE TO END!	25
SOME FATES ARE WORSE.	161	I'M HERE	16
WORSE THAN CASTOREUM OF MINK OR WEASELS,	187	THE LONGING	4
THAT MAKES AN OLD CONFUSION WORSE.	257	SANITARIUM	2
A LIKELY THING FOR THEY'RE NO WORSE	267	SAGINAW SONG	21
WORST			
WHERE THE WORST WIND WAS,	41	BIG WIND	16
IN THE WORST NIGHT OF MY WILL,	154	THE DYING MAN	31
ON LOVE'S WORST UGLY DAY,	157	FIRST MEDITATN	1
THE WORST SURPRISE A CORNER COULD HAVE,	161	I'M HERE	14
WHEN THE WORST IS ABOUT TO ARRIVE;	172	WHAT TELL BONES	35
FACED UP TO THE WORST.	223	ELEGY (2)	11
WHAT'S THE WORST PORTION IN THIS MORTAL LIFE?	246	THE MARROW	5
WORTH			
SAID THE WREN, YOUR SONG ISN'T WORTH 10¢.	177	KITTY-CAT BIRD	2
WOULD			
THE SECOND DAWN I WOULD NOT HAVE BELIEVED:	12	MID-CNTRY BLOW	5
AND WILLINGLY WOULD I DISPENSE	19	EPIDERM MACABRE	13
WOULD NOT RELEASE ONE RIVEN NOTE:	22	SILENCE	18
WOULD RATHER TAKE THAN DISH IT OUT.	23	AMOROUS LADY	4
WHEN AMOROUS ARTS WE WOULD PURSUE,	23	AMOROUS LADY	11
I WOULD PUT OFF MYSELF AND FLEE	24	BEFORE STUDY	5
THOSE DOTING AUNTIES NEVER WOULD HAVE BOTHERED.	25	DIM-WIT COUSIN	4
NOTHING WOULD SLEEP IN THAT CELLAR, DANK AS A DITCH,	38	ROOT CELLAR	1
NOTHING WOULD GIVE UP LIFE:	38	ROOT CELLAR	10
THEY PRAYED THE COGS WOULD CREEP;	46	PICKLE BELT	2
THAT'S THE WAY IT WOULD FEEL.	55	THE LOST SON	57
THE MOON WOULD NOT HAVE ME.	55	THE LOST SON	78
WHICH WOULD YOU RATHER?	77	BRING THE DAY!	4
THE GREEN GRASSES,--WOULD THEY?	77	BRING THE DAY!	6
SWAYING, WOULD YOU BELIEVE,	98	O, THOU OPENING	48
I WOULD HOLD HIGH CONVERSE	103	OLD LADY'S WRDS	14

	PAGE	TITLE	LINE
WOULD (CONTINUED)			
THAT CAME TO BE THE BEARS AND YEATS WOULD KNOW.	105	SIR JOHN DAVIES	24
THAT WOMAN WOULD SET SODDEN STRAW ON FIRE.	105	SIR JOHN DAVIES	28
IT WAS "WOULD YOU BELIEVE IT--FAWTHER'S TALL!"	111	SQUEEZE-BOX	14
BUT NOTHING WOULD SUIT.	115	THE SERPENT	18
WOULD NOT REJOICE?	122	ALL EARTH, AIR	30
WHEN SMALL BIRDS SIGHED, SHE WOULD SIGH BACK AT THEM;	127	I KNEW A WOMAN	2
BUT WHO WOULD COUNT ETERNITY IN DAYS?	127	I KNEW A WOMAN	26
STAYED BY WHAT WAS, AND PULLED BY WHAT WOULD BE.	129	SHE	16
WHAT GLORIES WOULD WE? MOTIONS OF THE SOUL?	135	THE RENEWAL	1
I WALK AS IF MY FACE WOULD KISS THE WIND.	135	THE RENEWAL	12
FOR I WOULD DROWN IN FIRE.	138	LOVE'S PROGRESS	25
AND SHE IS WHAT I WOULD. IN THIS LIGHT AIR,	140	THE SWAN	17
THERE WOULD BE REASON FOR ESSENTIAL SIN;	144	ELEGY (1)	2
OR BROKE, BUT WOULD NOT GO.	147	THE EXORCISM	18
BRING ME THE MEEK, FOR I WOULD KNOW THEIR WAYS;	149	IN LATE SUMMER	5
WOULD BLAKE CALL YOU HOLY?	151	SLUG	29
AND WOULD THE SAME AGAIN.	154	THE DYING MAN	33
DAWN'S WHERE THE WHITE IS. WHO WOULD KNOW THE DAWN	155	THE DYING MAN	52
BIRDS ARE AROUND. I'VE ALL THE SINGING I WOULD.	164	I'M HERE	93
A PRISONER OF SMELLS, I WOULD RATHER EAT THAN PRAY.	173	WHAT TELL BONES	79
I WISH YOU WOULD ACT LIKE A BIRD REALLY SHOULD,	177	KITTY-CAT BIRD	6
EVERY TIME I LET HIM, THE STRING WOULD BUST.	178	THE DONKEY	3
THAT HE WAS GONE, WOULD BE THE ROOF;	178	THE CEILING	4
HE WOULD ACT VERY SNIDE,	178	THE YAK	4
I THINK IT WOULD BE MOST REVEALING	178	THE CEILING	5
SHE WOULD EAT AT ONE GLUP	179	MYRTLE'S COUSIN	3
SHE WOULD SIT WITH A BOOK ON HER KNEES,--	179	MYRTLE	6
POOR MYRTLE WOULD SIGH, "SWEET MY COZ,	180	GOO-GIRL	1
WOULD FREQUENTLY TALK TO A BUSH,	182	BOY AND BUSH	2
AND THE BUSH WOULD SAY, "MAC,	182	BOY AND BUSH	3
I WOULD WITH THE FISH, THE BLACKENING SALMON, AND THE MAD LEMMINGS,	188	THE LONGING	39
I WOULD UNLEARN THE LINGO OF EXASPERATION, ALL THE DISTORTIONS OF MALICE AND HATRED;	188	THE LONGING	42
I WOULD BELIEVE MY PAIN: AND THE EYE QUIET ON THE GROWING ROSE;	188	THE LONGING	43
I WOULD DELIGHT IN MY HANDS, THE BRANCH SINGING, ALTERING THE EXCESSIVE BIRD:	188	THE LONGING	44
I WOULD BE A STREAM, WINDING BETWEEN GREAT STRIATED ROCKS IN LATE SUMMER;	188	THE LONGING	46
A LEAF, I WOULD LOVE THE LEAVES, DELIGHTING IN THE REDOLENT DISORDER OF THIS MORTAL LIFE,	188	THE LONGING	47
WITH THESE I WOULD BE.	190	AT OYSTER RIVER	30
AS HE WOULD OR WOULD NOT,--	209	HER RETICENCE	5
AS HE WOULD OR WOULD NOT,--	209	HER RETICENCE	5
(WOULD A CIGARETTE DISTURB HIM?)	226	THE LIZARD	13
WHO WOULD BE HALF POSSESSED	240	IN EVEING AIR	3
O WHO WOULD TAKE THE VISION FROM THE CHILD?--	243	THE MOTION	23
I WOULD BE NEAR; I SHUT MY EYES TO SEE;	246	THE MARROW	22
UPON THAT GOD WHO KNOWS WHAT I WOULD KNOW.	246	THE MARROW	24
WILLS WHAT HE WOULD, SURRENDERING HIS WILL	250	THE RIGHT THING	17
I WOULD BE A CHANTICLEER.	266	FOR STEVENS	12
RAISE UP WHEN YOU WOULD PEE.	267	SAGINAW SONG	24
IT WOULD BLOW THE PLACE APART,--	268	SAGINAW SONG	40
WOULDN'T			
THEY BOUGHT A DRUM. HE WOULDN'T WHACK IT.	115	THE SERPENT	14
I WOULDN'T BE YOU FOR EVEN A DAY,	177	KITTY-CAT BIRD	11
AND WHAT FOOL WOULDN'T, WHEN THINGS FROM SLEEP	273	SUPPR W LINDSAY	3
WOUND			
YOU WOUND THE WATCH IN AN OLD-FASHIONED LOCKET	29	THE REMINDER	7
FISHED IN AN OLD WOUND,	53	THE LOST SON	12
SKIN, A THING YOU CANNOT SAY TO WHISPER AND EQUAL A WOUND?	98	O, THOU OPENING	24
NOR THE MOSS, WOUND WITH THE LAST LIGHT.	102	ELEGY FOR JANE	17
I BARE A WOUND, AND DARE MYSELF TO BLEED.	155	THE DYING MAN	69
LOVE IS MY WOUND.	172	WHAT TELL BONES	48
WOUNDS			
WRIGGLING THROUGH WOUNDS	50	THE MINIMAL	7
WRAITH			
THE WRAITH	106	SIR JOHN DAVIES	ST
WRAPPED			
WRAPPED IN THE TATTERED ROBE OF DEATH,	136	THE SENSUALISTS	19

	PAGE	TITLE	LINE
WRAPS			
THE EVENING WRAPS ME, STEADY AS A FLAME.	150	IN LATE SUMMER	32
WRATH			
THE SPIRIT OF WRATH BECOMES THE SPIRIT OF BLESSING,	195	JOURNY INTERIOR	78
MY WRATH, WHERE'S THE EDGE	211	SONG (1)	1
HER WRATH	216	HER WRATH	T
BLESSED THE MEEK; THEY SHALL INHERIT WRATH;	244	INFIRMITY	17
WREATHES			
A WIND WREATHES ROUND A TREE.	126	WORDS FOR WIND	93
WRECKAGE			
THE SEASON'S WRECKAGE LIES ABOUT,	14	COMING OF COLD	26
SURROUNDED BY SAND, BROKEN SHELLS, THE WRECKAGE OF WATER.	197	THE LONG .WATERS	59
WREN			
A WREN, HAPPY, TAIL INTO THE WIND,	102	ELEGY FOR JANE	5
THE RABBIT, AND THE WREN;	137	LOVE'S PROGRESS	17
THE WREN, THE CATBIRD.	162	I'M HERE	34
THE LOVED FOX, AND THE WREN.	166	HER BECOMING	64
SAID THE WREN, YOUR SONG ISN'T WORTH 10¢.	177	KITTY-CAT BIRD	2
--SAID THE WREN TO THE KITTY-CAT BIRD.	177	KITTY-CAT BIRD	4
--SAID THE WREN TO THE KITTY-CAT BIRD.	177	KITTY-CAT BIRD	8
--SAID THE WREN TO THE KITTY-CAT BIRD.	177	KITTY-CAT BIRD	12
I LIVE BETWEEN THE HERON AND THE WREN,	239	IN A DARK TIME	5
WRENS			
THE WORMS WERE DELIGHTED AS WRENS.	63	FIELD OF LIGHT	50
WHILE THE WRENS BICKERED AND SANG IN THE HALF-GREEN HEDGEROWS,	200	THE FAR FIELD	36
AND THE WRENS SCOLD, AND THE CHICKADEES FRISK AND FROLIC,	234	ALL MORNING	24
WITH WRENS, SPARROWS, JUNCOS, CEDAR WAXWINGS, FLICKERS,	235	ALL MORNING	41
WREN'S			
THE WREN'S THROAT SHIMMERED,	51	THE WAKING (1)	6
WREN-SONG			
WREN-SONG IN TRELLIS: A LIGHT ECSTASY OF BUTTERFLIES COURTING,	255	LIGHT POEM	1
WRESTED			
WAS WRESTED FROM THE SUN;	18	GENESIS	2
WRESTLE			
THIS URGE, WRESTLE, RESURRECTION OF DRY STICKS,	37	CUTTINGS (LATE)	1
WRETCH			
A WRETCH NEEDS HIS WRETCHEDNESS. YES.	188	THE LONGING	24
A WRETCH NEEDS HIS WRETCHEDNESS. YES. BUT THIS SHAPE	260	THE CHANGELING	13
WRETCHEDNESS			
A WRETCH NEEDS HIS WRETCHEDNESS. YES.	188	THE LONGING	24
A WRETCH NEEDS HIS WRETCHEDNESS. YES. BUT THIS SHAPE	260	THE CHANGELING	13
WRIGGLING			
WRIGGLING THROUGH WOUNDS	50	THE MINIMAL	7
WRIGGLING LIKE A MINISCULE PUPPY.	227	MEADOW MOUSE	11
WRIGHT'S			
WHEN HATTIE WRIGHT'S ANGORA DIED AS WELL,	224	OTTO	29
WRINKLE			
CAN IT WRINKLE ITS NOSE?	54	THE LOST SON	51
WRINKLED			
A BIT OF WATER CAUGHT IN A WRINKLED CREVICE,	168	FOURTH MEDITATN	8
THE RIVER MOVES, WRINKLED BY MIDGES,	168	FOURTH MEDITATN	23
THE DRY BLOOM SPLITTING IN THE WRINKLED VALE,	197	THE LONG WATERS	30
WRINKLES			
THE LACELIKE WRINKLES OF THE WAKE WIDENING, THINNING OUT,	203	THE ROSE	33
WRINKLING			
TOWARD THE QUICK-WATER, WRINKLING AND RIPPLING.	54	THE LOST SON	39
WRINKLING BETWEEN REEDS IN SHALLOWER WATER,	93	I CRY, LOVE!	47
WRIST			
HAIR ON A NARROW WRIST BONE;	6	THE PREMONITION	9
THE HAND THAT HELD MY WRIST	45	MY PAPA'S WALTZ	9
"O IT'S WONDERFUL HOW WITH A FLICK OF YOUR WRIST,	117	LADY AND BEAR	21
WRISTS			
VINES TOUGHER THAN WRISTS	38	FORCING HOUSE	1
AND THEIR THORN-BITTEN WRISTS,	44	FRAU BAUMAN	34
HOPE'S HOLY WRISTS: THE LITTLE BURNING BOYS	143	SHIMMER OF EVIL	13
WRIST-THICK			
AND THAT WRIST-THICK CASCADE TUMBLING FROM A CLEFT ROCK,	191	AT OYSTER RIVER	44
WRITE			
THESE POETS, THEY WRITE LIKE I SNEEZE!"	179	MYRTLE	12
"WRITE ALL MY WHISPERS DOWN,"	208	HER WORDS	8

	PAGE	TITLE	LINE
WRITHE			
MOTHER OF QUARTZ, YOUR WORDS WRITHE INTO MY EAR.	65	SHAPE OF FIRE	54
WRITHER			
MY LIZARD, MY LIVELY WRITHER,	217	WISH YOUNG WIFE	1
WRITHING			
THE PSYCHE WRITHING AND SQUIRMING IN HEAVY WOOLEN,--	48	LAST WORDS	5
I SAW A VIRGIN WRITHING IN THE DIRT--	131	SENTENTIOUS MAN	2
WRITHING UNTIL THE LAST	147	THE EXORCISM	22
WRONG			
GOOD-BYE FOR BEING WRONG.	76	I NEED, I NEED	50
THESE WINGS ARE FROM THE WRONG NEST.	80	GIVE WAY, GATES	52
I'VE WAKED THE WRONG WIND:	82	SENSIBILITY! LA	29
ROCK ME TO SLEEP, THE WEATHER'S WRONG.	86	PRAISE TO END!	28
YOU'LL FIND I'M EITHER RIGHT OR WRONG	181	MONOTONY SONG	23
WROUGHT			
WHEREBY TRUE WORK IS WROUGHT.	20	REPL TO CENSURE	8
WUNDERKIND			
ALTES WUNDERKIND.	266	FOR STEVENS	16
WYANDOTTE			
IN ECORSE, TOLEDO, AND WYANDOTTE	111	SQUEEZE-BOX	11
YAK			
THE YAK	178	THE YAK	T
THERE WAS A MOST ODIOUS YAK	178	THE YAK	1
YANKING			
OR YANKING TOUGH FERN-SHAPES,	39	WEED PULLER	7
YARD			
FROM THE ONE BEAUTIFUL THING IN HER YARD, THE PEACHTREE;	223	ELEGY (2)	13
ALL IN MY YARD, OF A PERPETUAL SUNDAY,	235	ALL MORNING	46
YAWN			
HE STARTS TO YAWN--IT TAKES ALL DAY--	182	THE HIPPO	4
YAWNS			
WHEN OUR SPAYED FEMALE CAT YAWNS AND STRETCHES OUT IN THE SUNSHINE--	234	ALL MORNING	23
YE			
GIVE WAY, YE GATES	79	GIVE WAY, GATES	T
YE LITTLES, LIE MORE CLOSE!	240	IN EVEING AIR	7
YEA			
YEA, I HAVE GONE AND STAYED.	173	WHAT TELL BONES	96
YEA, I HAVE SLAIN MY WILL, AND STILL I LIVE;	246	THE MARROW	21
YEAR			
THE SHOOTS OF SPRING HAVE MELLOWED WITH THE YEAR.	12	SLOW SEASON	13
THE SKY TURNS DARK, THE YEAR GROWS OLD,	15	COMING OF COLD	36
HE THINKS ABOUT IT FOR A YEAR;	116	THE SLOTH	3
MY FRIENDS BECOME MORE CHRISTIAN, YEAR BY YEAR.	132	SENTENTIOUS MAN	38
MY FRIENDS BECOME MORE CHRISTIAN, YEAR BY YEAR.	132	SENTENTIOUS MAN	38
REMINDS ME I AM DYING WITH THE YEAR.	149	IN LATE SUMMER	24
IN A BLEAK TIME, WHEN A WEEK OF RAIN IS A YEAR,	187	THE LONGING	14
THE FIRST SNOW OF THE YEAR IN THE DARK FIR.	197	THE LONG WATERS	31
YEARNER			
I, STARVELING YEARNER, SEEM TO SEE	25	VERSE W ALLUSNS	11
YEARS			
YOU'RE LIKELY TO GO ON LIVING FOR YEARS,	23	ACADEMIC	2
THE VISIT OF VISION, LUCK YEARS OVERDUE,	29	THE GENTLE	6
WHO LIVED ABOVE A POTTING SHED FOR YEARS.	224	OTTO	4
OR FRENCHMEN KILLED A HUNDRED YEARS AGO,	224	OTTO	26
YEAR'S			
AND BOYS MOON AT GIRLS WITH LAST YEAR'S FATUOUS FACES,	24	VERNAL SENTIMNT	3
YEATS			
I TAKE THIS CADENCE FROM A MAN NAMED YEATS;	105	SIR JOHN DAVIES	19
THAT CAME TO BE THE BEARS AND YEATS WOULD KNOW.	105	SIR JOHN DAVIES	24
YELL			
"WHO CALLED ME POET OF THE COLLEGE YELL?	274	SUPPR W LINDSAY	40
YELLOW			
TWO YELLOW AND BLACK, AND ONE THAT LOOKS IN BETWEEN,--	24	VERNAL SENTIMNT	6
HUNG DOWN LONG YELLOW EVIL NECKS, LIKE TROPICAL SNAKES.	38	ROOT CELLAR	5
WINKIE WILL YELLOW I SANG.	72	WHERE KNOCK IS	35
MINNOWS CAN HEAR, AND BUTTERFLIES, YELLOW AND BLUE,	196	THE LONG WATERS	3
DROPPING A FINE YELLOW SILT WHERE THE SUN STAYS;	200	THE FAR FIELD	68
YELLOWISH			
OF GREEN, OR PLUNGED TO MY ELBOWS IN THE SPONGY YELLOWISH MOSS OF THE MARSHES:	40	MOSS-GATHERING	8
WHERE THE YELLOWISH PRONGS OF GRASS POKE THROUGH THE BLACKENED ASH,	196	THE LONG WATERS	15

	PAGE	TITLE	LINE

YELLOWISH-GREEN
AND THE YELLOWISH-GREEN FROM THE MOUNTAINY UPLAND,-- ..... 200 THE FAR FIELD 62
YELLOWY
ROTTEN LEAVES OR YELLOWY PETALS, ... 42 OLD FLORIST 5
EVEN THE HUSHED FORMS, THE BENT YELLOWY WEEDS .... 57 THE LOST SON 147
YELPING
A PENSIVE MISTRESS, AND A YELPING WIFE. .... 246 THE MARROW 6
YES
THE TROUBLE IS WITH NO AND YES .... 75 I NEED, I NEED 33
HER FEET SAID YES. .... 76 I NEED, I NEED 61
EXALTED? YES,-- .... 82 SENSIBILITY! LA 34
A SLOW SIGH SAYS YES. AND LIGHT SIGHS; .... 90 UNFOLD! UNFOLD! 49
YES. .... 98 O, THOU OPENING 40
YES, I WAS DANCING-MAD, AND HOW .... 105 SIR JOHN DAVIES 23
O PRINT IT, MY DEAR, DO PUBLISH IT, YES, ... 113 TO A LADY ED 9
YES, A BEAR HAS TO FISH WITH HIS PAW, PAW, PAW. ...... 117 LADY AND BEAR 19
GREAT BOEHME ROOTED ALL IN YES AND NO; .... 133 THE PURE FURY 13
MY SHAPE A LEVITY--YES!-- .... 165 HER BECOMING 4
A WRETCH NEEDS HIS WRETCHEDNESS. YES. .... 188 THE LONGING 24
A WRETCH NEEDS HIS WRETCHEDNESS. YES. BUT THIS SHAPE ..... 260 THE CHANGELING 13
YESTERDAY
ARE THOSE HORNS ON TOP OF THE HILL? YESTERDAY HAS A LONG
LOOK. .... 59 THE LONG ALLEY 13
WAS IT YESTERDAY I STRETCHED OUT THE THIN BONES OF MY
INNOCENCE? .... 168 FOURTH MEDITATN 12
YET
YET SUCH IS MY UNSEEMLINESS: .... 19 EPIDERM MACABRE 9
AND YET HIS HAPPINESS WAS NOT COMPLETE; .... 28 THE FAVORITE 11
YET WHEN I HEARD THE DRUNKARDS HOWLING, ... 48 JUDGE NOT 7
YET STILL? .... 58 THE LOST SON 168
FILLS AND TREMBLES AT THE EDGE YET DOES NOT FLOW OVER, ... 67 SHAPE OF FIRE 94
HAVE I COME TO ALWAYS? NOT YET. .... 74 WHERE KNOCK IS 86
YET STAYS: .... 101 LIGHT BREATHER 2
I TURNED MY FACE AWAY, AND YET SHE STAYED. ...... 119 THE DREAM 14
AND YET I ROAMED OUT WHERE .... 128 THE VOICE 7
DIMINISHED, YET STILL HEARD: .... 128 THE VOICE 10
YET STILL LAUGH IN MY SLEEP. .... 130 THE OTHER 24
EACH ONE'S HIMSELF, YET EACH ONE'S EVERYONE. .... 132 SENTENTIOUS MAN 36
YET, LIKE A TREE, ENDURE THE SHIFT OF THINGS. .... 135 THE RENEWAL 6
I KNOW I LOVE, YET KNOW NOT WHERE I AM; .... 135 THE RENEWAL 15
HER IMAGE FADES, YET DOES NOT DISAPPEAR-- .... 140 THE SWAN 2
YET WHISTLE BACK AT EVERY WHISTLING BIRD. .... 140 THE SWAN 11
CLOSE, AND YET FAR AWAY. .... 146 THE SONG 27
(AND YET I WAS NOT THERE, ... 147 THE EXORCISM 9
"WHAT'S DONE IS YET TO COME; .... 153 THE DYING MAN 6
I DIE INTO THIS LIFE, ALONE YET NOT ALONE. ...... 155 THE DYING MAN 59
YET DARED TO FIX HIS VISION ANYWHERE. .... 155 THE DYING MAN 65
THE VISION MOVES, AND YET REMAINS THE SAME. ..... 156 THE DYING MAN 94
WHO STOPS BEING A BIRD, YET BEATS HIS WINGS ..... 156 THE DYING MAN 100
YET REMAIN ONLY HALF AWARE OF THE INTRANSIENT GLORY? ..... 169 FOURTH MEDITATN 32
YET MOVES GENTLY AMONG THE BIRDS. .... 170 FOURTH MEDITATN 74
AND YET WAS STILL. .... 205 THE ROSE 105
WE ARE ONE, AND YET WE ARE MORE, ... 207 THE YOUNG GIRL 5
YET KEEP TO MYSELF MY OWN MIND; .... 208 HER WORDS 5
YET IF WE WAIT, UNAFRAID, BEYOND THE FEARFUL INSTANT, ... 221 THE ABYSS 57
AND YET SHE DIED IN AGONY, ... 223 ELEGY (2) 16
AND YET STILL VIOLENT MEN, WHOSE STACKED-UP GUNS .... 224 OTTO 27
AND YET MY THOUGHT TURNS BACK TO THEM, ... 225 THE CHUMS 3
THE WAVES NOT YET HIGH, BUT EVEN, ... 230 THE STORM 11
WHEN WE ABIDE YET GO .... 237 THE TRANCED 3
YET LOVE-LONGING OF A KIND .... 237 THE TRANCED 8
YET IT'S THE NATURE OF ALL LOVE TO RISE: .... 238 THE TRANCED 22
PURE AIMLESSNESS PURSUED AND YET PURSUED .... 241 THE SEQUEL 3
OH, TO BE SOMETHING ELSE, YET STILL TO BE! ...... 244 INFIRMITY 6
AND KNOWING THIS, I AM NOT YET UNDONE. .... 244 INFIRMITY 30
YET WHEN I SIGHED, I STOOD OUTSIDE MY LIFE, ... 248 THE TREE, BIRD 7
YET FOR THIS WE TRAVELLED .... 265 HARSH COUNTRY 13
YET FINE AS MAIDENHAIR, ... 271 THE REPLY 12
YICKETTY-YAK
AND GO HUMPING OFF, YICKETTY-YAK. .... 178 THE YAK 5
YIELDS
THE LATE PEACH YIELDS A SUBTLE MUSK, ... 14 COMING OF COLD 1

	PAGE	TITLE	LINE
YIELD'S			
THE YIELD'S HALF DOWN AND HALF IN AIR,	14	COMING OF COLD	8
YORK			
IT WASN'T THE JOINTS IN NEW YORK, NEW YORK;	111	SQUEEZE-BOX	9
IT WASN'T THE JOINTS IN NEW YORK, NEW YORK;	111	SQUEEZE-BOX	9
YOU (173)			
YOU'D			
YOU'D BETTER WATCH THE THINGS YOU DO.	114	DINKY	17
YOU'D BETTER WATCH THE THINGS YOU DO.	114	DINKY	18
YOU'D BETTER NOT LAUGH; AND DON'T SAY, "POOH!"	177	KITTY-CAT BIRD	18
YOU'D BE INSTITUTIONALIZED.	228	IN VIOLENT WARD	2
YOU'LL			
SOFTLY SOFTLY, YOU'LL WAKE THE CLAMS.	85	PRAISE TO END!	10
--OR YOU'LL END LIKE THE KITTY-CAT BIRD.	177	KITTY-CAT BIRD	21
YOU'LL FIND I'M EITHER RIGHT OR WRONG	181	MONOTONY SONG	23
YOUNG			
CORRUPTION REAPS THE YOUNG; YOU DREAD	4	FEUD	1
THE YOUNG FRUIT SWELL UPON THE PEAR-TREE BOUGH.	11	LIGHT BRIGHTER	16
AND YOUNG SHOOTS SPREAD UPON OUR INNER WORLD.	11	LIGHT BRIGHTER	20
TO KEEP INCLEMENT WEATHER FROM ITS YOUNG.	12	SLOW SEASON	6
ILLUSION'S TRINKETS, SPLENDID FOR THE YOUNG;	21	THE AUCTION	6
LIMP AND DAMP, DELICATE AS A YOUNG BIRD'S TONGUE;	39	ORCHIDS	5
LIFTING THE YOUNG PLANTS WITH TWO FINGERS,	42	TRANSPLANTING	3
THE YOUNG HORNS WINDING AND UNWINDING,	42	TRANSPLANTING	15
IF I WERE A YOUNG MAN,	104	OLD LADY'S WRDS	49
I AM NO LONGER YOUNG	125	WORDS FOR WIND	78
WE DID NOT FLY THE FLESH. WHO DOES, WHEN YOUNG?	131	SENTENTIOUS MAN	7
I SAW A YOUNG SNAKE GLIDE	150	SNAKE	1
SCUTTLING DOWN AND AROUND LIKE YOUNG SQUIRRELS,	152	THE SISKINS	17
THE SOUND OF VOICES, YOUNG VOICES, MIXED WITH SLEIGHBELLS,	161	I'M HERE	4
THE PRATTLE OF THE YOUNG NO LONGER PLEASES.	161	I'M HERE	9
IN THE SUN, BUSY AT A YOUNG BODY,	165	HER BECOMING	7
THE YOUNG, BROW-BEATEN EARLY INTO A BALEFUL SILENCE,	169	FOURTH MEDITATN	44
ALIVE WITH TINY STRIPED FISH, AND YOUNG CRABS CLIMBING IN AND OUT OF THE WATER.	190	AT OYSTER RIVER	5
THE YOUNG SNAKE, POISED IN GREEN LEAVES, WAITING FOR ITS FLY,	190	AT OYSTER RIVER	28
IN TIME WHEN THE TROUT AND YOUNG SALMON LEAP FOR THE LOW-FLYING INSECTS,	197	THE LONG WATERS	33
I SUFFERED FOR BIRDS, FOR YOUNG RABBITS CAUGHT IN THE MOWER,	199	THE FAR FIELD	24
HANGING, BUNCHED LIKE YOUNG FRUIT, BENDING THE END BRANCHES,	199	THE FAR FIELD	32
THE YOUNG GIRL	207	THE YOUNG GIRL	T
A YOUNG MOUTH LAUGHS AT A GIFT.	208	HER WORDS	1
WHEN SO YOUNG, WHEN SO YOUNG?	211	SONG (1)	4
WHEN SO YOUNG, WHEN SO YOUNG?	211	SONG (1)	4
WISH FOR A YOUNG WIFE	217	WISH YOUNG WIFE	T
HAD SLAUGHTERED GAME, AND CUT YOUNG FIR TREES DOWN.	224	OTTO	21
TO DISTRACT ATTENTION FROM THE SHORT-TAILED RIDICULOUS YOUNG ONES	234	ALL MORNING	19
A BIRD KEPT HAUNTING ME WHEN I WAS YOUNG--	245	THE DECISION	3
YOUNGEST			
HE WAS THE YOUNGEST SON OF A STRANGE BROOD,	224	OTTO	1
YOUNGLING			
IMPERIOUS YOUNGLING, THOUGH APPROACHING FORTY;	264	THREE EPIGRAMS	2
YOUNGLINGS			
YOUNGLINGS, THE SMALL FISH KEEP HEADING INTO THE CURRENT.	170	FOURTH MEDITATN	75
YOUR (48)			
YOU'RE			
YOU'RE LIKELY TO GO ON LIVING FOR YEARS,	23	ACADEMIC	2
EAT WHERE YOU'RE AT. I'M NOT A MOUSE.	72	WHERE KNOCK IS	40
YOU'RE NOT VERY NICE,--	75	I NEED, I NEED	29
YOU'RE BLISTERED ALL OVER	89	UNFOLD! UNFOLD!	14
BAGS? WHO EVER SAID GOD SANG IN YOUR FAT SHAPE? YOU'RE NOT THE ONLY	98	O, THOU OPENING	27
KEEPER OF HAY. THAT'S A SPRATLING'S PRATTLE. AND DON'T BE THINKING YOU'RE	98	O, THOU OPENING	28
IT WAS STAND ON YOUR FEET AS LONG AS YOU'RE ABLE,	112	SQUEEZE-BOX	35
YOU'RE PART OF HIM; HE'S PART OF YOU	114	DINKY	19
YOU'RE A FAKE, YOUR'RE A FRAUD, YOU'RE A HOR-RID PRETENSE!	177	KITTY-CAT BIRD	3
YOU'RE A FAKE, YOUR'RE A FRAUD, YOU'RE A HOR-RID PRETENSE!	177	KITTY-CAT BIRD	3
AND SAID, OLD BOY, YOU'RE SHEDDING HAIR,	181	MONOTONY SONG	6
--UNLESS YOU'RE HUGH OR HARRY!	181	MONOTONY SONG	28
ARE YOU? YOU'RE JUMPING TOO!	182	THE LAMB	4

	PAGE	TITLE	LINE
YOU'RE (CONTINUED)			
YOU'RE BECOMING THAT HORROR, A TWO-LEGGED PIG	272	DUET	3
YOUR'RE			
YOU'RE A FAKE, YOUR'RE A FRAUD, YOU'RE A HOR-RID PRETENSE!	177	KITTY-CAT BIRD	3
YOURS (1)			
YOURSELF			
AND SHOULD HE ARRIVE, WHY JUST LEAN YOURSELF BACK	113	TO A LADY ED	7
IT IS FATAL TO WOO YOURSELF, ...	172	WHAT TELL BONES	36
OR STAY BY YOURSELF DOWN DEEP IN THE WOOD, ...	177	KITTY-CAT BIRD	7
YOURSELF AWAKE UNTIL YOU SLEEP, ...	181	MONOTONY SONG	26
YOU'S			
DAN CUPID, I TELL YOU'S A BRAW LADDIE-BUCK;	113	TO A LADY ED	5
YOU'VE			
YOU'VE SEEN ME, PRINCE OF STINKS, ...	82	SENSIBILITY! LA	32
YOU'VE TOO MANY TUNES, AND NONE OF THEM GOOD:	177	KITTY-CAT BIRD	5
ZEALOT			
THE FURY OF THE HATE-DRIVEN ZEALOT, THE MEANNESS OF THE			
HUMAN WEASEL;	170	FOURTH MEDITATN	68
ZEN			
A MISTRESS OF ZEN, I'LL BITE YOUR THUMB, ...	272	DUET	18
ZEPHYR-HAUNTED			
A TRUE ZEPHYR-HAUNTED WOODIE.	81	SENSIBILITY! LA	7
10¢			
SAID THE WREN, YOUR SONG ISN'T WORTH 10¢.	177	KITTY-CAT BIRD	2

COMPONENTS OF HYPHENATED COMPOUNDS

	PAGE	TITLE	LINE
A (3)			
ABANDONED			
THE LAST-ABANDONED STALK ALWAYS QUIVERING	152	THE SISKINS	14
ACHE			
WHAT A BONE-ACHE I HAVE.	85	PRAISE TO END!	3
ADDER			
ADDER-MOUTHED,	39	ORCHIDS	2
AFTER			
TO STARE INTO THE AFTER-LIGHT, THE GLITTER LEFT ON THE LAKE'S SURFACE,	67	SHAPE OF FIRE	88
THE AFTER-IMAGE NEVER STAYS THE SAME.	132	SENTENTIOUS MAN	20
OR AFTER-IMAGE OF THE INNER EYE.	155	THE DYING MAN	57
THE EYES REJOICE IN THE ACT OF SEEING AND THE FRESH AFTER-IMAGE;	163	I'M HERE	79
THE AFTER-LIGHT UPON ICE-BURDENED PINES;	201	THE FAR FIELD	97
ALIVE			
MY DARLING, MY DEAREST, MOST-HONEST-ALIVE,	113	TO A LADY ED	13
FLESH-AWKWARD, HALF-ALIVE,	162	I'M HERE	27
ALL			
YOU ALL-OF-A-SUDDEN GODS,	82	SENSIBILITY! LA	26
ALMOST			
ITS ALMOST-INVISIBLE WINGS, BUZZING, HITTING THE LOOSE LEAVES INTERMITTENTLY--	234	ALL MORNING	32
AND (1)			
ANIMAL			
HALF-BIRD, HALF-ANIMAL.	141	MEMORY	6
ANKLE			
THE WALKER TRUDGES ANKLE-DEEP IN LEAVES;	12	SLOW SEASON	11
ARBUTUS			
SWAN-HEART, ARBUTUS-CALM,	124	WORDS FOR WIND	51
AS			
A MOST EX-AS-PER-AT-ING LUG.	116	THE SLOTH	7
AT (2)			
AWKWARD			
FLESH-AWKWARD, HALF-ALIVE,	162	I'M HERE	27
BACK			
OR PINCHING-BACK ASTERS, OR PLANTING AZALEAS,	42	OLD FLORIST	2
I KNOW THE BACK-STREAM'S JOY, AND THE STONE'S ETERNAL PULSELESS LONGING.	88	PRAISE TO END!	82
NUDGES INTO A BACK-EDDY, A SANDY INLET,	159	FIRST MEDITATN	69
BACKED			
ACROSS MY LAWN THE SOFT-BACKED CREATURES COME;	149	IN LATE SUMMER	3
BAG			
I'M TIRED OF ALL THAT, BAG-FOOT. I CAN HEAR SMALL ANGELS ANYTIME. WHO	98	O, THOU OPENING	25
BANKED			
MY BANKED-UP VERTIGO	213	THE HAPPY THREE	26
BAR			
ONLY TO FLY OVER TO HIS FAVORITE PERCH, THE CROSS-BAR OF A TELEPHONE POLE;	234	ALL MORNING	9
BARLEY			
BUT BARLEY-BREAK AND SQUEEZE.	60	THE LONG ALLEY	38
BARS			
THE WAVES, ALTERED BY SAND-BARS, BEDS OF KELP, MISCELLANEOUS DRIFTWOOD,	191	AT OYSTER RIVER	32
BAT			
AS HIS HEAD; HIS BAT-LIKE EARS	227	MEADOW MOUSE	15
BE (1)			
BEACH			
THE DEW REVIVES ON THE BEACH-GRASS;	190	AT OYSTER RIVER	20
BEAR			
THE SHE-BEAR MOPES UNDER THE HILL.	64	SHAPE OF FIRE	15
BEAST			
SEA-BEAST OR BIRD FLUNG TOWARD THE RAVAGED SHORE?	107	SIR JOHN DAVIES	68
BEAT			
THE LOVE-BEAT OF A BIRD.	212	LIGHT LISTENED	9
BEATEN			
THE YOUNG, BROW-BEATEN EARLY INTO A BALEFUL SILENCE,	169	FOURTH MEDITATN	44
THEIR WOODEN STORES OF SILVERY PINE AND WEATHER-BEATEN RED COURTHOUSES,	193	JOURNY INTERIOR	31
HER FACE LIKE A RAIN-BEATEN STONE ON THE DAY SHE ROLLED OFF	223	ELEGY (2)	1
ITS BEVY OF BEES, AND ITS WIND-BEATEN RICKETY SUN-CHAIRS.	226	THE LIZARD	29

	PAGE	TITLE	LINE
BED			
MY DIM-WIT COUSIN, SAVED BY A DEATH-BED QUAVER, ...	25	DIM-WIT COUSIN	1
NOW IN THE MISERY OF BED-SITTING ROOM CONFUSION, ...	29	THE REMINDER	9
BEETLES			
AND IN THE SHRUNKEN FACE OF A DEAD RAT, EATEN BY RAIN AND GROUND-BEETLES	199	THE FAR FIELD	19
BETWEEN			
AN IN-BETWEEN TIME,	58	THE LOST SON	150
BIRD			
HALF-BIRD, HALF-ANIMAL.	141	MEMORY	6
NERVOUS AND COLD, BIRD-FURTIVE, WHISKERY, ...	157	FIRST MEDITATN	16
LIKE A HUMMING-BIRD, ...	183	THE WAGTAIL	5
HAUNT OF THE CAT-BIRD, NESTING-PLACE OF THE FIELD-MOUSE,	199	THE FAR FIELD	15
MY BIRD-BLOOD READY.	207	THE YOUNG GIRL	12
BITTEN			
AND THEIR THORN-BITTEN WRISTS, ...	44	FRAU BAUMAN	34
THE ARROYO CRACKING THE ROAD, THE WIND-BITTEN BUTTES, THE CANYONS, ...	193	JOURNY INTERIOR	7
BLACK			
BLUE-BLACK FROM WHERE I AM SITTING, ...	190	AT OYSTER RIVER	12
BLOOD			
MY BIRD-BLOOD READY.	207	THE YOUNG GIRL	12
BLOSSOM			
THE HUMMINGBIRD, WHIRRING FROM QUINCE-BLOSSOM TO MORNING-GLORY--	190	AT OYSTER RIVER	29
BLOWN			
CHILDREN, THEIR BELLIES SWOLLEN LIKE BLOWN-UP PAPER BAGS,	48	JUDGE NOT	2
BLUE			
THEY FLICKER FASTER THAN A BLUE-TAILED SWIFT, ...	8	THE SIGNALS	5
BLUE-BLACK FROM WHERE I AM SITTING, ...	190	AT OYSTER RIVER	12
BO			
AND MY THOUGHT FLIES TO THE PLACE BY THE BO-TREE.	222	THE ABYSS	100
BOG			
BY THE MUDDY POND-EDGE, BY THE BOG-HOLES, ...	54	THE LOST SON	42
BOGEY			
WHOSE BOGEY-HAUNTED LOOK	7	ORDERS FOR DAY	16
BONE			
WHAT A BONE-ACHE I HAVE.	85	PRAISE TO END!	3
SPIRIT AND NATURE BEAT IN ONE BREAST-BONE--	131	SENTENTIOUS MAN	1
BONES			
ARCH MY BACK, PRETTY-BONES, I'M DEAD AT BOTH ENDS.	85	PRAISE TO END!	9
BOOK			
MY POETRY-BOOK, IF YOU PLEASE,--	179	MYRTLE	7
BORN			
THOU WERT MARMOREAN-BORN.	81	SENSIBILITY! LA	5
THE GENTLE AND BEAUTIFUL STILL-TO-BE-BORN;	170	FOURTH MEDITATN	65
BOTTLE			
NOW HE'S EATEN HIS THREE KINDS OF CHEESE AND DRUNK FROM HIS BOTTLE-CAP WATERING-TROUGH--	227	MEADOW MOUSE	12
BOTTOM			
BUMPING AGAINST STICKS AND BOTTOM-STONES, THEN SWINGING	159	FIRST MEDITATN	70
THE BOTTOM-STONES SHIMMER BACK THEIR IRREGULAR STRIATIONS,	233	THE PIKE	8
BOUND			
THE FLESH-BOUND SIGHING LOVER, ...	7	ORDERS FOR DAY	5
THE ICE PILING HIGH AGAINST THE IRON-BOUND SPILES, ...	191	AT OYSTER RIVER	50
BOW			
ITS SPRAY HOLDING A DOUBLE RAIN-BOW IN EARLY MORNING, ...	191	AT OYSTER RIVER	45
BOX			
INTO THE FLAT-BOX IT GOES, ...	42	TRANSPLANTING	12
SONG FOR THE SQUEEZE-BOX	111	SQUEEZE-BOX	T
BUT THIS MORNING THE SHOE-BOX HOUSE ON THE BACK PORCH IS EMPTY.	227	MEADOW MOUSE	20
BRANCH			
AND THE IVY-BRANCH, CAST TO THE GROUND, PUTS DOWN ROOTS INTO THE SAWDUST, ...	197	THE LONG WATERS	34
BREAK			
BUT BARLEY-BREAK AND SQUEEZE.	60	THE LONG ALLEY	38
THE SCRAGGLY WIND-BREAK OF A DUSTY RANCH-HOUSE.	194	JOURNY INTERIOR	45
BREAST			
SPIRIT AND NATURE BEAT IN ONE BREAST-BONE--	131	SENTENTIOUS MAN	1
BRIER			
AND MY DRESS CAUGHT ON ROSE-BRIER.	162	I'M HERE	47

	PAGE	TITLE	LINE
BROW			
THE YOUNG, BROW-BEATEN EARLY INTO A BALEFUL SILENCE,	169	FOURTH MEDITATN	44
BROWNISH			
AROUND, BACK INTO THE TINY MAINCURRENT, THE RUSH OF BROWNISH-WHITE WATER,	159	FIRST MEDITATN	71
BUCK			
DAN CUPID, I TELL YOU'S A BRAW LADDIE-BUCK;	113	TO A LADY ED	5
BUD			
STILL WET FROM ITS BUD-SHEATH,	101	LIGHT BREATHER	4
BUG			
DOWN AMONG THE RUBBISH, THE BUG-RIDDLED FOLIAGE,	54	THE LOST SON	41
A BUG-EYED EDIBLE ONE,	209	HER LONGING	8
BULB			
A SPIDER EASES HIMSELF DOWN FROM A SWAYING LIGHT-BULB,	231	THE STORM	34
BUM			
HE CAN PLINK THE SKITTER-BUM;	266	FOR STEVENS	6
BURDENED			
THE AFTER-LIGHT UPON ICE-BURDENED PINES;	201	THE FAR FIELD	97
BURIED			
IN YOUR SEA-BURIED EAR,	211	SONG (1)	11
BUTTERFLY			
A WHITE CABBAGE-BUTTERFLY DRIFTS IN,	226	THE LIZARD	20
BY (2)			
BYE			
GOOD-BYE FOR BEING WRONG.	76	I NEED, I NEED	50
CABBAGE			
A WHITE CABBAGE-BUTTERFLY DRIFTS IN,	226	THE LIZARD	20
CALM			
DESIRE WAS WINTER-CALM,	87	PRAISE TO END!	69
SWAN-HEART, ARBUTUS-CALM,	124	WORDS FOR WIND	51
CAN (1)			
CAP			
NOW HE'S EATEN HIS THREE KINDS OF CHEESE AND DRUNK FROM HIS BOTTLE-CAP WATERING-TROUGH--	227	MEADOW MOUSE	12
CARTOON			
HIS ABSURD WHISKERS STICKING OUT LIKE A CARTOON-MOUSE,	227	MEADOW MOUSE	7
CAT			
AND MIST LIFTING OUT OF THE BROWN CAT-TAILS;	67	SHAPE OF FIRE	87
THOSE CAT-LIKE IMMACULATE CREATURES	169	FOURTH MEDITATN	48
THE KITTY-CAT BIRD	177	KITTY-CAT BIRD	T
THE KITTY-CAT BIRD, HE SAT ON A FENCE.	177	KITTY-CAT BIRD	1
--SAID THE WREN TO THE KITTY-CAT BIRD.	177	KITTY-CAT BIRD	4
--SAID THE WREN TO THE KITTY-CAT BIRD.	177	KITTY-CAT BIRD	8
--SAID THE WREN TO THE KITTY-CAT BIRD.	177	KITTY-CAT BIRD	12
THE KITTY-CAT BIRD, HE MOPED AND HE CRIED.	177	KITTY-CAT BIRD	13
THAT THE KITTY-CAT BIRD JUST HOPPED INSIDE;	177	KITTY-CAT BIRD	15
--DID THE KITTY--THE KITTY-CAT BIRD.	177	KITTY-CAT BIRD	17
--OR YOU'LL END LIKE THE KITTY-CAT BIRD.	177	KITTY-CAT BIRD	21
THEIR CAT-MEWING OVER,	190	AT OYSTER RIVER	9
HAUNT OF THE CAT-BIRD, NESTING-PLACE OF THE FIELD-MOUSE,	199	THE FAR FIELD	15
AND THE TOM-CAT, CAUGHT NEAR THE PHEASANT-RUN,	199	THE FAR FIELD	21
TO LIVE BY COURTESY OF THE SHRIKE, THE SNAKE, THE TOM-CAT.	227	MEADOW MOUSE	25
CAUGHT			
LIKE THE EYE OF A NEW-CAUGHT FISH.	204	THE ROSE	88
CAVING			
BEFORE THE CAVING-IN OF ALL THAT IS;	149	IN LATE SUMMER	14
CHAIR			
US, UNDER THE CHAIR-RUNGS, TOWARD THE CELLAR DOOR.	273	SUPPR W LINDSAY	14
CHAIRS			
ITS BEVY OF BEES, AND ITS WIND-BEATEN RICKETY SUN-CHAIRS.	226	THE LIZARD	29
CHAMBERS			
DOWN LONG SEA-CHAMBERS OF THE INNER EAR.	129	SHE	6
CHANCE			
QUITE-BY-CHANCE BROUGHT ME MANY COOKIES.	90	UNFOLD! UNFOLD!	36
CHANGE			
THE DUBIOUS SEA-CHANGE, THE HEAVING SANDS, AND MY TENTACLED SEA-COUSINS.	196	THE LONG WATERS	23
CHANGING			
NOT TOO FAR AWAY FROM THE EVER-CHANGING FLOWER-DUMP,	199	THE FAR FIELD	16
CHICKEN			
AND THE FLICKER DRUMMED FROM HIS DEAD TREE IN THE CHICKEN-YARD.	200	THE FAR FIELD	37

	PAGE	TITLE	LINE
CHILD			
THEIR CHILD-WHIMPERING.	190	AT OYSTER RIVER	10
CHILL			
AND THE GROUND-CHILL COMES CLOSER TO US,	162	I'M HERE	55
CLIFF			
THEN RETIRE TO A ROCK HIGHER UP ON THE CLIFF-SIDE.	190	AT OYSTER RIVER	16
THE SUDDEN SHUDDER AS THE JUTTING SEA-CLIFF COLLAPSES,	231	THE STORM	42
CLIFFS			
PROTECTING THE SEA-CLIFFS.	209	HER LONGING	23
CLIP			
RITUAL OF MULTIGRAPH, PAPER-CLIP, COMMA,	46	DOLOR	7
CLOSE			
FAR AWAY, CLOSE-AT-HAND, HIS CALL FLOATING OVER THE ON-COMING TRAFFIC,	234	ALL MORNING	3
CLOUD			
THE MOON RETREATING INTO A VAGUE CLOUD-SHAPE	202	THE ROSE	18
COLD			
AND FROST IS MARROW-COLD, AND SOON	15	COMING OF COLD	51
COLORED			
OVER THE LOW, BARNACLED, ELEPHANT-COLORED ROCKS,	190	AT OYSTER RIVER	1
COMING			
IN THE SLOW COMING-OUT OF SLEEP,	162	I'M HERE	51
ALTERNATE SNOW AND SLEET, NO ON-COMING TRAFFIC,	199	THE FAR FIELD	6
THE ON-COMING WATER.	200	THE FAR FIELD	55
FAR AWAY, CLOSE-AT-HAND, HIS CALL FLOATING OVER THE ON-COMING TRAFFIC,	234	ALL MORNING	3
AS A MAN TURNS TO FACE ON-COMING SNOW.	245	THE DECISION	12
CONTEMPLATION			
SELF-CONTEMPLATION IS A CURSE	257	SANITARIUM	1
CORD			
A SWAYING LIGHT-CORD, THEN RAN HALF-WAY BACK.	273	SUPPR W LINDSAY	25
CORN			
I DAWDLE WITH GROUPS NEAR THE RICKETY POP-CORN STAND;	47	DOUBLE FEATURE	5
COUNTER			
SHE TAUGHT ME TURN, AND COUNTER-TURN, AND STAND;	127	I KNEW A WOMAN	9
COUNTRY			
MID-COUNTRY BLOW	12	MID-CNTRY BLOW	T
COUSINS			
THE DUBIOUS SEA-CHANGE, THE HEAVING SANDS, AND MY TENTACLED SEA-COUSINS.	196	THE LONG WATERS	23
CREST			
THEN DOWN, AS WE ROLL LIKE A BOAT FROM A WAVE-CREST.	158	FIRST MEDITATN	25
CRICKET			
THE CRICKET-VOICE DEEP IN THE MIDNIGHT FIELD,	196	THE LONG WATERS	27
CROOKED			
WING-CROOKED AND SURE,	93	I CRY, LOVE!	42
CROSS			
TOPPED BY CROSS-WINDS, TUGGED AT BY SINUOUS UNDERCURRENTS	191	AT OYSTER RIVER	33
SWIMMING SLOWLY, ITS BACK RUFFLED BY THE LIGHT CROSS-WINDS,	197	THE LONG WATERS	53
ONLY TO FLY OVER TO HIS FAVORITE PERCH, THE CROSS-BAR OF A TELEPHONE POLE;	234	ALL MORNING	9
CROSSING			
I REMEMBER THE CROSSING-TENDER'S GERANIUM BORDER	29	THE REMINDER	1
CROWNS			
OVER THE DRY SEED-CROWNS,	58	THE LOST SON	156
OR PERCH AND PECK AT LARGER FLOWER-CROWNS,	152	THE SISKINS	12
MY THIGHS BRUSHING AGAINST FLOWER-CROWNS;	161	I'M HERE	22
THE TOWNS WITH THEIR HIGH PITTED ROAD-CROWNS AND DEEP GUTTERS,	193	JOURNY INTERIOR	30
CRUMB			
NUDGES A SAND-CRUMB LOOSE,	37	CUTTINGS	6
CRUMBS			
FACES GREYING FASTER THAN LOAM-CRUMBS ON A HARROW;	48	JUDGE NOT	1
CULIAR			
WE BIDDLY'S ARE PEE-CULIAR BEARS.	117	LADY AND BEAR	7
CURB			
MAKING A SLOW JOURNEY AROUND THE WELL-CURB.	151	SLUG	3
CUT			
DEW DEEPENS ON THE FRESH-CUT LAWN;	33	IDYLL	7
DANCING			
I NEED A PLACE TO SING, AND DANCING-ROOM,	105	SIR JOHN DAVIES	4
YES, I WAS DANCING-MAD, AND HOW	105	SIR JOHN DAVIES	23

	PAGE	TITLE	LINE
DARK			
AND LIFT UP A PATCH, DARK-GREEN, THE KIND FOR LINING CEMETERY BASKETS,	40	MOSS-GATHERING	2
DAW			
FROM A CRAZY OLD JACK-DAW BIRD	183	THE WAGTAIL	7
DAZE			
ALONE, IN A SLEEP-DAZE, I STARED AT BILLBOARDS;	89	UNFOLD! UNFOLD!	24
DEAD			
LIKE THE HALF-DEAD, I HUG MY LAST SECRETS.	103	OLD LADY'S WRDS	5
AMONG THE HALF-DEAD TREES, I CAME UPON THE TRUE EASE OF MYSELF,	205	THE ROSE	99
PACING A ROOM, A ROOM WITH DEAD-WHITE WALLS;	242	THE SEQUEL	30
DEAF			
BEETLES IN CAVES, NEWTS, STONE-DEAF FISHES,	50	THE MINIMAL	3
DEATH			
MY DIM-WIT COUSIN, SAVED BY A DEATH-BED QUAVER,	25	DIM-WIT COUSIN	1
TO SLEEP IS ALL MY LIFE. IN SLEEP'S HALF-DEATH,	246	THE MARROW	14
DEE			
PITCHING LIGHTLY OVER THE HIGH HEDGEROWS, DEE-DEEING,	234	ALL MORNING	25
DEEING			
PITCHING LIGHTLY OVER THE HIGH HEDGEROWS, DEE-DEEING,	234	ALL MORNING	25
DEEP			
THE WALKER TRUDGES ANKLE-DEEP IN LEAVES;	12	SLOW SEASON	11
DEEP-HIDDEN EMBERS, SMOTHERED BY THE SCREEN	17	UNEXTINGUISHED	7
HIS DEEP-THROATED COOING PART OF THE EARLY MORNING,	234	ALL MORNING	2
DEFINED			
SO MUCH OF ADOLESCENCE IS AN ILL-DEFINED DYING,	162	I'M HERE	35
DELIGHTING			
A SELF-DELIGHTING CREATURE,	103	OLD LADY'S WRDS	40
DESTRUCTIVE			
THE SELF-DESTRUCTIVE SHAKE THE COMMON WALL;	250	THE RIGHT THING	14
DIM			
MY DIM-WIT COUSIN	25	DIM-WIT COUSIN	T
MY DIM-WIT COUSIN, SAVED BY A DEATH-BED QUAVER,	25	DIM-WIT COUSIN	1
DOWN			
WATCHING FOR DANGEROUS DOWN-HILL PLACES, WHERE THE WHEELS WHINED BEYOND EIGHTY--	193	JOURNY INTERIOR	19
DRENCHED			
A RAIN-DRENCHED FLY OR SPIDER.	151	SLUG	24
AND FRESH AS SALT-DRENCHED SKIN.	271	THE REPLY	9
DRIED			
(DRIED-OUT, SHE CREAKED LIKE A TULIP.)	228	THE GERANIUM	14
DRIVEN			
THE FURY OF THE HATE-DRIVEN ZEALOT, THE MEANNESS OF THE HUMAN WEASEL;	170	FOURTH MEDITATN	68
DROWSE			
STICKS-IN-A-DROWSE DROOP OVER SUGARY LOAM,	37	CUTTINGS	1
DUMP			
NOT TOO FAR AWAY FROM THE EVER-CHANGING FLOWER-DUMP,	199	THE FAR FIELD	16
EAGLE			
OR RISE WITH THE GAR-EAGLE, THE GREAT-WINGED CONDOR.	209	HER LONGING	16
EDDY			
NUDGES INTO A BACK-EDDY, A SANDY INLET,	159	FIRST MEDITATN	69
EDGE			
BY THE MUDDY POND-EDGE, BY THE BOG-HOLES,	54	THE LOST SON	42
EIGHT			
AMONG MY EIGHT-LEGGED FRIENDS,	209	HER LONGING	5
ELEPHANT			
OVER THE LOW, BARNACLED, ELEPHANT-COLORED ROCKS,	190	AT OYSTER RIVER	1
ELM			
UNDER THE EYE OF THE GREAT OWL WATCHING FROM THE ELM-TREE,	227	MEADOW MOUSE	24
ENCHANTED			
AT EASE WITH JOY, A SELF-ENCHANTED MAN.	248	THE TREE, BIRD	6
EVER			
NOT TOO FAR AWAY FROM THE EVER-CHANGING FLOWER-DUMP,	199	THE FAR FIELD	16
EX			
A MOST EX-AS-PER-AT-ING LUG.	116	THE SLOTH	7
MY EX-EXISTENTIALIST DARLING DEAR,	272	DUET	23
EXCITED			
A CHILD AT PLAY, A WIND-EXCITED BIRD.	165	HER BECOMING	23
EXISTENTIALIST			
MY EX-EXISTENTIALIST DARLING DEAR,	272	DUET	23

	PAGE	TITLE	LINE
EYED			
A BUG-EYED EDIBLE ONE,	209	HER LONGING	8
EYES			
SNAKE-EYES.	75	I NEED, I NEED	46
FACED			
I HAVE BEEN SOMEWHERE ELSE; I REMEMBER THE SEA-FACED UNCLES.	88	PRAISE TO END!	93
FAIR			
MORNING-FAIR, FOLLOW ME FURTHER BACK	66	SHAPE OF FIRE	64
FAR			
A FAR-OFF TRAIN BLOWS ITS ECHOING WHISTLE ONCE;	33	IDYLL	10
FARING			
WHO BUT THE LOVED KNOW LOVE'S A FARING-FORTH?	243	THE MOTION	13
FASHIONED			
YOU WOUND THE WATCH IN AN OLD-FASHIONED LOCKET	29	THE REMINDER	7
THICK AND CUSHIONY, LIKE AN OLD-FASHIONED DOORMAT,	40	MOSS-GATHERING	3
FEET			
LITTLE LIZARD-FEET,	227	MEADOW MOUSE	9
FERN			
OR YANKING TOUGH FERN-SHAPES,	39	WEED PULLER	7
FIELD			
HAUNT OF THE CAT-BIRD, NESTING-PLACE OF THE FIELD-MOUSE,	199	THE FAR FIELD	15
FINE			
OF YOUR FINE-HONED LAY	271	THE REPLY	3
FINGER			
A SURGEON GUIDES A SCALPEL WITH THUMB AND FINGER-TIPS.	28	CLAIRVOY WIDOW	20
FIR			
THE WAY BLOCKED AT LAST BY A FALLEN FIR-TREE,	193	JOURNY INTERIOR	15
THEY SIT, THREE OR FOUR, HIGH IN THE FIR-TREES BACK OF THE HOUSE,	234	ALL MORNING	6
FIRE			
SWINGING BY THE FIRE-PIT,	57	THE LOST SON	131
FISH			
WHAT FISH-WAYS YOU HAVE, LITTLEST FLOWERS,	61	THE LONG ALLEY	74
FISHING			
A NIGHT-FISHING OTTER.	220	THE ABYSS	43
FIVE			
A FIVE-FOOT DROP A VALLEY, SO TO SPEAK.	13	PRAISE PRAIRIE	2
JUST SEND ME ALONG THAT SWEET SEVENTY-FIVE;	113	TO A LADY ED	14
THE ROOM WAS THIRTY-FIVE BELOW;	114	DINKY	14
A FAT, FIVE-INCH APPENDAGE	151	SLUG	12
FLAD			
HE CAN PLAY THE FLITTER-FLAD;	266	FOR STEVENS	2
FLAP			
I'M UNDONE BY THE FLIP-FLAP OF ODIOUS PILLOWS.	86	PRAISE TO END!	45
FLASH			
CREEKS SWOLLEN IN MIDSUMMER FROM THE FLASH-FLOOD ROARING INTO THE NARROW VALLEY.	193	JOURNY INTERIOR	8
FLAT			
INTO THE FLAT-BOX IT GOES,	42	TRANSPLANTING	12
TIME FOR THE FLAT-HEADED MAN. I RECOGNIZE THAT LISTENER,	65	SHAPE OF FIRE	29
THE FLAT-ROOFED HOUSES, COMING DOWN IN GUSTS, BEATING	230	THE STORM	24
FLESH			
THE FLESH-BOUND SIGHING LOVER,	7	ORDERS FOR DAY	5
FLESH-AWKWARD, HALF-ALIVE,	162	I'M HERE	27
FLIGHT			
THEN PITCHING AWAY IN HALF-FLIGHT,	200	THE FAR FIELD	34
FLIP			
I'M UNDONE BY THE FLIP-FLAP OF ODIOUS PILLOWS.	86	PRAISE TO END!	45
FLITTER			
HE CAN PLAY THE FLITTER-FLAD;	266	FOR STEVENS	2
FLOOD			
CREEKS SWOLLEN IN MIDSUMMER FROM THE FLASH-FLOOD ROARING INTO THE NARROW VALLEY.	193	JOURNY INTERIOR	8
FLOWER			
OR PERCH AND PECK AT LARGER FLOWER-CROWNS,	152	THE SISKINS	12
MY THIGHS BRUSHING AGAINST FLOWER-CROWNS;	161	I'M HERE	22
NOT TOO FAR AWAY FROM THE EVER-CHANGING FLOWER-DUMP,	199	THE FAR FIELD	16
FLYING			
IN TIME WHEN THE TROUT AND YOUNG SALMON LEAP FOR THE LOW-FLYING INSECTS,	197	THE LONG WATERS	33
FOAM			
BACK ON THE SEA-FOAM;	263	FOLLIES OF ADAM	33

	PAGE	TITLE	LINE
FOOT			
A FIVE-FOOT DROP A VALLEY, SO TO SPEAK.	13	PRAISE PRAIRIE	2
I'M TIRED OF ALL THAT, BAG-FOOT. I CAN HEAR SMALL ANGELS ANYTIME. WHO	98	O, THOU OPENING	25
WHITE AND RED, IN THE WIDE SIX-HUNDRED-FOOT GREENHOUSES,	203	THE ROSE	52
LIFTING ME HIGH OVER THE FOUR-FOOT STEMS, THE MRS. RUSSELLS, AND HIS OWN ELABORATE HYBRIDS,	203	THE ROSE	54
FOOTED			
THE SOFT-FOOTED ONE	208	THE APPARITION	3
FOR (1)			
FORCE			
AND KNOW THAT TRUE LOVE IS MORE THAN A LIFE-FORCE	113	TO A LADY ED	3
FORGOTTEN			
ON A MOON-FORGOTTEN WAVE!	83	O LULL ME, LULL	13
FORTH			
WHO BUT THE LOVED KNOW LOVE'S A FARING-FORTH?	243	THE MOTION	13
FOUR			
THE BECHSTEIN PIANO, THE FOUR-POSTER BED,	32	SALE	10
LIFTING ME HIGH OVER THE FOUR-FOOT STEMS, THE MRS. RUSSELLS, AND HIS OWN ELABORATE HYBRIDS,	203	THE ROSE	54
WHILE I POKED WITH A STICK AT A STONE NEAR A FOUR-PRONGED FLOWER,	232	THE THING	21
FOX			
A STABLE AND PADDOCK, SOME FOX-HUNTING LAND,	32	SALE	6
FRAMES			
CREAKING THE CYPRESS WINDOW-FRAMES,	41	BIG WIND	17
FRESH			
DEW DEEPENS ON THE FRESH-CUT LAWN;	33	IDYLL	7
LIKE A FRESH-SALTED SKIN;	153	THE DYING MAN	4
FRIDAY			
KISS THE TROUGH, SWINE-ON-FRIDAY.	59	THE LONG ALLEY	24
FULL			
SIFTING IN A PALM-FULL OF FRESH LOAM,--	42	TRANSPLANTING	4
FUR			
THEIR INTRICATE STEM-FUR DRIES;	37	CUTTINGS	2
FURIOUS			
A COLD GOD-FURIOUS MAN	147	THE EXORCISM	21
FURTIVE			
NERVOUS AND COLD, BIRD-FURTIVE, WHISKERY,	157	FIRST MEDITATN	16
GAR			
OR RISE WITH THE GAR-EAGLE, THE GREAT-WINGED CONDOR.	209	HER LONGING	16
GATHERING			
MOSS-GATHERING	40	MOSS-GATHERING	T
THAT WAS MOSS-GATHERING.	40	MOSS-GATHERING	6
GIRL			
WITH A NURSE-MAID WADDLE AND A SHOP-GIRL SIMPER,	23	ACADEMIC	3
GOO-GIRL	180	GOO-GIRL	T
GLORY			
THE HUMMINGBIRD, WHIRRING FROM QUINCE-BLOSSOM TO MORNING-GLORY--	190	AT OYSTER RIVER	29
THE HELIOTROPE, VEINED LIKE A FISH, THE PERSISTENT MORNING-GLORY,	197	THE LONG WATERS	41
A SINGLE WILD ROSE, STRUGGLING OUT OF THE WHITE EMBRACE OF THE MORNING-GLORY,	203	THE ROSE	44
GOD			
A COLD GOD-FURIOUS MAN	147	THE EXORCISM	21
GOO			
GOO-GIRL	180	GOO-GIRL	T
GOOD			
GOOD-BYE FOR BEING WRONG.	76	I NEED, I NEED	50
GRASS			
THE DEW REVIVES ON THE BEACH-GRASS;	190	AT OYSTER RIVER	20
WHERE THE TURF DROPS OFF INTO A GRASS-HIDDEN CULVERT,	199	THE FAR FIELD	14
GRATE			
I SEE A BANKER'S MANSION WITH TWENTY WOOD-GRATE FIRES,	27	CLAIRVOY WIDOW	13
GREAT			
OR RISE WITH THE GAR-EAGLE, THE GREAT-WINGED CONDOR.	209	HER LONGING	16
GREEN			
AND LIFT UP A PATCH, DARK-GREEN, THE KIND FOR LINING CEMETERY BASKETS,	40	MOSS-GATHERING	2
WHILE THE WRENS BICKERED AND SANG IN THE HALF-GREEN HEDGEROWS,	200	THE FAR FIELD	36
AND THE YELLOWISH-GREEN FROM THE MOUNTAINY UPLAND,--	200	THE FAR FIELD	62

		PAGE	TITLE	LINE
GROOMED				
	AS DARKNESS CREEPS UP ON THE WELL-GROOMED SUBURBAN TOWN,	33	IDYLL	5
GROUND				
	AND THE GROUND-CHILL COMES CLOSER TO US,	162	I'M HERE	55
	AND IN THE SHRUNKEN FACE OF A DEAD RAT, EATEN BY RAIN AND GROUND-BEETLES	199	THE FAR FIELD	19
GROWN				
	THE HALF-GROWN CHRYSANTHEMUMS STARING UP LIKE ACCUSERS,	43	CHILD ON GRNHSE	3
	ITS ENTRAILS STREWN OVER THE HALF-GROWN FLOWERS,	199	THE FAR FIELD	22
HALF				
	MATCHING HIS STRIDE WITH HALF-STEPS	6	THE PREMONITION	5
	THE HALF-GROWN CHRYSANTHEMUMS STARING UP LIKE ACCUSERS,	43	CHILD ON GRNHSE	3
	LIKE THE HALF-DEAD, I HUG MY LAST SECRETS.	103	OLD LADY'S WRDS	5
	HALF-BIRD, HALF-ANIMAL.	141	MEMORY	6
	HALF-BIRD, HALF-ANIMAL.	141	MEMORY	6
	FLESH-AWKWARD, HALF-ALIVE,	162	I'M HERE	27
	THE SCENT OF THE HALF-OPENED BUDS CAME UP OVER ME.	162	I'M HERE	49
	BUT SHRINKS INTO A HALF-LIFE, LESS THAN ITSELF,	187	THE LONGING	20
	I'M LULLED INTO HALF-SLEEP	191	AT OYSTER RIVER	60
	ITS ENTRAILS STREWN OVER THE HALF-GROWN FLOWERS,	199	THE FAR FIELD	22
	THEN PITCHING AWAY IN HALF-FLIGHT,	200	THE FAR FIELD	34
	WHILE THE WRENS BICKERED AND SANG IN THE HALF-GREEN HEDGEROWS,	200	THE FAR FIELD	36
	IN A COUNTRY HALF-LAND, HALF-WATER.	201	THE FAR FIELD	76
	IN A COUNTRY HALF-LAND, HALF-WATER.	201	THE FAR FIELD	76
	AMONG THE HALF-DEAD TREES, I CAME UPON THE TRUE EASE OF MYSELF,	205	THE ROSE	99
	TO DRINK SOME HALF-AND-HALF	213	THE HAPPY THREE	15
	TO DRINK SOME HALF-AND-HALF	213	THE HAPPY THREE	15
	IN THIS, MY HALF-REST,	221	THE ABYSS	68
	RETIRING TO NUDGE HIS NECK HALF-WAY UNDER	226	THE LIZARD	16
	SO LONG ON GIN, BOBBIE PINS, HALF-SMOKED CIGARS, DEAD BEER,	228	THE GERANIUM	10
	BENDING THE TREES HALF-WAY DOWN TO THE GROUND,	231	THE STORM	31
	AND THE HALF-SUNKEN BRANCH BENDS AWAY FROM THE GAZER'S EYE.	233	THE PIKE	9
	TO SLEEP IS ALL MY LIFE. IN SLEEP'S HALF-DEATH,	246	THE MARROW	14
	AND SHE WAS HALF-UNDRESSED,	268	SAGINAW SONG	59
	WHEN THEY ARE HALF-UNDRESSED.	268	SAGINAW SONG	61
	"WHAT MOON?" HE CRIED, HALF-TURNING IN MOCK FURY.	273	SUPPR W LINDSAY	10
	A SWAYING LIGHT-CORD, THEN RAN HALF-WAY BACK.	273	SUPPR W LINDSAY	25
HALL				
	IT WAS JUMP-IN-THE-HEDGE; IT WAS WAIT-IN-THE-HALL;	111	SQUEEZE-BOX	13
HAND				
	THE HANDKERCHIEF TUCKED IN THE LEFT-HAND POCKET	29	THE REMINDER	5
	THE HAND-PAINTED WALL-PAPER, FINER THAN SKIN,	32	SALE	17
	WHO SPOKE FIRST IN THE COARSE SHORT-HAND OF THE SUBLIMINAL DEPTHS,	170	FOURTH MEDITATN	71
	FAR AWAY, CLOSE-AT-HAND, HIS CALL FLOATING OVER THE ON-COMING TRAFFIC,	234	ALL MORNING	3
HARPS				
	ON THE BANKS OF THE TOMBSTONE, THE WIND-HARPS HAVING THEIR SAY,	204	THE ROSE	60
HARRIED				
	TIME-HARRIED PRISONERS OF SHALL AND WILL--	250	THE RIGHT THING	2
HATE				
	THE FURY OF THE HATE-DRIVEN ZEALOT, THE MEANNESS OF THE HUMAN WEASEL;	170	FOURTH MEDITATN	68
HAUNTED				
	WHOSE BOGEY-HAUNTED LOOK	7	ORDERS FOR DAY	16
	A TRUE ZEPHYR-HAUNTED WOODIE.	81	SENSIBILITY! LA	7
HEADED				
	TIME FOR THE FLAT-HEADED MAN. I RECOGNIZE THAT LISTENER,	65	SHAPE OF FIRE	29
HEAPS				
	THE SLAG-HEAPS FUME AT THE EDGE OF THE RAW CITIES:	187	THE LONGING	15
HEART				
	SWAN-HEART, ARBUTUS-CALM,	124	WORDS FOR WIND	51
	AND SHE IS MY SWEET-HEART.	268	SAGINAW SONG	42
HEAT				
	WHILE, FARTHER AWAY, THE HEAT-LIGHTNING FLASHES.	194	JOURNY INTERIOR	41
	MY SOUL, LIKE SOME HEAT-MADDENED SUMMER FLY,	239	IN A DARK TIME	20
	I MOVED LIKE SOME HEAT-WEARY ANIMAL.	247	I WAITED	17
HEAVEN				
	HER HEAVEN-SENSE PURE AS A STONE.	260	THE CHANGELING	11

	PAGE	TITLE	LINE
HEAVY			
WITH MOTHERS, SLEEP-HEAVY CHILDREN, STALE PERFUME, PAST THE MANAGER'S SMILE	47	DOUBLE FEATURE	3
HEDGE			
IT WAS JUMP-IN-THE-HEDGE; IT WAS WAIT-IN-THE-HALL;	111	SQUEEZE-BOX	13
HIDDEN			
DEEP-HIDDEN EMBERS, SMOTHERED BY THE SCREEN	17	UNEXTINGUISHED	7
WHERE THE TURF DROPS OFF INTO A GRASS-HIDDEN CULVERT, ...	199	THE FAR FIELD	14
HIGH			
THE HIGH-PILED FLORAL OFFERINGS WITH SENTIMENTAL VERSES,	22	ROAD TO WDLAWN	3
IN THE HIGH-NOON OF THIGHS, ...	80	GIVE WAY, GATES	33
HILL			
WATCHING FOR DANGEROUS DOWN-HILL PLACES, WHERE THE WHEELS WHINED BEYOND EIGHTY--	193	JOURNY INTERIOR	19
HIPPETY			
THESE AIRY HIPPETY-HOP SKIPPERS, ...	152	THE SISKINS	20
HOLES			
BY THE MUDDY POND-EDGE, BY THE BOG-HOLES, ...	54	THE LOST SON	42
HONED			
OF YOUR FINE-HONED LAY	271	THE REPLY	3
HONEST			
MY DARLING, MY DEAREST, MOST-HONEST-ALIVE,	113	TO A LADY ED	13
HONEY			
IS NOW SEALED HONEY-TIGHT.	4	DEATH PIECE	4
HOP			
THESE AIRY HIPPETY-HOP SKIPPERS, ...	152	THE SISKINS	20
HOR			
YOU'RE A FAKE, YOUR'RE A FRAUD, YOU'RE A HOR-RID PRETENSE!	177	KITTY-CAT BIRD	3
HOT			
HAD THE RED-HOT SPOTS WHERE YOU FEEL A	111	SQUEEZE-BOX	20
HOUSE			
END OF THE ROSE-HOUSE, ...	41	BIG WIND	15
THAT OLD ROSE-HOUSE, ...	41	BIG WIND	22
THE SCRAGGLY WIND-BREAK OF A DUSTY RANCH-HOUSE.	194	JOURNY INTERIOR	45
HUMMING			
LIKE A HUMMING-BIRD, ...	183	THE WAGTAIL	5
HUNDRED			
WHITE AND RED, IN THE WIDE SIX-HUNDRED-FOOT GREENHOUSES,	203	THE ROSE	52
HUNTING			
A STABLE AND PADDOCK, SOME FOX-HUNTING LAND, ...	32	SALE	6
ICE			
THE AFTER-LIGHT UPON ICE-BURDENED PINES;	201	THE FAR FIELD	97
ILL			
ONLY A FEW BUBBLES LOOSENING FROM THE ILL-MATCHED TENTACLES,	159	FIRST MEDITATN	64
SO MUCH OF ADOLESCENCE IS AN ILL-DEFINED DYING, ...	162	I'M HERE	35
IMAGE			
THE AFTER-IMAGE NEVER STAYS THE SAME.	132	SENTENTIOUS MAN	20
OR AFTER-IMAGE OF THE INNER EYE.	155	THE DYING MAN	57
THE EYES REJOICE IN THE ACT OF SEEING AND THE FRESH AFTER-IMAGE;	163	I'M HERE	79
IN (5)			
INCH			
A FAT, FIVE-INCH APPENDAGE	151	SLUG	12
INFECTED			
THAT SELF-INFECTED LAIR;	47	THE RETURN	9
ING			
A MOST EX-AS-PER-AT-ING LUG.	116	THE SLOTH	7
INVISIBLE			
ITS ALMOST-INVISIBLE WINGS, BUZZING, HITTING THE LOOSE LEAVES INTERMITTENTLY--	234	ALL MORNING	32
INVOLVED			
I THINK OF THE SELF-INVOLVED:	169	FOURTH MEDITATN	35
IRON			
THE ICE PILING HIGH AGAINST THE IRON-BOUND SPILES, ...	191	AT OYSTER RIVER	50
IVY			
AND THE IVY-BRANCH, CAST TO THE GROUND, PUTS DOWN ROOTS INTO THE SAWDUST, ...	197	THE LONG WATERS	34
JACK			
FROM A CRAZY OLD JACK-DAW BIRD	183	THE WAGTAIL	7
JESUS			
AND NOW ARE WE TO HAVE THAT PELLUDIOUS JESUS-SHIMMER OVER ALL THINGS, ...	98	O, THOU OPENING	21

	PAGE	TITLE	LINE
JOCK			
WHERE'S ANN? WHERE'S LOU? WHERE'S JOCK-WITH-THE-WIND?	97	O, THOU OPENING	17
JOD			
THEIR HEADS JOD-JODDING LIKE PIGEONS;	235	ALL MORNING	35
JODDING			
THEIR HEADS JOD-JODDING LIKE PIGEONS;	235	ALL MORNING	35
JOHN			
JOHN-OF-THE-THUMB'S JUMPING;	81	SENSIBILITY! LA	19
JUMP			
IT WAS JUMP-IN-THE-HEDGE; IT WAS WAIT-IN-THE-HALL;	111	SQUEEZE-BOX	13
KITTEN			
BELIEVE ME, THERE'S NO ONE ELSE, KITTEN-LIMP SISTER.	59	THE LONG ALLEY	23
KITTY			
THE KITTY-CAT BIRD	177	KITTY-CAT BIRD	T
THE KITTY-CAT BIRD, HE SAT ON A FENCE.	177	KITTY-CAT BIRD	1
--SAID THE WREN TO THE KITTY-CAT BIRD.	177	KITTY-CAT BIRD	4
--SAID THE WREN TO THE KITTY-CAT BIRD.	177	KITTY-CAT BIRD	8
--SAID THE WREN TO THE KITTY-CAT BIRD.	177	KITTY-CAT BIRD	12
THE KITTY-CAT BIRD, HE MOPED AND HE CRIED.	177	KITTY-CAT BIRD	13
THAT THE KITTY-CAT BIRD JUST HOPPED INSIDE;	177	KITTY-CAT BIRD	15
--DID THE KITTY--THE KITTY-CAT BIRD.	177	KITTY-CAT BIRD	17
--OR YOU'LL END LIKE THE KITTY-CAT BIRD.	177	KITTY-CAT BIRD	21
KNOCK			
PIPE-KNOCK.	57	THE LOST SON	140
KNOWING			
AND NOT-KNOWING ENTERS, SILENT, ...	221	THE ABYSS	70
LADDIE			
DAN CUPID, I TELL YOU'S A BRAW LADDIE-BUCK;	113	TO A LADY ED	5
LADEN			
AND THEIR SNUFF-LADEN BREATH BLOWING LIGHTLY OVER ME IN MY FIRST SLEEP.	44	FRAU BAUMAN	35
THE ROAD LINED WITH SNOW-LADEN SECOND GROWTH, ...	199	THE FAR FIELD	4
THE OILY, TAR-LADEN WALLS	205	THE ROSE	94
AND MY SALT-LADEN HAIR	210	HER TIME	14
LAMP			
AND THE SMALL STREET-LAMP SWINGING AND SLAMMING AGAINST THE LAMP POLE.	230	THE STORM	7
LAND			
IN A COUNTRY HALF-LAND, HALF-WATER.	201	THE FAR FIELD	76
LARK			
A LARK-SWEET LOVER IF EVER THERE WAS.	258	SONG (3)	3
LAST			
THE LAST-ABANDONED STALK ALWAYS QUIVERING	152	THE SISKINS	14
LEAF			
LEAF-MOLD, MANURE, LIME, PILED AGAINST SLIPPERY PLANKS.	38	ROOT CELLAR	9
ONCE I FISHED FROM THE BANKS, LEAF-LIGHT AND HAPPY:	86	PRAISE TO END!	19
ONE LEAF-LIKE FOOT HUNG LAXLY	226	THE LIZARD	7
LEAPING			
A WINTER-LEAPING FROG.	83	O LULL ME, LULL	28
LEFT			
THE HANDKERCHIEF TUCKED IN THE LEFT-HAND POCKET	29	THE REMINDER	5
LEGGED			
A TWO-LEGGED DOG HUNTING A NEW HORIZON OF HOWLS.	65	SHAPE OF FIRE	38
AMONG MY EIGHT-LEGGED FRIENDS, ...	209	HER LONGING	5
YOU'RE BECOMING THAT HORROR, A TWO-LEGGED PIG	272	DUET	3
LESS			
(WHOM I LIKE NONE-THE-LESS), ...	213	THE HAPPY THREE	22
LICK			
AMONG THE SHY BEASTS, THE DEER AT THE SALT-LICK, ...	190	AT OYSTER RIVER	26
LIFE			
AND KNOW THAT TRUE LOVE IS MORE THAN A LIFE-FORCE	113	TO A LADY ED	3
BUT SHRINKS INTO A HALF-LIFE, LESS THAN ITSELF, ...	187	THE LONGING	20
HIS SEX-LIFE NEVER IS ONE-SIDED.	264	THREE EPIGRAMS	14
LIFTING			
A SLOW SNAIL-LIFTING, LIQUESCENT;	67	SHAPE OF FIRE	82
LIGHT			
TO STARE INTO THE AFTER-LIGHT, THE GLITTER LEFT ON THE LAKE'S SURFACE, ...	67	SHAPE OF FIRE	88
ONCE I FISHED FROM THE BANKS, LEAF-LIGHT AND HAPPY:	86	PRAISE TO END!	19
THE AFTER-LIGHT UPON ICE-BURDENED PINES;	201	THE FAR FIELD	97
A SPIDER EASES HIMSELF DOWN FROM A SWAYING LIGHT-BULB, ...	231	THE STORM	34
A SWAYING LIGHT-CORD, THEN RAN HALF-WAY BACK.	273	SUPPR W LINDSAY	25

		PAGE	TITLE	LINE
LIGHTNING				
	WHILE, FARTHER AWAY, THE HEAT-LIGHTNING FLASHES.	194	JOURNY INTERIOR	41
LIKE				
	THE BLOOD SLOWS TRANCE-LIKE IN THE ALTERED VEIN;	12	SLOW SEASON	15
	THOSE CAT-LIKE IMMACULATE CREATURES	169	FOURTH MEDITATN	48
	ONE LEAF-LIKE FOOT HUNG LAXLY	226	THE LIZARD	7
	A THREAD-LIKE FIRMNESS.	226	THE LIZARD	12
	AS HIS HEAD; HIS BAT-LIKE EARS	227	MEADOW MOUSE	15
LIMP				
	BELIEVE ME, THERE'S NO ONE ELSE, KITTEN-LIMP SISTER.	59	THE LONG ALLEY	23
LIZARD				
	LITTLE LIZARD-FEET,	227	MEADOW MOUSE	9
LOAM				
	FACES GREYING FASTER THAN LOAM-CRUMBS ON A HARROW;	48	JUDGE NOT	1
LONG				
	A THING CARVED OF STONE OR WOOD, WITH THE DULL IRIDESCENCE OF LONG-POLISHED WOOD,	234	ALL MORNING	11
LONGING				
	YET LOVE-LONGING OF A KIND	237	THE TRANCED	8
LOVE				
	NEXT DOOR THERE IS A LOVE-NEST OF PLASTER BOARD AND TIN,	27	CLAIRVOY WIDOW	15
	THE LOVE-BEAT OF A BIRD.	212	LIGHT LISTENED	9
	YET LOVE-LONGING OF A KIND	237	THE TRANCED	8
LOW				
	IN TIME WHEN THE TROUT AND YOUNG SALMON LEAP FOR THE LOW-FLYING INSECTS,	197	THE LONG WATERS	33
LURKING				
	IN A LURKING-PLACE I LURK,	122	ALL EARTH, AIR	26
MACHINE				
	SO WE DRAINED THE MANURE-MACHINE	41	BIG WIND	6
MAD				
	YES, I WAS DANCING-MAD, AND HOW	105	SIR JOHN DAVIES	23
MADDENED				
	MY SOUL, LIKE SOME HEAT-MADDENED SUMMER FLY,	239	IN A DARK TIME	20
MAID				
	WITH A NURSE-MAID WADDLE AND A SHOP-GIRL SIMPER,	23	ACADEMIC	3
MAKERS				
	MATCH-MAKERS, ARRANGERS OF PICNICS--	169	FOURTH MEDITATN	41
MAN				
	OF A MAN-TAILORED BLOUSE; THE LIST OF SHOPPING DONE;	29	THE REMINDER	6
MANURE				
	SO WE DRAINED THE MANURE-MACHINE	41	BIG WIND	6
MARMOREAN				
	THOU WERT MARMOREAN-BORN.	81	SENSIBILITY! LA	5
MARROW				
	AND FROST IS MARROW-COLD, AND SOON	15	COMING OF COLD	51
	MARROW-SOFT, DANCED IN THE SAND.	63	FIELD OF LIGHT	30
MATCH				
	MATCH-MAKERS, ARRANGERS OF PICNICS--	169	FOURTH MEDITATN	41
MATCHED				
	ONLY A FEW BUBBLES LOOSENING FROM THE ILL-MATCHED TENTACLES,	159	FIRST MEDITATN	64
ME (2)				
MEADOW				
	HOW ELSE, MEADOW-SHAPE?	258	SONG (3)	12
MEWING				
	THEIR CAT-MEWING OVER,	190	AT OYSTER RIVER	9
MID				
	MID-COUNTRY BLOW	12	MID-CNTRY BLOW	T
MILK				
	COME TO ME, MILK-NOSE. I NEED A LOAN OF THE QUICK.	59	THE LONG ALLEY	25
MIRROR				
	AND NO LIGHTS BEHIND, IN THE BLURRED SIDE-MIRROR,	199	THE FAR FIELD	7
MOLD				
	LEAF-MOLD, MANURE, LIME, PILED AGAINST SLIPPERY PLANKS.	38	ROOT CELLAR	9
MONKEY				
	THOSE LEWD MONKEY-TAILS HANGING FROM DRAINHOLES,--	39	WEED PULLER	3
MOON				
	ON A MOON-FORGOTTEN WAVE!	83	O LULL ME, LULL	13
MORNING				
	MORNING-FAIR, FOLLOW ME FURTHER BACK	66	SHAPE OF FIRE	64
	THE HUMMINGBIRD, WHIRRING FROM QUINCE-BLOSSOM TO MORNING-GLORY--	190	AT OYSTER RIVER	29

	PAGE	TITLE	LINE
MORNING (CONTINUED)			
THE HELIOTROPE, VEINED LIKE A FISH, THE PERSISTENT MORNING-GLORY,	197	THE LONG WATERS	41
A SINGLE WILD ROSE, STRUGGLING OUT OF THE WHITE EMBRACE OF THE MORNING-GLORY,	203	THE ROSE	44
MOSS			
MOSS-GATHERING	40	MOSS-GATHERING	T
THAT WAS MOSS-GATHERING.	40	MOSS-GATHERING	6
MOST			
MY DARLING, MY DEAREST, MOST-HONEST-ALIVE,	113	TO A LADY ED	13
MOTHER			
HOW DEEP THE MOTHER-ROOT OF THAT STILL CRY!	248	THE TREE, BIRD	17
MOUNTAIN			
ODOR OF BASSWOOD ON A MOUNTAIN-SLOPE,	201	THE FAR FIELD	98
MOUSE			
HAUNT OF THE CAT-BIRD, NESTING-PLACE OF THE FIELD-MOUSE,	199	THE FAR FIELD	15
HIS ABSURD WHISKERS STICKING OUT LIKE A CARTOON-MOUSE,	227	MEADOW MOUSE	7
TURNS, MOUSE-WARY,--	260	THE CHANGELING	2
MOUTHED			
ADDER-MOUTHED,	39	ORCHIDS	2
MOVING			
IN MOVING-SLOW HE HAS NO PEER.	116	THE SLOTH	1
MUMBLEY			
THE KIDS PLAY COPS AND ROBBERS, THE KIDS PLAY MUMBLEY-PEG,	27	CLAIRVOY WIDOW	9
MUSK			
OF MARSH GRASS HEAPED ABOVE A MUSK-RAT HOLE.	15	THE HERON	4
NEST			
NEXT DOOR THERE IS A LOVE-NEST OF PLASTER BOARD AND TIN,	27	CLAIRVOY WIDOW	15
NESTING			
HAUNT OF THE CAT-BIRD, NESTING-PLACE OF THE FIELD-MOUSE,	199	THE FAR FIELD	15
NEW			
I STEPPED CAREFULLY, LIKE A NEW-SHOD HORSE,	166	HER BECOMING	46
LIKE THE EYE OF A NEW-CAUGHT FISH.	204	THE ROSE	88
NIGHT			
A NIGHT-FISHING OTTER.	220	THE ABYSS	43
NONE			
(WHOM I LIKE NONE-THE-LESS),	213	THE HAPPY THREE	22
NOON			
IN THE HIGH-NOON OF THIGHS,	80	GIVE WAY, GATES	33
NOSE			
COME TO ME, MILK-NOSE. I NEED A LOAN OF THE QUICK.	59	THE LONG ALLEY	25
NOT (2)			
NURSE			
WITH A NURSE-MAID WADDLE AND A SHOP-GIRL SIMPER,	23	ACADEMIC	3
OF (2)			
OFF			
A FAR-OFF TRAIN BLOWS ITS ECHOING WHISTLE ONCE;	33	IDYLL	10
OLD			
YOU WOUND THE WATCH IN AN OLD-FASHIONED LOCKET	29	THE REMINDER	7
THICK AND CUSHIONY, LIKE AN OLD-FASHIONED DOORMAT,	40	MOSS-GATHERING	3
OF SIXTEEN-YEAR-OLD LUST.	46	PICKLE BELT	12
ON (5)			
ONE			
HIS SEX-LIFE NEVER IS ONE-SIDED.	264	THREE EPIGRAMS	14
OOZE			
STAY. STAY BY THE SLIP-OOZE. STAY.	100	THE VISITANT	4
OPENED			
THE SCENT OF THE HALF-OPENED BUDS CAME UP OVER ME.	162	I'M HERE	49
ORDER			
GOODBYE, GOODBYE, OLD STONES, THE TIME-ORDER IS GOING,	56	THE LOST SON	108
OUT			
IN THE SLOW COMING-OUT OF SLEEP,	162	I'M HERE	51
THERE ARE MANY DETOURS, WASHED-OUT INTERRUPTED RAW PLACES	193	JOURNY INTERIOR	2
(DRIED-OUT, SHE CREAKED LIKE A TULIP.)	228	THE GERANIUM	14
OVER			
TURNED-OVER ROOTS	43	FLOWER DUMP	6
PAIL			
IN THE SLOP-PAIL BY THE SINK;	269	GOB MUSIC	13
OH, THE SLOP-PAIL IS THE PLACE TO THINK	269	GOB MUSIC	16
OH, THE SLOP-PAIL IS THE PLACE TO THINK	270	GOB MUSIC	44
PAINTED			
THE HAND-PAINTED WALL-PAPER, FINER THAN SKIN,	32	SALE	17

		PAGE	TITLE	LINE
PALE				
	LILIES, PALE-PINK CYCLAMEN, ROSES,	39	WEED PULLER	12
PALM				
	SIFTING IN A PALM-FULL OF FRESH LOAM,--	42	TRANSPLANTING	4
	MY PALM-SWEAT FLASHES GOLD;	88	PRAISE TO END!	87
PAPA				
	WHAT'S THE TIME, PAPA-SEED?	72	WHERE KNOCK IS	20
PAPER				
	THE HAND-PAINTED WALL-PAPER, FINER THAN SKIN,	32	SALE	17
	NEAT IN THEIR BOXES, DOLOR OF PAD AND PAPER-WEIGHT,	46	DOLOR	2
	RITUAL OF MULTIGRAPH, PAPER-CLIP, COMMA,	46	DOLOR	7
PARCHED				
	NEAR THIS ROSE, IN THIS GROVE OF SUN-PARCHED, WIND-WARPED MADRONAS,	205	THE ROSE	98
PEA				
	THE SWEET-PEA TENDRILS, THE SMILAX,	44	FRAU BAUMAN	5
PEAR				
	THE YOUNG FRUIT SWELL UPON THE PEAR-TREE BOUGH.	11	LIGHT BRIGHTER	16
PEAS				
	OR FAN LIFE INTO WILTED SWEET-PEAS WITH HIS HAT,	42	OLD FLORIST	9
PEE				
	WE BIDDLY'S ARE PEE-CULIAR BEARS.	117	LADY AND BEAR	7
PEG				
	THE KIDS PLAY COPS AND ROBBERS, THE KIDS PLAY MUMBLEY-PEG,	27	CLAIRVOY WIDOW	9
PER				
	A MOST EX-AS-PER-AT-ING LUG.	116	THE SLOTH	7
PHEASANT				
	AND THE TOM-CAT, CAUGHT NEAR THE PHEASANT-RUN,	199	THE FAR FIELD	21
PILED				
	THE HIGH-PILED FLORAL OFFERINGS WITH SENTIMENTAL VERSES,	22	ROAD TO WDLAWN	3
PINCHING				
	OR PINCHING-BACK ASTERS, OR PLANTING AZALEAS,	42	OLD FLORIST	2
PINE				
	AND THE HURRICANE DRIVES THE DEAD STRAW INTO THE LIVING PINE-TREE.	231	THE STORM	43
PINK				
	LILIES, PALE-PINK CYCLAMEN, ROSES,	39	WEED PULLER	12
PIPE				
	PIPE-KNOCK.	57	THE LOST SON	140
PIT				
	SWINGING BY THE FIRE-PIT,	57	THE LOST SON	131
PLACE				
	IN A LURKING-PLACE I LURK,	122	ALL EARTH, AIR	26
	HAUNT OF THE CAT-BIRD, NESTING-PLACE OF THE FIELD-MOUSE,	199	THE FAR FIELD	15
POETRY				
	MY POETRY-BOOK, IF YOU PLEASE,--	179	MYRTLE	7
POLISHED				
	A THING CARVED OF STONE OR WOOD, WITH THE DULL IRIDESCENCE OF LONG-POLISHED WOOD,	234	ALL MORNING	11
POND				
	BY THE MUDDY POND-EDGE, BY THE BOG-HOLES,	54	THE LOST SON	42
	AS WHEN SILT DRIFTS AND SIFTS DOWN THROUGH MUDDY POND-WATER,	159	FIRST MEDITATN	60
POP				
	I DAWDLE WITH GROUPS NEAR THE RICKETY POP-CORN STAND;	47	DOUBLE FEATURE	5
POSTER				
	THE BECHSTEIN PIANO, THE FOUR-POSTER BED,	32	SALE	10
PRETTY				
	ARCH MY BACK, PRETTY-BONES, I'M DEAD AT BOTH ENDS.	85	PRAISE TO END!	9
PRICKLE				
	PRICKLE-ME, TICKLE-ME, CLOSE STEMS.	85	PRAISE TO END!	6
PRONGED				
	WHILE I POKED WITH A STICK AT A STONE NEAR A FOUR-PRONGED FLOWER,	232	THE THING	21
PROUD				
	ONCE ON RETURNING HOME, PURSE-PROUD AND HALE,	21	THE AUCTION	1
PURE				
	HER PURE-WHITE FEATHERINESS	213	THE HAPPY THREE	23
PURSE				
	ONCE ON RETURNING HOME, PURSE-PROUD AND HALE,	21	THE AUCTION	1
QUICK				
	TOWARD THE QUICK-WATER, WRINKLING AND RIPPLING.	54	THE LOST SON	39

	PAGE	TITLE	LINE
QUINCE			
THE HUMMINGBIRD, WHIRRING FROM QUINCE-BLOSSOM TO MORNING-GLORY--	190	AT OYSTER RIVER	29
QUITE			
QUITE-BY-CHANCE BROUGHT ME MANY COOKIES.	90	UNFOLD! UNFOLD!	36
RAIN			
AND A BEE SHAKING DROPS FROM A RAIN-SOAKED HONEYSUCKLE.	63	FIELD OF LIGHT	49
A RAIN-DRENCHED FLY OR SPIDER.	151	SLUG	24
ITS SPRAY HOLDING A DOUBLE RAIN-BOW IN EARLY MORNING,	191	AT OYSTER RIVER	45
HER FACE LIKE A RAIN-BEATEN STONE ON THE DAY SHE ROLLED OFF	223	ELEGY (2)	1
RANCH			
THE SCRAGGLY WIND-BREAK OF A DUSTY RANCH-HOUSE.	194	JOURNY INTERIOR	45
RAT			
OF MARSH GRASS HEAPED ABOVE A MUSK-RAT HOLE.	15	THE HERON	4
RED			
HAD THE RED-HOT SPOTS WHERE YOU FEEL A	111	SQUEEZE-BOX	20
REST			
IN THIS, MY HALF-REST,	221	THE ABYSS	68
REVEALED			
THIS ANGUISH SELF-REVEALED.	3	OPEN HOUSE	8
RICH			
PULPY STEMS, RANK, SILO-RICH,	38	ROOT CELLAR	8
RID			
YOU'RE A FAKE, YOUR'RE A FRAUD, YOU'RE A HOR-RID PRETENSE!	177	KITTY-CAT BIRD	3
RIDDLED			
DOWN AMONG THE RUBBISH, THE BUG-RIDDLED FOLIAGE,	54	THE LOST SON	41
RIPPLES			
COME THE FIRST TIDE-RIPPLES, MOVING, ALMOST WITHOUT SOUND, TOWARD ME,	190	AT OYSTER RIVER	2
ROAD			
THE TOWNS WITH THEIR HIGH PITTED ROAD-CROWNS AND DEEP GUTTERS,	193	JOURNY INTERIOR	30
ROCK			
UNDER EVEN THE ROCK-SHUT GROUND,	50	THE CYCLE	16
WHILE THE ROCK-SEAMS SWELL WITH THE SEA,	261	THE CHANGELING	33
ROOF			
FLINGING LONG STRINGS OF WET ACROSS THE ROOF-TOP,	41	BIG WIND	29
ROOFED			
THE FLAT-ROOFED HOUSES, COMING DOWN IN GUSTS, BEATING	230	THE STORM	24
ROOM			
I NEED A PLACE TO SING, AND DANCING-ROOM,	105	SIR JOHN DAVIES	4
ROOT			
HOW DEEP THE MOTHER-ROOT OF THAT STILL CRY!	248	THE TREE, BIRD	17
ROSE			
END OF THE ROSE-HOUSE,	41	BIG WIND	15
THAT OLD ROSE-HOUSE,	41	BIG WIND	22
AND MY DRESS CAUGHT ON ROSE-BRIER.	162	I'M HERE	47
RUN			
AND THE TOM-CAT, CAUGHT NEAR THE PHEASANT-RUN,	199	THE FAR FIELD	21
RUNGS			
US, UNDER THE CHAIR-RUNGS, TOWARD THE CELLAR DOOR.	273	SUPPR W LINDSAY	14
RUT			
ENDING AT LAST IN A HOPELESS SAND-RUT,	199	THE FAR FIELD	9
SAD			
A LOW VOICE, SUMMER-SAD.	90	UNFOLD! UNFOLD!	50
SALT			
THE SALT-SOAKED WOOD OF A FIRE CRACKLES;	190	AT OYSTER RIVER	21
AMONG THE SHY BEASTS, THE DEER AT THE SALT-LICK,	190	AT OYSTER RIVER	26
AND MY SALT-LADEN HAIR	210	HER TIME	14
AND FRESH AS SALT-DRENCHED SKIN.	271	THE REPLY	9
SALTED			
LIKE A FRESH-SALTED SKIN;	153	THE DYING MAN	4
SAND			
NUDGES A SAND-CRUMB LOOSE,	37	CUTTINGS	6
THE WAVES, ALTERED BY SAND-BARS, BEDS OF KELP, MISCELLANEOUS DRIFTWOOD,	191	AT OYSTER RIVER	32
ENDING AT LAST IN A HOPELESS SAND-RUT,	199	THE FAR FIELD	9
SEA			
I HAVE BEEN SOMEWHERE ELSE; I REMEMBER THE SEA-FACED UNCLES.	88	PRAISE TO END!	93
SEA-BEAST OR BIRD FLUNG TOWARD THE RAVAGED SHORE?	107	SIR JOHN DAVIES	68
DOWN LONG SEA-CHAMBERS OF THE INNER EAR.	129	SHE	6
AND THE SEA-WINDS MOVE THROUGH THE PINE TREES,	196	THE LONG WATERS	18

	PAGE	TITLE	LINE
SEA (CONTINUED)			
THE DUBIOUS SEA-CHANGE, THE HEAVING SANDS, AND MY TENTACLED SEA-COUSINS.	196	THE LONG WATERS	23
THE DUBIOUS SEA-CHANGE, THE HEAVING SANDS, AND MY TENTACLED SEA-COUSINS.	196	THE LONG WATERS	23
A SEA-SHAPE TURNING AROUND,--	201	THE FAR FIELD	84
BUT THIS ROSE, THIS ROSE IN THE SEA-WIND,	203	THE ROSE	39
CUT BY THE SEA-SLIME, FAR FROM THE CRASH	205	THE ROSE	92
AND IN THIS ROSE, THIS ROSE IN THE SEA-WIND,	205	THE ROSE	111
MINE AND THE SEA-WIND'S.	205	THE ROSE	114
PROTECTING THE SEA-CLIFFS.	209	HER LONGING	23
IN YOUR SEA-BURIED EAR,	211	SONG (1)	11
AS I WALKED BY THE HIGH SEA-WALL.	216	THE SHY MAN	4
AS I MOPED BY THE HIGH SEA-WALL.	216	THE SHY MAN	8
AS WE WALKED BY THE HIGH SEA-WALL.	216	THE SHY MAN	16
AS WE EMBRACE BY THE HIGH SEA-WALL.	216	THE SHY MAN	23
AS WE KISS BY THE HIGH SEA-WALL.	216	THE SHY MAN	26
I HAVE TAKEN COUNSEL OF THE CRAB AND THE SEA-URCHIN,	222	THE ABYSS	92
ALONG THE SEA-WALL, A STEADY SLOSHING OF THE SWELL,	230	THE STORM	10
THE FLAT BOOM ON THE BEACH OF THE TOWERING SEA-SWELL,	231	THE STORM	41
THE SUDDEN SHUDDER AS THE JUTTING SEA-CLIFF COLLAPSES,	231	THE STORM	42
A SEA-WIND PAUSING IN A SUMMER TREE.	235	MANIFESTATION	8
BACK ON THE SEA-FOAM;	263	FOLLIES OF ADAM	33
SEALED			
THOUGH STILL THE GUARDED SNOW IS WINTER-SEALED,	11	LIGHT BRIGHTER	6
SEAMS			
WHILE THE ROCK-SEAMS SWELL WITH THE SEA,	261	THE CHANGELING	33
SEED			
OVER THE DRY SEED-CROWNS,	58	THE LOST SON	156
WHAT'S THE TIME, PAPA-SEED?	72	WHERE KNOCK IS	20
SELF			
THIS ANGUISH SELF-REVEALED.	3	OPEN HOUSE	8
A DRUNK MAN STUMBLES BY, ABSORBED IN SELF-TALK.	33	IDYLL	2
THAT SELF-INFECTED LAIR;	47	THE RETURN	9
A SELF-DELIGHTING CREATURE,	103	OLD LADY'S WRDS	40
I THINK OF THE SELF-INVOLVED:	169	FOURTH MEDITATN	35
AT EASE WITH JOY, A SELF-ENCHANTED MAN.	248	THE TREE, BIRD	6
THE SELF-DESTRUCTIVE SHAKE THE COMMON WALL;	250	THE RIGHT THING	14
SELF-CONTEMPLATION IS A CURSE	257	SANITARIUM	1
SENSE			
HER HEAVEN-SENSE PURE AS A STONE.	260	THE CHANGELING	11
SETTLING			
WHITE UPON WHITE, SLOW-SETTLING ON A STONE;	149	IN LATE SUMMER	2
SEVENTY			
JUST SEND ME ALONG THAT SWEET SEVENTY-FIVE;	113	TO A LADY ED	14
SEX			
HIS SEX-LIFE NEVER IS ONE-SIDED.	264	THREE EPIGRAMS	14
SHAPE			
A SEA-SHAPE TURNING AROUND,--	201	THE FAR FIELD	84
THE MOON RETREATING INTO A VAGUE CLOUD-SHAPE	202	THE ROSE	18
HOW ELSE, MEADOW-SHAPE?	258	SONG (3)	12
SHAPES			
OR YANKING TOUGH FERN-SHAPES,	39	WEED PULLER	7
SHE (1)			
SHEATH			
I QUAIL, LEAN TO BEGINNINGS, SHEATH-WET.	37	CUTTINGS (LATE)	11
STILL WET FROM ITS BUD-SHEATH,	101	LIGHT BREATHER	4
SHIMMER			
AND NOW ARE WE TO HAVE THAT PELLUDIOUS JESUS-SHIMMER OVER ALL THINGS,	98	O, THOU OPENING	21
SHOD			
I STEPPED CAREFULLY, LIKE A NEW-SHOD HORSE,	166	HER BECOMING	46
SHOE			
BUT THIS MORNING THE SHOE-BOX HOUSE ON THE BACK PORCH IS EMPTY.	227	MEADOW MOUSE	20
SHOP			
WITH A NURSE-MAID WADDLE AND A SHOP-GIRL SIMPER,	23	ACADEMIC	3
SHORT			
WHO SPOKE FIRST IN THE COARSE SHORT-HAND OF THE SUBLIMINAL DEPTHS,	170	FOURTH MEDITATN	71
TO DISTRACT ATTENTION FROM THE SHORT-TAILED RIDICULOUS YOUNG ONES	234	ALL MORNING	19

	PAGE	TITLE	LINE
SHREW			
THE DESCENDANTS OF THE PLAYFUL TREE-SHREW THAT SURVIVED THE ARCHAIC KILLERS,	170	FOURTH MEDITATN	66
SHREWS			
A CONGRESS OF TREE-SHREWS AND RATS,	163	I'M HERE	66
SHUT			
UNDER EVEN THE ROCK-SHUT GROUND,	50	THE CYCLE	16
SHY			
ALL SMALL SHAPES, WILLOW-SHY,	90	UNFOLD! UNFOLD!	46
SIDE			
THEN RETIRE TO A ROCK HIGHER UP ON THE CLIFF-SIDE.	190	AT OYSTER RIVER	16
AND NO LIGHTS BEHIND, IN THE BLURRED SIDE-MIRROR,	199	THE FAR FIELD	7
SIDED			
HIS SEX-LIFE NEVER IS ONE-SIDED.	264	THREE EPIGRAMS	14
SIGH			
BIRD, SOFT-SIGH ME HOME,	53	THE LOST SON	9
SILO			
PULPY STEMS, RANK, SILO-RICH,	38	ROOT CELLAR	8
SING			
HIS LAUGHTER REDUCED THE SING-SONG OF PRATING,	29	THE GENTLE	7
SINGING			
SAD, IN A SINGING-TIME?	98	O, THOU OPENING	45
SITTING			
NOW IN THE MISERY OF BED-SITTING ROOM CONFUSION,	29	THE REMINDER	9
SIX			
WHITE AND RED, IN THE WIDE SIX-HUNDRED-FOOT GREENHOUSES,	203	THE ROSE	52
SIXTEEN			
OF SIXTEEN-YEAR-OLD LUST.	46	PICKLE BELT	12
SKELETONS			
WEEDS TURN TOWARD THE WIND WEED-SKELETONS.	173	WHAT TELL BONES	65
SKITTER			
HE CAN PLINK THE SKITTER-BUM;	266	FOR STEVENS	6
SLAG			
THE SLAG-HEAPS FUME AT THE EDGE OF THE RAW CITIES:	187	THE LONGING	15
SLEEP			
WITH MOTHERS, SLEEP-HEAVY CHILDREN, STALE PERFUME, PAST THE MANAGER'S SMILE	47	DOUBLE FEATURE	3
SING ME A SLEEP-SONG, PLEASE.	71	WHERE KNOCK IS	10
ALONE, IN A SLEEP-DAZE, I STARED AT BILLBOARDS;	89	UNFOLD! UNFOLD!	24
I'M LULLED INTO HALF-SLEEP	191	AT OYSTER RIVER	60
SLEEPING			
LAST NIGHT YOU LAY A-SLEEPING? NO!	114	DINKY	13
SLIME			
CUT BY THE SEA-SLIME, FAR FROM THE CRASH	205	THE ROSE	92
SLIP			
STAY. STAY BY THE SLIP-OOZE. STAY.	100	THE VISITANT	4
SLOP			
IN THE SLOP-PAIL BY THE SINK;	269	GOB MUSIC	13
OH, THE SLOP-PAIL IS THE PLACE TO THINK	269	GOB MUSIC	16
OH, THE SLOP-PAIL IS THE PLACE TO THINK	270	GOB MUSIC	44
SLOPE			
ODOR OF BASSWOOD ON A MOUNTAIN-SLOPE,	201	THE FAR FIELD	98
SLOW			
IN MOVING-SLOW HE HAS NO PEER.	116	THE SLOTH	1
WHITE UPON WHITE, SLOW-SETTLING ON A STONE;	149	IN LATE SUMMER	2
SLUG			
SLUG-SOFT STEMS,	43	FLOWER DUMP	2
SMOKED			
SO LONG ON GIN, BOBBIE PINS, HALF-SMOKED CIGARS, DEAD BEER,	228	THE GERANIUM	10
SNAIL			
A SLOW SNAIL-LIFTING, LIQUESCENT;	67	SHAPE OF FIRE	82
SNAKE			
SNAKE-EYES.	75	I NEED, I NEED	46
SNOW			
THE ROAD LINED WITH SNOW-LADEN SECOND GROWTH,	199	THE FAR FIELD	4
SNUFF			
AND THEIR SNUFF-LADEN BREATH BLOWING LIGHTLY OVER ME IN MY FIRST SLEEP.	44	FRAU BAUMAN	35
SOAKED			
AND A BEE SHAKING DROPS FROM A RAIN-SOAKED HONEYSUCKLE.	63	FIELD OF LIGHT	49
THE SALT-SOAKED WOOD OF A FIRE CRACKLES;	190	AT OYSTER RIVER	21
SOFT			
SLUG-SOFT STEMS,	43	FLOWER DUMP	2

	PAGE	TITLE	LINE
SOFT (CONTINUED)			
BIRD, SOFT-SIGH ME HOME,	53	THE LOST SON	9
MARROW-SOFT, DANCED IN THE SAND.	63	FIELD OF LIGHT	30
ACROSS MY LAWN THE SOFT-BACKED CREATURES COME;	149	IN LATE SUMMER	3
THE SOFT-FOOTED ONE	208	THE APPARITION	3
SONG			
HIS LAUGHTER REDUCED THE SING-SONG OF PRATING,	29	THE GENTLE	7
SING ME A SLEEP-SONG, PLEASE.	71	WHERE KNOCK IS	10
WREN-SONG IN TRELLIS: A LIGHT ECSTASY OF BUTTERFLIES COURTING,	255	LIGHT POEM	1
SPRING			
AND THE UP-SPRING OF THE PLANK WHEN A FOOT LEFT THE RUNWAY.	158	FIRST MEDITATN	47
SQUEEZE			
SONG FOR THE SQUEEZE-BOX	111	SQUEEZE-BOX	T
STACKED			
AND YET STILL VIOLENT MEN, WHOSE STACKED-UP GUNS	224	OTTO	27
STAND			
THE SOUL AT A STILL-STAND,	194	JOURNY INTERIOR	54
STEM			
THEIR INTRICATE STEM-FUR DRIES;	37	CUTTINGS	2
STEPS			
MATCHING HIS STRIDE WITH HALF-STEPS	6	THE PREMONITION	5
STICKS			
STICKS-IN-A-DROWSE DROOP OVER SUGARY LOAM,	37	CUTTINGS	1
STILL			
THE GENTLE AND BEAUTIFUL STILL-TO-BE-BORN;	170	FOURTH MEDITATN	65
THE SOUL AT A STILL-STAND,	194	JOURNY INTERIOR	54
STONE			
BEETLES IN CAVES, NEWTS, STONE-DEAF FISHES,	50	THE MINIMAL	3
STONES			
BUMPING AGAINST STICKS AND BOTTOM-STONES, THEN SWINGING	159	FIRST MEDITATN	70
THE BOTTOM-STONES SHIMMER BACK THEIR IRREGULAR STRIATIONS,	233	THE PIKE	8
STORM			
WHEN LIGHT DIVIDED ON A STORM-TOSSED TREE.	246	THE MARROW	20
STREAM'S			
I KNOW THE BACK-STREAM'S JOY, AND THE STONE'S ETERNAL PULSELESS LONGING.	88	PRAISE TO END!	82
STREET			
AND THE SMALL STREET-LAMP SWINGING AND SLAMMING AGAINST THE LAMP POLE.	230	THE STORM	7
STRUCK			
ROCKING IT, LIKE A SUN-STRUCK POND,	163	I'M HERE	84
SUDDEN			
YOU ALL-OF-A-SUDDEN GODS,	82	SENSIBILITY! LA	26
SUMMER			
A LOW VOICE, SUMMER-SAD.	90	UNFOLD! UNFOLD!	50
SUN			
ROCKING IT, LIKE A SUN-STRUCK POND,	163	I'M HERE	84
NEAR THIS ROSE, IN THIS GROVE OF SUN-PARCHED, WIND-WARPED MADRONAS,	205	THE ROSE	98
ITS BEVY OF BEES, AND ITS WIND-BEATEN RICKETY SUN-CHAIRS.	226	THE LIZARD	29
SUNKEN			
AND THE HALF-SUNKEN BRANCH BENDS AWAY FROM THE GAZER'S EYE.	233	THE PIKE	9
SWAN			
SWAN-HEART, ARBUTUS-CALM,	124	WORDS FOR WIND	51
SWAY			
MOVED IN A SLOW UP-SWAY.	57	THE LOST SON	148
SWEAT			
MY PALM-SWEAT FLASHES GOLD;	88	PRAISE TO END!	87
SWEET			
OR FAN LIFE INTO WILTED SWEET-PEAS WITH HIS HAT,	42	OLD FLORIST	9
THE SWEET-PEA TENDRILS, THE SMILAX,	44	FRAU BAUMAN	5
A LARK-SWEET LOVER IF EVER THERE WAS.	258	SONG (3)	3
AND SHE IS MY SWEET-HEART.	268	SAGINAW SONG	42
SWELL			
THE FLAT BOOM ON THE BEACH OF THE TOWERING SEA-SWELL,	231	THE STORM	41
SWINE			
KISS THE TROUGH, SWINE-ON-FRIDAY.	59	THE LONG ALLEY	24
TAIL			
WHO KNOWS HOW THE WAG-TAIL WOOS?	183	THE WAGTAIL	1
TAILED			
THEY FLICKER FASTER THAN A BLUE-TAILED SWIFT,	8	THE SIGNALS	5

	PAGE	TITLE	LINE
TAILED (CONTINUED)			
TO DISTRACT ATTENTION FROM THE SHORT-TAILED RIDICULOUS YOUNG ONES	234	ALL MORNING	19
TAILORED			
OF A MAN-TAILORED BLOUSE; THE LIST OF SHOPPING DONE;	29	THE REMINDER	6
TAILS			
THOSE LEWD MONKEY-TAILS HANGING FROM DRAINHOLES,--	39	WEED PULLER	3
AND MIST LIFTING OUT OF THE BROWN CAT-TAILS;	67	SHAPE OF FIRE	87
TALK			
A DRUNK MAN STUMBLES BY, ABSORBED IN SELF-TALK.	33	IDYLL	2
TAR			
THE OILY, TAR-LADEN WALLS	205	THE ROSE	94
TATTERED			
AN OLD WIND-TATTERED BUTTERFLY FLEW DOWN	243	THE MOTION	2
TENDER'S			
I REMEMBER THE CROSSING-TENDER'S GERANIUM BORDER	29	THE REMINDER	1
THE (5)			
THICK			
AND THAT WRIST-THICK CASCADE TUMBLING FROM A CLEFT ROCK,	191	AT OYSTER RIVER	44
THIRTY			
THE ROOM WAS THIRTY-FIVE BELOW;	114	DINKY	14
THORN			
AND THEIR THORN-BITTEN WRISTS,	44	FRAU BAUMAN	34
THRASHING			
A THRASHING-UP OF THE WHOLE POOL,	233	THE PIKE	17
THREAD			
A THREAD-LIKE FIRMNESS.	226	THE LIZARD	12
THROATED			
HIS DEEP-THROATED COOING PART OF THE EARLY MORNING,	234	ALL MORNING	2
THRUM			
THRUM-THRUM, WHO CAN BE EQUAL TO EASE?	97	O, THOU OPENING	13
THRUM-THRUM, WHO CAN BE EQUAL TO EASE?	97	O, THOU OPENING	13
THUMB'S			
JOHN-OF-THE-THUMB'S JUMPING;	81	SENSIBILITY! LA	19
TICKLE			
PRICKLE-ME, TICKLE-ME, CLOSE STEMS.	85	PRAISE TO END!	6
TIDE			
COME THE FIRST TIDE-RIPPLES, MOVING, ALMOST WITHOUT SOUND, TOWARD ME,	190	AT OYSTER RIVER	2
TIGHT			
IS NOW SEALED HONEY-TIGHT.	4	DEATH PIECE	4
TIME			
GOODBYE, GOODBYE, OLD STONES, THE TIME-ORDER IS GOING,	56	THE LOST SON	108
SAD, IN A SINGING-TIME?	98	O, THOU OPENING	45
TIME-HARRIED PRISONERS OF SHALL AND WILL--	250	THE RIGHT THING	2
TIPPED			
BEYOND THE SEA PINE, THE OAK, THE WIND-TIPPED MADRONA,	203	THE ROSE	47
TIPS			
A SURGEON GUIDES A SCALPEL WITH THUMB AND FINGER-TIPS.	28	CLAIRVOY WIDOW	20
TO (1)			
TOM			
AND THE TOM-CAT, CAUGHT NEAR THE PHEASANT-RUN,	199	THE FAR FIELD	21
TO LIVE BY COURTESY OF THE SHRIKE, THE SNAKE, THE TOM-CAT.	227	MEADOW MOUSE	25
TOP			
FLINGING LONG STRINGS OF WET ACROSS THE ROOF-TOP,	41	BIG WIND	29
TOSSED			
WHEN LIGHT DIVIDED ON A STORM-TOSSED TREE.	246	THE MARROW	20
TRANCE			
THE BLOOD SLOWS TRANCE-LIKE IN THE ALTERED VEIN;	12	SLOW SEASON	15
TRASH			
THREW HER, POT AND ALL, INTO THE TRASH-CAN,	228	THE GERANIUM	23
TREE			
THE YOUNG FRUIT SWELL UPON THE PEAR-TREE BOUGH.	11	LIGHT BRIGHTER	16
A CONGRESS OF TREE-SHREWS AND RATS,	163	I'M HERE	66
THE DESCENDANTS OF THE PLAYFUL TREE-SHREW THAT SURVIVED THE ARCHAIC KILLERS,	170	FOURTH MEDITATN	66
THE WAY BLOCKED AT LAST BY A FALLEN FIR-TREE,	193	JOURNY INTERIOR	15
AND MY THOUGHT FLIES TO THE PLACE BY THE BO-TREE.	222	THE ABYSS	100
UNDER THE EYE OF THE GREAT OWL WATCHING FROM THE ELM-TREE,	227	MEADOW MOUSE	24
AND THE HURRICANE DRIVES THE DEAD STRAW INTO THE LIVING PINE-TREE.	231	THE STORM	43

	PAGE	TITLE	LINE

TREES
> THEY SIT, THREE OR FOUR, HIGH IN THE FIR-TREES BACK OF THE
>> HOUSE, ... 234 ALL MORNING 6

TROUGH
> NOW HE'S EATEN HIS THREE KINDS OF CHEESE AND DRUNK FROM HIS
>> BOTTLE-CAP WATERING-TROUGH-- .... 227 MEADOW MOUSE 12

TURN
> SHE TAUGHT ME TURN, AND COUNTER-TURN, AND STAND; .... 127 I KNEW A WOMAN 9

TURNED
> TURNED-OVER ROOTS .... 43 FLOWER DUMP 6

TURNING
> "WHAT MOON?" HE CRIED, HALF-TURNING IN MOCK FURY. 273 SUPPR W LINDSAY 10

TWO
> A TWO-LEGGED DOG HUNTING A NEW HORIZON OF HOWLS. .... 65 SHAPE OF FIRE 38
> WHAT'S A THICK? TWO-BY-TWO'S A SHAPE. .... 92 I CRY, LOVE! 10
> YOU'RE BECOMING THAT HORROR, A TWO-LEGGED PIG .... 272 DUET 3

TWO'S
> WHAT'S A THICK? TWO-BY-TWO'S A SHAPE. .... 92 I CRY, LOVE! 10

UNDRESSED
> AND SHE WAS HALF-UNDRESSED, ... 268 SAGINAW SONG 59
> WHEN THEY ARE HALF-UNDRESSED. .... 268 SAGINAW SONG 61

UNPRAYED
> UNPRAYED-FOR, ... 173 WHAT TELL BONES 100

UP
> CHILDREN, THEIR BELLIES SWOLLEN LIKE BLOWN-UP PAPER BAGS, 48 JUDGE NOT 2
> MOVED IN A SLOW UP-SWAY. .... 57 THE LOST SON 148
> AND THE UP-SPRING OF THE PLANK WHEN A FOOT LEFT THE RUNWAY. 158 FIRST MEDITATN 47
> MY BANKED-UP VERTIGO 213 THE HAPPY THREE 26
> AND YET STILL VIOLENT MEN, WHOSE STACKED-UP GUNS 224 OTTO 27
> A THRASHING-UP OF THE WHOLE POOL, ... 233 THE PIKE 17

UPHOLSTERED
> ON WELL-UPHOLSTERED BUMS .... 31 LULL 10

URCHIN
> I HAVE TAKEN COUNSEL OF THE CRAB AND THE SEA-URCHIN, ... 222 THE ABYSS 92

VENT
> SHUTTLING ITS THROAT WHILE PERCHED ON A WIND-VENT, ... 158 FIRST MEDITATN 40

VENTS
> WHISTLING THINLY UNDER THE WIND-VENTS; .... 41 BIG WIND 31

VOICE
> THE CRICKET-VOICE DEEP IN THE MIDNIGHT FIELD, ... 196 THE LONG WATERS 27

WAG
> WHO KNOWS HOW THE WAG-TAIL WOOS? .... 183 THE WAGTAIL 1

WAIT
> IT WAS JUMP-IN-THE-HEDGE; IT WAS WAIT-IN-THE-HALL; .... 111 SQUEEZE-BOX 13

WALL
> THE HAND-PAINTED WALL-PAPER, FINER THAN SKIN, ... 32 SALE 17
> AS I WALKED BY THE HIGH SEA-WALL. .... 216 THE SHY MAN 4
> AS I MOPED BY THE HIGH SEA-WALL. .... 216 THE SHY MAN 8
> AS WE WALKED BY THE HIGH SEA-WALL. .... 216 THE SHY MAN 16
> AS WE EMBRACE BY THE HIGH SEA-WALL. .... 216 THE SHY MAN 23
> AS WE KISS BY THE HIGH SEA-WALL. .... 216 THE SHY MAN 26
> ALONG THE SEA-WALL, A STEADY SLOSHING OF THE SWELL, ... 230 THE STORM 10

WARPED
> NEAR THIS ROSE, IN THIS GROVE OF SUN-PARCHED, WIND-WARPED
>> MADRONAS, ... 205 THE ROSE 98

WARY
> TURNS, MOUSE-WARY,-- .... 260 THE CHANGELING 2

WASHED
> THERE ARE MANY DETOURS, WASHED-OUT INTERRUPTED RAW PLACES 193 JOURNY INTERIOR 2

WASP
> IN THE WINTER-WASP, PULSING ITS WINGS IN THE SUNLIGHT; ... 88 PRAISE TO END! 92

WATER
> TOWARD THE QUICK-WATER, WRINKLING AND RIPPLING. .... 54 THE LOST SON 39
> AS WHEN SILT DRIFTS AND SIFTS DOWN THROUGH MUDDY POND-WATER, 159 FIRST MEDITATN 60
> IN A COUNTRY HALF-LAND, HALF-WATER. .... 201 THE FAR FIELD 76

WATERING
> NOW HE'S EATEN HIS THREE KINDS OF CHEESE AND DRUNK FROM HIS
>> BOTTLE-CAP WATERING-TROUGH-- .... 227 MEADOW MOUSE 12

WAVE
> THEN DOWN, AS WE ROLL LIKE A BOAT FROM A WAVE-CREST. ..... 158 FIRST MEDITATN 25

WAVES
> BUCKING INTO THE WIND-WAVES .... 41 BIG WIND 26

	PAGE	TITLE	LINE
WAY			
RETIRING TO NUDGE HIS NECK HALF-WAY UNDER	226	THE LIZARD	16
BENDING THE TREES HALF-WAY DOWN TO THE GROUND,	231	THE STORM	31
A SWAYING LIGHT-CORD, THEN RAN HALF-WAY BACK.	273	SUPPR W LINDSAY	25
WAYS			
WHAT FISH-WAYS YOU HAVE, LITTLEST FLOWERS,	61	THE LONG ALLEY	74
WEARY			
I MOVED LIKE SOME HEAT-WEARY ANIMAL.	247	I WAITED	17
WEATHER			
THEIR WOODEN STORES OF SILVERY PINE AND WEATHER-BEATEN RED COURTHOUSES,	193	JOURNY INTERIOR	31
WEED			
WEEDS TURN TOWARD THE WIND WEED-SKELETONS.	173	WHAT TELL BONES	65
WEIGHT			
NEAT IN THEIR BOXES, DOLOR OF PAD AND PAPER-WEIGHT,	46	DOLOR	2
WELL			
ON WELL-UPHOLSTERED BUMS	31	LULL	10
AS DARKNESS CREEPS UP ON THE WELL-GROOMED SUBURBAN TOWN,	33	IDYLL	5
MAKING A SLOW JOURNEY AROUND THE WELL-CURB.	151	SLUG	3
WET			
I QUAIL, LEAN TO BEGINNINGS, SHEATH-WET.	37	CUTTINGS (LATE)	11
WHAT			
THE WHAT-NOT, THE SETTEE, THE CHIPPENDALE CHAIRS	32	SALE	3
WHIMPERING			
THEIR CHILD-WHIMPERING.	190	AT OYSTER RIVER	10
WHITE			
AROUND, BACK INTO THE TINY MAINCURRENT, THE RUSH OF BROWNISH-WHITE WATER,	159	FIRST MEDITATN	71
HER PURE-WHITE FEATHERINESS	213	THE HAPPY THREE	23
PACING A ROOM, A ROOM WITH DEAD-WHITE WALLS;	242	THE SEQUEL	30
WILLOW			
ALL SMALL SHAPES, WILLOW-SHY,	90	UNFOLD! UNFOLD!	46
WIND			
BUCKING INTO THE WIND-WAVES	41	BIG WIND	26
WHISTLING THINLY UNDER THE WIND-VENTS;	41	BIG WIND	31
WHERE'S ANN? WHERE'S LOU? WHERE'S JOCK-WITH-THE-WIND?	97	O, THOU OPENING	17
SHUTTLING ITS THROAT WHILE PERCHED ON A WIND-VENT,	158	FIRST MEDITATN	40
A CHILD AT PLAY, A WIND-EXCITED BIRD.	165	HER BECOMING	23
THE ARROYO CRACKING THE ROAD, THE WIND-BITTEN BUTTES, THE CANYONS,	193	JOURNY INTERIOR	7
THE SCRAGGLY WIND-BREAK OF A DUSTY RANCH-HOUSE.	194	JOURNY INTERIOR	45
BUT THIS ROSE, THIS ROSE IN THE SEA-WIND,	203	THE ROSE	39
BEYOND THE SEA PINE, THE OAK, THE WIND-TIPPED MADRONA,	203	THE ROSE	47
ON THE BANKS OF THE TOMBSTONE, THE WIND-HARPS HAVING THEIR SAY,	204	THE ROSE	60
NEAR THIS ROSE, IN THIS GROVE OF SUN-PARCHED, WIND-WARPED MADRONAS,	205	THE ROSE	98
AND IN THIS ROSE, THIS ROSE IN THE SEA-WIND,	205	THE ROSE	111
ITS BEVY OF BEES, AND ITS WIND-BEATEN RICKETY SUN-CHAIRS.	226	THE LIZARD	29
A SEA-WIND PAUSING IN A SUMMER TREE.	235	MANIFESTATION	8
AN OLD WIND-TATTERED BUTTERFLY FLEW DOWN	243	THE MOTION	2
WINDOW			
CREAKING THE CYPRESS WINDOW-FRAMES,	41	BIG WIND	17
WINDS			
TOPPED BY CROSS-WINDS, TUGGED AT BY SINUOUS UNDERCURRENTS	191	AT OYSTER RIVER	33
AND THE SEA-WINDS MOVE THROUGH THE PINE TREES,	196	THE LONG WATERS	18
SWIMMING SLOWLY, ITS BACK RUFFLED BY THE LIGHT CROSS-WINDS,	197	THE LONG WATERS	53
WIND'S			
MINE AND THE SEA-WIND'S.	205	THE ROSE	114
WING			
WING-CROOKED AND SURE,	93	I CRY, LOVE!	42
WINGED			
OR RISE WITH THE GAR-EAGLE, THE GREAT-WINGED CONDOR.	209	HER LONGING	16
WINTER			
THOUGH STILL THE GUARDED SNOW IS WINTER-SEALED,	11	LIGHT BRIGHTER	6
A WINTER-LEAPING FROG.	83	O LULL ME, LULL	28
DESIRE WAS WINTER-CALM,	87	PRAISE TO END!	69
IN THE WINTER-WASP, PULSING ITS WINGS IN THE SUNLIGHT;	88	PRAISE TO END!	92
WIT			
MY DIM-WIT COUSIN	25	DIM-WIT COUSIN	T
MY DIM-WIT COUSIN, SAVED BY A DEATH-BED QUAVER,	25	DIM-WIT COUSIN	1
WITH (1)			

	PAGE	TITLE	LINE
WOOD			
I SEE A BANKER'S MANSION WITH TWENTY WOOD-GRATE FIRES, ...	27	CLAIRVOY WIDOW	13
WREN			
WREN-SONG IN TRELLIS: A LIGHT ECSTASY OF BUTTERFLIES COURTING, ...	255	LIGHT POEM	1
WRIST			
AND THAT WRIST-THICK CASCADE TUMBLING FROM A CLEFT ROCK,	191	AT OYSTER RIVER	44
YAK			
AND GO HUMPING OFF, YICKETTY-YAK.	178	THE YAK	5
YARD			
AND THE FLICKER DRUMMED FROM HIS DEAD TREE IN THE CHICKEN-YARD.	200	THE FAR FIELD	37
YEAR			
OF SIXTEEN-YEAR-OLD LUST.	46	PICKLE BELT	12
YELLOWISH			
AND THE YELLOWISH-GREEN FROM THE MOUNTAINY UPLAND,--	200	THE FAR FIELD	62
YICKETTY			
AND GO HUMPING OFF, YICKETTY-YAK.	178	THE YAK	5
ZEPHYR			
A TRUE ZEPHYR-HAUNTED WOODIE.	81	SENSIBILITY! LA	7

TABLE OF WORD FREQUENCIES

(3323)
THE

(1539)
A

(1053)
AND

(1006)
OF

(991)
I

(738)
IN

(614)
TO

(548)
MY

(320)
WITH

(264)
IS

(258)
ON

(244)
ME

(219)
FROM

(213)
THAT

(210)
ALL

(193)
WAS

(192)
AS

(180)
FOR

(175)
IT

(173)
YOU

(170)
AT

(161)
WHAT

(151)
WHEN

(150)
LIGHT
LIKE
OUT

(149)
WE

(144)
HE

(142)
BY

(136)
HIS

(135)
SHE

(127)
BUT

(125)
OR

(124)
THIS

(120)
WIND

(116)
ONE

(115)
ARE
HER

(112)
DOWN

(111)
NOT

(107)
THEIR

(106)
BE
ITS
THEY

(105)
WHO

(102)
HAVE
INTO

(96)
OVER

(93)
THERE

(92)

SMALL

(90)
I'M

(89)
AN
CAN

(85)
LOVE
STILL

(84)
LONG
NO
UP
WHERE

(80)
WATER

(74)
BIRD

(70)
DARK
THAN

(68)
AIR
BACK
DEAD

(67)
DO
O

(65)
COME
MORE
SO

(64)
WOULD

(63)
MAN
TIME

(62)
AWAY

(60)
HOW

(59)
SUN

(58)
TREE

(57)
AM
STONE

(56)
KNOW

THING

(55)
THEN

(54)
HAS
OLD

(53)
EYE

(51)
DAY
WAY

(50)
OWN
SLOW

(49)
COULD
LEAVES
MOON

(48)
CAME
LAST
YOUR

(47)
ALONE
THROUGH

(46)
NIGHT
THINGS
UPON

(45)
FAR
FISH
HAD
MYSELF
SEE
SPIRIT
WILL

(44)
SLEEP
STONES

(43)
BIRDS
IF
NOW
PLACE
THINK

(42)
CLOSE
FIRE
GREAT
ROSE
YET

(41)
EYES

HEAR
HEART
OUR
UNDER
WHITE

(40)
ONCE
SING
SONG

(39)
BEFORE
FIELD
HIM
ONLY

(38)
BODY
LIFE
LIVE
SAID

(37)
BEYOND

(36)
BONES
FACE
HERE
PURE

(35)
ANOTHER
COLD
FLESH
SOME
SOUL
TOO

(34)
SEA
WITHOUT

(33)
NEVER
SANG
SHAPE
THOUGHT

(32)
AGAIN
COMES
GROUND
TOWARD

(31)
EDGE
GREEN
IT'S
MORNING
SOUND
THOSE

(30)
DID
ELSE
GO

ITSELF
LOOK
SKIN
SLOWLY
THESE
WORLD
YOUNG

(29)
AROUND
DEEP
I'LL
MIND
WAVES

(28)
DOES
GOD
HIGH
NEAR
SAW
UNTIL
WHAT'S

(27)
DRY
EVEN
FATHER
FIRST
HAND
MOUTH
RAIN
SAY
WERE

(26)
BETWEEN
GRASS
SUMMER

(25)
DEATH
HOUSE
LITTLE
RIGHT
RIVER
THEM
US

(24)
AGAINST
ALIVE
BEING
BREATH
CRY
FEET
GONE
I'VE
LOST
SOFT
TRUE
WOOD

(23)
CANNOT
EACH
HEAD
KEEP

MAY
MOTION
TAKE
TREES
TWO
WHILE
WITHIN

(22)
ALWAYS
BEAR
COMING
EARLY
HAPPY
LEFT
LOOSE
LOW
SHOULD
TELL
THIN
WEEDS
WHOLE

(21)
CAN'T
DREAM
DYING
END
MAKE
MANY
MOVES
NEED
NOR
OFF
REMEMBER
SILENCE
TURNED
WENT

(20)
ALONG
AMONG
CAT
ENOUGH
HAIR
KNOWS
LIPS
SINGLE
SNOW
SWEET
WINGS
WORM

(19)
EAR
FEEL
FINE
HANDS
HEARD
JOY
JUST
KISS
SHADE
SINGING
STREAM
WATERS

(18)

BLACK
CHILD
DUST
EAT
EVERY
FLAME
MOVE
NOSE
SAYS
SEED
SHADOW
SOMETHING
STAY
WIDE

(17)
ABOVE
ACROSS
BECOME
BEEN
BELIEVE
BENEATH
CLOUD
DANCE
DESIRE
DIE
FALL
GHOST
HALF
MONEY
MOVED
NOTHING
RUNNING
STOOD
TAIL
THOUGH
VOICE
WALK

(16)
BLOOD
CHANGE
CRIES
DRINK
FIND
FLOWERS
ICE
KEPT
KNEW
MADE
MOST
POND
ROCK
ROCKS
ROOTS
SHAPES
THERE'S
TURNS
WET

(15)
BEHIND
CLOSER
CRIED
EVER
FORWARD
FULL
HILL

LAY
LEAF
LET
LIVING
MOTHER
STAYED
SUCH
TURN
WALL
WARM

(14)
ABOUT
AFTER
ALMOST
CARE
DEAR
DIRT
KNEES
MIDNIGHT
NEITHER
PLAY
RAN
RISING
ROUND
RUNS
SAND
STAND
TONGUE
WHICH
WINDS
WISH
YOU'RE

(13)
BLUE
CHILDREN
DARE
DON'T
FAT
FEAR
GIVE
GOOD
KEEPS
LATE
LESS
LIVES
LONGER
MEN
OTHER
PART
PAST
PUT
ROAD
ROOM
SPEAK
STEM
THAT'S
TURNING
UPWARD
WALKED
WASN'T
WHERE'S
WHY

(12)
BED
BRIGHT

DANCED
DOG
DOOR
FELL
FISHING
FLY
FOUND
GOING
LAKE
LAUGH
LIE
LONELY
LOOKED
MEET
MOVING
MUCH
OH
ROSES
SAME
SHORE
SIGH
SIT
STEMS
WATCH
WAVE
WOMAN
YES

(11)
BEAUTIFUL
BREATHE
BRING
BROKEN
CALLED
CORNER
COUNTRY
DANCING
DIES
EARS
ETERNITY
FINAL
FURY
GARDEN
GOES
GOT
GREW
HARD
HAY
HOME
LAND
LEAN
LOVED
MOUSE
MUST
NOISE
PAIN
PATH
PLAIN
QUICK
SAD
SEEN
STRAIGHT
SWAYING
TOOK
TOUCH
VEINS
WAKE
WINDING

(10)
BEARS
BEATING
BREATHING
CLOUDS
DELIGHT
EARTH
EASE
EMBRACE
EVENING
GLASS
GRAVE
HARSH
HE'S
HIMSELF
LADY
LEARNED
LIVED
LORD
LOVELY
LOVE'S
MAKING
MET
MOMENT
NAKED
NEW
OPEN
OUTSIDE
POOL
QUIET
RETURN
ROOT
SHALL
SIGHS
SON
SOUL'S
TWICE
WEATHER
WHOM
WHO'S
WORDS

(9)
BEAST
BEES
BELOW
BIG
BLEAK
BONE
DUSTY
EASY
FALLEN
FALLING
FIELDS
FLAT
FLIES
FLOATING
GAZE
GIRL
HAT
HEAVEN
KITTY-CAT
KNOWING
KNOWN
LOG
NARROW
NOON

PLACES
POEM
PRAISE
RAGE
RISES
SALT
SAT
SELF
SHADOWS
SINGS
SKY
STARED
STARING
STAYS
STORM
STRETCH
SUNLIGHT
SWINGING
TAKES
THICK
THREE
VINE
WALLS
WATCHING
WATERY
WAYS
WINTER
WREN

(8)
ABYSS
ANY
ASKED
BEGIN
BOTH
BRANCH
BREAKING
BREAKS
BROKE
BURNING
CAUGHT
CENTER
CHOICE
DARKENING
DAWN
DOGS
DONE
ELM
FACES
FLOWER
FLOWING
FOOT
FROG
GREY
HARRY
HEAT
HOLE
I'D
INSTANT
JOURNEY
LEAP
LEAST
LIFTING
LIKES
LIMP
LINE
LIP
LIZARD

LOOKING
LUCK
MAKES
MIST
NEEDS
OURSELVES
PLAYED
REACH
RICH
RIPPLE
RUN
SECRET
SERPENT
SIGHT
SILL
SIMPLE
SLIDING
SNAKE
SOON
SPEECH
STARE
STICK
STRAW
SUDDEN
THEMSELVES
THROAT
TIMES
TINY
TOES
TOP
TRIED
UNDONE
VISION
WAITING
WAKING
WALKING
WEAR
WELL
WHISPER
WILD
WINDOWS
WISDOM
WORD
YEAR

(7)
AFRAID
ANIMAL
ARMS
ASK
BACKWARD
BARE
BEAT
BEGINS
BELLY
BLAKE
BLOSSOMS
BOY
BRIGHTER
BROUGHT
BUDS
CALL
CHAIR
CLEAR
COUSIN
DANGEROUS
DARLING
DELICATE

DIED
EITHER
ETERNAL
FAIR
FATHER'S
FERNS
FEW
FINGERS
FLEW
FLYING
FRESH
FRIEND
FROST
FRUIT
GULLS
HORSE
HUNG
INNER
KISSING
LEAPS
LEARN
LIGHTLY
LISTENED
LIVELY
LONGING
MAD
MEADOW
MOUNTAIN
NAME
NATURAL
NATURE
NECK
NOBODY
PAW
PERPETUAL
PIECE
PINE
POOR
PULSE
RISE
SAGINAW
SCENE
SENSUAL
SHAKING
SHARP
SHE'D
SHIFTING
SMELLS
SPRING
STAR
STICKS
SWAYS
SWEAT
TODAY
TOGETHER
WHATEVER
WHISTLE
WHOSE
WIFE
WORST

(6)
ANCIENT
APART
ASLEEP
ATE
AWAKE
BECAME

BECOMING
BEGINNING
BEGINNINGS
BENT
BESIDE
BETTER
BLOW
BOAT
BRAIN
BREAK
BUSH
CHANGES
CHILD'S
CINDERS
CORE
CRABS
CREAKING
CURRENT
DAH
DEW
DINKY
DIRTY
DOUBLE
DOVE
DREAD
DRIFTING
DROPS
EVERYONE
EVERYTHING
FALLS
FATE
FISHES
FLASH
FLAW
FOLLOW
FORM
FORMS
GLORY
GRASSES
HATE
HAZE
HEAVY
HELD
HIGHWAY
HOPE
HORN
HUGH
HUMAN
KIERKEGAARD
KIND
KISSED
LAUGHED
LEANING
LISTEN
LOAM
LOUD
MEAN
MIDDLE
MINNOWS
MOSSY
MUSIC
NOTES
NOWHERE
OBJECTS
OBSCURE
OFTEN
PIPES
PLANTS

POINT
PULSING
RAW
RED
REJOICE
REST
RIPPLES
ROCKING
RUBBLE
RUSH
SEA-WALL
SEEK
SEEMED
SEIZE
SEND
SENSE
SEVERAL
SHE'S
SHIFT
SHIMMER
SHINING
SHOOK
SHY
SIGHED
SISTER
SLIGHTLY
SNAIL
SNAKES
SOMETIMES
SONGS
STALK
STEADY
STRING
SUBSTANCE
SURE
SURFACE
SWAY
TALK
TALKED
TAUGHT
TEARS
TENDER
TENDRILS
TERRIBLE
THIGHS
THINKING
THUMB
TIRED
TRAFFIC
TREMBLING
TRUTH
UGLY
VALLEY
VISIBLE
WEAK
WE'LL
WHEELS
WHISTLING
WOODEN
WOUND

(5)
ACT
AFTERNOON
ALTERED
ANGEL
ANGELS
ANSWER

APPLES
BANKS
BATS
BECAUSE
BENDING
BILL
BITE
BLOOM
BOUGH
BRANCHES
BREAST
BRINGS
CALM
CAR
CARELESS
CAST
CAVE
CHANCE
CHEEK
CLAW
CLAY
CLOTHES
COLOR
COOL
CREATURE
CREATURES
CROWN
CURSE
CUT
CYCLAMEN
DAMP
DAYS
DEAREST
DROPPED
EASILY
EMPTY
ENDURE
EVIL
FEARFUL
FEATHERS
FINGER
FLING
FOLDS
FOND
FOREVER
FORGOTTEN
FRIENDS
FUME
GATE
GAVE
GET
GHOSTLY
GODS
GOD'S
GOOSE
GREENHOUSE
GROW
HAPPENS
HELLO
HERON
HOLD
HOLES
HOLY
HUNTING
IMAGE
IMMACULATE
IRON
ISN'T

KISSES
LANGUAGE
LAWN
LEAVE
LEAVING
LIES
LILIES
LINDSAY
LOOKS
LOVER
MAMMA
MICE
MINE
MOONLIGHT
MOTH
MOUTHS
NERVES
NONE
NORTH
OAK
OWL
PASS
PAWS
PERHAPS
PETALS
PLAYS
PLEASED
PLEASURE
POT
PRIDE
RAGGED
READ
READY
REASON
RECEDES
REMAIN
REPLY
RICKETY
RIDING
RIVER'S
ROLLING
SAINT
SALMON
SCENT
SHAKES
SHALE
SHELL
SHOE
SHOES
SHRUNKEN
SIDE
SIDEWAYS
SLEPT
SLIPPED
SLIPPERY
SOIL
SOMEWHERE
SPACE
SPARROWS
SPIDER
SPRAY
STAIR
STALE
STARS
STEP
SWAN
SWAYED
SWELL

TAKEN
TAKING
TILL
TOE
TOWN
TUNE
VAGUE
VEERING
VERY
WAIT
WAITED
WALKS
WALTZ
WEED
WEIGHT
WHENEVER
WIDENING
WIDOW
WIND'S
WINDY
WOKE
WORSE
WRONG
YELLOW

(4)
ABIDE
ADORE
AGING
ALL'S
ALTERING
APRIL
BARN
BEAK
BEATS
BECOMES
BEDS
BEHOLD
BENCHES
BEST
BIT
BITTER
BLAZE
BOLD
BOTTOM
BOYS
BRIDGE
BUSHES
BUSY
CALLING
CALLS
CARES
CARNATIONS
CATS
CAVES
CELLAR
CENTRAL
CHANGED
CHANGING
CHIN
CLIFFS
CLIMB
CLUMSY
COARSE
COMMON
CONDITION
CONFUSION
COURSE

CRAB
CREAM
CREEPING
CROSSING
CROW
DARKNESS
DELIGHTING
DEPTHS
DESCEND
DIMINISHED
DIPPING
DISAPPEAR
DISH
DIVING
DOESN'T
DONKEY
DRAINED
DRIFTS
DRINKING
DRIP
DRIVING
DROP
DROWN
DROWSE
EDGES
ELABORATE
ENEMIES
EYE'S
FAREWELL
FARTHER
FASTER
FEED
FEELING
FERN
FIGURE
FIGURES
FINCHES
FIR
FIVE
FLICKER
FLOOR
FLUNG
FOOL
FREE
GATHERED
GENTLY
GLITTER
GLITTERING
GRAVEL
GRIEF
GROWING
GROWS
GUESS
HANGING
HANGS
HEN
HERSELF
HID
HIGHER
HILLSIDE
HORNS
HORSES
HOUR
INVISIBLE
INWARD
IRREGULAR
JOHN
JUMPING

JUMPS	SHOOTS	WRENS	CONSTANT
KNOCK	SICK	YEARS	CONTAINED
LARK	SIDES	YOU'D	CONTENT
LARKS	SILT	YOURSELF	COPS
LEAPED	SILVER		COULDN'T
LET'S	SLEEPING	(3)	COUNTING
LEVEL	SLEEPS	ABSURD	CRACKING
LEWD	SLEEVE	AFTER-IMAGE	CRATERS
LIGHTS	SLIDES	AGES	CRAZY
LOOSENED	SLIME	AGO	CREEK
LOSE	SLOWED	AGONY	CRUMBLED
LOVES	SMELL	AHEAD	CRUMBLING
LUST	SMILE	AIRS	CRYING
MAN'S	SODDEN	ALAS	CURB
MARROW	SOFTLY	ALLEY	CURLED
MASTER	SOUTH	ALTERS	DANCES
MATCH	SPIDERS	ANIMALS	DANK
MEDITATION	SPIT	ARCH	DANTE
MICHIGAN	STANDING	ASH	DARED
MILK	STANDS	ASHES	DARES
MISERY	START	ASTRIDE	DAZZLE
MIXED	STEAM	ATTIC	DEEPENING
MOLE	STEEL	AUTUMNAL	DEEPER
MORTAL	STEPPED	BARK	DEEPEST
MOSS	STIFF	BAT	DENIED
MOTIONLESS	STIR	BATTERED	DESOLATION
MYRTLE	STIRRED	BAY	DEVIL
MYSTERY	STRANGE	BEARD	DIDN'T
NAKEDNESS	STREAMS	BEARING	DIPPED
NAMED	STREETS	BEASTS	DIVIDED
NEST	STRETCHED	BEE	DOE
NESTLING	STREWN	BEGAN	DOODLE
NICE	STUCK	BIGGER	DOORS
NOTE	STUDY	BILLOWING	DRAW
OILY	SUDDENLY	BLACKENED	DRAWS
ON-COMING	SUNKEN	BLEED	DRIED
ORCHARD	SWEAR	BLESS	DRIES
ORDER	SWIFT	BLESSED	DRIFT
PALM	SWUNG	BLOSSOM	DRIFTWOOD
PAPA	TEETH	BLOWING	DRINKS
PAPER	TELLS	BOOK	DRIPPING
PERCH	TEN	BORN	DUCK
PITCH	TERROR	BREATHES	EAST
PITCHING	THY	BROAD	EATEN
PLATEAU	TIDE	BRONZE	EATS
PLEASE	TIED	BROOD	ECHO
POKE	TILTING	BROODING	EEL
PRINCE	TOAD	BROOK	EELS
QUIETLY	TOSSED	BROWN	ELEGY
RANDOM	TRELLIS	BUFFALO	ELEMENT
RATHER	TWITTERING	BUNCHED	EMBANKMENT
REACHING	UNDERNEATH	BURNED	ENTERS
REALITY	USE	CAGE	ESCAPES
REPOSE	WAKES	CASUAL	EXTENDING
RIDE	WALLACE	CEILING	EXTREME
RIPPLING	WATCHED	CENTAUR	FACED
ROARING	WEEK	CERULEAN	FAMILIAR
ROLLED	WEEPING	CHERISH	FATHERS
ROMPED	WE'RE	CHILL	FAVORITE
SALE	WHEEL	CHOOSE	FEATHER
SECOND	WILLOW	CHRYSANTHEMUMS	FELT
SECRETS	WINDOW	CICADA	FEUD
SEEM	WIT	CIRCLES	FIELD'S
SEPTEMBER	WOMEN	CLEAREST	FILLS
SET	WOO	CLIMBING	FIXED
SHAKE	WOODS	CLOVER	FLICK
SHALLOW	WORK	COILED	FLOATED
SHINE	WRATH	COMPLETE	FLOATS

FLOW	LIGHT'S	PRESSED	SOURCE
FLOWED	LILY'S	PROW	SPECIAL
FLOWS	LIMBER	PULLED	SPOKE
FOOLISH	LINES	PUTS	SPREAD
FOOTIE	LION	QUAY	STARTS
FORCE	LOGS	RAGS	STEPS
FORTH	LOLL	RARE	STEVENS
FOUR	LONGED	RAT	STILLNESS
FRAU	LOT	RATS	STINKS
FROZEN	LOVERS	RAVINES	STIRS
FURTHER	LULL	REALLY	STOP
GENTLE	LYING	REALM	STOPPED
GERANIUM	MAIMED	RECALL	STREET
GIN	MATTER	REMEMBERS	STRETCHES
GLAD	MAYBE	REMINDED	STRICT
GLEAM	MEANING	RENEW	STUBBLE
GNU	MERCY	RETREATING	STUNNED
GOLD	MERELY	REVOLVING	SUCK
GRACE	METAL	RIBS	SUCKING
GRAIN	MIRROR	RIDGES	SUNDAY
GRISTLE	MISS	RINGS	SUNK
GROVE	MISTRESS	RIPE	SUPPOSE
GROWTH	MONOTONY	RIVERS	SURPRISE
GUNS	MORNING-GLORY	ROAR	SWALLOWS
HAG	MOTTLED	RODE	SWING
HALF-WAY	MOURN	ROLL	TALL
HATES	MUDDY	ROOF	TAMPING
HEART'S	NAILS	ROTTEN	TANGLED
HEAVEN'S	NARROWING	ROUT	TEACH
HEDGEROWS	NECKS	ROWS	TEARING
HEIGHO	NEIGHBORS	RUBBER	TEMPORAL
HERE'S	NEXT	SAIL	TENDERNESS
HIDDEN	NIBBLED	SAYING	THEREFORE
HIDE	NOTHINGNESS	SCRAPING	THINNED
HIT	NUDGE	SCRATCH	THORN
HOT	NUDGED	SCRATCHING	THOU
HOUSES	OBSCURES	SCUTTLING	THREW
HOWLS	ODIOUS	SEA'S	THROW
HUG	ONES	SEA-WIND	THRUSH
HUM	OOOMPH	SEEKING	THUS
HUMP	OPENING	SENT	TICKING
INANE	OPPOSITES	SERPENT'S	TIGHT
INNOCENCE	OTHERS	SHED	TIN
INSECTS	OTTER	SHEEP	TOADS
INSIDE	OYSTER	SHELLS	TOLD
INTERVALS	PALE	SHIMMERING	TONGUES
JAY	PARTAKE	SHIP	TOUCHED
JERK	PARTICULAR	SHIVER	TOWHEE
JIG	PASSED	SHORT	TREMBLED
JOURNEYS	PEBBLE	SHOW	TREMBLES
JUMP	PENSIVE	SHRIEK	TRIES
KIN	PHOEBE	SIGHING	TURTLES
KING	PICK	SILENT-	TWIST
KINGDOM	PICKED	SIN	UNAFRAID
KNOWLEDGE	PIECES	SINGULAR	UNDO
LA	PIERCE	SINUOUS	UPROSE
LACK	PIGEON	SLACK	VIOLENCE
LACKING	PILED	SLEEK	VIOLENT
LADIES	PIN	SLIGHT	VIREO'S
LAKES	PINNED	SLIPPING	VIRTUE
LAMB	PINS	SLOP-PAIL	VISIT
LAW	PIT	SLOWER	VULNERABLE
LEANED	POISE	SLUG	WAKENING
LEANS	POLE	SMILAX	WANDERS
LEAPING	POLISHED	SNOW'S	WANT
LEGS	PRAIRIE	SOLITUDE	WANTON
LIGHTED	PREFER	SOOT	WANTS
LIGHTER	PRESENT	SOULS	WASP

WASTED	BEACH	CARDS	CREVICE
WATER'S	BEACON	CARESS	CROSS
WESTERN	BEATRICE	CARESSES	CROSS-WINDS
WHALE	BEDROOM	CARNAL	CROWS
WHEELING	BEER	CARPET	CULVERT
WHENCE	BEETLES	CATBIRD	CUNNING
WHINE	BEGINNER	CATCH	CUP
WHISPERS	BELIEVED	CATERPILLAR	CURTAIN
WHITER	BELL	CAT'S	CUTTINGS
WING	BELOVED	CAUSE	DAILY
WISHES	BEND	CEMENT	DAKOTAS
WITCH	BENDS	CEMETERY	DANDY
WIZENED	BEWARE	CERTAIN	DAPPLED
WOE	BILLOWS	CHAOS	DARKER
WON	BITING	CHEEPING	DAUGHTER
WON'T	BLANKETS	CHERISHED	DAZZLED
WORE	BLAST	CHICKADEES	DEATH'S
WOULDN'T	BLAZING	CHILLY	DECAY
WRINKLED	BLEACHED	CHIMNEY	DECLARES
WRIST	BLESSEDNESS	CHING	DEEPENED
WRISTS	BLESSING	CHIP	DEEPENS
WRITHING	BLIND	CHORUS	DEER
YOU'LL	BLOWS	CHRIST	DELIGHTED
	BLUBBER	CIRCLED	DELIGHTS
(2)	BLURRED	CIRCUMSTANCE	DENIES
ABIDES	BOARD	CITIES	DENSE
ABSOLUTE	BOARDS	CITY	DENY
ACTING	BODIES	CLAIM	DEPTH
ACTIVE	BOFIN	CLAIRVOYANT	DESPAIR
ADD	BOOKS	CLAM	DEVOURING
ADVANCE	BOOR	CLEARLY	DIMENSIONS
ADVICE	BOTTOM-STONES	CLIMBS	DIM-WIT
AFTER-LIGHT	BOUND	CLINGING	DIRE
AH	BOWER	COAL	DISASTER
AIMLESS	BOWL	COAT	DISORDER
AIRY	BOX	COLDER	DITCH
ALACK	BOXES	COLLAPSES	DITCHES
ALDER	BREAKWATER	COMELY	DIVINITY
ALERT	BREATHER	COMFORT	DIZZY
ALREADY	BREEZE	CONCLUDE	DOCK
ALTER	BRIDE	CONCRETE	DOING
AMOROUS	BRIDGES	CONFINE	DOLOR
ANGUISH	BRITCHES	CONFUSION'S	DOLPHIN
ANTIC	BROODS	CONGRESS	DOORMAT
ANYTHING	BROTHER	CONTAIN	DOUBT
APPEAR	BROW	CONTINUE	DOVES
ARBOR	BRUISE	COO	DOVE'S
ARM	BRUSHING	COOKIES	DRAG
ARRANGED	BUCKLED	CORN	DRAIN
ARRIVE	BUD	CORNERS	DRANK
ART	BULB	COUNSEL	DREAM'S
ASSUME	BULK	COUNT	DREAMT
AUGUST	BULL	COURTING	DREARY
AUTUMN	BUMPS	COVE	DRESS
AWARE	BURDEN	COVER	DRIVERS
AWKWARD	BURN	COW	DROPPING
BABBLING	BURNT	COWS	DRUM
BABY	BURST	CRACK	DRUMMED
BACKS	BUSINESS	CRACKED	DRUNK
BAGS	BUTCHER	CRACKLES	DRUNKEN
BALANCED	BUTTERFLIES	CRAWL	DRYING
BALANCES	BUTTES	CRAWLING	DUBIOUS
BANG	BUZZ	CREAKED	DUCKS
BANK	BUZZING	CREAKS	DUSK
BARKED	CABBAGE	CREATION	EAGLE
BARREN	CAGED	CREEP	EAGLES
BASE	CANNAS	CREEPERS	EARTHLY
BASK	CANS	CREPT	EAVES

ECHOING	FOREST	HEMLOCK	LAPPING
ELEMENTS	FORGET	HEMLOCKS	LAPS
ELMS	FORGIVE	HIDING	LARK'S
ELSEWHERE	FORMAL	HIERATIC	LASHING
'EM	FREIGHT	HILLS	LATER
EMPTINESS	FRIGHTENED	HIND	LAUGHING
ENDING	FRISK	HISS	LAUGHS
ENDLESS	FUNNY	HO	LAUGHTER
ENDS	FUR	HOLDING	LAWYERS
ENDURED	FURIOUS	HOLDS	LAZILY
ENTRAILS	FURRED	HOLLOWS	LAZY
EPIDERMAL	GAIN	HONOR	LEADING
EQUAL	GANDER	HOOD	LEECH
ER	GARBAGE	HOOVES	LEEKS
ERRATIC	GASPING	HOPING	LEG
ESSENTIAL	GATES	HORROR	LICHEN
ETERNITY'S	GATHER	HOVER	LID
EVERYTHING'S	GATHERS	HOVERING	LIFT
EXCEEDS	GAY	HOWEVER	LIFTED
EXCESSIVE	GAZED	HUGS	LIFTS
EXISTENCE	GETTING	HUMMING	LIKELY
EXTENDED	GIFT	HUMMINGBIRD	LILY
EXTENT	GILLIFLOWER	HUMPED	LIMBS
EXULTATION	GIVES	HUNGER	LIME
EYELESS	GLASSY	HURRY	LIMPER
EYELIDS	GLEAMING	HUSH	LITTER
FAIL	GLIDES	HUTCH	LITTLEST
FAILED	GLINT	ILL	LOCKED
FAILS	GOLDEN	IMAGINED	LOLLING
FAILURE	GOO	IMMEDIATE	LONGEST
FAINT	GOODBYE	IMMENSE	LOO
FAITH	GRACEFUL	IMPULSE	LOOPS
FALSE	GRADUAL	INDIGNITY	LOOSEN
FAN	GRAPE	INFECTED	LOOSENING
FANG	GRASSY	INFIRMITY	LOOSENS
FANGS	GREASE	INNOCENT	LOUT
FANNING	GREENHOUSES	INSECT	LOVELESS
FARE	GREET	INSISTENT	LOVING
FAST	GRIEVE	INSTEAD	LULLED
FEARLESS	GRITTY	INTENSER	LUMINOUS
FEARS	GROUPS	INTERMITTENTLY	LUNCHES
FELICITY	GRUBS	INTIMATE	LUNGING
FETOR	GULPED	INTREPID	LURCH
FILLED	HA	INTRICATE	LUSH
FINALLY	HALF-DEAD	INVADES	MACHINES
FINDS	HALF-GROWN	INVENTION	MAID
FINER	HALF-UNDRESSED	IRE	MANNER
FIRES	HAMMER	ISLAND	MAPLE
FISHED	HANG	IST	MARE'S
FLAKE	HAPPENED	JERKS	MARIANNE
FLAP	HAPPINESS	JESUS	MARRIED
FLAPPING	HARDER	JOINTED	MATTERS
FLASHES	HARDLY	JUG	MAZE
FLASHING	HATRED	JUMPED	MEAL
FLATTENING	HAUNTING	KEEPER	MEANS
FLEE	HAVEN'T	KEEPING	MEASURE
FLOODS	HAVING	KELP	MEAT
FLORIST	HAWKS	KICK	MEEK
FLOWER-CROWNS	HEADLANDS	KIDS	MEEKNESS
FLOWERHEADS	HEADS	KILLDEER	MELT
FLUID	HEAVED	KILLED	MELTED
FLUSHED	HEAVILY	KINDS	MEMORY
FLUTTERS	HEAVING	KNIFE	MENTION
FOAM	HE'D	KNOCKED	MENTIONS
FOLLOWS	HEDGE	LAKE'S	MERRY
FONDLING	HEELS	LANDSCAPE	MIGHT
FOOD	HELL	LANE	MILE
FOOLS	HELP	LAP	MILLION

MIND'S	PILLOW	RAVAGES	SHIFTED
MINNOW	PINCH	REACHES	SHIMMERS
MINOR	PITCHED	REAL	SHOREBIRDS
MINUTE	PLAINT	REBORN	SHORELINE
MIRE	PLANK	REDUCED	SHOREWARD
MISCELLANEOUS	PLANKS	REEDS	SHOT
MISSED	PLANT	REFLECTED	SHOULDER
MISSION	PLATE	REFUSE	SHRINK
MOCK	PLATITUDES	REJECT	SHRINKING
MOCKED	PLAYING	RELEASE	SHUDDER
MOIST	PLUNGING	RELEASED	SHUT
MOOLY	POETS	RELIEF	SIFTED
MOORE	POINTING	REMEMBERED	SIFTING
MOPED	POINTS	REMIND	SILVERY
MOSS-GATHERING	POISED	REMINDER	SINK
MOTHER'S	POISONED	REMINDS	SIR
MOTIONS	POKES	RENEWAL	SISKINS
MOVEMENT	POKING	RENEWED	SKIES
MOWER	PONDS	REPTILIAN	SKINS
MUSCLES	POODLE	RHYTHM	SKIRTS
MUSTY	PORCH	RIDES	SKULL
MYRTLE'S	POSSESS	RIFLE	SKYWARD
NATURE'S	POSSESSIONS	RIND	SLAG
NEARLY	POTS	RING	SLAMMING
NEAT	PRATTLE	RIPENESS	SLAPPED
NEEDLE	PRAY	RIPPED	SLEEPY
NEEDLES	PRAYER	RIPPLED	SLIP
NEIGHBOR'S	PRESENCE	RITUAL	SLIPS
NESTLING'S	PRESERVE	RIVEN	SLOPED
NOTICE	PRESSURE	ROBES	SLOWING
NUDGES	PRETTY	ROCKY	SLOWS
NUMB	PRICKLING	ROMPING	SMALLEST
O'CONNELL'S	PRISONERS	ROOTED	SMELLED
ODD	PROGRESS	ROSE-HOUSE	SMOKY
OIL	PROMISE	RUBBISH	SMOTHER
OLD-FASHIONED	PROPER	RUSHING	SMOTHERED
ONE'S	PROVIDES	S	SNAILS
OOH	PRUSSIAN	SAKE	SNEEZE
ORDNUNG	PULL	SANDS	SOCRATES
ORIGINAL	PULLING	SANDY	SOFTER
OUTLEAPS	PULSED	SAPLING	SOLID
OVERWHELM	PURELY	SCALES	SOMEBODY
OWLS	PUREST	SCAMPERED	SOUNDS
PACE	PURGATORIAL	SCARCELY	SOVEREIGN
PAD	PURPOSE	SCHEME	SPARROW
PAILS	PURSUE	SCRAPE	SPILES
PANTS	PURSUED	SCREEN	SPILLED
PARTNER	QUAIL	SCUM	SPINE
PASSING	QUAKING	SCURRY	SPIRAL
PASTURE	QUEEN	SEALED	SPIRIT'S
PATCH	QUESTION	SEASON	SPITTING
PEACH	QUICKER	SEAT	SPLIT
PEAR	QUIESCENT	SECURE	SPONGY
PEBBLY	QUIVER	SEEDS	SPOON
PECULIAR	QUIVERED	SEEMS	SPRINGING
PEN	RABBITS	SEES	SQUEAKS
PENINSULA	RACE	SELVES	STABLE
PERCHED	RACKET	SERENE	STARES
PERFUME	RAGED	SERIOUS	STARVES
PERILS	RAGING	SEVEN	STEEP
PERPLEX	RAISED	SHAGINAW	STENCH
PERPLEXED	RANG	SHARPENED	STICKING
PETAL	RAPT	SHARPER	STINGY
PHILANDER	RARELY	SHEAVES	STINK
PICKLE	RASP	SHEDDING	STIRRING
PIERCING	RATTLING	SHEEN	STONE'S
PIGEONS	RAUCOUS	SHELF	STONY
PIKE	RAVAGED	SHELVES	STORM'S

STREAM'S
STRIKES
STRINGS
STRUCK
STRUGGLED
STRUGGLING
SUBSIDES
SUFFERING
SUGAR
SUNLESS
SUNLIT
SUNNY
SURF
SURLY
SURVIVED
SURVIVING
SWAMP
SWEATING
SWEETENED
SWEETLY
SWEETNESS
SWIMMING
SWINGS
SWIRL
SWOLLEN
SYLLABLES
TABLE
TASTE
TEACHES
TELEPHONE
TERRACE
TETHERED
THEE
THEME
THEREBY
THEY'LL
THICKET
THICKETS
THIGH
THINNING
THIRST
THOUSAND
THUMBS
THUNDER
TILT
TILTED
TILTS
TIPS
TIRES
TOM
TOM-CAT
TOMORROW
TOPPLING
TOWARDS
TRAILING
TRAIN
TRANSCEND
TRANSPLANTING
TRAPPED
TREMBLE
TRICK
TRICKSY
TROUBLE
TUB
TUCKED
TULIP
TUMBLING
TUNES

TURTLE
TWIG
TWIGS
TWILIGHT
TWINKLING
TWO-LEGGED
ULTIMATE
UMBRELLA
UNBORN
UNDEFILED
UNDERGROUND
UNDERSTAND
UNDULANT
UNFOLD
UNFOLDING
UNIVERSE
UNNATURAL
UNSEEN
UPLAND
USED
USUAL
USUALLY
VALE
VARIOUS
VAST
VEIN
VEINED
VERNAL
VERSE
VIEW
VIGIL
VINES
VOICES
WADDLE
WAITS
WAKING'S
WALKER
WANING
WARD
WARY
WAVER
WEASELS
WEBBY
WEEDY
WEEP
WELTER
WENCH
WEPT
WEST
WE'VE
WHEAT
WHEREFORE
WHETHER
WHINED
WHIPPING
WHIRLING
WHIRRING
WHISKERS
WHISKEY
WHITECAPS
WHITELY
WHO'D
WIDENS
WILLS
WINDBREAK
WINDERS
WINGBEAT
WINK

WINKING
WIRES
WITS
WOMAN'S
WONDER
WOODLAWN
WORMS
WRECKAGE
WRETCH
WRETCHEDNESS
WRIGGLING
WRINKLING
WRITE
YAK
YARD
YE
YEA
YEATS
YELLOWISH
YELLOWY
YESTERDAY
YORK
YOU'VE

(1)
AARDVARK
ABETTOR
ABIDING
ABJURE
ABLE
ABOMINABLE
ABSENT
ABSOLUTES
ABSORBED
ABSTRACT
ACADEMIC
ACCELERATION
ACCENTS
ACCEPT
ACCORDING
ACCOUNTING
ACCOUTERMENTS
ACCUSERS
ACHE
ACHIN'
ACKNOWLEDGE
ACQUIRES
ACRES
ACRID
ACTIVITY
ACTUAL
ADAM
ADAMANT
ADDER-MOUTHED
ADDLED
ADDS
ADIEU
ADMIRE
ADOLESCENCE
ADOLESCENT
ADORES
ADVANCING
ADVANTAGE
ADVERB
AFFIRMATIONS
AFFRIGHTED
AFLAME
AFRESH

AFTERLIGHT
AFTERNOONS
AFTERWARDS
AGED
AGENCY
AGITATION
AGONIES
AIMING
AIMLESSLY
AIMLESSNESS
AIR'S
AISLE
ALARM
ALBINO
ALDERMAN
ALGAE
ALGY'S
ALICE
ALIEN
ALKALINE
ALLEYS
ALL-OF-A-SUDDEN
ALLOW
ALLUSIONS
ALLUVIAL
ALMOST-INVISIBLE
ALOFT
ALOUD
ALSO
ALTERNATE
ALTES
AMBUSH
AMERICAN
AMISS
AMORPHOUS
ANALOGIES
ANATOMY
ANCESTORS
ANCESTRAL
ANGER
ANGORA
ANIMAL'S
ANISETTE
ANKLE-DEEP
ANKLES
ANN
ANNOUNCE
ANNOUNCED
ANONYMOUS
ANTIMACASSAR
ANTS
ANXIETY
ANXIOUS
ANYBODY
ANYTIME
ANYWHERE
APHORIST
APPALL
APPARENT
APPARITION
APPEARANCES
APPEARED
APPENDAGE
APPETITE
APPLAUSE
APPLEWORMS
APPREHENDED
APPROACHING

APPROVE
ARBITRATORS
ARBORS
ARBUTUS
ARBUTUS-CALM
ARCHAIC
ARCHED
ARCHNESS
ARDENT
ARDOR
ARDORS
ARID
ARISES
ARISTOCRACY
AROUSE
ARRANGERS
ARRIVALS
ARROYO
ARSENICAL
ARTS
ASKER
ASKEW
ASKS
A-SLEEPING
ASPECT
ASSEMBLE
ASSISTANT
ASSYRIAN
ASTER
ASTERS
ASTIR
ASTONISHED
ASTONISHMENT
ASTOUNDED
ASTOUNDS
ATTACKS
ATTAINED
ATTEND
ATTENDANT
ATTENDED
ATTENTION
AUCTION
AUCTIONEER
AUDACIOUSLY
AUK
AUNT
AUNTIES
AUSGEPOOPEN
AUTHENTIC
AWAKENS
AWFUL
AWL
AXLE
AZALEAS
AZURE
BABBLE
BABIES
BACKED
BACK-EDDY
BACKING
BACKLOTS
BACK-STREAM'S
BACTERIAL
BAD
BAG-FOOT
BAIT
BALEFUL
BALL

BALLAD
BALM
BALTIMORE
BAMBOO
BANANAS
BAND
BANDANNAS
BANKED-UP
BANKER'S
BANTER
BARED
BAREFOOT
BAREST
BARGAINS
BARLEY
BARLEY-BREAK
BARNACLED
BAROQUE
BARRIER
BARRIERS
BARSTOOLS
BASSWOOD
BARTENDERS
BARTER
BASALT
BASIN
BASKETS
BASSWOOD
BATHTUB
BAT-LIKE
BAUMAN
BAYS
BEACHES
BEACH-GRASS
BEACHY
BEADS
BEANS
BEARDED
BEAST'S
BEATEN
BECHSTEIN
BECKON
BECKONED
BECKONING
BEDRAGGLED
BED-SITTING
BEDSTEAD
BEEF
BEFALL
BEG
BEGETS
BEGONIA
BEGUILE
BEHAVED
BEING'S
BELCHES
BELIEVING
BELLIES
BELLS
BELONG
BELT
BEMUSED
BEMUSEDLY
BENCH
BENIGN
BENZEDRINE
BERRIES
BERTH
BESET

BESIDES
BESTOW
BET
BETOOK
BETRAY
BETRAYED
BETRAYERS
BETRAYING
BEVY
BEWILDERS
BEWITCHED
BIBBLE
BICKER
BICKERED
BID
BIDDERS
BIDDLY
BIDDLY'S
BIDS
BIGGEST
BIKE
BILLBOARDS
BILLS
BIN
BINDINGS
BIRCHTREES
BIRD-BLOOD
BIRD-FURTIVE
BIRDLESS
BIRD'S
BIRTH
BISCUIT
BISHOP
BITTEN
BLAB
BLACKBERRY
BLACKBURNIAN
BLACKENING
BLACKNESS
BLAND
BLASTED
BLASTING
BLASTS
BLAZES
BLEEDS
BLENCH
BLESSINGS
BLINDING
BLISTERED
BLIZZARD
BLOCKED
BLOND
BLOOD'S
BLOODSUCKER
BLOODSUCKERS
BLOODY
BLOOMING
BLOSSOMED
BLOUSE
BLOWN-UP
BLUEBIRD
BLUE-BLACK
BLUE-TAILED
BLUNDERING
BLURS
BOAST
BOBBIE
BOBOLINK

BOBOLINKS
BOEHME
BOG
BOGEY-HAUNTED
BOG-HOLES
BOGS
BOILED
BOILER
BOILERS
BOLDLY
BOLSTER
BOLT
BONE-ACHE
BONNY
BONY
BOOGER
BOOM
BOOMS
BOOPS
BOOT
BOOTS
BOOZE
BORDER
BORDERS
BORE
BORED
BOSOM
BOTHERED
BO-TREE
BOTTLE-CAP
BOTTOMS
BOUGHT
BOUNCE
BRACING
BRACKISH
BRAMBLE
BRASS
BRAVE
BRAW
BRAYED
BREAST-BONE
BREASTS
BREATHED
BREATHERS
BREED
BREEDS
BRIAR
BRIARS
BRIARY
BRICK
BRICKS
BRIDEGROOM
BRIDGEHEADS
BRIEF
BRIGHTLY
BRIM
BRIMMING
BRINGING
BRISK
BRISKED
BRISTLED
BROW-BEATEN
BROWNISH
BROWNISH-WHITE
BRUISED
BRUSHES
BUBBLES
BUCK

BUCKING	CARGO	CHIMNEYS	COILS
BUCKLE	CARIBBEAN	CHINK	COLLAPSE
BUCKSHOT	CAROLINA	CHINKS	COLLECTIVE
BUD-SHEATH	CARP	CHINS	COLLECTOR
BUG	CARPETS	CHIPPENDALE	COLLECTORS
BUG-EYED	CARRIAGES	CHIPPEWA	COLLEGE
BUG-RIDDLED	CARRIED	CHIPS	COLLOPED
BUGS	CARRION	CHIRPING	COLONY
BUILD	CARROTS	CHIRR	COLUMN
BUILT	CARRYING	CHOICES	COMBINE
BULBS	CARS	CHOKED	COMETH
BULGE	CARTOON-MOUSE	CHORTLING	COMING-OUT
BULKS	CARVED	CHRISTIAN	COMMA
BULLDOZER	CASCADE	CHRISTOPHER	COMMAND
BULLHEAD	CASE	CHRYSANTHEMUM	COMMINGLED
BULLHEADS	CASEMENT	CHUMS	COMMITTED
BUM	CASTOREUM	CHUNK	COMMODIOUS
BUMBLING	CASTRATI	CHURN	COMMODITIES
BUMPING	CATALOGUES	CHURNING	COMMOTION
BUMPKIN	CAT-BIRD	CICADAS	COMPANY
BUMS	CATCHER	CICERO	COMPLEMENT
BUNCHES	CATCHING	CIGARETTE	COMPREHENSIVE
BUNCHING	CAT-LIKE	CIGARETTES	COMPRESSION
BUNION	CAT-MEWING	CIGARS	CONCRETENESS
BUNYAN	CAT-TAILS	CINDERY	CONDEMN
BURDOCK	CATTLE	CIRCUIT	CONDONES
BURLAP	CAUSED	CIRCULAR	CONDONING
BURNISHED	CAVE'S	CIRCULARITY	CONDOR
BURNS	CAVING-IN	CIRCUMFERENCE	CONDUCTING
BURR	CAW	CIRCUMVENT	CONFLAGRATION
BURROWS	CEDAR	CISTERN	CONFLICTING
BURY	CEDARS	CLAMS	CONFORM
BUS	CEILING'S	CLAP	CONFUSING
BUSKS	CELESTIAL	CLAPS	CONGEALED
BUST	CELL	CLARE	CONNOISSEUR
BUTCHER'S	CELLS	CLAWS	CONSIDERED
BUTTER	CENSURE	CLEAN	CONSOLE
BUTTERFLY	CENTERED	CLEANING	CONSTANCY
BUTTERFLY'S	CENTRIPETAL	CLEARED	CONSTRICTED
BUTTERNUTS	CERTAINTY	CLEARER	CONSTRICTION
C	CERTITUDE	CLEFT	CONSUME
CABBAGE-BUTTERFLY	CESSATION	CLIFF	CONSUMED
CABBAGES	CHAINS	CLIFF-SIDE	CONTAINER
CADENCE	CHAIR-RUNGS	CLIMBED	CONTEMPLATION
CADGED	CHAIRS	CLINGS	CONTENDING
CAKE	CHALK	CLINKERS	CONTINUES
CAKED	CHANGELESS	CLOAK	CONTRARIES
CALIFORNIA	CHANGELING	CLOCK	CONTRIBUTIONS
CALLERS	CHANNEL	CLOSE-AT-HAND	CONVERGE
CANCEL	CHANTICLEER	CLOSED	CONVERSE
CANDID	CHAPTER	CLOSELY	CONVINCED
CANDOR	CHAR	CLOSET	COOING
CANKER	CHARGE	CLOSING	COOLER
CANNON	CHARITY	CLOUD'S	COOLNESS
CANT	CHARRED	CLOUD-SHAPE	COPLEY
CANYONS	CHASING	CLUB	CORAL
CAP	CHASTENED	CLUE	CORINTHIAN
CAPE	CHEAP	CLUMP	CORMORANT
CAPER	CHECK	CLUTCHING	CORNBREAD
CAPTAINS	CHEEKBONES	COALS	CORRECT
CARD	CHEESE	COAXING	CORRESPONDENCES
CARDPLAYERS	CHERRIES	COCKALORUM	CORRIDOR
CARED	CHEWS	COCKROACH	CORRIDORS
CAREENING	CHICKEN-YARD	COCKROACHES	CORRUPTION
CAREER	CHILDHOOD	COFFEE	CORTISONE
CAREFULLY	CHILD-WHIMPERING	COGS	COSMOS
CARELESSNESS	CHILLS	COHERE	COST
CARESSING	CHILL'S	COILING	COTTONWOODS

COUGH
COULDLY
COUNTED
COUNTENANCE
COUNTER-TURN
COURSING
COURTESY
COURTHOUSES
COVERLET
COWARD
COW'S
COZ
CRACKLING
CRADLE
CRADLED
CRADLES
CRAGS
CRANE
CRANED
CRASH
CRASS
CRATER
CRATES
CRAVENS
CRAWLED
CRAWLS
CRAZED
CRAZILY
CREAK
CREATE
CREATED
CREATURELY
CREEKS
CREEPS
CRETIN
CRICKET-VOICE
CRIME
CRISP
CRITIC
CROCUSES
CRONES
CRONE'S
CROOKS
CROONS
CROSS-BAR
CROSSING-TENDER'S
CROUCHED
CRUCIFIXION
CRUMBLES
CRUSH
CRUST
CRUSTS
CRYPTIC
CRYSTAL
CUBA
CUD
CUE
CULTURAL
CUPID
CUR
CURIOUS
CURLEW'S
CURLING
CURRENTS
CURSED
CURVE
CURVED
CURVES

CURVING
CUSHION
CUSHIONY
CUTS
CYCLE
CYPRESS
DABBLE
DAEMON
DAFT
DAISIES
DALLIANCE
DALLY
DAME
DAMES
DAN
DANCING-MAD
DANCING-ROOM
DANDELION
DANGER
DANGEROUSLY
DANGLED
DARKEN
DARKENED
DARKEST
DARK-GREEN
DART
DAVIES
DAWDLE
DAWDLES
DAWN'S
DAY'S
DAYTIME
DAZEDLY
DAZZLES
DAZZLING
DEAD-WHITE
DEAL
DEALT
DEARIE
DEARLY
DEARS
DEATH-BED
DEATHLY
DEBRIS
DECEIVES
DECEMBER
DECENTLY
DECEPTIVE
DECIDED
DECISION
DECISION'S
DECLARE
DECLARED
DECREASED
DEED
DEE-DEEING
DEEP-HIDDEN
DEEP-THROATED
DEFAMERS
DEFEAT
DEFEND
DEFER
DEFILES
DEFINED
DEIGN
DELAYED
DELIBERATELY
DELIRIUM

DELIVER
DELIVERED
DELVE
DEMANDS
DEN
DENSER
DENTED
DEPARTING
DESCENDANTS
DESCENDING
DESECRATION
DESERT
DESERTS
DESIRES
DESIRE'S
DESOLATE
DESPISE
DESSERT
DESTROY
DESTRUCTION
DETACH
DETERIORATION'S
DETOUR
DETOURS
DEVIL'S
DEVOURED
DICTATES
DIDDLE
DIET
DIFFICULT
DIFFUSE
DIGGING
DIGITS
DIGNITY
DILL
DIM
DIMENSION
DIMINISHING
DIMINUTIVES
DIN
DINING
DIOCESE
DIP
DIPPERS
DIPS
DIRECTION
DIRECTIONS
DIRT'S
DISCIPLINE
DISCOVER
DISEMBODIED
DISENGAGE
DISGUISE
DISK
DISMAL
DISMAY
DISMAYED
DISORDERED
DISPENSE
DISPERSED
DISPOSITION
DISREPAIR
DISSECTION
DISSEMBLING
DISTANCE
DISTANT
DISTENDED
DISTILLS

DISTORTIONS
DISTRACT
DISTRICT
DISTURB
DISTURBED
DIVE
DIVERGENT
DIVIDE
DIVINE
DOCTORS
DOLPHIN'S
DONKEY'S
DONNE
DOOM
DOORSTEPS
DOTING
DOUGH
DOUGHNUTS
DOWNDRAFT
DOWN-HILL
DOWNWARD
DOWNY
DOXIE
DOZEN
DRAFT
DRAGGING
DRAINHOLES
DRAINPIPES
DRAWING
DRAWN
DREAMILY
DREAMING
DREAMS
DREARILY
DREW
DRIED-OUT
DRINKERS
DRIPPY
DRIVE
DRIVER.
DRIVES
DROOP
DROOPED
DROOPS
DROSS
DROUGHT
DROVE
DROWSING
DRUMS
DRUNKARD
DRUNKARDS
DUET
DUG
DUKE
DULL
DUMB
DUMP
DUNES
DUNG
DUNK
DUPLICATE
DUPLICATION
DURING
DUTCHMAN
DUTIES
DUTY
DYED
DYNAMITE

EARN	EXALTED	FIDDLED	FOLD
EAR'S	EXAMPLES	FIELD-MOUSE	FOLDERS
EASES	EX-AS-PER-AT-ING	FIEND'S	FOLIAGE
EASTWARD	EXASPERATION	FIFTY	FOLLIES
EATING	EXCEED	FIGURED	FOLLOWING
EBBED	EXCEPT	FILM	FOLLY
ECORSE	EXCESSES	FILMY	FONDLING'S
ECSTASY	EXCHANGING	FILTH	FOOLISHNESS
EDDYING	EX-EXISTENTIALIST	FILTHY	FOOL'S
EDIBLE	EXHAUSTED	FINE-HONED	FOOTMAN
EDICT	EXHAUSTION	FINELY	FOOTSTEP
EDITOR	EXIT	FINES	FORCING
EERIE	EXORCISM	FINGERING	FOREBODING
EFFLORESCENCE	EXPENSIVE	FINGER-TIPS	FOREHEAD'S
EGG	EXPLODES	FINITE	FOREKNOWN
EGGS	EXPLORERS	FINN	FOREPAWS
EIGHT-LEGGED	EXQUISITE	FIREMAN	FOREVER'S
EIGHTY	EXTEND	FIRE-PIT	FORK
ELBOWS	EXTERNALS	FIRMNESS	FORNICATES
ELEMENTAL	EXTREMEST	FIR-TREE	FORSAKEN
ELEPHANT-COLORED	EXTREMITY	FIR-TREES	FORTITUDE
ELEPHANTS	EXULTING	FISHERMAN	FORTUNATE
ELF	EXULTS	FISHERMEN	FORTUNE'S
ELM-TREE	EYEBROWS	FISH-WAYS	FORTY
ELMTREES	FABRIC	FISSURE	FORWARD'S
ELUSIVE	FADE	FIT	FOUNTAIN
ELVERS	FADED	FITFULLY	FOUR-FOOT
EMBANKMENTS	FADES	FITLY	FOUR-POSTER
EMBER	FAINTLY	FIVE-FOOT	FOUR-PRONGED
EMBERS	FAIREST	FIVE-INCH	FOURS
EMBRACED	FAKE	FIX	FOURTH
EMBRACES	FALLING'S	FLAILING	FOWL
EMBRACING	FALTERED	FLAKES	FOX
EMINENCE	FANCIES	FLAMES	FOX-HUNTING
ENCIRCLED	FANCY'S	FLARE	FRAGRANCE
ENCOMPASSING	FARING-FORTH	FLARES	FRAUD
ENCRUSTED	FAR-OFF	FLASHED	FRAUDS
ENDURING	FART	FLASH-FLOOD	FRAYED
ENGLISH	FARTHEST	FLAT-BOX	FREEDOM
ENORMOUS	FASTIDIOUS	FLAT-HEADED	FREEZE
ENSHROUD	FATAL	FLAT-ROOFED	FREEZES
ENTER	FATES	FLAVOR	FREEZING
ENTERED	FATIGUES	FLEAS	FRENCH
ENTERTAINED	FATTENS	FLEDGLING	FRENCHMEN
ENTIRE	FATUOUS	FLESH-AWKWARD	FREQUENTLY
ENTITIES	FAUCET	FLESH-BOUND	FRESH-CUT
ENTRANCES	FAUCETS	FLESHLESS	FRESHENED
ENVY	FAVOR	FLESHY	FRESHLY
ENVY'S	FAWN	FLICKERS	FRESH-SALTED
EPIC	FAWTHER'S	FLICKER'S	FRIDAY
EPIGRAMS	FEATHERINESS	FLICKING	FRIGHTFUL
EPILEPTIC	FEATHERY	FLIGHT	FRIGIDAIRES
EQUALLY	FEATS	FLINGING	FRINGE
EQUIPPED	FEATURE	FLIP-FLAP	FRINGES
ERNEST	FEBRILE	FLIT	FRISKS
ERRAND	FED	FLITTER-FLAD	FRO
ERRANT	FEEDING	FLITTERMICE	FROGBIT
ERROR	FEELS	FLOODED	FROGS
ERRORS	FELLOWS	FLORAL	FROG'S
ESCAPE	FELLOWSHIP	FLORIST'S	FROLIC
ESCAPED	FEMALE	FLOUR	FROLICKS
ESTUARY	FENCE	FLOURISHING	FRONT
EURIPIDES	FENCEPOST	FLOWER-DUMP	FROSTED
EVER-CHANGING	FERN-SHAPES	FLOWERING	FROSTY
EVERYWHERE	FERNY	FLUTE	FROTH
EVILS	FERVENT	FLUTTER	FROWN
EXACT	FEVER	FLUTTERY	FROWNED
EXACTIOUS	FIDDLE	FOAMED	FUMING

FUN	GOAT	GUILD	HAWK'S
FUNERAL	GOATS	GUILT	HAWTHORN
FUNGUS	GOAT'S	GUINNESS	HEADED
FUNNIER	GOB	GULFS	HEADING
FURLED	GOD-FURIOUS	GULL	HEADLIGHTS
FURNISHED	GODHEAD	GULLIES	HEADLINES
FURNITURE	GOGGLES	GUMPTION	HEADY
FURROWS	GOLDY	GURGLE	HEALED
FURTIVE	GONG	GUST	HEALING
FUSE	GOOD-BYE	GUSTS	HEAP
FUTILE	GOODNESS	GUTTERS	HEAPED
FUZZY	GOO-GIRL	HACKING	HEAPS
GABBED	GORGE	HADN'T	HEARING
GAIETY	GOSSAMER	HAGS	HEARKENING
GAINSAYING	GRACELESS	HAIR'S	HEARS
GAIT	GRACIOUS	HAIRY	HEARSE
GAME	GRAINS	HALE	HEARSES
GAR-EAGLE	GRAMMAR	HALF-ALIVE	HEARTS
GARISH	GRAND	HALF-AND-HALF	HEATED
GARMENT	GRANDEUR	HALF-ANIMAL	HEAT-LIGHTNING
GARMENTS	GRANDFATHER'S	HALF-BIRD	HEAT-MADDENED
GARNISHED	GRANDMOTHER'S	HALF-DEATH	HEAT-WEARY
GARTER	GRANDPA	HALF-FLIGHT	HEAVEN-SENSE
GATHERING	GRANDPA'S	HALF-GREEN	HEAVINESS
GAUGE	GRANITE	HALF-LAND	HEDGEWREN'S
GAZER'S	GRANITIC	HALF-LIFE	HEIFER
GAZING	GRAPES	HALF-OPENED	HEIGHT
GEARS	GRASS-HIDDEN	HALF-REST	HEIGHTENED
GEESE	GRATE	HALF-SLEEP	HEIGHTS
GENERALS	GRATEFUL	HALF-SMOKED	HEIRS
GENERATIONS	GRAVES	HALF-STEPS	HELIOTROPE
GENESIS	GRAVY	HALF-SUNKEN	HE'LL
GENIUS	GRAY	HALF-TURNING	HELL'S
GENTLENESS	GRAYING	HALF-WATER	HELPED
GENTLES	GRAZED	HALL	HELPS
GENTLEST	GRAZING	HALLOO	HERO
GEORGE	GREATER	HALLS	HEROES
GESTURES	GREAT-WINGED	HALLWAYS	HERONS
GETS	GREEK	HAMMER'S	HERON'S
GHOSTS	GREENEST	HANDKERCHEE	HERRINGS
GHOULIE	GREENISH	HANDKERCHIEF	HERS
GIBBER	GREENS	HAND-PAINTED	HIDES
GILD	GREENY	HAPLESS	HIGHEST
GILDS	GREYING	HAR	HIGH-NOON
GILLS	GREYISH	HARBOR	HIGH-PILED
GIRLS	GRIEVING	HARBORS	HIKER
GIVING	GRILL	HARDENED	HILARIOUS
GIZZARD	GRIM	HARDENS	HINT
GLACIAL	GRIMACES	HARDEST	HIP
GLANCE	GRIND	HARDIHOOD	HIPPETY-HOP
GLAZED	GRINDING	HARDNESS	HIPPO
GLAZING	GROANING	HARE	HIPS
GLIB	GROANS	HARM	HISSED
GLIDDERED	GROIN	HARP	HITCHED
GLIDE	GROOVE	HARPY	HITTING
GLIDING	GROPE	HARRIED	HIVE
GLINTED	GROTESQUE	HARROW	HOAR
GLISTEN	GROUND-BEETLES	HARVEST	HOARD
GLISTENING	GROUND-CHILL	HARVESTING	HOARDED
GLISTENS	GROUND'S	HATED	HOE
GLISTER	GROWL	HATE-DRIVEN	HOG
GLITTERED	GROWN	HATH	HOLIEST
GLITTERS	GRRR	HATRED'S	HOLLOW
GLORIES	GRUBBY	HATS	HONEY
GLOVE	GUARD	HATTIE	HONEYMOON
GLOW	GUARDED	HAUNT	HONEYSUCKLE
GLUP	GUBBLE	HAUNTED	HONEY-TIGHT
GLUTTONY	GUIDES	HAVOC	HONORABLE

HONORED	IMAGINATION'S	INTOLERABLE	KINDLY
HONORS	IMAGINE	INTRANSIENT	KINGDOMS
HOO	IMAGINING	INTUITION	KINGFISHER
HOOK	IMMEASURABLE	INVADE	KINGFISHER'S
HOOKED	IMMEDIACY	INVENTED	KINSHIP
HOORAY	IMMENSITY	INVETERATE	KITCHEN
HOPED	IMMODERATELY	INVIOLATE	KITCHENS
HOPELESS	IMMODESTLY	INWARDNESS	KITE
HOPES	IMPACT	IRIDESCENCE	KITH
HOPE'S	IMPALED	IRIDESCENT	KITTEN
HOPPED	IMPERIOUS	IRISH	KITTEN-LIMP
HOPS	IMPERISHABLE	IRON-BOUND	KITTENS
HORACE	IMPLACABLE	IROQUOIS	KITTY
HORIZON	IMPORTANCE	IRRATIONAL	KNAVE
HORIZONS	IMPORTANT	IRREVOCABLE	KNEE
HORIZON'S	IMPOSSIBLE	ISLAMIC	KNEELED
HORRIBLE	IMPOTENT	ISLANDS	KNELT
HORRID	IMPURE	ITCH	KNITTED
HOR-RID	INACCESSIBILITY	ITCHES	KNIVES
HORRORS	INACCESSIBLE	ITEMS	KNOCKING
HORSE'S	IN-BETWEEN	IVY	KNOCKS
HOSTILE	INCARNADINE	IVY-BRANCH	KNOT
HOUND	INCH	JACKASS	KNOUT
HOUND'S	INCIDENT	JACK-DAW	KNUCKLE
HOURS	INCIPIENT	JACKPINE	LACE
HOUSEHOLD	INCLEMENT	JACKRABBITS	LACELIKE
HOVE	INCOMMENSURATE	JADED	LADDERS
HOWL	INCOMPREHENSIBLE	JANE	LADDIE-BUCK
HOWLED	INCREASING	JAUNTIER	LADEN
HOWLING	INCREDIBLE	JAYS	LADIES'
HUDDLE	INDEED	JERKED	LADLE
HUES	INDELICATE	JESUS-SHIMMER	LADY'S
HUMILITY	INDIAN	JIGGLE	LAG
HUMMED	INDIANS	JIGGLING	LAIR
HUMMING-BIRD	INDICATING	JOCKEY	LAMP
HUMMINGBIRD'S	INDICTMENTS	JOCK-WITH-THE-WIND	LANDLOCKED
HUMPBACKED	INDIFFERENT	JOD-JODDING	LANES
HUMPING	INDIGNANT	JOGGING	LANGUISHED
HUNCHES	INDIGNATION	JOGGLES	LANTERN
HUNDRED	INDIRECTION	JOGS	LAPFUL
HUNT	INDOORS	JOHN-OF-THE-	LAPSES
HUNTED	INDUCE	THUMB'S	LAPSING
HUNTER'S	INEXORABLE	JOIN	LARCHY
HUNTS	INFANTS	JOINED	LARGE
HURRICANE	INFINITUDE	JOINTS	LARGER
HURT	INFINITY	JOKES	LARGEST
HUSHED	INFIRM	JOLLY	LARK-SWEET
HUSK	INFLAME	JOLTS	LASH
HUZZA	INHERIT	JOTS	LASHED
HYACINTHINE	INLET	JOYLESS	LAST-ABANDONED
HYBRIDS	INLETS	JOYS	LATEST
HYDROTHERAPY	INSATIATE	JOY'S	LAUNDRY
HYSTERIA	INSENTIENT	JUDGE	LAURISCH
ICE-BURDENED	INSIST	JUGS	LAVATORY
IDENTITY	INSISTENCE	JUICE	LAVE
IDIOT	INSOLENCE	JUMP-IN-THE-HEDGE	LAWNMOWER
IDLING	INSOUCIANCE	JUNCOS	LAWS
IDYLL	INSTEP	JUNGLE	LAXLY
IGNORANCE	INSTINCT	JUTTING	LEADEN
ILL-DEFINED	INSTITUTIONALIZED	KATE	LEADS
ILL-MATCHED	INSTITUTIONS	KELLY'S	LEAF-LIGHT
ILLUMINATED	INSTRUMENT	KEROSENE	LEAF-LIKE
ILLUMINATION	INTENSE	KETTLES	LEAF-MOLD
ILLUSION	INTENT	KEY	LEAFY
ILLUSION'S	INTERIOR	KID	LEARNING
ILLUSTRIOUS	INTERLUDE	KIDNEYS	LEATHER
IMAGES	INTERRUPTED	KILL	LEATHERY
IMAGINATION	INTERVAL	KILLERS	LECHERS

LECHERY	LOOPING	MARROW-COLD	MINISCULE
LED	LOPING	MARROW-SOFT	MINK
LEE	LOPPED	MARRY	MINNOW'S
LEER	LOQUACIOUS	MARSALA	MINNOWY
LEFT-HAND	LORDLY	MARSH	MINSTREL
LEGACY	LORDS	MARSHES	MINUTES
LEISURELY	LOSING	MARSHLAND	MIPS
LEMMINGS	LOU	MARTYR	MIRACULOUS
LENGTHEN	LOUDER	MASCULINE	MIRRORS
LENGTHS	LOUDLY	MASKS	MIRY
LENT	LOUIS	MATCHING	MISFORTUNE
LESSENING	LOUT'S	MATCHLESS	MISLAID
LESSER	LOVE-BEAT	MATCH-MAKERS	MISSHAPEN
LETTER	LOVELIEST	MATCHSTICKS	MISSING
LEVELS	LOVE-LONGING	MATING	MISSTEP
LEVITY	LOVE-NEST	MATTED	MISTAKE
LIBERTIES	LOVER'S	MATTRESS	MISTS
LIBRARY	LOVINGLY	MATUNA	MIXES
LICE	LOWERED	MAX	MIXTURE
LICKING	LOW-FLYING	MEADOW-SHAPE	MNETHA
LIFE-FORCE	LOWLY	MEAGER	MOANS
LIGHT-BULB	LUBBER	MEANINGFUL	MOBILE
LIGHT-CORD	LUCIA	MEANINGLESS	MOCKER
LIGHTNING	LUG	MEANNESS	MOLD
LIKED	LUGGAGE	MEASURED	MOLDS
LIKELIEST	LUGUBRIOUSLY	MEASURES	MOLD'S
LILAC	LULLS	MEDIOCRE	MOLLUSKS
LILACS	LUMINESCENT	MEDITATE	MOMENTOUSLY
LILTING	LUMPS	MEDITERRANEAN	MOMENTS
LILTS	LUNGS	MEEKLY	MONKEY-TAILS
LIMESTONE	LURK	MELLOWED	MONONGAHELA
LINDSAY'S	LURKING-PLACE	MELTING	MONSTROUS
LINEAMENTS	LURKS	MELTS	MONUMENTAL
LINED	MA	MEMBERS	MOO
LINGER	MAC	MENACE	MOON-FORGOTTEN
LINGERS	MACABRE	MENSCH	MOONLESS
LINGO	MACHINE	MENTAL	MOONS
LINING	MACHINERY	MERE	MOON'S
LINKS	MADDENS	MERGED	MOORED
LINOLEUM	MADMAN	MERIT	MOPES
LINT	MADNESS	MESSAGES	MOPING
LINTEL	MADRONA	METAPHOR	MORAL
LIQUESCENT	MADRONAS	METER	MORAN
LIQUIDS	MAGNIFIED	MEW	MORGUES
LIQUOR	MAGNIFIES	MICA	MORLEYS
LIST	MAIDENHAIR	MICKEY	MORNING-FAIR
LISTENER	MAINCURRENT	MICROPHONES	MORNING'S
LISTENING	MAKER	MIDCHANNEL	MORRIS
LISTING	MALICE	MID-COUNTRY	MOST-HONEST-ALIVE
LITHE	MALIGN	MIDGE	MOSTLY
LITTLES	MALIGNANT	MIDGES	MOTES
LIZARD-FEET	MAMMALIAN	MIDST	MOTHER-ROOT
LIZARDS	MANAGER'S	MIDSUMMER	MOTHERS
LIZARD'S	MANHOOD	MIGHTY	MOTHS
LOAM-CRUMBS	MANIA	MIGRATING	MOULD
LOAN	MANIFEST	MILDEW	MOUND
LOATHE	MANIFESTATION	MILDEWED	MOUNTAINS
LOATHES	MANIFOLD	MILDEWS	MOUNTAIN'S
LOCKET	MANILLA	MILKED	MOUNTAIN-SLOPE
LOGGING	MANNERS	MILK-NOSE	MOUNTAINY
LOGIC	MANSION	MILKWEED	MOUNTING
LOITER	MAN-TAILORED	MIMETIC	MOURNERS'
LONELIEST	MANURE	MINCING	MOUSE-WARY
LONELINESS	MANURE-MACHINE	MINDFUL	MOVING-SLOW
LONESOME	MARKED	MINDLESS	MOW
LONGINGS	MARL	MINERAL	MOWING
LONG-POLISHED	MARMOREAN-BORN	MINIMAL	MR
LONGS	MARRED	MINIONS	MRS

MUCILAGE	NUMINOUS	PALE-PINK	PERISHES
MUCK	NURSE	PALLBEARERS	PERISHING
MUDDLE	NURSE-MAID	PALM-FULL	PERMISSION
MUFFLED	NURSES	PALM-SWEAT	PERMITS
MULTIGRAPH	NUTS	PANE	PERPETUALLY
MULTIPLE	NUZZLED	PANES	PERPETUATE
MUMBLEY-PEG	NYLON	PANS	PERSISTENT
MURDERED	NYMPH	PAPA'S	PERSISTS
MURMUR	OAR	PAPA-SEED	PERSUADE
MUSES	OATS	PAPER-CLIP	PERVERSE
MUSK	OBEY	PAPERS	PETROLEUM
MUSK-RAT	OBJECT	PAPER-WEIGHT	PHANTASIES
MUSKRATS	OBLIGATION	PARALDEHYDE	PHASE
MUSKY	OBLIVION	PARALYTIC	PHEASANT
MUSTN'T	OBSCENE	PARAQUET	PHEASANT-RUN
MUTILATED	OBSCENELY	PARCEL	PHILOSOPHERS
MUTTONY	OBSCENITY	PARCHED	PHILOSOPHICAL
MYSTERIOUS	OBSCURITY	PARE	PHLOX
NAMELESS	OBSEQUIOUS	PARK	PHOBIAS
NAMES	OBVIOUS	PARLORS	PHOEBE'S
NASTURTIUMS	OCCUR	PARMENIDES	PHOENIX
NATURES	ODDS	PARSNIP	PIANO
NEARED	ODOR	PARTICLES	PICKEREL
NECESSARY	OFFEND	PARTICULARS	PICKLED
NECESSITY	OFFERINGS	PARTING	PICNIC
NECKCURLS	OGALALA	PARTLY	PICNICS
NEEDLE'S	OLDER	PARTRIDGE	PICTURE
NEEDN'T	OMINOUS	PARTS	PIECEMEAL
NEIGHBORHOOD	ONE-SIDED	PASSENGER	PIFFLEBOB
NEMESIS	OOZE	PASSIONATE	PIG
NERVE	OPAQUE	PASSION'S	PILE
NERVELESS	OPENINGS	PASTURES	PILING
NERVOUS	OPERATES	PATHOS	PILLOWS
NESTING	OPINION	PATIENCE	PINCHING
NESTING-PLACE	ORANGES	PAUL	PINCHING-BACK
NESTS	ORCHIDS	PAUSE	PINES
NETHER	ORDERS	PAUSED	PINE-TREE
NETS	ORIOLE	PAUSING	PINK
NEW-CAUGHT	ORIOLES	PAVEMENT	PIPE-KNOCK
NEWLY	ORIOLE'S	PAWN	PIPLING
NEWS	OSPREY	PAY	PISSOIR
NEW-SHOD	OTHERLY	PAYS	PISTONS
NEWSMEN	OTHER'S	PEACE	PITCHER
NEWSPRINT	OTHERWISE	PEACHTREE	PITCHERS
NEWTS	OTTO	PEAK	PITH
NIBBLE	OULD	PEAKS	PITS
NICELY	OUTER	PEANUTS	PITTED
NIEMALS	OUTLEAP	PEARL	PITTING
NIGHT-FISHING	OUTPOURINGS	PEAR-TREE	PITY
NIGHTMARE	OUTRAGEOUS	PECK	PLAGUES
NIGHTS	OUTWARD	PECKED	PLAINS
NIMBLE	OVENBIRD	PECKING	PLAINTIVE
NIPPY	OVERDUE	PECKS	PLANET
NOBILITY	OVERFLOWS	PEDANTRY	PLANGENT
NOBLE	OVERHEAD	PEE	PLANTING
NOISELESS	OVERHUNG	PEE-CULIAR	PLASTER
NOISES	OWED	PEEL	PLATO
NONE-THE-LESS	OWLY	PEEP	PLATONIC
NOSES	OX'S	PEER	PLATTER
NOSING	OYSTER'S	PELLUDIOUS	PLAYFUL
NOSTRILS	PACED	PENCILS	PLEASES
NOTHINGS	PACING	PENNY	PLEASURES
NOTION	PADDOCK	PEOPLE	PLEDGE
NOT-KNOWING	PAGEANTRY	PEPPERMINTS	PLENTY
NOVEMBER	PAID	PERFORM	PLINK
NUB	PAIL	PERIMETER	PLOTTED
NUDGERS	PAINTED	PERIPHERAL	PLOUGHING
NUDGING	PAIR	PERISHED	PLUM

PLUME
PLUMPING
PLUMS
PLUNGE
PLUNGED
PLUNGER
POACHERS
POCKET
POD
PODS
POET
POETASTER
POETESS
POETRY-BOOK
POISONOUS
POKED
POLISH
POLO
POND-EDGE
POND-WATER
POOF
POOH
POOLS
POP-CORN
PORTION
PORTMANTEAU
POSEIDON'S
POSITION
POSSESSED
POSSIBILITIES
POSSIBLES
POSTURE
POTTED
POTTING
POUND
POURED
POURING
POWDER
POWER
POWERFUL
PRACTICALLY
PRAISING
PRANCING
PRATING
PRAYED
PRECEDES
PRECEPT
PRECISION
PREEN
PREMONITION
PRESS
PRESUMPTUOUS
PRETENDS
PRETENSE
PRETTY-BONES
PRICKLE-ME
PRICKLES
PRIMAL
PRIMEVAL
PRIMORDIAL
PRINCIPLE
PRINT
PRISON
PRISONER
PRIVACY
PRIVATE
PRIVILEGE
PRIVILEGED

PRIVY
PROBE
PROBING
PROCESSION
PROCLAIM
PRODIGIOUS
PRODUCTION
PROFESSORS
PROFFERED
PROFITS
PROGNOSIS
PRONE
PRONGS
PROOF
PROPINQUITY
PROPINQUITY'S
PROPOUNDED
PROSE
PROTECT
PROTECTING
PROTEST
PROUD
PROVERBS
PROWLING
PROXIMITY
PSYCHE
PUBLIC
PUBLISH
PUDDLE'S
PUFF
PULLER
PULLMAN
PULPY
PULSELESS
PULSES
PUMPED
PUMPING
PUMPKINS
PUNCH
PUNGENCE
PUPILS
PUPPIES
PUPPY
PURE-WHITE
PURIFIED
PURITY
PURPLE
PURSED
PURSE-PROUD
PURSUERS
PURSUING
PURSUIT
PUSH
PUSHING
PUTTING
PUTTY
QUAGMIRE
QUAILS
QUAKE
QUAKER
QUARRY'S
QUARTER
QUARTS
QUARTZ
QUAVER
QUEER
QUESTING
QUESTIONER

QUICKENED
QUICKENING
QUICKSAND
QUICKSILVER
QUICK-WATER
QUINCE
QUINCE-BLOSSOM
QUITE
QUITE-BY-CHANCE
QUIVERING
QUIVERS
RABBIT
RAGES
RAGGEDY
RAIL
RAILING
RAIN-BEATEN
RAINBOW
RAIN-BOW
RAIN-DRENCHED
RAIN-SOAKED
RAISE
RAISES
RAKE
RALLY
RAMBLING
RANCH-HOUSE
RANGES
RANK
RANSOM
RANT
RAPE
RAPID
RAPIDS
RAPPING
RAPS
RASPING
RATIONAL
RAT'S
RATTLES
RAVAGE
RAVE
RAVEN
RAVENOUS
RAVENS
RAVINE
RAZORS
REACHED
READS
REAPS
REARRANGES
REASONS
RECEDING
RECEIVE
RECEIVED
RECEPTION
RECITE
RECKONING
RECOGNIZE
RECOILING
RECOUNT
RECOVER
RECOVERED
RECUMBENCY
RECURRING
REDEEM
REDEEMER
RED-HOT

REDOLENT
REDOUBLES
REEKING
REFITS
REFLECTION
REFLECTIONS
REFLECTS
REGIONS
REGULAR
REHEARSE
REJOICED
RELATE
RELATIVES
RELICS
RELUCTANT
REMAINING
REMAINS
REMARK
REMARKS
REMEMBERING
RENDERED
RENE
RENOWN
REPEAT
REPEATEDLY
REPENT
REPLANT
REPLIED
REPRESSION
REPULSE
REQUIRE
RESEMBLES
RESERVED
RESIDES
RESIST
RESOUND
RESOUNDED
RESTIVE
RESTLESS
RESTORED
RESURRECTION
RETAIN
RETICENCE
RETIRE
RETIRING
RETREAT
RETREATS
RETURNING
REVEAL
REVEALING
REVEALS
REVELATION
REVERSED
REVILED
REVIVED
REVIVES
RHODODENDRON
RHULE
RIBBONING
RICHES
RID
RIDDLING
RIDGE
RIDICULOUS
RIFFLE
RIFFLED
RIFT
RIGHTS

RIGID	SALT-DRENCHED	SEA-FOAM	SHAPED
RIMMED	SALT-LADEN	SEAL	SHAPELESS
RINGED	SALT-LICK	SEAMS	SHAPELY
RIPENING	SALT-SOAKED	SEA-SHAPE	SHARDS
RIPS	SALVATION	SEA-SLIME	SHARE
RISINGS	SAMOOTS	SEASONS	SHARPLY
RISK	SAND-BARS	SEASON'S	SHAVING
RITUALISTS	SANDBLASTER	SEA-SWELL	SHEATH
RIVERMOUTH	SAND-CRUMB	SEATS	SHEATH-WET
RIVERY	SANDGRAINS	SEA-URCHIN	SHE-BEAR
RIVULET	SANDPIPER	SEAWARD	SHEDS
RIVULETS	SANDPIPER'S	SEA-WINDS	SHEEPISHLY
ROADBED	SAND-RUT	SEA-WIND'S	SHEETS
ROAD-CROWNS	SANITARIUM	SECRETING	SHELTER
ROADSIDE	SANK	SECRETION	SHEPHERD
ROADWAY	SANTA	SECURELY	SHIELD
ROAM	SATURDAY	SEED-CROWNS	SHIELDS
ROAMED	SAVAGE	SEEDY	SHIFTS
ROARED	SAVE	SEEING	SHIMMERED
ROARS	SAVED	SEEKS	SHINGLES
ROAST	SAVES	SEEMINGLY	SHINY
ROBBERS	SAWDUST	SEEPING	SHIPS
ROBE	SAXIFRAGE	SELDOM	SHIRT
ROBERT	SCALED	SELF-CONTEMPLATION	SHIVERED
ROBINS	SCALPEL	SELF-DELIGHTING	SHIVERS
ROCKED	SCARAB	SELF-DESTRUCTIVE	SHOAL
ROCKER	SCARE	SELF-ENCHANTED	SHOCK
ROCK-SEAMS	SCARF	SELF-INFECTED	SHOCKS
ROCK-SHUT	SCARLET	SELF-INVOLVED	SHOE-BOX
ROLLS	SCARS	SELF-REVEALED	SHOOTING
ROMP	SCARY	SELF-TALK	SHOP
ROOF-TOP	SCATTERING	SEMBLANCE	SHOP-GIRL
ROSE-BRIER	SCENTED	SENSES	SHOPPING
ROTTED	SCENTS	SENSIBILITY	SHORT-HAND
ROTTING	SCEPTER	SENSIBLE	SHORT-TAILED
ROUGH	SCHMIDT	SENSITIVE	SHOULDERS
ROUNDS	SCHOLAR	SENSUALISTS	SHOULDER'S
ROUNDY	SCHOOLBOYS	SENSUALITY	SHOUTING
ROUSE	SCHOOLED	SENSUOUS	SHOVE
ROUTINE	SCHWARTZE	SENTENTIOUS	SHOWED
ROWER	SCOLD	SENTIMENT	SHOWERED
RUB	SCOOP	SENTIMENTAL	SHRANK
RUBBERS	SCORN	SENTRY	SHRED
RUBBERY	SCOTER	SEPARATE	SHRIEKING
RUBBING	SCOTERS	SEPARATENESS	SHRIKE
RUBBLESTONES	SCOTT	SEPTET	SHRILLEST
RUDE	SCOW	SEQUEL	SHRINKS
RUFFLED	SCRAGGLY	SEQUENCE	SHRIVELED
RUIN	SCRAGGY	SERE	SHUDDERED
RUMBLE	SCRAP	SERENELY	SHUDDERING
RUMINANT	SCRAPED	SERIES	SHULE
RUNE	SCRATCHED	SERPENTING	SHUNDAY
RUNG	SCROLLS	SERPENTS	SHUTTLING
RUNNEL	SCRUBBING	SERVANT	SIBYL
RUNWAY	SCRUBBY	SERVE	SICKLE
RUSSELLS	SCRUPULOUS	SERVED	SIDEBOARD
RUSSIAN	SCULPTURE	SETTEE	SIDELONG
RUSTED	SCUMS	SETTLES	SIDE-MIRROR
RUSTLES	SCUTTLED	SETTLING	SIDE'S
RUSTLING	SEA-BEAST	SEVENTY-FIVE	SIFT
RUSTY	SEA-BURIED	SEWED	SIFTS
SACK	SEA-CHAMBERS	SEX-LIFE	SIGN
SACKED	SEA-CHANGE	SHAFTS	SIGNALS
SADNESS	SEA-CLIFF	SHAG	SIGNED
SAGGED	SEA-CLIFFS	SHALLOWER	SILENCES
SAILED	SEA-COUSINS	SHALLOWS	SILICA
SAILS	SEA-FACED	SHAME	SILKEN
SALIVA	SEAFOAM	SHANTY	SILKS

SILLY	SLUGGISH	SPEAKS	STEEPER
SILO	SLUGGISHLY	SPECTER	STELLER
SILO-RICH	SLUG-SOFT	SPEECHES	STEM-FUR
SILTED	SLURP	SPEED	STERN
SIMILAR	SLY	SPELL	STETHOSCOPE
SIMILITUDE	SMALLER	SPENT	STEVEN
SIMPER	SMART	SPIDER'S	STICKLEBACK
SIMPLICITY'S	SMILED	SPIDERY	STICKS-IN-A-DROWSE
SIMPLY	SMOKE	SPIEL	STIFFENED
SINCE	SMOKED	SPIES	STIFFENING
SINGING-TIME	SMOKELESS	SPIKEY	STILE
SINGLENESS	SMOKES	SPILLAGE	STILL-STAND
SING-SONG	SMOKE'S	SPILLS	STILL-TO-BE-BORN
SINISTER	SMOKING	SPINAL	STING
SINKING	SMOLDERING	SPINDLY	STINGS
SINKS	SMUDGY	SPINES	STITCHED
SINS	SMUG	SPINNING	STOCKING
SINUOSITY	SMUTS	SPINY	STONE-DEAF
SINUOUSNESS	SNAIL-LIFTING	SPIRITS	STOOL
SIREN'S	SNAIL'S	SPIRITUAL	STOOP
SISTERS	SNAKE-EYES	SPITE	STOPPING
SITS	SNEER	SPITTLE	STOPS
SITTING	SNIDE	SPITTOON	STORE
SIX	SNIFF	SPLENDID	STORED
SIX-HUNDRED-FOOT	SNIFFING	SPLINTERS	STOREROOM
SIXTEEN-YEAR-OLD	SNIGGERED	SPLITTING	STORES
SKEIN	SNIVEL	SPOIL	STORK
SKELETON	SNORE	SPOILED	STORM-TOSSED
SKINNED	SNORING	SPOKEN	STOVE
SKINNY	SNORT	SPORT	STRAIGHTEN
SKIN'S	SNORTS	SPORTIVE	STRAIGHTNESS
SKIPPED	SNOUT	SPOT	STRAIN
SKIPPERS	SNOWDRIFT	SPOTS	STRAINED
SKIPS	SNOW-LADEN	SPOUT	STRAINING
SKIRRING	SNUFF-LADEN	SPRATLING'S	STRANGELY
SKIRT	SNUFFLING	SPRAWL	STRANGENESS
SKIRTING	SOAKED	SPRINGTIME	STRANGER
SKITTER	SOB	SPRINKLED	STRAWBERRY
SKITTER-BUM	SOBBING	SPROUTS	STRAYED
SKITTERY	SOFA	SPRUCE	STREAK
SLACKENING	SOFT-BACKED	SQUASH	STREAKED
SLACKENS	SOFTENING	SQUASHY	STREET-LAMP
SLAG-HEAPS	SOFTEST	SQUAWKING	STRENGTHENS
SLAIN	SOFT-FOOTED	SQUEAK	STRETCHING
SLAPPING	SOFT-SIGH	SQUEEZE	STRETCHINGS
SLATTED	SOLACE	SQUEEZE-BOX	STRIATED
SLAUGHTERED	SOLD	SQUIRMERS	STRIATIONS
SLEDGE	SOLDIER	SQUIRMING	STRIDE
SLEEP-DAZE	SOLEMN	SQUIRRELS	STRIDES
SLEEPERS	SOLITARINESS	ST	STRIDING
SLEEP-HEAVY	SOMBER	STACKED-UP	STRIKE
SLEEPLESS	SOMEONE	STAG'S	STRIP
SLEEP'S	SOMEWHAT	STAID	STRIPED
SLEEP-SONG	SOOTHE	STAIRS	STRIPES
SLEET	SOOTY	STAIR'S	STROKED
SLEIGH	SOREN	STALKING	STROKES
SLEIGHBELLS	SORES	STALKS	STROLLED
SLICK	SORROW	STALLS	STRONGER
SLID	SOUP	STAMPING	STRUGGLE
SLIDE	SOUPS	STANDARD	STUDIED
SLIP-OOZE	SOURCES	STARER	STUFF
SLIPPER	SOURED	STARTLED	STUFFED
SLITHER	SOUTHERN	STARVELING	STUFFING
SLOBBERS	SPANIEL	STARVING	STUFFS
SLOSHING	SPANNED	STEADIES	STUMBLES
SLOTH	SPARE	STEADILY	STUMP
SLOWNESS	SPAYED	STEAK	STUNTED
SLOW-SETTLING	SPEAKING	STEAL	STUPOR

STY	SWEPT	THOUGHTS	TRAINS
STYLE	SWERVING	THRASH	TRANCED
SUBDUED	SWINE-ON-FRIDAY	THRASHED	TRANCE-LIKE
SUBJECT	SWINGE	THRASHING-UP	TRANSCENDED
SUBLIMINAL	SWIRLING	THREAD	TRASH-CAN
SUBMERGE	SWITCHBOARD	THREADBARE	TRAVELED
SUBTERRANEAN	SWOOPING	THREAD-LIKE	TRAVELER'S
SUBTLE	SWOOPS	THRESHOLDS	TRAVELLED
SUBTRACT	SWORD	THRICE	TREASURE
SUBURBAN	SYMBOL	THRILL	TREELESS
SUCKED	SYMBOLICAL	THROTTLE	TREE-SHREW
SUDDENNESS	SYMBOLS	THROWING	TREE-SHREWS
SUFFER	SYNCO	THRUM-THRUM	TRELLISED
SUFFERED	TAINT	THRUST	TREMENDOUS
SUFFICES	TALE	THRUSTS	TREMORS
SUFFICIENT	TALKING	THUMP	TREMULOUS
SUGARY	TALUS	TICK	TRICYCLE
SUIT	TAME	TICKET	TRINKETS
SULLEN	TAMES	TICKLE	TRIUMPHS
SULPHUROUS	TANGLE	TICKLE-ME	TRIVIA
SUM	TAPPING	TICKLING	TROPICAL
SUMMERS	TARFACE	TICKS	TROUGH
SUMMER'S	TAR-LADEN	TIDE-RIPPLES	TROUT
SUMMER-SAD	TASK	TIERS	TRUCKS
SUMMERY	TATTERED	TIGER	TRUDGES
SUMMIT	TEACHER	TIGHTER	TRULY
SUMMON	TEAR	TIGHTLY	TRUNKS
SUN-CHAIRS	TEARLESS	TILLY	TRUST
SUN-PARCHED	TEASED	TIME-HARRIED	TRUSTING
SUNSHINE	TEDIUM	TIME-ORDER	TRUTHS
SUN-STRUCK	TEDIUM'S	TIME'S	TRY
SUPERMARKET	TEETER	TIP	TRYING
SUPPER	TELESCOPE	TIPPED	TUBA
SUPPLEMENT	TELLING	TIPPING	TUFTY
SUPPRESS	TEMPESTS	TIPTOED	TUGGED
SURELY	TEMPTATION	TITS	TUGGING
SURETY	TENDED	TITTEBAWASEE	TUMULTUOUS
SURFACES	TENDEREST	TOBACCO	TUNNEL
SURFEIT	TENDRIL	TOIL	TUNNELED
SURGEON	TENDRILOUS	TOLEDO	TURF
SURRENDERING	TENSIONS	TOMBSTONE	TURNED-OVER
SURROUND	TENTACLED	TOOL	TWENTY
SURROUNDED	TENTACLES	TOOTLE	TWICED
SURROUNDINGS	TENTATIVE	TOPMOST	TWIGGY
SURVEY	TENTS	TOPPED	TWINE
SURVIVE	TERMS	TORMENT	TWINED
SUSTAINS	TERRACES	TORN	TWINKLED
SUSTENANCE	TERRIBLY	TORPOR	TWINY
SUTURES	TETONS	TORRENT	TWIRL
SWAGGERING	THANK	TORRENTIAL	TWITCH
SWALE	THAW	TORTURED	TWITCHING
SWAMPLAND	THEE'S	TOSSING	TWITTERED
SWAMPS	THEY'RE	TOUCHES	'TWIXT
SWAN-HEART	THEY'VE	TOUCHING	TWO-BY-TWO'S
SWAN'S	THICKENS	TOUGH	UDDER
SWARMS	THICKER	TOUGHENED	UNALTERABLE
SWART	THIEVING	TOUGHER	UNALTERED
SWEATS	THINGY	TOUGHEST	UNBLOOD
SWEEPS	THINKS	TOWER	UNBLOODY
SWEETER	THINLY	TOWERING	UNBOUND
SWEETHEART	THINNER	TOWHEES	UNBROKEN
SWEET-HEART	THIRD	TOWNS	UNCERTAIN
SWEETHEART'S	THIRDS	TOWN'S	UNCLE
SWEET-PEA	THIRTEEN	TOY	UNCLES
SWEET-PEAS	THIRTY-FIVE	TOYS	UNCLE'S
SWELLED	THISTLE	TRACE	UNCONSCIOUS
SWELLING	THISTLES	TRACED	UNDECEIVED
SWELLS	THORN-BITTEN	TRACTABLE	UNDERBELLY

UNDERBRUSH	VAPOROUS	WARS	WHOLLY
UNDERCLOTHES	VARICOSE	WASHED	WHOOPER
UNDERCURRENTS	VARIOUSLY	WASHED-OUT	WHORE
UNDERLEAVES	VARNISH	WASHES	WHORLS
UNDERSIDE	VASE	WASHING	WICKED
UNDERSONG	VASTY	WASHINGTON	WIDELY
UNDERSTANDABLE	VAT	WASPS	WIDEN
UNDERSTOOD	VEAL	WASTE	WIDENED
UNDERTAKER'S	VEER	WATCHER	WIDER
UNDERWEAR	VEGETABLE	WATCHMAN	WIGGLES
UNDID	VEIL	WATCHMAN'S	WILDEST
UNDIMINISHED	VEILED	WATERED	WILDLY
UNDIVIDED	VELVETY	WATERFALL	WILLIAM
UNDULATING	VENERY	WATERING	WILLIAMS
UNEASY	VERB	WATERING-TROUGH	WILLIE
UNEMPLOYED	VERBENAS	WAVE-CREST	WILLING
UNEMPLOYMENT	VERMIN	WAVED	WILLINGLY
UNENCUMBERED	VERSES	WAVERS	WILLOWS
UNEQUAL	VERTIGO	WAVING	WILLOW-SHY
UNESSENTIAL	VESPERAL	WAXWINGS	WILTED
UNEXTINGUISHED	VESSEL	WEAKLY	WIND-BEATEN
UNFROWN	VESTIGES	WEARING	WIND-BITTEN
UNFURL	VESTIGIAL	WEASEL	WIND-BREAK
UNGUARDED	VESTURE	WEATHER-BEATEN	WIND-EXCITED
UNHINGE	VIADUCT	WEATHER'S	WIND-HARPS
UNHOLY	VIBRATION	WEAVE	WINDLESS
UNIMPORTANT	VICE	WEAVES	WINDOW-FRAMES
UNISON	VICIOUS	WEB	WINDOW'S
UNKNOWN	VILLAGE	WEBS	WINDSHIELD
UNLEARN	VIOLATED	WE'D	WIND-TATTERED
UNLEAVE	VIREO	WEDGE	WIND-TIPPED
UNLESS	VIRGIN	WEEDS'	WIND-VENT
UNLIKE	VIRTUES	WEED-SKELETONS	WIND-VENTS
UNLOCKS	VIRULENT	WEEKS	WIND-WARPED
UNMEASURED	VISCID	WEIGHTLESS	WIND-WAVES
UNMELODIC	VISITANT	WEIRD	WINE
UNMINDFUL	VISITOR	WELL-CURB	WING-CROOKED
UNMOVING	VITAMINS	WELL-GROOMED	WINKIE
UNNECESSARY	VIVID	WELLS	WINSOME
UNPERPLEXED	VOCABLES	WELL-UPHOLSTERED	WINTER-CALM
UNPRAYED-FOR	VOCAL	WERT	WINTERGREEN
UNPROTECTED	VULTURE	WETNESS	WINTER-LEAPING
UNRAVELS	WAGS	WETTER	WINTER-SEALED
UNREFINED	WAGTAIL	WHACK	WINTER-WASP
UNSEALED	WAG-TAIL	WHAT-NOT	WIPING
UNSEEMLINESS	WAILED	WHEELBARROWS	WISEST
UNSINGING	WAIT-IN-THE-HALL	WHELM	WISHING
UNSTILLING	WAKED	WHEREBY	WISPS
UNTANGLE	WALKER'S	WHEREIN	WITCHES
UNTIED	WALL-PAPER	WHEREVER	WITHER
UNTRUE	WALTZED	WHETS	WITLESS
UNWILLING	WALTZING	WHIFFET	WITNESS
UNWIND	WAN	WHINES	WIVES
UNWINDING	WANDER	WHIPPOORWILL	WO
UNWRINKLING	WANDERED	WHIRL	WOMBS
UPPER	WANDERING	WHIRLS	WONDERFUL
UPSIDE	WANE	WHISKERY	WOODED
UP-SPRING	WANES	WHISKS	WOOD-GRATE
UP-SWAY	WANTED	WHISPERED	WOODIE
URGE	WANTING	WHISPERING	WOOD'S
URINALS	WAR	WHITENESS	WOOED
USURPS	WARBLERS	WHITENING	WOOL
UTTERED	WARLIKE	WHITENS	WOOLEN
UTTERLY	WARMED	WHITEWASHED	WOOS
VAGUELY	WARMING	WHITEY	WORDLESS
VAIN	WARMS	WHITISH	WORKERS
VALLEYS	WARNINGS	WHITMAN	WORKS
VANISHED	WARPS	WHITMAN'S	WORM'S

WORN
WORTH
WOUNDS
WRAITH
WRAPPED
WRAPS
WREATHES
WREN'S
WREN-SONG
WRESTED
WRESTLE
WRIGHT'S
WRINKLE
WRINKLES
WRIST-THICK
WRITHE
WRITHER
WROUGHT
WUNDERKIND
WYANDOTTE
YANKING
YAWN
YAWNS
YEARNER
YEAR'S
YELL
YELLOWISH-GREEN
YELPING
YICKETTY-YAK
YIELDS
YIELD'S
YOUNGEST
YOUNGLING
YOUNGLINGS
YOUR'RE
YOURS
YOU'S
ZEALOT
ZEN